W9-AQI-347

Index of American Periodical Verse: 1988

Rafael Catalá
and
James D. Anderson

assisted by

Sarah Park Anderson
and
Martha Park Sollberger

The Scarecrow Press, Inc.
Metuchen, N.J., & London
1990

Library of Congress Catalog Card No. 73-3060
ISBN 0-8108-2334-9

Manufactured in the United States of America

Contents

Preface

This, the eighteenth annual volume of the ***Index of American Periodical Verse***, was produced with the cooperation of 260 participating English and Spanish language periodicals from Canada, the United States, and the Caribbean. Nearly 6,000 entries for individual poets and translators are included, with more than 16,500 entries for individual poems and the same number of title or first line entries.

The importance of the ***Index*** grows as its necessity becomes more apparent in circles of contemporary poetry research. The increasing demand for inclusion corroborates this fact. The ***Index*** constitutes an objective measure of poetry in North America, recording not only the publication of our own poets in Canada, the U.S. and the Caribbean, but also those from other lands and cultures and from other times. Of course, the ***Index***'s primary purpose is to show what poems have been published by particular poets, what poems have been translated by particular translators, and who wrote poems with particular titles or first lines. But taken together, the ***Index*** reveals trends and influences: the ebb and flow of particular poets, as well as the influence of cultures of other lands and times as represented by their poets published in North American journals.

James D. Anderson has made a major contribution to the ***Index*** by designing and refining computer programs that have greatly facilitated the indexing process, control of necessary cross-references, and typesetting. Also, I want to express my sincere appreciation to Sarah Park Anderson and Martha Park Sollberger for their valuable assistance.

Rafael Catalá
Co-Editor

Introduction

Scope

The ***Index of American Periodical Verse*** indexes poems published in a broad cross-section of poetry, literary, scholarly, popular, general, and "little" magazines and journals published in the United States, Canada, and the Caribbean. The journals and magazines included are listed in the "Periodicals Indexed" section, together with name of editor(s), address, issues indexed in this volume, and subscription information. Selection of journals and magazines is the responsibility of the editors, based on recommendations of poets, librarians, literary scholars and publishers. Journal and magazine publishers agree to participate by supplying copies of all issues to the editors. Criteria for inclusion include the quality of poems and their presentation and the status or reputation of poets. Within these very broad and subjective guidelines, the editors attempt to include a cross-section of journals and magazines by type of publisher and/or publication, place of publication, and type of poetry. Journals published outside of North America may be included only if they have North American editors.

Compilation

The 1988 volume saw the transition from Osborne CP/M computers to a 286 MS/DOS computer for the compilation of the ***Index.*** We continued to use WordStar for data entry, but "moved up" to version 4 to take advantage of "shorthand" macro programs to repeat author headings for multiple poems by the same poet, create translator entries from author entries for translated poems, and transform complex author names into cross-reference entries. Sorting was done by "IOTA Big Sort," a fast program for sorting very large files written by Fred A. Rowley. Title entries were extracted from the original author entries and sorted, and formatted author and title entries were transferred to a Macintosh computer with lazer printer for typesetting and page formatting using MacWrite and PageMaker programs.

Persons interested in the precise details of compilation, including the computer programs used for error checking, sorting and formatting, should write to the editors at P.O. Box 38, New Brunswick, NJ 08903-0038. The ***Indexes*** for 1982 through 1988 are available from the editors on 5-1/4" floppy disks.

Names and Cross References

With the addition of many more poets with compound surnames and surnames containing various prefixes, we have recognized the need for systematic cross references from alternative forms of surname to the form chosen for entry in the ***Index.*** We have included cross references whenever the form used for entry does not fall under the last part or element of the name. In addition, many poets publish under different forms of the same name, for example, with or without a middle initial. When poets are known to use different forms of the same name, alternative forms may be indicated using the format authorized by the *Anglo-American Cataloguing Rules*, Second Edition. For example:

WHEATLEY, Pat (Patience)

This heading indicates that this poet has poems published under two forms of name: Pat Wheatley and Patience Wheatley.

When two or more different names refer to the same poet, one name will be chosen, with "see" references to the chosen name from other names. When it is not possible to determine with assurance whether a single poet is using variant forms of name or different poets have similar names, both names will be used. In such cases, "see also" references may be added to headings to remind users to check the variant name forms which might possibly refer to the same poet.

Format and Arrangement of Entries

The basic format and style of the ***Index*** remain unchanged. Poets are arranged alphabetically by surname and forenames. In creating this alphabetical sequence, we have adopted principles of the filing rules issued in 1980 by the American Library Association and the Library of Congress. Names are arranged on the basis of their spelling, rather than their pronunciation, so that, for example, names beginning with 'Mac' and 'Mc' are no longer interfiled. Similarly, the space consistently counts as a filing element, so that similar compound and prefixed surnames are often separated by some distance, as illustrated in the following examples. Note that "De BOLT" precedes "DeBEVOISE" by a considerable number of entries.

De ANGELIS
De BOLT
De GRAVELLES
De LOACH
De PALCHI
De RONSARD
De VAUL
DEAL
DeBEVOISE
DeFOE
DEGUY
Del VECCHIO
DeLISLE
DeMOTT
DENNISON
Der HOVANESSIAN
DESY
DeYOUNG

Van BRUNT
Van DUYN
Van HALTEREN
Van TOORN
Van TROYER
Van WERT
Van WINCKEL
VANCE
Vander DOES
VANDERBEEK
VanDEVENTER

Abbreviations are also arranged on the basis of spelling, rather than pronunciation, so that "ST. JOHN" is *not* filed as "SAINT JOHN", but as "S+T+space+JOHN". Punctuation, signs and symbols other than alphabetic letters and numerals are not considered; a hyphen is filed as if it were a space and apostrophes and accents are ignored for purposes of filing. In title entries, initial articles are also ignored. Numerals are arranged in numerical order preceding alphabetical letters rather than as if they were spelled out.

Under each poet's name, poems are arranged alphabetically by title or, if there is no title, by first line. Poem titles and first lines are placed within quotation marks. All significant words of titles are capitalized, but in first lines, only the first word and proper nouns are capitalized. Incomplete excerpts from larger works are followed by the note "Excerpt" or, if they consist of complete sections, by "Selection". The title, first line or number of the excerpt may follow if given in the publication. For example:

WALCOTT, Derek
"Midsummer" (Selections: XXXIV-XXXVI). [Agni] (18) 83, p. 5-7.

WEBB, Phyllis
"The Vision Tree" (Selection: "I Daniel"). [PoetryCR] (5:2) Wint 83-84, p. 11.

WAINWRIGHT, Jeffrey
"Heart's Desire" (Excerpt: "Some Propositions and Part of a Narrative"). [Agni] (18) 83, p. 37.

WATTEN, Barret
"One Half" (Excerpts). [ParisR] (24:86) Wint 82, p. 112-113.

If an excerpt is treated as a complete "sub-work", it receives an independent entry, with reference to the larger work in a note. For example:

ANDERSON, Jack
"Magnets" (from The Clouds of That Country). [PoNow] (7:2, #38) 83, p. 23.

Notes about dedications, joint authors, translators, and sources follow the title, enclosed in parentheses. A poem with more than one author is entered under each author. Likewise, a translated poem is entered under each translator, as well as its author(s). Each entry includes the names of all authors and all translators. Multiple authors or translators are indicated by the abbreviation "w.", standing for "with". Translators are indicated by the abbreviation "tr. by", standing for "translated by", and original authors are indicated by the abbreviation "tr. of", standing for "translation of". For example:

AGGESTAM, Rolf
"Old Basho" (tr. by Erland Anderson and Lars Nordström). [NewRena] (16) Spr 83, p. 25.

ANDERSON, Erland
"Old Basho" (tr. of Rolf Aggestam, w. Lars Nordström). [NewRena] (16) Spr 83, p. 25.

NORDSTRÖM, Lars
"Old Basho" (tr. of Rolf Aggestam, w. Erland Anderson). [NewRena] (16) Spr 83, p. 25.

The journal citation includes an abbreviation standing for the journal title, followed by volume and issue numbers, date, and pages. The journal abbreviation is enclosed in square brackets. An alphabetical list of these journal abbreviations is included at the front of the volume, followed by the full journal title, name of editor(s), address, the numbers of the issues indexed for this volume of the ***Index***, and subscription information. A separate list of indexed periodicals is arranged by full journal title, with a reference to the abbreviated title. Volume and issue numbers are included within parentheses, e.g., (16:5) stands for volume 16, number 5; (21) refers to issue 21 for a journal which does not use volume numbers. Dates are given using abbreviations for months and seasons. Year of publication is indicated by the last two digits of the year, e.g., 88. Please see the separate list of abbreviations at the front of the volume.

Compiling this year's ***Index*** has been an adventure into the wealth and variety of poetry published in U. S., Caribbean and Canadian periodicals as well as the intricacies of bringing this richness together and organizing it into a consistent index. The world of poetry publication is a dynamic one, with new journals appearing, older journals declining, dying, reviving and thriving. This year saw the loss of 10 journals and the addition of 14 new ones, with a net gain of 4 journals. Both deleted and newly added journals are listed at the front of the volume. Keeping up with these changes is a big job, and we solicit our readers' suggestions as to journals which should be included in future volumes of the ***Index***, and also, journals which could be dropped. Editors who would like their journals considered for inclusion in future volumes should send sample issues to:

Rafael Catalá, Editor
Index of American Periodical Verse
P.O. Box 38
New Brunswick, NJ 08903-0038

Although indexing is indispensable for the organization of any literature so that particular works can be found when needed and scholarship and research facilitated, it is a tedious business. I know that we have made mistakes. We solicit your corrections and suggestions, which you may send to me at the above address.

James D. Anderson
Co-Editor

Abbreviations

dir., dirs.	director, directors
ed., eds.	editor, editors
(for.)	price for foreign countries
(ind.)	price for individuals
(inst.)	price for institutions
(lib.)	price for libraries
NS	new series
p.	page, pages
po. ed.	poetry editor
pub.	publisher
(stud.)	price for students
tr. by	translated by
tr. of	translation of
U.	University
w.	with

Months

Ja	January	Jl	July
F	February	Ag	August
Mr	March	S	September
Ap	April	O	October
My	May	N	November
Je	June	D	December

Seasons

Aut	Autumn	Spr	Spring
Wint	Winter	Sum	Summer

Years

85	1985	87	1987
86	1986	88	1988

Periodicals Added

Periodical acronyms are followed by the titles. Full information may be found in the list of periodicals indexed.

ArtfulD: ARTFUL DODGE

ChamLR: CHAMINADE LITERARY REVIEW

CinPR: CINCINNATI POETRY REVIEW

GettyR: GETTYSBURG REVIEW

KeyWR: KEY WEST REVIEW

LittleBR: THE LITTLE BALKANS REVIEW

PacificR: THE PACIFIC REVIEW

Plain: PLAINSONGS

Rohwedder: ROHWEDDER

SwampR: SWAMP ROOT

Talisman: TALISMAN

TampaR: TAMPA REVIEW

Timbuktu: TIMBUKTU

Turnstile: TURNSTILE

Periodicals Deleted

ConcPo: CONCERNING POETRY, Ellwood Johnson, L. L. Lee, eds., Robert Huff, po. ed., Dept. of English, Western Washington U., Bellingham, WA 98225. Terminated publication with number 20 (1987).

GreenfR: GREENFIELD REVIEW, Joseph Bruchac III, ed., 2 Middle Grove Road, Greenfield Center, NY 12833. No longer published.

GWR: THE G. W. REVIEW, The Editor, Box 20, Marvin Center, The George Washington U., 800 21st St., N.W., Washington, DC 20052 (Editor changes annually). No 1987 or 1988 issues received.

OP: OPEN PLACES, Eleanor M. Bender, ed., Box 2085, Stephens College, Columbia, MO 65215. Summer 87 was final issue.

OroM: ORO MADRE, Loss and Jan Glazier, eds., 4429 Gibraltar Dr., Fremont, CA 94536. No issues received since 1985.

Raccoon: RACCOON, David Spicer, ed., 3387 Poplar Ave., Suite 205, Memphis, TN 38111. Issues indexed: No 1988 issues received; mail returned.

RevICP: REVISTA DEL INSTITUTO DE CULTURA PUERTORRIQUEÑA, Marta Aponte Alsina, Directora, Apartado 4184, San Juan, PR. Issues indexed: No 1987 or 1988 issues received.

Waves: WAVES, Bernice Lever, ed., Gay Allison, po. ed., 79 Denham Drive, Richmond Hill, Ontario L4C 6H9 Canada. Issues indexed: 14:4, 15:1/2, 3-4). Ceased publication following v. 15, no. 4.

WoosterR: WOOSTER REVIEW, Stuart Safford, Carrie Allison, Jonathan Barclay, eds., The College of Wooster, Wooster, OH 44691. No longer published.

YetASM: YET ANOTHER SMALL MAGAZINE, Candace Catlin Hall, ed., Andrew Mountain Press, Box 14353, Hartford, CT 06114. Issues indexed: No 1987 or 1988 issues received.

Periodicals Indexed

Arranged by acronym, with names of editors, addresses, issues indexed, and subscription information. New titles added to the *Index* in 1988 are marked with an asterisk (*).

Abraxas: ABRAXAS, Ingrid Swanberg, ed., 2518 Gregory St., Madison, WI 53711. Issues indexed: (37). Subscriptions: $12/4 issues; Single issues: $3; Double issues: $6.

Acts: ACTS: A Journal of New Writing, David Levi Strauss, ed. & pub., 514 Guerrero St., San Franisco, CA 94110. Issues indexed: (8/9). Subscriptions: $12/yr. (2 issues, ind.), $16/yr. (2 issues, inst. & for.); $20/2 yrs. (4 issues, ind.), $28/2 yrs. (4 issues, inst. & for.); Single issues: $8.

Agni: AGNI, Askold Melnyczuk, ed., Creative Writing Program, Boston U., 236 Bay State Rd., Boston, MA 02115. Issues indexed: (26-27). Subscriptions: $12/yr., $23/2 yrs., plus $2/yr. (for.); Single issues: $6.

AlphaBS: ALPHA BEAT SOUP, Dave Christy, ed., 5110 Adams St., Montreal, PQ H1V 1W8 Canada. Issues indexed: (3-4). Subscriptions: $5/yr. (2 issues); Single issues: $3.

Amelia: AMELIA, Frederick A. Raborg, Jr., ed., 329 "E" St., Bakersfield, CA 93304. Issues indexed: (4:4, 5:1-2, issues 11-13). Subscriptions: US, Canada, Mexico, $20/yr. (4 issues), $38/2 yrs., $56/3 yrs.; $36/yr., $70/2 yrs., $104/3 yrs. (for. air mail); Single issues: $6.50, $10 (for. air mail).

Americas: THE AMERICAS REVIEW, A Review of Hispanic Literature and Art of the USA (formerly Revista Chicano-Riqueña), Julián Olivares, ed., U. of Houston, Houston, TX 77204-2090. Issues indexed: (16:1-3/4). Subscriptions: $15/yr. (ind.), $20/yr. (inst.); Single issues: $5.

AmerPoR: THE AMERICAN POETRY REVIEW, David Bonanno, Stephen Berg, Arthur Vogelsang, eds., 1704 Walnut St., Philadelphia, PA 19103. Issues indexed: (17:1-6). Subscriptions: $26/3 yrs., $31/3 yrs. (for.), $19/2 yrs., $23/2 yrs. (for.), $11/yr., $13/yr. (for.); classroom rate $6/yr. per student; Single issues: $2.25.

AmerS: THE AMERICAN SCHOLAR, Joseph Epstein, ed., United Chapters of Phi Beta Kappa, 1811 Q St. NW, Washington, DC 20009. Issues indexed: (57:1-4). Subscriptions: $18/yr., $32/2 yrs., $42/3 yrs. plus $3/yr. (for.); Single issues: $5.

AmerV: THE AMERICAN VOICE, Sallie Bingham, Frederick Smock, eds., The Kentucky Foundation for Women, Inc., 332 West Broadway, Suite 1215, Louisville, KY 40202. Issues indexed: (10-13). Subscriptions: $12/yr. Single issues: $4.

AnotherCM: ANOTHER CHICAGO MAGAZINE, Lee Webster, Barry Silesky, eds., Box 11223, Chicago, IL 60611. Issues indexed: (18). Subscriptions: $15/yr., $60/5 yrs., $149.95/lifetime; Single issues: $8.

Antaeus: ANTAEUS, Daniel Halpern, ed., The Ecco Press, 26 W. 17th St., New York, NY 10011. Issues indexed: (60). Subscriptions: $20/4 issues, $37/8 issues, $53/12 issues; plus $3 per issue (for., surface mail), $6 per issue (for. air mail); Single issues: $10.

AntigR: THE ANTIGONISH REVIEW, George Sanderson, ed., St. Francis Xavier U., Antigonish, Nova Scotia B2G 1C0 Canada. Issues indexed: (73, 74/75). Subscriptions: $16/4 issues; Single issues: $4.50.

Periodicals Indexed

AntR: THE ANTIOCH REVIEW, Robert S. Fogarty, ed., David St. John, po. ed., P.O. Box 148, Yellow Springs, OH 45387. Issues indexed: (46:1-4). Subscriptions: $20/yr. (4 issues), $38/2 yrs., $54/3 yrs. (ind.); $30/yr., $58/2 yrs., $86/3 yrs. (inst.); plus $5/yr. (for.); Single issues: $5.

Areíto: AREÍTO, Andrés Gómez, Director, P.O. Box 44-1403, Miami, FL 33144. Issues indexed: Segunda Epoca (1:2-4). Subscriptions: $20/yr. (inst.), $30/yr. (for. inst.), $12/yr. (ind)., $18/yr. (ind. for.).

ArizQ: ARIZONA QUARTERLY, Albert Frank Gegenheimer, ed., U. of Arizona, Main Library B-541, Tucson, AZ 85721. Issues indexed: (41:1). No further issues will be indexed: "Under a change of editorial policy and staff, Arizona Quarterly is now exclusively a journal of American literature, culture and theory, and will no longer publish poetry or fiction" -- 21 May 1989. Subscriptions: $10/3 yrs., $5/yr.; Single issues: $1.50.

*ArtfulD: ARTFUL DODGE, Daniel Bourne, ed., Dept. of English, College of Wooster, Wooster, OH 44691. Issues indexed: (14/15). Subscriptions: $10/4 issues (ind.), $16/4 issues (inst.); Soingle issues: $5.

Ascent: ASCENT, Daniel Curley, et al ., eds., English Dept., U. of Illinois, 608 South Wright St., Urbana, IL 61801. Issues indexed: (13:2-3, 14:1-2). Subscriptions: $3/yr. (3 issues), $4.50/yr. (for.); Single issues: $1 (bookstore), $1.50 (mail).

Atlantic: THE ATLANTIC, William Whitworth, ed., Peter Davison, po. ed., 8 Arlington St., Boston, MA 02116. Issues indexed: (261:1-6, 262:1-6). Subscriptions: $14.95/yr., $27.95/2 yrs., $39.95/3 yrs., plus $4/yr. (Canada), $6/yr. (for.); Single issues: $2. Subscription address: Atlantic Subscription Processing Center, Box 2547, Boulder, CO 80322.

BallSUF: BALL STATE UNIVERSITY FORUM, Bruce W. Hozeski, ed., Darlene Mathis-Eddy, po. ed., Ball State U., Muncie, IN 47306. Issues indexed: (29:1-4). Subscriptions: $20/yr. (4 issues), Single issues: $6.

BambooR: BAMBOO RIDGE: The Hawaii Writers' Quarterly, Eric Chock, Darrell H. Y Lum, eds., P.O. Box 61781, Honolulu, HI 96822-8781. Issues indexed: (37/38-39/40). Subscriptions: $12/yr., $22/2 yrs., $30/3 yrs.; Single issues, $3-$9.

BellArk: BELLOWING ARK, Robert R. Ward, ed., P.O. Box 45637, Seattle, WA 98145. Issues indexed: (4:1-6). Subscriptions: $12/yr., $20/2 yrs.; Single issues: $2.

BellR: THE BELLINGHAM REVIEW, Shelley Rozen, ed., P.O. Box 4065, Bellingham, WA 98227. Issues indexed: (11:1-2). Subscriptions: $4/yr. (2 issues), $7.50/2 yrs., $10.50/3 yrs.; Single issues: $2.

BelPoJ: THE BELOIT POETRY JOURNAL, Marion K. Stocking, ed., RFD 2, Box 154, Ellsworth, ME 04605. Issues indexed: (38:3-4, 39:1-2). Subscriptions: $8/yr. (4 issues, ind.), $22/3 yrs.; $12/yr., $33/3 yrs. (inst.); plus $2.96/yr. (Canada), $3.20 (for.); Single issues: $2-5.

BilingR: THE BILINGUAL REVIEW / LA REVISTA BILINGÜE, Gary D. Keller, ed., Hispanic Research Center, Arizona State U., Tempe, AZ 85287. Issues indexed: (13:1/2), Ja-Ag 86, c1988. Subscriptions: $15/yr., $28/2 yrs., $39/3 yrs. (ind.); $24/yr. (inst.).

BlackALF: BLACK AMERICAN LITERATURE FORUM, Division on Black American Literature and Culture, Modern Language Association, Joe Weixlmann, ed., Thadious David, Pinkie Gordon Lane, Sterling Plumpp, po. eds., Parsons Hall 237, Indiana State U., Terre Haute, IN 47809. Issues indexed: (22:1-4). Subscriptions: $17/yr. (ind.), $25/yr. (inst.), $21/yr. (for.), $29 (for. inst.). Single issues: $6.50.

BlackWR: BLACK WARRIOR REVIEW, Jeff Mock, ed., Michelle Elise, po. ed., U. of Alabama, P.O. Box 2936, Tuscaloosa, AL 35487-2936. Issues indexed: (14:2, 15:1). Subscriptions: $7.50/yr. (ind.), $11/yr. (inst.); Single issues: $4.

BlueBldgs: BLUE BUILDINGS: An International Magazine of Poetry and Translations, Tom Urban, Ruth Doty, Michaela Haberkern, David Smith, Cathy Colver, eds., Dept. of English, Drake U., Des Moines, IA 50311. Issues indexed: No 1988 issues published. Subscriptions: $4/2 issues; Single issues: $2; Back issues: $1.50.

Blueline: BLUELINE, Anthony Tyler, ed., English Dept., Potsdam College, SUNY, Potsdam, NY 13676. Issues indexed: (9:1/2]). Subscriptions: $6/yr., $10/2 yrs.; Single issues: $5.75.

Bogg: BOGG, John Elsberg, ed., 422 N. Cleveland St., Arlington, VA 22201. Issues indexed: (59-60). Subscriptions: $10/3 issues; Single issues: $4.

Bomb: BOMB MAGAZINE, Betsy Sussler, ed. & pub., Roland Legiardi-Laura, po. ed., New Art Publications, P.O. Box 2003, Canal Station, New York, NY 10013. Issues indexed: (22-26). Subscriptions: $18/yr., $35/2 yrs.; $26/yr. (for.); Single issues: $5.

BostonR: BOSTON REVIEW, Margaret Ann Roth, ed. & pub., 33 Harrison Ave., Boston, MA 02111. Issues indexed: (13:1-6). Subscriptions: $12/yr., $20/2 yrs. (ind.); $15/yr., $25/2 yrs. (inst.); plus $6/yr. (for.); Single issues: $3.

Boulevard: BOULEVARD, David Brezovic, executive ed., Richard Burgin, ed., Opojaz, Inc., 4 Washington Square Village #9-R, New York, NY 10012. Issues indexed: (3:2/3). Subscriptions: $12/yr., $20/2 yrs., $25/3 yrs.; Single issues: $4-$4.50.

Bound: BOUNDARY 2, William V. Spanos, ed., Dept. of English, State U. of New York, Binghamton, NY 13901. Issues indexed: (15:3/16:1). Subscriptions: $25/yr. (inst.), $15/yr. (ind.), $13/yr (stud.), plus $2 (for.); Single issues: $8, Double issues: $10.

Caliban: CALIBAN, Lawrence R. Smith, ed., P.O. Box 4321, Ann Arbor, MI 48106. Issues indexed: (4-5). Subscriptions: $8/yr., 2 issues (ind.), $15/yr. (inst.); $11/yr. (ind.), $15/yr. (inst.), Canadian currency; $12/yr. (for. ind.), $21/yr. (for. inst.). Single issues: $5.

Callaloo: CALLALOO: A Journal of Afro-American and African Arts and Letters, Charles H. Rowell, ed., Dept. of English, Wilson Hall, U. of Virginia, Charlottesville, VA 22903. Issues indexed: (10:4, 11:1-4; #33-37). Subscriptions: $18/yr. (ind.), $38/yr. (inst.); plus $5.00 (Canada, Mexico); plus $11 (outside North America); The Johns Hopkins University Press, Journals Publishing Division, 701 W. 40th St., Suite 275, Baltimore, MD 21211.

CalQ: CALIFORNIA QUARTERLY, Elliot L. Gilbert, ed., Carlos Rodriguez, po. ed., 100 Sproul Hall, U. of California, Davis, CA 95616. Issues indexed: No 1988 issues received. Subscriptions: $10/yr. (4 issues); Single issues: $2.50.

Calyx: CALYX: A Journal of Art and Literature by Women, Margarita Donnelly, Lisa Domitrovich, Managing eds., P.O. Box B, Corvallis, OR 97339-0539. Issues indexed: (10:2/3, 11:1). Subscriptions: $18/yr., $32/2 yrs., $42/3 yrs., plus $4/yr. (for.), $9/yr. (for. airmail); $22.50/yr. (inst.); $15/yr. (low income individual); Single issue: $6.50-$12.

CanLit: CANADIAN LITERATURE, W. H. New, ed., U. of British Columbia, 2029 West Mall, Vancouver, B.C. V6T 1W5 Canada. Issues indexed: (117-119). Subscriptions: $25/yr. (ind.), $30/yr. (inst.) plus $5/yr. outside Canada; Single issues: $7.50.

CapeR: THE CAPE ROCK, Harvey Hecht, ed., Southeast Missouri State U., Cape Girardeau, MO 63701. Issues indexed: (23:1-2). Subscriptions: $3/yr. (2 issues); Single issues: $2.

CapilR: THE CAPILANO REVIEW, Dorothy Jantzen, ed., Sharon Thesen, po. ed., Capilano College, 2055 Purcell Way, North Vancouver, B.C. V7J 3H5 Canada. Issues indexed: (46-49). Subscriptions: $22/8 issues (ind.), $12/4 issues (ind.), $14/4 issues (lib.); plus $1/4 issues (for.); Single issues: $5.

Periodicals Indexed

CarolQ: CAROLINA QUARTERLY, Allison Bulsterbaum, ed., Jon Wike, po. ed., Greenlaw Hall CB#3520, U. of North Carolina, Chapel Hill, NC 27599-3520. Issues indexed: (40:2-3, 41:1). Subscriptions: $12/yr. (3 issues) (inst.), $10/yr. (ind.), $11/yr. (for.); Single issues: $4, plus $1 postage.

CentR: THE CENTENNIAL REVIEW, Linda Wagner-Martin, ed., 110 Morril Hall, Michigan State U., East Lansing, MI 48824-1036. Issues indexed: (32:1-4). Subscriptions: $7/yr., $10/2 yrs., plus $3/yr. (for.); Single issues: $2.

CentralP: CENTRAL PARK, Stephen-Paul Martin, Richard Royal, Eve Ensler, eds., Box 1446, New York, NY 10023. Issues indexed: (13-14). Subscriptions: $9/yr., 2 issues (ind.), $10/yr. (inst.); Single issues: $5 (ind), $5.50 (inst).

*ChamLR: CHAMINADE LITERARY REVIEW, Loretta Petrie, ed., Jim Kraus, po. ed., Chaminade U. of Honolulu, 3140 Waialae Ave., Honolulu, HI 96816. Issues indexed: (1:1-1, 2:1; #1-3). Subscriptions: $10/yr.; $18/2 yrs.; plus $2 (for.).; Single issues: $5.

CharR: THE CHARITON REVIEW, Jim Barnes, ed., Division of Language and Literature, Northeast Missouri State U., Kirksville, MO 63501. Issues indexed: (14:1-2). Subscriptions: $9/4 issues; Single issues: $2.50.

ChatR: THE CHATTAHOOCHEE REVIEW, Lamar York, ed., DeKalb College, 2101 Womack Road, Dunwoody, GA 30338-4497. Issues indexed: (8:2-4, 9:1). Subscriptions: $15/yr. (4 issues), $25/2 yrs.; Single issues: $3.50.

Chelsea: CHELSEA, Sonia Raiziss, ed., P.O. Box 5880, Grand Central Station, New York, NY 10163. Issues indexed: (47). Subscriptions: $11/2 issues or double issue, $13 (for.); Single issues: $6, $7 (for.).

ChiR: CHICAGO REVIEW, Elizabeth Arnold, Jenny Mueller, eds., Paul Baker, Jane Hoogestraat, po. eds., 5801 South Kenwood, Chicago, IL 60637. Issues indexed: (36:1-2). Subscriptions: $14/ yr. (ind.), $18/yr. (inst.); $36/2 yrs., $54/3 yrs., plus $4/yr. (for.); Single issues: $4.50.

ChrC: THE CHRISTIAN CENTURY, James M. Wall, ed., 407 S. Dearborn St., Chicago, IL 60605. Issues indexed: (105:1-39). Subscriptions: $28/yr.; Single issues: $1.50.

CimR: CIMARRON REVIEW, John Kenny Crane, ed., Nuala Archer, Rochelle Owens, po. eds., 205 Morrill Hall, Oklahoma State U., Stillwater, OK 74078-0135. Issues indexed: (82-85). Subscriptions: $12/yr., $15 (Canada); $30/3 yrs., $40 (Canada); plus $2.50/yr. (for.); Single issues: $3.

*CinPR: CINCINNATI POETRY REVIEW, Dallas Wiebe, ed., Department of English, U. of Cincinnati, Cincinnati, OH 45221. Issues indexed: (17-18). Subscriptions: $9/4 issues; Single issues: $3.

ClockR: CLOCKWATCH REVIEW: A Journal of the Arts, James Plath, ed., 737 Penbrook Way, Hartland, WI 53029. Issues indexed: (4:2). Subscriptions: $6/yr.; Single issues: $3.

ColEng: COLLEGE ENGLISH, National Council of Teachers of English, James C. Raymond, ed., James Tate, po. ed., P.O. Drawer AL, Tuscaloosa, AL 35487. Issues indexed: (50:1-8). Subscriptions: $40/yr. (inst.), $35/yr. (ind.), plus $4/yr. (for.); Single issues: $4.50; NCTE, 1111 Kenyon Rd., Urbana, IL 61801.

ColR: COLORADO REVIEW, Bill Tremblay, ed., English Dept., Colorado State U., 360 Eddy Bldg., Fort Collins, CO 80523. Issues indexed: (NS 15:1-2). Subscriptions: $9/yr. (2 issues), $17.50/2 yrs.; Single issues: $5.

Colum: COLUMBIA: A Magazine of Poetry & Prose, Jill Birdsall, Peter B. Erdmann, eds., Lucy Logsdon, po. eds., 404 Dodge Hall, Columbia Univ., New York, NY 10027. Issues indexed: (13). Subscriptions: $4.50/yr.

Comm: COMMONWEAL, Margaret O'Brien Steinfels, ed., Rosemary Deen, po. ed., 15 Dutch St., New York, NY 10038. Issues indexed: (115:1-22). Subscriptions: $32/yr., $34/yr. (Canada), $37/yr. (for.); $57/2 yrs., $61/2 yrs. (Canada), $67/2 yrs. (for.), ; Single issues: $1.50.

Cond: CONDITIONS: A Feminist Magazine of Writing by Women with an Emphasis on Writing by Lesbians, Cheryl Clarke, Melinda Goodman, Dorothy Randall Gray, Pam A. Parker, Mariana Romo-Carmona, eds., P.O. Box 159046, Van Brunt Station, Brooklyn, NY 11215-9046. Issues indexed: (15). Subscriptions: $24/3 issues (ind.), $34/3 issues (inst.), $32 (for.); Single issues: $8.95 (ind.), $10.95 (inst.); Back issues: $7-10.

Confr: CONFRONTATION, Martin Tucker, ed., English Dept., C. W. Post Campus of Long Island U., Brookville, NY 11548. Issues indexed: (37/38, plus special issue *The World of Brooklyn*). Subscriptions: $10/yr., $20/2 yrs., $30/3 yrs.; Single issues: $6-7.

Conjunc: CONJUNCTIONS: Bi-Annual Volumes of New Writing, Bradford Morrow, ed., 33 West 9th St., New York, NY 10011. Issues indexed: (12). Subscriptions: $16/yr. (2 issues), $30/2 yrs.; $20/yr., $40/2 yrs. (inst., for.); $45/yr., $85/ 2 yrs. (cloth binding); Single issues: $9.95.

ConnPR: THE CONNECTICUT POETRY REVIEW, J. Clair White, James Wm. Chichetto, eds., P.O. Box 3783, Amity Station, New Haven, CT 06525. Issues indexed: (7:1). Single issues: $3 (including postage).

Contact: CONTACT II: A Poetry Review, Maurice Kenny, J. G. Gosciak, eds., P.O. Box 451, Bowling Green, New York, NY 10004. Issues indexed: (9:47/48/49). Subscriptions: $8/yr. (ind.); $14/yr. (inst.); Single issues: $6.

CrabCR: CRAB CREEK REVIEW, Linda Clifton, ed., 4462 Whitman Ave. N., Seattle WA 98103. Issues indexed: (5:1-3). Subscriptions: $8/yr., $15/2 yrs.; Single issues: $3.

Crazy: CRAZYHORSE, Zabelle Derounian, managing ed., Ralph Burns, po. ed., Dept. of English, U. of Arkansas, Little Rock, AR 72204. Issues indexed: (34-35). Subscriptions: $8/yr., $15/2 yrs., $22/3 yrs. Single issues: $4.

CreamCR: CREAM CITY REVIEW, Ron Tanner, ed., Renee Deljon, Mary Anne Gavin, po. ed., Dept. of English, U. of Wisconsin, P.O. Box 413, Milwaukee, WI 53201. Issues indexed: (12:1-2). Subscriptions: $8/yr. (2 issues), $14/2 yrs.; Single issues: $4; Double issues: $5.

CrescentR: THE CRESCENT REVIEW, Guy Neal Williams, ed., P.O. Box 15065, Winston-Salem, NC 27113. Issues indexed: (6:1). Subscriptions: $7.50/yr. (2 issues); Single issues: $4.

CrossC: CROSS-CANADA WRITERS' MAGAZINE, Ted Plantos, ed., George Swede, po. ed., Box 277, Station F, Toronto, Ontario M4Y 2L7 Canada. Issues indexed: (10:1-3). Subscriptions: $12/yr., $20/2 yrs. (ind.); $18/yr. (for. inst.), $21/yr (for.); Single issues: $3.

CrossCur: CROSSCURRENTS, Linda Brown Michelson, ed., Elizabeth Bartlett, po. ed., 2200 Glastonbury Road, Westlake Village, CA 91361. Issues indexed: (7:4, 8:1). Subscriptions: $15/yr., $22.50/2 yrs.; Single issues: $6.

CuadP: CUADERNOS DE POÉTICA, Diógenes Céspedes, Director, Apartado Postal 1736, Santo Domingo, República Dominicana; US Editors: Kate Nickel, 111 Oldfather Hall, U. of Nebraska, Lincoln, NE 68588-0315, Rafael Catalá, P.O. Box 450, Corrales, NM 87048. Issues indexed: (5:14-16). Subscriptions: $25/yr. (ind.), $30/yr. (inst.).

CumbPR: CUMBERLAND POETRY REVIEW, Ingram Bloch, Bob Darrell, Sherry Bevins Darrell, Malcolm Glass, Jeanne Gore, Thomas Heine, Michael Kreyling, Laurence Lerner, Alison Reed, Eva Touster, eds., Poetics, Inc., P.O. Box 120128, Acklen Station, Nashville, TN 37212. Issues indexed: (7:2, 8:1). Subscriptions: $12/yr, $22/2 yrs. (ind.); $15/yr., $27/2 yrs. (inst.); $21/yr., $33/2 yrs. (for.); Single issue: $6.

Periodicals Indexed

CutB: CUTBANK, Piper, Paul S. ed., Dept. of English, U. of Montana, Missoula, MT 59812. Issues indexed: (29/30-31/32). Subscriptions: $9/yr.

Dandel: DANDELION, Robert Hilles, managing eds., Claire Harris, John McDowell, po eds., Alexandra Centre, 922 - 9th Ave., S.E., Calgary, Alberta T2G 0S4 Canada. Issues indexed: (15:1-2). Subscriptions: $10/yr. (2 issues), $18/2 yrs.;$15/yr. (inst.); Single issues: $5.

DeKalbLAJ: THE DEKALB LITERARY ARTS JOURNAL, Frances S. Ellis, ed., DeKalb College, 555 N. Indian Creek Dr., Clarkston, GA 30021. Issues indexed: (21:1-3/4). Subscriptions: $15/volume, $17/volume (for.); Single issues: $5.

DenQ: DENVER QUARTERLY, Donald Revell, ed., U. of Denver, Denver, CO 80208. Issues indexed: (22:2-4, 23:1-2). Subscriptions: $15/yr., $18/yr. (inst.); $28/2 yrs.; plus $1/yr. (for.); Single issues: $5.

Descant: DESCANT, Karen Mulhallen, ed., P.O. Box 314, Station P, Toronto M5S 2S8, Ontario, Canada. Issues indexed: (19:1-4, issues 60-63). Subscriptions: $21/yr., $38/2 yrs. (ind.); $29/yr., $58/2 yrs. (inst.); plus $4/yr. (for.); Single issues: $7.50-$9.95.

Electrum: ELECTRUM MAGAZINE, Roger Suva, ed., 2222 Silk Tree Drive, Tustin, CA 92680-7129. Issues indexed: No 1988 issues received. Subscriptions: $10/4 issues, $17/8 issues, plus $5 (for.); Single issues: $3.

EngJ: ENGLISH JOURNAL, National Council of Teachers of English, Ben F. Nelms, ed., 215-216 Townsend Hall, U. of Missouri, Columbia, MO 65211; Paul Janeczko, po. ed., P.O. Box 1079, Gray, ME 04039. Issues indexed: (77:1-8). Subscriptions: $40/yr. (inst.), $35/yr. (ind.), plus $4/yr. (for.); Single issues: $4.50; NCTE, 1111 Kenyon Rd., Urbana, IL 61801.

Epoch: EPOCH, C. S. Giscombe, ed., 251 Goldwin Smith Hall, Cornell U., Ithaca, NY 14853-3201. Issues indexed: (37:1-3). Subscriptions: $9.50/yr.; Single issues: $3.50.

Event: EVENT: The Douglas College Review, Dale Zieroth, ed., Douglas College, P.O. Box 2503, New Westminster, B.C., V3L 5B2 Canada. Issues indexed: (17:1-3). Subscriptions: $9/yr., $17/2 yrs.; $17/2 yrs. (lib.); Single issue: $4.

Farm: FARMER'S MARKET, Jean C. Lee, John E. Hughes, Gail Nichols, Susan Swartwout, eds., Midwest Farmer's Market, Inc., P.O. Box 1272, Galesburg, IL 61402. Issues indexed: (5:1-2); 5:1 has "Vol. 4, No. 1" on cover. Subscriptions: $7/yr. (2 issues).

Field: FIELD: Contemporary Poetry and Poetics, Stuart Friebert, David Young, eds., Rice Hall, Oberlin College, Oberlin, OH 44074. Issues indexed: (38-39). Subscriptions: $10/yr., $16/2 yrs.; Single issues: $5.; Back issues: $10.

FiveFR: FIVE FINGERS REVIEW, Lori Callies, Elizabeth Claman, Carol Dorf, John High, Clifford Hunt, eds., 553 - 25th Ave., San Francisco, CA 94121. Issues indexed: (6). Subscriptions: $20/4 issues, $11/2 issues, plus $5 (for.); Single issues: $7.

FloridaR: THE FLORIDA REVIEW, Pat Rushin, ed., Tom George, po. ed., Dept. of English, U. of Central Florida, Orlando, FL 32816. Issues indexed: (16:1). Subscriptions: $7/yr., $11/2 yrs.; Single issues: $4.50.

Footwork: FOOTWORK, A Literary Collection of Contemporary Poetry, Short Fiction, and Art, Maria Gillan, ed., Passaic County Community College, College Boulevard, Paterson, NJ 07509. Issues indexed: (1988). Subscriptions: $5/issue + $1 for postage and handling.

FourQ: FOUR QUARTERS, John J. Keenan, ed., La Salle U., Philadelphia, PA 19141. Issues indexed: Second Series (2:1-2). Subscriptions: $8/yr. (2 issues), $13/2 yrs.; Single issues: $4.

Gambit: GAMBIT MAGAZINE: A Journal of the Ohio Valley, a joint publication of the Ohio Valley Literary Group and Parkersburg Community College, Jane Somerville, ed., P.O. Box 1122, Marietta, OH 45750. Issues Indexed: (22). Single issues: $3.

Gargoyle: GARGOYLE MAGAZINE, Richard Peabody, Peggy Pfeiffer, eds., Paycock Press, P.O. Box 30906, Bethesda, MD 20814. Issues indexed: (35); (34) was not received. Subscriptions: $15/2 issues (ind.), $20/2 issues (inst.). Single issues: $5.95-7.95.

GeoR: GEORGIA REVIEW, Stanley W. Lindberg, ed., U. of Georgia, Athens, GA 30602. Issues indexed: (41:1-4). Subscriptions: $12/ yr., $20/2 yrs., plus $3/yr. (for.); Single issues: $5, $6 (for.).

Germ: GERMINATION, Allan Cooper, ed. & pub., Leigh Faulkner, Assoc. ed., 428 Yale Ave., Riverview, New Brunswick E1B 2B5, Canada. Issues indexed: No 1988 issues received. Subscriptions: $6/2 issues (ind.), $8/2 issues (inst.); Single issues: $3.50.

*GettyR: GETTYSBURG REVIEW, Peter Stitt, ed., Gettysburg College, Gettysburg, PA 17325-1491. Issues indexed: (1:1-4). Subscriptions: $12/yr., $22/2 yrs., $30/3 yrs., plus $4 (for.); Single issues: $4.

GrahamHR: GRAHAM HOUSE REVIEW, Peter Balakian & Bruce Smith, eds., Colgate U. Press, Box 5000, Colgate U., Hamilton, NY 13346; Issues indexed: (11). Subscriptions: $17/2 yrs; Single issues: $4.50.

Grain: GRAIN, Saskatchewan Writers Guild, Mick Burrs, ed., Mary Shepperd, po. ed., Box 1154, Regina, Saskatchewan S4P 3B4 Canada. Issues indexed: (16:1-4). Subscriptions: $12/yr., $20/2 yrs.; Single issues: $4.

GrandS: GRAND STREET, Ben Sonnenberg, ed., 50 Riverside Dr., New York, NY 10024. Issues indexed: (7:2-4, 8:1). Subscriptions: $24/yr. (ind.), $28/yr. (for.); $28/yr. (inst.), $32/yr. (for. inst.); Single issues: $6; Back issues, $8.

GreensboroR: THE GREENSBORO REVIEW, Jim Clark, ed., Martha Zettlemoyer, po. ed., Dept. of English, U. of North Carolina, Greensboro, NC 27412. Issues indexed: (44-45). Subscriptions: $5/yr. (2 issues), $12/3 yrs.; Single issues: $2.50.

HampSPR: THE HAMPDEN-SYDNEY POETRY REVIEW, Tom O'Grady, ed., P.O. Box 126, Hampden-Sydney, VA 23943. Issues indexed: 1988. Subscriptions: $5/yr. (single issue).

HangL: HANGING LOOSE, Robert Hershon, Dick Lourie, Mark Pawlak, Ron Schreiber, eds., 231 Wyckoff St., Brooklyn, NY 11217. Issues indexed: (52-53). Subscriptions: $9/3 issues, $17.50/6 issues, $25/9 issues (ind.); $10.50/3 issues, $21/6 issues, $31.50/9 issues (inst.); Single issues: $3.50 plus $1 postage and handling.

Harp: HARPER'S MAGAZINE, Lewis H. Lapham, ed., 666 Broadway, New York, NY 10012. Issues indexed: (276:1652-1657, 277:1658-1663). Subscriptions: $18/yr., plus $2/yr. (USA possessions, Canada), plus $3/yr. (for.); Single issues: $2; P.O. Box 1937, Marion, OH 43305.

HarvardA: THE HARVARD ADVOCATE, Emily Greenley, Managing ed., Andrew Osborn, po. ed., 21 South St., Cambridge, MA 02138. Issues indexed: (122:3-4, 123:1, plus New Yorker spoof issue). Subscriptions: $15/yr. (ind.), $17/yr. (inst.), $20/yr. (for.).

HawaiiR: HAWAII REVIEW, Jeannie Thompson, ed., Zdenek Kluzak, po. ed., U. of Hawaii at Manoa, Dept. of English, 1733 Donaghho Rd., Honolulu, HI 06822. Issues indexed: (12:1-2, #23-24). Subscriptions: $6/yr. (2 issues); Single issue: $4.

HayF: HAYDEN'S FERRY REVIEW, Becky Turnbull, Managing ed., Kevin Dobbs, Susan L. Krevitsky, Gary Short, po. eds., Student Publications, Matthews Center, Arizona State U., Tempe, AZ 85287. Issues indexed: (3). Subscriptions: $5/yr. (1 issue) plus $1 postage & handling.

HeliconN: HELICON NINE: The Journal of Women's Arts & Letters, Gloria Vando Hickok, ed., P.O. Box 22412, Kansas City, MO 64113. Issues indexed: (19). Subscriptions: $18/yr. (3 issues), $33/2 yrs., $22/yr. (inst)., plus $1/issue (for.); Single issues: $8-12.

HighP: HIGH PLAINS LITERARY REVIEW, Robert O. Greer, Jr., ed., Joy Harjo, po. ed., 180 Adams St., Suite 250, Denver, CO 80206. Issues indexed: (3:1-3). Subscriptions: $20/yr. (3 issues), $38/2 yrs., plus $5/yr. (for.); Single issues: $7.

HiramPoR: HIRAM POETRY REVIEW, English Dept., Hiram College, Hale Chatfield & Carol Donley, eds., P.O. Box 162, Hiram, OH 44234. Issues indexed: (44/45) plus supplements #8-9. Subscriptions: $4/yr. (2 issues); Single issues: $2; Supplements, $4.

HolCrit: THE HOLLINS CRITIC, John Rees Moore, ed., Hollins College, VA 24020. Issues indexed: (25:1-5). Subscriptions: $6/yr., $10/2 yrs., $14/3 yrs.; $7.50/yr., $11.50/2 yrs., $15.50/3 yrs. (for.).

Hudson: THE HUDSON REVIEW, Paula Deitz, Frederick Morgan, eds., 684 Park Ave., New York, NY 10021. Issues indexed: (40:4, 41:1-3). Subscriptions: $20/yr., $38/2 yrs., $56/3 yrs., plus $4/yr. (for.); Single issues: $6; Recent back issues: $5.

IndR: INDIANA REVIEW, Kim McKinney, ed., Donna Strickland, Rick Madigan, Joe Like, po. eds., 316 N. Jordan Ave., Bloomington, IN 47405. Issues indexed: (11:2-3, 12:1). Subscriptions: $10/3 issues, $12/3 issues (inst.); $18/6 issues (ind.), $20/6 issues (inst.); plus $5/3 issues (for.). Single issues: $4.

Interim: INTERIM, A. Wilber Stevens, ed., Dept. of English, U. of Nevada, Las Vegas, NV 89154. Issues indexed: (7:1-2). Subscriptions: $5/yr. (2 issues), $8/2 yrs., $10/3 yrs. (ind.); $8/yr. (lib.), $10/yr. (for.); Single issues: $3, $5 (for.).

InterPR: INTERNATIONAL POETRY REVIEW, Evalyn P. Gill, ed., Box 2047, Greensboro, NC 27402. Issues indexed: (14:1-2). Subscriptions: $7/yr. (2 issues); Single issues: $3.50.

Inti: INTI, Revista de Literatura Hispánica, Roger B. Carmosino, ed., Dept. of Modern Languages, Providence College, Providence, RI 02918. Issues indexed: (26/27, 28). Subscriptions: $20/yr. (2 issues, ind.), $25/yr. (for.); $30/yr. (inst.); Single issues: $15, $25 (double issues).

Iowa: IOWA REVIEW, David Hamilton, ed., 308 EPB, U. of Iowa, Iowa City, IA 52242. Issues indexed: (18:1-3). Subscriptions: $15/yr. (3 issues, ind.), $20/yr. (inst.), plus $3/yr. (for.); Single issues: $6.95.

Jacaranda: THE JACARANDA REVIEW, Cornel Bonca, ed., Dept. of English, U. of California, Los Angeles, 90024. Issues indexed: (3:1-2). Subscriptions: $8/yr. (2 issues, ind.), $12/yr. (inst.).

JamesWR: THE JAMES WHITE REVIEW, A Gay Men's Literary Journal, Greg Baysans, David Lindahl, eds., P.O. Box 3356, Traffic Station, Minneapolis, MN 55403. Issues indexed: (5:2-3, 6:1). Subscriptions: $10/yr., $17/2 yrs.; $12/yr. (Canada); $15/yr. (other for.); Single issues: $2.50; Back issues, $3.

JlNJPo: THE JOURNAL OF NEW JERSEY POETS, Sander Zulauf, ed., County College of Morris, Route 10 & Center Grove Rd., Randolph, NJ 07869. Issues indexed: (10:1/2). Subscriptions: $5/2 issues; Single issues: $4.

Kaleid: KALEIDOSCOPE, International Magazine of Literature, Fine Arts, and Disability, Darshan Perusek, ed., Chris Hewitt (228 W. 71 St., Apt. F, New York, NY 10023), po. ed., United Cerebral Palsy and Services for the Handicapped, 326 Locust St., Akron, OH 44302. Issues indexed: (16-17). Subscriptions: $8/yr. (2 issues, ind.), $10/yr. (inst.), plus $4/yr. (for.); Single issues: $4, $6 (for.); Sample issue: $2.

KanQ: KANSAS QUARTERLY, Harold Schneider, Ben Nyberg, W. R. Moses, John Rees, eds., Dept. of English, Denison Hall, Kansas State U., Manhattan, KS 66506. Issues indexed: (20:1/2-4). Subscriptions: $20/yr., $35/2 yrs. (USA, Canada, Latin America); $21/yr., $37/2 yrs. (other countries); Single issues: $5; Double issues: $7.50.

KenR: KENYON REVIEW, T. R. Hummer, ed., Kenyon College, Gambier, OH 43022. Issues indexed: (NS 10:1-4). Subscriptions: Kenyon Review, P.O. Box 1308 L, Fort Lee, NJ 07024; $15/yr., $28/2 yrs., $39/3 yrs. (ind.); $18/yr. (inst.); plus $5 (for.); Single issues: $6.50; Back issues: $10.

*KeyWR: KEY WEST REVIEW, William J. Schlicht, Jr., ed., 9 Ave. G, Key West, FL 33040. Issues indexed: (1:1-2). Subscriptions: $18/yr. (4 issues); Single issues: $5.

Lactuca: LACTUCA, Mike Selender, ed., P.O. Box 621, Suffern, NY 10901. Issues indexed: (9-11). Subscriptions: $10/yr. (3 issues), plus $4/yr. (for.); Single issues: $3.50, plus $1 (for.).

LakeSR: THE LAKE STREET REVIEW, Kevin FitzPatrick, ed., Box 7188, Minneapolis, MN 55407. Issues indexed: (22). Subscriptions: $4/2 yrs. (2 issues); Single issues: $2.

LaurelR: LAUREL REVIEW, Craig Goad, ed., Green Tower Press, Dept. of English, Northwest Missouri State U., Maryville, MO 64468. Issues indexed: (22:1-2). Subscriptions: $8/yr. (2 issues), $14/2 yrs.; Single issues: $4.50.

LetFem: LETRAS FEMENINAS, Asociación de Literatura Femenina Hispánica, Adelaida López de Martínez, ed., Dept. of Modern Languages, U. of Nebraska-Lincoln, Lincoln, NE 68588-0315. Issues indexed: 14:1/2. Membership/Subscription: $20/yr; $25/yr. (lib.).

LightY: LIGHT YEAR: The Biennial of Light Verse & Witty Poems, Robert Wallace, ed., Bits Press, Dept. of English, Case Western Reserve U., Cleveland, OH 44106. Issues indexed: ('88/9). Subscriptions: '87, $13.95; '88/9, $15.95.

LindLM: LINDEN LANE MAGAZINE, Heberto Padilla, Belkis Cuza Malé, eds., P.O. Box 2384, Princeton, NJ 08543-2384. Issues indexed: (7:1-2/4). Subscriptions: $12/yr. (ind.), $18/yr. (inst.), $22/yr. (Latin America), $20/yr. (Europe); Single issues: $2.

Lips: LIPS, Laura Boss, ed., P.O. Box 1345, Montclair, NJ 07042. Issues indexed: (14). Subscriptions: $9/yr. (3 issues), $12/yr. (inst).; Single issues: $3, $4 (inst.).

LitR: THE LITERARY REVIEW, Walter Cummins, ed., Fairleigh Dickinson U., 285 Madison Ave., Madison, NJ 07940. Issues indexed: (31:2-4, 32:1). Subscriptions: $18/yr., $21/yr. (for.); $30/2 yrs., $36/2 yrs. (for.); Single issues: $5, $6 (for.).

*LittleBR: THE LITTLE BALKANS REVIEW: A Southeast Kansas Literary and Graphics Quarterly, Gene DeGruson, ed., 601 Grandview Heights Terrace, Pittsburgh, KS 66762. Issues indexed: (5:2). Subscriptions: $15/yr.; Single issues: $4.

LittleM: THE LITTLE MAGAZINE, Kathryn Cramer, et al ., eds, Dragon Press, P.O. Box 78, Pleasantville, NY 10570. Issues Indexed: (15:3/4) "last issue".

Lyra: LYRA, Lourdes Gil, Iraida Iturralde, eds., P.O. Box 3188, Guttenberg, NJ 07093. Issues indexed: (1:3-4). Subscriptions: $15/yr. (4 issues, ind.), $20/yr. (inst.), plus $5/yr. (for.); Single issues: $4, $6 (for.).

Mairena: MAIRENA: Revista de Crítica y Poesía, Manuel de la Puebla, director, Himalaya 257, Urbanización Monterrey, Río Piedras, PR 00926. Issues indexed: (10:25). Subscriptions: $6/yr., $10/yr. (inst.), $10/yr. (for.), $15/yr. (for. inst.).

MalR: THE MALAHAT REVIEW, Constance Rooke, ed., P.O. Box 1700, Victoria, B. C., Canada V8W 2Y2. Issues indexed: (82-85). Subscriptions: $15/yr., $40/3 yrs., (ind., USA, Canada); $25/yr. (inst., USA, Canada); $20/yr., $50/3 yrs. (other countries); $10/yr. (stud., USA, Canada); Single issues: $7 (USA, Canada), $8 (other countries).

ManhatPR: MANHATTAN POETRY REVIEW, Elaine Reiman-Fenton, ed., P.O. Box 8207, New York, NY 10150. Issues indexed: (10). Subscriptions: $12/yr. (2 issues); Single issues: $7.

ManhatR: THE MANHATTAN REVIEW, Philip Fried, ed., 304 Third Ave., Suite 4A, New York, NY 10010. Issues indexed: (4:2). Subscriptions: $8/2 issues (ind.), $12/2 issues (inst.), plus $2.50/2 issues (outside USA & Canada); Back issues: $4 (ind.), $6 (inst).

Margin: MARGIN: A Quarterly Magazine for Imaginative Writing and Ideas, Robin Magowan, ed., James Magowan, USA ed., 46 Shepard St., #42, Cambridge, MA 02138. Issues indexed: (6-7). Subscriptions: $20/4 issues; $24/4 issues (Canada); Single issues: $7.

MassR: THE MASSACHUSETTS REVIEW, Mary Heath, PAUL JENKINS, Fred Robinson, eds., Anne Halley, Paul Jenkins, po. eds., Memorial Hall, U. of Massachusetts, Amherst, MA 01003. Issues indexed: (29:1-4). Subscriptions: $12/yr. (ind.), $15/yr. (lib.), $17/yr. (for.); Single issues: $4.

MemphisSR: MEMPHIS STATE REVIEW, Sharon Bryan, faculty ed., Dept. of English, Memphis State U., Memphis, TN 38152. Issues indexed: (8:2). Subscriptions: $5/yr. (ind., 2 issues), $6/yr. (inst).; Single issues: $3.

Mester: MESTER, Silvia Rosa Zamora, ed., Dept. of Spanish and Portuguese, U. of California, Los Angeles, CA 90024. Issues indexed: (17:1-2). Subscriptions: $17/yr. (2 issues, inst.), $10/yr. (ind.), $6/yr. (stud.), plus $2/yr. outside U.S., Canada, Mexico; Single issues: $7 (inst.), $4 (ind.)

MichQR: MICHIGAN QUARTERLY REVIEW, Laurence Goldstein, ed., 3032 Rackham Bldg., U. of Michigan, Ann Arbor, MI 48109. Issues indexed: (27:1-4). Subscriptions: $13/yr., $24/2 yrs. (ind.), $15/yr. (inst.); Single issues: $3.50; Back issues: $2.

MidAR: MID-AMERICAN REVIEW, Robert Early, ed., Ken Letko, po. ed., 106 Hanna Hall, Dept. of English, Bowling Green State U., Bowling Green, OH 43403. Issues indexed: (8:1-2). Subscriptions: $6/yr. (2 issues), $10/2 yrs., $14/3 yrs.

MidwQ: THE MIDWEST QUARTERLY: A Journal of Contemporary Thought, James B. M. Schick, ed., Stephen E. Meats, po. ed., Pittsburg State U., Pittsburg, KS 66762-5889. Issues indexed: (29:2-4, 30:1). Subscriptions: $8/yr. plus $2 (for.); Single issues: $2.50.

MinnR: THE MINNESOTA REVIEW, Helen Cooper, Marlon Ross, Michael Sprinker, Susan Squier, eds, Helen Cooper, Billy Joe Harris, po. eds., Dept. of English, State U. of New York, Stony Brook, NY 11794-5350. Issues Indexed: (NS 30/31). Subscriptions: $7/yr. (2 issues), $12/2 yrs. (ind.); $14/yr., $24/2 yrs. (inst. & for.); Single issues: $4.

MissouriR: THE MISSOURI REVIEW, Speer Morgan, ed., Sherod Santos, Garrett Kaoru Hongo, Lunne McMahon, po. eds., Dept. of English, 107 Tate Hall, U. of Missouri, Columbia, MO 65211. Issues indexed: (11:1-3). Subscriptions: $12/yr. (3 issues), $21/2 yrs.; Single issues: $5.

MissR: MISSISSIPPI REVIEW, Frederick Barthelme, ed., The Center for Writers, U. of Southern Mississippi, Southern Station, Box 5144, Hattiesburg, MS 39406-5144. Issues indexed: (15:1-2/3, issues 46, 47/48). Subscriptions: $10/yr. (2 issues), $18/2 yrs., $26/3 yrs., plus $2/yr. (for.); Single issues: usually $5.

MoodySI: MOODY STREET IRREGULARS, Joy Walsh, ed., P.O. Box 157, Clarence Center, NY 14032. Issues indexed: No 1988 issues published. Subscriptions: $10/4 single, 2 double issues (ind.), $15/4 single, 2 double issues (lib.); Single issues: $3, double issues: $5.

MSS: MSS, L. M. Rosenberg, ed., Box 530, State U. of NY at Binghamton, Binghamton, NY 13901. Issues indexed: (6:2). Subscriptions: $10/yr. (3 issues), $18/2 yrs. (ind.); $20/yr., $35/2 yrs. (lib.); Single issues: $4., Double issues: $6.

Nat: THE NATION, Victor Navasky, ed., Grace Schulman, po. ed., 72 Fifth Ave., New York, NY 10011. Issues indexed: (246:1-25, 247:1-20). Subscriptions: $36/yr., $64/2 yrs., plus $14/yr. (for.); Single issues: $1.75; Back issues: $3, $4 (for.). Send subscription correspondence to: P.O. Box 1953, Marion, OH 43305.

NegC: NEGATIVE CAPABILITY, Sue Walker, ed., 62 Ridgelawn Dr. East, Mobile, AL 36608. Issues indexed: (8:1/2-4). Subscriptions: $12/yr. (ind.), $16/yr. (inst., for.); Single issues: $5.

NewAW: NEW AMERICAN WRITING, Maxine Chernoff, Paul Hoover, eds., OINK! Press, 2920 West Pratt, Chicago, IL 60645. Issues indexed: (3-4). Subscriptions: $12/yr. (2 issues); Single issues: $6.

NewEngR: NEW ENGLAND REVIEW AND BREAD LOAF QUARTERLY, Sydney Lea, Maura High, eds., Middlebury College, Middlebury, VT 05753. Issues indexed: (10:3-4, 11:1-2). Subscriptions: $12/yr. (4 issues), $22/2 yrs., $33/3 yrs. (ind.); $18/yr., $26/2 yrs., $33/3 yrs. (inst.); plus $3/yr. (for.); Single issues: $4.

NewL: NEW LETTERS, James McKinley, ed., U. of Missouri-Kansas City, 5216 Rockhill Rd., Kansas City, MO 64110. Issues indexed: (54:2-4, 55:1-2). Subscriptions: $15/yr. (4 issues), $25/2 yrs., $50/5 yrS. (ind.); $18/yr., $30/2 yrs., $60/5 yrS. (lib.); Single issues: $4.

NewOR: NEW ORLEANS REVIEW, John Biguenet, John Mosier, eds., Box 195, Loyola U., New Orleans, LA 70118. Issues indexed: (15:1-4). Subscriptions: $25/yr. (ind.), $30/yr. (inst.), $35/yr. (for.); Single issues: $9.

NewRena: THE NEW RENAISSANCE, Louise T. Reynolds, ed., Stanwood Bolton, po. ed., 9 Heath Road, Arlington, MA 02174. Issues indexed: (7:2, #22). Subscriptions: $11.50/3 issues, $22/6 issues; $13.50/3 issues, $25/6 issues (Canada, Mexico, Europe); $14.50/3 issues, $27/6 issues (elsewhere); Single issues: $5.

NewRep: THE NEW REPUBLIC, Martin Peretz, ed., Richard Howard, po. ed., 1220 19th St. N.W., Washington, DC 20036. Issues indexed: (198:1-26, 199:1-26). Subscriptions: $56/yr., $70/yr. (Canada), $81/yr. (elsewhere). Back issues: $2.50. Single issues: $2.25. Subscription Service Dept., The New Republic, P.O. Box 56515, Boulder, CO 80322.

NewYorker: THE NEW YORKER, 25 W. 43rd St., New York, NY 10036. Issues indexed: (63:46-52, 64:1-45). Subscriptions: $32/yr., $52/2 yrS.; $50/yr. (Canada); $56/yr. (other for.); Single issues: $1.75; Subscription correspondence to: Box 56447, Boulder, CO 80322.

NewYRB: THE NEW YORK REVIEW OF BOOKS, Robert B. Silvers, Barbara Epstein, eds., 250 W. 57th St., New York, NY 10107. Issues indexed: (34:21/22, 35:1-20). Subscriptions: $37.50/yr.; Single issues: $2.25; NY Review of Books, Subscription Service Dept., P.O. Box 940, Farmingdale, NY 11737.

Nimrod: NIMROD, Francine Ringold, ed., Joan Flint, Manly Johnson, Dee Ann Short, po. eds., Arts and Humanities Council of Tulsa, 2210 S. Main St., Tulsa, OK 74114. Issues indexed: (31:2, 32:1). Subscriptions: $10/yr. (2 issues), $13/yr. (for.); Single issues: $5.50, $7 (for.).

NoAmR: THE NORTH AMERICAN REVIEW, Robley Wilson, Jr., ed., Peter Cooley, po. ed., U. of Northern Iowa, Cedar Falls, IA 50614. Issues indexed: (273:1-4). Subscriptions: $11/yr., $13/yr. (Canada, Latin America), $15/yr. (elsewhere); Single issues: $3.

NoDaQ: NORTH DAKOTA QUARTERLY, Robert W. Lewis, ed., Jay Meek, po. ed., Box 8237, U. of North Dakota, Grand Forks, ND 58202. Issues indexed: (56:1-4). Subscriptions: $10/yr., $14/yr. (for.); Single issues: $5.

Northeast: NORTHEAST, John & Judson, ed., Juniper Press, 1310 Shorewood Dr., La Crosse, WI 54601. Issues indexed: (Ser. 4:7-8). Subscriptions: $30 (2 issues, ind.), $35 (inst.), includes 2-4 books in addition to NORTHEAST; Single issues: $3.

Notus: NOTUS, New Writing, Pat Smith, ed., 2420 Walter Dr., Ann Arbor, MI 48103. Issues indexed: (3:1-2). Subscriptions: $10/yr. (2 issues, U.S. & Canada, ind.), $14/yr. (elsewhere), $20/yr. (inst.).

NowestR: NORTHWEST REVIEW, John Witte, ed. & po. ed., 369 PLC, U. of Oregon, Eugene, OR 97403. Issues indexed: (26:1-3). Subscriptions: $11/yr. (3 issues), $21/2 yrs., $30/3 yrs.; $10/yr., $20/2 yrs. (stud.); plus $2/yr. (for.); Single issues: $4.

Obs: OBSIDIAN II: Black Literature in Review, Gerald Barrax, ed., Dept. of English, Box 8105, North Carolina State University, Raleigh, NC 27695-8105. Issues indexed: No 1987 or 1988 issues received. Subscriptions: $10/yr., $18/2 yrs.; $11/yr. (Canada), $13/yr. (other for.); Single issues: $4; Double issues: $8.

OhioR: THE OHIO REIVEW, Wayne Dodd, ed., Ellis Hall, Ohio U., Athens, OH 45701-2979. Issues indexed: (40-42). Subscriptions: $12/yr. (3 issues), $30/3 yrs.; Single issues: $4.25.

OntR: ONTARIO REVIEW, Raymond J. Smith, ed., 9 Honey Brook Dr., Princeton, NJ 08540. Issues indexed: (28-29). Subscriptions: $10/yr. (2 issues), $18/2 yrs., $24/3 yrs., plus $1/yr. (for.); Single issues: $4.95.

Os: OSIRIS, Andrea Moorhead, ed., Box 297, Deerfield, MA 01342. Issues indexed: (26-26) plus "Special Supplement". Subscriptions: $7/2 issues, $10/2 issues (inst.). Single issues: $3.50.

Outbr: OUTERBRIDGE, Charlotte Alexander, ed., Linda Principe, po. ed., English Dept. (A323), College of Staten Island, 715 Ocean Terrace, Staten Island, NY 10301. Issues indexed: No 1988 issues published. Subscriptions: $5/yr. (1 issue); double issues: $2.

*PacificR: THE PACIFIC REVIEW: A Magazine of Poetry and Prose, Kellie R. Rayburn, ed., Viktoria Norbert, Po. ed., B. H. Fairchild, faculty ed., Dept. of English, California State U., 5500 University Parkway, San Bernardino, CA 92407. Issues indexed: (6). Single issues: $4.

Paint: PAINTBRUSH: A Journal of Poetry, Translations, and Letters, Ben Bennani, ed., Division of Language and Literature, Northeast Missouri State U., Kirksville, MO 63501. Issues indexed: (14:29-30). Subscriptions: $9/yr. (2 issues, ind.), $12/yr. (inst.); Single issues: $7; Back issues: $7.

PaintedB: PAINTED BRIDE QUARTERLY, Louis Camp, Joanna DiPaolo, eds., Painted Bride Arts Center, 230 Vine St., Philadelphia, PA 19106. Issues indexed: (32/33-36). Subscriptions: $12/yr. (4 issues), $20/2 yrs., $16/yr. (lib, inst.); Single issues: $4. Distributed free to inmates.

ParisR: THE PARIS REVIEW, George A. Plimpton, Peter Matthiessen, Donald Hall, Robert B. Silvers, Blair Fuller, Maxine Groffsky, eds., Patricia Storace, po. ed., 541 East 72nd St., New York, NY 10021. Issues indexed: (30:106-109). Subscriptions: $20/4 issues, $40/8 issues, $60/12 issues, $1000/life, plus $4/4 issues (for.); Single issues: $6; Subscription address: 45-39 171 Place, Flushing, NY 11358.

PartR: PARTISAN REVIEW, William Phillips, ed., Boston U., 141 Bay State Rd., Boston, MA 02215. Issues indexed: (55:1-4). Subscriptions: $18/yr. (4 issues), $33/2 yrs., $33/2 yrs., $47/3 yrs.; $21/yr., $36/2 yrs. (for.); $28/yr. (inst.); Single issues: $5 plus $1 per issue postage and handling.

PassN: PASSAGES NORTH, Elinor Benedict, ed., Bay Arts Writers' Guild of the William Bonifas Fine Arts Center, Inc., Escanaba, MI 49829. Issues indexed: (9:1-2). Subscriptions: $2/yr., $5/3 yrs; Single issues: $1.50.

Pax: PAX: A Journal for Peace through Culture, Bryce Milligan, ed., Center for Peace through Culture, 217 Pershing Ave., San Antonio, TX 78209. Issues indexed: No 1987 or 1988 issues received. Subscriptions: $15/3 issues (U.S., Canada, Mexico); $20/3 issues (inst.); $25/3 issues (other for.).

Pembroke: PEMBROKE MAGAZINE, Shelby Stephenson, ed., Box 60, Pembroke State U., Pembroke, NC 28372. Issues indexed: (20). Subscriptions: $3/issue (USA, Canada, Mexico), $3.50/issue (for.).

PennR: THE PENNSYLVANIA REVIEW, Ed Ochester, executive ed., Jan Beatty, po. ed., 526 Cathedral of Learning, U. of Pittsburgh, Pittsburgh, PA 15260. Issues indexed: (4:1). Subscriptions: $9/yr., $15/2 yrs.; Single issues: $5.

Pequod: PEQUOD, Mark Rudman, ed., Dept. of English, Room 200, New York U., 19 University Place, New York, NY 10003. Issues indexed: (25). Subscriptions: $10/yr. (2 issues, ind.), $18/2 yrs.; $17/yr., $30/2 yrs. (inst).; plus $3/yr. (for.); Single issues: $5.

Phoenix: PHOENIX, Joan Shaddox Isom, ed., Division of Arts & Letters, Northeastern State U., Tahlequah, OK 74464. Issues indexed: (9:1/2); vol. 8 not received. Subscriptions: $9.50/yr. (2 issues), $11/yr. (for.); Single issues: $5, $6.50 (for.).

Pig: PIG IRON, Rose Sayre & Jim Villani, eds., Pig Iron Press, P.O. Box 237, Youngstown, OH 44501. Issues indexed: No 1988 issues received. Single issues: $6.95.

PikeF: THE PIKESTAFF FORUM, Robert D. Sutherland, James R. Scrimgeour, eds./pubs., P.O. Box 127, Normal, IL 61761. Issues indexed: (9). Subscriptions: $10/6 issues; Single issues: $2.

*Plain: PLAINSONGS, Dwight Marsh, ed., Dept. of English, Hastings College, Hastings, NE 68902. Issues indexed: (8:1-3, 9:1). Subscriptions: $8/yr. (3 issues).

Ploughs: PLOUGHSHARES, DeWitt Henry, Peter O'Malley, Directors, Div. of Writing, Publishing and Literature, Emerson College, 100 Beacon St., Boston, MA 02116; send manuscripts to Box 529, Cambridge, MA 02139-0529. Issues indexed: (14:1, 2/3, 4). Subscriptions: $15/yr. (ind.), $18/yr. (for. ind.); $18/yr. (inst.), $21/yr. (for. inst.). Single issues: $5.95.

Poem: POEM, Huntsville Literary Association, Nancy Frey Dillard, eds., c/o English Dept., U. of Alabama, Huntsville, AL 35899. Issues indexed: (59-60). Subscriptions: $10/yr.; Back issues: $5; subscription address: Huntsville Literary Association, P.O. Box 919,, Huntsville, AL 35804.

PoetC: POET AND CRITIC, Neal Bowers, ed., 203 Ross Hall, Iowa State U., Ames, IA 50011. Issues indexed: (19:2-3, 20:1). Subscriptions: Iowa State U. Press, South State St., Ames, IA 50010, $12/yr., plus $3/yr. (for.); Single issues: $4; .

PoeticJ: POETIC JUSTICE: Contemporary American Poetry, Alan Engebretsen, ed., 8220 Rayford Dr., Los Angeles, CA 90045. Issues indexed: No 1988 issues received. Subscriptions: $10/4 issues (irregular); Single issues: $3.

PoetL: POET LORE, Philip K. Jason, Barbara Lefcowitz, Roland Flint, Executive eds., The Writer's Center, 7815 Old Georgetown Rd., Bethesda, MD 20814. Issues Indexed: (83:1-4). Subscriptions: $8/yr. (Writer's Center members); $12/yr. (ind.); $20/yr. (inst.), plus $5/yr. (for.); Single issues: $4.50.

Poetry: POETRY, Joseph Parisi, ed., 60 W. Walton St., Chicago, IL 60610. Issues indexed: (151:4-6, 152:1-6, 153:1/2-3). Subscriptions: $25/yr. (ind.); $31/yr. (for.); $27/yr. (inst.); $33/yr. (for. inst.); Single issues: $2.50 plus $1 postage; Back issues: $3 plus $1 postage.

PoetryE: POETRY EAST, Richard Jones, Kate Daniels, eds., Dept. of English, 802 W. Belden Ave., DePaul Univ., Chicago, IL 60614. Issues indexed: (25-26). Subscriptions: $10/yr.; Single issues: $6.

PoetryNW: POETRY NORTHWEST, David Wagoner, ed., U. of Washington, 4045 Brooklyn Ave., NE, Seattle, WA 98105. Issues indexed: (28:1-4). Subscriptions: $10/yr., $12/yr. (for.); Single issues: $3, $3.50 (for.).

PottPort: THE POTTERSFIELD PORTFOLIO, Peggy Amirault, Barbara Cottrell, Donalee Moulton-Barrett, eds., Crazy Quilt Press, c/o 19 Oakhill Drive, Halifax, Nova Scotia B3M 2V3 Canada. Issues indexed: (9-10). Subscriptions: $12/3 yrs. (ind.), $15/3 yrs. (inst.); $15/3 yrs. (USA, for. ind.), $18/3 yrs. (USA, for. inst., USA); Single issues: $4.50.

PraF: PRAIRIE FIRE, Andris Taskans, managing ed., Kristjana Gunnars, po. ed., 208-100 Arthur Street, Winnipeg, Manitoba R3B 1H3 Canada. Issues indexed: (9:1-4). Subscriptions: $20/yr. (ind.), $28/yr. (inst.), plus $8 (for.); Single issues: $6.95.

PraS: PRAIRIE SCHOONER, Hilda Raz, ed., Sally Herrin, Marcia Southwick, po. readers, 201 Andrews Hall, U. of Nebraska, Lincoln, NE 68588-0334. Issues indexed: (62:1-4). Subscriptions: $15/yr., $28/2 yrs., $39/3 yrs. (ind.); $19/yr. (lib.); Single issues: $4.

Prima: PRIMAVERA, Joline Gitis, Lisa Grayson, Elizabeth Harter, Jeanne Krinsley, Ruth Young, eds., U. of Chicago, 1212 East 59th, Chicago, IL 60637. Issues indexed: (11/12). Single issues: $6; Back issues: $5.

Puerto: PUERTO DEL SOL, Joe Somoza, po. ed., English Dept., Box 3E, New Mexico State U., Las Cruces, NM 88003. Issues indexed: No 1988 issues received. Subscriptions: $7.75/yr. (2 issues), $15/2 yrs., $22/3 yrs.; Single issues: $4.

Quarry: QUARRY, Bob Hilderley, ed., Box 1061, Kingston, Ontario K7L 4Y5 Canada. Issues indexed: (37:1-4). Subscriptions: $18/yr. (4 issues), $30/2 yrs. (8 issues); Single issues: $5.

QRL: QUARTERLY REVIEW OF LITERATURE, T. & R. Weiss, 26 Haslet Ave., Princeton, NJ 08540. Issues indexed: No 1988 issues received. Series IX, Vol. 28/29 published in 1989. Subscriptions: $15/2 volumes (paper), $20/volume (cloth, inst.).

QW: QUARTERLY WEST, Tom Hazuka, Kevin J. Ryan, eds.; Kevin Cantwell, po. ed., 317 Olpin Union, U. of Utah, Salt Lake City, UT 84112. Issues indexed: (26-27). Subscriptions: $8.50/yr. (2 issues), $16/2 yrs.; $12.50/yr., $24/2 yrs. (for.); Single issues: $4.50.

RagMag: RAG MAG, Beverly Voldseth, ed., Box 12, Goodhue, MN 55027. Issues indexed: (6:1-2). Subscriptions: $7/yr.; Single issues: $3 plus $1 postage.

Rampike: RAMPIKE, Karl Jirgens, ed., 95 Rivercrest Road, Toronto, Ontario M6S 4H7 Canada. Issues indexed: No 1988 issues received. Subscriptions: $12/yr. (2 issues); Single issues: $6.

Raritan: RARITAN, Richard Poirier, ed., Rutgers U., 165 College Ave., New Brunswick, NJ 08903. Issues indexed: (7:3-4, 8:1-2). Subscriptions: $16/yr., $26/2 yrs. (ind.); $20/yr., $30/2 yrs. (inst.); plus $4/yr (for.); Single issues: $5; Back issues: $6.

RedBass: RED BASS, Jay Murphy, ed., 2425 Burgundy St., New Orleans, LA 70117. Issues indexed: (13). Subscriptions: $10/3 issues (ind.), $15 (inst., for.); Single issues: $4.

RiverS: RIVER STYX, Carol J. Pierman, ed., 14 South Euclid, St. Louis, MO 63108. Issues indexed: (25-27). Subscriptions: $14/3 issues (ind.); $24/3 issues (inst.); Single issues: $5.

*Rohwedder: ROHWEDDER, Nancy L. Antell, Robert Dassanowsky-Harris, Nancy A. Locke, Hans Jurgen Schacht, eds., P.O. Box 29490, Los Angeles, CA 90029. Issues indexed: (3-4). Subscriptions: $12/4 issues (USA, Canada, Mexico, ind.); $18/4 issues (inst.); $16/4 issues (other for., surface mail, plus $1/copy airmail); Single issues: $4.

Salm: SALMAGUNDI, Robert Boyers, ed., Skidmore College, Saratoga Springs, NY 12866. Issues indexed: (78/79, 80). Subscriptions: $12/yr., $18/2 yrs. (ind.); $16/yr., $25/2 yrs. (inst.); Plus $2/yr. (for.); Single issues: $4-6.

SenR: SENECA REVIEW, Deborah Tall, ed., Hobart & William Smith Colleges, Geneva, NY 14456. Issues indexed: (18:1-2). Subscriptions: $6/yr. (2 issues), $10/2 yrs.; Single issues: $3.50.

Sequoia: SEQUOIA, Marianne Burke, Sam Harris, eds., Storke Publications Building, Stanford, CA 94305. Issues indexed: (31:2, 32:1). Subscriptions: $10/yr. (2 issues), $11/yr. (for.), $15/yr. (inst.); Single issues: $4.

SewanR: THE SEWANEE REVIEW, George Core, ed., U. of the South, Sewanee, TN 37375. Issues indexed: (96:1-4). Subscriptions: $12/yr., $20/2 yrs., $28/3 yrs. (ind.); $18/yr., $33/2 yrs., $48/3 yrs. (inst.); plus $3/yr. (for.); Single issues: $4; Back issues: $5-10, plus $1/copy postage & handling.

Shen: SHENANDOAH, Dabney Stuart, ed., Richard Howard, po. ed., Washington and Lee U., Box 722, Lexington, VA 24450. Issues indexed: (38:1-4). Subscriptions: $11/yr., $18/2 yrs., $25/3 yrs.; $14/yr., $24/2 yrs., $33/3 yrs. (for.); Single issues: $3.50; Back issues: $6.

SilverFR: SILVERFISH REVIEW, Rodger Moody, ed., P.O. Box 3541, Eugene, OR 97403. Issues indexed: (15). Subscriptions: $9/3 issues (ind.), $12/3 issues (inst.), Single issues: $4.

SingHM: SING HEAVENLY MUSE!: Women's Poetry and Prose, Sue Ann Martinson, Carol Masters, eds., P.O. Box 13299, Minneapolis, MN 55414. Issues indexed: (15). Subscriptions: $17/3 issues (ind.), $21/3 issues (inst.); Single issues: $7 + $2 postage & handling.

Sink: SINK, Spencer Selby, ed., P.O. Box 590095, San Francisco, CA 94159. Issues indexed: (3). Subscriptions: $15/3 issues; Single issues: $5.

SinW: SINISTER WISDOM, Elana Dykewomon, ed. & pub., P.O. Box 3252, Berkeley, CA 94703. Issues indexed: (32-36). Subscriptions: $17/yr. (4 issues), $30/2 yrs. (ind.); $30/yr. (inst.); $20/yr. (for.); $6/yr. (hardship); Free on request to women in prisons and mental institutions; Single issues: $5.

SlipS: SLIPSTREAM, Robert Borgatti, Dan Sicoli, eds., Box 2071, New Market Station, Niagara Falls, NY 14301. Issues indexed: (8). Subscriptions: $5.50/2 issues; Single issues: $3.

SmPd: THE SMALL POND MAGAZINE OF LITERATURE, Napoleon St. Cyr, ed./pub., P.O. Box 664, Stratford, CT 06497. Issues indexed: (25:1-3, issues 66-68). Subscriptions: $7/yr. (3 issues), $12.25/2 yrs., $17.50/3 yrs.; Single issues: $2.50.

SnapD: SNAPDRAGON, Gail Eckwright, D'Wayne Hodgin, Ron McFarland, Tina Foriyes, eds., Dept. of English, U. of Idaho, Moscow, ID 83843. Issues indexed: No 1988 issues received. Subscriptions: Karen Buxton, c/o Library, U. of Idaho, Moscow, ID 83843, $3.50 (ind.), $4.50 (inst.).

Sonora: SONORA REVIEW, Heather Aronson, Michael Magoolaghan, eds, William Marsh, po. ed., Dept. of English, U. of Arizona, Tucson, AZ 85721. Issues indexed: (14/15-16). Subscriptions: $6/yr. (2 issues); Single issues: $4.

SoCaR: SOUTH CAROLINA REVIEW, Richard J. Calhoun, ed., Dept. of English, Clemson U., Clemson, SC 29634-1503. Issues indexed: (20:2, 21:1). Subscriptions: $5/yr., $9/2 yrs. (USA, Canada, Mexico); $5.50/yr., $10/2 yrs. (elsewhere); Back issues: $5.

SoDakR: SOUTH DAKOTA REVIEW, John R. Milton, ed., Dept. of English, U. of South Dakota, Box 111, U. Exchange, Vermillion, SD 57069. Issues indexed: (26:1-4). Subscriptions: $10/yr., $17/2 yrs. (USA, Canada); $12/yr., $20/2 yrs. (elsewhere); Single issues: $3-$5.

SouthernHR: SOUTHERN HUMANITIES REVIEW, Dan R. Latimer, Thomas L. Wright, eds., R. T. Smith, po. ed., 9088 Haley Center, Auburn U., AL 36849. Issues indexed: (22:1-4). Subscriptions: $12/yr.; Single issues: $4.

SouthernPR: SOUTHERN POETRY REVIEW, Robert Grey, ed., English Dept., U. of North Carolina, Charlotte, NC 28223. Issues indexed: (28:1-2). Subscriptions: $6 yr.; Single issues: $3.50.

SouthernR: SOUTHERN REVIEW, Fred Hobson, James Olney, eds., Louisiana State U., 43 Allen Hall, Baton Rouge, LA 70803. Issues indexed: (24:1-4). Subscriptions: $12/yr., $21/2 yrs., $30/3 yrs.; $30/yr., $52/2 yrs., $75/3 yrs. (inst.); Single issues: $5, $10 (inst.).

SouthwR: SOUTHWEST REVIEW, Willard Spiegelman, ed., Southern Methodist U., 6410 Airline Rd., Dallas, TX 75275. Issues indexed: (73:1-4). Subscriptions: $16/yr., $32/2 yrs., $40/3 yrs.; $20/yr. (inst.); Single issues: $5.

Sparrow: SPARROW POVERTY PAMPHLETS, Felix Stefanile, ed./pub., Sparrow Press, 103 Waldron St., West Lafayette, IN 47906. Issues indexed: (54-55); No. 53 not received. Subscriptions: $7.50/3 issues; Single issues: $2.50.

Spirit: THE SPIRIT THAT MOVES US, Morty Sklar, ed./pub., P.O. Box 1585, Iowa City, IA 52244. Issues indexed: (9:1-2). Subscriptions: Vol. 9 -- $10.80 (paper), $20.40 (cloth).

SpiritSH: SPIRIT, David Rogers, ed., Seton Hall U., South Orange, NJ 07079. Issues indexed: (54). Subscriptions: $4/yr.; Single issues: $2.

SpoonRQ: THE SPOON RIVER QUARTERLY, Lucia Cordell Getsi, ed., English Dept., Illinois State U., Normal, IL 61761. Issues indexed: (12:4, 13:1-4). Subscriptions: $10/yr.; $12/yr. (inst.); Single issues: $3.

Stand: STAND, Jack and Pam Kingsbury, U.S.A. ed., P.O. Box 1161, Florence, AL 35631-1161; Howard Fink, Canadian ed., 4054 Melrose Ave., Montreal, Quebec H4A 2S4 Canada. Issues indexed: (29:1-4). Subscriptions: $16/yr.; $14/yr. (students, unwaged); Single issues: $4; U.S.A. distributor: Anton J. Mikovsky, 57 West 84th St., #1-C, New York, NY 10024.

StoneC: STONE COUNTRY, Judith Neeld, ed., The Nathan Mayhew Seminars of Martha's Vineyard, P.O. Box 132, Menemsha, MA 02552. Issues indexed: (15:3/4, 16:1/2). Subscriptions: $9/2 issues, $17/4 issues; Single issues: $5; Back issues: $3.50.

Sulfur: SULFUR, Clayton Eshleman, ed., English Dept., Eastern Michigan U., Ypsilanti, MI 48197. Issues indexed: (7:3, 8:1-2, issues 21-23). Subscriptions: $15/yr., 3 issues (ind.), $22/yr., 3 issues (inst.), plus $3/yr. (for.) or $12 for airmail postage; Single issues: $6.

*SwampR: SWAMP ROOT, Al Masarik, ed., Route 2, Box 1098, Hiwassee One, Jacksboro, TN 37757. Issues indexed: (1-2/3). Subscriptions: $12/3 issues; $15/3 issues (libs.); Single issues: $5.

*Talisman: TALISMAN: A Journal of Contemporary Poetry and Poetics, Edward Foster, ed., Box 1117, Hoboken, NJ 07030. Issues indexed: (1). Subscriptions: $9/yr. (2 issues); $13/yr. (inst.); plus $2/yr. (for.); Single issues: $5.

*TampaR: TAMPA REVIEW: Literary Journal of the University of Tampa, Richard Mathews, ed., Donald Morrill, Kathryn Van Spanckeren, po. eds., Box 19-F, U. of Tampa, 401 W. Kennedy Blvd., Tampa, FL 33606-1490. Issues indexed: (1). Subscriptions: $5/yr. (2 issues); plus $2/yr. (for.)

TarRP: TAR RIVER POETRY, Peter Makuck, ed., Dept. of English, General Classroom Bldg., East Carolina U., Greenville, NC 27858-4353. Issues indexed: (27:2, 28:1). Subscriptions: $6/yr (2 issues), $10/2 yrs.; Single issues: $3.

Temblor: TEMBLOR, Contemporary Poets, Leland Hickman, ed., 4624 Cahuenga Blvd., #307, North Hollywood, CA 91602. Issues indexed: (7-8). Subscriptions: $16/2 issues, $30/4 issues (ind.); $20/2 issues, $40/4 issues (inst.); plus $2.50/issue (for.); Single issues: $7.50.

TexasR: TEXAS REVIEW, Paul Ruffin, ed., Division of English and Foreign Languages, Sam Houston State U., Huntsville, TX 77341. Issues indexed: (9:1/2; 9:3/4 = "special release: Contemporary New England Poetry: A Sampler, Vol. II"). Subscriptions: $6/yr., $6.25/yr. (Canada), $6.50/yr. (for.); Single issues: $2.

ThRiPo: THREE RIVERS POETRY JOURNAL, Gerald Costanzo, ed., Three Rivers Press, P.O. Box 21, Carnegie-Mellon U., Pittsburgh, PA 15213. Issues indexed: No 1988 issues received. Subscriptions: $10/4 issues; Single issues: $2.50; Double issues: $5.

Thrpny: THE THREEPENNY REVIEW, Wendy Lesser, ed., pub., P.O. Box 9131, Berkeley, CA 94709. Issues indexed: (32-35). Subscriptions: $10/yr., $16/2 yrs., $18/yr. (surface for.), $24/yr. (airmail for.); Single issues: $3.

*Timbuktu: TIMBUKTU, Molly Turner, pub., P.O. Box 469, Charlottesville, VA 22902. Issues indexed: (1-2). Subscriptions: $6/yr. (2 issues); Single issues: $4.

Trans: TRANSLATION, The Journal of Literary Translation, Frank MacShane, Franklin D. Reeve, William Jay Smith, eds., The Translation Center, 307-A Mathematics Bldg., Columbia U., New York, NY 10027. Issues indexed: (20). Subscriptions: $17/yr. (2 issues), $30/2 yrs., $42/3 yrs., plus $1.50/yr. (for., except Canada, Mexico); Single issues: $8.

TriQ: TRIQUARTERLY, Reginald Gibbons, ed., Northwestern U., 2020 Ridge, Evanston, IL 60208. Issues indexed: (71-73). Subscriptions: $18/yr., $32/2 yrs., $250/life (ind.); $26/yr., $44/2 yrs., $300/life (inst.), plus $4/yr. (for.); Single issues: usually $7.95; Sample copies: $4.

*Turnstile: TURNSTILE, Jill Benz, Lindsey Crittenden, Ann Biester Deane, Twisne Fan, Sara Gordonson, Mitchell Nauffts, Paolo Pepe, Lisa Samson, Amit Shah, eds., 175 Fifth Avenue, Suite 2348, New York, NY 10010. Issues indexed: (1:1-2). Subscriptions: $12/2 issues, $24/4 issues; Single issues: $6.50.

US1: US 1 WORKSHEETS, Cynthia Gooding, ed., Lynn Powell, Mark Scott, po eds., US 1 Poets' Cooperative, 21 Lake Dr., Roosevelt, NJ 08555. Issues indexed: No issues published in 1988. Subscriptions: $5/4 issues; Single issues: $2; Back issues: Prices on request.

Verse: VERSE, Henry Hart, U. S. ed., Dept. of English, College of William and Mary, Williamsburg, VA 23185. Issues indexed: (5:1-3). Subscriptions: $9/yr. (3 issues); Single issues: $3.

VirQR: THE VIRGINIA QUARTERLY REVIEW, Staige D. Blackford, ed., Gregory Orr, po. consultant, One West Range, Charlottesville, VA 22903. Issues indexed: (64:1-4). Subscriptions: $15/yr., $22/2 yrs., $30/3 yrs. (ind.); $22/yr., $30/2 yrs., $50/3 yrs. (inst.); plus $3/yr. (for.); Single issues: $5.

Vis: VISIONS, Bradley R. Strahan, po. ed./pub., Black Buzzard Press, 4705 South 8th Rd., Arlington, VA 22204. Issues indexed: (26-28). Subscriptions: $11/yr., $21/2 yrs. (ind.); $33/3 yrs. (lib).; Single issues: $3.75-4.00.

WeberS: WEBER STUDIES: An Interdisciplinary Humanities Journal, Neila Seshachari, ed., Weber State College, Ogden, UT 84408. Issues indexed: (5:1-2). Subscriptions: $5/yr. (2 issues), $10/yr. (inst.); plus actual postage extra per year (for.); Back issues: $5; Single issues: $2.75.

WebR: WEBSTER REVIEW, Nancy Schapiro, ed., Pamela White Hadas & Jerred Metz, po. eds., Webster U., 470 E. Lockwood, Webster Groves, MO 63119. Issues indexed: (13:1-2). Subscriptions: $5/yr. (2 issues); Single issues: $2.50.

WestB: WEST BRANCH, Karl Patten & Robert Taylor, eds., Dept. of English, Bucknell U., Lewisburg, PA 17837. Issues indexed: (21/22). Subscriptions: $5/yr. (2 issues), $8/2 yrs.; Single issues: $3; double issues $5.

WestCR: WEST COAST REVIEW, a Literary Quarterly, Harvey De Roo, ed., Charles Watts, po. ed., Dept. of English, Simon Fraser U., Burnaby, B.C. V5A 1S6 Canada. Issues indexed: (22:3-4, 23:2). Subscriptions: $14/yr. (ind., 4 issues), $18/yr. (inst.); Single issues: $4.

WestHR: WESTERN HUMANITIES REVIEW, Barry Weller, ed., Larry Levis, po. ed., U. of Utah, Salt Lake City, UT 84112. Issues indexed: (42:1-4). Subscriptions: $18/yr. (4 issues, ind.), $24/yr. (inst.); Single issues: $5.

Periodicals Indexed

WilliamMR: THE WILLIAM AND MARY REVIEW, William Clark, ed., Robert Dilworth, Susan Taylor, po. eds., College of William and Mary, Williamsburg, VA 23185. Issues indexed: (26:1). Subscriptions: $4.50/issue, plus $1.50 (for.); Single issues: $5.

WillowS: WILLOW SPRINGS, Gillian Conoley, ed., Michael Gill, po. ed., PUB P.O. Box 1063, MS-1, Eastern Washington U., Cheney, WA 99004. Issues Indexed: (21-22). Subscriptions: $7/yr. (2 issues), $13/2 yrs.; Single issues: $4.

Wind: WIND, Quentin R. Howard, ed., RFD Route 1, Box 809K, Pikeville, KY 41501. Issues indexed: (18:62-63). Subscriptions: $7/3 issues (ind.), $8/3 issues (inst.), $12/3 issues (for.); Single issues: $2.50; $5 (for.).

WindO: THE WINDLESS ORCHARD, Robert Novak, ed., English Dept., Indiana-Purdue U., Fort Wayne, IN 46805. Issues indexed: (50). Subscriptions: $8/yr. (4 issues), $20/3 yrs.; Single issues: $3.

Witness: WITNESS, Peter Stine, ed., 31000 Northwestern Highway, P.O. Box 9079, Farmington Hills, MI 48333-9079. Issues indexed: 1988 issues received too late for indexing; will be included in 1989 volume. Subscriptions: $16/yr. (4 issues), $28/2 yrs.; $22/yr., $40/2 yrs. (inst.); plus $4/yr. (for.); Single copies: $5.

WorldO: WORLD ORDER, Firuz Kazemzadeh, Betty J. Fisher, Howard Garey, James D. Stokes, eds., National Spiritual Assembly of the Baha'is of the United States, 415 Linden Ave., Wilmette, IL 60091. Issues indexed: (20:3/4-21:1/2). Subscriptions: $10/yr., $18/2 yrs. (USA, Canada, Mexico); $15/yr., $28/2 yrs. (elsewhere); $20/yr., $38/2 yrs. (for. airmail); Single issues: $3.

WormR: THE WORMWOOD REVIEW, Marvin Malone, ed., P.O. Box 8840, Stockton, CA 95208-0840. Issues indexed: (28:1, 2/3, 4, #109, 110/111, 112). Subscriptions: $8/4 issues (ind.), $9/4 issues (inst.); Single issues: $4.

Writ: WRIT, Roger Greenwald, ed., Innis College, U. of Toronto, 2 Sussex Ave., Toronto, Canada M5S 1J5. Issues indexed: (20). Subscriptions: $12/2 issues (US funds outside Canada); Back issues: $5-10.

Writer: THE WRITER, Sylvia K. Burack, ed. & pub., 120 Boylston St., Boston, MA 02116. Issues indexed: (103:3, 6, 8-12); no. 1-2, 4-5, 7 not received. Subscriptions: $22/yr., $43/2 yrs., $63/3 yrs.; plus $8/yr. (for.); $10/6 issues for new subscribers; Single issues: $1.75.

WritersF: WRITERS' FORUM, Alexander Blackburn, Victoria McCabe, Craig Lesley, Bret Lott, eds., P.O. Box 7150, U. of Colorado, Colorado Springs, CO 80933-7150. Issues indexed: (14). Subscriptions: $8.95/yr; Back issue sample: $5.95.

YaleR: THE YALE REVIEW, Kai Erikson, ed., J. D. McClatchy, po. ed., Yale U., 1902 A Yale Station, New Haven, CT 06520. Issues indexed: (77:2-4, 78:1). Subscriptions: $16/yr. (ind.), $25/yr. (inst.), plus $3/yr. (for.); Single issues: $6; Back issues: Prices on request; Subscription office: Yale University Press, 92A Yale Station, New Haven, CT 06520.

YellowS: YELLOW SILK, Journal of Erotic Arts, Lily Pond, ed., P.O. Box 6374, Albany, CA 94706. Issues indexed: (26-28). Subscriptions: $20/yr. (ind.), $24/yr. (lib., inst.), plus $6/yr. (for. surface) or $20/yr. (for. air). Single issues: $5.

Zyzzyva: ZYZZYVA: The Last Word, West Coast Writers & Artists, Howard Junker, ed, 41 Sutter St., Suite 1400, San Francisco, CA 94104. Issues indexed: (4:1-4, #13-16). Subscriptions: $20/yr. (4 issues), $32/2 yrs; $28/yr. (inst.); $30/yr. (for.); Single copies: $8 post paid.

Alphabetical List of Journals Indexed, with Acronyms

Abraxas : Abraxas
Acts: A Journal of New Writing : Acts
The Agni Review : Agni
Alpha Beat Soup : AlphaBS
Amelia : Amelia
The American Poetry Review : AmerPoR
The American Scholar : AmerS
The American Voice : AmerV
The Americas Review : Americas
Another Chicago Magazine : AnotherCM
Antaeus : Antaeus
The Antigonish Review : AntigR
The Antioch Review : AntR
Areíto : Areíto
Arizona Quarterly : ArizQ
Artful Dodge : ArtfulD
Ascent : Ascent
The Atlantic : Atlantic

Ball State University Forum : BallSUF
Bamboo Ridge : BambooR
The Bellingham Review : BellR
Bellowing Ark : BellArk
The Beloit Poetry Journal : BelPoJ
The Bilingual Review/La Revista Bilingüe : BilingR
Black American Literature Forum : BlackALF
Black Warrior Review : BlackWR
Blue Buildings: An International Magazine of Poetry and Translations : BlueBldgs
Blueline : Blueline
Bogg : Bogg
Bomb Magazine : Bomb
Boston Review : BostonR
Boulevard : Boulevard
Boundary 2 : Bound

Caliban : Caliban
California Quarterly : CalQ
Callaloo: A Tri-annual Journal of Afro-american and African Arts and Letters : Callaloo
Calyx: A Journal of Art and Literature by Women : Calyx
Canadian Literature : CanLit
The Cape Rock : CapeR
The Capilano Review : CapilR
Carolina Quarterly : CarolQ
The Centennial Review : CentR
Central Park : CentralP
Chaminade Literary Review : ChamLR
The Chariton Review : CharR
The Chattahoochee Review : ChatR
Chelsea : Chelsea
Chicago Review : ChiR
The Christian Century : ChrC
Cimarron Review : CimR
Cincinnati Poetry Review : CinPR
Clockwatch Review : ClockR
College English : ColEng
Colorado Review : ColR
Columbia : Colum
Commonweal : Comm

Alphabetical List of Journals

Colorado Review : ColR
Columbia : Colum
Commonweal : Comm
Conditions : Cond
Confrontation : Confr
Conjunctions : Conjunc
The Connecticut Poetry Review : ConnPR
Contact II : Contact
Crab Creek Review : CrabCR
Crazyhorse : Crazy
Cream City Review : CreamCR
The Crescent Review : CrescentR
Cross-Canada Writers' Quarterly : CrossC
Crosscurrents : CrossCur
Cuadernos de Poética : CuadP
Cumberland Poetry Review : CumbPR
Cutbank : CutB

Dandelion : Dandel
The Dekalb Literary Arts Journal : DekalbLAJ
Denver Quarterly : DenQ
Descant : Descant

Electrum Magazine : Electrum
English Journal : EngJ
Epoch : Epoch
Event: Journal of the Contemporary Arts : Event

Farmer's Market : Farm
Field: Contemporary Poetry and Poetics : Field
Five Fingers Riview : FiveFR
The Florida Review : FloridaR
Footwork : Footwork
Four Quarters : FourQ

Gambit Magazine : Gambit
Gargoyle Magazine : Gargoyle
Georgia Review : GeoR
Germination : Germ
Gettysburg Review : GettyR
Graham House Review : GrahamHR
Grain : Grain
Grand Street : GrandS
The Greensboro Review : GreensboroR

The Hampden-Sydney Poetry Reivew : HampSPR
Hanging Loose : HangL
Harper's Magazine : Harp
The Harvard Advocate : HarvardA
Hawaii Review : HawaiiR
Hayden's Ferry Review : HayF
Helicon Nine: The Journal of Women's Arts & Letters : HeliconN
High Plains Literary Review : HighP
Hiram Poetry Review : HiramPoR
The Hollins Critic : HolCrit
The Hudson Review : Hudson

Indiana Review : IndR
Interim : Interim
International Poetry Review : InterPR
Inti : Inti
Iowa Review : Iowa

The Jacaranda Review : Jacaranda
The James White Review : JamesWR

The Journal Of New Jersey Poets : JINJPo

Kaleidoscope : Kaleid
Kansas Quarterly : KanQ
Kenyon Review : KenR
Key West R3eview : KeyWR

Lactuca : Lactuca
The Lake Street Review : LakeSR
Laurel Review : LaurelR
Letras Femeninas : LetFem
Light Year : LightY
Linden Lane Magazine : LindLM
Lips : Lips
The Literary Review : LitR
The Little Balkans Review : LittleBR
The Little Magazine : LittleM
Lyra : Lyra

Mairena : Revista de Crítica y Poesía
The Malahat Review : MalR
Manhattan Poetry Review : ManhatPR
The Manhattan Review : ManhatR
Margin : MarginMARGIN
The Massachusetts Review : MassR
Memphis State Review : MemphisSR
Mester : Mester
Michigan Quarterly Review : MichQR
Mid-American Review : MidAR
The Midwest Quarterly : MidwQ
The Minnesota Review : MinnR
Mississippi Review : MissR
The Missouri Review : MissouriR
Moody Street Irregulars : MoodySI
Mss : MSS

The Nation : Nat
Negative Capability : NegC
New American Writing : NewAW
New England Review And Bread Loaf Quarterly : NewEngR
New Letters : NewL
New Orleans Review : NewOR
The New Renaissance : NewRena
The New Republic : NewRep
The New York Review Of Books : NewYRB
The New Yorker : NewYorker
Nimrod : Nimrod
The North American Review : NoAmR
North Dakota Quarterly : NoDaQ
Northeast : Northeast
Northwest Review : NowestR
Notus : Notus

Obsidian Ii: Black Literature in Review : Obs
The Ohio Reivew : OhioR
Ontario Review : OntR
Osiris : Os
Outerbridge : Outbr

Pacific Review : PacificR
Paintbrush: A Journal of Poetry : Paint
Painted Bride Quarterly : PaintedB
The Paris Review : ParisR
Partisan Review : PartR
Passages North : PassN

Alphabetical List of Journals

The Pennsylvania Review : PennR
Pequod : Pequod
Phoenix : Phoenix
Pig Iron : Pig
The Pikestaff Forum : PikeF
Plainsongs : Plain
Ploughshares : Ploughs
Poem : Poem
Poet And Critic : PoetC
Poet Lore : PoetL
Poetic Justice: Contemporary American Poetry : PoeticJ
Poetry : Poetry
Poetry East : PoetryE
Poetry Northwest : PoetryNW
The Pottersfield Portfolio : PottPort
Prairie Fire : PraF
Prairie Schooner : PraS
Primavera : Prima
Puerto del Sol : Puerto

Quarry : Quarry
Quarterly Review of Literature : QRL
Quarterly West : QW

Rag Mag : RagMag
Rampike : Rampike
Raritan : Raritan
Red Bass : RedBass
River Styx : RiverS
Rohwedder : Rohwedder

Salmagundi : Salm
Seneca Review : SenR
Sequoia : Sequoia
The Sewanee Review : SewanR
Shenandoah : Shen
Silverfish Review : SilverFR
Sing Heavenly Muse!: Women's Poetry and Prose : SingHM
Sink : Sink
Sinister Wisdom : SinW
Slipstream : SlipS
The Small Pond Magazine of Literature : SmPd
Snapdragon : SnapD
Sonora Review : Sonora
South Carolina Review : SoCaR
South Dakota Review : SoDakR
Southern Humanities Review : SouthernHR
Southern Poetry Review : SouthernPR
Southern Review : SouthernR
Southwest Review : SouthwR
Sparrow Press Poverty Pamphlets : Sparrow
Spirit : SpiritSH
The Spirit That Moves Us : Spirit
The Spoon River Quarterly : SpoonRQ
Stand : Stand
Stone Country : StoneC
Sulfur : Sulfur
Swamp Root : SwampR

Talisman : Talisman
Tampa Review : TampaR
Tar River Poetry : TarRP
Temblor : Temblor
Texas Review : TexasR
Three Rivers Poetry Journal : ThRiPo

Texas Review : TexasR
Three Rivers Poetry Journal : ThRiPo
The Threepenny Review : Thrpny
Timbuktu : Timbuktu
Translation : Translation
Triquarterly : TriQ
Turnstile : Turnstile

Us 1 Worksheets : US1

Verse : Verse
The Virginia Quarterly Review : VirQR
Visions : Vis

Weber Studies : WeberS
Webster Review : WebR
West Branch : WestB
West Coast Review : WestCR
Western Humanities Review : WestHR
The William and Mary Review : WilliamMR
Willow Springs : WillowS
Wind : Wind
The Windless Orchard : WindO
Witness : Witness
World Order : WorldO
The Wormwood Review : WormR
Writ : Writ
The Writer : Writer
Writers' Forum : WritersF

The Yale Review : YaleR
Yellow Silk : YellowS

Zyzzyva: The Last Word : Zyzzyva

The Author Index

1. AAL, Katharyn Machan
"Away." [SwampR] (1:2/3) D 88, p. 77.
"Black Spring." [Footwork] ('88) 88, p. 29.
"Elf Owl." [BellR] (11:1) Spr 88, p. 31-32.
"Emely Dunton (1888)." [SinW] (36) Wint 88-89, p. 30.
"Her Mouth a Promise Still." [ChamLR] (2:1, #3) Fall 88, p. 42.
"Hope's Poem." [Footwork] ('88) 88, p. 29.
"In Your Absence." [ChamLR] (2:1, #3) Fall 88, p. 43.
"Jane Ann Dunton (1888)." [SinW] (36) Wint 88-89, p. 29.
"Leda's Sister and the Geese." [HolCrit] (25:4) O 88, back cover.
"Leda's Sister and the Geese." [LightY] ('88/9) 88, p. 120.
2. AALFS, Janet
"Branded." [SinW] (36) Wint 88-89, p. 123-124.
3. AARNES, William
"Final Chore." [PoetC] (19:3) Spr 88, p. 37-38.
"Making Twilight." [SouthernR] (24:2) Spr 88, p. 343-344.
4. AARON, Jonathan
"Below Argentina." [WestHR] (42:4) Wint 88, p. 306.
"The Consultation." [WestHR] (42:4) Wint 88, p. 303.
"Death, the Philosopher." [WestHR] (42:4) Wint 88, p. 310.
"The White Room." [WestHR] (42:4) Wint 88, p. 308-309.
"Your Angela." [WestHR] (42:4) Wint 88, p. 304-305.
5. ABERNETHY, Hugh C., Jr.
"Drifting from Paradise." [KanQ] (20:3) Sum 88, p. 158.
"Next to Nowhere and Close to Everything." [MidAR] (8:1) 88, p. 10.
"Remote Station." [KanQ] (20:3) Sum 88, p. 157.
6. ABRAMSON, Neal
"Be Dazzled to Ceci." [Lactuca] (11) O 88, p. 34.
7. ABSE, Dannie
"Of Itzig and the Horse." [Antaeus] (60) Spr 88, p. 236.
"A Prescription." [NewEngR] (10:4) Sum 88, p. 435-436.
"Smiling Through." [Poetry] (151:6) Mr 88, p. 469-470.
8. ACEVEDO, Diana
"Icarus' Absence." [PacificR] (6) Spr 88, p. 9.
"Xochitl." [PacificR] (6) Spr 88, p. 8.
9. ACKERMAN, Diane
"At Walt Whitman's Birthplace, Huntington, Long Island." [KenR] (NS 10:1) Wint 88, p. 42-43.
"Aviatrix." [KenR] (NS 10:1) Wint 88, p. 41.
"Beija-Flor" (Hummingbird). [Poetry] (152:4) Jl 88, p. 200-201.
"Letter of Retainer" (For Morton Janklow). [Poetry] (152:1) Ap 88, p. 32-34.
"Nightletter to Loren Eiseley." [MichQR] (27:3) Sum 88, p. 446.
"Roll Top Desk." [MichQR] (27:3) Sum 88, p. 447.
"Soft Lens." [KenR] (NS 10:1) Wint 88, p. 40-41.
"Transition." [GettyR] (1:4) Aut 88, p. 723.
"Wanderlust." [GettyR] (1:4) Aut 88, p. 724.
"We Are Listening." [Poetry] (151:4) Ja 88, p. 346.
10. ACOSTA POSADA, Armando
"Breach." [PaintedB] (36) 88, p. 55-57.
"Oceanic Elegy" (for P.M.S.). [PaintedB] (36) 88, p. 52-53.
11. ADAMS, B. B.
"Giving Up." [Amelia] (4:4, #11) 88, p. 85.
12. ADAMS, Chelsea
"Caroline." [Wind] (18:62) 88, p. 45.
13. ADAMS, Coralie
"Bad, Dirty Poems." [Bogg] (59) 88, p. 29.
"Version #1." [Bogg] (60) 88, p. 9.

14. ADAMS, LaVerne
"Leaving Banff." [Dandel] (15:1) Spr-Sum 88, p. 34.
15. ADAMS, Michael E.
"Cutting Through." [HiramPoR] (44/45) Spr-Wint 88, p. 7.
16. ADAMS, Neil
"Beneath His Finger." [DenQ] (22:3) Wint 88, p. 251.
17. ADAN CASTELAR, Jose
"Moises Moreira." [Mairena] (10:25) 88, p. 27-28.
18. ADCOCK, Betty
"Digression on the Nuclear Age." [TriQ] (71) Wint 88, p. 117.
"One of a Kind." [TarRP] (28:1) Fall 88, p. 30.
"Rent House." [TriQ] (71) Wint 88, p. 113-116.
19. ADCOCK, Fleur
"The Blackbird." [Antaeus] (60) Spr 88, p. 193-194.
"Heliopsis Scabra." [Antaeus] (60) Spr 88, p. 192.
"My Father." [PartR] (55:1) Wint 88, p. 62-63.
20. ADDIEGO, John
"Mission Nuestra Señora de la Soledad." [NowestR] (26:2) 88, p. 63-64.
"Mission San Francisco de Asís." [NowestR] (26:2) 88, p. 61-62.
21. ADDONIZIO, Kim
"The Night Princess." [FiveFR] (6) 88, p. 76.
22. ADILMAN, Mona Elaine
"The Pomegranate Widow." [Quarry] (37:4) Aut 88, p. 58-59.
23. ADLER, Carol
"Matins — Coup D'Oeil" (For Doug Dempster). [BallSUF] (29:4) Aut 88, p. 24-25.
24. ADLER, Cori
"*Panahaiko* by Motorcycle." [PoetL] (83:4) Wint 88-89, p. 41-42.
25. ADRIAN, Vonna
"By Yon Bonny Banks or Thereabout." [LightY] ('88/9) 88, p. 166.
"Clerihews" (2 poems). [LightY] ('88/9) 88, p. 73.
26. AFAMADO, Gladys
"Las botellas se alinean en los estantes." [Mairena] (10:25) 88, p. 130.
27. AFROUZ, Novin
"A Country" (tr. by the author). [Vis] (26) 88, p. 14.
"Words" (tr. by the author). [Vis] (26) 88, p. 15.
28. AGNYATSVET, Edzi
"The 'Appassionata'" (tr. by Walter May). [NegC] (8:1/2) 88, p. 26-27.
29. AGOOS, Julie
"Bois de Boulogne." [YaleR] (78:1) Aut 88, p. 116-117.
"Lake in Rain." [YaleR] (78:1) Aut 88, p. 117-118.
"Where I Was." [Boulevard] (3:2/3) Fall 88, p. 139-140.
30. AGOSIN, Marjorie
"Beyond the Dawn" (tr. by Cola Franzen). [HangL] (52) 88, p. 49.
"Blood Nest" (tr. by Cola Franzen). [Vis] (26) 88, p. 48.
"Disappeared Woman III" (tr. by Cola Franzen). [Vis] (26) 88, p. 48.
"Si Me Permiten." [HangL] (52) 88, p. 50, 52.
"Tras el Alba." [HangL] (52) 88, p. 48.
"With Your Permission" (tr. by Cola Franzen). [HangL] (52) 88, p. 51, 53.
31. AGRICOLA, Sandra
"Gyroscope." [OhioR] (42) 88, p. 23.
32. AGTE, Bruce
"Birds." [Sequoia] (32:1) Spr-Sum 88, p. 7.
33. AGUEROS, Jack
"Sonnet for Angelo Monterosa." [HangL] (52) 88, p. 56.
"Sonnet Substantially Like the Words of Fulano Rodriguez One Position Ahead of Me on the Unemployement Line." [HangL] (52) 88, p. 54.
34. AGUILAR DIAZ, Gaspar
"Alguien Sabe Dónde Pasó la Última Noche Roque Dalton?" [Rohwedder] (3) Spr 88, p. 8-9.
"Does Anyone Know Where Roque Dalton Spent His Final Night?" (tr. by John Oliver Simon). [Rohwedder] (3) Spr 88, p. 8-9.
35. AGUIRRE, Mirta
"Canción Antigua a Che Guevara." [Areíto] (1:2) F 88, p. 35.
"Elegías." [Areíto] (1:2) F 88, inside front cover.
"Historia" (Recuerdo de Juan Ruiz, Arcipreste de Hita). [Areíto] (1:2) F 88, inside back cover.

36. AHLSCHWEDE, Margrethe
"Honda FM." [Plain] (8:1) Fall 87, p. 10.
"I Remember Yesterday Asking About Snow." [Plain] (9:1) Fall 88, p. 20.
"June Rain." [Plain] (8:2) Wint 88, p. 23.
37. AHO, Margaret
"Alyssum." [BelPoJ] (38:3) Spr 88, p. 38.
"Foxglove (Digitalis)." [BelPoJ] (38:3) Spr 88, p. 39.
38. AI
"The Resurrection of Elvis Presley." [Chelsea] (47) 88, p. 82-84.
39. AICHINGER, Ilse
"Bobinger's Complaint" (tr. by Patricia Dobler). [MidAR] (8:2) 88, p. 189.
"Part of the Question" (tr. by Patricia Dobler). [MidAR] (8:2) 88, p. 190.
40. AIELLO, Kate
"Salud." [Bogg] (59) 88, p. 19.
41. AISENBERG, Katy
"Something Borrowed" (for T.C. d. 10/84). [PartR] (55:4) Fall 88, p. 623-625.
42. AISENBERG, Nadya
"Hope" (for Nadezhda Mandelstam). [AntR] (46:2) Spr 88, p. 238-239.
"The Universe Carries the Egg the World Desires." [Ploughs] (14:1) 88, p. 62-63.
43. AKHMADULINA, Bella
"Another" (tr. by Diana Senechal). [Trans] (20) Spr 88, p. 208.
"The Christmas Tree in the Hospital Corridor" (tr. by William Jay Smith and Svetlana Kluge). [AmerPoR] (17:3) My-Je 88, p. 40.
"The Death of the Owl" (tr. by William Jay Smith and Svetlana Kluge). [AmerPoR] (17:3) My-Je 88, p. 38.
"Don't Devote Much Time to Me" (tr. by Diana Senechal). [Trans] (20) Spr 88, p. 207.
"A New Notebook" (tr. by Diana Senechal). [Trans] (20) Spr 88, p. 209.
"Raphael Day" (tr. by William Jay Smith and Svetlana Kluge). [AmerPoR] (17:3) My-Je 88, p. 39.
"The Resort" (tr. by William Jay Smith and Svetlana Kluge). [AmerPoR] (17:3) My-Je 88, p. 39.
"The Theater" (tr. by F. D. Reeve). [AmerPoR] (17:3) My-Je 88, p. 40.
"Who Knows If I May Roam the Earth" (tr. by Diana Senechal). [Trans] (20) Spr 88, p. 208.
44. AKHMATOVA, Anna
"223. Little Song" (tr. by Judith Hemschemeyer). [SouthernR] (24:3) Sum 88, p. 537.
"224. And here, left alone, I" (tr. by Judith Hemschemeyer). [SouthernR] (24:3) Sum 88, p. 535-536.
"229. Long years I waited for him in vain" (tr. by Judith Hemschemeyer). [SouthernR] (24:3) Sum 88, p. 536.
"551. *De profundis*, My generation" (tr. by Judith Hemschemeyer). [SouthernR] (24:3) Sum 88, p. 537.
"561. They will forget? — How astonishing!" (tr. by Judith Hemschemeyer). [SouthernR] (24:3) Sum 88, p. 538.
"568. Inscription on a Book" (tr. by Judith Hemschemeyer). [SouthernR] (24:3) Sum 88, p. 538.
"Evening" (tr. by Lenore Mayhew). [Field] (39) Fall 88, p. 8.
"Everything Promised Him to Me" (tr. by Judith Hemschemeyer). [TriQ] (73) Fall 88, p. 93.
"Flowers and Non-Living Things" (tr. by Lenore Mayhew). [Field] (39) Fall 88, p. 12.
"I Don't Speak with Anyone for a Week" (tr. by Richard McKane). [Field] (39) Fall 88, p. 17.
"It's Not with a Lover's Lyre" (tr. by Lyn Coffin). [Field] (39) Fall 88, p. 40.
"The Neighbor, Out of Pity" (tr. by Judith Hemschemeyer). [TriQ] (73) Fall 88, p. 94.
"Northern Elegies" (Selection: "Four," tr. by Liza Tucker). [Field] (39) Fall 88, p. 32-33.
"So We Lowered Our Eyes" (tr. by Judith Hemschemeyer). [NewEngR] (11:2) Wint 88, p. 141.
"Terror, Fingering Things in the Dark" (tr. by Judith Hemschemeyer). [Field] (39) Fall 88, p. 21.
"To the Memory of V. S. Sreznevskaya" (tr. by Judith Hemschemeyer). [TriQ] (73) Fall 88, p. 95.
"White Night" (tr. by Judith Hemschemeyer). [NewEngR] (11:2) Wint 88, p. 140.
45. AKLILU, Atlabachew
"America." [Vis] (26) 88, p. 8.

46. AL-KINANI, Al-Shaddakh
"On Death" (tr. by Arthur Wormhoudt). [Paint] (15:30) Aut 88, p. 43.
47. AL-MUSHAFI
"The Quince" (tr. from the Spanish of Emilio García Gómez by Christopher Middleton and Leticia Garza-Falcón). [NewYorker] (64:29) 5 S 88, p. 22.
48. AL-TURTUSI, Abu Kakr
"Absence" (tr. from the Spanish of Emilio García Gómez by Christopher Middleton and Leticia Garza-Falcón). [NewYorker] (64:29) 5 S 88, p. 23.
49. ALABAU, Magaly
"Poemas de Electra, Clitemnestra" (IX, III). [Lyra] (1:3) 88, p. 25.
50. ALARCON, Francisco X.
"Antigua Canción." [FiveFR] (6) 88, p. 34.
"Cuarto Oscuro." [FiveFR] (6) 88, p. 32.
"Dark Room" (tr. by Francisco Aragon). [FiveFR] (6) 88, p. 33.
"Old Song" (tr. by Francisco Aragon). [FiveFR] (6) 88, p. 35.
51. ALBA, Alicia Gaspar de
"After 21 Years, a Postcard from My Father." [Americas] (16:3/4) Fall-Wint 88, p. 49-50.
"Bamba Basilica." [Americas] (16:3/4) Fall-Wint 88, p. 55.
"Crooked Foot Speaks / Habla Pata Chueca." [Americas] (16:3/4) Fall-Wint 88, p. 56.
"From Dust to Dust." [Americas] (16:3/4) Fall-Wint 88, p. 54.
"Holy Ground." [Americas] (16:3/4) Fall-Wint 88, p. 52-53.
"In the Shadow of Greater Things." [Americas] (16:3/4) Fall-Wint 88, p. 512.
52. ALBERT, Sam
"I Said Girl to a Woman Eighty Years Old." [TexasR] (9:3/4) Fall-Wint 88, p. 1.
53. ALBERTI, Antonio
"Autorretrato." [Inti] (28) Otoño 88, p. 147.
"Código." [Inti] (28) Otoño 88, p. 148-149.
"Los Perros." [Inti] (28) Otoño 88, p. 149.
"Sobre los Sueños." [Inti] (28) Otoño 88, p. 148.
54. ALCALAY, Ammiel
"I Had Thought of Writing a Play Based on the Following Facts." [Caliban] (4) 88, p. 144-147.
55. ALCOSSER, Sandra
"Beauty Is the Sun's Daughter." [CutB] (29/30) 88, p. 12-13.
"Michael's Wine." [YaleR] (77:2) Wint 88, p. 297-298.
"The Stray Sod." [CutB] (29/30) 88, p. 11.
"Woodpecker." [NoAmR] (273:3) S 88, p. 48.
56. ALDRICH, Marcia
"As When" (for David Hart Isomaki). [GreensboroR] (45) Wint 88-89, p. 76-77.
"Baby Reaching for an Apple" (from an 1893 Mary Cassatt painting). [GreensboroR] (45) Wint 88-89, p. 78-79.
"Blackberrying." [GreensboroR] (45) Wint 88-89, p. 73-75.
57. ALDRIDGE, Richard
"The Siege" (to my father at 89). [PoetC] (19:3) Spr 88, p. 30.
58. ALEGRIA, Claribel
"Documentary" (tr. by the author and Darwin T. Flakoll). [ParisR] (30:108) Fall 88, p. 156-159.
"Little Cambray Tamales" (for Eduardo and Helena, tr. by the author and Darwin T. Flakoll). [ParisR] (30:108) Fall 88, p. 155.
"Mortally Wounded" (tr. by Darwin J. Flakoll). [Bomb] (24) Sum 88, p. 68.
"My City" (tr. by Darwin J. Flakoll). [Bomb] (24) Sum 88, p. 68.
"The Procession" (tr. by Darwin J. Flakoll). [Bomb] (24) Sum 88, p. 68.
"The Return" (tr. by Darwin J. Flakoll). [Bomb] (24) Sum 88, p. 69.
"Summing Up" (tr. by the author and Darwin T. Flakoll). [ParisR] (30:108) Fall 88, p. 154.
59. ALESHIRE, Joan
"Engrams." [Poetry] (152:5) Ag 88, p. 279-280.
"Healing." [Poetry] (152:5) Ag 88, p. 280-281.
60. ALEXANDER, Charles
"Remains" (part 3 of a series). [Sonora] (16) Fall 88, p. 63.
61. ALEXANDER, Elizabeth
"Bearden." [AmerPoR] (17:2) Mr-Ap 88, p. 39.
"Monet at Giverny." [SouthernR] (24:3) Sum 88, p. 576.
"Penmanship." [SouthernR] (24:3) Sum 88, p. 576-577.
"Van DerZee" (1886-1983). [AmerPoR] (17:2) Mr-Ap 88, p. 39.

62. ALEXANDER, Meena
"Aunt Chinna." [MassR] (29:4) Wint 88-89, p. 625-627.
"Passion." [MassR] (29:4) Wint 88-89, p. 628-631.
"The Storm: A Poem in Five Parts" (For U.R. Anantha Murthy. Selections). [Nimrod] (31:2) Spr-Sum 88, p. 39-49.
"Under the Incense Tree." [MassR] (29:4) Wint 88-89, p. 627-628.
63. ALEXANDER, Pamela
"Audubon Remembers American Falls." [Field] (39) Fall 88, p. 64-65.
"Table of Elements." [Poetry] (153:3) D 88, p. 144-145.
64. ALEXANDER, Will
"Lightning" (Selection: Part I: "Stepped Leader"). [Temblor] (8) 88, p. 146-154.
ALGECIRAS, Ben Ani Ruh of
See BEN ANI RUH OF ALGECIRAS
65. ALI, Agha Shahid
"Be Near Me" (tr. of Faiz Ahmed Faiz). [NewRena] (7:2, #22) Spr 88, p. 51.
"Before You Came" (tr. of Faiz Ahmed Faiz). [NewRena] (7:2, #22) Spr 88, p. 23.
"The City from Here" (tr. of Ahmed Faiz Faiz). [Nimrod] (31:2) Spr-Sum 88, p. 104.
"Evening" (tr. of Faiz Ahmed Faiz). [NewRena] (7:2, #22) Spr 88, p. 25.
"Evening in the Asylum." [QW] (26) Wint 88, p. 115.
"Ghazal: In the sun's last embers, the evening star burns to ash" (tr. of Faiz Ahmed Faiz). [NewRena] (7:2, #22) Spr 88, p. 30.
"The Heart Gives Up" (tr. of Faiz Ahmed Faiz). [NewRena] (7:2, #22) Spr 88, p. 27.
"I Dream I Return to Tucson in the Monsoons." [MassR] (29:4) Wint 88-89, p. 717-720.
"It Is Spring" (tr. of Faiz Ahmed Faiz). [QW] (26) Wint 88, p. 114.
"A Last Speaker" (tr. of Ahmed Faiz Faiz). [Nimrod] (31:2) Spr-Sum 88, p. 106-107.
"Snow on the Desert." [ParisR] (30:107) Sum 88, p. 202-205.
"Solitary Confinement" (tr. of Faiz Ahmed Faiz). [NewRena] (7:2, #22) Spr 88, p. 29.
"Vista" (tr. of Faiz Ahmed Faiz). [NewRena] (7:2, #22) Spr 88, p. 49.
66. ALIESAN, Jody
"Fate." [CrabCR] (5:1) Wint 88, p. 16.
67. ALISHAN, Leonardo P.
"Anahit As Armenia." [Vis] (26) 88, p. 11.
68. ALKALAY-GUT, Karen
"Hostage Crisis." [PraS] (62:2) Sum 88, p. 77-79.
"I Guard the Children in the School Yard" (tr. of Yehuda Amichai). [PraS] (62:2) Sum 88, p. 79-80.
"New York University" (tr. of Yehuda Amichai). [PraS] (62:2) Sum 88, p. 80.
"Transportation." [Lips] (14) 88, p. 26.
69. ALLAN, A. T.
"Dreaming." [ChamLR] (1:2, #2) Spr 88, p. 94.
"Temporary." [ChamLR] (1:2, #2) Spr 88, p. 95.
70. ALLARDT, Linda
"Is It Because the Light." [NegC] (8:3) 88, p. 137.
"Mine." [GeoR] (42:1) Spr 88, p. 129.
71. ALLBERY, Debra
"Sentiment." [KenR] (NS 10:1) Wint 88, p. 82.
"Sherwood Anderson Walks Out." [KenR] (NS 10:1) Wint 88, p. 80-81.
"Tour of Duty." [YaleR] (77:2) Wint 88, p. 240-241.
72. ALLEGRUCCI, Scott
"A Discovery in Winter." [LittleBR] (5:2) Wint 88-89, p. 17.
73. ALLEN, Annette
"A Season Begins" (for Charles). [Footwork] ('88) 88, p. 59.
74. ALLEN, Cheryl
"Autumn Whispers." [PottPort] (10) 88, p. 41.
75. ALLEN, Deborah
"Salt Marsh." [PaintedB] (36) 88, p. 46.
76. ALLEN, Dick
"The Flutist." [TexasR] (9:3/4) Fall-Wint 88, p. 2.
"Lost Friends." [Boulevard] (3:2/3) Fall 88, p. 37-38.
77. ALLEN, Edward
"Look." [PoetryNW] (29:4) Wint 88-89, p. 40-41.
"Next Door." [PoetryNW] (29:4) Wint 88-89, p. 39.
"The Night Is Made of Numbers." [PoetryNW] (29:4) Wint 88-89, p. 37-38.
78. ALLEN, Gilbert
"The Flickering Jungle of Paris." [Wind] (18:62) 88, p. 2.

"In Old Salem" (Winston-Salem, North Carolina). [Interim] (7:1) Spr 88, p. 37.
"Signs" (for Bill Aarnes). [Wind] (18:62) 88, p. 1.
"What We Cannot Imagine." [SouthernPR] (28:2) Fall 88, p. 31-32.

79. ALLEN, Jeffrey Renard
"Grinding Names." [ChrC] (105:34) 16 N 88, p. 1034.

80. ALLEN, Jo Nan
"Bourbon Street." [Phoenix] (9:1/2) 88, p. 60.

81. ALLEN, Kathy
"Possessions." [Wind] (18:63) 88, p. 5.

82. ALLEN, Paul
"For the Uncommon Conditions." [CimR] (82) Ja 88, p. 40.
"My Daughter's House." [Crazy] (34) Spr 88, p. 52.
"Natural Causes." [PoetryNW] (29:3) Aut 88, p. 40-41.
"Pickup." [Crazy] (34) Spr 88, p. 49-51.

83. ALLISON, Gay
"Love, on the Bus to Haliburton." [PraF] (9:4) Wint 88-89, p. 54-55.

84. ALLMAN, John
"A House." [PoetryNW] (29:4) Wint 88-89, p. 18.
"The Planets." [BelPoJ] (38:3) Spr 88, p. 22-37.
"Reading Proust to Wild Donkeys in the Caribbean." [WilliamMR] (26:1) Spr 88, p. 95.
"Reading *The Times* in the Car Wash." [PoetryNW] (29:4) Wint 88-89, p. 16-17.

ALMERIA, Ben Safar al-Marini of
See BEN SAFAR AL-MARINI OF ALMERIA

85. ALMON, Bert
"Connoisseurship of Stones" (glacial valley, Battle River). [PraF] (9:4) Wint 88-89, p. 49-50.
"Restoring a Photograph" (Mary Lora Smith, 1854-1928). [ChiR] (36:2) Aut 88, p. 35-36.
"This Windy Morning." [MidwQ] (29:3) Spr 88, p. 333.

86. ALPIZAR, Juan Alberto
"Elegía de Mí Mismo." [Mairena] (10:25) 88, p. 141.

87. ALTIZER, Nell
"Letter." [MassR] (29:2) Sum 88, p. 224.
"Letter to Karma." [MassR] (29:2) Sum 88, p. 225-226.

88. ALURISTA
"Bartolo's Kuilmas." [BilingR] (13:1/2) Ja-Ag 86, c1988, p. 92-94.
"It Has Been Said." [BilingR] (13:1/2) Ja-Ag 86, c1988, p. 152.
"Southwestern Treck in Four Part Harmony." [RedBass] (13) 88, p. 13-14.

89. ALVARADO DE RICORD, Elsie
"Humani Sumus." [Mairena] (10:25) 88, p. 181.

90. ALVAREZ, Julia
"The Weekend." [Spirit] (9:1) 88, p. 30.

91. ALVAREZ, Maria Auxiliadora
"Ella me abre las piernas." [Mairena] (10:25) 88, p. 62.

92. ALVAREZ, Soledad
"Duda." [CuadP] (5:14) Enero-Abril 88, p. 34.
"Odio de la Ciudad." [CuadP] (5:14) Enero-Abril 88, p. 35.
"Pasaje de Sueño." [CuadP] (5:14) Enero-Abril 88, p. 33-34.
"El Sur" (A Pedro Vergés). [CuadP] (5:14) Enero-Abril 88, p. 34.

ALVEZ, Delia Cazarre de
See CAZARRE DE ALVEZ, Delia

AMAT, Carlos Oquendo de
See OQUENDO DE AMAT, Carlos

93. AMBRUSO, Diane
"Afternoons." [Amelia] (5:2, #13) 88, p. 120.

94. AMICHAI, Yehuda
"How Do You Manage a Rowdy Child?" (tr. by Chana Bloch). [Zyzzyva] (4:2) Sum 88, p. 81.
"I Guard the Children in the School Yard" (tr. by Karen Alkalay-Gut). [PraS] (62:2) Sum 88, p. 79-80.
"It's a Shame. We Were a Fine Invention" (tr. by Bernhard Frnak). [ColR] (NS 15:2) Fall-Wint 88, p. 75.
"New York University" (tr. by Karen Alkalay-Gut). [PraS] (62:2) Sum 88, p. 80.
"Sleep in Jerusalem" (tr. by Matt Steinglass). [HarvardA] (122:4) My 88, p. 27.

95. AMICK, Steve
"From the Top." [AnotherCM] (18) 88, p. 7.

"They Bully You Around in Detroit." [AnotherCM] (18) 88, p. 6.
96. AMMONS, A. R.
"All's All." [Poetry] (143, i.e. 153:1) O 88, p. 4.
"Anxiety's Prosody." [Poetry] (143, i.e. 153:1) O 88, p. 2.
"Boon." [NewRep] (199:5) 1 Ag 88, p. 48.
"Ceppagna." [NewYorker] (64:5) 21 Mr 88, p. 40.
"Coming Clearing." [Poetry] (143, i.e. 153:1) O 88, p. 1-2.
"Commissary." [PraS] (62:2) Sum 88, p. 36.
"The Damned." [YaleR] (77:3) Spr 88, p. 435-436.
"The Deep Slow." [GrandS] (7:4) Sum 88, p. 81.
"The Incomplete Life." [OhioR] (41) 88, p. 106.
"Readings by Ways." [PartR] (55:4) Fall 88, p. 611.
"Roselie." [NewRep] (198:10) 7 Mr 88, p. 34.
"Sparklings." [GrandS] (7:4) Sum 88, p. 83.
"Spot Check." [GrandS] (7:4) Sum 88, p. 82.
"Strings" (for Don Randel). [TarRP] (28:1) Fall 88, p. 60-61.
"The Surprise of an Ending." [Poetry] (143, i.e. 153:1) O 88, p. 3.
"Tenure's Pleasures." [Abraxas] (37) 88, p. 77-78.
"Time after Time." [OhioR] (41) 88, p. 105.
"What Was That Again." [OhioR] (41) 88, p. 107.
97. AMPRIMOZ, Alexandre L.
"Comedy of Nostalgia." [CanLit] (117) Sum 88, p. 23.
"The Fiction of Poems." [CanLit] (117) Sum 88, p. 71.
98. ANANIA, Michael
"Gin Music." [TriQ] (73) Fall 88, p. 96-97.
99. ANAPORTE, J.
"The Space Between." [PaintedB] (32/33) 88, p. 55.
100. ANDERSEN, Marguerite
"Les framboises sauvages, délice des voyages d'été." [PottPort] (10) 88, p. 43.
101. ANDERSON, Bobby
"Hard Light." [Thrpny] (33) Spr 88, p. 22.
102. ANDERSON, Chris
"Burke-Gilman." [CrabCR] (5:1) Wint 88, p. 28.
"Feeder." [CrabCR] (5:3) Fall 88, p. 14.
"Harbor." [CrabCR] (5:1) Wint 88, p. 28.
103. ANDERSON, Daniel
"Fingertips." [CinPR] (17) Spr 88, p. 73.
104. ANDERSON, Ellen
"County Scandal" (The 14th Kansas Poetry Contest, prize winner). [LittleBR] (5:2) Wint 88-89, p. 62.
105. ANDERSON, Jack
"Mysteries." [AnotherCM] (18) 88, p. 8.-9.
"The Paradise of the Shopping Mall." [Spirit] (9:1) 88, p. 78-80.
"Raving." [Spirit] (9:1) 88, p. 81-82.
106. ANDERSON, James
"The Flickering Lights of a Winter Afternoon." [LittleM] (15:3/4) 88, p. 54-55.
"The Next Life." [LittleM] (15:3/4) 88, p. 53.
"The Toledo Museum." [LittleM] (15:3/4) 88, p. 51-52.
107. ANDERSON, Jon
"CNN." [Sonora] (16) Fall 88, p. 45-46.
"Good Morning Little Schoolgirl." [Sonora] (16) Fall 88, p. 48.
"Winnepasaukee." [Sonora] (16) Fall 88, p. 47.
108. ANDERSON, Linda
"Anna Jameson in Canada to Her Friend Ottilie von Goethe in Germany, 1834." [LittleM] (15:3/4) 88, p. 101-102.
109. ANDERSON, Maggie
"As Long As I Can." [PoetryE] (25) Spr 88, p. 46.
"Black Raspberries." [PoetryE] (25) Spr 88, p. 50-52.
"The End of Summer in a Small Garden." [PoetryE] (25) Spr 88, p. 45.
"The Memory of Venetian Evening." [PoetryE] (25) Spr 88, p. 48-49.
"Profligacy." [PoetryE] (25) Spr 88, p. 47.
110. ANDERSON, Mia
"Elegy for Myself" (for Harriet). [Quarry] (37:4) Aut 88, p. 32-33.
"The Saugeen Sonata." [MalR] (84) S 88, p. 43-64.
111. ANDERSON, Michael
"The Walks" (Excerpt). [Sink] (3) 88, p. 50-54.

112. ANDERSON, Nathalie
"Aulophobia, Fear of Flues." [ParisR] (30:107) Sum 88, p. 57.
"Cymophobia, Fear of Waves." [ParisR] (30:107) Sum 88, p. 56.
"Erythrophobia, Fear of Blushing." [ParisR] (30:107) Sum 88, p. 58.
"Nephophobia, Fear of Clouds." [ParisR] (30:107) Sum 88, p. 59.
113. ANDERSON, Rod
"Diagnostics." [Grain] (16:2) Sum 88, p. 54.
114. ANDERSON, Sallie
"Redbird." [NewYorker] (64:26) 15 Ag 88, p. 78.
115. ANDERSON, T. J., III
"Better Get It in Yo' Soul" (Charles Mingus). [Notus] (3:2) Fall 88, p. 45.
116. ANDRADA, María del Rosario
"Eva." [LetFem] (14:1/2) Primavera-Otoño 88, p. 145.
117. ANDRADE, Carlos Drummond de
"The Hand" (tr. by Ron Horning). [NewYorker] (64:37) 31 O 88, p. 40.
"Innocents of Leblon" (tr. by Ron Horning). [NewYorker] (64:21) 11 Jl 88, p. 26.
"Secret" (tr. by Stan Rose). [CutB] (31/32) 88, p. 79.
"Untitled: I missed the bus and lost hope" (tr. by Stan Rose). [CutB] (31/32) 88, p. 80.
"Within a Budding Grove" (tr. by Ron Horning). [NewYorker] (64:21) 11 Jl 88, p. 26.
118. ANDRADE, Eugenio de
"Come Closer" (tr. by Alexis Levitin). [Amelia] (4:4, #11) 88, p. 89.
"Solar Matter" (Selections: 1, 4, 6, 7, 11, 14, in English, tr. by Alexis Levitin). [Rohwedder] (4) [Wint 88-89], p. 15-16.
"Solar Matter" (Selections: 1, 4, 6, 7, 11, 14, in Portugese). [Rohwedder] (4) [Wint 88-89], p. 15-16.
ANDRADE, Jorge Carrera
See CARRERA ANDRADE, Jorge
119. ANDRE, Michael
"I feel like I am playing chess against Samuel Beckett." [Abraxas] (37) 88, p. 56.
120. ANDREA, Marianne
"Odyssey." [MidwQ] (29:2) Wint 88, p. 215.
"Weather Report." [MidwQ] (29:2) Wint 88, p. 214.
"Where the Road Veers Off." [Crosscur] (7:4) 88, p. 51-52.
121. ANDREWS, Bruce
"Saliva Valentines." [Sink] (3) 88, p. 17-20.
"Strictly Confidential" (Selections: Two Sections). [NewAW] (4) Fall 88, p. 63-64.
122. ANDREWS, Michael
"Oatmeal Cookies." [Jacaranda] (3:2) Fall-Wint 88, p. 66-67.
"Riverrun." [Amelia] (5:1, #12) 88, p. 62.
"The Road." [Amelia] (5:1, #12) 88, p. 58-61.
123. ANDREWS, Nancy
"To the Creatures of Galapagos." [KanQ] (20:3) Sum 88, p. 246.
124. ANDREWS, Tom
"The Brother's Country" (John Andrews, 1956-80). [PoetryE] (25) Spr 88, p. 39-44.
"A Language of Hemophilia" (Selections: 5-11). [Timbuktu] (1) Wint-Spr 88, p. 65-70.
125. ANDROLA, Ron
"I Am Not Writing Poems." [Bogg] (60) 88, p. 38.
"Poem for My Father." [Bogg] (60) 88, p. 35.
"Sitting in Antarctica." [Bogg] (60) 88, p. 36.
"Stereo Windows & What A." [Bogg] (60) 88, p. 37.
126. ANDRYCHUK, Kristin
"Addressing the Rocks." [Event] (17:3) Fall 88, p. 72-73.
"Relations." [Event] (17:3) Fall 88, p. 74.
127. ANGELL, Roger
"Greetings, Friends." [NewYorker] (64:45) 26 D 88, p. 26.
128. ANGLESEY, Zoë
"America" (tr. of Ruben Vela). [ColR] (NS 15:2) Fall-Wint 88, p. 88.
"Explain to Me" (tr. of Ana Maria Rodas). [RedBass] (13) 88, p. 16.
"I Didn't Ask for the War" (tr. of Ana Istaru). [ColR] (NS 15:1) Spr-Sum 88, p. 73-74.
"Minute Death in Bed" (tr. of Ana Istaru). [FiveFR] (6) 88, p. 38-39.
"Prison Poem" (tr. of Reyna Hernandez). [ColR] (NS 15:1) Spr-Sum 88, p. 75.
"Scab" (tr. of Ana María Rodas). [CrabCR] (5:1) Wint 88, p. 25.
"We Are" (tr. of Ana Istaru). [CrabCR] (5:1) Wint 88, p. 25.

129. ANNENSKY, Innokenty
"Anguish of White Stone" (tr. by Devon Miller-Duggan and Nancy Tittler). [Paint] (15:30) Aut 88, p. 31.
"January Fairy Tale" (tr. by Devon Miller-Duggan and Nancy Tittler). [Paint] (15:30) Aut 88, p. 30.

130. ANONYMOUS
"An Anchor Lifts" (tr. from the Mediaeval Korean by Constantine Contogenis and Wolhee Choe). [NewEngR] (11:2) Wint 88, p. 180.
"The Black Crow" (tr. from the Mediaeval Korean by Constantine Contogenis and Wolhee Choe). [NewEngR] (11:2) Wint 88, p. 180.
"Crying Ospreys" (From the *Book of Songs*, tr. by Shiguang Hu). [AntR] (46:2) Spr 88, p. 135.
"Freedom makes new tyrants out of old slaves" (from Bogg 30, 1975). [Bogg] (59) 88, p. 41.
"Gathasaptashati" (Selections: 3 Prakrit Verses, English tr. by Martha Ann Selby). [Nimrod] (31:2) Spr-Sum 88, p. 16.
"Haiku: Full of honey" (tr. by Sneharashmi). [Nimrod] (31:2) Spr-Sum 88, p. 72.
"Hainteny" (49 poems in Malagasy and English, tr. by Leonard Fox). [InterPR] (14:2) Fall 88, p. 10-57.
"Invocación en Lengua Yoruba" (Spanish tr. by Alira Muñoz). [Areíto] (1:3) Jl 88, inside front cover.
"Iyuba" (Reiterando homenaje, Spanish tr. by Alira Muñoz). [Areíto] (1:3) Jl 88, inside back cover.
"Kindlings" (tr. from the Korean by Graeme Wilson). [LitR] (32:1) Fall 88, p. 68.
"Memento" (tr. of anonymous Korean poet by Graeme Wilson). [Jacaranda] (3:2) Fall-Wint 88, p. 144.
"Papago Deer Songs" (tr. by Donald Bahr and Brian Swann). [SouthernHR] (22:3) Sum 88, p. 238-240.
"Prakrit Verses" (2 verses, selected by Amritjit Singh, English tr. by David Ray). [Nimrod] (31:2) Spr-Sum 88, p. 17.
"Quince" (From the *Book of Songs*, tr. by Shiguang Hu). [AntR] (46:2) Spr 88, p. 156.
"The Reeds" (From the *Book of Songs*, tr. by Shiguang Hu). [AntR] (46:2) Spr 88, p. 165.
"Sing Along with Rehnquist" (from "Old Favorites with the Chief Justice"). [Harp] (277:1661) O 88, p. 23.
"Subhashitaratnakosha" (Selections: 2 Sanskrit poems collected by Vidyakara, tr. by Martha Ann Selby). [Nimrod] (31:2) Spr-Sum 88, p. 18.

131. ANSTETT, Aaron
"Before the Frost." [RagMag] (6:2) Fall 88, p. 6.
"Here and There." [RagMag] (6:2) Fall 88, p. 7.
"Surrender." [RagMag] (6:2) Fall 88, p. 8.

132. ANTHONY, Anthony Michael
"A Bronx Threnody" (tr. from the New Englandish by the author). [HarvardA] (The New Yorker spoof issue) 88?, p. 11.

133. ANTHONY, Pat
"Reserved" (Seaton Honorable Mention Poem 1988). [KanQ] (20:3) Sum 88, p. 25.

134. ANTIEAU, David K.
"Crazy." [ChrC] (105:29) 12 O 88, p. 893.

ANTIN, Carolina d'
See D'ANTIN, Carolina

135. ANTLER
"Paleolithic Consciousness Orbited by TVs." [RiverS] (27) 88, p. 75.
"Underwater Lake Michigan Socrates." [LightY] ('88/9) 88, p. 162-163.
"Your Poetry's No Good Because It's Too Easy to Understand." [RiverS] (27) 88, p. 76-78.

136. ANZALDUA, Gloria
"That Dark Shining Thing" (for Sandra Rounds, Bessie Jo Faris, & Denise Brugman). [SinW] (33) Fall 87, p. 73-74.

137. APPEL, Dori
"Escape Artist." [ChamLR] (2:1, #3) Fall 88, p. 44.
"Giraffe Between Earth and Sky." [ChamLR] (2:1, #3) Fall 88, p. 46.
"Novice." [ChamLR] (2:1, #3) Fall 88, p. 45.

138. APPLEBY, Frank W.
"Stolen Dreams." [DeKalbLAJ] (21:3/4) 88, p. 46.

139. APPLEMAN, Philip
"Fleas." [LightY] ('88/9) 88, p. 205-206.
"Heavenly Body" (Halley's Comet, 1986). [Poetry] (151:5) F 88, p. 417-418.
140. APPLEWHITE, James
"Clear Winter." [Writer] (101:8) Ag 88, p. 25.
"A Conversation." [SouthernR] (24:3) Sum 88, p. 567-570.
"Grob, That Improbable Bird" (for Roger Hivert). [VirQR] (64:1) Wint 88, p. 75-76.
"The Snow's Code." [KenR] (NS 10:1) Wint 88, p. 73.
"The War Against Nature." [VirQR] (64:1) Wint 88, p. 74.
141. APRIL, Susan
"Egress." [Vis] (27) 88, p. 28.
142. ARAGON, Francisco
"Dark Room" (tr. of Francisco X. Alarcon). [FiveFR] (6) 88, p. 33.
"Old Song" (tr. of Francisco X. Alarcon). [FiveFR] (6) 88, p. 35.
143. ARAKELIAN, Caroline
"A Baby Rocks Me Now." [ArtfulD] (14/15) Fall 88, p. 79.
ARANGO, Jorge Valls
See VALLS ARANGO, Jorge
144. ARATANI, Mariko
"The autumn night" (tr. of Ono no Komachi, w. Jane Hirshfield). [AmerPoR] (17:1) Ja-F 88, p. 16.
"I know it must be this way" (tr. of Ono no Komachi, w. Jane Hirshfield). [AmerPoR] (17:1) Ja-F 88, p. 16.
"If the one I've waited for" (tr. of Izumi Shikibu, w. Jane Hirshfield). [AmerPoR] (17:1) Ja-F 88, p. 16.
"Love-soaked, rain soaked" (tr. of Izumi Shikibu, w. Jane Hirshfield). [AmerPoR] (17:1) Ja-F 88, p. 16.
"Lying alone" (tr. of Izumi Shikibu, w. Jane Hirshfield). [AmerPoR] (17:1) Ja-F 88, p. 16.
"The seaweed gatherer's weary feet" (tr. of Ono no Komachi, w. Jane Hirshfield). [AmerPoR] (17:1) Ja-F 88, p. 16.
"The way I must enter" (tr. of Izumi Shikibu, w. Jane Hirshfield). [AmerPoR] (17:1) Ja-F 88, p. 16.
"We live in a tide-swept inlet" (tr. of Izumi Shikibu, w. Jane Hirshfield). [AmerPoR] (17:1) Ja-F 88, p. 16.
"When my desire" (tr. of Ono no Komachi, w. Jane Hirshfield). [AmerPoR] (17:1) Ja-F 88, p. 16.
145. ARAUZ, Susan
"Sweet Chocolate." [Footwork] ('88) 88, p. 59-60.
146. ARB, Jan
"Black Garments" (tr. by Ellen Watson). [Antaeus] (60) Spr 88, p. 285.
147. ARBELECHE, Jorge
"La llama es nada más que la ceniza." [Mairena] (10:25) 88, p. 132.
148. ARBOGAST, Johnny
"Chatanuga Cafe." [Os] (26) 88, p. 13.
149. ARBOGAST, Karen
"Megathoughts." [AlphaBS] (3) Je 88, p. 92-94.
150. ARBOR, Arbor
"Smoking People: Encountering the New Chinese Poetry" (Chapbook 19, tr. by Arbor Arbor et al.). [BelPoJ] (39:2) Wint 88-89, 76 p.
151. ARCHER, Anne
"Noches de Adrenalina" (6 selections: i, xiii-xvii, tr. of Carmen Ollé). [AmerPoR] (17:6) N-D 88, p. 41-43.
152. ARCHER, Nuala
"Before the Call, This Beginning." [Phoenix] (9:1/2) 88, p. 21.
"From a Mobil Home: Through the Os of Booger Holler" (for Emmeca). [CreamCR] (12:2) Sum 88, p. 149-150.
"From a Mobile Home: Through the Os of Booger Holler" (for Emmeca). [SenR] (18:2) 88, p. 60-61.
"Hollywood, Panama." [CreamCR] (12:2) Sum 88, p. 151-153.
"Star*mapping My Trans*atlantic Com*mutes." [CreamCR] (12:2) Sum 88, p. 154-155.
153. ARDERY, Julia
"The Joke." [Caliban] (4) 88, p. 28.
154. AREVALO, Marta de
"Canto a la Palabra." [LetFem] (14:1/2) Primavera-Otoño 88, p. 141.

155. AREVALO, Reyes Gilberto
"Todo Hecho de Amor Es Subversivo." [Mairena] (10:25) 88, p. 155.
156. ARGÜELLES, Ivan
"Lazarus." [GreensboroR] (44) Sum 88, p. 22.
"Desolation Angel." [Abraxas] (37) 88, p. 14.
"Koré." [YellowS] (27) Aut 88, p. 35.
"Naked Brains." [RedBass] (13) 88, p. 25.
"Orphic Fragment." [Abraxas] (37) 88, p. 15.
"The Red Swan." [YellowS] (28) D 88, p. 8-9.
"Text." [Caliban] (4) 88, p. 94-95.
"Translation to Heaven." [ArtfulD] (14/15) Fall 88, p. 83.
"Untitled Diorama" (for christina). [Caliban] (4) 88, p. 96-97.
"Ventura Freeway." [Bogg] (59) 88, p. 53.
"White Lightning." [RedBass] (13) 88, p. 15-16.
157. ARGUETA, Manlio
"Cárcel." [Mairena] (10:25) 88, p. 154-155.
158. ARGYROS, Alex
"Being Somewhere." [Poem] (59) My 88, p. 15.
"Carolina Jessamine." [Grain] (16:3) Fall 88, p. 88.
"Legacy." [Poem] (59) My 88, p. 14.
"Ogygia." [Poem] (59) My 88, p. 17.
"Upon Hearing of a Lover's Death." [Poem] (59) My 88, p. 16.
159. ARIZA, René
"Soneto." [LindLM] (7:2/4) Ap-D 88, p. 12.
160. ARKELL, Chris
"I Had Rubbed Myself with a Towel" (tr. of Eugene Dubnov, w. John Heath-Stubbs). [MissR] (16:1, #46) 88, p. 43.
161. ARMANTROUT, Rae
"Attention." [Sulfur] (8:2, #23) Fall 88, p. 62.
"The Book." [NewAW] (4) Fall 88, p. 35.
"Family Resemblances." [NewAW] (4) Fall 88, p. 36.
"Getting Warm." [Sulfur] (8:2, #23) Fall 88, p. 61.
"Necromance" (Selections: 3 poems). [Temblor] (7) 88, p. 150-154.
162. ARMENTROUT, Anne
"Shower." [Amelia] (4:4, #11) 88, p. 16.
163. ARMITAGE, Barri
"Family Tree" (to my father, 87). [GeoR] (42:2) Sum 88, p. 386-387.
164. ARMITAGE, Simon
"Advertisement." [Verse] (5:3) N 88, p. 60.
165. ARMOUR, Richard
"Say Id Isn't So." [LightY] ('88/9) 88, p. 61.
166. ARMSTRONG, Gene
"Afternoon Visit Late in the Semester." [BellArk] (4:6) N-D 88, p. 10.
"Calendar." [BellArk] (4:6) N-D 88, p. 6.
"Close to Nature." [BellArk] (4:6) N-D 88, p. 4.
"Del Mar and California." [BellArk] (4:5) S-O 88, p. 1.
"A Piece at a Time, I Take You In." [Spirit] (9:1) 88, p. 40.
"Stepping Through." [BellArk] (4:6) N-D 88, p. 3.
167. ARMSTRONG, Patricia Mees
"Unfinished Book." [Writer] (101:6) Je 88, p. 24.
168. ARMSTRONG, Peter
"A Deaf Woman in Her Old Age." [Stand] (29:4) Aut 88, p. 7.
169. ARNDT, Walter
"Experience of Death" (tr. of Rainer Maria Rilke). [Thrpny] (35) Fall 88, p. 14.
170. ARNETT, H.
"Burial." [SoDakR] (26:3) Aut 88, p. 54.
171. ARNETT, Harold
"Late Summer Nightfall." [Wind] (18:63) 88, p. 1.
172. ARRIZON, María Alicia
"A Don Tomás Rivera." [BilingR] (13:1/2) Ja-Ag 86, c1988, p. 102.
173. ARROYO, Rane
"Seascape." [SpoonRQ] (13:1) Wint 88, p. 19.
"Try Angles." [Lactuca] (9) F 88, p. 4.
"Voices Await." [SpoonRQ] (13:1) Wint 88, p. 18.
174. ARTAUD, Antonin
"Gebet" (tr. into German by Paul Celan). [Acts] (8/9) 88, p. 165.

"Prayer" (English tr. of Paul Celan's German tr. by Pierre Joris). [Acts] (8/9) 88, p. 165.
"Prayer" (tr. by Pierre Joris). [Acts] (8/9) 88, p. 164.
"Prière." [Acts] (8/9) 88, p. 164.

175. ARTEGA, Alfred
"Mammon." [YellowS] (27) Aut 88, p. 36.

176. ARVILLA, Mark
"Day at the Cabin." [RagMag] (6:2) Fall 88, p. 10.
"Mother's Day 1985." [RagMag] (6:2) Fall 88, p. 11.

177. ASCHMANN, Charles
"The Graduation Party" (for Yuko Ogasawara, who wrote a thesis for me). [DeKalbLAJ] (21:3/4) 88, p. 46.

178. ASH, John
"Methodical Sonatas." [ParisR] (30:107) Sum 88, p. 116-117.
"My Egypt." [ParisR] (30:107) Sum 88, p. 120-121.
"Smoke." [ParisR] (30:107) Sum 88, p. 122-123.
"Weekends in West Connecticut." [ParisR] (30:107) Sum 88, p. 118-119.

179. ASHLEY, Renée A.
"The Last Night You Are Gone." [SouthernPR] (28:2) Fall 88, p. 6-7.
"Not the First Snow." [MidAR] (8:1) 88, p. 11.
"Wild Radish." [GreensboroR] (44) Sum 88, p. 38-40.

180. ASIM, Jabari
"Dumas." [BlackALF] (22:2) Sum 88, p. 158.

181. ASPENBERG, Gary
"The Choir" (for Robert Bly). [Vis] (27) 88, p. 23.
"For Olga Korbut." [CapeR] (23:1) Spr 88, p. 46.

182. ASPENSTRÖM, Werner
"The Scream" (tr. by D. L. Emblen). [ArtfulD] (14/15) Fall 88, p. 82.

183. ASTHANA, Ghanshyam
"Direction" (tr. of Kedarnath Singh). [Nimrod] (31:2) Spr-Sum 88, p. 78.

184. ATKINS, Kathleen
"Half Moon" (for Michelle). [MemphisSR] (8:2) Spr 88, p. 14.
"Interlude." [ArtfulD] (14/15) Fall 88, p. 5.
"Suspended Pleasure." [MemphisSR] (8:2) Spr 88, p. 15.

185. ATKINS, Priscilla
"Still Life Overlooking Lake Michigan." [HawaiiR] (12:1, #23) Spr 88, p. 32.

186. ATKINSON, Alan
"Forest." [WritersF] (14) Fall 88, p. 116.

187. ATKINSON, Charles
"After David's Layoff." [RiverS] (25) 88, p. 70.
"Almost Like Touching Him." [SouthernPR] (28:2) Fall 88, p. 69.
"Babysitting for Friends." [WebR] (13:2) Fall 88, p. 78-79.
"The Essential Blindness of Parents." [RiverS] (25) 88, p. 71.
"First of Fall, with Thunderheads." [PennR] (4:1) 88, p. 85.
"Morning Grace." [NegC] (8:3) 88, p. 149.
"When the Spirit Was All Body." [WebR] (13:2) Fall 88, p. 80.

188. ATKINSON, Jennifer
"Birds of the Air" (for Eric). [CinPR] (18) Fall 88, p. 8.
"Chestnut Blight." [CinPR] (18) Fall 88, p. 9.
"Daughters of Jerusalem" (Luke 23:28-30). [CinPR] (18) Fall 88, p. 12.
"For the Love of Nina Ruth." [CinPR] (18) Fall 88, p. 10-11.
"Prosperity." [RiverS] (26) 88, p. 54-55.
"The Words Would Have Us." [CinPR] (18) Fall 88, p. 7.

189. ATKINSON, Michael
"A Circus on Long Island, Summer 1986." [SenR] (18:2) 88, p. 74-75.

190. ATKINSON, Thomas M.
"I-86." [CinPR] (17) Spr 88, p. 58.
"Menu Please?" [CinPR] (17) Spr 88, p. 59.

191. ATLEE, Champ
"Mirabile Dictu." [Amelia] (4:4, #11) 88, p. 86-87.

192. ATLIN, Gary N.
"A Second Hypothesis Concerning the Murder of Muñoz, the Marxist Mayor of Huancayo." [NewL] (55:1) Fall 88, p. 52.

193. AUBERT, Jimmy
"The Dinosaur's Hipbone Undergoes Cosmetic Preparation." [KanQ] (20:4) Fall 88, p. 21.

"Dorothy's First Gunfighter" (From the Borders of Ozland). [KanQ] (20:4) Fall 88, p. 22.
194. AUER, Benedict
"Answering the Silence." [Rohwedder] (4) [Wint 88-89], p. 34.
"An Aztec Legend." [KanQ] (20:4) Fall 88, p. 48.
"The Confessor." [Plain] (8:2) Wint 88, p. 25.
"A Heron Spotted by Oberweis Pond." [Rohwedder] (4) [Wint 88-89], p. 34.
"Making Love in Public." [ManhatPR] (10) Ja 88, p. 54.
"Merlin's Moon." [BallSUF] (29:4) Aut 88, p. 41.
"A Monet Morning." [KanQ] (20:1/2) Wint-Spr 88, p. 113.
"Night Frescoes." [Rohwedder] (4) [Wint 88-89], p. 34.
"The Sky Probe." [Amelia] (5:2, #13) 88, p. 129.
"Two Buddhas." [Footwork] ('88) 88, p. 62.
"A Whiff of Cinnamon." [ChamLR] (1:2, #2) Spr 88, p. 123.
"You in Me." [Footwork] ('88) 88, p. 62.
"Zap!" [ChamLR] (2:1, #3) Fall 88, p. 72.
195. AUGUSTYN, Dennis
"Hart Crane (1899-1932)." [Ascent] (14:2) 88, p. 40.
196. AURA, Alejandro
"Hermano." [Mairena] (10:25) 88, p. 167.
197. AUSLANDER, Bonnie
"Aster and Iris." [Field] (39) Fall 88, p. 53.
"My Mother Admires the Hat." [Field] (39) Fall 88, p. 54.
198. AUSTEN, Catherine
"Hanging Pictures." [Quarry] (37:1) Wint 88, p. 16.
199. AUSTIN, David Craig
"Children's Hospital." [SouthernR] (24:1) Wint 88, p. 167-168.
"The Gifts." [PoetryNW] (29:2) Sum 88, p. 24-25.
"A Perfectible Curse" (for Robin Nemlich). [CinPR] (18) Fall 88, p. 35.
200. AUSTIN, Jerry
"Andrés Segovia." [BellArk] (4:3) My-Je 88, p. 9.
"Andrés Segovia." [BellArk] (4:4) Jl-Ag 88, p. 7.
"The Animal Remembering to Be Glad." [BellArk] (4:4) Jl-Ag 88, p. 9.
"At Church Camp, Near Gold Bar." [BellArk] (4:2) Mr-Ap 88, p. 9.
"Careful, A Dove May Flutter from This Poem." [BellArk] (4:1) Ja-F 88, p. 6.
"Grandfather's Pumpkins." [BellArk] (4:6) N-D 88, p. 10.
201. AUSTIN, Penelope
"Wilno." [QW] (26) Wint 88, p. 116-120.
AVE JEANNE
See JEANNE, Ave
202. AVERILL, Diane
"Bow, Horsehair." [PoetC] (19:3) Spr 88, p. 36.
"Center for Delinquent Girls." [SinW] (36) Wint 88-89, p. 23-24.
"Dreams Garbage." [CutB] (31/32) 88, p. 99.
203. AVI-RAM, Amitai F.
"Beauty's Imperative." [CentralP] (14) Fall 88, p. 43-44.
204. AVILES, Luis
"Mar de los Sargazos." [Inti] (28) Otoño 88, p. 152-153.
"Melibea y el Poeta." [Inti] (28) Otoño 88, p. 153-154.
"Oscares." [Inti] (28) Otoño 88, p. 153.
"Retorno del Cine." [Inti] (28) Otoño 88, p. 151-152.
205. AXELROD, David
"In the Foothills." [CreamCR] (12:2) Sum 88, p. 156-157.
"Waking in September." [CreamCR] (12:2) Sum 88, p. 158.
206. AXELROD, David B.
"Mallards in the Mill Pond Inlet." [Footwork] ('88) 88, p. 83.
"Poems for We Who Keep Lasting." [Footwork] ('88) 88, p. 83.
207. AXELROD, M. R.
"Ionun Union" (concrete poem). [Spirit] (9:1) 88, p. 29.
208. AYGI, Gennady
"Phloxes in the Beginning" (tr. by Peter France). [Verse] (5:1) F 88, p. 67.
"Winds-and-Radiance: Departures" (to L. N. and M. Roginsky, tr. by Peter France). [Verse] (5:1) F 88, p. 66.
209. AYHAN, Ece
"A Blind Cat Black" (tr. by Murat Nemet-Nejat). [Trans] (20) Spr 88, p. 286.
"Epitafio" (tr. by Murat Nemet-Nejat). [Trans] (20) Spr 88, p. 287.

210. AYRES, Gail
"Fouling the Nest" (The 14th Kansas Poetry Contest, First Honorable Mention). [LittleBR] (5:2) Wint 88-89, p. 65.
211. AYRES, Noreen
"That Place for Bluegrass Music." [Vis] (28) 88, p. 13.
212. AYUKAWA, Nobuo
"The Dean Man" (tr. by Tomoyuki Iino). [Stand] (29:3) Sum 88, p. 23.
213. AZRAEL, Mary
"The Double." [SpoonRQ] (13:3) Sum 88, p. 53-54.
"Fish, Doubled." [Chelsea] (47) 88, p. 75.
"Near Harper's Ferry." [PaintedB] (36) 88, p. 9.
"Necessity." [NowestR] (26:2) 88, p. 56.
214. AZZOUNI, Jodi
"Losing My Marbles." [HolCrit] (25:3) Je 88, p. 19.
BAASTAD, Erling Friis
See FRIIS-BAASTAD, Erling
215. BAATZ, Ronald
"100 Laps." [WormR] (28:4, #112) 88, p. 123-124.
"Christmas Lights." [WormR] (28:4, #112) 88, p. 121.
"A Good Sign." [YellowS] (28) D 88, p. 19.
"Living Alone." [WormR] (28:4, #112) 88, p. 122-123.
"Snow Poem." [WormR] (28:4, #112) 88, p. 121.
"Standing in the Kitchen Eating Out of a Box of Leftover Chinese Food." [WormR] (28:4, #112) 88, p. 120.
"These Cold Mountains." [WormR] (28:4, #112) 88, p. 121-122.
"What Happened on My Visit to the Seashore." [YellowS] (28) D 88, p. 18.
216. BABB, Sanora
"Above Malpaso Creek." [HawaiiR] (12:2, #24) Fall 88, p. 54-55.
217. BABCOX, Emilie
"Fireflies." [MalR] (85) D 88, p. 29.
"Old Men Swimming." [MalR] (85) D 88, p. 30.
"Winter Trees." [ChrC] (105:5) 17 F 88, p. 163.
218. BACH, Emmon
"Amnestic." [MassR] (29:2) Sum 88, p. 330.
"Paranerdicks." [MassR] (29:2) Sum 88, p. 331.
219. BACHMANN, Evelyn
"Summertime" (The 14th Kansas Poetry Contest, Third Honorable Mention). [LittleBR] (5:2) Wint 88-89, p. 67.
220. BACKEN, Bud
"Mr. Winner Worries About All the Sperm." [SlipS] (8) 88, p. 6-7.
221. BAGG, Robert
"Muscongus Bay Sloop." [TexasR] (9:3/4) Fall-Wint 88, p. 3-4.
222. BAGGETT, Rebecca
"Snow White Awake" (for Leslie and Celeste). [NegC] (8:3) 88, p. 183-185.
223. BAGLOW, John
"Continental Drift." [Quarry] (37:1) Wint 88, p. 51.
224. BAHAN, Lee Harlin
"Teach's Hole, Ocracoke." [FloridaR] (16:1) Spr-Sum 88, p. 122.
"Wyndham Lewis, 1917." [CapeR] (23:2) Fall 88, p. 20.
225. BAHLER, Beth
"It's Curious." [Footwork] ('88) 88, p. 49.
226. BAHM, Jim
"Lonely Happiness." [Plain] (8:2) Wint 88, p. 34.
"Moonlight Explosions." [Plain] (8:1) Fall 87, p. 31.
"Sobering Up." [Plain] (9:1) Fall 88, p. 10.
227. BAHR, Ali
"Hildegund." [Jacaranda] (3:2) Fall-Wint 88, p. 146-147.
228. BAHR, Donald
"Papago Deer Songs" (tr. of anonymous songs, w. Brian Swann). [SouthernHR] (22:3) Sum 88, p. 238-240.
229. BAILEY, Alice Morrey
"Death of James." [Amelia] (5:1, #12) 88, p. 84-85.
230. BAILEY, Don
"Homeless Heart" (a persona prose-poem play). [Quarry] (37:2) Spr 88, p. 5-13.
231. BAILEY-WOFFORD, Jan
"The Abbey at Rievaulx." [SoCaR] (20:2) Spr 88, p. 16.

"Balm." [KenR] (NS 10:4) Fall 88, p. 96.
"Encounter." [IndR] (12:1) Wint 88, p. 11.
"Outliving My Son." [KenR] (NS 10:4) Fall 88, p. 95.

232. BAIRD, Bonnie
"In the Moment of Birth." [PottPort] (9) 88, p. 51.
"Lucifer As Cat." [PottPort] (9) 88, p. 51.
"Night Rains." [PottPort] (10) 88, p. 11.
"Period." [PottPort] (10) 88, p. 11.
"This Body." [PottPort] (10) 88, p. 11.

233. BAKER, Brenda
"Tribute to Grain in Four Movements" (Perfomred at the Grain Celebration in Regina, Nov. 21st, 1987). [Grain] (16:1) Spr 88, p. 5-8.

234. BAKER, David
"Forms of Joy." [PoetryNW] (29:3) Aut 88, p. 20-21.
"Generation" (imagining a son). [KenR] (NS 10:2) Spr 88, p. 60-61.
"November: The End of Myth." [WestHR] (42:2) Sum 88, p. 116.
"Our August Moon" (for Ann). [PoetryNW] (29:3) Aut 88, p. 21-22.
"Volunteers" (picture postcard from afar). [KenR] (NS 10:2) Spr 88, p. 61-62.

235. BAKER, Donald W.
"Ben's Garden." [LaurelR] (22:2) Sum 88, p. 40-41.
"Capsules." [LaurelR] (22:2) Sum 88, p. 42-43.

236. BAKKEN, Dick
"Old Bamboo Fishing Pole." [Abraxas] (37) 88, p. 78.

237. BAKOWSKI, Peter
"Of Trains and Hearts and Students of the Dream." [AlphaBS] (4) D 88, p. 51-54.
"Old Men in the Lobby of the Huntington Hotel" (old Los Angeles, for Edward Hopper). [AlphaBS] (4) D 88, p. 55-56.

238. BAKUCZ, Joseph J.
"Professional Angel" (tr. by the author). [Vis] (26) 88, p. 25.

239. BALABAN, John
"Agua Fría y las Chicharras." [PoetL] (83:3) Fall 88, p. 9-11.
"For My Sister in Warmister General Hospital." [PoetL] (83:3) Fall 88, p. 5-6.
"For the Missing in Action." [Ploughs] (14:1) 88, p. 14.
"Lovers Near Jemez Springs." [PoetL] (83:3) Fall 88, p. 7-8.
"Mangy Sparrow among McCallum's Chickens." [PoetL] (83:3) Fall 88, p. 12.
"Mr. Giai's Poem." [TriQ] (72) Spr-Sum 88, p. 157-158.
"Thoughts Before Dawn" (for Mary Bui Thi Khuy, 1944-1969). [ColR] (NS 15:1) Spr-Sum 88, p. 93.
"Words for My Daughter." [Ploughs] (14:1) 88, p. 15-17.

240. BALAKIAN, Peter
"To Arshile Gorky." [Agni] (26) 88, p. 49-50.
"A Version of Paolo and Francesca." [Agni] (26) 88, p. 47-48.

241. BALASHOVA, Elena
"Instructing Clarity in a Confusion" (tr. of Arkadii Dragomoshchenko, w. Lyn Hejinian). [NewAW] (4) Fall 88, p. 8-11.
"The Islands of Sirens" (tr. of Arkadii Dragomoshchenko, w. Lyn Hejinian). [Zyzzyva] (4:1) Spr 88, p. 87-106.

242. BALAZ, Joseph P.
"All the Luck." [ChamLR] (1) Fall 87, p. 89-90.
"Anything You Kill You Gada Eat." [HawaiiR] (12:2, #24) Fall 88, p. 44.
"Beneath the Underground." [ChamLR] (2:1, #3) Fall 88, p. 114-115.
"Just Call Me Nero." [HawaiiR] (12:1, #23) Spr 88, p. 120-121.
"Regarding Waffles." [ChamLR] (1:2, #2) Spr 88, p. 114-115.

243. BALAZS, Mary
"The Man on the Front Stoop." [Wind] (18:62) 88, p. 3-4.
"Mole" (Honorable Mention Poem, 1987/1988). [KanQ] (20:1/2) Wint-Spr 88, p. 44.

244. BALBO, Ned
"At the Aerodrome." [KanQ] (20:3) Sum 88, p. 112-113.
"A Villanelle." [KanQ] (20:3) Sum 88, p. 112.

245. BALCOM, John
"The Turkey" (tr. of Ch'in Shang). [NowestR] (26:3) 88, p. 56.
"Water Hyacinths" (tr. of Ch'in Shang). [NowestR] (26:3) 88, p. 57.

246. BALDERSTON, Jean
"Garbo Stepping In." [LightY] ('88/9) 88, p. 83.

247. BALDOCK, Robert
"Ferocious Cage" (tr. of Nancy Morejon, w. Kathleen Weaver). [Callaloo] (11:1, #34) Wint 88, p. 37.
248. BALDWIN, Joseph
"Dora." [KanQ] (20:3) Sum 88, p. 119.
"Shelter." [KanQ] (20:1/2) Wint-Spr 88, p. 98.
"Visitant." [KanQ] (20:1/2) Wint-Spr 88, p. 97.
249. BALK, Christianne
"Why I Did It." [Crazy] (35) Wint 88, p. 34-37.
250. BALL, Angela
"Ancient Skills." [Boulevard] (3:2/3) Fall 88, p. 94.
"Autobiography." [MalR] (85) D 88, p. 46-47.
"A Fall Day." [NewAW] (4) Fall 88, p. 75.
"Generosity." [NewAW] (4) Fall 88, p. 74.
"The Kiss." [MalR] (85) D 88, p. 45.
251. BALL, David
"Weather Report." (Excerpts, w. Tom Raworth). [Notus] (3:2) Fall 88, p. 20-21.
252. BALL, Joseph H.
"Father's Morning." [CreamCR] (12:1) Wint 88, p. 87.
"The Woman Who Had the Dream." [StoneC] (15:3/4) Spr-Sum 88, p. 17.
253. BALL, Richard
"Lost Brotherhood" (For Henry Moore, Sculptor, who died, 31.8.1986). [Pembroke] (20) 88, p. 197.
"Marshland." [Pembroke] (20) 88, p. 19.
"Return Home." [Pembroke] (20) 88, p. 198.
254. BALLARD, Rae
"Joseph Remembers the Annunciation." [ChrC] (105:39) 21-28 D 88, p. 1182-1183.
255. BALLARD, Sheila
"Setting Up Housekeeping." [KanQ] (20:3) Sum 88, p. 213.
256. BALLENTINE, Lee
"Chain-of-Command." [Caliban] (4) 88, p. 152.
"The Cultural Revolution." [AnotherCM] (18) 88, p. 10.
257. BALLINGER, Franchot
"Closings." [CinPR] (17) Spr 88, p. 62.
"A Winter Evening" (After Trakl). [CinPR] (17) Spr 88, p. 63.
258. BALTENSPERGER, Peter
"Beachcombing." [PottPort] (9) 88, p. 45.
259. BAMBOO, Billy
"Billy Bamboo" (Aboriginal Narrative of New South Wales, Collected by Roland Robinson). [PraS] (62:4) Wint 88-89, p. 18-19.
260. BANANI, Amin
"The Rose and the Nightingale" (tr. of Nader Naderpour, w. Jascha Kessler). [Vis] (26) 88, p. 11.
261. BANDHYOPADHYAY, Manohar
"Run Away Cow" (tr. of Sati Kumar). [Nimrod] (31:2) Spr-Sum 88, p. 95.
262. BANERIAN, James
"Bougainvillea" (tr. of Tan Cao). [Vis] (26) 88, p. 17.
"Letter from Home" (tr. of Tan Cao). [Vis] (26) 88, p. 16-17.
263. BANERJEE, Paramita
"The Blaze" (tr. of Pratima Ray, w. Carolyne Wright). [Nimrod] (31:2) Spr-Sum 88, p. 33.
"Man" (tr. of Mallika Sengupta, w. Carolyne Wright). [SenR] (18:2) 88, p. 29.
"Month of Honey" (tr. of Mallika Sengupta, w. Carolyne Wright). [SenR] (18:2) 88, p. 25-26.
"Peace" (tr. of Anuradha Mahapatra, w. Carolyne Wright). [Nimrod] (31:2) Spr-Sum 88, p. 35.
"The Poor Fund" (tr. of Nabaneeta Dev Sen, w. Carolyne Wright and the author). [Nimrod] (31:2) Spr-Sum 88, p. 37.
"Recovery" (tr. of Nabaneeta Dev Sen, w. Carolyne Wright and the author). [Nimrod] (31:2) Spr-Sum 88, p. 36.
"Simile" (tr. of Pratima Ray, w. Carolyne Wright). [Nimrod] (31:2) Spr-Sum 88, p. 33.
"Son of Air" (tr. of Mallika Sengupta, w. Carolyne Wright). [SenR] (18:2) 88, p. 28.
"Two Golden Airplanes" (tr. of Mallika Sengupta, w. Carolyne Wright). [SenR] (18:2) 88, p. 27.

"Worshipping the Tree" (tr. of Mallika Sengupta, w. Carolyne Wright). [SenR] (18:2) 88, p. 24.

264. BANKS, Loy
"Photograph: The Neota Wilderness" (for botanist Fred Hermann, remembered). [Blueline] (9:1/2) 88, p. 94.

265. BANUS, Maria
"November" (tr. by Diana Der Hovanessian). [GrahamHR] (11) Spr 88, p. 96.

266. BARABAS, Gabor
"Biko Poems" (4 poems). [Lactuca] (11) O 88, p. 24-25.

267. BARADULIN, Rygor
"Eternity" (tr. by Walter May). [NegC] (8:1/2) 88, p. 39.

268. BARAKA, Amiri
"The Pause of Joe." [Sulfur] (8:1, #22) Spr 88, p. 25-39.

269. BARAN, Susan
"Lobster Telephone." [NewAW] (3) Spr 88, p. 93.

270. BARANCZAK, Stanislaw
"29-77-02" (tr. of Artur Miedzyrzecki, w. Clare Cavanagh). [ManhatR] (4:2) Spr 88, p. 35.
"After Gloria Was Done" (tr. by the author and Reginald Gibbons). [TriQ] (71) Wint 88, p. 145-146.
"Among Us, the Unclean Ones" (tr. of Jan Polkowski, w. Clare Cavanagh). [ManhatR] (4:2) Spr 88, p. 40.
"Archaeology" (tr. of Wislawa Szymborska, w. Clare Cavanagh). [TriQ] (71) Wint 88, p. 147-148.
"At the Cave" (tr. of Artur Miedzyrzecki, w. Clare Cavanagh). [TriQ] (71) Wint 88, p. 151.
"Before Dawn" (tr. of Julia Hartwig, w. Clare Cavanagh). [ManhatR] (4:2) Spr 88, p. 36.
"But of Course" (tr. of Julia Hartwig, w. Clare Cavanagh). [TriQ] (71) Wint 88, p. 154.
"Funeral" (tr. of Wislawa Szymborska, w. Clare Cavanagh). [TriQ] (71) Wint 88, p. 150.
"The Golden Age" (tr. of Artur Miedzyrzecki, w. Clare Cavanagh). [ManhatR] (4:2) Spr 88, p. 35.
"Hitler's First Photograph" (tr. of Wislawa Szymborska, w. Clare Cavanagh). [TriQ] (71) Wint 88, p. 149.
"I Am Not Worthy" (tr. of Ryszard Krynicki, w. Clare Cavanagh). [ManhatR] (4:2) Spr 88, p. 39.
"In this slough becoming stone" (tr. of Wiktor Woroszylski, w. Clare Cavanagh). [ManhatR] (4:2) Spr 88, p. 38.
"In Your Eyes" (tr. of Julia Hartwig, w. Clare Cavanagh). [TriQ] (71) Wint 88, p. 153.
"Plotting with the Dead" (tr. of Wislawa Szymborska, w. Clare Cavanagh). [ManhatR] (4:2) Spr 88, p. 33-34.
"Rain outside a window, a glass of tea on the table" (tr. of Bronislaw Maj, w. Clare Cavanagh). [ManhatR] (4:2) Spr 88, p. 41-42.
"Roommates" (tr. of Wiktor Woroszylski, w. Clare Cavanagh). [TriQ] (71) Wint 88, p. 155-156.
"So What If" (tr. of Ryszard Krynicki, w. Clare Cavanagh). [ManhatR] (4:2) Spr 88, p. 39.
"Stage Fright" (tr. of Wislawa Szymborska, w. Clare Cavanagh). [ManhatR] (4:2) Spr 88, p. 31-32.
"Suddenly" (tr. of Ryszard Krynicki, w. Clare Cavanagh). [ManhatR] (4:2) Spr 88, p. 39.
"These are strong, calm words" (tr. of Bronislaw Maj, w. Clare Cavanagh). [ManhatR] (4:2) Spr 88, p. 41.
"They" (tr. of Artur Miedzyrzecki, w. Clare Cavanagh). [ManhatR] (4:2) Spr 88, p. 34.
"Though Mortal, I Desired You" (tr. of Jan Polkowski, w. Clare Cavanagh). [ManhatR] (4:2) Spr 88, p. 40-41.
"To Grazyna" (tr. by the author and Reginald Gibbons). [TriQ] (71) Wint 88, p. 143-144.
"Towards the End" (tr. of Julia Hartwig, w. Clare Cavanagh). [ManhatR] (4:2) Spr 88, p. 36-37.
"View with a Grain of Sand" (tr. of Wislawa Szymborska, w. Clare Cavanagh). [ManhatR] (4:2) Spr 88, p. 32-33.

"The Wall" (tr. of Ryszard Krynicki, w. Clare Cavanagh). [ManhatR] (4:2) Spr 88, p. 40.
"What a Poem Is Allowed" (tr. of Wiktor Woroszylski, w. Clare Cavanagh). [ManhatR] (4:2) Spr 88, p. 37.
"What Does the Political Scientist Know" (tr. of Artur Miedzyrzecki, w. Clare Cavanagh). [TriQ] (71) Wint 88, p. 152.
"The world: whole and indivisible, begins where" (tr. of Bronislaw Maj, w. Clare Cavanagh). [TriQ] (71) Wint 88, p. 157.

271. BARBARESE, J. T.
"Broken Windows." [DenQ] (23:1) Sum 88, p. 35-37.
"Downtown Ronny Smash." [PaintedB] (36) 88, p. 63-64.
"Eclipse." [PaintedB] (36) 88, p. 69.
"God." [PaintedB] (36) 88, p. 70.
"The Jets in the Dirt." [DenQ] (23:1) Sum 88, p. 32-34.
"The Middle Class Enter Heaven." [PaintedB] (36) 88, p. 65-66.
"Phnom Penh." [KanQ] (20:3) Sum 88, p. 113.
"South Street." [PaintedB] (36) 88, p. 67-68.
"Strange and Wonderful." [Atlantic] (261:2) F 88, p. 60.
"The Sunbeam" (for Jesse). [PaintedB] (36) 88, p. 60.
"Testament." [PaintedB] (36) 88, p. 61-62.
"Windy." [SouthwR] (73:2) Spr 88, p. 252.
"Winter Dawn." [NoAmR] (273:3) D 88, p. 40.

272. BARBER, David
"The Earth Is Round." [GeoR] (42:3) Fall 88, p. 607-608.
"Elegy for the Bad Uncles." [Ploughs] (14:4) 88, p. 125-126.
"First Light, False Dawn." [AntR] (46:3) Sum 88, p. 360-361.
"Prospectus." [Ploughs] (14:4) 88, p. 127-128.

273. BARBER, Jennifer
"95 [degrees] F." [Pequod] (25) 88, p. 7.
"M4." [Pequod] (25) 88, p. 8.

274. BARBOSA, Jorge Pedro
"Island" (tr. by Michael Platzer). [Vis] (27) 88, p. 21.

275. BARDEN, Tom
"Picasso's 'Woman with Crow'." [PoetL] (83:3) Fall 88, p. 19-20.

276. BARDSLEY, Beverly
"Helen" (tr. of Yannis Ritsos, w. Peter Green). [GrandS] (8:1) Aut 88, p. 65-85.

277. BARGEN, Walter
"Age of Extinction." [Ascent] (13:3) 88, p. 11.
"Another Hour." [Ascent] (13:3) 88, p. 10.
"Handmade Table." [SpoonRQ] (13:3) Sum 88, p. 52.
"Internal Exile." [Farm] (4:1, i.e. 5:1) Wint 88, p. 69.
"Mark of Cain." [KanQ] (20:1/2) Wint-Spr 88, p. 219.
"Power Outage." [RiverS] (26) 88, p. 68.
"Reign of Nails." [HangL] (53) 88, p. 6-7.
"Self-Inflicted Postcard from Paris." [CharR] (14:2) Fall 88, p. 79-80.

278. BARGER, Kim R.
"The Mirror As Text." [HolCrit] (25:5) D 88, p. 15.

279. BARKAN, Stanley H.
"Angel's Descent" (for Bebe). [Footwork] ('88) 88, p. 49.
"The Cats and Dogs of Tel Aviv." [Lips] (14) 88, p. 30.
"Cockroaches" (for David B. Axelrod). [Footwork] ('88) 88, p. 49.
"Karen's Dog." [Lips] (14) 88, p. 31.
"The Worm in the Book" (for Alfred Van Loen). [Footwork] ('88) 88, p. 49.

280. BARKER, Wendy
"Foundation." [SouthernPR] (28:1) Spr 88, p. 65-66.
"Identifying Things." [Poetry] (152:5) Ag 88, p. 266-267.

281. BARKS, Coleman
"Some Orange Juice." [PaintedB] (36) 88, p. 10.
"Vigil Notes." [PaintedB] (36) 88, p. 11.

282. BARNES, C. F.
"The Aluminum Woman." [MidAR] (8:2) 88, p. 2-3.
"Dancing at Johnson's Corner." [SouthernPR] (28:2) Fall 88, p. 20.
"Pearl I See You Rescue" (for LJC). [HawaiiR] (12:2, #24) Fall 88, p. 75.

283. BARNES, G.
"Five Winter Slides." [Plain] (8:2) Wint 88, p. 27.

284. BARNES, Jane
"Cleaning Squid." [TexasR] (9:3/4) Fall-Wint 88, p. 5.
"Vietnam in the South End." [RiverS] (27) 88, p. 46.
285. BARNES, Jim
"Bombardier." [QW] (27) Sum-Fall 88, p. 119-122.
"Deer Camp: Blue Mountain." [RiverS] (27) 88, p. 49.
"Going After the Milch Cow." [HayF] (3) Spr 88, p. 68.
"The La Plata Cantata" (Selections: vi, vii). [Confr] (37/38) Spr-Sum 88, p. 76-77.
"La Plata, Missouri: Heavy Metal." [Paint] (15:29) Spr 88, p. 7.
"La Plata, Missouri: Savage Country." [Paint] (15:29) Spr 88, p. 6.
"La Plata, Missouri: The Light Above the Store." [Paint] (15:29) Spr 88, p. 5.
"La Plata, Missouri: The Palace Cafe." [Paint] (15:29) Spr 88, p. 8.
"The Sawdust War." [Nat] (247:16) 28 N 88, p. 572.
"Souvenirs." [HayF] (3) Spr 88, p. 69.
"Wolf Watch: Winding Stair Mountains, 1923." [WebR] (13:2) Fall 88, p. 53-58.
286. BARNES, Kate
"The Barn in December." [TexasR] (9:3/4) Fall-Wint 88, p. 6-7.
287. BARNES, Michael
"Flying Dreams." [Plain] (8:1) Fall 87, p. 13.
288. BARNES, Richard
"The Vanity." [SlipS] (8) 88, p. 9.
289. BARNETT, Ruth Anderson
"Eagle on the Roof: Oraibi, Arizona." [ArizQ] (44:1) Spr 88, p. 94-95.
290. BARNSTONE, Tony
"About Old Age, in Answer to a Poem by Zhang Shaofu" (tr. of Wang Wei, w. Willis Barnstone and Xu Haixin). [ArtfulD] (14/15) Fall 88, p. 81.
"Drifting on the Lake" (tr. of Wang Wei, w. Willis Barnstone and Xu Haixin). [ArtfulD] (14/15) Fall 88, p. 81.
"East River Moon" (tr. of Wang Wei, w. Willis Barnstone and Xu Haixin). [ArtfulD] (14/15) Fall 88, p. 80.
"Lazy about Writing Poems" (tr. of Wang Wei, w. Willis Barnstone and Xu Haixin). [ArtfulD] (14/15) Fall 88, p. 80.
"Red Peonies" (tr. of Wang Wei, w. Willis Barnstone and Xu Haixin). [ArtfulD] (14/15) Fall 88, p. 81.
291. BARNSTONE, Willis
"About Old Age, in Answer to a Poem by Zhang Shaofu" (tr. of Wang Wei, w. Tony Barnstone and Xu Haixin). [ArtfulD] (14/15) Fall 88, p. 81.
"Apprenticeship" (tr. of Dorin Tudoran, w. M. Calinescu). [Vis] (26) 88, p. 41.
"Christ on the Cross" (tr. of Jorge Luis Borges). [AmerPoR] (17:5) S-O 88, p. 21.
"Drifting on the Lake" (tr. of Wang Wei, w. Tony Barnstone and Xu Haixin). [ArtfulD] (14/15) Fall 88, p. 81.
"East River Moon" (tr. of Wang Wei, w. Tony Barnstone and Xu Haixin). [ArtfulD] (14/15) Fall 88, p. 80.
"Lazy about Writing Poems" (tr. of Wang Wei, w. Tony Barnstone and Xu Haixin). [ArtfulD] (14/15) Fall 88, p. 80.
"On His Blindness" (tr. of Jorge Luis Borges). [AmerPoR] (17:5) S-O 88, p. 21.
"Red Peonies" (tr. of Wang Wei, w. Tony Barnstone and Xu Haixin). [ArtfulD] (14/15) Fall 88, p. 81.
"Winter Came" (tr. of Bronislava Volek, w. the author). [Vis] (26) 88, p. 21.
292. BARR, John
"The Brotherhood of Morticians." [IndR] (11:3) Sum 88, p. 14-16.
"The Dial Painters." [MichQR] (27:4) Fall 88, p. 617-619.
293. BARR, Tina
"Circe." [Poetry] (152:6) S 88, p. 336-337.
"Folding Laundry." [AmerPoR] (17:1) Ja-F 88, p. 47.
"For Don." [SwampR] (1:1) Ja 88, p. 26.
"For Etheridge." [PaintedB] (32/33) 88, p. 113.
"Lines." [SwampR] (1:2/3) D 88, p. 26.
"Pipersville, Bucks County." [SwampR] (1:1) Ja 88, p. 27.
"The Shearing Force." [SwampR] (1:1) Ja 88, p. 28-29.
294. BARRAX, Gerald
"Haunted House." [Callaloo] (11:3, #36) Sum 88, p. 449-450.
"Polar's TV Fantasy." [Callaloo] (11:3, #36) Sum 88, p. 453.
"Strangers Like Us: Pittsburgh, Raleigh, 1945-1985." [Callaloo] (11:3, #36) Sum 88, p. 448.
"Uniforms" (For Martin Luther King, Jr.). [Callaloo] (11:3, #36) Sum 88, p. 451-452.

"Universe." [Callaloo] (11:3, #36) Sum 88, p. 454-455.
295. BARRESI, Dorothy
"At the Pioneer Valley Legal Clinic." [CreamCR] (12:2) Sum 88, p. 159-160.
"Chin Music." [Poetry] (152:3) Je 88, p. 139-140.
"Group Therapy Lounge, Columbia, South Carolina." [PoetryNW] (29:3) Aut 88, p. 38-39.
"Honeymoon Ocean, 1939." [WillowS] (22) Spr 88, p. 29-30.
"To the Tomboys, to Make Much of Time." [PoetryNW] (29:3) Aut 88, p. 35-37.
296. BARRETT, Carol
"Driving the Last Hour." [KanQ] (20:1/2) Wint-Spr 88, p. 232.
"Making Ready" (For Sharon). [Verse] (5:3) N 88, p. 20.
"Rendezvous." [SoDakR] (26:3) Aut 88, p. 84-85.
"The Sunflower Setback" (from an article by Jean Hays in the *Wichita Eagle-Beacon*). [KanQ] (20:1/2) Wint-Spr 88, p. 230-231.
297. BARRETT, Lou
"The Shakespeare Class." [EngJ] (77:2) F 88, p. 87.
298. BARRINGTON, Judith
"La Bruja del Sueño." [SinW] (35) Sum-Fall 88, p. 15.
299. BARRIOS, Marilyn Horton
"Wife Kills Hubby & Mails Head to His Mistress" (headline from *The Sun*). [ColR] (NS 15:2) Fall-Wint 88, p. 59.
300. BARROWS, Roy F.
"Father and Son." [LitR] (31:2) Wint 88, p. 188.
301. BARRY, Sebastian
"Fanny Hawke Goes to the Mainland Forever." [Iowa] (18:2) 88, p. 109-110.
"Fanny Hawke Goes to the Mainland Forever." [Stand] (29:4) Aut 88, p. 46.
"The Only True History of Lizzy Finn, by Herself." [Iowa] (18:2) 88, p. 108-109.
"The Only True History of Lizzy Finn, by Herself." [Stand] (29:4) Aut 88, p. 45.
"Trooper O'Hara at the Indian Wars." [Stand] (29:4) Aut 88, p. 44.
"Voyage to Azania" (A letter to James Mathews of Athlone [Cape Town]). [Antaeus] (60) Spr 88, p. 228-230.
302. BARST, Fran
"Black Sun." [Footwork] ('88) 88, p. 59.
"Death in the Mountains." [Lactuca] (10) Je 88, p. 7-8.
"Eskamege (to Eat Raw Fish)." [Lactuca] (10) Je 88, p. 9-10.
"Rape." [Lactuca] (10) Je 88, p. 8-9.
"A Song." [Lactuca] (10) Je 88, p. 7.
"The Ward." [CarolQ] (40:2) Wint 88, p. 79-80.
303. BARTELETTI, Rob
"The Making of a White Liberal: 1969." [Thrpny] (34) Sum 88, p. 24.
304. BARTH, R. L.
"Cyclops" (Variations on Rimbaud, for John Finlay). [CinPR] (17) Spr 88, p. 76.
305. BARTHOLOMEW, Hillary
"Lullaby on 84th." [GreensboroR] (44) Sum 88, p. 116-117.
306. BARTLETT, Brian
"All Fall You Wrote Me about the Desert." [MalR] (84) S 88, p. 78-84.
"The Multiplication of Windows." [MalR] (84) S 88, p. 74-75.
"On the Bus from Beer-Sheba" (December 1986). [MalR] (84) S 88, p. 76-77.
307. BARTLOW, Bruce G.
"Interlude." [KanQ] (20:3) Sum 88, p. 245.
308. BARTON, John
"At Wimbledon." [Dandel] (15:1) Spr-Sum 88, p. 24.
"Crepusculaire." [Descant] (19:2, #61) Sum 88, p. 9-10.
"In Tristan's House." [Descant] (19:2, #61) Sum 88, p. 11-12.
"Lazaro Screamed." [Descant] (19:2, #61) Sum 88, p. 13-14.
"The Reverse Side of a Picture Postcard." [Descant] (19:2, #61) Sum 88, p. 7-8.
309. BARTOW, Stuart
"An Hallucination of Gardeners." [JINJPo] (10:1/2) 88, p. 6.
"Stereo." [JINJPo] (10:1/2) 88, p. 5.
310. BASINSKI, Michael
"Song of the Check Out Line in Freshmart." [AlphaBS] (3) Je 88, p. 38-39.
311. BASSEN, Lois Shapley
"Twentieth Anniversary." [AmerS] (57:4) Aut 88, p. 514.
312. BATES, Scott
"B Is for Baseball." [LightY] ('88/9) 88, p. 122.

313. BATHANTI, Joseph
"Relic." [SouthernPR] (28:1) Spr 88, p. 33.
"The Sabbath." [TexasR] (9:1/2) Spr-Sum 88, p. 48-49.
314. BATISTA, Liony (Liony E.)
"Origins." [Lips] (14) 88, p. 3-5.
"Remembrance." [Lips] (14) 88, p. 6.
"Southern Images" (series of poems based on the Southern Coast of Dominican Republic). [FiveFR] (6) 88, p. 9-11.
315. BATTRAM, Michael R.
"Gary." [CapeR] (23:2) Fall 88, p. 22.
316. BAUDELAIRE, Charles
"Exotic Perfume" (tr. by James McGowan). [HiramPoR] (44/45) Spr-Wint 88, p. 69.
"Harmonie du Soir." [HiramPoR] (44/45) Spr-Wint 88, p. 70.
"Harmony of the Evening" (tr. by James McGowan). [HiramPoR] (44/45) Spr-Wint 88, p. 70.
"Parfum Exotique." [HiramPoR] (44/45) Spr-Wint 88, p. 69.
317. BAUER, Grace
"Dancing on the Bar at the Blue Goose Saloon." [PoetL] (83:1) Spr 88, p. 32.
"Las Madres de los Desaparecidos." [ColR] (NS 15:2) Fall-Wint 88, p. 58.
318. BAUER, Steven
"Evening." [IndR] (11:3) Sum 88, p. 55.
"White Cedar Swamp." [SouthwR] (73:3) Sum 88, p. 401.
319. BAUMEL, Judith
"Herschel's Milk" (for my godson, James Stephen Gilbert Yarrow). [Pequod] (25) 88, p. 37-39.
"Malleus Maleficarum." [IndR] (11:3) Sum 88, p. 22.
"The Monk and the Udayana Statue of Buddha." [Pequod] (25) 88, p. 40.
"Samuel." [Pequod] (25) 88, p. 36.
320. BAWER, Bruce
"Saxophone." [Pequod] (25) 88, p. 29.
321. BAXTER, Charles
"Unused Words." [Colum] (13) 88, p. 65-66.
322. BAXTER, David
"A Kind of Eden" (from Bogg 30, 1975). [Bogg] (59) 88, p. 41.
323. BAY, Marisa
"Corazón de Papel." [LetFem] (14:1/2) Primavera-Otoño 88, p. 136-137.
324. BAYSA, Fred
"Dieffenbachia" (for Daniel). [ChamLR] (1:2, #2) Spr 88, p. 93.
325. BAYSANS, Greg
"Cutting Room Floor." [JamesWR] (5:2) Wint 88, p. 10.
"Passion Concentrate." [JamesWR] (5:2) Wint 88, p. 10.
326. BEADELL, Robert M., Jr.
"Ain't Nothin' Fancy." [Plain] (8:1) Fall 87, p. 32.
327. BEAM, Jeffery
"The Beautiful Tendons" (Selections). [YellowS] (28) D 88, p. 38.
"No One Else Will Do" (with a nod to Gertrude Stein). [YellowS] (27) Aut 88, p. 18.
328. BEAM, Mary Ernestine
"Oranges." [Amelia] (4:4, #11) 88, p. 41.
329. BEANLAND, Josie
"Pavan for a Dead Infant." [Bogg] (59) 88, p. 28.
"Thinking of You." [Bogg] (59) 88, p. 20.
BEAR, Ray A. Young
See YOUNG BEAR, Ray A.
330. BEARD, Cathy
"Hands." [RagMag] (6:1) [88], p. 5.
"I See." [RagMag] (6:1) [88], p. 5.
"Remembrance." [RagMag] (6:1) [88], p. 4.
331. BEASLEY, Bruce
"Eternal Spring" (for my sister). [PoetryE] (25) Spr 88, p. 65.
"Limbo." [WestHR] (42:3) Aut 88, p. 206-207.
332. BEATTY, Sheila Aileen
"Fuma Nera." [DenQ] (22:3) Wint 88, p. 267.
333. BEAUCHAMP, Lincoln T.
"Brother Henry" (for Henry Dumas). [BlackALF] (22:2) Sum 88, p. 175-176.
334. BEAUCHAMP, Steve
"Bird Books Can Be Wrong." [KanQ] (20:1/2) Wint-Spr 88, p. 111.

335. BEAUMONT, Jeanne
"Like a Fist." [BellArk] (4:1) Ja-F 88, p. 3.
"Women Poets Come of Age." [BellArk] (4:1) Ja-F 88, p. 1.
336. BECERRA, Jose Carlos
"Oscura Palabra (2)." [Mairena] (10:25) 88, p. 172.
337. BECK, Art
"All Saints Morning" (for Al Masarik). [PaintedB] (36) 88, p. 22.
"Angel Rain." [SwampR] (1:2/3) D 88, p. 34.
"Broken April." [SwampR] (1:1) Ja 88, p. 12.
"Eden." [SwampR] (1:2/3) D 88, p. 33.
"Transaction." [SwampR] (1:1) Ja 88, p. 10-11.
338. BECK, Rachel
"The Wrong Line." [LightY] ('88/9) 88, p. 48.
339. BECKER, Robin
"Betrayal of the Animals." [Ploughs] (14:1) 88, p. 126.
"Bodies We Will Never Know." [Ploughs] (14:1) 88, p. 125.
"The Deaths of Animals." [Ploughs] (14:1) 88, p. 127.
"The Gardener." [PraS] (62:2) Sum 88, p. 44-45.
"On Vashon." [PraS] (62:2) Sum 88, p. 43-44.
"The Problem of Magnification." [PraS] (62:2) Sum 88, p. 45.
340. BECKETT, Larry
"Southern Girl" (after Li Po). [BellR] (11:2) Fall 88, p. 37.
341. BECKMAN, Madeleine D.
"Take Out." [SouthernPR] (28:2) Fall 88, p. 21.
342. BEDFORD, William
"The Last Red Squirrel" (Grantham: 1948). [MalR] (85) D 88, p. 60.
343. BEEDE, Gayle Jansen
"Dancing with the Disabled." [PacificR] (6) Spr 88, p. 22-23.
344. BEGGS, Marck L.
"Our Tendency to Trust Strangers." [DenQ] (22:3) Wint 88, p. 22-23.
345. BEGLEY, Carl E.
"Supraliminal." [KeyWR] (1:2) Fall 88, p. 75.
346. BEHM, Richard
"The Non-Custodial Parent Takes His Children to the Nature Preserve." [CreamCR] (12:2) Sum 88, p. 161.
"Winter Ball." [CreamCR] (12:2) Sum 88, p. 162.
347. BEHN, Robin
"Angels." [Poetry] (152:2) My 88, p. 90-91.
"Birch Island." [NewL] (54:3) Spr 88, p. 59.
"Etiquette." [Iowa] (18:1) 88, p. 119-120.
"Fogging the Bees." [OhioR] (42) 88, p. 82.
"In That Year." [DenQ] (22:4) Spr 88, p. 10-11.
"Letter Via Stars." [Iowa] (18:1) 88, p. 120-121.
"Not East." [NewL] (54:3) Spr 88, p. 58.
"Open Heart." [Poetry] (152:2) My 88, p. 88-89.
"Quintet for Flute and Strings." [Iowa] (18:1) 88, p. 121-122.
"Recovery." [Iowa] (18:1) 88, p. 123.
"The Waders." [DenQ] (22:4) Spr 88, p. 12-15.
348. BEHRENDT, Stephen C.
"Drought." [Footwork] ('88) 88, p. 47.
"Ice Fishing" (A Plainsongs Award Poem). [Plain] (8:2) Wint 88, p. 4.
"Jannie." [LitR] (31:2) Wint 88, p. 192-193.
"Norway Maples at the Reflecting Pool." [MidwQ] (29:3) Spr 88, p. 334-335.
"Pilgrimage." [Plain] (8:3) Spr-Sum 88, p. 29.
349. BEI, Dao
"Ancient Temple" (tr. by Donald Finkel and Xueliang Chen). [AmerPoR] (17:4) Jl-Ag 88, p. 42.
"Bodhisattva" (tr. by Edward Morin and Dennis Ding). [WebR] (13:2) Fall 88, p. 18.
"A Day" (tr. by Donald Finkel and Xueliang Chen). [AmerPoR] (17:4) Jl-Ag 88, p. 42.
"Everything" (in Chinese & English). [BelPoJ] (39:2) Wint 88-89, p. 16-17.
"Habit" (tr. by Donald Finkel and Xueliang Chen). [AmerPoR] (17:4) Jl-Ag 88, p. 43.
"Hello Mountain of a Hundred Flowers" (tr. by Donald Finkel and Xueliang Chen). [AmerPoR] (17:4) Jl-Ag 88, p. 42.
"Island" (in Chinese & English). [BelPoJ] (39:2) Wint 88-89, p. 10-13.
"Island" (tr. by Donald Finkel and Xueliang Chen). [AmerPoR] (17:4) Jl-Ag 88, p. 44.

"Memory" (tr. by Donald Finkel and Xueliang Chen). [AmerPoR] (17:4) Jl-Ag 88, p. 43.
"Nightmare" (tr. by Donald Finkel and Xueliang Chen). [AmerPoR] (17:4) Jl-Ag 88, p. 43.
"Notes on the City of the Sun" (tr. by Donald Finkel and Xueliang Chen). [AmerPoR] (17:4) Jl-Ag 88, p. 43.
"A Reply" (in Chinese & English). [BelPoJ] (39:2) Wint 88-89, p. 14-15.
"The Tale Goes On" (tr. by Donald Finkel and Xueliang Chen). [AmerPoR] (17:4) Jl-Ag 88, p. 43.
"Unfamiliar Shore" (tr. by Donald Finkel and Xueliang Chen). [AmerPoR] (17:4) Jl-Ag 88, p. 44.
"You Say" (tr. by Donald Finkel and Xueliang Chen). [AmerPoR] (17:4) Jl-Ag 88, p. 44.

350. BEINING, Guy R.
"Beige Copy" (Excerpt). [Caliban] (4) 88, p. 105-106.

351. BEISCH, June
"Continental Drift." [LitR] (31:2) Wint 88, p. 177.

352. BEISPIEL, David
"December." [Plain] (8:2) Wint 88, p. 22.
"The Wanderers." [Plain] (8:3) Spr-Sum 88, p. 22.

353. BELIEU, Erin
"The Green That Never Leaves the Skin." [LaurelR] (22:2) Sum 88, p. 49-50.

354. BELITT, Ben
"Papermill Graveyard" (North Bennington, Vermont). [TexasR] (9:3/4) Fall-Wint 88, p. 10-11.
"Thoreau on Paran Creek" (for Bernard Malamud). [TexasR] (9:3/4) Fall-Wint 88, p. 8-9.

355. BELL, Kathryn
"Ester." [Phoenix] (9:1/2) 88, p. 50.

356. BELL, Marvin
"An American Anthem." [NewRep] (198:23) 6 Je 88, p. 38.
"Elegy of a Morning Walk." [Nat] (246:18) 7 My 88, p. 653.
"Headlines." [OhioR] (42) 88, p. 70.
"Music Lessons." [MemphisSR] (8:2) Spr 88, p. 80.
"Not Joining the Wars." [Nat] (246:25) 25 Je 88, p. 908.
"Of a Day in June." [Boulevard] (3:2/3) Fall 88, p. 70.
"Pages" (Excerpt). [OhioR] (42) 88, p. 71.
"These Green-Going-to-Yellow." [MemphisSR] (8:2) Spr 88, p. 76-77.
"To No One in Particular." [MemphisSR] (8:2) Spr 88, p. 78-79.

357. BELL, Richard
"Orchis Nigra." [Phoenix] (9:1/2) 88, p. 43.

358. BELLAMY, Joe David
"Education." [CinPR] (17) Spr 88, p. 15.
"Memory of Singing." [CinPR] (17) Spr 88, p. 14.

359. BELLI, Carlos German
"Algún Día el Amor." [Inti] (26/27) Otoño 87-Primavera 88, p. 18.
"Amanuense." [Inti] (26/27) Otoño 87-Primavera 88, p. 21.
"Asir la Forma Que Se Va." [Inti] (26/27) Otoño 87-Primavera 88, p. 16.
"El Atarantado." [Inti] (26/27) Otoño 87-Primavera 88, p. 23-24.
"Boda de la Pluma y la Letra." [Inti] (26/27) Otoño 87-Primavera 88, p. 26-27.
"La Cara de Mis Hijas." [Inti] (26/27) Otoño 87-Primavera 88, p. 25.
"Cepo de Lima." [Inti] (26/27) Otoño 87-Primavera 88, p. 21.
"Cuánta Existencia Menos!" [Inti] (26/27) Otoño 87-Primavera 88, p. 20.
"Fisco." [Inti] (26/27) Otoño 87-Primavera 88, p. 22.
"Las Fórmulas Mágicas." [Inti] (26/27) Otoño 87-Primavera 88, p. 17.
"Ha Llegado el Domingo." [Inti] (26/27) Otoño 87-Primavera 88, p. 19-20.
"Mis Ajos." [Inti] (26/27) Otoño 87-Primavera 88, p. 22-23.
"Oh Alma Mía Empedrada!" [Inti] (26/27) Otoño 87-Primavera 88, p. 18.
"Oh Hada Cibernética!" [Inti] (26/27) Otoño 87-Primavera 88, p. 20.
"Oh Padres, Sabedlo Bien!" [Inti] (26/27) Otoño 87-Primavera 88, p. 19.
"Papá, Mamá." [Inti] (26/27) Otoño 87-Primavera 88, p. 18-19.
"Poema: Nuestro amor no está en nuestros respectivos." [Inti] (26/27) Otoño 87-Primavera 88, p. 16.
"Segregación No. 1" (a modo de un pintor primitivo culto). [Inti] (26/27) Otoño 87-Primavera 88, p. 17.
"Sextina de los Desiguales." [Inti] (26/27) Otoño 87-Primavera 88, p. 24-25.

"Villanela." [Inti] (26/27) Otoño 87-Primavera 88, p. 27.

360. BELTON, Julia
"Our Family Doctor." [SpoonRQ] (12:4) Fall 87, p. 55-56.

361. BEN AL-TALLA OF MAHDIA
"Artichoke Heart" (tr. from the Spanish of Emilio García Gómez by Christopher Middleton and Leticia Garza-Falcón). [NewYorker] (64:29) 5 S 88, p. 23.

362. BEN ANI RUH OF ALGECIRAS
"Honey River" (tr. from the Spanish of Emilio García Gómez by Christopher Middleton and Leticia Garza-Falcón). [NewYorker] (64:29) 5 S 88, p. 22.

363. BEN BILLITA, Al-Asad Ibrahim
"The Rooster" (tr. from the Spanish of Emilio García Gómez by Christopher Middleton and Leticia Garza-Falcón). [NewYorker] (64:29) 5 S 88, p. 23.

364. BEN HARIQ OF VALENCIA, Ali
"Galley Oars" (tr. from the Spanish of Emilio García Gómez by Christopher Middleton and Leticia Garza-Falcón). [NewYorker] (64:29) 5 S 88, p. 22.

365. BEN HISN, Abul Hasan Ali
"The Dove" (tr. from the Spanish of Emilio García Gómez by Christopher Middleton and Leticia Garza-Falcón). [NewYorker] (64:29) 5 S 88, p. 22.
"Reflection of Wine" (tr. from the Spanish of Emilio García Gómez by Christopher Middleton and Leticia Garza-Falcón). [NewYorker] (64:29) 5 S 88, p. 22.

366. BEN JARAF OF CAIRUAN
"Satire" (tr. from the Spanish of Emilio García Gómez by Christopher Middleton and Leticia Garza-Falcón). [NewYorker] (64:29) 5 S 88, p. 22.

367. BEN SAFAR AL-MARINI OF ALMERIA
"The Guadalquivir in Flood" (tr. from the Spanish of Emilio García Gómez by Christopher Middleton and Leticia Garza-Falcón). [NewYorker] (64:29) 5 S 88, p. 23.

368. BEN SAID, Abu Jafar Ahmad
"The Procuress" (tr. from the Spanish of Emilio García Gómez by Christopher Middleton and Leticia Garza-Falcón). [NewYorker] (64:29) 5 S 88, p. 23.

369. BEN SARA OF SANTAREN
"A Pool with Turtles" (tr. from the Spanish of Emilio García Gómez by Christopher Middleton and Leticia Garza-Falcón). [NewYorker] (64:29) 5 S 88, p. 23.

370. BEN-TOV, S.
"The Foucault Pendulum at Hanover." [ParisR] (30:106) Spr 88, p. 196.
"Pauses in Indian Flute Music." [ParisR] (30:107) Sum 88, p. 40.

371. BENADE, Judi
"Poems of Religious Ecstacy" (2 poems, tr. of Kabir). [Nimrod] (31:2) Spr-Sum 88, p. 20.
"Prayer One" (tr. of Sarveshvar Dayal Saksena). [Nimrod] (31:2) Spr-Sum 88, p. 76.
"Prayer Two" (tr. of Sarveshvar Dayal Saksena). [Nimrod] (31:2) Spr-Sum 88, p. 77.
"Worshipping God As a Baby" (3 poems, tr. of Surdas). [Nimrod] (31:2) Spr-Sum 88, p. 21-23.

372. BENAVIDEZ, Max
"Durango." [Jacaranda] (3:2) Fall-Wint 88, p. 68-71.

373. BENDALL, Molly
"Black Tulips." [AntR] (46:1) Wint 88, p. 72-73.
"Conversation with Mary Cassatt." [MissouriR] (11:1) 88, p. 54-55.
"Goose Feathers." [Sonora] (14/15) Spr 88, p. 24.
"Waiting." [WestHR] (42:3) Aut 88, p. 245-246.

374. BENDON, Chris
"The Children's Newspaper." [NewEngR] (10:4) Sum 88, p. 462.
"High Victorian." [Bogg] (59) 88, p. 24.

375. BENEDETTI, Mario
"Pebbles at the Window" (tr. by Richard Zenith). [ColR] (NS 15:2) Fall-Wint 88, p. 85.

376. BENEDIKTSSON, Tom
"Professor Narcisso Thinks of Death." [JlNJPo] (10:1/2) 88, p. 7.

377. BENEVENTO, Joe
"Telephone Line." [Footwork] ('88) 88, p. 73.
"You Bet Your Life." [Footwork] ('88) 88, p. 73.

378. BENEY, Zsuzsa
"Shimmering, But Darkening" (tr. by Zsuzsanna Ozsvath and Martha Satz). [LitR] (31:2) Wint 88, p. 160-161.

379. BENJAMIN, Jeanne Clark
"Bottoming Out at Damariscove." [TexasR] (9:3/4) Fall-Wint 88, p. 12.

"Harbor Seal in the Harraskeeket." [TexasR] (9:3/4) Fall-Wint 88, p. 13.

380. BENKSO, Rosemary
"Seeing the Dark." [ColR] (NS 15:2) Fall-Wint 88, p. 60-61.

381. BENNANI, Ben
"Psalm Sixteen" (tr. of Mahmud Darwish). [CharR] (14:1) Spr 88, p. 37.
"Psalm Thirteen" (tr. of Mahmud Darwish). [CharR] (14:1) Spr 88, p. 36.

382. BENNETT, Bruce
"Box Step." [LightY] ('88/9) 88, p. 122.
"The Experience." [LightY] ('88/9) 88, p. 210.
"The Form." [LightY] ('88/9) 88, p. 48-49.
"The Garden." [TarRP] (28:1) Fall 88, p. 46.
"Norman, or, The Fungus Among Us." [LightY] ('88/9) 88, p. 134.
"A Political Animal." [LightY] ('88/9) 88, p. 224.
"Spilled." [TarRP] (28:1) Fall 88, p. 46.
"Travis Licked Me." [LightY] ('88/9) 88, p. 94.

383. BENNETT, Debbie
"Illness." [CapilR] (49) 88, p. 74-75.
"Last Mortgage Payment." [CapilR] (49) 88, p. 76-77.

384. BENNETT, John
"The Answer." [CentralP] (14) Fall 88, p. 120.

385. BENNETT, John M.
"The Blur." [Caliban] (4) 88, p. 155.
"The Current." [Caliban] (4) 88, p. 155.
"Horse." [Abraxas] (37) 88, p. 65.
"Liquidator." [Bogg] (59) 88, p. 27.
"Stuttering." [Bogg] (60) 88, p. 39.

386. BENNETT, Karen
"I Would Like All Effort to Cease." [FourQ] (2d series 2:2) Fall 88, p. 43.

387. BENNETT, Maria
"The History of Darkness" (Commended, 15th Anniversary Competition). [StoneC] (16:1/2) Fall-Wint 88-89, unpaged front matter.

388. BENSEN, Robert
"Caprice." [ParisR] (30:107) Sum 88, p. 44-45.

389. BENSKO, John
"Away from It All." [Chelsea] (47) 88, p. 86-87.
"The Children of Goodwill." [NewOR] (15:2) Sum 88, p. 10.
"In the Everglades." [Chelsea] (47) 88, p. 85.
"The Progress of Love" (a suite of poems). [BlackWR] (14:2) Spr 88, p. 49-63.

390. BENSON, Judith
"Sky." [Grain] (16:4) Wint 88, inside front cover.

391. BENTLEY, Beth
"Afterword: Felicia" (from Posthumous Letters). [NegC] (8:3) 88, p. 65-67.
"Almost Landscapes" (Eight Ghazels). [BellArk] (4:6) N-D 88, p. 4.
"Heron Country." [BellArk] (4:5) S-O 88, p. 1.
"Little Fires: Camille and Gwen" (Second Place, 1987 Eve of Saint Agnes Poetry Competition). [NegC] (8:3) 88, p. 18-23.
"Northern Idylls." [GettyR] (1:4) Aut 88, p. 661-662.

392. BENTLEY, Nelson
"Tracking the Transcendental Moose" (Book 11: Apocalypses, Epics, and Castalia). [BellArk] (4:1) Ja-F 88, p. 10-19.
"Tracking the Transcendental Moose" (Book 12: Moose Call and Concord). [BellArk] (4:2) Mr-Ap 88, p. 10-19.
"Tracking the Transcendental Moose" (Book 13: Iron Man of the Hoh & Snoqualmie Falls Apocalypse). [BellArk] (4:3) My-Je 88, p. 10-18.
"Tracking the Transcendental Moose" (Book 14: the Moose and the Bellowing Ark). [BellArk] (4:4) Jl-Ag 88, p. 11-24.

393. BENTLEY, Roy
"The Country of the Dead." [MidAR] (8:2) 88, p. 191-192.
"Lighted Jesus" (for Claire). [CinPR] (18) Fall 88, p. 64-65.
"View from the Great Southern Hotel." [IndR] (11:3) Sum 88, p. 53-54.

394. BENTTINEN, Ted
"Blue Flame and the Red Weight of Wings." [LitR] (31:2) Wint 88, p. 218-219.
"Death of a Young Son." [SouthernR] (24:1) Wint 88, p. 153.
"Grebe Feathers Are Painted by Hydrogen." [ManhatPR] (10) Ja 88, p. 60.
"Looking North, Looking South." [BallSUF] (29:4) Aut 88, p. 53.

395. BERG, Clair
"Mid-Canal, Antwerp." [TriQ] (71) Wint 88, p. 159-160.
"The Storm." [TriQ] (71) Wint 88, p. 161.
396. BERG, Lora
"A Flower Clock." [ConnPR] (7:1) 88, p. 24-26.
397. BERG, Nancy
"I Could Have Danced All Night If I Hadn't Spontaneously Combusted." [NegC] (8:3) 88, p. 58-61.
398. BERG, Stephen
"My Door." [Field] (39) Fall 88, p. 25-26.
"One Listener." [PoetryE] (26) Fall 88, p. 88.
399. BERGAMIN, José
"She Asks for a Sonnet" (tr. by David Garrison). [PoetryE] (25) Spr 88, p. 127.
400. BERGER, Bruce
"Facing the Music." [Poetry] (143, i.e. 153:1) O 88, p. 10-11.
"Impressionists." [Poetry] (143, i.e. 153:1) O 88, p. 12.
"Tallulah at the Schubert." [LightY] ('88/9) 88, p. 82-83.
"These Arias." [Poetry] (143, i.e. 153:1) O 88, p. 11.
401. BERGER, Don
"Quality Hill." [Caliban] (5) 88, p. 79-81.
402. BERGER, Linda-Ruth
"What the Sun Provided." [AmerV] (12) Fall 88, p. 61-62.
403. BERGER, Margi
"Jens Jensen." [BellR] (11:2) Fall 88, p. 34.
404. BERGER, Suzanne E. (Suzanne F.?)
"Four Girls in a Red Room" (after a painting by John Singer Sargent). [TexasR] (9:3/4) Fall-Wint 88, p. 16.
"In the Evening of Creatures." [TexasR] (9:3/4) Fall-Wint 88, p. 14-15.
"Keep." [Ploughs] (14:1) 88, p. 65.
405. BERGHASH, Rachel
"A Small Man Is Greater Than a Starry Dome." [ChiR] (36:2) Aut 88, p. 61-62.
406. BERGLAND, Martha
"Four Answers to the Same Question" ("Why do you eat so much?"). [Prima] (11/12) 88, p. 67-68.
407. BERGMAN, David
"A Dream of Nightingales" (In memory of Jerry Thompson). [AmerS] (57:2) Spr 88, p. 200.
408. BERGMAN, Mara
"My Sister's Pregnant." [PoetryE] (25) Spr 88, p. 69.
"Waiting for the Baby." [PoetryE] (25) Spr 88, p. 70.
409. BERGMAN, Susan
"Presents." [PraS] (62:1) Spr 88, p. 110-112.
410. BERGON, Holly St. John
"Chamula Dolls." [Sequoia] (31:2) Wint 88, p. 16.
411. BERGSTROM, Vera
"Joie." [Bogg] (60) 88, p. 28.
412. BERKE, Judith
"Completely Open." [NewL] (54:3) Spr 88, p. 53.
"Dionysus." [BlackWR] (14:2) Spr 88, p. 25.
"Discovery" (after the painting by Magritte). [Field] (39) Fall 88, p. 59.
"Family Tree." [KenR] (NS 10:3) Sum 88, p. 121.
"The Last Supper." [Field] (39) Fall 88, p. 60.
"Midnight Sun." [Field] (39) Fall 88, p. 61.
"Old Woman." [Iowa] (18:2) 88, p. 114-115.
"Persephone." [BlackWR] (14:2) Spr 88, p. 27.
"Poem Beginning in the Bed of My Mother and Father." [NewRep] (198:6) 8 F 88, p. 39.
"Quasimodo." [BlackWR] (14:2) Spr 88, p. 26.
"Repression in the Age of Aquarius." [Iowa] (18:2) 88, p. 113.
"Scheherazade." [KenR] (NS 10:3) Sum 88, p. 120.
"Visiting Borges." [Iowa] (18:2) 88, p. 115-116.
"Vizcaya (the Deering estate)." [AntR] (46:2) Spr 88, p. 247.
413. BERKE, Nancy
"The Diver." [Footwork] ('88) 88, p. 59.

414. BERKES, Ulrich
"Exaggerated Self-Portrait" (tr. by George Kane). [ParisR] (30:106) Spr 88, p. 289-291.
"I Was Icarus" (tr. by George Kane). [ParisR] (30:106) Spr 88, p. 292.
"Orpheus" (tr. by George Kane). [ParisR] (30:106) Spr 88, p. 294.
"Remington Portable" (tr. by George Kane). [ParisR] (30:106) Spr 88, p. 293.
"Theocritus" (tr. by George Kane). [ParisR] (30:106) Spr 88, p. 295.
415. BERLIND, Bruce
"Cynthia Lodgepole's Bum Rap." [LightY] ('88/9) 88, p. 131-132.
BERMUDEZ, Federico Jovine
See JOVINE BERMUDEZ, Federico
416. BERNAL LABRADA, Emilio
"The Nightingale" (tr. of Jorge Valls Arango). [Vis] (26) 88, p. 51.
"There Is No Light" (tr. of Jorge Valls Arango). [Vis] (26) 88, p. 51.
417. BERNARD, April
"Boyacá Is the Land of Liberty." [ParisR] (30:108) Fall 88, p. 213-214.
418. BERNHARD, Jim
"Esther Phillips." [BellArk] (4:6) N-D 88, p. 6.
"Film Noir." [BellArk] (4:5) S-O 88, p. 10.
419. BERNSTEIN, Charles
"Applied Monk: Preliminary Notes." [Caliban] (4) 88, p. 53-59.
"Artifice of Absorption" (special issue). [PaperAir] (4:1) 87, 71 p.
"Desalination." [Caliban] (4) 88, p. 128-130.
"Polynesian Days" (Variations on Nichole Brossard's "Polynèse Des Yeux", Notus 2:2, 1987). [Notus] (3:2) Fall 88, p. 22-23.
420. BERNSTEIN, Lisa
"After He Left Her." [Spirit] (9:1) 88, p. 66.
"A Rescue." [Zyzzyva] (4:3) Fall 88, p. 118-119.
421. BERRETT, Jean
"The Difference in Mass." [NewL] (55:1) Fall 88, p. 82.
"Teh River That Rises in My Bones." [Spirit] (9:1) 88, p. 147-148.
422. BERRY, Paul
"Heroes." [Bogg] (59) 88, p. 17.
423. BERRYMAN, Tony
"Denouement." [PottPort] (10) 88, p. 35.
424. BERSSENBRUGGE, Mei-Mei
"Chronicle." [Calyx] (11:2/3) Fall 88, p. 148-149.
"Duration of Water." [Calyx] (11:2/3) Fall 88, p. 147.
425. BERTOLINO, James
"Indra's Falls." [BellR] (11:1) Spr 88, p. 46-47.
"Spring Crocus." [PikeF] (9) Fall 88, p. 7.
426. BERTRAND, Claudine
"Une Fiction au Noir Lunaire." [Os] (26) 88, p. 10.
"Vue d'un Rêve." [Os] (26) 88, p. 11.
427. BESCHTA, Jim
"Luke Waking: First Birthday." [BellR] (11:1) Spr 88, p. 29.
"Night Sounds." [DeKalbLAJ] (21:1) Wint 88, p. 43.
428. BEST, Michael
"Message." [CanLit] (119) Wint 88, p. 72.
429. BETHANY
"Untitled: I've never had a masturbatory fantasy and now I probably never will." [SinW] (36) Wint 88-89, p. 22.
430. BETTENCOURT, Michael
"Boundary Walls." [BallSUF] (29:4) Aut 88, p. 22-23.
"Conch." [DeKalbLAJ] (21:1) Wint 88, p. 44.
431. BEUM, Robert
"The Coiffure." [SewanR] (96:3) Sum 88, p. 408.
"December Night." [ChrC] (105:38) 14 D 88, p. 1140.
"In Four Acres." [CanLit] (117) Sum 88, p. 125.
"Notes Toward an Inventory." [SewanR] (96:3) Sum 88, p. 407.
432. BEVERIDGE, Judith
"Flamingo Park." [NewAW] (4) Fall 88, p. 111-112.
"Flower of Flowers." [NewAW] (4) Fall 88, p. 110.
"In the Park." [NewAW] (4) Fall 88, p. 109.
"Reels." [NewAW] (4) Fall 88, p. 112-113.
"The Workday." [NewAW] (4) Fall 88, p. 110-111.

433. BEYER, Catharine Hoffman
"Continental Drift." [CrabCR] (5:2) Sum 88, p. 25.
434. BEYER, Richard G.
"Greek Tragedy." [DeKalbLAJ] (21:3/4) 88, p. 47.
"Line to Jimmy Collins" (Drowned in the Tennessee River, alone, Dec. 1986). [Wind] (18:63) 88, p. 16.
435. BEZIAT, Richard
"Running the Projector in Reverse." [AmerS] (57:1) Wint 88, p. 48-49.
436. BEZNER, Kevin
"On This, a Holy Night." [PassN] (9:1) Wint 88, p. 21.
437. BHARATI, Subramania
"In Time of the Breaking of the Worlds" (Oozhi-K-Koothu, tr. by Prema Nandakumar). [Nimrod] (31:2) Spr-Sum 88, p. 98-99.
438. BHATT, Sujata
"Go to Ahmedabad." [Calyx] (11:2/3) Fall 88, p. 25-27.
"Muliebrity." [Calyx] (11:2/3) Fall 88, p. 28.
439. BIANCHI, Matilde
"Mi Noche Triste." [Mairena] (10:25) 88, p. 131.
440. BICH, Nguyen Ngoc
"Picking Tea Leaves Under a July Rain" (tr. of Tran Kha). [Vis] (27) 88, p. 18.
441. BICHET, Yves
"Le Ciel de Montines" (à la mémoire de Jacques Bussy). [Os] (26) 88, p. 25-31.
442. BIDGOOD, Ruth
"Above Rhulen." [NewEngR] (10:4) Sum 88, p. 416.
"Night Ride." [NewEngR] (10:4) Sum 88, p. 416.
443. BIEHL, Michael
"Coastal Farmland." [Interim] (7:1) Spr 88, p. 41-42.
"The Hermits." [Plain] (8:3) Spr-Sum 88, p. 36.
"A Natural Reconciliation." [BellArk] (4:2) Mr-Ap 88, p. 1.
"Pentecost." [Plain] (9:1) Fall 88, p. 35.
444. BIERDS, Linda
"The Anatomy Lesson of Dr. Nicolaas Tulp, Amsterdam, 1632." [NewYorker] (63:50) 1 F 88, p. 30.
"Wedding" (From the Painting by Jan van Eyck). [NewYorker] (64:36) 24 O 88, p. 44.
445. BIESPIEL, David
"Driving along the Connecticut River at Dawn." [EngJ] (77:6) O 88, p. 87.
446. BIGGINS, Michael
"The Arm" (tr. of Tomaz Salamun, w. John Engels). [NewEngR] (10:3) Spr 88, p. 279-280.
"Birds" (tr. of Tomaz Salamun). [NewEngR] (10:3) Spr 88, p. 278.
"Judas Iscariot" (tr. of Tomaz Salamun). [Agni] (27) 88, p. 206.
"Oops!" (tr. of Tomaz Salamun). [Agni] (27) 88, p. 205.
"Red Cliff" (tr. of Tomaz Salamun). [NewEngR] (10:3) Spr 88, p. 278.
447. BIGGS, Fred
"The Child Who Had No Father" (Aboriginal Narrative of New South Wales, Collected by Roland Robinson). [PraS] (62:4) Wint 88-89, p. 20-21.
448. BILGERE, George
"The Children." [KenR] (NS 10:3) Sum 88, p. 123.
"Coyote Mort." [KanQ] (20:3) Sum 88, p. 135.
"The Last Snapshot." [SouthwR] (73:2) Spr 88, p. 253-254.
"Major Bennett." [KenR] (NS 10:3) Sum 88, p. 122-123.
"A Postcard" (In thanks for a gift). [KenR] (NS 10:3) Sum 88, p. 122.
449. BILICKE, Tom
"Untitled #1." [Wind] (18:63) 88, p. 2.
"Via Appia." [Bogg] (59) 88, p. 39.
"West Hollywood." [Wind] (18:63) 88, p. 2-3.
BILLITA, Al-Asad Ibrahim ben
See BEN SAID, Al-Asad Ibrahim
450. BINGHAM, Sallie
"Two Girls." [NegC] (8:3) 88, p. 125-126.
451. BINKINS, Robert
"For My Grandfather" (In Memoriam: August 1, 1913 — September 4, 1986). [MSS] (6:2) 88, p. 34-35.
BISHOP, Annick Perrot
See PERROT-BISHOP, Annick

452. BISHOP, Elizabeth
"It is marvellous to wake up together." [AmerPoR] (17:1) Ja-F 88, p. 35.
453. BISHOP, W.
"Vanessa." [HolCrit] (25:5) D 88, p. 14.
454. BISHOP, Wendy
"Our Animals." [MinnR] (NS 30/31) Spr-Fall 88, p. 36.
"Pension" (Lake Chapala, Mexico). [Wind] (18:62) 88, p. 5-6.
"V-Mail" (A found poem from WWII correspondences). [AmerPoR] (17:5) S-O 88, p. 7-8.
455. BISSONETTE, David
"Horoscope" (for R.R.). [JamesWR] (6:1) Fall 88, p. 8.
456. BITAR, Walid
"Bad Western." [Quarry] (37:1) Wint 88, p. 43.
457. BITZ, Gregory W.
"If I Could Only Believe You" (Selection from War Hangover). [LakeSR] (22) 88, p. 21-22.
458. BIXLER, Berniece
"Western Cut." [Phoenix] (9:1/2) 88, p. 49.
459. BIZZARO, Patrick
"Swimming the Earth." [SpoonRQ] (13:3) Sum 88, p. 12.
460. BJORNVIG, Thorkild
"Space Dog" (tr. by Marilyn Wanick). [ColR] (NS 15:2) Fall-Wint 88, p. 72-73.
461. BLACK, Candace
"Housewarming." [SoDakR] (26:3) Aut 88, p. 86-87.
"Letter in Spring." [SoDakR] (26:3) Aut 88, p. 88.
462. BLACK, Patricia Rodgers
"The Text." [CentR] (32:2) Spr 88, p. 152.
463. BLACK, Ralph
"Cadenza." [SewanR] (96:3) Sum 88, p. 411-412.
"View from the Boggeragh Mountains." [SewanR] (96:3) Sum 88, p. 409-410.
464. BLACK, Ralph W.
"Nightsong on the Salmon River." [CarolQ] (41:1) Fall 88, p. 77.
465. BLACK, Sharon
"What to Be Made Of." [Jacaranda] (3:1) Wint 88, p. 94.
466. BLACK, Sophie Cabot
"The Body Still Wanting." [Agni] (27) 88, p. 35.
"The Converted." [Agni] (27) 88, p. 36.
"On the Last Day of the World." [Pequod] (25) 88, p. 55-57.
"The Wait." [Agni] (27) 88, p. 34.
467. BLACK, Star
"Lava." [Sequoia] (31:2) Wint 88, p. 62.
"Sigh." [Sequoia] (31:2) Wint 88, p. 63.
468. BLACKBULL, Jefferson
"Little-Flower-Killer Moon." [Phoenix] (9:1/2) 88, p. 8.
"Osage War Dance." [Phoenix] (9:1/2) 88, p. 9.
469. BLACKFORD, Anne
"Twins." [KanQ] (20:3) Sum 88, p. 192.
470. BLACKSTONE, Alice
"Birthday Song." [Plain] (8:3) Spr-Sum 88, p. 29.
"Maverick." [Plain] (9:1) Fall 88, p. 11.
471. BLADES, Joe
"Cycle." [SlipS] (8) 88, p. 19.
"Humming Wires." [PottPort] (9) 88, p. 3.
"Ode by Harold Robbins." [SlipS] (8) 88, p. 18-19.
"Twinning the Trans-Canada." [PottPort] (9) 88, p. 3.
472. BLAICH, Beryl
"Apparition." [ChamLR] (2:1, #3) Fall 88, p. 14-15.
"Reading an Anthology of Contemporary American Poetry." [ChamLR] (1:2, #2) Spr 88, p. 141-142.
473. BLAIR, Sam
"Dog." [PoetryNW] (29:3) Aut 88, p. 47.
474. BLAKE, Jonathan
"Her Lover's Departure." [PikeF] (9) Fall 88, p. 29.
475. BLAKER, Margaret
"Clerihews" (2 poems). [LightY] ('88/9) 88, p. 75-76.

"Minerva Cheevy" (Granddaughter of E. A. Robinson's "Miniver Cheevy"). [Amelia] (4:4, #11) 88, p. 55.

476. BLANCHARD, David
"Roll Tide." [DeKalbLAJ] (21:3/4) 88, p. 48.

477. BLANCO, Alberto
"Black Tryptich" (tr. by John Oliver Simon). [Rohwedder] (3) Spr 88, p. 17.
"A Skeptical Noah" (tr. by John Oliver Simon). [Zyzzyva] (4:3) Fall 88, p. 129-130.
"Triptico Negro." [Rohwedder] (3) Spr 88, p. 18.

478. BLANKENBURG, Gary
"After All." [Bogg] (59) 88, p. 34.

479. BLAUNER, Laurie
"Memoirs of a Painter's Model, 1929." [DeKalbLAJ] (21:2) Spr 88, p. 32.
"Where the Body Ends." [GeoR] (42:4) Wint 88, p. 754.

480. BLAZEK, Douglas
"Birthday Field Map." [Abraxas] (37) 88, p. 26-27.
"A Bundle of Tongues." [Abraxas] (37) 88, p. 26.
"A Tentative Silence." [SwampR] (1:2/3) D 88, p. 57.

481. BLEA, Irene I.
"Generation." [BilingR] (13:1/2) Ja-Ag 86, c1988, p. 98.
"Losing." [BilingR] (13:1/2) Ja-Ag 86, c1988, p. 99.

482. BLEHERT, Dean
"Your moans of pleasure reward." [Bogg] (59) 88, p. 33.

483. BLESSING, Marlene
"The Coat." [TarRP] (28:1) Fall 88, p. 52-53.
"Our Summer Reunions." [TarRP] (28:1) Fall 88, p. 51.
"A Show of Magic." [TarRP] (28:1) Fall 88, p. 50.

484. BLIZARD, Robert Bruce
"East." [BellR] (11:1) Spr 88, p. 25.

485. BLOCH, Chana
"How Do You Manage a Rowdy Child?" (tr. of Yehuda Amichai). [Zyzzyva] (4:2) Sum 88, p. 81.
"Rough Draft" (tr. of Dahlia Ravikovitch). [GrahamHR] (11) Spr 88, p. 107.
"Survivors" (in memory of N. K.). [GrahamHR] (11) Spr 88, p. 36.
"The Window" (tr. of Dahlia Ravikovitch). [GrahamHR] (11) Spr 88, p. 106.

486. BLOCK, Laurie
"Angel in the Snow." [PraF] (9:4) Wint 88-89, p. 21.
"Churchill Manitoba." [PraF] (9:4) Wint 88-89, p. 21.
"Forty Years in the Desert." [PraF] (9:4) Wint 88-89, p. 20.

487. BLOMAIN, Karen
"The Dancers." [PassN] (9:1) Wint 88, p. 17.

488. BLOOMER, Andrew
"The River" (Poetry Contest Winner). [HarvardA] (122:3) Mr 88, p. 11.

489. BLOOMFIELD, Maureen
"Dies Irae." [CinPR] (17) Spr 88, p. 16.

490. BLOSSOM, Laurel
"Things to Say When You Quit Smoking." [LightY] ('88/9) 88, p. 221-222.

491. BLOUNT, Chriscinthia
"42nd Street Scan." [CentralP] (14) Fall 88, p. 55-56.

492. BLOUNT, Roy, Jr.
"Still Life." [LightY] ('88/9) 88, p. 189.

493. BLUE, Ophelia
"After all this time." [Writer] (101:12) D 88, p. 24.

494. BLUESTONE, Stephen
"Bewildering Clarity of Tongues" (for Aaron Lebedeff, performer on the Yiddish stage). [GreensboroR] (45) Wint 88-89, p. 5-6.
"A Circumstance of the Porch." [GreensboroR] (45) Wint 88-89, p. 7.
"First Voices." [GreensboroR] (45) Wint 88-89, p. 3-4.

495. BLUME, Jillian
"How Far." [LitR] (31:3) Spr 88, p. 332.

496. BLUMENREICH, Julia
"Flowery prints." [CentralP] (13) Spr 88, p. 177-178.
"Ingathering Text 1 Jan - Feb 88." [CentralP] (14) Fall 88, p. 127-129.

497. BLUMENTHAL, Jay (Jay A.)
"Annus Mirabilis, 1969-1970." [GreensboroR] (45) Wint 88-89, p. 26.
"Breakfast in Pavonia." [JlNJPo] (10:1/2) 88, p. 8.
"Cary Grant's Last Role." [ChamLR] (1:2, #2) Spr 88, p. 122.

"Circe." [Vis] (28) 88, p. 8.
"The Dover Sole." [GreensboroR] (45) Wint 88-89, p. 25-26.
"A Dwarf's Intimation of Christmas." [Interim] (7:1) Spr 88, p. 22.
"Groucho." [Footwork] ('88) 88, p. 46.
"Lazarus, O Lazarus." [LitR] (32:1) Fall 88, p. 90.
"Random Thoughts on Falling Out of an Office Building." [Footwork] ('88) 88, p. 46.
"A Remarkable Dream of Harpo." [ChamLR] (2:1, #3) Fall 88, p. 113.
"A Remarkable Dream of Harpo." [Footwork] ('88) 88, p. 46.
"The Revised City of God." [GreensboroR] (45) Wint 88-89, p. 27.
"The Revised City of God." [JINJPo] (10:1/2) 88, p. 9.
"Richard Burton: An Appreciation." [CumbPR] (7:2) Spr 88, p. 1-2.

498. BLUMENTHAL, Michael
"The Art of Poetry." [TexasR] (9:3/4) Fall-Wint 88, p. 18-19.
"Garments." [NewRep] (198:4) 25 Ja 88, p. 35.
"God Loves You, and So Do I." [AmerS] (57:3) Sum 88, p. 392.
"The Pleasures of Old Age." [Poetry] (151:5) F 88, p. 413.
"Stamps" (after Bruno Schultz). [TexasR] (9:3/4) Fall-Wint 88, p. 17.

499. BLY, Robert
"Windy Night in Summer." [CreamCR] (12:1) Wint 88, p. 81.

500. BOBRICK, James
"Lines for Mike." [Lactuca] (11) O 88, p. 4-5.
"McGeorge Bundy at Harvard, 1965." [Lactuca] (11) O 88, p. 5.
"Olympia Market, New Bedford." [Lactuca] (11) O 88, p. 4.

501. BOBYSHEV, Dmitry
"The Other World" (For O.S.-B., tr. by Michael Van Walleghen). [Vis] (26) 88, p. 44.
"Return" (tr. by Michael Van Walleghen). [Vis] (26) 88, p. 45, 47.
"Trotsky in Mexico" (tr. by Michael Van Walleghen). [Vis] (26) 88, p. 43.

502. BOCCANERA, Jorge
"I Say Inside Me" (tr. by John Oliver Simon). [Rohwedder] (3) Spr 88, p. 32.
"Yo Digo Adentro Mio." [Rohwedder] (3) Spr 88, p. 32.

503. BOCKES, Zan
"The Knife Is Mine." [Plain] (8:2) Wint 88, p. 16.
"Resurrecting the Fire." [Plain] (8:1) Fall 87, p. 34.

504. BOE, Marilyn J.
"Visit in December." [ChrC] (105:39) 21-28 D 88, p. 1180.

505. BOES, Don
"Heaven and Earth." [SpoonRQ] (13:1) Wint 88, p. 24.

506. BOGAN, James
"Between the Lines" (tr. of Max Martins). [CharR] (14:1) Spr 88, p. 37.

507. BOGEN, Don
"Examination." [CinPR] (18) Fall 88, p. 22-23.
"The Moon in the Water." [CinPR] (17) Spr 88, p. 36-37.
"Rain Forest." [Nat] (247:4) 13-20 Ag 88, p. 144.
"This Far." [Stand] (29:3) Sum 88, p. 51.

508. BOGEN, Laurel Ann
"Brand New Dandy." [Spirit] (9:1) 88, p. 25.
"Detective Supremo." [Jacaranda] (3:2) Fall-Wint 88, p. 72-73.

509. BOGGS, William
"Bottle of Beer." [HiramPoR] (44/45) Spr-Wint 88, p. 8.
"Dead Man." [HiramPoR] (44/45) Spr-Wint 88, p. 9.
"Gritch." [ColR] (NS 15:1) Spr-Sum 88, p. 95.

510. BOGIN, George
"At the Graves of My Grandparents." [Confr] (37/38) Spr-Sum 88, p. 216-217.

511. BOGIN, Magda
"Parca" (tr. of Salvador Espriu). [Boulevard] (3:2/3) Fall 88, p. 141.
"The Wind" (Homage to Pablo Neruda, tr. of Salvador Espriu). [Boulevard] (3:2/3) Fall 88, p. 142.

512. BOHM, Robert
"Going Down Low Enough to Need the Moon" (for Mafundi). [NegC] (8:3) 88, p. 134-136.

513. BOISSEAU, Michelle
"The Melancholia of Pleasure." [CinPR] (17) Spr 88, p. 17.

514. BOLAND, Eavan
"The Achill Woman." [Atlantic] (262:2) Ag 88, p. 45.
"The Glass King." [PartR] (55:1) Wint 88, p. 57-59.
"Mountain Time." [NewYorker] (64:16) 6 Je 88, p. 40.

"The River." [NewYorker] (64:39) 14 N 88, p. 120.
"The Shadow Doll." [YaleR] (77:2) Wint 88, p. 241-242.
"Spring at the Edge of the Sonnet." [NewYorker] (64:6) 28 Mr 88, p. 32.

515. BOLLS, Imogene
"Cave of the Hands." [CinPR] (18) Fall 88, p. 63.

516. BOLSTRIDGE, Alice
"Fire." [CinPR] (17) Spr 88, p. 50-51.
"Water Color." [CinPR] (17) Spr 88, p. 52-54.

517. BOLT, Jeffrey
"Numbers to a Young Poet." [Interim] (7:2) Fall 88, p. 12.
"We Seldom Speak of the Governor." [Interim] (7:2) Fall 88, p. 11.

518. BOLT, Thomas
"1971 Pontiac LeMans." [ParisR] (30:109) Wint 88, p. 59.

519. BOLTON, Joe (Joseph Edward)
"Autumn Fugue" (To Amy Wallace). [Crazy] (34) Spr 88, p. 38-39.
"Fathers and Sons." [BlackWR] (14:2) Spr 88, p. 31-32.
"Fin de Siècle." [DenQ] (22:4) Spr 88, p. 35.
"A Hymn to the Body." [Crazy] (35) Wint 88, p. 38-40.
"In Pieces." [TampaR] (1) 88, p. 60.
"Landscapes I." [WestHR] (42:1) Spr 88, p. 72.
"Recitative" (tr. of Enrique Huaco). [ColR] (NS 15:2) Fall-Wint 88, p. 86.
"The Seasons: A Quartet." [BlackWR] (14:2) Spr 88, p. 28-30.
"The Story" (after Vallejo). [StoneC] (16:1/2) Fall-Wint 88-89, p. 23.
"Tall Palms." [YaleR] (77:4) Sum 88, p. 607.
"Tropical Lament" (after Vallejo). [MidAR] (8:2) 88, p. 194.

520. BOLZ, Jody
"The Word Asia." [Ascent] (13:3) 88, p. 22-24.

521. BOMBACH, Jean Jandel
"Praise Gods." [ChatR] (8:3) Spr 88, p. 7.

522. BONAFFINI, Luigi
"Song of Evening Falling" (tr. of Salvidor Espiru). [Vis] (27) 88, p. 12.

523. BONAZZOLI, Laura M.
"Playing by the Rules." [Writer] (101:12) D 88, p. 23.

524. BOND, Adrienne
"Burial." [SouthernR] (24:2) Spr 88, p. 322-324.
"On the Fall Line." [SouthernR] (24:2) Spr 88, p. 320-321.

525. BOND, Bruce
"The Art of Memory: Neighborhoods." [CharR] (14:1) Spr 88, p. 62.
"Bartok." [KanQ] (20:4) Fall 88, p. 67.
"The Consolation of Open Spaces." [CharR] (14:1) Spr 88, p. 62-63.
"The Day the Tumor Moves In." [SouthernPR] (28:2) Fall 88, p. 52.
"The Drowning." [InterPR] (14:1) Spr 88, p. 106.
"The Elephants of Kitum." [InterPR] (14:1) Spr 88, p. 105.
"Jean Returns from Wintering in Phoenix." [LaurelR] (22:21) Wint 88, p. 48-49.
"Nocturne for Marie Curie." [HighP] (3:2) Fall 88, p. 106.
"Ravel." [PacificR] (6) Spr 88, p. 14.
"Red Weather." [LaurelR] (22:21) Wint 88, p. 49.
"Satie." [DenQ] (23:2) Fall 88, p. 35.
"Shostakovich." [KanQ] (20:4) Fall 88, p. 68.
"Small Talk." [LaurelR] (22:21) Wint 88, p. 48.
"That the Future Is Not What Frees Us" (for Wray, -1982). [StoneC] (16:1/2) Fall-Wint 88-89, p. 62.
"Varese." [PacificR] (6) Spr 88, p. 15.
"Webern." [PacificR] (6) Spr 88, p. 16.

526. BOND, Cynthia
"Ode." [Epoch] (37:1) 88, p. 6.
"Some Things I'll Try to Do." [Epoch] (37:1) 88, p. 5.

527. BONENFANT, Joseph
"Mer." [Os] (26) 88, p. 24.

528. BONNEFOY, Yves
"The Quickness of Clouds" (tr. by Joyce Oliver Lowrie). [AmerPoR] (17:4) Jl-Ag 88, p. 46.
"The Well" (tr. by Joyce Oliver Lowrie). [AmerPoR] (17:4) Jl-Ag 88, p. 46.

BONTÉ, Karen la
See LaBONTÉ, Karen

529. BOOK, M. K.
"Twelve Postulates Regarding One's Head, Art and Science." [WormR] (28:1, #109) 88, p. 36-38.
530. BOOTH, Philip
"Kim's Dreamsong, 1987" (w. Kim Waller, in memory of Gabrielle Ladd, 1937-1960). [CreamCR] (12:2) Sum 88, p. 303.
"Marches." [AmerPoR] (17:5) S-O 88, p. 48.
"Sixty." [Atlantic] (261:3) Mr 88, p. 80.
"Wanting." [Ploughs] (14:1) 88, p. 42-44.
531. BORAN, Pat
"The Catherine-Wheel." [BellR] (11:2) Fall 88, p. 9.
"The House." [BellR] (11:2) Fall 88, p. 10.
BORBON, Rafael Diaz
See DIAZ BORBON, Rafael
532. BORCHERS, Elisabeth
"Es ist wahr, dass es um Mitternacht." [StoneC] (16:1/2) Fall-Wint 88-89, p. 65.
"Yes, it's true, at midnight" (tr. by Anneliese Wagner). [StoneC] (16:1/2) Fall-Wint 88-89, p. 64.
BORDA, J. G. Cobo
See COBO BORDA, J. G.
533. BORDEN, William
"At the Crossroads Inn." [Farm] (5:2) Fall 88, p. 42.
"Balloon." [SoDakR] (26:3) Aut 88, p. 36.
"Bisbee, North Dakota." [Farm] (5:2) Fall 88, p. 41.
"Bisbee, North Dakota." [GreensboroR] (44) Sum 88, p. 92.
"Bisbee, North Dakota." [Vis] (27) 88, p. 24.
"Driving Across North Dakota." [GreensboroR] (44) Sum 88, p. 92.
"Escargot." [SlipS] (8) 88, p. 30.
"On the Way to Ucross, Wyoming." [SoDakR] (26:3) Aut 88, p. 34-35.
"Prowling." [Farm] (5:2) Fall 88, p. 40.
"Winter Thoughts." [SlipS] (8) 88, p. 31-32.
534. BORGES, Jorge Luis
"Christ on the Cross" (tr. by Willis Barnstone). [AmerPoR] (17:5) S-O 88, p. 21.
"On His Blindness" (tr. by Willis Barnstone). [AmerPoR] (17:5) S-O 88, p. 21.
535. BORICH, Barrie Jean
"The Disappeared." [SinW] (32) Sum 87, p. 10-12.
536. BORKHUIS, Charles
"Digesting the Data." [Caliban] (4) 88, p. 148.
"The Living." [Caliban] (4) 88, p. 149.
BORKOWSKI, Miriam Halliday
See HALLIDAY-BORKOWSKI, Miriam
537. BORMAN, Kevin
"Chipboard Offcuts" (from Bogg 30, 1975). [Bogg] (59) 88, p. 41.
538. BORN, Anne
"Vanishing Days" (tr. of Pia Tafdrup). [ColR] (NS 15:2) Fall-Wint 88, p. 80-81.
539. BORSON, Roo
"2 a.m." [WestCR] (22:4) Spr 87, i.e. 88, p. 25.
"About the Cat." [MalR] (85) D 88, p. 102-103.
"And." [WestCR] (22:4) Spr 87, i.e. 88, p. 19-20.
"Close to the Beginning." [WestCR] (22:4) Spr 87, i.e. 88, p. 18.
"Finding Halley's Comet." [MalR] (85) D 88, p. 107.
"Grief." [WestCR] (22:4) Spr 87, i.e. 88, p. 17.
"House." [WestCR] (22:4) Spr 87, i.e. 88, p. 21.
"Leaving the Island." [MalR] (85) D 88, p. 110.
"The Limits of Knowledge, Tilton School, New Hampshire." [WestCR] (22:4) Spr 87, i.e. 88, p. 22-23.
"Snowlight on the Northwood Path." [MalR] (85) D 88, p. 108-109.
"Spring Poem." [MalR] (85) D 88, p. 104-105.
"Sympathetic Magic." [MalR] (85) D 88, p. 106.
"Working and Getting to Sleep on Time." [WestCR] (22:4) Spr 87, i.e. 88, p. 24.
540. BORST, Steve
"Jug-Bitten." [CapeR] (23:1) Spr 88, p. 24.
541. BORUCH, Marianne
"1957." [PraS] (62:1) Spr 88, p. 73-74.
"Bleeding Heart." [GrahamHR] (11) Spr 88, p. 52.

"A Corner of the Artist's Room in Paris" (after the painting by Gwen John, 1907). [AntR] (46:1) Wint 88, p. 65.
"A Deck of Cards Thrown to Wind." [Field] (38) Spr 88, p. 37.
"The Flood Plain." [KenR] (NS 10:2) Spr 88, p. 84.
"The Fox." [Field] (38) Spr 88, p. 38.
"The Hand Itself." [LitR] (31:2) Wint 88, p. 210.
"House Moving." [DenQ] (23:1) Sum 88, p. 39.
"In Starlight." [DenQ] (23:1) Sum 88, p. 38.
"A Night in Florida." [GrahamHR] (11) Spr 88, p. 54.
"Perennial Garden." [KenR] (NS 10:2) Spr 88, p. 83.
"Reasons." [PraS] (62:1) Spr 88, p. 71-73.
"Roof." [GrahamHR] (11) Spr 88, p. 53.
"The Window." [Field] (38) Spr 88, p. 36.

542. BOSCH, Daniel
"Domestic Problems of a Blind Man." [Shen] (38:4) 88, p. 85.
"Tinder." [Shen] (38:4) 88, p. 84.

BOSE, Melisa du
See DuBOSE, Melisa

543. BOSKOVSKI, Jozo T.
"Coming Come" (tr. by Cynthia Keeson). [Lips] (14) 88, p. 37.
"Jackals." [Lips] (14) 88, p. 36.
"Masks." [Lips] (14) 88, p. 38-39.

544. BOSLEY, Deborah
"No Woman Is Ever Prepared." [SpoonRQ] (12:4) Fall 87, p. 57.

545. BOSS, Laura
"After the Funeral." [Abraxas] (37) 88, p. 30.
"The Knife Sharpening Man." [Footwork] ('88) 88, p. 22.
"My Car Thinks It's Elvis Presley." [Footwork] ('88) 88, p. 20.
"My Father's Class Picture." [Talisman] (1) Fall 88, p. 85.
"Sometimes I Worry That I'm Not Writing More Poems." [Footwork] ('88) 88, p. 21.
"Trying to Write a Love Poem." [Footwork] ('88) 88, p. 22.

546. BOSTON, B. H.
"Processional." [Ploughs] (14:4) 88, p. 120.
"When the Train Comes" (for Cecil Allouise Knott, my grandmother). [Ploughs] (14:4) 88, p. 121-122.

547. BOSTROM, Annette
"October Dawn on Lake Lashaway." [Bogg] (59) 88, p. 16.

548. BOSWELL, Robin Mary
"Winter Ballet." [MassR] (29:2) Sum 88, p. 273-276.

549. BOTTOMS, David
"Barriers" (For Kelly). [Poetry] (152:3) Je 88, p. 151.
"In the Kitchen, Late." [Poetry] (152:3) Je 88, p. 150.

550. BOUCHER, Alan
"Primal Symbol" (tr. of Olafur Johann Sigurdsson). [Vis] (27) 88, p. 6.
"Words Fell" (tr. of Steinn Steinarr). [Vis] (28) 88, p. 28.

551. BOUCHERON, Robert
"Ode 1,5: To Pyrrha" (tr. of Horace). [NewEngR] (10:3) Spr 88, p. 351.
"Poem 22: On Suffenus" (tr. of Catullus). [NewEngR] (10:3) Spr 88, p. 352.

BOUCHET, André du
See Du BOUCHET, André

552. BOURGEOIS, Bruce
"New, and Improved." [Amelia] (4:4, #11) 88, p. 84.

553. BOURNE, Daniel
"Age" (tr. of Bronislaw Maj). [Paint] (15:30) Aut 88, p. 35.
"The Air We Share Between Us" (Wspólne powietrze, Selections, tr. of Bronislaw Maj). [BelPoJ] (38:4) Sum 88, p. 22-27.
"Another Language" (tr. of Bronislaw Maj). [Paint] (15:30) Aut 88, p. 34.
"Atmosphere." [ClockR] (4:2) 88, p. 62.
"Bottom Fish." [AmerPoR] (17:6) N-D 88, p. 49.
"Children and Soldiers" (tr. of Tomasz Jastrun). [Vis] (28) 88, p. 25.
"Chile" (tr. of Bronislaw Maj). [CentralP] (13) Spr 88, p. 63-70.
"Dry Lightning." [RiverS] (27) 88, p. 5.
"Exodus" (tr. of Tomasz Jastrun). [WillowS] (21) Wint 88, p. 65.
"The Fall" (tr. of Tomasz Jastrun). [Abraxas] (37) 88, p. 21.
"Father and Son" (tr. of Tomasz Jastrun). [WillowS] (21) Wint 88, p. 67.
"The Fertile Cancer." [AnotherCM] (18) 88, p. 56-58.

"Fog" (tr. of Tomasz Jastrun). [PoetL] (83:3) Fall 88, p. 24.
"From a Letter of Bertolt Brecht to His Son" (tr. of Krzysztof Karasek). [LitR] (31:2) Wint 88, p. 143.
"Him" (tr. of Tomasz Jastrun). [Abraxas] (37) 88, p. 21.
"I Haven't Forgotten a Thing" (tr. of Bronislaw Maj). [Spirit] (9:1) 88, p. 75.
"Leaving the House" (tr. of Tomasz Jastrun). [RiverS] (25) 88, p. 68.
"Little Fears, Big Fears" (tr. of Krzysztof Karasek). [LitR] (31:2) Wint 88, p. 145.
"Orpheus in the Diner" (tr. of Krzysztof Karasek). [LitR] (31:2) Wint 88, p. 144-145.
"Our Black Madonna of Czestochowa" (tr. of Tomasz Jastrun). [WillowS] (21) Wint 88, p. 66.
"Picturing the Disaster." [RiverS] (27) 88, p. 4.
"Preparing for Bed" (tr. of Tomasz Jastrun). [QW] (27) Sum-Fall 88, p. 100.
"Pulp Fiction" (tr. of Tomasz Jastrun). [Vis] (28) 88, p. 25.
"Refraction." [CharR] (14:2) Fall 88, p. 96.
"A School in No One's Name" (tr. of Tomasz Jastrun). [QW] (27) Sum-Fall 88, p. 101.
"Seven Scenes from the Life of Men" (tr. of Krystyna Lars). [LitR] (31:2) Wint 88, p. 146-153.
"Shipwreck" (tr. of Tomasz Jastrun). [Abraxas] (37) 88, p. 20.
"Sleigh Ride" (tr. of Tomasz Jastrun). [QW] (27) Sum-Fall 88, p. 102.
"The Top and Bottom of Every Board in Existence." [CharR] (14:2) Fall 88, p. 95.
"What Is It Like in Paradise?" (tr. of Ryszard Holzer). [LitR] (31:2) Wint 88, p. 154.
"The Year 1864" (tr. of Tomasz Jastrun). [RiverS] (25) 88, p. 68.

554. BOURNE, Lesley-Anne
"Signs." [Event] (17:3) Fall 88, p. 37.

555. BOUVARD, Marguerite
"Blessings." [LitR] (31:2) Wint 88, p. 166.
"The Fresco at the Duomo." [LitR] (31:2) Wint 88, p. 165.
"Portrait." [LitR] (31:2) Wint 88, p. 164.
"White Out." [WestB] (21/22) 88, p. 93.

556. BOVETT, David
"Mom broke her back (as incredible as it seemed." [PacificR] (6) Spr 88, p. 54.

557. BOWEN, Euros
"Reredos" (in Welsh). [NewEngR] (10:4) Sum 88, p. 476.
"Reredos" (tr. by the author). [NewEngR] (10:4) Sum 88, p. 477.

BOWERS, Cathy Smith
See SMITH-BOWERS, Cathy

558. BOWERS, Edgar
"The Devereux Slough." [RedBass] (13) 88, p. 36-37.
"Elegy: Walking the Line." [SouthernR] (24:3) Sum 88, p. 557-560.
"For Louis Pasteur." [Thrpny] (34) Sum 88, p. 5.
"A Meditation on 'The Devereux Slough'." [RedBass] (13) 88, p. 37-38.
"On Robert Wells' Moving from Tours to Blois." [RedBass] (13) 88, p. 33-34.
"Thomas." [RedBass] (13) 88, p. 35.

559. BOWERS, Neal
"Black Walnuts." [NoAmR] (273:2) Je 88, p. 19.
"Door to Door Salvation." [TarRP] (27:2) Spr 88, p. 37.
"Eden Revisited." [SewanR] (96:1) Wint 88, p. f 36.
"Flower Talk." [Iowa] (18:2) 88, p. 55.
"Insomnia." [Hudson] (41:3) Aut 88, p. 494.
"Kitchen Secrets." [Hudson] (41:3) Aut 88, p. 495.
"Late Innings" (for Marianne Moore). [HeliconN] (19) 88, p. 45.
"Losing Paris." [Hudson] (41:3) Aut 88, p. 496.
"Methods of Attachment." [SewanR] (96:1) Wint 88, p. 35-36.
"Night Vision." [SewanR] (96:4) Fall 88, p. 548-549.
"On a Sidewalk." [SewanR] (96:1) Wint 88, p. 35.
"Ovations." [MichQR] (27:3) Sum 88, p. 461.
"Produce." [TarRP] (27:2) Spr 88, p. 36.
"Readings." [AmerS] (57:1) Wint 88, p. 129.
"Shapes and Shadows." [Hudson] (41:3) Aut 88, p. 493.
"Stump Speech." [Poetry] (152:4) Jl 88, p. 219.
"The Suitor." [AntR] (46:1) Wint 88, p. 84.
"The Y-Chromosome." [NewL] (54:3) Spr 88, p. 87.

560. BOWIE, Robert
"Four Letter Word." [Ascent] (14:2) 88, p. 11-12.

561. BOWMAN, Catherine
"The Bed." [ParisR] (30:109) Wint 88, p. 131-132.
"The Foot People." [RiverS] (25) 88, p. 65-66.
"Jackie in Cambodia." [RiverS] (25) 88, p. 64.
"Twins of a Gazelle Which Feed Among the Lilies." [ParisR] (30:109) Wint 88, p. 129-130.
562. BOWMAN, P. C.
"1957." [LitR] (31:4) Sum 88, p. 416.
"The Convalescence." [LitR] (31:4) Sum 88, p. 416.
"The First Stage of Grief." [KanQ] (20:3) Sum 88, p. 229.
"The Porch." [KanQ] (20:3) Sum 88, p. 228-229.
"Prolegomena to Any Future Ethics." [LitR] (31:4) Sum 88, p. 417.
"Six Short Meditations on Dissecting Earthworms." [LitR] (31:2) Wint 88, p. 206-207.
563. BOWMAN, R. L.
"Advance Scouts." [RagMag] (6:2) Fall 88, p. 9.
564. BOYCHUK, Bohdan
"Almost a Lullaby" (tr. by Mark Rudman). [Pequod] (25) 88, p. 113.
565. BOYD, Greg
"Bonjour." [Lactuca] (10) Je 88, p. 23.
"The Lip Worm." [CreamCR] (12:1) Wint 88, p. 80.
566. BOYD, Megan
"Evening, Young Woman Sewing." [ManhatPR] (10) Ja 88, p. 44-45.
"Grandmother Fox, Fowler, Colorado." [ManhatPR] (10) Ja 88, p. 45-46.
"The Power Quickens in the Smallest Center." [ManhatPR] (10) Ja 88, p. 46.
567. BOYD, Robert
"Holding on in a Howling Wind." [RiverS] (27) 88, p. 3.
"Snapshots from My Family Album #3: Uncle Herman, the Rake." [RiverS] (27) 88, p. 1.
"Snapshots from My Family Album #6: My Father Fishing." [RiverS] (27) 88, p. 2.
568. BOYLE, Kay
"For Marianne Moore's Birthday, November 15, 1967." [HeliconN] (19) 88, p. 29.
569. BOZANIC, Nick
"Woodchuck." [HawaiiR] (12:1, #23) Spr 88, p. 6-7.
570. BRACHO, Coral
"On the Facets: The Flashing" (tr. by Thomas Hoeksema). [Sulfur] (8:1, #22) Spr 88, p. 5-8.
"Water" (tr. by Thomas Hoeksema and Romelia Enríquez). [MidAR] (8:2) 88, p. 81-82.
571. BRACKENRIDGE, Valery
"The Gallop." [Footwork] ('88) 88, p. 74.
"Grandmother." [Footwork] ('88) 88, p. 74-75.
"His Side." [Footwork] ('88) 88, p. 74.
"So Many Times." [Footwork] ('88) 88, p. 74.
"Time Past." [Footwork] ('88) 88, p. 74.
572. BRADLEY, George
"The Blue Cage." [GrandS] (8:1) Aut 88, p. 91.
"Chaos, the Theory." [GrandS] (8:1) Aut 88, p. 92.
"Deformation Professionnelle." [GrandS] (8:1) Aut 88, p. 93.
"Keat's Handkerchief." [NewRep] (198:24) 13 Je 88, p. 31.
"Lives of the Chinese Poets." [SouthwR] (73:3) Sum 88, p. 343.
"Loihi" (for T. N. Danforth). [Verse] (5:2) Jl 88, p. 50.
"Of the Knowledge of Good and Evil." [NewYorker] (64:1) 22 F 88, p. 40.
"The Panic at Gonesse." [SouthwR] (73:3) Sum 88, p. 344-346.
573. BRADLEY, Jerry
"The Astrologer Consults His Chart." [SouthernHR] (22:4) Fall 88, p. 387.
"Cursing the Photos." [HighP] (3:2) Fall 88, p. 82.
"Winter Flight." [SouthernHR] (22:4) Fall 88, p. 321.
574. BRADLEY, Robert
"Milk Ghosts." [SenR] (18:1) 88, p. 56-58.
"Necessity." [SouthernPR] (28:2) Fall 88, p. 59.
575. BRADUNAS, Jurgis
"At the Inn by the Road to Vilnius" (tr. of Kazys Bradunas). [Vis] (26) 88, p. 29.
"On the Nemunas River" (tr. of Kazys Bradunas). [Vis] (26) 88, p. 30.
576. BRADUNAS, Kazys
"At the Inn by the Road to Vilnius" (tr. by Jurgis Bradunas). [Vis] (26) 88, p. 29.
"On the Nemunas River" (tr. by Jurgis Bradunas). [Vis] (26) 88, p. 30.

577. BRADY, Philip
"Baptizing David." [Footwork] ('88) 88, p. 43.
"Hunger's Painting." [Abraxas] (37) 88, p. 48-51.
578. BRAHMABHATT, Aniruddha
"Would One Believe?" (tr. by Digish Mehta). [Nimrod] (31:2) Spr-Sum 88, p. 71.
579. BRAND, Alice G.
"While Trees Bend into Fields." [Paint] (15:29) Spr 88, p. 9.
580. BRANDENBURG, John H.
"The Language of Yawns" (For L.H.B., the author's mother who has Alzheimer's Syndrome). [Phoenix] (9:1/2) 88, p. 42.
581. BRANNEN, Jonathan
"Miscarriage." [SoCaR] (20:2) Spr 88, p. 41.
582. BRASCH, Charles
"Daily Wages" (tr. of Amrita Pritam). [Nimrod] (31:2) Spr-Sum 88, p. 96.
583. BRASFIELD, James
"The Autumn Sea." [ColEng] (50:5) S 88, p. 518.
"The Granite Steps." [ColEng] (50:5) S 88, p. 519.
"If Someone Could Write" (tr. of Arturo Fontaine, w. the author). [WebR] (13:2) Fall 88, p. 30.
"Lecturer." [ColEng] (50:5) S 88, p. 519.
"Mediacy." [ColEng] (50:5) S 88, p. 517.
"The Noblemen" (tr. of Arturo Fontaine, w. the author). [WebR] (13:2) Fall 88, p. 30.
584. BRASON, Maris
"Cleaning." [AmerPoR] (17:3) My-Je 88, p. 37.
"On the Steps." [AmerPoR] (17:3) My-Je 88, p. 37.
"Rooms." [AmerPoR] (17:3) My-Je 88, p. 36.
"That Church on Hudson Street." [AmerPoR] (17:3) My-Je 88, p. 36.
585. BRATHWAITE, Edward Kamau
"Clips" (for Frank Collymore, 1893-1980). [Callaloo] (11:1, #34) Wint 88, p. 52-73.
586. BRAULT, Jacques
"Rue Saint-Denis" (tr. by F. R. Scott). [Trans] (20) Spr 88, p. 173-174.
587. BRAUNLICH, Phyllis
"Tulsa Autumn, Fog-Rise." [Phoenix] (9:1/2) 88, p. 48.
588. BRAVERMAN, Kate
"Vodka." [Jacaranda] (3:2) Fall-Wint 88, p. 74-75.
589. BRAVO, Dolores
"Exile Boulevard" (tr. of Juan Felipe Herrera, w. Sesshu Foster). [Rohwedder] (3) Spr 88, p. 1-3.
"Poetic Report: On Servants: Toward a Model for Urban Hispaniks, USA" (tr. of Juan Felipe Herrera, w. Sesshu Foster). [Rohwedder] (3) Spr 88, p. 30-31.
590. BREBNER, Diana
"Radiant Life Forms." [Event] (17:3) Fall 88, p. 71.
"That Covenant, Terrible and Binding." [Event] (17:3) Fall 88, p. 70.
591. BRECHT, Stefan
"The Plant." [Confr] (37/38) Spr-Sum 88, p. 194.
592. BREEDEN, David
"Buying Crickets." [Turnstile] (1:1) Wint 88, p. 22.
"Calf-Killing." [Turnstile] (1:1) Wint 88, p. 21.
"Docking the Lamb." [LaurelR] (22:2) Sum 88, p. 46.
"O, Cafe." [SpiritSH] (54) Fall-Wint 88, p. 27-28.
593. BREEN, Nancy
"Green." [CinPR] (17) Spr 88, p. 19.
"Morgan Tours Greater Cincinnati." [CinPR] (17) Spr 88, p. 18.
"Old-Tyme Photos — $4 Each." [Amelia] (5:2, #13) 88, p. 42.
"One Mother's Story." [Amelia] (5:2, #13) 88, p. 43.
594. BREGA, Jorge
"Flight" (tr. by Thorpe Running). [ColR] (NS 15:1) Spr-Sum 88, p. 76-77.
595. BREINIG, Jeane
"Mood Music." [BellArk] (4:4) Jl-Ag 88, p. 7.
596. BREMSER, Ray
"Mumbling Burroughs Blues / Rice-Burroughs" (riffs for unbelieving coolies). [AlphaBS] (3) Je 88, p. 49-53.
597. BRENNAN, Karen
"Irresistibly, the Heart Opens." [BlackWR] (14:2) Spr 88, p. 33.
"Tucson Oranges." [Sequoia] (32:1) Spr-Sum 88, p. 26.

"The World, You Think, Wants to Be More Graceful." [Sequoia] (32:1) Spr-Sum 88, p. 27.

598. BRENNAN, Matthew
"In the Midnight Darkness." [PoetL] (83:3) Fall 88, p. 38.

599. BRESLIN, Paul
"In a Rowboat, Once, By Night." [Agni] (27) 88, p. 37-38.

600. BRETON, Mara
"Phylum: Arthropoda." [Iowa] (18:3) 88, p. 59.
"Yetzer Hara." [Iowa] (18:3) 88, p. 60.

601. BRETT, Doris
"For My Mother." [PraS] (62:4) Wint 88-89, p. 119-120.

602. BRETT, Peter
"Edge." [Lactuca] (10) Je 88, p. 31-32.
"The Ghost of God." [Lactuca] (9) F 88, p. 28.
"Road Kills." [Lactuca] (10) Je 88, p. 32.
"Snake Dance." [Lactuca] (9) F 88, p. 27.
"Town of Woodacre, Ca." [Lactuca] (9) F 88, p. 27-28.
"Visiting Grandmother." [Lactuca] (10) Je 88, p. 33.

603. BREWER, Kenneth W.
"Belly of the Mouse." [KanQ] (20:3) Sum 88, p. 233-234.
"Burning the House." [WeberS] (5:2) Fall 88, p. 16-17.
"Flood." [WeberS] (5:2) Fall 88, p. 14-16.
"Paranoia, Maybe." [WeberS] (5:2) Fall 88, p. 18-19.
"Writers and Falling Bodies." [KanQ] (20:3) Sum 88, p. 233.

604. BREWTON, Catherine
"Abbottwitch Court." [Confr] (37/38) Spr-Sum 88, p. 265.
"The Constant Heart." [HampSPR] Wint 88, p. 34.
"A Game of Relativity." [Poetry] (143, i.e. 153:1) O 88, p. 22-23.
"Muse." [NoDaQ] (56:3) Sum 88, p. 71-72.
"Natural Selection." [SouthernPR] (28:2) Fall 88, p. 25.
"Waiting for the Storm to Pass." [HampSPR] Wint 88, p. 35.
"White Tigers." [SouthernPR] (28:1) Spr 88, p. 31.
"Woman Dancing Without Music." [HampSPR] Wint 88, p. 33-34.

605. BRICCETTI, Lee Ellen
"Aria." [NegC] (8:3) 88, p. 111-112.
"Second Baptism." [HangL] (53) 88, p. 7.

606. BRIDGFORD, Kim
"For Sylvia Plath." [CentR] (32:3) Sum 88, p. 266.
"The Habit of Longing." [BallSUF] (29:4) Aut 88, p. 14.

607. BRIEFS, E. Castendyk
"Fat Mama at Swensen's." [LightY] ('88/9) 88, p. 220-221.

608. BRIEGER, Randy
"Communion" (for Angela Ball). [HawaiiR] (12:2, #24) Fall 88, p. 123.

609. BRINSON-CURIEL, Barbara
"Accident." [HangL] (52) 88, p. 58.
"Garfield Pool, 1965." [HangL] (52) 88, p. 57.

610. BROADHURST, Nicole
"Letter to My Brother." [PoetL] (83:3) Fall 88, p. 13-14.
"Letter to My Grandfather, While Waiting for the Train." [PoetL] (83:3) Fall 88, p. 17-18.
"To My Father, Sparing Him." [PoetL] (83:3) Fall 88, p. 15-16.

611. BROCK, James
"Girl at the Hotel Exile." [Jacaranda] (3:1) Wint 88, p. 3.

612. BROCK, Van K.
"Ossabaw Tabby." [AmerV] (11) Sum 88, p. 52-60.

613. BROCK-BROIDO, Lucie
"And So Long, I've Had You Fame." [Agni] (27) 88, p. 14-15.
"Elective Mutes." [Harp] (276:1656) My 88, p. 38-39.
"Evolution." [SouthwR] (73:1) Wint 88, p. 96-97.
"The Future as a Cow." [Harp] (277:1663) D 88, p. 39.
"I Wish You Love." [Agni] (27) 88, p. 11-13.
"Jessica, From the Well." [VirQR] (64:3) Sum 88, p. 443-448.
"Kid Flash." [Agni] (27) 88, p. 16-17.
"Playing Havoc." [GrahamHR] (11) Spr 88, p. 60.
"Trouble Child." [GrahamHR] (11) Spr 88, p. 59.
"What You Want." [GrahamHR] (11) Spr 88, p. 57-58.

614. BROCKWELL, Stephen
"Pullets." [Event] (17:1) Spr 88, p. 30-35.
615. BRODINE, Karen
"Driving Home." [CrabCR] (5:1) Wint 88, p. 3.
"No Words or Names." [CrabCR] (5:1) Wint 88, p. 4-5.
"Survivors." [CrabCR] (5:1) Wint 88, p. 5-6.
"Two Pages of the Book." [CrabCR] (5:1) Wint 88, p. 3-4.
616. BRODKEY, Harold
"Susan's Field." [NewYorker] (64:40) 21 N 88, p. 52.
617. BRODSKY, Joseph
"Allenby Road." [NewYRB] (35:2) 18 F 88, p. 16.
"Centaurs I-V" (5 poems). [WestHR] (42:4) Wint 88, p. 267-271.
"Exeter Revisited." [NewYRB] (35:14) 20 S 88, p. 14.
"North Baltic" (tr. by the author). [NewYRB] (35:2) 18 F 88, p. 16.
"Seven Strophes" (tr. by Paul Graves). [WestHR] (42:1) Spr 88, p. 18.
618. BRODSKY, Louis Daniel
"Cracow, Now!" (For Darlene Mathis-Eddy). [BallSUF] (29:4) Aut 88, p. 1-2.
"Crossword Learning" (For Troika's Third-Grade Class at Glenridge School). [BallSUF] (29:4) Aut 88, p. 65.
"Emigré in the Promised Land." [BallSUF] (29:4) Aut 88, p. 3-4.
"Surviving Another Fall." [BallSUF] (29:4) Aut 88, p. 5.
619. BRODY, Harry
"Root Canal." [Lactuca] (11) O 88, p. 29.
620. BRODY, Michal
"Transit Waltz." [SinW] (33) Fall 87, p. 112.
BROIDO, Lucie Brock
See BROCK-BROIDO, Lucie
621. BROMLEY, Anne (Anne C.)
"Aubade for Coconino County." [TampaR] (1) 88, p. 20.
"Bone Messages." [DenQ] (23:1) Sum 88, p. 40-41.
"The Breakfast Club's Next to Last Meeting." [NoDaQ] (56:1) Wint 88, p. 95.
"The Fast." [LaurelR] (22:2) Sum 88, p. 68-69.
"Midnight Fugue." [CimR] (84) Jl 88, p. 78.
"Night of the Blue Moon." [CimR] (84) Jl 88, p. 79.
622. BROOKER, Gregory J.
"Failure in Trolling." [Jacaranda] (3:1) Wint 88, p. 34.
623. BROOKLYN, Igor
"May 11th 1988." [AlphaBS] (4) D 88, p. 42.
624. BROOKS, Connie
"No Equity in Love." [Bogg] (59) 88, p. 36.
625. BROOKS, Paula
"Arousing the Poem." [SinW] (33) Fall 87, p. 41.
626. BROSMAN, Catharine Savage
"Chaco Canyon: The Fire." [Interim] (7:2) Fall 88, p. 15.
"Crossing to Evian." [SouthernR] (24:4) Aut 88, p. 944.
"Destin: Swimming on Easter Day." [SouthernR] (24:4) Aut 88, p. 945-946.
"Driving to Vézelay." [Interim] (7:2) Fall 88, p. 16.
"Peaches." [SewanR] (96:1) Wint 88, p. 37-38.
"Vézelay." [SewanR] (96:1) Wint 88, p. 38-39.
627. BROSNAN, Michael
"About Men." [Footwork] ('88) 88, p. 18.
628. BROUGHTON, T. Alan
"African Violets" (for Lyn Camire Tisdale). [Confr] (37/38) Spr-Sum 88, p. 63.
"Amish Market." [TexasR] (9:3/4) Fall-Wint 88, p. 20.
"Barbera D'Asti." [TarRP] (27:2) Spr 88, p. 19.
"A Curse for Dictators." [Confr] (37/38) Spr-Sum 88, p. 64.
"Palatine." [TarRP] (27:2) Spr 88, p. 20.
629. BROUMAS, Olga
"Anoint the Ariston" (16 selections, tr. of Odysseas Elytis). [AmerPoR] (17:1) Ja-F 88, p. 13-15.
"Etymology." [TexasR] (9:3/4) Fall-Wint 88, p. 21.
"The Massacre." [AmerV] (12) Fall 88, p. 50-53.
"With Light and Death" (Selections: 9, 15-21, tr. of Odysseas Elytis). [Agni] (27) 88, p. 176-183.
630. BROWN, Alan
"The Closed Room" (tr. of Anne Hebert). [Trans] (20) Spr 88, p. 129-130.

"A Small Dead Girl" (tr. of Anne Hebert). [Trans] (20) Spr 88, p. 131.

631. BROWN, Betsy
"Dignity in the Home." [AmerPoR] (17:5) S-O 88, p. 8.
"Endo." [ColEng] (50:6) O 88, p. 638.
"It Never Comes Out of Nowhere." [AmerPoR] (17:5) S-O 88, p. 8.
"Music." [DenQ] (22:4) Spr 88, p. 36.
"No Deliberate Tributary." [SenR] (18:1) 88, p. 34.
"Other Math." [ColEng] (50:6) O 88, p. 639.

632. BROWN, Bill
"Awake with the Frogs." [PassN] (9:1) Wint 88, p. 28.
"Her Silence." [DeKalbLAJ] (21:2) Spr 88, p. 33.
"Home for the Holidays." [PassN] (9:1) Wint 88, p. 28.
"Migration." [Poem] (59) My 88, p. 67.
"Pact" (1988 Poetry Competition, First Prize). [PassN] (9:2) Sum 88, p. 16.
"Sonnet for an Appalachian Werewolf." [Poem] (59) My 88, p. 68.

633. BROWN, D. F.
"Eyeball Television." [ColR] (NS 15:1) Spr-Sum 88, p. 16.
"More." [ColR] (NS 15:1) Spr-Sum 88, p. 30-31.
"The Nam." [ColR] (NS 15:1) Spr-Sum 88, p. 32.
"Sonic." [ColR] (NS 15:1) Spr-Sum 88, p. 29.
"Sonnet: You're in this someplace else you dream." [ColR] (NS 15:1) Spr-Sum 88, p. 28.

634. BROWN, Harriet
"Fall" (for Vivian Langan). [PraS] (62:3) Fall 88, p. 54.
"Misguided." [PraS] (62:3) Fall 88, p. 53.

635. BROWN, Harry
"Paint Lick Pastoral." [Poem] (60) N 88, p. 28.
"The Straight and Their Reward." [Wind] (18:62) 88, p. 7.
"What I Heard in Maaco's Body Shop, Half of Which I Believe, or, Bless Blake and Black." [Poem] (60) N 88, p. 27.

636. BROWN, Robert
"Chaos." [PoetryNW] (29:4) Wint 88-89, p. 4-5.
"The Chess Players." [PoetryNW] (29:4) Wint 88-89, p. 3-4.
"The Dream at Half Moon Bay." [CreamCR] (12:2) Sum 88, p. 163-164.
"The Geometry of Justice." [PoetryNW] (29:4) Wint 88-89, p. 6.
"Salamanca: Siesta." [CreamCR] (12:2) Sum 88, p. 165-166.
"Shadows on the Brain." [KanQ] (20:3) Sum 88, p. 136.
"Stockmen's Bar." [KanQ] (20:4) Fall 88, p. 62.
"Without Pleasure." [KanQ] (20:3) Sum 88, p. 136-137.

637. BROWN, Simon
"Sydney, 1942." [Bogg] (59) 88, p. 9.

638. BROWN, Stephanie
"Parts of the Eye." [AmerPoR] (17:1) Ja-F 88, p. 15.
"The Slow Hours." [Jacaranda] (3:2) Fall-Wint 88, p. 31.

639. BROWN, Steven Ford
"A Fall Day, Texas" (tr. of Angel Gonzalez, w. Pedro Gutierrez Revuelta). [LitR] (31:2) Wint 88, p. 220.
"Order (Poetics That Others Follow)" (tr. of Angel Gonzalez, w. Pedro Gutierrez Revuelta). [Paint] (15:30) Aut 88, p. 37.
"Poetics That I Sometimes Try to Follow" (tr. of Angel Gonzalez, w. Pedro Gutierrez Revuelta). [Paint] (15:30) Aut 88, p. 36.
"To Poetry" (tr. of Angel Gonzalez, w. Pedro Gutierrez Revuelta). [Gargoyle] (35) 88, p. 9.

640. BROWN, Susan M.
"Autopsychography" (tr. of Fernando Pessoa, w. Edwin Honig). [ConnPR] (7:1) 88, p. 44.
"I Never Kept Sheep" (From "The Keeper of Sheep": I, tr. of Fernando Pessoa, w. Edwin Honig). [ConnPR] (7:1) 88, p. 41.
"Now Ashen Gray Tinges the Balding Brow" (tr. of Fernando Pessoa, w. Edwin Honig). [ConnPR] (7:1) 88, p. 42.
"Oblique Rain" (Excerpt, II, tr. of Fernando Pessoa, w. Edwin Honig). [ConnPR] (7:1) 88, p. 44.
"Salutation to Walt Whitman" (tr. of Fernando Pessoa, w. Edwin Honig). [ConnPR] (7:1) 88, p. 43.
"Written in a Book Abandoned on the Trip" (Excerpt, tr. of Fernando Pessoa, w. Edwin Honig). [ConnPR] (7:1) 88, p. 43.

"You men who raised stone pillars . . ." (from "Maritime Ode," tr. of Fernando Pessoa, w. Edwin Honig). [ConnPR] (7:1) 88, p. 42.

641. BROWN, Sylvia
"Eric." [Confr] (37/38) Spr-Sum 88, p. 222.

642. BROWN, Thomas J.
"Siblings." [InterPR] (14:1) Spr 88, p. 96.
"Silverflier." [InterPR] (14:1) Spr 88, p. 94-96.
"Temptation." [InterPR] (14:1) Spr 88, p. 96.

643. BROWN, Victor H.
"Mother." [Pembroke] (20) 88, p. 215.

644. BROWNE, Michael Dennis
"Heaven." [LightY] ('88/9) 88, p. 206.
"Paycheck." [LightY] ('88/9) 88, p. 44.

645. BROWNELL, Mary Legato
"On Wondering about Teaching Well." [EngJ] (77:1) Ja 88, p. 102.

646. BROWNING, Barbara
"When I Gave You the Unpleasant Gift." [LitR] (31:2) Wint 88, p. 214.

647. BROWNING, Preston
"It Was a Scattered Squadron (September, 1978)" (tr. of Daisy Zamora, w. Lang Gomez). [AnotherCM] (18) 88, p. 195.
"Love Until Now" (tr. of Rosario Murillo, w. Lang Gomez). [AnotherCM] (18) 88, p. 138.

648. BROX, Jane
"Supper Time." [Hudson] (41:3) Aut 88, p. 498.
"Understanding the Time." [Hudson] (41:3) Aut 88, p. 497.

649. BROYLES, Nancy
"Prophecy." [Amelia] (5:2, #13) 88, p. 134.
"Search" (sense of porpoise). [Amelia] (5:2, #13) 88, p. 134.

650. BRUCE, Debra
"An Argument About a Tree." [Poetry] (152:3) Je 88, p. 138.
"My Father Refuses to Read the Obituaries." [VirQR] (64:1) Wint 88, p. 76-78.
"Young Wife Waiting for the Results of Her Husband's Biopsy." [VirQR] (64:1) Wint 88, p. 78-79.

651. BRUCE, Lennart
"Indications Are." [Caliban] (5) 88, p. 64.
"Reaching for My Loved Ones." [Caliban] (5) 88, p. 65.

652. BRUCHAC, Joseph
"Heathens." [Lips] (14) 88, p. 29.
"Inupiaq — the Whalers." [Abraxas] (37) 88, p. 22-24.

653. BRUCK, Julie
"Connection." [DenQ] (22:3) Wint 88, p. 91-92.

654. BRUGALETTA, John
"Dead Friends Bury Dead Friends." [CharR] (14:2) Fall 88, p. 99.

655. BRUNK, Juanita
"All Sweet Things, Like Forgiveness, Are a Falling." [PoetL] (83:3) Fall 88, p. 41.
"Can." [PoetL] (83:3) Fall 88, p. 39.
"My Father's Tongue." [PoetL] (83:3) Fall 88, p. 40.

BRUNT, H. L. van
See Van BRUNT, Lloyd

BRUNT, Lloyd van
See Van BRUNT, Lloyd

656. BRUSH, Thomas
"Artificial Heart." [PoetryNW] (29:1) Spr 88, p. 40.

657. BRUTUS, Dennis
"Beginning to Think." [Vis] (26) 88, p. 9.
"For the Prisoners in South Africa." [PaintedB] (32/33) 88, p. 99.
"For the Prisoners in South Africa." [RiverS] (26) 88, p. 69.
"Wilkinsburg." [Vis] (26) 88, p. 9.

658. BRYAN, Sharon
"Kid Gloves." [GeoR] (42:4) Wint 88, p. 838-839.

659. BUCHANAN, Carl
"Faust Keeps Talking." [KanQ] (20:1/2) Wint-Spr 88, p. 96.
"In the Castle." [KanQ] (20:1/2) Wint-Spr 88, p. 96.
"The Quiet Town." [KanQ] (20:1/2) Wint-Spr 88, p. 97.
"Three Jack the Ripper Poems." [KanQ] (20:3) Sum 88, p. 110-111.

660. BUCK, Paula Closson
"To the Sea in Hard Shoes" (Chapbook: 8 Poems, for J. H. B.). [OhioR] (40) 88, p. 65-80.
661. BUCKHOLTS, Claudia
"In a Time of Abundance." [MidwQ] (29:2) Wint 88, p. 224.
"In the Garden." [ConnPR] (7:1) 88, p. 33.
"Two Travelers." [KanQ] (20:3) Sum 88, p. 80-81.
662. BUCKLEY, Christopher
"Another Place and Time." [Ploughs] (14:4) 88, p. 77-78.
"Beauty in the World" (Washington Court House, 1954). [GettyR] (1:4) Aut 88, p. 509-510.
"Blackbirds in a Parking Lot, Southern California." [Ploughs] (14:4) 88, p. 79-80.
"Dead Cottonwood Tree, Abiquiu, New Mexico, 1943." [QW] (26) Wint 88, p. 99.
"Giotto's 'St. Franics Preaching to the Birds'." [Nat] (246:19) 14 My 88, p. 688.
"Homage to Canaletto." [MissouriR] (11:1) 88, p. 152.
"Last Night at Akrotiri." [Poetry] (151:4) Ja 88, p. 351-352.
"The Lost Catechism of the Clouds" (Santa Barbara, 1957). [Crazy] (35) Wint 88, p. 41-42.
"Photograph of Myself by Modigliani's Grave, Père Lachaise 1984." [DenQ] (23:1) Sum 88, p. 42-44.
"Ranchos Church No. 1." [QW] (26) Wint 88, p. 100.
"Red Hills and the Sun, Lake George." [QW] (26) Wint 88, p. 101.
"Speculation in Dark Air." [GettyR] (1:4) Aut 88, p. 611-613.
663. BUCKLEY, Joy
"Paper Guards & Ultra Violet." [AlphaBS] (4) D 88, p. 23.
664. BUCKNER, Sally
"Burial." [Pembroke] (20) 88, p. 190-191.
"Clouds." [Pembroke] (20) 88, p. 191.
"Joseph." [Pembroke] (20) 88, p. 192.
"Mahalia Jackson Gets Ready to Go on Stage." [Pembroke] (20) 88, p. 193.
"Night Watchman." [Pembroke] (20) 88, p. 193-194.
665. BUDY, Andrea Hollander
"Bachelor." [Farm] (5:2) Fall 88, p. 38.
"Broom." [Farm] (4:1, i.e. 5:1) Wint 88, p. 67.
"On the Death of James Wright." [CharR] (14:1) Spr 88, p. 10.
"Song of Sixpence." [Farm] (4:1, i.e. 5:1) Wint 88, p. 66.
666. BUELL, T. C.
"Hwai-Yuen 1910." [Amelia] (5:1, #12) 88, p. 49.
667. BUGEJA, Michael J.
"Asylum, at Least on Paper." [CapeR] (23:1) Spr 88, p. 31.
"For All I Knew." [DenQ] (22:3) Wint 88, p. 33-34.
"Hove" (for Leon Daniel). [Nimrod] (32:1) Fall-Wint 88, p. 22-25.
"Liebe und Literatur." [CharR] (14:1) Spr 88, p. 21.
"Patient." [CapeR] (23:1) Spr 88, p. 32.
"The Resurrection of Small Pox." [DenQ] (22:3) Wint 88, p. 32-33.
"South." [PoetL] (83:3) Fall 88, p. 25.
"The Visionary." [HolCrit] (25:5) D 88, p. 18.
668. BUHROW, Bonnie
"The Act of Eating a Whole Black Radish." [Abraxas] (37) 88, p. 41.
"Evelyn Nesbit in Minnesota." [CapeR] (23:2) Fall 88, p. 49.
669. BUKOWSKI, Charles
"40 Years Ago in That Hotel Room." [WormR] (28:2/3, #110/111) 88, p. 44-46.
"1988." [Jacaranda] (3:2) Fall-Wint 88, p. 79-80.
"Beauti - ful & Other Long Poems" (A Wormwood Chapbook: 19 poems). [WormR] (28:2/3, #110/111) 88, p. 41-88.
"Beauti-ful." [WormR] (28:2/3, #110/111) 88, p. 86-88.
"Bright Boy." [WormR] (28:2/3, #110/111) 88, p. 51-55.
"Duck and Forget It." [AlphaBS] (3) Je 88, p. 78-79.
"The End of an Era." [WormR] (28:2/3, #110/111) 88, p. 71-74.
"Fingernails." [WormR] (28:2/3, #110/111) 88, p. 57.
"Fooling Marie." [WormR] (28:2/3, #110/111) 88, p. 59-61.
"Gertrude Up the Stairway." [SlipS] (8) 88, p. 8-9.
"Good Morning, How Are You?" [WormR] (28:4, #112) 88, p. 129.
"Hemingway's Shadow." [WormR] (28:2/3, #110/111) 88, p. 61-63.
"I Been Working on the Railroad." [WormR] (28:2/3, #110/111) 88, p. 47-51.
"In a Room." [AlphaBS] (4) D 88, p. 24-25.

"It's All So Clearly Simple." [WormR] (28:2/3, #110/111) 88, p. 55-56.
"Joe." [Gargoyle] (35) 88, p. 88-91.
"Letter to a Friend with a Domestic Problem." [WormR] (28:2/3, #110/111) 88, p. 41-43.
"Macho Man." [WormR] (28:2/3, #110/111) 88, p. 70-71.
"The Main Course." [WormR] (28:2/3, #110/111) 88, p. 74-76.
"The Movie Actors." [Jacaranda] (3:2) Fall-Wint 88, p. 77-79.
"No Gain, No Loss." [AlphaBS] (4) D 88, p. 26.
"No Man Is an Island, Especially Around Hollywood Park." [WormR] (28:2/3, #110/111) 88, p. 79-80.
"Non-Walking Papers." [AlphaBS] (3) Je 88, p. 76.
"One Out." [WormR] (28:2/3, #110/111) 88, p. 58-59.
"Put Out the Candles." [Jacaranda] (3:2) Fall-Wint 88, p. 76-77.
"Red Mercedes." [WormR] (28:2/3, #110/111) 88, p. 69-70.
"A Sad Poem." [WormR] (28:4, #112) 88, p. 128-129.
"Save the Trees." [WormR] (28:1, #109) 88, p. 39.
"Swivel." [WormR] (28:2/3, #110/111) 88, p. 63-66.
"Talking to a Part of My Mailbox." [WormR] (28:1, #109) 88, p. 38-39.
"The Tax Consultant." [WormR] (28:2/3, #110/111) 88, p. 80-86.
"Transformation and Disfiguration at the P.O." [WormR] (28:2/3, #110/111) 88, p. 66-69.
"Wandering in the Cage." [PaintedB] (36) 88, p. 79-83.
"White!" [AlphaBS] (3) Je 88, p. 77.
"The Yellow Pencil." [WormR] (28:2/3, #110/111) 88, p. 76-78.

670. BULLOCK, Michael
"In a Summer Garden." [CrossC] (10:2) 88, p. 8.

671. BULLOCK, Teresa
"How Gentle Women Commit Mayhem at the Monthly Poetry Coterie." [CrabCR] (5:3) Fall 88, p. 26.
"Offspring." [CrabCR] (5:3) Fall 88, p. 26.

672. BUMGARDNER, Karin
"I'll Say I Knew Her Then." [BellArk] (4:2) Mr-Ap 88, p. 1.
"Water Emotion." [BellArk] (4:2) Mr-Ap 88, p. 7.

673. BUNGE, Patricia
"Clerihew." [LightY] ('88/9) 88, p. 75.

674. BURCH, Brian
"Still Life / Allison." [Dandel] (15:2) Fall-Wint 88, p. 25.

675. BURCH, F. F.
"X-Rated." [LightY] ('88/9) 88, p. 135.

676. BURCH, Shelley
"Regeneration." [BallSUF] (29:4) Aut 88, p. 63.

677. BURCH, Wendy Jeanne
"A Passenger." [RiverS] (27) 88, p. 72.
"Pod." [RiverS] (27) 88, p. 73.

678. BURD, Jennifer J.
"Therapy." [BellR] (11:1) Spr 88, p. 38-39.

679. BURDEN, Jean
"Between Seasons." [GeoR] (42:3) Fall 88, p. 534.

680. BURDIGE, Lisa
"Evening Song." [Lactuca] (9) F 88, p. 15.
"Promises." [Lactuca] (9) F 88, p. 15.
"Understanding Chekov." [Lactuca] (9) F 88, p. 16.

681. BURK, Ronnie
"Decalcomania." [Caliban] (5) 88, p. 69.
"The Getaway" (poem to a junkie). [Americas] (16:3/4) Fall-Wint 88, p. 44.
"Hazards of the Day (NYC)." [Americas] (16:3/4) Fall-Wint 88, p. 43.
"Letter to Miguel Piñero." [Americas] (16:3/4) Fall-Wint 88, p. 39-41.
"Millie." [Caliban] (5) 88, p. 67.
"NYC Collage." [Americas] (16:3/4) Fall-Wint 88, p. 42.
"NYC Collage." [Caliban] (5) 88, p. 68.
"Poem: To be delicate yet contain light as an orchid amid dream." [Caliban] (4) 88, p. 114.

682. BURKARD, Michael
"Child at Anchor." [WillowS] (21) Wint 88, p. 9.
"Elizabeth." [Sonora] (16) Fall 88, p. 59-62.
"Hotel Tropicana." [Epoch] (37:1) 88, p. 12.

"My Brother the Reader." [WestHR] (42:3) Aut 88, p. 216.
"The Night Is a Sea." [WillowS] (21) Wint 88, p. 10.
"On a Train Approaching Midnight" (after a line by Louis Simpson). [QW] (26) Wint 88, p. 110.
"Red Leaf." [NoAmR] (273:3) S 88, p. 43.
"Shortage of Memory." [SouthernPR] (28:2) Fall 88, p. 37.
"To Rose." [WillowS] (21) Wint 88, p. 7-8.
"Total Strangers." [WestHR] (42:3) Aut 88, p. 217-218.
"The Weight of Escape." [Epoch] (37:1) 88, p. 10-11.
"Zane Grey." [QW] (26) Wint 88, p. 111.

683. BURKE, Brian
"Let's Face the Music & Dance: *Follow the Fleet* Starring Fred Astaire & Ginger Rogers." [Quarry] (37:4) Aut 88, p. 44-46.
"She Reads You a Poem About Rape." [CanLit] (118) Aut 88, p. 82.

684. BURKE, C.
"Did You Ever Hear the Like." [Grain] (16:4) Wint 88, p. 52.
"What Is the Difference Between Man and Woman." [Grain] (16:4) Wint 88, p. 52.

685. BURKE, Daniel
"Christmas Cards." [FourQ] (2d series 2:2) Fall 88, p. 23.

686. BURKE, Marianne
"Starlings" (for my brother). [SouthernPR] (28:2) Fall 88, p. 67.

687. BURKETT, Thomas D.
"Rehearsal." [SoDakR] (26:2) Sum 88, p. 133.

688. BURNETT, Gary
"Glacial." [Sink] (3) 88, p. 33-34.
"In Voice." [Sink] (3) 88, p. 32.

689. BURNHAM, Deborah
"Again." [Prima] (11/12) 88, p. 15.
"Provide." [WestB] (21/22) 88, p. 107.
"The Stolen Child." [WestB] (21/22) 88, p. 107.

690. BURNHAM, Gregory
"Subtotals." [Turnstile] (1:1) Wint 88, p. 68-69.

691. BURNINGHAM, Bradd
"Nights with My Father." [PottPort] (9) 88, p. 4.
"Winter in Saskatoon." [PottPort] (9) 88, p. 4.

692. BURNS, Gerald
"The Myth of Accidence, Book VII." [Sulfur] (7:3, #21) Wint 88, p. 114-117.
"Socrates Dying in Widener." [Temblor] (7) 88, p. 44-49.

693. BURNS, Michael
"Bedtime Stories." [MidwQ] (29:2) Wint 88, p. 217.
"A Drunken Satyr from Newton County Tells How He Met Daphne and Nearly Lost a Good Tree Nymph." [LightY] ('88/9) 88, p. 126.
"October." [MidwQ] (29:2) Wint 88, p. 216.
"Trying to Know." [Poetry] (143, i.e. 153:2) N 88, p. 69-70.
"The Widow on Route Three." [Poetry] (143, i.e. 153:2) N 88, p. 69.

694. BURNS, Ralph
"Influence." [Field] (39) Fall 88, p. 48-51.
"Lullaby." [Poetry] (143, i.e. 153:2) N 88, p. 105.

695. BURNS, William
"Alcoholic: The Morning Beckon." [Interim] (7:2) Fall 88, p. 39.
"All Out." [TexasR] (9:1/2) Spr-Sum 88, p. 67.
"A View From the Top" (San Jose Del Cabo, Mexico, 1986). [Interim] (7:2) Fall 88, p. 40.
"Wasted." [Interim] (7:2) Fall 88, p. 38.

696. BURNSIDE, John
"At Blackheath." [Verse] (5:3) N 88, p. 12.
"Cow Parsley." [Verse] (5:3) N 88, p. 11.
"Metaphysics." [Verse] (5:3) N 88, p. 11.
"Sea Slug." [Verse] (5:3) N 88, p. 10.

697. BURR, Gray
"Prisms" (for Ellen, 20 poems). [Sparrow] (55) 88, 24 p.
"The Selkies." [Vis] (28) 88, p. 46.

698. BURRIS, Sidney
"The Epiphany of Ponce de Leon." [CharR] (14:1) Spr 88, p. 88.
"The Fiddle in the Corner." [VirQR] (64:1) Wint 88, p. 79-80.
"The Queen and Her Court." [CharR] (14:1) Spr 88, p. 86-87.

699. BURROWS, E. G.
"Endangered Species." [Ascent] (14:2) 88, p. 43.
"Half and Half." [Plain] (9:1) Fall 88, p. 38.
"In Marysville Meadow." [BlackWR] (14:2) Spr 88, p. 16-17.
"The Language About to Be Lost." [HawaiiR] (12:1, #23) Spr 88, p. 52.
"Moles." [Plain] (8:3) Spr-Sum 88, p. 19.
"The River Birch." [Ascent] (14:2) 88, p. 44.
"Road Kill." [GettyR] (1:3) Sum 88, p. 438-439.
"Running to Hedges." [HawaiiR] (12:1, #23) Spr 88, p. 53.
"Scripture" (A Plainsongs Award Poem). [Plain] (8:2) Wint 88, p. 20.
"Sunday Falls." [Ascent] (14:2) 88, p. 45.
"Where Cows Grazed." [SwampR] (1:2/3) D 88, p. 67.
700. BURSK, Christopher
"What Do You Need?" [WilliamMR] (26:1) Spr 88, p. 90-91.
"You Are Going to Die." [Crazy] (34) Spr 88, p. 24-26.
701. BURT, Kathryn
"In a Country We Didn't Know." [CinPR] (17) Spr 88, p. 78.
"Infecundity." [OhioR] (41) 88, p. 96.
"Winter Betrothal." [AntR] (46:3) Sum 88, p. 363.
702. BUSAILAH, Reja-e
"Baby with the Bathwater." [DeKalbLAJ] (21:3/4) 88, p. 49.
703. BUSH, Duncan
"Old Master." [NewEngR] (10:4) Sum 88, p. 419-420.
704. BUSH, George F.
"Forbid a Stillborn Earth." [TexasR] (9:3/4) Fall-Wint 88, p. 22.
705. BUSHKOWSKY, Aaron
"Motherly Advice." [Quarry] (37:1) Wint 88, p. 23.
"Muse." [Quarry] (37:1) Wint 88, p. 22.
706. BUTCHER, Grace
"Amelia." [HiramPoR] (44/45) Spr-Wint 88, p. 53.
"Chernobyl." [MidwQ] (29:4) Sum 88, p. 451.
"The Crazy Old Woman Who Lives Alone." [MidwQ] (29:4) Sum 88, p. 449-450.
"Flight #117." [PassN] (9:1) Wint 88, p. 21.
"In the Waiting Room at the Mental Health Clinic." [Vis] (28) 88, p. 44.
"Mound Cemetery" (Marietta, Ohio). [HiramPoR] (44/45) Spr-Wint 88, p. 54.
"The Watcher." [LitR] (31:2) Wint 88, p. 231.
707. BUTLER, Erika M.
"Ways to Pray." [PassN] (9:2) Sum 88, p. 24.
708. BUTLER, Jack
"The Key to Nothing." [Poetry] (152:2) My 88, p. 66-67.
"The Lord Is Down in the Greek Theatre Again." [Poetry] (151:6) Mr 88, p. 468.
"Opening Movement." [NewOR] (15:2) Sum 88, p. 62.
"Practice." [Poetry] (152:2) My 88, p. 67.
709. BUTLER, Lynne
"Estate Sale" (for C.E.B. 1907-1986). [PraS] (62:2) Sum 88, p. 118-119.
"Forever Is Easy." [CentR] (32:1) Wint 88, p. 41.
"Visiting Hours." [CimR] (82) Ja 88, p. 61.
"When the Electrician Comes to Change the Wiring." [PraS] (62:2) Sum 88, p. 117-118.
710. BUTLER, Michele J.
"Shady Lane Farm / Grampa Schumacher." [PacificR] (6) Spr 88, p. 26.
"Shady Lane Farm / Pictures for a Catholic Child." [PacificR] (6) Spr 88, p. 27.
"Suzie Makes the *L.A. Times*." [PacificR] (6) Spr 88, p. 28.
711. BUTSON, Barry
"When I Was No Longer Blind." [Dandel] (15:2) Fall-Wint 88, p. 17.
712. BUTTRESS, Derrick
"The Warning" (from Bogg 30, 1975). [Bogg] (59) 88, p. 41.
713. BUTZ, Sharon
"For Etheridge Knight." [PaintedB] (32/33) 88, p. 87.
714. BYLES, Joan Montgomery
"Babuska." [Wind] (18:63) 88, p. 4.
"Old Man and Blue Heron" (For my Father). [Blueline] (9:1/2) 88, p. 4.
"Winter Solstice." [Wind] (18:63) 88, p. 4-5.
715. BYRNE, Kevin O.
"Exit Interview." [PoetC] (20:1) Fall 88, p. 28-29.

716. BYRNE, Ted
"Centripetal Song." [WestCR] (23:1) Spr, i.e. Sum 88, p. 13.
CABRAL de MELO NETO, João
See NETO, João Cabral de Melo
717. CADER, Teresa
"Ice Fishing." [Ploughs] (14:1) 88, p. 146-147.
"The Odalisques of Matisse." [Ploughs] (14:1) 88, p. 144-145.
718. CADNUM, Michael
"Burning Ivy." [LitR] (31:2) Wint 88, p. 178.
"Buying Lottery Tickets." [PikeF] (9) Fall 88, p. 28.
"Camille on Her Death Bed" (Musée D'Orsay, Paris). [GeoR] (42:4) Wint 88, p. 809-810.
"Climbing a Tree." [CentR] (32:1) Wint 88, p. 39.
"The Eighteenth-Century Room" (Palace of the Legion of Honor, San Francisco). [LitR] (31:2) Wint 88, p. 179.
"Ghost." [Comm] (115:4) 26 F 88, p. 114.
"Growing Up." [Poem] (59) My 88, p. 55.
"It's Wonderful Here at Little Riding." [AntR] (46:3) Sum 88, p. 349.
"Oaxaca." [Poem] (59) My 88, p. 56.
"Parallel Texts." [Poem] (59) My 88, p. 54.
"Queen Inez of Alcobaca." [PoetryNW] (29:4) Wint 88-89, p. 25.
"Try to Find the Thirty-three Things Wrong with This Picture" (from a restaurant placemat). [NoDaQ] (56:3) Sum 88, p. 146-147.
"When Death Was a Little Boy." [PoetryNW] (29:1) Spr 88, p. 39.
"Winter, Knight's Valley." [StoneC] (16:1/2) Fall-Wint 88-89, p. 53.
719. CADOU, René Guy
"Le Chant de Solitude." [HayF] (3) Spr 88, p. 84, 86.
"Song of Solitude" (tr. by Dorothy Neil Cohen). [HayF] (3) Spr 88, p. 85, 87.
CAEIRO, Alberto
See PESSOA, Fernando
720. CAFAGNA, Marcus
"After the Divorce." [Abraxas] (37) 88, p. 9.
721. CAI, Qi-jiao
"Distance" (tr. by Edward Morin and Dennis Ding). [TriQ] (71) Wint 88, p. 130.
"The Pearl" (in Chinese and English, tr. by Edward Morin and Dennis Ding). [HawaiiR] (12:1, #23) Spr 88, p. 90-91.
"Poetry" (tr. by Edward Morin and Dai Fang). [TriQ] (72) Spr-Sum 88, p. 171.
722. CAICEDO, Rosario
"Letter from a Friend." [SinW] (36) Wint 88-89, p. 25-26.
"Near Plymouth Rock." [Spirit] (9:1) 88, p. 68.
723. CAIN, Kathleen
"A Charm." [HighP] (3:1) Spr 88, p. 50.
"Postcards from Ireland." [HighP] (3:1) Spr 88, p. 51-53.
724. CAINE, Shulamith Wechter
"World and Local News." [AmerPoR] (17:4) Jl-Ag 88, p. 47.
725. CAIRNES, Thomas J.
"The Connection." [TarRP] (27:2) Spr 88, p. 4.
726. CAIRNS, Barbara
"Greenscapes" (for M.M.). [WestB] (21/22) 88, p. 158-159.
727. CAIRNS, Scott
"Chore." [CharR] (14:2) Fall 88, p. 92.
"Imperial Theology" (for Jerry Falwell). [CharR] (14:2) Fall 88, p. 92-93.
"Leaving Florinopolis." [Shen] (38:4) 88, p. 65-66.
728. CAIRNS, Thomas J.
"Bless Me Father — a Tenth Confession." [Wind] (18:63) 88, p. 6.
CAIRUAN, Ben Jaraf of
See BEN JARAF OF CAIRUAN
729. CALBERT, Cathleen
"Cajun Wings and Loaded Skins." [Shen] (38:2) 88, p. 16-17.
"Dad" (from "Lessons in Space"). [Nimrod] (32:1) Fall-Wint 88, p. 54-55.
"Garden Grove" (from "Lessons in Space"). [Nimrod] (32:1) Fall-Wint 88, p. 52-53.
"Lessons in Space" (from "Lessons in Space"). [Nimrod] (32:1) Fall-Wint 88, p. 61.
"Lessons in Space" (Selections. Pablo Neruda Prize for Poetry, Second Prize). [Nimrod] (32:1) Fall-Wint 88, p. 52-61.
"The Limits of Mercy." [PoetryNW] (29:2) Sum 88, p. 39-40.

"Losing His Mother" (from "Lessons in Space"). [Nimrod] (32:1) Fall-Wint 88, p. 58-60.
"Mysterious Weather" (from "Lessons in Space"). [Nimrod] (32:1) Fall-Wint 88, p. 56-58.
"On Mowing." [TarRP] (27:2) Spr 88, p. 35.
"A Train Is Going to Germany." [PoetryNW] (29:2) Sum 88, p. 40-41.
"When Forever Began" (from "Lessons in Space"). [Nimrod] (32:1) Fall-Wint 88, p. 53.

730. CALDNUM, Michael
"Yes, They Have a Room." [SouthernPR] (28:2) Fall 88, p. 56.

731. CALERO, Carlos
"During Holy Week there's a strong sun" (tr. by Nancy Esposito). [AmerPoR] (17:2) Mr-Ap 88, p. 29.
"In the Masaya Lagoon" (tr. by Nancy Esposito). [AmerPoR] (17:2) Mr-Ap 88, p. 29.

732. CALINESCU, M.
"Apprenticeship" (tr. of Dorin Tudoran, w. Willis Barnstone). [Vis] (26) 88, p. 41.

733. CALLAGHAN, Barry
"Stone Blind Love" (Selections: 8 poems). [OntR] (29) Fall-Wint 88-89, p. 39-46.

734. CALLAHAN, Jeff
"Like Thunder." [DenQ] (22:3) Wint 88, p. 86-88.

735. CALLAHAN, Stephen Daniel
"Elements" (Selections: XXIV, XXI, XI). [Bogg] (60) 88, p. 54.

736. CALMAN, Mercedes U.
"The Prophet Goes Swimming." [Plain] (9:1) Fall 88, p. 16-17.

737. CALTELVECCHI, Gladys
"Oracion por Elimelec." [Mairena] (10:25) 88, p. 128.

738. CALVERT, Winter O.
"Waiting." [Wind] (18:63) 88, p. 33.

739. CAMAJ, Martin
"Atje Ku S'na Njeh Kush." [InterPR] (14:1) Spr 88, p. 30.
"Drekë Malsore." [InterPR] (14:1) Spr 88, p. 26.
"The Evening Is Distant" (tr. by Leonard Fox). [InterPR] (14:1) Spr 88, p. 35.
"Gjarpni e Fëmija." [InterPR] (14:1) Spr 88, p. 24.
"The Jacket" (tr. by Leonard Fox). [InterPR] (14:1) Spr 88, p. 37.
"Mbramja Asht Larg." [InterPR] (14:1) Spr 88, p. 34.
"Mimosas" (tr. by Leonard Fox). [InterPR] (14:1) Spr 88, p. 39.
"Mimozat." [InterPR] (14:1) Spr 88, p. 38.
"Mountain Wake" (tr. by Leonard Fox). [InterPR] (14:1) Spr 88, p. 27.
"Rain on the River" (tr. by Leonard Fox). [InterPR] (14:1) Spr 88, p. 33.
"Shiu Mbi Lum." [InterPR] (14:1) Spr 88, p. 32.
"Sibaris." [InterPR] (14:1) Spr 88, p. 28.
"Snake and Child" (tr. by Leonard Fox). [InterPR] (14:1) Spr 88, p. 25.
"Sybaris" (tr. by Leonard Fox). [InterPR] (14:1) Spr 88, p. 29.
"Where No One Knows Us" (tr. by Leonard Fox). [InterPR] (14:1) Spr 88, p. 31.
"Xhaketa." [InterPR] (14:1) Spr 88, p. 36.

740. CAMERON, Juan
"Bolero" (tr. by Cola Franzen). [Vis] (26) 88, p. 49.
"Bridge" (tr. by Cola Franzen). [Vis] (26) 88, p. 49.
"Perro de Circo" (Selections: 4 poems, tr. by Cola Franzen). [Bound] (15:3/16:1) Spr-Fall 88, p. 41-44.

741. CAMERON, Mary
"A Lotus Fog." [Grain] (16:3) Fall 88, inside back cover.
"Vision." [Grain] (16:3) Fall 88, inside front cover.

742. CAMILLO, Victor
"After Reading James Wright." [Farm] (5:2) Fall 88, p. 47.
"K-Mart." [Vis] (28) 88, p. 10.

743. CAMP, James
"Claritas" (A skip-rope song). [LightY] ('88/9) 88, p. 89-90.
"The Fruits of Retirement" (With a nod to X. J. Kennedy). [LightY] ('88/9) 88, p. 154.
"Transformers." [Paint] (15:29) Spr 88, p. 13.

744. CAMPANA, Dino
"To a Whore with Iron-Gray Eyes" (tr. by Michael L. Johnson). [QW] (26) Wint 88, p. 112.

745. CAMPBELL, Anne
"I Wait for the Day." [Dandel] (15:2) Fall-Wint 88, p. 28.

"Today Is Love." [Dandel] (15:2) Fall-Wint 88, p. 29.
746. CAMPBELL, B. D.
"This Page." [Grain] (16:4) Wint 88, p. 46.
747. CAMPBELL, Carolyn E.
"Daughter I Never Had." [Plain] (8:3) Spr-Sum 88, p. 6.
748. CAMPBELL, Mary (Mary B.)
"Drugs." [ParisR] (30:107) Sum 88, p. 222.
"Fear of Travel." [PartR] (55:2) Spr 88, p. 282-283.
"The Loneliness of Men Bathing." [ParisR] (30:107) Sum 88, p. 223.
749. CAMPBELL, Mary Belle
"Later, She Remembers" (from "My Mother's Days, a Longpoem"). [StoneC] (16:1/2) Fall-Wint 88-89, p. 57.
750. CAMPBELL, Nicholas
"The Artist." [Pembroke] (20) 88, p. 195.
"A Prayer It Will Snow Before Morning." [Pembroke] (20) 88, p. 195.
751. CAMPION, Dan
"An Ode by Benjamin Franklin, Recently Discovered." [Timbuktu] (2) Sum-Fall 88, p. 59-60.
"Partners." [Timbuktu] (2) Sum-Fall 88, p. 58.
CAMPOS, Alvaro de
See PESSOA, Fernando
752. CAMRUD, Madelyn
"June Morning." [NoDaQ] (56:4) Fall 88, p. 46.
753. CANIZARO, Vincent, Jr.
"Cold Moon." [BallSUF] (29:4) Aut 88, p. 15.
"Silent Pearl." [BallSUF] (29:4) Aut 88, p. 66.
754. CANNON, Maureen
"Gift in October." [Amelia] (5:1, #12) 88, p. 52.
755. CANNON, Melissa
"Ikeedo" (Second Runner Up, 1987 Narrative Poetry Contest). [PoetL] (83:1) Spr 88, p. 19-23.
756. CANTWELL, Kevin
"Border States" (for Ralph Wilson). [MemphisSR] (8:2) Spr 88, p. 24-26.
"The Fossilized Dog." [KanQ] (20:1/2) Wint-Spr 88, p. 110-111.
"In the Third Month" (for B.). [MemphisSR] (8:2) Spr 88, p. 17-18.
757. CANTWELL, Sandra
"Some Nights Are for the Squid." [PottPort] (9) 88, p. 21.
758. CAO, Tan
"Bougainvillea" (tr. by James Banerian). [Vis] (26) 88, p. 17.
"Letter from Home" (tr. by James Banerian). [Vis] (26) 88, p. 16-17.
759. CAPUTO, Geri
"In a Foster Home, U.S.A." [Footwork] ('88) 88, p. 81.
"No More Birthdays for You, Nana" (to Katie, my grandmother through marriage: 1898-1987). [Footwork] ('88) 88, p. 80-81.
CARBEAU, Mitchell les
See LesCARBEAU, Mitchell
760. CARDEA, Caryatis
"Class" (to white feminists of class privilege). [SinW] (35) Sum-Fall 88, p. 27-28.
761. CARDENAS, Alejandra
"Hubo una Vez Algien Llamado Alicia." [Inti] (28) Otoño 88, p. 157-158.
"Manifestación de Acratas." [Inti] (28) Otoño 88, p. 155.
"Medusa Espera a Príncipe Azul." [Inti] (28) Otoño 88, p. 155-156.
"Una Pareja hace el Amor bajo el Agua." [Inti] (28) Otoño 88, p. 156-157.
762. CARDILLO, Joe
"Passion." [Lactuca] (10) Je 88, p. 20.
763. CARDOZO, Nancy
"Crazy April." [Confr] (37/38) Spr-Sum 88, p. 95.
764. CAREY, Barbara
"Against the Clock." [MalR] (85) D 88, p. 50-51.
"Arms." [WestCR] (22:3) Wint 87, p. 12-13.
"As Cells Are." [WestCR] (22:3) Wint 87, p. 5-6.
"Making a Wish." [WestCR] (22:3) Wint 87, p. 7-8.
"Psychology Today." [WestCR] (22:3) Wint 87, p. 9.
"Wishbone." [MalR] (85) D 88, p. 49.
"Without Incident." [WestCR] (22:3) Wint 87, p. 10-11.
"Wobble." [Dandel] (15:2) Fall-Wint 88, p. 14.

765. CAREY, Michael (Michael A.)
"Absolute Zero" (for Jim Richmond). [StoneC] (15:3/4) Spr-Sum 88, p. 54-55.
"Appreciated." [DeKalbLAJ] (21:1) Wint 88, p. 46-47.
"Bright Lives: Queens 1957." [JlNJPo] (10:1/2) 88, p. 10.
"The Distant Hills" (for Chuck Offenburger). [PoetC] (19:3) Spr 88, p. 21.
"Honest Effort." [PoetC] (19:3) Spr 88, p. 20.
"The Mad Steer" (for Helen Beadle, a Plainsongs Award Poem). [Plain] (8:3) Spr-Sum 88, p. 4.
"The Milky Way." [LaurelR] (22:2) Sum 88, p. 33.
"What the Earth Gives." [LaurelR] (22:2) Sum 88, p. 32.
"Witness." [PoetC] (19:3) Spr 88, p. 22-23.
766. CAREY, Steve
"The Dancer." [Talisman] (1) Fall 88, p. 84.
767. CARLILE, Henry
"November 4, 1985: A Sequence." [Crazy] (35) Wint 88, p. 15-19.
"Winter Raven, Summer Crow." [Crazy] (35) Wint 88, p. 7-14.
768. CARLSON, Barbara Siegel
"Sister." [KanQ] (20:1/2) Wint-Spr 88, p. 220.
769. CARLSON, R. S.
"Aversion." [HolCrit] (25:5) D 88, p. 17.
"Elements." [CapeR] (23:1) Spr 88, p. 28.
770. CARMEN, Crystall
"Riot." [PikeF] (9) Fall 88, p. 20.
771. CARNERO, Guillermo
"Brummel" (tr. by Frederick H. Fornoff). [LitR] (32:1) Fall 88, p. 63.
"Departure for Cythera" (tr. by Gina Sconza and Alexis Levitin). [WebR] (13:1) Spr 88, p. 34.
"Melancholy of Paul Scarron, Burlesque Poet" (tr. by Frederick H. Fornoff). [LitR] (32:1) Fall 88, p. 62.
772. CARNEY, Jeanne
"The Rabbit" (Honorable Mention, 15th Anniversary Competition). [StoneC] (16:1/2) Fall-Wint 88-89, unpaged front matter.
773. CARPENTER, Anne
"The American Museum of Natural History." [Ploughs] (14:1) 88, p. 82-83.
"The Owl." [Ploughs] (14:1) 88, p. 81.
774. CARPENTER, David
"Brown's Pond." [CanLit] (118) Aut 88, p. 58.
775. CARPENTER, Lucas
"The World Is Not a Text." [ChatR] (8:3) Spr 88, p. 54.
776. CARPER, Thomas
"At the Sistine Chapel: A View from the Floor." [Poetry] (152:1) Ap 88, p. 3.
"Children at Play." [TexasR] (9:3/4) Fall-Wint 88, p. 24.
"Fugue." [Poetry] (152:1) Ap 88, p. 3.
"Have I Not Played Well, Robert?" [AmerS] (57:2) Spr 88, p. 272.
"Nobody at Treblinka." [Poetry] (151:6) Mr 88, p. 493.
"On Sitting Down to Read the Dust Jacket Once Again." [Poetry] (152:1) Ap 88, p. 4-5.
"Perspective." [TexasR] (9:3/4) Fall-Wint 88, p. 23.
"The Resident Poet." [Poetry] (152:1) Ap 88, p. 4.
777. CARR, Mark
"Direct Current." [CimR] (85) O 88, p. 28.
778. CARRACINO, Nicholas
"A Child's Toy." [JlNJPo] (10:1/2) 88, p. 11.
"Just Like Me." [JlNJPo] (10:1/2) 88, p. 12.
779. CARRANZA, Eduardo
"El Insomne." [Mairena] (10:25) 88, p. 43.
780. CARRERA ANDRADE, Jorge
"Dining-Room Mirror" (tr. by Michael L. Johnson). [WebR] (13:2) Fall 88, p. 31-32.
781. CARRIER, Constance
"A Lost Village." [TexasR] (9:3/4) Fall-Wint 88, p. 25-26.
782. CARRINO, Michael
"Summer School." [PoetC] (19:3) Spr 88, p. 17.
783. CARROLL, Joyce Armstrong
"August Pickings." [EngJ] (77:6) O 88, p. 87.
784. CARROLL, Rhoda
"Briefing from the Ozone Layer." [Vis] (27) 88, p. 47.

"Small Rain." [Vis] (27) 88, p. 45.
"What We Called Love in Vermont." [Vis] (27) 88, p. 46.

785. CARRUTH, Hayden
"Absoluteness." [ParisR] (30:109) Wint 88, p. 133.
"Depression." [OhioR] (40) 88, p. 48.
"Essay on Death." [AmerPoR] (17:5) S-O 88, p. 17-19.
"Insert X." [PartR] (55:4) Fall 88, p. 617.
"Instructions." [ParisR] (30:109) Wint 88, p. 134.

786. CARSON, Jo
"Her Apples." [AmerV] (11) Sum 88, p. 79-80.

787. CARSON, Julia
"Out of Body." [Spirit] (9:1) 88, p. 41.

788. CARSON, Malcolm
"The Pauper 1830." [Stand] (29:2) Spr 88, p. 60.

789. CARSON, Meredith S.
"Negative Pegs" (The 14th Kansas Poetry Contest, prize winner). [LittleBR] (5:2) Wint 88-89, p. 63.
"The Oleander Sphinx Moth." [ManhatPR] (10) Ja 88, p. 50.
"Pre-Columbian Whistle." [ChamLR] (2:1, #3) Fall 88, p. 37.

790. CARSON, Mike
"Black Autumn." [SpoonRQ] (12:4) Fall 87, p. 7-8.
"Closer." [SpoonRQ] (12:4) Fall 87, p. 9-10.
"Prophet." [SpoonRQ] (12:4) Fall 87, p. 5.
"Return." [SpoonRQ] (12:4) Fall 87, p. 6.

791. CARSON, Ricks
"A Prayer to the Fates." [KanQ] (20:1/2) Wint-Spr 88, p. 140.
"The Refusal of Self-Denial." [KanQ] (20:1/2) Wint-Spr 88, p. 139.
"To the Miami Pillowcase Rapist." [KanQ] (20:1/2) Wint-Spr 88, p. 138.

792. CARTER, Brad
"Big Brother." [PikeF] (9) Fall 88, p. 20.

793. CARTER, David H.
"Letter from the Queen City." [CinPR] (18) Fall 88, p. 19.

794. CARTER, Ian
"Sleetstorm." [PottPort] (9) 88, p. 41.

795. CARTER, Jared
"Errata Slip." [LightY] ('88/9) 88, p. 196.
"Moiré." [Ascent] (14:1) 88, p. 11-14.
"Soul Sleeping." [Poetry] (153:3) D 88, p. 157-158.
"Sunnyland Slim Remembers the Muse" (a found poem — for Etheridge Knight). [PaintedB] (32/33) 88, p. 137.

796. CARTIER, Marie
"The Naturopath" (for Jody Shevins, N.D.). [SinW] (36) Wint 88-89, p. 118.

797. CARUSO, Gina Maria
"I Move Away from You." [Turnstile] (1:2) 88, p. 22.

798. CARVER, Raymond
"Gravy." [NewYorker] (64:28) 29 Ag 88, p. 28.
"Margo." [Poetry] (151:5) F 88, p. 416.
"The Moon, the Train." [Zyzzyva] (4:4) Wint 88, p. 63-64.

799. CASAL, Lourdes
"La Habana 1968." [Areíto] (1:4) D 88, inside front cover.
"Mi Barrio — Version No. 2." [Areíto] (1:4) D 88, inside back cover.

800. CASARJIAN, Bethany
"In Time." [NewRena] (7:2, #22) Spr 88, p. 93.
"Simply Rolling." [NewRena] (7:2, #22) Spr 88, p. 94.

801. CASCORBI, H. F.
"Clerihew." [LightY] ('88/9) 88, p. 74.

802. CASE, David
"Autobiography." [Jacaranda] (3:2) Fall-Wint 88, p. 34-35.

803. CASERIO, Dave
"How Close the Child to the Skin." [Footwork] ('88) 88, p. 43.
"I Want to Talk About the Place." [Footwork] ('88) 88, p. 42-43.

804. CASEY, Deb
"Sisters." [GrahamHR] (11) Spr 88, p. 13.

805. CASEY, Michael
"Iliad." [LightY] ('88/9) 88, p. 200.

806. CASEY, Robbie
"Julio." [Writer] (101:3) Mr 88, p. 18.
807. CASPERS, Nona
"Litany, Amy of." [NegC] (8:3) 88, p. 189-190.
808. CASSELMAN, Barry
"Somersault Collar." [AnotherCM] (18) 88, p. 61.
"Undernoise Rise Zeppelins." [AnotherCM] (18) 88, p. 59-60.
"You Wrote This." [KanQ] (20:1/2) Wint-Spr 88, p. 114.
809. CASSIAN, Nina
"The Escape" (tr. by Naomi Lazard). [AmerPoR] (17:2) Mr-Ap 88, p. 48.
"Farce" (tr. by Christopher Hewitt). [NewYorker] (64:27) 22 Ag 88, p. 60.
"Temptation" (tr. by Andrea Deletant and Brenda Walker). [AmerPoR] (17:2) Mr-Ap 88, p. 48.
"The Widow" (tr. by Christopher Hewitt). [NewYorker] (63:46) 4 Ja 88, p. 26.
810. CASSIDY, Christine
"In Flight." [BelPoJ] (38:3) Spr 88, p. 14-17.
811. CASSIDY, John
"Kafka's Funeral." [Stand] (29:2) Spr 88, p. 61.
812. CASSIN, Maxine
"Eating Animal Crackers in the Dark." [NewOR] (15:1) Spr 88, p. 10.
813. CASSITY, Turner
"How Jazz Came up the Elbe." [YaleR] (77:4) Sum 88, p. 607-608.
"The Last Tauber-Lied" (Budapest). [Poetry] (152:1) Ap 88, p. 18.
"Other-Directed." [Poetry] (152:1) Ap 88, p. 20.
"Persistence of Memory." [Poetry] (152:1) Ap 88, p. 19.
"Preservation News." [YaleR] (77:4) Sum 88, p. 608-609.
"The Virus Treks." [Shen] (38:3) 88, p. 96-103.
CASTELAR, Jose Adan
See ADAN CASTELAR, Jose
814. CASTILLO, Inés del
"Asilado de la Calle." [Os] (27) 88, p. 32.
815. CASTLE, Gregory
"Coming Down." [Jacaranda] (3:2) Fall-Wint 88, p. 28-29.
816. CASTLE, Sandie
"Warning" (Inspired by Nina Rota). [Gargoyle] (35) 88, p. 231.
817. CASTLEMAN, D. (David)
"The Rainbow Is a Symbol of the Resurrection." [ArtfulD] (14/15) Fall 88, p. 90.
"The Rainbow Is a Symbol of the Resurrection." [Pembroke] (20) 88, p. 105.
818. CASTRO, Michael
"Closing Down the Bars" (For George Barlow). [TampaR] (1) 88, p. 91.
"For Katherine Dunham." [Vis] (27) 88, p. 8, 10.
CASTRO, Tania Diaz
See DIAZ CASTRO, Tania
819. CASTRO, Tomas
"Fundidos." [Mairena] (10:25) 88, p. 107.
820. CASTRO JO, Carlos
"North American Woman" (tr. by Nancy Esposito). [AmerPoR] (17:2) Mr-Ap 88, p. 27.
821. CASWELL, Donald
"The Business of His Life." [Wind] (18:63) 88, p. 3.
"Carswell Reads in St. Petersburg." [ChatR] (8:2) Wint 88, p. 4.
"The Edge." [DeKalbLAJ] (21:1) Wint 88, p. 49-50.
822. CATHERS, Ken
"Edward Curtis." [WestCR] (22:3) Wint 87, p. 45-50.
823. CATINA, Ray
"Rungs." [CapeR] (23:1) Spr 88, p. 18.
"Standing Guard." [CapeR] (23:1) Spr 88, p. 17.
824. CATLIN, Alan
"Breaking the Code, London." [Bogg] (59) 88, p. 8.
"The Good Old Days: Pounding a Beat." [WormR] (28:1, #109) 88, p. 32.
"Mahler in the House That Ruth Built." [WindO] (50) Aut 88, p. 32.
"The Michael Jackson Special." [Lactuca] (9) F 88, p. 38-39.
"People Are Strange." [Lactuca] (9) F 88, p. 38.
"Salsa." [Lactuca] (9) F 88, p. 37.
"Short Fat Man with the Broken Right Wrist." [RagMag] (6:2) Fall 88, p. 13.
"Sick Time." [Interim] (7:1) Spr 88, p. 15.

"Songs of the Earth: The Bellvue Mahler." [WindO] (50) Aut 88, p. 33.
"The Streets of Boston." [WormR] (28:1, #109) 88, p. 32-33.
"Undercover Man." [RagMag] (6:2) Fall 88, p. 12.

825. CATTO, Brenda
"Ocean Out Over Ohio." [GeoR] (42:1) Spr 88, p. 130-131.

826. CATULLUS (Gaius Valerius)
"9. Veranius, the best of all my friends" (tr. by Peter Glassgold). [NoDaQ] (56:1) Wint 88, p. 20.
"11. Furius and Aurelius, companions of Catullus" (tr. by Peter Glassgold). [NoDaQ] (56:1) Wint 88, p. 20-21.
"13. My own Fabullus, you'll dine well at my place" (tr. by Peter Glassgold). [NoDaQ] (56:1) Wint 88, p. 21-22.
"15. I give into your keeping, Aurelius, myself" (tr. by Peter Glassgold). [NoDaQ] (56:1) Wint 88, p. 22.
"17. The town of Verona wants a long bridge" (tr. by Peter Glassgold). [NoDaQ] (56:1) Wint 88, p. 22-23.
"Poem 22: On Suffenus" (tr. by Robert Boucheron). [NewEngR] (10:3) Spr 88, p. 352.

827. CAULFIELD, Carlota
"Anonymous" (To Osip Mandelstam, tr. by Terry Clarke). [Vis] (26) 88, p. 50.
"Cibeles." [Lyra] (1:3) 88, p. 5.
"Echidna." [Lyra] (1:3) 88, p. 5.
"A Fall Celebration" (tr. by Terry Clarke). [Vis] (26) 88, p. 50.
"Poemas Muertos de Egipto y Sumeria." [Lyra] (1:3) 88, p. 4.

828. CAVAFY, C. P. (Constantine)
"December of 1903" (in Greek and English, tr. by Tommy Nitis). [InterPR] (14:1) Spr 88, p. 74-75.
"Melancholy of Jason Kleander, . . ." (in Greek and English, tr. by Tommy Nitis). [InterPR] (14:1) Spr 88, p. 74-75.
"Poseidonians" (in Greek and English, tr. by Tommy Nitis). [InterPR] (14:1) Spr 88, p. 72-73.

829. CAVALIERI, Grace
"Beads" (For Abigail Cutter). [Footwork] ('88) 88, p. 17.
"The First." [Footwork] ('88) 88, p. 17.

830. CAVANAGH, Clare
"29-77-02" (tr. of Artur Miedzyrzecki, w. Stanislaw Baranczak). [ManhatR] (4:2) Spr 88, p. 35.
"Among Us, the Unclean Ones" (tr. of Jan Polkowski, w. Stanislaw Baranczak). [ManhatR] (4:2) Spr 88, p. 40.
"Archaeology" (tr. of Wislawa Szymborska, w. Stanislaw Baranczak). [TriQ] (71) Wint 88, p. 147-148.
"At the Cave" (tr. of Artur Miedzyrzecki, w. Stanislaw Baranczak). [TriQ] (71) Wint 88, p. 151.
"Before Dawn" (tr. of Julia Hartwig, w. Stanislaw Baranczak). [ManhatR] (4:2) Spr 88, p. 36.
"But of Course" (tr. of Julia Hartwig, w. Stanislaw Baranczak). [TriQ] (71) Wint 88, p. 154.
"Funeral" (tr. of Wislawa Szymborska, w. Stanislaw Baranczak). [TriQ] (71) Wint 88, p. 150.
"The Golden Age" (tr. of Artur Miedzyrzecki, w. Stanislaw Baranczak). [ManhatR] (4:2) Spr 88, p. 35.
"Hitler's First Photograph" (tr. of Wislawa Szymborska, w. Stanislaw Baranczak). [TriQ] (71) Wint 88, p. 149.
"I Am Not Worthy" (tr. of Ryszard Krynicki, w. Stanislaw Baranczak). [ManhatR] (4:2) Spr 88, p. 39.
"In this slough becoming stone" (tr. of Wiktor Woroszylski, w. Stanislaw Baranczak). [ManhatR] (4:2) Spr 88, p. 38.
"In Your Eyes" (tr. of Julia Hartwig, w. Stanislaw Baranczak). [TriQ] (71) Wint 88, p. 153.
"Plotting with the Dead" (tr. of Wislawa Szymborska, w. Stanislaw Baranczak). [ManhatR] (4:2) Spr 88, p. 33-34.
"Rain outside a window, a glass of tea on the table" (tr. of Bronislaw Maj, w. Stanislaw Baranczak). [ManhatR] (4:2) Spr 88, p. 41-42.
"Roommates" (tr. of Wiktor Woroszylski, w. Stanislaw Baranczak). [TriQ] (71) Wint 88, p. 155-156.

"So What If" (tr. of Ryszard Krynicki, w. Stanislaw Baranczak). [ManhatR] (4:2) Spr 88, p. 39.
"Stage Fright" (tr. of Wislawa Szymborska, w. Stanislaw Baranczak). [ManhatR] (4:2) Spr 88, p. 31-32.
"Suddenly" (tr. of Ryszard Krynicki, w. Stanislaw Baranczak). [ManhatR] (4:2) Spr 88, p. 39.
"These are strong, calm words" (tr. of Bronislaw Maj, w. Stanislaw Baranczak). [ManhatR] (4:2) Spr 88, p. 41.
"They" (tr. of Artur Miedzyrzecki, w. Stanislaw Baranczak). [ManhatR] (4:2) Spr 88, p. 34.
"Though Mortal, I Desired You" (tr. of Jan Polkowski, w. Stanislaw Baranczak). [ManhatR] (4:2) Spr 88, p. 40-41.
"Towards the End" (tr. of Julia Hartwig, w. Stanislaw Baranczak). [ManhatR] (4:2) Spr 88, p. 36-37.
"View with a Grain of Sand" (tr. of Wislawa Szymborska, w. Stanislaw Baranczak). [ManhatR] (4:2) Spr 88, p. 32-33.
"The Wall" (tr. of Ryszard Krynicki, w. Stanislaw Baranczak). [ManhatR] (4:2) Spr 88, p. 40.
"What a Poem Is Allowed" (tr. of Wiktor Woroszylski, w. Stanislaw Baranczak). [ManhatR] (4:2) Spr 88, p. 37.
"What Does the Political Scientist Know" (tr. of Artur Miedzyrzecki, w. Stanislaw Baranczak). [TriQ] (71) Wint 88, p. 152.
"The world: whole and indivisible, begins where" (tr. of Bronislaw Maj, w. Stanislaw Baranczak). [TriQ] (71) Wint 88, p. 157.

831. CAWLEY, Kevin
"Walking." [KanQ] (20:3) Sum 88, p. 230.

832. CAY, Marilyn
"The Day We Picked the Apartment." [CrossC] (10:1) 88, p. 10.
"The Interview." [CrossC] (10:1) 88, p. 10.
"Passing Through" (A Gordon Lightfoot Song). [CrossC] (10:1) 88, p. 10.

833. CAYLE
"Breath" (for T. S. C. Fay). [Crosscur] (7:4) 88, p. 105.

834. CAZARRE DE ALVEZ, Delia
"Espantapajaros." [LetFem] (14:1/2) Primavera-Otoño 88, p. 142-143.

835. CECIL, Richard
"Life Studies." [Crazy] (35) Wint 88, p. 57-58.
"Little World." [Crazy] (35) Wint 88, p. 54-56.
"Miracles." [Chelsea] (47) 88, p. 65-67.
"Sonnet for Singles." [Crazy] (35) Wint 88, p. 59.

836. CEE, Steve
"Stepfather." [Lips] (14) 88, p. 8.

837. CELAN, Paul
"Décimale Blanche" (1 poem, German tr. of Jean Daive). [Acts] (8/9) 88, p. 54.
"Décimale Blanche" (2 poems, German tr. of Jean Daive). [Acts] (8/9) 88, p. 50-53.
"Décimale Blanche" (4 poems, German tr. of Jean Daive). [Acts] (8/9) 88, p. 32-39.
"Eis, Eden" (From *Niemandsrose*). [AntigR] (73) Spr 88, p. 20.
"Es wird etwas sein, später" (From *Zeitgehöff*). [AntigR] (73) Spr 88, p. 24.
"Gebet" (Germn translation of Antonin Artaud). [Acts] (8/9) 88, p. 165.
"Ein Grab" (tr. of Marianne Moore). [Acts] (8/9) 88, p. 120.
"Huhediblu." [Acts] (8/9) 88, p. 168, 170.
"Ice, Eden" (From *Niemandsrose*, tr. by Bernhard Frank). [AntigR] (73) Spr 88, p. 21.
"Later there will be something" (From *Zeitgehöff*, tr. by Bernhard Frank). [AntigR] (73) Spr 88, p. 25.
"Oo-oo-the Blue" (tr. by Joel Golb). [Acts] (8/9) 88, p. 169, 171.
"Prayer" (English tr. by Pierre Joris of Celan's German tr. of Antonin Artaud). [Acts] (8/9) 88, p. 165.
"Psalm." [AntigR] (73) Spr 88, p. 22.
"Psalm" (tr. by Bernhard Frank). [AntigR] (73) Spr 88, p. 23.
"Zeitgehöft" (7 poems from "Timesteaded," tr. by Cid Corman, w. Günther Nitschke). [Acts] (8/9) 88, p. 123-129.
"Zeitgehöft" (8 poems from "Timesteaded," tr. by Cid Corman, w. Günther Nitschke). [Acts] (8/9) 88, p. 218-221.

CERDA, Hernan Lavin
See LAVIN CERDA, Hernan

838. CERENIO, Virginia R.
"Family Photos: Black and White, 1960." [Calyx] (11:2/3) Fall 88, p. 77.
839. CERRUTO, Oscar
"Patria de Sal Cautiva." [Mairena] (10:25) 88, p. 76.
840. CERVO, Nathan
"Canticle." [SpiritSH] (54) Fall-Wint 88, p. 11-12.
"Logos." [SpiritSH] (54) Fall-Wint 88, p. 12.
"Root Canal." [SpiritSH] (54) Fall-Wint 88, p. 13.
"This Is My Body." [SpiritSH] (54) Fall-Wint 88, p. 14.
841. CÉSAIRE, Aimé
"Genesis for Wilfredo" (tr. by Clayton Eshleman and Annette Smith). [Caliban] (5) 88, p. 18.
"Léon G. Damas Feu Sombre Toujours" (in memoriam). [Epoch] (37:2) 88, p. 103-104.
"Leon G. Damas Somber Fire Always" (in memoriam, tr. by Clayton Eshleman and Annette Smith). [Epoch] (37:2) 88, p. 105.
"Let Us Offer Its Heart to the Sun" (tr. by Clayton Eshleman and Annette Smith). [Caliban] (5) 88, p. 19.
"Link of the Chain-Gang" (tr. by Clayton Eshleman and Annette Smith). [Epoch] (37:2) 88, p. 109.
"Macumba Word" (tr. by Clayton Eshleman and Annette Smith). [Caliban] (5) 88, p. 15.
"Maillon de la Cadène." [Epoch] (37:2) 88, p. 108.
"Mangrove Swamp" (tr. by Clayton Eshleman and Annette Smith). [Caliban] (5) 88, p. 14.
"Nights" (tr. by Clayton Eshleman and Annette Smith). [Caliban] (5) 88, p. 16.
"Ribbon" (tr. by Clayton Eshleman and Annette Smith). [Caliban] (5) 88, p. 17.
"Test." [Epoch] (37:2) 88, p. 106.
"Testing" (tr. by Clayton Eshleman and Annette Smith). [Epoch] (37:2) 88, p. 107.
842. CETRANO, Sal
"To Linda, at Creedmore." [Wind] (18:63) 88, p. 7-8.
843. CHABAS, Dan
"First Year." [EngJ] (77:5) S 88, p. 106.
844. CHADWICK, Jerah
"After the Aleut." [MidAR] (8:2) 88, p. 74-75.
"Attu, 1943: from the Diary of Dr. Nebu Tatsuguchi." [WritersF] (14) Fall 88, p. 63.
"The Seal People." [BellR] (11:2) Fall 88, p. 40.
845. CHAFFIN, Lillie D.
"Under Pressure." [Footwork] ('88) 88, p. 77.
846. CHAHIN, Plinio
"Poemas de los Tres Momentos del Olvido." [CuadP] (5:14) Enero-Abril 88, p. 57-58.
847. CHALAKEE, Helen
"In the Custody of Ezekiel." [Phoenix] (9:1/2) 88, p. 43.
848. CHALIFOUX, Kristine
"A Postcard, Reinvented." [AntR] (46:3) Sum 88, p. 342.
849. CHALLENDER, Craig
"Song fo Louie." [TarRP] (27:2) Spr 88, p. 23.
850. CHALLIS, Chris
"Fifties Girls." [AlphaBS] (3) Je 88, p. 3.
851. CHALONER, David
"Tongues of Light." [Temblor] (7) 88, p. 178.
852. CHALPIN, Lila
"Mink Coat." [TexasR] (9:3/4) Fall-Wint 88, p. 27.
853. CHAMBERS, Carole
"Ravished on a Bed of Roses, Sky by Fragonard." [YellowS] (28) D 88, p. 10.
854. CHAMLEE, Ken
"That Long Delayed But Always Expected Something That We Life For" (— The Glass Menagerie). [GreensboroR] (44) Sum 88, p. 86.
855. CHANDLER, Tom
"Buffalo in the Basement." [WestB] (21/22) 88, p. 10.
"Potato." [WestB] (21/22) 88, p. 11.
856. CHANDRA, G. S. Sharat
"Attila Is Cosming." [PoetC] (19:3) Spr 88, p. 31-33.
"Country." [MassR] (29:4) Wint 88-89, p. 597-598.
"Fable of the Talker." [PoetC] (19:3) Spr 88, p. 34-35.
"India Association Plans a Newsletter." [MassR] (29:4) Wint 88-89, p. 596-597.

857. CHANG, Diana
"On Being in the Midwest." [Calyx] (11:2/3) Fall 88, p. 123.
"On the Fly." [Calyx] (11:2/3) Fall 88, p. 124-125.
"Under the Moon and Moving." [StoneC] (15:3/4) Spr-Sum 88, p. 46-49.
858. CHANG, Soo Ko
"By the River." [WebR] (13:1) Spr 88, p. 69.
"Dizziness" (tr. of Dong-Jip Shin). [WebR] (13:2) Fall 88, p. 14.
"Peasant and Ox" (tr. of Dong-Jip Shin). [WebR] (13:2) Fall 88, p. 15.
"The Sea" (tr. of Dong-Jip Shin). [WebR] (13:2) Fall 88, p. 16.
"Suburbs on Spring Day" (tr. of Dong-Jip Shin). [WebR] (13:2) Fall 88, p. 15.
CHANT, George A., Jr. de
See DeCHANT, George A., Jr.
859. CHAPMAN, Cynthia
"Between Dog 'n Suds and Tommy's Tavern." [MidwQ] (30:1) Aut 88, p. 84.
860. CHAPMAN, R. S.
"Shelter." [Northeast] (ser. 4:7) Sum 88, p. 33.
"There Is Something to Be Said." [PoetL] (83:3) Fall 88, p. 26.
"Waking to Asters." [Northeast] (ser. 4:7) Sum 88, p. 32.
861. CHAPPELL, Fred
"Relativity." [TarRP] (28:1) Fall 88, p. 34-35.
862. CHAR, René
"Escheat" (tr. by Charles Guenther). [AmerPoR] (17:3) My-Je 88, p. 25.
"Going Out" (tr. by Charles Guenther). [AmerPoR] (17:3) My-Je 88, p. 25.
"Haunted Gift" (tr. by Charles Guenther). [AmerPoR] (17:3) My-Je 88, p. 24.
"Lost Nakedness" (tr. by Charles Guenther). [AmerPoR] (17:3) My-Je 88, p. 24.
"Silent Game" (tr. by Charles Guenther). [AmerPoR] (17:3) My-Je 88, p. 25.
"Slow Pace of the Future" (tr. by Charles Guenther). [AmerPoR] (17:3) My-Je 88, p. 24.
"Song of the Fig Tree" (tr. by Charles Guenther). [AmerPoR] (17:3) My-Je 88, p. 24.
"Traced on the Gulf" (tr. by Charles Guenther). [AmerPoR] (17:3) My-Je 88, p. 24.
"Troublesome Simplicity" (tr. by Charles Guenther). [AmerPoR] (17:3) My-Je 88, p. 24.
"The Vertical Village" (tr. by Charles Guenther). [AmerPoR] (17:3) My-Je 88, p. 25.
"Welcome" (tr. by Charles Guenther). [AmerPoR] (17:3) My-Je 88, p. 24.
"With a Common Bond" (tr. by Charles Guenther). [AmerPoR] (17:3) My-Je 88, p. 24.
863. CHARLOT, John
"Three Poems for Terri." [HawaiiR] (12:2, #24) Fall 88, p. 42.
864. CHARLTON, James
"To Governor George Arthur in Heaven." [PraS] (62:4) Wint 88-89, p. 66-67.
865. CHASE, Aleka
"New England Postcard." [FiveFR] (6) 88, p. 13.
866. CHASE, Naomi Feigelson
"Marriage." [Amelia] (5:2, #13) 88, p. 126.
"Why I Love St. Francis." [Ploughs] (14:1) 88, p. 34-35.
867. CHATFIELD, Hale
"Antipodes." [HiramPoR] (44/45) Spr-Wint 88, p. 55-58.
"At Home" (Poems, Second Edition). [HiramPoR] (Suppl. #9) 88, p. 5-65.
"Even. Now." [SpoonRQ] (13:3) Sum 88, p. 20-21.
"A New Poem." [KanQ] (20:3) Sum 88, p. 48.
"Roman Sapphics: Via del Corso di Luna." [SpoonRQ] (13:3) Sum 88, p. 19-20.
868. CHATTERJEE, Enakshi
"To a Cowherd Boy" (tr. of Kabita Sinha, w. Carolyne Wright). [Nimrod] (31:2) Spr-Sum 88, p. 30.
869. CHATTOPADHYAY, Shakti
"The Cat" (in Bengali and English, tr. by Jayanta Mahapatra). [Nimrod] (31:2) Spr-Sum 88, p. 29.
870. CHATTORAJ, Partha
"The Sudbury Aqueduct." [HarvardA] (123:1) N 88, p. 16.
871. CHAVARRIA, Gabriela
"La Amante" (Cuerpo No. 15). [Mairena] (10:25) 88, p. 144.
872. CHEATHAM, Karyn
"Drinking Straight." [PikeF] (9) Fall 88, p. 11.
CHEN, Gu
See GU, Chen

CHEN, Rajandaye Ramkissoon
See RAMKISSOON-CHEN, Rajandaye
873. CHEN, Xueliang
"Ancient Temple" (tr. of Bei Dao, w. Donald Finkel). [AmerPoR] (17:4) Jl-Ag 88, p. 42.
"A Day" (tr. of Bei Dao, w. Donald Finkel). [AmerPoR] (17:4) Jl-Ag 88, p. 42.
"Habit" (tr. of Bei Dao, w. Donald Finkel). [AmerPoR] (17:4) Jl-Ag 88, p. 43.
"Hello Mountain of a Hundred Flowers" (tr. of Bei Dao, w. Donald Finkel). [AmerPoR] (17:4) Jl-Ag 88, p. 42.
"Island" (tr. of Bei Dao, w. Donald Finkel). [AmerPoR] (17:4) Jl-Ag 88, p. 44.
"Memory" (tr. of Bei Dao, w. Donald Finkel). [AmerPoR] (17:4) Jl-Ag 88, p. 43.
"Nightmare" (tr. of Bei Dao, w. Donald Finkel). [AmerPoR] (17:4) Jl-Ag 88, p. 43.
"Notes on the City of the Sun" (tr. of Bei Dao, w. Donald Finkel). [AmerPoR] (17:4) Jl-Ag 88, p. 43.
"The Tale Goes On" (tr. of Bei Dao, w. Donald Finkel). [AmerPoR] (17:4) Jl-Ag 88, p. 43.
"Unfamiliar Shore" (tr. of Bei Dao, w. Donald Finkel). [AmerPoR] (17:4) Jl-Ag 88, p. 44.
"You Say" (tr. of Bei Dao, w. Donald Finkel). [AmerPoR] (17:4) Jl-Ag 88, p. 44.
CHENG, Gu
See GU, Cheng
874. CHENG, Pan-ch'iao
"Bamboo Growing Out of a Rock" (1693-1765 — Ch'ing Dynasty, tr. by Wang Zhihuan). [AntR] (46:2) Spr 88, p. 221.
875. CHERKOVSKI, Neeli
"Lord." [JamesWR] (6:1) Fall 88, p. 7.
"On Hollywood Boulevard." [JamesWR] (6:1) Fall 88, p. 7.
876. CHERRY, Kelly
"Anniversary." [Crosscur] (7:4) 88, p. 34-35.
"Emphysema." [SouthernR] (24:3) Sum 88, p. 561.
"Gethsemane." [Atlantic] (261:4) Ap 88, p. 42.
"The Letter." [SouthernR] (24:3) Sum 88, p. 562.
"Lunch at the Lake." [CumbPR] (7:2) Spr 88, p. 3.
"My Mother's Swans." [SouthernR] (24:3) Sum 88, p. 562-563.
"Receiving the Gift." [NewL] (54:3) Spr 88, p. 61.
877. CHESS, Richard
"Eve in Florida." [NewEngR] (10:3) Spr 88, p. 272.
"Sarah's Divorce." [TampaR] (1) 88, p. 37.
"Saturday on the Itchetucknee." [MissouriR] (11:2) 88, p. 186.
"The Tenth Emanation of Creation" (Amsterdam, 1656). [TampaR] (1) 88, p. 36.
878. CHETWYND, Richard
"Count Rzewuski's Deliberations on Betrayal" (tr. of Grzegorz Musial). [PoetL] (83:4) Wint 88-89, p. 23-24.
"Death of an Actress, Berlin, 1937" (tr. of Grzegorz Musial). [PoetL] (83:4) Wint 88-89, p. 22.
"The End of the World at Breakfast" (tr. of Grzegorz Musial). [PoetL] (83:4) Wint 88-89, p. 25.
"Isadora Duncan Dances in Her Red Scarf, 1918" (for Zbigniew Herbert, tr. of Grzegorz Musial). [PoetL] (83:4) Wint 88-89, p. 20.
"Lotte Lenya Sings Brecht, 1932" (tr. of Grzegorz Musial). [PoetL] (83:4) Wint 88-89, p. 21.
879. CHEYFITZ, Eric
"Terminal." [AntR] (46:1) Wint 88, p. 81.
880. CHICHETTO, James (James Wm.)
"Abused." [ManhatR] (4:2) Spr 88, p. 54.
"Battered Woman." [ManhatR] (4:2) Spr 88, p. 53.
"For Anne Frank." [Footwork] ('88) 88, p. 62.
"From KKK Poems, Steve Biko and Isaiah." [ConnPR] (7:1) 88, p. 28.
"The John Lennon Memorial, Dec. 14, 1980." [ManhatR] (4:2) Spr 88, p. 54.
"Under Fire in Asia, 1972." [Footwork] ('88) 88, p. 62-63.
881. CHILDERS, Joanne
"Snowstorm: Atlanta, Georgia, 1988" (In Memoriam — Christopher Griffin — 1973-1988). [DeKalbLAJ] (21:1) Wint 88, p. 48.
882. CHILDRESS, William
"Mother Goose for Our Time." [CharR] (14:2) Fall 88, p. 97.

883. CHIN, Marilyn
"The Administrator." [Caliban] (5) 88, p. 66.
"Gruel." [Ploughs] (14:1) 88, p. 61.
"Its Name." [FiveFR] (6) 88, p. 18.
"Reggae Renga." [FiveFR] (6) 88, p. 19.
"Urban Love Poem." [Zyzzyva] (4:3) Fall 88, p. 45-46.
"We Are Americans Now, We Live in the Tundra." [Calyx] (11:2/3) Fall 88, p. 17.
CHIN, Woon Ping
See PING, Chin Woon
884. CHINN, Daryl
"Hanging in the Shop." [FloridaR] (16:1) Spr-Sum 88, p. 35.
"A Small Part in *Annie Get Your Gun.*" [FloridaR] (16:1) Spr-Sum 88, p. 36-37.
"Three." [FloridaR] (16:1) Spr-Sum 88, p. 38-40.
885. CHIRNSIDE, Carolyn H.
"Of English Teachers." [EngJ] (77:4) Ap 88, p. 87.
886. CHITWOOD, Michael
"A History of the Country" (Chapbook: 6 Poems). [OhioR] (42) 88, p. 49-64.
887. CHMIELARZ, Sharon
"Homecoming." [LakeSR] (22) 88, p. 31.
888. CHOCK, Eric
"Ghislaine's Quilt." [ChamLR] (1:2, #2) Spr 88, p. 57.
"Pua'a: Nuuanu." [ChamLR] (1:2, #2) Spr 88, p. 56.
889. CHOE, Wolhee
"Ah, What Have I Done" (tr. of Hwang Jinie, w. Constantine Contogenis). [TriQ] (72) Spr-Sum 88, p. 183.
"An Anchor Lifts" (tr. of anonymous Mediaeval Korean, w. Constantine Contogenis). [NewEngR] (11:2) Wint 88, p. 180.
"At Cold Solstice" (tr. of Hwang Jinie, w. Constantine Contogenis). [TriQ] (72) Spr-Sum 88, p. 183.
"The Black Crow" (tr. of anonymous Mediaeval Korean, w. Constantine Contogenis). [NewEngR] (11:2) Wint 88, p. 180.
"Whenever Did I" (tr. of Hwang Jinie, w. Constantine Contogenis). [TriQ] (72) Spr-Sum 88, p. 183.
890. CHOO, Mary E.
"Festival of Ghosts." [CrossC] (10:2) 88, p. 10.
"Incarnate." [CrossC] (10:2) 88, p. 10.
"Sentinel." [Amelia] (5:2, #13) 88, p. 135.
891. CHORLTON, David
"Between the Dunes." [Pembroke] (20) 88, p. 217.
"Between Trains." [Lactuca] (11) O 88, p. 30.
"Breath." [ChamLR] (2:1, #3) Fall 88, p. 33.
"Coyote." [Abraxas] (37) 88, p. 59.
"Cross Visions." [Lactuca] (11) O 88, p. 32.
"The Disinherited Country." [Pembroke] (20) 88, p. 216.
"The Emperor, Ling Ti." [Lactuca] (11) O 88, p. 32.
"How to Cross a Border." [Pembroke] (20) 88, p. 216.
"Kein-Wu's Journey." [Lactuca] (11) O 88, p. 31.
"Kiev." [Abraxas] (37) 88, p. 58.
"Mezzogiorno." [Lactuca] (11) O 88, p. 33.
"New Clothes." [Lactuca] (11) O 88, p. 31.
"La Plage." [Pembroke] (20) 88, p. 216.
892. CHOYCE, Lesley
"The Man Who Borrowed th Bay of Fundy." [PottPort] (10) 88, p. 48.
"Xerox Lovers Anonymous." [PottPort] (10) 88, p. 48.
893. CHRISTENSEN, Erleen J.
"Facts of Life." [Amelia] (5:1, #12) 88, p. 32.
894. CHRISTHILF, Mark
"Flowers." [MidwQ] (29:3) Spr 88, p. 336.
"Ocean." [KanQ] (20:3) Sum 88, p. 194.
895. CHRISTIANSON, Kevin
"Houses of the Poor." [MinnR] (NS 30/31) Spr-Fall 88, p. 21.
"Potato." [Turnstile] (1:1) Wint 88, p. 95-100.
896. CHRISTINA, Martha
"To Serengeti and Back." [Prima] (11/12) 88, p. 65-66.
897. CHRISTINA-MARIE
"For Those Who Have Died." [Caliban] (5) 88, p. 108.

898. CHRISTOPHER, G. B.
"How to Take It." [SouthernHR] (22:3) Sum 88, p. 262.
899. CHRISTOPHER, Nicholas
"Circe in Love." [Nat] (246:18) 7 My 88, p. 653.
"Map." [SouthwR] (73:1) Wint 88, p. 80-81.
"Mrs. Luna." [NewYorker] (64:25) 8 Ag 88, p. 34.
"Nocturne for Miranda." [Shen] (38:4) 88, p. 35-36.
"Voyeur." [Shen] (38:1) 88, p. 67-68.
900. CHRYSTOS
"I Am Not Your Princess" (especially for Dee Johnson). [SinW] (33) Fall 87, p. 18-19.
901. CHRZANOWSKI, J.
"El Velorio" (A Margarita). [LindLM] (7:2/4) Ap-D 88, p. 12.
902. CHU, Meng-dan
"Smoking People: Encountering the New Chinese Poetry" (Chapbook 19, tr. by Chu Meng-dan et al.). [BelPoJ] (39:2) Wint 88-89, 76 p.
903. CHUDAKOV, Sergei
"Suicide Is a Duel With Yourself" (tr. by Daniel Weissbort). [NegC] (8:1/2) 88, p. 24.
904. CHUTE, Robert M.
"Balance Point." [LitR] (31:4) Sum 88, p. 415.
"Dear Friend Ricketson" (Based on a letter dated November 4, 1860 from Henry Thoreau). [StoneC] (15:3/4) Spr-Sum 88, p. 73.
"Designing Simplicity" (Based on letters from Thoreau to H.G.O. Blake, March/April, 1850). [StoneC] (15:3/4) Spr-Sum 88, p. 73.
"Election Day, Mount Vernon, Maine." [CapeR] (23:2) Fall 88, p. 25.
"Fox Business." [LitR] (31:2) Wint 88, p. 230.
"From Fire Island, Aug. 9, 1850" (from Thoreau's Journal). [Northeast] (ser. 4:7) Sum 88, p. 29.
"Going Back." [CapeR] (23:1) Spr 88, p. 10.
"March, 1724." [TexasR] (9:3/4) Fall-Wint 88, p. 28-29.
"Rosh Ha-Shanah at Upper Range Pond." [KanQ] (20:3) Sum 88, p. 135.
"Shopping Center in May." [SmPd] (25:2) Spr 88, p. 23.
905. CIARDI, John
"Dear Sir." [NewL] (55:1) Fall 88, p. 8.
"Elegy for a Cave Full of Bones" (Saipan, December 16, 1944). [Poetry] (151:6) Mr 88, p. 471-472.
"God." [NewL] (55:1) Fall 88, p. 5.
"One Betty — Five Skulls." [KeyWR] (1:1) Spr 88, p. 14-15.
"Psalm." [NewL] (55:1) Fall 88, p. 6-8.
"Return." [KeyWR] (1:1) Spr 88, p. 11.
"A Traffic Victim Sends a Sonnet of Confused Thanks to God As the Sovereign Host." [NewL] (55:1) Fall 88, p. 9.
"Visibility Zero." [KeyWR] (1:1) Spr 88, p. 12-13.
906. CIRINO, Leonard
"A Fact: The Quickest Win." [Amelia] (5:1, #12) 88, p. 99.
"A Kind of Politic." [CapeR] (23:2) Fall 88, p. 10.
"Sorting Kingdoms." [CapeR] (23:2) Fall 88, p. 8.
"Twilight at Noon." [CapeR] (23:2) Fall 88, p. 9.
"A Woman." [Paint] (15:30) Aut 88, p. 18.
907. CISNEROS, Antonio
"Arte Poética." [Inti] (26/27) Otoño 87-Primavera 88, p. 39-40.
"Contemplación del Mediterráneo + Leonard Cohen." [Inti] (26/27) Otoño 87-Primavera 88, p. 41-42.
"De Vuelta a la Casona (Papá y Mamá)." [Inti] (26/27) Otoño 87-Primavera 88, p. 43.
"Heme Aquí, el Perfil de Mi Cabeza En." [Inti] (26/27) Otoño 87-Primavera 88, p. 43-44.
"Una Madre Habla de su Muchacho." [Inti] (26/27) Otoño 87-Primavera 88, p. 46-47.
"Una Muchachita en Domingo." [Inti] (26/27) Otoño 87-Primavera 88, p. 45-46.
"Una Muerte del Niño Jesús." [Inti] (26/27) Otoño 87-Primavera 88, p. 45.
"No Puede Ser. La Felicidad (una Buena." [Inti] (26/27) Otoño 87-Primavera 88, p. 44-45.
"Otra Muerte del Niño Jesús." [Inti] (26/27) Otoño 87-Primavera 88, p. 46.
"Postal para Lima." [Inti] (26/27) Otoño 87-Primavera 88, p. 41.
"Un Soneto Donde Digo Que Mi Hijo Está Muy Lejos Hace Ya Más de un Año." [Inti] (26/27) Otoño 87-Primavera 88, p. 40-41.

908. CITINO, David
"At the Hotel Giotto." [Salm] (80) Fall 88, p. 122-123.
"Ballad of the Northland Mall." [CreamCR] (12:2) Sum 88, p. 167-168.
"Charcoal Sketch of Aged Couple in Peasant Dress, Circa 1880." [Poetry] (152:2) My 88, p. 95-96.
"The Discipline." [KanQ] (20:3) Sum 88, p. 62-63.
"The Father and the Son." [CreamCR] (12:2) Sum 88, p. 170.
"The Fathers." [AntR] (46:1) Wint 88, p. 85.
"The First Poem" (for Maria). [LaurelR] (22:21) Wint 88, p. 6-7.
"Having No Gods at All." [KanQ] (20:3) Sum 88, p. 63.
"Homage to Hildegarde of Bingen." [LitR] (31:3) Spr 88, p. 312-313.
"In the Kitchen, He Recalls a Passage from Suetonius." [Poetry] (152:2) My 88, p. 96-97.
"On His Daughter's Second Birthday." [CreamCR] (12:2) Sum 88, p. 169.
"The Quantum Mechanics of Fathers and Sons." [LaurelR] (22:21) Wint 88, p. 7-8.
"The Salvage." [LaurelR] (22:21) Wint 88, p. 5.
"Sister Mary Appassionata Lectures the Journalism Class: Homage to the Paparazzi." [LightY] ('88/9) 88, p. 197.
"Sister Mary Appassionata Lectures the Sociobiology Class." [SouthernPR] (28:2) Fall 88, p. 29.
"Sister Mary Appassionata to the Human Awareness Class: Notes Toward the Perfection of Sex." [WestB] (21/22) 88, p. 5-7.
"Walking in the Piazza San Marco, I Remember Ascension of our Lord Elementary School . . ." [TarRP] (28:1) Fall 88, p. 16-17.
909. CLAESON, Eva
"At the Window" (tr. of Margareta Ekström). [GrahamHR] (11) Spr 88, p. 108-109.
"In the Morning" (tr. of Margareta Ekström). [GrahamHR] (11) Spr 88, p. 110-111.
910. CLAIR, Maxine
"Daily Paper." [Callaloo] (11:2, #35) Spr 88, p. 212.
"Deja Vu." [Callaloo] (11:2, #35) Spr 88, p. 213.
"Lone Lily beside the Road." [Prima] (11/12) 88, p. 33-34.
911. CLAIRMAN, Gary
"Au Coin." [AlphaBS] (3) Je 88, p. 35-37.
912. CLAMPITT, Amy
"Alders." [NewYorker] (64:9) 18 Ap 88, p. 38.
"Dejection: A Footnote." [YaleR] (77:4) Sum 88, p. 512-513.
"Dorset, August 27, 1985." [MidwQ] (30:1) Aut 88, p. 63.
"High Noon." [NewYorker] (64:19) 27 Je 88, p. 32.
"Iola, Kansas." [SouthwR] (73:4) Aut 88, p. 482-483.
"A Minor Tremor." [Boulevard] (3:2/3) Fall 88, p. 48.
"Mulciber at West Egg." [CreamCR] (12:2) Sum 88, p. 171.
"Pure Pathos." [Boulevard] (3:2/3) Fall 88, p. 47.
"A Winter Burial." [MidwQ] (30:1) Aut 88, p. 61-62.
913. CLANCY, Joseph P.
"Rituals." [ManhatPR] (10) Ja 88, p. 36-37.
914. CLARK, Alison
"Pathetic Fallacy." [NewAW] (4) Fall 88, p. 120.
"Reading Novels I." [NewAW] (4) Fall 88, p. 121.
"Reading Novels III — Romance." [NewAW] (4) Fall 88, p. 122.
"The Sailors Passed and the Ocean Vanished." [NewAW] (4) Fall 88, p. 121.
"The Unhealthy Mists of Lammermoor." [NewAW] (4) Fall 88, p. 119.
"With How Sad Steps." [NewAW] (4) Fall 88, p. 119-120.
915. CLARK, Arthur
"The Dead." [Dandel] (15:1) Spr-Sum 88, p. 19.
916. CLARK, Irene Grayce
"Juvenile Delinquent." [Plain] (9:1) Fall 88, p. 7.
917. CLARK, J. Wesley
"Bordertown." [Bogg] (59) 88, p. 5.
"For James Wright." [Bogg] (60) 88, p. 15.
"Ghost Dancer." [Notus] (3:1) Spr 88, p. 84.
"Walt Bell's World View." [Notus] (3:1) Spr 88, p. 83.
"Yaquitepec." [Notus] (3:1) Spr 88, p. 85.
918. CLARK, Mary
"Celebrations." [Lips] (14) 88, p. 2.
919. CLARK, Naomi
"Believing Water: In the Time of Famine." [PraS] (62:1) Spr 88, p. 86-87.

920. CLARK, Patricia
"Two Bodies." [PennR] (4:1) 88, p. 29.
921. CLARK, Tom
"Eternity Time Share Rebus." [Zyzzyva] (4:4) Wint 88, p. 93.
"Trebizond." [Talisman] (1) Fall 88, p. 86.
922. CLARKE, Amanda (Amanda M.)
"The Dream." [Jacaranda] (3:2) Fall-Wint 88, p. 25.
"One Year the Milkweed Died." [Jacaranda] (3:1) Wint 88, p. 42.
"Zoo." [Jacaranda] (3:1) Wint 88, p. 43.
923. CLARKE, D. A.
"And Everywhere Unicorns." [SinW] (35) Sum-Fall 88, p. 8-11.
924. CLARKE, George Elliott
"Cora's Testament." [PottPort] (9) 88, p. 35.
"Each Moment Is Magnificent." [PottPort] (10) 88, p. 33.
925. CLARKE, Gillian
"At One Thousand Feet." [NewEngR] (10:4) Sum 88, p. 417.
"Neighbours." [NewEngR] (10:4) Sum 88, p. 418.
926. CLARKE, Ian
"Earth and Air in August." [SouthernPR] (28:1) Spr 88, p. 46.
927. CLARKE, Terry
"Anonymous" (To Osip Mandelstam, tr. of Carlota Caulfield). [Vis] (26) 88, p. 50.
"A Fall Celebration" (tr. of Carlota Caulfield). [Vis] (26) 88, p. 50.
928. CLARVOE, Jennifer S.
"Adams's Hand" ("or Michael taking Adam by the wrist"). [Verse] (5:1) F 88, p. 3.
929. CLAUSEN, Christopher
"Being and Becoming at Cape Hatteras." [SouthwR] (73:1) Wint 88, p. 81-82.
930. CLEARY, Michael
"Bumper Hopping and the Transmigration of Souls." [SouthernPR] (28:2) Fall 88, p. 41-42.
"January Crossing, Lake Champlain" (Third Place, 1987 Eve of Saint Agnes Poetry Competition). [NegC] (8:3) 88, p. 24-26.
"John Wayne, Freddie Freihofer, and the Buckskin Mare." [Blueline] (9:1/2) 88, p. 72-73.
"My Mother Wonders, What Do I have to Do Before You Write About Me? Die?" [NegC] (8:3) 88, p. 68-69.
931. CLEARY, Suzanne
"Labyrinthitis." [OhioR] (41) 88, p. 108-109.
932. CLEAVER, Darcy Jane
"Ropeburn." [PoetL] (83:1) Spr 88, p. 31.
CLEMENT, Dymphny Koenig
See KOENIG-CLEMENT, Dymphny
933. CLEMENT, Jennifer
"Lady of the Haystack." [AmerV] (13) Wint 88, p. 27-28.
"A World in Which the Clouds Are the Shadows" (— Villaurrutia). [AmerPoR] (17:2) Mr-Ap 88, p. 39.
934. CLEMENTS, Arthur L.
"In This Cold." [Footwork] ('88) 88, p. 15.
"Neither Flight Nor Song." [Footwork] ('88) 88, p. 14.
"Some Poems." [Footwork] ('88) 88, p. 15.
"Sun Water Woman." [Footwork] ('88) 88, p. 14.
935. CLEMENTS, Susan
"Blue Boxcar." [Footwork] ('88) 88, p. 8-9.
"Custer's Revenge." [Footwork] ('88) 88, p. 8.
"Halloween, Oakland, New Jersey." [Footwork] ('88) 88, p. 8.
"Mummy Cat in the British Museum." [CumbPR] (7:2) Spr 88, p. 4.
"The Orange Cat of Portofino." [Footwork] ('88) 88, p. 9.
"White Angels." [Footwork] ('88) 88, p. 9.
936. CLENMAN, Donia Blumenfeld
"Friendship in the Afternoon." [PraF] (9:4) Wint 88-89, p. 30-31.
937. CLEWELL, David
"Why Certain Poets Have No Business at the Track" (for Pete G.). [Abraxas] (37) 88, p. 68-69.
938. CLIMENHAGA, Joel
"Yoke on My Heart, Wanderlust, Options" (Selections: 4 poems). [KanQ] (20:1/2) Wint-Spr 88, p. 122-124.

939. CLINCH, Brad
"Sixty Years of Dogs." [BellArk] (4:4) Jl-Ag 88, p. 7.
940. CLINTON, D. (DeWitt)
"Casting into Blue." [CapeR] (23:2) Fall 88, p. 4.
"Church" (from a manuscript, "The Collected Writings of Our Lady of Cortez"). [RiverS] (26) 88, p. 78-79.
"Dental Appointment." [Contact] (9:47/48/49) Spr 88, p. 54-55.
"Evening." [CapeR] (23:2) Fall 88, p. 5.
"This Last Place" (from a manuscript entitled "The Collected Writings of Our Lady of Cortez"). [Contact] (9:47/48/49) Spr 88, p. 55.
941. CLINTON, Michèlle T.
"007." [Jacaranda] (3:2) Fall-Wint 88, p. 81-82.
CLUE, Charlotte de
See DeCLUE, Charlotte
942. CLUTE, Mitchell
"The Apothecary's Grave." [HawaiiR] (12:1, #23) Spr 88, p. 97.
943. COBO BORDA, J. G.
"Al Recuerdo de un Escritor." [Inti] (26/27) Otoño 87-Primavera 88, p. 58.
"Elogio de la Superficialidad." [Inti] (26/27) Otoño 87-Primavera 88, p. 58-59.
"Hecha por Todos: la Poesía." [Inti] (26/27) Otoño 87-Primavera 88, p. 61.
"Letanía." [Inti] (26/27) Otoño 87-Primavera 88, p. 60.
"Los Viejos Trucos." [Inti] (26/27) Otoño 87-Primavera 88, p. 59-60.
944. COBURN, Teresa Lloyd
"The Cruellest Month" (for Win Brown). [Quarry] (37:1) Wint 88, p. 26-27.
"Half Drowned." [Quarry] (37:1) Wint 88, p. 24-25.
945. COCHRAN, Leonard
"Abundance." [ChrC] (105:27) 28 S 88, p. 837.
"Matthew 4:19." [ChrC] (105:21) 6-13 Jl 88, p. 637.
"Three Riddles." [SpiritSH] (54) Fall-Wint 88, p. 10.
946. COCHRANE, Guy R.
"Branded New." [WormR] (28:4, #112) 88, p. 119.
"Digital." [WormR] (28:4, #112) 88, p. 119.
"Not Inclined." [WormR] (28:4, #112) 88, p. 119.
"Pinned." [WormR] (28:4, #112) 88, p. 119.
947. COCHRANE, Shirley G.
"Grandmother." [ColR] (NS 15:2) Fall-Wint 88, p. 47.
948. CODRESCU, Andrei
"Casino Pierre" (for Alice Notley). [Talisman] (1) Fall 88, p. 76.
"Circle Jerk." [Chelsea] (47) 88, p. 123-125.
"Demands of Exile." [Vis] (26) 88, p. 41.
949. COE, Dina
"Deer Season." [PraS] (62:3) Fall 88, p. 55-57.
"The Moon." [HolCrit] (25:3) Je 88, p. 18.
"Window II." [PraS] (62:3) Fall 88, p. 57-58.
950. COFER, Judith Ortiz
"The Bleeder." [DeKalbLAJ] (21:2) Spr 88, p. 34.
"Fulana." [Americas] (16:2) Sum 88, p. 42.
"The Hour of the Siesta." [Americas] (16:2) Sum 88, p. 45.
"How to Get a Baby." [SouthernPR] (28:2) Fall 88, p. 22.
"The Life of an Echo." [AntR] (46:3) Sum 88, p. 359.
"La Negra." [Americas] (16:2) Sum 88, p. 44.
"Paciencia." [Americas] (16:2) Sum 88, p. 43.
"Penelope's Journal" (Selections: "Learning to Walk Alone," "The Drowned Sailor"). [KenR] (NS 10:4) Fall 88, p. 80-81.
951. COFFEY, Kathy
"Gift Wrap with Thunder and Cadence, Please." [EngJ] (77:3) Mr 88, p. 88.
952. COFFIN, Lawrence
"Monk" (below Gangotri Glacier). [CinPR] (17) Spr 88, p. 64.
"Picnic at West Fork." [CinPR] (17) Spr 88, p. 65.
953. COFFIN, Lyn
"It's Not with a Lover's Lyre" (tr. of Anna Akhmatova). [Field] (39) Fall 88, p. 40.
"Lady Godiva" (tr. of Irina Ratushinskaya, w. Serge Shishkoff). [MichQR] (27:3) Sum 88, p. 395-396.
"Whale's Song" (tr. of Jaroslav Seifert). [Spirit] (9:1) 88, p. 157-160.
954. COGEOS, Stephanie
"Untitled: Sunlight dancing on ocean waves." [Wind] (18:62) 88, p. 37.

955. COGSWELL, Fred
"Letter to Milton Acorn." [CrossC] (10:2) 88, p. 8.
"To Hesiod." [PraF] (9:2) Sum 88, p. 42-43.
956. COHEN, Allen
"Letter to the Editor" (January 27, 1987). [AlphaBS] (3) Je 88, p. 32.
"Poets — Legislators of the World." [AlphaBS] (3) Je 88, p. 33-34.
957. COHEN, Andrea
"No Segue In, Out of This World." [DenQ] (22:3) Wint 88, p. 148-149.
958. COHEN, Carole
"Pollen" (for Louis Cohen, 1897-). [CapeR] (23:2) Fall 88, p. 27.
959. COHEN, Dorothy Neil
"Song of Solitude" (tr. of René Guy Cadou). [HayF] (3) Spr 88, p. 85, 87.
960. COHEN, Gerald
"British Museum Library." [Amelia] (5:2, #13) 88, p. 133.
961. COHEN, Jonathan
"Oquendo's 'Rain': A Choral Rendering." [AmerV] (10) Spr 88, p. 83-85.
962. COHEN, Marc
"As the Crow Flies." [Verse] (5:2) Jl 88, p. 11.
"The Gordian Knot." [NewAW] (3) Spr 88, p. 94-95.
963. COHN, Jim
"Glacier Park Journal." [Lactuca] (9) F 88, p. 5-6.
964. COKINOS, Chris (Christopher)
"Diogenes Addresses the Trustees of Indiana University . . . ." [ArtfulD] (14/15) Fall 88, p. 66.
"Failed Experiment 1." [AnotherCM] (18) 88, p. 77.
965. COLANDER, Valerie (Valerie Nieman)
"Brush-Burning." [SingHM] (15) 88, p. 64-65.
"Farm Wife." [SingHM] (15) 88, p. 42.
"First Generation." [SingHM] (15) 88, p. 66-67.
"Firstfruits." [SingHM] (15) 88, p. 60-61.
"Hanging Up Clothes." [SingHM] (15) 88, p. 44.
"I Am Converted by Anna." [SingHM] (15) 88, p. 69.
"The Increase of the Earth." [SingHM] (15) 88, p. 53-56.
"A Moment's Peace." [SingHM] (15) 88, p. 47-51.
"Necessity Is the Poor Woman's Doctor." [SingHM] (15) 88, p. 62-63.
"Other People's Children." [SingHM] (15) 88, p. 52.
"Pond." [SingHM] (15) 88, p. 41.
"Pond." [Vis] (27) 88, p. 17.
"A Raccoon Saved." [SingHM] (15) 88, p. 43.
"Reclamation: Washing Machine." [SingHM] (15) 88, p. 68.
"Three Lectures on Bird Songs." [SingHM] (15) 88, p. 45-46.
"When Things Were in Good Order." [SingHM] (15) 88, p. 58-59.
"Wichita, Kan. (UPI)" ("Triplets separated . . . 57 years ago have met for the first time."). [SingHM] (15) 88, p. 57.
966. COLBY, Joan
"The Art of Dying." [Poetry] (152:5) Ag 88, p. 259-260.
967. COLBY, R.
"The Nicaraguan children." [GrahamHR] (11) Spr 88, p. 34.
968. COLE, Barbara S.
"I get a kiss." [Amelia] (5:1, #12) 88, p. 115.
"We are two-toned shadows." [Amelia] (5:1, #12) 88, p. 114.
"You're best when just from your dreams." [Amelia] (5:1, #12) 88, p. 114.
969. COLE, E. R.
"Summer Company." [CumbPR] (7:2) Spr 88, p. 5-6.
970. COLE, Henri
"A Half-Life." [Poetry] (152:5) Ag 88, p. 255-256.
"Papilloma." [SouthwR] (73:3) Sum 88, p. 402-403.
"Vanessa." [ParisR] (30:108) Fall 88, p. 148-151.
"West Point Remembered." [ParisR] (30:108) Fall 88, p. 146-147.
971. COLE, James
"The Banquet." [Interim] (7:1) Spr 88, p. 10.
"Bicycles." [Interim] (7:1) Spr 88, p. 12.
"The Greenhouse." [Interim] (7:1) Spr 88, p. 11.
"In the Queue: London." [HolCrit] (25:5) D 88, back cover.
"The Remains of Cong Abbey." [Comm] (115:14) 12 Ag 88, p. 431.

972. COLE, Kevin
"Homage to Heat in Winter." [ArtfulD] (14/15) Fall 88, p. 28-29.
"New Names." [ArtfulD] (14/15) Fall 88, p. 30.
973. COLE, Lyllian D.
"Lay-About." [Amelia] (5:2, #13) 88, p. 116.
974. COLE, Norma
"Itinerary's Control." [Conjunc] (12) 88, p. 29-36.
"Notes on Translation" (tr. of André Du Bouchet). [Acts] (8/9) 88, p. 199-217.
975. COLE, Peter
"Ambit." [Conjunc] (12) 88, p. 252-266.
976. COLE, Richard
"Waiting for Money." [DenQ] (23:2) Fall 88, p. 36-37.
977. COLE, Robert
"Funeral." [Interim] (7:2) Fall 88, p. 20.
"Opting Out." [Interim] (7:2) Fall 88, p. 19.
"Red Skirt." [Bogg] (60) 88, p. 27.
978. COLE, William Rossa
"Dirty Work on the appellation Trail, or, I Can't Remember the Mnemoniker." [LightY] ('88/9) 88, p. 38-39.
"Marriage Toast." [LightY] ('88/9) 88, p. 140.
"A Mini-Samizdat of New River Rhymes." [LightY] ('88/9) 88, p. 163-164.
979. COLEMAN, Jane
"Bird Women" (The Bitterroots, 1805). [SoDakR] (26:3) Aut 88, p. 33.
"Lullabye" (Kansas, 1874). [SoDakR] (26:3) Aut 88, p. 24.
"Mid-Life Crisis." [PassN] (9:2) Sum 88, p. 30.
980. COLEMAN, John
"Bedstead Square." [SouthernR] (24:3) Sum 88, p. 543-548.
"Diving In." [PaintedB] (36) 88, p. 8.
981. COLEMAN, Mary Ann
"April: Recognizing the Angel." [ChatR] (8:3) Spr 88, p. 50.
982. COLEMAN, Wanda
"Billy Jones." [SlipS] (8) 88, p. 54-56.
"I.S. in the Purple Felt Hat (2)." [SlipS] (8) 88, p. 56.
"Syndesis." [SlipS] (8) 88, p. 57.
983. COLES, Katharine
"August." [PoetryNW] (29:3) Aut 88, p. 11-12.
"Father." [QW] (26) Wint 88, p. 108-109.
"Kudzu." [PraS] (62:3) Fall 88, p. 114-115.
"My Mother's Lesson." [MemphisSR] (8:2) Spr 88, p. 93-94.
"Not a Storytelling Family." [MemphisSR] (8:2) Spr 88, p. 91-92.
984. COLETTI, Ed
"Mourning a Lost Poem." [LightY] ('88/9) 88, p. 192.
COLLADO, Alfredo Villanueva
See VILLANUEVA-COLLADO, Alfredo
985. COLLADO, Hector M.
"Asterisco" (fragmentos). [Mairena] (10:25) 88, p. 181.
986. COLLIER, Michael
"Skimming." [Ploughs] (14:4) 88, p. 57-58.
"Territory." [Ploughs] (14:4) 88, p. 55-56.
987. COLLIER, Phyllis K.
"Crossing to a New Latitude." [ColEng] (50:2) F 88, p. 156.
"The Elusive Lights." [ColEng] (50:2) F 88, p. 155.
"How the Earth Shifts Her Patterns." [SoDakR] (26:3) Aut 88, p. 9.
"Rite of Spring." [SoDakR] (26:3) Aut 88, p. 7-8.
"Rosie Has Her Baby — Frederick, Oklahoma, 1933." [PoetL] (83:2) Sum 88, p. 17-18.
"Summer Again." [PoetL] (83:2) Sum 88, p. 19-20.
988. COLLINS, Andrea
"Wig Blues." [ColEng] (50:6) O 88, p. 635.
989. COLLINS, Billy
"Aphorism." [BlackWR] (15:1) Fall 88, p. 109.
"Books." [Poetry] (152:1) Ap 88, p. 22.
"A History of Weather." [Poetry] (152:1) Ap 88, p. 23.
"The History Teacher." [KanQ] (20:1/2) Wint-Spr 88, p. 256-257.
"Horseman, Pass By!" [KanQ] (20:1/2) Wint-Spr 88, p. 256.
"Questions About Angels." [GeoR] (42:4) Wint 88, p. 714-715.

"Student of Clouds." [Poetry] (143, i.e. 153:1) O 88, p. 24.
"Vade Mecum." [BlackWR] (15:1) Fall 88, p. 108.
"Winter Syntax." [Poetry] (152:1) Ap 88, p. 21.

990. COLLINS, Floyd
"A Blues Funeral Mood." [DenQ] (22:3) Wint 88, p. 234.

991. COLLINS, Jennifer
"The Day After." [Footwork] ('88) 88, p. 82.
"Imperfection." [Footwork] ('88) 88, p. 82.
"In Reverence to Dr. Martin Luther King, Jr." [Footwork] ('88) 88, p. 82-83.

992. COLLINS, Martha
"After." [WestB] (21/22) 88, p. 70.
"Beauty." [DenQ] (23:1) Sum 88, p. 45.
"Bodies." [PraS] (62:3) Fall 88, p. 89-90.
"The Border." [Field] (39) Fall 88, p. 87.
"Cleft." [Field] (39) Fall 88, p. 86.
"Complicity." [DenQ] (23:1) Sum 88, p. 46.
"Images of Women in American Literature Part One" (Runner Up, 1988 Narrative Poetry Contest). [PoetL] (83:4) Wint 88-89, p. 5-13.
"In a Northern State." [PraS] (62:3) Fall 88, p. 90-91.
"The Language It Would Speak." [GrahamHR] (11) Spr 88, p. 55.
"Last Things." [PraS] (62:3) Fall 88, p. 88-89.
"On the Train." [WestB] (21/22) 88, p. 71.
"Over." [MSS] (6:2) 88, p. 63.
"Phase Three." [Field] (39) Fall 88, p. 84-85.

993. COLLOM, Jack
"The Formalist's Compleynt." [NewAW] (3) Spr 88, p. 101.
"Whites." [NewAW] (3) Spr 88, p. 100.

994. COLLUMS, Magdalene
"Haiku: They passed this morning" (The 14th Kansas Poetry Contest, Third Prize). [LittleBR] (5:2) Wint 88-89, p. 69.

995. COLONNESE, Michael
"At a Dealers-Only Auction." [CarolQ] (41:1) Fall 88, p. 72.
"At a Roadside Spring in Marathon." [PoetL] (83:4) Wint 88-89, p. 44.

996. COLTMAN, Paul
"War: 1917-1982." [CumbPR] (7:2) Spr 88, p. 7-8.

997. COMANN, Brad
"Across the Waters." [KanQ] (20:1/2) Wint-Spr 88, p. 302.
"Kites, Balloons, Jets." [KanQ] (20:1/2) Wint-Spr 88, p. 294.

998. COMBELLICK, Hank
"Grandfather and Brids." [AntR] (46:1) Wint 88, p. 88.

999. COMENA, Anna
"Men." [GrandS] (7:3) Spr 88, p. 185.

1000. CONKLING, Helen
"Veterans" (1946). [ChiR] (36:2) Aut 88, p. 65-66.

1001. CONLEY, Toni
"Someday I Will Tell." [CimR] (83) Ap 88, p. 42.

1002. CONN, Jan
"I Am a Visitor in My Mother's House." [MalR] (84) S 88, p. 18.
"Learning to Be My Father's Daughter." [MalR] (84) S 88, p. 16-17.
"One View from the Lookout Tower." [MalR] (84) S 88, p. 19.
"To My Father at Age Nine." [MalR] (84) S 88, p. 20.

1003. CONN, Stewart
"Aria." [Verse] (5:1) F 88, p. 63.

1004. CONNELLY, Karen
"Learning Colour and Demons" (Northern Thailand). [Grain] (16:2) Sum 88, p. 7-12.

1005. CONNELLY, Michele
"Deliverance." [Footwork] ('88) 88, p. 28.

1006. CONNER, Ann
"Fossils." [KanQ] (20:3) Sum 88, p. 194.

1007. CONNOLLY, Carol
"A Hole in the Night." [LakeSR] (22) 88, p. 17.

1008. CONNOLLY, Geraldine
"At Mimi's Style Shop." [GettyR] (1:4) Aut 88, p. 600.
"A Chinese Bowl." [AntR] (46:2) Spr 88, p. 237.
"In the Blue Train." [PoetryNW] (29:1) Spr 88, p. 3-4.
"In the Family Scene." [PoetryNW] (29:1) Spr 88, p. 4-5.

"Lydia." [Poetry] (152:3) Je 88, p. 131-132.
"My Uncles." [PoetryNW] (29:1) Spr 88, p. 6.
"Sunset." [CentR] (32:1) Wint 88, p. 37-38.

1009. CONOLEY, Gillian
"The Last Aunt." [IndR] (11:3) Sum 88, p. 51-52.

1010. CONOVER, Carl
"Composition." [TexasR] (9:1/2) Spr-Sum 88, p. 55.
"Excavation." [LitR] (32:1) Fall 88, p. 85.
"Night Stand." [LitR] (32:1) Fall 88, p. 84-85.
"Off Stage with the Messenger" (After Euripides). [SouthernHR] (22:2) Spr 88, p. 169.
"The Passive Voice." [Shen] (38:4) 88, p. 45.
"Periphery." [PoetL] (83:2) Sum 88, p. 35.
"Someone Else." [Shen] (38:4) 88, p. 45-46.

1011. CONRAD, Nick
"Epistle to a Newborn." [Jacaranda] (3:2) Fall-Wint 88, p. 149.

1012. CONTENT, Rob
"Aviary." [AntR] (46:4) Fall 88, p. 488.

1013. CONTI, Edmund
"Aping." [Bogg] (59) 88, p. 7.
"Clerihews" (3 poems). [LightY] ('88/9) 88, p. 74.
"Flesti, Selfit" (circular poem). [Bogg] (60) 88, p. 32.
"Haiku: OK, all you frogs." [HawaiiR] (12:2, #24) Fall 88, p. 89.
"How to Write a Sestina." [SmPd] (25:3) Fall 88, p. 36.

1014. CONTOGENIS, Constantine
"Ah, What Have I Done" (tr. of Hwang Jinie, w. Wolhee Choe). [TriQ] (72) Spr-Sum 88, p. 183.
"An Anchor Lifts" (tr. of anonymous Mediaeval Korean, w. Wolhee Choe). [NewEngR] (11:2) Wint 88, p. 180.
"At Cold Solstice" (tr. of Hwang Jinie, w. Wolhee Choe). [TriQ] (72) Spr-Sum 88, p. 183.
"The Black Crow" (tr. of anonymous Mediaeval Korean, w. Wolhee Choe). [NewEngR] (11:2) Wint 88, p. 180.
"Whenever Did I" (tr. of Hwang Jinie, w. Wolhee Choe). [TriQ] (72) Spr-Sum 88, p. 183.

1015. CONWAY, Jack
"Brothers Don't Wear No Cowboy Boots." [CrabCR] (5:2) Sum 88, p. 10.
"Ditties." [CrabCR] (5:2) Sum 88, p. 9.

1016. CONWAY, Tina Marie
"Why I Believe in the American Dream." [SlipS] (8) 88, p. 43.

1017. COOK, Albert
"Modes" (Selection: XVIII). [Interim] (7:1) Spr 88, p. 45.
"The Time of Afterthought Is Now Upon Me." [Interim] (7:1) Spr 88, p. 43-44.

1018. COOK, Jane W.
"Minnie Pierson." [CapeR] (23:1) Spr 88, p. 6.
"Reading the Rings." [CapeR] (23:1) Spr 88, p. 5.
"Secrets of Bouffant." [Footwork] ('88) 88, p. 43.
"Yolk Poking." [CapeR] (23:1) Spr 88, p. 7.

1019. COOK-DARBY, Candice
"Late Mourning." [Confr] (37/38) Spr-Sum 88, p. 93.
"Slaughter." [Confr] (37/38) Spr-Sum 88, p. 94.

1020. COOKE, Robert P.
"Indiana Salmon." [CapeR] (23:2) Fall 88, p. 26.
"North Woods Cabin." [SouthernPR] (28:1) Spr 88, p. 34.
"Thankful." [SouthernPR] (28:2) Fall 88, p. 68.

1021. COOKSHAW, Marlene
"Green Plums." [PraF] (9:4) Wint 88-89, p. 48.
"What the Air Has Washed Under." [Grain] (16:4) Wint 88, p. 45-46.

1022. COOLEY, Peter
"The Choices." [WillowS] (21) Wint 88, p. 87.
"Cities of the Dead." [SouthernR] (24:3) Sum 88, p. 578.
"A Dream of Childhood." [WillowS] (21) Wint 88, p. 86.
"Holy Family: Audubon Zoo, New Orleans." [Poetry] (143, i.e. 153:2) N 88, p. 91.
"Lovemaking of the Dead." [SouthwR] (73:2) Spr 88, p. 274.
"Madrigal." [MissouriR] (11:1) 88, p. 154.
"Mother and Child." [Atlantic] (261:2) F 88, p. 62-63.

"The Soul." [Poetry] (143, i.e. 153:2) N 88, p. 92.
"To a Child Facing Out to Sea." [SouthernR] (24:3) Sum 88, p. 579.

1023. COOLIDGE, Clark
"At Egypt" (Selection: Section III). [Sulfur] (7:3, #21) Wint 88, p. 144-151.
"Credo." [Epoch] (37:3) 88, p. 147.
"Literal Landscapes" (Selections: 7 poems). [NewAW] (4) Fall 88, p. 1-7.
"Monk, a Head." [Caliban] (4) 88, p. 42-43.
"Prepare for the Tongue to Be Fraught." [Epoch] (37:3) 88, p. 146.
"Scatters Where the Avenue Mocks the Street." [Sequoia] (31:2) Wint 88, p. 58.
"Stardust." [Epoch] (37:3) 88, p. 148.
"Viable Withheld." [Epoch] (37:3) 88, p. 145.

1024. COONEY, Ellen
"John the Raker Cleaning London Streets in a Year of Great Stink 1357." [Turnstile] (1:2) 88, p. 59.

1025. COOPER, Charles
"The Prodigal Son." [CapeR] (23:2) Fall 88, p. 12.

1026. COOPER, Darius
"Beyond the Chameleon's Skill." [MassR] (29:4) Wint 88-89, p. 671-672.

1027. COOPER, David
"Rescue Party." [HarvardA] (122:4) My 88, p. 23.

1028. COOPER, M. Truman (Marsha Truman)
"Catching Your Death." [HawaiiR] (12:2, #24) Fall 88, p. 78-79.
"The Elements of Communion." [SoDakR] (26:3) Aut 88, p. 137.
"A Faith in Trees." [SoDakR] (26:3) Aut 88, p. 136.
"Lovesong for an Old Shadow." [WebR] (13:2) Fall 88, p. 83.
"A Nickel's Worth." [WestB] (21/22) 88, p. 50.
"Quality Control." [PoetryNW] (29:2) Sum 88, p. 31-32.
"Raw Materials." [WestB] (21/22) 88, p. 51.
"The Reappearance of Jessie." [WebR] (13:2) Fall 88, p. 84.
"Slipping Away." [KanQ] (20:1/2) Wint-Spr 88, p. 211.
"Solemn Vows." [SoDakR] (26:3) Aut 88, p. 134-135.
"True North." [Blueline] (9:1/2) 88, p. 65.

1029. COOPER, Wyn
"All or Nothing." [CimR] (83) Ap 88, p. 15-16.
"From the Outback." [QW] (27) Sum-Fall 88, p. 123-124.
"Truth: A Way to End." [QW] (27) Sum-Fall 88, p. 125.

1030. COOPER-FRATRIK, Julie
"While Reading Neruda, I Think of Some Things." [Footwork] ('88) 88, p. 65.

1031. COOPERMAN, Robert
"Anna Isabella Millbank, Estranged Wife of George Gordon, Lord Byron." [Event] (17:2) Sum 88, p. 54-55.
"At Such Times." [LitR] (31:2) Wint 88, p. 162-163.
"Benjamin Franklin at Versailles." [CapeR] (23:1) Spr 88, p. 36-37.
"A Bitter Ending." [MemphisSR] (8:2) Spr 88, p. 45.
"Charity Sinclair, Daughter of Homesteaders, Colorado Territory." [PikeF] (9) Fall 88, p. 29.
"The Divine Comdy." [KanQ] (20:1/2) Wint-Spr 88, p. 190.
"Extravagant Endings." [StoneC] (16:1/2) Fall-Wint 88-89, p. 37.
"George Eliot Remembers Attending a Concert with G. H. Lewes." [CreamCR] (12:1) Wint 88, p. 92-93.
"The Guinness Book of Records." [WebR] (13:2) Fall 88, p. 67-68.
"Handiwork" (To Dave Cather). [DeKalbLAJ] (21:2) Spr 88, p. 35-36.
"In England, Sophia Starling Hears of the Death of John Sprockett." [HolCrit] (25:4) O 88, p. 18.
"Isabella Bird Rides in a Round-Up, Colorado Territory, 1873." [WebR] (13:2) Fall 88, p. 68-69.
"Language Lesson." [SlipS] (8) 88, p. 75.
"The Lower East Side, 1903." [AmerPoR] (17:2) Mr-Ap 88, p. 46.
"Making the Rounds." [CapeR] (23:2) Fall 88, p. 32.
"Painting Jesus Black." [PennR] (4:1) 88, p. 31.
"A Question of Origin." [Pembroke] (20) 88, p. 237-238.
"Remembering." [PassN] (9:1) Wint 88, p. 21.
"Self-Inflicted Wounds." [Footwork] ('88) 88, p. 28.
"Snow." [SwampR] (1:2/3) D 88, p. 32.
"The Sorrows of the Emperor Diocletian." [ColEng] (50:7) N 88, p. 755.
"Tempting Fate." [Footwork] ('88) 88, p. 28.

"Thomas Alva Edison's Last Words." [ColEng] (50:7) N 88, p. 756.
"Twister." [ChamLR] (1) Fall 87, p. 390-391.
"Under the Dome at St. Paul's." [Crosscur] (7:4) 88, p. 132.
"A Videotaping." [KanQ] (20:1/2) Wint-Spr 88, p. 189.
"Views of the General, His Chief Aide-de-Camp." [Lactuca] (11) O 88, p. 9-10.
"Watching Out for the Neighbors." [HiramPoR] (44/45) Spr-Wint 88, p. 10.
"What They Don't Know." [AmerPoR] (17:2) Mr-Ap 88, p. 46.
"Whittling." [HampSPR] Wint 88, p. 6-7.
"The Widow's Guest." [AmerPoR] (17:2) Mr-Ap 88, p. 46.
"A Wounded Woman in a Recent Paris Bombing." [CapeR] (23:1) Spr 88, p. 35.
"Your Only Escape." [Grain] (16:3) Fall 88, p. 48.

1032. COOVER, Robert
"The Asian Lectures" (In anticipation of the question: "Why do you write?"). [Conjunc] (12) 88, p. 87-88.

1033. COPE, David
"At the Summit." [Lactuca] (9) F 88, p. 3.
"Hospital Windows." [Lactuca] (9) F 88, p. 4.
"Planting." [Lactuca] (9) F 88, p. 2.
"September." [Lactuca] (9) F 88, p. 2.
"Sky Spread Out with Stars." [Lactuca] (9) F 88, p. 1.
"Two Boys." [Lactuca] (9) F 88, p. 2.

1034. COPE, Steven R.
"Bells on the Mountain." [InterPR] (14:1) Spr 88, p. 84.
"The Country in Which All Others Are But States of Mind." [Poem] (60) N 88, p. 53.
"The Fall of '86." [InterPR] (14:1) Spr 88, p. 81-83.
"Freud." [LitR] (32:1) Fall 88, p. 106-107.
"The Great Oak." [Poem] (60) N 88, p. 55.
"Man Song" (played on sticks). [Poem] (60) N 88, p. 54.

1035. COPE, Wendy
"Chaucerian Roundel." [Antaeus] (60) Spr 88, p. 212.
"English Weather." [LightY] ('88/9) 88, p. 165-166.
"The New Régime." [Antaeus] (60) Spr 88, p. 213.

1036. COPELAND, Helen M.
"The Year of the Elk." [Pembroke] (20) 88, p. 238.

1037. COPLAND, Jean
"Malibu Beach Notes." [ChatR] (8:3) Spr 88, p. 58.

1038. CORBETT, Michael
"Faith." [Spirit] (9:1) 88, p. 59.
"Independence Day-nemora." [Spirit] (9:1) 88, p. 57-58.
"Labor Day." [LitR] (31:2) Wint 88, p. 213.

1039. CORBETT, William
"My Father-in-Law's Coat." [Agni] (27) 88, p. 192-193.

1040. CORBIERE, Tristan
"Do, l'Enfant Do." [CumbPR] (7:2) Spr 88, p. 12.
"Little Corpse Good for a Laugh" (tr. by Peter Dale). [CumbPR] (7:2) Spr 88, p. 11.
"Petit Mort pour Rire." [CumbPR] (7:2) Spr 88, p. 10.
"Rock-a-Bye Baby" (tr. by Peter Dale). [CumbPR] (7:2) Spr 88, p. 13.

1041. CORBUS, Patricia
"Coda: The Fourteenth Waltz." [GreensboroR] (44) Sum 88, p. 41.
"Gladys Among the Azaleas." [GreensboroR] (44) Sum 88, p. 42.

1042. CORDING, Robert
"Assisi." [AmerS] (57:1) Wint 88, p. 90.
"Fazenda: Darwin in Rio de Janeiro." [SewanR] (96:2) Spr 88, p. 205.
"Feeding the Birds." [Poetry] (152:6) S 88, p. 325-326.
"For an Anniversary." [Crazy] (34) Spr 88, p. 43-44.
"The Gravity of Anonymity." [Poetry] (151:6) Mr 88, p. 464-465.
"Insomnia." [SouthwR] (73:3) Sum 88, p. 374-375.
"The Naming." [SewanR] (96:2) Spr 88, p. 206-207.
"Noli Me Tangere: San Marco, Florence." [TarRP] (27:2) Spr 88, p. 15.
"Rounds." [SewanR] (96:2) Spr 88, p. 207-208.
"Ruffed Grouse." [Poetry] (152:6) S 88, p. 327-328.
"The Story of Oisin." [QW] (26) Wint 88, p. 102-103.

1043. COREY, Chet
"A Cafe Story." [SpoonRQ] (12:4) Fall 87, p. 18.
"Hunger." [SpoonRQ] (12:4) Fall 87, p. 17.
"Loss." [SpoonRQ] (12:4) Fall 87, p. 17.

1044. COREY, Stephen
"Attacking the *Pietà*." [KenR] (NS 10:4) Fall 88, p. 22-30.
"Blank Page." [AntR] (46:3) Sum 88, p. 348.
"Complicated Shadows." [Poetry] (151:5) F 88, p. 391.
"Failure to Be Priests: a Modern Harvest." [TarRP] (28:1) Fall 88, p. 40.
"Instant Stories." [TarRP] (28:1) Fall 88, p. 41.
"Inventing the Black Bees of Love." [YellowS] (27) Aut 88, p. 8.
"Not for Clennie (1901-)." [TarRP] (28:1) Fall 88, p. 42.
"Purity." [NoAmR] (273:3) S 88, p. 53.
"Taking the Light Whitely." [Ploughs] (14:1) 88, p. 135-136.
1045. CORISH, Denis
"Seeing." [NewYorker] (64:24) 1 Ag 88, p. 36.
1046. CORLEY, Elisabeth Lewis
"Making Money." [CarolQ] (40:2) Wint 88, p. 7.
1047. CORMAN, Cid
"Zeitgehöft" (7 poems from "Timesteaded," tr. of Paul Celan, w. Günther Nitschke). [Acts] (8/9) 88, p. 123-129.
"Zeitgehöft" (8 poems from "Timesteaded," tr. of Paul Celan, w. Günther Nitschke). [Acts] (8/9) 88, p. 218-221.
CORMIER-SHEKERJIAN, Regina de
See DeCORMIER-SHEKERJIAN, Regina
1048. CORN, Alfred
"Assistances" (for David Kalstone). [NewRep] (198:3) 18 Ja 88, p. 32.
CORNIS, Marcel Pop
See POP-CORNIS, Marcel
CORRAIN, Donncha O
See O CORRAIN, Donncha
1049. CORRIE, Daniel
"The Dancing Bear." [VirQR] (64:1) Wint 88, p. 81-82.
"Golden Touch." [Pembroke] (20) 88, p. 196.
"Ground." [SouthernPR] (28:2) Fall 88, p. 44-49.
"The Years." [Nat] (246:25) 25 Je 88, p. 904.
1050. CORRINGTON, John William
"Translations" (Pan Am Flight 759, New Orleans, 9 July 1982). [SouthernR] (24:1) Wint 88, p. 150-152.
1051. CORTES, Carlos
"Do Veces Alicia." [Mairena] (10:25) 88, p. 145.
1052. CORTEZ, Jayne
"For the Poets" (Christopher Okigbo and Henry Dumas). [BlackALF] (22:2) Sum 88, p. 200-201.
1053. CORY, Cynthia Jay
"On Pierre Cecile Puvis de Chavannes (1824-1898)" (Untitled: Twilight). [Shen] (38:1) 88, p. 52.
"The Wait." [PassN] (9:1) Wint 88, p. 4.
1054. COSENS, Susan M.
"Juncos at Feeder." [RagMag] (6:2) Fall 88, p. 16.
1055. COSIER, Tony
"Jock River at Cedarview: The Ghost Poem." [Farm] (5:2) Fall 88, p. 68-69.
"Swamp." [Blueline] (9:1/2) 88, p. 66.
1056. COSTANZA, Natalie J.
"Ryder Beach" (Wellfleet, Massachusetts). [ChamLR] (1) Fall 87, p. 393-394.
1057. COSTANZO, Gerald
"Carl Yastrzemski" (Harwich, Massachusetts 1981). [WillowS] (22) Spr 88, p. 74-75.
"Fatty Arbuckle." [WillowS] (22) Spr 88, p. 76-77.
"In the Blood." [LightY] ('88/9) 88, p. 112.
"The Rise of the Sunday School Movement." [NoAmR] (273:1) Mr 88, p. 14.
"Seeing My Name in *TV Guide*." [LightY] ('88/9) 88, p. 193.
1058. COSTLEY, Bill
"Hammered Silver" (Sonnets, the K series written to Kate White, 7 selections). [SmPd] (25:1) Wint 88, p. 32-35.
"Terrazzo" (Selections: T.7, T.11, T.14). [SmPd] (25:1) Wint 88, p. 30-31.
"Yuppies (West-Suburban-Boston Sonnets)" (Selections: Y.IV, Y.VI). [SmPd] (25:1) Wint 88, p. 29.
1059. COULEHAN, Jack
"Bursting with Danger and Music." [KanQ] (20:3) Sum 88, p. 66.

"The Empress of Ireland." [BellR] (11:1) Spr 88, p. 22-23.
"Harbor Seals." [CinPR] (18) Fall 88, p. 31.
"The Knitted Glove." [ManhatPR] (10) Ja 88, p. 49.
"Labrador." [ManhatPR] (10) Ja 88, p. 48.

COURCY, Lynne H. de
See DeCOURCY, Lynne H.

1060. COURSEN, H. R.
"30 November, 1987." [SmPd] (25:3) Fall 88, p. 37.

1061. COURT, Wesli
"The Cave Painters." [KanQ] (20:3) Sum 88, p. 64.
"Sirvente of the Linden Tree." [LightY] ('88/9) 88, p. 139-140.

1062. COUTEAU, Bob
"Beethoveniana Edda Marie." [Footwork] ('88) 88, p. "67, 69.
"Edda in Argentina." [Footwork] ('88) 88, p. 67.

1063. COVEY, Patricia
"Trajectory." [Sonora] (14/15) Spr 88, p. 8-9.

1064. COVINO, Michael
"In the Poor Part of Town." [ParisR] (30:107) Sum 88, p. 41-43.

1065. COWING, Sue
"Frau Becker Remembers the Last Day with Paula, November, 1907." [ChamLR] (1:2, #2) Spr 88, p. 136-137.
"Homestead" (After a photograph by Wright Morris). [ChamLR] (1:2, #2) Spr 88, p. 135.
"*Saturday Review* Interviews a Clarinet and a Flute." [ChamLR] (1:2, #2) Spr 88, p. 138-140.

1066. COX, Larry
"Charlie Pavik's Gone." [CreamCR] (12:1) Wint 88, p. 75.
"Forty-One." [Plain] (8:1) Fall 87, p. 13.
"Fringe Area." [CreamCR] (12:1) Wint 88, p. 74.
"Lesser Game." [CapeR] (23:1) Spr 88, p. 19.
"Vessels." [CreamCR] (12:1) Wint 88, p. 73.

1067. COX, Mark
"Divorce." [PoetryNW] (29:2) Sum 88, p. 10-11.
"Donald." [WillowS] (22) Spr 88, p. 26-28.
"Putting On My Coat." [PoetryNW] (29:2) Sum 88, p. 9-10.
"Simile at the Side of the Road." [Poetry] (152:2) My 88, p. 79-80.

1068. COX, Nancy
"Expatriate." [KanQ] (20:3) Sum 88, p. 81.

1069. COX, Rosemary D.
"Pantoum: For Billy" (To Floyd Watkins). [ChatR] (8:3) Spr 88, p. 35.

CRABBE, Chris Wallace
See WALLACE-CRABBE, Chris

1070. CRAIG, Ford M.
"On Planting a Pear Tree Near the Property Line." [Plain] (8:2) Wint 88, p. 15.

1071. CRAIG, Peter
"The Statesman." [Bogg] (59) 88, p. 36.

1072. CRAINER, Stuart
"Darkly She Feared." [Stand] (29:1) Wint 87-88, p. 62.
"Talking with the Dead." [Stand] (29:1) Wint 87-88, p. 63.

1073. CRAM, David
"Boomerang." [LightY] ('88/9) 88, p. 57.
"Cricket Match." [LightY] ('88/9) 88, p. 166.
"An Urban Lad." [LightY] ('88/9) 88, p. 227.

1074. CRAMER, Steven
"The Hospitals." [Poetry] (152:5) Ag 88, p. 261.

1075. CRAWFORD, Lynn
"Bordercrossing: Emissary from a Nightmare, Speaking to Me in a Dream." [SinW] (32) Sum 87, p. 13-15.
"Just That Would Be Enough." [SinW] (32) Sum 87, p. 109-110.

1076. CRAWFORD, Tom
"Letter from a Psychic." [PoetryE] (25) Spr 88, p. 59.
"Song of the Carpenter" (For Brother Mark). [PoetryE] (25) Spr 88, p. 60-61.
"Untitled: The frustrated boy." [PoetryE] (25) Spr 88, p. 57-58.

1077. CREELEY, Robert
"Echoes." [CutB] (31/32) 88, p. 82.
"Talking of Age." [NewAW] (3) Spr 88, p. 20-22.

"You." [Bound] (15:3/16:1) Spr-Fall 88, p. 97-98.

1078. CRENNER, James
"The Dance in the School Gym." [AntR] (46:1) Wint 88, p. 79.
"Others." [NoAmR] (273:1) Mr 88, p. 35.

1079. CRESPO, Luis Alberto
"Las Cinco." [Mairena] (10:25) 88, p. 61.

1080. CREWS, Judson
"My Saddest Commentary on the Human." [WritersF] (14) Fall 88, p. 71.
"A Pen of Wet Fibers, Almost a Brush." [WritersF] (14) Fall 88, p. 71-72.

1081. CROCKETT, Andy (Andrew P.)
"Feet." [Jacaranda] (3:1) Wint 88, p. 72.
"Going Home." [DenQ] (22:3) Wint 88, p. 66-67.

1082. CROOKER, Barbara
"The Autistic Boy." [Footwork] ('88) 88, p. 27.
"Autumn Sonata." [JlNJPo] (10:1/2) 88, p. 14.
"Celestial Navigation." [Footwork] ('88) 88, p. 27.
"Dieting." [StoneC] (15:3/4) Spr-Sum 88, p. 16.
"Dieting" (The Phillips Award — Spring/Summer, 1988). [StoneC] (16:1/2) Fall-Wint 88-89, p. 2.
"Gardening in a Dry Year." [PaintedB] (36) 88, p. 7.
"January." [PaintedB] (36) 88, p. 6.
"Modern Photography." [Footwork] ('88) 88, p. 27.
"Obbligato." [NegC] (8:3) 88, p. 108-109.
"On the Last Morning." [JlNJPo] (10:1/2) 88, p. 13.
"Ordinary Life." [PassN] (9:1) Wint 88, p. 17.
"Tenth Anniversary." [WestB] (21/22) 88, p. 142-143.

1083. CROSSLEY-HOLLAND, Kevin
"Here, at the Tide's Turning." [Antaeus] (60) Spr 88, p. 234-235.

1084. CROW, Mary
"Blind Date." [Abraxas] (37) 88, p. 34-35.
"Country Road" (tr. of Jorge Teillier). [BlackWR] (15:1) Fall 88, p. 95.
"The Initiative of My Shadow" (tr. of Roberto Juarroz). [MidAR] (8:1) 88, p. 44.
"The Key" (tr. of Jorge Teillier). [BlackWR] (15:1) Fall 88, p. 93.
"Love Poem." [Abraxas] (37) 88, p. 33.
"A Man Who Lives Alone in Athens." [Abraxas] (37) 88, p. 35.
"Moving On." [GrahamHR] (11) Spr 88, p. 82-83.
"A Net of Looking" (tr. of Roberto Juarroz). [MidAR] (8:1) 88, p. 45.

1085. CROW, Steve
"Distant Fishing." [Caliban] (5) 88, p. 76.
"Post-Traumatic Stress Disorder." [ColR] (NS 15:1) Spr-Sum 88, p. 85.
"Untitled: I want to walk." [Caliban] (5) 88, p. 77.

1086. CROZIER, Lorna
"Childhood Landscapes." [Descant] (19:2, #61) Sum 88, p. 28.
"The Oldest Song." [CrossC] (10:3) 88, p. 5.
"Red Sweater." [Event] (17:3) Fall 88, p. 34-35.
"Remembering You." [Descant] (19:2, #61) Sum 88, p. 29.
"Sometimes Flying." [Event] (17:3) Fall 88, p. 32-33.
"Turning into Flesh." [Descant] (19:2, #61) Sum 88, p. 27.
"Ways of Leaving." [Event] (17:3) Fall 88, p. 36.
"A Woman's Shoe." [CanLit] (119) Wint 88, p. 54-55.

1087. CRUNK, T.
"For Sallie Youngs." [PoetryNW] (29:3) Aut 88, p. 11.

1088. CRUSOE, Edwin, IV
"Blue Norther." [KeyWR] (1:1) Spr 88, p. 69.
"With Apologies to T. S. Eliot." [KeyWR] (1:1) Spr 88, p. 67-68.

1089. CRUSZ, Rienzi
"Resolve to Be Always Beginning — To Be a Beginner: Rilke." [CanLit] (117) Sum 88, p. 79.

1090. CRUZKATZ, Ida
"Calling to My Husband from the Lawn." [ManhatPR] (10) Ja 88, p. 47.

1091. CSAMER, Mary Ellen
"Night Sounds." [Event] (17:3) Fall 88, p. 81.
"One O'Clock on the Ward." [Event] (17:3) Fall 88, p. 80.

1092. CUCULLU, Lois
"Letter to My Husband in Vietnam, 1972." [ColR] (NS 15:1) Spr-Sum 88, p. 45.

1093. CUDDIHY, Michael
"The Pendulum." [VirQR] (64:3) Sum 88, p. 436.
1094. CUDDY, Dan
"Requiem." [Vis] (28) 88, p. 16.
1095. CULLY, Barbara
"Desert Avenue." [Sonora] (14/15) Spr 88, p. 2-4.
"In Memory." [Sonora] (14/15) Spr 88, p. 5-6.
"Speedway." [Sonora] (14/15) Spr 88, p. 1.
"Where One Sings a Wild Song." [AmerPoR] (17:4) Jl-Ag 88, p. 37.
"World Without End." [Sonora] (14/15) Spr 88, p. 7.
1096. CULVER, Ralph
"Lyric." [DenQ] (22:3) Wint 88, p. 231.
1097. CUMBERLAND, Sharon
"Ars Poetica." [Iowa] (18:3) 88, p. 126-128.
"On the Darien Train." [Contact] (9:47/48/49) Spr 88, p. 58.
"The Speechwriter Speaks His Peace." [Contact] (9:47/48/49) Spr 88, p. 59.
"The Speechwriter Takes Action." [Contact] (9:47/48/49) Spr 88, p. 59.
"Unreasonable Woman." [Iowa] (18:3) 88, p. 128.
1098. CUMMING, Patricia
"Martin Luther King's Funeral on Television." [RedBass] (13) 88, p. 20.
1099. CUMMINS, Jim
"The Novelist Manque." [CinPR] (17) Spr 88, p. 55.
1100. CUMPIANO, Ida
"Downfall." [PassN] (9:2) Sum 88, p. 23.
1101. CUNNINGHAM, Michael
"Doll in the Lime Street Cutting." [Verse] (5:3) N 88, p. 63-64.
CURIEL, Barbara Brinson
See BRINSON-CURIEL, Barbara
1102. CURNOW, Allen
"The Vespiary: A Fable." [PartR] (55:4) Fall 88, p. 619-620.
1103. CURRY, Duncan C.
"Loaded." [Bogg] (59) 88, p. 40.
"Ties." [Bogg] (59) 88, p. 12.
1104. CURTIS, David F.
"Galilean Sonnets." [FourQ] (2d series 2:1) Spr 88, p. 62.
"Parasite." [FourQ] (2d series 2:1) Spr 88, p. 61.
1105. CURTIS, Jack
"Cahuama" (La Cachora). [StoneC] (15:3/4) Spr-Sum 88, p. 6.
1106. CURTIS, Tony
"Games with My Daughter." [Confr] (37/38) Spr-Sum 88, p. 224.
"Thoughts from the Holiday Inn" (For John Tripp). [NewEngR] (10:4) Sum 88, p. 447-453.
"Villanelle for a Photographer" (O. Winston Link: Hot Shot East at Iaeger, West Virginia, August 1956). [Verse] (5:3) N 88, p. 58.
1107. CURZON, David
"A Marriage." [NewRep] (198:16) 18 Ap 88, p. 38.
"A Marriage." [Shen] (38:2) 88, p. 17.
1108. CUSAC, Anne-Marie
"The Knitting Lesson." [AmerS] (57:2) Spr 88, p. 218.
1109. CUSHING, James
"You Go to My Head." [Plain] (9:1) Fall 88, p. 18.
1110. CUSHMAN, Stephen
"Bellydancer." [GreensboroR] (44) Sum 88, p. 87.
"Blood and Snow." [Timbuktu] (2) Sum-Fall 88, p. 39.
"Therapy." [Timbuktu] (2) Sum-Fall 88, p. 38.
1111. CUTLER, Bruce
"Defensive Driving." [PoetryNW] (29:3) Aut 88, p. 30-31.
"Grandfather's Tale" (From: *The Book of Naples*). [BelPoJ] (39:1) Fall 88, p. 18-22.
"Prognosis." [Poetry] (153:3) D 88, p. 156.
"Sand Creek!" (The Attack, November 29, 1984). [KanQ] (20:4) Fall 88, p. 116-124.
"Time Now for Some Inertia." [PoetryNW] (29:3) Aut 88, p. 31.
"Wisteria." [Shen] (38:4) 88, p. 46.
1112. CUZA MALÉ, Belkis
"Anne Sexton." [Inti] (26/27) Otoño 87-Primavera 88, p. 67-68.
"Biografía del Poeta." [Inti] (26/27) Otoño 87-Primavera 88, p. 72.
"Las Cenicientas." [Inti] (26/27) Otoño 87-Primavera 88, p. 72-73.

"De la Naturaleza de la Vida." [Inti] (26/27) Otoño 87-Primavera 88, p. 68-69.
"Desayuno en el Club Universitario." [LindLM] (7:2/4) Ap-D 88, p. 8.
"Homenaje a Jose Cid" (Pintor español muerto en Cuba el 21 de diciembre de 1979). [LindLM] (7:2/4) Ap-D 88, p. 8.
"Oh, Mi Rimbaud." [Inti] (26/27) Otoño 87-Primavera 88, p. 71-72.
"La Patria de Mi Madre." [Inti] (26/27) Otoño 87-Primavera 88, p. 69.
"Poética." [Inti] (26/27) Otoño 87-Primavera 88, p. 70.
"El Tiempo." [Inti] (26/27) Otoño 87-Primavera 88, p. 69.
"Yo Virginia Woolf Desbocada en la Muerte." [Inti] (26/27) Otoño 87-Primavera 88, p. 70-71.

1113. CUZMA, Greg
"Ball Practice" (A Plainsongs Award Poem). [Plain] (9:1) Fall 88, p. 4.

1114. CZAPLA, Cathy
"My Heart Is a Forest." [SinW] (33) Fall 87, p. 84.

1115. CZYZ, Vince
"Washington Square Park." [Footwork] ('88) 88, p. 70.

1116. DACEY, Florence
"Pieces of God." [Vis] (28) 88, p. 37.

1117. DACEY, Philip
"The Movie: A Book of Poems" (Excerpt). [Jacaranda] (3:1) Wint 88, p. 29.
"Renoir & Co." [Jacaranda] (3:1) Wint 88, p. 28-29.
"Thomas Eakins: The Secret Whitman Sitting." [Hudson] (41:3) Aut 88, p. 489-492.
"Thoreau's Last Words." [TarRP] (28:1) Fall 88, p. 38-39.
"Translated from the." [PoetryNW] (29:2) Sum 88, p. 21.
"Windfall Windhovers." [TarRP] (28:1) Fall 88, p. 39.

1118. DACHEVA, Svezha
"The Flesh of Air" (tr. by Atanas Slavov). [Vis] (26) 88, p. 18, 20.

DAFYDD AP GWILYM
See GWILYM, Dafydd ap

1119. DaGAMA, Steven
"The Island." [YellowS] (27) Aut 88, p. 4.
"Magic." [YellowS] (27) Aut 88, p. 4.
"Modern Poet." [YellowS] (28) D 88, p. 5.
"Prayer." [YellowS] (27) Aut 88, p. 4.
"Sunday Morning." [YellowS] (26) Spr 88, p. 22.

1120. DAHL, Chris
"At the Depleted Mine." [BellR] (11:1) Spr 88, p. 27.

1121. DAHL, David
"Saigon Split." [Abraxas] (37) 88, p. 55.

1122. DAHLEN, Beverly
"The Givens" (Excerpts). [Sonora] (16) Fall 88, p. 66-68.

1123. DAHM, Kathy Hohn
"Driving Through the Bottoms." [CapeR] (23:1) Spr 88, p. 25.

DAI, Fang
See FANG, Dai

1124. DAIGON, Ruth
"Artifact." [Blueline] (9:1/2) 88, p. 50.
"Refuge." [SouthernPR] (28:1) Spr 88, p. 35.
"Winter." [Blueline] (9:1/2) 88, p. 50.

1125. DAIVE, Jean
"Décimale Blanche" (1 poem, tr. into German by Paul Celan, into English by Joel Golb). [Acts] (8/9) 88, p. 54.
"Décimale Blanche" (2 poems, tr. into German by Paul Celan, into English by Joachim Neugroschel). [Acts] (8/9) 88, p. 50-53.
"Décimale Blanche" (4 poems, tr. into German by Paul Celan, into English by Joachim Neugroschel). [Acts] (8/9) 88, p. 32-39.

1126. DALDORPH, Brian
"Muse." [Bogg] (60) 88, p. 30.

1127. DALE, Jo Anna
"Cleaning the Gutters." [KanQ] (20:3) Sum 88, p. 199.

1128. DALE, Peter
"Little Corpse Good for a Laugh" (tr. of Tristan Corbiere). [CumbPR] (7:2) Spr 88, p. 11.
"Rock-a-Bye Baby" (tr. of Tristan Corbiere). [CumbPR] (7:2) Spr 88, p. 13.

1129. DALEY, Michael
"Yes & No" (Commended, 15th Anniversary Competition). [StoneC] (16:1/2) Fall-Wint 88-89, unpaged front matter.
1130. DALTON, Gaylia
"Inside the Lines." [KeyWR] (1:1) Spr 88, p. 35-36.
"Nursing Home on Sunday." [KeyWR] (1:1) Spr 88, p. 37.
"Picture of a Wedding." [KeyWR] (1:1) Spr 88, p. 34.
1131. DALTON, Roque
"Alta Hora de la Noche." [Rohwedder] (3) Spr 88, p. 10-11.
"Alta Hora de la Noche" (English tr. by James Graham). [Bomb] (24) Sum 88, p. 67.
"Como Tu." [Mairena] (10:25) 88, p. 154.
"El Gran Despecho" (The Great Despair, English tr. by James Graham). [Bomb] (24) Sum 88, p. 67.
"The Late Hour of the Night" (tr. by Ruben Martinez). [Rohwedder] (3) Spr 88, p. 10-11.
"El Mar" (for Tati, Meri, Margarita, with whom I rode a wave, English tr. by James Graham). [Bomb] (24) Sum 88, p. 66-67.
1132. DALY, Daniel
"Day 39." [Plain] (8:3) Spr-Sum 88, p. 38.
"The Pillowed Mouse." [LaurelR] (22:2) Sum 88, p. 10.
"Transported." [Plain] (9:1) Fall 88, p. 32.
1133. DALY, Patrick
"Singing." [FiveFR] (6) 88, p. 31.
1134. DAME, Enid
"Brighton Beach." [Confr] (Special issue: The World of Brooklyn) 88, p. 41-42.
"Interim Report." [NegC] (8:3) 88, p. 70-71.
"Untenanted" (Third Place, 1987 Eve of Saint Agnes Poetry Competition). [NegC] (8:3) 88, p. 27-28.
1135. DANAHY, Michael P.
"Brooklyn, 1960." [Contact] (9:47/48/49) Spr 88, p. 42.
"Touch." [Contact] (9:47/48/49) Spr 88, p. 42.
1136. DANIEL, Hal J., III
"Academic Poem." [ChatR] (8:2) Wint 88, p. 22-23.
"Diastema." [HiramPoR] (44/45) Spr-Wint 88, p. 11.
"Light Bulbs and Bananas." [LightY] ('88/9) 88, p. 117.
"Paternity." [Pembroke] (20) 88, p. 222-223.
1137. DANIEL, John
"Beginnings." [SouthernR] (24:1) Wint 88, p. 162.
"December in the Oregon Desert." [SouthernR] (24:1) Wint 88, p. 163.
"The Meal." [Poetry] (143, i.e. 153:2) N 88, p. 94.
"Of Earth" (for Wallace Stegner). [NoAmR] (273:3) S 88, p. 47.
"To the Scrub Jay on My Office Mate's Desk." [Poetry] (143, i.e. 153:2) N 88, p. 95.
1138. DANIELS, Jim
"Avalanche." [LaurelR] (22:21) Wint 88, p. 34.
"The Bookkeepers Talk Baseball." [LightY] ('88/9) 88, p. 56.
"Bush's Story." [CutB] (31/32) 88, p. 83.
"Detroit Hymns, Christmas Eve." [LightY] ('88/9) 88, p. 153-154.
"Digger's Territory." [Gargoyle] (35) 88, p. 190.
"Factory Stud." [NewL] (55:1) Fall 88, p. 80.
"Hard Rock." [WestB] (21/22) 88, p. 108-109.
"Polish-American Night, Tiger Stadium." [CentR] (32:2) Spr 88, p. 150-151.
"Still Lives in Detroit #6: Benitau St." [MichQR] (27:2) Spr 88, p. 284.
"Sweeping Stoned." [NewEngR] (11:2) Wint 88, p. 209.
1139. DANIELS, Kate
"Bus Ride." [MassR] (29:2) Sum 88, p. 262.
"The Niobe Poems" (Selections: 8 poems). [NewEngR] (10:3) Spr 88, p. 328-336.
"War Photography." [MassR] (29:2) Sum 88, p. 263.
1140. DANIELSEN, Al
"3AM Reststop." [KanQ] (20:3) Sum 88, p. 119.
"LA Bus Driver." [KanQ] (20:3) Sum 88, p. 118.
"Night Journey." [KanQ] (20:3) Sum 88, p. 118.
1141. DANON, Ruth
"Nightwatch" (for David Spry). [GettyR] (1:4) Aut 88, p. 646.
"Sex and Death on Sullivan Street." [BostonR] (13:1) F 88, p. 29.
1142. DANTE
"Paradiso, First Canto" (Lines 100-143 in Italian). [AntigR] (73) Spr 88, p. 96, 98.

"Paradiso, First Canto, in Scots" (Lines 100-143, tr. by William S. Milne). [AntigR] (73) Spr 88, p. 97, 99.

1143. D'ANTIN, Carolina
"Aquella Fecha, un Día." [LetFem] (14:1/2) Primavera-Otoño 88, p. 118-119.
"Grito Gris." [LetFem] (14:1/2) Primavera-Otoño 88, p. 117-118.
"El Niño Mudo." [LetFem] (14:1/2) Primavera-Otoño 88, p. 119.

DAO, Bei
See BEI, Dao

DARBY, Candice Cook
See COOK-DARBY, Candice

1144. DARGAN, Joan
"Tree." [Blueline] (9:1/2) 88, p. 99.

1145. DARLING, Charles
"Arturo and Stella." [CumbPR] (7:2) Spr 88, p. 15.
"Astronomy Lesson." [GreensboroR] (44) Sum 88, p. 107.
"Bees at the Class Reunion" (August, 1987, Charlemont, Massachusetts). [DeKalbLAJ] (21:3/4) 88, p. 50.
"Drowning at Age Twelve." [DeKalbLAJ] (21:3/4) 88, p. 51.
"Frost in the Outlying Areas." [CumbPR] (7:2) Spr 88, p. 14.
"July 11, 1864." [TexasR] (9:3/4) Fall-Wint 88, p. 30.
"Saturday Morning with Mrs. Wash." [GreensboroR] (44) Sum 88, p. 108.
"Trifles." [NoDaQ] (56:1) Wint 88, p. 150-151.

1146. DARLINGTON, Andrew
"A Brief Aromatic Poem (This Poem Stinks)." [SlipS] (8) 88, p. 48.

1147. DARNELL, Marc
"Unborn Children." [Plain] (8:2) Wint 88, p. 36.
"The Whippoorwill." [Plain] (8:1) Fall 87, p. 24.

1148. DARR, Ann
"At Lunch You Talked About a Shoeshine in Chicago." [Ploughs] (14:1) 88, p. 141.

1149. DARRACOTT, Marion J.
"A Cause for War." [ChatR] (8:3) Spr 88, p. 51.
"Mama Cried." [KanQ] (20:3) Sum 88, p. 176.

1150. DARUWALLA, Keki N.
"Migrations." [Nimrod] (31:2) Spr-Sum 88, p. 50.
"You, Slipping Past." [Nimrod] (31:2) Spr-Sum 88, p. 51.

1151. DARWISH, Mahmud
"Psalm Sixteen" (tr. by Ben Bennani). [CharR] (14:1) Spr 88, p. 37.
"Psalm Thirteen" (tr. by Ben Bennani). [CharR] (14:1) Spr 88, p. 36.

1152. DASGUPTA, Pranabendu
"Carignano Dak Bungalow." [Vis] (28) 88, p. 26.
"Love, Jadavpur, Time." [Vis] (27) 88, p. 23.

1153. DASSANOWSKY-HARRIS, Robert
"Muse" (in German and English, tr. by the author). [Rohwedder] (4) [Wint 88-89], p. 33.
"Pens Bring Down the Berlin Wall" (An Interview, Over Beer, With the Expert). [Vis] (28) 88, p. 22-23.
"Viennese Impressionism" (In memory of my Grandfather, F.v.D., tr. by the author). [Os] (27) 88, p. 18.
"Wertherie" (After Goethe, in German and English, tr. by the author). [Rohwedder] (4) [Wint 88-89], p. 33.
"Wiener Impressionismus" (Meinem Grossvater, F.v.D. zum Gedächtnis). [Os] (27) 88, p. 19.

1154. DATTA, Jyotirmoy
"Second Planet Earth" (tr. of Anuradha Mahapatra, w. Carolyne Wright). [Nimrod] (31:2) Spr-Sum 88, p. 34.
"Spell" (tr. of Anuradha Mahapatra, w. Carolyne Wright). [Nimrod] (31:2) Spr-Sum 88, p. 34.

1155. DAUENHAUER, Richard
"Frame of Reference." [CrabCR] (5:1) Wint 88, p. 17.

1156. DAUENHAUER, William
"Pandemic." [LitR] (31:2) Wint 88, p. 194.

1157. DAUPHIN, Jacques
"Liebesfugue: Lying in Love's Stupor" (After Celan, tr. by Ron Offen). [Vis] (27) 88, p. 43.

1158. DAURIO, Beverly
"Flagellants." [Quarry] (37:1) Wint 88, p. 52-53.

1159. DAVIDSON, Ian
"Night Flight." [GettyR] (1:3) Sum 88, p. 451.
1160. DAVIDSON, Michael
"Beyond the Alps." [NewAW] (3) Spr 88, p. 58-60.
"A Descriptive Method" (tr. of Claude Royet-Journoud). [Temblor] (7) 88, p. 61-71.
"Elsewhere." [NewAW] (3) Spr 88, p. 61-62.
"The Last Word on the Sign." [Conjunc] (12) 88, p. 246.
"Lords Over Fact." [Conjunc] (12) 88, p. 243-245.
"The Second Word." [Conjunc] (12) 88, p. 247.
"Sonnet: One who speaks of the multifariousness of voices." [Conjunc] (12) 88, p. 245.
1161. DAVIDSON, Phebe E.
"Water Bearer." [Amelia] (5:1, #12) 88, p. 36.
1162. DAVIDSON, Phoebe
"To My Mother, Sleeping." [Footwork] ('88) 88, p. 66.
1163. DAVIE, Donald
"After the Match." [CumbPR] (8:1) Fall 88, p. 19.
"The Aspirant" (after Seneca). [CumbPR] (8:1) Fall 88, p. 18.
"Black Hoyden." [CumbPR] (8:1) Fall 88, p. 15.
"Hermes and Mr. Shaw." [CumbPR] (8:1) Fall 88, p. 22-23.
"Homage to George Whitefield (1714-1770)." [CumbPR] (8:1) Fall 88, p. 14.
"On Edmund Spenser's House in Ireland." [CumbPR] (8:1) Fall 88, p. 16.
"Savannah" (for Alex Heard, administrator). [CumbPR] (8:1) Fall 88, p. 11-12.
"They, to Me." [CumbPR] (8:1) Fall 88, p. 13.
"Two Widows in Tashkent." [CumbPR] (8:1) Fall 88, p. 17.
"West Virginia's Auburn." [CumbPR] (8:1) Fall 88, p. 20-21.
1164. DAVIES, Blair
"Two Critics." [KanQ] (20:1/2) Wint-Spr 88, p. 224.
1165. DAVIES, Hilary
"From the Chinese of Cho Chi Yen" (fl. 1150 A.D.). [Verse] (5:3) N 88, p. 67.
"From the Chinese of Li Bai Ying" (fl. 700 A.D.). [Verse] (5:3) N 88, p. 67.
"Winchester Diver." [Verse] (5:3) N 88, p. 66.
1166. DAVIES, John
"The Beach." [NewEngR] (10:4) Sum 88, p. 408-409.
"Country." [SoDakR] (26:2) Sum 88, p. 103.
"Sand People." [SoDakR] (26:2) Sum 88, p. 102.
"Starting Place." [TarRP] (27:2) Spr 88, p. 40.
"Sunday Fishing." [NewEngR] (10:4) Sum 88, p. 409.
"What Doesn't End When the Year Ends." [TarRP] (27:2) Spr 88, p. 41.
1167. DAVIS, B.
"June Heat." [Plain] (8:2) Wint 88, p. 13.
1168. DAVIS, Barbara
"Doldrums." [BellArk] (4:5) S-O 88, p. 10.
1169. DAVIS, Becky
"I Spent the Night in Custer County." [Plain] (8:1) Fall 87, p. 25.
1170. DAVIS, Carol V.
"After My Mother's Death." [BellR] (11:1) Spr 88, p. 53.
"After the First Night." [BellR] (11:1) Spr 88, p. 52.
1171. DAVIS, Christopher
"And the Third Part of the Sea Became Blood." [JamesWR] (5:3) Spr-Sum 88, p. 10.
"The Angels of Earth." [BostonR] (13:6) D 88, p. 15.
"At the Bar (His Soul Talking)." [ConnPR] (7:1) 88, p. 22.
"Can This Fear of the Deaf Rose Keep God Immortal?" [NoAmR] (273:1) Mr 88, p. 20-21.
"Clarence White Escapes His Demon Lover." [BostonR] (13:6) D 88, p. 15.
"Clarence White Exposed by High Noon." [Sonora] (14/15) Spr 88, p. 14-15.
"Clarence White Seduced by an Icecube." [Sonora] (14/15) Spr 88, p. 16.
"If We Can't Surrender Greed to Love We'll Murder Earth" (In the Post Office). [JamesWR] (5:3) Spr-Sum 88, p. 10.
"Jack Frost's Question" (for R.S.). [BostonR] (13:6) D 88, p. 15.
"Jojo's." [BostonR] (13:6) D 88, p. 15.
"Look at the Obese Loser Trying Not to Pray" (to my dead brother). [NoAmR] (273:3) S 88, p. 47.
"Lust." [BostonR] (13:6) D 88, p. 15.
"O I Am Very Sick and Sorrowful." [BostonR] (13:6) D 88, p. 15.
"The Only Pasture We Can Graze In." [BostonR] (13:6) D 88, p. 15.

"Patience." [JamesWR] (5:3) Spr-Sum 88, p. 10.
"Riverfront, Coming Down." [ConnPR] (7:1) 88, p. 21.
"Taps." [Crazy] (34) Spr 88, p. 34.
"To Amelia Earhart." [Agni] (26) 88, p. 179.
"(Unfinished Poem about Mary Queen of Scots)." [Crazy] (34) Spr 88, p. 35-36.

1172. DAVIS, DeeAnne
"We Come from Iowa." [SinW] (35) Sum-Fall 88, p. 61-64.

1173. DAVIS, Donna
"The Black Iris." [EngJ] (77:1) Ja 88, p. 103.

1174. DAVIS, Jennifer
"Incident on Alto Road." [DeKalbLAJ] (21:3/4) 88, p. 52.

1175. DAVIS, John
"Possibilities." [Wind] (18:63) 88, p. 20.

1176. DAVIS, Jon
"Essay on Joy Beginning with Mozart's *Sinfonia Concertante in E-Flat Major*." [Poetry] (151:4) Ja 88, p. 359.
"Essay: The Yearbook." [Poetry] (151:6) Mr 88, p. 463.
"Those Dying Generations." [CutB] (29/30) 88, p. 18-21.

1177. DAVIS, Kate
"Hermitage." [GrahamHR] (11) Spr 88, p. 77-78.

1178. DAVIS, Kevin
"Highline: Eastern Montana." [CapeR] (23:2) Fall 88, p. 23.

1179. DAVIS, Margo
"Southern Tradition." [PassN] (9:2) Sum 88, p. 19.

1180. DAVIS, Michael C.
"Woodcraft." [PoetL] (83:2) Sum 88, p. 25-26.

1181. DAVIS, R. M. (Robert M.)
"Hunting in the Wichita Mountains." [Phoenix] (9:1/2) 88, p. 19.
"Terence Bay Cemetery." [PottPort] (9) 88, p. 36.

1182. DAVIS, Thadious M.
"Conversations with Home." [NewOR] (15:1) Spr 88, p. 38.

1183. DAVIS, Tim
"Love Poem #1." [YellowS] (26) Spr 88, p. 38.

1184. DAVIS, William Virgil
"Another Night." [ConnPR] (7:1) 88, p. 40.
"Autumn Equinox" (for Carol). [CrabCR] (5:1) Wint 88, p. 21.
"Distanced." [WritersF] (14) Fall 88, p. 92.
"Home." [CimR] (82) Ja 88, p. 39.
"Legacy." [CimR] (82) Ja 88, p. 38.
"On an Unknown Japanese Painting." [CimR] (82) Ja 88, p. 39.
"The River Moving." [MidwQ] (29:4) Sum 88, p. 452.
"The Spring." [PoetC] (20:1) Fall 88, p. 23-24.
"Tour." [CimR] (82) Ja 88, p. 38.
"Walden." [PassN] (9:2) Sum 88, p. 28.
"White Light." [CrabCR] (5:1) Wint 88, p. 21.
"Windows." [GettyR] (1:3) Sum 88, p. 520.

1185. DAVISON, Peter
"Emerald." [IndR] (11:3) Sum 88, p. 23.
"Mother & Child #3." [Poetry] (152:5) Ag 88, p. 277.
"The War of the Pelicans." [Poetry] (152:4) Jl 88, p. 194.

1186. DAVITT, Michael
"Disillusion Street" (tr. by Paul Muldoon). [Antaeus] (60) Spr 88, p. 296.

1187. DAWE, Bruce
"Old Wood." [PraS] (62:4) Wint 88-89, p. 30.
"On the Fall from Grace of a Well-Known Politician." [PraS] (62:4) Wint 88-89, p. 31.

1188. DAWIT, Seble
"Neighbors and Other Selves." [Vis] (26) 88, p. 7.

1189. DAY-ROBERTS, Cynthia
"Elizabeth Park." [KanQ] (20:1/2) Wint-Spr 88, p. 152.
"That You Should Know Me When I Least Want to Knos Myself" (for Hayden). [KanQ] (20:1/2) Wint-Spr 88, p. 151.

De . . .
See also names beginning with "De" without the following space, filed below in their alphabetic positions, e.g., DeFOE.

De ALBA, Alicia Gaspar
See ALBA, Alicia Gaspar de
De ALVEZ, Delia Cazarre
See CAZARRE DE ALVEZ, Delia
De AMAT, Carlos Oquendo
See OQUENDO DE AMAT, Carlos
De ANDRADE, Carlos Drummond
See ANDRADE, Carlos Drummond de
De ANDRADE, Eugenio
See ANDRADE, Eugenio de
De AREVALO, Marta
See AREVALO, Marta de
De CAMPOS, Alvaro
See PESSOA, Fernando
1190. De KORVIN, André
"The Drowned Man." [BallSUF] (29:4) Aut 88, p. 56-62.
1191. De MARIS, Ron
"Pizarro." [SewanR] (96:2) Spr 88, p. 209.
"Turtle." [SewanR] (96:2) Spr 88, p. 210.
De MELO NETO, João Cabral
See NETO, João Cabral de Melo
De PASTORINI, Eloísa Perez
See PEREZ DE PASTORINI, Eloísa
De RICORD, Elsie Alvarado
See ALVARADO DE RICORD, Elsie
1192. De VINCK, Christopher
"From the North." [AmerS] (57:2) Spr 88, p. 290.
1193. De VITO, E. B.
"Circle." [AmerS] (57:2) Spr 88, p. 250.
"How Many Doors." [AmerS] (57:1) Wint 88, p. 50.
De WIT, Johan
See WIT, Johan de
1194. DEAGON, Ann
"All Saints." [SouthernHR] (22:4) Fall 88, p. 346.
"Traditional Music." [SouthernHR] (22:3) Sum 88, p. 250.
1195. DEAL, Susan Strayer
"Lithograph." [Plain] (8:1) Fall 87, p. 26.
1196. DEAN, Mick
"Picnic at the Mausoleum." [Ascent] (14:1) 88, p. 25-27.
1197. DEANOVICH, Connie
"55% Icelandic." [NewAW] (4) Fall 88, p. 70.
1198. DEAVEL, Christine
"The Geography of a Divorce." [PoetryNW] (29:4) Wint 88-89, p. 42-43.
"Than Never." [PoetryNW] (29:4) Wint 88-89, p. 44-45.
"A Visitation During Lawn Care." [PoetryNW] (29:4) Wint 88-89, p. 41-42.
1199. DECARNIN, Camilla
"Dreamtender." [LittleM] (15:3/4) 88, p. 106.
1200. DECEMBER, John
"Snow: A Letter." [PassN] (9:1) Wint 88, p. 11.
1201. DeCHANT, George A., Jr.
"Life Is That Apple." [SlipS] (8) 88, p. 44.
1202. DeCLUE, Charlotte
"The Needle." [Phoenix] (9:1/2) 88, p. 60-61.
1203. DeCORMIER-SHEKERJIAN, Regina
"The First Telling." [Comm] (115:17) 7 O 88, p. 530.
"Kinship." [Comm] (115:18) 21 O 88, p. 565.
"Letters from the Coast." [NegC] (8:3) 88, p. 35-36.
"Paloma." [Comm] (115:11) 3 Je 88, p. 366.
"The Runner's Wife Calls Long Distance." [KanQ] (20:1/2) Wint-Spr 88, p. 92.
"The Woman Who Steals Ham Bones." [Comm] (115:11) 3 Je 88, p. 335.
1204. DeCOURCY, Lynne H.
"Changing the Gown." [MidAR] (8:1) 88, p. 12.
"Generations." [CimR] (83) Ap 88, p. 40-41.
"The River." [Nimrod] (32:1) Fall-Wint 88, p. 129-131.
1205. DEERY, Alice
"Learning to Make Makah Baskets." [MinnR] (NS 30/31) Spr-Fall 88, p. 12-15.

1206. DeFOE, Mark
"The Aging Divorcée at Solitaire." [TarRP] (28:1) Fall 88, p. 15.
"Body Language." [PikeF] (9) Fall 88, p. 28.
"The Call" (Phone booths / Ft. Campbell, KY / 1967). [PoetL] (83:1) Spr 88, p. 25.
"The Former Miner Returns from His First Day As a Service Worker" (at McDonald's — somewhere in Appalachia). [SouthernHR] (22:1) Wint 88, p. 34.
"The House by the Interstate." [CreamCR] (12:2) Sum 88, p. 172-173.
"Setting Free the Bird." [PikeF] (9) Fall 88, p. 25.
1207. DeFORD, Sheri
"Mill Street Tunnel." [KanQ] (20:4) Fall 88, p. 103-104.
1208. DeFREES, Madeline
"Blueprints." [MemphisSR] (8:2) Spr 88, p. 13.
"Imaginary Ancestors: Marianne Moore." [HeliconN] (19) 88, p. 36-37.
"Swimming in Categories." [CrabCR] (5:3) Fall 88, p. 25.
"This Paper White Narcissus." [WillowS] (21) Wint 88, p. 23-24.
1209. DeGRAVELLES, Charles
"The Healing." [FloridaR] (16:1) Spr-Sum 88, p. 61.
1210. DeGUZMAN, Maria
"Substitution." [CapeR] (23:2) Fall 88, p. 45.
1211. DeHAAN, Jayne
"Riverrun." [Plain] (8:1) Fall 87, p. 32.
1212. DEHN, Olive
"The Last Platform" (tr. of Yuri Galanskov). [NegC] (8:1/2) 88, p. 40.
Del CASTILLO, Inés
See CASTILLO, Inés del
1213. Del VALLE, Pompeyo
"Estudio de Mi Madre." [Mairena] (10:25) 88, p. 26.
1214. DELANO, Page Dougherty
"Electricity." [TarRP] (28:1) Fall 88, p. 37.
"Mercury Sestina." [WestB] (21/22) 88, p. 94-95.
1215. DELETANT, Andrea
"Temptation" (tr. of Nina Cassian, w. Brenda Walker). [AmerPoR] (17:2) Mr-Ap 88, p. 48.
1216. DELGADO, Juan
"Quarrels." [PacificR] (6) Spr 88, p. 17.
1217. DellaROCCA, L.
"Half." [Poem] (60) N 88, p. 26.
1218. DELP, Mike (Michael)
"American Male" (for Jack, Nick and Terry). [Spirit] (9:1) 88, p. 13-15.
"Rising Poem." [PassN] (9:1) Wint 88, p. 14.
1219. DeMARS, Douglas
"The Duncan Man." [TarRP] (27:2) Spr 88, p. 24.
"Man Versus Nature." [StoneC] (16:1/2) Fall-Wint 88-89, p. 51.
1220. DEMING, Alison
"First Encounter Beach" (Eastham, Massachusetts). [Sequoia] (32:1) Spr-Sum 88, p. 28-30.
"Island Stars." [DenQ] (23:2) Fall 88, p. 38-39.
1221. DENBERG, Ken
"Of Two Minds, Like a Tree." [SouthernPR] (28:2) Fall 88, p. 26.
1222. DeNIORD, Chard
"From the Apocrypha of David." [Iowa] (18:1) 88, p. 127-130.
"Hester." [Iowa] (18:1) 88, p. 126.
"The Wind and the Door." [Iowa] (18:1) 88, p. 126-127.
1223. DENNIS, Carl
"The Bill of Rights." [DenQ] (23:1) Sum 88, p. 49-50.
"Haven." [DenQ] (23:1) Sum 88, p. 47-48.
"I Have Years on My Back Forty-Eight." [SenR] (18:1) 88, p. 15-16.
"On Niagara Street." [SenR] (18:1) 88, p. 14.
"Shelter." [SenR] (18:1) 88, p. 17-18.
1224. DENNISON, Matt
"Raising the Dead." [Vis] (27) 88, p. 29, 31.
1225. DENNY, Alma
"The Birds of 9th Ave." [LightY] ('88/9) 88, p. 161.
"Lettuce Pause." [LightY] ('88/9) 88, p. 216.
"Thought While Dressing to Meet the 'Girls'." [LightY] ('88/9) 88, p. 221.

1226. DEPTA, Victor
"Get Out of Yourself." [WestB] (21/22) 88, p. 72.
"It's All in the Mind." [WestB] (21/22) 88, p. 73.
1227. DEPUTY, Allison
"Starlet." [PacificR] (6) Spr 88, p. 44-45.
1228. DER-HOVANESSIAN, Diana
"Annunciation" (14th Century painting by Simone Martini). [GrahamHR] (11) Spr 88, p. 72.
"The Astonomer." [TexasR] (9:3/4) Fall-Wint 88, p. 31.
"Couples." [PartR] (55:2) Spr 88, p. 283-284.
"Envy" (tr. of Medaksé). [GrahamHR] (11) Spr 88, p. 95.
"Feathers" (tr. of Bedros Khourasanjian). [LitR] (32:1) Fall 88, p. 66.
"It's No Secret" (tr. of Medaksé). [GrahamHR] (11) Spr 88, p. 94.
"Keri's Curse." [GrahamHR] (11) Spr 88, p. 73-74.
"November" (tr. of Maria Banus). [GrahamHR] (11) Spr 88, p. 96.
"The Poet Who Wrote on Glass" (for Mary Mattafield). [InterPR] (14:2) Fall 88, p. 87.
"Statues of Haig." [InterPR] (14:2) Fall 88, p. 86-87.
"Sunset." [GrahamHR] (11) Spr 88, p. 75.
"Time Out" (tr. of Bedros Khourasanjian). [LitR] (32:1) Fall 88, p. 67.
"Young." [LitR] (31:2) Wint 88, p. 208.
1229. DERRICK, Curtis
"The Afflictions of Desire." [CumbPR] (7:2) Spr 88, p. 16-17.
1230. DERRICOTTE, Toi
"Blackbottom, 1945." [MassR] (29:2) Sum 88, p. 230.
"Books." [NewL] (54:3) Spr 88, p. 97.
"New Jersey Diner." [Footwork] ('88) 88, p. 84.
"A Note on My Son's Face." [Callaloo] (10:4 #33) Fall 87, p. 561-562.
"Squeaky Bed." [PaintedB] (34) 88, p. 46.
"The Struggle." [MassR] (29:2) Sum 88, p. 231.
"Stuck." [Footwork] ('88) 88, p. 84.
"Touching / Not Touching: My Mother." [AmerPoR] (17:4) Jl-Ag 88, p. 21.
1231. DERRY, Alice
"Still Life." [Prima] (11/12) 88, p. 36-37.
1232. DeRUGERIS, C. K.
"Help Wanted." [JamesWR] (6:1) Fall 88, p. 5.
"Horseshit." [PaintedB] (34) 88, p. 82.
"Monday Morning." [PaintedB] (34) 88, p. 81.
"Spaghetti for Breakfast." [PaintedB] (34) 88, p. 81.
"Understudy." [PaintedB] (34) 88, p. 82.
1233. DESIDERATO, Adrian
"Sketch of Ingmar Bergman" (tr. by John Oliver Simon). [Rohwedder] (3) Spr 88, p. 28.
1234. DESILETS, E. Michael
"Daddy's Home." [JINJPo] (10:1/2) 88, p. 17.
"A Little Slip." [JINJPo] (10:1/2) 88, p. 16.
"Something to Look At." [JINJPo] (10:1/2) 88, p. 15.
1235. DESMOND, Walter
"Child's Fare." [MemphisSR] (8:2) Spr 88, p. 90.
"No Mail for the Dead." [WebR] (13:2) Fall 88, p. 92.
1236. DESNOS, Robert
"Coming Down Hillsides in the Spring" (tr. by William Kulik). [Antaeus] (60) Spr 88, p. 268.
"The Equinox" (tr. by William Kulik). [Antaeus] (60) Spr 88, p. 267.
"From the Marble Rose to the Iron Rose" (tr. by Edouard Roditi). [Antaeus] (60) Spr 88, p. 265-266.
"Men on Earth" (tr. by William Kulik). [Antaeus] (60) Spr 88, p. 269-270.
1237. DesRUISSEAUX, Pierre
"J'ai tracé seul." [Os] (26) 88, p. 2.
"Près de la matière." [Os] (26) 88, p. 3.
1238. DESY, Peter
"Aunt Nell." [HampSPR] Wint 88, p. 15.
"How We Ended." [Spirit] (9:1) 88, p. 129.
"In Our Time." [Nimrod] (32:1) Fall-Wint 88, p. 126.
"In Our Time." [StoneC] (16:1/2) Fall-Wint 88-89, p. 46.
"A Letter to My Sister: The Weather Here Is Fine." [HampSPR] Wint 88, p. 14-15.

"Resurrection." [BellR] (11:2) Fall 88, p. 17.
"Seasonal." [Nimrod] (32:1) Fall-Wint 88, p. 127.
"The Touch." [DeKalbLAJ] (21:2) Spr 88, p. 36.

1239. DETOUR, Vera
"La Mar — A Praise Poem to Times Passed By." [BellArk] (4:3) My-Je 88, p. 3.

1240. DEUTSCH, Laynie Tzena
"Directions." [NegC] (8:3) 88, p. 90-93.

1241. DEVENISH, Alan
"Silver Heart Over Chevy Chase Maryland." [Gargoyle] (35) 88, p. 126.
"Toucans." [LittleM] (15:3/4) 88, p. 6-8.

1242. DEVET, Rebecca McClanahan
"Produce Aisle." [CarolQ] (40:2) Wint 88, p. 31.
"Snow Woman." [SouthernPR] (28:1) Spr 88, p. 62-63.

1243. DEWDNEY, Christopher
"Elora Gorge Idyll." [Descant] (19:1, #60) Spr 88, p. 59-71.

1244. DeWINTER, Corrine
"Museum of Fine Arts." [Writer] (101:6) Je 88, p. 24.

DeWITT, Susan Kelly
See KELLY-DeWITT, Susan

1245. DEY, Richard Morris
"Archipelago" (for David Perkins). [HawaiiR] (12:1, #23) Spr 88, p. 103.
"At Hill House." [HawaiiR] (12:1, #23) Spr 88, p. 102.
"Boats at Anchor, Out on Their Moorings." [HawaiiR] (12:1, #23) Spr 88, p. 104-105.

1246. DHARWADKER, Vinay
"The Red Bicycle" (tr. of Sarveshvar Dayal Saksena). [Nimrod] (31:2) Spr-Sum 88, p. 75.

1247. DHOMHNAILL, Nuala Ní
"Bone" (tr. by Joe Malone). [WebR] (13:2) Fall 88, p. 23.
"Confession" (tr. by Joe Malone). [WebR] (13:2) Fall 88, p. 24.

Di . . .
See also names beginning with "Di" without the following space, filed below in their alphabetic positions, e.g., DiPALMA

1248. Di PIERO, W. S.
"Augustine on the Beach." [SouthernR] (24:3) Sum 88, p. 564-565.
"The Caverns." [TriQ] (72) Spr-Sum 88, p. 169-170.
"Dreaming the Pacific." [Thrpny] (33) Spr 88, p. 20.
"Emmaus." [Pequod] (25) 88, p. 59-60.
"Frankie's Birthday Party." [Zyzzyva] (4:3) Fall 88, p. 78-79.
"The Hotel Room Mirror." [Pequod] (25) 88, p. 58.
"In Calbria." [TriQ] (72) Spr-Sum 88, p. 167-168.
"Leopardi's 'Il Sabato del Villaggio'." [SouthernR] (24:3) Sum 88, p. 565-566.
"Natural History." [Pequod] (25) 88, p. 64-65.
"The Speech in the Middle of the Night." [Pequod] (25) 88, p. 61-63.
"Starlings." [Thrpny] (35) Fall 88, p. 30.

1249. Di PRIMA, Diane
"Dawn Poems." [AlphaBS] (4) D 88, p. 30.
"Swallow Sequence." [AlphaBS] (4) D 88, p. 29.

1250. Di STEFANO, John
"Rainy Day in Potomac, Maryland." [Wind] (18:62) 88, p. 8.

DIAZ, Gaspar Aguilar
See AGUILAR DIAZ, Gaspar

1251. DIAZ BORBON, Rafael
"Relato de Bucaneros." [Mairena] (10:25) 88, p. 44-45.

1252. DIAZ CASTRO, Tania
"Poeta en la Habana" (2 poems). [LindLM] (7:1) Ja-Mr 88, p. 4.

1253. DIAZ RODRIGUEZ, Ernesto
"Poemas Desde la Prision" (3 poems). [LindLM] (7:1) Ja-Mr 88, p. 3.

1254. DICKEY, James
"Basics." [AmerPoR] (17:2) Mr-Ap 88, p. 37.
"Expanses." [AmerPoR] (17:2) Mr-Ap 88, p. 38.
"Moon Flock." [AmerPoR] (17:2) Mr-Ap 88, p. 38.
"Night Bird." [AmerPoR] (17:2) Mr-Ap 88, p. 37.
"The One." [AmerPoR] (17:2) Mr-Ap 88, p. 36.
"Sea." [AmerPoR] (17:2) Mr-Ap 88, p. 38.
"Sleepers." [AmerPoR] (17:2) Mr-Ap 88, p. 37.

"Snow Thickets." [AmerPoR] (17:2) Mr-Ap 88, p. 38.
"The Three." [AmerPoR] (17:2) Mr-Ap 88, p. 36.
"Weeds." [AmerPoR] (17:2) Mr-Ap 88, p. 36.

1255. DICKEY, R. P.
"Browsing in *Roget's Thesaurus*." [LightY] ('88/9) 88, p. 113.

1256. DICKEY, William
"Indirect Discourse." [Sonora] (14/15) Spr 88, p. 18-19.
"A Wild Thing." [Zyzzyva] (4:2) Sum 88, p. 68-69.

1257. DICKSON, Charles B.
"No More Hard Times." [Pembroke] (20) 88, p. 106.

1258. DICKSON, John
"The Bats." [LitR] (31:2) Wint 88, p. 199.
"Scheherazade." [TriQ] (71) Wint 88, p. 173.
"Self Portrait." [PikeF] (9) Fall 88, p. 11.
"Victory Celebration." [TriQ] (71) Wint 88, p. 171-172.

1259. DICKSON, Ray Clark
"The Eclipse." [BelPoJ] (39:1) Fall 88, p. 32-34.
"Thank You Very Much for the Last Time." [YellowS] (28) D 88, p. 43.

1260. DIETMEIER, Richard
"Death at the Drive-In." [WormR] (28:1, #109) 88, p. 34.
"Winning." [WormR] (28:1, #109) 88, p. 33-34.

1261. DIGGES, Deborah
"For the Second Millenium." [NewYorker] (64:27) 22 Ag 88, p. 26.
"The Sea with Doors" (For John Hartnal and crew, lost at sea, buried in the Antarctic, 1844 . . .). [Field] (39) Fall 88, p. 62-63.

1262. DIGMAN, Steven M
"The Idol." [SlipS] (8) 88, p. 46.

1263. DiLALLO, Robert
"Brown Horses at Sunset." [Poem] (59) My 88, p. 33.
"Evening by the Sea." [Poem] (59) My 88, p. 34.
"The Ferry at Shelter Island, 1979." [LitR] (31:3) Spr 88, p. 297.
"Trenton Local" (The Death of Marc Chagall). [Poem] (59) My 88, p. 35.
"When Next It Grows Cold." [Poem] (59) My 88, p. 32.

1264. DILLARD, Jennifer O.
"Open Window." [CrabCR] (5:3) Fall 88, p. 20.

1265. DILLHUNT, C. X.
"Aster." [CreamCR] (12:2) Sum 88, p. 174-175.

1266. DILLON, Andrew
"At the School Gym on a Frozen Morning." [PoetC] (20:1) Fall 88, p. 12.
"Berengarius of Tours" (1000-1088 A.D.). [KanQ] (20:1/2) Wint-Spr 88, p. 153.
"Hard Days at School." [PoetC] (20:1) Fall 88, p. 13.
"Letters." [NoDaQ] (56:3) Sum 88, p. 98.
"Marvin Bell and the Route to Being Anyone." [KanQ] (20:3) Sum 88, p. 78.
"Neighborhood." [Poem] (59) My 88, p. 25.
"Once Nothing Had a History Behind It." [SoDakR] (26:1) Spr 88, p. 30.
"Reading a Paper — Cleveland, Last Day." [Poem] (59) My 88, p. 23.
"To My Daughter — Across One of Our Arguments." [Poem] (59) My 88, p. 24.
"Virginia Battlefield." [KanQ] (20:3) Sum 88, p. 77.
"Winter Morning." [KanQ] (20:1/2) Wint-Spr 88, p. 152-153.

1267. DILSAVER, Paul
"Confession." [WritersF] (14) Fall 88, p. 116-117.
"Morgue Song." [WritersF] (14) Fall 88, p. 117-118.

1268. DiMAGGIO, Jill
"Hi-rise Living." [Lactuca] (9) F 88, p. 27.
"Labor Day Blackout." [PaintedB] (36) 88, p. 84.
"The Retired Soldier — For Chester." [Lactuca] (9) F 88, p. 26.
"Widow." [Lactuca] (9) F 88, p. 27.

1269. DiMICHELE, Bill
"Burnhole" (Excerpt). [Sink] (3) 88, p. 59-62.

1270. DIMITROVA, Blaga
"Bulgarian Woman from the Old Days" (tr. by Heather McHugh and Nikolai B. Popov). [Antaeus] (60) Spr 88, p. 280.
"Forbidden Sea" (Selections: 14, 16, tr. by Heather McHugh and Nikolai B. Popov). [Thrpny] (33) Spr 88, p. 18.
"In the Balance" (tr. by Heather McHugh and Nikolai B. Popov). [Antaeus] (60) Spr 88, p. 279.

"Portrait with Soap Bubbles" (tr. by Heather McHugh and Nikolai B. Popov). [Antaeus] (60) Spr 88, p. 283-284.
"Who Cares for the Blind Stork" (tr. by Heather McHugh and Nikolai B. Popov). [Antaeus] (60) Spr 88, p. 277-278.
"The Women Who Are Poets in My Land" (tr. by Heather McHugh and Nikolai B. Popov). [Antaeus] (60) Spr 88, p. 281-282.

1271. DINE, Carol
"The Diver." [CreamCR] (12:2) Sum 88, p. 176.

1272. DING, Dennis
"Bodhisattva" (tr. of Bei Dao, w. Edward Morin). [WebR] (13:2) Fall 88, p. 18.
"Distance" (tr. of Cai Qi-jiao, w. Edward Morin). [TriQ] (71) Wint 88, p. 130.
"Going Astray" (tr. of Wang Xiao-ni, w. Edward Morin). [WebR] (13:2) Fall 88, p. 17.
"The Pearl" (in Chinese and English, tr. of Cai Qi-jiao, w. Edward Morin). [HawaiiR] (12:1, #23) Spr 88, p. 90-91.
"Repairing the Wall" (tr. of Min Zhen, w. Edward Morin). [WebR] (13:1) Spr 88, p. 40.
"Scenery" (tr. of Gu Cheng, w. Edward Morin). [WindO] (50) Aut 88, p. 39.
"A Self-Portrait" (tr. of Shu Ting, w. Edward Morin). [TriQ] (72) Spr-Sum 88, p. 156.
"The Wind Is Roaring" (tr. of Xiao-ni Wang, w. Edward Morin). [Spirit] (9:1) 88, p. 100.

1273. DINGS, Fred
"At a Cemetery in the Smoky Mountains." [HighP] (3:3) Wint 88-89, p. 102-103.

1274. DIOGENES, Rochelle
"Ergo Sumus" (tr. of Anna Frajlich-Zajac, w. the author). [Vis] (26) 88, p. 37.

1275. DIORIO, Margaret T.
"The Man Behind the Wheel." [CentR] (32:3) Sum 88, p. 274.

1276. DiPALMA, Ray
"Mirage or moan point." [NewAW] (3) Spr 88, p. 74.
"Musing stupefied by indiscretions." [NewAW] (3) Spr 88, p. 73.
"Territory" (Excerpts). [Sink] (3) 88, p. 45-49.
"The work shoots along." [NewAW] (3) Spr 88, p. 74.
"The zero is glass grey." [NewAW] (3) Spr 88, p. 73.

1277. DIPPEL, Kim
"The Sunset." [DeKalbLAJ] (21:2) Spr 88, p. 71.

1278. DISCH, Thomas M.
"Koch on Broadway." [GrandS] (7:4) Sum 88, p. 84-92.

1279. DISCH, Tom
"At the Grave of Amy Clampitt." [Shen] (38:4) 88, p. 34.
"The Dirt and the Willow." [ParisR] (30:106) Spr 88, p. 253-254.
"Donna Anna Writes to Her Sister." [LightY] ('88/9) 88, p. 159.
"Dueling Platitudes." [LightY] ('88/9) 88, p. 58-60.
"Economy, Convenience, Good Taste." [LightY] ('88/9) 88, p. 51-52.
"March." [Boulevard] (3:2/3) Fall 88, p. 121.
"More Good Advice for the Young." [Salm] (78/79) Spr-Sum 88, p. 175.
"October." [Boulevard] (3:2/3) Fall 88, p. 121-122.
"Ode to Equanimity." [Salm] (78/79) Spr-Sum 88, p. 172-174.
"Rules of Order for New Conservatives." [Salm] (78/79) Spr-Sum 88, p. 174-175.
"A Stroll Through Moscow." [Poetry] (152:1) Ap 88, p. 16-17.
"Theseus to Hippolyta." [Salm] (78/79) Spr-Sum 88, p. 172.
"What's Left Unsaid, or the Dodo's Joy." [Boulevard] (3:2/3) Fall 88, p. 122-123.
"Why This Tie, Why That." [Poetry] (152:1) Ap 88, p. 15-16.
"Yorick's Reply." [Shen] (38:4) 88, p. 34-35.

1280. DISLER, Jacqui
"Blue T.V. Idyll." [NewAW] (4) Fall 88, p. 80.
"Church Within the Bar." [NewAW] (4) Fall 88, p. 81.

1281. DITCHOFF, Pamela
"Interim." [Amelia] (5:1, #12) 88, p. 55.

1282. DITSKY, John
"Bites." [Comm] (115:13) 15 Jl 88, p. 405.
"Last Words." [OntR] (28) Spr-Sum 88, p. 61-62.

1283. DITTBERNER-JAX, Norita
"It Was Like This." [Comm] (115:13) 15 Jl 88, p. 405.
"Sunrise on Lombard." [LakeSR] (22) 88, p. 27.

1284. DIVAKARUNI, Chitra
"At Muktinath." [Calyx] (11:2/3) Fall 88, p. 29-30.
"Bengal Night." [BelPoJ] (38:4) Sum 88, p. 2-3.
"Burning Bride" (for the victims of dowry deaths in India). [Prima] (11/12) 88, p. 18-20.
"The House Serpents." [ColR] (NS 15:2) Fall-Wint 88, p. 45-46.
"In the Hinglaj Desert." [ColR] (NS 15:2) Fall-Wint 88, p. 44.
"My Mother at Maui." [Prima] (11/12) 88, p. 47-48.
"The Reason for Nasturtiums." [BelPoJ] (38:4) Sum 88, p. 6.
"The Robbers' Cave." [BelPoJ] (38:4) Sum 88, p. 3-5.

1285. DIXON, C. E., III
"Adman" (for Bill Yost). [ChatR] (8:3) Spr 88, p. 46.

1286. DIXON, Kent R.
"Arcadia." [GreensboroR] (45) Wint 88-89, p. 121-122.

1287. DIXON, Melvin
"Hands." [SouthernR] (24:2) Spr 88, p. 339-340.
"Winter Without Snow" (Dakar, Senegal). [SouthernR] (24:2) Spr 88, p. 340.

1288. DJANIKIAN, Gregory
"The Boy Who Had Eleven Toes." [Poetry] (152:2) My 88, p. 70-71.
"Late at Night in Bed." [Poetry] (152:2) My 88, p. 71-73.

1289. DJERASSI, Carl
"Why Are Chemists Seldom Poets?" [SoDakR] (26:2) Sum 88, p. 128-129.

1290. DOBLER, Patricia
"Bobinger's Complaint" (tr. of Ilse Aichinger). [MidAR] (8:2) 88, p. 189.
"Part of the Question" (tr. of Ilse Aichinger). [MidAR] (8:2) 88, p. 190.
"Train Platform: Munich to Dachau." [Ploughs] (14:1) 88, p. 38-40.

1291. DOBSON, Rosemary
"Private Soldier" (from a Series: "Untold Lives"). [PraS] (62:4) Wint 88-89, p. 107.
"Who?" (from a Series: "Untold Lives"). [PraS] (62:4) Wint 88-89, p. 105.
"The Widow" (from a Series: "Untold Lives"). [PraS] (62:4) Wint 88-89, p. 106.

1292. DOBYNS, Stephen
"Brink." [Poetry] (152:2) My 88, p. 94.
"Freight Cars." [Poetry] (152:2) My 88, p. 93.
"Thoughts at Thirty-Thousand Feet." [Poetry] (152:2) My 88, p. 92-93.

1293. DODD, Wayne
"Hands." [DenQ] (23:1) Sum 88, p. 52.
"Homage to Marcel Duchamp." [DenQ] (23:1) Sum 88, p. 51.
"Late Afternoon Light." [TarRP] (27:2) Spr 88, p. 32-33.
"Late Summer Song." [GettyR] (1:2) Spr 88, p. 308-312.
"Seasonal." [DenQ] (23:1) Sum 88, p. 53.

1294. DODGE, Robert
"Readings." [CharR] (14:1) Spr 88, p. 82.

1295. DODSON, Keith
"The Dog." [Lactuca] (10) Je 88, p. 22.
"It's Tough Living at Home." [Lactuca] (10) Je 88, p. 22.
"The Men's Room at System M." [Lactuca] (10) Je 88, p. 22.
"On the Proud Bird." [Lactuca] (10) Je 88, p. 23.

1296. DODSON, Keith A.
"A Reading at the Works Gallery, Long Beach, California." [Bogg] (60) 88, p. 33.
"Teresa." [Bogg] (59) 88, p. 5.

1297. DOHERTY, Berlie
"Three." [Stand] (29:4) Aut 88, p. 50-51.

1298. DOLA, Ken
"Opal Creek." [VirQR] (64:2) Spr 88, p. 287-288.

1299. DOLAN, John
"Poem of the End" (tr. of Marina Tsvetayeva). [Sulfur] (8:2, #23) Fall 88, p. 6-30.

1300. DOLAN, Kathleen Hunt
"Aluminum Cocktails." [PaintedB] (36) 88, p. 17-18.
"Nocturne." [PaintedB] (36) 88, p. 19.
"Two Still-Lifes in August." [Vis] (27) 88, p. 16.
"Two Still-Lifes in January." [Vis] (28) 88, p. 34.

1301. DOLCIMASCOLO, Gelia
"Narcissus" (Third Place, Creative Writing Club Contest). [DeKalbLAJ] (21:2) Spr 88, p. 53.

1302. DOLIN, Sharon
"Sketch of Paula Modersohn-Becker Dying After Childbirth." [Thrpny] (35) Fall 88, p. 11.
1303. DOLL, Selva
"Viaje." [LetFem] (14:1/2) Primavera-Otoño 88, p. 144.
1304. DOMEK, Tom
"The Medicine Bow Mountains." [NoDaQ] (56:4) Fall 88, p. 45.
1305. DOMINA, Lynn
"Dancers at Rest." [NegC] (8:3) 88, p. 168-169.
"The Easy Good-Bye." [MemphisSR] (8:2) Spr 88, p. 66.
"The One You Never Get Over." [MemphisSR] (8:2) Spr 88, p. 64.
"Taking Leave." [NowestR] (26:2) 88, p. 65.
"With My Husband." [MemphisSR] (8:2) Spr 88, p. 65.
1306. DOMINGO, Jose
"Carmen" (tr. by Kent Johnson). [MidAR] (8:1) 88, p. 143.
1307. DONAGHY, Michael
"Deceit." [ChiR] (36:1) 88, p. 48.
"The Light Verse of the Damned." [ChiR] (36:1) 88, p. 49.
"Machines." [Poetry] (152:6) S 88, p. 341.
"Ramon Fernandez?" [ChiR] (36:2) Aut 88, p. 33-34.
"Remembering Steps to Dances Learned Last Night." [ChiR] (36:1) 88, p. 46-47.
"Shibboleth." [Poetry] (152:6) S 88, p. 342.
"Square Dressed Stone." [ChiR] (36:1) 88, p. 50.
1308. DONAHUE, Joseph
"Errand Immanent." [Notus] (3:1) Spr 88, p. 90.
"Thunderclap." [CentralP] (14) Fall 88, p. 182.
"Zango." [Notus] (3:1) Spr 88, p. 91.
1309. DONALDSON, Jeffery
"Word from Niagara Falls" (Gustav Mahler, 1910). [YaleR] (77:4) Sum 88, p. 513-518.
1310. DONLAN, John
"For the King of Naples." [NewAW] (3) Spr 88, p. 97.
"Hellhound on My Trail." [NewAW] (3) Spr 88, p. 98.
"Peasant Life." [CapilR] (47) 88, p. 76.
"Practical." [NewAW] (4) Fall 88, p. 66.
"Sleep." [CapilR] (47) 88, p. 77.
"Stable." [Dandel] (15:2) Fall-Wint 88, p. 33.
"Unacted." [NewAW] (4) Fall 88, p. 65.
1311. DONNELLY, J. R.
"A Light." [AntigR] (73) Spr 88, p. 26.
1312. DONOHUE, Sheila P.
"Visiting Hours" (for Henry Korson). [GreensboroR] (45) Wint 88-89, p. 92.
1313. DONOVAN, Karen
"Courtyard of the Gardner Museum, Boston." [ColR] (NS 15:2) Fall-Wint 88, p. 55.
"Every Direction Continues" (from "The Plumber's Begun to Notice). [Nimrod] (32:1) Fall-Wint 88, p. 81-82.
"Fishing the Swift." [ColR] (NS 15:2) Fall-Wint 88, p. 56.
"Flight of Starlings" (from "The Plumber's Begun to Notice). [Nimrod] (32:1) Fall-Wint 88, p. 86.
"Getting in Trouble" (from "The Plumber's Begun to Notice). [Nimrod] (32:1) Fall-Wint 88, p. 83-84.
"The Middle Child Wakes Up at Night" (from "The Plumber's Begun to Notice). [Nimrod] (32:1) Fall-Wint 88, p. 84.
"Nothing by Mouth" (from "The Plumber's Begun to Notice). [Nimrod] (32:1) Fall-Wint 88, p. 83.
"The Plumber's Begun to Notice" (from "The Plumber's Begun to Notice). [Nimrod] (32:1) Fall-Wint 88, p. 81.
"The Plumber's Begun to Notice" (Selections. Pablo Neruda Prize for Poetry, Honorable Mention). [Nimrod] (32:1) Fall-Wint 88, p. 81-86.
"Roadkill" (from "The Plumber's Begun to Notice). [Nimrod] (32:1) Fall-Wint 88, p. 85-86.
"Travel Silk." [GeoR] (42:3) Fall 88, p. 554.
1314. DONOVAN, Laurence
"Changes: Miami, 1988." [KeyWR] (1:2) Fall 88, p. 61-62.
"The House of Stone and Branch." [LindLM] (7:1) Ja-Mr 88, p. 20.
"In the Long Run." [KanQ] (20:1/2) Wint-Spr 88, p. 291.

"This Time Around." [LindLM] (7:1) Ja-Mr 88, p. 20.
1315. DONOVAN, Stewart
"Knight Inlet, B. C." [AntigR] (73) Spr 88, p. 69-70.
"Saturday Night in Sydney." [AntigR] (73) Spr 88, p. 71.
1316. DOOLEY, David
"Letter." [Turnstile] (1:1) Wint 88, p. 51.
"Proust Poem." [HolCrit] (25:5) D 88, p. 14.
DOREN, John van
See Van DOREN, John
1317. DORESKI, William
"The Book of Mormon." [Poem] (59) My 88, p. 19.
"Brockway Gorge." [LitR] (31:2) Wint 88, p. 180-181.
"Gondola, Tank Car." [Poem] (59) My 88, p. 20-21.
"Nursing Home." [Poem] (59) My 88, p. 18.
"Sunday Brunch." [ClockR] (4:2) 88, p. 12.
1318. DORF, Carol
"Daybook." [Contact] (9:47/48/49) Spr 88, p. 38-39.
"A Single Gesture." [Contact] (9:47/48/49) Spr 88, p. 39.
1319. DORF, Marilyn
"Fall." [Plain] (9:1) Fall 88, p. 38.
"A Tin Roof." [Plain] (8:3) Spr-Sum 88, p. 14.
"The Wind Knows." [Plain] (9:1) Fall 88, p. 28.
1320. DORFMAN, Ariel
"Cost of Living" (for Isabel Letelier). [AmerPoR] (17:2) Mr-Ap 88, p. 47.
"First We Set Up the Chairs" (tr. by the author and Edith Grossman). [Harp] (276:1653) F 88, p. 33.
"Red Tape." [AmerPoR] (17:2) Mr-Ap 88, p. 47.
1321. DORN, Alfred
"Accidents." [LightY] ('88/9) 88, p. 66.
"Apparition." [Hudson] (40:4) Wint 88, p. 636.
"At Mirror Lake." [Amelia] (5:2, #13) 88, p. 112.
"Ballade of Bones." [LightY] ('88/9) 88, p. 212.
"A careless young farmer named Howe." [Amelia] (5:2, #13) 88, p. 94.
"In Afternoon Light." [Hudson] (40:4) Wint 88, p. 635.
1322. DORSETT, Robert
"Cassandra." [BallSUF] (29:4) Aut 88, p. 8.
"The Fayum." [Sequoia] (32:1) Spr-Sum 88, p. 55.
"Memory for a Native Speaker." [PoetC] (19:3) Spr 88, p. 24.
1323. DORSETT, Thomas
"Although Spacetime's Expanding Clock." [PikeF] (9) Fall 88, p. 18.
"Franz Rosen." [CrabCR] (5:3) Fall 88, p. 17.
"His Smile." [Footwork] ('88) 88, p. 41.
"The Outcaste." [PikeF] (9) Fall 88, p. 18.
"The Smile." [Paint] (15:29) Spr 88, p. 18.
1324. DOTY, Mark
"63rd Street Y." [IndR] (11:3) Sum 88, p. 48-50.
"Adonis Theatre." [PoetryNW] (29:2) Sum 88, p. 4-6.
"Ararat." [Poetry] (152:1) Ap 88, p. 24.
"In the Form of Snow." [MissouriR] (11:1) 88, p. 184-185.
"Independence Day." [TexasR] (9:3/4) Fall-Wint 88, p. 32-34.
"Playland." [Agni] (26) 88, p. 54-56.
"Sideshow." [TexasR] (9:3/4) Fall-Wint 88, p. 35.
"Six Thousand Terracotta Men and Horses." [Agni] (26) 88, p. 57-58.
1325. DOUBIAGO, Sharon
"The Other Woman." [Spirit] (9:1) 88, p. 132-133.
1326. DOUGHERTY, Jay
"About Writing." [Amelia] (5:1, #12) 88, p. 98.
"Arena." [Lactuca] (9) F 88, p. 25.
"Etymological Poem." [Amelia] (5:1, #12) 88, p. 98.
"For My Friend Roderick, the Process Poet, or: And I Started Only with Words (& 1/4 Ounce)." [Amelia] (5:1, #12) 88, p. 99.
"Happy Birthday." [Amelia] (5:1, #12) 88, p. 98.
"'I don't Like a Saxophone in the Morning,' She Said." [Lactuca] (9) F 88, p. 26.
"Unpleasant Surprise." [Amelia] (5:1, #12) 88, p. 99.
1327. DOUGLAS, Jim
"Night Reconnaissance." [MidwQ] (29:2) Wint 88, p. 225.

1328. DOUGLASS, Karen
"Duet." [Ascent] (14:2) 88, p. 47.
"Retreat." [Ascent] (14:2) 88, p. 46.
"Seeing My Shadow." [PassN] (9:2) Sum 88, p. 7.
1329. DOVE, Rita
"Backyard, 6 a.m." [HighP] (3:2) Fall 88, p. 16.
"The Buckeye." [PraS] (62:1) Spr 88, p. 32-33.
"Dedication" (after Czeslaw Milosz). [YaleR] (78:1) Aut 88, p. 84.
"The Great Piece of Turf" (after Albrecht Dürer's *Das Grosse Rasenstück*, 1503). [GeoR] (42:2) Sum 88, p. 250.
"The Ground We Walk On." [ClockR] (4:2) 88, p. 35.
"Horse and Tree." [GeoR] (42:2) Sum 88, p. 251.
"In the Museum." [GrahamHR] (11) Spr 88, p. 80.
"The Late Notebooks of Albrecht Dürer." [GettyR] (1:1) Wint 88, p. 166-168.
"Mississippi." [ClockR] (4:2) 88, p. 36.
"The Other Side of the House." [PraS] (62:1) Spr 88, p. 31.
"Ozone." [HighP] (3:2) Fall 88, p. 17-18.
"The Passage" (Corporal Orval E. Peyton, 372nd Infantry, 93rd Division, A.E.J.). [OhioR] (42) 88, p. 7-14.
"Pastoral." [GrahamHR] (11) Spr 88, p. 81.
"Persephone, Falling." [Sequoia] (32:1) Spr-Sum 88, p. 24.
"Persephone Underground." [Sequoia] (32:1) Spr-Sum 88, p. 25.
"Stitches." [ClockR] (4:2) 88, p. 32.
"Untitled: Blown apart by loss, she let herself go." [HighP] (3:2) Fall 88, p. 15.
1330. DOW, Mark
"With." [Thrpny] (33) Spr 88, p. 25.
1331. DOW, Philip
"Love Poem." [Bound] (15:3/16:1) Spr-Fall 88, p. 99-109.
1332. DOWD, Amanda
"From the Collections fo an Amnesiac." [CentralP] (14) Fall 88, p. 125.
1333. DOWDEN, Kaviraj George
"L.A. to San Fran." [AlphaBS] (4) D 88, p. 9-11.
1334. DOWELL, Season Harper
"A Blade of Grass." [Plain] (8:3) Spr-Sum 88, p. 15.
"A Blade of Grass." [Plain] (9:1) Fall 88, p. 25.
1335. DOWNES, G. V.
"Subtext for Evensong." [Event] (17:1) Spr 88, p. 74.
1336. DOWNS, Stuart
"Just Reflected." [VirQR] (64:2) Spr 88, p. 284-287.
1337. DOYLE, James
"The Cemetery." [BallSUF] (29:4) Aut 88, p. 17.
"The Clock." [Amelia] (4:4, #11) 88, p. 83.
"Saying Grace." [WestB] (21/22) 88, p. 92.
"The Ship." [Ascent] (14:1) 88, p. 49.
"Soliloquies from the House of Pilate." [Amelia] (4:4, #11) 88, p. 68.
1338. DOYLE, Lynn
"Proverbs" (Excerpt). [Timbuktu] (1) Wint-Spr 88, p. 20-21.
"Tropical Depression — Carla, 1961." [Timbuktu] (2) Sum-Fall 88, p. 36.
1339. DOYLE, Mike
"Incident in Late Winter" (for Ivor Roberts). [MalR] (84) S 88, p. 132-134.
"Len Stokes's Concert" (for Carol Johnson). [MalR] (84) S 88, p. 135.
"Put Yourself in His Place." [MalR] (84) S 88, p. 130-131.
"Winter Ball" (found, in a sports magazine). [MalR] (84) S 88, p. 136.
1340. DRAGOMOSHCHENKO, Arkadii
"Instructing Clarity in a Confusion" (tr. by Lyn Hejinian and Elena Balashova). [NewAW] (4) Fall 88, p. 8-11.
"The Islands of Sirens" (tr. by Lyn Hejinian and Elena Balashova). [Zyzzyva] (4:1) Spr 88, p. 87-106.
1341. DRAKE, Barbara
"The Buzzard." [StoneC] (16:1/2) Fall-Wint 88-89, p. 26.
"The Smell of Man." [StoneC] (16:1/2) Fall-Wint 88-89, p. 26-28.
1342. DRAKE, James
"Naked Manikins." [Caliban] (5) 88, p. 136-143.
1343. DREW, Bettina
"Music." [AnotherCM] (18) 88, p. 94-95.

1344. DREW, George
"Fattucci." [QW] (27) Sum-Fall 88, p. 107-108.
"Febo" (Letter to Aretino, undated: 1546). [QW] (27) Sum-Fall 88, p. 109-110.
"Leda and Her Sister's Geese" (For Katharyn). [HolCrit] (25:1) F 88, p. 16.
"Riding the Black Man-killer." [CimR] (83) Ap 88, p. 91-92.
"Trapping Muskrat in Roe Park with Scudder Bates." [Blueline] (9:1/2) 88, p. 80-81.
1345. DREXEL, John
"Deserted Houses, County Galway." [SenR] (18:1) 88, p. 61.
"Remembering Killybegs" (for Rosemary Allen). [SenR] (18:1) 88, p. 59-60.
1346. DRISCOLL, Frances
"Donor Mentality" (for Craig). [MassR] (29:3) Fall 88, p. 556.
1347. DRISCOLL, Jack
"American Myth." [Spirit] (9:1) 88, p. 18-19.
"Bounty Hunting for Snappers." [PassN] (9:1) Wint 88, p. 15.
"Inadmissable Evidence." [OhioR] (40) 88, p. 94-97.
"Returning Only Part Way Home" (w. Bill Meissner). [PassN] (9:1) Wint 88, p. 29.
"Strip Poker." [MichQR] (27:2) Spr 88, p. 300.
"Winter Fishing" (w. Bill Meissner). [PassN] (9:1) Wint 88, p. 29.
"Woman Has a Baby in Her Sleep" (Headline from the *National Enquirer*). [LightY] ('88/9) 88, p. 137-138.
1348. DROMEY, John H.
"Perspective." [LightY] ('88/9) 88, p. 220.
1349. DRUMMEY, Jenny
"Avalanche." [WilliamMR] (26:1) Spr 88, p. 77.
DRUMMOND de ANDRADE, Carlos
See ANDRADE, Carlos Drummond de
1350. DRURY, John
"The Agency Mural." [Pequod] (25) 88, p. 50.
"Consignment." [MemphisSR] (8:2) Spr 88, p. 44.
"The Double Spires." [Pequod] (25) 88, p. 51.
"Lake Shore Limited." [CinPR] (17) Spr 88, p. 23.
"Little Diamond Island." [CinPR] (17) Spr 88, p. 22.
"Retreat." [NewRep] (199:16) 17 O 88, p. 42.
"Thinking of Easter." [MemphisSR] (8:2) Spr 88, p. 43.
1351. DU, Fu
"After Solstice" (tr. by Sam Hamill). [AmerPoR] (17:4) Jl-Ag 88, p. 25.
"Another Spring" (tr. by Sam Hamill). [AmerPoR] (17:4) Jl-Ag 88, p. 25.
"Becoming a Farmer" (tr. by Sam Hamill). [AmerPoR] (17:4) Jl-Ag 88, p. 26.
"Ch'iang Village" (tr. by Sam Hamill). [AmerPoR] (17:4) Jl-Ag 88, p. 26.
"Clear After Rain" (tr. by Sam Hamill). [CrabCR] (5:3) Fall 88, p. 8.
"Crooked River Meditation" (tr. by Sam Hamill). [AmerPoR] (17:4) Jl-Ag 88, p. 26.
"Dragon Gate Gorge" (tr. by Sam Hamill). [AmerPoR] (17:4) Jl-Ag 88, p. 26.
"Drinking at Crooked River" (tr. by Sam Hamill). [AmerPoR] (17:4) Jl-Ag 88, p. 25.
"Expanding the Frontiers" (tr. by Graeme Wilson). [Jacaranda] (3:2) Fall-Wint 88, p. 144.
"Farewell Rhyme" (tr. by Sam Hamill). [AmerPoR] (17:4) Jl-Ag 88, p. 25.
"Homecoming — Late at Night" (tr. by Kenneth Rexroth). [Blueline] (9:1/2) 88, p. 54.
"Impromptu" (tr. by Sam Hamill). [AmerPoR] (17:4) Jl-Ag 88, p. 26.
"In a Village by the River" (tr. by Sam Hamill). [AmerPoR] (17:4) Jl-Ag 88, p. 25.
"In Praise of Rain" (tr. by Sam Hamill). [CrabCR] (5:3) Fall 88, p. 9.
"In Seclusion" (tr. by Sam Hamill). [AmerPoR] (17:4) Jl-Ag 88, p. 26.
"Leaving Ch'in-chou" (tr. by Sam Hamill). [AmerPoR] (17:4) Jl-Ag 88, p. 26.
"Ni-Kung Mountain" (tr. by Lee Gerlach). [Agni] (27) 88, p. 175.
"Poems for Mr. Li in Early Spring" (tr. by Sam Hamill). [AmerPoR] (17:4) Jl-Ag 88, p. 25.
"Seven Songs at T'ung-ku" (tr. by David Hinton). [AmerPoR] (17:4) Jl-Ag 88, p. 23-24.
"Thinking of Li Po" (tr. by Sam Hamill). [AmerPoR] (17:4) Jl-Ag 88, p. 24.
"To Abbot Min the Compassionate" (tr. by Sam Hamill). [AmerPoR] (17:4) Jl-Ag 88, p. 24.
"Watching the Distances" (tr. by Sam Hamill). [CrabCR] (5:3) Fall 88, p. 9.
"Word from My Brothers" (tr. by Sam Hamill). [CrabCR] (5:3) Fall 88, p. 9.
Du . . .
See also names beginning with "Du" without the following space, filed below in their alphabetic positions, e.g., DuPLESSIS.

1352. Du BOUCHET, André
"Notes on Translation" (tr. by Norma Cole). [Acts] (8/9) 88, p. 199-217.
1353. Du TOIT, Basil
"Home Truths in Harsh Surroundings." [Verse] (5:3) N 88, p. 18.
"Little Heidi's Cheese." [Verse] (5:1) F 88, p. 57-58.
"The Nature of the Far Country." [Verse] (5:1) F 88, p. 58.
"The Sadness of Biographies." [Verse] (5:1) F 88, p. 57.
"Social Anthropology (1908-)" (on what there must continue to be). [Verse] (5:3) N 88, p. 17.
1354. DUBIE, Norman
"Amen." [AmerPoR] (17:1) Ja-F 88, p. 48.
"An American Scene." [QW] (26) Wint 88, p. 95-96.
"Encanto's Ferry." [MissR] (16:1, #46) 88, p. 32-33.
"Fever" (for my wife). [HayF] (3) Spr 88, p. 49.
"First Wednesday at Heater Lawns." [QW] (26) Wint 88, p. 97.
"The Great Polar Expedition" (circa 1912). [QW] (26) Wint 88, p. 98.
"New Age at Airport Mesa." [HayF] (3) Spr 88, p. 47-48.
"Northwind Escarpment." [GettyR] (1:1) Wint 88, p. 98.
"Safe Conduct." [HayF] (3) Spr 88, p. 52.
"The Saints of Negativity." [HayF] (3) Spr 88, p. 50-51.
"Shipwreck." [GettyR] (1:1) Wint 88, p. 99.
"Shrine." [MissR] (16:1, #46) 88, p. 40-41.
"They Are the Queens of the Bird's Body" (—Eddie Miguel). [QW] (26) Wint 88, p. 93-94.
"Union Ushers at the Norcross Farm — 1863." [WestHR] (42:1) Spr 88, p. 46-47.
1355. DUBNOV, Eugene
"Define this as you choose" (tr. of Boris Pasternak, w. John Heath-Stubbs). [StoneC] (16:1/2) Fall-Wint 88-89, p. 29.
"A Dream" (tr. by the author and John Heath-Stubbs). [MissR] (16:1, #46) 88, p. 44-45.
"From Sextus Propertius." [ChiR] (36:2) Aut 88, p. 79.
"The Gardener Said" (for Raymond and Pamela Harper, tr. by the author and John Heath-Stubbs). [MissR] (16:1, #46) 88, p. 42.
"I Had Rubbed Myself with a Towel" (tr. by Chris Arkell and John Heath-Stubbs). [MissR] (16:1, #46) 88, p. 43.
1356. DuBOSE, Melisa
"Fringes." [DeKalbLAJ] (21:2) Spr 88, p. 72.
1357. DUBRAVA, Patricia
"Postcards Featuring Aborigines." [Spirit] (9:1) 88, p. 117.
1358. DUDIS, Ellen Kirvin
"Rose." [CreamCR] (12:2) Sum 88, p. 177.
"Spring, Accomack County." [Vis] (28) 88, p. 32.
1359. DUDLEY, Betty
"White-Trash Cooking." [SinW] (35) Sum-Fall 88, p. 65.
1360. DUEMER, Joseph
"Island Universe" (Selections: "Teleological Argument," "Evening Primrose"). [KanQ] (20:3) Sum 88, p. 94-95.
1361. DUER, David
"Combs." [LittleM] (15:3/4) 88, p. 14-15.
1362. DUFER, Dennis
"Disciple." [PaintedB] (36) 88, p. 78.
"In Fall the Newsboys Burn." [WestB] (21/22) 88, p. 25.
"What Became of Irving." [PaintedB] (36) 88, p. 77.
1363. DUFFIN, K. E.
"Buffleheads in Winter Sea." [Verse] (5:3) N 88, p. 22.
"'Chiryu: Horse Fair in Early Summer' by Hiroshige." [CarolQ] (41:1) Fall 88, p. 19.
"Excavations." [CumbPR] (7:2) Spr 88, p. 20.
"Headstone: Lost at Sea." [GrahamHR] (11) Spr 88, p. 11.
"'Narumi' by Hiroshige." [CarolQ] (41:1) Fall 88, p. 19.
"Pangaea." [CumbPR] (7:2) Spr 88, p. 19.
"Reading Cyrillic." [GrahamHR] (11) Spr 88, p. 10.
"Transatlantic Telegraph." [Verse] (5:2) Jl 88, p. 16.
1364. DUFFORD, Elizabeth M.
"The Sugar Bowl Emptied." [LittleM] (15:3/4) 88, p. 140.
DUGGAN, Devon Miller
See MILLER-DUGGAN, Devon

1365. DUGGAN, Laurie
"Academic Poem." [NewAW] (4) Fall 88, p. 100-101.
"Blue Hills 2." [NewAW] (4) Fall 88, p. 98.
"Blue Hills 13." [NewAW] (4) Fall 88, p. 98-99.
"In Perigord." [NewAW] (4) Fall 88, p. 99-100.
"Poem: Looking out over the beds of tram lines." [NewAW] (4) Fall 88, p. 97.
"Three Found Poems." [NewAW] (4) Fall 88, p. 101-102.
1366. DUGGIN, Lorraine
"A Sunday at Neale Woods" (For Carl Jonas). [Plain] (8:1) Fall 87, p. 28.
"Umbilicus." [Plain] (8:3) Spr-Sum 88, p. 24.
1367. DUHAMEL, Denise
"The Day the First Grade Voted for the Death Penalty." [MassR] (29:1) Spr 88, p. 39.
"Mother." [Footwork] ('88) 88, p. 42.
1368. DUMARAN, Adele
"Desire" (Captain Cook's Bay, Moorea, July 1986, For Bill and the rest of us). [ChamLR] (1) Fall 87, p. 56-57.
"For the Man of a Hundred Half Songs." [HawaiiR] (12:1, #23) Spr 88, p. 3.
"The World Is a Wedding" (for my father). [HawaiiR] (12:1, #23) Spr 88, p. 1-2.
1369. DUMARS, Denise
"The Harrowing of Hell" (after the painting by Jonathan Falk). [Jacaranda] (3:2) Fall-Wint 88, p. 83-84.
"Red." [WormR] (28:4, #112) 88, p. 120.
"The Village Coffee Shop." [WormR] (28:4, #112) 88, p. 119.
1370. DUMAS, Henry
"East Saint Hell: Up from the Ghetto." [RiverS] (26) 88, p. 25-26.
"I Will Be Singing in the Morning!" (behind Forest Flower blowing me on and on). [RiverS] (26) 88, p. 23-24.
"Our King Is Dead." [BlackALF] (22:2) Sum 88, p. 245-246.
"Take This River!" [BlackALF] (22:2) Sum 88, p. 241-244.
1371. DUMBRAVEANU, Anghel
"Daca Voi Intilni O Fintina." [NewRena] (7:2, #22) Spr 88, p. 72.
"Dreaming with Snow" (for Adam Puslojic, tr. by Adam J. Sorkin and Irina Grigorescu). [NowestR] (26:3) 88, p. 53.
"Fereastra Corabierului." [NewRena] (7:2, #22) Spr 88, p. 74.
"If I'll Meet Any Fountain" (tr. by Robert J. Ward and Marcel Pop-Cornis). [NewRena] (7:2, #22) Spr 88, p. 73.
"The News from Chimaera Land" (tr. by Adam J. Sorkin and Irina Grigorescu). [NowestR] (26:3) 88, p. 54.
"The Seaman's Window" (tr. by Robert J. Ward and Marcel Pop-Cornis). [NewRena] (7:2, #22) Spr 88, p. 75.
1372. DUNCAN, Graham
"Crooked Hypotenuse." [Blueline] (9:1/2) 88, p. 64.
1373. DUNCAN, Julia Nunnally
"Good Old Joe." [Lactuca] (11) O 88, p. 37.
"Rattlesnake." [Lactuca] (11) O 88, p. 35.
"Sister Rose." [Lactuca] (11) O 88, p. 37-38.
"Terriers." [Footwork] ('88) 88, p. 42.
1374. DUNCAN, Robert
"A Song from the Structures of Rime Ringing As the Poet Paul Celan Sings." [Acts] (8/9) 88, p. 7.
1375. DUNGEY, Christopher
"Two-a-Day Drills." [RiverS] (27) 88, p. 54.
1376. DUNLOP, Ethel
"Imayo." [Amelia] (5:1, #12) 88, p. 74.
1377. DUNMORE, Helen
"On Drinking Lime-Juice in September" (for Patrick Dunn and Patrick Charnley). [Verse] (5:3) N 88, p. 62.
1378. DUNN, Ann
"Aphrodite." [HiramPoR] (44/45) Spr-Wint 88, p. 12.
"January." [DeKalbLAJ] (21:1) Wint 88, p. 50.
"Medea." [HiramPoR] (44/45) Spr-Wint 88, p. 13.
1379. DUNN, Douglas
"In-Flight Entertainment." [Antaeus] (60) Spr 88, p. 195-197.
1380. DUNN, Ethel
"First Fruit." [Kaleid] (16) Wint-Spr 88, p. 19.
"Separation." [Kaleid] (16) Wint-Spr 88, p. 19.

"Springtime." [Kaleid] (16) Wint-Spr 88, p. 19.
"Sunday." [Kaleid] (16) Wint-Spr 88, p. 19.

1381. DUNN, Millard
"Eating Out." [KanQ] (20:1/2) Wint-Spr 88, p. 164-165.
"Hunting Frogs." [KanQ] (20:1/2) Wint-Spr 88, p. 164.

1382. DUNN, Stephen
"Almost Home." [PraS] (62:3) Fall 88, p. j84-85.
"Always a Citizen." [Pequod] (25) 88, p. 54.
"At the Atlantic City Bus Station." [Pequod] (25) 88, p. 52-53.
"Between Angels." [NewYorker] (64:39) 14 N 88, p. 40.
"Beyond Hammonton." [PoetryNW] (29:1) Spr 88, p. 44-45.
"Biographia Literaria: The Hofstra Basketball Team Goes to Central Pennsylvania." [NoDaQ] (56:1) Wint 88, p. 24.
"Bitterness." [TampaR] (1) 88, p. 89.
"Competition." [DenQ] (22:4) Spr 88, p. 6-7.
"Dancing with God." [VirQR] (64:3) Sum 88, p. 433-434.
"Father, Mother, Robert Henley Who Hanged Himself in the Ninth Grade, *et. Al.*" [PraS] (62:3) Fall 88, p. 83.
"Happiness." [Poetry] (153:3) D 88, p. 152.
"A Kind of Blindness and a Kind of Warmth." [NewEngR] (10:3) Spr 88, p. 281.
"Kindness." [Poetry] (153:3) D 88, p. 152-153.
"Leaving the Polite Party." [VirQR] (64:3) Sum 88, p. 434-436.
"Let Me Introduce Myself." [JINJPo] (10:1/2) 88, p. 39.
"Letting the Puma Go." [Poetry] (153:3) D 88, p. 150-151.
"Luck." [TriQ] (72) Spr-Sum 88, p. 172.
"The Man Who Closed Shop." [TriQ] (72) Spr-Sum 88, p. 173.
"Naturally." [Poetry] (153:3) D 88, p. 150.
"An Orchestration of Dream." [HayF] (3) Spr 88, p. 9-10.
"The Search." [TampaR] (1) 88, p. 35.
"Seriousness." [PraS] (62:3) Fall 88, p. 79-80.
"To a Terrorist." [PoetryNW] (29:1) Spr 88, p. 47.
"Trouble." [HayF] (3) Spr 88, p. 7-8.
"Urgencies." [PraS] (62:3) Fall 88, p. 80-82.
"Walking the Marshland" (Brigantine Wildlife Refuge, 1987). [PoetryNW] (29:1) Spr 88, p. 45-46.
"Withdrawal." [DenQ] (22:4) Spr 88, p. 8-9.

1383. DUNNING, Stephen
"You Might Say, This Is the Story of My Life." [Spirit] (9:1) 88, p. 26-28.

1384. DUNSMORE, Roger
"Nuclear Peach" (for Meng Qingshi). [CutB] (31/32) 88, p. 23-25.

1385. DUNWOODY, Michael
"The Life in a Day." [Event] (17:1) Spr 88, p. 91-94.

1386. DUO, Duo
"The Production of Language Is in the Kitchen" (in Chinese & English). [BelPoJ] (39:2) Wint 88-89, p. 6-7.
"When People Rise from Cheese, Statement #1" (in Chinese & English). [BelPoJ] (39:2) Wint 88-89, p. 4-5.

1387. DUPIN, Jacques
"Thirst" (tr. by Elton Glaser). [Paint] (15:30) Aut 88, p. 40.
"The Truce" (tr. by Elton Glaser). [Paint] (15:30) Aut 88, p. 40.

1388. DuPLESSIS, Rachel Blau
"Draft #6: Midrush." [Temblor] (7) 88, p. 50-55.

1389. DUPRE, Louise
"Evidence." [Os] (27) 88, p. 33-37.

1390. DUPREE, Edison
"Exhortation to Political Invertebrates" (for Chuck Oglesby). [Ploughs] (14:1) 88, p. 89.
"Girl Spinner in Carolina Cotton Mill, 1909" (after Lewis Hine). [Ploughs] (14:1) 88, p. 88.

DURAN, Jorge Gaitan
See GAITAN DURAN, Jorge

1391. DURBIN, M. B.
"I'll Only Wake Up If You Kiss My Hair." [Amelia] (5:2, #13) 88, p. 127.

1392. DURHAM, Sandra
"Tresa and Me." [ChatR] (8:3) Spr 88, p. 36.

1393. DUTTON, G. F.
"Carmen Mortis." [Verse] (5:1) F 88, p. 62.
"Crossing Over." [Verse] (5:1) F 88, p. 62.
"Crossing the Tundra." [Verse] (5:1) F 88, p. 61.
1394. DUVAL, Quinton
"Mudflats at Cley." [CharR] (14:2) Fall 88, p. 106-107.
"On Weight." [KanQ] (20:3) Sum 88, p. 242.
"Summer Nights in Boulogne." [CharR] (14:2) Fall 88, p. 106.
DUYN, Mona van
See Van DUYN, Mona
1395. DWYER, David
"Elsewhere." [NoDaQ] (56:4) Fall 88, p. 274.
"Old Recipe for a Meadow." [NoDaQ] (56:4) Fall 88, p. 273.
"An Old Story." [NoDaQ] (56:4) Fall 88, p. 273.
"Quantum Mechanics: Another Love Poem." [Agni] (27) 88, p. 187-188.
1396. DWYER, William
"Acceptance." [CapeR] (23:2) Fall 88, p. 46.
"Driftwood." [SewanR] (96:2) Spr 88, p. 212-213.
"Man O'War." [CapeR] (23:2) Fall 88, p. 47.
"Xylophone Trees." [SewanR] (96:2) Spr 88, p. 211-212.
1397. DYBEK, Stuart
"Farmer" (corrected reprint). [PassN] (9:2) Sum 88, p. 18.
"Farmer" (corrected version on insert). [PassN] (9:1) Wint 88, p. 15.
"Nydia's Alba." [ClockR] (4:2) 88, p. 21.
"Smelt Fishers." [ClockR] (4:2) 88, p. 20.
1398. DYC, Gloria
"Somehow We Managed" (for Ollie Napesni). [PassN] (9:1) Wint 88, p. 4.
1399. DYE, Bru
"Black Shirts" (Vita Volta 1910). [JamesWR] (5:3) Spr-Sum 88, p. 12.
"What Happened" (after Jim Dine). [JamesWR] (6:1) Fall 88, p. 5.
1400. DYE, Vesna Markulin
"House with Venetian Blinds." [InterPR] (14:1) Spr 88, p. 49.
"Kuca Sa Venecijskim Zavjesama." [InterPR] (14:1) Spr 88, p. 48.
"The Time We Picked Blackberries" (tr. by the author). [InterPR] (14:1) Spr 88, p. 41, 43.
"Tvoj Nacin Odlaska." [InterPR] (14:1) Spr 88, p. 44, 46.
"Vrijème Kad Smo Brali Kupine." [InterPR] (14:1) Spr 88, p. 40, 42.
"Your Way of Departure" (tr. by the author). [InterPR] (14:1) Spr 88, p. 45, 47.
1401. DYER, Lynda
"In the Drought, We Only Sleep." [PaintedB] (34) 88, p. 29-30.
1402. DYKEWOMON, Elana
"From My Journal: The Night That Willow Died." [SinW] (32) Sum 87, p. 52-54.
"The Real Fat Womon Poems." [SinW] (33) Fall 87, p. 85-93.
1403. EADY, Cornelius
"False Arrest." [SenR] (18:2) 88, p. 38-39.
"The Grin." [SenR] (18:2) 88, p. 37.
"June 14th, 1988." [SenR] (18:2) 88, p. 40.
"The Mouse." [SenR] (18:2) 88, p. 36.
"Pastoral." [WilliamMR] (26:1) Spr 88, p. 36-37.
"Sherbet." [Crazy] (34) Spr 88, p. 58-59.
"Sherbet." [Harp] (277:1659) Ag 88, p. 35.
"Song." [Crazy] (34) Spr 88, p. 56-57.
"William Carlos Williams." [WilliamMR] (26:1) Spr 88, p. 35.
1404. EANES, Linda
"At the Woodpile." [Callaloo] (11:2, #35) Spr 88, p. 272.
1405. EARLE, Karen
"In Their Town." [DenQ] (22:3) Wint 88, p. 181.
1406. EARLY, Gerald
"Below Zero on the Installment Plan." [AmerPoR] (17:4) Jl-Ag 88, p. 32.
"Country or Western Music" (for tenor saxophonist John Coltrane). [AmerPoR] (17:4) Jl-Ag 88, p. 32.
"Dumbo's Ears or How We Begin" (for Linnet, my daughter). [NowestR] (26:2) 88, p. 57-58.
"Innocency or Not Song X" (for jazz pianist Bud Powell). [AmerPoR] (17:4) Jl-Ag 88, p. 31.
"Lear and His Daughter." [AmerPoR] (17:4) Jl-Ag 88, p. 33.

"Some Memories of an American Girlhood." [AmerPoR] (17:4) Jl-Ag 88, p. 33.
"Southern Belle and Boy." [NowestR] (26:2) 88, p. 59-60.

1407. EARLY, Lynn
"Excuses (for Not Doing Homework) I Have Heard." [EngJ] (77:8) D 88, p. 81.

1408. EATON, Charles Edward
"Against the Grain." [CharR] (14:2) Fall 88, p. 86-87.
"The Cove." [Salm] (78/79) Spr-Sum 88, p. 154-155.
"The Drawbridge." [DeKalbLAJ] (21:1) Wint 88, p. 51-52.
"Dumbbells." [Salm] (78/79) Spr-Sum 88, p. 153-154.
"The Gangplank." [BostonR] (13:4) Ag 88, p. 3.
"The Grommet." [AnotherCM] (18) 88, p. 96.
"Harlequin Head." [HiramPoR] (44/45) Spr-Wint 88, p. 14.
"The Hook." [CharR] (14:2) Fall 88, p. 88-89.
"Jowls." [Poem] (59) My 88, p. 22.
"The Knocker." [SouthernPR] (28:2) Fall 88, p. 60-61.
"Last Straw." [DenQ] (22:4) Spr 88, p. 55-56.
"Meteorite." [CharR] (14:2) Fall 88, p. 89.
"The Pistol." [FourQ] (2d series 2:2) Fall 88, p. 58.
"Quetzal." [MidwQ] (29:2) Wint 88, p. 218-219.
"The Reef." [CrabCR] (5:3) Fall 88, p. 5.
"The Stereoscope." [CharR] (14:1) Spr 88, p. 61.
"The Sun Says Grace." [Amelia] (4:4, #11) 88, p. 23.
"Sword of Damocles." [Salm] (78/79) Spr-Sum 88, p. 152-153.
"Tongue Twister." [CharR] (14:1) Spr 88, p. 60.
"Trial Runs." [CharR] (14:2) Fall 88, p. 87.
"Truffles." [KanQ] (20:1/2) Wint-Spr 88, p. 142.

1409. EBERHART, Richard
"The Blunting." [AmerPoR] (17:4) Jl-Ag 88, p. 22.
"The Body and the Book." [KeyWR] (1:2) Fall 88, p. 19-20.
"Change." [KeyWR] (1:2) Fall 88, p. 21.
"Chart Indent." [AmerPoR] (17:4) Jl-Ag 88, p. 22.
"Eight Lines About Everything." [KeyWR] (1:2) Fall 88, p. 24.
"Football." [KeyWR] (1:2) Fall 88, p. 26.
"The Immortal Picture." [AmerPoR] (17:4) Jl-Ag 88, p. 22.
"Just So Everybody Comes Up to Bat." [KeyWR] (1:2) Fall 88, p. 25.
"Little Glass Box." [KeyWR] (1:2) Fall 88, p. 22.
"Power House Gift that Startles." [KeyWR] (1:2) Fall 88, p. 23.

1410. EBERT, Gwen
"Twigs for Tools." [CreamCR] (12:1) Wint 88, p. 84.

1411. ECHAVARREN, Roberto
"Aguas Primaverales." [Inti] (26/27) Otoño 87-Primavera 88, p. 86-87.
"Amores." [Inti] (26/27) Otoño 87-Primavera 88, p. 88-89.
"El Claro." [Inti] (26/27) Otoño 87-Primavera 88, p. 84-85.
"Cuando el Sol Se Hunde." [Inti] (26/27) Otoño 87-Primavera 88, p. 89-90.
"Doble Sueño." [Inti] (26/27) Otoño 87-Primavera 88, p. 83-84.
"Justo el Treintaiuno." [Inti] (26/27) Otoño 87-Primavera 88, p. 85-86.
"Nostalgia." [Inti] (26/27) Otoño 87-Primavera 88, p. 90-91.
"Para Esta Noche." [Inti] (26/27) Otoño 87-Primavera 88, p. 86.
"Relámpago." [Inti] (26/27) Otoño 87-Primavera 88, p. 84.
"Ultimo Tango." [Inti] (26/27) Otoño 87-Primavera 88, p. 87-88.

1412. ECHELES, Justi
"The Woman on the Amtrak." [DenQ] (22:3) Wint 88, p. 46-47.

1413. ECKEL, Martha Charlier
"In the Next Building." [Amelia] (5:2, #13) 88, p. 122.

1414. ECONOMOU, George
"A Five in One Wedding Song" (for Charis & John). [Contact] (9:47/48/49) Spr 88, p. 49.

1415. EDELSTEIN, Carol
"Open." [DenQ] (23:2) Fall 88, p. 40.
"Small Charms." [YellowS] (28) D 88, p. 28.

1416. EDMANDS, Trevor
"The Gift." [Bogg] (60) 88, p. 23.

1417. EDMOND, Lauris
"Separate Development" (tr. of Tanja Sassor). [Verse] (5:3) N 88, p. 68.
"The Written Word." [CumbPR] (7:2) Spr 88, p. 9.

1418. EDMUNDS, Martin
"Gaea." [Agni] (26) 88, p. 169.
1419. EDSON, Russell
"The Afternoon Tea." [Caliban] (4) 88, p. 81.
"The Dancing Lesson." [Gambit] (22) 88, p. 63.
"Little Edward." [Caliban] (4) 88, p. 82.
"The Mountain Guide." [Gambit] (22) 88, p. 62.
"Nice." [Caliban] (4) 88, p. 80.
"Of Distant Stars." [WillowS] (21) Wint 88, p. 46.
"The Rabbit Story." [WillowS] (21) Wint 88, p. 45.
"Recipes for a Brain Disguised as a Wig." [Caliban] (4) 88, p. 82.
"Structure and Sense." [Caliban] (4) 88, p. 81.
"That Day." [WillowS] (21) Wint 88, p. 47.
"The Vegetable Kings." [Caliban] (4) 88, p. 80.
EDWARDS, Luis Carlos Philips
See PHILIPS EDWARDS, Luis Carlos
1420. EDWARDS, Stephanie
"Wonder." [RagMag] (6:2) Fall 88, p. 15.
1421. EDWARDS, Susan
"Binocular Vision." [Blueline] (9:1/2) 88, p. 29.
1422. EDWARDS, Thomas S.
"Oriental Carpet" (tr. of Reiner Kunze, w. Ken Letko). [ColR] (NS 15:2) Fall-Wint 88, p. 87.
1423. EGERMEIER, Virginia
"Hopscotch." [Jacaranda] (3:2) Fall-Wint 88, p. 85-86.
"When the Wind Blows This Hard." [LitR] (31:3) Spr 88, p. 298.
1424. EHRHART, W. D.
"Adoquinas" (Masaya, Nicaragua, July 22nd, 1986). [PaintedB] (36) 88, p. 98.
"Chasing Locomotives." [ColR] (NS 15:1) Spr-Sum 88, p. 22.
"In San Jose de los Remates" (Nicaragua, July 1986). [PaintedB] (36) 88, p. 97.
"Nicaragua Libre" (for Flavio Galo). [AmerPoR] (17:2) Mr-Ap 88, p. 35.
"Second Thoughts" (for Nyugen Van Hung). [ColR] (NS 15:1) Spr-Sum 88, p. 20.
"Starting Over" (for Nguyen Thi Kim Thanh). [ColR] (NS 15:1) Spr-Sum 88, p. 21.
"The Trouble with Poets." [StoneC] (16:1/2) Fall-Wint 88-89, p. 68.
"Why I Don't Mind Rocking Leela to Sleep." [AmerPoR] (17:2) Mr-Ap 88, p. 35.
1425. EHRLICH, Shelley
"About Blankets." [MemphisSR] (8:2) Spr 88, p. 88-89.
"The Chronically Ill" (after a line by Auden). [MemphisSR] (8:2) Spr 88, p. 87.
"The Generation's Flood." [Wind] (18:62) 88, p. 9.
"Mailbox on Linden Street." [Wind] (18:62) 88, p. 9.
"Small Victories." [WestB] (21/22) 88, p. 23.
"Summer Is Tumbling Down." [TexasR] (9:3/4) Fall-Wint 88, p. 36.
"Winter Trees" (In memory of Shelley Ehrlich: b. 1931 d. March, 1988). [Northeast] (ser. 4:7) Sum 88, inside back cover.
1426. EIBEL, Deborah
"Divorce." [CanLit] (118) Aut 88, p. 95-96.
"Later." [CanLit] (118) Aut 88, p. 59-60.
1427. EICH, Gunther
"In Conclusion" (tr. by Francis Golffing). [SpiritSH] (54) Fall-Wint 88, p. 30.
"October" (tr. by Francis Golffing). [SpiritSH] (54) Fall-Wint 88, p. 29.
"Untitled: Meditation on justice to fishes" (tr. by Francis Golffing). [SpiritSH] (54) Fall-Wint 88, p. 28.
1428. EIELSON, Jorge Eduardo
"A un Ciervo Otra Vez Herido." [Inti] (26/27) Otoño 87-Primavera 88, p. 106-107.
"Cámara Luciente." [Inti] (26/27) Otoño 87-Primavera 88, p. 106.
"La Ciudad." [Inti] (26/27) Otoño 87-Primavera 88, p. 100-101.
"Dalí." [Inti] (26/27) Otoño 87-Primavera 88, p. 105.
"Los Ebrios." [Inti] (26/27) Otoño 87-Primavera 88, p. 101.
"Extranjera." [Inti] (26/27) Otoño 87-Primavera 88, p. 104.
"Genitales Bajo el Vino." [Inti] (26/27) Otoño 87-Primavera 88, p. 107.
"Llanto." [Inti] (26/27) Otoño 87-Primavera 88, p. 105.
"Mi Familia Ha Muerto." [Inti] (26/27) Otoño 87-Primavera 88, p. 105.
"Poema para Leer de Pie en el Autobús entre la Puerta Flaminia y el Tritone." [Inti] (26/27) Otoño 87-Primavera 88, p. 109-114.
"Primera Muerte de María." [Inti] (26/27) Otoño 87-Primavera 88, p. 107-109.
"Los Que Velan." [Inti] (26/27) Otoño 87-Primavera 88, p. 102.

"Recuerdo." [Inti] (26/27) Otoño 87-Primavera 88, p. 103.
"Soneto a un Ebrio de la Antigua Roma." [Inti] (26/27) Otoño 87-Primavera 88, p. 103-104.
"Tableta Arcaica." [Inti] (26/27) Otoño 87-Primavera 88, p. 105.

1429. EIFERMAN, Sharon Rees
"Ontology of Rain." [Writer] (101:9) S 88, p. 25-26.

1430. EIMERS, Nancy
"Where We Came From, Where We Are Going." [IndR] (12:1) Wint 88, p. 112-116.

1431. EISELE, Midge
"Savannah." [GettyR] (1:2) Spr 88, p. 374.

1432. EISELE, Thomas
"The distance between us is hard to explain." [PoetryE] (25) Spr 88, p. 122.
"I am who am." [PoetryE] (25) Spr 88, p. 120.
"She is an angel and I am a snail" (for Martha Margarita Tamez). [PoetryE] (25) Spr 88, p. 123.
"We both knew there wasn't any point." [PoetryE] (25) Spr 88, p. 121.

1433. EISNER
"The Anniversary of the Cambodia Bombings." [MinnR] (NS 30/31) Spr-Fall 88, p. 50.
"Red and God." [MinnR] (NS 30/31) Spr-Fall 88, p. 51.

1434. EISNER, Cliff
"At the Party." [Margin] (6) Sum 88, p. 85.
"The Silence Calls You Back" (for Henry Miller). [Margin] (6) Sum 88, p. 84.

1435. EKELUND, Louise
"Den Ljusa Underjorden" (Excerpt, tr. by Ulla Nätterqvist-Sawa). [LitR] (31:3) Spr 88, p. 300.

1436. EKSTRÖM, Margareta
"At the Window" (tr. by Eva Claeson). [GrahamHR] (11) Spr 88, p. 108-109.
"In the Morning" (tr. by Eva Claeson). [GrahamHR] (11) Spr 88, p. 110-111.

1437. ELDER, Karl
"The Cockroach." [HighP] (3:1) Spr 88, p. 48-49.
"Constanza." [BelPoJ] (38:4) Sum 88, p. 20-21.
"A Life." [HighP] (3:1) Spr 88, p. 44.
"Miracle." [HighP] (3:1) Spr 88, p. 45.
"The Rock." [HighP] (3:1) Spr 88, p. 46-47.

1438. ELDRED, Charlotte
"Home." [MSS] (6:2) 88, p. 38.

1439. ELDRIDGE, Kevin Joe
"The Meaning of Hillbilly Music." [Agni] (27) 88, p. 214-216.

1440. ELEISH, Parinaz
"As Good As Any Other Day." [InterPR] (14:2) Fall 88, p. 88.

1441. ELIAS, Megan
"The doctor is young and eager." [HangL] (53) 88, p. 56.
"Not Tomorrow." [HangL] (53) 88, p. 57.

1442. ELIZABETH, Martha
"Manon Considers Leaving Her Lover." [PassN] (9:2) Sum 88, p. 19.

1443. ELKIN, Roger
"Deaf-and-Dumb Man's Hands" (for Graham, for Jo). [Crosscur] (7:4) 88, p. 121.

1444. ELKIND, Sue Saniel
"Always There's a Moving Away." [Turnstile] (1:1) Wint 88, p. 73.
"Crossing the Street." [CentR] (32:1) Wint 88, p. 40.
"Grandmother." [CentR] (32:1) Wint 88, p. 40-41.
"Jerusalem of My Dream." [SpoonRQ] (13:3) Sum 88, p. 15.
"Killing Birds." [SpoonRQ] (13:3) Sum 88, p. 13.
"Summer." [SpoonRQ] (13:3) Sum 88, p. 14.

1445. ELLEDGE, Jim
"Equinox." [DenQ] (22:4) Spr 88, p. 54.
"Homage." [PoetryE] (25) Spr 88, p. 117.
"Olly Olly Oxen Free" (For Jim Stark). [SpoonRQ] (12:4) Fall 87, p. 54.
"Station to Station." [SpoonRQ] (12:4) Fall 87, p. 52-53.
"Vital Signs." [PoetC] (19:2) Wint 88, p. 3.

1446. ELLEFSON, J. C.
"The Blacksmith's Dog Story." [CrabCR] (5:1) Wint 88, p. 20.

1447. ELLEN
"The Confession." [Footwork] ('88) 88, p. 71.

"I Would Gather Up the Nomads." [Footwork] ('88) 88, p. 71.
"Maybe I should Take a Morning Job in the Sahara." [Turnstile] (1:1) Wint 88, p. 71-72.
"Soft." [Footwork] ('88) 88, p. 70.

1448. ELLENBOGEN, George
"An Artist with Seven Fingers." [Amelia] (5:1, #12) 88, p. 33.

1449. ELLINGSON, Alice Olds
"William Carlos Williams." [PikeF] (9) Fall 88, p. 3.

1450. ELLIOT, Alistair
"Arthur Rimbaud: Girls Looking for Lice." [Margin] (6) Sum 88, p. 73.
"José-Maria de Heredia: Antony and Cleopatra." [Margin] (6) Sum 88, p. 74.
"Paul Valéry: The Footsteps." [Margin] (6) Sum 88, p. 74.

1451. ELLIOTT, William I.
"Clockwise." [CrabCR] (5:2) Sum 88, p. 19.
"Hymn" (tr. of Shuntaro Tanikawa, w. Kazuo Kawamura). [CrabCR] (5:2) Sum 88, p. 14.
"Some Questions" (tr. of Shuntaro Tanikawa, w. Kazuo Kawamura). [CrabCR] (5:2) Sum 88, p. 15-16.
"A Study of the Tactile Sense" (tr. of Shuntaro Tanikawa, w. Kazuo Kawamura). [CrabCR] (5:2) Sum 88, p. 16-19.
"The Window" (tr. of Shuntaro Tanikawa, w. Kazuo Kawamura). [CrabCR] (5:2) Sum 88, p. 14.

1452. ELLIS, Linda
"After." [PacificR] (6) Spr 88, p. 20.
"Saying Goodbye." [PacificR] (6) Spr 88, p. 18-19.
"Someone New." [PacificR] (6) Spr 88, p. 21.

1453. ELLIS, Ron
"Canto 65." [PoetryNW] (29:3) Aut 88, p. 32-33.
"Performers." [FloridaR] (16:1) Spr-Sum 88, p. 51.

1454. ELLSWORTH, Priscilla
"Cave in the Dordogne." [Nimrod] (32:1) Fall-Wint 88, p. 119.
"Shadows." [PoetL] (83:4) Wint 88-89, p. 38.

1455. ELMAN, Richard
"For Tomas Borge." [Pequod] (25) 88, p. 22-24.
"Post Time" (Belmont Park). [Confr] (37/38) Spr-Sum 88, p. 221.

1456. ELMSLIE, Kenward
"Haikus" (6 poems). [NewAW] (3) Spr 88, p. 42-53.

1457. ELON, Florence
"The Name for Moustache." [Vis] (28) 88, p. 11.
"Place Not Taken." [ParisR] (30:106) Spr 88, p. 255.
"Securities." [Pembroke] (20) 88, p. 134.
"You." [Pembroke] (20) 88, p. 133.

1458. ELOVIC, Barbara
"Hibernation." [HighP] (3:1) Spr 88, p. 110.
"How He Left Me." [PassN] (9:2) Sum 88, p. 29.
"Maybe." [MSS] (6:2) 88, p. 40.

1459. ELROD, John
"Driving Known Roads in the Dark." [BellArk] (4:6) N-D 88, p. 4.
"Drought's End." [BellArk] (4:6) N-D 88, p. 10.
"Geode." [BellArk] (4:5) S-O 88, p. 16.
"Secrets." [BellArk] (4:6) N-D 88, p. 17.
"Songbird." [BellArk] (4:4) Jl-Ag 88, p. 1.
"Swing Low." [BellArk] (4:1) Ja-F 88, p. 6.
"The Tent." [BellArk] (4:3) My-Je 88, p. 3.
"Therapy." [BellArk] (4:1) Ja-F 88, p. 8.

1460. ELSBERG, John
"Fragment." [Gargoyle] (35) 88, p. 153.

1461. ELUARD, Paul
"Fish" (tr. by Deborah Waters). [StoneC] (15:3/4) Spr-Sum 88, p. 27.
"Poisson." [StoneC] (15:3/4) Spr-Sum 88, p. 26.

1462. ELYTIS, Odysseus (Odysseas)
"Anoint the Ariston" (16 selections, tr. by Olga Broumas). [AmerPoR] (17:1) Ja-F 88, p. 13-15.
"The Little Seafarer" (Selections: 6 poems). [TriQ] (71) Wint 88, p. 118-126.
"With Light and Death" (Selections: 9, 15-21, tr. by Olga Broumas). [Agni] (27) 88, p. 176-183.

1463. EMANS, Elaine V.
"The Frog." [KanQ] (20:3) Sum 88, p. 234.
"Note to Janie, Unsent." [KanQ] (20:1/2) Wint-Spr 88, p. 177.
"Pumps." [KanQ] (20:1/2) Wint-Spr 88, p. 178.
"Wilde in the Highest City in the United States, 1882." [KanQ] (20:1/2) Wint-Spr 88, p. 178.
1464. EMANUEL, Lynn
"The Technology of Inspiration." [LightY] ('88/9) 88, p. 145-146.
1465. EMBLEN, D. L.
"The Scream" (tr. of Werner Aspenström). [ArtfulD] (14/15) Fall 88, p. 82.
1466. EMERY, Michael J.
"The 3rd Movement." [WindO] (50) Aut 88, p. 5.
"The Auction of the Mind." [WindO] (50) Aut 88, p. 8.
"Basketball & Others." [WindO] (50) Aut 88, p. 9.
"I Can't Feel You, Rain." [WindO] (50) Aut 88, p. 7.
"Up." [WindO] (50) Aut 88, p. 6.
"We Are the Deaf." [WindO] (50) Aut 88, p. 5.
1467. EMERY, Thomas
"Lou Labonte's Inn." [Ploughs] (14:4) 88, p. 118-119.
1468. EMIN, Gevork
"In Moments Rare of Inspiration" (tr. by Olga Shartse). [NegC] (8:1/2) 88, p. 49.
1469. EMMANUEL, Lenny
"The Blonde and the Yellow Catawba Trees." [WindO] (50) Aut 88, p. 28-29.
1470. ENDO, Russell S.
"Ode" (to a Poet). [PaintedB] (32/33) 88, p. 115-116.
1471. ENEMARK, Brett
"Another Adam" (Pablo Armando Fernández, tr. for Paul de Barros). [WestCR] (22:4) Spr 87, i.e. 88, p. 59.
1472. ENGBLOM, Philip C.
"Ajanta, February 1962" (tr. of P. S. Rege). [Nimrod] (31:2) Spr-Sum 88, p. 88.
"Line" (tr. of P. S. Rege). [Nimrod] (31:2) Spr-Sum 88, p. 90.
"Lord Thousand-Eyes" (tr. of P. S. Rege). [Nimrod] (31:2) Spr-Sum 88, p. 89.
"Vision" (tr. of P. S. Rege). [Nimrod] (31:2) Spr-Sum 88, p. 91.
1473. ENGEL, Mary
"Apparition in the Afternoon." [CreamCR] (12:2) Sum 88, p. 178.
1474. ENGELBERT, Jo Anne
"The Brutal Lovers" (To F. Díaz Chávez, J. A. Medina Durón & C. S. Toro, tr. of Roberto Sosa). [Bomb] (24) Sum 88, p. 70.
"Military Secret" (Answer to Rafael Heliodoro Valle, tr. of Roberto Sosa). [Bomb] (24) Sum 88, p. 70.
"Stroessner or the Mask" (tr. of Roberto Sosa). [Bomb] (24) Sum 88, p. 70.
"Urgent" (tr. of Roberto Sosa). [Bomb] (24) Sum 88, p. 70.
1475. ENGELS, John
"The Arm" (tr. of Tomaz Salamun, w. Michael Biggins). [NewEngR] (10:3) Spr 88, p. 279-280.
"In Cedar Grove Cemetery." [GeoR] (42:3) Fall 88, p. 483-484.
"The Planet." [TexasR] (9:3/4) Fall-Wint 88, p. 38.
"A Watercolor." [TexasR] (9:3/4) Fall-Wint 88, p. 37.
1476. ENGLAND, Gerald
"And after his neighbors complained he." [Bogg] (60) 88, p. 14.
"Croick Churchyard." [Lactuca] (11) O 88, p. 19.
1477. ENGLE, John D., Jr.
"Reminder." [LightY] ('88/9) 88, p. 229.
1478. ENGMAN, John
"The Basho Doll." [NewEngR] (11:2) Wint 88, p. 176-179.
"Staff." [VirQR] (64:4) Aut 88, p. 623-624.
"Stones That Seem to Have Grown from the Lawn." [VirQR] (64:4) Aut 88, p. 622-623.
1479. ENRIQUEZ, Romelia
"Water" (tr. of Coral Bracho, w. Thomas Hoeksema). [MidAR] (8:2) 88, p. 81-82.
1480. ENSLIN, Theodore
"Axes" (Excerpt). [Bound] (15:3/16:1) Spr-Fall 88, p. 111-115.
1481. ENTREKIN, Gail Rudd
"The Nothing." [Abraxas] (37) 88, p. 25.

1482. ENZENSBERGER, Hans Magnus
"Death of a Poet" (For Rainer M. Gerhardt, tr. by Reinhold Grimm). [NowestR] (26:2) 88, p. 43.
"Finnish Tango" (In memory of Felix Pollak, tr. by Reinhold Grimm). [NowestR] (26:2) 88, p. 42.
1483. EPSTEIN, Daniel Mark
"The Rivals." [ParisR] (30:106) Spr 88, p. 115.
1484. EQUI, Elaine
"A Date with Robbe-Grillet." [NewAW] (3) Spr 88, p. 91.
"Fire." [NewAW] (4) Fall 88, p. 28.
"'Round Midnight." [NewAW] (3) Spr 88, p. 90.
1485. ERDRICH, Louise
"Angels." [Caliban] (5) 88, p. 9.
"Avila." [Caliban] (5) 88, p. 10.
"Immaculate Conception." [Caliban] (5) 88, p. 8.
"Orozco's Christ." [Caliban] (5) 88, p. 7.
1486. EREMENKO, Aleksandr
"A horizontal country" (tr. by John High and Katya Olmsted). [FiveFR] (6) 88, p. 30.
1487. ERHARD, Nancie
"Bridge Over a Utah Gorge." [PottPort] (9) 88, p. 41.
"An Immigrant Garden." [PottPort] (9) 88, p. 41.
1488. ERICKSON, Marsha
"The Road to Kawaikoi" (for Sabra, Nani Kaua'i, Mark, Laua'e, and Mana'o'io). [HawaiiR] (12:2, #24) Fall 88, p. 52-53.
1489. ERLANGER, Liselotte
"Love on the Horizon" (tr. of Ursula Krechel). [Rohwedder] (4) [Wint 88-89], p. 20.
"To Meet with Peace" (tr. of Carl Guesmer). [Rohwedder] (4) [Wint 88-89], p. 21.
1490. ERNST, Matthew
"Not Far From Salt Lake City." [Caliban] (5) 88, p. 92-93.
1491. ERNST, Myron
"Another Way." [Crosscur] (7:4) 88, p. 46-47.
"Another Way." [MidwQ] (29:3) Spr 88, p. 337.
"Autumn." [PikeF] (9) Fall 88, p. 29.
"Autumn" (for Shirley). [HampSPR] Wint 88, p. 41.
"The Brownstones on Foster Avenue, Brooklyn, 1950." [GreensboroR] (44) Sum 88, p. 56.
"Florida." [Poem] (60) N 88, p. 9.
"Florida, the Pathetic Fallacy." [CumbPR] (7:2) Spr 88, p. 23-24.
"Four from Brooklyn." [WebR] (13:1) Spr 88, p. 72-74.
"From the Porch." [Poem] (60) N 88, p. 10-11.
"In the Perfect Poem." [HampSPR] Wint 88, p. 40.
"Nile." [HolCrit] (25:5) D 88, p. 17.
"The Other Way." [CumbPR] (7:2) Spr 88, p. 21-22.
"The Pavilion." [CumbPR] (7:2) Spr 88, p. 25-26.
"Vermeer." [MSS] (6:2) 88, p. 26.
"The Wife in the Mural at Pompeii." [Poem] (60) N 88, p. 8.
"A Witch." [HampSPR] Wint 88, p. 39.
1492. ESCOTT, Beth
"July Passes Easter in St. Louis." [Timbuktu] (2) Sum-Fall 88, p. 55-56.
1493. ESCUDERO, Ernesto
"Dialogo al Muerto." [LindLM] (7:2/4) Ap-D 88, p. 7.
"Diapositiva." [LindLM] (7:2/4) Ap-D 88, p. 7.
1494. ESHLEMAN, Clayton
"At the Speed of Wine." [Temblor] (8) 88, p. 172-177.
"Galactite" (In Memory of Ana Mendieta). [Sulfur] (8:1, #22) Spr 88, p. 106-110.
"Genesis for Wilfredo" (tr. of Aimé Césaire, w. Annette Smith). [Caliban] (5) 88, p. 18.
"Leon G. Damas Somber Fire Always" (in memoriam, tr. of Aimé Césaire, w. Annette Smith). [Epoch] (37:2) 88, p. 105.
"Let Us Offer Its Heart to the Sun" (tr. of Aimé Césaire, w. Annette Smith). [Caliban] (5) 88, p. 19.
"Link of the Chain-Gang" (tr. of Aimé Césaire, w. Annette Smith). [Epoch] (37:2) 88, p. 109.
"Macumba Word" (tr. of Aimé Césaire, w. Annette Smith). [Caliban] (5) 88, p. 15.

ESHLEMAN
"Mangrove Swamp" (tr. of Aimé Césaire, w. Annette Smith). [Caliban] (5) 88, p. 14.
"A Memorial to the Grand." [OhioR] (42) 88, p. 67.
"The Night Against Its Lit Elastic." [ParisR] (30:109) Wint 88, p. 73-75.
"Nights" (tr. of Aimé Césaire, w. Annette Smith). [Caliban] (5) 88, p. 16.
"Our Journey Around the Drowned City of Is" (Excerpts). [Notus] (3:1) Spr 88, p. 65-66.
"Re. Closure." [Caliban] (5) 88, p. 78.
"Ribbon" (tr. of Aimé Césaire, w. Annette Smith). [Caliban] (5) 88, p. 17.
"Testing" (tr. of Aimé Césaire, w. Annette Smith). [Epoch] (37:2) 88, p. 107.

1495. ESPADA, Martín
"The Chota and the Patron." [HangL] (52) 88, p. 59-60.
"The Promised Land" (Selection: 29, tr. of Clemente Soto Vélez, w. Camilo Pérez). [HangL] (52) 88, p. 73, 75.

1496. ESPAILLAT, Rhina P.
"Translation." [Amelia] (5:2, #13) 88, p. 26.

1497. ESPINA, Eduardo
"En Uso Moderno de la Fábula" (Reflejos, días, Marilin Monroe). [Inti] (26/27) Otoño 87-Primavera 88, p. 126.
"Funerales de Don Góngora en Pleno Madrid" (Con fusas, infusas y semi corcheas). [Inti] (26/27) Otoño 87-Primavera 88, p. 127-128.
"Muros de Guernica." [Inti] (26/27) Otoño 87-Primavera 88, p. 129-131.
"Noche de Búlgaros." [Inti] (26/27) Otoño 87-Primavera 88, p. 128-129.
"Tres Versos por Fedor D." [Inti] (26/27) Otoño 87-Primavera 88, p. 128.

1498. ESPIRU, Salvidor
"Song of Evening Falling" (tr. by Luigi Bonaffini). [Vis] (27) 88, p. 12.

1499. ESPOSITO, Nancy
"During Holy Week there's a strong sun" (tr. of Carlos Calero). [AmerPoR] (17:2) Mr-Ap 88, p. 29.
"In Somoza's Time" (tr. of Juan Ramón Falcón). [AmerPoR] (17:2) Mr-Ap 88, p. 29.
"In the Masaya Lagoon" (tr. of Carlos Calero). [AmerPoR] (17:2) Mr-Ap 88, p. 29.
"Laid in the Tomb" (tr. of Carlos Martínez Rivas). [AmerPoR] (17:2) Mr-Ap 88, p. 28.
"Mirror" (tr. of Luis Rocha). [AmerPoR] (17:2) Mr-Ap 88, p. 31.
"North American Woman" (tr. of Carlos Castro Jo). [AmerPoR] (17:2) Mr-Ap 88, p. 27.
"Reflection About My Feet" (tr. of Daisy Zamora). [AmerPoR] (17:2) Mr-Ap 88, p. 30.
"Street in Summer" (tr. of Ana Ilce Gomez). [AmerPoR] (17:2) Mr-Ap 88, p. 31.
"The Tiger in the Garden" (tr. of Ernesto Mejía Sanchez). [AmerPoR] (17:2) Mr-Ap 88, p. 30.
"Turtle" (tr. of Ana Ilce Gomez). [AmerPoR] (17:2) Mr-Ap 88, p. 31.
"What Hands in My Hands" (tr. of Daisy Zamora). [AmerPoR] (17:2) Mr-Ap 88, p. 30.

1500. ESPRIU, Salvador
"Parca" (tr. by Magda Bogin). [Boulevard] (3:2/3) Fall 88, p. 141.
"The Wind" (Homage to Pablo Neruda, tr. by Magda Bogin). [Boulevard] (3:2/3) Fall 88, p. 142.

1501. ESPY, Willard R.
"Can We Make It Next Weekend Instead?" [LightY] ('88/9) 88, p. 109.
"Did She Say 'Hmp-mp' Instead of 'Mp-hmp'?" [LightY] ('88/9) 88, p. 115.
"A Graduation of Pasta." [LightY] ('88/9) 88, p. 218.
"An Inelegant Proposal." [LightY] ('88/9) 88, p. 132.

1502. ESTESS, Sybil
"The Woman Who Married Her Brother-in-Law." [NewRep] (198:9) 29 F 88, p. 30.

1503. ESTEVES, Sandra María
"From the Ferrybank." [HangL] (52) 88, p. 62.

ESTRADA, Alfredo Silva
See SILVA ESTRADA, Alfredo

1504. ETTER, Dave
"Brother." [EngJ] (77:7) N 88, p. 78.
"Composition." [Abraxas] (37) 88, p. 74-75.
"Jazz Night." [CreamCR] (12:2) Sum 88, p. 179.
"Summer of 1932." [OhioR] (42) 88, p. 80.

1505. EVANS, David
"Nude." [CutB] (29/30) 88, p. 85.
"Uncle Columbus." [CutB] (29/30) 88, p. 92.
1506. EVANS, George
"Bond." [Sulfur] (8:2, #23) Fall 88, p. 38.
"The Missing Sunflower." [Sulfur] (8:2, #23) Fall 88, p. 37.
"Nara." [Zyzzyva] (4:1) Spr 88, p. 76-77.
"Nuclear Sonnet." [Sulfur] (8:2, #23) Fall 88, p. 36-37.
"Revelation in the Mother Lode." [Sulfur] (8:2, #23) Fall 88, p. 34-35.
1507. EVANS, Jack
"The Opposite of Life." [LitR] (31:2) Wint 88, p. 205.
1508. EVANS, Lee
"In This Room." [HighP] (3:3) Wint 88-89, p. 64.
1509. EVANS, M. Jerome
"Settling In: Lake Ming / Late in the Day / Late Summer." [Amelia] (5:2, #13) 88, p. 33.
1510. EVATT, Julia
"Blood Kin." [Poem] (60) N 88, p. 22-23.
"The Way to Climb a Mountain." [Poem] (60) N 88, p. 24-25.
1511. EVERDING, Kelly
"Pregnant." [ColEng] (50:7) N 88, p. 757.
"Soup." [ColEng] (50:7) N 88, p. 758-759.
1512. EWALD, Mary
"The Gold of Asia." [AmerS] (57:2) Spr 88, p. 172.
1513. EWART, Gavin
"Country Matters." [LightY] ('88/9) 88, p. 36.
"Jabberwocky." [GrandS] (7:2) Wint 88, p. 86-87.
"The Laureate's Complaint" (An Inspirational Poem). [LightY] ('88/9) 88, p. 188.
"The Premature Coronation." [GrandS] (8:1) Aut 88, p. 131-132.
"The Rivals." [GrandS] (8:1) Aut 88, p. 129-130.
"The Wages of Sin." [GrandS] (7:2) Wint 88, p. 88-89.
1514. EXLER, Samuel
"Green." [PoetryE] (25) Spr 88, p. 72.
"India." [PoetryE] (25) Spr 88, p. 71.
"A Place We Want to Go." [PoetryE] (25) Spr 88, p. 73.
1515. EYUBOGLU, Bedri Rahmi
"Salt" (tr. by Ozcan Yalim, William A. Fielder, and Dionis Coffin Riggs). [StoneC] (16:1/2) Fall-Wint 88-89, p. 40.
"Tuz" (in Turkish). [StoneC] (16:1/2) Fall-Wint 88-89, p. 40.
1516. EZEKIEL, Nissim
"Edinburgh Interlude — Lightly" (Selection: 7). [Nimrod] (31:2) Spr-Sum 88, p. 52.
1517. FABIAN, R. Gerry
"P.M.S." [RagMag] (6:2) Fall 88, p. 15.
1518. FACKINA, Edward Paul
"In My Sister's Shadow." [Lips] (14) 88, p. 20.
1519. FAGERLUND, Frances
"Dust." [HawaiiR] (12:1, #23) Spr 88, p. 96.
"House at Poipu Beach." [HawaiiR] (12:1, #23) Spr 88, p. 94-95.
1520. FAGET, Rolando
"No del Todo." [Mairena] (10:25) 88, p. 132.
1521. FAGLES, Robert
"Helen Reviews the Champions" (The Illiad, Book III, tr. of Homer). [GrandS] (8:1) Aut 88, p. 50-64.
1522. FAHEY, W. A.
"The Elbow." [WormR] (28:4, #112) 88, p. 95-96.
"Fennel." [WormR] (28:4, #112) 88, p. 95.
"Fingers." [WormR] (28:4, #112) 88, p. 96.
"Ides of March '88." [Confr] (37/38) Spr-Sum 88, p. 239.
"Long Island Twilight" (For Chas. Wright). [Confr] (37/38) Spr-Sum 88, p. 239.
"The Neck." [WormR] (28:4, #112) 88, p. 96.
"Strawberries." [WormR] (28:4, #112) 88, p. 95.
1523. FAHRBACH, Helen
"Body Language." [RagMag] (6:1) [88], p. 7.
1524. FAINLIGHT, Ruth
"The European Story." [Thrpny] (34) Sum 88, p. 12.

"The Pleiades." [GrahamHR] (11) Spr 88, p. 85.
"The Yellow Plate." [NewYorker] (64:42) 5 D 88, p. 48.

1525. FAIRCHILD, B. H.
"The Drunk Foreman." [SouthernPR] (28:1) Spr 88, p. 13.
"The Family Altar." [Jacaranda] (3:2) Fall-Wint 88, p. 87.
"Kansas." [Jacaranda] (3:2) Fall-Wint 88, p. 88.
"There Is Constant Movement in My Head." [GeoR] (42:2) Sum 88, p. 262-263.
"Work." [TriQ] (73) Fall 88, p. 103-105.

1526. FAIZ, Faiz Ahmed
"Be Near Me" (in Urdu and English, tr. by Agha Shahid Ali). [NewRena] (7:2, #22) Spr 88, p. 50-51.
"Before You Came" (in Urdu and English, tr. by Agha Shahid Ali). [NewRena] (7:2, #22) Spr 88, p. 22-23.
"The City from Here" (in Urdu and English, tr. by Agha Shahid Ali). [Nimrod] (31:2) Spr-Sum 88, p. 104-105.
"Evening" (in Urdu and English, tr. by Agha Shahid Ali). [NewRena] (7:2, #22) Spr 88, p. 24-25.
"Ghazal: In the sun's last embers, the evening star burns to ash" (tr. by Agha Shahid Ali). [NewRena] (7:2, #22) Spr 88, p. 30.
"The Heart Gives Up" (in Urdu and English, tr. by Agha Shahid Ali). [NewRena] (7:2, #22) Spr 88, p. 26-27.
"It Is Spring" (tr. by Agha Shahid Ali). [QW] (26) Wint 88, p. 114.
"A Last Speaker" (tr. by Agha Shahid Ali). [Nimrod] (31:2) Spr-Sum 88, p. 106-107.
"Solitary Confinement" (in Urdu and English, tr. by Agha Shahid Ali). [NewRena] (7:2, #22) Spr 88, p. 28-29.
"Vista" (in Urdu and English, tr. by Agha Shahid Ali). [NewRena] (7:2, #22) Spr 88, p. 48-49.

1527. FALCO, Edward
"Possessions." [NewL] (55:1) Fall 88, p. 49.

1528. FALCON, Juan Ramón
"In Somoza's Time" (tr. by Nancy Esposito). [AmerPoR] (17:2) Mr-Ap 88, p. 29.

FALCON, Leticia Garza
See GARZA-FALCON, Leticia

1529. FANDEL, John
"Endangered Species." [Comm] (115:4) 26 F 88, p. 114.
"Incident at Damascus, Ark." [Comm] (115:4) 26 F 88, p. 114.

1530. FANG, Dai
"Poetry" (tr. of Cai Qi-jiao, w. Edward Morin). [TriQ] (72) Spr-Sum 88, p. 171.

1531. FANTHORPE, U. A.
"Friends' Meeting House, Frenchay, Bristol." [Antaeus] (60) Spr 88, p. 237.

1532. FARALLO, Livio
"Morning." [SlipS] (8) 88, p. 92.

1533. FARGAS, Laura
"October 15th." [GeoR] (42:3) Fall 88, p. 591.
"Rendezvous." [MSS] (6:2) 88, p. 61.
"Translations." [MSS] (6:2) 88, p. 62.
"What I Wait For Might Not Happen." [IndR] (11:3) Sum 88, p. 27.

1534. FARLEY, Blanche
"Inheritance." [SouthernHR] (22:1) Wint 88, p. 48.

1535. FARMER, Rod
"The toolmaker." [Lactuca] (10) Je 88, p. 33.

1536. FARNSWORTH, Robert
"Blueprint." [TexasR] (9:3/4) Fall-Wint 88, p. 42.
"Destination." [SenR] (18:2) 88, p. 67.
"Museum." [AntR] (46:4) Fall 88, p. 477.
"A Night in St. Cloud" (after Edvard Munch). [SenR] (18:2) 88, p. 66.
"The Pose." [TexasR] (9:3/4) Fall-Wint 88, p. 39-41.
"A Postcard in Memory of Donald Evans." [MissouriR] (11:1) 88, p. 56.
"Toward Hallowe'en." [AmerPoR] (17:6) N-D 88, p. 50.
"Upon a Fit of Laughter." [SenR] (18:2) 88, p. 68-69.

1537. FARQUHAR, Dion (Farquahar, Dion)
"Eats of Eden." [CreamCR] (12:2) Sum 88, p. 180.
"Empire Stake." [PoetL] (83:2) Sum 88, p. 23-24.
"Second City." [PoetL] (83:2) Sum 88, p. 22.
"Siracusa." [CreamCR] (12:2) Sum 88, p. 181-184.

"Treading Culture 5." [Vis] (28) 88, p. 24.
1538. FARR, Judith
"Monologue: Hester Prynne to Arthur Dimmesdale" (In Tribute to R.Motherwell's "Reconciliation Elegy"). [ManhatPR] (10) Ja 88, p. 27-28.
"Old Song for My Uncle's Death" (For James Henry Knox, Voyager, Philanthropist). [ManhatPR] (10) Ja 88, p. 29-31.
1539. FARRELL, Kate
"First Cat Poem." [AntigR] (73) Spr 88, p. 74.
1540. FARRELL, Mary Ann
"The Dreams of Garbage Collectors." [Pembroke] (20) 88, p. 132.
"Mary Ann Lamb at Seventy-Four." [Pembroke] (20) 88, p. 131.
1541. FASULO, Anne
"Hiding Places" (for Jane and Jennifer). [BellArk] (4:4) Jl-Ag 88, p. 1.
1542. FAUCHER, Real
"Flirting with the Enemy." [Wind] (18:63) 88, p. 9-10.
"From First Growth." [Wind] (18:63) 88, p. 10.
"Knowing What You've Got & How to Use It." [Bogg] (59) 88, p. 35.
"Playing Doctor." [SlipS] (8) 88, p. 30.
"When She Dies." [Wind] (18:63) 88, p. 9.
1543. FAULHABER, Claire Will
"Ballad of Male Hegemony." [Comm] (115:15) 9 S 88, p. 466.
1544. FAULKNER, Pete
"1910" (I.M. Count Luchino Visconti). [Bogg] (59) 88, p. 7.
1545. FAVILLA, Candice
"The Canon." [NewRep] (199:10) 5 S 88, p. 38.
1546. FAY, Julie
"Dear Marilyn." [SenR] (18:2) 88, p. 30-32.
"Flowers." [GettyR] (1:3) Sum 88, p. 489-490.
"Prisms" (for my mother). [NewL] (55:2) Wint 88-89, p. 78.
1547. FE, Marina
"Duelo." [Mairena] (10:25) 88, p. 170.
1548. FEDERHART, Douglas
"The Song of the Fan." [JamesWR] (6:1) Fall 88, p. 11.
1549. FEDERMAN, Raymond
"Last Night's Dream." [Caliban] (4) 88, p. 107-108.
1550. FEENY, Thomas
"Cealie's Saturday Night." [Plain] (8:3) Spr-Sum 88, p. 37.
1551. FEIERSTEIN, Ricardo
"Argentina 1983" (tr. by J. Kates and Stephen A. Sadow). [MinnR] (NS 30/31) Spr-Fall 88, p. 47.
1552. FEIN, Richard
"Mass Extinction." [CapeR] (23:1) Spr 88, p. 21.
1553. FEINGOLD, Michael
"Afraid of the Light" (tr. of Henrik Ibsen). [Bomb] (24) Sum 88, p. 51.
"Bird and Birdcatcher" (tr. of Henrik Ibsen). [Bomb] (24) Sum 88, p. 51.
"Burned Ships" (tr. of Henrik Ibsen). [Bomb] (24) Sum 88, p. 51.
"The Murder of Abraham Lincoln" (tr. of Henrik Ibsen). [Bomb] (24) Sum 88, p. 50.
"The Stormy Petrel" (tr. of Henrik Ibsen). [Bomb] (24) Sum 88, p. 51.
"A Swan" (tr. of Henrik Ibsen). [Bomb] (24) Sum 88, p. 51.
"A Verse" (tr. of Henrik Ibsen). [Bomb] (24) Sum 88, p. 51.
1554. FEINSTEIN, Robert N.
"Heaven Can't Wait." [LightY] ('88/9) 88, p. 213.
"High Tech Sick Bed." [Bogg] (59) 88, p. 8.
"Uneasy Riders." [LightY] ('88/9) 88, p. 156.
1555. FEIRSTEIN, Frederick
"Window Frame" (for Leon Klinghoffer). [SouthernR] (24:2) Spr 88, p. 341-342.
1556. FEITLOWITZ, Marguerite
"The Taking of the Winter Palace" (tr. of Pere Gimferrer). [LitR] (32:1) Fall 88, p. 64-65.
1557. FELDMAN, Alan
"I Come Up Before the Board of Numbers to Talk About My Son." [TexasR] (9:3/4) Fall-Wint 88, p. 43.
"One of My Daughter's Drawings." [TexasR] (9:3/4) Fall-Wint 88, p. 45.
"Self-Portrait." [TexasR] (9:3/4) Fall-Wint 88, p. 44.

1558. FELDMAN, Irving
"The Dream." [NewRep] (199:3/4) 18-25 Jl 88, p. 34.
"Entrances." [PartR] (55:2) Spr 88, p. 277-280.
"No Big Deal." [GrandS] (8:1) Aut 88, p. 33-34.
"Poem of the Old Avant-Garde." [PartR] (55:2) Spr 88, p. 276-277.
"Street Scene" (Greenwich Village, Summer 1979). [ParisR] (30:106) Spr 88, p. 106-109.
1559. FELDMAN, Ruth
"Age: A Collage." [TexasR] (9:3/4) Fall-Wint 88, p. 47.
"Autobiography" (tr. of Primo Levi). [MissR] (16:1, #46) 88, p. 50-51.
"Collapse" (tr. of Margherita Guidacci). [WebR] (13:1) Spr 88, p. 24.
"For Adolf Eichmann" (tr. of Primo Levi, w. Brian Swann). [ParisR] (30:108) Fall 88, p. 206.
"The Girl-Child of Pompeii" (tr. of Primo Levi). [WebR] (13:2) Fall 88, p. 29.
"Huayna Capac" (Inca emperor, died in 1527, tr. of Primo Levi). [PartR] (55:4) Fall 88, p. 612.
"Illumination." [TexasR] (9:3/4) Fall-Wint 88, p. 48.
"The Old Man" (tr. of Margherita Guidacci). [WebR] (13:1) Spr 88, p. 25.
"The Piano Lesson." [TexasR] (9:3/4) Fall-Wint 88, p. 46.
"Pliny" (tr. of Primo Levi). [SouthernR] (24:2) Spr 88, p. 315.
"They're Talking about Eichmann on a Radio" (—Mario Luzi. Tr. of Elio Fiore). [StoneC] (15:3/4) Spr-Sum 88, p. 11.
"Waiting Room" (tr. of Margherita Guidacci). [WebR] (13:1) Spr 88, p. 26.
"The Wise Are Always Right" (tr. of Margherita Guidacci). [WebR] (13:1) Spr 88, p. 25.
1560. FELGENHAUER, H. R.
"Lenny's Law." [AlphaBS] (4) D 88, p. 40.
1561. FELL, Alison
"Cornfield with Skylark." [PartR] (55:1) Wint 88, p. 66-68.
"The Mistresses." [PartR] (55:3) Sum 88, p. 479-480.
1562. FELLMAN, Stanley A.
"What Bird Song Remains." [MidAR] (8:1) 88, p. 13.
1563. FERGUSON, Moira
"Mandarins Give Ground in Johannesburg." [MinnR] (NS 30/31) Spr-Fall 88, p. 49.
1564. FERGUSON, Penny
"Soliloquy." [PottPort] (10) 88, p. 33.
1565. FERNANDEZ, Angel Jose
"Yo no inventé nada." [Mairena] (10:25) 88, p. 170.
1566. FERNANDEZ, Guillermo
"Invencion de la Noche." [Mairena] (10:25) 88, p. 142.
1567. FERNANDEZ, Pablo Armando
"Pequeña Oda de Amor a la Patria" (X Aniversario de la "Brigada Antonio Maceo"). [Areíto] (1:2) F 88, p. 39.
1568. FERRARELLI, Rina
"Crows" (For a friend at the women's shelter). [LaurelR] (22:21) Wint 88, p. 17.
"December at Porta Nuova" (tr. of Leonardo Sinisgalli). [WebR] (13:1) Spr 88, p. 31.
"Reaching My Father's Age." [MSS] (6:2) 88, p. 60.
"Where the Age of the Rose Burned Proudly" (tr. of Leonardo Sinisgalli. Translation Chapbook Series). [MidAR] (8:2) 88, p. 129-153.
1569. FERRE, Rosario
"Contracanto." [Inti] (26/27) Otoño 87-Primavera 88, p. 137-140.
FERRER, Juan José Prat
See PRAT FERRER, Juan José
1570. FERTIG, Nelle
"There was a roue from Bengal." [Amelia] (5:2, #13) 88, p. 138.
"Understanding You Perfectly." [Amelia] (5:2, #13) 88, p. 132.
FICK, Karen Ohnesorge
See OHNESORGE-FICK, Karen
1571. FICOCIELLO, John
"Between Three Thirty Six and Nine and a Half." [CinPR] (17) Spr 88, p. 39.
"The Fish" (for van Tilburg). [ClockR] (4:2) 88, p. 60-61.
"Literature." [CinPR] (17) Spr 88, p. 38.

1572. FIELD, Gregory K.
"After Watching a Man Playing with His Dog in the Grass." [NewL] (55:1) Fall 88, p. 70.
"In the Waiting Room." [NewL] (55:1) Fall 88, p. 71.
"Nothing and No One." [NewL] (55:1) Fall 88, p. 69.
"The Sea Is the Longest Breath" (for Crystal). [NewL] (55:1) Fall 88, p. 68.
1573. FIELDER, William A.
"Salt" (tr. of Bedri Rahmi Eyuboglu, w. Ozcan Yalim and Dionis Coffin Riggs). [StoneC] (16:1/2) Fall-Wint 88-89, p. 40.
1574. FIELDS, Leslie Leyland
"After a Day in Which We Catch 6,489 Fish." [BellR] (11:2) Fall 88, p. 27.
"Making the Dream Right." [BellR] (11:2) Fall 88, p. 27.
1575. FIGMAN, Elliot
"Big Spring." [Pequod] (25) 88, p. 42.
"The Issue." [Pequod] (25) 88, p. 41.
1576. FILES, Meg
"Island." [MidAR] (8:2) 88, p. 193.
1577. FILIP, Raymond
"Europapa." [PraF] (9:1) Spr 88, p. 29.
"What Cezanne's Bathers Were Whispering." [PraF] (9:1) Spr 88, p. 28.
1578. FILIPOWSKA, Patricia
"According to Guinness." [SinW] (33) Fall 87, p. 72.
"The Well." [PoetC] (19:3) Spr 88, p. 39-40.
1579. FILKINS, Peter
"Beet Weeding." [HiramPoR] (44/45) Spr-Wint 88, p. 60-61.
"Meditation" (for Ilona & Neil). [HiramPoR] (44/45) Spr-Wint 88, p. 59.
1580. FINALE, Frank
"Tale End, Summer." [DeKalbLAJ] (21:1) Wint 88, p. 52.
1581. FINCH, Annie
"Rain Birth." [Sequoia] (31:2) Wint 88, p. 66.
1582. FINCH, Casey
"Midnight." [OhioR] (42) 88, p. 22.
"Rome." [Iowa] (18:2) 88, p. 56-57.
1583. FINCH, Peter
"Hills." [NewEngR] (10:4) Sum 88, p. 414-415.
1584. FINCH, Roger
"Arriving at Mandalay." [WormR] (28:1, #109) 88, p. 7-8.
"Church of St. John of the Kings." [CarolQ] (40:3) Spr 88, p. 49.
"The Evening Air Turns." [CapeR] (23:1) Spr 88, p. 9.
"A Father Watches Boys Play Baseball." [WindO] (50) Aut 88, p. 23.
"Floating Downstream." [Poem] (60) N 88, p. 2.
"Flower Market." [Chelsea] (47) 88, p. 158.
"Greco's House: The Garden." [Event] (17:2) Sum 88, p. 60.
"In the Picture None of Us Are Missing." [CimR] (83) Ap 88, p. 32.
"An Inca Silver Figurine of an Alpaca." [LaurelR] (22:21) Wint 88, p. 74.
"Oh, Calcutta." [KanQ] (20:3) Sum 88, p. 133.
"One Middle-Aged Woman Opening Christmas Gifts." [WormR] (28:1, #109) 88, p. 9.
"The Peasant Stank As Did the Priest." [Poem] (60) N 88, p. 1.
"The Ruins of Sukhotai." [DeKalbLAJ] (21:3/4) 88, p. 53.
"September Morn." [BelPoJ] (38:4) Sum 88, p. 31.
"The Snow Queen's Kiss." [Chelsea] (47) 88, p. 158.
"Street of St. Elizabeth." [CarolQ] (40:3) Spr 88, p. 50.
"Studies on Arden's *Tamil Grammar*, Chapter 2: Rules Concerning the Combination and Changes of Letters." [WindO] (50) Aut 88, p. 22.
"The Sweet Potato Vendor." [Chelsea] (47) 88, p. 159.
"Tourists See Him Shave." [WormR] (28:1, #109) 88, p. 8.
"The *Transparente* Chapel, Toledo Cathedral." [KanQ] (20:3) Sum 88, p. 132.
"The Undertaker of Trunyan." [AntigR] (73) Spr 88, p. 126.
"Watching the *Wayang Kulit* from the Wrong Side." [AntigR] (73) Spr 88, p. 127.
"Woman Seated at the Spinet." [Poem] (60) N 88, p. 3.
1585. FINCKE, Gary
"After Work." [PraS] (62:3) Fall 88, p. 104-105.
"The Anencephalic Donor." [CapeR] (23:2) Fall 88, p. 39.
"August 16, 1987." [LitR] (32:1) Fall 88, p. 83.
"The Boat People Honorees." [ColR] (NS 15:1) Spr-Sum 88, p. 49.

"Bomb Drill." [WestB] (21/22) 88, p. 67-68.
"The Book of Numbers." [PoetryNW] (29:1) Spr 88, p. 26-27.
"Callback." [KanQ] (20:3) Sum 88, p. 200-201.
"The Congestive Failure of Belief." [PoetryNW] (29:1) Spr 88, p. 27-28.
"Every Year." [Amelia] (4:4, #11) 88, p. 74-75.
"Four-Way Stop." [CapeR] (23:2) Fall 88, p. 38.
"Heading, with Rain, to Harrisburg." [PoetL] (83:2) Sum 88, p. 32.
"In Montana, a Substitute Teacher Is Killed by Mistake." [ColR] (NS 15:1) Spr-Sum 88, p. 48.
"In Philadelphia." [SlipS] (8) 88, p. 68.
"Junior Blackface." [WestB] (21/22) 88, p. 68-69.
"Like She Was One of Us." [ColR] (NS 15:1) Spr-Sum 88, p. 46-47.
"Malthus Season." [LaurelR] (22:2) Sum 88, p. 111-112.
"Naming the Sky." [PoetryNW] (29:3) Aut 88, p. 17.
"Parables." [PoetryNW] (29:3) Aut 88, p. 16-17.
"The Reabsorbed Twins." [PoetL] (83:4) Wint 88-89, p. 39.
"Rounds." [PoetL] (83:4) Wint 88-89, p. 40.
"Scratch Test." [Amelia] (4:4, #11) 88, p. 73.
"Tube Time." [LaurelR] (22:2) Sum 88, p. 112-113.
"Waiting for the Names." [LaurelR] (22:2) Sum 88, p. 110.
"The Warmest Fall on Record." [LitR] (31:2) Wint 88, p. 182.
"What the Builders Left." [GettyR] (1:2) Spr 88, p. 350.
"What You Can Do Blindfolded." [PaintedB] (36) 88, p. 20.

1586. FINK, Janie
"October: Deep South." [PoetryE] (25) Spr 88, p. 107.
"Weather Vane." [PoetryE] (25) Spr 88, p. 106.

1587. FINKEL, Donald
"Ancient Temple" (tr. of Bei Dao, w. Xueliang Chen). [AmerPoR] (17:4) Jl-Ag 88, p. 42.
"A Day" (tr. of Bei Dao, w. Xueliang Chen). [AmerPoR] (17:4) Jl-Ag 88, p. 42.
"Deshabille." [DenQ] (23:2) Fall 88, p. 43.
"Dry Time." [DenQ] (23:2) Fall 88, p. 41.
"Errata." [Chelsea] (47) 88, p. 146.
"For Whose Use." [DenQ] (23:2) Fall 88, p. 42.
"Four Portraits of the Artist As an Old Man." [OntR] (28) Spr-Sum 88, p. 57-60.
"Habit" (tr. of Bei Dao, w. Xueliang Chen). [AmerPoR] (17:4) Jl-Ag 88, p. 43.
"Hello Mountain of a Hundred Flowers" (tr. of Bei Dao, w. Xueliang Chen). [AmerPoR] (17:4) Jl-Ag 88, p. 42.
"Heroic Measures." [GrandS] (8:1) Aut 88, p. 46.
"In Dickens' House." [Poetry] (152:6) S 88, p. 343.
"Interval." [GrandS] (8:1) Aut 88, p. 45.
"Island" (tr. of Bei Dao, w. Xueliang Chen). [AmerPoR] (17:4) Jl-Ag 88, p. 44.
"Lot's Wife." [Chelsea] (47) 88, p. 147.
"Memory" (tr. of Bei Dao, w. Xueliang Chen). [AmerPoR] (17:4) Jl-Ag 88, p. 43.
"The Natural History of Dryads." [LaurelR] (22:2) Sum 88, p. 47-48.
"Nightmare" (tr. of Bei Dao, w. Xueliang Chen). [AmerPoR] (17:4) Jl-Ag 88, p. 43.
"Notes on the City of the Sun" (tr. of Bei Dao, w. Xueliang Chen). [AmerPoR] (17:4) Jl-Ag 88, p. 43.
"The Tale Goes On" (tr. of Bei Dao, w. Xueliang Chen). [AmerPoR] (17:4) Jl-Ag 88, p. 43.
"Unfamiliar Shore" (tr. of Bei Dao, w. Xueliang Chen). [AmerPoR] (17:4) Jl-Ag 88, p. 44.
"Waiting for the Monarchs." [LaurelR] (22:2) Sum 88, p. 48.
"You Say" (tr. of Bei Dao, w. Xueliang Chen). [AmerPoR] (17:4) Jl-Ag 88, p. 44.

1588. FINKELSTEIN, Caroline
"Spring." [Verse] (5:2) Jl 88, p. 16.

1589. FINKELSTEIN, Norman
"Moldavanka." [DenQ] (23:2) Fall 88, p. 45-46.
"Sketch for a Portrait." [DenQ] (23:2) Fall 88, p. 44.

1590. FINLAY, John
"In the Time of the Civil War." [SouthernR] (24:4) Aut 88, p. 934-937.
"Through a Glass Darkly." [SouthernR] (24:4) Aut 88, p. 937-938.

1591. FINLEY, L. D.
"My Brother in the Fields." [Phoenix] (9:1/2) 88, p. 44-45.

1592. FINNEGAN, James
"Because It's Raining on Robert Johnson's Birthday." [CutB] (31/32) 88, p. 20.
"In the Dollhouse." [Ascent] (14:1) 88, p. 42-43.
"The Roofer." [KanQ] (20:3) Sum 88, p. 244-245.
"A Sad Story." [Ascent] (14:1) 88, p. 40-42.
"Seeing in the Dark." [Ploughs] (14:4) 88, p. 117.
"The Sunshine Inheritance." [SouthernPR] (28:1) Spr 88, p. 54.
"The Tidepool." [Ploughs] (14:4) 88, p. 115-116.
1593. FINOL, Zita
"Alerta." [LetFem] (14:1/2) Primavera-Otoño 88, p. 132.
"Crecer." [LetFem] (14:1/2) Primavera-Otoño 88, p. 131.
"Los Niños de Mi Tiempo." [LetFem] (14:1/2) Primavera-Otoño 88, p. 131.
1594. FIORE, Elio
"Dicono a una Radio di Eichmann" (—Mario Luzi). [StoneC] (15:3/4) Spr-Sum 88, p. 10.
"They're Talking about Eichmann on a Radio" (—Mario Luzi. Tr. by Ruth Feldman). [StoneC] (15:3/4) Spr-Sum 88, p. 11.
1595. FIRER, Susan
"Breath & Bone at the Milwaukee County Zoo." [Abraxas] (37) 88, p. 64.
1596. FISCHER, Allen C.
"By Night." [SouthwR] (73:4) Aut 88, p. 525.
"Highnotes." [Poetry] (143, i.e. 153:1) O 88, p. 9.
"An Idea Without Wings." [Poetry] (143, i.e. 153:1) O 88, p. 6.
"Ménage à Trois." [Poetry] (143, i.e. 153:1) O 88, p. 8.
"Rare Earths." [Poetry] (143, i.e. 153:1) O 88, p. 7.
"Two Tubas in the Morning." [IndR] (11:3) Sum 88, p. 12.
1597. FISCHER, Norman
"Fish." [Temblor] (7) 88, p. 161.
"On Whether or Not to Believe in Your Mind" (Excerpts). [Sink] (3) 88, p. 63-65.
"The Tooting." [Notus] (3:2) Fall 88, p. 46-50.
"Untitled Poem #37." [Temblor] (7) 88, p. 162-163.
"Working Title." [Temblor] (7) 88, p. 159-161.
1598. FISCHER, Stephen
"Shelf Life for Apples." [BellArk] (4:3) My-Je 88, p. 9.
1599. FISCHEROVA, Sylva
"Black Tiger" (tr. by Jarmila and Ian Milner). [Field] (38) Spr 88, p. 10-11.
"Jasmine Wind" (tr. by Jarmila and Ian Milner). [Field] (38) Spr 88, p. 9.
"Necessary" (tr. by Jarmila and Ian Milner). [Field] (38) Spr 88, p. 13-14.
"The Primer" (tr. by Jarmila and Ian Milner). [Field] (38) Spr 88, p. 12.
1600. FISHER, David
"For Nikita Koloff" (Russian translation of Virginia Love Long). [InterPR] (14:1) Spr 88, p. 52, 54.
"We Shall Not Escape Hell" (for Marina Tsvetayeva, Russian translation of Virginia Love Long). [InterPR] (14:1) Spr 88, p. 50.
1601. FISHER, Lori
"America, the Treeway" (tr. of Reiner Kunze). [Rohwedder] (4) [Wint 88-89], p. 37.
"Bells All Too Near" (tr. of Reiner Kunze). [Rohwedder] (4) [Wint 88-89], p. 40.
"Clearing Tree Stumps" (for H.W.M. in the Thuringer Forest, tr. of Reiner Kunze). [Rohwedder] (4) [Wint 88-89], p. 39.
"Empty Snowposts, Norway, Middle of September" (tr. of Reiner Kunze). [Rohwedder] (4) [Wint 88-89], p. 39.
"Letter from Prague 1980" (tr. of Reiner Kunze). [Rohwedder] (4) [Wint 88-89], p. 41.
1602. FISHER, Sally
"The Letter A." [Chelsea] (47) 88, p. 150.
"My Early Religious Education." [LightY] ('88/9) 88, p. 205.
"Trombone Ghazal." [Chelsea] (47) 88, p. 151.
"Wind and Zen Ghazal." [Chelsea] (47) 88, p. 151.
1603. FISHER, Steve
"The First Few Hours, Alone After Prison." [TriQ] (73) Fall 88, p. 110-111.
1604. FISHMAN, Charles
"Fiery Oven" (tr. of Sarah Kirsch, w. Marina L. Roscher). [Rohwedder] (4) [Wint 88-89], p. 8.
"The Geese Flew Inland" (tr. of Sarah Kirsch, w. Marina L. Roscher). [Rohwedder] (4) [Wint 88-89], p. 6.

"The Geologists" (tr. of Sarah Kirsch, w. Marina L. Roscher). [Rohwedder] (4) [Wint 88-89], p. 5.
"The Green Double" (tr. of Sarah Kirsch, w. Marina L. Roscher). [Rohwedder] (4) [Wint 88-89], p. 4.
"Hoarfrost Harvest" (tr. of Sarah Kirsch, w. Marina L. Roscher). [Rohwedder] (4) [Wint 88-89], p. 7.
"Moorland" (tr. of Sarah Kirsch, w. Marina L. Roscher). [Rohwedder] (4) [Wint 88-89], p. 8.
"War Story, 1942." [LaurelR] (22:21) Wint 88, p. 18.
"When the Ice Floats" (tr. of Sarah Kirsch, w. Marina L. Roscher). [Rohwedder] (4) [Wint 88-89], p. 3.

1605. FISTER, Mary
"For a Few Trees." [CreamCR] (12:2) Sum 88, p. 185-186.

1606. FITCH, Brian
"A Musician Leaves Music for the Third and Possibly Last Time." [SewanR] (96:4) Fall 88, p. 601.
"Railroad Icehouse." [SewanR] (96:4) Fall 88, p. 602.

1607. FITCH, David
"Go Fish." [Writer] (101:12) D 88, p. 24.

1608. FITCH, Patrick
"Tanzanian Night." [Phoenix] (9:1/2) 88, p. 20.

1609. FITZPATRICK, Winnie E.
"Autumn Winter Raindrops." [Amelia] (5:1, #12) 88, p. 79.

1610. FLAHERTY, Doug
"Love Poem" (for Ms. Violet Light). [Farm] (4:1, i.e. 5:1) Wint 88, p. 58-59.

1611. FLAKOLL, Darwin J. (Darwin T.)
"Documentary" (tr. of Claribel Alegria, w. the author). [ParisR] (30:108) Fall 88, p. 156-159.
"Little Cambray Tamales" (for Eduardo and Helena, tr. of Claribel Alegria, w. the author). [ParisR] (30:108) Fall 88, p. 155.
"Mortally Wounded" (tr. of Claribel Alegria). [Bomb] (24) Sum 88, p. 68.
"My City" (tr. of Claribel Alegria). [Bomb] (24) Sum 88, p. 68.
"The Procession" (tr. of Claribel Alegria). [Bomb] (24) Sum 88, p. 68.
"The Return" (tr. of Claribel Alegria). [Bomb] (24) Sum 88, p. 69.
"Summing Up" (tr. of Claribel Alegria, w. the author). [ParisR] (30:108) Fall 88, p. 154.

1612. FLAMM, Matthew
"Al's Tune." [PoetryE] (25) Spr 88, p. 17.
"Miss Park" (Seoul). [PoetryE] (25) Spr 88, p. 18-19.
"Tokyo." [Pequod] (25) 88, p. 48-49.

1613. FLANAGAN, Katherine
"A Pair of Twos." [SlipS] (8) 88, p. 45.

1614. FLANDERS, Jane
"Grand Central." [PraS] (62:2) Sum 88, p. 93.
"The Handbell Choir." [AmerS] (57:1) Wint 88, p. 80.
"Horse Kiss." [PraS] (62:2) Sum 88, p. 89-90.
"Mantises." [NewYorker] (64:17) 13 Je 88, p. 36.
"Mozart." [PraS] (62:2) Sum 88, p. 91-92.
"On the IRT." [PraS] (62:2) Sum 88, p. 92.
"Other Lives of the Romantics." [LightY] ('88/9) 88, p. 184-185.
"Two Sisters." [PraS] (62:2) Sum 88, p. 90.

1615. FLECK, Richard (Richard F.)
"By Ontario's Wintry Shore." [CharR] (14:1) Spr 88, p. 93.
"Encloistered." [CharR] (14:1) Spr 88, p. 93.
"Glacial Ghost" (In Memory of John Muir). [Paint] (15:29) Spr 88, p. 11.
"Lake Ontario in an Arctic Mood." [CharR] (14:1) Spr 88, p. 93.
"Late November Sundown." [Paint] (15:29) Spr 88, p. 10.

1616. FLEMING, Harold
"Lisa Turns on a Dime." [WestB] (21/22) 88, p. 157.
"So Lisa Goes." [WestB] (21/22) 88, p. 156.
"The Watchdogs" (—The Towamencin Poems). [StoneC] (15:3/4) Spr-Sum 88, p. 18.

1617. FLETCHER, Ann
"Off Dennis." [QW] (27) Sum-Fall 88, p. 118.

1618. FLETCHER, Lynne Yamaguchi
"After Delivering Your Lunch." [Calyx] (11:2/3) Fall 88, p. 119.

"Higashiyama Crematorium, November 16, 1983." [Calyx] (11:2/3) Fall 88, p. 120-121.
"The Way April Leads to Autumn." [Calyx] (11:2/3) Fall 88, p. 122.

1619. FLINT, Roland
"Black Sea, Mother and Son." [TriQ] (73) Fall 88, p. 121-123.
"Chop." [TriQ] (73) Fall 88, p. 126.
"Hallelujah!" [TriQ] (73) Fall 88, p. 124.

1620. FLOCK, Miriam
"California Landscape with Figures." [HighP] (3:2) Fall 88, p. 88-91.

1621. FLOOK, Maria
"The Orphan, 1917." [NewYorker] (64:38) 7 N 88, p. 42.
"Useless Days." [MichQR] (27:4) Fall 88, p. 564-565.

1622. FLORES, Charles
"Watching the Goggle Box" (tr. by the author). [Vis] (28) 88, p. 19.

1623. FLORES Y ASCENCIO, Daniel
"Homosapiens" (tr. by the author). [Bomb] (24) Sum 88, p. 72.
"Mi Cuerpo." [Bomb] (24) Sum 88, p. 72.
"My Body" (tr. by the author). [Bomb] (24) Sum 88, p. 72.

FLORIDO, Jorge J. Rodriguez
See RODRIGUEZ-FLORIDO, Jorge J.

1624. FLOSDORF, Jim
"The Cabin." [Blueline] (9:1/2) 88, p. 17.
"Deer." [Blueline] (9:1/2) 88, p. 16.
"In the Rain." [Blueline] (9:1/2) 88, p. 15.

1625. FLOWERDAY, Charlie
"Beatitude" (Martha's Vineyard, Thumb Point). [PraS] (62:2) Sum 88, p. 115-116.

1626. FLYNN, David
"In the Poem." [Wind] (18:62) 88, p. 2.
"The Settled Life." [Wind] (18:62) 88, p. 28.

FOE, Mark de
See DeFOE, Mark

1627. FOERSTER, Richard
"Again." [KeyWR] (1:2) Fall 88, p. 63.
"Isaac." [ManhatR] (4:2) Spr 88, p. 46.
"On the Train from Brighton." [SouthernHR] (22:4) Fall 88, p. 353.
"Playland." [Poetry] (151:5) F 88, p. 400.
"Spring Tide" (York, Maine). [StoneC] (15:3/4) Spr-Sum 88, p. 21.
"That Other." [HolCrit] (25:4) O 88, p. 17.

1628. FOGARTY, Mark
"Fine Line." [Footwork] ('88) 88, p. 72.

1629. FOGEL, Aaron
"BW." [WestHR] (42:3) Aut 88, p. 220-228.

1630. FOGEL, Alice
"Conspiracy." [Ascent] (14:1) 88, p. 15.

1631. FOLEY, Louis
"Lost." [Bogg] (59) 88, p. 42.
"A Midnight Scene from the World's Smallest Play: Through the Wink of an Eye." [Bogg] (60) 88, p. 49.

1632. FOLLIN-JONES, Elizabeth
"Coming of Age." [PoetL] (83:3) Fall 88, p. 23.
"Passing By." [Footwork] ('88) 88, p. 26.

1633. FONTAINE, Arturo
"If Someone Could Write" (tr. by the author and James Brasfield). [WebR] (13:2) Fall 88, p. 30.
"The Noblemen" (tr. by the author and James Brasfield). [WebR] (13:2) Fall 88, p. 30.

1634. FONTENOT, Ken
"A Study of Two Girls." [Lactuca] (11) O 88, p. 29-30.
"Wondering: All the Way Home." [KanQ] (20:1/2) Wint-Spr 88, p. 302-303.

1635. FOOTE, Gerry
"Honor and Gold" (for Phuc Vinh Truong). [EngJ] (77:5) S 88, p. 107.

1636. FORBES, Duncan
"Disaster Movie." [Verse] (5:3) N 88, p. 34-35.

1637. FORBES, John
"The Age of Plastic" (after Ovid). [NewAW] (4) Fall 88, p. 104-105.
"Death, an Ode." [PraS] (62:4) Wint 88-89, p. 73.

"Drugs." [NewAW] (4) Fall 88, p. 107-108.
"Egyptian Reggae." [NewAW] (4) Fall 88, p. 106.
"Floating." [NewAW] (4) Fall 88, p. 103.
"A Loony Tune." [NewAW] (4) Fall 88, p. 104.
"Lullaby." [NewAW] (4) Fall 88, p. 105.
"Missing Persons." [NewAW] (4) Fall 88, p. 103.
"Speed, a Pastoral." [PraS] (62:4) Wint 88-89, p. 72-73.

1638. FORCE, Kathy
"Waking Up Poor." [ChamLR] (1) Fall 87, p. 389.

1639. FORCHÉ, Carolyn
"The Angel of History" (Selections: I.i.-II.xii, In memory of Terrence Des Pres). [GrahamHR] (11) Spr 88, p. 23-30.

1640. FORD, John M.
"III: Complex Gardens." [LittleM] (15:3/4) 88, p. 73.

1641. FORD, Mark
"Cross-Section." [Verse] (5:3) N 88, p. 61.
"If You Could Only See Me Now!" [Verse] (5:3) N 88, p. 61.

FORD, Sheri de
See DeFORD, Sheri

1642. FORD, William
"At Mt. Rushmore." [Poetry] (151:6) Mr 88, p. 459.
"The Missionary on Furlough." [PennR] (4:1) 88, p. 30.
"The Summer of Twelve." [Poetry] (151:6) Mr 88, p. 460.

1643. FORNI, Regina
"Glacier Noon." [DeKalbLAJ] (21:1) Wint 88, p. 53-54.
"In Time I Slip." [Footwork] ('88) 88, p. 40.
"Where I Lived." [Footwork] ('88) 88, p. 40-41.

1644. FORNOFF, Frederick H.
"Brummel" (tr. of Guillermo Carnero). [LitR] (32:1) Fall 88, p. 63.
"Melancholy of Paul Scarron, Burlesque Poet" (tr. of Guillermo Carnero). [LitR] (32:1) Fall 88, p. 62.
"This Song Be Your Shroud" (tr. of Silvina Saldaña). [MichQR] (27:2) Spr 88, p. 240-241.
"To Dream Death" (tr. of Silvina Saldaña). [MichQR] (27:2) Spr 88, p. 242-244.

1645. FORSYTHE-MOORE, Anne
"On the Road Again." [PottPort] (9) 88, p. 35.

1646. FORTUNATO, Peter
"April Fools (a Mad Song)." [AnotherCM] (18) 88, p. 97.
"The Good Waitress." [Footwork] ('88) 88, p. 26.
"Hurry (a Mad Song)." [AnotherCM] (18) 88, p. 98.
"Little Joe." [Footwork] ('88) 88, p. 25-26.
"Piebald Music." [Footwork] ('88) 88, p. 25.

1647. FOSS, Phillip
"Prescriptive Equinox." [Notus] (3:2) Fall 88, p. 70-71.
"The Usual." [Notus] (3:2) Fall 88, p. 68-69.

1648. FOSS, Vanessa
"The Thirst of a Sprout." [BellArk] (4:1) Ja-F 88, p. 3.

1649. FOSTER, Edward
"Marianne Moore in Egypt" (Lips (13) 87, p. 37: erratum note). [Lips] (14) 88, p. 57.

1650. FOSTER, Leslie
"Academic Nighttown." [Lactuca] (11) O 88, p. 26-28.
"No Bleedin' 'Arts." [Lactuca] (11) O 88, p. 28.

1651. FOSTER, Linda Nemec
"The Change." [Vis] (28) 88, p. 39.
"Heat Lightning" (for Therese Becker). [Farm] (4:1, i.e. 5:1) Wint 88, p. 60-61.
"Instinct." [PassN] (9:1) Wint 88, p. 18.
"My Son Expounds on His Theory of Creation" (1988 Poetry Competition, Second Prize). [PassN] (9:2) Sum 88, p. 17.
"Song of Red Candles." [Farm] (4:1, i.e. 5:1) Wint 88, p. 62.

1652. FOSTER, Nick
"The Paris Phase." [Margin] (7) 88, p. 80.

1653. FOSTER, Sesshu
"The Corpse of a Forgetful Man Will Suddenly Sit Up and Look Around." [RedBass] (13) 88, p. 24.

"Exile Boulevard" (tr. of Juan Felipe Herrera, w. Dolores Bravo). [Rohwedder] (3) Spr 88, p. 1-3.
"Poetic Report: On Servants: Toward a Model for Urban Hispaniks, USA" (tr. of Juan Felipe Herrera, w. Dolores Bravo). [Rohwedder] (3) Spr 88, p. 30-31.

1654. FOUNTAIN, Paula A.
"42nd Street." [Wind] (18:62) 88, p. 4.

1655. FOWLER, Anne Carroll
"At Allen's Cay" (1988 Second Prize in Poetry). [Lyra] (1:4) 88, p. 7.
"At the Copley Plaza." [LitR] (31:2) Wint 88, p. 209.
"At the Table." [KanQ] (20:1/2) Wint-Spr 88, p. 150-151.
"Autumnal." [Footwork] ('88) 88, p. 75.
"Granny's Lawn in August." [KanQ] (20:1/2) Wint-Spr 88, p. 150.
"Hauntings." [LitR] (31:4) Sum 88, p. 418.
"Items." [Vis] (27) 88, p. 43.
"When You Came Back." [Footwork] ('88) 88, p. 75.

1656. FOWLER, Bret
"Snapshot." [EngJ] (77:7) N 88, p. 98.

1657. FOWLER, Connie May
"Kateland." [MidwQ] (29:4) Sum 88, p. 453.
"There Is a Black Man in My Dreams." [MidwQ] (29:4) Sum 88, p. 455-456.
"Ybor City Number One." [MidwQ] (29:4) Sum 88, p. 454.

1658. FOWLER, Russell
"Dixieyarn." [ColEng] (50:1) Ja 88, p. 52.

1659. FOWLER, Ruth
"Retirement." [Writer] (101:12) D 88, p. 25-26.

1660. FOWLER, Sandra
"White Tune." [MidwQ] (29:4) Sum 88, p. 457.

1661. FOX, Hannah
"Adam's Ex-." [LightY] ('88/9) 88, p. 141.

1662. FOX, Hugh
"Darker and darker earlier and earlier." [SwampR] (1:2/3) D 88, p. 37.
"Drifting." [CrabCR] (5:1) Wint 88, p. 28.
"He advances through the day sampling lint and." [SwampR] (1:2/3) D 88, p. 39.
"Hitchhiker's Guide to Times Square" (Excerpt). [Bogg] (60) 88, p. 14.
"Pleasure Dome." [SlipS] (8) 88, p. 78-79.
"Recollected in Tranquility." [SlipS] (8) 88, p. 79-81.
"Song of Christopher" (Excerpt). [Abraxas] (37) 88, p. 44-45.
"Wuwuchim." [SwampR] (1:2/3) D 88, p. 38.

1663. FOX, Leonard
"Distant lightning flickers" (tr. of Ramantoanina). [InterPR] (14:2) Fall 88, p. 59.
"The Evening Is Distant" (tr. of Martin Camaj). [InterPR] (14:1) Spr 88, p. 35.
"Flute Players" (tr. of Jean-Joseph Rabearivelo). [InterPR] (14:2) Fall 88, p. 67.
"Hainteny" (49 poems, tr. from the Malagasy). [InterPR] (14:2) Fall 88, p. 10-57.
"The Jacket" (tr. of Martin Camaj). [InterPR] (14:1) Spr 88, p. 37.
"Lofty Forest" (tr. of Jean-Joseph Rabearivelo). [InterPR] (14:2) Fall 88, p. 69, 71.
"Mimosas" (tr. of Martin Camaj). [InterPR] (14:1) Spr 88, p. 39.
"Mountain Wake" (tr. of Martin Camaj). [InterPR] (14:1) Spr 88, p. 27.
"The Poem" (tr. of Jean-Joseph Rabearivelo). [InterPR] (14:2) Fall 88, p. 63.
"Rain on the River" (tr. of Martin Camaj). [InterPR] (14:1) Spr 88, p. 33.
"Reading" (tr. of Jean-Joseph Rabearivelo). [InterPR] (14:2) Fall 88, p. 61.
"Snake and Child" (tr. of Martin Camaj). [InterPR] (14:1) Spr 88, p. 25.
"Sybaris" (tr. of Martin Camaj). [InterPR] (14:1) Spr 88, p. 29.
"Translated from the Night" (Selections: 1, 2, 4, 21, tr. of Jean-Joseph Rabearivelo). [InterPR] (14:2) Fall 88, p. 77-83.
"Valiha" (tr. of Jean-Joseph Rabearivelo). [InterPR] (14:2) Fall 88, p. 75.
"Where No One Knows Us" (tr. of Martin Camaj). [InterPR] (14:1) Spr 88, p. 31.
"The White Bull" (tr. of Jean-Joseph Rabearivelo). [InterPR] (14:2) Fall 88, p. 65.
"Zebu" (tr. of Jean-Joseph Rabearivelo). [InterPR] (14:2) Fall 88, p. 73.

1664. FOX, Lucía
"Los Rinocerontes y el Unicornio." [LetFem] (14:1/2) Primavera-Otoño 88, p. 135.

1665. FOX, Marilyn
"The Willow Trees." [Cond] (15) 88, p. 138.

1666. FOX, Robert
"It's My Fault." [LightY] ('88/9) 88, p. 206-207.

FOX, Sandra Inskeep
See INSKEEP-FOX, Sandra

1667. FOY, John
"Rue des Martyrs Sonnets." [AntigR] (73) Spr 88, p. 32-34.
1668. FRAJLICH-ZAJAC, Anna
"Beautiful Is My Mother" (tr. by Jakub Pogoda). [Vis] (26) 88, p. 36.
"Emigration" (tr. by Regina Grol-Prokopczyk). [Vis] (26) 88, p. 36.
"Ergo Sumus" (tr. by the author and Rochelle Diogenes). [Vis] (26) 88, p. 37.
FRAN, Brad la
See LaFRAN, Brad
1669. FRANÇOIS, Jocelyne
"Living" (tr. by Marguerite Le Clézio). [Cond] (15) 88, p. 113.
"Pouvoir du Poeme." [Cond] (15) 88, p. 110.
"The Power of a Poem" (tr. by Marguerite Le Clézio). [Cond] (15) 88, p. 111.
"Vivre." [Cond] (15) 88, p. 112.
1670. FRANCE, Peter
"Phloxes in the Beginning" (tr. of Gennady Aygi). [Verse] (5:1) F 88, p. 67.
"Winds-and-Radiance: Departures" (to L. N. and M. Roginsky, tr. of Gennady Aygi). [Verse] (5:1) F 88, p. 66.
1671. FRANCES, Linda
"Family Ritual." [SinW] (35) Sum-Fall 88, p. 85.
1672. FRANCIA, Luis H.
"Fairly should the future blacken god's grey hair." [LindLM] (7:2/4) Ap-D 88, p. 25.
"Measured Infinity." [LindLM] (7:2/4) Ap-D 88, p. 25.
1673. FRANCIS, Robert
"Late Fire Late Snow" (33 poems). [PaintedB] (35) 88, p. 9-44.
"Light Against Light." [PaintedB] (35) 88, p. 61.
"Poem-in-Progress: Light Against Light." [PaintedB] (35) 88, p. 59-60.
"A Touch of Italy." [PaintedB] (35) 88, p. 45-49.
1674. FRANCIS, Scott
"Coal in the Stove" (For my Motherland, tr. of Guo Mo Ruo). [Paint] (15:29) Spr 88, p. 58.
"Phoenix Dying: A Chorus of Birds Celebrate" (tr. of Guo Mo Ruo). [Paint] (15:29) Spr 88, p. 59.
1675. FRANCISCO, Edward
"Anniversary" (for Edna Gann Francisco, 1925-1977). [SouthernR] (24:1) Wint 88, p. 160-161.
"Neighbor." [NoDaQ] (56:1) Wint 88, p. 149.
"One for You." [NoDaQ] (56:1) Wint 88, p. 148.
1676. FRANK, Bernhard
"From Day to Night" (tr. of Daliah Ravikovich). [ColR] (NS 15:2) Fall-Wint 88, p. 76.
"Ice, Eden" (From *Niemandsrose*, tr. of Paul Celan). [AntigR] (73) Spr 88, p. 21.
"Later there will be something" (From *Zeitgehöff*, tr. of Paul Celan). [AntigR] (73) Spr 88, p. 25.
"My Sister Sits Smiling" (tr. of Abba Kovner). [ColR] (NS 15:2) Fall-Wint 88, p. 74.
"Psalm" (tr. of Paul Celan). [AntigR] (73) Spr 88, p. 23.
1677. FRANKEL, Lillian
"Ten Years After She Dies My Mother Teaches Me How to Sew." [PoetL] (83:2) Sum 88, p. 33-34.
1678. FRANTOM, Marcy
"Song of the Seamstress." [HolCrit] (25:2) Ap 88, p. 13.
1679. FRANZEN, Cola
"Beyond the Dawn" (tr. of Marjorie Agosin). [HangL] (52) 88, p. 49.
"Blood Nest" (tr. of Marjorie Agosin). [Vis] (26) 88, p. 48.
"Bolero" (tr. of Juan Cameron). [Vis] (26) 88, p. 49.
"Bridge" (tr. of Juan Cameron). [Vis] (26) 88, p. 49.
"Disappeared Woman III" (tr. of Marjorie Agosin). [Vis] (26) 88, p. 48.
"Perro de Circo" (Selections: 4 poems, tr. of Juan Cameron). [Bound] (15:3/16:1) Spr-Fall 88, p. 41-44.
"With Your Permission" (tr. of Marjorie Agosin). [HangL] (52) 88, p. 51, 53.
1680. FRASER, Sanford
"Isabel Weeds." [Wind] (18:63) 88, p. 11-12.
"My Passionate Part." [Turnstile] (1:2) 88, p. 24.
"Supper Out." [Wind] (18:63) 88, p. 11.

1681. FRASER, Wallace
"Just Another Casualty." [Writer] (101:12) D 88, p. 25.
1682. FRATE, Frank C.
"Primeval." [Wind] (18:62) 88, p. 11.
"Shut-in." [Wind] (18:62) 88, p. 10.
FRATRIK, Julie Cooper
See COOPER-FRATRIK, Julie
1683. FRATUS, David
"The Nazi Night Fighter Pilot Envisions His Death." [HiramPoR] (44/45) Spr-Wint 88, p. 62.
"A Short Guide to Proper Names." [HiramPoR] (44/45) Spr-Wint 88, p. 63.
1684. FRAZEE, James
"At an Exhibition of Photographs by Harry Callahan." [SenR] (18:1) 88, p. 7-8.
"Bougainvillea." [SenR] (18:1) 88, p. 5-6.
"Playback" (for Elsie Clisbee). [MissouriR] (11:2) 88, p. 217-219.
1685. FRAZIER, Alexander
"Patience Please" (The 14th Kansas Poetry Contest, Fourth Honorable Mention). [LittleBR] (5:2) Wint 88-89, p. 68.
1686. FREDERIKSEN, Nancy
"Braided Rugs." [RagMag] (6:2) Fall 88, p. 18.
"Skinning Muskrats with Dad in the Basement." [RagMag] (6:2) Fall 88, p. 19.
1687. FREEDMAN, Martha H.
"Clerihews" (2 poems). [LightY] ('88/9) 88, p. 75.
1688. FREEDMAN, Robert D.
"More." [WestB] (21/22) 88, p. 96.
1689. FREEMAN, Jan
"Comedian" (for R. T.). [AmerV] (13) Wint 88, p. 31-33.
"Contemplating the Latest Departure." [AmerPoR] (17:2) Mr-Ap 88, p. 42.
"Gravity." [AmerV] (10) Spr 88, p. 43-45.
1690. FREEMAN, Keller Cushing
"The First and Last Poem of the Woman Who Thought She Was Sylvia Plath's Daughter." [Amelia] (5:2, #13) 88, p. 12-13.
"Walking Like a Waterspider." [KenR] (NS 10:4) Fall 88, p. 92-94.
1691. FREEMAN, Sunil
"Dream Girl." [Vis] (28) 88, p. 14.
1692. FREERICKS, Mary
"Russian Bride." [NegC] (8:3) 88, p. 172-178.
FREES, Madeline de
See DeFREES, Madeline
1693. FREIDINGER, Paul
"Chicago July." [Lactuca] (10) Je 88, p. 16.
"Emptiness Has a Face." [Crosscur] (7:4) 88, p. 120.
"The Mist in August." [Farm] (5:2) Fall 88, p. 66-67.
1694. FREISINGER, Randall R.
"Thoughts on a Child's Nose Swallowed by a Dog." [LaurelR] (22:21) Wint 88, p. 65-68.
FRENCH, Dayv James
See JAMES-FRENCH, Dayv
1695. FRENCH, Joe
"Blank Verse." [LittleBR] (5:2) Wint 88-89, p. 52.
1696. FRENCH, Kimberly
"Untitled: A pumpkin face droops." [CapilR] (49) 88, p. 67.
"Untitled: You are wearing the amber I put around your neck" (for V.M.). [CapilR] (49) 88, p. 66.
1697. FRETWELL, Kathy
"Flash Up in Drydock." [CapilR] (48) 88, p. 14.
"Hiatus." [CapilR] (48) 88, p. 15.
"The Leap." [CapilR] (48) 88, p. 16.
1698. FREUND, Edith
"How to Come Back." [Prima] (11/12) 88, p. 35.
1699. FRIEBERT, Stuart
"Afterclap." [Footwork] ('88) 88, p. 46.
"Chest-Pounders." [Footwork] ('88) 88, p. 45-46.
"Chokedamp." [Confr] (37/38) Spr-Sum 88, p. 228.
"Cripes, I've Lost My Glasses Again." [Footwork] ('88) 88, p. 45.
"The Cross and the Kiss." [SouthernPR] (28:2) Fall 88, p. 41.

"Death As Snowman" (tr. of Karl Krolow). [InterPR] (14:1) Spr 88, p. 7.
"If Not disposed to Go by Sea." [ArtfulD] (14/15) Fall 88, p. 15.
"Illusion" (tr. of Karl Krolow). [Field] (39) Fall 88, p. 79.
"Life" (for Siegfried Unseld, tr. of Karl Krolow). [InterPR] (14:1) Spr 88, p. 9.
"Next Door" (tr. of Karl Krolow). [Field] (39) Fall 88, p. 80.
"Night-Watches" (tr. of Karl Krolow). [Field] (39) Fall 88, p. 78.
"Only for an Hour" (for SK). [NewL] (54:3) Spr 88, p. 95.
"The Order of Things" (tr. of Karl Krolow). [InterPR] (14:1) Spr 88, p. 11.
"The Smallest Snail." [MinnR] (NS 30/31) Spr-Fall 88, p. 37-38.
"Two Views" (for MH & JB). [AntR] (46:2) Spr 88, p. 248.
"While We Watch." [ArtfulD] (14/15) Fall 88, p. 14.

1700. FRIED, Elliot
"As If There Were No Such Thing As Death." [Jacaranda] (3:2) Fall-Wint 88, p. 89.

1701. FRIED, Philip
"Messiah Cycle" (2 poems: "Contemporary Prayer," "When grandma died in God's dream"). [ConnPR] (7:1) 88, p. 30-31.
"Old Camp Songs." [PoetC] (20:1) Fall 88, p. 3-4.

1702. FRIEDLANDER, Benjamin
"Muthoplokon." [Sulfur] (8:2, #23) Fall 88, p. 118.
"My Emily Dickinson" (for Susan Howe's). [Sulfur] (8:2, #23) Fall 88, p. 117-118.
"Retrospectively, for Primo Levi." [Sulfur] (8:2, #23) Fall 88, p. 117.

1703. FRIEDMAN, Daisy
"There's Just No Richer Red Than Beet." [Confr] (37/38) Spr-Sum 88, p. 75.

1704. FRIEDMAN, Dorothy
"Drifting." [Wind] (18:63) 88, p. 13.
"Peers." [Wind] (18:63) 88, p. 13-14.

1705. FRIEDMAN, Jeff
"Sunday Walk" (after my father's stroke). [Boulevard] (3:2/3) Fall 88, p. 161-162.
"The Teacher." [PassN] (9:1) Wint 88, p. 16.

1706. FRIEDSON, Tony
"Holy Deadline." [ChamLR] (1) Fall 87, p. 83.
"Traditional Japanese Proverbs on Long Poetry Readings" (after an interminable reading). [HawaiiR] (12:2, #24) Fall 88, p. 135.

1707. FRIES, Kenny
"In These Times." [FiveFR] (6) 88, p. 95-97.

1708. FRIESEN, Patrick
"Anna" (4 Selections). [Dandel] (15:1) Spr-Sum 88, p. 5-8.

1709. FRIGGIERI, Joe
"Berlin" (tr. by Oliver Friggieri). [Vis] (28) 88, p. 23.

1710. FRIGGIERI, Oliver
"Berlin" (tr. of Joe Friggieri). [Vis] (28) 88, p. 23.

1711. FRIIS-BAASTAD, Erling
"Answers to a High School Reunion Questionnaire." [AlphaBS] (3) Je 88, p. 18-20.
"Beat." [AlphaBS] (4) D 88, p. 36-37.

1712. FRIMAN, Alice
"Another Windfall." [WebR] (13:2) Fall 88, p. 62.
"Asking Directions" (Pine Ridge Indian Reservation, South Dakota). [NoDaQ] (56:4) Fall 88, p. 27-28.
"The Composer and the Dancer." [LitR] (31:2) Wint 88, p. 211.
"Dance Lesson." [WebR] (13:2) Fall 88, p. 61.
"The Fish." [CarolQ] (40:2) Wint 88, p. 89.
"Footprint Lake, Canada 1985" (for Michelle). [PikeF] (9) Fall 88, p. 28.
"Last Riff" (for Les). [PaintedB] (32/33) 88, p. 138.
"Love Song to a Surgeon." [TexasR] (9:1/2) Spr-Sum 88, p. 68-69.
"The Shirt." [NoDaQ] (56:1) Wint 88, p. 96-97.
"The Train" (for Molly Peacock). [SouthernPR] (28:1) Spr 88, p. 18-19.
"Watching the Newlyweds." [Paint] (15:29) Spr 88, p. 22-23.

1713. FRISARDI, Andrew
"The Vocation." [Verse] (5:1) F 88, p. 64.

1714. FRNAK, Bernhard
"It's a Shame. We Were a Fine Invention" (tr. of Yehudah Amichai). [ColR] (NS 15:2) Fall-Wint 88, p. 75.

1715. FROST, Carol
"Alto." [GeoR] (42:4) Wint 88, p. 782.
"Eating the Whole." [Crazy] (35) Wint 88, p. 20.
"Graduation." [TarRP] (28:1) Fall 88, p. 54.

"The Hunt." [TarRP] (28:1) Fall 88, p. 53-54.
"The Landscapes." [AntR] (46:3) Sum 88, p. 350.
"Music for Death." [PraS] (62:3) Fall 88, p. 21.
"The Table Garden." [PraS] (62:3) Fall 88, p. 21-22.
"This Early." [GettyR] (1:2) Spr 88, p. 330.

1716. FROST, Kenneth
"Bombardment." [ChamLR] (2:1, #3) Fall 88, p. 62.
"Flash Compounds." [Salm] (78/79) Spr-Sum 88, p. 170-171.
"Fundamental Gothic." [Interim] (7:1) Spr 88, p. 42.
"Learning to Read." [ChamLR] (2:1, #3) Fall 88, p. 63.
"The mind is everywhere." [StoneC] (16:1/2) Fall-Wint 88-89, p. 61.

1717. FROST, Richard
"The Hawk." [SenR] (18:2) 88, p. 59.
"Mephisto's Flea Song" (Goethe, *Faust*, Part I, Scene 5). [LightY] ('88/9) 88, p. 101.
"New Tooth." [LitR] (31:3) Spr 88, p. 278.
"Sen-Sen." [AmerS] (57:3) Sum 88, p. 438.
"Sen-Sen." [LightY] ('88/9) 88, p. 207-208.

1718. FROST, Robert A.
"Hoover Salesman." [Farm] (4:1, i.e. 5:1) Wint 88, p. 56.

1719. FRUMKIN, Gene
"Baptism." [ChamLR] (2:1, #3) Fall 88, p. 65.
"Closure." [Contact] (9:47/48/49) Spr 88, p. 57.
"The Dandy." [Bound] (15:3/16:1) Spr-Fall 88, p. 150.
"A Good Story." [Bound] (15:3/16:1) Spr-Fall 88, p. 148.
"Harlem Table." [ChamLR] (2:1, #3) Fall 88, p. 67.
"Outlines." [ChamLR] (2:1, #3) Fall 88, p. 68.
"Outnumbering Any One Way." [Caliban] (4) 88, p. 131-140.
"Patterns in the Cloth." [ChamLR] (2:1, #3) Fall 88, p. 66.
"The Shape of Things." [Contact] (9:47/48/49) Spr 88, p. 56.
"There Is No Reason To It." [Bound] (15:3/16:1) Spr-Fall 88, p. 149.
"White Fedora Woman." [ChamLR] (2:1, #3) Fall 88, p. 69.

1720. FRY, D.
"Making Me Live There." [JlNJPo] (10:1/2) 88, p. 18-19.

1721. FRY, Nan
"All My Mothers." [NegC] (8:3) 88, p. 54.
"The Female Subject Addresses the Male Critic." [LittleM] (15:3/4) 88, p. 124.
"Fern Hill Quick Bread." [LittleM] (15:3/4) 88, p. 125.
"Our Going." [NegC] (8:3) 88, p. 167.

1722. FRYE, Nancy
"Bending to the Field." [LitR] (31:2) Wint 88, p. 215-217.
"For to Them Remind." [StoneC] (15:3/4) Spr-Sum 88, p. 13.

FU, Du
See DU ,Fu

FU, Tu
See DU ,Fu

1723. FUKUMOTO, Curt
"About Summer in 1915." [HawaiiR] (12:2, #24) Fall 88, p. 30.
"Debts." [ChamLR] (2:1, #3) Fall 88, p. 61.
"December." [HawaiiR] (12:2, #24) Fall 88, p. 28.
"The Long Drive." [HawaiiR] (12:2, #24) Fall 88, p. 29.

1724. FULKER, Tina
"In Early March." [Bogg] (59) 88, p. 37.
"A January morning." [Bogg] (60) 88, p. 22.
"Love is a borrowed book." [Bogg] (59) 88, p. 12.

1725. FULLER, William
"Fraud Partitions" (Mendocino, California). [NewAW] (3) Spr 88, p. 77.

1726. FULTON, Alice
"Art Thou the Thing I Wanted." [ParisR] (30:108) Fall 88, p. 41-44.
"Cusp." [ParisR] (30:108) Fall 88, p. 37-40.
"Hardware." [MichQR] (27:4) Fall 88, p. 561-563.
"Losing It." [Epoch] (37:1) 88, p. 7-9.
"Powers of Congress." [Atlantic] (262:6) D 88, p. 63.
"Self-Storage." [Poetry] (143, i.e. 153:2) N 88, p. 79-81.
"Small Objects Within Reach." [MichQR] (27:4) Fall 88, p. 558-560.
"Traveling Light" (from *Palladium*'). [PassN] (9:1) Wint 88, p. 8.

"A Union House." [Poetry] (143, i.e. 153:2) N 88, p. 82-83.
1727. FULTON, Graham
"Mammoth Tasks for the Evening." [Verse] (5:3) N 88, p. 15.
1728. FULTON, Leah Shelleda
"A Casting of Shadows." [InterPR] (14:2) Fall 88, p. 89.
"Current Events." [SoDakR] (26:3) Aut 88, p. 171-172.
"Deep Purple." [PikeF] (9) Fall 88, p. 28.
"Sir Gawain at Table." [InterPR] (14:2) Fall 88, p. 90.
"Speaking to the Leaves of Nasturtium." [SoDakR] (26:3) Aut 88, p. 169-170.
1729. FUNGE, Robert
"The Cream Song." [Paint] (15:29) Spr 88, p. 28.
"The Death of Henry." [BallSUF] (29:4) Aut 88, p. 48-50.
"Holdings Back." [HolCrit] (25:1) F 88, p. 18.
"One Way to Get Through a Summer Day." [CimR] (83) Ap 88, p. 90.
"The Pulitzer Prize Winning Refrigerator." [LightY] ('88/9) 88, p. 198-199.
"To the Stone" (for Richard Shelton). [MidwQ] (29:3) Spr 88, p. 338.
"Untitled: Pondering whether poems are really important." [Paint] (15:29) Spr 88, p. 29.
1730. FUNK, Allison
"This Scar." [Poetry] (152:3) Je 88, p. 134-135.
1731. FUNKHOUSER, Erica (Erika)
"Earth Day in Provincetown." [TexasR] (9:3/4) Fall-Wint 88, p. 50.
"The Evening of the Stillborn Calf" (for Danielle). [Ploughs] (14:1) 88, p. 84-85.
"Fishing for Flounder." [TexasR] (9:3/4) Fall-Wint 88, p. 49.
1732. FUQUA, C. S.
"Old Games." [Bogg] (60) 88, p. 39.
1733. FURUTA, Soichi
"But I Saw It, in Venice." [Pembroke] (20) 88, p. 194.
1734. FUSEK, Serena
"At Last, a Woman on Paper!" [PoetL] (83:4) Wint 88-89, p. 33-34.
"Weekend." [Vis] (27) 88, p. 20.
"The Young O'Keeffe in Stieglitz's Photograph." [PoetL] (83:4) Wint 88-89, p. 35.
1735. GABBARD, G. N.
"News from the Basement Laundromat." [LightY] ('88/9) 88, p. 180-181.
"Philosophiae Consolationis" (tr. of Paul Scarron). [LightY] ('88/9) 88, p. 70.
1736. GAITAN DURAN, Jorge
"Amantes." [Mairena] (10:25) 88, p. 46.
1737. GALANSKOV, Yuri
"The Last Platform" (tr. by Olive Dehn). [NegC] (8:1/2) 88, p. 40.
1738. GALASSI, Jonathan
"The Lake." [ParisR] (30:107) Sum 88, p. 230-232.
"Presentism." [Thrpny] (34) Sum 88, p. 21.
1739. GALEF, David
"Loosely from the Latin." [LightY] ('88/9) 88, p. 80.
1740. GALIMOV, Ruslan
"Autumn has lowered" (tr. by Diana Russell). [NegC] (8:1/2) 88, p. 46.
"He sat, one leg drawn up" (tr. by Diana Russell). [NegC] (8:1/2) 88, p. 46.
"Today I thought about death" (tr. by Diana Russell). [NegC] (8:1/2) 88, p. 47.
1741. GALLER, David
"Ghosts." [Chelsea] (47) 88, p. 148-149.
1742. GALVAN, Kyra
"Contradicciones Ideológicas al Lavar un Plato." [Sonora] (14/15) Spr 88, p. 98, 100.
"Ideological Contradictions on Washing a Plate" (tr. by Thomas Hoeksema). [Sonora] (14/15) Spr 88, p. 99, 101-102.
1743. GALVAN, Roberto A.
"Un Acróstico a la Memoria de Tomás Rivera." [BilingR] (13:1/2) Ja-Ag 86, c1988, p. 95.
1744. GALVIN, Brendan
"Donegal." [Nat] (247:20) 26 D 88, p. 730.
"Dune Shacks" (Cape Cod National Seashore). [Pembroke] (20) 88, p. 163.
"Great Horned Owls." [Pembroke] (20) 88, p. 161-162.
"A Holy Well." [TarRP] (28:1) Fall 88, p. 2-3.
"Hurricane Warning." [Pembroke] (20) 88, p. 163.
"In Ireland I Remembered the Foxes of Truro, Massachusetts." [TarRP] (28:1) Fall 88, p. 1-2.

"Kale Soup." [Poetry] (143, i.e. 153:2) N 88, p. 84-85.
"The Knot Hole Gang." [Pembroke] (20) 88, p. 164.
"Mayflies." [Pembroke] (20) 88, p. 157-158.
"Swallow." [Atlantic] (262:3) S 88, p. 65.
"War in the Garden." [Poetry] (143, i.e. 153:2) N 88, p. 85-86.
"Warmth." [TexasR] (9:3/4) Fall-Wint 88, p. 51.
"Wild Apple Trees." [GeoR] (42:4) Wint 88, p. 807-808.
"Young Owls." [TexasR] (9:3/4) Fall-Wint 88, p. 52-53.

1745. GALVIN, James
"The Heart." [Field] (38) Spr 88, p. 26.
"Reading the Will." [Sonora] (14/15) Spr 88, p. 29.
"Time Optics." [Field] (38) Spr 88, p. 24.
"Trapper's Cabin." [Field] (38) Spr 88, p. 25.
"The Uncertainty Principle." [Sonora] (14/15) Spr 88, p. 30.

1746. GALVIN, Martin
"Apple Wine." [Poem] (59) My 88, p. 70.
"Iron Bed." [Poem] (59) My 88, p. 69.

GAMA, Steven da
See DaGAMA, Steven

1747. GANASSI, Ian
"Oxymoron." [AnotherCM] (18) 88, p. 99.

1748. GANGEMI, Kenneth
"Confessions of an Ailurophile." [Abraxas] (37) 88, p. 36-37.
"First Marriage." [PoetryE] (25) Spr 88, p. 53-56.
"Politics After Forty." [Abraxas] (37) 88, p. 38.
"Waiting for the Biopsy." [Chelsea] (47) 88, p. 88.

1749. GANICK, Peter
"*160" (from "Remove a Concept," part three). [Os] (27) 88, p. 38.
"*1411" (from "Remove a Concept," part twenty-seven). [Os] (27) 88, p. 38.

1750. GANSZ, David C.D.
"Animadversions" (Selections: VI). [Notus] (3:1) Spr 88, p. 52-53.

1751. GARBER, D. L.
"Depending." [Crosscur] (7:4) 88, p. 73.

1752. GARCIA, Albert
"The Lure." [CutB] (29/30) 88, p. 83.

1753. GARCIA, Carlos Ernesto
"On the Death of a Private Mayor." [Rohwedder] (3) Spr 88, p. 32.

1754. GARCIA, Richard
"The Death of Zorro." [FiveFR] (6) 88, p. 3.
"The Shadow Captain." [FiveFR] (6) 88, p. 1-2.

1755. GARCIA BIDO, Rafael
"Palabras Que Dijo el Viento para una Muchacha Triste." [Mairena] (10:25) 88, p. 106.

1756. GARCIA GOMEZ, Emilio
"Absence" (Spanish tr. of Abu Kakr al-Turtusi, tr. into Enlish by Christopher Middleton and Leticia Garza-Falcón). [NewYorker] (64:29) 5 S 88, p. 23.
"Artichoke Heart" (Spanish tr. of Ben al-Talla of Mahdía, tr. into Enlish by Christopher Middleton and Leticia Garza-Falcón). [NewYorker] (64:29) 5 S 88, p. 23.
"The Dove" (Spanish tr. of Abul Hasan Ali ben Hisn, tr. into Enlish by Christopher Middleton and Leticia Garza-Falcón). [NewYorker] (64:29) 5 S 88, p. 22.
"Galley Oars" (Spanish tr. of Ali ben Hariq of Valencia, tr. into Enlish by Christopher Middleton and Leticia Garza-Falcón). [NewYorker] (64:29) 5 S 88, p. 22.
"The Guadalquivir in Flood" (Spanish tr. of Ben Safar al-Marini of Almería, tr. into Enlish by Christopher Middleton and Leticia Garza-Falcón). [NewYorker] (64:29) 5 S 88, p. 23.
"Honey River" (Spanish tr. of Ben Ani Ruh of Algeciras, tr. into Enlish by Christopher Middleton and Leticia Garza-Falcón). [NewYorker] (64:29) 5 S 88, p. 22.
"A Pool with Turtles" (Spanish tr. of Ben Sara of Santaren, tr. into Enlish by Christopher Middleton and Leticia Garza-Falcón). [NewYorker] (64:29) 5 S 88, p. 23.
"The Procuress" (Spanish tr. of Abu Jafar Ahmad ben Said, tr. into Enlish by Christopher Middleton and Leticia Garza-Falcón). [NewYorker] (64:29) 5 S 88, p. 23.

"The Quince" (Spanish tr. of Al-Mushafi, tr. into Enlish by Christopher Middleton and Leticia Garza-Falcón). [NewYorker] (64:29) 5 S 88, p. 22.
"Reflection of Wine" (Spanish tr. of Abul Hasan Ali ben Hisn, tr. into Enlish by Christopher Middleton and Leticia Garza-Falcón). [NewYorker] (64:29) 5 S 88, p. 22.
"The Rooster" (Spanish tr. of Al-Asad Ibrahim ben Billita, tr. into Enlish by Christopher Middleton and Leticia Garza-Falcón). [NewYorker] (64:29) 5 S 88, p. 23.
"Satire" (Spanish tr. of Ben Jaraf of Cairuán, tr. into Enlish by Christopher Middleton and Leticia Garza-Falcón). [NewYorker] (64:29) 5 S 88, p. 22.

1757. GARCIA LORCA, Federico
"Abandoned Church" (Ballad of the Great War, tr. by Greg Simon and Steven F. White). [NowestR] (26:1) 88, p. 88.
"Childhood and Death" (tr. by Greg Simon and Steven F. White). [Antaeus] (60) Spr 88, p. 254-255.
"Christmas on the Hudson" (tr. by Greg Simon and Steven F. White). [NowestR] (26:1) 88, p. 89.
"Earth and Moon" (tr. by Greg Simon and Steven F. White). [Antaeus] (60) Spr 88, p. 252-253.
"Fable of Three Friends, to Be Sung in Rounds" (tr. by Greg Simon and Steven F. White). [NowestR] (26:1) 88, p. 86-87.
"In the Forest of Clocks" (a suite, tr. by Jerome Rothenberg). [Sulfur] (8:2, #23) Fall 88, p. 141-145.
"Little Infinite Poem" (For Luis Cardoza y Aragón, tr. by Greg Simon and Steven F. White). [Antaeus] (60) Spr 88, p. 256-257.
"Mirror Suite" (tr. by Jerome Rothenberg). [Sulfur] (8:2, #23) Fall 88, p. 134-140.

1758. GARDINIER, Suzanne
"The International Meteorological Committee Reports." [MichQR] (27:2) Spr 88, p. 301-302.
"Voyage." [GrandS] (7:3) Spr 88, p. 25-29.

1759. GARDNER, Eric
"Harvest of Stones." [PikeF] (9) Fall 88, p. 3.

1760. GARDNER, Geoffrey
"Change." [Paint] (15:30) Aut 88, p. 10.
"Starksboro." [AmerPoR] (17:2) Mr-Ap 88, p. 55.

1761. GARDNER, Grant "Raindance"
"Ghost Poem." [CapilR] (49) 88, p. 56.
"With My Fingers in the Busy Window Light I Let the Blind Down a Bit." [CapilR] (49) 88, p. 54-55.

1762. GARDUÑO, Raul
"Suelo de la Cercania." [Mairena] (10:25) 88, p. 171.

1763. GARGANO, Elizabeth
"Buy This Ticket." [LittleM] (15:3/4) 88, p. 96.
"Driving Home." [LittleM] (15:3/4) 88, p. 97.
"My Demon." [LittleM] (15:3/4) 88, p. 95.

1764. GARIN, Marita
"For David." [KanQ] (20:3) Sum 88, p. 150.

1765. GARNEAU, Saint-Denys
"Bird Cage" (tr. by F. R. Scott). [Trans] (20) Spr 88, p. 155.
"Spectacle of the Dance" (tr. by F. R. Scott). [Trans] (20) Spr 88, p. 154-155.

1766. GARRETT, George
"Fall Landscape, New England." [TexasR] (9:3/4) Fall-Wint 88, p. 56.
"Figure of Speech." [CreamCR] (12:2) Sum 88, p. 189.
"Long & Short of It: A Letter to Brendan Galvin." [CreamCR] (12:2) Sum 88, p. 187-188.
"Main Weathers." [TexasR] (9:3/4) Fall-Wint 88, p. 54-55.
"Splitting Wood." [TexasR] (9:3/4) Fall-Wint 88, p. 57.

1767. GARRETT, Nola
"Absurd." [ChrC] (105:15) 4 My 88, p. 445.
"Georgia O'Keefe and the Bag Ladies." [HiramPoR] (44/45) Spr-Wint 88, p. 15.
"Maid of the Mist." [HiramPoR] (44/45) Spr-Wint 88, p. 16.
"Surd." [ChrC] (105:15) 4 My 88, p. 445.

1768. GARRISON, David
"The Business of Water." [CentR] (32:1) Wint 88, p. 42.
"John Keats, Baseball Player" (for Paul Kendall). [LaurelR] (22:21) Wint 88, p. 19.
"She Asks for a Sonnet" (tr. of José Bergamin). [PoetryE] (25) Spr 88, p. 127.

"Sweeping the Cemetery." [LaurelR] (22:21) Wint 88, p. 19.

1769. GARRISON, Deborah Gottlieb
"Long Weekend at Your House." [NewYorker] (64:30) 12 S 88, p. 34.
"Love on Ives Street." [Ploughs] (14:1) 88, p. 107-108.

1770. GARTON, Victoria
"The Human Beeper." [Vis] (28) 88, p. 19.

1771. GARZA-FALCON, Leticia
"Absence" (tr. of Abu Kakr al-Turtusi from the Spanish of Emilio García Gómez, w. Christopher Middleton). [NewYorker] (64:29) 5 S 88, p. 23.
"Artichoke Heart" (tr. of Ben al-Talla of Mahdía from the Spanish of Emilio García Gómez, w. Christopher Middleton). [NewYorker] (64:29) 5 S 88, p. 23.
"The Dove" (tr. of Abul Hasan Ali ben Hisn from the Spanish of Emilio García Gómez, w. Christopher Middleton). [NewYorker] (64:29) 5 S 88, p. 22.
"Galley Oars" (tr. of Ali ben Hariq of Valencia from the Spanish of Emilio García Gómez, w. Christopher Middleton). [NewYorker] (64:29) 5 S 88, p. 22.
"The Guadalquivir in Flood" (tr. of Ben Safar al-Marini of Almería from the Spanish of Emilio García Gómez, w. Christopher Middleton). [NewYorker] (64:29) 5 S 88, p. 23.
"Honey River" (tr. of Ben Ani Ruh of Algeciras from the Spanish of Emilio García Gómez, w. Christopher Middleton). [NewYorker] (64:29) 5 S 88, p. 22.
"A Pool with Turtles" (tr. of Ben Sara of Santaren from the Spanish of Emilio García Gómez, w. Christopher Middleton). [NewYorker] (64:29) 5 S 88, p. 23.
"The Procuress" (tr. of Abu Jafar Ahmad ben Said from the Spanish of Emilio García Gómez, w. Christopher Middleton). [NewYorker] (64:29) 5 S 88, p. 23.
"The Quince" (tr. of Al-Mushafi from the Spanish of Emilio García Gómez, w. Christopher Middleton). [NewYorker] (64:29) 5 S 88, p. 22.
"Reflection of Wine" (tr. of Abul Hasan Ali ben Hisn from the Spanish of Emilio García Gómez, w. Christopher Middleton). [NewYorker] (64:29) 5 S 88, p. 22.
"The Rooster" (tr. of Al-Asad Ibrahim ben Billita from the Spanish of Emilio García Gómez, w. Christopher Middleton). [NewYorker] (64:29) 5 S 88, p. 23.
"Satire" (tr. of Ben Jaraf of Cairuán from the Spanish of Emilio García Gómez, w. Christopher Middleton). [NewYorker] (64:29) 5 S 88, p. 22.

1772. GASH, Sondra
"Enough Poems." [Footwork] ('88) 88, p. 34.
"My Mother Comes to Her First Poetry Reading." [Footwork] ('88) 88, p. 35.
"Primary Colors." [Footwork] ('88) 88, p. 35.
"Remnants." [Footwork] ('88) 88, p. 34.

1773. GASPAR, Frank X.
"The Bullet Hole in the Twelfth-Street Door." [Nat] (247:14) 14 N 88, p. 506.
"Catwalk." [Nat] (247:19) 19 D 88, p. 698.
"Golden Colt Ranch." [KenR] (NS 10:4) Fall 88, p. 98-99.
"Tía Joanna." [KenR] (NS 10:4) Fall 88, p. 97-98.

GASPAR DE ALBA, Alicia
See ALBA, Alicia Gaspar de

1774. GASPARINI, Len
"In the Tropics (II)." [Quarry] (37:4) Aut 88, p. 74.
"Out of Time" (for Donna). [Quarry] (37:4) Aut 88, p. 73.
"Streets That Follow Us." [Quarry] (37:4) Aut 88, p. 73.

1775. GATES, Rosemary
"Going Home." [SouthernR] (24:4) Aut 88, p. 954-955.

1776. GAVIN, Gaynell
"Artifacts." [KanQ] (20:3) Sum 88, p. 180-181.

1777. GELETA, Greg
"La Bamba" (for Michael, whom I slept with). [PaintedB] (36) 88, p. 73.
"Etheridge in High School." [PaintedB] (32/33) 88, p. 85.

1778. GELLAND, Carolyn
"Ishmael." [LaurelR] (22:21) Wint 88, p. 30-31.
"There Are No Pockets in the Cerement." [GreensboroR] (44) Sum 88, p. 57.

1779. GEMMELL, Kathleen
"The Sight of Portugal." [PoetL] (83:4) Wint 88-89, p. 32.

1780. GENEGA, Paul
"The Courier" (for Jan Karski, the Polish courier sent . . . to inform the world of the Holocaust). [Nat] (247:18) 12 D 88, p. 656.

1781. GENG, Wei
"In Autumn Days" (in Chinese and 3 English versions, tr. by Tang Zhao-jian, Wang Qing-ling, and Xing Yong-zhen). [MidAR] (8:1) 88, p. 14-15.
1782. GENT, Andrew
"Sonnet: Dislanguage me." [PaintedB] (36) 88, p. 102.
"Sonnet: Each shoosh of tire and road." [PaintedB] (36) 88, p. 100.
"Sonnet: That Blob of green is 'tree'." [PaintedB] (36) 88, p. 101.
1783. GEORGE, Beth
"Buttons." [SoDakR] (26:3) Aut 88, p. 68-69.
"Purple." [SoDakR] (26:3) Aut 88, p. 70.
1784. GEORGE, Diana Hume
"The Phantom Breast" (Selections: 6 poems). [SpoonRQ] (12:4) Fall 87, p. 11-15.
1785. GEORGE, Emery
"Admonition" (tr. of János Pilinszky). [AntigR] (73) Spr 88, p. 82.
"At the Philadelphia Flower Show." [SoDakR] (26:3) Aut 88, p. 166-168.
"The Ballad of Shaky Jake." [PoetryNW] (29:2) Sum 88, p. 22-23.
"Cattle Brand" (tr. of János Pilinszky). [AntigR] (73) Spr 88, p. 81.
"Homunculus As Architect." [SoDakR] (26:3) Aut 88, p. 161-165.
"Poem for Hallowe'en." [SoDakR] (26:3) Aut 88, p. 156-160.
"White Pietà" (tr. of János Pilinszky). [AntigR] (73) Spr 88, p. 81.
1786. GEORGE, Gerald
"Arcadia" (tr. of J. Slauerhoff). [KanQ] (20:1/2) Wint-Spr 88, p. 75.
1787. GEORGE, Jan Huesgen
"Life on the Prairie: Those Who Follow." [NoDaQ] (56:4) Fall 88, p. 152.
1788. GEORGE, Tom
"Canterbury Bookstore" (Pieces of Nicole). [Footwork] ('88) 88, p. 77.
1789. GERBER, Dan
"Sail Baby Sail." [PassN] (9:1) Wint 88, p. 4.
"Sail Baby Sail" (corrected reprint). [PassN] (9:2) Sum 88, p. 18.
1790. GERHARD, Kathryn R.
"Flying." [Vis] (27) 88, p. 32.
1791. GERLACH, Lee
"V. The black acadias drop a loose shade, green." [Agni] (27) 88, p. 189.
"VII. My Rome has happened, huddles in a bright, brass cage." [Agni] (27) 88, p. 190.
"City Nights" (Selection: 17). [PartR] (55:2) Spr 88, p. 281-282.
"Ni-Kung Mountain" (tr. of Du Fu). [Agni] (27) 88, p. 175.
GERMAIN, Sheryl St.
See ST. GERMAIN, Sheryl
1792. GERMAN, Greg
"The Limestone Cowboy's Luck Runs Out." [LightY] ('88/9) 88, p. 95.
1793. GERMAN, Norman
"Bobby German Courts the Fat Lady." [DeKalbLAJ] (21:1) Wint 88, p. 54-56.
"The Gift Giver." [LitR] (31:2) Wint 88, p. 212.
1794. GERRY, David
"Allergies." [KanQ] (20:3) Sum 88, p. 227.
"Glass." [KanQ] (20:3) Sum 88, p. 228.
"Root Cellar." [PaintedB] (36) 88, p. 74.
1795. GERSTLE, Val
"After Florida." [CinPR] (17) Spr 88, p. 32.
"Reminders." [CinPR] (17) Spr 88, p. 30-31.
1796. GERSTLER, Amy
"Christmas." [Colum] (13) 88, p. 143.
"Haiku" (4 poems). [Jacaranda] (3:2) Fall-Wint 88, p. 90.
"Russian Lullaby." [Gargoyle] (35) 88, p. 107.
"Wish in a War Zone." [Gargoyle] (35) 88, p. 106.
1797. GERTLER, Pesha
"What Happens When Bag Ladies Sign Up for Your Classes" (for Pat Pederson and Pat Andrus). [CrabCR] (5:3) Fall 88, p. 27.
1798. GERVASIO, Michael
"Waking Up Nemo." [PoetryNW] (29:4) Wint 88-89, p. 31-32.
1799. GERY, John
"For the People of Lesbos." [Poem] (59) My 88, p. 58.
"Pandora's Gift." [Poem] (59) My 88, p. 57.
"What It's Like to Travel Long Distance Alone on the Train" (for Addison H. Gery, 1923-1985). [SouthwR] (73:3) Sum 88, p. 403-404.

1800. GESSNER, Richard
"The Battery Song." [AnotherCM] (18) 88, p. 100.
1801. GETSI, Lucia
"Woman Hanging from Lightpole, Illinois Route 136." [AnotherCM] (18) 88, p. 101-102.
1802. GEWANTER, David
"Muse of Reminders." [Verse] (5:1) F 88, p. 4.
1803. GHIGNA, Charles
"Father of the Bride." [LightY] ('88/9) 88, p. 136.
"When Howard Flew into His Resurrection." [MSS] (6:2) 88, p. 91.
"When Howard Gave First Blood." [MSS] (6:2) 88, p. 92.
"When Howard Learned of the Guile of God." [MSS] (6:2) 88, p. 90.
1804. GHISELIN, Brewster
"Elegy for Jon." [WestHR] (42:2) Sum 88, p. 90.
"Honor and Honors." [Poetry] (152:1) Ap 88, p. 5.
1805. GIAMBRESE, Beverly
"Gonna Be an Early Winter." [Footwork] ('88) 88, p. 77.
1806. GIANNINI, David
"Hand Pump." [TexasR] (9:3/4) Fall-Wint 88, p. 58.
1807. GIBB, Robert
"Crossing the Meadow." [Wind] (18:62) 88, p. 12.
"Gazing In from the Outer Light." [CumbPR] (7:2) Spr 88, p. 28.
"Lightning." [CumbPR] (7:2) Spr 88, p. 27.
"On a Winter Night." [Wind] (18:62) 88, p. 12-13.
"Sparrow Hawk." [Wind] (18:62) 88, p. 13.
"The World in the Present Tense." [CumbPR] (7:2) Spr 88, p. 29.
1808. GIBBENS, John
"A Question." [Stand] (29:3) Sum 88, p. 50.
1809. GIBBONS, Reginald
"After Gloria Was Done" (tr. of Stanislaw Baranczak, w. the author). [TriQ] (71) Wint 88, p. 145-146.
"The Cycle." [PoetL] (83:1) Spr 88, p. 27-28.
"Hark." [OntR] (29) Fall-Wint 88-89, p. 66.
"I Want to Try." [PoetL] (83:1) Spr 88, p. 26.
"To Grazyna" (tr. of Stanislaw Baranczak, w. the author). [TriQ] (71) Wint 88, p. 143-144.
1810. GIBIAN, Ruth
"Data Entry." [PoetryNW] (29:2) Sum 88, p. 32-33.
1811. GIBSON, Becky Gould
"Dark Sits Down" (In Memoriam, Grace Marie Griffin, 1902-1977). [NegC] (8:3) 88, p. 153-156.
"Poetry Is a Plentiful Preserve" (1987 Second Prize in Poetry). [Lyra] (1:3) 88, p. 8.
1812. GIBSON, Grace
"What's Left." [Pembroke] (20) 88, p. 132.
1813. GIBSON, Joe
"Chariot." [Grain] (16:4) Wint 88, p. 62.
1814. GIBSON, Margaret
"Cactus Blooms" (for Jean). [MidAR] (8:2) 88, p. 4-5.
"Double Vision." [AntR] (46:4) Fall 88, p. 482-483.
"In the Desert" (for David, Death Valley, 1987). [GrahamHR] (11) Spr 88, p. 43-47.
"In the Mountains." [TarRP] (28:1) Fall 88, p. 70-71.
"Making Salad" (after Eihei Dogen). [MidAR] (8:2) 88, p. 6-7.
"Rings of Fire." [PraS] (62:3) Fall 88, p. 59-62.
"Things Unseen" (for Jacqueline). [TarRP] (28:1) Fall 88, p. 72-73.
1815. GIGUERE, Roland
"The Age of the Word" (tr. by D. G. Jones). [Trans] (20) Spr 88, p. 106.
"Greener Than Nature" (tr. by F. R. Scott). [Trans] (20) Spr 88, p. 107.
"Landscape Estranged" (tr. by F. R. Scott). [Trans] (20) Spr 88, p. 108.
"Rose and Thorn" (tr. by Donald Winkler). [Trans] (20) Spr 88, p. 103-105.
1816. GIL, Lourdes
"Ana." [Inti] (28) Otoño 88, p. 159-160.
"Concebido el Hombre." [Inti] (28) Otoño 88, p. 159.
"Family Album: Snapshots" (Selections: 3 poems, tr. of José Triana, w. Iraida Iturralde). [Lyra] (1:4) 88, p. 22-23.
"Sería Inútil la Noche, y Errátil." [Inti] (28) Otoño 88, p. 161-162.

"Su Rugido Anoche." [Inti] (28) Otoño 88, p. 160-161.

1817. GILBERT, Celia
"After-Image." [Poetry] (152:5) Ag 88, p. 284.
"The Death of St. Francis" (Santa Maria Novella). [Poetry] (152:5) Ag 88, p. 283.
"One Sounding for a Final Note." [NewYorker] (64:31) 19 S 88, p. 84.
"Requiem." [Poetry] (152:5) Ag 88, p. 282-283.
"The Sabbath." [Poetry] (143, i.e. 153:2) N 88, p. 63-66.
"September, Running, with Birds." [Ploughs] (14:1) 88, p. 41.

1818. GILBERT, Gregory W.
"Sinews." [PacificR] (6) Spr 88, p. 56.
"Tongzhi." [PacificR] (6) Spr 88, p. 57.

1819. GILBERT, Mary
"Canoe." [RagMag] (6:1) [88], p. 10.
"It Has Been Here for Years." [RagMag] (6:1) [88], p. 11.

1820. GILBERT, Sandra M.
"Memory Fails." [Poetry] (152:5) Ag 88, p. 286-287.
"Rain / Insomnia / North Coast." [Poetry] (152:5) Ag 88, p. 288.
"Seizure." [Poetry] (152:5) Ag 88, p. 285.

1821. GILDNER, Gary
"Cabbage in Polish." [Poetry] (153:3) D 88, p. 129.
"In Puerto Rico, She Says" (for Miss LaToosh). [CentR] (32:1) Wint 88, p. 45-47.
"My Mother and the Touched Old Woman." [CentR] (32:1) Wint 88, p. 47-49.
"My Mother and the Touched Old Woman." [LightY] ('88/9) 88, p. 105-107.
"Poems." [PassN] (9:1) Wint 88, p. 8.
"Some Summer Afternoon in the Country." [CentR] (32:1) Wint 88, p. 43-45.
"String." [Poetry] (153:3) D 88, p. 127-128.
"Sunday Morning: Marilee Combs Her Red Hair." [PoetryNW] (29:1) Spr 88, p. 20-23.
"To Live in Warsaw." [GeoR] (42:3) Fall 88, p. 605-606.

1822. GILEVICH, Nil
"Far Off Afield in Varna's Foothill Area" (tr. by Walter May). [NegC] (8:1/2) 88, p. 29.

1823. GILGUN, John
"In Which Niki Fails a Biology Exam." [JamesWR] (5:3) Spr-Sum 88, p. 7.

1824. GILL, Evalyn P.
"Five Poems." [InterPR] (14:2) Fall 88, p. 91-92.
"Politics of Mind." [InterPR] (14:2) Fall 88, p. 92.

1825. GILLAN, Maria
"The Leavetaking" (To my son). [Lips] (14) 88, p. 18-19.
"The River at Dusk." [Lips] (14) 88, p. 17.

1826. GILLETT, Michelle
"Fixed Bodies." [PassN] (9:2) Sum 88, p. 26.

1827. GILLILAND, Mary
"Charms for Children." [Footwork] ('88) 88, p. 39-40.
"Poem for Carolyn." [HighP] (3:2) Fall 88, p. 108.
"That the Sun Would Fade." [Footwork] ('88) 88, p. 39.
"When One Romantic Touches Another." [Footwork] ('88) 88, p. 39.

1828. GILLIS, Don
"The Cartesian Water Pipes." [PottPort] (9) 88, p. 11.
"Milton Acorn." [PottPort] (9) 88, p. 11.
"Post Literacy Classroom." [PottPort] (10) 88, p. 44.

1829. GILMORE, Patricia
"For Etty Hillesum, 1914-1943: The Thinking Heart of the Barracks." [PassN] (9:2) Sum 88, p. 24.
"The Twisted Granny." [SouthernPR] (28:1) Spr 88, p. 55.

1830. GIMFERRER, Pere
"The Taking of the Winter Palace" (tr. by Marguerite Feitlowitz). [LitR] (32:1) Fall 88, p. 64-65.

1831. GINSBERG, Louis
"Thinking of a Heart Attack." [JINJPo] (10:1/2) 88, p. 40.

1832. GIOIA, Dana
"The Other Side of Mirrors." [WilliamMR] (26:1) Spr 88, p. 64-65.

1833. GIOSEFFI, Daniela
"As When Some Long Silenced Singer Hears Her Aria" (after Vittoria Colona, 1492-1547). [Confr] (37/38) Spr-Sum 88, p. 223.

1834. GIOVANETTI VIOLA, Hugo
"Anunciacion." [Mairena] (10:25) 88, p. 132.
1835. GIRAULT, Norton
"Dreaming Blind." [KeyWR] (1:2) Fall 88, p. 42-43.
1836. GIROUX, Roger
"And I'm Wearing Myself Out Standing" (tr. by Richard Zenith). [WebR] (13:1) Spr 88, p. 32-33.
"Legacy" (tr. by Richard Zenith). [WebR] (13:1) Spr 88, p. 33.
1837. GISCOMBE, C. S.
"Dayton, O. — the 50s & 60s." [SenR] (18:2) 88, p. 5-9.
1838. GIZZI, Michael
"At First Glance." [Sulfur] (8:2, #23) Fall 88, p. 120-121.
"In My Ivanhoe." [Sulfur] (8:2, #23) Fall 88, p. 119-120.
1839. GLADE, Jon Forrest
"Trout Fishing in Viet Nam." [ColR] (NS 15:2) Fall-Wint 88, p. 48-49.
1840. GLANCY, Diane
"Amelia's Breakfast." [ArtfulD] (14/15) Fall 88, p. 67-69.
"The Dead Wife Speaks." [RagMag] (6:1) [88], p. 12-13.
"Great Plains Museum, Lawton, Oklahoma." [Phoenix] (9:1/2) 88, p. 17.
"Landscape of Light." [Phoenix] (9:1/2) 88, p. 15-17.
"Leftover." [FiveFR] (6) 88, p. 14.
"Portrait of Crow Dog." [Timbuktu] (2) Sum-Fall 88, p. 7.
"Primer." [Jacaranda] (3:2) Fall-Wint 88, p. 30.
"Remembering Kona." [ChamLR] (2:1, #3) Fall 88, p. 16-17.
"Snake Meat." [PaintedB] (36) 88, p. 90.
"Upright Piano." [SwampR] (1:2/3) D 88, p. 78.
"Wagon III (a Sculpture on Wheels), David Smith, Nelson Art Gallery, Kansas City, Mo." [Phoenix] (9:1/2) 88, p. 18.
"What the Mutt?" [Phoenix] (9:1/2) 88, p. 18.
1841. GLANG, Gabriele
"Consider the Horseradish" (For Gillian, In Memoriam). [NegC] (8:3) 88, p. 191.
"Consider the Horseradish" (for Gillian, In Memoriam). [Quarry] (37:4) Aut 88, p. 57.
"Plumblood" (for Trevor). [Quarry] (37:4) Aut 88, p. 56.
"Stark Naked on a Cold Irish Morning." [NegC] (8:3) 88, p. 139.
1842. GLASER, Elton
"Confluences at San Francisco" (M.L.A., 1987). [Poetry] (153:3) D 88, p. 131.
"Elegy with Sideburns." [PoetryNW] (29:2) Sum 88, p. 23.
"Epiphany Stick." [SouthernPR] (28:2) Fall 88, p. 70.
"Hibernation" (for Elton). [SouthernPR] (28:1) Spr 88, p. 61.
"Ragdoll Raga." [LittleM] (15:3/4) 88, p. 94.
"Redwing Blackbirds." [Lips] (14) 88, p. 52-53.
"The Return of Hoon." [NoDaQ] (56:1) Wint 88, p. 195-196.
"Somniloquy." [FloridaR] (16:1) Spr-Sum 88, p. 18.
"Thirst" (tr. of Jacques Dupin). [Paint] (15:30) Aut 88, p. 40.
"Three Poems About Pumps." [FloridaR] (16:1) Spr-Sum 88, p. 16-17.
"The Truce" (tr. of Jacques Dupin). [Paint] (15:30) Aut 88, p. 40.
1843. GLASS, Jesse
"Gnosis M." [CreamCR] (12:2) Sum 88, p. 190-193.
1844. GLASS, Jesse, Jr.
"At a Reading of Local Poets." [Bogg] (59) 88, p. 26-27.
1845. GLASS, Malcolm
"Children of Blackout." [PoetC] (19:3) Spr 88, p. 45.
"Crows." [HighP] (3:3) Wint 88-89, p. 48.
"First Meeting" (In memoriam, Lowell Lee Lotspeich). [PoetC] (19:3) Spr 88, p. 43.
"Incident" (for R, my student). [PoetC] (19:3) Spr 88, p. 44.
"Legerdemain" (For Mont Davis). [Poetry] (152:4) Jl 88, p. 188-189.
"Living on Light." [Poetry] (152:4) Jl 88, p. 187-188.
"Newlyweds." [HighP] (3:1) Spr 88, p. 101.
"Risks." [LightY] ('88/9) 88, p. 168.
"Soaring: Goal and Return." [Poetry] (152:4) Jl 88, p. 189-190.
"Warning." [Ascent] (13:2) 88, p. 41.
1846. GLASSCO, John
"The Reign of Winter" (tr. of Gaston Miron). [Trans] (20) Spr 88, p. 172.

1847. GLASSGOLD, Peter
"9. Veranius, the best of all my friends" (tr. of Gaius Valerius Catullus). [NoDaQ] (56:1) Wint 88, p. 20.
"11. Furius and Aurelius, companions of Catullus" (tr. of Gaius Valerius Catullus). [NoDaQ] (56:1) Wint 88, p. 20-21.
"13. My own Fabullus, you'll dine well at my place" (tr. of Gaius Valerius Catullus). [NoDaQ] (56:1) Wint 88, p. 21-22.
"15. I give into your keeping, Aurelius, myself" (tr. of Gaius Valerius Catullus). [NoDaQ] (56:1) Wint 88, p. 22.
"17. The town of Verona wants a long bridge" (tr. of Gaius Valerius Catullus). [NoDaQ] (56:1) Wint 88, p. 22-23.
1848. GLAZER, Jane
"Easter Walk with Nan." [BellArk] (4:1) Ja-F 88, p. 3.
1849. GLAZIER, Loss Pequeño
"Autumn in the South Land." [Jacaranda] (3:2) Fall-Wint 88, p. 91.
"Bienfait." [Os] (27) 88, p. 23.
"In Amersfoort." [Os] (26) 88, p. 12.
"Instinct." [Os] (27) 88, p. 22.
1850. GLAZKOV, Nikolai
"Khikhimora" (Excerpt, tr. by Daniel Weissbort). [NegC] (8:1/2) 88, p. 20-22.
"Poetograd" (Selections: 1-2, tr. by Daniel Weissbort). [NegC] (8:1/2) 88, p. 17-19.
"The Raven" (tr. by Daniel Weissbort). [NegC] (8:1/2) 88, p. 23.
1851. GLAZNER, Greg
"After the Rains in Chimayó." [HighP] (3:3) Wint 88-89, p. 100-101.
1852. GLEASON, Kathi
"Tango, Tangle." [LittleM] (15:3/4) 88, p. 31-32.
1853. GLEASON, Marian
"Near Myth." [LightY] ('88/9) 88, p. 81.
"The Ritual." [ChrC] (105:36) 30 N 88, p. 1084.
"Treasure Trove." [ChrC] (105:34) 16 N 88, p. 1040.
1854. GLEN, Emilie
"Mobile." [Confr] (37/38) Spr-Sum 88, p. 263.
"Tears Hard." [Lactuca] (10) Je 88, p. 33.
1855. GLENN, Laura
"Potpourri." [FloridaR] (16:1) Spr-Sum 88, p. 57.
1856. GLICKSTEIN, Gloria
"The Sibyl." [Boulevard] (3:2/3) Fall 88, p. 97-98.
1857. GLOEGGLER, Tony
"45 RPMS." [Bogg] (60) 88, p. 27.
"Blue Collar." [Bogg] (59) 88, p. 14.
"Grandpa's Hands." [Turnstile] (1:2) 88, p. 100.
1858. GLÜCK, Louise
"All Hallows." [LitR] (31:3) Spr 88, p. 263-264.
"Departure." [LitR] (31:3) Spr 88, p. 266.
"For My Mother." [LitR] (31:3) Spr 88, p. 264-265.
"The Gift." [LitR] (31:3) Spr 88, p. 269.
"Love Poem." [LitR] (31:3) Spr 88, p. 266.
"Memo from the Cave." [LitR] (31:3) Spr 88, p. 261-262.
"Nurse's Song." [LitR] (31:3) Spr 88, p. 262.
"The Reproach." [LitR] (31:3) Spr 88, p. 271.
1859. GNANAKKOOTHAN
"The Street" (tr. by Nakulan). [Nimrod] (31:2) Spr-Sum 88, p. 97.
1860. GOCKER, Paula
"True Stories" (Selection: Number 5). [CarolQ] (40:3) Spr 88, p. 44.
1861. GODIN, Deborah
"Confluence: The Water Cycle." [PraF] (9:4) Wint 88-89, p. 28.
"Mid September." [Dandel] (15:1) Spr-Sum 88, p. 22.
"S.E.T.I." [PraF] (9:4) Wint 88-89, p. 29.
1862. GOEDICKE, Patricia
"The Charge." [NewEngR] (11:1) Aut 88, p. 78-79.
"Dad's Ashes." [OntR] (29) Fall-Wint 88-89, p. 21-23.
"Dear Presence." [GrahamHR] (11) Spr 88, p. 61-63.
"The General's Digel." [TarRP] (28:1) Fall 88, p. 20-21.
"Lost in Translation." [GettyR] (1:2) Spr 88, p. 274-275.
"The Man and the Woman in the Sky." [CutB] (29/30) 88, p. 22-23.
"The Marriage Tub." [OntR] (29) Fall-Wint 88-89, p. 24-26.

"Mountainside Farm." [GettyR] (1:2) Spr 88, p. 271-273.
"On Second Thought." [NewEngR] (11:1) Aut 88, p. 75-77.
"Phantom Limb." [TarRP] (27:2) Spr 88, p. 9-11.
"Ubi Leones." [CutB] (29/30) 88, p. 24-25.
"Weight Bearing." [GettyR] (1:2) Spr 88, p. 276-277.
"Whatever Gray Grid." [NoAmR] (273:2) Je 88, p. 51.

1863. GOHAIN, Hiren
"Poems" (4 selections, tr. of Nilmani Phookan). [Nimrod] (31:2) Spr-Sum 88, p. 25-27.

1864. GOINS, J.
"Mid-Atlantic Monodies." [PacificR] (6) Spr 88, p. 52.
"Running with Deer." [PacificR] (6) Spr 88, p. 50.
"West Wind." [PacificR] (6) Spr 88, p. 51.

1865. GOLB, Joel
"Décimale Blanche" (1 poem, English tr. of Jean Daive). [Acts] (8/9) 88, p. 54.
"Oo-oo-the Blue" (tr. of Paul Celan). [Acts] (8/9) 88, p. 169, 171.

1866. GOLD, Arthur
"1944." [ParisR] (30:109) Wint 88, p. 58.

1867. GOLD, Sid
"Silver Bullets." [SouthernPR] (28:1) Spr 88, p. 8.

1868. GOLDBARTH, Albert
"All About." [BlackWR] (15:1) Fall 88, p. 44-48.
"Famous Bridges." [TarRP] (28:1) Fall 88, p. 27-28.
"Going In Coming Out." [OhioR] (42) 88, p. 78-79.
"Gold / Silk." [SouthwR] (73:1) Wint 88, p. 127-128.
"How We Do It." [TarRP] (28:1) Fall 88, p. 29.
"The Multiverse." [Poetry] (151:4) Ja 88, p. 329-332.
"Of Two Things at My Door This Morning." [CutB] (29/30) 88, p. 7.
"Places Where Worlds Meet in Passing." [DenQ] (23:1) Sum 88, p. 56-57.
"Powers." [CutB] (29/30) 88, p. 8-10.
"Predictopoem." [IndR] (12:1) Wint 88, p. 67-68.
"Qebehseneuf." [OntR] (28) Spr-Sum 88, p. 81-90.
"The Quest for the Source of the Nile." [Poetry] (151:4) Ja 88, p. 332-336.
"Shangri-La: A Mystery Story." [BelPoJ] (38:3) Spr 88, p. 5-13.
"The Whole Earth Catalogue." [PoetryNW] (29:3) Aut 88, p. 3-5.
"Why I Believe in Ghosts." [DenQ] (23:1) Sum 88, p. 54-55.

1869. GOLDBERG, Barbara
"Border Dispatch." [SenR] (18:1) 88, p. 52-53.
"The Miracle of Bubbles" (International Poetry Contest, Third Prize). [WestB] (21/22) 88, p. 41.
"What I Dwell On." [AntR] (46:2) Spr 88, p. 246.
"When I Learn My Friend Must Lose Her Breast to Cancer" (First Runner Up, 1987 Poetry Contest). [PoetL] (83:1) Spr 88, p. 14-18.

1870. GOLDBERG, Beckian Fritz
"First Love." [VirQR] (64:2) Spr 88, p. 283-284.
"Refraction" (for my brother). [CutB] (29/30) 88, p. 89-91.

1871. GOLDBERGER, Iefke
"Last Steps" (in memory of a classmate). [Spirit] (9:1) 88, p. 61-62.

1872. GOLDBLATT, Eli
"58 Nabaj, 1980." [AnotherCM] (18) 88, p. 103.
"Troop Ships Land Men." [AnotherCM] (18) 88, p. 104.

1873. GOLDEN, Renny
"Messenger." [AmerV] (12) Fall 88, p. 82.

1874. GOLDENHAR, Edith
"A Sabbath." [IndR] (11:3) Sum 88, p. 18-20.
"Unabashed." [YellowS] (27) Aut 88, p. 29.

1875. GOLDENSOHN, Lorrie
"Anesthesia." [Poetry] (152:5) Ag 88, p. 291.
"Practice Run." [Salm] (78/79) Spr-Sum 88, p. 150-151.
"Promises." [Poetry] (152:5) Ag 88, p. 289-290.
"Rooms and Pictures." [Salm] (78/79) Spr-Sum 88, p. 146-148.
"Soap Opera." [Salm] (78/79) Spr-Sum 88, p. 149.
"The World As Conscious Will." [Poetry] (152:5) Ag 88, p. 292-293.

1876. GOLDMAN, Kathleen Zeisler
"About Flowers." [Northeast] (ser. 4:7) Sum 88, p. 28.

1877. GOLDOWSKY, Barbara
"Observing Andromeda." [Confr] (37/38) Spr-Sum 88, p. 240.
1878. GOLDSTEIN, Darra
"Fir Trees Clanked Like Green Metal!" (tr. of Viktor Sosnora, w. Kathryn Hellerstein). [NewYRB] (35:15) 13 O 88, p. 47.
"Letter" (tr. of Viktor Sosnora, w. Kathryn Hellerstein). [NewYRB] (35:15) 13 O 88, p. 47.
1879. GOLDSTEIN, Henry
"The House with the Blue Door." [Confr] (Special issue: The World of Brooklyn) 88, p. 53.
1880. GOLDSTEIN, Laurence
"Firmament on High." [Iowa] (18:2) 88, p. 63.
"The Silent Movie Theater" (in memoriam). [Iowa] (18:2) 88, p. 58-62.
1881. GOLDSTEIN, Marion
"Rain Room." [Footwork] ('88) 88, p. 40.
"September." [Footwork] ('88) 88, p. 40.
1882. GOLFFING, Francis
"In Conclusion" (tr. of Gunther Eich). [SpiritSH] (54) Fall-Wint 88, p. 30.
"October" (tr. of Gunther Eich). [SpiritSH] (54) Fall-Wint 88, p. 29.
"Sibylline Leaves." [Shen] (38:1) 88, p. 21.
"The Tomb of Paul Verlaine" (After Mallarmé). [Shen] (38:1) 88, p. 21-22.
"Untitled: Meditation on justice to fishes" (tr. of Gunther Eich). [SpiritSH] (54) Fall-Wint 88, p. 28.
1883. GOLL, Yvan
"The Mill of Death" (tr. by Joel Spector). [Agni] (27) 88, p. 43-44.
"The Sacred Body" (tr. by Joel Spector). [Agni] (27) 88, p. 45.
GOMEZ, Ana Ilce
See ILCE GOMEZ, Ana
GOMEZ, Emilio García
See GARCIA GOMEZ, Emilio
1884. GOMEZ, Juan Antonio
"Aguas para el Olvido." [Mairena] (10:25) 88, p. 184.
1885. GOMEZ, Lang
"It Was a Scattered Squadron (September, 1978)" (tr. of Daisy Zamora, w. Preston Browning). [AnotherCM] (18) 88, p. 195.
"Love Until Now" (tr. of Rosario Murillo, w. Preston Browning). [AnotherCM] (18) 88, p. 138.
1886. GOMEZ-PEÑA, Guillermo
"Good Morning, This Is Radio Latino Spoiling Your Breakfast As Always." [Zyzzyva] (4:3) Fall 88, p. 49.
1887. GOMEZ ROSA, A.
"Banquete de Familia II." [Inti] (28) Otoño 88, p. 166-167.
"El Espejo del Minotauro." [Inti] (28) Otoño 88, p. 164-165.
"Inspiración de Hoy en Ocho." [Inti] (28) Otoño 88, p. 165-166.
"Momificando los Días del Idiota." [Inti] (28) Otoño 88, p. 163-164.
1888. GOMORI, George
"Found Images" (tr. by the author and Clive Wilmer). [Vis] (26) 88, p. 25.
1889. GOMRINGER, Eugen
"Avenidas." [Mairena] (10:25) 88, p. 79.
1890. GONET, Jill
"The Shells." [BlackWR] (15:1) Fall 88, p. 120.
GONGORA, Helcías Martan
See MARTAN GONGORA, Helcías
1891. GONZALES, Merrill Ann
"Holding Fast." [RagMag] (6:2) Fall 88, p. 20.
"The Unlocking." [RagMag] (6:2) Fall 88, p. 21.
1892. GONZALEZ, Angel
"A la Poesia." [Gargoyle] (35) 88, p. 8.
"A Fall Day, Texas" (tr. by Pedro Gutierrez Revuelta and Steven Ford Brown). [LitR] (31:2) Wint 88, p. 220.
"Order (Poetics That Others Follow)" (tr. by Steven Ford Brown and Pedro Gutierrez Revuelta). [Paint] (15:30) Aut 88, p. 37.
"Poetics That I Sometimes Try to Follow" (tr. by Steven Ford Brown and Pedro Gutierrez Revuelta). [Paint] (15:30) Aut 88, p. 36.
"To Poetry" (tr. by Steven Ford Brown and Pedro Gutierrez Revuelta). [Gargoyle] (35) 88, p. 9.

1893. GONZALEZ, Sonia
"Espejo." [Mairena] (10:25) 88, p. 63.
1894. GONZALEZ FERRER, Campo Elias
"Escrito suavemente." [Mairena] (10:25) 88, p. 180.
1895. GOODENOUGH, J. B.
"Bass Harbor." [TexasR] (9:3/4) Fall-Wint 88, p. 59.
"Door." [HiramPoR] (44/45) Spr-Wint 88, p. 17.
"Forty Days and Forty Nights." [HiramPoR] (44/45) Spr-Wint 88, p. 18.
"Neighbors." [PaintedB] (36) 88, p. 42.
"Perennial." [PaintedB] (36) 88, p. 43.
"Planting." [Farm] (5:2) Fall 88, p. 56.
"Spells." [ArtfulD] (14/15) Fall 88, p. 16.
"Th Inutility of Anger." [Confr] (37/38) Spr-Sum 88, p. 227.
"The Way Out." [TexasR] (9:3/4) Fall-Wint 88, p. 61.
"Weather Watch." [TexasR] (9:3/4) Fall-Wint 88, p. 60.
"Years of Mornings." [LitR] (31:2) Wint 88, p. 233.
1896. GOODMAN, Jenny
"Trying to Explain Don Juan." [FiveFR] (6) 88, p. 70.
1897. GOODMAN, Michael
"The Metamorphosis." [SenR] (18:2) 88, p. 77-79.
"The Trespasser's Tale." [Agni] (27) 88, p. 200-201.
1898. GOODMAN, Ryah Tumarkin
"A Coat Can Walk." [Confr] (37/38) Spr-Sum 88, p. 168.
"The End." [Crosscur] (7:4) 88, p. 45.
1899. GOODSWAN, William
"Poem from Lunar Base." [Writer] (101:9) S 88, p. 23.
1900. GOODWIN, Douglas
"Barking for Fish." [Bogg] (60) 88, p. 12.
"End of the Year." [Lactuca] (10) Je 88, p. 18-19.
"Good Morning." [Lactuca] (10) Je 88, p. 20.
"Idiot Victory." [Lactuca] (10) Je 88, p. 19.
1901. GOODWIN, June
"Applause." [CentR] (32:3) Sum 88, p. 272-273.
"Conventions." [GettyR] (1:1) Wint 88, p. 116.
1902. GOODWIN, Leigh Clifton
"Suicide 1962-1981." [CrabCR] (5:2) Sum 88, p. 21.
1903. GORCZYNSKI, Renata
"Alma Mater" (tr. of Adam Zagajewski, w. C. K. Williams). [TriQ] (71) Wint 88, p. 142.
"September Afternoon in the Abandoned Barracks" (tr. of Adam Zagajewski, w. C. K. Williams). [TriQ] (71) Wint 88, p. 141.
"Seventeen Years Old" (tr. of Adam Zagajewski). [WestHR] (42:4) Wint 88, p. 273.
"When Death Came" (tr. of Adam Zagajewski, w. C. K. Williams). [TriQ] (71) Wint 88, p. 139-140.
1904. GORDETT, Marea
"Patience." [Ploughs] (14:1) 88, p. 86-87.
1905. GORDON, Benjamin L.
"A Middle-aged Teacher Sees His Head." [EngJ] (77:1) Ja 88, p. 102.
1906. GORDON, Carol
"Bundy." [CrabCR] (5:1) Wint 88, p. 6.
1907. GORDON, Elizabeth
"Looking for Home." [CutB] (31/32) 88, p. 84.
1908. GORDON, John
"I seek poetry here in this forest" (tr. of Olga Lebedushkina). [NegC] (8:1/2) 88, p. 48.
1909. GORDON, Kirpal
"Beware: You Are//OR//Be Where You Are Not: It's Descending Anyway." [CentralP] (13) Spr 88, p. 159-162.
"The Catholic Imprint: Lustrum at the RKO." [SlipS] (8) 88, p. 23-24.
"City Words." [Amelia] (4:4, #11) 88, p. 66.
"The Poverty of Their Desire." [SlipS] (8) 88, p. 22.
1910. GORDON, Sarah
"The Daughters." [ChatR] (8:3) Spr 88, p. 55.
1911. GOREN, Judith
"On Eating an Artichoke." [PassN] (9:1) Wint 88, p. 10.

1912. GORHAM, Sarah
"Oval." [NewL] (55:1) Fall 88, p. 67.
"Walkingstick." [TexasR] (9:3/4) Fall-Wint 88, p. 62.
1913. GORMAN, LeRoy
"Ina her yli." [Bogg] (60) 88, p. 16.
"Service Club Fund Raiser" (Or, Where Have All the o's Gone?). [Bogg] (59) 88, p. 46.
1914. GORSKI, Andrew
"A Filmframe" (tr. of Piotr Sommer). [Os] (27) 88, p. 8-9.
"Fragility" (tr. of Piotr Sommer). [Os] (27) 88, p. 28-31.
"Landscape with a Branch" (tr. of Piotr Sommer). [Os] (27) 88, p. 6-7.
"Medicine" (tr. of Piotr Sommer). [Os] (27) 88, p. 12-13.
"Street Songs" (tr. of Piotr Sommer). [Os] (27) 88, p. 10-11.
1915. GOTO, T. M.
"After Pastel Sky." [ChamLR] (1) Fall 87, p. 52.
"Lovewave." [ChamLR] (1) Fall 87, p. 51.
"One Lanai at the Halfmoon." [HawaiiR] (12:2, #24) Fall 88, p. 109.
1916. GOTT, George
"Always." [Paint] (15:29) Spr 88, p. 20.
"Un Peu Moisi." [Paint] (15:29) Spr 88, p. 21.
"The Third Day." [MidwQ] (29:2) Wint 88, p. 223.
1917. GOTTSCHALK, Elin K.
"DP Camp Child." [Vis] (26) 88, p. 24.
"Pictures." [Vis] (26) 88, p. 23.
1918. GOULD, Alan
"New Holland" (Excerpt from a section of "The Commonwealth of James Cook"). [PraS] (62:4) Wint 88-89, p. 67-72.
1919. GOULD, Roberta
"From *Educacion Publica* with Diego Rivera Murals." [ChamLR] (2:1, #3) Fall 88, p. 73.
1920. GOULD, Scott
"Remington's Statue." [CarolQ] (40:2) Wint 88, p. 16.
"Running the Dogs." [CarolQ] (40:2) Wint 88, p. 15.
1921. GOUMAS, Yannis
"Loneliness." [Verse] (5:3) N 88, p. 68.
1922. GOURGOURIS, Stathis
"My Father." [Jacaranda] (3:2) Fall-Wint 88, p. 148.
1923. GOW, Ruth
"Death Valley." [SmPd] (25:2) Spr 88, p. 14.
1924. GOWLAND, M. L.
"At Home Abroad." [RagMag] (6:2) Fall 88, p. 23.
"Dating a Man with a Broken Heart." [RagMag] (6:2) Fall 88, p. 23.
"Orange Juice." [RagMag] (6:2) Fall 88, p. 22.
"She Writes a Poem." [RagMag] (6:2) Fall 88, p. 24-25.
"The Slumber Party." [RagMag] (6:2) Fall 88, p. 25.
1925. GRABILL, James (Jim)
"Belt Drive." [Caliban] (4) 88, p. 124-125.
"The Finches." [MidAR] (8:1) 88, p. 18.
"In the Scent of Earth." [Caliban] (4) 88, p. 127.
"Opening the Lens." [MidAR] (8:1) 88, p. 16-17.
"Saturday Morning." [Spirit] (9:1) 88, p. 38.
"What It Does to Him." [Caliban] (4) 88, p. 126.
1926. GRAFF, E. J.
"Daphne." [Thrpny] (34) Sum 88, p. 13.
"Psyche." [Thrpny] (34) Sum 88, p. 13.
1927. GRAFF, Herman
"Baskets of War." [Lactuca] (10) Je 88, p. 13.
"The Ghosts of War." [Lactuca] (10) Je 88, p. 11, 13.
"The Host." [Lactuca] (10) Je 88, p. 11.
"Unseen Realm." [Lactuca] (10) Je 88, p. 14-15.
1928. GRAFTON, Grace
"Legs." [BellArk] (4:4) Jl-Ag 88, p. 9.
"Tuolomne Meadow, Yosemite National Park." [BellArk] (4:1) Ja-F 88, p. 3.
"Waking with You." [BellArk] (4:1) Ja-F 88, p. 6.
"A Woman at Home Cooks Beets." [BellArk] (4:3) My-Je 88, p. 3.

1929. GRAHAM, David
"The Fox, a Most Cat-like Dog." [PraS] (62:2) Sum 88, p. 110-111.
"Lucky Man." [PraS] (62:2) Sum 88, p. 112-113.
"My Father Standing at the Door." [LaurelR] (22:2) Sum 88, p. 107.
"My Parents at Home." [PraS] (62:2) Sum 88, p. 111-112.
"Sara Who Fucked Like a Horse." [Spirit] (9:1) 88, p. 154-155.
"Wedding Gift." [PraS] (62:2) Sum 88, p. 113.

1930. GRAHAM, Desmond
"Change" (tr. of Anna Kamienska, w. Tomasz P. Krzeszowski). [Verse] (5:2) Jl 88, p. 13.
"A Thirteen Year Old Girl" (tr. of Anna Kamienska, w. Tomasz P. Krzeszowski). [Verse] (5:2) Jl 88, p. 14.

1931. GRAHAM, James
"Alta Hora de la Noche" (English tr. of Roque Dalton). [Bomb] (24) Sum 88, p. 67.
"El Gran Despecho" (The Great Despair, English tr. of Roque Dalton). [Bomb] (24) Sum 88, p. 67.
"El Mar" (for Tati, Meri, Margarita, with whom I rode a wave, English tr. of Roque Dalton). [Bomb] (24) Sum 88, p. 66-67.

1932. GRAHAM, Jorie
"Desire." [LitR] (31:3) Spr 88, p. 355.
"The Region of Unlikeness" (Selections: 7 poems). [BlackWR] (15:1) Fall 88, p. 49-71.

1933. GRANDBOIS, Alain
"Let Us Close the Cupboard" (tr. by D. G. Jones). [Trans] (20) Spr 88, p. 144-146.

1934. GRANT, Craig
"The Butcher's Daughter" (Selections from a suite of poems). [Grain] (16:2) Sum 88, p. 62-74.

1935. GRANT, Jamie
"Daylight Moon." [PraS] (62:4) Wint 88-89, p. 95-97.
"The Hospital Bell-Tower." [PraS] (62:4) Wint 88-89, p. 93-95.

1936. GRANT, Paul
"Casting the Movie." [ColEng] (50:2) F 88, p. 157.
"Equal Rights." [PoetL] (83:2) Sum 88, p. 39-40.
"Farmhouse: Liberty, Indiana." [PoetL] (83:2) Sum 88, p. 41.
"The Ghost of Buck Jones' Horse, Silver, Talks to Reporters about Fire Prevention." [Gargoyle] (35) 88, p. 28.
"Grand Terrace Shuffle" (for Richard Hugo). [Gargoyle] (35) 88, p. 29.
"In the Mood." [ColEng] (50:2) F 88, p. 158.
"Linoleum." [NegC] (8:3) 88, p. 120-121.
"Natural Science." [PoetL] (83:2) Sum 88, p. 38.

1937. GRANT, Ray
"Identity." [Iowa] (18:2) 88, p. 54.
"Syeeda's Song Flute (Coltrane 1959)." [Iowa] (18:2) 88, p. 53.

1938. GRANTHAM, R. F.
"Death of a Flowerbed." [Writer] (101:3) Mr 88, p. 19.

1939. GRAPES, Jack
"A Deed of Light." [Jacaranda] (3:2) Fall-Wint 88, p. 92-94.

GRAVELLES, Charles de
See DeGRAVELLES, Charles

1940. GRAVES, Paul
"The Decanter" (tr. of Aleksandr Kushner). [Confr] (37/38) Spr-Sum 88, p. 24.
"Seven Strophes" (tr. of Joseph Brodsky). [WestHR] (42:1) Spr 88, p. 18.
"Sheltering Thoughts" (tr. of Aleksandr Kushner). [Confr] (37/38) Spr-Sum 88, p. 23.

1941. GRAVES, Thomas West
"A Puzzle Usually." [PoetryE] (25) Spr 88, p. 5.

1942. GRAY, Alice Wirth
"Lines After Marianne Moore." [HeliconN] (19) 88, p. 35.
"The Man with a Child for Each of His Fingers" (Runner Up, 1988 Narrative Poetry Contest). [PoetL] (83:4) Wint 88-89, p. 14-19.

1943. GRAY, Elizabeth
"At Five." [BellArk] (4:1) Ja-F 88, p. 5.

1944. GRAY, Jennifer
"On the Other Side." [HangL] (53) 88, p. 58.
"The Roof." [HangL] (53) 88, p. 59.

1945. GRAY, Patrick Worth
"Daydreaming in Church" (for Richard Wyatt). [WebR] (13:2) Fall 88, p. 85-86.
"Flying to the 1987 David B. Steinman Festival of the Arts" ("Art and the Vietnam Era"). [CapeR] (23:2) Fall 88, p. 1.
1946. GRAY, Robert
"Black Landscape." [PraS] (62:4) Wint 88-89, p. 108-109.
"A Winter Morning." [PraS] (62:4) Wint 88-89, p. 110.
1947. GRAZIDE, Richard
"All the dead animals." [Notus] (3:1) Spr 88, p. 87.
"Bound among fish." [Notus] (3:1) Spr 88, p. 89.
"I can see how I didn't make myself clear." [Notus] (3:1) Spr 88, p. 88.
GRECA, T. R. la
See LaGRECA, T. R.
1948. GREEN, David
"We, the Real." [Crosscur] (7:4) 88, p. 53.
1949. GREEN, David H.
"Down East Drama." [LightY] ('88/9) 88, p. 133-134.
1950. GREEN, Jessie L.
"Haiku: Smooth water dappled" (The 14th Kansas Poetry Contest, Fifth Honorable Mention). [LittleBR] (5:2) Wint 88-89, p. 70.
1951. GREEN, Peter
"Helen" (tr. of Yannis Ritsos, w. Beverly Bardsley). [GrandS] (8:1) Aut 88, p. 65-85.
1952. GREEN, William H.
"Crimes Against Nature." [DeKalbLAJ] (21:3/4) 88, p. 54.
"Two Women in Half Light." [Wind] (18:62) 88, p. 35.
1953. GREENBERG, Alex M.
"Footprints on the Sand." [ManhatPR] (10) Ja 88, p. 56.
1954. GREENBERG, Alvin
"Breathing Easy." [GettyR] (1:3) Sum 88, p. 469.
"Conversion." [LittleM] (15:3/4) 88, p. 127.
"Flood Stage." [CinPR] (17) Spr 88, p. 9.
"In the Graveyard, My Father." [GettyR] (1:3) Sum 88, p. 472.
"Into the Orthodox Jewish Home for the Aged." [CinPR] (17) Spr 88, p. 8.
"Natural Science: Daily Lesson." [LittleM] (15:3/4) 88, p. 126.
"Thanacopia" (Pablo Neruda Prize for Poetry, First Prize). [Nimrod] (32:1) Fall-Wint 88, p. 1-4.
"What With." [GettyR] (1:3) Sum 88, p. 470-471.
1955. GREENBURG, Candace
"Adam Musing." [PassN] (9:1) Wint 88, p. 29.
"Le Lieu des Morts." [Event] (17:2) Sum 88, p. 47-49.
"Noon in the Hackberry Tree." [Event] (17:2) Sum 88, p. 46.
1956. GREENE, Ben
"Hiking Up from Dawson's Pass" (Glacier National Park, Montana). [InterPR] (14:2) Fall 88, p. 94-95.
"Kaleidoscope." [InterPR] (14:2) Fall 88, p. 93.
"Thistle in May." [HiramPoR] (44/45) Spr-Wint 88, p. 19.
1957. GREENE, James
"Black Earth" (tr. of Osip Mandelstam). [WillowS] (22) Spr 88, p. 24.
"Help me, O Lord, to survive this night" (tr. of Osip Mandelstam). [WillowS] (22) Spr 88, p. 22.
"I drink to the blossoming epaulette" (tr. of Osip Mandelstam). [WillowS] (22) Spr 88, p. 20.
"I was only in a childish way connected with the world of power" (tr. of Osip Mandelstam). [WillowS] (22) Spr 88, p. 21.
"In my disgrace I shall perform a smoky rite" (tr. of Osip Mandelstam). [WillowS] (22) Spr 88, p. 23.
"My country conversed with me" (tr. of Osip Mandelstam). [WillowS] (22) Spr 88, p. 23.
"The people need pale-blue air and light" (tr. of Osip Mandelstam). [WillowS] (22) Spr 88, p. 25.
"Return to the incestuous lap" (tr. of Osip Mandelstam). [WillowS] (22) Spr 88, p. 17.
"Those hundred-carat ingots, Roman nights" (tr. of Osip Mandelstam). [WillowS] (22) Spr 88, p. 22.

"Where can I go this January?" (tr. of Osip Mandelstam). [WillowS] (22) Spr 88, p. 25.
"Whoever's been kissing time's tortured crown" (tr. of Osip Mandelstam). [WillowS] (22) Spr 88, p. 18-19.
"Your narrow shoulders are to redden under scourges" (tr. of Osip Mandelstam). [WillowS] (22) Spr 88, p. 22.

1958. GREENE, Jeffrey
"The Horses of Autumn" (to my cousin). [SenR] (18:2) 88, p. 64-65.
"The Love of Daughters." [IndR] (11:3) Sum 88, p. 56-57.
"The Subtender." [AmerS] (57:1) Wint 88, p. 31-32.

1959. GREENE, Robin
"August 1474: The Basilisk." [Sequoia] (31:2) Wint 88, p. 72.

1960. GREENING, John
"Pluto." [Verse] (5:2) Jl 88, p. 13.
"Portrait of Henry V by an Unknown Artist." [Stand] (29:4) Aut 88, p. 30.

1961. GREENLEAF, Constance
"A Different Perspective." [ChiR] (36:1) 88, p. 60.
"Elegy." [ChiR] (36:1) 88, p. 59.
"A Single Light." [ChiR] (36:1) 88, p. 61-62.

1962. GREENLEE, Marie
"Flamingos." [Sonora] (14/15) Spr 88, p. 69.
"I Don't Think I'd Stay." [Sonora] (14/15) Spr 88, p. 67.
"Perry." [Sonora] (14/15) Spr 88, p. 70.
"Waiting for Roses." [Sonora] (14/15) Spr 88, p. 68.

1963. GREENLEY, Emily
"Dog." [HarvardA] (122:4) My 88, p. 24.
"Now Begin Without." [HarvardA] (123:1) N 88, p. 13.

1964. GREENWALD, Roger
"Blood Poisoning" (tr. of Gunnar Harding). [Writ] (20) 88, p. 34-35.
"Guarding the Air" (tr. of Gunnar Harding). [Writ] (20) 88, p. 39-43.
"I Saw You." [Spirit] (9:1) 88, p. 119.
"The National Hospital, Oslo, September 1976" (tr. of Gunnar Harding). [Writ] (20) 88, p. 36-38.
"Star-Goalie" (tr. of Gunnar Harding). [Writ] (20) 88, p. 32-33.

1965. GREENWAY, William
"Boomers." [Poetry] (152:3) Je 88, p. 130.
"Entrance." [Poetry] (152:3) Je 88, p. 129.
"Small Road to Nowhere." [Poetry] (152:3) Je 88, p. 130.

1966. GREGER, Debora
"After Iceland, William Morris Dreams of Panama." [BostonR] (13:2) Ap 88, p. 19.
"Book of Hours." [BostonR] (13:2) Ap 88, p. 19.
"Don Giovanni in Florida." [WilliamMR] (26:1) Spr 88, p. 50.
"Foolscap." [WilliamMR] (26:1) Spr 88, p. 51.
"A Guide to the Gods." [SouthwR] (73:1) Wint 88, p. 57-58.
"In Violet." [GettyR] (1:3) Sum 88, p. 568.
"The Man Who Writes Dialogue for a Living." [SouthwR] (73:1) Wint 88, p. 56-57.
"The Married State." [YaleR] (78:1) Aut 88, p. 142-143.
"The Painter's Model." [BostonR] (13:2) Ap 88, p. 19.
"Piranesi in L.A." [BostonR] (13:2) Ap 88, p. 19.
"Preface to the Collected Works." [YaleR] (78:1) Aut 88, p. 143-144.
"The Shallows." [BostonR] (13:2) Ap 88, p. 19.
"Sleeping Beauty." [Poetry] (153:3) D 88, p. 139-140.
"The Snow Woman." [Poetry] (153:3) D 88, p. 138.
"St. Jerome on the Virgin's Profession." [GettyR] (1:3) Sum 88, p. 566-567.

1967. GREGERMAN, Debra
"Silent Globe." [AntR] (46:4) Fall 88, p. 489.

1968. GREGG, Linda
"A Dangerous Trade." [MassR] (29:1) Spr 88, p. 20.
"A Dark Thing Inside the Day." [AmerPoR] (17:4) Jl-Ag 88, p. 37.
"Glistening." [MassR] (29:1) Spr 88, p. 21.
"The Invention of Writing." [AmerPoR] (17:4) Jl-Ag 88, p. 36.
"The Letter" (for Jerry). [PoetryE] (26) Fall 88, p. 159.
"Ordinary Songs." [AmerPoR] (17:4) Jl-Ag 88, p. 36.
"Overcast." [AmerPoR] (17:4) Jl-Ag 88, p. 37.
"The Small Thing Love Is." [MassR] (29:1) Spr 88, p. 20.
"Tokens of What She Is." [AmerPoR] (17:4) Jl-Ag 88, p. 36.

1969. GREGOR, Arthur
"On Another Departure, Châtillon 1987." [Nat] (246:10) 12 Mr 88, p. 354.
1970. GREGORY, Dennis
"Night Embroidery." [CapeR] (23:2) Fall 88, p. 48.
1971. GREGORY, Gina
"I'll See You Around" (from Bogg 30, 1975). [Bogg] (59) 88, p. 41.
1972. GREGORY, Michael
"Mole Hunting: A Triptych." [CapeR] (23:1) Spr 88, p. 14-15.
"The Shield" (To Alesa). [CapeR] (23:1) Spr 88, p. 16.
1973. GREGORY, Mike
"Shorelines." [DenQ] (22:3) Wint 88, p. 106-107.
1974. GREGORY, Robert
"After-Grass" (Excerpts). [CentralP] (14) Fall 88, p. 141-144.
"There Is No Such Thing As Solitude." [PennR] (4:1) 88, p. 13.
1975. GREIG, Andrew
"The Maid & I." [Verse] (5:2) Jl 88, p. 15.
1976. GRENIER, Robert
"Beauty." [Talisman] (1) Fall 88, p. 68.
"Le Jardin Artistic" (August 4/87). [Talisman] (1) Fall 88, p. 69.
"Your Garden." [Talisman] (1) Fall 88, p. 68.
1977. GRENNAN, Eamon
"Kitchen Vision." [NewYorker] (64:45) 26 D 88, p. 32.
"Sea Dog." [NewYorker] (64:13) 16 My 88, p. 38.
"Two Climbing." [NewYorker] (64:4) 14 Mr 88, p. 36.
"Uphill Home." [NewYorker] (64:36) 24 O 88, p. 38.
GRESTY, David Price
See PRICE-GRESTY, David
1978. GREY, John
"1959 and Cafe Rita Was the Place to Be." [Lactuca] (9) F 88, p. 21.
"Contact." [Lactuca] (9) F 88, p. 20.
"Dance to the Window." [CapeR] (23:2) Fall 88, p. 13.
"Fisherman." [Blueline] (9:1/2) 88, p. 83.
"From Your Planet." [SpoonRQ] (13:2) Spr 88, p. 14.
"I Cannot Hold It Back." [Lactuca] (10) Je 88, p. 21.
"Just the Hand Left." [GreensboroR] (45) Wint 88-89, p. 105.
"Love Song Thick As Night." [SpoonRQ] (13:2) Spr 88, p. 13.
"The Mall Legends." [Lactuca] (9) F 88, p. 20.
"Not Dragging the River in the Right Place." [Plain] (9:1) Fall 88, p. 36-37.
"The Pretty One Glides by Unharmed." [Lactuca] (10) Je 88, p. 21.
"The River Joins, Unjoins." [GreensboroR] (45) Wint 88-89, p. 106-107.
"Secret Blood." [GreensboroR] (45) Wint 88-89, p. 104.
1979. GREY, Lucinda
"Ritual." [Pembroke] (20) 88, p. 118.
1980. GRICE, Dorsey
"There Is a Water Moccasin in My Cistern." [KanQ] (20:1/2) Wint-Spr 88, p. 234.
"Unreclaimed." [KanQ] (20:1/2) Wint-Spr 88, p. 234.
1981. GRIFFIN, Larry D.
"Set." [Phoenix] (9:1/2) 88, p. 7.
1982. GRIFFIN, Shaun
"Beneath a Pacific Moon." [Interim] (7:2) Fall 88, p. 21.
1983. GRIFFIN, Walter
"After the Inner Sanctum and the Last Drink of Water, 1945." [LitR] (31:3) Spr 88, p. 345.
"After the Inner Sanctum and the Last Drink of Water, 1945." [SouthernR] (24:4) Aut 88, p. 964-965.
"Corvus." [Poetry] (143, i.e. 153:2) N 88, p. 98.
"Dirt." [SouthernR] (24:4) Aut 88, p. 965-966.
"Respite." [ChatR] (8:3) Spr 88, p. 34.
"Stanley Smith Is Dead." [Poetry] (143, i.e. 153:2) N 88, p. 99.
1984. GRIGORESCU, Irina
"Dreaming with Snow" (for Adam Puslojic, tr. of Anghel Dumbraveanu, w. Adam J. Sorkin). [NowestR] (26:3) 88, p. 53.
"The News from Chimaera Land" (tr. of Anghel Dumbraveanu, w. Adam J. Sorkin). [NowestR] (26:3) 88, p. 54.

1985. GRIMM, Reinhold
"Death of a Poet" (For Rainer M. Gerhardt, tr. of Hans Magnus Enzensberger). [NowestR] (26:2) 88, p. 43.
"Finnish Tango" (In memory of Felix Pollak, tr. of Hans Magnus Enzensberger). [NowestR] (26:2) 88, p. 42.
"Hotel Room in Mestre" (tr. of Gunter Kunert). [NewL] (54:3) Spr 88, p. 23.
"Three Cretan Poems" (tr. of Gunter Kunert). [NewL] (54:3) Spr 88, p. 22.
"Venice Lost" (tr. of Gunter Kunert). [NewL] (54:3) Spr 88, p. 23.

1986. GRISWOLD, Jay
"Depth." [Plain] (9:1) Fall 88, p. 17.
"The Insomnia of the Heart." [Spirit] (9:1) 88, p. 39.
"The Man Whose Eyes See Only Real Things." [Gargoyle] (35) 88, p. 180.
"Meditations on a Starry Night." [MidAR] (8:2) 88, p. 83.
"Parable." [LitR] (31:4) Sum 88, p. 450.
"Petit Mal." [CrabCR] (5:2) Sum 88, p. 21.
"Scribe." [DeKalbLAJ] (21:1) Wint 88, p. 57.
"The Swallows." [HawaiiR] (12:2, #24) Fall 88, p. 37.
"Table." [Plain] (8:3) Spr-Sum 88, p. 30.
"The Widow." [CapeR] (23:2) Fall 88, p. 50.

1987. GRIVNINA, Irina
"In Memory of Dima Leontev" (2 excerpts, tr. by Daniel Weissbort). [NegC] (8:1/2) 88, p. 53-56.
"Parting" (tr. by Daniel Weissbort). [NegC] (8:1/2) 88, p. 57-59.
"To J.D. Salinger — One Who Understood the Vanity of Human Relations . . ." (tr. by Daniel Weissbort). [NegC] (8:1/2) 88, p. 62.
"To V. Bukovsky" (tr. by Daniel Weissbort). [NegC] (8:1/2) 88, p. 60-61.
"Verses on the Back of a Photograph of an Old Town" (dedicated to B.V., tr. by Daniel Weissbort). [NegC] (8:1/2) 88, p. 52.
"A word in your ear" (tr. by Daniel Weissbort). [NegC] (8:1/2) 88, p. 50-51.

1988. GROFF, David
"Proving Ground." [AmerPoR] (17:4) Jl-Ag 88, p. 6.

1989. GROL-PROKOPCZYK, Regina
"Emigration" (tr. of Anna Frajlich-Zajac). [Vis] (26) 88, p. 36.

1990. GROLMES, Sam
"Derivations." [Abraxas] (37) 88, p. 18.

1991. GROSHOLZ, Emily
"Prothalamia." [Hudson] (41:1) Spr 88, p. 161-166.

1992. GROSS, Pamela
"Blessed Coming Off Ladders" (For the carpenter, whose eye wants level, heart wants plumb). [GeoR] (42:3) Fall 88, p. 567-568.

1993. GROSSMAN, Allen
"The Gate." [TexasR] (9:3/4) Fall-Wint 88, p. 63.

1994. GROSSMAN, Andrew J.
"Ghosts." [Wind] (18:63) 88, p. 15-16.
"Honeymoon." [Wind] (18:63) 88, p. 15.
"Mr. Jones Dodges the Bullet." [RagMag] (6:2) Fall 88, p. 27.
"Mr. Jones' Last Flicker of Jock Fever." [RagMag] (6:2) Fall 88, p. 28.
"Porcelain." [RagMag] (6:2) Fall 88, p. 26-27.
"Shade." [BallSUF] (29:4) Aut 88, p. 33-34.
"Sometime the Cow Kick Your Head." [LightY] ('88/9) 88, p. 92.

1995. GROSSMAN, Edith
"First We Set Up the Chairs" (tr. of Ariel Dorfman, w. the author). [Harp] (276:1653) F 88, p. 33.

1996. GROSSMAN, Florence
"Forecast." [SouthwR] (73:4) Aut 88, p. 545.
"Surveying." [SouthwR] (73:4) Aut 88, p. 544.

1997. GROTH, Patricia Celley
"Dream, Spring." [JlNJPo] (10:1/2) 88, p. 41.

1998. GROVE, C. L.
"A 5th Stanza for Dr. Johnson, Donald Hall, Louis Phillips, & X. J. Kennedy" (who wrote stanzas 1-4). [LightY] ('88/9) 88, p. 182-183.

1999. GROVE, Rex
"Hallucinations." [EngJ] (77:3) Mr 88, p. 89.

2000. GRUMMER, Greg
"Intimate Gesture." [RagMag] (6:1) [88], p. 14.
"Love Poem." [RagMag] (6:1) [88], p. 16.

"Running Laps Inside Riverside Cemetery." [RagMag] (6:1) [88], p. 15.
2001. GRUNDY, Jeff
"Inquiry into the Origins of Hatred." [OhioR] (40) 88, p. 100.
2002. GRYMES, Morrey
"Reflection." [KanQ] (20:3) Sum 88, p. 177.
2003. GRYNBERG, Henryk
"Nostalgia" (tr. by the author). [Vis] (26) 88, p. 39.
"The Shtetl Resurrected" (Williamsburg, NY, 1985, tr. by the author). [Vis] (26) 88, p. 38-39.
2004. GU, Chen
"A Generation" (in Chinese & English). [BelPoJ] (39:2) Wint 88-89, p. 8-9.
2005. GU, Cheng
"Scenery" (tr. by Edward Morin and Dennis Ding). [WindO] (50) Aut 88, p. 39.
2006. GUAURA, Alberto
"Es sentir miedo de un secreto." [Mairena] (10:25) 88, p. 62-63.
2007. GUDAS, Eric
"En Route." [Sonora] (16) Fall 88, p. 51.
"He's No Good." [Sonora] (16) Fall 88, p. 52-54.
"I Lost It at the Movies." [Sonora] (16) Fall 88, p. 50.
2008. GUDE, Michael
"Each of Us." [NegC] (8:3) 88, p. 128-129.
"The Heart of Anything." [PennR] (4:1) 88, p. 79.
"How We Begin to Remember." [PennR] (4:1) 88, p. 80-81.
"White Birches." [SouthernPR] (28:1) Spr 88, p. 30.
2009. GUEL, Richard
"Remembrance of Tomás Rivera." [BilingR] (13:1/2) Ja-Ag 86, c1988, p. 84.
2010. GUENTHER, Charles
"Escheat" (tr. of René Char). [AmerPoR] (17:3) My-Je 88, p. 25.
"Going Out" (tr. of René Char). [AmerPoR] (17:3) My-Je 88, p. 25.
"Haunted Gift" (tr. of René Char). [AmerPoR] (17:3) My-Je 88, p. 24.
"Lost Nakedness" (tr. of René Char). [AmerPoR] (17:3) My-Je 88, p. 24.
"Silent Game" (tr. of René Char). [AmerPoR] (17:3) My-Je 88, p. 25.
"Slow Pace of the Ruture" (tr. of René Char). [AmerPoR] (17:3) My-Je 88, p. 24.
"Song of the Fig Tree" (tr. of René Char). [AmerPoR] (17:3) My-Je 88, p. 24.
"Traced on the Gulf" (tr. of René Char). [AmerPoR] (17:3) My-Je 88, p. 24.
"Troublesome Simplicity" (tr. of René Char). [AmerPoR] (17:3) My-Je 88, p. 24.
"The Vertical Village" (tr. of René Char). [AmerPoR] (17:3) My-Je 88, p. 25.
"Welcome" (tr. of René Char). [AmerPoR] (17:3) My-Je 88, p. 24.
"With a Common Bond" (tr. of René Char). [AmerPoR] (17:3) My-Je 88, p. 24.
2011. GUEREÑA, Jacinto Luis
"Ojos ofuscados por exceso de luz." [Os] (26) 88, p. 6.
2012. GUERIN, Christopher D.
"I-70." [MidwQ] (29:3) Spr 88, p. 339.
2013. GUERNSEY, Bruce
"The Compass." [SpoonRQ] (12:4) Fall 87, p. 51.
"The Father." [SpoonRQ] (12:4) Fall 87, p. 48.
"Looking Back." [MissouriR] (11:1) 88, p. 178.
"Me and Hitler at the Rhine." [TriQ] (71) Wint 88, p. 162.
"Shaving Without a Mirror." [SpoonRQ] (12:4) Fall 87, p. 49.
"The Snake." [SpoonRQ] (12:4) Fall 87, p. 50.
2014. GUERNSEY, Julia
"The Man with the Paisley Tie." [PoetL] (83:3) Fall 88, p. 34.
2015. GUESMER, Carl
"Den Frieden Anzutreffen." [Rohwedder] (4) [Wint 88-89], p. 21.
"To Meet with Peace" (tr. by Liselotte Erlanger). [Rohwedder] (4) [Wint 88-89], p. 21.
2016. GUEST, Barbara
"Chalk." [Temblor] (8) 88, p. 3-8.
"Ilex." [Conjunc] (12) 88, p. 106-108.
"Words of the Theatre." [NewAW] (4) Fall 88, p. 23-24.
2017. GUIDACCI, Margherita
"A Febo per l'Amicizia di Lefteris." [InterPR] (14:1) Spr 88, p. 60.
"Collapse" (tr. by Ruth Feldman). [WebR] (13:1) Spr 88, p. 24.
"Euridice" (Al poeta Febo Delfi, nel ricordo della sua Maria). [InterPR] (14:1) Spr 88, p. 58.

"Eurydice" (To the poet Phoebus Delphi, in remembrance of his Marie, tr. by Renata Treitel). [InterPR] (14:1) Spr 88, p. 59.
"For a Gift of Loukoumi" (tr. by Renata Treitel). [InterPR] (14:1) Spr 88, p. 61.
"In Mezzo ai Telchini." [InterPR] (14:1) Spr 88, p. 56.
"In the Midst of the Telchines" (tr. by Renata Treitel). [InterPR] (14:1) Spr 88, p. 57.
"The Old Man" (tr. by Ruth Feldman). [WebR] (13:1) Spr 88, p. 25.
"Per un Dono di Lukumi." [InterPR] (14:1) Spr 88, p. 60.
"Slava Raskaj" (tr. by Renata Treitel, w. Manly Johnson). [GrahamHR] (11) Spr 88, p. 98-99.
"To Phoebus for Lefteris's Friendship" (tr. by Renata Treitel). [InterPR] (14:1) Spr 88, p. 61.
"Virius" (tr. by Renata Treitel, w. Manly Johnson). [GrahamHR] (11) Spr 88, p. 97.
"Waiting Room" (tr. by Ruth Feldman). [WebR] (13:1) Spr 88, p. 26.
"The Wise Are Always Right" (tr. by Ruth Feldman). [WebR] (13:1) Spr 88, p. 25.

2018. GUILFORD, Charles
"The Awakening." [CrabCR] (5:1) Wint 88, p. 21.

2019. GUILLEN, Jorge
"Names" (tr. by Stan Rose). [CutB] (31/32) 88, p. 78.

2020. GUILLÉN, Nicolás
"El Abuelo." [InterPR] (14:1) Spr 88, p. 66.
"Can You?" (tr. by Bill Siegel). [InterPR] (14:1) Spr 88, p. 63, 65.
"The Grandfather" (tr. by Bill Siegel). [InterPR] (14:1) Spr 88, p. 67.
"Puedes?" [InterPR] (14:1) Spr 88, p. 62, 64.
"Sensemayá." [InterPR] (14:1) Spr 88, p. 68.
"Sensemayá: A Chant for Killing a Snake" (tr. by Bill Siegel). [InterPR] (14:1) Spr 88, p. 69.

2021. GULLANS, Charles
"American History." [SouthernR] (24:2) Spr 88, p. 345.

2022. GUNDY, Jeff
"Easy Secrets." [LaurelR] (22:2) Sum 88, p. 71.
"In Response to Inquiries on the Dialectics of Consumption." [BelPoJ] (39:1) Fall 88, p. 2-3.
"Inquiry into Keeping Time." [CinPR] (18) Fall 88, p. 76-77.
"Inquiry into Pipes Filled with Steam." [HiramPoR] (44/45) Spr-Wint 88, p. 20.
"Inquiry into the Existential Maneuvers of Avians, or Honkers." [CinPR] (18) Fall 88, p. 78.
"Inquiry into the Nature of Beauty, or The Tale of the King of the Cats." [SpoonRQ] (13:2) Spr 88, p. 7.
"Loose Women." [LaurelR] (22:2) Sum 88, p. 70.
"Ode for a Little Knife." [HiramPoR] (44/45) Spr-Wint 88, p. 22-23.
"The Seal Despair." [ArtfulD] (14/15) Fall 88, p. 3-4.
"The Universe Is a Safe Place for Souls." [HiramPoR] (44/45) Spr-Wint 88, p. 21.

2023. GUNN, Genni
"We Have Been Friends." [Quarry] (37:1) Wint 88, p. 66.
"You Still Speak of Me." [Quarry] (37:1) Wint 88, p. 65.

2024. GUNN, Thom
"Improvisation." [Thrpny] (32) Wint 88, p. 6.
"The Missing." [Verse] (5:1) F 88, p. 5.
"Sacred Heart." [ParisR] (30:106) Spr 88, p. 112-113.
"To the Dead Owner" (of Chelsea Gym, NYC). [Verse] (5:1) F 88, p. 6.
"Words for Some Ash." [ParisR] (30:106) Spr 88, p. 114.

2025. GUNTER, Susan Elizabeth
"Sestina for Esther." [PoetL] (83:2) Sum 88, p. 29-30.
"Sour Cherries." [PoetL] (83:2) Sum 88, p. 31.

2026. GÜNTHER, Thomas
"Balkan Nights" (tr. by Roderick Iverson). [Trans] (20) Spr 88, p. 260.
"Over the Blue Mountains" (tr. by Roderick Iverson). [Trans] (20) Spr 88, p. 261.

2027. GURLEY, James
"Clearing." [Wind] (18:63) 88, p. 17.

2028. GUSS, David M.
"Rain" (tr. of Carlos Oquendo de Amat). [AmerV] (10) Spr 88, p. 83.

2029. GUSTAFSON, Jim
"Memo: Re." [Notus] (3:1) Spr 88, p. 82.

2030. GUSTAFSSON, Lars
"Ballad of a Chinese Picture" (dedicated to Ho Tsien, Peking, tr. by Robert Hedin). [ColR] (NS 15:2) Fall-Wint 88, p. 82-83.
"Border Zone, Minefield, Snow East of Bebra" (tr. by Christopher Middleton). [NewYorker] (64:4) 14 Mr 88, p. 40.
"Flight of Cranes over Skane at Dawn in April" (tr. by Christopher Middleton and the author). [SouthernHR] (22:1) Wint 88, p. 18.
"Notes on the 1860s" (tr. by Christopher Middleton). [NewYorker] (64:16) 6 Je 88, p. 36.
"On All That Glides in the Air" (tr. by Christopher Middleton and the author). [SouthernHR] (22:1) Wint 88, p. 17-18.

GUT, Karen Alkalay
See ALKALAY-GUT, Karen

2031. GUTIERREZ REVUELTA, Pedro
"A Fall Day, Texas" (tr. of Angel Gonzalez, w. Steven Ford Brown). [LitR] (31:2) Wint 88, p. 220.
"Order (Poetics That Others Follow)" (tr. of Angel Gonzalez, w. Steven Ford Brown). [Paint] (15:30) Aut 88, p. 37.
"Poetics That I Sometimes Try to Follow" (tr. of Angel Gonzalez, w. Steven Ford Brown). [Paint] (15:30) Aut 88, p. 36.
"To Poetry" (tr. of Angel Gonzalez, w. Steven Ford Brown). [Gargoyle] (35) 88, p. 9.

2032. GUZLOWSKI, John
"How Early Fall Came This Year." [Farm] (4:1, i.e. 5:1) Wint 88, p. 63.

GUZMAN, Maria de
See DeGUZMAN, Maria

2033. GWILYM, Dafydd ap
"The Dream (Y Breuddwyd)" (tr. from the Welsh by Leslie Morris). [Atlantic] (261:6) Je 88, p. 92.

2034. GWYNN, R. S.
"Among Philistines." [LightY] ('88/9) 88, p. 78-80.
"Snow White and the Seven Deadly Sins." [LightY] ('88/9) 88, p. 107-108.

HA, Jin
See JIN, Ha

2035. HAAKENSON, Bergine
"At Your Going" (1988 Poetry Competition, Third Prize). [PassN] (9:2) Sum 88, p. 17.

HAAN, Jayne de
See DeHAAN, Jayne

2036. HAAS, Robert
"A Chant" (Wilno, 1934, tr. of Czeslaw Milosz). [RiverS] (27) 88, p. 69-71.
"Dawns" (Wilno, 1932, tr. of Czeslaw Milosz). [RiverS] (27) 88, p. 67-68.

2037. HACKER, Marilyn
"Against Silence." [Boulevard] (3:2/3) Fall 88, p. 41-45.
"Country and Western." [PraS] (62:3) Fall 88, p. 64-65.
"Country and Western II" (for Julie Fay). [PraS] (62:3) Fall 88, p. 65-66.
"Days of 1944: Three Friends." [GrandS] (7:3) Spr 88, p. 72-73.
"Dear Jool, I Miss You in St. Saturnin." [ParisR] (30:107) Sum 88, p. 227-229.
"For K.J., Leaving and Coming Back." [Ploughs] (14:1) 88, p. 130-132.
"From Orient Point." [GrahamHR] (11) Spr 88, p. 22.
"From Orient Point." [ManhatPR] (10) Ja 88, p. 14.
"Languedocienne." [GrahamHR] (11) Spr 88, p. 21.
"Letter from Goose Creek: April" (For K.J.). [YellowS] (26) Spr 88, p. 20-21.
"Little Unsent Letter from L'Herault." [ManhatPR] (10) Ja 88, p. 15.
"Reposte" (from Saratoga Springs). [ManhatPR] (10) Ja 88, p. 16-17.

2038. HACTHOUN, A.
"Los Perros Ladraron Toda la Noche." [Americas] (16:3/4) Fall-Wint 88, p. 69-71.
"Regresarán una Vez Más los Angeles." [Americas] (16:3/4) Fall-Wint 88, p. 72.

2039. HADAS, Rachel
"Art" (Selections: iv, vii, ix, xi, xvi, xvii). [LitR] (31:2) Wint 88, p. 202-203.
"At the Beach." [Shen] (38:3) 88, p. 95.
"Desire II." [BostonR] (13:5 [sic]) Je 88, p. 3.
"Double Elegy." [Shen] (38:2) 88, p. 74-75.
"Fix It" (Selections: iv, v). [Sequoia] (31:2) Wint 88, p. 10-11.
"Invitation Withdrawn." [Confr] (37/38) Spr-Sum 88, p. 120.
"Love" (Selections: 1-5, 8-12, 14). [Margin] (6) Sum 88, p. 51-54.

"On Poetry." [DenQ] (23:1) Sum 88, p. 62-64.
"Over the Edge" (to Mark Rudman). [DenQ] (23:1) Sum 88, p. 58-61.
"The Whale." [NewRep] (199:21) 21 N 88, p. 44.

2040. HADLEY, Drummond
"A Colt 45 and a Chili Queen." [Sonora] (14/15) Spr 88, p. 75-76.
"Prospecting the Mother Lode." [Sonora] (14/15) Spr 88, p. 74.
"Rustlers." [Sonora] (14/15) Spr 88, p. 73.

2041. HAGAN, Fred
"All I Know." [DenQ] (22:3) Wint 88, p. 136.

2042. HAGEDORN, Jessica
"All Shook Up." [Sonora] (14/15) Spr 88, p. 103-108.
"The Song of Bullets." [Calyx] (11:2/3) Fall 88, p. 144-146.

2043. HAGIWARA, Sakutaro
"Cracksman" (tr. by Graeme Wilson). [SenR] (18:2) 88, p. 42.
"Howling at the Moon" (tr. by Graeme Wilson). [SenR] (18:2) 88, p. 45.
"Parting" (tr. by Tomoyuki Iino). [Stand] (29:3) Sum 88, p. 22.
"Rotten Chrysanthemum" (tr. by Graeme Wilson). [SenR] (18:2) 88, p. 44.
"Scene of the Crime" (tr. by Graeme Wilson). [SenR] (18:2) 88, p. 41.
"Sparrows" (tr. by Graeme Wilson). [SenR] (18:2) 88, p. 43.

2044. HAGUE, Richard
"Reading Him to Sleep." [CinPR] (17) Spr 88, p. 67.
"Those Who Return" (for Bob Collins and Joe Enzweiler). [CinPR] (17) Spr 88, p. 66.

2045. HAHN, Kimiko
"The Avocado." [HangL] (53) 88, p. 20.
"The Gladiolas." [HangL] (53) 88, p. 21.
"Imagination." [HangL] (53) 88, p. 16-18.
"Nora." [Contact] (9:47/48/49) Spr 88, p. 12-16.
"The Operation." [HangL] (53) 88, p. 22-23.
"Sponge." [HangL] (53) 88, p. 19-20.

2046. HAHN, Oscar
"A la Una Mi Fortuna, a las Dos Tu Reloj." [Inti] (26/27) Otoño 87-Primavera 88, p. 146-147.
"A Mi Bella Enemiga." [Inti] (26/27) Otoño 87-Primavera 88, p. 146.
"El Centro del Dormitorio." [Inti] (26/27) Otoño 87-Primavera 88, p. 148-149.
"Cometa." [Inti] (26/27) Otoño 87-Primavera 88, p. 149-150.
"Con Pasíon sin Compasión." [Inti] (26/27) Otoño 87-Primavera 88, p. 148.
"Misterio Gozoso." [Inti] (26/27) Otoño 87-Primavera 88, p. 147.
"Paisaje Ocular." [Inti] (26/27) Otoño 87-Primavera 88, p. 146.
"Rocío de los Prados." [Inti] (26/27) Otoño 87-Primavera 88, p. 148.
"Sábana de Arriba." [Inti] (26/27) Otoño 87-Primavera 88, p. 149.
"Sobre los Hemisferios." [Inti] (26/27) Otoño 87-Primavera 88, p. 147.

2047. HAHN, Robert
"Monk's *'Round Midnight* Deconstructed." [Agni] (27) 88, p. 212-213.
"A Shelburne Farms. Coachyard. Swallows. Schubert." [DenQ] (23:2) Fall 88, p. 47-48.

2048. HAHN, S. C.
"Disenfranchisement." [WormR] (28:4, #112) 88, p. 93-94.
"More Effects of Uncle George's Trunk" (Photograph dated September 10, 1910). [WormR] (28:4, #112) 88, p. 93.
"Mortise." [KanQ] (20:3) Sum 88, p. 201.
"Pets." [WormR] (28:4, #112) 88, p. 94.

2049. HAHN, Steven
"Pope Gregory Recalls." [LaurelR] (22:2) Sum 88, p. 72-75.
"Powers of Two." [Confr] (37/38) Spr-Sum 88, p. 237.

2050. HAHN, Susan
"At the Intersection." [PoetryE] (25) Spr 88, p. 78.
"The Blue Porcelain Bird." [PoetryE] (25) Spr 88, p. 76-77.
"Feuerstein." [RiverS] (26) 88, p. 3.
"The Picture I Never Gave Her." [PoetryNW] (29:3) Aut 88, p. 23.
"The Second of the Seven Warnings." [RiverS] (26) 88, p. 4.
"Sex Primer, Circa 1960." [PoetryE] (25) Spr 88, p. 74-75.
"Shavings." [NoAmR] (273:3) S 88, p. 56.
"Since Then" (from G. to N. — Dec. '83). [RiverS] (26) 88, p. 1-2.

2051. HAI-JEW, Shalin
"Father's Belt." [Calyx] (11:2/3) Fall 88, p. 91.

"No Regrets." [Footwork] ('88) 88, p. 18-19.
2052. HAINES, John
"Farm." [SwampR] (1:1) Ja 88, p. 33.
"The Fates." [TriQ] (71) Wint 88, p. 127-129.
2053. HAINES, John Francis
"Ancient Wisdom." [Bogg] (59) 88, p. 10.
2054. HAJEK, Louise
"Final Decree" (The 14th Kansas Poetry Contest, Second Honorable Mention). [LittleBR] (5:2) Wint 88-89, p. 66.
HAKUSHU, Kitahara
See KITAHARA, Hakushu
2055. HALES, Corrinne
"Street Ball Catcher" (for Peter Clegg, 1946-1967). [WestHR] (42:2) Sum 88, p. 138-139.
2056. HALEY, Vanessa
"Pavlova's Mother, in Her Old Age, Speaks of Her Daughter's Death." [Pembroke] (20) 88, p. 230-231.
2057. HALL, Donald
"A 5th Stanza for Dr. Johnson, Donald Hall, Louis Phillips, & X. J. Kennedy" (who wrote stanzas 1-4). [LightY] ('88/9) 88, p. 182-183.
"The Calvinist's Caribbean." [LightY] ('88/9) 88, p. 149.
"Carlotta's Confession." [Hudson] (41:1) Spr 88, p. 143-146.
"Eclogue." [GettyR] (1:2) Spr 88, p. 348-349.
"History." [NewYorker] (64:11) 2 My 88, p. 34-35.
"Match." [Ploughs] (14:1) 88, p. 66.
"Proverbs." [LightY] ('88/9) 88, p. 58.
"The Table." [TexasR] (9:3/4) Fall-Wint 88, p. 64-65.
"To Build a House." [Iowa] (18:1) 88, p. 27-39.
2058. HALL, James Baker
"Dividing Ridge." [KenR] (NS 10:3) Sum 88, p. 100.
"For the Scattering of My Ashes." [PoetryE] (25) Spr 88, p. 63.
"In the Garden of Children." [PoetryE] (25) Spr 88, p. 62.
"Monet." [SewanR] (96:3) Sum 88, p. 347-349.
"The Window." [KenR] (NS 10:3) Sum 88, p. 101.
2059. HALL, Judith
"A Letter." [NewRep] (199:19) 7 N 88, p. 32.
2060. HALL, K. Graehm
"Messages." [ChamLR] (1) Fall 87, p. 394-396.
2061. HALL, Karen J.
"Misdemeanor" (for Radclyffe Hall, 1886-1943). [SinW] (33) Fall 87, p. 103.
2062. HALL, William Keith
"Gathering." [Pembroke] (20) 88, p. 174.
2063. HALLAMAN, E. G.
"The Exploding Poem." [LightY] ('88/9) 88, p. 194-195.
2064. HALLER, Amelia
"Claymore Apartments." [BellR] (11:2) Fall 88, p. 32.
2065. HALLERMAN, Victoria
"Beneath the Interstate." [Poetry] (152:2) My 88, p. 77.
2066. HALLEY, Anne
"Elsa's Story" (Leipzig, Dresden, München, Bayreuth, Hannover, et al. c. 1860-1933). [StoneC] (15:3/4) Spr-Sum 88, p. 41-43.
2067. HALLIDAY, Mark
"64 Elmgrove." [NewEngR] (11:1) Aut 88, p. 39.
"Chinese Leftovers." [DenQ] (23:1) Sum 88, p. 65-66.
"Forty-Two." [TampaR] (1) 88, p. 62.
"Girl in a Nightgown." [TampaR] (1) 88, p. 61.
"Grief." [VirQR] (64:2) Spr 88, p. 283.
"Mistress." [MichQR] (27:3) Sum 88, p. 460.
"My Strange New Poetry." [Colum] (13) 88, p. 62.
"Springtime for You." [GettyR] (1:3) Sum 88, p. 551.
"What Will Suffice." [GettyR] (1:3) Sum 88, p. 552-553.
2068. HALLIDAY-BORKOWSKI, Miriam
"Jo Ann Yellow Bird Jazz Poem: Manifesto" (Selection). [Colum] (13) 88, p. 63-64.
2069. HALMAN, Talat (Talat S.)
"Ending" (tr. of Lutfu Ozkok). [Vis] (28) 88, p. 35.
"Like Kissing a Wound" (tr. of Kemal Ozer). [Vis] (27) 88, p. 28.

2070. HALME, Kathleen
"In Situ." [ChamLR] (2:1, #3) Fall 88, p. 38-39.
2071. HALPERN, Daniel
"Cliché Domestique." [IndR] (11:3) Sum 88, p. 25-26.
"A Note." [TarRP] (28:1) Fall 88, p. 7-8.
2072. HALPERN, Nick
"Christmas in July." [AmerPoR] (17:6) N-D 88, p. 9.
"Maritime Medicine." [AmerPoR] (17:6) N-D 88, p. 9.
"Standing Room Only." [AmerPoR] (17:6) N-D 88, p. 9.
2073. HAMEL, Joseph
"Unfamiliar Relatives." [LittleBR] (5:2) Wint 88-89, p. 53.
2074. HAMILL, Sam
"After Solstice" (tr. of Tu Fu). [AmerPoR] (17:4) Jl-Ag 88, p. 25.
"Another Spring" (tr. of Tu Fu). [AmerPoR] (17:4) Jl-Ag 88, p. 25.
"Becoming a Farmer" (tr. of Tu Fu). [AmerPoR] (17:4) Jl-Ag 88, p. 26.
"Ch'iang Village" (tr. of Tu Fu). [AmerPoR] (17:4) Jl-Ag 88, p. 26.
"Clear After Rain" (tr. of Fu Du). [CrabCR] (5:3) Fall 88, p. 8.
"Crooked River Meditation" (tr. of Tu Fu). [AmerPoR] (17:4) Jl-Ag 88, p. 26.
"Dragon Gate Gorge" (tr. of Tu Fu). [AmerPoR] (17:4) Jl-Ag 88, p. 26.
"Drinking at Crooked River" (tr. of Tu Fu). [AmerPoR] (17:4) Jl-Ag 88, p. 25.
"Farewell Rhyme" (tr. of Tu Fu). [AmerPoR] (17:4) Jl-Ag 88, p. 25.
"Impromptu" (tr. of Tu Fu). [AmerPoR] (17:4) Jl-Ag 88, p. 26.
"In a Village by the River" (tr. of Tu Fu). [AmerPoR] (17:4) Jl-Ag 88, p. 25.
"In Praise of Rain" (tr. of Fu Du). [CrabCR] (5:3) Fall 88, p. 9.
"In Seclusion" (tr. of Tu Fu). [AmerPoR] (17:4) Jl-Ag 88, p. 26.
"Leaving Ch'in-chou" (tr. of Tu Fu). [AmerPoR] (17:4) Jl-Ag 88, p. 26.
"Poems for Mr. Li in Early Spring" (tr. of Tu Fu). [AmerPoR] (17:4) Jl-Ag 88, p. 25.
"Thinking of Li Po" (tr. of Tu Fu). [AmerPoR] (17:4) Jl-Ag 88, p. 24.
"To Abbot Min the Compassionate" (tr. of Tu Fu). [AmerPoR] (17:4) Jl-Ag 88, p. 24.
"Watching the Distances" (tr. of Fu Du). [CrabCR] (5:3) Fall 88, p. 9.
"Word from My Brothers" (tr. of Fu Du). [CrabCR] (5:3) Fall 88, p. 9.
2075. HAMILTON, Alfred Starr
"Africa and Greece." [Footwork] ('88) 88, p. 65.
"A Drifting Cloud." [Lips] (14) 88, p. 22.
"The Month of Maine." [Lips] (14) 88, p. 23.
"Poetry." [WormR] (28:1, #109) 88, p. 10.
"Yes." [WormR] (28:1, #109) 88, p. 9.
2076. HAMILTON, Carol
"Anonymity." [Phoenix] (9:1/2) 88, p. 1.
"Apothegm." [Phoenix] (9:1/2) 88, p. 7.
"At the Clothesline." [Phoenix] (9:1/2) 88, p. 4.
"The Earth Is Still Flat." [Phoenix] (9:1/2) 88, p. 6.
"Famadihana." [CapeR] (23:1) Spr 88, p. 26-27.
"Heliotrope (Definition)." [GreensboroR] (44) Sum 88, p. 23-24.
"Instruction." [Phoenix] (9:1/2) 88, p. 2.
"Past Leanings." [Phoenix] (9:1/2) 88, p. 4.
"Recorded Fireworks at the Vietnamese Festival." [Phoenix] (9:1/2) 88, p. 3.
2077. HAMILTON, Fritz
"Baby Raccoon." [PaintedB] (34) 88, p. 33.
"A Beach Ceremony." [Wind] (18:62) 88, p. 16.
"The Bones." [SmPd] (25:2) Spr 88, p. 33.
"Cool in the Park." [KanQ] (20:3) Sum 88, p. 243.
"Ennobled." [DeKalbLAJ] (21:1) Wint 88, p. 58.
"Her Kiss" (for Phoebe). [Kaleid] (16) Wint-Spr 88, p. 37.
"Illusions Flashing." [SmPd] (25:2) Spr 88, p. 32.
"Inspiration!" [ChatR] (8:2) Wint 88, p. 13.
"It Never Stops." [SmPd] (25:2) Spr 88, p. 34.
"Just Like Us." [CrabCR] (5:3) Fall 88, p. 10.
"A Last Flowering." [Wind] (18:62) 88, p. 15-16.
"A Late Understanding." [PikeF] (9) Fall 88, p. 3.
"My Awareness." [KanQ] (20:1/2) Wint-Spr 88, p. 126.
"Overheating the Economy." [SmPd] (25:2) Spr 88, p. 35.
"Penny." [DeKalbLAJ] (21:2) Spr 88, p. 37.
"Pingpong Toss at the Carnival." [ArtfulD] (14/15) Fall 88, p. 31.

"Saturday Night Oblivion!" [Wind] (18:62) 88, p. 14-15.
"Time to Defy." [Lips] (14) 88, p. 44-45.
"Two in a Row." [PikeF] (9) Fall 88, p. 3.

2078. HAMILTON, J. A.
"The America Poems." [MalR] (84) S 88, p. 88-99.

2079. HAMILTON, Kitty
"The Queen's Sister." [BelPoJ] (39:1) Fall 88, p. 23.
"True Story." [DenQ] (22:3) Wint 88, p. 175-176.

2080. HAMMER, Jonathan
"Interlaid." [Notus] (3:2) Fall 88, p. 73-74.
"The Legend of Suran." [Notus] (3:2) Fall 88, p. 72.

2081. HAMMER, Langdon
"The Divining." [Shen] (38:4) 88, p. 43-44.
"A Troika for Rachmaninoff." [Shen] (38:4) 88, p. 44.

2082. HAMMER, Margaret
"Bus Ride, New York." [PottPort] (10) 88, p. 31.
"Challenge." [PottPort] (9) 88, p. 45.
"The Trouble with Dusting." [PottPort] (10) 88, p. 31.

2083. HAMMER, Patrick, Jr.
"At 30." [Footwork] ('88) 88, p. 77.
"It Was a June." [StoneC] (16:1/2) Fall-Wint 88-89, p. 66.

2084. HAMMIAL, Philip
"Gumbo." [ArtfulD] (14/15) Fall 88, p. 88.
"Taxation." [ArtfulD] (14/15) Fall 88, p. 89.

2085. HAMMOND, Elise
"Martin's Pond." [DenQ] (22:3) Wint 88, p. 183-184.

2086. HAMMOND, Karla M.
"Knowledge of Resin." [Footwork] ('88) 88, p. 77.
"Sunday Poem" (For Al). [Footwork] ('88) 88, p. 79.

2087. HANAN, Deborah
"Munich, I." [PraS] (62:2) Sum 88, p. 74.
"Munich, II." [PraS] (62:2) Sum 88, p. 75.
"Munich, III." [PraS] (62:2) Sum 88, p. 75.
"Munich, IV." [PraS] (62:2) Sum 88, p. 76.

2088. HANCOCK, James H.
"Aphorisms." [Bogg] (59) 88, p. 20.
"Night Prayer." [Bogg] (59) 88, p. 24.

2089. HANDLIN, Jim
"Hugh." [Footwork] ('88) 88, p. 27.

2090. HANDY, Nixeon Civille
"Antigonish, Nova Scotia" (for Catherine Isabel Handy 1871-1971). [BellArk] (4:6) N-D 88, p. 5.
"It Will Be Dark in Here." [StoneC] (16:1/2) Fall-Wint 88-89, p. 52.
"Listening to Dolphins: Orinoco River, Guiana Highlands, S. America." [BellArk] (4:1) Ja-F 88, p. 3.
"Seattle's Skidrow." [BellArk] (4:1) Ja-F 88, p. 20.
"Street Song." [DeKalbLAJ] (21:3/4) 88, p. 55.
"Stressed, Unstressed." [BellArk] (4:2) Mr-Ap 88, p. 4.

2091. HANFORD, Mary
"Aftermath." [SwampR] (1:2/3) D 88, p. 54.
"A Faint Chopin." [SwampR] (1:2/3) D 88, p. 55.
"Renaissance." [SwampR] (1:2/3) D 88, p. 52-53.

2092. HANFORD, Mary (Barnes)
"A Last Swim." [SpoonRQ] (13:3) Sum 88, p. 23.
"A Summit." [SpoonRQ] (13:3) Sum 88, p. 22.

2093. HANIFAN, Jil
"Pain/Craft: The Sundance." [Contact] (9:47/48/49) Spr 88, p. 44.

2094. HANLEY, Aedan
"Louanne, Sitting Nude" (Inspired by Matisse's *Seated Nude*). [CreamCR] (12:2) Sum 88, p. 194.

2095. HANNAN, T. C.
"Lady Lovus." [PacificR] (6) Spr 88, p. 55.

2096. HANSELL, Susan
"Epilogue: You, He" (Excerpt). [FiveFR] (6) 88, p. 40.
"If one night were the Limit." [FiveFR] (6) 88, p. 41.
"The moon exactly." [FiveFR] (6) 88, p. 42.

"Poem for a Goodbye Never Spoken" (para Silva, doquiera que esté). [SinW] (32) Sum 87, p. 16-17.
"The Wolf." [SinW] (32) Sum 87, p. 76-78.

2097. HANSEN, Tom
"And Now for a Few Words from Shiva." [WebR] (13:1) Spr 88, p. 61.
"Assembling the Crumbs: Four Found Fortunes." [WebR] (13:1) Spr 88, p. 59-60.
"A Little Poem About the Shadow." [KanQ] (20:3) Sum 88, p. 120.
"Other Father Wynken." [KanQ] (20:3) Sum 88, p. 120.
"Poem of Falling Snow." [LitR] (32:1) Fall 88, p. 86-87.
"Sunlight Snowfall." [AmerS] (57:1) Wint 88, p. 89.

2098. HANSEN, Twyla
"How to Live in the Heartland." [SoDakR] (26:3) Aut 88, p. 25.
"Love Poem From the Prairie" (for D.B.). [CimR] (85) O 88, p. 60.
"My Brother Randall Teaches Me to Ride a Bicycle." [Wind] (18:62) 88, p. 6.
"Suppose." [Plain] (9:1) Fall 88, p. 15.
"Suppose" (A Plainsongs Award Poem). [Plain] (8:3) Spr-Sum 88, p. 32.
"View from I-80." [SoDakR] (26:3) Aut 88, p. 26.

HANSON, Sharon Kinney
See KINNEY-HANSON, Sharon

2099. HANZLICEK, C. G.
"Adrenalin." [Poetry] (143, i.e. 153:1) O 88, p. 20.
"Heart" (For Peter). [Poetry] (143, i.e. 153:1) O 88, p. 18-20.
"Imagination" (For John Haines). [Poetry] (143, i.e. 153:1) O 88, p. 21.

2100. HARDENBROOK, Yvonne
"Thunderclap!" [Amelia] (5:2, #13) 88, p. 8.
"Vesper bells." [Amelia] (5:1, #12) 88, p. 8.

2101. HARDIN, Rob
"Fistic Hermaphrodites." [MissR] (16:2/3, #47/48) 88, p. 156.
"Microbes" (For Tristan Avakian). [MissR] (16:2/3, #47/48) 88, p. 157.
"Nerve Terminals." [MissR] (16:2/3, #47/48) 88, p. 158.

2102. HARDING, Deborah
"Untold History." [AntR] (46:3) Sum 88, p. 362.

2103. HARDING, Gunnar
"Blood Poisoning" (tr. by Roger Greenwald). [Writ] (20) 88, p. 34-35.
"Guarding the Air" (tr. by Roger Greenwald). [Writ] (20) 88, p. 39-43.
"The National Hospital, Oslo, September 1976" (tr. by Roger Greenwald). [Writ] (20) 88, p. 36-38.
"Star-Goalie" (tr. by Roger Greenwald). [Writ] (20) 88, p. 32-33.

2104. HARDING, Robert
"She's Snowed In." [CanLit] (119) Wint 88, p. 99.

2105. HARDING-RUSSELL, Gillian
"Finding My Voice (Lost) with the Help of an Actress." [Quarry] (37:1) Wint 88, p. 17-19.
"Scared Spineless." [CanLit] (119) Wint 88, p. 42-43.
"When I Hear." [Dandel] (15:2) Fall-Wint 88, p. 30-32.

2106. HARDY, Jan
"Independence Day." [SinW] (33) Fall 87, p. 58.
"Memorial Day, Three Years After." [SinW] (33) Fall 87, p. 56-57.

2107. HARER, Katharine
"Galia's Piñata." [FiveFR] (6) 88, p. 4.
"Nicaraguan Bananas." [FiveFR] (6) 88, p. 5.

2108. HARJO, Joy
"Autobiography." [Cond] (15) 88, p. 108-109.
"The Book of Myths." [Cond] (15) 88, p. 21-22.

2109. HARKNESS, Edward
"Spain, 1938." [CrabCR] (5:1) Wint 88, p. 26.

2110. HARMES, James
"Between Lives We Write the History." [DenQ] (22:4) Spr 88, p. 57-58.

2111. HARMON, William
"One Bagatelle for a Dead Friend." [Agni] (27) 88, p. 191.
"That Tense Is Time." [CarolQ] (40:3) Spr 88, p. 14-15.

2112. HARMS, James
"Breakfast on the Patio." [SouthernPR] (28:2) Fall 88, p. 10-11.
"Everywhere at Once." [MissouriR] (11:2) 88, p. 104-105.
"Penance." [Poetry] (152:3) Je 88, p. 146-147.
"Salzburg Cathedral." [Jacaranda] (3:2) Fall-Wint 88, p. 95-96.

2113. HARNACK, Curtis
"Wearing a Noise Protector in Manhattan." [OntR] (29) Fall-Wint 88-89, p. 86-87.
2114. HARP, Jerry
"Gathering." [MidAR] (8:1) 88, p. 41.
"The Idea of Mick Jagger at a Concert." [LightY] ('88/9) 88, p. 84-85.
2115. HARPER, Juana
"Words to Chew." [ChatR] (8:2) Wint 88, p. 49.
2116. HARPER, L. L.
"Favoring Andy." [KanQ] (20:3) Sum 88, p. 204.
"In Pennsylvania Spring Comes Hard." [KanQ] (20:3) Sum 88, p. 204.
"Vanities." [HawaiiR] (12:1, #23) Spr 88, p. 77.
2117. HARPER, Michael S.
"Songwriting from a Tessera(e) Journal: Romare Bearden, 1912-1988)." [Callaloo] (11:3, #36) Sum 88, p. 403-408.
2118. HARRINGTON, Raquel Mendieta
"A nuestra Madre Universal, la inspiración de Ana." [Sulfur] (8:1, #22) Spr 88, p. 92-93.
2119. HARRIS, Bill
"Two Moons of Luvernia" (Third Movement, from Suite for Reclining Nudes). [Callaloo] (11:2, #35) Spr 88, p. 275-276.
2120. HARRIS, Jana
"The Ascent of Everest" (notes from a social climber). [CrabCR] (5:1) Wint 88, p. 18-19.
"The Assurances of Eve Svenson." [Lips] (14) 88, p. 24.
"Tales from Useless Bay" (3 poems). [OntR] (28) Spr-Sum 88, p. 43-46.
2121. HARRIS, Joseph
"The Butterfly." [Kaleid] (17) Sum-Fall 88, p. 26.
"Landscape with Barn." [DeKalbLAJ] (21:3/4) 88, p. 55.
"On Straightening Utrillo." [HolCrit] (25:3) Je 88, p. 17.
2122. HARRIS, Mary M.
"Personal Effects" (for my grandmother Mary Margaret Gleason). [Amelia] (4:4, #11) 88, p. 80-81.
2123. HARRIS, Michael D.
"Nights at Ned's." [Phoenix] (9:1/2) 88, p. 28.
2124. HARRIS, Peter
"Back Down Morrill Avenue" (for Natalie). [BelPoJ] (38:4) Sum 88, p. 18-19.
"China Lake." [BelPoJ] (38:4) Sum 88, p. 16-17.
HARRIS, Robert Dassanowsky
See DASSANOWSKY-HARRIS, Robert
2125. HARRIS, Will
"The Austin Revelations." [WritersF] (14) Fall 88, p. 72-74.
2126. HARRISON, Devin
"Divination." [Poem] (60) N 88, p. 16.
"Estate Auctions." [SoDakR] (26:3) Aut 88, p. 66-67.
"In Memoriam" (Yang Mulia Bapak: 1901-1987). [Poem] (60) N 88, p. 12.
"Repeating the Pattern." [PassN] (9:2) Sum 88, p. 28.
"Roofs." [Poem] (60) N 88, p. 14-15.
"Shabbat Shalom, Kibbutz Dovrat." [Poem] (60) N 88, p. 13.
"Witness." [SoDakR] (26:3) Aut 88, p. 65.
2127. HARRISON, Jeffrey
"Bathtubs, Three Varieties." [Poetry] (152:2) My 88, p. 86.
"A Field Guide to Mosses." [Verse] (5:1) F 88, p. 63.
"Graveyard." [CinPR] (17) Spr 88, p. 20.
"How the Ginkgo Got Its Smell" (Sapporo, Japan). [AntR] (46:1) Wint 88, p. 80.
"The Light Cure." [CinPR] (17) Spr 88, p. 21.
"The One that Got Away" (For Julie). [Poetry] (152:2) My 88, p. 87.
"Slaughter Cows." [OntR] (28) Spr-Sum 88, p. 104.
2128. HARRISON, Jim
"Counting Birds" (for Gerald Vizenor). [Caliban] (5) 88, p. 12-13.
2129. HARRISON, Richard
"Leonard vs Hagler for the Championship of the World." [CrossC] (10:2) 88, p. 3.
2130. HARROD, Lois Marie
"I Cannot Buy." [LitR] (31:3) Spr 88, p. 277.
2131. HARSHAM, Tom
"The Cover Letter." [CinPR] (17) Spr 88, p. 74.

2132. HART, Henry
"Columbus in El Otro Mundo." [CreamCR] (12:2) Sum 88, p. 196.
"King Philip's Ghost." [CreamCR] (12:2) Sum 88, p. 195.
2133. HART, Jack
"Contrary to Verlaine." [Poem] (60) N 88, p. 36.
"Don't Turn Your head." [Poem] (60) N 88, p. 37.
"Survey of Literature." [YellowS] (26) Spr 88, p. 38.
2134. HART, Kathy
"Star Search." [Sequoia] (32:1) Spr-Sum 88, p. 31.
2135. HART, Kevin
"The Gift." [PraS] (62:4) Wint 88-89, p. 98-99.
"The Gift." [Verse] (5:3) N 88, p. 4.
"Making a Rat." [Verse] (5:3) N 88, p. 5.
"The Map." [PraS] (62:4) Wint 88-89, p. 99-100.
2136. HARTER, Penny
"The Clown Car." [Footwork] ('88) 88, p. 30.
"My Father and Jocko at the Staten Island Zoo." [Footwork] ('88) 88, p. 31.
"Why I Don't Wear Fur Coats." [Footwork] ('88) 88, p. 30.
2137. HARTMAN, Charles O.
"Alarm." [PraS] (62:2) Sum 88, p. 94-95.
"Glass Enclosure." [Temblor] (8) 88, p. 135-145.
"Love Song: Accidental Species." [Ploughs] (14:1) 88, p. 142-143.
"Waking Up." [PraS] (62:2) Sum 88, p. 93-94.
2138. HARTNER, Johnny
"When We Learned What 69 Meant." [Gargoyle] (35) 88, p. 105.
2139. HARTOG, Diana
"The Art of Sleeping Alone." [Trans] (20) Spr 88, p. 39.
"Bannock Point." [MalR] (83) Je 88, p. 145.
"The Coldness of Shakespeare." [WestCR] (22:4) Spr 87, i.e. 88, p. 41.
"The Color of Blindfolds." [Trans] (20) Spr 88, p. 38.
"Common Knowledge." [WestCR] (22:4) Spr 87, i.e. 88, p. 40.
"Courtesy of Texaco." [Trans] (20) Spr 88, p. 42.
"The Difference Between Prose and Poetry." [Trans] (20) Spr 88, p. 40.
"The Flight of Three White Boulders." [MalR] (83) Je 88, p. 141-142.
"The Guest." [MalR] (83) Je 88, p. 145.
"In America the Silence Is Very Tiny" (for Jane). [MalR] (83) Je 88, p. 146.
"Oasis." [MalR] (83) Je 88, p. 147-160.
"A Peridot." [MalR] (83) Je 88, p. 144.
"Sleeves." [MalR] (83) Je 88, p. 143.
"Tiny Black Periods." [Trans] (20) Spr 88, p. 40.
"Water." [Trans] (20) Spr 88, p. 41.
2140. HARTWIG, Julia
"Before Dawn" (tr. by Stanislaw Baranczak and Clare Cavanagh). [ManhatR] (4:2) Spr 88, p. 36.
"But of Course" (tr. by Stanislaw Baranczak and Clare Cavanagh). [TriQ] (71) Wint 88, p. 154.
"In Your Eyes" (tr. by Stanislaw Baranczak and Clare Cavanagh). [TriQ] (71) Wint 88, p. 153.
"Towards the End" (tr. by Stanislaw Baranczak and Clare Cavanagh). [ManhatR] (4:2) Spr 88, p. 36-37.
2141. HARVEY, Anne-Marie
"Seattle to Spokane with Cousin Erika." [BellR] (11:1) Spr 88, p. 5.
2142. HARVEY, Gayle Elen
"Adam and Eve." [LaurelR] (22:21) Wint 88, p. 33.
"Letter from the Asylum." [HolCrit] (25:2) Ap 88, p. 11.
"Mantis" (The Phillips Award, Fall/Winter 1987/88). [StoneC] (15:3/4) Spr-Sum 88, p. 2.
2143. HARVEY, Jack D.
"Fancy Woman." [Vis] (28) 88, p. 9.
2144. HARVEY, Ken J.
"Overcast Sky on a Sunny Day." [Event] (17:2) Sum 88, p. 38-39.
2145. HARVEY, Suzanne R.
"The Land of Skulls." [Vis] (27) 88, p. 27.
2146. HARWAY, Judith
"Aubade: In His Voice." [CapeR] (23:2) Fall 88, p. 30.
"Because It's There." [CapeR] (23:2) Fall 88, p. 31.

"Flying Blind." [CarolQ] (40:3) Spr 88, p. 72.
2147. HARWIN, Patricia
"Education." [SmPd] (25:1) Wint 88, p. 8.
2148. HARWOOD, Gwen
"Carapace." [PraS] (62:4) Wint 88-89, p. 54.
"Crow-Call." [PraS] (62:4) Wint 88-89, p. 48.
"Forty Years On" (to Peter Bennie). [PraS] (62:4) Wint 88-89, p. 49-50.
"Picture a Brisbane Afternoon." [PraS] (62:4) Wint 88-89, p. 52-43.
"Resurrection." [PraS] (62:4) Wint 88-89, p. 50-52.
2149. HASAN, Rabiul
"In Winter." [Wind] (18:62) 88, p. 20.
2150. HASEGAWA, Ryusei
"People Who Get Off" (tr. by Graeme Wilson). [Jacaranda] (3:1) Wint 88, p. 5.
2151. HASHIMOTO, Sharon
"Eleven A.M. on My Day Off, My Sister Phones Desperate for a Babysitter." [Calyx] (11:2/3) Fall 88, p. 199.
"Standing in the Doorway, I Watch the Young Child Sleep." [Calyx] (11:2/3) Fall 88, p. 198.
2152. HASHMI, Alamgir
"Lot's Wife." [Vis] (28) 88, p. 18.
"Nine Tankas Out of Time." [NewL] (54:3) Spr 88, p. 84-85.
2153. HASKINS, Lola
"The Confrontation." [WestB] (21/22) 88, p. 53-54.
"Cookery: To Truss Small Birds." [Iowa] (18:2) 88, p. 112.
"Fashion: How to Wear the Veil." [Iowa] (18:2) 88, p. 112.
"The Gift." [WestB] (21/22) 88, p. 53.
"Marriage Customs in Patagonia." [LitR] (31:3) Spr 88, p. 276-277.
"The Prairie Woman Tells." [WestB] (21/22) 88, p. 52.
"Six Cairns for Mary." [NewEngR] (11:1) Aut 88, p. 2-4.
"Xtofer and Elizabeth." [MidwQ] (29:2) Wint 88, p. 205-213.
2154. HASS, Robert
"1945" (tr. of Czeslaw Milosz, w. the author). [Antaeus] (60) Spr 88, p. 264.
"An Appeal" (Brie-Compte-Robert, 1954, tr. of Czeslaw Milosz). [Verse] (5:1) F 88, p. 12-13.
"Ballad of Levallois" (Barracks for the unemployed . . . , tr. of Czeslaw Milosz, w. the author). [Antaeus] (60) Spr 88, p. 258-259.
"How It Should Be in Heaven" (tr. of Czeslaw Milosz, w. the author). [Antaeus] (60) Spr 88, p. 261.
"In Milan" (tr. of Czeslaw Milosz, w. the author). [Antaeus] (60) Spr 88, p. 260.
"On Parting with My Wife, Janina" (tr. of Czeslaw Milosz, w. the author). [Antaeus] (60) Spr 88, p. 262-263.
"Privilege of Being." [Verse] (5:1) F 88, p. 7.
"Tahoe in August." [Zyzzyva] (4:3) Fall 88, p. 33-34.
"A Treatise on Poetry" (2 fragments, tr. of Czeslaw Milosz, w. the author). [AmerPoR] (17:3) My-Je 88, p. 7-8.
2155. HASSELSTROM, Linda (Linda M.)
"After the Storm." [Spirit] (9:1) 88, p. 11-12.
"Apologies to Frost's Neighbor." [NoDaQ] (56:4) Fall 88, p. 35-36.
"The Blind Corral." [Spirit] (9:1) 88, p. 11.
"Dawn, After Hearing William Stafford." [NoDaQ] (56:4) Fall 88, p. 36.
"Drowning." [SwampR] (1:2/3) D 88, p. 25.
"Fourteen." [SwampR] (1:1) Ja 88, p. 34-35.
"Hang Gliding." [SwampR] (1:1) Ja 88, p. 36.
2156. HASSNA, Steve
"One Each, Combat Tour" (Excerpt). [ColR] (NS 15:1) Spr-Sum 88, p. 89-90.
2157. HATHAWAY, Jeanine
"Two Poets in the Family." [RiverS] (25) 88, p. 48.
2158. HATHAWAY, William
"Below Houston" (for Bill Mills). [SouthernR] (24:2) Spr 88, p. 332-338.
"No Direction Known." [TarRP] (28:1) Fall 88, p. 77-78.
"Peach Pit." [Salm] (80) Fall 88, p. 124-125.
"Spit." [AntR] (46:3) Sum 88, p. 356-357.
"Vacationer." [AmerPoR] (17:2) Mr-Ap 88, p. 40.
"Wan Hope" (For Robert Pinsky). [NewEngR] (11:2) Wint 88, p. 191-193.
"Why That's Bob Hope." [Verse] (5:3) N 88, p. 49.

2159. HATTA, Mari
"Senility." [Boulevard] (3:2/3) Fall 88, p. 124.
2160. HATTERSLEY, Geoff
"Unrequited Love." [Bogg] (59) 88, p. 53.
2161. HAUG, James
"Clear." [PoetryE] (25) Spr 88, p. 94.
"Driving Around." [PoetryE] (25) Spr 88, p. 93.
"Dry Ice." [PoetryE] (25) Spr 88, p. 97-98.
"Meeting Walter." [Ploughs] (14:4) 88, p. 81.
"Nightswimmer." [Confr] (37/38) Spr-Sum 88, p. 277.
"Passing Through Barre." [PoetryE] (25) Spr 88, p. 92.
"Pool Is a Godless Sport." [PoetryE] (25) Spr 88, p. 87.
"A Song for Stolen Bread." [Ploughs] (14:4) 88, p. 82.
"The Stolen Car." [PoetryE] (25) Spr 88, p. 95-96.
"The Tennessee Waltz." [PoetryE] (25) Spr 88, p. 88-89.
"White Dust." [PoetryE] (25) Spr 88, p. 90-91.
2162. HAUK, Barbara
"The Graduate Watch." [CapeR] (23:1) Spr 88, p. 22.
2163. HAUPTMAN, Terry
"Kaiya on the Night of Her Grandma's Death." [Caliban] (4) 88, p. 156.
"Persistent Heat." [PaintedB] (36) 88, p. 47.
"Teaching in the Prison." [Caliban] (4) 88, p. 157.
"Ward's Island." [Caliban] (4) 88, p. 157.
2164. HAVEN, Stephen
"Change of Shift." [KanQ] (20:1/2) Wint-Spr 88, p. 266.
"Edge of a Watershed" (for Byll). [KanQ] (20:1/2) Wint-Spr 88, p. 272-273.
"For My Brother's Decision to Join the Navy." [Blueline] (9:1/2) 88, p. 30.
2165. HAVIRD, David
"Habit of the Heart." [KanQ] (20:3) Sum 88, p. 176.
2166. HAWKINS, Hunt
"Honeymoon." [GeoR] (42:2) Sum 88, p. 340-341.
2167. HAWKINS, Rose Furuya
"Proud Upon an Alien Shore" (Excerpts). [Calyx] (11:2/3) Fall 88, p. 21-24.
2168. HAWLEY, Beatrice
"The New House." [Atlantic] (262:2) Ag 88, p. 58.
2169. HAXTON, Brooks
"Canon" (to Caroline Beasley-Baker). [BelPoJ] (39:1) Fall 88, p. 11-13.
"Commencement" (to George Tatge). [BelPoJ] (39:1) Fall 88, p. 4-5.
"Compline." [ParisR] (30:108) Fall 88, p. 45.
"Fall." [SenR] (18:2) 88, p. 70-71.
"Graveyard Pond, Adams County, Mississippi." [SenR] (18:2) 88, p. 72-73.
"Horae Paganicae" (Selections: "Lauds," "Sext," "None"). [MissouriR] (11:1) 88, p. 148-150.
"Horae Paganicae" (Selections: "Prime," "Terce," "Matins"). [NewEngR] (11:1) Aut 88, p. 58-62.
"Three Letters." [BelPoJ] (39:1) Fall 88, p. 4-13.
"Wingnut" (to my brother Richard). [BelPoJ] (39:1) Fall 88, p. 6-10.
2170. HAYDEN, Dolores
"The Line Striper" (for Lita Albuquerque, who wanted to turn the street blue). [ManhatPR] (10) Ja 88, p. 57.
"Pickers' Market" (Brimfield, Massachusetts." [PoetryNW] (29:2) Sum 88, p. 38-39.
2171. HAYDEN, Robert
"And All the Atoms Cry Aloud." [WorldO] (21:1/2) Fall-Wint 86-87, c89, p. 50-52.
2172. HAYDON, Rich
"Angina Pectoris." [CapeR] (23:2) Fall 88, p. 17.
"Burning the Plum Tree." [CapeR] (23:2) Fall 88, p. 16.
2173. HAYES, Aidan
"A Line." [LakeSR] (22) 88, p. 16.
2174. HAYES, Jack
"American Dreams." [Timbuktu] (1) Wint-Spr 88, p. 28-29.
"Angelology, or the Black Rose Cafe." [Timbuktu] (2) Sum-Fall 88, p. 64.
"Aubade." [Timbuktu] (1) Wint-Spr 88, p. 31.
"Easter's Good News." [Timbuktu] (2) Sum-Fall 88, p. 66-67.
"L'Envoi." [Timbuktu] (1) Wint-Spr 88, p. 30.
"The Goat-Boy's Bucolic." [Timbuktu] (1) Wint-Spr 88, p. 29-30.

"Heavenly Bodies." [Timbuktu] (2) Sum-Fall 88, p. 65.
"Muskrat Trapper." [Ascent] (14:2) 88, p. 41.
"Mutant Heroes." [Timbuktu] (1) Wint-Spr 88, p. 34-35.
"My Gloria, or Translate This Song." [Timbuktu] (2) Sum-Fall 88, p. 63.
"Night-Sea Journey." [Timbuktu] (1) Wint-Spr 88, p. 17.
"Under Heaven." [Timbuktu] (2) Sum-Fall 88, p. 61.
"Up-to-Date (or Ancient) Gothic." [Timbuktu] (1) Wint-Spr 88, p. 32-33.
"Waffle House Fantasy." [Ascent] (14:2) 88, p. 42.
"Window-Shopping as Paradise." [Timbuktu] (2) Sum-Fall 88, p. 62.

HAYES, Reine Thomas
See THOMAS-HAYES, Reine

2175. HAYES, Robert
"Cattle Truck." [DeKalbLAJ] (21:3/4) 88, p. 56.

2176. HAYMAN, Patrick
"Words for Painting." [Margin] (6) Sum 88, p. 13-15.

2177. HAYMON, Ava Leavell
"The Baby Meets the Three Kings." [BellR] (11:2) Fall 88, p. 14.
"Heat." [NowestR] (26:2) 88, p. 24.
"Hi-Tech Diagnostics." [NowestR] (26:2) 88, p. 26.
"January 6: American Calendar." [BellR] (11:2) Fall 88, p. 15.
"Return." [BellR] (11:2) Fall 88, p. 11-12.
"Sestina in Gratitude for a Southern Baptist Upbringing." [NowestR] (26:2) 88, p. 27-28.
"Troublemakers." [BellR] (11:2) Fall 88, p. 13-14.
"Verdict." [Hudson] (41:2) Sum 88, p. 323-328.
"Warning." [Bogg] (59) 88, p. 12.
"What the Magnolias Say." [NowestR] (26:2) 88, p. 25.

2178. HAYN, Annette
"Landmarks." [Wind] (18:62) 88, p. 17.
"Secrets." [Wind] (18:62) 88, p. 17-18.

2179. HAYNES, Mary
"Hard Kernels" (9 poems). [Temblor] (8) 88, p. 113-119.

2180. HAYNES, Robert E.
"The Bathing Dinosaur." [CapeR] (23:1) Spr 88, p. 4.
"Failed Flight." [CapeR] (23:1) Spr 88, p. 3.
"Happiness in Poetry." [Vis] (28) 88, p. 20.
"Still Life with Dancer." [Wind] (18:63) 88, p. 24.
"The Visit." [Wind] (18:63) 88, p. 31.

2181. HAYNES, Tony
"The Evolution of the Bazaar" (The Seaton Third Award Poem 1988). [KanQ] (20:3) Sum 88, p. 18.

2182. HAYWARD, Camille
"Little." [BellArk] (4:1) Ja-F 88, p. 5.
"Naming" (After Margaret Wise Brown's *Goodnight Moon*). [BellArk] (4:1) Ja-F 88, p. 5.

2183. HAZARD, James
"The Industrial Room of the Illiana Hotel, Whiting, Indiana." [CutB] (29/30) 88, p. 103.
"The Way of the Cross in Whiting, Indiana." [CutB] (29/30) 88, p. 102.

2184. HAZEN, James
"The Dancing Professors." [Poem] (59) My 88, p. 27.
"Granted." [ChatR] (9:1) Fall 88, p. 40.
"Hartfield." [HawaiiR] (12:1, #23) Spr 88, p. 17.
"The River." [Poem] (59) My 88, p. 28.
"Spring Southwest." [Poem] (59) My 88, p. 26.
"Teller She's Lovely." [Farm] (5:2) Fall 88, p. 65.

2185. HAZO, Samuel
"Mediterraneans." [TarRP] (28:1) Fall 88, p. 73-74.
"Song for the Flies of Fire." [TarRP] (28:1) Fall 88, p. 75-76.
"Update." [Comm] (115:10) 20 My 88, p. 303.

2186. HEAD, Robert
"First i got the feather." [Bogg] (60) 88, p. 50.
"Hokouzaï and the Wife of the Fisherman" (tr. of Yorges Pavlópoulos). [Bogg] (59) 88, p. 52.
"Hwen darlene opens the millet bread." [Bogg] (60) 88, p. 50.
"I believe that Persephone." [Bogg] (60) 88, p. 51.

"If you do not see signs & wonders you will not believe." [Bogg] (60) 88, p. 51.
"Thank you for your company I said." [WormR] (28:4, #112) 88, p. 104.
"White-Watering on the River of Death." [WormR] (28:4, #112) 88, p. 104.

HEALY, Eloise Klein
See KLEIN-HEALY, Eloise

2187. HEANEY, Seamus
"The Ash Plant." [Antaeus] (60) Spr 88, p. 184.
"The Pitchfork." [Antaeus] (60) Spr 88, p. 183.
"The Sound of Rain" (i.m. Richard Ellmann). [GeoR] (42:3) Fall 88, p. 481-482.

2188. HEAP, Chad
"A Note for Plath" (Poetry Contest Honorable Mention). [HarvardA] (122:3) Mr 88, p. 13.

2189. HEARD, Georgia
"What We Hoped For." [Agni] (27) 88, p. 199.

2190. HEARD, Karen
"And It Came to Pass." [ChrC] (105:39) 21-28 D 88, p. 1182.

2191. HEATH, Elaine
"To: Chuck, Dead of Lung Cancer at 44." [EngJ] (77:2) F 88, p. 86.

2192. HEATH-STUBBS, John
"Define this as you choose" (tr. of Boris Pasternak, w. Eugene Dubnov). [StoneC] (16:1/2) Fall-Wint 88-89, p. 29.
"A Dream" (tr. of Eugene Dubnov, w. the author). [MissR] (16:1, #46) 88, p. 44-45.
"The Gardener Said" (for Raymond and Pamela Harper, tr. of Eugene Dubnov, w. the author). [MissR] (16:1, #46) 88, p. 42.
"The Great Yahoo Revolution." [Interim] (7:1) Spr 88, p. 3-6.
"I Had Rubbed Myself with a Towel" (tr. of Eugene Dubnov, w. Chris Arkell). [MissR] (16:1, #46) 88, p. 43.

2193. HEBERT, Anne
"The Closed Room" (tr. by Alan Brown). [Trans] (20) Spr 88, p. 129-130.
"Manor Life" (tr. by F. R. Scott). [Trans] (20) Spr 88, p. 132.
"A Small Dead Girl" (tr. by Alan Brown). [Trans] (20) Spr 88, p. 131.
"The Tomb of the Kings" (tr. by F. R. Scott). [Trans] (20) Spr 88, p. 133-135.

2194. HEDGES, Ben
"This will sound a little trite." [PottPort] (10) 88, p. 38.

2195. HEDGES, David
"Jobless on the First of June." [BellArk] (4:2) Mr-Ap 88, p. 20.

2196. HEDIN, Robert
"Ballad of a Chinese Picture" (dedicated to Ho Tsien, Peking, tr. of Lars Gustafsson). [ColR] (NS 15:2) Fall-Wint 88, p. 82-83.
"Bells" (For M. L., killed in Viet Nam). [MissouriR] (11:2) 88, p. 187.
"May on the Windowpane" (tr. of Rolf Jacobsen). [InterPR] (14:1) Spr 88, p. 23.
"Moon Before It Becomes Dark" (tr. of Rolf Jacobsen). [InterPR] (14:1) Spr 88, p. 21.
"Night Music" (tr. of Rolf Jacobsen). [PoetryE] (25) Spr 88, p. 126.
"Play" (tr. of Rolf Jacobsen). [InterPR] (14:1) Spr 88, p. 21.
"Seabird" (tr. of Rolf Jacobsen). [InterPR] (14:1) Spr 88, p. 23.
"The Sky" (tr. of Stein Mehren). [ColR] (NS 15:2) Fall-Wint 88, p. 84.
"Teeth." [CharR] (14:2) Fall 88, p. 110.
"Winter Solstice in Lourdes." [MissouriR] (11:2) 88, p. 188.

2197. HEDLEY, Leslie Woolf
"Places." [WormR] (28:1, #109) 88, p. 7.
"There Is No Future." [WormR] (28:1, #109) 88, p. 6.

2198. HEFFERNAN, Donald J.
"Ancestors on Hillsides." [Paint] (15:29) Spr 88, p. 14-15.

2199. HEFFERNAN, Michael
"Babies, Babies." [CharR] (14:1) Spr 88, p. 64.
"The Dancing Ground." [CharR] (14:1) Spr 88, p. 64.
"The Facts in the Ground." [NoAmR] (273:1) Mr 88, p. 37.
"Halfway in the Journey." [CharR] (14:1) Spr 88, p. 63.
"In the Forum at Lugdunum." [GettyR] (1:1) Wint 88, p. 86.
"The Journey to Brindisi." [GettyR] (1:1) Wint 88, p. 87.
"The Last Man." [PoetryNW] (29:1) Spr 88, p. 13-14.
"Left." [Crazy] (35) Wint 88, p. 60.
"On the Beach at Saugatuck." [Crazy] (35) Wint 88, p. 61.
"The Sun Comes Out in South Haven." [MissouriR] (11:2) 88, p. 100-101.

"Why We Forget the Things We Thought We Wouldn't." [PoetryNW] (29:1) Spr 88, p. 12-13.

2200. HEFFERNAN, Thomas
"Liam's Fall into a Ditch." [StoneC] (15:3/4) Spr-Sum 88, p. 67.
"Poem for Liam Dall O Heffernan, 1715-1802." [StoneC] (15:3/4) Spr-Sum 88, p. 66.

2201. HEIGHTON, Steven
"Annotation of a Fragment" (from The Collected Works). [Dandel] (15:2) Fall-Wint 88, p. 20-22.
"In the Terminal." [Event] (17:1) Spr 88, p. 71.
"Scholar in November." [Dandel] (15:2) Fall-Wint 88, p. 24.
"The Scholar's Dream." [Dandel] (15:2) Fall-Wint 88, p. 23.
"Song of the Cynical Missionary." [Event] (17:1) Spr 88, p. 70.

2202. HEILBRONN, Monica
"Branch." [Confr] (37/38) Spr-Sum 88, p. 252.
"Sanctum." [Confr] (37/38) Spr-Sum 88, p. 253.

2203. HEINE-KOEHN, Lala
"The Cameo." [PraF] (9:4) Wint 88-89, p. 32-33.
"The Little Christmas Breadlet." [Grain] (16:4) Wint 88, p. 32-34.

2204. HEINRICH, Peggy
"Finding Mother." [Footwork] ('88) 88, p. 26-27.
"Moon Goddess." [TexasR] (9:3/4) Fall-Wint 88, p. 66.

2205. HEISLER, Eva
"Into the Fire" (Katherine Mansfield, 1923). [GettyR] (1:4) Aut 88, p. 689-690.
"Katherine Mansfield, Italy, 1919." [GettyR] (1:4) Aut 88, p. 687-688.

2206. HEJINIAN, Lyn
"The Cell." [Sink] (3) 88, p. 35-38.
"Instructing Clarity in a Confusion" (tr. of Arkadii Dragomoshchenko, w. Elena Balashova). [NewAW] (4) Fall 88, p. 8-11.
"The Islands of Sirens" (tr. of Arkadii Dragomoshchenko, w. Elena Balashova). [Zyzzyva] (4:1) Spr 88, p. 87-106.

2207. HELFMAN, Suzanne
"Rose Water." [FiveFR] (6) 88, p. 75.
"Two Kinds of Birdseed on Identical Blue." [FiveFR] (6) 88, p. 74.

2208. HELLER-ZBLOKI, Chiah
"For Michiyo Fukayo, April 25, 1953-July 9, 1987." [SinW] (36) Wint 88-89, p. 59-61.
"To the Women Who Weep." [SinW] (36) Wint 88-89, p. 62-63.

2209. HELLERSTEIN, Kathryn
"Fir Trees Clanked Like Green Metal!" (tr. of Viktor Sosnora, w. Darra Goldstein). [NewYRB] (35:15) 13 O 88, p. 47.
"Letter" (tr. of Viktor Sosnora, w. Darra Goldstein). [NewYRB] (35:15) 13 O 88, p. 47.

2210. HELLMAN, Sheila
"Anarchy Is Swallowed with Chopped Liver" (from a sequence, "Lower East Side: 1940"). [StoneC] (16:1/2) Fall-Wint 88-89, p. 48-49.
"A Woman's Face." [Footwork] ('88) 88, p. 72-73.

2211. HELLMUTH, Elane Summers
"The Barn" (Commended, 15th Anniversary Competition). [StoneC] (16:1/2) Fall-Wint 88-89, unpaged front matter.

2212. HEMMING, Dianna
"Player." [SpoonRQ] (13:3) Sum 88, p. 51.

2213. HEMPEL, Wes
"I Try to Change." [HangL] (52) 88, p. 6.

2214. HEMSCHEMEYER, Judith
"223. Little Song" (tr. of Anna Akhmatova). [SouthernR] (24:3) Sum 88, p. 537.
"224. And here, left alone, I" (tr. of Anna Akhmatova). [SouthernR] (24:3) Sum 88, p. 535-536.
"229. Long years I waited for him in vain" (tr. of Anna Akhmatova). [SouthernR] (24:3) Sum 88, p. 536.
"551. *De profundis*, My generation" (tr. of Anna Akhmatova). [SouthernR] (24:3) Sum 88, p. 537.
"561. They will forget? — How astonishing!" (tr. of Anna Akhmatova). [SouthernR] (24:3) Sum 88, p. 538.
"568. Inscription on a Book" (tr. of Anna Akhmatova). [SouthernR] (24:3) Sum 88, p. 538.

"Everything Promised Him to Me" (tr. of Anna Akhmatova). [TriQ] (73) Fall 88, p. 93.
"The Neighbor, Out of Pity" (tr. of Anna Akhmatova). [TriQ] (73) Fall 88, p. 94.
"So We Lowered Our Eyes" (tr. of Anna Akhmatova). [NewEngR] (11:2) Wint 88, p. 141.
"Terror, Fingering Things in the Dark" (tr. of Anna Akhmatova). [Field] (39) Fall 88, p. 21.
"To the Memory of V. S. Sreznevskaya" (tr. of Anna Akhmatova). [TriQ] (73) Fall 88, p. 95.
"White Night" (tr. of Anna Akhmatova). [NewEngR] (11:2) Wint 88, p. 140.

2215. HENDERSON, Heather
"Denver landing." [SoDakR] (26:1) Spr 88, p. 108.

2216. HENDRICKS, Brent
"A Baseball Story." [PoetryE] (25) Spr 88, p. 86.

2217. HENKE, Mark
"West from the Avalon Ballroom." [Writer] (101:9) S 88, p. 25.

2218. HENN, Mary Ann
"The Angels' Wings." [Footwork] ('88) 88, p. 81-82.
"Chimera." [LightY] ('88/9) 88, p. 124-125.
"Little Brother." [Bogg] (59) 88, p. 26.
"The Sting." [Wind] (18:62) 88, p. 41.

2219. HENNING, Barbara
"City Porches." [Lactuca] (11) O 88, p. 23.
"Detroit 1967." [Lactuca] (11) O 88, p. 23.
"Grenada: Petty Cash Flow." [Ascent] (14:1) 88, p. 45-47.
"Real Life." [Ascent] (14:1) 88, p. 44-45.
"Spattered with White." [Vis] (28) 88, p. 43.

2220. HENRIE, Carol
"For the Sake of the Argument." [PoetryNW] (29:1) Spr 88, p. 11-12.
"Regret." [PoetryNW] (29:1) Spr 88, p. 9-11.
"T*E*X." [PoetryNW] (29:1) Spr 88, p. 7-9.
"What the Wind Knew." [PraS] (62:2) Sum 88, p. 88-89.

2221. HENRY, Daniel
"Birthday Poem." [EngJ] (77:3) Mr 88, p. 88.

2222. HENRY, Laurie
"At the Writers' Conference." [CinPR] (17) Spr 88, p. 48-49.

2223. HENSON, Kelly
"Sweets & Fruits." [Amelia] (4:4, #11) 88, p. 20.

2224. HENSON, Sandy
"A Dream After Avoiding a Fight Through Silence." [Poem] (59) My 88, p. 50-51.
"The White Lie." [Poem] (59) My 88, p. 52-53.

2225. HERBECK, Ernst
"The Fire-Eater" (tr. by Melissa Monroe). [BlackWR] (14:2) Spr 88, p. 65.

2226. HERBERT, W. N.
"From a Picaresque Tale in Verse." [Verse] (5:1) F 88, p. 46-47.
"Icaro, 1931." [Verse] (5:3) N 88, p. 16.
"Keelie's Een." [Verse] (5:3) N 88, p. 16.

2227. HERBERT, Zbigniew
"Fish" (tr. by Ioanna-Veronika Warwick). [Thrpny] (35) Fall 88, p. 26.

2228. HERMS, George
"January Juggernaut." [Zyzzyva] (4:1) Spr 88, p. 51.

2229. HERMSEN, Terry
"Burning the Trash" (from "Eight Sonnets for My Daughter). [Nimrod] (32:1) Fall-Wint 88, p. 93.

2230. HERNANDEZ, Francisco
"19. The bed slides through a sleepless sea" (tr. by Linda Scheer). [Caliban] (5) 88, p. 97.
"About How Robert Schumann Was Defeated by His Demons" (tr. by Linda Scheer). [Caliban] (5) 88, p. 96.

2231. HERNANDEZ, Miguel
"Lullaby of the Onion" (Dedicated to his son, tr. by Don Share). [ParisR] (30:107) Sum 88, p. 198-200.

2232. HERNANDEZ, Reyna
"Prison Poem" (tr. by Zoe Anglesey). [ColR] (NS 15:1) Spr-Sum 88, p. 75.

2233. HERRERA, Juan Felipe
"Exile Boulevard" (tr. by Sesshu Foster and Dolores Bravo). [Rohwedder] (3) Spr 88, p. 1-3.
"Foreign Inhabitant." [HangL] (52) 88, p. 64-65.
"Inside the Jacket." [HangL] (52) 88, p. 63.
"Poetic Report: On Servants: Toward a Model for Urban Hispaniks, USA" (tr. by Sesshu Foster and Dolores Bravo). [Rohwedder] (3) Spr 88, p. 30-31.
"World Artist: Critical Gazing." [Zyzzyva] (4:1) Spr 88, p. 29-35.
2234. HERRIN, Sally
"Jeremiah" (Reagan II: Day 2. Fargo). [MidwQ] (29:3) Spr 88, p. 341-344.
"The Whole Code Is Everywhere." [MidwQ] (29:3) Spr 88, p. 340.
"Why I Begged You to Leave." [StoneC] (16:1/2) Fall-Wint 88-89, p. 59.
2235. HERRON, Elizabeth
"Driving West." [CapilR] (47) 88, p. 4-5.
"Fetal Demise." [CapilR] (47) 88, p. 9.
"Mysteries." [CapilR] (47) 88, p. 6-7.
"Since I Said It." [CapilR] (47) 88, p. 8.
2236. HERSCH, Greer
"Blind Girl" (Poetry Contest Honorable Mention). [HarvardA] (122:3) Mr 88, p. 12.
"Our Shyness." [HarvardA] (123:1) N 88, p. 13.
2237. HERSCHEL, John
"Monet's Feet." [AmerPoR] (17:6) N-D 88, p. 34.
2238. HERSHEY, Laura
"Progress." [SinW] (34) Spr 88, p. 41-42.
2239. HERSHON, Robert
"Humphrey Bogart." [NewAW] (3) Spr 88, p. 106.
"Laird Cregar and the Academic Exercise." [PoetryNW] (29:1) Spr 88, p. 31.
"October" (for Larry Zirlin). [PoetryNW] (29:1) Spr 88, p. 30-31.
"Whimsy Hit by Truck." [Turnstile] (1:1) Wint 88, p. 50.
2240. HESS, Sonya
"Mirth." [Caliban] (4) 88, p. 141-142.
2241. HESSLER, Ole
"Memory Game" (tr. by the author). [Vis] (27) 88, p. 19.
2242. HESTER, Beth
"The Swimmer" (after David Hockney). [HolCrit] (25:1) F 88, p. 15.
2243. HETRICK, Lawrence
"Some Red Arrowheads." [SouthernHR] (22:3) Sum 88, p. 222.
2244. HETTICH, Michael
"Anniversary" (for Colleen). [Spirit] (9:1) 88, p. 23.
"At the Beach." [LittleM] (15:3/4) 88, p. 131.
"The Earth Went Out." [LittleM] (15:3/4) 88, p. 134-135.
"Mercy, Mercy." [Spirit] (9:1) 88, p. 22.
"Near Inverness, Florida." [LittleM] (15:3/4) 88, p. 132-133.
HEUREUX, Maurice l'
See L'HEUREUX, Maurice
2245. HEWITT, Christopher
"Farce" (tr. of Nina Cassian). [NewYorker] (64:27) 22 Ag 88, p. 60.
"The Widow" (tr. of Nina Cassian). [NewYorker] (63:46) 4 Ja 88, p. 26.
2246. HEWITT, Greg
"Ode to a Penis." [JamesWR] (5:3) Spr-Sum 88, p. 7.
2247. HEYEN, William
"Brockport Sunflowers." [IndR] (11:2) Spr 88, p. 71.
"Futures." [CreamCR] (12:1) Wint 88, p. 79.
"If You Know Me at All." [OntR] (28) Spr-Sum 88, p. 40.
"Parabola." [Sequoia] (31:2) Wint 88, p. 50.
"Wildflower" (John Logan 1923-1987). [OntR] (28) Spr-Sum 88, p. 41.
2248. HEYER, Paul
"Blue Monk." [AlphaBS] (3) Je 88, p. 47.
2249. HEYMAN, Ann
"In Careless Wonder." [DeKalbLAJ] (21:2) Spr 88, p. 72.
2250. HIBBERD, Tom
"Doomsday Comedy." [PaintedB] (34) 88, p. 87.
"Headlines." [PaintedB] (34) 88, p. 87.
2251. HICKS, John V.
"Lines." [Grain] (16:4) Wint 88, p. 44.
"Outburst." [Grain] (16:4) Wint 88, p. 40.

2252. HIESTAND, Emily
"Candlepower." [Nat] (246:17) 30 Ap 88, p. 610.
2253. HIGGINS, Dick
"Tenebrae Pslam." [Notus] (3:2) Fall 88, p. 76-89.
2254. HIGH, John
"A horizontal country" (tr. of Aleksandr Eremenko, w. Katya Olmsted). [FiveFR] (6) 88, p. 30.
"Quiet of the Chestnuts" (Excerpts, tr. of Aleksandr Tkachenko, w. Katya Olmsted). [FiveFR] (6) 88, p. 87-88.
"Six Days Gone." [FiveFR] (6) 88, p. 66.
2255. HILBERT, Donna
"In the Garden Beyond Ourselves." [PassN] (9:2) Sum 88, p. 27.
2256. HILDEBIDLE, John
"Addie Grace." [BelPoJ] (39:1) Fall 88, p. 29.
"After One Year." [StoneC] (16:1/2) Fall-Wint 88-89, p. 14-15.
"The Disasters of War" (for John Hodgen). [BelPoJ] (39:1) Fall 88, p. 24-25.
"House Sparrow." [StoneC] (16:1/2) Fall-Wint 88-89, p. 13-14.
"Passing." [TexasR] (9:3/4) Fall-Wint 88, p. 67-68.
"A Quilt for a Lost Daughter." [BelPoJ] (39:1) Fall 88, p. 25-28.
"The Window in Springtime." [BelPoJ] (39:1) Fall 88, p. 30.
2257. HILDERLEY, Jeri
"Essence." [Sequoia] (32:1) Spr-Sum 88, p. 54.
"Sheepish." [Sequoia] (32:1) Spr-Sum 88, p. 53.
"Tragedy Comes in Pews." [Sequoia] (32:1) Spr-Sum 88, p. f53.
2258. HILE, Sharon E.
"Light Snow." [Plain] (8:2) Wint 88, p. 32.
"Through the Windowpane." [Plain] (8:3) Spr-Sum 88, p. 23.
"Where Winter Began." [Plain] (9:1) Fall 88, p. 28.
2259. HILL, Crag
"Dict" (Excerpt). [Sink] (3) 88, p. 21-25.
2260. HILL, Daniel
"Bones Beneath a Granite Eagle Feather." [MinnR] (NS 30/31) Spr-Fall 88, p. 16-17.
"Poem with a Disclaimer." [NoDaQ] (56:4) Fall 88, p. 190-191.
"Struck Dumb." [PoetL] (83:2) Sum 88, p. 21.
"Visiting the Bismarck Heritage Center." [KanQ] (20:1/2) Wint-Spr 88, p. 293.
2261. HILL, Elizabeth M.
"The Magical Valentina." [PikeF] (9) Fall 88, p. 20.
2262. HILL, Gerald
"House Mountain, British Columbia, Elevation 4,118 Feet, Admiralty Chart." [Dandel] (15:2) Fall-Wint 88, p. 38.
"Low, Quebec, Elevation 412 Feet, C.P.R." [Dandel] (15:2) Fall-Wint 88, p. 39.
2263. HILL, R. Nemo
"Volunteer." [LittleM] (15:3/4) 88, p. 77-78.
2264. HILLARD, Jeff
"The Big Picture." [CinPR] (17) Spr 88, p. 26-27.
"Once Ending." [CinPR] (17) Spr 88, p. 24-25.
2265. HILLER, Tobey
"Glossalalia." [Abraxas] (37) 88, p. 67.
"Landscape & Cabin." [Caliban] (5) 88, p. 127-129.
"Night." [Caliban] (5) 88, p. 125-126.
"Not Like." [Caliban] (5) 88, p. 130.
2266. HILLES, Robert
"Foothills in Winter." [Grain] (16:2) Sum 88, p. 36-37.
"A Gentle Look." [Grain] (16:2) Sum 88, p. 34-35.
"My Father Waits in the Country." [Grain] (16:2) Sum 88, inside back cover.
"The Problem of Seeing" (After a day at the beach). [CanLit] (118) Aut 88, p. 45-46.
"A Shaman Sings Opera to His Bride." [Spirit] (9:1) 88, p. 72-73.
"Sometime You Wake Afraid." [Grain] (16:2) Sum 88, inside front cover.
"Stumblings." [Grain] (16:2) Sum 88, p. 32-33.
"Training Camp, Gallipoli." [PraF] (9:2) Sum 88, p. 55-56.
"Trill of the Moon" (Guatemala). [PraF] (9:2) Sum 88, p. 56.
"You Stand Still Against a Cemetery's Memory." [PraF] (9:2) Sum 88, p. 57.
2267. HILLILA, Bernhard
"Shore Thing." [LightY] ('88/9) 88, p. 149.

2268. HILLIS, Rick
"Bob and Bing Visit Saskatchewan." [MalR] (84) S 88, p. 86-87.
"Memory Boy." [Event] (17:2) Sum 88, p. 56-59.
"What Else Don't You Know?" [MalR] (84) S 88, p. 85.
2269. HILLMAN, Brenda
"Adult Joy." [AmerPoR] (17:6) N-D 88, p. 8-9.
"At a Motel." [AmerPoR] (17:6) N-D 88, p. 7.
"Bookstore." [Pequod] (25) 88, p. 14-17.
"Contest." [AmerPoR] (17:6) N-D 88, p. 8.
"Gnostic Heaven." [AmerPoR] (17:3) My-Je 88, p. 48.
"The Goats." [MissouriR] (11:1) 88, p. 52-53.
"Little Furnace." [AmerPoR] (17:6) N-D 88, p. 7.
"Magdalene." [AmerPoR] (17:6) N-D 88, p. 6-7.
"Meridian Plinth." [ParisR] (30:107) Sum 88, p. 50-51.
"Night and Day." [AmerPoR] (17:6) N-D 88, p. 8.
"Pavane at Dusk." [AmerPoR] (17:6) N-D 88, p. 7-8.
"Twelve Dawns." [AmerPoR] (17:6) N-D 88, p. 3-5.
2270. HILLMAN, Brent
"Mer de Lune." [Thrpny] (33) Spr 88, p. 28.
2271. HILLMAN, Elizabeth
"Otherworld." [Plain] (8:2) Wint 88, p. 6.
2272. HILLRINGHOUSE, Mark
"Lost at Sunrise." [Footwork] ('88) 88, p. 75.
"Penn Station." [PassN] (9:2) Sum 88, p. 3.
"That Horrible Color Again" (for Fred Duignan). [Talisman] (1) Fall 88, p. 80-81.
2273. HILTON, David
"33rd & Greenmount, Baltimore." [Lips] (14) 88, p. 32.
"The Barmaid in the Wigwam." [Abraxas] (37) 88, p. 40-41.
"Investigation." [Lips] (14) 88, p. 33.
"'Pachuco Hop' — Chuck Higgins, 1954." [Spirit] (9:1) 88, p. 46-51.
2274. HILTY, Peter
"Hiroko Plays a Chopin Nocturne on the Violin." [CapeR] (23:1) Spr 88, p. 48.
2275. HINDLEY, Chris
"Chinese Aunty" (for M. Y. M.). [HawaiiR] (12:1, #23) Spr 88, p. 78.
"Mrs. Mitchell." [HawaiiR] (12:1, #23) Spr 88, p. 79.
2276. HINDLEY, Norman
"Autograph Tree." [ChamLR] (1:2, #2) Spr 88, p. 6.
"Billy's." [HawaiiR] (12:1, #23) Spr 88, p. 58.
"The Character of Glass." [ChamLR] (1:2, #2) Spr 88, p. 9-10.
"Shopping the Liquor Barn in Alameda with Tom." [HawaiiR] (12:1, #23) Spr 88, p. 56-57.
"Soft Drinks." [ChamLR] (1:2, #2) Spr 88, p. 7-8.
2277. HINDS, Stephen
"The Knot Undone." [Phoenix] (9:1/2) 88, p. 38.
2278. HINE, Daryl
"Postscripts." [YaleR] (78:1) Aut 88, p. 113-115.
2279. HINES, Debra
"As a Young Youth." [MassR] (29:3) Fall 88, p. 473-475.
"At Gitcheegoomee, Cake for One." [MassR] (29:3) Fall 88, p. 475-476.
"From Lamp to Tall Green Lamp." [KanQ] (20:3) Sum 88, p. 231-232.
"Ghazal Del Dia." [ColEng] (50:3) Mr 88, p. 289.
"The Piano Player Wants to Dance." [ColEng] (50:3) Mr 88, p. 288.
2280. HINKLE, Ann
"Appalachian Portrait." [MidAR] (8:2) 88, p. 76-77.
2281. HINOSTROZA, Rodolfo
"Nudo Borromeo." [Inti] (26/27) Otoño 87-Primavera 88, p. 158-164.
2282. HINRICHSEN, Dennis
"The Fields, the Sky" (after Beckett. In Memoriam: Hans Hinrichsen, 1926-1982). [Crazy] (35) Wint 88, p. 21.
"For a Bluesman." [Crazy] (35) Wint 88, p. 23-24.
"Ode." [Crazy] (35) Wint 88, p. 30-31.
"One Wing." [Agni] (27) 88, p. 184-185.
"Recurring Sound." [Crazy] (34) Spr 88, p. 32-33.
"Signatures." [Crazy] (35) Wint 88, p. 25-26.
"The Straight Natural Blues." [Crazy] (34) Spr 88, p. 27-31.
"Template." [Crazy] (35) Wint 88, p. 27-29.

"Unlit Courts" (to T.M., 1952-1968). [IndR] (12:1) Wint 88, p. 69-70.
"Water Touching Water." [Agni] (27) 88, p. 186.

2283. HINSHELWOOD, Nigel
"The Saxophone Player Who Was Tired of Jazz." [Gargoyle] (35) 88, p. 218.

2284. HINTON, David
"Seven Songs at T'ung-ku" (tr. of Tu Fu). [AmerPoR] (17:4) Jl-Ag 88, p. 23-24.

2285. HINTON, Matheu
"Sherade" (Written with Keisha Lynette Woodford). [Footwork] ('88) 88, p. 54-55.

2286. HIRAIDE, Takashi
"Ecstasy of a Solitary Cheiropter" (tr. by Tomoyuki Iino). [Stand] (29:3) Sum 88, p. 25.

HIROSHI, Yoshino
See YOSHINO, Hiroshi

2287. HIRSCH, Edward
"Cemetery by the Sea: Kahuku" (for Garrett Hongo). [WestHR] (42:1) Spr 88, p. 75-76.
"Complaint." [NewEngR] (11:2) Wint 88, p. 143-144.
"Family Stories." [OntR] (29) Fall-Wint 88-89, p. 57-66.
"In the Underground Garage." [Nat] (246:18) 7 My 88, p. 653.
"Incandescence at Dusk." [NewYorker] (64:31) 19 S 88, p. 38-39.
"My Father's Back." [NewEngR] (11:2) Wint 88, p. 142-143.
"A Photograph Ripped in Half." [WestHR] (42:1) Spr 88, p. 73-74.
"A Short Lexicon of Torture in the Eighties." [NewRep] (199:14) 3 O 88, p. 40.
"Siblings." [GettyR] (1:1) Wint 88, p. 122-125.
"Skywriting" (Harper-Grace Hospital, July 15, 1984). [AmerPoR] (17:6) N-D 88, p. 26.
"When Skyscrapers Were Invented in Chicago." [YaleR] (77:3) Spr 88, p. 399-401.

2288. HIRSCHMAN, Jack
"Endless Threshold." [AmerPoR] (17:5) S-O 88, p. 6.
"The Jacket" (In memory of Leopoldo Fiorenzato, suicided 1987). [AmerPoR] (17:5) S-O 88, p. 3.
"Madrid" (Commune, 1937, tr. of Jacques Roumain). [RedBass] (13) 88, p. 22-23.
"The New Palestine Arcane." [AmerPoR] (17:5) S-O 88, p. 4-5.
"The Rabbit." [AmerPoR] (17:5) S-O 88, p. 5.
"Sunsong." [AmerPoR] (17:5) S-O 88, p. 5.
"What Can Stop It?" [AmerPoR] (17:5) S-O 88, p. 3.

2289. HIRSHFIELD, Jane
"1973." [YellowS] (26) Spr 88, p. 49.
"Autumn." [ParisR] (30:109) Wint 88, p. 57.
"The autumn night" (tr. of Ono no Komachi, w. Mariko Aratani). [AmerPoR] (17:1) Ja-F 88, p. 16.
"I know it must be this way" (tr. of Ono no Komachi, w. Mariko Aratani). [AmerPoR] (17:1) Ja-F 88, p. 16.
"If the one I've waited for" (tr. of Izumi Shikibu, w. Mariko Aratani). [AmerPoR] (17:1) Ja-F 88, p. 16.
"Love-soaked, rain soaked" (tr. of Izumi Shikibu, w. Mariko Aratani). [AmerPoR] (17:1) Ja-F 88, p. 16.
"Lying alone" (tr. of Izumi Shikibu, w. Mariko Aratani). [AmerPoR] (17:1) Ja-F 88, p. 16.
"The Mesmer." [ParisR] (30:109) Wint 88, p. 54.
"The seaweed gatherer's weary feet" (tr. of Ono no Komachi, w. Mariko Aratani). [AmerPoR] (17:1) Ja-F 88, p. 16.
"The Stone of Heaven." [ParisR] (30:109) Wint 88, p. 55-56.
"Under the River." [AmerPoR] (17:4) Jl-Ag 88, p. 17.
"The way I must enter" (tr. of Izumi Shikibu, w. Mariko Aratani). [AmerPoR] (17:1) Ja-F 88, p. 16.
"We live in a tide-swept inlet" (tr. of Izumi Shikibu, w. Mariko Aratani). [AmerPoR] (17:1) Ja-F 88, p. 16.
"When my desire" (tr. of Ono no Komachi, w. Mariko Aratani). [AmerPoR] (17:1) Ja-F 88, p. 16.

HISN, Abul Hasan Ali ben
See BEN HISN, Abul Hasan Ali

2290. HITCHCOCK, George
"Fourteen Stanzas in Search of." [Caliban] (4) 88, p. 83-88.

2291. HIX, H. Edgar
"Alien Artifact." [Writer] (101:9) S 88, p. 26.

"Calling." [LightY] ('88/9) 88, p. 135.
2292. HIX, H. L.
"Grackles Roosting." [StoneC] (16:1/2) Fall-Wint 88-89, p. 58.
"Service Station Restroom: Wink, Texas." [Timbuktu] (2) Sum-Fall 88, p. 5.
2293. HIX, Hubert
"Dolls." [Phoenix] (9:1/2) 88, p. 67.
2294. HOAGLAND, Tony
"The Collaboration." [Ploughs] (14:1) 88, p. 111-112.
"Easter." [TriQ] (71) Wint 88, p. 175-176.
"History of Desire." [IndR] (11:2) Spr 88, p. 51-52.
"The Miracle." [Poetry] (153:3) D 88, p. 148-149.
"Proud." [Crazy] (34) Spr 88, p. 45-46.
"Rising and Falling" (for Gibb Windahl). [Crazy] (34) Spr 88, p. 47-48.
"Volunteer." [Poetry] (153:3) D 88, p. 146-148.
2295. HOBBS, Blair
"Mimi's Hobby." [Poem] (60) N 88, p. 46.
"Painting My Father." [Poem] (60) N 88, p. 44-45.
"Reading." [Poem] (60) N 88, p. 47.
"Snapshot" (for Edward). [Poem] (60) N 88, p. 43.
2296. HOBERMAN, Denny
"The Way Toward Sleep." [AntR] (46:2) Spr 88, p. 240.
2297. HOBROCK, P. J. M.
"On Walking with My Husband Through St. James Park." [Plain] (8:3) Spr-Sum 88, p. 11.
2298. HOBSON, Christopher Z.
"Eternal City." [PraS] (62:1) Spr 88, p. 28-29.
"The Radetzky March" (for Richard F. Sterba, M.D.). [PraS] (62:1) Spr 88, p. 24-25.
"Seated Male Nude" (Study for the Sistine Chapel ceiling). [PraS] (62:1) Spr 88, p. 27-28.
"Victor Serge (1890-1947)." [PraS] (62:1) Spr 88, p. 26-27.
2299. HOCHMAN, Benjamin
"Genetics." [Amelia] (4:4, #11) 88, p. 34.
2300. HODGE
"Now and Then." [SpiritSH] (54) Fall-Wint 88, p. 7.
2301. HODGE, David G.
"Spirit." [KanQ] (20:3) Sum 88, p. 182.
2302. HODGE, Margaret
"By Waves Drawing Gravel" (for Mike). [BellArk] (4:6) N-D 88, p. 6.
"Photograph Taken by My Son, Age Eight." [BellArk] (4:1) Ja-F 88, p. 4.
2303. HODGE, Marion
"Scope." [SouthernPR] (28:1) Spr 88, p. 41-42.
2304. HODGEN, John
"Catching Our Deaths." [LitR] (32:1) Fall 88, p. 104.
"Flying." [LitR] (32:1) Fall 88, p. 105.
"For the Woman Whose Husband Fell Seven Stories to His Death Trying to Get in . . . Their Locked Apartment." [PennR] (4:1) 88, p. 36.
2305. HODGINS, Philip
"The Bull." [Verse] (5:3) N 88, p. 33-34.
"Chopped Prose with Pigs." [PraS] (62:4) Wint 88-89, p. 23-26.
"The Cow." [PraS] (62:4) Wint 88-89, p. 26-27.
"An Early Mistake." [PraS] (62:4) Wint 88-89, p. 27-29.
"Shooting the Dogs." [PraS] (62:4) Wint 88-89, p. 22-23.
2306. HODGSON, Pamela
"Shared E/space Partagé" (w. Annick Perrot-Bishop). [PottPort] (10) 88, p. 9-10.
2307. HOEFER, David
"Western Swing." [Interim] (7:1) Spr 88, p. 46.
2308. HOEKSEMA, Thomas
"Blue Mouth" (tr. of Vera Larrosa). [Sonora] (14/15) Spr 88, p. 91, 93.
"Details About the Muse Who Was Ten Times a Woman" (fragment, 2, 3, tr. of Herminio Martinez). [Sonora] (14/15) Spr 88, p. 95, 97.
"Ideological Contradictions on Washing a Plate" (tr. of Kyra Galvan). [Sonora] (14/15) Spr 88, p. 99, 101-102.
"On the Facets: The Flashing" (tr. of Coral Bracho). [Sulfur] (8:1, #22) Spr 88, p. 5-8.
"Water" (tr. of Coral Bracho, w. Romelia Enríquez). [MidAR] (8:2) 88, p. 81-82.

2309. HOEY, Allen
"A Father Speaks." [MidwQ] (29:2) Wint 88, p. 226-231.
"Winter Light." [Blueline] (9:1/2) 88, p. 84.
2310. HOFER, Mariann
"Flash Point." [CinPR] (18) Fall 88, p. 33.
"Why She Lives in the Country." [CinPR] (18) Fall 88, p. 32.
2311. HOFFMAN, Daniel
"August." [Boulevard] (3:2/3) Fall 88, p. 229.
"The Cape Racer." [NewYorker] (64:18) 20 Je 88, p. 30.
"New Wine." [GettyR] (1:2) Spr 88, p. 263-264.
"Saturday." [LightY] ('88/9) 88, p. 87.
"Who Done It?" [LightY] ('88/9) 88, p. 99.
2312. HOFFMAN, Fred
"Convict Lake." [MissR] (16:1, #46) 88, p. 47.
"Mona Lisa Jumping." [MissR] (16:1, #46) 88, p. 46.
"Tornado Dreams." [MissR] (16:1, #46) 88, p. 48-49.
2313. HOFFMAN, Michael
"Day in the Netherlands." [BostonR] (13:1) F 88, p. 16.
"Dependants." [BostonR] (13:1) F 88, p. 16.
"Fine Adjustments." [BostonR] (13:1) F 88, p. 16.
"The Magic of Mantovani for Simon Korner." [BostonR] (13:1) F 88, p. 16.
"Touring Company." [BostonR] (13:1) F 88, p. 16.
"A Western Pastoral." [BostonR] (13:1) F 88, p. 16.
2314. HOFFMANN, Roald
"Evolution." [SouthwR] (73:2) Spr 88, p. 273-274.
"Grand Unification." [TriQ] (72) Spr-Sum 88, p. 150-151.
"In Need of Mending." [Nimrod] (32:1) Fall-Wint 88, p. 121-122.
"Stretch Marks." [NegC] (8:3) 88, p. 37-39.
2315. HOFMANN, Michael
"Continental Summer." [Antaeus] (60) Spr 88, p. 185.
"Kurt Schwitters in Lakeland." [Antaeus] (60) Spr 88, p. 186-187.
"Up in the Air." [PartR] (55:1) Wint 88, p. 68.
2316. HOFMANNSTHAL, Hugo von
"The Two" (tr. by Leonard Kress). [WestB] (21/22) 88, p. 74.
2317. HOFRANKO, Michael
"Happy to Have It." [Ploughs] (14:4) 88, p. 103-104.
2318. HOGAN, Linda
"Rain." [AmerV] (11) Sum 88, p. 65-66.
2319. HOGAN, Wayne
"Latest Word from My Editor." [CrabCR] (5:2) Sum 88, p. 2.
"Seriousness on the Rise." [LightY] ('88/9) 88, p. 49.
2320. HOGG, Ian
"Farmhands at 5 A.M." [Bogg] (59) 88, p. 15.
2321. HOGGARD, James
"Endurance." [KanQ] (20:3) Sum 88, p. 82.
"Improvisation Before the Introit." [HampSPR] Wint 88, p. 24-26.
"July." [SouthwR] (73:4) Aut 88, p. 554-555.
2322. HOGUE, Cynthia
"In Denmark Fish Can Sing." [NegC] (8:3) 88, p. 118-119.
"Mother of Light." [NegC] (8:3) 88, p. 42-43.
2323. HOHMANN, Marti
"Ledger: After." [SinW] (35) Sum-Fall 88, p. 66.
2324. HOKANSON, Alicia
"Leaving the Island." [CrabCR] (5:2) Sum 88, p. 6.
2325. HOLAHAN, Susan
"In the Lower Business District." [LittleM] (15:3/4) 88, p. 16.
2326. HOLDEN, Jonathan
"After Closing Luigi Cremona's *Projective Geometry*." [Poetry] (151:4) Ja 88, p. 353-354.
"The Candyman." [GeoR] (42:2) Sum 88, p. 273-274.
2327. HOLDER, Barbara
"Valhalla Cemetery." [Footwork] ('88) 88, p. 75.
2328. HOLDT, David
"Cremation Myths." [Amelia] (5:2, #13) 88, p. 87-89.
"The River at High Summer: August at the Turn." [Amelia] (5:2, #13) 88, p. 86.
"The River at High Summer: Thunderstorm." [Amelia] (5:2, #13) 88, p. 86-87.

2329. HOLINGER, Richard
"Arcimboldo's Faces" (Summer, Winter, Water, Fire). [Chelsea] (47) 88, p. 133.
"Climbing Railings" (after reading Nemerov's "Remembering the Way" in *The Southern Review*). [StoneC] (15:3/4) Spr-Sum 88, p. 65.
"Nesting Blue." [BallSUF] (29:4) Aut 88, p. 12-13.
"Paradise Shattered." [Chelsea] (47) 88, p. 132.
2330. HOLLAHAN, Eugene
"Pound Foolish: A Trilogy." [KanQ] (20:1/2) Wint-Spr 88, p. 177.
"Two Look at Each Other." [KanQ] (20:1/2) Wint-Spr 88, p. 176.
HOLLAND, Kevin Crossley
See CROSSLEY-HOLLAND, Kevin
2331. HOLLAND, Larry
"Essence." [Plain] (8:2) Wint 88, p. 7.
"Fallout." [Plain] (8:3) Spr-Sum 88, p. 25.
"Friday Night" (for Beck. A Plainsongs Award Poem). [Plain] (8:1) Fall 87, p. 18.
"Sand." [KanQ] (20:1/2) Wint-Spr 88, p. 198.
"Walk on Water" (for Paul and Jim). [KanQ] (20:1/2) Wint-Spr 88, p. 199.
2332. HOLLAND, Michelle
"That's How Guilt Is." [Footwork] ('88) 88, p. 72.
"A Week Before Christmas at Mario's." [Footwork] ('88) 88, p. 72.
2333. HOLLANDER, Benjamin
"Onome." [Sulfur] (8:2, #23) Fall 88, p. 111-112.
2334. HOLLANDER, Jean
"Snowfall." [KanQ] (20:3) Sum 88, p. 93.
2335. HOLLANDER, John
"Again after an Old Text." [WestHR] (42:4) Wint 88, p. 317.
"Edward Hopper's Seven A.M. (1948)." [NewRep] (198:5) 1 F 88, p. 37.
"For a Tall Headstone." [Poetry] (152:1) Ap 88, p. 8.
"Green-Shadowed Rocks." [WestHR] (42:4) Wint 88, p. 316.
"Island Pond." [GrandS] (7:2) Wint 88, p. 14-15.
"The Mad Potter." [NewYorker] (63:48) 18 Ja 88, p. 27.
2336. HOLLANDER, Martha
"Difficult Movie." [ParisR] (30:108) Fall 88, p. 208-209.
2337. HOLLEY, Monelle
"Out Near the Lake." [Amelia] (5:2, #13) 88, p. 130.
2338. HOLLO, Anselm
"The Art Through the Ages." [WestCR] (23:1) Spr, i.e. Sum 88, p. 6.
"Bro Hipponax" (Pentti Saarikoski, 1937-1983). [WestCR] (23:1) Spr, i.e. Sum 88, p. 5.
"Home on the Shelf." [WestCR] (23:1) Spr, i.e. Sum 88, p. 12.
"It Was All About." [WestCR] (23:1) Spr, i.e. Sum 88, p. 9.
"The Jump." [Abraxas] (37) 88, p. 71.
"The Missing Page." [WestCR] (23:1) Spr, i.e. Sum 88, p. 11.
"Naming a Ship." [Talisman] (1) Fall 88, p. 46-47.
"Rosalie." [Abraxas] (37) 88, p. 70.
"La Vida" (for Janey, mi vida). [WestCR] (23:1) Spr, i.e. Sum 88, p. 10.
"Western Thought." [WestCR] (23:1) Spr, i.e. Sum 88, p. 7-8.
2339. HOLLOWAY, Glenna
"Quitting." [PikeF] (9) Fall 88, p. 10.
2340. HOLLOWAY, John
"The Deed Is Done." [KenR] (NS 10:1) Wint 88, p. 100-101.
"The Hermit Wordman." [KenR] (NS 10:1) Wint 88, p. 99.
"Villanelle: Success Story at Sea." [KenR] (NS 10:1) Wint 88, p. 99-100.
2341. HOLLOWAY, Marcella M.
"Let Be, Let Be!" [Paint] (15:29) Spr 88, p. 19.
2342. HOLMAN, Bob
"Des Moines Dawn." [Talisman] (1) Fall 88, p. 4.
2343. HOLMES, Diane
"Painting Your Brother from Memory." [CinPR] (18) Fall 88, p. 21.
2344. HOLMES, Elizabeth
"Explanation." [SouthernPR] (28:1) Spr 88, p. 48.
2345. HOLMES, Janet
"Chez Persephone." [HayF] (3) Spr 88, p. 82-83.
"Hibiscus." [HayF] (3) Spr 88, p. 81.
2346. HOLMES, John Clellon
"At 'Arrowhead', Pittsfield, Massachusetts." [TexasR] (9:3/4) Fall-Wint 88, p. 69.

2347. HOLMES, Nancy
"The Disordered Lyric." [MalR] (85) D 88, p. 52.
"Jennie E. McDonald, 20th Birthday, Aug. 26, 1898." [MalR] (85) D 88, p. 53.
"The Marriage of Reverend Charles Kingsley." [MalR] (85) D 88, p. 54-55.
"Victorian." [MalR] (85) D 88, p. 56-57.
"You Search for History, I Read Jane Austen." [MalR] (85) D 88, p. 58-59.
2348. HOLMGREN, Mark
"Resolutions." [Grain] (16:3) Fall 88, p. 16.
2349. HOLST-WARHALF, Gail
"The Difficult Hour" (tr. of Tasos Leivaditis). [Paint] (15:30) Aut 88, p. 33.
"Family Warmth" (tr. of Tasos Leivaditis). [Paint] (15:30) Aut 88, p. 32.
2350. HOLSTEIN, Michael
"Charley's Green Guide" (at the Mobil Station). [LightY] ('88/9) 88, p. 157.
2351. HOLTAN, Peder
"Chronology." [HiramPoR] (44/45) Spr-Wint 88, p. 24.
"Like the Rain." [HiramPoR] (44/45) Spr-Wint 88, p. 25.
2352. HOLZER, Ryszard
"What Is It Like in Paradise?" (tr. by Daniel Bourne). [LitR] (31:2) Wint 88, p. 154.
2353. HOMAYOUNJAM, Haleh
"A Door to Madess" (tr. of Nader Naderpour). [Vis] (26) 88, p. 12.
"A Meteor in Darkness" (tr. of Nader Naderpour). [Vis] (26) 88, p. 12-13.
2354. HOMER
"Helen Reviews the Champions" (The Illiad, Book III, tr. by Robert Fagles). [GrandS] (8:1) Aut 88, p. 50-64.
"The Iliad" (the opening lines of the first book, tr. by Christopher Logue). [ParisR] (30:106) Spr 88, p. 221-227.
2355. HOMER, Art
"The Doctor Drives His Unfaithful Wife Home from Her Surgery." [LaurelR] (22:21) Wint 88, p. 28-29.
2356. HONEYCUTT, Irene Blair
"On Seeing Huston's Film of Joyce's *The Dead*." [Nimrod] (32:1) Fall-Wint 88, p. 113-114.
HONG, Zuo
See ZUO, Hong
2357. HONGO, Garrett Kaoru
"Ancestral Graves, Kahuku" (for Edward Hirsch). [AmerPoR] (17:1) Ja-F 88, p. 33-34.
"Billboard: Portrait of a Lady." [TriQ] (71) Wint 88, p. 109-110.
"Four Chinatown Figures." [TriQ] (71) Wint 88, p. 111-112.
"Jigoku: On the Glamour of Self-Hate." [Zyzzyva] (4:1) Spr 88, p. 116-121.
"O-Bon: Dance for the Dead." [ChamLR] (1:2, #2) Spr 88, p. 98-99.
"The Pier." [ChamLR] (1:2, #2) Spr 88, p. 100-103.
"The Pier." [Chelsea] (47) 88, p. 57-59.
2358. HONIG, Edwin
"Autopsychography" (tr. of Fernando Pessoa, w. Susan M. Brown). [ConnPR] (7:1) 88, p. 44.
"I Never Kept Sheep" (From "The Keeper of Sheep": I, tr. of Fernando Pessoa, w. Susan M. Brown). [ConnPR] (7:1) 88, p. 41.
"Minotaur." [SewanR] (96:4) Fall 88, p. 603-604.
"Now Ashen Gray Tinges the Balding Brow" (tr. of Fernando Pessoa, w. Susan M. Brown). [ConnPR] (7:1) 88, p. 42.
"Oblique Rain" (Excerpt, II, tr. of Fernando Pessoa, w. Susan M. Brown). [ConnPR] (7:1) 88, p. 44.
"Pessoa's Last Masquerade." [ConnPR] (7:1) 88, p. 34-35.
"Salutation to Walt Whitman" (Excerpt, tr. of Fernando Pessoa, w. Susan M. Brown). [ConnPR] (7:1) 88, p. 43.
"Under Sirius." [SouthernPR] (28:1) Spr 88, p. 37.
"Written in a Book Abandoned on the Trip" (tr. of Fernando Pessoa, w. Susan M. Brown). [ConnPR] (7:1) 88, p. 43.
"You men who raised stone pillars . . ." (from "Maritime Ode," tr. of Fernando Pessoa, w. Susan M. Brown). [ConnPR] (7:1) 88, p. 42.
2359. HOOD, Michael
"The Leaves" (Burrillville, from a sequence of Rhode Island poems). [StoneC] (15:3/4) Spr-Sum 88, p. 28.
2360. HOOGESTRAAT, Jane
"Shared Quarters." [NoDaQ] (56:2) Spr 88, p. 93.

2361. HOOGLAND, Joan
"In the Gallery" (after seeing Marcia Perkins' drawings, Studies From Life). [Dandel] (15:1) Spr-Sum 88, p. 14-18.
"The Man I Love Is Going." [Event] (17:2) Sum 88, p. 61.
2362. HOOLIHAN, Patricia
"On Returning Home." [BellR] (11:1) Spr 88, p. 6.
2363. HOOPER, Edward L.
"When the Tracks Are Gone." [Kaleid] (17) Sum-Fall 88, p. 29.
2364. HOOPER, Patricia
"At Dinner." [SouthernPR] (28:1) Spr 88, p. 69.
2365. HOOVER, Carmen
"Song to Vermin Town." [Spirit] (9:1) 88, p. 44-45.
2366. HOOVER, Paul
"The Dog." [Caliban] (4) 88, p. 119.
"The Novel" (Selections: "Twenty-four," "Twenty-five"). [NewAW] (4) Fall 88, p. 15-22.
"Water." [Caliban] (4) 88, p. 119.
2367. HOPE, Tryna
"In Her Voice." [SinW] (36) Wint 88-89, p. 11-12.
2368. HOPES, David
"Eurydice." [StoneC] (15:3/4) Spr-Sum 88, p. 50-51.
"Georges de la Tour: *The Penitent Magdalen*, circa 1640." [HiramPoR] (44/45) Spr-Wint 88, p. 64-66.
"Photographs of Mother As A Girl." [StoneC] (15:3/4) Spr-Sum 88, p. 51-52.
2369. HOPPER, Edward
"Gary Zebrun." [SewanR] (96:1) Wint 88, p. 54.
2370. HORACE
"I.23. You shun me, Chloe, like a young fawn" (tr. by Joseph S. Salemi). [HolCrit] (25:5) D 88, p. 15.
"Ode 1,5: To Pyrrha" (tr. by Robert Boucheron). [NewEngR] (10:3) Spr 88, p. 351.
"Ode III:13" (tr. by Joe Malone). [CharR] (14:1) Spr 88, p. 91-92.
2371. HORNER, Jan
"Sculpture Class." [PraF] (9:3) Aut 88, p. 68-69.
2372. HORNING, Ron
"The Hand" (tr. of Carlos Drummond de Andrade). [NewYorker] (64:37) 31 O 88, p. 40.
"Innocents of Leblon" (tr. of Carlos Drummond de Andrade). [NewYorker] (64:21) 11 Jl 88, p. 26.
"Within a Budding Grove" (tr. of Carlos Drummond de Andrade). [NewYorker] (64:21) 11 Jl 88, p. 26.
2373. HORNOSTY, Cornelia C.
"A Cautionary Note." [Descant] (19:2, #61) Sum 88, p. 19-20.
"Counter Intelligence." [Descant] (19:2, #61) Sum 88, p. 22-23.
"Questionnaire." [Descant] (19:2, #61) Sum 88, p. 21.
"A Sunny Day." [CanLit] (117) Sum 88, p. 61.
2374. HOROWITZ, Mikhail
"Thembi" (writ listening to pharoah sanders' *thembi*). [AlphaBS] (3) Je 88, p. 48.
2375. HORST, JoAnn
"Twenty-Five Cents." [SlipS] (8) 88, p. 5.
2376. HORTON, Barbara
"The Bedroom Window Frames." [KanQ] (20:3) Sum 88, p. 187.
2377. HORTON, Batista
"The One That Didn't Get Away." [DenQ] (22:3) Wint 88, p. 109.
2378. HORVATH, Margaret
"Painting of Lady Playing Violin." [CapilR] (48) 88, p. 12.
"Water." [CapilR] (48) 88, p. 13.
2379. HOSKIN, Laurie J.
"Eulogy in Three Parts." [SinW] (32) Sum 87, p. 49-51.
"Release." [SinW] (32) Sum 87, p. 47-48.
2380. HOSKIN, William
"Old Mountain House." [Blueline] (9:1/2) 88, p. 18.
2381. HOSKIN, William D.
"Blur of Red Fox." [HiramPoR] (44/45) Spr-Wint 88, p. 68.
"Yo Yo Ma at the Eastman." [HiramPoR] (44/45) Spr-Wint 88, p. 67.
2382. HOSPITAL, Carolina
"Images." [Amelia] (5:2, #13) 88, p. 66.

2383. HOSTETLER, Marianne
"Spiders." [Plain] (8:2) Wint 88, p. 22.
2384. HOTALING, Debra
"At the Holiday." [Spirit] (9:1) 88, p. 54.
"Late Afternoon, Late 30s." [SouthernR] (24:2) Spr 88, p. 319.
"News of the World." [SouthernR] (24:2) Spr 88, p. 318.
2385. HOTCHKISS, Joanne
"From My Window." [Footwork] ('88) 88, p. 73.
"Lullaby." [Footwork] ('88) 88, p. 74.
"The Wedding 1954." [Footwork] ('88) 88, p. 73.
2386. HOUGEN, Judith
"Why the Young Girl Dreams of Horses." [GeoR] (42:1) Spr 88, p. 70.
2387. HOUGHTON, Barbara C.
"Return to Vermont." [Blueline] (9:1/2) 88, p. 27.
2388. HOUGHTON, Timothy
"Omen." [Turnstile] (1:2) 88, p. 99.
"Visit." [ColEng] (50:1) Ja 88, p. 51.
2389. HOUSE, Elizabeth
"Haiku: A cardboard coffin" (The 14th Kansas Poetry Contest, First Prize). [LittleBR] (5:2) Wint 88-89, p. 69.
"He'd abused his health all he dared to." [Amelia] (5:2, #13) 88, p. 119.
2390. HOUSE, Tom
"The Madman's Resume." [Pembroke] (20) 88, p. 172.
2391. HOUSTON, Beth
"Delusion." [LitR] (31:3) Spr 88, p. 311.
"Fall's End." [Poem] (60) N 88, p. 50-51.
"Indian Summer." [Poem] (60) N 88, p. 49.
"An Old Book." [Poem] (60) N 88, p. 48.
"Snake in the Cellar." [MinnR] (NS 30/31) Spr-Fall 88, p. 39-40.
"Transmigration." [Poem] (60) N 88, p. 52.
2392. HOUSTON, Peyton
"Instructions in Navigation." [TexasR] (9:3/4) Fall-Wint 88, p. 70.
HOUTEN, Lois van
See Van HOUTEN, Lois
HOVANESSIAN, Diana Der
See DER-HOVANESSIAN, Diana
2393. HOWARD, Ben
"In Irishtown." [KenR] (NS 10:3) Sum 88, p. 118.
"The Makers." [MidwQ] (29:4) Sum 88, p. 458.
"No Parking" (For Paul Strong). [KenR] (NS 10:3) Sum 88, p. 119.
2394. HOWARD, David
"South Africa." [PottPort] (10) 88, p. 38.
2395. HOWARD, Eugene (Eugene C.)
"If I Could I Would and I'm Working On It" (for the circle). [PaintedB] (32/33) 88, p. 145-146.
"Still Blue Above the Stormy Weather" (Selections: 13-14). [PaintedB] (34) 88, p. 45.
2396. HOWARD, Richard
"Always With You." [CinPR] (17) Spr 88, p. 5-7.
"Colored Stones" (Occidental haiku for the painter Robin Utterback). [YaleR] (77:3) Spr 88, p. 397-399.
"Concerning K." [NewYorker] (64:15) 30 My 88, p. 32.
"For James Boatwright" (died of AIDS, 1937-1988). [WestHR] (42:4) Wint 88, p. 318-319.
"Mademoiselle's Last Sunday." [Nat] (246:18) 7 My 88, p. 654.
"A Sorcerer's Apprentice." [GrandS] (8:1) Aut 88, p. 17-20.
"Triangulations" (For Stephen Orgel." [Poetry] (151:5) F 88, p. 402-406.
2397. HOWE, Fanny
"11/11." [Ploughs] (14:4) 88, p. 59.
"The Border." [Sulfur] (8:1, #22) Spr 88, p. 40-45.
2398. HOWE, Marie
"The Good Reason for Our Forgetting." [PartR] (55:2) Spr 88, p. 280-281.
"The Good Thief." [GrahamHR] (11) Spr 88, p. 65-66.
"Letter to My Sister." [GrahamHR] (11) Spr 88, p. 64.
"Mary's Argument." [Agni] (26) 88, p. 188.

2399. HOWE, Susan
"History Professor Emeritus." [KanQ] (20:4) Fall 88, p. 5.
"On a [p <suddenly . . ." [Sulfur] (8:1, #22) Spr 88, p. 9-16.
"Outpost itinerant." [Sequoia] (32:1) Spr-Sum 88, p. 42.
"The Stolen Television Set." [GreensboroR] (45) Wint 88-89, p. 72.
"We see liberty." [Sequoia] (32:1) Spr-Sum 88, p. 43.
"Why I Am a Witch." [KanQ] (20:4) Fall 88, p. 5.
2400. HOWELL, Christopher
"The Imp of the Unquestionable." [CutB] (31/32) 88, p. 46-47.
"Lyric with Blue Horses" (For David Luckert). [CutB] (31/32) 88, back cover.
"Mean and Stupid." [MidwQ] (30:1) Aut 88, p. 71-72.
"September in a Line Shack Outside Girard, Kansas." [MidwQ] (30:1) Aut 88, p. 72.
"Sweat Socks from Hell." [CutB] (31/32) 88, p. 45.
2401. HOWES, Barbara
"Among Shells." [TexasR] (9:3/4) Fall-Wint 88, p. 71.
2402. HOWLAND, John, Jr.
"Nothing on rth." [Timbuktu] (1) Wint-Spr 88, p. 36.
2403. HU, Meng-jie
"Smoking People: Encountering the New Chinese Poetry" (Chapbook 19, tr. by Hu Meng-jie et al.). [BelPoJ] (39:2) Wint 88-89, 76 p.
2404. HU, Shiguang
"Crying Ospreys" (tr. of anonymous poem form the *Book of Songs*). [AntR] (46:2) Spr 88, p. 135.
"Quince" (tr. of anonymous poem form the *Book of Songs*). [AntR] (46:2) Spr 88, p. 156.
"The Reeds" (tr. of anonymous poem form the *Book of Songs*). [AntR] (46:2) Spr 88, p. 165.
HUA, Li Min
See LI, Min Hua
2405. HUACO, Enrique
"Recitative" (tr. by Joe Bolton). [ColR] (NS 15:2) Fall-Wint 88, p. 86.
2406. HUDDLE, David
"Things I Know, Things I Don't." [PraS] (62:1) Spr 88, p. 48-67.
2407. HUDGINS, Andrew
"Against Gardens." [SouthernR] (24:4) Aut 88, p. 939-940.
"All of Us Beneath Red Cowbowy Hats." [CinPR] (17) Spr 88, p. 12.
"Bewilderments of the Eye." [Hudson] (40:4) Wint 88, p. 612-613.
"Compost: An Ode." [CinPR] (17) Spr 88, p. 10-11.
"The Cult of the Lost Cause" (Camp Robin, near Ashville, August, 1882). [MSS] (6:2) 88, p. 3-7.
"A Father on the Marsh." [SouthernR] (24:1) Wint 88, p. 147-149.
"Fruit." [Hudson] (40:4) Wint 88, p. 613.
"The Garden Changes." [SouthernR] (24:4) Aut 88, p. 942-943.
"Green Inside the Door: A Memory." [Hudson] (40:4) Wint 88, p. 610-612.
"Heat Lightning in a Time of Drought." [GeoR] (42:3) Fall 88, p. 506-509.
"The Hereafter." [Hudson] (40:4) Wint 88, p. 609-610.
"How Shall We Sing the Lord's Song in a Strange Land?" [GeoR] (42:3) Fall 88, p. 504-506.
"A Husband on the Marsh." [MissouriR] (11:1) 88, p. 99-101.
"Mostly My Nightmares Are Dull." [ParisR] (30:107) Sum 88, p. 124.
"A Soldier on the Marsh." [SouthernR] (24:1) Wint 88, p. 145-147.
"Sufficient Witness." [MissouriR] (11:1) 88, p. 104.
"The Ugly Flowers." [SouthernR] (24:4) Aut 88, p. 941-942.
"What Light Destroys." [MissouriR] (11:1) 88, p. 102-103.
"Worlds." [Hudson] (40:4) Wint 88, p. 614.
2408. HUDSON, David
"Of the Sad Immortality of Matter." [Ascent] (14:1) 88, p. 47-48.
"The River So Far." [Ascent] (14:1) 88, p. 48.
2409. HUDSON, Marc
"A Figure for Time." [SewanR] (96:2) Spr 88, p. 214-215.
2410. HUDZIK, Robert
"The Farmer's Daughter." [CinPR] (17) Spr 88, p. 40-41.
2411. HUERTA, David
"November Notebook — 1976" (Excerpt, tr. by Linda Scheer). [Caliban] (5) 88, p. 98-99.

2412. HUETER, Diane
"At Nine." [KanQ] (20:3) Sum 88, p. 243.
2413. HUEZO MIXCO, Miguel
"Para Que lo Entiendas de una Vez." [Mairena] (10:25) 88, p. 158.
2414. HUFF, Steven
"August." [PaintedB] (34) 88, p. 12.
2415. HUFFMAN, Heather Marie
"Glass Dreams." [Footwork] ('88) 88, p. 82.
2416. HUFFSTICKLER, Albert
"Evva." [HolCrit] (25:2) Ap 88, p. 12.
"Girl from the Border." [Lactuca] (10) Je 88, p. 24-25.
"Journey's End." [RagMag] (6:2) Fall 88, p. 50-51.
"Making Do." [Lactuca] (10) Je 88, p. 25.
"My Mother Watched Wrestling." [Lactuca] (9) F 88, p. 42.
"Not What It's All About." [Lactuca] (10) Je 88, p. 28-29.
"Outsider." [Lactuca] (10) Je 88, p. 26.
"Small Graces" (Mar. 26, 1988, Cafe du Jour). [SwampR] (1:2/3) D 88, p. 58.
"Songs I Grew Up On." [Lactuca] (10) Je 88, p. 27-28.
2417. HUGGINS, Peter
"Choctaw Point." [CreamCR] (12:2) Sum 88, p. 197.
2418. HUGHES, Henry J.
"In Honor of This Church." [HiramPoR] (44/45) Spr-Wint 88, p. 26.
2419. HUGHES, Sophie
"So Much Dying." [Interim] (7:1) Spr 88, p. 38.
2420. HUGHES, Ted
"The Black Rhino." [Antaeus] (60) Spr 88, p. 176-182.
2421. HULL, Barbara
"Absence of Heart." [Footwork] ('88) 88, p. 20.
"Hermes." [Footwork] ('88) 88, p. 20.
"Leaving Together." [Interim] (7:2) Fall 88, p. 14.
"Portrait of a Former Husband." [Interim] (7:2) Fall 88, p. 13.
2422. HULL, C. E.
"The Dead Sea Along 1153." [PraS] (62:4) Wint 88-89, p. 127.
2423. HULL, David
"Shield." [CanLit] (119) Wint 88, p. 99-100.
2424. HULL, Lynda
"Adagio" (for Mark Doty). [GettyR] (1:3) Sum 88, p. 454-455.
"Black Mare." [Agni] (27) 88, p. 24-26.
"Magical Thinking." [Agni] (27) 88, p. 27-28.
"Midnight Reports." [Agni] (27) 88, p. 29-30.
"Shore Leave." [Poetry] (143, i.e. 153:2) N 88, p. 75-76.
"Slick Packages." [Poetry] (143, i.e. 153:2) N 88, p. 77-78.
"Visiting Hour." [Agni] (27) 88, p. 22-23.
2425. HULL, Robert
"Crocuses." [CumbPR] (7:2) Spr 88, p. 32-33.
"Gnome's Tale." [CumbPR] (7:2) Spr 88, p. 36-38.
"The Harbour's." [CumbPR] (7:2) Spr 88, p. 30-31.
"Reassurance by Tadpole." [CumbPR] (7:2) Spr 88, p. 34-35.
2426. HULSE, Michael
"Addressed to Shave." [AntigR] (73) Spr 88, p. 8-9.
"Sundown, Landing the Catch" (Pangandaran, Java). [AntigR] (73) Spr 88, p. 7.
"Tum Ti Tum" (after Goethe). [AntigR] (73) Spr 88, p. 9.
2427. HUMES, Harry
"My Wife Vanishes in a Field of Sunflowers." [WestB] (21/22) 88, p. 20-21.
"One Afternoon at the End of the Year the Baboon Yawns." [Salm] (80) Fall 88, p. 114.
"Opening Day" (for Roger Edelman, 1st Prize, 15th Anniversary Competition). [StoneC] (16:1/2) Fall-Wint 88-89, unpaged front matter.
"Potatoes and Time in November." [WestB] (21/22) 88, p. 22.
"The Tulpehocken." [Salm] (80) Fall 88, p. 112-113.
"Waiting in the Crow Roost, He Thinks of the Woman Who Went Back to the City." [Salm] (80) Fall 88, p. 115-116.
"You Cannot Quite Get to the Bottom of a Morning with Clouds." [PoetryNW] (29:2) Sum 88, p. 3.
2428. HUMMER, T. R.
"The March Personifications." [WestHR] (42:3) Aut 88, p. 244.

"Salt Flats Crossing: Homage ot Vachel Lindsay." [WestHR] (42:2) Sum 88, p. 112-114.
2429. HUMPHREY, Paul
"Seasoning." [LightY] ('88/9) 88, p. 124.
2430. HUMPHREY, Ron
"Delta Sunset." [PikeF] (9) Fall 88, p. 29.
"White Ao Dai." [PikeF] (9) Fall 88, p. 29.
2431. HUMPHREYS, Helen
"Always." [Event] (17:3) Fall 88, p. 85-88.
"From Windows." [Event] (17:3) Fall 88, p. 82-85.
2432. HUMPHRIES, Dwight E.
"Broken Bone." [Wind] (18:63) 88, p. 18.
"Tableau with Red Car." [DeKalbLAJ] (21:1) Wint 88, p. 59.
"Tableau with Red Car." [DeKalbLAJ] (21:2) Spr 88, p. 38-39.
2433. HUMPHRIES, Jefferson
"Christmas Party." [SouthernR] (24:4) Aut 88, p. 958-961.
"Poe As Cause and Effect of the Civil War, or, Why the South Is a Nation of Liars." [SoCaR] (20:2) Spr 88, p. 2-3.
2434. HUNT, Leigh
"Smile." [Amelia] (5:1, #12) 88, p. 93.
"Stomping the Blues." [NegC] (8:3) 88, p. 186-187.
"To Your Native Intelligence." [Amelia] (5:2, #13) 88, p. 49.
2435. HUNT, William
"Ancient Light." [YellowS] (27) Aut 88, p. 8.
2436. HUNTER, Donnell
"Cows." [CrabCR] (5:3) Fall 88, p. 10.
"Gentians." [HawaiiR] (12:2, #24) Fall 88, p. 51.
"A Stone Bird." [Vis] (27) 88, p. 33.
2437. HUNTINGTON, Cynthia
"Off-Season Motel Room." [PacificR] (6) Spr 88, p. 7.
2438. HUNTINGTON, Jack
"Untitled: The rotation method." [JlNJPo] (10:1/2) 88, p. 20.
2439. HUNTINGTON, Rania
"The First Words" (Poetry Contest Winner). [HarvardA] (122:3) Mr 88, p. 11.
"For Li He" (tinted with others, Poetry Contest Honorable Mention). [HarvardA] (122:3) Mr 88, p. 13.
2440. HUNTLEY, David
"Love of Weather." [GettyR] (1:3) Sum 88, p. 456.
2441. HURFORD, Chris
"The Dumbless Beast." [Verse] (5:2) Jl 88, p. 18.
2442. HURLEY, Maureen
"Exodus, Exile and Desire." [ChamLR] (2:1, #3) Fall 88, p. 49.
2443. HURLOW, Marcia L.
"A Letter from the Outcrops." [CinPR] (18) Fall 88, p. 18.
"Unrequited at the Longdistance Diner." [PaintedB] (36) 88, p. 38.
"Unrequited at the Longdistance Diner." [Plain] (8:2) Wint 88, p. 8.
2444. HUSTON, Robert
"Folly Pool." [Bogg] (60) 88, p. 40.
2445. HUTCHINSON, Ann
"The Intensity of Our Loving." [SinW] (33) Fall 87, p. 111.
2446. HUTCHISON, Joseph
"Homage to William Matthews." [CharR] (14:1) Spr 88, p. 85.
"Journey with Music." [HighP] (3:3) Wint 88-89, p. 73.
"Vander Meer at Sundown." [KanQ] (20:3) Sum 88, p. 137.
"The Voice." [CharR] (14:1) Spr 88, p. 86.
2447. HUTH, Geof A.
"Blackberrying Summer." [Poem] (59) My 88, p. 5-6.
"Clay Todd & the Idea of Stone Arabia." [BellArk] (4:6) N-D 88, p. 3.
"Deafsong." [Poem] (59) My 88, p. 9.
"The Fruiterer." [KanQ] (20:3) Sum 88, p. 149.
"Two Receipts." [Poem] (59) My 88, p. 7-8.
2448. HUTTON, Virgil
"Haiku" (5 poems). [PikeF] (9) Fall 88, p. 7.
2449. HWANG, Jinie
"Ah, What Have I Done" (tr. by Constantine Contogenis and Wolhee Choe). [TriQ] (72) Spr-Sum 88, p. 183.

"At Cold Solstice" (tr. by Constantine Contogenis and Wolhee Choe). [TriQ] (72) Spr-Sum 88, p. 183.
"Whenever Did I" (tr. by Constantine Contogenis and Wolhee Choe). [TriQ] (72) Spr-Sum 88, p. 183.

2450. HYDE, Janine
"The Tracks." [HangL] (52) 88, p. 80.

2451. HYETT, Barbara Helfgott
"Horseshoe Crabs." [SouthernPR] (28:2) Fall 88, p. 23.

2452. HYLAND, Gary
"Becoming Dead." [Grain] (16:4) Wint 88, p. 67-69.
"Case History 3." [CapilR] (47) 88, p. 74.
"Her Choice." [PraF] (9:4) Wint 88-89, p. 11.
"Making Place." [PraF] (9:4) Wint 88-89, p. 14.
"The Same Old Story." [PraF] (9:4) Wint 88-89, p. 13.
"Self-Defence." [CapilR] (47) 88, p. 75.
"Telling Fortunes." [PraF] (9:4) Wint 88-89, p. 10.
"Wrecks." [PraF] (9:4) Wint 88-89, p. 12.

2453. IBAÑEZ ROSAZZA, Mercedes
"Cansancio." [Inti] (26/27) Otoño 87-Primavera 88, p. 170.
"Metáfora." [Inti] (26/27) Otoño 87-Primavera 88, p. 169-170.

2454. IBN DHARIH, Qais, Majnun
"Lubna's Word" (tr. by Arthur Wormhoudt). [Paint] (15:30) Aut 88, p. 42.

2455. IBRAHIM, Huma
"Kamala Das." [MassR] (29:4) Wint 88-89, p. 682.

2456. IBSEN, Henrik
"Afraid of the Light" (tr. by Michael Feingold). [Bomb] (24) Sum 88, p. 51.
"Bird and Birdcatcher" (tr. by Michael Feingold). [Bomb] (24) Sum 88, p. 51.
"Burned Ships" (tr. by Michael Feingold). [Bomb] (24) Sum 88, p. 51.
"The Murder of Abraham Lincoln" (tr. by Michael Feingold). [Bomb] (24) Sum 88, p. 50.
"The Stormy Petrel" (tr. by Michael Feingold). [Bomb] (24) Sum 88, p. 51.
"A Swan" (tr. by Michael Feingold). [Bomb] (24) Sum 88, p. 51.
"A Verse" (tr. by Michael Feingold). [Bomb] (24) Sum 88, p. 51.

2457. IERODIACONOU, Andriana
"Going to New York" (after Cavafy, tr. by the author). [GrahamHR] (11) Spr 88, p. 105.
"The Heart of Nicosia" (tr. by the author). [GrahamHR] (11) Spr 88, p. 102-103.
"Kyrie Eleison" (tr. by the author). [GrahamHR] (11) Spr 88, p. 100.
"Love Song" (tr. by the author). [GrahamHR] (11) Spr 88, p. 104.
"An Orange" (tr. by the author). [GrahamHR] (11) Spr 88, p. 101.

2458. IGNATOW, David
"Epitaph for a City." [PaintedB] (32/33) 88, p. 93.
"From Time to Time." [PaintedB] (32/33) 88, p. 94.
"If." [ManhatPR] (10) Ja 88, p. 25.
"If." [Poetry] (151:5) F 88, p. 399.
"In Life." [ManhatPR] (10) Ja 88, p. 24.
"Its Power." [PoetryE] (25) Spr 88, p. 114.
"Leaves." [ManhatPR] (10) Ja 88, p. 25.
"The Life." [PaintedB] (32/33) 88, p. 93.
"Neighborhood." [WilliamMR] (26:1) Spr 88, p. 66.
"Notes, 198- ." [BlackWR] (14:2) Spr 88, p. 100-101.
"Notes, 1982." [BlackWR] (14:2) Spr 88, p. 98-99.
"Of the Living." [BlackWR] (14:2) Spr 88, p. 104.
"Sequence I." [BlackWR] (14:2) Spr 88, p. 102.
"A Sequence I." [GettyR] (1:2) Spr 88, p. 261-262.
"Six Love Poems" (Selections: 1, 4, 6). [Poetry] (151:5) F 88, p. 398-399.
"Suburbia II." [ManhatPR] (10) Ja 88, p. 25.
"Summary." [ManhatPR] (10) Ja 88, p. 24.
"Summer." [ManhatPR] (10) Ja 88, p. 26.
"Sunset." [ManhatPR] (10) Ja 88, p. 24.
"Surface." [PaintedB] (32/33) 88, p. 94.
"These Words." [BlackWR] (14:2) Spr 88, p. 103.

2459. IINO, Tomoyuki
"The Dean Man" (tr. of Nobuo Ayukawa). [Stand] (29:3) Sum 88, p. 23.
"Ecstasy of a Solitary Cheiropter" (tr. of Takashi Hiraide). [Stand] (29:3) Sum 88, p. 25.

"In the Morning, Why?" (tr. of Ryuichi Tamura). [Stand] (29:3) Sum 88, p. 21.
"The Man Who Read Homer" (tr. of Junzaburo Nishiwaki). [Stand] (29:3) Sum 88, p. 22.
"Parting" (tr. of Sakutaro Hagiwara). [Stand] (29:3) Sum 88, p. 22.
"Spring" (tr. of Machiko Kishimoto). [Stand] (29:3) Sum 88, p. 24.
"Summer Letter" (tr. of Ryuichi Tamura). [Stand] (29:3) Sum 88, p. 20.

2460. ILCE GOMEZ, Ana
"Street in Summer" (tr. by Nancy Esposito). [AmerPoR] (17:2) Mr-Ap 88, p. 31.
"Turtle" (tr. by Nancy Esposito). [AmerPoR] (17:2) Mr-Ap 88, p. 31.

2461. INADA, Lawson Fusao
"Monk's Prosody." [Caliban] (4) 88, p. 60.
"Two Variations (Linear and Percussive) on a Theme by Thelonious Monk as Inspired by Mal Waldron." [Caliban] (4) 88, p. 61-66.

2462. INEZ, Colette
"Aubade." [Ploughs] (14:4) 88, p. 113.
"Autumn Notes." [TarRP] (28:1) Fall 88, p. 6.
"The Bequest." [NoAmR] (273:3) S 88, p. 45.
"Contentions." [LaurelR] (22:2) Sum 88, p. 6.
"Early June Meditation at Lakeside." [PoetryNW] (29:1) Spr 88, p. 16-17.
"Just Dessert." [LightY] ('88/9) 88, p. 186.
"Midwest Albas." [Ploughs] (14:4) 88, p. 14.
"Setting Out from the Lowlands." [Boulevard] (3:2/3) Fall 88, p. 177-178.
"Spinoza Doesn't Come Here Any More." [Boulevard] (3:2/3) Fall 88, p. 175-176.
"Taking Calls in Freeport, New York." [LaurelR] (22:2) Sum 88, p. 5.

2463. INGERSON, Martin I.
"Bald Knob Summit and On." [BellArk] (4:5) S-O 88, p. 8.
"Bright Clouds in Transit, Texas." [BellArk] (4:2) Mr-Ap 88, p. 9.
"Day Breaks Over the Cascades." [BellArk] (4:4) Jl-Ag 88, p. 10.
"Kelcema Lake." [BellArk] (4:6) N-D 88, p. 4.
"Morphic Fields." [BellArk] (4:6) N-D 88, p. 17.
"Red Blonde Dancing the Process Proceeds" (for my daughter Ingrid). [BellArk] (4:1) Ja-F 88, p. 4.
"Solar Winds." [BellArk] (4:3) My-Je 88, p. 3.

2464. INMAN, Will
"Recognitions." [Abraxas] (37) 88, p. 51.
"Writing Board." [WindO] (50) Aut 88, p. 24.

2465. INSKEEP-FOX, Sandra
"All Thing Trivial Are Woman's." [CentR] (32:3) Sum 88, p. 277.
"My Ma Speaks Like a Poem." [CimR] (82) Ja 88, p. 62.
"Star Struck." [LightY] ('88/9) 88, p. 42.

2466. IRAHETA SANTOS, Julio
"El Poeta y la Esposa." [Mairena] (10:25) 88, p. 156.

2467. IRIE, Kevin
"Autumnal." [Quarry] (37:1) Wint 88, p. 72-73.
"Baited." [Quarry] (37:1) Wint 88, p. 74.

2468. IRION, Mary Jean
"Early Morning: Driving Through." [SouthernHR] (22:1) Wint 88, p. 33.

2469. IRWIN, Mark
"Arcadia" (Selection: Part Nine). [SenR] (18:1) 88, p. 35-37.
"Cheese." [LightY] ('88/9) 88, p. 131.
"Church." [CinPR] (18) Fall 88, p. 69.
"Evergreen." [CinPR] (18) Fall 88, p. 70.
"It's Tough Being American." [LightY] ('88/9) 88, p. 43-44.
"Prayer." [CinPR] (18) Fall 88, p. 68.
"Tomato Soup." [Atlantic] (261:5) My 88, p. 46.

2470. ISERMAN, Bruce
"The Clasp of Love." [Grain] (16:1) Spr 88, p. 24-25.
"Eulogy." [Grain] (16:1) Spr 88, p. 23.
"Moving." [CanLit] (117) Sum 88, p. 80.

2471. ISSENHUTH, Jean-Pierre
"Le Jardin Parle." [Os] (27) 88, p. 2.
"Pin d'Ecosse." [Os] (27) 88, p. 16.

2472. ISTARU, Ana
"I Didn't Ask for the War" (tr. by Zoe Anglesey). [ColR] (NS 15:1) Spr-Sum 88, p. 73-74.
"Minute Death in Bed" (tr. by Zoë Anglesey). [FiveFR] (6) 88, p. 38-39.

"Muerte Mínima en una Cama." [FiveFR] (6) 88, p. 36-37.
"Por Mi Libertad." [Mairena] (10:25) 88, p. 141.
"We Are" (tr. by Zoë Anglesey). [CrabCR] (5:1) Wint 88, p. 25.

2473. ITO, Sally
"Begging Bowl." [Grain] (16:3) Fall 88, p. 87.
"Like Stones." [Grain] (16:3) Fall 88, p. 86.

2474. ITURRALDE, Iraida
"Family Album: Snapshots" (Selections: 3 poems, tr. of José Triana, w. Lourdes Gil). [Lyra] (1:4) 88, p. 22-23.

2475. IUPPA, M. J.
"Familiarity." [YellowS] (26) Spr 88, p. 10.
"Windfall." [StoneC] (16:1/2) Fall-Wint 88-89, p. 58.

2476. IVERSON, Roderick
"Balkan Nights" (tr. of Thomas Günther). [Trans] (20) Spr 88, p. 260.
"Emergency Exit" (tr. of Richard Pietrass). [Trans] (20) Spr 88, p. 259.
"Over the Blue Mountains" (tr. of Thomas Günther). [Trans] (20) Spr 88, p. 261.
"Shadow Algae" (tr. of Richard Pietrass). [Trans] (20) Spr 88, p. 258.

2477. IVIMY, May
"Flying a Kite." [Pembroke] (20) 88, p. 105.

IZUMI, Shikibu
See SHIKIBU, Izumi

2478. JACKSON, Angela
"The Love of Travellers" (Doris, Sandra and Sheryl). [Callaloo] (11:2, #35) Spr 88, p. 211.

2479. JACKSON, Haywood
"Le Jour de l'An, 1982." [LittleM] (15:3/4) 88, p. 30.
"The Reviewing Stand." [StoneC] (15:3/4) Spr-Sum 88, p. 19.

2480. JACKSON, Laura (Riding)
"Lamenting the Terms of Modern Praise" (A Private Statement). [Chelsea] (47) 88, p. 3.

2481. JACKSON, Leslie M.
"With Mother in the Morning." [CanLit] (119) Wint 88, p. 44.

2482. JACKSON, Reuben M.
"Big Chill Variations." [Vis] (28) 88, p. 21.
"Edward" (after Etheridge Knight). [PaintedB] (32/33) 88, p. 111-112.
"Voyeurs — 1969." [Gargoyle] (35) 88, p. 119.

2483. JACKSON, Richard
"Eight Ball." [Poetry] (151:6) Mr 88, p. 487-489.
"A Hand in the Tree." [Poetry] (151:6) Mr 88, p. 484-487.
"Hobbies." [PraS] (62:3) Fall 88, p. 34-35.
"Hope." [PraS] (62:3) Fall 88, p. 29-33.
"The Other Day." [BlackWR] (15:1) Fall 88, p. 118-119.
"The Sum of the Drafts Exceeds the Whole." [NoAmR] (273:2) Je 88, p. 12-13.

2484. JACOB, Catherine
"The Kitchen Dance." [PottPort] (10) 88, p. 37.

2485. JACOB, John
"The Girl with One Arm." [SpoonRQ] (13:1) Wint 88, p. 25.

2486. JACOBIK, Gray
"Biker." [OntR] (28) Spr-Sum 88, p. 103-104.
"The Country Road." [Blueline] (9:1/2) 88, p. 36.
"The End of August." [CreamCR] (12:2) Sum 88, p. 200.
"Honeymoon" (Rosebud, Alabama, 1966). [OntR] (28) Spr-Sum 88, p. 102-103.
"The Man Who Feared Women." [BallSUF] (29:4) Aut 88, p. 10.
"Night and Day." [CreamCR] (12:2) Sum 88, p. 195.
"The Old Story." [HolCrit] (25:1) F 88, p. 14.
"Postcard Photograph." [BellR] (11:2) Fall 88, p. 31.
"The Soft Light." [CreamCR] (12:2) Sum 88, p. 194.
"The Turn." [Blueline] (9:1/2) 88, p. 36.
"The Woodstove." [Blueline] (9:1/2) 88, p. 37.

2487. JACOBITZ, Regina
"Magic Lantern." [Plain] (8:2) Wint 88, p. 12.

2488. JACOBOWITZ, Judah (Judah L.)
"Artists Models at the Fair." [JlNJPo] (10:1/2) 88, p. 42.
"French Hotel Mystery." [PaintedB] (36) 88, p. 92.
"Life Urges." [DeKalbLAJ] (21:3/4) 88, p. 57.
"Model Apple." [PaintedB] (36) 88, p. 93.

"The Sun and the Moon." [Plain] (8:2) Wint 88, p. 35.
"Tomorrow's Promotions." [JlNJPo] (10:1/2) 88, p. 21.

2489. JACOBS, Jennifer
"Russell." [HangL] (52) 88, p. 79.

2490. JACOBSEN, Josephine
"The Chinese Insomniacs." [Nat] (247:10) 17 O 88, p. 353.
"The Parthenon Frieze." [Nat] (247:10) 17 O 88, p. 353.
"Pondicherry Blues" (for voice and snare-drum). [Nat] (247:10) 17 O 88, p. 353.
"The Shade-Seller" (for A.R. Ammons). [Nat] (247:10) 17 O 88, p. 352.
"Swimmer's Tide." [Poetry] (152:4) Jl 88, p. 208.

2491. JACOBSEN, Rolf
"Lek." [InterPR] (14:1) Spr 88, p. 20.
"Mai Pá Ruten." [InterPR] (14:1) Spr 88, p. 22.
"Máne Før Det Blir Mørkt." [InterPR] (14:1) Spr 88, p. 20.
"May on the Windowpane" (tr. by Robert Hedin). [InterPR] (14:1) Spr 88, p. 23.
"Moon Before It Becomes Dark" (tr. by Robert Hedin). [InterPR] (14:1) Spr 88, p. 21.
"Night Music" (tr. by Robert Hedin). [PoetryE] (25) Spr 88, p. 126.
"Play" (tr. by Robert Hedin). [InterPR] (14:1) Spr 88, p. 21.
"Seabird" (tr. by Robert Hedin). [InterPR] (14:1) Spr 88, p. 23.
"Sjøfugl." [InterPR] (14:1) Spr 88, p. 22.

2492. JACOBSON, Bonnie
"Head Table Wives." [LightY] ('88/9) 88, p. 140.
"Introductions, or, What's in a Name." [LightY] ('88/9) 88, p. 73.
"Sitting Around Waiting for Your Cat to Die." [LaurelR] (22:2) Sum 88, p. 77.
"Sitting Around Waiting for Your Cat to Die." [LightY] ('88/9) 88, p. 96.
"Someday Somebody Might Like to Know this." [LaurelR] (22:2) Sum 88, p. 76.
"The Young Writer Smells a Rat." [LightY] ('88/9) 88, p. 189.

2493. JACOBSON, Jean Alice
"The Amateur." [NewYorker] (64:24) 1 Ag 88, p. 28.
"Persian Shrubs." [NewYorker] (64:13) 16 My 88, p. 34.

2494. JAEGER, Lowell
"At the Vietnam Memorial" (Washington D.C., 1983). [ColR] (NS 15:1) Spr-Sum 88, p. 91-92.
"Autonomic Nerves." [MinnR] (NS 30/31) Spr-Fall 88, p. 41-42.
"E.E.G." [CutB] (29/30) 88, p. 26-27.
"Warning." [HighP] (3:3) Wint 88-89, p. 49-50.
"Where We Went Wrong." [Spirit] (9:1) 88, p. 34-35.

2495. JAFFE, Dan
"The Middle-Aged Man Looks Out into the Gulf." [NewL] (54:3) Spr 88, p. 78-79.
"Of Marianne Moore and Jim Thorpe." [HeliconN] (19) 88, p. 62.
"They Would Be My Poems." [NewL] (54:3) Spr 88, p. 79.
"Waiting for You to Reappear in the House We Never Left." [NewL] (54:3) Spr 88, p. 80-81.

2496. JAFFE, Harold
"Foucault the Cyberpunks." [MissR] (16:2/3, #47/48) 88, p. 45.

2497. JAMES, Colin
"Heir." [RagMag] (6:2) Fall 88, p. 40.

2498. JAMES, David
"Always Here." [CimR] (85) O 88, p. 19.
"Think Death" (for Richard Shelton). [PassN] (9:2) Sum 88, p. 23.

2499. JAMES, Norberto
"Extranjero." [CuadP] (6:16) Sept.-Dic. 88, p. 52.
"Poema: Las estatuas." [CuadP] (6:16) Sept.-Dic. 88, p. 52.
"Prioridades." [CuadP] (6:16) Sept.-Dic. 88, p. 51.

2500. JAMES, Stewart
"Her Bread." [CarolQ] (41:1) Fall 88, p. 41.
"Tangerine" (for Robert Hass). [AntR] (46:3) Sum 88, p. 352-353.
"What I Know Is Beauty" (for Virginia). [AntR] (46:3) Sum 88, p. 351.

2501. JAMES, Winston Churchill
"Hermanos Negros." [Mairena] (10:25) 88, p. 183.

2502. JAMES-FRENCH, Dayv
"On Showing Early Promise." [PottPort] (10) 88, p. 47.

2503. JAMIESON, Scot
"Nuclear Submarine." [PottPort] (10) 88, p. 25.

2504. JAMIS, Fayad
"A Tu Luz, A Tu Gente, A Tu Galaxia." [Rohwedder] (3) Spr 88, p. 27.
"To Your Light, To Your People, To your Galaxy" (tr. by John Oliver Simon). [Rohwedder] (3) Spr 88, p. 26.
2505. JAMMES, Francis
"Come, I'll Give You" (tr. by Antony Oldknow). [Antaeus] (60) Spr 88, p. 272.
"Confucius" (tr. by Antony Oldknow). [Antaeus] (60) Spr 88, p. 275-276.
"In Hot Sun" (tr. by Antony Oldknow). [Antaeus] (60) Spr 88, p. 271.
"There Will Be Snow" (tr. by Antony Oldknow). [Antaeus] (60) Spr 88, p. 274.
"When Shall I See the Islands" (tr. by Antony Oldknow). [Antaeus] (60) Spr 88, p. 273.
2506. JANES, Ed
"Inventory of Fear" (w. Warren Woessner). [Lips] (14) 88, p. 25.
2507. JANIK, E. M.
"Office Dancing." [Vis] (28) 88, p. 45.
2508. JANO
"Stalin's Big Brush Mustache." [SinW] (35) Sum-Fall 88, p. 33-34.
2509. JANOWITZ, Phyllis
"The Mage at the Sea." [WilliamMR] (26:1) Spr 88, p. 75-76.
"Soliloquy in an Empty Hall." [Jacaranda] (3:1) Wint 88, p. 32-33.
2510. JANSEN, Walfried
"As the Season's." [Quarry] (37:1) Wint 88, p. 75.
"Spruce Shadows." [Quarry] (37:1) Wint 88, p. 76.
2511. JANZEN, Jean
"Peaches in Minnesota." [PraS] (62:2) Sum 88, p. 47.
"To Will One Thing" (for my brother). [PraS] (62:2) Sum 88, p. 46.
2512. JANZEN, Rhoda
"Father Junipero Serra Leans Back." [AntR] (46:3) Sum 88, p. 343.
2513. JARAMILLO LEVI, Enrique
"Bruja." [Mairena] (10:25) 88, p. 184.
2514. JARMAN, Mark
"The Cuckoo." [TarRP] (28:1) Fall 88, p. 59.
"Days of '74." [Poetry] (151:5) F 88, p. 392-393.
"The Death of God." [Ploughs] (14:4) 88, p. 18-20.
"Ground Swell." [IndR] (12:1) Wint 88, p. 12-13.
"Hawk." [SewanR] (96:4) Fall 88, p. 605-606.
"The Man Who Knew." [TarRP] (28:1) Fall 88, p. 58-59.
"Patriarch." [SewanR] (96:4) Fall 88, p. 607.
"The Shrine and the Burning Wheel." [MissouriR] (11:2) 88, p. 66-68.
"Shyness of the Muse in an Almond Orchard." [Poetry] (152:4) Jl 88, p. 220.
"Story Hour." [PartR] (55:2) Spr 88, p. 286-291.
"The Tuba Lesson." [Ploughs] (14:4) 88, p. 16-17.
2515. JARVIS, Edward
"An Offering" (for Nicole). [AmerV] (12) Fall 88, p. 17-18.
2516. JASTERMSKY, Karen
"Es Bonita Senorita." [SmPd] (25:1) Wint 88, p. 17.
2517. JASTRUN, Tomasz
"Children and Soldiers" (tr. by Daniel Bourne). [Vis] (28) 88, p. 25.
"Exodus" (tr. by Daniel Bourne). [WillowS] (21) Wint 88, p. 65.
"The Fall" (tr. by Daniel Bourne). [Abraxas] (37) 88, p. 21.
"Father and Son" (tr. by Daniel Bourne). [WillowS] (21) Wint 88, p. 67.
"Fog" (tr. by Daniel Bourne). [PoetL] (83:3) Fall 88, p. 24.
"Him" (tr. by Daniel Bourne). [Abraxas] (37) 88, p. 21.
"Leaving the House" (tr. by Daniel Bourne). [RiverS] (25) 88, p. 68.
"On." [Abraxas] (37) 88, p. 20.
"Our Black Madonna of Czestochowa" (tr. by Daniel Bourne). [WillowS] (21) Wint 88, p. 66.
"Preparing for Bed" (tr. by Daniel Bourne). [QW] (27) Sum-Fall 88, p. 100.
"Pulp Fiction" (tr. by Daniel Bourne). [Vis] (28) 88, p. 25.
"Rozbitkowie." [Abraxas] (37) 88, p. 20.
"A School in No One's Name" (tr. by Daniel Bourne). [QW] (27) Sum-Fall 88, p. 101.
"Shipwreck" (tr. by Daniel Bourne). [Abraxas] (37) 88, p. 20.
"Sleigh Ride" (tr. by Daniel Bourne). [QW] (27) Sum-Fall 88, p. 102.
"Spadanie." [Abraxas] (37) 88, p. 21.
"The Year 1864" (tr. by Daniel Bourne). [RiverS] (25) 88, p. 68.

JAX, Norita Dittberner
See DITTBERNER-JAX, Norita
2518. JEANNE, Ave
"Black Hat & Madness." [PaintedB] (36) 88, p. 34.
"Motions / Movements Movements." [PaintedB] (32/33) 88, p. 27.
"Portrait / Old Men in Charcoal." [Amelia] (4:4, #11) 88, p. 72.
"Staying in the Exit / Saturday." [PaintedB] (36) 88, p. 35.
2519. JECH, Jon
"A Death in White Center." [BellArk] (4:5) S-O 88, p. 5-7.
2520. JEFFERSON, Jennifer
"Country Weekend." [ColR] (NS 15:1) Spr-Sum 88, p. 43-44.
2521. JENKINS, Lee C.
"Twoy Boy." [ColEng] (50:6) O 88, p. 636.
2522. JENKINS, Louis
"The All-Night Chinese Cafe." [Abraxas] (37) 88, p. 69.
"Campsite." [Abraxas] (37) 88, p. 70.
"Winter Clothes." [Colum] (13) 88, p. 5.
2523. JENKINS, Mike
"Bob Marley." [NewEngR] (10:4) Sum 88, p. 464.
"Creature." [NewEngR] (10:4) Sum 88, p. 463.
2524. JENKINS, Paul
"Bluejay." [MidwQ] (30:1) Aut 88, p. 64.
"Contrary." [Chelsea] (47) 88, p. 128-130.
"The Second Hand." [Chelsea] (47) 88, p. 127.
"Things." [Chelsea] (47) 88, p. 126.
"What Makes Us Human." [MidwQ] (30:1) Aut 88, p. 67.
"Where You Live Do Buildings." [MidwQ] (30:1) Aut 88, p. 65-66.
2525. JENKINS, Robin David
"Bigfoot." [DeKalbLAJ] (21:1) Wint 88, p. 60.
2526. JENNINGS, Kate
"Dominica." [LittleM] (15:3/4) 88, p. 74-75.
"Layette" (for James). [Wind] (18:62) 88, p. 19-20.
"The Road to Roseau." [LittleM] (15:3/4) 88, p. 76.
"Spell" (for Lou). [Wind] (18:62) 88, p. 19.
2527. JENNINGS, Lane
"To His Cool Mistress." [Amelia] (5:2, #13) 88, p. 128.
2528. JENSEN, Jeffry
"Father's Day." [Plain] (8:1) Fall 87, p. 15.
"Running Down." [Plain] (8:2) Wint 88, p. 17.
2529. JENSEN, Laura
"85 — Sympathy." [CutB] (29/30) 88, p. 15.
"Black History Month" (St. Paul, February 1988). [Field] (39) Fall 88, p. 46-47.
"Dresses." [MichQR] (27:2) Spr 88, p. 280-281.
"Ryecatcher's Song." [Epoch] (37:2) 88, p. 116.
"We Sell My Mother's Dolls." [Field] (39) Fall 88, p. 45.
2530. JENTZ, Paul
"The Tradition That Seeks Us Out." [NoDaQ] (56:4) Fall 88, p. 116.
2531. JEROME, Judson
"A Flight Within" (for Julian Blau, 1917-1987). [HampSPR] Wint 88, p. 4.
"The Hunk." [Amelia] (5:1, #12) 88, p. 12-14.
"The Hunk." [LightY] ('88/9) 88, p. 127-130.
"Our Just Desserts." [HampSPR] Wint 88, p. 4.
"Philander's Pitch for Open Marriage." [HampSPR] Wint 88, p. 5.
"A Private Feast." [LightY] ('88/9) 88, p. 123.
2532. JEROZAL, Gregory
"Antique Thieves." [HampSPR] Wint 88, p. 21.
"Chichikov's Driver." [HampSPR] Wint 88, p. 20.
JEW, Shalin Hai
See HAI-JEW, Shalin
2533. JEWELL, Terry L.
"Night Hush for Sister." [Cond] (15) 88, p. 87.
"She Who Bears the Thorn." [Cond] (15) 88, p. 35.
2534. JHAVERI, Hansa
"Whirlwind" (tr. of Ravaji Patel). [Nimrod] (31:2) Spr-Sum 88, p. 74.
2535. JILES, Paulette
"Ragtime." [MalR] (83) Je 88, p. 101-114.

2536. JIN, Ha
"The Dead Soldier's Talk." [BostonR] (13:4) Ag 88, p. 12.
"The Haircut." [BostonR] (13:4) Ag 88, p. 12.
"A Hero's Mother Blames Her Daughter." [BostonR] (13:4) Ag 88, p. 12.
"An Older Scholar's Advice." [BostonR] (13:4) Ag 88, p. 12.
"A Sacred Mango." [BostonR] (13:4) Ag 88, p. 12.

JIN, Xuefei
See JIN, Ha

JINIE, Hwang
See HWANG, Jinie

JO, Carlos Castro
See CASTRO JO, Carlos

2537. JOANS, Ted
"Him the Bird." [Gargoyle] (35) 88, p. 219.

2538. JOHANSSEN, Kerry
"Critique of Impure Reason." [PoetryNW] (29:3) Aut 88, p. 7.
"Eye That Dries the Fruit." [NegC] (8:3) 88, p. 132-133.
"Fog Seen from the Sardis Firetower at Dawn." [PoetryNW] (29:3) Aut 88, p. 6-7.

2539. JOHN, Roland
"Keeping a Record." [Pembroke] (20) 88, p. 247.

2540. JOHNSON, Clifford S.
"What Do Ugly People Do on Saturday Night." [CapeR] (23:1) Spr 88, p. 2.

2541. JOHNSON, Colin
"Talking Author." [PraS] (62:4) Wint 88-89, p. 125-126.

2542. JOHNSON, Don
"Dolls at the Fish Springs Store and Filling Station." [PraS] (62:2) Sum 88, p. 50-51.
"Energy" (for Jack Higgs). [PraS] (62:2) Sum 88, p. 48-50.
"Mammoth Cave: Good Friday, 1986" (For Doris). [SouthernPR] (28:2) Fall 88, p. 39-40.

2543. JOHNSON, Elizabeth
"Alderbaran." [Prima] (11/12) 88, p. 74.

2544. JOHNSON, Frank
"Delphinium." [BlackWR] (15:1) Fall 88, p. 107.

2545. JOHNSON, Greg
"The Foreign Element." [Poetry] (152:5) Ag 88, p. 258.
"Visiting the Sick." [Poetry] (152:5) Ag 88, p. 257.

2546. JOHNSON, Honor
"At the University." [MassR] (29:1) Spr 88, p. 67-68.
"The Other." [MassR] (29:1) Spr 88, p. 66.

2547. JOHNSON, Judith E.
"Body Politic." [PartR] (55:2) Spr 88, p. 283.
"How It Was in Frost Country." [Shen] (38:2) 88, p. 41.
"I Found Last Night As I Walked Alone, a Dying." [Abraxas] (37) 88, p. 60.
"Press Conference." [MassR] (29:2) Sum 88, p. 264-265.
"Say Norse's Saying." [Abraxas] (37) 88, p. 61.

2548. JOHNSON, Kent
"Carmen" (tr. of Jose Domingo). [MidAR] (8:1) 88, p. 143.
"I Wonder" (tr. of Carlos Pacheco). [MidAR] (8:1) 88, p. 143.
"Sandino" (tr. of Javier Ortez). [MidAR] (8:1) 88, p. 143.

2549. JOHNSON, Larry
"Agrippina." [Lips] (14) 88, p. 7.

2550. JOHNSON, Linnea
"Advice." [SpoonRQ] (12:4) Fall 87, p. 35-36.
"Advice." [SpoonRQ] (13:4) Fall 88, p. 21-22.
"Birch Wood, Summer." [SpoonRQ] (12:4) Fall 87, p. 41.
"Birch Wood, Summer." [SpoonRQ] (13:4) Fall 88, p. 26-27.
"A Call, an Offer, an Invitation." [SpoonRQ] (12:4) Fall 87, p. 42-43.
"Caught Back Returning." [SpoonRQ] (12:4) Fall 87, p. 23.
"Caught Back Returning." [SpoonRQ] (13:4) Fall 88, p. 12-13.
"Chicago Sestina." [SpoonRQ] (12:4) Fall 87, p. 46-47.
"Chicago Sestina." [SpoonRQ] (13:4) Fall 88, p. 30-31.
"For My Son Alone in an Old Fiat, Route 80, December." [SpoonRQ] (12:4) Fall 87, p. 36.
"For My Son Alone in an Old Fiat, Route 80, December." [SpoonRQ] (13:4) Fall 88, p. 22.

"From the Window." [SpoonRQ] (12:4) Fall 87, p. 24-25.
"From the Window." [SpoonRQ] (13:4) Fall 88, p. 14-15.
"Gulf." [SpoonRQ] (12:4) Fall 87, p. 37.
"Gulf." [SpoonRQ] (13:4) Fall 88, p. 23.
"Harbor." [SpoonRQ] (12:4) Fall 87, p. 26.
"Harbor." [SpoonRQ] (13:4) Fall 88, p. 13.
"I Have Found What Would Have Kept You Alive." [SpoonRQ] (12:4) Fall 87, p. 44-45.
"I Have Found What Would Have Kept You Alive." [SpoonRQ] (13:4) Fall 88, p. 28-29.
"Iowa." [SpoonRQ] (12:4) Fall 87, p. 27.
"Long Enough." [SpoonRQ] (12:4) Fall 87, p. 38-39.
"Maine for the Weekend." [SpoonRQ] (12:4) Fall 87, p. 32.
"Marriage Manual." [SpoonRQ] (12:4) Fall 87, p. 33-34.
"Marriage Manual." [SpoonRQ] (13:4) Fall 88, p. 19-20.
"Piano Man." [SpoonRQ] (12:4) Fall 87, p. 30.
"Piano Man." [SpoonRQ] (13:4) Fall 88, p. 17.
"Reprise." [SpoonRQ] (12:4) Fall 87, p. 40.
"Reprise." [SpoonRQ] (13:4) Fall 88, p. 24-25.
"Translation from the Cryptography Handbook You Keep, One Surely Thinks, By Your Beddybyeside." [SpoonRQ] (12:4) Fall 87, p. 29-30.
"Translation from the Cryptography Handbook You Keep, One Surely Thinks, by You Beddybyeside." [SpoonRQ] (13:4) Fall 88, p. 16-17.
"Waking Up to It." [SpoonRQ] (12:4) Fall 87, p. 31.
"Waking Up to It." [SpoonRQ] (13:4) Fall 88, p. 18.
"White Paint." [SpoonRQ] (12:4) Fall 87, p. 28.

2551. JOHNSON, Manly
"House with Garden." [Phoenix] (9:1/2) 88, p. 51.
"A Man Is" (Geoge O'Brien). [Phoenix] (9:1/2) 88, p. 52.
"Slava Raskaj" (tr. of Margherita Guidacci, w. Renata Treitel). [GrahamHR] (11) Spr 88, p. 98-99.
"Virius" (tr. of Margherita Guidacci, w. Renata Treitel). [GrahamHR] (11) Spr 88, p. 97.

2552. JOHNSON, Mark
"The Astronomer Watches Birds." [DenQ] (22:3) Wint 88, p. 64.

2553. JOHNSON, Mark Allan
"Field Guide." [BellArk] (4:6) N-D 88, p. 6.
"Spring's Promise: A Wedding Song." [BellArk] (4:2) Mr-Ap 88, p. 7.
"Upon Reading the Morrow Anthology of Younger American Poets." [BellArk] (4:5) S-O 88, p. 8.

2554. JOHNSON, Markham
"Voices." [CimR] (83) Ap 88, p. 30-31.

2555. JOHNSON, Michael (Michael L.)
"Dining-Room Mirror" (tr. of Jorge Carrera Andrade). [WebR] (13:2) Fall 88, p. 31-32.
"Epileptic." [Wind] (18:63) 88, p. 29.
"First Time." [Wind] (18:63) 88, p. 34.
"The Great Horned Owl." [MidAR] (8:1) 88, p. 42-43.
"Insomnia" (tr. of José Juan Tablada). [WebR] (13:2) Fall 88, p. 32.
"Nadia." [KanQ] (20:3) Sum 88, p. 35.
"Peacock" (tr. of José Juan Tablada). [WebR] (13:2) Fall 88, p. 32.
"Smoke-Out." [DeKalbLAJ] (21:2) Spr 88, p. 40.
"To a Whore with Iron-Gray Eyes" (tr. of Dino Campana). [QW] (26) Wint 88, p. 112.
"Tunnels." [TexasR] (9:1/2) Spr-Sum 88, p. 66.
"What Does This Poem Mean?" [Amelia] (5:1, #12) 88, p. 85.
"Woman in Pisa" (tr. of Mario Luzi). [QW] (26) Wint 88, p. 113.
"Xmas Eve." [KanQ] (20:3) Sum 88, p. 35.

2556. JOHNSON, Nancy
"Nationalism." [AntR] (46:4) Fall 88, p. 485.

2557. JOHNSON, Peter
"Marital Metaphors." [FloridaR] (16:1) Spr-Sum 88, p. 84-85.
"Private Citizen." [Iowa] (18:3) 88, p. 139-140.
"The Provider." [Iowa] (18:3) 88, p. 138.
"A Ritual As Old As Time Itself." [Iowa] (18:3) 88, p. 138-139.
"Somebody's Fool." [Iowa] (18:3) 88, p. 139.

2558. JOHNSON, Pyke, Jr.
"Picnic at the Beach." [LightY] ('88/9) 88, p. 148.
"Report After a Walk Along the Avenue." [LightY] ('88/9) 88, p. 47.
2559. JOHNSON, Robert K.
"A Waste of Time." [Wind] (18:62) 88, p. 22.
"A Year Later." [Vis] (27) 88, p. 33.
2560. JOHNSON, Samuel
"A 5th Stanza for Dr. Johnson, Donald Hall, Louis Phillips, & X. J. Kennedy" (who wrote stanzas 1-4). [LightY] ('88/9) 88, p. 182-183.
2561. JOHNSON, Sandi
"How He Entered." [CapilR] (49) 88, p. 20.
"The Naked Man at a Western Movie." [CapilR] (49) 88, p. 22.
"What the Naked Man Saw." [CapilR] (49) 88, p. 21.
2562. JOHNSON, Steven
"What Moves." [Gargoyle] (35) 88, p. 181.
2563. JOHNSON, Susan Marie
"Piecing It." [Nimrod] (32:1) Fall-Wint 88, p. 73-76.
2564. JOHNSON, Tom
"All I Can Say to You" (after Heisenberg). [GettyR] (1:1) Wint 88, p. 108.
"L'Envoi" (for Tinkum Brooks). [SouthernR] (24:2) Spr 88, p. 316.
"Falling Asleep in the Car" (after Einstein). [GettyR] (1:1) Wint 88, p. 107.
"My Brother's Child." [SouthernR] (24:2) Spr 88, p. 316-317.
"Poems for My Daughters" (3 poems). [SewanR] (96:1) Wint 88, p. 40-44.
2565. JOHNSON, Virginia
"For My Grandmother." [Pembroke] (20) 88, p. 122.
"A Hymn to the Apposable Thumb." [Pembroke] (20) 88, p. 122.
"To My Father." [Pembroke] (20) 88, p. 121.
2566. JOHNSON, W. R.
"Caesar Dividing Gaul." [LitR] (31:4) Sum 88, p. 470.
"The Death of Cicero." [LitR] (31:4) Sum 88, p. 470.
2567. JOHNSON, William R.
"Ice at the Heart." [StoneC] (15:3/4) Spr-Sum 88, p. 13.
2568. JOHNSON, Wotring
"Memory." [Amelia] (5:1, #12) 88, p. 18.
2569. JOHNSTON, Arnie
"Thirteen Ways of Looking at a Telephone" (After Wallace Stevens). [HiramPoR] (44/45) Spr-Wint 88, p. 27-28.
2570. JOHNSTON, Fred
"The Angels of the City Fold Away and Sleep." [PoetC] (19:3) Spr 88, p. 19.
2571. JOHNSTON, George
"For Astrid" (at five weeks). [MalR] (82) Mr 88, p. 58.
"Haste." [MalR] (82) Mr 88, p. 58.
"In Air." [MalR] (82) Mr 88, p. 59.
"Old Tune." [MalR] (82) Mr 88, p. 59.
2572. JOHNSTON, Jerry
"French Pound." [Plain] (8:2) Wint 88, p. 31.
"On First Looking into James Merrill's 'Sandover'." [Plain] (8:2) Wint 88, p. 16.
2573. JOHNSTON, Mark
"Contortionist." [PaintedB] (36) 88, p. 94.
"The Question of the Trash." [ChamLR] (1) Fall 87, p. 388.
2574. JOHNSTON, Stella
"Ball Lightning: Palestine, Texas, 1952." [Shen] (38:1) 88, p. 18-20.
2575. JOINER, Ardell Carpenter
"Thirteen Ways of Looking at 8th Grade: Tract C." [EngJ] (77:2) F 88, p. 87.
2576. JONES, Arlene
"Night Vigil: Kyrenia, Cyprus, in August 1964." [Wind] (18:63) 88, p. 19.
2577. JONES, B. S.
"Regalo." [Sequoia] (31:2) Wint 88, p. 59-61.
2578. JONES, D. G.
"The Age of the Word" (tr. of Roland Giguere). [Trans] (20) Spr 88, p. 106.
"And We Loved" (tr. of Fernand Ouellette). [Trans] (20) Spr 88, p. 141-142.
"Let Us Close the Cupboard" (tr. of Alain Grandbois). [Trans] (20) Spr 88, p. 144-146.
"The Sun" (tr. of Fernand Ouellette). [Trans] (20) Spr 88, p. 143.
JONES, Elizabeth Follin
See FOLLIN-JONES, Elizabeth

2579. JONES, Jean
"Prufrock by the Sea." [KanQ] (20:1/2) Wint-Spr 88, p. 138.
2580. JONES, Paul
"That Kind of Night." [SouthernHR] (22:2) Spr 88, p. 170.
2581. JONES, Peter Thabit
"Hurrying Down Pant Street." [NewEngR] (10:4) Sum 88, p. 461.
2582. JONES, Richard
"After the Divorce." [Pequod] (25) 88, p. 20.
"My Painting." [Poetry] (153:3) D 88, p. 132-133.
"Singing in Church." [Pequod] (25) 88, p. 21.
"The Spider." [Pequod] (25) 88, p. 20.
"Things." [Poetry] (153:3) D 88, p. 132.
"White Towels." [Pequod] (25) 88, p. 20.
2583. JONES, Robert C.
"Delphi: Phaedriades." [NewL] (55:1) Fall 88, p. 81.
2584. JONES, Rodney
"Academic Subjects." [GeoR] (42:3) Fall 88, p. 583-584.
"Caught." [GeoR] (42:2) Sum 88, p. 384-385.
"Every Day There Are New Memos." [GeoR] (42:3) Fall 88, p. 581-582.
"Just So." [PoetryNW] (29:2) Sum 88, p. 16-18.
"Mimosa." [NoAmR] (273:3) S 88, p. 50.
"Mule." [Atlantic] (261:2) F 88, p. 62-63.
"My Manhood." [RiverS] (27) 88, p. 65-66.
"News of the Cranes." [MissouriR] (11:1) 88, p. 10-11.
"Pure Mathematics." [PoetryNW] (29:2) Sum 88, p. 13-14.
"The Weepers." [PoetryNW] (29:2) Sum 88, p. 15-16.
"Winter Retreat: Homage to Martin Luther King." [MissouriR] (11:1) 88, p. 8-9.
2585. JONES, Roger
"The Drill." [KanQ] (20:1/2) Wint-Spr 88, p. 46.
"Gold." [HawaiiR] (12:2, #24) Fall 88, p. 12-13.
"Making My Peace." [CimR] (84) Jl 88, p. 70.
"Resignation" (Honorable Mention Poem, 1987/1988). [KanQ] (20:1/2) Wint-Spr 88, p. 45.
"Summer Run in the Country." [CimR] (84) Jl 88, p. 71.
2586. JONES, Tom
"Gandhi's Ocean." [InterPR] (14:2) Fall 88, p. 95.
"Maharaja Murders Two Thousand Dancers" (For Tom, on his 21st Birthday). [InterPR] (14:2) Fall 88, p. 95.
2587. JONES INGRAM, Nida E.
"Haiku: Balmy spring twilight" (The 14th Kansas Poetry Contest, First Honorable Mention). [LittleBR] (5:2) Wint 88-89, p. 69.
2588. JORDAN, Dennis
"Foreplay." [SlipS] (8) 88, p. 6.
2589. JORDAN, Johanna
"Paradox." [BellArk] (4:4) Jl-Ag 88, p. 24.
"Procession." [BellArk] (4:3) My-Je 88, p. 1.
"Procession." [BellArk] (4:4) Jl-Ag 88, p. 9.
"To Moon (Crescent)." [BellArk] (4:4) Jl-Ag 88, p. 10.
2590. JORIS, Pierre
"The Circulation of Our Discontent." [Notus] (3:1) Spr 88, p. 40.
"The Horses of Lalla Fatima." [Bound] (15:3/16:1) Spr-Fall 88, p. 207-213.
"Listening to glenn gould." [Notus] (3:1) Spr 88, p. 43.
"Prayer" (tr. of Antonin Artaud). [Acts] (8/9) 88, p. 164.
"Prayer" (tr. of Paul Celan's German tr. of Antonin Artaud). [Acts] (8/9) 88, p. 165.
"The Shrill Knowledge." [Notus] (3:1) Spr 88, p. 41-42.
"Winnetou Old" (Selections: Stanzas). [Notus] (3:2) Fall 88, p. 60-61.
"The Work of Al-Ishk." [Notus] (3:1) Spr 88, p. 37-39.
2591. JORNS, Rebecca Ann
"Waiting." [EngJ] (77:3) Mr 88, p. 89.
2592. JOSEPH, Lawrence
"An Awful Lot Was Happening." [Poetry] (152:2) My 88, p. 68-69.
2593. JOSEPHS, Laurence
"Cat." [Salm] (78/79) Spr-Sum 88, p. 160.
"The Gardener's Wife" (For Terence Diggory). [Salm] (78/79) Spr-Sum 88, p. 158-159.
"On Finding an Old Letter in a Book." [Salm] (78/79) Spr-Sum 88, p. 159.

2594. JOSHI, Rachna
"The Death of My Grandmother." [Nimrod] (31:2) Spr-Sum 88, p. 53-54.
"Periplum." [Nimrod] (31:2) Spr-Sum 88, p. 54.
2595. JOTAMARIO
"Dictionary of the Rose-Colored Wizard" (tr. by Ellen Watson). [Antaeus] (60) Spr 88, p. 286-289.
JOURNOUD, Claude Royet
See ROYET-JOURNOUD, Claude
2596. JOVINE BERMUDEZ, Federico
"Tres Cantos a Vivian Revere." [Mairena] (10:25) 88, p. 107-108.
2597. JOWETT, Derek
"(1940) France. Dunkirk." [PottPort] (10) 88, p. 37.
2598. JOYCE, Dianne
"Saturday Matinee." [Grain] (16:4) Wint 88, p. 23.
"Twelve." [Grain] (16:4) Wint 88, p. 22.
2599. JOYCE, William
"For a Mouth That Never Resigns Itself to Sorrow." [Vis] (27) 88, p. 39.
2600. JUARROZ, Roberto
"The creatures of afternoon" (tr. by W. S. Merwin). [AmerPoR] (17:1) Ja-F 88, p. 26.
"Death is another way of looking" (tr. by W. S. Merwin). [AmerPoR] (17:1) Ja-F 88, p. 25.
"Each thing makes hands for itself" (tr. by W. S. Merwin). [AmerPoR] (17:1) Ja-F 88, p. 26.
"Embrace your head" (tr. by W. S. Merwin). [AmerPoR] (17:1) Ja-F 88, p. 26.
"The faces that you've discarded" (tr. by W. S. Merwin). [AmerPoR] (17:1) Ja-F 88, p. 26.
"Forms are born of an open hand" (tr. by W. S. Merwin). [AmerPoR] (17:1) Ja-F 88, p. 25.
"A glass of water" (tr. by W. S. Merwin). [AmerPoR] (17:1) Ja-F 88, p. 26.
"The Initiative of My Shadow" (tr. by Mary Crow). [MidAR] (8:1) 88, p. 44.
"Life is a necessary precaution" (tr. by W. S. Merwin). [AmerPoR] (17:1) Ja-F 88, p. 24.
"A long tunnel is coming closer to my mouth" (tr. by W. S. Merwin). [AmerPoR] (17:1) Ja-F 88, p. 25.
"The memories leap out of the eyes" (tr. by W. S. Merwin). [AmerPoR] (17:1) Ja-F 88, p. 25.
"A Net of Looking" (tr. by Mary Crow). [MidAR] (8:1) 88, p. 45.
"The other who bears my name" (tr. by W. S. Merwin). [AmerPoR] (17:1) Ja-F 88, p. 25.
"The stone is a clenched lap" (tr. by W. S. Merwin). [AmerPoR] (17:1) Ja-F 88, p. 25.
"There are footprints that do not coincide with their foot" (tr. by W. S. Merwin). [AmerPoR] (17:1) Ja-F 88, p. 24.
"An uncommitted gesture, a rapt expression" (tr. by W. S. Merwin). [AmerPoR] (17:1) Ja-F 88, p. 25.
"Unique each night" (tr. by W. S. Merwin). [AmerPoR] (17:1) Ja-F 88, p. 26.
2601. JUDA
"Shayla." [JamesWR] (5:3) Spr-Sum 88, p. 1.
2602. JUDGE, Joseph M.
"Watching the Hurricane Arrive." [StoneC] (16:1/2) Fall-Wint 88-89, p. 55.
2603. JUDSON, John
"Psalm Above Santa Fe" (16 March 1987). [Poetry] (151:4) Ja 88, p. 347.
2604. JUHASZ, Ferenc
"The Biography of a Woman." [Sulfur] (7:3, #21) Wint 88, p. 66-76.
2605. JULAVITS, Virginia
"Doll Shop on Rodeo Drive." [KanQ] (20:3) Sum 88, p. 114.
2606. JULIANO, Gary
"Future Funerals." [Wind] (18:63) 88, p. 8.
2607. JULLICH, Jeffrey
"Calligraphy." [JINJPo] (10:1/2) 88, p. 23.
"Plain." [JINJPo] (10:1/2) 88, p. 22.
"Visa of Foreign Gender." [AnotherCM] (18) 88, p. 105.
2608. JUNKINS, Donald
"Crossing by Ferry." [TexasR] (9:3/4) Fall-Wint 88, p. 72-73.

"Swans Island, the Late 70's: Middle Age." [TexasR] (9:3/4) Fall-Wint 88, p. 74-75.
JUNZABURO, Nishiwaki
See NISHIWAKI, Junzaburo
2609. JUSSAWALLA, Adil
"Bats." [Nimrod] (31:2) Spr-Sum 88, p. 52.
2610. JUST, Julia
"Home." [VirQR] (64:1) Wint 88, p. j82.
2611. JUSTICE, Donald
"The Conspirators Make Their Vows" (Act I, Scene 3 of the libretto for Edwin London's opera). [MichQR] (27:4) Fall 88, p. 586-593.
2612. JUSTICE, Jack
"Please Write Soon." [Spirit] (9:1) 88, p. 60.
2613. KABIR
"Poems of Religious Ecstacy" (2 poems, tr. by Judi Benade). [Nimrod] (31:2) Spr-Sum 88, p. 20.
2614. KAFKA, Paul
"Sejour." [CinPR] (18) Fall 88, p. 34.
2615. KALAMARAS, George
"When Anger Became a Man." [Caliban] (4) 88, p. 143.
"Where the Wind Ended" (for William Stafford). [StoneC] (16:1/2) Fall-Wint 88-89, p. 17.
2616. KALINA, Gail
"Restoring *The Last Suppe*r." [SpoonRQ] (13:1) Wint 88, p. 62-63.
2617. KALLET, Marilyn
"The Adulterer Tells Her to Write Him 'Open, Friendly letters,' and She Complies." [Spirit] (9:1) 88, p. 55.
"The Dream." [DenQ] (23:2) Fall 88, p. 49.
"The Great Complaint of My Obscurity Three" (tr. of Tristan Tzara). [Sonora] (14/15) Spr 88, p. 11.
"Sentimental Talk." [GreensboroR] (44) Sum 88, p. 93-94.
"Wheat and Chaff" (A Partially Recovered Proclamation, tr. of Tristan Tzara). [Sonora] (14/15) Spr 88, p. 12-13.
2618. KALLSEN, T. J.
"For Too-Personal Poets." [KanQ] (20:3) Sum 88, p. 133.
2619. KAMAL, Daud
"Exile." [Vis] (26) 88, inside front cover.
"Horizons" (tr. of Munir Niazi). [Vis] (28) 88, p. 31.
"The Other Shore." [Vis] (27) 88, inside front cover.
2620. KAMENETZ, Rodger
"After Benjamin Whorf." [Shen] (38:2) 88, p. 61.
"An Angelology." [SouthernR] (24:2) Spr 88, p. 325-329.
"Daylight Savings Time." [NewRep] (198:15) 11 Ap 88, p. 36.
"Homage: Anselm Kiefer, the Order of Angels." [Shen] (38:2) 88, p. 60-61.
"In Print." [Shen] (38:2) 88, p. 60.
"Joe Steps Out." [NoAmR] (273:3) S 88, p. 49.
"The Landing." [Shen] (38:2) 88, p. 59.
"Meg and Joe: Five Poems." [WillowS] (21) Wint 88, p. 83-85.
2621. KAMIENSKA, Anna
"Change" (tr. by Tomasz P. Krzeszowski and Desmond Graham). [Verse] (5:2) Jl 88, p. 13.
"A Thirteen Year Old Girl" (tr. by Tomasz P. Krzeszowski and Desmond Graham). [Verse] (5:2) Jl 88, p. 14.
2622. KAMPLEY, Linda
"Channel Markings." [CreamCR] (12:2) Sum 88, p. 201.
"Family History." [Pembroke] (20) 88, p. 223.
2623. KANABUS, Henry
"Bishop Bampopo in Corfu." [NewAW] (3) Spr 88, p. 103.
"In All Your Dwellings." [NewAW] (3) Spr 88, p. 102.
2624. KANDL, John
"Thoreau in the Morning." [NoDaQ] (56:3) Sum 88, p. 54.
2625. KANE, George
"Did You Notice That the American Soldier" (tr. of Steffen Mensching). [ParisR] (30:106) Spr 88, p. 296.
"Exaggerated Self-Portrait" (tr. of Ulrich Berkes). [ParisR] (30:106) Spr 88, p. 289-291.

"I Was Icarus" (tr. of Ulrich Berkes). [ParisR] (30:106) Spr 88, p. 292.
"In a Hotel Room in Meissen I Read" (tr. of Steffen Mensching). [ParisR] (30:106) Spr 88, p. 296.
"Official Telephone Book, Reich Postal District Berlin, 1941" (tr. of Steffen Mensching). [ParisR] (30:106) Spr 88, p. 297-298.
"Orpheus" (tr. of Ulrich Berkes). [ParisR] (30:106) Spr 88, p. 294.
"Remington Portable" (tr. of Ulrich Berkes). [ParisR] (30:106) Spr 88, p. 293.
"So White Was the Morning" (tr. of Steffen Mensching). [ParisR] (30:106) Spr 88, p. 296.
"Theocritus" (tr. of Ulrich Berkes). [ParisR] (30:106) Spr 88, p. 295.
"Torn and Tattered Elegy in Black" (tr. of Steffen Mensching). [ParisR] (30:106) Spr 88, p. 299.

2626. KANGAS, J. R.
"At the Art Museum." [Bogg] (59) 88, p. 18.
"Early Summer." [BellR] (11:2) Fall 88, p. 33.

KAORU, Maruyama
See MARUYAMA, Kaoru

2627. KAPLAN, Robert
"Full Moon Over Main Street." [Lips] (14) 88, p. 49-50.
"Several Steps Toward a Voice." [Lips] (14) 88, p. 51.

2628. KAPLAN, Susan
"Titled Poem." [Boulevard] (3:2/3) Fall 88, p. 64.

2629. KARASEK, Krzysztof
"From a Letter of Bertolt Brecht to His Son" (tr. by Daniel Bourne). [LitR] (31:2) Wint 88, p. 143.
"Little Fears, Big Fears" (tr. by Daniel Bourne). [LitR] (31:2) Wint 88, p. 145.
"Orpheus in the Diner" (tr. by Daniel Bourne). [LitR] (31:2) Wint 88, p. 144-145.

2630. KARP, Vickie
"Getting Dressed in the Dark." [NewYRB] (35:17) 10 N 88, p. 20.
"Goodbye." [NewYorker] (64:7) 4 Ap 88, p. 32.

2631. KARR, Mary
"Bad Family." [Ploughs] (14:4) 88, p. 76.
"In Illo Tempore" (for Tom Johnson, 1951-1986). [Colum] (13) 88, p. 113.

2632. KARR, Muriel
"Swallowing the Bone." [YellowS] (27) Aut 88, p. 21.

2633. KASDORF, Julia Spicher
"How to Think of Danger" (for David). [WestB] (21/22) 88, p. 110.

2634. KASISCHKE, Laura
"The Cyclone." [SpoonRQ] (13:2) Spr 88, p. 57-58.
"Duration" (after Octavio Paz). [ChamLR] (2:1, #3) Fall 88, p. 82-83.
"The Man with Cancer in the Park." [ChamLR] (2:1, #3) Fall 88, p. 84.
"Parade" (Michigan Sesquicentennial Poetry Competition, First Prize). [PassN] (9:1) Wint 88, p. 3.
"Photograph with My Mother, 1961." [SpoonRQ] (13:2) Spr 88, p. 61.
"We Seal Our Daughter in a Tower." [SpoonRQ] (13:2) Spr 88, p. 59-60.

2635. KASSELMANN, Barbara C.
"Shower." [SlipS] (8) 88, p. 14.

2636. KATES, J.
"Argentina 1983" (tr. of Ricardo Feierstein, w. Stephen A. Sadow). [MinnR] (NS 30/31) Spr-Fall 88, p. 47.
"Letter to Etheridge." [PaintedB] (32/33) 88, p. 79.
"Pastorale." [TexasR] (9:3/4) Fall-Wint 88, p. 77-78.
"Places of Permanent Shade." [Spirit] (9:1) 88, p. 43.
"Seductions of the Buddha" (for Jon Silkin). [StoneC] (15:3/4) Spr-Sum 88, p. 7-9.
"Still-Life" (tr. of Tatyana Shcherbina). [MinnR] (NS 30/31) Spr-Fall 88, p. 46.
"Three Weeks" (to and from L.B.). [TexasR] (9:3/4) Fall-Wint 88, p. 76.
"Waiting My Turn." [Spirit] (9:1) 88, p. 42.
"Winterlied." [StoneC] (15:3/4) Spr-Sum 88, p. 9.
"The Wrist." [BellR] (11:2) Fall 88, p. 36.

2637. KATROVAS, Richard
"Ed's Gun." [WillowS] (21) Wint 88, p. 60-61.
"Jewels." [IndR] (12:1) Wint 88, p. 5-6.
"My Friends the Pigeons." [NewEngR] (10:3) Spr 88, p. 273.
"Shifting." [WillowS] (21) Wint 88, p. 62-63.

2638. KATZ, David M.
"Prospero in August." [Shen] (38:1) 88, p. 62-66.

2639. KATZ, Vincent
"Shopping." [NewAW] (4) Fall 88, p. 82.
"Window Life." [Bomb] (25) Fall 88, p. 72-73.
2640. KAUFMAN, Andrew
"Sonnets" (#12-16, 18-19). [Crazy] (35) Wint 88, p. 62-68.
"The Taryn Sonnets" (Selections: 1, 2, 8, 11). [SouthernPR] (28:2) Fall 88, p. 8-9.
"The Taryn Sonnets" (Selection: #18). [BlackWR] (15:1) Fall 88, p. 13.
"Water." [HolCrit] (25:2) Ap 88, p. 12.
"Writers' Anonymous." [LittleM] (15:3/4) 88, p. 45.
2641. KAUFMAN, Debra
"Confession." [SpoonRQ] (13:3) Sum 88, p. 18.
"Once Again, I Write What I Can't Say." [SpoonRQ] (13:3) Sum 88, p. 17.
2642. KAUFMAN, Ellen
"After the Hockney Retrospective." [Verse] (5:3) N 88, p. 21.
2643. KAUFMAN, Shirley
"Jealousy." [Field] (39) Fall 88, p. 58.
"The Temples of Khajuraho." [Ploughs] (14:1) 88, p. 29-31.
2644. KAULICH, R.
"A Letter to a Deaf Girl." [Kaleid] (17) Sum-Fall 88, p. 38.
2645. KAUNE, Gayle Rogers
"Michigan Autumn." [PassN] (9:1) Wint 88, p. 12.
2646. KAUTZMANN, María Eunice
"Criança: Universo do Amor." [LetFem] (14:1/2) Primavera-Otoño 88, p. 146-148.
"Maria do Beco." [LetFem] (14:1/2) Primavera-Otoño 88, p. 149-150.
2647. KAVANAGH, P. J.
"Morning." (For Douglas Dunn and his Elegies). [GrandS] (7:3) Spr 88, p. 123.
2648. KAWAMURA, Kazuo
"Hymn" (tr. of Shuntaro Tanikawa, w. William I. Elliott). [CrabCR] (5:2) Sum 88, p. 14.
"Some Questions" (tr. of Shuntaro Tanikawa, w. William I. Elliott). [CrabCR] (5:2) Sum 88, p. 15-16.
"A Study of the Tactile Sense" (tr. of Shuntaro Tanikawa, w. William I. Elliott). [CrabCR] (5:2) Sum 88, p. 16-19.
"The Window" (tr. of Shuntaro Tanikawa, w. William I. Elliott). [CrabCR] (5:2) Sum 88, p. 14.
2649. KAY, Jackie
"Generations." [Cond] (15) 88, p. 95-96.
"Mother in Exile" (for Lorna). [Cond] (15) 88, p. 88-90.
2650. KAYLOR, Keri
"Poem for Etheridge Knight." [PaintedB] (32/33) 88, p. 88.
2651. KAZEL, Maggie
"Scarves" (To Michelle and the Lexington Control Unit inmates). [SinW] (36) Wint 88-89, p. 19-20.
KAZUO, Kawamura
See KAWAMURA, Kazuo
KE, Man
See MAN, Ke
2652. KEARNS, Lionel
"Beyond Resurrection." [ChamLR] (1:2, #2) Spr 88, p. 3-4.
"Caution." [ColEng] (50:8) D 88, p. 878.
"Corpulence." [ChamLR] (1:2, #2) Spr 88, p. 2.
"Insight." [ColEng] (50:8) D 88, p. 877.
"Open Form." [ColEng] (50:8) D 88, p. 879.
"Origins." [ChamLR] (2:1, #3) Fall 88, p. 105.
"Origins." [ColEng] (50:8) D 88, p. 876.
"Realism." [ColEng] (50:8) D 88, p. 877.
"Rhapsody." [ColEng] (50:8) D 88, p. 878.
"Self Reference." [ChamLR] (2:1, #3) Fall 88, p. 104.
"Sociopathology." [ChamLR] (2:1, #3) Fall 88, p. 102.
"Time." [ChamLR] (2:1, #3) Fall 88, p. 103.
"Warning." [ChamLR] (1:2, #2) Spr 88, p. 1.
KEATING, Helane Levine
See LEVINE-KEATING, Helane
2653. KEELER, Greg
"Duct Tape Psalm." [LightY] ('88/9) 88, p. 204.
"Epiphany at Goofy's Gas, Missoula, MT." [TarRP] (27:2) Spr 88, p. 27.

"The Guilt Bug." [SpoonRQ] (13:1) Wint 88, p. 7.

2654. KEEN, Suzanne
"April Elegy: The Best Place to Keep It." [Notus] (3:2) Fall 88, p. 58.
"August Elegy: The Truth about Play." [Notus] (3:2) Fall 88, p. 57.
"Small Wind Bring Down Rain." [Notus] (3:2) Fall 88, p. 59.

2655. KEENAN, Deborah
"Stigmata." [PaintedB] (34) 88, p. 43.

2656. KEENEY, Patricia
"A Plea for My Daughter." [CrossC] (10:3) 88, p. 9.

2657. KEESON, Cynthia
"Coming Come" (tr. of Jozo T. Boskovski). [Lips] (14) 88, p. 37.

2658. KEIDA, Yusuke
"Out of the Gogo-An" (for John Solt). [AlphaBS] (3) Je 88, p. 64-65.

2659. KEIN, Sybil
"Soulangai." [NewOR] (15:1) Spr 88, p. 32-33.

2660. KEITHLEY, George
"Supper." [LightY] ('88/9) 88, p. 97.

2661. KEIZER, Garret
"The Forming of Monsters." [TexasR] (9:3/4) Fall-Wint 88, p. 80.
"Leafletting with Father Castle." [TexasR] (9:3/4) Fall-Wint 88, p. 79.

2662. KELLER, David
"At the Anger Reunion." [AnotherCM] (18) 88, p. 106-107.
"A Funeral Early in May." [Footwork] ('88) 88, p. 12.
"It's Not Safe to Send a Man Out for Rosebuds." [Footwork] ('88) 88, p. 12.
"Sharing the Secrets." [Footwork] ('88) 88, p. 12.

2663. KELLER, Tsipi Edith
"A Lesson in Weeping" (tr. of Dan Pagis). [PoetL] (83:4) Wint 88-89, p. 26.
"A True Story" (tr. of Dan Pagis). [PoetL] (83:4) Wint 88-89, p. 27-28.

2664. KELLEY, Janine
"Los Desaparecidos" (por las madres de Argentina). [CentR] (32:3) Sum 88, p. 269-270.
"The Fence." [MinnR] (NS 30/31) Spr-Fall 88, p. 9-10.

2665. KELLEY, Karen
"Freud's Wish." [Sulfur] (8:2, #23) Fall 88, p. 122-125.

2666. KELLEY, Tina
"Dance of the Firefly Catchers." [LitR] (31:4) Sum 88, p. 432.
"The Species Evolving Along with Us." [StoneC] (16:1/2) Fall-Wint 88-89, p. 21.

2667. KELLMAN, Tony
"Bajan." [Vis] (27) 88, p. 13.

2668. KELLY, Brigit Pegeen
"Landscape." [PraS] (62:1) Spr 88, p. 30.
"The Teacher." [WestB] (21/22) 88, p. 90.
"The Visitation." [WestB] (21/22) 88, p. 91-92.
"The White Deer." [WestB] (21/22) 88, p. 89.

2669. KELLY, Mary Lee
"The Egg Trick" (for L.H.). [Amelia] (4:4, #11) 88, p. 70.
"In Balboa Park." [Amelia] (4:4, #11) 88, p. 71.

2670. KELLY, Robert
"A Grave" (tr. of Paul Celan's German translation of Marianne Moore). [Acts] (8/9) 88, p. 121.
"In the Light." [Conjunc] (12) 88, p. 75-77.
"The Inequalities." [Notus] (3:2) Fall 88, p. 24-29.
"Poem Beginning with Lines from Ted Enslin's *The Weather Within*." [Notus] (3:1) Spr 88, p. 47-49.
"The Second Elegy." [Temblor] (8) 88, p. 42-48.

2671. KELLY-DeWITT, Susan
"Chernobyl." [SpoonRQ] (13:3) Sum 88, p. 60-61.
"Fireweed" (Epilobium augustifolium). [CimR] (84) Jl 88, p. 38-39.
"Flowering Plum." [SpoonRQ] (13:3) Sum 88, p. 58-59.
"Freeway Noise." [StoneC] (16:1/2) Fall-Wint 88-89, p. 34-35.
"Fungi." [ClockR] (4:2) 88, p. 9.
"In the Tradition of the Drinking Song." [Nimrod] (32:1) Fall-Wint 88, p. 128-129.
"Loquat." [SpoonRQ] (13:3) Sum 88, p. 56-57.
"Toward the Music." [CutB] (29/30) 88, p. 36.
"The War Mother." [StoneC] (16:1/2) Fall-Wint 88-89, p. 35.
"When the Angel." [SpoonRQ] (13:3) Sum 88, p. 62.

2672. KEMF, Elizabeth
"Primavera." [HolCrit] (25:3) Je 88, p. 12.
2673. KEMP, Carolyn
"Weighted and pulled." [FiveFR] (6) 88, p. 43.
2674. KEMPA, Rick
"Invitation" (for Fern). [YellowS] (26) Spr 88, p. 33.
"Travelling With My Old Man." [DenQ] (22:3) Wint 88, p. 141-142.
2675. KEMPHER, Ruth Moon
"A Reply to the Rhetorical Question." [Bogg] (59) 88, p. 23.
2676. KENDALL
"Like Your Other Callers." [SinW] (36) Wint 88-89, p. 27-28.
2677. KENDALL, John
"The Cyndi Lauper Tree." [EngJ] (77:6) O 88, p. 87.
2678. KENDALL, Robert
"Octoberfest." [RiverS] (27) 88, p. 43.
"Payoff." [Contact] (9:47/48/49) Spr 88, p. 48.
2679. KENDIG, Diane
"Scrimshaw." [CinPR] (18) Fall 88, p. 62.
2680. KENDLER, Helene
"I Knew a Woman Who Conjured God" (Maharashtra, India). [SouthernHR] (22:4) Fall 88, p. 344-345.
"On a Train Through Maharashtra." [SouthernHR] (22:4) Fall 88, p. 345.
"To My Brother Who Took His Own Life." [SouthernHR] (22:4) Fall 88, p. 354.
2681. KENNEDY, Alexandra
"Taking Off." [GrahamHR] (11) Spr 88, p. 84.
2682. KENNEDY, Monique M.
"Anyway" (tr. of Pia Tafdrup, w. Thomas E. Kennedy). [Spirit] (9:1) 88, p. 165.
"Came to You" (tr. of Pia Tafdrup, w. Thomas E. Kennedy). [StoneC] (16:1/2) Fall-Wint 88-89, p. 54.
"The Dream about the Reader" (tr. of Pia Tafdrup, w. Thomas E. Kennedy). [Rohwedder] (4) [Wint 88-89], p. 36.
"Glazed Eyes" (tr. of Pia Tafdrup, w. Thomas E. Kennedy). [ColR] (NS 15:2) Fall-Wint 88, p. 78.
"The Many Lives" (tr. of Pia Tafdrup, w. Thomas E. Kennedy). [Rohwedder] (4) [Wint 88-89], p. 36.
"Panorama" (tr. of Pia Tafdrup, w. Thomas E. Kennedy). [ColR] (NS 15:2) Fall-Wint 88, p. 79.
"Silent Explosion" (tr. of Pia Tafdrup, w. Thomas E. Kennedy). [ColR] (NS 15:2) Fall-Wint 88, p. 77.
"Snowpins" (tr. of Pia Tafdrup, w. Thomas E. Kennedy). [Spirit] (9:1) 88, p. 164.
2683. KENNEDY, Thomas E.
"Anyway" (tr. of Pia Tafdrup, w. Monique M. Kennedy). [Spirit] (9:1) 88, p. 165.
"Came to You" (tr. of Pia Tafdrup, w. Monique M. Kennedy). [StoneC] (16:1/2) Fall-Wint 88-89, p. 54.
"The Dream about the Reader" (tr. of Pia Tafdrup, w. Monique M. Kennedy). [Rohwedder] (4) [Wint 88-89], p. 36.
"Fevered Lillies" (tr. of Pia Tafdrup). [Vis] (28) 88, p. 32.
"Five Tributes." [SlipS] (8) 88, p. 77.
"Glazed Eyes" (tr. of Pia Tafdrup, w. Monique M. Kennedy). [ColR] (NS 15:2) Fall-Wint 88, p. 78.
"The Many Lives" (tr. of Pia Tafdrup, w. Monique M. Kennedy). [Rohwedder] (4) [Wint 88-89], p. 36.
"Panorama" (tr. of Pia Tafdrup, w. Monique M. Kennedy). [ColR] (NS 15:2) Fall-Wint 88, p. 79.
"Silent Explosion" (tr. of Pia Tafdrup, w. Monique M. Kennedy). [ColR] (NS 15:2) Fall-Wint 88, p. 77.
"Snowpins" (tr. of Pia Tafdrup, w. Monique M. Kennedy). [Spirit] (9:1) 88, p. 164.
"Transit Passenger." [PassN] (9:2) Sum 88, p. 7.
2684. KENNEDY, X. J.
"A 5th Stanza for Dr. Johnson, Donald Hall, Louis Phillips, & X. J. Kennedy" (who wrote stanzas 1-4). [LightY] ('88/9) 88, p. 182-183.
"At the Body Club." [LightY] ('88/9) 88, p. 143-144.
"City Churchyard." [Poetry] (152:1) Ap 88, p. 6-7.
"Fresh Brats." [LightY] ('88/9) 88, p. 40-41.
"Long Distance." [TexasR] (9:3/4) Fall-Wint 88, p. 83.

"Nonsense Poems for Children" (5 poems). [Timbuktu] (2) Sum-Fall 88, p. 78-79.
"On Being Accused of Wit." [TexasR] (9:3/4) Fall-Wint 88, p. 82.
"On Finding That the Dickinson House in Amherst Has an Answering Machine." [TexasR] (9:3/4) Fall-Wint 88, p. 81.
"People." [LightY] ('88/9) 88, p. 71-72.

2685. KENNEY, Paige
"Ars Poetica." [PoetryNW] (29:2) Sum 88, p. 7-8.
"To My Lover Going Into the Army." [PoetryNW] (29:2) Sum 88, p. 6.
"When You Left Me Again." [PoetryNW] (29:2) Sum 88, p. 8-9.

2686. KENNEY, Richard
"Asphyxiation Sapphics." [CreamCR] (12:2) Sum 88, p. 202.
"Shadow." [TexasR] (9:3/4) Fall-Wint 88, p. 87-88.
"Slater (Equinox)." [TexasR] (9:3/4) Fall-Wint 88, p. 85.
"Speed of Light." [TexasR] (9:3/4) Fall-Wint 88, p. 84.
"Up Chimney." [TexasR] (9:3/4) Fall-Wint 88, p. 86.

2687. KENNY, Adele
"For a Little While." [Footwork] ('88) 88, p. 66.
"The Other Side" (for Bill). [Footwork] ('88) 88, p. 65.

2688. KENT, Rolly
"Children of the Forties." [Thrpny] (32) Wint 88, p. 19.

2689. KENYON, Jane
"After the Hurricane." [AmerV] (10) Spr 88, p. 79.
"At the Winter Solstice." [OhioR] (42) 88, p. 83.
"Heavy Summer Rain." [NewYorker] (64:19) 27 Je 88, p. 28.
"Letter to Alice." [TexasR] (9:3/4) Fall-Wint 88, p. 89.
"Private Beach." [NewYorker] (63:47) 11 Ja 88, p. 34.
"Taking Down the Tree." [Ploughs] (14:1) 88, p. 128.
"Three Songs at the End of Summer." [Poetry] (152:6) S 88, p. 311-312.
"Waking in January Before Dawn." [Ploughs] (14:1) 88, p. 129.
"Work." [MissouriR] (11:1) 88, p. 57.

2690. KERLEY, Gary
"History." [GettyR] (1:4) Aut 88, p. 736.
"The Sun Door." [GettyR] (1:4) Aut 88, p. 737.

2691. KERLIKOWSKE, Elizabeth
"Brother / Sister." [PassN] (9:2) Sum 88, p. 6.

KEROSENE, Gene
See RONAN, Stephen

2692. KERR, Debra
"Grandpa Speaks." [Grain] (16:3) Fall 88, p. 39.
"To a Bus Driver." [Grain] (16:3) Fall 88, p. 40.

2693. KERR, Louella
"On the Third Day of January." [CrossC] (10:3) 88, p. 10.
"Second Opinion." [CrossC] (10:3) 88, p. 10.

2694. KERR, Walter H.
"She Walks in Ugly" (Lard Byron Meets William Butler Yeti). [LightY] ('88/9) 88, p. 181-182.

2695. KERRIGAN, T. S.
"Ashes." [KanQ] (20:1/2) Wint-Spr 88, p. 210.
"Nocturne." [KanQ] (20:1/2) Wint-Spr 88, p. 209.

2696. KERSCHNER, Larry
"Dying Light." [CrabCR] (5:3) Fall 88, p. 18.

2697. KERSHNER, Brandon
"Living Room." [TampaR] (1) 88, p. 21.
"Tantrum." [TampaR] (1) 88, p. 63.

2698. KERSHNER, Ivan
"Farm Accident." [Plain] (8:3) Spr-Sum 88, p. 17.
"Home from School, Smithwick, SD — 1958." [Plain] (8:1) Fall 87, p. 9.

2699. KESLER, Russell
"Elegy for J.D.B." [FloridaR] (16:1) Spr-Sum 88, p. 118.
"Screech Owl at Two A.M." [SouthernPR] (28:1) Spr 88, p. 12.

2700. KESSLER, Clyde
"Ghost." [DeKalbLAJ] (21:3/4) 88, p. 58.

2701. KESSLER, Ellen Terry
"Sugar & Spice." [SlipS] (8) 88, p. 67.

2702. KESSLER, Jascha
"Air Granma" (tr. of Ottó Orban, w. Maria Körösy). [LitR] (31:2) Wint 88, p. 157.

"Ancestors" (tr. of Ottó Orban, w. Maria Körösy). [LitR] (31:2) Wint 88, p. 159.
"Chile" (tr. of Ottó Orban, w. Maria Körösy). [MSS] (6:2) 88, p. 83.
"Cosmic Tapestry" (tr. of Anna Kiss, w. Maria Korosy). [Spirit] (9:1) 88, p. 161-163.
"Cradle" (tr. of Ottó Orban, w. Maria Körösy). [MSS] (6:2) 88, p. 85.
"Earth Granma" (tr. of Ottó Orban, w. Maria Körösy). [LitR] (31:2) Wint 88, p. 158.
"Harbach 1944" (tr. of János Pilinzsky, w. Maria Körösy). [MSS] (6:2) 88, p. 86-87.
"Miniatures" (tr. of Anna Kiss, w. Maria Körösy). [Nimrod] (32:1) Fall-Wint 88, p. 142-146.
"A Poem on Theater" (tr. of Sándor Weöres, w. Maria Körösy). [Nimrod] (32:1) Fall-Wint 88, p. 141.
"A Preface to Dying" (tr. of György Rába, w. Maria Körösy). [MSS] (6:2) 88, p. 88-89.
"The Rose and the Nightingale" (tr. of Nader Naderpour, w. Amin Banani). [Vis] (26) 88, p. 11.
"A Strange City" (tr. of Sándor Weöres, w. Maria Körösy). [MSS] (6:2) 88, p. 84.
"The Uses of Poetry" (tr. of Ottó Orban, w. Maria Körösy). [LitR] (31:2) Wint 88, p. 156.
"A Vision" (tr. of Sándor Weöres, w. Maria Körösy). [Nimrod] (32:1) Fall-Wint 88, p. 140.

2703. KESSLER, Rod
"Doing Without." [Interim] (7:2) Fall 88, p. 37.
"January Thaw" (North Hadley, Mass.). [Interim] (7:2) Fall 88, p. 37.

2704. KESTENBAUM, Stuart
"A Cold Rain the Day Before Spring." [BelPoJ] (38:4) Sum 88, p. 7.

2705. KETTNER, M.
"Alone." [SlipS] (8) 88, p. 52.
"A Mile Away." [AlphaBS] (3) Je 88, p. 59.
"Nocturne." [Amelia] (5:2, #13) 88, p. 36.
"Time." [Lactuca] (9) F 88, p. 35.
"We fear what we might gain and we fear what we might lose." [SlipS] (8) 88, p. 48.
"Winter." [RagMag] (6:2) Fall 88, p. 55.

2706. KEYES, Claire
"Canoe Trip." [SpoonRQ] (13:2) Spr 88, p. 15-16.
"German Shepherd." [SpoonRQ] (13:2) Spr 88, p. 18.
"Inside Haleakala." [SpoonRQ] (13:2) Spr 88, p. 16-17.

2707. KEYES, Scott
"Interference." [LightY] ('88/9) 88, p. 151.

2708. KEYS, Kerry Shawn
"And She Is Loved by the People." [PaintedB] (34) 88, p. 47.

2709. KHA, Tran
"Picking Tea Leaves Under a July Rain" (tr. by Nguyen Ngoc Bich). [Vis] (27) 88, p. 18.

2710. KHAW, Brian
"'Nalo Chicken Fights." [HawaiiR] (12:2, #24) Fall 88, p. 80-81.

2711. KHOSLA, Maya
"Fruitseller." [Wind] (18:63) 88, p. 20.

2712. KHOURASANJIAN, Bedros
"Feathers" (tr. by Diana Der-Hovanessian). [LitR] (32:1) Fall 88, p. 66.
"Time Out" (tr. by Diana Der-Hovanessian). [LitR] (32:1) Fall 88, p. 67.

2713. KICH, Martin
"Requiem for a Parish Priest." [Wind] (18:63) 88, p. 21-22.

2714. KIEFER, Rita
"Certain Words" (for Sister Dorothy Kazel). [WeberS] (5:2) Fall 88, p. 58-61.
"Childless Poet." [WeberS] (5:2) Fall 88, p. 62.
"Convergence." [WeberS] (5:2) Fall 88, p. 58.
"From Your Unknown Friend Across the World" (for Irina Ratushinskaya). [WeberS] (5:2) Fall 88, p. 62.

2715. KIJEWSKI, Bruce
"Your Operator-Safe-Reliable-Courteous." [Jacaranda] (3:2) Fall-Wint 88, p. 97-99.

2716. KIKEL, Rudy
"My Eyes." [MassR] (29:3) Fall 88, p. 428-429.
"My Penis." [MassR] (29:3) Fall 88, p. 429-430.

"My Soul." [MassR] (29:3) Fall 88, p. 430-431.

2717. KILLIAN, Kevin
"Neutral." [Sink] (3) 88, p. 57-58.
"Plum Tree." [Sink] (3) 88, p. 58.
"Tell." [Sink] (3) 88, p. 55-56.

2718. KILLIAN, Natasha
"Irkutsk — Three Centuries" (tr. of Mark Sergeyev). [NegC] (8:1/2) 88, p. 70-71.
"Priceless Minutes and Lost Hours" (tr. of Boris Kopaligin). [NegC] (8:1/2) 88, p. 188-194.
"The Sacred Tambourine" (tr. of Andrei Passar). [NegC] (8:1/2) 88, p. 68-69.

2719. KILLIAN, Sean
"Atmospherics." [Notus] (3:1) Spr 88, p. 73.
"Serif." [Notus] (3:1) Spr 88, p. 72.

2720. KIM, Alison
"Sewing Woman." [Calyx] (11:2/3) Fall 88, p. 203.

2721. KIM, Myung Mi
"Into Such Assembly." [Calyx] (11:2/3) Fall 88, p. 18-19.
"A Rose of Sharon." [Calyx] (11:2/3) Fall 88, p. 20.

2722. KIM, Sabina
"In the Owltime." [Grain] (16:4) Wint 88, p. 11.

2723. KIM, Yuhn-Bok
"The Epitaph on the Snow." [Confr] (37/38) Spr-Sum 88, p. 119.
"On the Road to the Old Shoe-Shaped Village." [Confr] (37/38) Spr-Sum 88, p. 118.

2724. KIMBALL, Arthur
"Act." [CrabCR] (5:1) Wint 88, p. 14.
"Fall." [CrabCR] (5:1) Wint 88, p. 14.

2725. KIME, Peter
"Accidents." [RiverS] (25) 88, p. 49.
"Incinerators." [RiverS] (25) 88, p. 50.
"A Suicide." [LitR] (31:2) Wint 88, p. 183.

2726. KIMMET, Gene
"Christmas Baroque." [SpoonRQ] (12:4) Fall 87, p. 59.
"In the London Underground." [SpoonRQ] (12:4) Fall 87, p. 58.

2727. KIMMICH, Flora
"Aubade (Second Asclepiadean Stanzas: Dithyrambs)." [LitR] (31:4) Sum 88, p. 447.

2728. KINCAID, Joan Payne
"Demise of Why I." [Crosscur] (7:4) 88, p. 106-107.
"Hearing Mahler in the Distance." [WindO] (50) Aut 88, p. 21.
"Lying Low." [WindO] (50) Aut 88, p. 19.
"Talk about Making Love." [Bogg] (60) 88, p. 13.
"Why Write Poetry Even If You Never Are Published?" [WindO] (50) Aut 88, p. 20.

2729. KING, Kenneth
"Concrete Poem." [GreensboroR] (45) Wint 88-89, p. 103.
"Dog Barking at Fireflies." [PoetryNW] (29:2) Sum 88, p. 46-47.
"If It Came, If It Played." [GreensboroR] (45) Wint 88-89, p. 102.
"Our Failure to Cancel Fireworks Displays in a Fire-Prone Season." [PoetryNW] (29:4) Wint 88-89, p. 22-23.

2730. KING, R. D.
"Style." [NowestR] (26:3) 88, p. 17.

2731. KING, Robert
"Walking at Dusk." [KanQ] (20:3) Sum 88, p. 114.

2732. KING, T. A.
"February, 1987." [JamesWR] (6:1) Fall 88, p. 9.

2733. KINGSLEY, Chris
"Waiting for the Ferry to Le Havre." [LittleM] (15:3/4) 88, p. 123.

2734. KINNELL, Galway
"Brother of My Heart" (for Etheridge Knight). [PaintedB] (32/33) 88, p. 59.

2735. KINNEY, Jeanne (Jeanne Kawelolani)
"Something like the Speed of Light." [Ascent] (14:1) 88, p. 24.
"Something Like the Speed of Light." [Jacaranda] (3:2) Fall-Wint 88, p. 151.
"What Nancy Said." [HawaiiR] (12:2, #24) Fall 88, p. 11.

2736. KINNEY-HANSON, Sharon
"Marianne Moore: A Bit of History in a Modern Mode." [HeliconN] (19) 88, p. 72-73.

2737. KINSELLA, Thomas
"St. Catherine's Clock" (Excerpts). [ManhatR] (4:2) Spr 88, p. 26-29.
2738. KINSLEY, Robert
"Faint-light" (for Tristan). [IndR] (11:2) Spr 88, p. 16-17.
"Trilling." [IndR] (11:2) Spr 88, p. 15.
2739. KINSOLVING, Susan
"August Island." [HighP] (3:2) Fall 88, p. 44-45.
"Beginning." [TexasR] (9:3/4) Fall-Wint 88, p. 90.
"Elegy." [NewRep] (199:17) 24 O 88, p. 36.
"Ode." [HighP] (3:2) Fall 88, p. 43.
"Our Fields." [HighP] (3:2) Fall 88, p. 41-42.
"Snow Sleep." [TexasR] (9:3/4) Fall-Wint 88, p. 91.
"Walking After Winter." [NewRep] (198:19) 9 My 88, p. 36.
2740. KINZIE, Mary
"Autumn Eros." [TriQ] (71) Wint 88, p. 132-136.
"The Clover Cross." [NewYorker] (64:14) 23 My 88, p. 32.
"The Current." [Shen] (38:2) 88, p. 18-19.
"Dark Carol." [Sequoia] (32:1) Spr-Sum 88, p. 51-52.
"Diner." [Salm] (80) Fall 88, p. 105-107.
"Drawing Through Fever." [Shen] (38:2) 88, p. 19-20.
"On the Actor Edward Petherbridge." [YaleR] (77:4) Sum 88, p. 566-568.
"Reading an Old Poem of Mine." [NewYorker] (64:25) 8 Ag 88, p. 64.
"Ringing Words." [NewRep] (198:27, i.e. 199:1) 4 Jl 88, p. 36.
2741. KIRBY, Barney
"The Crying Tree." [AmerPoR] (17:2) Mr-Ap 88, p. 45.
"Untitled: Those bleached lavender flowers." [AmerPoR] (17:2) Mr-Ap 88, p. 45.
2742. KIRBY, David
"A Comb and a Nickel." [Timbuktu] (2) Sum-Fall 88, p. 57.
"La Forza del Destino in the Tri-State Area." [SouthernR] (24:3) Sum 88, p. 582-583.
"Nocturne." [LightY] ('88/9) 88, p. 135-136.
"Unable to Wait for Godot." [BelPoJ] (38:3) Spr 88, p. 18-19.
2743. KIRBY, Mark
"Confirmation." [Comm] (115:13) 15 Jl 88, p. 405.
2744. KIRCHWEY, Karl
"Child's Ballad by Lake Geneva." [PraS] (62:1) Spr 88, p. 34-36.
"Hat Blocks in Loco" (Canton Ticino). [PraS] (62:1) Spr 88, p. 33-34.
"House Lights Down." [ParisR] (30:107) Sum 88, p. 196.
"An Irish Girl on the Lake of Geneva." [Shen] (38:2) 88, p. 39-40.
"John Howland's Lyric." [SouthwR] (73:4) Aut 88, p. 526-528.
"Lost Wax" (Reading Cellini's *Autobiography*). [MassR] (29:3) Fall 88, p. 519-520.
"Two Legends of Salvation." [YaleR] (77:2) Wint 88, p. 295-296.
"A Wandering Island." [Nat] (247:15) 21 N 88, p. 542.
2745. KIRK, Laurie
"Bridging the Dark." [Footwork] ('88) 88, p. 11.
"Dressing for Bed." [Footwork] ('88) 88, p. 11.
"High School Teacher." [HayF] (3) Spr 88, p. 32-33.
"In the Whispered Dark." [Footwork] ('88) 88, p. 11.
2746. KIRKEBY, Cindy
"How Can I Keep from Dancing?" [RagMag] (6:1) [88], p. 18.
2747. KIRKLAND, Leigh
"Paper Sculpture." [ChatR] (8:3) Spr 88, p. 59.
"Playgrounds." [CutB] (29/30) 88, p. 35.
2748. KIRMAYER, Laurence J.
"For Penfield." [Quarry] (37:1) Wint 88, p. 71.
2749. KIRSCH, Sarah
"Feuerofen." [Rohwedder] (4) [Wint 88-89], p. 8.
"Fiery Oven" (tr. by Marina L. Roscher and Charles Fishman). [Rohwedder] (4) [Wint 88-89], p. 8.
"Die Gänse Flogen Landeinwärts." [Rohwedder] (4) [Wint 88-89], p. 6.
"The Geese Flew Inland" (tr. by Marina L. Roscher and Charles Fishman). [Rohwedder] (4) [Wint 88-89], p. 6.
"Die Geologen." [Rohwedder] (4) [Wint 88-89], p. 5.
"The Geologists" (tr. by Marina L. Roscher and Charles Fishman). [Rohwedder] (4) [Wint 88-89], p. 5.

"The Green Double" (tr. by Marina L. Roscher and Charles Fishman). [Rohwedder] (4) [Wint 88-89], p. 4.
"Der Grüne Doppelgänger." [Rohwedder] (4) [Wint 88-89], p. 4.
"Hoarfrost Harvest" (tr. by Marina L. Roscher and Charles Fishman). [Rohwedder] (4) [Wint 88-89], p. 7.
"Moorland." [Rohwedder] (4) [Wint 88-89], p. 8.
"Moorland" (tr. by Marina L. Roscher and Charles Fishman). [Rohwedder] (4) [Wint 88-89], p. 8.
"Reif." [Rohwedder] (4) [Wint 88-89], p. 7.
"Wenn das Eis Geht." [Rohwedder] (4) [Wint 88-89], p. 3.
"When the Ice Floats" (tr. by Marina L. Roscher and Charles Fishman). [Rohwedder] (4) [Wint 88-89], p. 3.

2750. KIRSCHENBAUM, Blossom S.
"Portrait of the Consort to Louis XIV." [LightY] ('88/9) 88, p. 67.
"Realpolitik." [LightY] ('88/9) 88, p. 67.

2751. KISHIMOTO, Machiko
"Spring" (tr. by Tomoyuki Iino). [Stand] (29:3) Sum 88, p. 24.

2752. KISHKAN, Theresa
"Mysteries." [Event] (17:2) Sum 88, p. 52.
"You Have Loved Them." [Event] (17:2) Sum 88, p. 53.

2753. KISS, Anna
"Cosmic Tapestry" (tr. by Jascha Kessler, w. Maria Korosy). [Spirit] (9:1) 88, p. 161-163.
"Miniatures" (tr. by Jascha Kessler, w. Maria Körösy). [Nimrod] (32:1) Fall-Wint 88, p. 142-146.

2754. KITAHARA, Hakushu
"Master Fall" (tr. by Graeme Wilson). [Jacaranda] (3:1) Wint 88, p. 6-7.

2755. KITTELL, Ronald Edward
"Small Female Things & Jewels." [Plain] (8:1) Fall 87, p. 15.

2756. KLANDER, Sharon
"By Being Still." [NewL] (55:2) Wint 88-89, p. 44.
"Extreme Unction." [NewL] (55:2) Wint 88-89, p. 46-47.
"Five Senses." [NewL] (55:2) Wint 88-89, p. 48.
"Grandfather." [NewL] (55:2) Wint 88-89, p. 45-46.
"The Landscape Going Home" (for my sister). [NewL] (55:2) Wint 88-89, p. 43-44.
"Secrets We Keep." [NewL] (55:2) Wint 88-89, p. 49.
"Therapy." [DenQ] (22:3) Wint 88, p. 138.
"To Mother on My Birthday." [Shen] (38:3) 88, p. 77.
"Turning to Morning" (Selections. Pablo Neruda Prize for Poetry, Honorable Mention). [Nimrod] (32:1) Fall-Wint 88, p. 89-93.

2757. KLASSEN, Sarah
"Incarnation." [Dandel] (15:2) Fall-Wint 88, p. 16.
"Inheritance." [Dandel] (15:2) Fall-Wint 88, p. 15.

2758. KLAUKE, Amy
"Epiphanies." [CimR] (84) Jl 88, p. 25.
"Under the Flight Path." [CimR] (84) Jl 88, p. 26.

2759. KLAVAN, Andrew
"Margaret Love." [KanQ] (20:1/2) Wint-Spr 88, p. 64.

2760. KLAWITTER, George
"Nature Over Art." [PoetryNW] (29:3) Aut 88, p. 30.
"Recital a la Carte." [PoetryNW] (29:3) Aut 88, p. 29.

2761. KLEIN, Michael
"Naming the Elements" (for Michael S., for John W.). [JamesWR] (5:2) Wint 88, p. 10.
"Positive." [CentralP] (14) Fall 88, p. 9-11.
"Staying Stopped." [CutB] (29/30) 88, p. 93.
"Tracings from Belmont." [CutB] (29/30) 88, p. 94-95.

2762. KLEIN-HEALY, Eloise
"After Seeing the Hockney Retrospective." [Jacaranda] (3:2) Fall-Wint 88, p. 100-101.
"Artemis." [Jacaranda] (3:1) Wint 88, p. 1.
"The Valley of the Amazons." [Jacaranda] (3:1) Wint 88, p. 2.

2763. KLEINSCHMIDT, Edward
"All of the Above." [PoetryNW] (29:4) Wint 88-89, p. 36.
"At the Drowning Every Afternoon." [Sonora] (14/15) Spr 88, p. 10.
"A Disturbance in Mirrors." [AnotherCM] (18) 88, p. 116.

"Just Stop and Think." [PoetC] (19:3) Spr 88, p. 12.
"Mumbo Jumbo." [MassR] (29:3) Fall 88, p. 450.
"Nothing Is But What Is Not." [Poetry] (143, i.e. 153:1) O 88, p. 5.
"Past Living (Beyond the Power, Scope, Extent)." [AnotherCM] (18) 88, p. 117-118.
"The Sympathetic Nervous System." [PoetC] (19:3) Spr 88, p. 14-15.
"While Walking in the Garden, the Garlic Considers Sainthood." [PoetC] (19:3) Spr 88, p. 13.

2764. KLEINZAHLER, August
"April Before Gehenna." [Thrpny] (33) Spr 88, p. 22.
"Before Winter, Part II." [Sulfur] (8:2, #23) Fall 88, p. 79-80.
"Disappointment." [Sulfur] (8:2, #23) Fall 88, p. 79.
"Earthquake Weather." [NewAW] (4) Fall 88, p. 33-34.
"Ebenezer Californicus." [NewAW] (4) Fall 88, p. 29.
"February on the Palisades" (8 poems). [Thrpny] (32) Wint 88, p. 20-21.
"Friends Through at New Year's." [Zyzzyva] (4:4) Wint 88, p. 104-105.
"Like Cities, Like Storms." [NewAW] (4) Fall 88, p. 32.
"A Little July Something." [NewAW] (4) Fall 88, p. 30.
"The Lunatic of Lindley Meadow." [NewAW] (4) Fall 88, p. 31.
"Since You Didn't Phone." [NewYorker] (64:25) 8 Ag 88, p. 30.
"Sunset in Chinatown." [Sulfur] (8:2, #23) Fall 88, p. 80-81.
"The Tree." [Harp] (276:1654) Mr 88, p. 34.

2765. KLOEFKORN, William
"1943." [SoDakR] (26:2) Sum 88, p. 134-135.
"Easter Sunday." [SpoonRQ] (13:2) Spr 88, p. 62-63.
"Independent" (for Gary Gildner). [LaurelR] (22:2) Sum 88, p. 65-67.
"Last Summer and the One Before." [CreamCR] (12:2) Sum 88, p. 210-211.
"Odyssey." [SwampR] (1:2/3) D 88, p. 80-81.
"The Price of Admission." [Spirit] (9:1) 88, p. 144-146.
"Spring." [SwampR] (1:2/3) D 88, p. 82.
"The Understanding." [CreamCR] (12:2) Sum 88, p. 203-209.

2766. KLOKKER, Jay
"Dangerous Facts." [HangL] (53) 88, p. 26.
"Ghazal." [HangL] (53) 88, p. 25.
"Remembering the Skykomish" (for Richard Hugo). [BellR] (11:2) Fall 88, p. 35.
"Whale Watch: Beyond the Harbor." [HangL] (53) 88, p. 24.

2767. KLOPFENSTEIN, Helen
"Anniversary." [BellArk] (4:3) My-Je 88, p. 3.
"Rabbits & a Blue-Ribbon Goose." [BellArk] (4:4) Jl-Ag 88, p. 1.

2768. KLUGE, Ian
"Out of the Siyah-Chal." [WorldO] (20:3/4) Spr-Sum 86, c89, p. 42-43.

2769. KLUGE, Svetlana
"The Christmas Tree in the Hospital Corridor" (tr. of Bella Akhmadulina, w. William Jay Smith). [AmerPoR] (17:3) My-Je 88, p. 40.
"The Death of the Owl" (tr. of Bella Akhmadulina, w. William Jay Smith). [AmerPoR] (17:3) My-Je 88, p. 38.
"Raphael Day" (tr. of Bella Akhmadulina, w. William Jay Smith). [AmerPoR] (17:3) My-Je 88, p. 39.
"The Resort" (tr. of Bella Akhmadulina, w. William Jay Smith). [AmerPoR] (17:3) My-Je 88, p. 39.

2770. KLUKOFF, Philip
"Einstein at Christmas." [NewAW] (3) Spr 88, p. 99.

2771. KLUTTS, Randy
"Because It's There." [SlipS] (8) 88, p. 20.
"Hot Wax." [SlipS] (8) 88, p. 20-21.
"In the Attic." [RagMag] (6:1) [88], p. 19.

2772. KNAUTH, S. (Stephen)
"The Blue Cedar." [CinPR] (18) Fall 88, p. 71.
"Crossing the Nantahala (Her Sorrel Hair Undoes Me)." [CarolQ] (41:1) Fall 88, p. 71.
"Sunday Evening." [YellowS] (27) Aut 88, p. 36.
"Winter Blossom." [KanQ] (20:3) Sum 88, p. 179.

2773. KNIGHT, Arthur Winfield
"The Big Things." [WormR] (28:1, #109) 88, p. 27-28.
"The Biker." [Amelia] (4:4, #11) 88, p. 63.
"Billy the Kid: Last Words." [SpoonRQ] (13:1) Wint 88, p. 60.

"Blood on the Moon." [Turnstile] (1:1) Wint 88, p. 52-53.
"Breaking Things." [Amelia] (5:1, #12) 88, p. 47.
"Buckskin Frank Leslie: Loner." [Footwork] ('88) 88, p. 32.
"Buffalo Bill's Last Dream, 1917." [SpoonRQ] (13:1) Wint 88, p. 61.
"Chief Joseph: Defeated" (A Found Poem). [Bogg] (59) 88, p. 52.
"A Christmas Letter to Mom and Dad." [Wind] (18:62) 88, p. 23-25.
"Cole Younger: Dreams." [CinPR] (18) Fall 88, p. 42.
"The Dissatisfied." [WormR] (28:1, #109) 88, p. 28-29.
"Dog Tags." [WormR] (28:1, #109) 88, p. 29.
"The Happiest Man Alive." [CinPR] (18) Fall 88, p. 40-41.
"Instant Winner." [SlipS] (8) 88, p. 47.
"The Pencil." [CinPR] (18) Fall 88, p. 39.
"Rapture." [SlipS] (8) 88, p. 46.
"Tell Me an Erotic Story." [SlipS] (8) 88, p. 48.
"The Unpardonable Sin." [CinPR] (18) Fall 88, p. 38-39.

2774. KNIGHT, Denis
"In Limogne Square." [Stand] (29:2) Spr 88, p. 27.
"The Town Hall at Montpezat." [Stand] (29:2) Spr 88, p. 26.
"Twelve Police-Horses" (At the miners' march, February 1985). [Stand] (29:4) Aut 88, p. 47.
"Two Things, Said Noe Marty." [Stand] (29:2) Spr 88, p. 27.

2775. KNIGHT, Etheridge
"The Bones of My Father." [PaintedB] (32/33) 88, p. 25-26.
"Cell Song." [PaintedB] (32/33) 88, p. 48.
"Dearly / — Beloved / — Mizzee" (for Elizabeth Gordon McKim). [PaintedB] (32/33) 88, p. 141.
"Feeling Fucked Up." [PaintedB] (32/33) 88, p. 74.
"For Langston Hughes." [PaintedB] (32/33) 88, p. 62.
"Haiku: Making jazz swing in." [PaintedB] (32/33) 88, p. 136.
"Hip/Notes to My/Self." [PaintedB] (32/33) 88, p. 81.
"The Keeping of a Promise" (for Charlene Blackburn). [PaintedB] (32/33) 88, p. 92.
"Memo #75." [PaintedB] (32/33) 88, p. 101.
"A Poem to Galway Kinnell." [PaintedB] (32/33) 88, p. 60-61.
"The Sun Came." [PaintedB] (32/33) 88, p. 10.
"Things Awfully Quiet in America" (Song of the Mwalimu Nkosi Ajanaku). [PaintedB] (32/33) 88, p. 100.
"Upon Your Leaving" (for Sonia). [PaintedB] (32/33) 88, p. 73.
"Various Protestations from Various People." [PaintedB] (32/33) 88, p. 86.
"Who Knows ? ? ?" [PaintedB] (32/33) 88, p. 97.

2776. KNIGHT, Kit
"Jacking Off the Rhino." [SlipS] (8) 88, p. 25.

2777. KNIGHT, Sondra
"Sisters." [SinW] (35) Sum-Fall 88, p. 59.

2778. KNIGHTS, Maudeen
"West Seattle Alley." [BellArk] (4:6) N-D 88, p. 3.

2779. KNOEPFLE, John
"I Weep Before My Angel." [Paint] (15:30) Aut 88, p. 24.

2780. KNOPPOW, Susan
"Summer 1987." [Crosscur] (7:4) 88, p. 27.

2781. KNOTT, Bill
"Alfonsina Storni." [Caliban] (4) 88, p. 11-12.
"Endless Evening: My Life at Il Vittoriale." [Caliban] (4) 88, p. 11.
"For Claudia." [Caliban] (4) 88, p. 13.
"My Plea for Sanctum in the Sculpture Garden of Medusa." [Caliban] (4) 88, p. 13.
"Refusing an Invitation to the Masked Ball." [Caliban] (4) 88, p. 12.

2782. KNOTT, Kip
"Honeymoon, Burr Oak." [SoDakR] (26:3) Aut 88, p. 83.
"The Sounding." [Vis] (27) 88, p. 16.
"Van Gogh, 'Self Portrait with Pipe'." [MidAR] (8:2) 88, p. 84.

2783. KNOX, Caroline
"Emblem Poem: Scallop Shell." [CreamCR] (12:2) Sum 88, p. 212.
"Log of the Snow Star." [NewRep] (198:1/2) 4-11 Ja 88, p. 38.
"Pantoum du Chat." [Ploughs] (14:1) 88, p. 113-114.
"Reggae Blue Sweater." [LightY] ('88/9) 88, p. 62.

KO, Chang Soo
See CHANG, Soo Ko

2784. KOCH, Claude
"The Hidden." [FourQ] (2d series 2:2) Fall 88, p. 44.
2785. KOCH, James
"A Fitness Center Chant." [LightY] ('88/9) 88, p. 55.
2786. KOCH, Kenneth
"Alexander." [NewAW] (3) Spr 88, p. 15.
"Cook." [NewAW] (3) Spr 88, p. 4.
"Crêpe de Chine." [NewAW] (3) Spr 88, p. 17.
"Four Loves." [NewAW] (3) Spr 88, p. 5-7.
"Mahx Bruddahs." [NewAW] (3) Spr 88, p. 18-19.
"Mary Magdalene's Song." [NewAW] (3) Spr 88, p. 9.
"Olive Oyl Commandeers Popeye's Gunboat and Sails Off to Attack Russia." [NewAW] (3) Spr 88, p. 16.
"The Party." [NewAW] (3) Spr 88, p. 8.
"Permanently." [NewAW] (3) Spr 88, p. 11-12.
"Stuck in Now." [NewAW] (3) Spr 88, p. 10.
"Time and His Trumpet." [NewAW] (3) Spr 88, p. 1-2.
"Transposed Hamlet." [NewAW] (3) Spr 88, p. 13.
"Two Tall Individuals." [NewAW] (3) Spr 88, p. 3.
"Wittgenstein, or Bravo, Dr. Wittgenstein." [NewAW] (3) Spr 88, p. 14.
2787. KOCH, Michael
"Ensemble." [FiveFR] (6) 88, p. 62.
2788. KODOLANYI, Gyula
"The Sea and John Smith." [Sulfur] (7:3, #21) Wint 88, p. 85-90.
"Tract on Rhyme." [Sulfur] (7:3, #21) Wint 88, p. 91-92.
KOEHN, Lala Heine
See HEINE-KOEHN, Lala
2789. KOENIG-CLEMENT, Dymphny
"Mistakes." [Grain] (16:4) Wint 88, p. 37.
2790. KOERNER, Edgar
"Mid-March." [ManhatPR] (10) Ja 88, p. 38.
"Shoe Laces All Tied." [LittleM] (15:3/4) 88, p. 33-34.
"Solo." [ManhatPR] (10) Ja 88, p. 38-39.
"Working Up to a Daisy." [LittleM] (15:3/4) 88, p. 35.
2791. KOERTGE, Ron
"Jealousy." [Jacaranda] (3:2) Fall-Wint 88, p. 102.
2792. KOESTENBAUM, Wayne
"The Babysitter in the Ham Radio." [Jacaranda] (3:2) Fall-Wint 88, p. 26-27.
"Doctor Type." [Shen] (38:1) 88, p. 89-91.Ward, Robert "Sunflowers." [Shen] (38:1) 88, p. 91-92.
"The Ornate and Lovely Corner House." [Boulevard] (3:2/3) Fall 88, p. 187-188.
"Relics of the True Cross." [AntR] (46:4) Fall 88, p. 486-487.
2793. KOETHE, John
"The Realm of Ends." [Boulevard] (3:2/3) Fall 88, p. 206.
"The Third Wish." [GrandS] (7:2) Wint 88, p. 32-33.
2794. KOHLER, Sandra
"Last Poem from Squaw Valley." [AmerPoR] (17:4) Jl-Ag 88, p. 38.
"Trying to Talk About Sex — II." [AmerPoR] (17:4) Jl-Ag 88, p. 38.
2795. KOHN, Deborah
"Aix-en-Provence from our Window and at Tabac Le Grimaldier." [Interim] (7:1) Spr 88, p. 40.
2796. KOLAKOWSKI, Denny
"Moving Water." [SmPd] (25:1) Wint 88, p. 26-28.
2797. KOLODINSKY, Alison
"The Chipping Sparrow." [FloridaR] (16:1) Spr-Sum 88, p. 119.
2798. KOLODZIEJ, Krysia
"Venezuela, 1984: Impasse in Four Parts." [LindLM] (7:1) Ja-Mr 88, p. 21-22.
2799. KOLUMBAN, Nicholas
"Before Long You'll Turn 28. You'll Live to See the Axe" (tr. of Tibor Zalan). [CharR] (14:2) Fall 88, p. 101.
"I'm with My Most Supple Poems Now When You Don't Love Me" (tr. of Tibor Zalan). [CharR] (14:2) Fall 88, p. 102-103.
"New York." [HawaiiR] (12:1, #23) Spr 88, p. 116.
"Returning from the Capital of a Small Country to a Small Town in America." [HawaiiR] (12:1, #23) Spr 88, p. 118.
"The Voyager." [HawaiiR] (12:1, #23) Spr 88, p. 117.

"When It's Not Fashionable to Write Silence, I'll Portray Your Silence" (tr. of Tibor Zalan). [CharR] (14:2) Fall 88, p. 102.
"You Can Do Anything to Me But One Thing: Don't Love Me" (tr. of Tibor Zalan). [CharR] (14:2) Fall 88, p. 100.

2800. KOMACHI, Ono no
"The autumn night" (tr. by Jane Hirshfield, w. Mariko Aratani). [AmerPoR] (17:1) Ja-F 88, p. 16.
"I know it must be this way" (tr. by Jane Hirshfield, w. Mariko Aratani). [AmerPoR] (17:1) Ja-F 88, p. 16.
"The seaweed gatherer's weary feet" (tr. by Jane Hirshfield, w. Mariko Aratani). [AmerPoR] (17:1) Ja-F 88, p. 16.
"When my desire" (tr. by Jane Hirshfield, w. Mariko Aratani). [AmerPoR] (17:1) Ja-F 88, p. 16.

2801. KOMUNYAKAA, Yusef
"Boxing Day." [Callaloo] (11:2, #35) Spr 88, p. 223-224.
"The Cops Call Him Charlie." [WillowS] (21) Wint 88, p. 20.
"The Edge." [Callaloo] (11:2, #35) Spr 88, p. 225-226.
"February in Sydney." [WillowS] (21) Wint 88, p. 22.
"In the Mirror." [Callaloo] (11:2, #35) Spr 88, p. 222.
"It's Always Night." [Caliban] (4) 88, p. 52.
"Jungle Surrender" (after Don Cooper's painting). [ColR] (NS 15:1) Spr-Sum 88, p. 14-15.
"Maps Drawn in the Dust." [ColR] (NS 15:1) Spr-Sum 88, p. 13.
"Oaths & Debts." [Callaloo] (11:2, #35) Spr 88, p. 227.
"The Plea." [Caliban] (4) 88, p. 50-51.
"Protection of Movable Cultural Heritage." [WillowS] (21) Wint 88, p. 21.
"Report from the Lucky Country" ([In] memory of numerous black men killed in Australia). [Callaloo] (11:2, #35) Spr 88, p. 220-221.
"Rocks Push." [Crazy] (34) Spr 88, p. 41-42.
"Rollcall." [Callaloo] (11:2, #35) Spr 88, p. 228.
"Venus's-Flytraps." [Ploughs] (14:4) 88, p. 150-151.

2802. KONDOS, Yannis
"The End of the Day" (tr. by James Stone). [Agni] (27) 88, p. 209.

2803. KONO, Juliet S.
"Hilo Rains" (40 poems). [BambooR] (37/38) Spr 88, 103 p.
"Pearls." [HawaiiR] (12:1, #23) Spr 88, p. 54-55.

2804. KONRAD, Linda
"Father's Fall." [JlNJPo] (10:1/2) 88, p. 24.
"Upon the Renovation of Saint Leo's." [JlNJPo] (10:1/2) 88, p. 25.

KOON, Woon
See WOON, Koon

2805. KOONTZ, Haven
"My Daughter Cannot Stand to See Me Cry." [BallSUF] (29:4) Aut 88, p. 6-7.

2806. KOONTZ, Tom
"Etheridge" (Indianapolis 5/1/84). [PaintedB] (32/33) 88, p. 70-71.
"Form Is Emptiness." [PaintedB] (34) 88, p. 9.
"Waves Coming In." [PaintedB] (34) 88, p. 9.

2807. KOOSER, Ted
"In Tennessee." [LightY] ('88/9) 88, p. 151.
"The Mouse in the Piano." [PoetryE] (25) Spr 88, p. 6 repeated on back cover.

2808. KOPALIGIN, Boris
"Priceless Minutes and Lost Hours" (tr. by Natasha Killian). [NegC] (8:1/2) 88, p. 188-194.

2809. KOPELKE, Kendra
"Poetry Reading." [PassN] (9:2) Sum 88, p. 23.

2810. KOROLYOV, Sergei
"Flights in a Dream" (tr. by Leonid S. Polevoy). [NegC] (8:1/2) 88, p. 66.

2811. KÖRÖSY, Maria
"Air Granma" (tr. of Ottó Orban, w. Jascha Kessler). [LitR] (31:2) Wint 88, p. 157.
"Ancestors" (tr. of Ottó Orban, w. Jascha Kessler). [LitR] (31:2) Wint 88, p. 159.
"Chile" (tr. of Ottó Orban, w. Jascha Kessler). [MSS] (6:2) 88, p. 83.
"Cosmic Tapestry" (tr. of Anna Kiss, w. Jascha Kessler). [Spirit] (9:1) 88, p. 161-163.
"Cradle" (tr. of Ottó Orban, w. Jascha Kessler). [MSS] (6:2) 88, p. 85.
"Earth Granma" (tr. of Ottó Orban, w. Jascha Kessler). [LitR] (31:2) Wint 88, p. 158.

"Harbach 1944" (tr. of János Pilinzsky, w. Jascha Kessler). [MSS] (6:2) 88, p. 86-87.
"Miniatures" (tr. of Anna Kiss, w. Jascha Kessler). [Nimrod] (32:1) Fall-Wint 88, p. 142-146.
"A Poem on Theater" (tr. of Sándor Weöres, w. Jascha Kessler). [Nimrod] (32:1) Fall-Wint 88, p. 141.
"A Preface to Dying" (tr. of György Rába, w. Jascha Kessler). [MSS] (6:2) 88, p. 88-89.
"A Strange City" (tr. of Sándor Weöres, w. Jascha Kessler). [MSS] (6:2) 88, p. 84.
"The Uses of Poetry" (tr. of Ottó Orban, w. Jascha Kessler). [LitR] (31:2) Wint 88, p. 156.
"A Vision" (tr. of Sándor Weöres, w. Jascha Kessler). [Nimrod] (32:1) Fall-Wint 88, p. 140.

2812. KORSTANGE, Gordon
"California Achievement Tests." [EngJ] (77:6) O 88, p. 86.

2813. KORT, Betty
"The French Quarter" (New Orleans, 1987). [CapeR] (23:1) Spr 88, p. 12-13.

KORVIN, André de
See De KORVIN, André

2814. KOSSOWSKY, Sari
"Desire." [FiveFR] (6) 88, p. 8.

2815. KOST, Holly Hunt
"(reAtriX." [FloridaR] (16:1) Spr-Sum 88, p. 78-81.

2816. KOSTELANETZ, Richard
"0 6 4 5 0 5." [Pembroke] (20) 88, p. 137.
"1024." [Pembroke] (20) 88, p. 138.
"Epiphanies." [CentralP] (13) Spr 88, p. 119-123.
"Epiphanies." [PoetryE] (25) Spr 88, p. 124-125.
"Epiphanies" (Excerpts). [Notus] (3:1) Spr 88, p. 86.
"More Portraits from Memory." [Lips] (14) 88, p. 46-48.
"Partitions." [PaintedB] (32/33) 88, p. 102-103.

2817. KOVACIK, Karen
"Rachel and Leah." [StoneC] (16:1/2) Fall-Wint 88-89, p. 16.

2818. KOVACS, Edna
"Crossing the hills." [Amelia] (5:1, #12) 88, p. 95.
"Dream Sequences." [BellArk] (4:5) S-O 88, p. 3.
"I wait for someone." [Amelia] (5:2, #13) 88, p. 60.
"Mackinac Island." [BellArk] (4:6) N-D 88, p. 3.

2819. KOVANDA, William James
"Last Rites." [Plain] (8:1) Fall 87, p. 11.

2820. KOVNER, Abba
"My Sister Sits Smiling" (tr. by Bernhard Frank). [ColR] (NS 15:2) Fall-Wint 88, p. 74.

2821. KOYAMA, Tina
"Currents." [Calyx] (11:2/3) Fall 88, p. 128.
"Downtown Seattle in the Fog." [Calyx] (11:2/3) Fall 88, p. 129.

2822. KOZAK, Roberta
"The Old Country." [AntR] (46:1) Wint 88, p. 82-83.
"View from Sweetgrass." [DenQ] (22:3) Wint 88, p. 179-180.

2823. KOZER, José
"Amor para una Joven Aspirante a Poeta." [Inti] (26/27) Otoño 87-Primavera 88, p. 189-190.
"La Guerra en los Bosques." [Inti] (26/27) Otoño 87-Primavera 88, p. 188-189.
"Holocausto." [Inti] (26/27) Otoño 87-Primavera 88, p. 186-188.
"Púber." [Inti] (26/27) Otoño 87-Primavera 88, p. 189.
"Tríptico de los Británicos" (Para Julián Ríos). [Inti] (26/27) Otoño 87-Primavera 88, p. 190-195.

2824. KRAEHE, Claudia
"Looking Back." [FiveFR] (6) 88, p. 44.

2825. KRAFFT, Charles
"The Peruvian Nap" (The Exciting sequel to The Offhanded Refill). [Margin] (6) Sum 88, p. 90-92.

2826. KRAFT, Doris
"Arte Moderno." [LetFem] (14:1/2) Primavera-Otoño 88, p. 130.
"Blanco" (Tres Etapas de Me Vida). [LetFem] (14:1/2) Primavera-Otoño 88, p. 125.
"Círculo Vicioso." [LetFem] (14:1/2) Primavera-Otoño 88, p. 125.

"Cuatro Estaciones." [LetFem] (14:1/2) Primavera-Otoño 88, p. 129-130.
"En el Parque." [LetFem] (14:1/2) Primavera-Otoño 88, p. 126.
"El Escritor." [LetFem] (14:1/2) Primavera-Otoño 88, p. 127.
"Gaviota." [LetFem] (14:1/2) Primavera-Otoño 88, p. 127.
"Loa Guadalupana." [LetFem] (14:1/2) Primavera-Otoño 88, p. 128.
"No Se Vende." [LetFem] (14:1/2) Primavera-Otoño 88, p. 129.
"Reencuentro." [LetFem] (14:1/2) Primavera-Otoño 88, p. 129.
"Tu Cuerpo" (A me Hija). [LetFem] (14:1/2) Primavera-Otoño 88, p. 126.

2827. KRAFT, Eugene
"The Portrait of a Woman." [Paint] (15:29) Spr 88, p. 24-25.

2828. KRAMER, Aaron
"A Black Man Has Fallen Asleep" (tr. of Rajzel Zychlinska). [Vis] (27) 88, p. 26.
"Blizzard." [KenR] (NS 10:2) Spr 88, p. 110.
"Charlie." [WritersF] (14) Fall 88, p. 118.
"I Look into Rembrandt's Eyes" (tr. of Rajzel Zychlinska). [Vis] (26) 88, p. 35.
"Neighbors." [NewEngR] (10:3) Spr 88, p. 282.
"On My Sixtieth Birthday." [Confr] (37/38) Spr-Sum 88, p. 238.
"Passengers." [KenR] (NS 10:2) Spr 88, p. 111.
"Reflections." [KenR] (NS 10:2) Spr 88, p. 110.
"A Snow Falls" (tr. of Rajzel Zychlinska). [Vis] (26) 88, p. 35.
"This Is Not the Road" (Book of Kings II, tr. of Rajzel Zychlinska). [Vis] (26) 88, p. 35.
"Two Stones" (tr. of Rajzel Zychlinska). [Vis] (27) 88, p. 27.

2829. KRATT, Mary
"Wherever I Look, They Are Waving." [PoetL] (83:3) Fall 88, p. 30-31.

2830. KRAUJIETE, Aina
"Fairytales and Myths" (tr. by Valters Nollendorfs). [Vis] (26) 88, p. 27.

2831. KRAUS, Jim
"The Fountain of Youth: Hawaii / Florida." [HawaiiR] (12:2, #24) Fall 88, p. 120-122.
"Island." [HawaiiR] (12:2, #24) Fall 88, p. 119.
"True North." [ChamLR] (1:2, #2) Spr 88, p. 14-16.

2832. KRAUS, Susan
"The Original Mariners." [HawaiiR] (12:2, #24) Fall 88, p. 39.
"Photosynthesis." [ChamLR] (1:2, #2) Spr 88, p. 134.

2833. KRAUSE, Judith
"Localizing the Pain." [PraF] (9:4) Wint 88-89, p. 19.
"Mother's Day." [PraF] (9:4) Wint 88-89, p. 17.
"Night Terrors." [PraF] (9:4) Wint 88-89, p. 16.
"Portrait" (Warsaw, 1939). [PraF] (9:4) Wint 88-89, p. 18.
"We'll See." [PraF] (9:4) Wint 88-89, p. 20.

2834. KRAUSE, Richard
"Shower." [Confr] (37/38) Spr-Sum 88, p. 230-231.

2835. KRAUSHAAR, Mark
"Personal Reasons." [PoetryNW] (29:3) Aut 88, p. 33-34.
"Why Is L&M Import Giving Away Famous Nationally Advertised Watches for Only . . . ?" (Magazine Ad). [PoetryNW] (29:3) Aut 88, p. 34.

2836. KRAUSS, Janet
"Before the Moment: Forli's *Annunciation*, Uffizi." [Jacaranda] (3:1) Wint 88, p. 98-99.
"Eye to Eye We Begin to Rock" (Rachel, 4 months old). [SpoonRQ] (13:3) Sum 88, p. 7.

2837. KREBS, Sylvia
"Viewing a Comet on a Moonlit Night." [DeKalbLAJ] (21:3/4) 88, p. 59.

2838. KRECHEL, Ursula
"Liebe am Horizont." [Rohwedder] (4) [Wint 88-89], p. 20.
"Love on the Horizon" (tr. by Liselotte Erlanger). [Rohwedder] (4) [Wint 88-89], p. 20.

2839. KREITER-KURYLO, Carolyn
"Apples." [PraS] (62:1) Spr 88, p. 39-40.
"Dream: Catching the Air." [PraS] (62:1) Spr 88, p. 37-39.

2840. KRESH, David
"The Convalescent." [MSS] (6:2) 88, p. 82.

2841. KRESS, Leonard
"The Two" (tr. of Hugo von Hofmannsthal). [WestB] (21/22) 88, p. 74.

2842. KRETZ, Thomas
"Back in Days Before McDonald's." [BellR] (11:2) Fall 88, p. 4.
"Brothels under Franco." [Plain] (9:1) Fall 88, p. 10.
"Chauvinistic Exchange." [KanQ] (20:1/2) Wint-Spr 88, p. 89.
"Coming Down Hard." [Paint] (15:30) Aut 88, p. 17.
"Fold in the Cold." [Amelia] (5:2, #13) 88, p. 103.
"Priceless Creation Unsold." [LitR] (31:2) Wint 88, p. 204.
"Round and Warm." [Paint] (15:30) Aut 88, p. 16.
"Seeking Auroral Relief from Duty." [NegC] (8:3) 88, p. 192.
"Twenty-Second of December." [Bogg] (59) 88, p. 39.

2843. KRICORIAN, Nancy
"The Clock." [GrahamHR] (11) Spr 88, p. 19.
"Fishing in the Cape Cod Canal." [GrahamHR] (11) Spr 88, p. 17.
"My Father Said That's the Devil's Work." [GrahamHR] (11) Spr 88, p. 20.
"The Rapture." [GrahamHR] (11) Spr 88, p. 18.

2844. KRIKAU, Kathy
"Monday, Tuesday, Wednesday." [PikeF] (9) Fall 88, p. 22.

2845. KRINSLEY, Jeanne
"After an Act of God" (For Lori). [Prima] (11/12) 88, p. 94-95.

2846. KROLL, Ernest
"Crossing the Tred Avon River" (from Bellevue to Oxford, Md.). [WebR] (13:2) Fall 88, p. 89.
"Genesis" (Awakening near Osawatomie). [MidwQ] (29:2) Wint 88, p. 222.
"The Grove." [WebR] (13:2) Fall 88, p. 88.
"Windows on the Mississippi." [WebR] (13:2) Fall 88, p. 89.
"Winter Race Meeting" (Bowie in February). [LightY] ('88/9) 88, p. 57.

2847. KROLL, Judith
"First Rumors." [ConnPR] (7:1) 88, p. 36.

2848. KROLOW, Karl
"Death As Snowman" (tr. by Stuart Friebert). [InterPR] (14:1) Spr 88, p. 7.
"Illusion" (tr. by Stuart Friebert). [Field] (39) Fall 88, p. 79.
"Leben" (Für Siegfried Unseld). [InterPR] (14:1) Spr 88, p. 8.
"Life" (for Siegfried Unseld, tr. by Stuart Friebert). [InterPR] (14:1) Spr 88, p. 9.
"Next Door" (tr. by Stuart Friebert). [Field] (39) Fall 88, p. 80.
"Night-Watches" (tr. by Stuart Friebert). [Field] (39) Fall 88, p. 78.
"The Order of Things" (tr. by Stuart Friebert). [InterPR] (14:1) Spr 88, p. 11.
"Die Ordnung der Dinge." [InterPR] (14:1) Spr 88, p. 10.
"Tod Als Schneemann." [InterPR] (14:1) Spr 88, p. 16.

2849. KRONEN, Steve
"After Viewing Twelve Versions of Madonna and Child." [Thrpny] (32) Wint 88, p. 14.
"The Reverend Falwell Describes the Bakkers' Swimming Pool." [Ploughs] (14:4) 88, p. 107.
"Think of the Blackouts." [Ploughs] (14:4) 88, p. 108.

2850. KRONENBERG, Mindy (Mindy H.)
"After Fighting." [RagMag] (6:1) [88], p. 20.
"Circular Motion" (for my father). [HawaiiR] (12:2, #24) Fall 88, p. 14-15.
"Dismantling the Playground." [BallSUF] (29:4) Aut 88, p. 36.
"Dismantling the Playground." [FloridaR] (16:1) Spr-Sum 88, p. 110-111.
"Inkberries." [ChamLR] (1:2, #2) Spr 88, p. 5.
"Inquire Within." [Lactuca] (11) O 88, p. 21.
"Laura Talking." [BallSUF] (29:4) Aut 88, p. 64.
"My Mother's Fruitbowl." [RagMag] (6:1) [88], p. 21.

2851. KRUGOVOY, Anna C.
"On Viewing Monet." [PaintedB] (36) 88, p. 37.
"Two Young Italians." [PaintedB] (36) 88, p. 36.

2852. KRUMBERGER, John
"The Color of Dusk." [Farm] (5:2) Fall 88, p. 62.

2853. KRUSOE, James
"Further." [Jacaranda] (3:2) Fall-Wint 88, p. 103.
"Horses in Fire." [AmerPoR] (17:5) S-O 88, p. 28.

2854. KRYNICKI, Ryszard
"I Am Not Worthy" (tr. by Stanislaw Baranczak and Clare Cavanagh). [ManhatR] (4:2) Spr 88, p. 39.
"So What If" (tr. by Stanislaw Baranczak and Clare Cavanagh). [ManhatR] (4:2) Spr 88, p. 39.

"Suddenly" (tr. by Stanislaw Baranczak and Clare Cavanagh). [ManhatR] (4:2) Spr 88, p. 39.
"The Wall" (tr. by Stanislaw Baranczak and Clare Cavanagh). [ManhatR] (4:2) Spr 88, p. 40.

2855. KRYSS, T. L.
"Nocturnal Picnic." [SwampR] (1:2/3) D 88, p. 65.

2856. KRZESZOWSKI, Tomasz P.
"Change" (tr. of Anna Kamienska, w. Desmond Graham). [Verse] (5:2) Jl 88, p. 13.
"A Thirteen Year Old Girl" (tr. of Anna Kamienska, w. Desmond Graham). [Verse] (5:2) Jl 88, p. 14.

2857. KUBACH, David
"Animals of My Life: A Sequence." [PaintedB] (34) 88, p. 5-8.

2858. KUBY, Lolette
"For Philip Larkin." [AmerS] (57:3) Sum 88, p. 430.

2859. KUHNLEY, Debbie Phillips
"Furrows." [EngJ] (77:3) Mr 88, p. 89.
"Maverick." [EngJ] (77:2) F 88, p. 87.

2860. KULAK, Lorne
"The Carpenter." [Grain] (16:4) Wint 88, p. 19.
"Driving." [Grain] (16:4) Wint 88, p. 18.
"Glare of the Sun." [Grain] (16:4) Wint 88, p. 20.
"My Father's Motors." [Grain] (16:4) Wint 88, p. 18.
"Notes on My Growing." [Grain] (16:4) Wint 88, p. 21.

2861. KULIK, William
"Coming Down Hillsides in the Spring" (tr. of Robert Desnos). [Antaeus] (60) Spr 88, p. 268.
"The Equinox" (tr. of Robert Desnos). [Antaeus] (60) Spr 88, p. 267.
"Men on Earth" (tr. of Robert Desnos). [Antaeus] (60) Spr 88, p. 269-270.

2862. KULIKOV, Boris
"The Sound of Fall" (tr. by Leonid S. Polevoy). [NegC] (8:1/2) 88, p. 65.

2863. KULYCKY, Michael
"Bite Your Tongue, Sweetie, and Realize." [KanQ] (20:1/2) Wint-Spr 88, p. 282-283.
"Some of My Students Are." [KanQ] (20:1/2) Wint-Spr 88, p. 283.

2864. KUMAR, Sati
"Run Away Cow" (tr. by Manohar Bandhyopadhyay). [Nimrod] (31:2) Spr-Sum 88, p. 95.

2865. KUMAR, Shiv
"I'm a Vegetarian." [Nimrod] (31:2) Spr-Sum 88, p. 55.
"Thou Shalt Not Commit Adultery." [Nimrod] (31:2) Spr-Sum 88, p. 55.

2866. KUMIN, Maxine
"The Accolade of the Animals." [CreamCR] (12:2) Sum 88, p. 213.
"Custodian." [OntR] (28) Spr-Sum 88, p. 52-53.
"A Game of Monopoly in Chavannes." [NewYorker] (64:40) 21 N 88, p. 56.
"In the Park." [NewYorker] (63:51) 8 F 88, p. 70.
"In Warm Rooms, Before a Blue Light." [NewYorker] (63:48) 18 Ja 88, p. 34.
"'Primitivism' Exhibit" (Museum of Modern Art, 1984). [TexasR] (9:3/4) Fall-Wint 88, p. 92.
"Repent." [Nat] (247:18) 12 D 88, p. 664.
"Sleeping with Animals." [OntR] (29) Fall-Wint 88-89, p. 19-20.
"Turning the Garden in Middle Age." [OntR] (28) Spr-Sum 88, p. 54.
"We Stood There Singing." [GrahamHR] (11) Spr 88, p. 7.

2867. KUNERT, Gunter
"Hotel Room in Mestre" (tr. by Reinhold Grimm). [NewL] (54:3) Spr 88, p. 23.
"Three Cretan Poems" (tr. by Reinhold Grimm). [NewL] (54:3) Spr 88, p. 22.
"Venice Lost" (tr. by Reinhold Grimm). [NewL] (54:3) Spr 88, p. 23.

2868. KUNTZ, Laurie
"Coming Out" (for K. P.). [Spirit] (9:1) 88, p. 31.

2869. KUNZE, Reiner
"America, the Treeway" (tr. by Lori Fisher). [Rohwedder] (4) [Wint 88-89], p. 37.
"Amerika, der Autobaum." [Rohwedder] (4) [Wint 88-89], p. 37.
"Bells All Too Near" (tr. by Lori Fisher). [Rohwedder] (4) [Wint 88-89], p. 40.
"Brief aus Prag 1980." [Rohwedder] (4) [Wint 88-89], p. 41.
"Clearing Tree Stumps" (for H.W.M. in the Thuringer Forest, tr. by Lori Fisher). [Rohwedder] (4) [Wint 88-89], p. 39.

"Empty Snowposts, Norway, Middle of September" (tr. by Lori Fisher). [Rohwedder] (4) [Wint 88-89], p. 39.
"Glocken Allzu Nah." [Rohwedder] (4) [Wint 88-89], p. 40.
"Leere Schneestangen, Norwegen, Mitte September." [Rohwedder] (4) [Wint 88-89], p. 38.
"Letter from Prague 1980" (tr. by Lori Fisher). [Rohwedder] (4) [Wint 88-89], p. 41.
"Oriental Carpet" (tr. by Thomas S. Edwards and Ken Letko). [ColR] (NS 15:2) Fall-Wint 88, p. 87.
"Stöckeroden" (für H.W.M. im Thüringer Wald). [Rohwedder] (4) [Wint 88-89], p. 38.

2870. KUPFERBERG, Tuli
"Hold the AIDS cure back." [AlphaBS] (4) D 88, p. 8.

2871. KUPPNER, Frank
"Cloud Formations: A Node." [Verse] (5:1) F 88, p. 48-55.
"Eclogue Four." [Verse] (5:2) Jl 88, p. 9-10.
"Kelvinbridge. A Node." [Verse] (5:3) N 88, p. 12-14.

2872. KURIS, Edward S.
"If You Ever See My Heart." [PottPort] (9) 88, p. 41.
"Recital." [Dandel] (15:1) Spr-Sum 88, p. 23.

KURYLO, Carolyn Kreiter
See KREITER-KURYLO, Carolyn

2873. KUSHNER, Aleksandr
"The Decanter" (tr. by Paul Graves). [Confr] (37/38) Spr-Sum 88, p. 24.
"Sheltering Thoughts" (tr. by Paul Graves). [Confr] (37/38) Spr-Sum 88, p. 23.

2874. KUTCHINS, Laurie
"Minneapolis, Almost April." [DenQ] (22:3) Wint 88, p. 65-66.

2875. KUUSISTO, Stephen
"August, 1959." [AntR] (46:3) Sum 88, p. 345.
"Snow Melts" (tr. of Pentti Saarikoski). [SenR] (18:1) 88, p. 21.
"Today I Go by Another Route" (tr. of Pentti Saarikoski). [SenR] (18:1) 88, p. 20.
"You Couldn't See Through the Snow Squall" (tr. of Pentti Saarikoski). [SenR] (18:1) 88, p. 22.

2876. KUZMA, Greg
"After the August Birthdays." [KanQ] (20:3) Sum 88, p. 97.
"Burying the Dog." [MidAR] (8:1) 88, p. 46-48.
"Claire Hill." [ClockR] (4:2) 88, p. 10-11.
"Dreams." [LitR] (31:2) Wint 88, p. 167.
"Elegy." [LitR] (31:2) Wint 88, p. 168-169.
"Father" (after Kees). [MSS] (6:2) 88, p. 1.
"High Water, Fish Creek, August 1986." [ConnPR] (7:1) 88, p. 27.
"Lives." [PoetryNW] (29:3) Aut 88, p. 42-43.
"Pheasant Season." [KenR] (NS 10:4) Fall 88, p. 86.
"Softball." [MSS] (6:2) 88, p. 2.
"The Summer." [SouthwR] (73:4) Aut 88, p. 553.
"Sunday, Reading Late, September 28." [KenR] (NS 10:4) Fall 88, p. 84-85.
"The Table." [CharR] (14:1) Spr 88, p. 83.
"Where the Dogs Lie Down with the Cats" (for Claire Hill). [KanQ] (20:3) Sum 88, p. 96.
"Wilber." [Paint] (15:30) Aut 88, p. 14-15.

2877. KVAM, Wayne
"O my, Mika." [Amelia] (5:2, #13) 88, p. 17.

2878. KVASNICKA, Mellanee
"Myth." [Plain] (8:1) Fall 87, p. 33.

2879. KYLE, Carol
"Easter Sunday Morning." [SpoonRQ] (13:2) Spr 88, p. 28-29.
"Easter Sunday Morning." [SpoonRQ] (13:4) Fall 88, p. 59-60.
"Five Windows in the Red Light District." [SpoonRQ] (13:2) Spr 88, p. 38-43.
"Five Windows in the Red Light District." [SpoonRQ] (13:4) Fall 88, p. 67-72.
"A Poem Sonata for Harpsichord and Flute" (for René). [SpoonRQ] (13:2) Spr 88, p. 33-37.
"A Poem Sonata for Harpsichord and Flute" (for René). [SpoonRQ] (13:4) Fall 88, p. 62-66.
"Sleeping Together" (for John). [SpoonRQ] (13:2) Spr 88, p. 30.
"Sleeping Together" (for John). [SpoonRQ] (13:4) Fall 88, p. 61.
"Tuning the Harpsichord." [SpoonRQ] (13:2) Spr 88, p. 31-32.

"The Valentine." [SpoonRQ] (13:2) Spr 88, p. 44.
"Visiting My Mother in Late Summer." [SpoonRQ] (13:2) Spr 88, p. 45-46.
"Visiting My Mother in Late Summer." [SpoonRQ] (13:4) Fall 88, p. 73-74.
"Windmills at Kinderdijk" (for Koos Petterson). [SpoonRQ] (13:2) Spr 88, p. 26-27.
"Windmills at Kinderdijk" (for Koos Petterson). [SpoonRQ] (13:4) Fall 88, p. 57-58.

2880. KYLE, Moira
"The Organ Grinder's Monkey." [FiveFR] (6) 88, p. 15-17.

KYOKO, Mori
See MORI, Kyoko

La . . .
See also names beginning with "La" without the following space, filed below in their alphabetic positions, e.g., LaSALLE.

2881. LA LOCA
"The Mayan" (Excerpt). [Jacaranda] (3:2) Fall-Wint 88, p. 104-105.

2882. LABINSKI, Marek
"I cannot be only a human being" (tr. of Halina Poswiatowska). [Rohwedder] (4) [Wint 88-89], p. 31.
"I come from the flowing water" (tr. of Halina Poswiatowska). [Rohwedder] (4) [Wint 88-89], p. 30.
"In My Barbaric Language" (tr. of Halina Poswiatowska). [MidAR] (8:2) 88, p. 8.
"A Mirror" (tr. of Halina Poswiatowska). [Rohwedder] (4) [Wint 88-89], p. 30.
"My shadow is a woman" (tr. of Halina Poswiatowska). [Rohwedder] (4) [Wint 88-89], p. 30.
"The sliver of my imagination" (tr. of Halina Poswiatowska). [Rohwedder] (4) [Wint 88-89], p. 29.
"These words have always been" (tr. of Halina Poswiatowska). [Rohwedder] (4) [Wint 88-89], p. 29.
"We don't believe in hell" (tr. of Halina Poswiatowska). [Rohwedder] (4) [Wint 88-89], p. 29.

2883. LaBONTÉ, Karen
"Blood Bushes" (for J., who came back). [CimR] (83) Ap 88, p. 20-22.
"Listless Passengers." [DenQ] (22:3) Wint 88, p. 150-152.

LABRADA, Emilio Bernal
See BERNAL LABRADA, Emilio

2884. LACHOWSKI, Cheryl Schaff
"Mass for 5 Voices." [SouthernPR] (28:2) Fall 88, p. 18-19.

2885. LADIN, Jay
"The Old God at the Urinal." [Vis] (28) 88, p. 17.

2886. LaFRAN, Brad
"Edgar Sees the Train of Love and Lets His Wife Go." [DenQ] (22:3) Wint 88, p. 20-21.

2887. LAGIER, Jennifer
"Autumn Cadaver: Ancient Cow Barn in French Camp." [ColEng] (50:1) Ja 88, p. 48.
"Backyard Mausoleum." [ColEng] (50:1) Ja 88, p. 49.
"Central Valley November." [ColEng] (50:1) Ja 88, p. 49.

2888. LAGOMARSINO, Nancy
"Duration." [QW] (27) Sum-Fall 88, p. 91.

2889. LaGRECA, T. R.
"The Newlywed." [HolCrit] (25:2) Ap 88, p. 10.

2890. LAHEY, Ed
"A Different Price." [MidAR] (8:2) 88, p. 79.

2891. LAINSBURY, G. P.
"Omnigomp." [Dandel] (15:1) Spr-Sum 88, p. 25.

2892. LAKE, Kathleen
"To Rise." [PaintedB] (34) 88, p. 90.

2893. LAKE, Paul
"Additions." [YaleR] (77:3) Spr 88, p. 439-440.

LALLO, Robert di
See DiLALLO, Robert

2894. LAMBERT, Jean Clarence
"Night of Tepoztlan — Five" (tr. by Julia Older). [Vis] (27) 88, p. 42.
"Night of Tepoztlan — One" (To Cecilia, tr. by Julia Older). [Vis] (27) 88, p. 41.

2895. LaMERS, Joyce
"Observation by a Formerly Rose-Lipt Maiden." [LightY] ('88/9) 88, p. 141.
"The River Nile." [LightY] ('88/9) 88, p. 160.
2896. LAMKIN, Kurt
"Little Heavens." [Contact] (9:47/48/49) Spr 88, p. 48.
2897. LAMMON, Martin
"Elegy." [CharR] (14:1) Spr 88, p. 56-57.
"Naming Day" (In memoriam: Wilhelm Lichtenwald). [CharR] (14:1) Spr 88, p. 57.
2898. LAMPE, Sandra
"Midnight, Pisces Ascending." [SouthernPR] (28:1) Spr 88, p. 38-39.
2899. LAMPORT, Felicia
"Buck Up." [LightY] ('88/9) 88, p. 228.
2900. LAN, Se
"The Chinese: Back View" (in Chinese & English). [BelPoJ] (39:2) Wint 88-89, p. 36-37.
"Christmas" (in Chinese & English). [BelPoJ] (39:2) Wint 88-89, p. 38-39.
"City in Ruins" (in Chinese & English). [BelPoJ] (39:2) Wint 88-89, p. 34-35.
2901. LAND, Thomas Grover
"4:39am March 21, 1988." [Plain] (8:3) Spr-Sum 88, p. 39.
"Nothing Is Always." [Vis] (28) 88, p. 36.
2902. LANDALE, Zoë
"Birth." [CanLit] (118) Aut 88, p. 80-81.
"The Colour of Winter Air." [WestCR] (22:4) Spr 87, i.e. 88, p. 43.
"Portrait: Trail Islands in Winter." [WestCR] (22:4) Spr 87, i.e. 88, p. 42.
2903. LANDGRAF, Susan
"Accidents." [SmPd] (25:2) Spr 88, p. 29.
"I Am a Blue Bowl." [BellR] (11:2) Fall 88, p. 41.
"Onion Poem." [SmPd] (25:2) Spr 88, p. 27.
"Woman Who Had Thought She Was Alone." [Prima] (11/12) 88, p. 69.
"The Yolk and the White of It." [SmPd] (25:2) Spr 88, p. 28.
2904. LANDIS, Geoffrey A.
"To Live in Hell (The Terraforming of Venus, 2045-2128 A.D.)." [Writer] (101:9) S 88, p. 24.
2905. LANE, Alycee J.
"It Came to Her Children." [MinnR] (NS 30/31) Spr-Fall 88, p. 18-19.
2906. LANE, Dixie
"Naked Ladies." [GrahamHR] (11) Spr 88, p. 42.
"You Are the Distance." [Ploughs] (14:4) 88, p. 69-70.
2907. LANE, Donna M.
"Wild Cats." [SwampR] (1:2/3) D 88, p. 61.
2908. LANE, John
"Along the Little Betsie" (For Nikki and Dan). [CimR] (84) Jl 88, p. 89-90.
2909. LANE, M. Travis
"Ave Maters." [CanLit] (119) Wint 88, p. 7.
2910. LANE, Pinkie Gordon
"Negotiations" (For Gordon). [NewOR] (15:1) Spr 88, p. 61.
"Reading Poetry by Henry Dumas While Listening to *Cool Jazz*." [BlackALF] (22:2) Sum 88, p. 275.
2911. LANG, Leonard
"When My Father Still Wore the Grey Mustache." [Vis] (27) 88, p. 14.
2912. LANG, Warren
"And Again." [RagMag] (6:2) Fall 88, p. 53.
"Elegy in Spring." [RagMag] (6:2) Fall 88, p. 52.
"In the Suburbs." [RagMag] (6:2) Fall 88, p. 53.
2913. LANGLAS, James
"Marking Time." [CutB] (31/32) 88, p. 100-101.
2914. LANGMAN, Peter
"Neighbors" (A response, with all due respect, to Robert Frost's "Mending Wall"). [SpiritSH] (54) Fall-Wint 88, p. 20.
"Setting Forth." [SpiritSH] (54) Fall-Wint 88, p. 21.
2915. LANSDOWNE, Andrew
"Pine and Poem." [Verse] (5:3) N 88, p. 41.
2916. LANSING, Gerrit
"In Erasmus Darwin's Generous Light" (for Thorpe Feidt). [Sulfur] (8:2, #23) Fall 88, p. 31-33.

2917. LANZA, Carmela Delia
"On Our Mother's 60th Birthday Party." [Turnstile] (1:2) 88, p. 112-114.
2918. LANZIT, Robert
"Sand Dollars." [CinPR] (17) Spr 88, p. 72.
2919. LAO-TZU
"Tao Te Ching" (Selections: 46, 53, 57, 60, 61, 62, tr. by Stephen Mitchell). [Zyzzyva] (4:3) Fall 88, p. 87-90.
2920. LAPIDUS, Jacqueline
"All Hallows Eve." [Cond] (15) 88, p. 75.
"Promisetown." [Cond] (15) 88, p. 118-122.
2921. LAPINGTON, S. C.
"Girl, Eleven." [Stand] (29:1) Wint 87-88, p. 57.
"Summer Canvas." [Stand] (29:1) Wint 87-88, p. 56.
2922. LAPOINTE, Paul-Marie
"Poem for Winter" (tr. by G. V. Downes). [Trans] (20) Spr 88, p. 153.
2923. LARAQUE, Paul
"The Grand Guignol of Countries, or, Country of the Grand Guignol" (tr. by Rosemary Manno). [RedBass] (13) 88, p. 6.
2924. LARDAS, Constance
"My Ancestors" (tr. of Armando Romero). [CinPR] (17) Spr 88, p. 46-47.
2925. LARDAS, Konstantinos
"Langour." [Sequoia] (31:2) Wint 88, p. 79.
"Smyrna, 1922." [Sequoia] (31:2) Wint 88, p. 78.
2926. LARDNER, Ted
"Drought News." [Caliban] (5) 88, p. 122.
"Magpies and a Stroke of Jet." [Caliban] (5) 88, p. 123.
"The Nightgown." [Caliban] (5) 88, p. 124.
2927. LaRIVIERE, G. M.
"By the South Gate." [ChamLR] (1:2, #2) Spr 88, p. 96.
"Dried Basil." [ChamLR] (1:2, #2) Spr 88, p. 97.
"Journey on Ash Wednesday." [ChamLR] (2:1, #3) Fall 88, p. 70.
"Sonnets of Lent." [ChamLR] (2:1, #3) Fall 88, p. 71.
2928. LARKIN, Philip
"The Whitsun Weddings." [BostonR] (13:5 [sic]) Je 88, p. 17.
2929. LARROSA, Vera
"Blue Mouth" (tr. by Thomas Hoeksema). [Sonora] (14/15) Spr 88, p. 91, 93.
"Boca Azul." [Sonora] (14/15) Spr 88, p. 90, 92.
2930. LARS, Krystyna
"Seven Scenes from the Life of Men" (tr. by Daniel Bourne). [LitR] (31:2) Wint 88, p. 146-153.
2931. LARSEN, Deborah
"New Litany for the Disguised Brother Benedetto de Gofs . . ." (for Aimee Larsen, my daughter). [GettyR] (1:4) Aut 88, p. 676-677.
"Rain in Advent." [WestHR] (42:3) Aut 88, p. 205.
"Stitching Porcelain" (After Ricci in Sixteenth-Century China). [Nat] (246:17) 30 Ap 88, p. 609.
2932. LARSEN, Jeanne
"Her Life." [WilliamMR] (26:1) Spr 88, p. 89.
"To E.D." [WilliamMR] (26:1) Spr 88, p. 7.
2933. LARSEN, Lance
"Moon." [LitR] (31:3) Spr 88, p. 331.
2934. LARSEN, Wendy Wilder
"Mites on the Iceplant in the Middle of the Freeway." [LittleM] (15:3/4) 88, p. 142.
"Pulling Them In." [Confr] (37/38) Spr-Sum 88, p. 183.
"Single Again at 43." [LittleM] (15:3/4) 88, p. 142.
2935. LARSON, Michael
"Learning Young to Love the Graveyard." [PassN] (9:1) Wint 88, p. 25.
2936. LARSON, Rustin
"The Invalid." [PoetryE] (25) Spr 88, p. 36.
"The Lamp." [PoetryE] (25) Spr 88, p. 38.
"The Lawn." [PoetryE] (25) Spr 88, p. 37.
2937. LaRUE, Dorie
"After *An American Bestiary*." [AmerPoR] (17:4) Jl-Ag 88, p. 20.
"Ceiling Stains." [AmerPoR] (17:4) Jl-Ag 88, p. 19.
"The Coroner." [AmerPoR] (17:4) Jl-Ag 88, p. 19.
"The Footprint." [AmerPoR] (17:4) Jl-Ag 88, p. 18.

"Recomposition" (Ponce de Leon Springs, Fla.). [AmerPoR] (17:4) Jl-Ag 88, p. 18.
"Thoughts While Cruising on the Amite." [AmerPoR] (17:4) Jl-Ag 88, p. 20.
"The Woman and the Gargoyles." [AmerPoR] (17:4) Jl-Ag 88, p. 19.

2938. LaSALLE, Peter
"Mrs. R.'s Mall Problem." [ColEng] (50:6) O 88, p. 637.

2939. LASDUN, James
"Cello Music." [Pequod] (25) 88, p. 34-35.
"A Jump Start." [Pequod] (25) 88, p. 30-31.
"The Refugees" (a variation on "Les Eléphants" by Leconte de Lisle). [Pequod] (25) 88, p. 32-33.

2940. LASHER, Susan
"The Act of Love in the Age of Mechanical Reproduction." [Verse] (5:2) Jl 88, p. 19.
"The Poet." [Verse] (5:2) Jl 88, p. 20.
"Sometimes a Man Takes a Good Look at Himself." [PartR] (55:2) Spr 88, p. 285-286.

2941. LASKEY, Michael
"Liberal Studies." [Stand] (29:1) Wint 87-88, p. 41-43.

2942. LASKIN, Pamela L.
"Grandmother." [Amelia] (5:1, #12) 88, p. 20.

2943. LASTRA, Pedro
"Conversación con Mary Anna en 'La Casa de la Cima'." [Inti] (26/27) Otoño 87-Primavera 88, p. 201-202.
"De Pequeñas Ururas." [Inti] (26/27) Otoño 87-Primavera 88, p. 203.
"Diario (1o de Octubre, 1972)." [Inti] (26/27) Otoño 87-Primavera 88, p. 204.
"Los Días Contados" (A Patricia Isabel). [Inti] (26/27) Otoño 87-Primavera 88, p. 205.
"Disolución de la Memoria." [Inti] (26/27) Otoño 87-Primavera 88, p. 202-203.
"Escribo el Nombre de Nerval." [Inti] (26/27) Otoño 87-Primavera 88, p. 204.
"Instantánea." [Inti] (26/27) Otoño 87-Primavera 88, p. 202.
"Nota para el Poema 'André Breton y Nosotros'." [Inti] (26/27) Otoño 87-Primavera 88, p. 204.
"La Otra Versión". [Inti] (26/27) Otoño 87-Primavera 88, p. 205.
"El Sexto Sentido." [Inti] (26/27) Otoño 87-Primavera 88, p. 202.
"Sueño en Busca de Personaje." [Inti] (26/27) Otoño 87-Primavera 88, p. 203-204.

2944. LATTIMORE, Richmond
"Five Last Poems." [Hudson] (41:2) Sum 88, p. 319-322.

2945. LAU, Alan Chong
"Water That Springs from a Rock." [Contact] (9:47/48/49) Spr 88, p. 17-21.

2946. LAU, Barbara
"Truth Like Enormous Flakes of Snow." [SpoonRQ] (13:1) Wint 88, p. 13.

2947. LAU, Carolyn
"Emily Dickinson Harvesting T'ao Ch'ien." [AmerPoR] (17:6) N-D 88, p. 32.
"Friday Night, Saturday Morning." [AmerPoR] (17:6) N-D 88, p. 31.
"Mencius Fulfilled by Escher." [AmerPoR] (17:6) N-D 88, p. 31.
"Psyche's Waltz" (for Charlotte). [AmerPoR] (17:6) N-D 88, p. 31.
"Three Measures of Horse" (A Foonote to Gong Sun Long). [AmerPoR] (17:6) N-D 88, p. 32.
"Zhoukoudian Bride's Harvest." [Calyx] (11:2/3) Fall 88, p. 126-127.

2948. LAU, Evelyn
"Bobby-Pin Scratches." [HangL] (52) 88, p. 81.
"John." [HangL] (52) 88, p. 82.
"The Quiet Room" (Psychiatric Assessment Unit, Vancouver General Hospital). [HangL] (52) 88, p. 83.

2949. LAUBY, Adrienne
"Job Description: Disabled (3)." [SinW] (35) Sum-Fall 88, p. 25.

2950. LAUGHLIN, James
"An Anginal Equivalent." [ParisR] (30:106) Spr 88, p. 148.
"The Drawing Lesson." [NewAW] (3) Spr 88, p. 54.
"The Envelopes." [Interim] (7:1) Spr 88, p. 35-36.
"Her Letters." [ParisR] (30:106) Spr 88, p. 154.
"The Heretic." [ParisR] (30:106) Spr 88, p. 147.
"The Kiss." [ParisR] (30:106) Spr 88, p. 152.
"The Lament of Professor Turbojet." [LightY] ('88/9) 88, p. 202.
"The Limper." [ParisR] (30:106) Spr 88, p. 151.
"News from Planet Earth." [ParisR] (30:106) Spr 88, p. 156.

"Our Bicycles." [YaleR] (77:3) Spr 88, p. 438-439.
"Prolepsis." [ParisR] (30:106) Spr 88, p. 149.
"The Ritual." [ParisR] (30:106) Spr 88, p. 153.
"A Shard of History." [ParisR] (30:106) Spr 88, p. 150.
"The Sorrows of Smindyrides." [ParisR] (30:106) Spr 88, p. 155.
"Thumbs Up!." [Interim] (7:1) Spr 88, p. 35.

2951. LAUTERBACH, Ann
"Annotation." [AntR] (46:4) Fall 88, p. 496.
"Clamor." [AntR] (46:4) Fall 88, p. 492-493.
"Excessive Innuendo." [CreamCR] (12:2) Sum 88, p. 216.
"Frame of Reference" (for Doug Swift). [CreamCR] (12:2) Sum 88, p. 214.
"Further Thematics." [AntR] (46:4) Fall 88, p. 494-495.
"Local Branch." [NewAW] (3) Spr 88, p. 25.
"Night Rehearsal." [NewAW] (3) Spr 88, p. 23-24.
"Stipend." [CreamCR] (12:2) Sum 88, p. 215.
"Tribe (Stamina of the Unseen)." [AntR] (46:4) Fall 88, p. 490-491.
"Werner Herzog 68 / Iowa City 88." [NewAW] (3) Spr 88, p. 26.

2952. LAUTERMILCH, Steven
"1.4. O, you innocents, go out now and then" (tr. of Rainer Maria Rilke). [InterPR] (14:1) Spr 88, p. 19.
"Autumn Day" (tr. of Rainer Maria Rilke). [InterPR] (14:1) Spr 88, p. 15.
"Mary's Annunciation" (tr. of Rainer Maria Rilke). [InterPR] (14:1) Spr 88, p. 17.
"My life is not this steep and dizzy hour" (tr. of Rainer Maria Rilke). [InterPR] (14:1) Spr 88, p. 13.
"To Say While Falling Asleep" (tr. of Rainer Maria Rilke). [InterPR] (14:1) Spr 88, p. 15.

2953. LAUX, Dorianne
"On the Back Porch." [Zyzzyva] (4:4) Wint 88, p. 77.

2954. LAVIN CERDA, Hernan
"Aviso en Los Angeles." [Inti] (26/27) Otoño 87-Primavera 88, p. 221.
"El Cuello del Pelícano." [Inti] (26/27) Otoño 87-Primavera 88, p. 219.
"Divertimiento." [Inti] (26/27) Otoño 87-Primavera 88, p. 218.
"El Espantapájaros." [Inti] (26/27) Otoño 87-Primavera 88, p. 215.
"Garfio en la Funeraria." [Inti] (26/27) Otoño 87-Primavera 88, p. 221.
"Heredero de Van Gogh." [Inti] (26/27) Otoño 87-Primavera 88, p. 220.
"Historia de la Lengua." [Inti] (26/27) Otoño 87-Primavera 88, p. 216-217.
"Una Mariposa en la Nariz." [Inti] (26/27) Otoño 87-Primavera 88, p. 218.
"Pajarito." [Inti] (26/27) Otoño 87-Primavera 88, p. 215-216.
"Sombra." [Inti] (26/27) Otoño 87-Primavera 88, p. 220.
"Soy Poeta Místico." [Inti] (26/27) Otoño 87-Primavera 88, p. 222-223.
"El Tecolote." [Inti] (26/27) Otoño 87-Primavera 88, p. 222.
"El Viaje." [Inti] (26/27) Otoño 87-Primavera 88, p. 219.

2955. LAW, L. Bradley
"Home Cooking." [Plain] (8:3) Spr-Sum 88, p. 7.
"January." [Plain] (9:1) Fall 88, p. 37.

2956. LAWDER, Donald
"Evening in the Country." [NewEngR] (11:1) Aut 88, p. 107.

2957. LAWLER, Patrick
"Dead Mom Speaks to Son Through Talking Teddy." [CentralP] (14) Fall 88, p. 169.
"Miracle Boy Cures the Sick by Taking on Their Illnesses." [CentralP] (14) Fall 88, p. 171.
"Scientists Discover Herb That Will Make Us Immortal." [CentralP] (14) Fall 88, p. 170.

2958. LAWRENCE, Sean A.
"Sally's Secular Saga." [SlipS] (8) 88, p. 15.

2959. LAWRY, Mercedes
"Simple as Shadows." [MidAR] (8:2) 88, p. 195.
"Tides." [SouthernPR] (28:1) Spr 88, p. 40.

2960. LAWSON, D. S.
"Listing Paul and Anton." [FiveFR] (6) 88, p. 94.

2961. LAWSON, Paul
"Choice View." [Chelsea] (47) 88, p. 91.
"The Message." [Chelsea] (47) 88, p. 90.
"The Shrew." [Chelsea] (47) 88, p. 89-90.

2962. LAYTON, Irving
"Birthday Poem for John Newlove." [CanLit] (119) Wint 88, p. 56.
2963. LAZARD, Naomi
"The Escape" (tr. of Nina Cassian). [AmerPoR] (17:2) Mr-Ap 88, p. 48.
2964. LAZARUS, A. L.
"Questions & Answers." [LightY] ('88/9) 88, p. 196-197.
2965. LAZARUS, K. F.
"Bragatelle." [LightY] ('88/9) 88, p. 68.
2966. LAZER, Hank
"Displayspace 1." [Temblor] (8) 88, p. 91-94.
"Leaving Charlottesville." [SouthernR] (24:1) Wint 88, p. 158-159.
"Number Theory." [SouthernR] (24:1) Wint 88, p. 159.
Le . . .
See also names beginning with "Le" without the following space, filed below in their alphabetic positions, e.g., LeFEVRE.
2967. Le CLÉZIO, Marguerite
"Living" (tr. of Jocelyne François). [Cond] (15) 88, p. 113.
"The Power of a Poem" (tr. of Jocelyne François). [Cond] (15) 88, p. 111.
2968. LEA, Sydney
"After the Deacon's Funeral, I Want to Say Something." [LaurelR] (22:21) Wint 88, p. 11-13.
"Insomnia: The Distances." [DenQ] (23:1) Sum 88, p. 67-70.
"Midway." [TexasR] (9:3/4) Fall-Wint 88, p. 93-95.
"On Munson Island" (in mem. MKL). [Crazy] (35) Wint 88, p. 32-33.
"Two Chets." [LaurelR] (22:21) Wint 88, p. 13-16.
2969. LEALE, B. C.
"Highly Intoxicated Clerks." [Gargoyle] (35) 88, p. 191.
2970. LEASE, Joseph
"Acteon to Sappho." [LittleM] (15:3/4) 88, p. 41.
"For All the Wrong Reasons." [LittleM] (15:3/4) 88, p. 43.
"Letter to Another Young Poet." [LittleM] (15:3/4) 88, p. 44.
"Michael Kolhaas." [Pequod] (25) 88, p. 43-44.
"No More Surrealism." [LittleM] (15:3/4) 88, p. 43.
"Rime to Jonathan." [LittleM] (15:3/4) 88, p. 42.
2971. LEAVELL, Jeff
"He was standing in the window." [HangL] (52) 88, p. 85.
"Mona." [HangL] (52) 88, p. 84.
2972. LEAX, John
"Winter Spring." [CreamCR] (12:2) Sum 88, p. 217.
"Women's Work." [CreamCR] (12:2) Sum 88, p. 218-219.
2973. LEBEDUSHKINA, Olga
"I seek poetry here in this forest" (tr. by John Gordon). [NegC] (8:1/2) 88, p. 48.
2974. LECLERC, Félix
"Hommes au Travail" (From *Rêves à vendre*). [AntigR] (73) Spr 88, p. 72.
"Men at Work" (From *Rêves à vendre*, tr. by John Palander). [AntigR] (73) Spr 88, p. 73.
2975. LEDBETTER, J. T.
"Aubade for Nine Sparrows, Seward, Nebraska." [ManhatPR] (10) Ja 88, p. 55.
"Setting of Stems" (for Dolores). [Spirit] (9:1) 88, p. 121-123.
2976. LEDDY, Phillipa K.
"San Miguel de Allenda." [KeyWR] (1:2) Fall 88, p. 104-106.
2977. LEE, David
"Arthritis" (For Ken and Bobbie). [WeberS] (5:1) Spr 88, p. 55-60.
"Coda." [Plain] (8:3) Spr-Sum 88, p. 12-13.
2978. LEE, Josephine
"The Maine Coon Cat." [Blueline] (9:1/2) 88, p. 97.
2979. LEE, Susan K. C.
"Letter from Turtle Beach." [Calyx] (11:2/3) Fall 88, p. 202.
2980. LEER, Norman
"Cape Ann Heat Wave." [SpoonRQ] (13:1) Wint 88, p. 52.
"A Dream in Rockport." [SpoonRQ] (13:1) Wint 88, p. 53.
2981. LEET, Judith
"Mission." [Agni] (27) 88, p. 217-218.
2982. LEFCOWITZ, Barbara F.
"The Command." [WebR] (13:2) Fall 88, p. 64.
"Fans." [WebR] (13:2) Fall 88, p. 63-64.

"For Mirjam Lenka" (born 1/15/1935, Prague, died 1/6/1944, Auschwitz). [FloridaR] (16:1) Spr-Sum 88, p. 114-117.
"Microwave." [WebR] (13:2) Fall 88, p. 65-66.

2983. LEFEBURE, Stephen
"The Death of God." [LitR] (31:2) Wint 88, p. 232.

2984. LEFKOWITZ, Larry
"Inversion." [LitR] (31:3) Spr 88, p. 314.

2985. LeFLORE, Shirley Bradley
"Double Birthright" (for Q. Troupe). [RiverS] (25) 88, p. 63.
"Dumas Is Necessary" (For Henry Dumas, Poet-Extraordinaire). [BlackALF] (22:2) Sum 88, p. 276-280.
"Healing." [RiverS] (25) 88, p. 62.

2986. LEGARE, Andrew P.
"Dreamscape #11: Within Reach" (for Mary Ann). [Wind] (18:62) 88, p. 22.

2987. LEGENDRE, Janis
"While Waiting for the Teacups to Arrive." [BallSUF] (29:4) Aut 88, p. 31.

2988. LEGGO, Carl
"O." [Dandel] (15:2) Fall-Wint 88, p. 13.

2989. LEGLER, Philip
"An Old Home Movie." [PassN] (9:1) Wint 88, p. 14.

2990. LEHMAN, David
"The Answering Stranger." [YaleR] (77:4) Sum 88, p. 518-520.
"Arrival at Kennedy." [NewAW] (3) Spr 88, p. 96.
"An English Summer." [Boulevard] (3:2/3) Fall 88, p. 65-66.
"Heaven." [NewAW] (4) Fall 88, p. 37.
"Museum, 1980." [Boulevard] (3:2/3) Fall 88, p. 67-69.
"Mythologies." [ParisR] (30:106) Spr 88, p. 60-79.
"Rejection Slip." [NewRep] (198:26) 27 Je 88, p. 32.
"Spontaneous Combustion." [Shen] (38:2) 88, p. 58-59.
"Spontaneous Generation." [Shen] (38:2) 88, p. 57-58.
"The Square Root of Minus One." [OntR] (28) Spr-Sum 88, p. 55-56.
"Travel Notes." [Boulevard] (3:2/3) Fall 88, p. 66-67.

2991. LEHNER, Frank
"Handsel." [PennR] (4:1) 88, p. 44-45.
"Whis Is What I Did." [PennR] (4:1) 88, p. 42-43.

2992. LEIBLEIN, Adelle
"Talking to the Moon While Cooking From Scratch." [DenQ] (22:3) Wint 88, p. 152-153.

2993. LEIMBACHER, Ed
"Lunchbreak." [PoetryNW] (29:3) Aut 88, p. 24.

2994. LEINART, Virginia
"My Neighbors in Port Angeles." [BellArk] (4:6) N-D 88, p. 20.
"The Teacherage Door." [BellArk] (4:6) N-D 88, p. 5.

2995. LEIPER, Esther M.
"An Old Man's Early Sleep." [Amelia] (5:2, #13) 88, p. 111.
"The Wars of Faery" (for C.S. Lewis — Book 1, Canto V-VI). [Amelia] (4:4, #11) 88, p. 25-34.
"The Wars of Faery" (for C.S. Lewis — Book 1, Cantos VII-VIII). [Amelia] (5:1, #12) 88, p. 23-32.
"The Wars of Faery" (for C.S. Lewis — Book 1, Cantos IX-X). [Amelia] (5:2, #13) 88, p. 51-60.

2996. LEITHAUSER, Brad
"The Mail from Anywhere." [NewYorker] (64:23) 25 Jl 88, p. 30-31.
"Old Bachelor Brother." [Atlantic] (262:1) Jl 88, p. 71.
"Signalled." [NewYRB] (35:10) 16 Je 88, p. 12.
"A Worded Welcome." [NewYorker] (64:6) 28 Mr 88, p. 28.

2997. LEIVADITIS, Tasos
"The Difficult Hour" (tr. by Gail Holst-Warhaft). [Paint] (15:30) Aut 88, p. 33.
"Family Warmth" (tr. by Gail Holst-Warhaft). [Paint] (15:30) Aut 88, p. 32.

2998. LEMM, Richard
"After You Left." [PottPort] (10) 88, p. 34.
"That Moment." [PottPort] (10) 88, p. 34.
"When You Ask for More." [PottPort] (10) 88, p. 35.

2999. LENHART, Michael
"Daydream." [Bogg] (59) 88, p. 14.

3000. LENIHAN, Dan
"The Back Yard." [Bogg] (60) 88, p. 34.
"The Lawnmower." [Bogg] (59) 88, p. 25-26.
3001. LENIHAN, Edmund
"Observation Tower, Detroit Airport." [KanQ] (20:1/2) Wint-Spr 88, p. 78.
3002. LENSON, David
"Spy Novel" (After John Le Carre). [WillowS] (22) Spr 88, p. 94-96.
3003. LEONE, Dan
"The Bug's Good Attitude." [PaintedB] (36) 88, p. 99.
"Susan's Thing." [PaintedB] (36) 88, p. 99.
3004. LEPORE, Dominick J.
"My Father's House." [Footwork] ('88) 88, p. 66-67.
3005. LEPOVETSKY, Lisa
"Clown." [SpoonRQ] (13:1) Wint 88, p. 64.
3006. LERNER, Betsy
"Taking Flight" (for Barbara, 1962-1964). [Sonora] (14/15) Spr 88, p. 27-28.
3007. LERNER, Linda
"A Helluva Night for Love." [Vis] (27) 88, p. 40.
3008. LesCARBEAU, Mitchell
"Mockingbird." [Interim] (7:2) Fall 88, p. 18.
"The Undertaker, Drunk." [Colum] (13) 88, p. 7.
3009. LESLIE, Naton
"Above Ground." [DenQ] (22:3) Wint 88, p. 107-108.
3010. LESSER, Rika
"The Center of Unheard-Of" (tr. of Göran Sonnevi). [MissouriR] (11:1) 88, p. 41.
"Poems with No Order" (Excerpt, tr. of Göran Sonnevi). [Boulevard] (3:2/3) Fall 88, p. 180.
"There Is Life That" (tr. of Göran Sonnevi). [MissouriR] (11:1) 88, p. 37.
"Unfinished Poems" (Excerpt, tr. of Göran Sonnevi). [Boulevard] (3:2/3) Fall 88, p. 179-180.
3011. LESSING, Karin
"Bee-orchis, fluted up from the root." [Conjunc] (12) 88, p. 110.
"Forcalquier, Candlemas 1986." [Conjunc] (12) 88, p. 109-110.
"Night-Ark, Adrift." [Conjunc] (12) 88, p. 109.
"Under Sirius." [Sulfur] (7:3, #21) Wint 88, p. 141-143.
3012. LESTER-MASSMAN, Gordon
"Density." [Confr] (37/38) Spr-Sum 88, p. 233.
"The Generous Man." [HampSPR] Wint 88, p. 8-9.
3013. LETKO, Ken
"Oriental Carpet" (tr. of Reiner Kunze, w. Thomas S. Edwards). [ColR] (NS 15:2) Fall-Wint 88, p. 87.
3014. LEURGANS, Lois
"Olympic Event." [LightY] ('88/9) 88, p. 57.
3015. LEV, Donald
"History as Theatre." [Footwork] ('88) 88, p. 32.
"The Human Condition in Brighton Beach." [NegC] (8:3) 88, p. 127.
"Introspection." [Footwork] ('88) 88, p. 32.
"Trailing Off." [Lips] (14) 88, p. 13.
"Waters: Three Poems for My Mother." [Lips] (14) 88, p. 12.
3016. LEVANT, Jonathan
"The Comedian Cracks." [Footwork] ('88) 88, p. 31.
"Portrait of Dandan Zhang Who Will Say: 'Wow the Country Western Music'." [Turnstile] (1:1) Wint 88, p. 70.
"Remember by the Firelight When We Were Apes?" [Footwork] ('88) 88, p. 31.
"Trading Tricks for Tricks." [Grain] (16:2) Sum 88, p. 53.
"The Ungelded God." [ChatR] (8:2) Wint 88, p. 14.
3017. LEVENDOSKY, Charles
"Aunt Lily Speaks Her Piece." [ConnPR] (7:1) 88, p. 46.
3018. LEVERING, Donald
"From a Rainy Window." [HiramPoR] (44/45) Spr-Wint 88, p. 29.
"Meteorite Anvil." [Amelia] (5:1, #12) 88, p. 116-117.
"Water Witch." [PoetryE] (25) Spr 88, p. 67.
3019. LEVERTOV, Denise
"In California: Morning, Evening, Late January." [Sequoia] (32:1) Spr-Sum 88, p. 10-11.
"The Life of Art." [AmerPoR] (17:2) Mr-Ap 88, p. 24.

"A Sound." [Abraxas] (37) 88, p. 5.

3020. LEVI, Corona Morgan
"While Packing to Leave Oklahoma." [Phoenix] (9:1/2) 88, p. 59.

LEVI, Enrique Jaramillo
See JARAMILLO LEVI, Enrique

3021. LEVI, Primo
"Autobiography" (tr. by Ruth Feldman). [MissR] (16:1, #46) 88, p. 50-51.
"For Adolf Eichmann" (tr. by Ruth Feldman and Brian Swann). [ParisR] (30:108) Fall 88, p. 206.
"The Girl-Child of Pompeii" (tr. by Ruth Feldman). [WebR] (13:2) Fall 88, p. 29.
"Huayna Capac" (Inca emperor, died in 1527, tr. by Ruth Feldman). [PartR] (55:4) Fall 88, p. 612.
"Into the Valley" (tr. by M. L. Rosenthal). [Nat] (246:22) 4 Je 88, p. 802.
"Plinio." [SouthernR] (24:2) Spr 88, p. 314.
"Pliny" (tr. by Ruth Feldman). [SouthernR] (24:2) Spr 88, p. 315.

3022. LEVI STRAUSS, David
"Some Real Ones." [CentralP] (13) Spr 88, p. 107-117.

3023. LEVIN, Jeffrey
"Three Sheets to the Wind." [DenQ] (22:3) Wint 88, p. 218-219.

3024. LEVIN, Phillis
"Another Defence of Poetry." [Pequod] (25) 88, p. 105.
"The Cricket." [Nat] (247:9) 10 O 88, p. 324.
"Inscriptions." [Boulevard] (3:2/3) Fall 88, p. 159-160.
"Ore." [Pequod] (25) 88, p. 104.
"Prisoners' Round" (After the etching by Gustave Doré and the painting by Vincent van Gogh). [PartR] (55:4) Fall 88, p. 614.
"The Ransom." [GrandS] (7:4) Sum 88, p. 194-195.
"Regions Off the Chart." [DenQ] (23:1) Sum 88, p. 73.
"Springtime Soliloquy." [DenQ] (23:1) Sum 88, p. 71-72.
"The Stairwell." [Agni] (27) 88, p. 39-42.

3025. LEVINE, Miriam
"Nor Seven-Months Pregnant." [AmerPoR] (17:4) Jl-Ag 88, p. 35.

3026. LEVINE, Philip
"Coming Close." [NewYorker] (64:26) 15 Ag 88, p. 30.
"Dog Poem." [GettyR] (1:1) Wint 88, p. 190-191.
"During Rain and Wind." [NewYorker] (64:33) 3 O 88, p. 42.
"Every Blessed Day." [NewYorker] (64:42) 5 D 88, p. 44.
"Fear and Fame." [NewYorker] (64:1) 22 F 88, p. 36.
"In a Light Time." [WestHR] (42:1) Spr 88, p. 44-45.
"The Right Cross." [Poetry] (152:3) Je 88, p. 125-128.
"These Streets." [Hudson] (40:4) Wint 88, p. 625-627.

3027. LEVINE, Rhonda
"Through Gritted Teeth and a Tight Stomach." [Footwork] ('88) 88, p. 51.

3028. LEVINE-KEATING, Helane
"Mother's Nails." [GrahamHR] (11) Spr 88, p. 41.
"The Woman Who Lived in Trees." [GrahamHR] (11) Spr 88, p. 39-40.

3029. LEVITIN, Alexis
"Come Closer" (tr. of Eugenio de Andrade). [Amelia] (4:4, #11) 88, p. 89.
"Departure for Cythera" (tr. of Guillermo Carnero, w. Gina Sconza). [WebR] (13:1) Spr 88, p. 34.
"Solar Matter" (Selections: 1, 4, 6, 7, 11, 14, tr. of Eugenio de Andrade). [Rohwedder] (4) [Wint 88-89], p. 15-16.

3030. LEVITT, Peter
"When the world of its own breaks apart." [Jacaranda] (3:2) Fall-Wint 88, p. 106.

3031. LEVITZ, Linda
"Stone Soup." [Vis] (28) 88, p. 36.

3032. LEVY, Andrew
"Indiana" (Selections). [Temblor] (8) 88, p. 120-134.

3033. LEVY, Ellen
"Film on the Point of Disintegrating." [Raritan] (7:3) Wint 88, p. 33.
"Your Present Moment." [Raritan] (7:3) Wint 88, p. 32.

3034. LEVY, Heather
"$4.40." [PottPort] (10) 88, p. 37.

3035. LEVY, Robert J.
"Bypassed." [RiverS] (27) 88, p. 26.
"Cat and Mouse." [GettyR] (1:2) Spr 88, p. 390-391.

"Church." [RiverS] (27) 88, p. 27.
"The Dialectical Pigeon." [Confr] (37/38) Spr-Sum 88, p. 254.

3036. LEWIS, Bill
"And." [WormR] (28:1, #109) 88, p. 12.
"Fox." [WormR] (28:1, #109) 88, p. 12.
"Metro" (Paris, 1983). [Bogg] (59) 88, p. 35-36.
"El thou art in Electri City." [WormR] (28:1, #109) 88, p. 11.
"The World's Full of Writers Who Don't Write, Painters Who Don't Paint." [WormR] (28:1, #109) 88, p. 13.

3037. LEWIS, Dan
"For the Bones in Your Hands." [Amelia] (4:4, #11) 88, p. 50.

3038. LEWIS, Gwyneth
"The Bad Shepherd." [Verse] (5:3) N 88, p. 58.
"Dameg y Ferch Chwithig." [NewEngR] (10:4) Sum 88, p. 404, 406.
"Parable of the Awkward Woman" (tr. by the author). [NewEngR] (10:4) Sum 88, p. 405, 407.

3039. LEWIS, J. Patrick
"Notes from Leningrad at Forty Below" (For Lida). [KanQ] (20:3) Sum 88, p. 98.
"The Red Army Colonel, Drunk on New Year's Eve." [GettyR] (1:2) Spr 88, p. 243.

3040. LEWIS, Jeffery
"Abortion" (for Lydia). [YellowS] (26) Spr 88, p. 24-29.
"The Lake Is Open." [YellowS] (28) D 88, p. 26.

3041. LEWIS, Jim
"Reunion." [SpoonRQ] (12:4) Fall 87, p. 16.

3042. LEWIS, Joel
"Semi-Multicolored Caucasian." [Talisman] (1) Fall 88, p. 10.

3043. LEWIS, Katherine Greene
"Long Distance." [LakeSR] (22) 88, p. 28.
"Thoughts on the Birth of My Daughter with Down's Syndrome." [LakeSR] (22) 88, p. 29.

3044. LEWIS, Lisa
"Election Day's Eve." [KenR] (NS 10:2) Spr 88, p. 87-88.
"Measure of Control." [KenR] (NS 10:2) Spr 88, p. 86-87.
"Pastoral with Horses." [KenR] (NS 10:2) Spr 88, p. 85-86.

3045. L'HEUREUX, Maurice
"The Jake Trilogy" (A minimalist primer for life in the suburbs). [SmPd] (25:1) Wint 88, p. 11-16.

3046. LI, Min Hua
"Tick, Tock, Tick, Tock, Tick, Tock." [PoetryE] (25) Spr 88, p. 118-119.

3047. LI, Po
"Green Mountain Mind" (tr. by Graeme Wilson). [Jacaranda] (3:2) Fall-Wint 88, p. 145.

3048. LI, Shang-yin
"Untitled: So hard for us to meet" (A.D. 813-858 — T'ang Dynasty, tr. by Wang Zhihuan). [AntR] (46:2) Spr 88, p. 203.

LI, Sun
See SUN, Li

3049. LI, Yi-dong
"Smoking People: Encountering the New Chinese Poetry" (Chapbook 19, tr. by Li Yi-dong et al.). [BelPoJ] (39:2) Wint 88-89, 76 p.

3050. LIATSOS, Sandra
"To My Sick Brother." [Crosscur] (7:4) 88, p. 167-168.
"Wrinkles We Wear." [CapeR] (23:1) Spr 88, p. 29.

3051. LIBBEY, Elizabeth
"The Morning After." [PraS] (62:1) Spr 88, p. 68.
"Quiche of the Day." [PraS] (62:1) Spr 88, p. 69-70.

3052. LIBERA, Sharon
"My Mother's Way." [Ploughs] (14:1) 88, p. 64.

3053. LIEBERMAN, Laurence
"Balconies of the Coffee Houses." [SewanR] (96:3) Sum 88, p. 416-417.
"The Creole Mephistopheles." [AmerPoR] (17:6) N-D 88, p. 46-48.
"Mayhem and Romance in a Crop Duster Fuselage" (Dominica, West Indies. 16: Conclusion). [Boulevard] (3:2/3) Fall 88, p. 71-78.
"Mayhem and Romance in a Crop-Duster Fuselage" (Selection: Part 9). [CharR] (14:2) Fall 88, p. 81-84.

"Mayhem and Romance in a Cropduster Fuselage" (Dominica, West Indies. Selections: 10-11). [NewEngR] (11:2) Wint 88, p. 157-167.
"Mayhem and Romance in a Cropduster Fuselage" (Selections: 1-2, 4-5, 7-8). [KenR] (NS 10:2) Spr 88, p. 113-126.
"The Sailworks Cistern." [Hudson] (41:2) Sum 88, p. 329-332.
"Self Catch." [TarRP] (28:1) Fall 88, p. 67-70.
"The Skateboard Throne: An Ode to Citizen Amputees" (Jacmel, Haiti, Christmas 1983). [AmerPoR] (17:6) N-D 88, p. 44-46.
"Swimming Pool Pastoral." [KenR] (NS 10:1) Wint 88, p. 58-62.

3054. LIEBERT, Daniel
"First Fight." [LakeSR] (22) 88, p. 30.
"The Heart Fund." [LitR] (32:1) Fall 88, p. 120.
"Household." [LitR] (32:1) Fall 88, p. 119.
"Hunger in America." [SlipS] (8) 88, p. 26.
"The Innocence." [SlipS] (8) 88, p. 25.
"The Lord's Day." [SlipS] (8) 88, p. 26.
"Night Thought." [NewOR] (15:2) Sum 88, p. 75.

3055. LIFSHIN, Lyn
"1945 Dispatch: War Correspondent James McGlincy Who Visited Hiroshima Several Days After It Was Destroyed." [Lactuca] (11) O 88, p. 22.
"After the Visit." [Amelia] (4:4, #11) 88, p. 39.
"Afterward." [NewL] (55:1) Fall 88, p. 79.
"Alexandra with Her Bruised Toes." [DeKalbLAJ] (21:3/4) 88, p. 59.
"Anita." [Footwork] ('88) 88, p. 29.
"Annie Her Last Days." [Footwork] ('88) 88, p. 30.
"Annie, Those Last Days in the Hospital in a Snow of Morphine." [WebR] (13:1) Spr 88, p. 67.
"Aprils, Jackson Avenue." [Wind] (18:62) 88, p. 26.
"Artemis Goes Out on the Prowl." [DeKalbLAJ] (21:1) Wint 88, p. 61.
"As the Water Rose Higher." [Grain] (16:4) Wint 88, p. 36.
"Ballet Class Madonna." [WormR] (28:1, #109) 88, p. 14.
"The Bath House." [WindO] (50) Aut 88, p. 17.
"Becoming What You're Called." [Gargoyle] (35) 88, p. 229-230.
"Blue Leaks Out." [Caliban] (4) 88, p. 7.
"Candles in Us." [WindO] (50) Aut 88, p. 17.
"Denim Madonna." [WormR] (28:1, #109) 88, p. 14.
"Depression Like Fat." [ConnPR] (7:1) 88, p. 18.
"Desert Wind Madonna." [WormR] (28:1, #109) 88, p. 14.
"Dream of Emeralds and Mesh Printed Front Page Rolling Stone." [Caliban] (4) 88, p. 10.
"The Engineer on Her Sculpture, Terra Cotta Torsos." [Lactuca] (11) O 88, p. 21.
"Facing Away from Where You Are Going." [Gargoyle] (35) 88, p. 228-229.
"February Monday." [Footwork] ('88) 88, p. 29.
"February Tuesday." [ChamLR] (2:1, #3) Fall 88, p. 40.
"The First Night." [Spirit] (9:1) 88, p. 63-64.
"Fitzi in the Year Book." [SlipS] (8) 88, p. 54.
"He Said He Thought Somehow He'd Caught It, the." [LittleM] (15:3/4) 88, p. 145-146.
"He Said There Were Frogs." [ChamLR] (1:2, #2) Spr 88, p. 13.
"Hearing About the Poem My Sister Wrote That I Hadn't." [LittleM] (15:3/4) 88, p. 144.
"Hearing My Sister." [PikeF] (9) Fall 88, p. 7.
"The Heat." [Amelia] (5:2, #13) 88, p. 39.
"The Hostage in the Room with No Window." [Farm] (4:1, i.e. 5:1) Wint 88, p. 57.
"I Wish Honey." [Bogg] (59) 88, p. 17.
"In That House." [BellR] (11:1) Spr 88, p. 26.
"In the Cafe More Than 20 Years Later." [Footwork] ('88) 88, p. 30.
"In the Canoe Fire Crackers Exploding." [DeKalbLAJ] (21:1) Wint 88, p. 62.
"In the Parking Lot After Small Claims Court." [SlipS] (8) 88, p. 62.
"In the Soaps." [Grain] (16:2) Sum 88, p. 42.
"Jump Start Madonna." [WormR] (28:1, #109) 88, p. 14.
"Lace Madonna." [WormR] (28:1, #109) 88, p. 14.
"Letter to B." [Wind] (18:62) 88, p. 27-28.
"Lie, I Tell Them." [BellR] (11:2) Fall 88, p. 38-39.
"The Mad Girl Dreams of Dreams She Had as a Child of Children in German and Polish Tunnels." [AnotherCM] (18) 88, p. 119.

"The Mad Girl Dreams of New Mexico, Wakes Up Shaking." [Confr] (37/38) Spr-Sum 88, p. 169.
"The Mad Girl Dreams of Two Men in the Car That's Her." [Caliban] (4) 88, p. 8.
"The Mad Girl Finds 'Boring Shot in the Fifth with Colors'." [Caliban] (4) 88, p. 9.
"The Mad Girl Watches the Walnuts Big as Limes in Rain." [WindO] (50) Aut 88, p. 18.
"Madonna of the Paper Romances." [Grain] (16:4) Wint 88, p. 35.
"Modern Dance Club Photo in a High School Year Book." [AlphaBS] (4) D 88, p. 50.
"My Mother at 72." [Lips] (14) 88, p. 9-11.
"My Mother Rubbing My Back." [LittleM] (15:3/4) 88, p. 143-144.
"My Mother, Who Was Never Bored or Lonely." [Abraxas] (37) 88, p. 29.
"My Mother Writes, I Used to Call You Joy for What You Brought Me." [RagMag] (6:1) [88], p. 22.
"My Sister's Diaries." [Wind] (18:62) 88, p. 26.
"Night Soft as Pine." [Grain] (16:2) Sum 88, p. 43.
"Oh Yes." [Wind] (18:62) 88, p. 27.
"The Old Man Posing." [Confr] (37/38) Spr-Sum 88, p. 169.
"Old Men, Hotel Brenner." [Farm] (5:2) Fall 88, p. 39.
"On Rapple Drive." [AnotherCM] (18) 88, p. 120.
"On the Edge Madonna: 1-2." [WormR] (28:1, #109) 88, p. 14.
"On the Way to the Bus Station." [Grain] (16:1) Spr 88, p. 61.
"Penthouse Playboy" (from "Naked Charm"). [SlipS] (8) 88, p. 63-64.
"The Photographs with My Hair Up." [RagMag] (6:1) [88], p. 23.
"Record Cold." [Grain] (16:4) Wint 88, p. 35.
"Ronnie Says He's Worried Draws Red Oozing North Coming Out of Central America Toward Florida . . ." [Grain] (16:1) Spr 88, p. 62-63.
"Sabotage Madonna." [Bogg] (59) 88, p. 45.
"Science Contests." [NewL] (55:1) Fall 88, p. 78-79.
"Sometimes It's Like Talking to Someone in a Casket." [SwampR] (1:2/3) D 88, p. 56.
"Sonny Terry Is Dead." [Contact] (9:47/48/49) Spr 88, p. 45.
"T Bird Madonna." [WormR] (28:1, #109) 88, p. 14.
"That April." [Footwork] ('88) 88, p. 29.
"That Thanksgiving 1980." [WebR] (13:1) Spr 88, p. 66.
"Thirty Miles West of Chicago." [BallSUF] (29:4) Aut 88, p. 16.
"To Get Rid of It." [Grain] (16:4) Wint 88, p. 36.
"Two Streets Past the Green House." [SlipS] (8) 88, p. 62.
"Two Weeks Dreaming of My Ex Husband." [DeKalbLAJ] (21:3/4) 88, p. 60.
"Under This White Silk." [Footwork] ('88) 88, p. 29.
"When Jesse Helms Buys CBS." [Lactuca] (11) O 88, p. 22.
"Why Aerograms Are Always Blue." [HawaiiR] (12:1, #23) Spr 88, p. 34.
"Workshop." [Grain] (16:1) Spr 88, p. 60.

3056. LIFSHITZ, Leatrice
"First Wife" (the wives of John Brown and Dangerfield Newby, abolishionists, a 3-part series). [StoneC] (15:3/4) Spr-Sum 88, p. 58.

3057. LIFSON, Martha Ronk
"Dark Tonight." [AmerPoR] (17:2) Mr-Ap 88, p. 43.
"Looking at a Reproduction of *Ladies of the Village* in T.J. Clark, A Letter." [AmerPoR] (17:2) Mr-Ap 88, p. 43.
"One Needs." [AmerPoR] (17:2) Mr-Ap 88, p. 43.

3058. LIGI
"A Cunt." [SlipS] (8) 88, p. 81-82.

3059. LIGNELL, Kathleen
"Anticipating Your Visit." [TexasR] (9:3/4) Fall-Wint 88, p. 97.
"Departure." [TexasR] (9:3/4) Fall-Wint 88, p. 96.
"Night of the Iguana." [Colum] (13) 88, p. 110-111.

3060. LILBURNE, Geoffrey R.
"The Veteran Swimmers." [ChrC] (105:37) 7 D 88, p. 1124.

3061. LILLARD, Charles
"Small Daylight in Green Shade." [Grain] (16:2) Sum 88, p. 15.
"Stikine Plateau." [Quarry] (37:4) Aut 88, p. 35.

LILLYWHITE, Eileen Silver
See SILVER-LILLYWHITE, Eileen

3062. LILLYWHITE, Harvey
"Once More." [KanQ] (20:3) Sum 88, p. 203.

3063. LIM, Genny
"Children Are Color-Blind." [Calyx] (11:2/3) Fall 88, p. 196-197.
3064. LIM, Shirley Geok-lin
"Mean Confession." [MassR] (29:3) Fall 88, p. 422.
"Pantoun for Chinese Women." [Calyx] (11:2/3) Fall 88, p. 204-205.
"Starlight Haven." [MassR] (29:3) Fall 88, p. 421-422.
"Visiting Malacca." [Calyx] (11:2/3) Fall 88, p. 206.
3065. LINCOLN, Kenneth
"Two Rivers Away" (Written by flashlight at the Fragrant Brook Pavilion, Wuhan, 4/21/88). [Jacaranda] (3:2) Fall-Wint 88, p. 107.
3066. LINDEMAN, Jack
"Growing Deaf." [Comm] (115:6) 25 Mr 88, p. 173.
3067. LINDEN, Dianne
"About My Husband Walt." [Grain] (16:2) Sum 88, p. 40.
"Litany." [Grain] (16:2) Sum 88, p. 38.
"Oncoming Train." [Grain] (16:2) Sum 88, p. 39.
3068. LINDHOLDT, Paul
"Benediction." [CapeR] (23:1) Spr 88, p. 38.
"Buck Meadows." [CapeR] (23:1) Spr 88, p. 39.
"Centuries Inland." [CapeR] (23:1) Spr 88, p. 40.
"Trainer." [CapeR] (23:1) Spr 88, p. 41.
3069. LINDNER, April
"Vegetable Suite." [SwampR] (1:2/3) D 88, p. 68-71.
3070. LINDNER, Carl
"Bête Noire." [KanQ] (20:1/2) Wint-Spr 88, p. 173.
"Boomerang." [MidAR] (8:2) 88, p. 1.
"Caulking in Late Fall." [Wind] (18:62) 88, p. 30-31.
"Hand." [LitR] (31:2) Wint 88, p. 189.
"How I Got Here." [Wind] (18:62) 88, p. 29.
"Sailing: First Lesson." [Wind] (18:62) 88, p. 30.
"Windfall." [BellR] (11:1) Spr 88, p. 28.
3071. LINEHAN, Don
"Narrow Road." [PottPort] (9) 88, p. 51.
3072. LINETT, Deena
"Letter from Yaddo in May." [Blueline] (9:1/2) 88, p. 6.
3073. LING, Greg
"Mid-December, Northern Hills." [KanQ] (20:3) Sum 88, p. 216.
3074. LINTERMANS, Tony
"Stone Wall About to Fall." [MassR] (29:2) Sum 88, p. 266.
"Two Brothers Renovate the Farmhouse." [MassR] (29:2) Sum 88, p. 266.
3075. LINTHICUM, John
"Licking the Blade of Unfaithfulness." [SenR] (18:2) 88, p. 33-35.
3076. LINTON, David
"The Dropped." [PoetC] (19:2) Wint 88, p. 9.
3077. LINTON, M. E.
"Floaters." [SouthernPR] (28:2) Fall 88, p. 61.
3078. LIOTTA, P. H.
"The Story I Can't Tell." [Poetry] (151:6) Mr 88, p. 473-477.
3079. LIPKIND, A. (Arnold)
"Hot Tub Yuppies." [JINJPo] (10:1/2) 88, p. 27.
"In a World Uncouth." [Bogg] (60) 88, p. 49.
"I've Never Understood You" (Notes Taken While Being Driven Over the Pali by My Estranged Wife). [Amelia] (5:2, #13) 88, p. 72-77.
"To Richard." [JINJPo] (10:1/2) 88, p. 26.
3080. LIPSCOMB, James
"Robbing the Organ Bank." [Wind] (18:62) 88, p. 33.
LIPSINER-VERSENYI, Sue
See VERSENYI, Sue Lipsiner
3082. LIPSITZ, Lewis
"On the Declaration of Martial Law in Poland, December 13, 1981." [NegC] (8:3) 88, p. 40-41.
3083. LIPSITZ, Lou
"The Dugout" (from "The Grief"). [Nimrod] (32:1) Fall-Wint 88, p. 111.
"The Grief" (from "The Grief"). [Nimrod] (32:1) Fall-Wint 88, p. 110-111.
"Summer Night." [Caliban] (4) 88, p. 92-93.

3084. LISCANO, Juan
"Cresta." [Inti] (26/27) Otoño 87-Primavera 88, p. 233-234.
"Dictado." [Inti] (26/27) Otoño 87-Primavera 88, p. 232.
"Luz." [Inti] (26/27) Otoño 87-Primavera 88, p. 231.
"No Pasa el Tiempo." [Inti] (26/27) Otoño 87-Primavera 88, p. 234.
"Siempre" (A Carmen Teresa). [Inti] (26/27) Otoño 87-Primavera 88, p. 232-233.
3085. LISOWSKI, Joseph
"Chrysanthemums." [StoneC] (15:3/4) Spr-Sum 88, p. 15.
"Pepper Plant Garden" (tr. of P'ei Ti). [HiramPoR] (44/45) Spr-Wint 88, p. 30.
"Pepper Plant Garden" (tr. of Wang Wei). [HiramPoR] (44/45) Spr-Wint 88, p. 31.
3086. LITTLE, Geraldine C.
"Beyond the Boxwood Comb: Six Women's Voices from Japan" (linked haiku on six women poets of Japan). [Sparrow] (54) 88, 31 p.
"The Exceptional Child." [JlNJPo] (10:1/2) 88, p. 43.
"Revelations: Rosa Bonheur." [MassR] (29:2) Sum 88, p. 227-229.
"Vision." [SenR] (18:1) 88, p. 44.
3087. LITTLE, Jack
"Poème de Terre, or, Love Song to a Potato." [LightY] ('88/9) 88, p. 218-219.
3088. LOCKARD, Amy
"The Concept of Grace." [Spirit] (9:1) 88, p. 36-37.
3089. LOCKARD, Rosemary S.
"Riverbottom Rust." [ChatR] (8:3) Spr 88, p. 60.
3090. LOCKE, Duane
"Sanibel Notes, 1-6" (6 poems). [Pembroke] (20) 88, p. 182-183.
3091. LOCKE, Edward
"Miscounting." [GeoR] (42:1) Spr 88, p. 152. Reprinted with correction, [GeoR] (42:2) Sum 88, p. 399.
3092. LOCKE, John
"A Festival Play" (For the Inauguration of the Art Center, Bremen, 1902, tr. of Rainer Maria Rilke). [Paint] (15:30) Aut 88, p. 26-29.
3093. LOCKLIN, Gerald
"Are We Speaking the Same Language, Dear?" [WormR] (28:1, #109) 88, p. 4-5.
"Black Monday, Tuesday, Wednesday, etc." [WormR] (28:4, #112) 88, p. 127.
"The Carrot and the Whip." [WormR] (28:1, #109) 88, p. 6.
"Dick and Jane." [SlipS] (8) 88, p. 83-84.
"Don't I Wish They Did." [WormR] (28:1, #109) 88, p. 3.
"For the Time Capsule." [WormR] (28:4, #112) 88, p. 127.
"A Guy I Think I Would Have Liked, Even Though He Wouldn't Have Liked Me." [WormR] (28:1, #109) 88, p. 5.
"Happy Ending." [Abraxas] (37) 88, p. 72-73.
"A Man for No Seasons." [WormR] (28:1, #109) 88, p. 4.
"A Man's Home Is His Castle Is." [WormR] (28:4, #112) 88, p. 127.
"Otto Dix: *Soldier with Pipe*, 1918." [WormR] (28:4, #112) 88, p. 127.
"Our Mother Who Art in Heaven." [WormR] (28:4, #112) 88, p. 128.
"Out-Flanked." [SlipS] (8) 88, p. 83.
"Rake's Progress." [SlipS] (8) 88, p. 83.
"Touché." [WormR] (28:1, #109) 88, p. 5.
"We All Sleep Well at Night." [WormR] (28:4, #112) 88, p. 127.
3094. LOCKWOOD, Margo
"Things I Wouldn't Have Known About Russia" (for Galina Gabay). [Ploughs] (14:1) 88, p. 27-28.
3095. LODEN, Rachel
"The Wedding Journey." [ChamLR] (1) Fall 87, p. 392.
3096. LOEBER, Lynne
"Even This Late." [GrahamHR] (11) Spr 88, p. 8-9.
3097. LOGAN, William
"The Age of Ballroom Dining." [Poetry] (151:6) Mr 88, p. 483.
"Haddocks' Eyes." [ParisR] (30:106) Spr 88, p. 256-257.
"Racial Prejudice in Imperial Rome." [Crazy] (34) Spr 88, p. 37.
"The Underground." [SewanR] (96:2) Spr 88, p. 236-242.
"Westport After the Hurricane." [WilliamMR] (26:1) Spr 88, p. 21.
3098. LOGUE, Christopher
"The Iliad" (the opening lines of the first book, tr. of Homer). [ParisR] (30:106) Spr 88, p. 221-227.
3099. LOHMANN, Jeanne (Jeanne A.)
"Olallieberry." [Farm] (4:1, i.e. 5:1) Wint 88, p. 38.

"Toward Morning the Inuit Grandmother Talks to Herself." [PassN] (9:2) Sum 88, p. 30.
"Water Lily." [PassN] (9:1) Wint 88, p. 29.
"Wild Honey" (after a photograph in National Geographic). [ColR] (NS 15:2) Fall-Wint 88, p. 50.

3100. LOMAS, Herbert
"Assisi and Back." [Hudson] (41:3) Aut 88, p. 483-484.
"Chanson Triste." [Hudson] (41:3) Aut 88, p. 481.
"First Kisses." [Hudson] (41:3) Aut 88, p. 482-483.
"In Spite of Everything." [Hudson] (41:3) Aut 88, p. 484-485.
"Other Life." [Hudson] (41:3) Aut 88, p. 482.
"Suffolk Evenings." [Hudson] (41:3) Aut 88, p. 485-488.

3101. LONDON, Jonathan
"The Etruscan Shiver" (for Maureen). [SlipS] (8) 88, p. 42.
"Like Salamanders Meandering" (for Maureen). [SlipS] (8) 88, p. 42-43.
"Tearing Down the Old Wall." [SpoonRQ] (13:3) Sum 88, p. 16.

3102. LONG, John Wingo
"Believe It or Not." [Amelia] (5:1, #12) 88, p. 107.
"Coffee Break." [Amelia] (5:1, #12) 88, p. 108.

3103. LONG, Priscilla
"The Return." [NoDaQ] (56:1) Wint 88, p. 94.

3104. LONG, Robert
"Terminal Cafe." [AntR] (46:4) Fall 88, p. 484.
"The Wrong Word." [SouthernPR] (28:1) Spr 88, p. 52-53.

3105. LONG, Robert Hill
"Grandfather Long the Last Time." [VirQR] (64:1) Wint 88, p. 83-88.
"The Streets of the Muses." [PoetryE] (25) Spr 88, p. 7-16.

3106. LONG, Virginia Love
"For Mule." [Pembroke] (20) 88, p. 120-121.
"For Nikita Koloff" (in English with Russian translation by David Fisher). [InterPR] (14:1) Spr 88, p. 52-55.
"Six Nikitas." [InterPR] (14:1) Spr 88, p. 78-80.
"We Shall Not Escape Hell" (for Marina Tsvetayeva, with Russian translation by David Fisher). [InterPR] (14:1) Spr 88, p. 50-51.

3107. LONGLEY, Michael
"Cathedral." [PartR] (55:3) Sum 88, p. 475.
"Detour." [PartR] (55:1) Wint 88, p. 55.
"The Shack." [PartR] (55:3) Sum 88, p. 475-476.

3108. LOOMIS, Sabra
"The Grandmother." [CinPR] (17) Spr 88, p. 60.
"Green" (Harbor Point, 1942). [CinPR] (17) Spr 88, p. 61.

3109. LOONEY, George
"Diving Cold into This Life." [CinPR] (18) Fall 88, p. 74-75.
"Threatening Light." [CimR] (84) Jl 88, p. 91-92.

3110. LOOSELEAF, Victoria
"Radical Queen." [RagMag] (6:1) [88], p. 26.
"Smile, Freeze." [RagMag] (6:1) [88], p. 24-25.

3111. LOOTS, Barbara
"Squaw Creek" (for Linda). [NewL] (55:1) Fall 88, p. 48-49.

3112. LOPEZ MARIN, Olga
"Sensaciones." [LetFem] (14:1/2) Primavera-Otoño 88, p. 133.

LORCA, Federico García
See GARCIA LORCA, Federico

3113. LOTT, Clarinda Harriss
"Tangerines for Mother's Day." [CimR] (83) Ap 88, p. 61-64.

3114. LOTT, Rick
"The Flyer" (In Memory of Clarence Davis). [DenQ] (22:3) Wint 88, p. 232.
"The Man Who Loved Distance." [KenR] (NS 10:1) Wint 88, p. 86.
"Shooting for Shape." [KenR] (NS 10:1) Wint 88, p. 85.
"Vision at Wheeler Lake." [DenQ] (22:3) Wint 88, p. 233.

3115. LOUTER, David
"In the Stands" (For Paul Zarzyski). [CutB] (29/30) 88, p. 88.

3116. LOUTHAN, Robert
"Letter Written on a Paper Mountain" (to W. E. Butts). [Agni] (26) 88, p. 177-178.

3117. LOVE, B. D.
"Chuck Berry." [Vis] (27) 88, p. 7.

"Fat Lady Stuck in New Sports Car" (Tabloid Headline, March, 1986). [ChamLR] (2:1, #3) Fall 88, p. 106-108.
"Lungs" (for David Faulkner). [BelPoJ] (39:1) Fall 88, p. 16-17.
"Mick Jagger." [Vis] (27) 88, p. 7.
"Starlight and Milk." [BelPoJ] (39:1) Fall 88, p. 14-15.

3118. LOW, Denise
"Skipping Stones at Clinton." [MidwQ] (30:1) Aut 88, p. 77.

3119. LOW, Jackson Mac
"6th Merzgedicht" (in Memoriam Kurt Schwitters). [Notus] (3:1) Spr 88, p. 11-14.
"7th Merzgedicht" (in Memoriam Kurt Schwitters). [Notus] (3:1) Spr 88, p. 15-16.
"8th Merzgedicht in Memoriam Kurt Schwitters." [Temblor] (7) 88, p. 3-10.
"11th Merzgedicht *in Memoriam* Kurt Schwitters." [Sonora] (14/15) Spr 88, p. 110.
"21st Merzgedicht *in Memoriam* Kurt Schwitters." [Sonora] (14/15) Spr 88, p. 111-112.
"Briggflatts 2." [Sonora] (14/15) Spr 88, p. 109.
"Pieces o' Six" (Selections: XXXI, XXXIII, with computer graphics by Anne Tardos). [Temblor] (7) 88, p. 72-84.
"Progress I." [CentralP] (13) Spr 88, p. 145-146.
"Progress 2." [CentralP] (13) Spr 88, p. 146-147.
"Silence" (Selection: Poem for John Cage's 75th Birthday). [Notus] (3:1) Spr 88, p. 10.

3120. LOWE, Bia
"Blue." [Caliban] (4) 88, p. 89.
"Horse." [BelPoJ] (38:4) Sum 88, p. 14.
"Purple." [Caliban] (4) 88, p. 90.
"Sarasvati (Consonants and Vowels)." [BelPoJ] (38:4) Sum 88, p. 15.

3121. LOWENSTEIN, Robert
"The First Leaf." [CapeR] (23:1) Spr 88, p. 43.
"Fruit of Victory." [Wind] (18:62) 88, p. 32.
"Odysseus Sets the Record Straight." [SpoonRQ] (13:1) Wint 88, p. 59.
"Picture That." [Wind] (18:62) 88, p. 32-33.
"Rite of Passage." [SpoonRQ] (13:1) Wint 88, p. 58.

3122. LOWERY, Joanne
"Color January." [SpoonRQ] (13:1) Wint 88, p. 54.
"A Couple of Poets." [CumbPR] (7:2) Spr 88, p. 39-40.
"Escape." [Plain] (8:2) Wint 88, p. 29.
"Nightfall." [SpoonRQ] (13:1) Wint 88, p. 55.
"Running Cows." [KanQ] (20:1/2) Wint-Spr 88, p. 176.
"Second Moon." [Plain] (8:3) Spr-Sum 88, p. 34.
"Thursday." [ChamLR] (1) Fall 87, p. 396.
"Walking in the Rain." [SpoonRQ] (13:1) Wint 88, p. 55.
"Wishbones." [Crosscur] (7:4) 88, p. 11.

3123. LOWRIE, Joyce Oliver
"Cuevas Blues" (with drawings by José-Luis Cuevas, tr. of André Pieyre de Mandiargues). [AmerPoR] (17:5) S-O 88, p. 30-31.
"Finger of God" (tr. of André Pieyre de Mandiargues). [AmerPoR] (17:5) S-O 88, p. 32.
"From Geranium to Fire" (tr. of André Pieyre de Mandiargues). [AmerPoR] (17:5) S-O 88, p. 32.
"The Hunter" (tr. of André Pieyre de Mandiargues). [AmerPoR] (17:5) S-O 88, p. 32.
"In Celebration of the Birth of Sibylle" (tr. of André Pieyre de Mandiargues). [AmerPoR] (17:5) S-O 88, p. 32.
"Pearl" (tr. of André Pieyre de Mandiargues). [AmerPoR] (17:5) S-O 88, p. 32.
"The Quickness of Clouds" (tr. of Yves Bonnefoy). [AmerPoR] (17:4) Jl-Ag 88, p. 46.
"Rebellion" (tr. of André Pieyre de Mandiargues). [AmerPoR] (17:5) S-O 88, p. 32.
"Silkworm" (tr. of André Pieyre de Mandiargues). [AmerPoR] (17:5) S-O 88, p. 32.
"Spanish Café" (tr. of André Pieyre de Mandiargues). [AmerPoR] (17:5) S-O 88, p. 32.
"The Well" (tr. of Yves Bonnefoy). [AmerPoR] (17:4) Jl-Ag 88, p. 46.
"Withdrawal" (tr. of André Pieyre de Mandiargues). [AmerPoR] (17:5) S-O 88, p. 32.

3124. LOWRY, John
"Early Sunday Morning." [HangL] (53) 88, p. 27.

3125. LOYD, Marianne
"Elegy for Sean Kelly." [CrabCR] (5:1) Wint 88, p. 27.
"Marriage: The Words." [CrabCR] (5:1) Wint 88, p. 27.
3126. LOZANO, Orieta
"Rito." [Mairena] (10:25) 88, p. 45.
3127. LU, Wen
"Smoking People: Encountering the New Chinese Poetry" (Chapbook 19, tr. by Lu Wen et al.). [BelPoJ] (39:2) Wint 88-89, 76 p.
3128. LU, Yiu
"Written During a Storm" (A.D. 1192, at 68 years of age, in retirement in Chekiang Prov., tr. by Wang Zhihuan). [AntR] (46:2) Spr 88, p. 196.
3129. LUCERO, Jaime
"A Certain Kind of Wife." [DenQ] (22:3) Wint 88, p. 182.
3130. LUCHS, Evelyn
"Eve." [StoneC] (15:3/4) Spr-Sum 88, p. 74.
3131. LUCINA, Mary
"In a Car Covered with Snow." [GreensboroR] (44) Sum 88, p. 106.
"Spinal Tap." [LaurelR] (22:21) Wint 88, p. 47.
3132. LUDVIGSON, Susan
"Now Is the Silence of Sleeping Doves." [RiverS] (25) 88, p. 16.
"Woman on a Bridge." [RiverS] (25) 88, p. 17.
3133. LUEBBE, James
"November." [KanQ] (20:1/2) Wint-Spr 88, p. 89.
3134. LUECKE, Janemarie
"Cancer Poem 1987." [NegC] (8:3) 88, p. 76-86.
3135. LUKASIK, Gail
"Daughter Suite." [Northeast] (ser. 4:7) Sum 88, p. 24-25.
"Terce." [Northeast] (ser. 4:7) Sum 88, p. 25.
3136. LUKIN, Liliana
"Barrerla." [Inti] (26/27) Otoño 87-Primavera 88, p. 239-240.
"Bonyumadam." [Inti] (26/27) Otoño 87-Primavera 88, p. 242-243.
"Carne." [Inti] (26/27) Otoño 87-Primavera 88, p. 241-242.
"Frutos." [Inti] (26/27) Otoño 87-Primavera 88, p. 238-239.
"La Máquina Infernal." [Inti] (26/27) Otoño 87-Primavera 88, p. 241.
"Para Que Estés Más Cerca." [Inti] (26/27) Otoño 87-Primavera 88, p. 240.
3137. LUM, Wing Tek
"And We Kept On Chatting." [ChamLR] (1:2, #2) Spr 88, p. 60.
"Coloring a Rainbow." [ChamLR] (1:2, #2) Spr 88, p. 58-59.
"This Visit." [ChamLR] (1:2, #2) Spr 88, p. 61.
3138. LUMMIS, Suzanne
"Why Life Is Worth Living." [Jacaranda] (3:2) Fall-Wint 88, p. 108-109.
3139. LUMSDEN, Roddy
"Vanity." [Verse] (5:2) Jl 88, p. 18.
3140. LUND, Orval
"The One Night Marlyce Jacobsen Expressed Herself." [Farm] (5:2) Fall 88, p. 63.
3141. LUNDAY, Robert
"A Child Caught in the Forked Branch of a Tree." [SouthernHR] (22:4) Fall 88, p. 321.
"Fort Bragg." [SouthernPR] (28:1) Spr 88, p. 43-44.
"Fort Jackson." [PraS] (62:2) Sum 88, p. 62.
"It Snows Here." [HampSPR] Wint 88, p. 30.
3142. LUNDE, David
"Villon's Quatrain" (tr. of François Villon). [LightY] ('88/9) 88, p. 70.
3143. LUNDE, Diane
"Love Poem II." [Vis] (27) 88, p. 44.
3144. LUNDQUIST, Kaye
"Two Painters." [BellArk] (4:3) My-Je 88, p. 20.
3145. LUNDY, Gary
"At the Y." [Spirit] (9:1) 88, p. 65.
"Everlasting Peace." [Bound] (15:3/16:1) Spr-Fall 88, p. 275.
"Mirror." [Bound] (15:3/16:1) Spr-Fall 88, p. 274.
"This Making I Tore the Sight From." [Bound] (15:3/16:1) Spr-Fall 88, p. 273.
"We All Walk Were the Image Fails." [Bound] (15:3/16:1) Spr-Fall 88, p. 217-272.
3146. LUOMA, Bill
"Piazza della Radio" (a sequence of visual poems: Selections). [CentralP] (13) Spr 88, p. 138-144.

3147. LUSCHEI, Glenna
"For the Women." [NegC] (8:3) 88, p. 170-171.
3148. LUSH, Laura
"Joanna." [Grain] (16:1) Spr 88, p. 44.
"Turnips." [Grain] (16:1) Spr 88, p. 45.
3149. LUSK, Daniel
"Any Morning." [AmerPoR] (17:6) N-D 88, p. 33.
"Children Sleeping." [AmerPoR] (17:6) N-D 88, p. 33.
"Daydream with Scissor Accompaniment." [KanQ] (20:3) Sum 88, p. 138.
"Samuel." [SouthernPR] (28:1) Spr 88, p. 51.
3150. LUX, Thomas
"Fever Ship." [Field] (39) Fall 88, p. 81.
"The Fracture Family." [WillowS] (21) Wint 88, p. 39.
"Fundamental." [Iowa] (18:1) 88, p. 59-60.
"The Garden." [Iowa] (18:1) 88, p. 58-59.
"Institute of Defectology." [Field] (39) Fall 88, p. 82.
"Irreconcilabilia." [WestHR] (42:1) Spr 88, p. 66.
"Missing Persons." [Colum] (13) 88, p. 8.
"Motel Seedy." [WestHR] (42:1) Spr 88, p. 68-69.
"Mr. Pope." [Iowa] (18:1) 88, p. 57-58.
"On a High Branch." [WillowS] (21) Wint 88, p. 40.
"Peevish." [WillowS] (21) Wint 88, p. 38.
"Please Don't Touch the Ruins." [Iowa] (18:1) 88, p. 56-57.
"Post Mortem Menu." [Field] (39) Fall 88, p. 83.
"So You Put the Dog to Sleep." [Colum] (13) 88, p. 9.
"The Sudd as Metaphor." [Agni] (27) 88, p. 33.
"Summer Evening, 1864, Andersonville, Georgia." [WestHR] (42:1) Spr 88, p. 67.
"Walt Whitman's Brain Dropped on Laboratory Floor." [Agni] (27) 88, p. 31-32.
3151. LUZI, Mario
"Woman in Pisa" (tr. by Michael L. Johnson). [QW] (26) Wint 88, p. 113.
3152. LYLE, Joy
"Grace." [PoetryNW] (29:3) Aut 88, p. 8.
"Planting Trees in the Rain." [PoetryNW] (29:3) Aut 88, p. 8.
"The Woman Agnes." [PoetryNW] (29:3) Aut 88, p. 9.
3153. LYLE, K. Curtis
"Henry Dumas Walking through Subway Skulls." [BlackALF] (22:2) Sum 88, p. 281-285.
3154. LYLES, Peggy Willis
"Divisions" (Excerpts). [StoneC] (15:3/4) Spr-Sum 88, p. 14-15.
3155. LYNCH, Annette
"Fresh Is Good, Live Is Better." [PoetL] (83:3) Fall 88, p. 22.
3156. LYNCH, Janice
"To Steven, in Critical Condition" (for Michele). [Vis] (27) 88, p. 34-35.
3157. LYNCH, Michael
"Cry." [NewRep] (198:11) 14 Mr 88, p. 44.
3158. LYNCH, Thomas
"The Mid-life of Bill Childers." [SouthwR] (73:4) Aut 88, p. 484-487.
3159. LYNSKEY, Edward C.
"After the Dinner Guests." [Paint] (15:30) Aut 88, p. 19.
"Building a Fencerow." [RagMag] (6:2) Fall 88, p. 54.
"Choptank Oyster Dredgers." [SouthwR] (73:2) Spr 88, p. 219.
"Death of Cold." [HiramPoR] (44/45) Spr-Wint 88, p. 32.
"The Duck Corps Rupture." [KanQ] (20:3) Sum 88, p. 230.
"Home from the Lobster Shift." [PikeF] (9) Fall 88, p. 3.
"Kiss of Kin." [Turnstile] (1:1) Wint 88, p. 20.
"Little Boy Blue." [Farm] (5:2) Fall 88, p. 16.
"Mrs. Lincoln Enters Bellevue Place." [SouthernPR] (28:1) Spr 88, p. 9.
"Mrs. Lincoln Winters in Nice." [DeKalbLAJ] (21:3/4) 88, p. 61.
"Shade Tree Mechanics." [HampSPR] Wint 88, p. 13.
"The Tree Surgeon's Alibi." [WebR] (13:2) Fall 88, p. 70.
"The Tree Surgeon's Curse." [Blueline] (9:1/2) 88, p. 100.
"The Tree Surgeon's Ladder." [Writer] (101:6) Je 88, p. 22.
"The Tree Surgeon's Overtime." [KanQ] (20:3) Sum 88, p. 231.
"Windless Orchards." [Vis] (27) 88, p. 44.
3160. LYON, Hillary
"The Roots of a Red Tulip." [LitR] (31:3) Spr 88, p. 346.

3161. LYON, Rick
"Paradise." [TarRP] (27:2) Spr 88, p. 16.
3162. LYONS, Edward
"Looking at Canaan." [Pembroke] (20) 88, p. 173.
3163. LYONS, Kimberly
"Aphra." [NewAW] (3) Spr 88, p. 107-109.
"Lynn's Dream." [Colum] (13) 88, p. 112.
3164. LYONS, Richard
"Charon's Boat" (after Patinier). [NewRep] (199:2) 11 Jl 88, p. 34.
3165. LYONS, Robert
"A Walk in the Woods." [BellArk] (4:2) Mr-Ap 88, p. 7.
3166. LYONS, Stephen
"Hermiston." [Grain] (16:4) Wint 88, p. 73.
"Women Out West." [Grain] (16:4) Wint 88, p. 72.
Mac . . .
See also names beginning with Mc . . .
3167. MAC, Kathy
"Insubstantial Lover." [AntigR] (73) Spr 88, p. 122.
"Woman Reaching." [PottPort] (9) 88, p. 47.
Mac LOW, Jackson
See LOW, Jackson Mac
3168. MacAFEE, Norman
"Italy '76" (for Pasolini, Rossellini, Visconti dead within a year of each other). [LittleM] (15:3/4) 88, p. 107-111.
3169. MACCABEE, Lillian
"A Love Letter to Lillian." [HangL] (53) 88, p. 60-62.
3170. MacDONALD, Frank
"El Salvador (1971)." [PottPort] (10) 88, p. 46-47.
3171. MACDONALD, Lorne
"A New Conception of Karma" (for Richard). [Quarry] (37:1) Wint 88, p. 42.
3172. MacFARLANE, Myra
"After the Market." [WestCR] (22:3) Wint 87, p. 40.
"Animal Market, Momostenango." [WestCR] (22:3) Wint 87, p. 39.
"Leaving." [WestCR] (22:3) Wint 87, p. 43-44.
"Serafina's Hand." [WestCR] (22:3) Wint 87, p. 41-42.
3173. MACFIE, Jenny
"Rules of War." [Wind] (18:62) 88, p. 51.
3174. MacGUIRE, James
"Cambridge: Winter Dawn." [SouthernR] (24:1) Wint 88, p. 154-155.
"Katmandu." [KanQ] (20:3) Sum 88, p. 134.
"Raking Leaves." [KanQ] (20:3) Sum 88, p. 134.
"Sleep." [SouthernR] (24:1) Wint 88, p. 156-157.
"White Mountains." [SouthernR] (24:1) Wint 88, p. 155-156.
3175. MACHADO, Antonio
"I Have Walked Down Many Roads" (tr. by Don Share). [Agni] (27) 88, p. 9-10.
MACHIKO, Kishimoto
See KISHIMOTO, Machiko
3176. MACIOCI, R. Nikolas
"Desired Image." [WindO] (50) Aut 88, p. 11.
"Gustav Mahler Discovers His Grandmother's Piano." [WindO] (50) Aut 88, p. 10.
"Kamikaze." [Amelia] (4:4, #11) 88, p. 67.
"Pen Ethics." [WindO] (50) Aut 88, p. 15.
"Port Clinton Portrait." [WindO] (50) Aut 88, p. 12.
"Rabbit Hunter." [WindO] (50) Aut 88, p. 13.
"Rain Is Our Significance." [WindO] (50) Aut 88, p. 14.
"Sea Gull Survival." [WindO] (50) Aut 88, p. 14.
3177. MACK, Robin Rebecca
"Love Is a Lot Like Quicksand." [AmerPoR] (17:3) My-Je 88, p. 8.
3178. MACKAY, Neil
"Pensées Volées." [Margin] (7) 88, p. 65-71.
3179. MacKENZIE, Ginny
"He Paints a Picture of His House." [NegC] (8:3) 88, p. 143-145.
"Thinking About Going Out." [Boulevard] (3:2/3) Fall 88, p. 116.
3180. MACKENZIE, Robert
"Reformation." [Verse] (5:2) Jl 88, p. 12.

3181. MACKEY, Nathaniel
"Knotted Highness" ("mu" sixth part). [Epoch] (37:2) 88, p. 125-128.
MACKINNON, Margaret Shaw
See SHAW-MacKINNON, Margaret
3182. MACKLIN, Elizabeth
"Chiding the Very-God." [NewYorker] (64:24) 1 Ag 88, p. 22.
"Ornament in a Port City." [NewYorker] (64:15) 30 My 88, p. 36.
"Seeking to Account to a Fisherman Thief." [NewYorker] (64:3) 7 Mr 88, p. 40.
"The Sorry Creatures in This Country-Side." [NewYorker] (64:35) 17 O 88, p. 44.
"The Two Scenes in Color." [NewYorker] (64:43) 12 D 88, p. 44.
3183. MacLAINE, Wendell
"An Angry Shadow." [PottPort] (9) 88, p. 30.
"The Streetsweeper." [PottPort] (9) 88, p. 30.
3184. MacLEAN, Alasdair
"Cloud Shout." [Antaeus] (60) Spr 88, p. 208.
"Northeast Poem." [Antaeus] (60) Spr 88, p. 207.
3185. MacLEAN, Sorley
"Hallaig." [Antaeus] (60) Spr 88, p. 305-306.
3186. MacLEOD, Colin
"Questions Posed to the Foreigners Out Germans" (tr. of Peter Schneider, w. Hans-Jurgen Schacht). [Rohwedder] (4) [Wint 88-89], p. 13.
3187. MACLEOD, Norman
"Harry Forgot to Tell Us." [Pembroke] (20) 88, p. 246.
"What the Big Boss Is About." [Pembroke] (20) 88, p. 246.
MacLOW, Jackson
See LOW, Jackson Mac
3188. MacMANUS, Mariquita
"In the Fast Lane." [PoetL] (83:3) Fall 88, p. 29.
3189. MacPHERSON, Jennifer B.
"Demolition: Halfway Through at Quitting Time." [Footwork] ('88) 88, p. 31.
"Family Album." [CapeR] (23:1) Spr 88, p. 23.
"In Memory of a Misanthrope." [Plain] (9:1) Fall 88, p. 34.
"Winter in Three Movements." [Plain] (8:3) Spr-Sum 88, p. 30.
3190. MacSWAIN, James
"Ruins." [PottPort] (10) 88, p. 33.
3191. MADDOX, Everette
"New Orleans" (for Ralph Adamo). [SouthernPR] (28:1) Spr 88, p. 14.
3192. MADDUX, Robert E.
"Ozark Hotel." [Phoenix] (9:1/2) 88, p. 26.
3193. MADGETT, Naomi Long
"On Corcovado Mountain." [MichQR] (27:2) Spr 88, p. 245.
3194. MADIGAN, Mark
"I Have Not Forgotten." [KanQ] (20:1/2) Wint-Spr 88, p. 154.
3195. MADSON, Arthur
"Class of '45." [SoCaR] (20:2) Spr 88, p. 55.
"Onions and Elbows." [PoetC] (19:3) Spr 88, p. 16.
3196. MAERZ, Florence D.
"Resignation." [Amelia] (5:2, #13) 88, p. 131.
3197. MAGARRELL, Elaine
"The Joy of Cooking." [LightY] ('88/9) 88, p. 142.
3198. MAGEE, Kevin
"The Break of Day." [Caliban] (4) 88, p. 167-168.
"Happy Face" (Excerpt). [NewAW] (4) Fall 88, p. 84.
"Slave Rhymes" (for my superiors). [NewAW] (4) Fall 88, p. 83.
3199. MAGER, Donald
"Old Shop Signs" (tr. of Jaroslav Seifert). [MidAR] (8:1) 88, p. 102-103.
"Song at Evening" (tr. of Jaroslav Seifert). [MidAR] (8:1) 88, p. 102-104.
MAGGIO, Jill di
See DiMAGGIO, Jill
3200. MAHANTA, Keshab
"The Empty Pitcher Lying Over Dry Ground" (in Assamese and English, tr. by Emdad Ullah). [Nimrod] (31:2) Spr-Sum 88, p. 28.
"Sketches" (Excerpt, tr. by the author). [Nimrod] (31:2) Spr-Sum 88, p. 28.
3201. MAHAPATRA, Anuradha
"Peace" (in Bengali and English, tr. by Paramita Banerjee and Carolyne Wright). [Nimrod] (31:2) Spr-Sum 88, p. 35.

"Second Planet Earth" (tr. by Jyotirmoy Datta and Carolyne Wright). [Nimrod] (31:2) Spr-Sum 88, p. 34.
"Spell" (tr. by Jyotirmoy Datta and Carolyne Wright). [Nimrod] (31:2) Spr-Sum 88, p. 34.

3202. MAHAPATRA, Jayanta
"Another Hour's Bell." [Poetry] (152:5) Ag 88, p. 278.
"The Cat" (tr. of Shakti Chattopadhyay). [Nimrod] (31:2) Spr-Sum 88, p. 29.
"Consolations." [Nimrod] (31:2) Spr-Sum 88, p. 58.
"Letter." [Nimrod] (31:2) Spr-Sum 88, p. 57.
"Song of the Bones." [Nimrod] (31:2) Spr-Sum 88, p. 56-57.

MAHDIA, Ben al-Talla of
See BEN AL-TALLA OF MAHDIA

3203. MAHER, Jan
"Birds and Cats." [BellArk] (4:6) N-D 88, p. 5.

3204. MAHLE, Benj
"The Design Inside." [RagMag] (6:2) Fall 88, p. 56.
"My Mother Made Lemon Meringue Pies." [RagMag] (6:2) Fall 88, p. 57.

3205. MAHON, Jeanne
"The Anthropologist." [CimR] (82) Ja 88, p. 12.

3206. MAHON, Robert L. (Robert Lee)
"The Deer Hunter." [SmPd] (25:3) Fall 88, p. 19.
"The Reunion." [Amelia] (4:4, #11) 88, p. 42.

3207. MAHOOD, Geri
"Sex Education." [BellR] (11:2) Fall 88, p. 25.
"Undertow." [BellR] (11:2) Fall 88, p. 25.

3208. MAIDEN, Jennifer
"Psalm." [PraS] (62:4) Wint 88-89, p. 139.
"A Summer Emotion." [PraS] (62:4) Wint 88-89, p. 139.

3209. MAIN, Pamela A.
"Hare Hunter." [PennR] (4:1) 88, p. 12.
"Why We Live." [PennR] (4:1) 88, p. 11.

3210. MAINO, Jeannette
"Hidden January." [KanQ] (20:1/2) Wint-Spr 88, p. 199.
"Subdivision." [KanQ] (20:1/2) Wint-Spr 88, p. 200.

3211. MAIO, Samuel
"6th Avenue, L.A." [SoDakR] (26:2) Sum 88, p. 104.
"Gathering Fungi." [CimR] (85) O 88, p. 69.
"Winter Story." [SoDakR] (26:2) Sum 88, p. 105-106.

3212. MAIRE, Mark
"March." [Farm] (4:1, i.e. 5:1) Wint 88, p. 11.

3213. MAISEL, Carolyn
"For a Composer Beset by Admirers." [WillowS] (21) Wint 88, p. 36-37.
"Tarbaby in the Briar Patch." [WillowS] (21) Wint 88, p. 35.
"A Woman Is Missing." [WillowS] (21) Wint 88, p. 33-34.

3214. MAJ, Bronislaw
"Age" (tr. by Daniel Bourne). [Paint] (15:30) Aut 88, p. 35.
"The Air We Share Between Us" (Wspólne powietrze, Selections, tr. by Daniel Bourne). [BelPoJ] (38:4) Sum 88, p. 22-27.
"Another Language" (tr. by Daniel Bourne). [Paint] (15:30) Aut 88, p. 34.
"Chile" (tr. by Daniel Bourne). [CentralP] (13) Spr 88, p. 63-70.
"I Haven't Forgotten a Thing" (tr. by Daniel Bourne). [Spirit] (9:1) 88, p. 75.
"Rain outside a window, a glass of tea on the table" (tr. by Stanislaw Baranczak and Clare Cavanagh). [ManhatR] (4:2) Spr 88, p. 41-42.
"These are strong, calm words" (tr. by Stanislaw Baranczak and Clare Cavanagh). [ManhatR] (4:2) Spr 88, p. 41.
"The world: whole and indivisible, begins where" (tr. by Stanislaw Baranczak and Clare Cavanagh). [TriQ] (71) Wint 88, p. 157.

MAJNUN, Qais ibn Dharih
See IBN DHARIH, Qais, Majnun

3215. MAKGOLIS, Gary
"Angels and the Jews." [PraS] (62:2) Sum 88, p. 73-74.
"Autumn Bees on Broccoli Blossoms Gone By." [PraS] (62:2) Sum 88, p. 67-68.
"Most Likely." [PraS] (62:2) Sum 88, p. 69-70.
"Nothing More." [PraS] (62:2) Sum 88, p. 70-71.
"Road Lulav." [PraS] (62:2) Sum 88, p. 71-72.

3216. MAKOFSKE, Mary
"Hexenschuss." [CumbPR] (7:2) Spr 88, p. 41-42.
3217. MAKUCK, Peter
"Backwaters." [OhioR] (42) 88, p. 68-69.
3218. MALANGA, Gerard
"Poems in the Key of G" (Excerpt). [Caliban] (4) 88, p. 169-179.
MALÉ, Belkis Cuza
See CUZA MALÉ, Belkis
3219. MALINOWITZ, Michael
"In Darragh's Garden." [NewAW] (4) Fall 88, p. 76.
"That Greater Hubris of the Twentieth Century." [AnotherCM] (18) 88, p. 121-123.
3220. MALKUS, Steven W.
"Nuclear Winter" (after Sankai Juku, Butoh Dancers). [SouthernHR] (22:1) Wint 88, p. 18.
3221. MALONE, Eileen
"Overworked Poetic Expressions." [Amelia] (4:4, #11) 88, p. 62-63.
"A Sight of Swans." [Vis] (27) 88, p. 18.
3222. MALONE, Jacquelyn
"Spring Trees." [NegC] (8:3) 88, p. 148.
3223. MALONE, Joe
"Amores, I:5" (tr. of Ovid). [CharR] (14:1) Spr 88, p. 91.
"Bone" (tr. of Nuala Ní Dhomhnaill). [WebR] (13:2) Fall 88, p. 23.
"Confession" (tr. of Nuala Ní Dhomhnaill). [WebR] (13:2) Fall 88, p. 24.
"Ode III:13" (tr. of Horace). [CharR] (14:1) Spr 88, p. 91-92.
3224. MALONE, Pamela Altfeld
"Summer's End." [BellArk] (4:1) Ja-F 88, p. 9.
3225. MALONEY, Jim
"Donner Party." [PacificR] (6) Spr 88, p. 29.
"Johnson Ranch" (For Colleen, 1931-1982). [PacificR] (6) Spr 88, p. 30-31.
3226. MALYON, Carol
"Iris" (from a watercolour by Eric Freifeld. Editors' Second Prize Winner). [CrossC] (10:1) 88, p. 17.
3227. MAMET, David
"What was it?" (One April, 1988). [ParisR] (30:107) Sum 88, p. 197.
3228. MAN, Ke
"The City" (in Chinese & English). [BelPoJ] (39:2) Wint 88-89, p. 40-43.
"Growing Old Even After Death" (in Chinese & English). [BelPoJ] (39:2) Wint 88-89, p. 44-47.
MANCERON, Katherine Smith
See SMITH-MANCERON, Katherine
3229. MANCHESTER, Susan A.
"Eyewitness." [Footwork] ('88) 88, p. 38.
"Study in Still Life." [Blueline] (9:1/2) 88, p. 28.
3230. MANDEL, Charlotte
"Collecting Tinfoil." [RiverS] (27) 88, p. 47-48.
"The Grauballe Man" (For historisk Museum Moesgard, Aarhus, Denmark). [JINJPo] (10:1/2) 88, p. 44-45.
"Table for Four." [SenR] (18:2) 88, p. 62.
3231. MANDEL, Tom
"The Answers." [Temblor] (8) 88, p. 78-80.
"Four Strange Books." [Sulfur] (8:2, #23) Fall 88, p. 53-60.
"Four Strange Books" (Selections: 5-9). [Temblor] (8) 88, p. 81-85.
"Twenty One Sonnets" (Selections: IV, V). [Acts] (8/9) 88, p. 90-91.
3232. MANDELSTAM, Osip
"8. This body given to me — what shall I do" (tr. by R. H. Morrison). [SouthernR] (24:3) Sum 88, p. 539.
"9. Sadness beyond expression" (tr. by R. H. Morrison). [SouthernR] (24:3) Sum 88, p. 540.
"175. You went by through a cloud of mist" (tr. by R. H. Morrison). [SouthernR] (24:3) Sum 88, p. 540.
"341. Mounds of human heads recede into the distance" (tr. by R. H. Morrison). [SouthernR] (24:3) Sum 88, p. 541.
"352. Don't make comparisons: what lives" (tr. by R. H. Morrison). [SouthernR] (24:3) Sum 88, p. 541.
"457 (xv). Prophetic breath of my verses' life-giving spirit" (tr. by R. H. Morrison). [SouthernR] (24:3) Sum 88, p. 541.

"Black Earth" (tr. by James Greene). [WillowS] (22) Spr 88, p. 24.
"Help me, O Lord, to survive this night" (tr. by James Greene). [WillowS] (22) Spr 88, p. 22.
"Here Toads That Fill One with Disgust" (tr. by R. H. Morrison). [LitR] (31:2) Wint 88, p. 155.
"I drink to the blossoming epaulette" (tr. by James Greene). [WillowS] (22) Spr 88, p. 20.
"I was only in a childish way connected with the world of power" (tr. by James Greene). [WillowS] (22) Spr 88, p. 21.
"In my disgrace I shall perform a smoky rite" (tr. by James Greene). [WillowS] (22) Spr 88, p. 23.
"In My Perception Winter" (tr. by R. H. Morrison). [LitR] (31:4) Sum 88, p. 449.
"In the Mist I Could Not Feel Your Image" (tr. by R. H. Morrison). [LitR] (31:2) Wint 88, p. 155.
"Let the Names of Flourishing Cities" (tr. by R. H. Morrison). [LitR] (31:4) Sum 88, p. 448.
"Light Vapor Was Melting Away in the Frosty Air" (tr. by R. H. Morrison). [LitR] (31:4) Sum 88, p. 449.
"My country conversed with me" (tr. by James Greene). [WillowS] (22) Spr 88, p. 23.
"My Silent Dream, My Every Minute's Dream" (tr. by R. H. Morrison). [LitR] (31:4) Sum 88, p. 448.
"The people need pale-blue air and light" (tr. by James Greene). [WillowS] (22) Spr 88, p. 25.
"Return to the incestuous lap" (tr. by James Greene). [WillowS] (22) Spr 88, p. 17.
"Those hundred-carat ingots, Roman nights" (tr. by James Greene). [WillowS] (22) Spr 88, p. 22.
"Where can I go this January?" (tr. by James Greene). [WillowS] (22) Spr 88, p. 25.
"Whoever's been kissing time's tortured crown" (tr. by James Greene). [WillowS] (22) Spr 88, p. 18-19.
"Your narrow shoulders are to redden under scourges" (tr. by James Greene). [WillowS] (22) Spr 88, p. 22.

3233. MANDIARGUES, André Pieyre de
"Cuevas Blues" (with drawings by José-Luis Cuevas, tr. by Joyce Oliver Lowrie). [AmerPoR] (17:5) S-O 88, p. 30-31.
"Finger of God" (tr. by Joyce Oliver Lowrie). [AmerPoR] (17:5) S-O 88, p. 32.
"From Geranium to Fire" (tr. by Joyce Oliver Lowrie). [AmerPoR] (17:5) S-O 88, p. 32.
"The Hunter" (tr. by Joyce Oliver Lowrie). [AmerPoR] (17:5) S-O 88, p. 32.
"In Celebration of the Birth of Sibylle" (tr. by Joyce Oliver Lowrie). [AmerPoR] (17:5) S-O 88, p. 32.
"Pearl" (tr. by Joyce Oliver Lowrie). [AmerPoR] (17:5) S-O 88, p. 32.
"Rebellion" (tr. by Joyce Oliver Lowrie). [AmerPoR] (17:5) S-O 88, p. 32.
"Silkworm" (tr. by Joyce Oliver Lowrie). [AmerPoR] (17:5) S-O 88, p. 32.
"Spanish Café" (tr. by Joyce Oliver Lowrie). [AmerPoR] (17:5) S-O 88, p. 32.
"Withdrawal" (tr. by Joyce Oliver Lowrie). [AmerPoR] (17:5) S-O 88, p. 32.

3234. MANDRAKE, Jill
"Circus Days." [WestCR] (23:1) Spr, i.e. Sum 88, p. 29-31.

3235. MANESIOTIS, Joy
"Behind Anger." [AmerPoR] (17:5) S-O 88, p. 38.

3236. MANFRED, Freya
"On Attachment." [HighP] (3:1) Spr 88, p. 111-112.

3237. MANGAN, Gerald
"Wasp Nest." [Verse] (5:3) N 88, p. 64.

3238. MANGAN, Kathy
"On 661" (for L.M.). [TarRP] (28:1) Fall 88, p. 55.

3239. MANICOM, David
"Birds, Flight." [MalR] (82) Mr 88, p. 70-71.
"Daily Bread." [MalR] (82) Mr 88, p. 68-69.
"December 27th, 1938" (near Vladivostock, perhaps). [MalR] (82) Mr 88, p. 72-73.
"Facing Switzerland." [MalR] (82) Mr 88, p. 74-75.

3240. MANILLA, Saul
"The Archibald Mc." [WormR] (28:1, #109) 88, p. 13.
"The Edna St. Vincent." [WormR] (28:1, #109) 88, p. 13.
"The Ernest." [WormR] (28:1, #109) 88, p. 13.

"The Gary." [WormR] (28:1, #109) 88, p. 14.
"The Gertrude." [WormR] (28:1, #109) 88, p. 13.
"The Steven Vincent." [WormR] (28:1, #109) 88, p. 14.

3241. MANN, Barbara
"Grafting." [CimR] (85) O 88, p. 68.

3242. MANN, Charles
"Linda Mann" (for my daughter). [PaintedB] (36) 88, p. 76.

3243. MANNER, Eeva-Liisa
"The Forest" (tr. by Ritva Poom). [ManhatR] (4:2) Spr 88, p. 43.
"The Moon" (tr. by Ritva Poom). [ManhatR] (4:2) Spr 88, p. 44.
"Seeing" (tr. by Ritva Poom). [ManhatR] (4:2) Spr 88, p. 44-45.

3244. MANNERS, Tyler
"The Diner." [PacificR] (6) Spr 88, p. 25.

3245. MANNING, Nancy
"Everyone Thinkin It Mine." [MidAR] (8:2) 88, p. 188.

3246. MANNO, Rosemary
"The Grand Guignol of Countries, or, Country of the Grand Guignol" (tr. of Paul Laraque). [RedBass] (13) 88, p. 6.

3247. MANOS, Kenna Creer
"Homage to British Columbia." [ColEng] (50:8) D 88, p. 875.
"Identity." [ColEng] (50:8) D 88, p. 875.
"A Marriage Poem." [ColEng] (50:8) D 88, p. 874.

3248. MANOUSOS, Anthony
"At the Providence Zen Center." [PaintedB] (36) 88, p. 44-45.

3249. MANUEL, G. C.
"Un Texto." [CuadP] (5:14) Enero-Abril 88, p. 51-52.

3250. MANUS, Fay Whitman
"Astaire and Me." [NewL] (54:3) Spr 88, p. 90-91.

3251. MAPANJE, Jack
"Moving into Monkey Bay (Balamanja North)." [Stand] (29:3) Sum 88, p. 38.

3252. MAR, Richard DeLos
"Jekyll Island, 1942." [GreensboroR] (45) Wint 88-89, p. 55.
"Skylight." [GreensboroR] (45) Wint 88-89, p. 56.
"Trinity, 1945." [GreensboroR] (45) Wint 88-89, p. 55.

3253. MARCELLO, Leo Luke
"Warm Bitter Aginst the Cold" (St. Davids, Wales). [Vis] (27) 88, p. 22.

3254. MARCHANT, Fred
"Viet Name Era." [ConnPR] (7:1) 88, p. 52.

3255. MARCHANT, Frederick J.
"The Frost Place." [Poem] (59) My 88, p. 43.
"Your Tears." [Poem] (59) My 88, p. 42.

3256. MARCONI, Catherine (Catie)
"The Job." [HayF] (3) Spr 88, p. 54-55.
"The Nest." [BellArk] (4:2) Mr-Ap 88, p. 4.
"Peace Offering." [Amelia] (4:4, #11) 88, p. 64-65.

3257. MARCUS, Jacqueline
"Discord on Aki No Kure." [SouthernHR] (22:1) Wint 88, p. 46.
"Magnolia." [Wind] (18:63) 88, p. 23-24.

3258. MARCUS, Mordecai
"Always Back There." [PoetL] (83:4) Wint 88-89, p. 29-30.
"April Overcast." [DeKalbLAJ] (21:2) Spr 88, p. 40.
"Bindings." [Agni] (27) 88, p. 197-198.
"From a Considerable Distance." [Plain] (8:1) Fall 87, p. 20.
"In Place of a Prayer" (Seaton Honorable Mention Poem 1988). [KanQ] (20:3) Sum 88, p. 26.
"Neighborly News." [KanQ] (20:3) Sum 88, p. 27.
"Reflections in an Empty House." [PoetC] (19:3) Spr 88, p. 41-42.
"Snow Cones." [SoDakR] (26:3) Aut 88, p. 98-99.

3259. MARCUS, Morton
"The Gift." [Zyzzyva] (4:3) Fall 88, p. 110-111.
"The Immigrant." [CreamCR] (12:2) Sum 88, p. 220-222.

3260. MARCUS, Stanley
"Juden." [PoetryE] (25) Spr 88, p. 115.

3261. MARGOLIS, Gary
"Between Us." [Crazy] (35) Wint 88, p. 50-51.
"The Groves of Argos." [Poetry] (151:6) Mr 88, p. 478-479.

"Like Fireflies." [Crazy] (35) Wint 88, p. 49.
"Some Nation Who's Been Slighted." [Poetry] (143, i.e. 153:2) N 88, p. 71.

3262. MARGUERITTE
"Variation on a Theme by William Carlos Williams" (Desert Music). [RagMag] (6:2) Fall 88, p. 55.

3263. MARGULIES, Stephen
"Medical Report." [Timbuktu] (2) Sum-Fall 88, p. 70.

3264. MARIANI, Paul
"The Coming Changes" (For Czeslaw Milosz). [TampaR] (1) 88, p. 77.
"Fog Warning." [TampaR] (1) 88, p. 76.

MARIN, Olga López
See LOPEZ MARIN, Olga

3265. MARINARA, Martha
"Reflection in a Well House: Tuscumbia, Alabama 1887." [NegC] (8:3) 88, p. 142.

3266. MARINELLI, Joanne
"Ab Ovo Fertilla." [AlphaBS] (4) D 88, p. 38-39.

3267. MARION, A. T.
"Footpaths Home." [PottPort] (9) 88, p. 28-30.

3268. MARION, Jeff Daniel
"Jonquils." [SouthernHR] (22:2) Spr 88, p. 112.

3269. MARIS, Maria R.
"Fern, She Thought." [KanQ] (20:3) Sum 88, p. 180.

MARIS, Ron de
See De MARIS, Ron

3270. MARKERT, Lawrence
"Almost Dressed." [Wind] (18:62) 88, p. 34.

3271. MARKHAM, E. A.
"Letter to a Lover, to Be Treated with Suspicion." [Stand] (29:4) Aut 88, p. 12-15.

3272. MARKHAM, Jacquelyn
"A Mother's Story" (for Hawa Ali-Ethiopia). [Wind] (18:63) 88, p. 25.

3273. MARKS, Gigi
"Generation." [Farm] (5:2) Fall 88, p. 52.
"A Longer Day." [Farm] (5:2) Fall 88, p. 54.
"Moving Again." [Farm] (5:2) Fall 88, p. 53.
"Near My Mother's House." [SouthernPR] (28:2) Fall 88, p. 57.

3274. MARLIS, Stefanie
"15 1/2." [HayF] (3) Spr 88, p. 31.

3275. MARMOL, José
"Al Nombre de Alguna Mujer." [CuadP] (5:14) Enero-Abril 88, p. 48-49.
"Esquicio del Vuelo." [CuadP] (5:14) Enero-Abril 88, p. 47.
"El Extraño." [CuadP] (5:14) Enero-Abril 88, p. 49.
"La Invención del Día." [CuadP] (5:14) Enero-Abril 88, p. 49-50.
"Otra Vez un Poema." [CuadP] (5:14) Enero-Abril 88, p. 47.
"Poema 24 al Ozama: Acuarela." [CuadP] (5:14) Enero-Abril 88, p. 48.

3276. MARMON, Sharon
"Childhood Memories: Some Borderplace in Texas." [Rohwedder] (3) Spr 88, p. 16.
"Nostalgia." [Vis] (27) 88, p. 38.
"She Disappeared" (por las madres). [Rohwedder] (3) Spr 88, p. 17.

3277. MARQUARDT, Randall
"A Nebraskan Dreams His Death." [Plain] (9:1) Fall 88, p. 22.

3278. MARQUARDT, Stephen
"April 15." [Margin] (6) Sum 88, p. 7.
"Because we observe the rules of love." [Margin] (6) Sum 88, p. 10.
"For Charlie to Use for Walking with His Shadow." [Margin] (6) Sum 88, p. 11.
"Home by Noon." [Margin] (6) Sum 88, p. 9.
"I heard of a coach who bit." [Margin] (6) Sum 88, p. 12.
"J. T. Brown's Hardware Store in Craig, Alaska." [Margin] (6) Sum 88, p. 8.
"Lighthouse Guitar." [Margin] (6) Sum 88, p. 11.
"Long Path Walking Slow." [Margin] (6) Sum 88, p. 12.
"No One Is Riding the Donkey." [Margin] (6) Sum 88, p. 7.
"Toothbrush Poem." [Margin] (6) Sum 88, p. 10.

3279. MARQUEZ, Héctor P.
"Corrido de Tomás Rivera." [BilingR] (13:1/2) Ja-Ag 86, c1988, p. 87-88.

3280. MARQUINA, Mauricio
"Me Basta la Palabra." [Mairena] (10:25) 88, p. 4.

3281. MARQUIS, Don
"Boss I am disappointed in some of your readers." [LightY] ('88/9) 88, p. 5.
3282. MARRIOTT, Anne
"After a Death." [Quarry] (37:4) Aut 88, p. 17.
"Circles." [Quarry] (37:4) Aut 88, p. 18.
MARS, Douglas de
See DeMARS, Douglas
3283. MARSHALL, Jack
"Note." [FiveFR] (6) 88, p. 85.
"Shadow on Ice." [FiveFR] (6) 88, p. 86.
3284. MARSHALL, John
"Romance Language at Shilshole Bay." [CrabCR] (5:3) Fall 88, p. 28.
3285. MARSHALL, Peter
"Night in the Smokies." [Bogg] (60) 88, p. 14.
3286. MARSHBURN, Sandra
"Anecdotes of Music." [LaurelR] (22:2) Sum 88, p. 64.
"Field Guide." [TarRP] (27:2) Spr 88, p. 28.
"Postcards." [CinPR] (18) Fall 88, p. 20.
3287. MARTAN GONGORA, Helcías
"Cristo Negro." [Mairena] (10:25) 88, p. 44.
3288. MARTIN, Charles Casey
"Satellites." [Agni] (27) 88, p. 219-222.
3289. MARTIN, David
"Child Speech." [CreamCR] (12:2) Sum 88, p. 224-225.
"Ramón" (for Ramón Fernandez). [CreamCR] (12:2) Sum 88, p. 223.
3290. MARTIN, Grace B.
"Early Marriage." [SlipS] (8) 88, p. 73-74.
3291. MARTIN, J.
"The Death Process and Mishima, 1970." [Shen] (38:4) 88, p. 86-88.
3292. MARTIN, Joseph
"Faberge." [SoDakR] (26:3) Aut 88, p. 173.
"Hothouse." [Poem] (60) N 88, p. 4.
"Marie Feodorovna." [Poem] (60) N 88, p. 5.
3293. MARTIN, Lynn
"Mercy." [SinW] (32) Sum 87, p. 31.
"The Perils of Pauline." [SinW] (32) Sum 87, p. 32.
3294. MARTIN, Mairin
"All of a Piece." [LightY] ('88/9) 88, p. 84.
3295. MARTIN, Mary E.
"Hard Scrabble Pass, Custer County, Colorado." [KanQ] (20:3) Sum 88, p. 17.
"Meditation" (The Seaton Second Award Poem 1988). [KanQ] (20:3) Sum 88, p. 16.
3296. MARTIN, Paul
"When I'm Exhausted." [PassN] (9:2) Sum 88, p. 25.
3297. MARTIN, Reginald
"Media Transfer: Boots and Wurlitzer." [Callaloo] (11:2, #35) Spr 88, p. 214.
3298. MARTINEZ, Demetria
"September." [Colum] (13) 88, p. 107.
3299. MARTINEZ, Dionisio D.
"Carp." [SenR] (18:1) 88, p. 24-25.
"Chinese Carnations." [IndR] (12:1) Wint 88, p. 1-2.
"Folklore." [SenR] (18:1) 88, p. 23.
"How the News Repeats Itself." [MidwQ] (29:3) Spr 88, p. 345-347.
"Maps Don't Fold the Same Way Twice." [IndR] (12:1) Wint 88, p. 3-4.
3300. MARTINEZ, Herminio
"Details About the Muse Who Was Ten Times a Woman" (fragment, 2, 3, tr. by Thomas Hoeksema). [Sonora] (14/15) Spr 88, p. 95, 97.
"Detalles Acerca de la Musa Que Fue Diez Veces Mujer" (fragmento: 2, 3). [Sonora] (14/15) Spr 88, p. 94, 96.
3301. MARTINEZ, Ramón E.
"Borges." [Contact] (9:47/48/49) Spr 88, p. 40-41.
"Seashells." [Ascent] (13:3) 88, p. 28.
"Survivor of the Burning Cistern." [Ascent] (13:3) 88, p. 29.
"Xí-in Army." [Contact] (9:47/48/49) Spr 88, p. 41.
3302. MARTINEZ, Rubén
"Hotel Ontario." [Rohwedder] (3) Spr 88, p. 13.

"The Late Hour of the Night" (tr. of Roque Dalton). [Rohwedder] (3) Spr 88, p. 10-11.
"There's a War." [Rohwedder] (3) Spr 88, p. 6-7.
3303. MARTINEZ, Sara
"Coordinates" (tr. by Julia Stein). [RedBass] (13) 88, p. 28.
3304. MARTINEZ, Victor L.
"Hunger Isn't a Woman." [FiveFR] (6) 88, p. 6.
"National Geographic." [Zyzzyva] (4:2) Sum 88, p. 104-107.
3305. MARTINEZ OSTOS, Alicia
"El Lago." [LetFem] (14:1/2) Primavera-Otoño 88, p. 134.
3306. MARTINEZ RIVAS, Carlos
"Laid in the Tomb" (tr. by Nancy Esposito). [AmerPoR] (17:2) Mr-Ap 88, p. 28.
3307. MARTINS, Max
"Between the Lines" (tr. by James Bogan). [CharR] (14:1) Spr 88, p. 37.
3308. MARTINSON, Harry
"Below the Stars' Distant Glow" (tr. by William Jay Smith and Leif Sjoberg). [PaintedB] (36) 88, p. 27.
"The Butterfly" (tr. by William Jay Smith and Leif Sjoberg). [PaintedB] (36) 88, p. 24.
"The Forest of Childhood" (tr. by William Jay Smith and Leif Sjoberg). [PaintedB] (36) 88, p. 26.
"The Henhouse" (tr. by William Jay Smith and Leif Sjoberg). [PaintedB] (36) 88, p. 28.
"Late-Born Swarms of Flying Beings" (tr. by William Jay Smith and Leif Sjoberg). [PaintedB] (36) 88, p. 29.
"Leaf-Fall" (tr. by William Jay Smith and Leif Sjoberg). [PaintedB] (36) 88, p. 30.
"The Song of the Meadow" (tr. by William Jay Smith and Leif Sjoberg). [PaintedB] (36) 88, p. 25.
3309. MARTONE, Michael
"Species." [YellowS] (27) Aut 88, p. 21.
3310. MARUNYCZ, Jacki
"Family Album." [Lactuca] (11) O 88, p. 2.
3311. MARUYAMA, Kaoru
"Estuary Anchorage" (tr. by Graeme Wilson). [Jacaranda] (3:1) Wint 88, p. 7.
3312. MASARIK, Al
"Certain Words." [PaintedB] (36) 88, p. 12.
"Kokanee." [LittleM] (15:3/4) 88, p. 93.
"Round Mountain, Nevada." [PaintedB] (36) 88, p. 13-14.
"Winter Dream Frogs Courting." [PaintedB] (36) 88, p. 15-16.
3313. MASON, David
"Tourists Arriving." [CrabCR] (5:1) Wint 88, p. 24.
3314. MASON, James
"Sun Stroke." [Lactuca] (11) O 88, p. 8.
3315. MASON, Julian
"Extinction." [SoCaR] (20:2) Spr 88, p. 15.
3316. MASON, Kenneth C.
"Creation" (For Vahid). [Plain] (9:1) Fall 88, p. 26.
"Subdivision Eclogue." [NoDaQ] (56:3) Sum 88, p. 99-101.
"Weightlifter" (for David Moore, a Plainsongs Award Poem). [Plain] (8:2) Wint 88, p. 38.
MASSMAN, Gordon Lester
See LESTER-MASSMAN, Gordon
3317. MASTERSON, Dan
"Purple Finch." [PoetryNW] (29:1) Spr 88, p. 19.
3318. MATEO, Andrés L.
"La Infancia y el Signo." [CuadP] (5:14) Enero-Abril 88, p. 53-55.
3319. MATHEWS, Harry
"Condo Auction." [ParisR] (30:109) Wint 88, p. 64-72.
3320. MATHEWS, Marsha Caddell
"Leaving Home." [HampSPR] Wint 88, p. 43.
"The Rise Above the Water" (for Sandy). [Pembroke] (20) 88, p. 269-271.
3321. MATHIS, Cleopatra
"After Water." [NewEngR] (11:1) Aut 88, p. 40-41.
"The Competition." [GrahamHR] (11) Spr 88, p. 88.
"The Faithful." [GeoR] (42:3) Fall 88, p. 531-533.
"Flowers." [GrahamHR] (11) Spr 88, p. 89.

"The Gardener and Ghosts: For My Teacher." [GrahamHR] (11) Spr 88, p. 92-93.
"Grace: Two Versions." [GrahamHR] (11) Spr 88, p. 87.
"Signature in a House of Ghosts." [GrahamHR] (11) Spr 88, p. 90-91.
"Something in the Wall." [NewEngR] (11:1) Aut 88, p. 41.

3322. MATLIN, David
"Mother of ghosts." [Notus] (3:1) Spr 88, p. 67-69.

3323. MATSON, Suzanne
"Debussy." [AmerPoR] (17:2) Mr-Ap 88, p. 21.
"There Was a Temporary Accident." [AmerPoR] (17:2) Mr-Ap 88, p. 21.

3324. MATSUEDA, Pat
"The Anesthesiologist" (for A.M.). [HawaiiR] (12:2, #24) Fall 88, p. 134.
"Heir to the Highwire." [ChamLR] (2:1, #3) Fall 88, p. 1-2.
"Journey Through the Break" (for Matthew). [ChamLR] (1) Fall 87, p. 60-62.
"Love Poem for the Unchosen." [ChamLR] (1) Fall 87, p. 59.

3325. MATTHEWS, William
"Civics." [TarRP] (28:1) Fall 88, p. 22.
"Every Tub." [Atlantic] (262:4) O 88, p. 52.
"Homer's Seeing-Eye Dog." [Atlantic] (262:5) N 88, p. 62.
"Hope." [IndR] (11:2) Spr 88, p. 69-70.
"The Introduction." [LightY] ('88/9) 88, p. 46-47.

3326. MATTISON, Alice
"Chicks Hatching at the Friendly Farm, Dublin, New Hampshire." [BostonR] (13:3[sic]) O 88, p. 9.
"During the Night." [ParisR] (30:106) Spr 88, p. 205.
"The Phone." [BostonR] (13:3[sic]) O 88, p. 9.
"Riverton Fair." [BostonR] (13:3[sic]) O 88, p. 9.
"Secret Animals." [BostonR] (13:3[sic]) O 88, p. 9.

3327. MATUZAK, Joseph
"Detonating the Poem." [PassN] (9:2) Sum 88, p. 3.

3328. MAUCERI, Grace
"Stained Glass." [CapeR] (23:1) Spr 88, p. 45.

3329. MAVIGLIA, Joseph
"Ritual." [LittleM] (15:3/4) 88, p. 137-138.

3330. MAXSON, Gloria A.
"Epitaphs." [LightY] ('88/9) 88, p. 210.
"Walter Scott." [LightY] ('88/9) 88, p. 186.

3331. MAXWELL, Glyn
"County Event." [Verse] (5:2) Jl 88, p. 7.
"Death in a Mist." [Agni] (27) 88, p. 89-90.
"The High Achievers." [Agni] (27) 88, p. 86.
"In the Gap." [Agni] (27) 88, p. 91-93.
"Poisonfield." [Agni] (27) 88, p. 95-96.
"Push On, Amigo." [Agni] (27) 88, p. 94.
"School Holiday, South Wales." [Agni] (27) 88, p. 87-88.
"Sobrat." [Verse] (5:2) Jl 88, p. 6.
"Trouble #17." [Verse] (5:2) Jl 88, p. 8.
"Whatever Else." [Agni] (27) 88, p. 97.

3332. MAY, Doug
"The Truce." [NoDaQ] (56:2) Spr 88, p. 91-92.

3333. MAY, Farin
"White T.V." [ChamLR] (1) Fall 87, p. 84-87.

3334. MAY, Kathy
"Cows in the Snow." [KanQ] (20:1/2) Wint-Spr 88, p. 274.
"Hard Candy." [PoetC] (20:1) Fall 88, p. 10.
"The Purple Dress." [PoetC] (20:1) Fall 88, p. 9.
"Saved." [PoetC] (20:1) Fall 88, p. 8.

3335. MAY, Kerry Paul
"The Tourists." [NowestR] (26:1) 88, p. 28-29.

3336. MAY, Ron
"Public Buns." [Amelia] (5:2, #13) 88, p. 125.

3337. MAY, Walter
"The 'Appassionata'" (tr. of Edzi Agnyatsvet). [NegC] (8:1/2) 88, p. 26-27.
"Arise, Dead Tyrants" (tr. of Vasil Zuyonak). [NegC] (8:1/2) 88, p. 31-32.
"Eternity" (tr. of Rygor Baradulin). [NegC] (8:1/2) 88, p. 39.
"Far Off Afield in Varna's Foothill Area" (tr. of Nil Gilevich). [NegC] (8:1/2) 88, p. 29.

"Our Neighbor Pelagea" (tr. of Yaugenia Yanishchits). [NegC] (8:1/2) 88, p. 38.
"Requiem for Every Fourth" (tr. of Anatol Vyartsinski). [NegC] (8:1/2) 88, p. 33-36.
"Revelation" (tr. of Alyaksei Rusetski). [NegC] (8:1/2) 88, p. 30.
"Rye" (tr. of Vasil Vitka). [NegC] (8:1/2) 88, p. 37.

3338. MAYBERRY, Stephen
"Boy and Girl: Cielito Park." [PoetryNW] (29:1) Spr 88, p. 38.

3339. MAYER, Gerda
"Male Butterflies Court Falling Leaves." [Bogg] (60) 88, p. 24.
"The Poet Reclining" (Marc Chagall, 1915). [Bogg] (60) 88, p. 24.

3340. MAYERS, Dara
"Bullseye." [HangL] (53) 88, p. 64.
"Cold Beach." [HangL] (53) 88, p. 63.
"White Wax Burning." [HangL] (53) 88, p. 65.

3341. MAYHALL, Jane
"A Distant Trumpet." [NewYorker] (64:30) 12 S 88, p. 82.
"Seven Men on a Brooklyn Asphalt Truck." [Confr] (Special issue: The World of Brooklyn) 88, p. 18.
"Speech for Elizabeth Cady Stanton" (after reading *Eighty Years and More*). [ManhatPR] (10) Ja 88, p. 51.

3342. MAYHEW, Lenore
"Evening" (tr. of Anna Akhmatova). [Field] (39) Fall 88, p. 8.
"Flowers and Non-Living Things" (tr. of Anna Akhmatova). [Field] (39) Fall 88, p. 12.

3343. MAYHOOD, Clif
"The Fog." [JamesWR] (6:1) Fall 88, p. 3.

3344. MAYNE, Helen
"Key West Hand Print Fabrics." [KeyWR] (1:2) Fall 88, p. 44.

3345. MAYO, Cathy
"The Bearing Tree." [Plain] (8:2) Wint 88, p. 28.
"Prelude in F-Sharp Minor." [Plain] (8:1) Fall 87, p. 22.

3346. MAZER, Gina
"This Is What I Will Never Forget" (First Place, 1987 Eve of Saint Agnes Poetry Competition). [NegC] (8:3) 88, p. 13-17.

3347. MAZUR, Gail
"After the Storm, August." [Ploughs] (14:4) 88, p. 68.
"Afterthoughts, 4 A.M." (to my daughter). [Sequoia] (31:2) Wint 88, p. 49.
"Foliage." [Poetry] (152:6) S 88, p. 318.
"Groping Toward Entropy." [BostonR] (13:5 [sic]) Je 88, p. 19.
"Poem Ending with Three Lines from Wordsworth." [Ploughs] (14:4) 88, p. 66-67.
"Summer Afternoon." [Sequoia] (31:2) Wint 88, p. 48.
"Traces." [Ploughs] (14:1) 88, p. 148-149.

3348. MAZZARO, Jerome
"Here, Too, La Mettrie." [Shen] (38:1) 88, p. 38.
"Jerome Again." [CreamCR] (12:2) Sum 88, p. 226.

3349. MAZZOCCO, Robert
"Kidnapped." [NewYorker] (64:30) 12 S 88, p. 40.
"What the Night Is Like." [NewYorker] (64:2) 29 F 88, p. 34.

Mc . . .
See also names beginning with Mac . . .

3350. McADAMS, Janet
"Confessions of a Grown Woman." [SouthernPR] (28:1) Spr 88, p. 49-51.
"Nocturne." [Jacaranda] (3:1) Wint 88, p. 95.
"Vintage." [Jacaranda] (3:1) Wint 88, p. 96.

3351. McALEAVEY, David
"It's Early." [SouthernPR] (28:2) Fall 88, p. 30.

3352. McALPINE, Katherine
"Homecoming." [Footwork] ('88) 88, p. 35.
"Reflections on What's-His-Name #2." [BellR] (11:2) Fall 88, p. 30.
"Reflections on What's-His-Name #7." [BellR] (11:2) Fall 88, p. 30.
"Yellow Submarine Homesick Blues Revisited." [Amelia] (5:2, #13) 88, p. 43-44.

3353. McALPINE, Nathaniel
"An Island Created." [PikeF] (9) Fall 88, p. 20.

3354. McANALLY, Mary
"Conversations Overheard at Cain's Ballroom." [Phoenix] (9:1/2) 88, p. 62.

"The First Christmas" (or demythologizing the magnificat). [Phoenix] (9:1/2) 88, p. 63.

3355. McARTHUR, Mary
"Song of Granny Smith." [LightY] ('88/9) 88, p. 118.

3356. McBRIDE, David
"Blizzards of Siberia." [CrabCR] (5:1) Wint 88, p. 17.

3357. McBRIDE, Mekeel
"River." [SouthwR] (73:2) Spr 88, p. 250.
"The Solitary Map." [SouthwR] (73:2) Spr 88, p. 251-252.

3358. McBRIDE, Susan
"To Someone." [Kaleid] (17) Sum-Fall 88, p. 27.

3359. McCABE, Susan
"Circular." [Jacaranda] (3:1) Wint 88, p. 31.
"Frameless." [Jacaranda] (3:1) Wint 88, p. 30.
"Zen Master." [Jacaranda] (3:2) Fall-Wint 88, p. 154-155.

3360. McCABE, Victoria
"Bed-Time." [PraS] (62:1) Spr 88, p. 91.
"Beddoes." [Shen] (38:3) 88, p. 76-77.
"Disembodiment: Early Morning." [DenQ] (23:2) Fall 88, p. 50.
"Pain" (for Donald F. Drummond). [PraS] (62:1) Spr 88, p. 90.
"Transportations." [NewL] (55:1) Fall 88, p. 53.

3361. McCAFFERY, Steve
"Lag" (Excerpt). [Temblor] (8) 88, p. 36-39.

3362. McCANN, Janet
"Agents." [ColEng] (50:1) Ja 88, p. 50.
"Diologue with the Dogcatcher." [BellArk] (4:4) Jl-Ag 88, p. 3.
"The Hour Before Dawn." [SoDakR] (26:3) Aut 88, p. 152.
"In This Town." [BellArk] (4:3) My-Je 88, p. 1.
"Marianne Moore's Apartment." [HeliconN] (19) 88, p. 60.
"Party Sketch." [HiramPoR] (44/45) Spr-Wint 88, p. 33.
"Tallow Trees in Central Texas." [SoDakR] (26:3) Aut 88, p. 153.
"Texas Suburbs." [NegC] (8:3) 88, p. 150-152.

3363. McCARTHY, Fabian, Jr.
"Booze." [Bogg] (60) 88, p. 33.

3364. McCARTHY, Maureen
"Mr. Coin." [Event] (17:2) Sum 88, p. 51.
"The Tempests." [Event] (17:2) Sum 88, p. 50.

3365. McCASLIN, Susan
"A Child." [BellArk] (4:1) Ja-F 88, p. 4.
"Confirmation." [BellArk] (4:1) Ja-F 88, p. 6.
"Coyote." [BellArk] (4:2) Mr-Ap 88, p. 1.
"God Talk." [BellArk] (4:6) N-D 88, p. 5.
"In the Selkirks." [BellArk] (4:2) Mr-Ap 88, p. 9.
"Lark." [BellArk] (4:3) My-Je 88, p. 9.
"Lines on Sleeping." [BellArk] (4:4) Jl-Ag 88, p. 10.
"Lines on Waking." [BellArk] (4:4) Jl-Ag 88, p. 10.
"Recognition." [BellArk] (4:5) S-O 88, p. 8.

3366. McCLATCHY, J. D.
"Fog Tropes." [Poetry] (152:5) Ag 88, p. 249-254.
"The Landing." [CreamCR] (12:2) Sum 88, p. 227.
"An Old Song Ended." [FourQ] (2d series 2:1) Spr 88, p. 43.

3367. McCLOSKEY, Mark
"The Rude." [LightY] ('88/9) 88, p. 208.

3368. McCLURE, Michael
"Rebel Lions." [Zyzzyva] (4:2) Sum 88, p. 50-53.

3369. McCOMAS, Marilyn
"Clothespins." [Confr] (37/38) Spr-Sum 88, p. 96.
"Padding the Bones." [HampSPR] Wint 88, p. 23.

3370. McCOMBS, Judith
"Burden." [Poetry] (152:5) Ag 88, p. 270.

3371. McCONNEL, Frances
"To My New Granddaughter, at the End of My First Visit." [BellArk] (4:6) N-D 88, p. 9.

3372. McCORD, Howard
"Moral Theology." [RiverS] (25) 88, p. 18.

3373. McCORKLE, James
"The Great Blue Heron." [SenR] (18:1) 88, p. 48-49.
"Pine Burn." [SouthwR] (73:1) Wint 88, p. 129-130.
"Tereus." [SenR] (18:1) 88, p. 50-51.

3374. McCROSSIN, Dana L.
"A Pantoum." [CrabCR] (5:1) Wint 88, p. 14.

3375. McCUE, Frances
"Barn Raising." [PoetryNW] (29:2) Sum 88, p. 30.
"Doctor Doctor." [PoetryNW] (29:2) Sum 88, p. 29-30.
"Soundmaker." [PoetryNW] (29:2) Sum 88, p. 28-29.

3376. McCULLOH, Joel
"It Was Only a Moment we Touched." [Plain] (8:1) Fall 87, p. 35.

3377. McCULLOUGH, Ken
"Colleton County, S. C." (In memory of John Beecher, for Pamela). [Spirit] (9:1) 88, p. 96-97.
"Earl Miller." [StoneC] (15:3/4) Spr-Sum 88, p. 71.

3378. McCURDY, Harold (Harold G.)
"August 6, 1945." [SouthernHR] (22:3) Sum 88, p. 261.
"The Blue Garden." [Poem] (59) My 88, p. 60.
"Cos." [Poem] (59) My 88, p. 59.
"Revolution." [SewanR] (96:1) Wint 88, p. 46-47.
"A Rope End." [SewanR] (96:1) Wint 88, p. 45.

3379. McDADE, Thomas Michael
"River." [PikeF] (9) Fall 88, p. 29.

3380. McDANIEL, Kim I.
"Symmetry." [Writer] (101:6) Je 88, p. 23.

3381. McDANIEL, Wilma Elizabeth
"Conversion and Baptism of a Biker." [HangL] (52) 88, p. 7.
"Dustbowl Doxology." [WormR] (28:1, #109) 88, p. 25.
"Emptying the Wastebasket." [WormR] (28:1, #109) 88, p. 23.
"Essentials." [WormR] (28:1, #109) 88, p. 21.
"Fourteen and Feeling It." [WormR] (28:1, #109) 88, p. 16.
"Harley Joe Goes to Town." [WormR] (28:1, #109) 88, p. 23.
"Harvest Time." [WormR] (28:1, #109) 88, p. 19.
"The Interpreter." [WormR] (28:1, #109) 88, p. 17.
"Joe Cooley in Hardhat the Week After His Divorce." [WormR] (28:1, #109) 88, p. 22.
"Just Before the 1932 Presidential Elections." [WormR] (28:1, #109) 88, p. 21.
"Last Commandment." [WormR] (28:1, #109) 88, p. 24.
"Library Patrons." [HangL] (52) 88, p. 7.
"Misnomers." [WormR] (28:1, #109) 88, p. 26.
"Ownership." [WormR] (28:1, #109) 88, p. 25.
"Reading a Name Thought to Be Defunct." [HangL] (53) 88, p. 29.
"Reality." [WormR] (28:1, #109) 88, p. 17.
"Remembering a Cat's Funeral, 1926." [WormR] (28:1, #109) 88, p. 20.
"Remembering an Event from 1937." [WormR] (28:1, #109) 88, p. 22.
"To the Point." [WormR] (28:1, #109) 88, p. 24.
"Visiting Pioneer Village 4-5-'87." [WormR] (28:1, #109) 88, p. 18.
"Who Else." [HangL] (53) 88, p. 28.
"Writing Poetry on a Stolen Table." [WormR] (28:1, #109) 88, p. 16.
"Your Money Will be Refunded." [WormR] (28:1, #109) 88, p. 20.

3382. McDERMOTT, Maura
"Cantaloupes on Summer Nights." [Phoenix] (9:1/2) 88, p. 23.
"The First Train to Miami, 1896." [Phoenix] (9:1/2) 88, p. 22-23.
"An Oklahoma Arts and Crafts Show." [Phoenix] (9:1/2) 88, p. 25.
"The Starlings." [Phoenix] (9:1/2) 88, p. 24.

3383. McDONALD, Walter
"And Her Fans." [CutB] (29/30) 88, p. 86.
"Between Wars." [ColR] (NS 15:1) Spr-Sum 88, p. 24.
"Bunking with Veterans." [ColR] (NS 15:1) Spr-Sum 88, p. 26.
"Coming Home." [Poetry] (143, i.e. 153:2) N 88, p. 101.
"Dawn Runner." [CinPR] (18) Fall 88, p. 44.
"The Difference Between Night and Day." [ColR] (NS 15:1) Spr-Sum 88, p. 27.
"The Digs in Escondido Canyon." [ColEng] (50:6) O 88, p. 640.
"For a Child Trapped in a Cellar." [SpoonRQ] (13:2) Spr 88, p. 56.
"Found in the Alley Dumpster." [NoAmR] (273:3) S 88, p. 45.

"Goat Ranching on Hardscrabble." [SpoonRQ] (13:2) Spr 88, p. 54.
"Greenhorn." [CinPR] (18) Fall 88, p. 45.
"Hawks, When the Wind Dies." [Descant] (19:2, #61) Sum 88, p. 17.
"Hit and Run." [Confr] (37/38) Spr-Sum 88, p. 202.
"Hunting for a '55 Chevy." [TarRP] (27:2) Spr 88, p. 1.
"Hunting on Hardscrabble." [PraS] (62:3) Fall 88, p. 51.
"In a Dry Season." [Descant] (19:2, #61) Sum 88, p. 16.
"In Green Pastures." [MassR] (29:1) Spr 88, p. 69-70.
"Living on Hardscrabble." [KenR] (NS 10:3) Sum 88, p. 98.
"Looking for Friends from Childhood." [SpoonRQ] (13:2) Spr 88, p. 55.
"The Middle Years." [Descant] (19:2, #61) Sum 88, p. 15.
"The Middle Years." [LaurelR] (22:2) Sum 88, p. 108-109.
"The Middle Years." [TarRP] (27:2) Spr 88, p. 1.
"Night Flights." [Footwork] ('88) 88, p. 61-62.
"Night of the Power Outage." [ArtfulD] (14/15) Fall 88, p. 53.
"On the Farm." [Descant] (19:2, #61) Sum 88, p. 18.
"Praying for More Than Thunder." [PraS] (62:3) Fall 88, p. 52.
"The Price of Aviation Fuel." [ColR] (NS 15:1) Spr-Sum 88, p. 23.
"Reasons for Taking Risks." [DeKalbLAJ] (21:1) Wint 88, p. 64.
"Riding on Hardscrabble." [ColR] (NS 15:1) Spr-Sum 88, p. 25.
"Songs at Three Months." [CinPR] (18) Fall 88, p. 46-47.
"The Songs We Fought For." [Poetry] (143, i.e. 153:2) N 88, p. 100.
"Unloading Gold at Fort Knox." [HolCrit] (25:4) O 88, p. 17.
"When It Seemed Easy." [CutB] (29/30) 88, p. 87.
"When It Seemed Easy." [KenR] (NS 10:3) Sum 88, p. 99.
"The Witness of Dry Plains." [MalR] (82) Mr 88, p. 34.
"Wonders of the World." [MalR] (82) Mr 88, p. 33.

3384. McDOUGALL, Jo
"As Time Goes By." [MidwQ] (30:1) Aut 88, p. 70.
"Care." [LittleBR] (5:2) Wint 88-89, p. 27.
"Courtly Love." [MidwQ] (30:1) Aut 88, p. 69.
"Farewell, Dusky Seaside" (a found poem, *Time* magazine, June 19, 1987). [NewL] (54:3) Spr 88, p. 93.
"Her Story." [Spirit] (9:1) 88, p. 17.
"Her Town." [MidwQ] (30:1) Aut 88, p. 68.
"A Man Named Zeke." [NewL] (54:3) Spr 88, p. 92.
"She Feels Out of Place in Burl's Auto Service." [MidwQ] (30:1) Aut 88, p. 68.
"A Woman of Substance." [MidwQ] (30:1) Aut 88, p. 70.

3385. McDOUGALL, Maureen
"Luck." [LaurelR] (22:2) Sum 88, p. 11.

3386. McDOWELL, Robert
"The Fifties." [Hudson] (41:1) Spr 88, p. 147-155.
"What They Do at the New Church." [Ploughs] (14:4) 88, p. 105-106.

3387. McDUFF, David
"Old Soldier." [Stand] (29:1) Wint 87-88, p. 61.
"School Song." [Stand] (29:1) Wint 87-88, p. 60.

3388. McENTIRE, Norma
"I Miss You, Arthur." [Phoenix] (9:1/2) 88, p. 58.

3389. McEUEN, James
"The Gray Suit's Dreams." [PoetL] (83:2) Sum 88, p. 46.
"Jail Course Poetics." [PoetL] (83:2) Sum 88, p. 47-48.

3390. McEWEN, Christian
"Doubles." [SinW] (34) Spr 88, p. 66.

3391. McEWEN, R. F.
"To Yasmin." [SoDakR] (26:3) Aut 88, p. 97.

3392. McFARLAND, Ron
"At the Carnival." [CutB] (29/30) 88, p. 14.
"Heroics." [HayF] (3) Spr 88, p. 34.
"The Worley Club Cafe." [HayF] (3) Spr 88, p. 35.

3393. McFEE, Michael
"Bach, Beethoven, Brahms, Mendelssohn, Mozart, Schubert, and Schumann." [Poetry] (143, i.e. 153:2) N 88, p. 90.
"Passing the Corporate Forest." [LightY] ('88/9) 88, p. 200.
"Shooting Baskets at Dusk." [Poetry] (143, i.e. 153:2) N 88, p. 89.

3394. McFERRIN, Linda
"The Shell Game." [CapeR] (23:2) Fall 88, p. 34.

3395. McGAHAN, Martha
"Dakota Sunrise." [Plain] (9:1) Fall 88, p. 8.
McGILL, Deborah Root
See ROOT-McGILL, Deborah
3396. McGLYNN, Brian
"Awakening." [Wind] (18:62) 88, p. 35.
"Drab Mysteries." [Wind] (18:62) 88, p. 35.
3397. McGOVERN, Martin
"If the Light Could Kill Us." [GettyR] (1:4) Aut 88, p. 624.
"The Rainbow Diary." [NewRep] (198:22) 30 My 88, p. 38.
"Tonight the Lace Curtain." [Shen] (38:2) 88, p. 75.
3398. McGOWAN, James
"Exotic Perfume" (tr. of Charles Baudelaire). [HiramPoR] (44/45) Spr-Wint 88, p. 69.
"Harmony of the Evening" (tr. of Charles Baudelaire). [HiramPoR] (44/45) Spr-Wint 88, p. 70.
3399. McGOWAN, Whitman
"Catfish." [Margin] (7) 88, p. 25.
3400. McGRADY, Nell
"Navajo Woman." [CharR] (14:2) Fall 88, p. 105.
3401. McGRATH, Campbell
"Capitalist Poem #25." [TriQ] (71) Wint 88, p. 168-170.
"Dialectical Poem #1." [TriQ] (71) Wint 88, p. 167.
"Memphis." [Shen] (38:4) 88, p. 77-78.
"Torre dell'Orologia." [RiverS] (26) 88, p. 50.
"Where the Water Runs Down." [RiverS] (26) 88, p. 51-53.
3402. McGRATH, Kristina
"This Is Not Home but Navigation." [StoneC] (16:1/2) Fall-Wint 88-89, p. 55.
"Windfall." [StoneC] (15:3/4) Spr-Sum 88, p. 23-25.
3403. McGRATH, Thomas
"Birthdays." [NoDaQ] (56:3) Sum 88, p. 1.
"For Jimmy McGrath." [NoDaQ] (56:4) Fall 88, p. 22.
"For Joe McGrath." [NoDaQ] (56:4) Fall 88, p. 21.
"Poem for Martin McGrath: Tool and Die Maker." [NoDaQ] (56:4) Fall 88, p. 21.
"Poems by Tomasito." [NoDaQ] (56:4) Fall 88, p. 22.
"Song of the Open Road" (for Reg Gibbons). [NoDaQ] (56:3) Sum 88, p. 1.
"Suspicion of Some Kinds of Solitude." [NoDaQ] (56:3) Sum 88, p. 2.
"Welcome" (for Etheridge Knight). [PaintedB] (32/33) 88, p. 11.
3404. McGUCKIAN, Medbh
"Dear Rain." [Antaeus] (60) Spr 88, p. 198-199.
"The Dream-Language of Fergus." [YaleR] (77:2) Wint 88, p. 237.
"Head of a Woman." [Antaeus] (60) Spr 88, p. 201-202.
"Lighthouse with Dead Leaves." [PartR] (55:1) Wint 88, p. 64-65.
"The Lion Tamer." [YaleR] (77:2) Wint 88, p. 238-240.
"Mrs. Orchard." [Antaeus] (60) Spr 88, p. 200.
"Whimbrel." [YaleR] (77:2) Wint 88, p. 238.
"Yeastlight." [PartR] (55:3) Sum 88, p. 476-477.
3405. McGUINESS, Daniel
"Lemonade in Blue." [PoetC] (19:3) Spr 88, p. 9-11.
3406. McGUINN, Rex
"Habit Is Severe" (For Adrienne Rich). [Pembroke] (20) 88, p. 223.
3407. McGUIRK, Kevin
"October, Writing." [Grain] (16:2) Sum 88, p. 30.
"Poem Written One Hot September When Berry Juices Fermented on the Ground Outside the Stadium." [Event] (17:1) Spr 88, p. 72.
3408. McGURL, Mark
"A Rose Poem: this rose is not a rose." [HarvardA] (122:4) My 88, p. 7.
"A Rose Poem: what did you make of these birds." [HarvardA] (122:4) My 88, p. 7.
"A Short Story." [HarvardA] (123:1) N 88, p. 9.
3409. McHALE, D. Brett
"For a Black Poet's Arrival in a Small Town." [PaintedB] (32/33) 88, p. 65.
3410. McHALE, Elizabeth Anne
"Ego Confession." [GrahamHR] (11) Spr 88, p. 48-49.
3411. McHUGH, Heather
"Bulgarian Woman from the Old Days" (tr. of Blaga Dimitrova, w. Nikolai B. Popov). [Antaeus] (60) Spr 88, p. 280.

"Forbidden Sea" (Selections: 14, 16, tr. of Blaga Dimitrova, w. Nikolai B. Popov). [Thrpny] (33) Spr 88, p. 18.
"In the Balance" (tr. of Blaga Dimitrova, w. Nikolai B. Popov). [Antaeus] (60) Spr 88, p. 279.
"Portrait with Soap Bubbles" (tr. of Blaga Dimitrova, w. Nikolai B. Popov). [Antaeus] (60) Spr 88, p. 283-284.
"Who Cares for the Blind Stork" (tr. of Blaga Dimitrova, w. Nikolai B. Popov). [Antaeus] (60) Spr 88, p. 277-278.
"The Women Who Are Poets in My Land" (tr. of Blaga Dimitrova, w. Nikolai B. Popov). [Antaeus] (60) Spr 88, p. 281-282.

3412. McINNIS, Michael
"Larry Cdnt." [Bogg] (59) 88, p. 38.

3413. MCINTOSH, Joan
"Uncouplings." [Spirit] (9:1) 88, p. 128.

3414. McIRVIN, Michael
"Child's Game with a Blue Balloon." [PassN] (9:1) Wint 88, p. 25.

3415. McIVER, Mary
"Reading Poetry." [EngJ] (77:8) D 88, p. 80.

3416. McKAIN, David
"The Old Woman." [ColR] (NS 15:2) Fall-Wint 88, p. 51.

3417. MCKANE, Richard
"I Don't Speak with Anyone for a Week" (tr. of Anna Akhmatova). [Field] (39) Fall 88, p. 17.

3418. McKAY, Don
"Another Theory of Dusk" (for Jan). [Descant] (19:3, #62) Fall 88, p. 148.

3419. McKAY, Leo, Jr.
"Being Acadian." [AntigR] (73) Spr 88, p. 80.
"My Life: The Outside." [CapilR] (49) 88, p. 78.

3420. McKAY, Linda Back
"Dog Days." [Farm] (5:2) Fall 88, p. 34-35.
"I Wear My WOJB Radio Cap with the Feather to Embarrass the Children." [Farm] (4:1, i.e. 5:1) Wint 88, p. 64-65.
"Nam Man." [LakeSR] (22) 88, p. 23.

3421. McKEAN, James
"Joy Luck." [CinPR] (18) Fall 88, p. 24.
"The Ride Back" (After a line by Rilke). [SenR] (18:1) 88, p. 46.
"Splitting Wood." [CinPR] (18) Fall 88, p. 26.
"There's a Hawk in the Yard." [SenR] (18:1) 88, p. 47.
"Tornado Warning." [CinPR] (18) Fall 88, p. 27.
"The Try-Your-Strength Machine at the Tivoli Gardens." [CinPR] (18) Fall 88, p. 25.
"Whispering in Leo Kauf's Ear." [SenR] (18:1) 88, p. 45.

3422. McKEE, Glenn
"Walled." [Wind] (18:62) 88, p. 31.

3423. McKEE, Louis
"An Act of Faith." [BellR] (11:2) Fall 88, p. 16.
"Chores." [Interim] (7:1) Spr 88, p. 21.
"From the Greek." [SwampR] (1:2/3) D 88, p. 30-31.
"In My Dream." [Amelia] (5:1, #12) 88, p. 119.
"Last Call" (for Etheridge Knight). [PaintedB] (32/33) 88, p. 143.
"Resolved." [SwampR] (1:2/3) D 88, p. 28-29.
"Scrabble." [SwampR] (1:1) Ja 88, p. 18.

3424. McKENTY, Bob
"Andujar in the Pique of His Career." [LightY] ('88/9) 88, p. 55.
"General Custer." [LightY] ('88/9) 88, p. 81.
"Leo." [LightY] ('88/9) 88, p. 99.
"Mona Leo" (to the tune of "Mona Lisa"). [LightY] ('88/9) 88, p. 69.

3425. McKEOWN, Tom
"White Avenue by the Sea." [CreamCR] (12:2) Sum 88, p. 228.

3426. McKIERNAN, Ethna
"Fire" (from the "Manic/Depressive" Series). [LakeSR] (22) 88, p. 33.
"History of Proper Nouns" (At the Vietnam War Memorial, Washington, D.C.). [LakeSR] (22) 88, p. 24.
"Hospital." (from the "Manic/Depressive" Series). [LakeSR] (22) 88, p. 35.
"Letting Go the Wolves" (from the "Manic/Depressive" Series). [LakeSR] (22) 88, p. 34.

3427. McKIM, Elizabeth
"Muse." [PaintedB] (32/33) 88, p. 142.
McKINNEY, Michael A.
See RONDELL, Rat
3428. McKINNEY, Sandy
"The Sphere." [BlackWR] (14:2) Spr 88, p. 90.
3429. McKINNON, Barry
"Mrs Snowdon." [WestCR] (22:3) Wint 87, p. 15.
"The Petting Zoo." [WestCR] (22:3) Wint 87, p. 14.
"Sex at 38." [Descant] (19:3, #62) Fall 88, p. 149-153.
3430. McKINNON, Michelle
"Footsteps." [PottPort] (10) 88, p. 43.
3431. McKINNON, Patrick
"Connie Larson." [SlipS] (8) 88, p. 57.
"The Glasses Poem." [Gargoyle] (35) 88, p. 26-27.
"Old Al Scarpelli." [SlipS] (8) 88, p. 58.
3432. McKINSEY, Martin
"The Text." [RiverS] (25) 88, p. 43-44.
3433. McLAUGHLIN, John
"August Dance." [Footwork] ('88) 88, p. 15.
"New shoots." [Footwork] ('88) 88, p. 15.
3434. McLAUGHLIN, W. M.
"Darlene." [PottPort] (9) 88, p. 28.
"Our Field." [PottPort] (10) 88, p. 23.
"Saturday Morning." [PottPort] (9) 88, p. 28.
3435. McLAUGHLIN, Walt
"Finitude." [Wind] (18:63) 88, p. 22.
3436. McLAUGHLIN, William
"The Old Man of the Backyard Finds Coincidences of Autumn." [KanQ] (20:1/2) Wint-Spr 88, p. 90-91.
3437. McLAURIN, Ken
"Every Man's Dream." [SouthernR] (24:3) Sum 88, p. 584-585.
"Juanita Flesher." [SouthernR] (24:3) Sum 88, p. 585.
3438. McLEAN, Clara D.
"Two Eyes and a Mouth." [Turnstile] (1:1) Wint 88, p. 74.
3439. McLEAN, Roy W.
"An Illness." [PottPort] (10) 88, p. 47.
3440. McLEOD, Margaret
"The Apprentices." [PottPort] (9) 88, p. 10.
3441. McLEOD, Milt
"Only the Owl Understands Such Things." [KanQ] (20:1/2) Wint-Spr 88, p. 78.
"A Remembrance of Water." [PaintedB] (34) 88, p. 95.
3442. McLEOD, Stephen
"Angelus." [Agni] (27) 88, p. 207.
"The Goose" (for RJL). [Agni] (27) 88, p. 208.
"Michelangelo's *Pietà*." [Shen] (38:4) 88, p. 42.
"What Comes Through Hearing." [AmerPoR] (17:1) Ja-F 88, p. 47.
3443. McMAHON, Lynne
"Aubade." [Field] (38) Spr 88, p. 34.
"Dog Days." [ParisR] (30:106) Spr 88, p. 110-111.
"An Elvis for the Eighties." [WestHR] (42:2) Sum 88, p. 115.
"Of Serious Conversation." [Field] (38) Spr 88, p. 35.
3444. McMAHON, Michael
"Coyote Howls Beyond Patton's Corn Field." [Farm] (4:1, i.e. 5:1) Wint 88, p. 39.
"Picking Up the Bones of a Mouse in the Barn." [Farm] (4:1, i.e. 5:1) Wint 88, p. 34-35.
"Touching the First Apple Blossom" (for E.M.)." [Farm] (4:1, i.e. 5:1) Wint 88, p. 37.
3445. McMICHAEL, James
"Mrs. Elliott." [Verse] (5:1) F 88, p. 8.
"Seven Poems." [ParisR] (30:108) Fall 88, p. 137-139.
3446. McMILLAN, J. A.
"Dead Snake." [StoneC] (16:1/2) Fall-Wint 88-89, p. 44.
"To Wallace Stevens." [StoneC] (16:1/2) Fall-Wint 88-89, p. 45.
3447. McMILLAN, Peter
"Anchors Weighed." [LightY] ('88/9) 88, p. 86.

3448. McNAIR, Wesley
"The Abandonment." [Atlantic] (262:4) O 88, p. 72.
"After My Stepfather's Death." [Poetry] (152:3) Je 88, p. 148.
"Ghosts." [KenR] (NS 10:3) Sum 88, p. 95-97.
"The Hand." [KenR] (NS 10:3) Sum 88, p. 97.
"Killing the Animals." [NewEngR] (11:1) Aut 88, p. 80.
"The Last Time Shorty Towers Fetched the Cows." [TexasR] (9:3/4) Fall-Wint 88, p. 98.
"Memory of North Sutton" (Chile, 1978). [TexasR] (9:3/4) Fall-Wint 88, p. 99.
"The Revival." [Poetry] (152:5) Ag 88, p. 275-276.
"Sue Reed Walking." [CreamCR] (12:2) Sum 88, p. 229-230.

3449. McNALL, Sally Allen
"Builder." [KanQ] (20:3) Sum 88, p. 146.
"The Garden in the Machine." [KanQ] (20:3) Sum 88, p. 145.
"Occasional Poem." [KanQ] (20:3) Sum 88, p. 146-147.
"Sweet Basil" (for M. A.-R.). [KanQ] (20:3) Sum 88, p. 147-148.

3450. McNALLY, Stephen
"At the Town Where I Was Born." [SouthernPR] (28:1) Spr 88, p. 19-20.

3451. McNAMARA, Eugene
"Saying Grace" (for Jim Cooney). [CrossC] (10:1) 88, p. 8.

3452. McNAMARA, Robert
"After a Year, Some Words for You." [MassR] (29:2) Sum 88, p. 355.
"At My Daughter's School." [MassR] (29:2) Sum 88, p. 356.
"At the Savannah." [KanQ] (20:1/2) Wint-Spr 88, p. 13.
"In the Hearts of His Countrymen: L. B. J." [QW] (27) Sum-Fall 88, p. 94.
"Out of the Blue." [QW] (27) Sum-Fall 88, p. 93.
"Such Accomplishments" (for Douglas Shields Dix). [QW] (27) Sum-Fall 88, p. 92.
"The Wound" (First Award Poem, 1987/1988). [KanQ] (20:1/2) Wint-Spr 88, p. 12-13.

3453. McNAUGHTON, Duncan
"The Pilot" (Selections: 3 poems). [Temblor] (7) 88, p. 164-171.
"The Pilot" (Selections: 11 poems). [Temblor] (8) 88, p. 53-60.

3454. McNEIL, Maureen
"Glass Float." [LitR] (31:2) Wint 88, p. 190.

3455. McNERNEY, Joan
"Dividing Mind." [Wind] (18:63) 88, p. 26.

3456. McNULTY, Tim
"As a Heron Unsettles a Shallow Pool" (For Mary). [CrabCR] (5:2) Sum 88, p. 3.
"The Skagit Stone Owl." [Chelsea] (47) 88, p. 156-157.
"The Wind in Lost Basin." [CrabCR] (5:3) Fall 88, p. 28.

3457. McPHERSON, Michael
"A. J. W. MacKenzie & Son, 29 Miles Volcano" (for Garrett Hongo). [HawaiiR] (12:1, #23) Spr 88, p. 20.
"John Dalton." [ChamLR] (1) Fall 87, p. 71-72.
"Kiholo." [HawaiiR] (12:1, #23) Spr 88, p. 21.
"Kohala." [ChamLR] (1:2, #2) Spr 88, p. 75.
"My Uncles Surfing at Waikiki, Circa 1935." [HawaiiR] (12:2, #24) Fall 88, p. 91.
"Points." [HawaiiR] (12:1, #23) Spr 88, p. 19.
"Return to a Nameless Place." [HawaiiR] (12:2, #24) Fall 88, p. 90.
"Tapes." [HawaiiR] (12:1, #23) Spr 88, p. 18.

3458. McPHERSON, Sandra
"The Ability to Make a Face Like a Spider While Singing Blues: Junior Wells." [NewRep] (198:20) 16 My 88, p. 25.
"As She Left Their Home." [MissouriR] (11:2) 88, p. 154-155.
"Autumn on a Small Tree." [YaleR] (77:4) Sum 88, p. 613-614.
"Black Quilt from the '60s: Synthetics: the No Blocks." [WestHR] (42:3) Aut 88, p. 214.
"Blues in the Joy of the Fourth of July, Dusk, Crissy Field, San Francisco." [TriQ] (72) Spr-Sum 88, p. 188-189.
"Easter 1979." [MissouriR] (11:2) 88, p. 158.
"Elegy for Floating Things." [GrandS] (7:3) Spr 88, p. 96-97.
"Esther Mack's Utility Quilt with the Lights in It." [YaleR] (77:4) Sum 88, p. 610-611.
"Hawaiian Buddha." [TriQ] (72) Spr-Sum 88, p. 186-187.
"Kindness" (Albion River mouth at the Pacific). [Verse] (5:1) F 88, p. 9-11.

"Mrs. Longmire Builds a Picket Fence Quilt and Talks to It." [Field] (39) Fall 88, p. 88.
"Muskogee Quilter Explains: The Non-Shortcut Method." [Field] (39) Fall 88, p. 89-90.
"Quilt of Rights." [AmerV] (11) Sum 88, p. 33.
"Quilt Top Discovered at the Muskogee Flea Market and Found to Contain Blocks . . . ." [YaleR] (77:4) Sum 88, p. 609-610.
"Red Diamond Centers: Approximation." [WestHR] (42:3) Aut 88, p. 215.
"Some Metaphysics of Junior Wells" (18 September 1987). [YaleR] (77:4) Sum 88, p. 611-613.
"Some Schizophrenics." [MissouriR] (11:2) 88, p. 151-153.
"The Stranger Melody." [MissouriR] (11:2) 88, p. 156-157.
"Suspension: Junior Wells on a Small Stage in a Converted Barn." [TriQ] (72) Spr-Sum 88, p. 190-192.
"Tents-of-Armageddon Quilt, Black Improvisation, 1980s." [Field] (39) Fall 88, p. 91.
"Twelve Bar Quilt." [Field] (39) Fall 88, p. 93-94.
"Waterfall with Baskets, Summer Quilt" (Uncategorized Design, Probably Afro-American). [Field] (39) Fall 88, p. 92.

3459. McQUILKIN, Rennie
"Daphne in California." [CinPR] (18) Fall 88, p. 36-37.
"Flower Farmer." [MalR] (85) D 88, p. 119-120.
"Getting There." [MalR] (85) D 88, p. 116-118.
"Lines." [LitR] (31:4) Sum 88, p. 435-436.
"Peter Farr." [TexasR] (9:3/4) Fall-Wint 88, p. 100.

3460. McRAY, Paul
"Games with the Blind." [Interim] (7:1) Spr 88, p. 39.
"How It Doesn't Happen" (for Charles Rotmil). [CinPR] (18) Fall 88, p. 29.
"Mósa — Mohave." [Poetry] (152:4) Jl 88, p. 215-216.

3461. McROBBIE, Kenneth
"Inventing Others." [PraF] (9:3) Aut 88, p. 67.
"Still That Hair." [PraF] (9:3) Aut 88, p. 68.

3462. McROBERTS, Robert
"Opsprey." [Northeast] (ser. 4:7) Sum 88, p. 22.
"Real Estate." [Northeast] (ser. 4:7) Sum 88, p. 21.

3463. MEAD, Jane
"Maybe She Go." [Pequod] (25) 88, p. 45-47.

3464. MEAD, Philip
"Cinema Point." [NewAW] (4) Fall 88, p. 123.
"For Those Who Came In Late." [NewAW] (4) Fall 88, p. 124-125.
"Melbourne or the Bush." [NewAW] (4) Fall 88, p. 125-126.
"There." [NewAW] (4) Fall 88, p. 123-124.

3465. MEAD, S. E.
"Empathy." [BellArk] (4:2) Mr-Ap 88, p. 4.
"From a Burn Unit." [BellArk] (4:3) My-Je 88, p. 6.

3466. MEADS, Kat
"Going Under Tremors in Sight of the Bay Bridge Tunnel." [SwampR] (1:2/3) D 88, p. 35.
"The Winter of '82." [SwampR] (1:2/3) D 88, p. 36.

3467. MEDAKSÉ
"Envy" (tr. by Diana Der Hovanessian). [GrahamHR] (11) Spr 88, p. 95.
"It's No Secret" (tr. by Diana Der Hovanessian). [GrahamHR] (11) Spr 88, p. 94.

3468. MEDEARIS, Martha
"Fourth Child — Third Son." [Phoenix] (9:1/2) 88, p. 47.

3469. MEEHAN, Maude
"Maxima Culpa" (from *Chipping Bone*). [SinW] (32) Sum 87, p. 46.

3470. MEEK, Jay
"Vienna in the Rain." [KenR] (NS 10:2) Spr 88, p. 89-90.

3471. MEHLMAN, Robert
"Star Trek." [Spirit] (9:1) 88, p. 70.

3472. MEHREN, Stein
"The Sky" (tr. by Robert Hedin). [ColR] (NS 15:2) Fall-Wint 88, p. 84.

3473. MEHTA, Digish
"Would One Believe?" (tr. of Aniruddha Brahmabhatt). [Nimrod] (31:2) Spr-Sum 88, p. 71.

3474. MEIER, Kay
"Blueprint for Emotion." [EngJ] (77:2) F 88, p. 86.
"The Man Who Went to Tegucigalpa." [Vis] (27) 88, p. 35.
"Visit to the Nursing Home." [EngJ] (77:1) Ja 88, p. 103.
3475. MEIKSIN, Judy
"Tied." [SinW] (33) Fall 87, p. 59.
3476. MEINKE, Peter
"The Dead Tree." [Poetry] (152:3) Je 88, p. 136-137.
"Exodus with Children." [Poetry] (152:3) Je 88, p. 136.
"The Student." [LightY] ('88/9) 88, p. 38.
3477. MEISSNER, Bill
"Returning Only Part Way Home" (w. Jack Driscoll). [PassN] (9:1) Wint 88, p. 29.
"Winter Fishing" (w. Jack Driscoll). [PassN] (9:1) Wint 88, p. 29.
3478. MEISTER, Shirley Vogler
"Making Up after the Breaking Up." [Bogg] (59) 88, p. 45.
"The Prevaricator." [LightY] ('88/9) 88, p. 198.
"Sestina for Sparrow." [Amelia] (4:4, #11) 88, p. 88-89.
3479. MEJIA SANCHEZ, Ernesto
"The Tiger in the Garden" (tr. by Nancy Esposito). [AmerPoR] (17:2) Mr-Ap 88, p. 30.
3480. MELANÇON, Robert
"L'Avant-Printemps à Montréal." [Os] (27) 88, p. 17.
"Beginning of Summer" (tr. by Philip Stratford). [Trans] (20) Spr 88, p. 151.
"Blind Painting II" (tr. by Philip Stratford). [Trans] (20) Spr 88, p. 152.
"Jean-Aubert Loranger." [Os] (27) 88, p. 5.
3481. MELFI, Mary
"O Boy." [Quarry] (37:1) Wint 88, p. 69-70.
"Slave Owners." [Quarry] (37:1) Wint 88, p. 67-68.
3482. MELHEM, D. H.
"Coney Island." [Confr] (Special issue: The World of Brooklyn) 88, p. 39-40.
3483. MELNYCZUK, Askold
"Downer Forest Road." [PartR] (55:4) Fall 88, p. 621-622.
"The Usual Immigrant Uncle Poem." [Poetry] (153:3) D 88, p. 130.
MELO NETO, João Cabral de
See NETO, João Cabral de Melo
3484. MELVIN, John
"1207 Muscatine Avenue." [CutB] (31/32) 88, p. 61.
"Listen." [CutB] (31/32) 88, p. 62.
"Water." [CutB] (31/32) 88, p. 60-61.
3485. MEMON, Muhammad Umar
"Call from Above" (tr. of Shahryar). [Nimrod] (31:2) Spr-Sum 88, p. 107.
3486. MENASHE, Samuel
"Dominion." [Confr] (37/38) Spr-Sum 88, p. 96.
3487. MENDIETA, Ana
"Pain of Cuba." [Sulfur] (8:1, #22) Spr 88, p. 70-71.
3488. MENEBROKER, Ann
"Alley-House Thinking." [Bogg] (60) 88, p. 5.
"Going into the House of My Youth." [SwampR] (1:2/3) D 88, p. 49.
"If she was good." [Bogg] (60) 88, p. 8.
"Ohio Lust." [Bogg] (59) 88, p. 5.
"One Good Line." [Bogg] (60) 88, p. 7.
"Sales." [Bogg] (59) 88, p. 16.
"Slices" (Selections: 4 poems). [Bogg] (60) 88, p. 6.
"State-of-the-Art Cycle." [SwampR] (1:1) Ja 88, p. 22-23.
"Torch Song." [SwampR] (1:1) Ja 88, p. 24.
"Trying to Get Across." [SwampR] (1:1) Ja 88, p. 25.
"The Warped Notion of Romantic Love." [SwampR] (1:2/3) D 88, p. 50-51.
MENG-DAN, Chu
See CHU, Meng-dan
MENG-JIE, Hu
See HU, Meng-jie
3489. MENNIS, Bernice
"Without Will." [SinW] (34) Spr 88, p. 70.
3490. MENSCHING, Steffen
"Did You Notice That the American Soldier" (tr. by George Kane). [ParisR] (30:106) Spr 88, p. 296.

"In a Hotel Room in Meissen I Read" (tr. by George Kane). [ParisR] (30:106) Spr 88, p. 296.
"Official Telephone Book, Reich Postal District Berlin, 1941" (tr. by George Kane). [ParisR] (30:106) Spr 88, p. 297-298.
"So White Was the Morning" (tr. by George Kane). [ParisR] (30:106) Spr 88, p. 296.
"Torn and Tattered Elegy in Black" (tr. by George Kane). [ParisR] (30:106) Spr 88, p. 299.

3491. MEREDITH, Joseph
"All-Star" (for AMM in his tenth summer). [PaintedB] (36) 88, p. 96.
"Sunday Dusk" (for JMM). [PaintedB] (36) 88, p. 95.

3492. MERRIAM, Eve
"Rodomontade in the Menagerie." [LightY] ('88/9) 88, p. 98.

3493. MERRICLE, William
"1988." [SlipS] (8) 88, p. 7.
"Billy's Third Law of Astro-Intestinal Movement." [Abraxas] (37) 88, p. 63.
"VD Sheets." [SlipS] (8) 88, p. 7.

3494. MERRILL, Christopher
"Doppelgänger." [CinPR] (18) Fall 88, p. 59.
"The Guests." [CinPR] (18) Fall 88, p. 58.
"Lupines" (for Agha Shahid Ali). [AntR] (46:2) Spr 88, p. 249.
"Old Wives' Tales." [SenR] (18:2) 88, p. 55-58.
"Words." [ParisR] (30:108) Fall 88, p. 212.

3495. MERRILL, James
"Alabaster." [NewYorker] (64:34) 10 O 88, p. 37.
"Graffito." [Verse] (5:2) Jl 88, p. 3.
"November Ode." [NewYRB] (35:16) 27 O 88, p. 14.
"Storm." [KeyWR] (1:1) Spr 88, p. 10.
"Walks in Rome." [YaleR] (77:2) Wint 88, p. 168-171.

3496. MERRITT, Jonathan
"The Choice Which Is Constant." [FiveFR] (6) 88, p. 81.
"Tuesday Night." [FiveFR] (6) 88, p. 82.

MERS, Joyce la
See LaMERS, Joyce

3497. MERTON, Thomas
"Elegy for a Trappist" (Fr. M. Stephen, O.C.S.O.). [Comm] (115:21) 2 D 88, p. 651.

3498. MERWIN, W. S.
"Among Bells." [NewYorker] (64:35) 17 O 88, p. 38.
"The Archaic Maker." [AmerPoR] (17:2) Mr-Ap 88, p. 22.
"The Biology of Art." [AmerPoR] (17:2) Mr-Ap 88, p. 23.
"The Blind Seer of Ambon" (George Everard Rumpf, 1628?-1702, great Dutch naturalist). [Atlantic] (261:4) Ap 88, p. 49.
"Coming to Hear." [AmerPoR] (17:2) Mr-Ap 88, p. 23.
"Coming to the Morning." [AmerPoR] (17:2) Mr-Ap 88, p. 23.
"The creatures of afternoon" (tr. of Roberto Juarroz). [AmerPoR] (17:1) Ja-F 88, p. 26.
"Death is another way of looking" (tr. of Roberto Juarroz). [AmerPoR] (17:1) Ja-F 88, p. 25.
"Each thing makes hands for itself" (tr. of Roberto Juarroz). [AmerPoR] (17:1) Ja-F 88, p. 26.
"Embrace your head" (tr. of Roberto Juarroz). [AmerPoR] (17:1) Ja-F 88, p. 26.
"The faces that you've discarded" (tr. of Roberto Juarroz). [AmerPoR] (17:1) Ja-F 88, p. 26.
"For the Departure of a Stepson." [AmerPoR] (17:2) Mr-Ap 88, p. 23.
"Forms are born of an open hand" (tr. of Roberto Juarroz). [AmerPoR] (17:1) Ja-F 88, p. 25.
"A glass of water" (tr. of Roberto Juarroz). [AmerPoR] (17:1) Ja-F 88, p. 26.
"Knock." [AmerPoR] (17:2) Mr-Ap 88, p. 23.
"Life is a necessary precaution" (tr. of Roberto Juarroz). [AmerPoR] (17:1) Ja-F 88, p. 24.
"A long tunnel is coming closer to my mouth" (tr. of Roberto Juarroz). [AmerPoR] (17:1) Ja-F 88, p. 25.
"The memories leap out of the eyes" (tr. of Roberto Juarroz). [AmerPoR] (17:1) Ja-F 88, p. 25.

"The other who bears my name" (tr. of Roberto Juarroz). [AmerPoR] (17:1) Ja-F 88, p. 25.
"The Overpass." [Poetry] (152:2) My 88, p. 78.
"The Palms." [GrandS] (7:4) Sum 88, p. 118-119.
"The River." [GrandS] (7:4) Sum 88, p. 120.
"Sight." [AmerPoR] (17:2) Mr-Ap 88, p. 22.
"So Far." [Atlantic] (262:4) O 88, p. 64.
"The stone is a clenched lap" (tr. of Roberto Juarroz). [AmerPoR] (17:1) Ja-F 88, p. 25.
"The Superstition." [NewYorker] (63:52) 15 F 88, p. 36.
"There are footprints that do not coincide with their foot" (tr. of Roberto Juarroz). [AmerPoR] (17:1) Ja-F 88, p. 24.
"To the Insects." [AmerPoR] (17:2) Mr-Ap 88, p. 22.
"Tracing the Letters." [AmerPoR] (17:2) Mr-Ap 88, p. 22.
"An uncommitted gesture, a rapt expression" (tr. of Roberto Juarroz). [AmerPoR] (17:1) Ja-F 88, p. 25.
"Unique each night" (tr. of Roberto Juarroz). [AmerPoR] (17:1) Ja-F 88, p. 26.
"The Wars in New Jersey." [NewYorker] (64:14) 23 My 88, p. 28.

3499. MESA, Lauren
"American." [Amelia] (4:4, #11) 88, p. 47.
"Keeping Balance." [PoetC] (19:2) Wint 88, p. 11.
"Middle-Ground" (chapbook: 10 poems). [SilverFR] (15) 88, 24 p.
"The Years We Will Know Them." [Poetry] (151:4) Ja 88, p. 343.

3500. MESSERLI, Douglas
"The Magicians." [CentralP] (14) Fall 88, p. 152.
"Toast." [NewAW] (3) Spr 88, p. 76.
"Twas the Night." [NewAW] (3) Spr 88, p. 75.

3501. MESZOLY, Miklos
"Ode to the Elegy." [Sulfur] (7:3, #21) Wint 88, p. 63-65.

METER, Suzanne van
See Van METER, Suzanne

3502. METZGER, Deena
"Canta" (for Claribel Alegria). [Jacaranda] (3:2) Fall-Wint 88, p. 111-112.
"Owl" (For Michael Ortiz Hill). [Jacaranda] (3:2) Fall-Wint 88, p. 110.

3503. MEYER, Paul
"Time." [LaurelR] (22:2) Sum 88, p. 116.
"The Un-Lovers Say." [LaurelR] (22:2) Sum 88, p. 117.

3504. MEYER, Thomas
"The Hurry" (from "Sonnets & Tableaux). [Notus] (3:1) Spr 88, p. 3-9.

3505. MEYER, William, Jr.
"Cub Hypervisual American Eroticism." [SlipS] (8) 88, p. 16.
"The Speed oif Light." [SlipS] (8) 88, p. 16.

3506. MEYERS, Bert
"Daybreak." [SwampR] (1:1) Ja 88, p. 55.
"L. A." [SwampR] (1:1) Ja 88, p. 56.
"Landscapes." [SwampR] (1:1) Ja 88, p. 47-49.
"Ocean." [SwampR] (1:1) Ja 88, p. 50-51.
"Paris." [SwampR] (1:1) Ja 88, p. 57-61.
"Rainy Day." [SwampR] (1:1) Ja 88, p. 52.
"This Morning." [SwampR] (1:1) Ja 88, p. 53.
"Watercolor Days." [SwampR] (1:1) Ja 88, p. 54.

3507. MG
"The Exit." [CinPR] (17) Spr 88, p. 35.

3508. MICHAEL, Ann E.
"The Night Animals." [PaintedB] (34) 88, p. 41.

3509. MICHEAELS, Cathleen
"A Prayer for What Is Sacred and Silent." [SouthernPR] (28:2) Fall 88, p. 28.

MICHELE, Bill di
See DiMICHELE, Bill

3510. MICHELI, Linda
"One-Eye, Two-Eyes, Three-Eyes." [CentR] (32:2) Spr 88, p. 153.

3511. MICHELINE, Jack
"God Bless the Unknown." [AlphaBS] (3) Je 88, p. 61.
"Poem to the Freaks." [AlphaBS] (3) Je 88, p. 60.

3512. MICUS, Edward (Edward K.)
"Cemetery Near Cambria, Minnesota." [Vis] (28) 88, p. 33.

"Note." [KanQ] (20:1/2) Wint-Spr 88, p. 125.
"Photo: Boy in a Suit." [Farm] (5:2) Fall 88, p. 17.

3513. MIDDLETON, Christopher
"Absence" (tr. of Abu Kakr al-Turtusi from the Spanish of Emilio García Gómez, w. Leticia Garza-Falcón). [NewYorker] (64:29) 5 S 88, p. 23.
"Artichoke Heart" (tr. of Ben al-Talla of Mahdía from the Spanish of Emilio García Gómez, w. Leticia Garza-Falcón). [NewYorker] (64:29) 5 S 88, p. 23.
"Border Zone, Minefield, Snow East of Bebra" (tr. of Lars Gustafsson). [NewYorker] (64:4) 14 Mr 88, p. 40.
"Cybele." [Antaeus] (60) Spr 88, p. 226-227.
"The Dove" (tr. of Abul Hasan Ali ben Hisn from the Spanish of Emilio García Gómez, w. Leticia Garza-Falcón). [NewYorker] (64:29) 5 S 88, p. 22.
"Flight of Cranes over Skane at Dawn in April" (tr. of Lars Gustafsson, w. the author). [SouthernHR] (22:1) Wint 88, p. 18.
"Galley Oars" (tr. of Ali ben Hariq of Valencia from the Spanish of Emilio García Gómez, w. Leticia Garza-Falcón). [NewYorker] (64:29) 5 S 88, p. 22.
"The Guadalquivir in Flood" (tr. of Ben Safar al-Marini of Almería from the Spanish of Emilio García Gómez, w. Leticia Garza-Falcón). [NewYorker] (64:29) 5 S 88, p. 23.
"Honey River" (tr. of Ben Ani Ruh of Algeciras from the Spanish of Emilio García Gómez, w. Leticia Garza-Falcón). [NewYorker] (64:29) 5 S 88, p. 22.
"In Texas." [Antaeus] (60) Spr 88, p. 223-225.
"Notes on the 1860s" (tr. of Lars Gustafsson). [NewYorker] (64:16) 6 Je 88, p. 36.
"On All That Glides in the Air" (tr. of Lars Gustafsson, w. the author). [SouthernHR] (22:1) Wint 88, p. 17-18.
"A Pool with Turtles" (tr. of Ben Sara of Santaren from the Spanish of Emilio García Gómez, w. Leticia Garza-Falcón). [NewYorker] (64:29) 5 S 88, p. 23.
"The Procuress" (tr. of Abu Jafar Ahmad ben Said from the Spanish of Emilio García Gómez, w. Leticia Garza-Falcón). [NewYorker] (64:29) 5 S 88, p. 23.
"The Quince" (tr. of Al-Mushafi from the Spanish of Emilio García Gómez, w. Leticia Garza-Falcón). [NewYorker] (64:29) 5 S 88, p. 22.
"Reflection of Wine" (tr. of Abul Hasan Ali ben Hisn from the Spanish of Emilio García Gómez, w. Leticia Garza-Falcón). [NewYorker] (64:29) 5 S 88, p. 22.
"The Rooster" (tr. of Al-Asad Ibrahim ben Billita from the Spanish of Emilio García Gómez, w. Leticia Garza-Falcón). [NewYorker] (64:29) 5 S 88, p. 23.
"Satire" (tr. of Ben Jaraf of Cairuán from the Spanish of Emilio García Gómez, w. Leticia Garza-Falcón). [NewYorker] (64:29) 5 S 88, p. 22.

3514. MIDDLETON, David
"The Burning Fields" (South Louisiana). [SouthernR] (24:4) Aut 88, p. 952-953.

3515. MIDDLETON, Peter
"Portrait of an Unknown Man." [Temblor] (7) 88, p. 131-140.

3516. MIDDLETON, Polly
"Cloudy Every Day." [Footwork] ('88) 88, p. 47.
"Pictures Remember." [Footwork] ('88) 88, p. 47.

3517. MIEDZYRZECKI, Artur
"29-77-02" (tr. by Stanislaw Baranczak and Clare Cavanagh). [ManhatR] (4:2) Spr 88, p. 35.
"At the Cave" (tr. by Stanislaw Baranczak and Clare Cavanagh). [TriQ] (71) Wint 88, p. 151.
"The Golden Age" (tr. by Stanislaw Baranczak and Clare Cavanagh). [ManhatR] (4:2) Spr 88, p. 35.
"They" (tr. by Stanislaw Baranczak and Clare Cavanagh). [ManhatR] (4:2) Spr 88, p. 34.
"What Does the Political Scientist Know" (tr. by Stanislaw Baranczak and Clare Cavanagh). [TriQ] (71) Wint 88, p. 152.

3518. MIERAU, Maurice
"Buffalo Plains Hospital." [Grain] (16:2) Sum 88, p. 17.
"Grandfather, Retired." [Grain] (16:2) Sum 88, p. 16.

3519. MIHALYI, Marti
"The Woman in the Glass House Speaks." [PassN] (9:2) Sum 88, p. 29.

3520. MIHAN, Elizabeth
"Nightfear." [DenQ] (22:3) Wint 88, p. 85-86.

3521. MIHELARAKIS, Joseph
"The Poor Fisherman" (Pierre Puvis de Chavannes, 1824-1896). [Shen] (38:3) 88, p. 19.

3522. MIKITA, Nancy
"Tending the Garden in Winter." [CapeR] (23:2) Fall 88, p. 24.
3523. MIKKELSEN, Robert
"Falling at Fifty." [WeberS] (5:1) Spr 88, p. 36.
"What If." [WeberS] (5:1) Spr 88, p. 34-36.
3524. MIKORUSZ, Andrenske
"Finding Unused Tickets" (tr. from the Serbo-Croation by the author). [HarvardA] (The New Yorker spoof issue) 88?, p. 20.
3525. MIKULEC, Patrick (Patrick B.)
"Claims." [HawaiiR] (12:2, #24) Fall 88, p. 74.
"The Disappearance of Names" (Barlow Pioneer Cemetery, 1986). [WebR] (13:1) Spr 88, p. 76.
"The Escape" (for T.M.). [WebR] (13:1) Spr 88, p. 77.
"Lost Gold Mine." [WebR] (13:1) Spr 88, p. 78.
"Old Things That People Save" (On finding a broken, Klamath bowl in a junk store in Canby, Oregon). [Footwork] ('88) 88, p. 52-53.
"Skit." [ChamLR] (2:1, #3) Fall 88, p. 59.
3526. MILAN, Eduardo
"Decir Ahí Es una Flor Difícil." [Inti] (26/27) Otoño 87-Primavera 88, p. 251-252.
"Fragmentos Sobre el Futuro" (para J. A. Masoliver). [Inti] (26/27) Otoño 87-Primavera 88, p. 252-253.
"Nerval: Nervaduras" (A Horacio Costa). [Inti] (26/27) Otoño 87-Primavera 88, p. 250-251.
3527. MILBURN, Michael
"The Cruelty." [PraS] (62:3) Fall 88, p. 35-36.
"A Grip." [PraS] (62:3) Fall 88, p. 36-38.
3528. MILES, Ron
"Keaton." [CanLit] (118) Aut 88, p. 28-34.
3529. MILLAN, Gonzalo
"While" (tr. by Thorpe Running). [ColR] (NS 15:1) Spr-Sum 88, p. 78-79.
3530. MILLER, A. McA.
"Atthis, the 'Grape Girl,' to Sappho." [StoneC] (15:3/4) Spr-Sum 88, p. 64-65.
3531. MILLER, Bill
"Upon Arrival at Sing Sing." [HangL] (52) 88, p. 8.
3532. MILLER, Carol
"The Face." [CapeR] (23:2) Fall 88, p. 11.
3533. MILLER, Chuck
"After Watching 'The Times of Harvey Milk'." [Spirit] (9:1) 88, p. 107-109.
"How in the Morning: Poems 1962-1988" (Number 5 of the Outstanding Author Series). [Spirit] (9:2) 88, 80 p.
3534. MILLER, E. Ethelbert
"August Rain." [Gargoyle] (35) 88, p. 10.
"Bill Mazeroski Returns Home from the World Series." [Footwork] ('88) 88, p. 84.
"Chinatown." [Lips] (14) 88, p. 15.
"Growing Up." [Gargoyle] (35) 88, p. 11.
"Holiday." [Footwork] ('88) 88, p. 84.
"Poem for Seble." [Lips] (14) 88, p. 14.
"Rebecca." [Footwork] ('88) 88, p. 84.
"The Sea." [Lips] (14) 88, p. 16.
3535. MILLER, E. S.
"Ars Poetica." [HeliconN] (19) 88, p. 63.
"Loverse." [HeliconN] (19) 88, p. 63.
3536. MILLER, Errol
"Down the Boulevard." [Lactuca] (10) Je 88, p. 5.
"His Acre." [Lactuca] (10) Je 88, p. 4.
"The Horizon." [Lactuca] (10) Je 88, p. 2.
"Majestic." [Interim] (7:2) Fall 88, p. 24.
"The Man Who Believed in Nothing" (for New York City). [Lactuca] (10) Je 88, p. 3.
"Mars Hill." [Lactuca] (10) Je 88, p. 6.
"Star City." [Lactuca] (10) Je 88, p. 6.
3537. MILLER, Frances
"An Old Woman Speaks to the Young." [StoneC] (15:3/4) Spr-Sum 88, p. 29.
3538. MILLER, Greg
"Age of Reason" (for Kelly, 1957-1969). [Interim] (7:2) Fall 88, p. 44.
"Animals." [Thrpny] (35) Fall 88, p. 22.

"Downstream." [ChiR] (36:1) 88, p. 63-64.
"Story." [Verse] (5:1) F 88, p. 11.
"To His Wife." [Interim] (7:2) Fall 88, p. 43.
"Trophaeum Peccati." [Interim] (7:2) Fall 88, p. 46.
"Water" (after E.P.). [Interim] (7:2) Fall 88, p. 45.

3539. MILLER, James A.
"Atlantic, 1819: An Amish Progression." [BellArk] (4:5) S-O 88, p. 3.
"On the Salutary Effect of Coffee (Good Such) and Other Certain Cultural Digressions." [HawaiiR] (12:2, #24) Fall 88, p. 105-108.

3540. MILLER, Jane Ann
"September 9, 1901, Malromé." [PartR] (55:4) Fall 88, p. 613-614.

3541. MILLER, Jauren
"Homecoming." [Wind] (18:63) 88, p. 27-28.
"Kite Day" (for J.T.). [Wind] (18:63) 88, p. 27.

3542. MILLER, Jeanette
"Circulaire." [PoetC] (19:2) Wint 88, p. 18.
"Cyclical." [PoetC] (19:2) Wint 88, p. 14-15.
"Encore for My Aunt." [PoetC] (19:2) Wint 88, p. 12-13.
"Pods." [PoetC] (19:2) Wint 88, p. 16-17.
"Woman with a Crow, Picasso 1904." [PoetC] (19:2) Wint 88, p. 15.

3543. MILLER, Jeannette
"Amo Este Pueblo de Caminos Tranquilos." [CuadP] (5:14) Enero-Abril 88, p. 30-31.
"La Palabra Enemiga." [CuadP] (5:14) Enero-Abril 88, p. 27-28.
"Parada." [CuadP] (5:14) Enero-Abril 88, p. 31.
"El Pintalabios." [CuadP] (5:14) Enero-Abril 88, p. 32.
"La Turista." [CuadP] (5:14) Enero-Abril 88, p. 28-30.

3544. MILLER, John N.
"Hyphenating the Old Country." [WebR] (13:2) Fall 88, p. 95.
"Inside Story." [CharR] (14:1) Spr 88, p. 59.
"On the Trail of Marx in London" (with borrowings from Michael Buselmeier). [CharR] (14:1) Spr 88, p. 58-59.
"Par Avion" (for Ille). [HawaiiR] (12:1, #23) Spr 88, p. 35.

3545. MILLER, Judy Keyser
"The Woman He Never Told." [Plain] (8:1) Fall 87, p. 10.

3546. MILLER, Kevin J.
"Gifts." [BellArk] (4:4) Jl-Ag 88, p. 4.
"Minter Creek Heron." [CrabCR] (5:1) Wint 88, p. 14.

3547. MILLER, Leslie Adrienne
"After Dinner Story for Three Single Women" (for Eleanor Bender). [AmerPoR] (17:6) N-D 88, p. 10.
"Definition." [QW] (27) Sum-Fall 88, p. 99.
"Early Dark." [NewL] (55:2) Wint 88-89, p. 76-77.
"Flower Walk" (for Deb Pursifull). [QW] (26) Wint 88, p. 124-125.
"The Monkey." [AmerPoR] (17:6) N-D 88, p. 10.
"My Students Catch Me Dancing." [QW] (27) Sum-Fall 88, p. 95-96.
"The Weather of Invention." [QW] (27) Sum-Fall 88, p. 97-98.
"When I Come Back As a Younger Woman." [QW] (26) Wint 88, p. 122-123.
"William's Undershirts in the Wind." [QW] (26) Wint 88, p. 121.

3548. MILLER, Maureen Lee
"Lighthouse Park" (after a legend . . .). [GreensboroR] (44) Sum 88, p. 58.

3549. MILLER, Pamela
"Sonia Walks Out." [Prima] (11/12) 88, p. 13-14.

3550. MILLER, Patricia
"Point of View." [Thrpny] (34) Sum 88, p. 27.

3551. MILLER, Patricia Cleary
"Amy Was Born in Anchorage in Spring." [NewL] (55:1) Fall 88, p. 44-47.
"Mother Has Stopped Doing Her Sit-Ups." [NewL] (55:1) Fall 88, p. 43.

3552. MILLER, Philip
"Bric-a-brac." [LitR] (31:3) Spr 88, p. 329.
"In Deep October." [LitR] (31:3) Spr 88, p. 328.
"On the Wagon." [NewL] (54:3) Spr 88, p. 98.
"When You Hung Up." [RagMag] (6:1) [88], p. 31.

3553. MILLER, Raeburn
"Birthday Poem." [StoneC] (16:1/2) Fall-Wint 88-89, p. 28.
"The Return." [NoDaQ] (56:3) Sum 88, p. 92.

"Unclean." [CapeR] (23:1) Spr 88, p. 20.
3554. MILLER, Theresa W.
"Rescuing the Widower." [GreensboroR] (44) Sum 88, p. 67-69.
3555. MILLER, Tom
"San Francisco Star" (for George). [WebR] (13:2) Fall 88, p. 77.
3556. MILLER, William
"Shiloh Cemetery (Delta, Alabama)." [GreensboroR] (44) Sum 88, p. 115.
"The Vietnam Veteran in K-Mart." [FloridaR] (16:1) Spr-Sum 88, p. 50.
3557. MILLER-DUGGAN, Devon
"Anguish of White Stone" (tr. of Innokenty Annensky, w. Nancy Tittler). [Paint] (15:30) Aut 88, p. 31.
"Because on the Beach." [StoneC] (16:1/2) Fall-Wint 88-89, p. 47.
"January Fairy Tale" (tr. of Innokenty Annensky, w. Nancy Tittler). [Paint] (15:30) Aut 88, p. 30.
"The Work of the Hands." [CutB] (29/30) 88, p. 98-101.
3558. MILLETT, John
"Rape." [Bogg] (59) 88, p. 10.
3559. MILLIGAN, Paula
"Reflections on Gray and Other Patterns." [BellArk] (4:3) My-Je 88, p. 5.
"To Skate Away." [BellArk] (4:5) S-O 88, p. 1.
3560. MILLIRON, Kerry
"Godzilla Meets the Nuns." [Turnstile] (1:1) Wint 88, p. 48-49.
3561. MILLIS, Christopher
"Elegy." [SenR] (18:2) 88, p. 14.
"Invitation." [SenR] (18:2) 88, p. 17-18.
"Notice." [SenR] (18:2) 88, p. 16.
"Smelting" (for Ted). [SenR] (18:2) 88, p. 15.
"Still." [HangL] (53) 88, p. 30.
3562. MILLS, George
"Island." [TexasR] (9:3/4) Fall-Wint 88, p. 101.
3563. MILLS, Joe
"Winter." [Plain] (8:2) Wint 88, p. 27.
3564. MILLS, Ralph J., Jr.
"7/9." [TarRP] (28:1) Fall 88, p. 61.
"7/25." [Ascent] (14:2) 88, p. 15.
"8/10." [TarRP] (28:1) Fall 88, p. 62.
"Wind's Coming." [Ascent] (14:2) 88, p. 14-15.
3565. MILLS, Sparling
"Aunt Elizabeth 1880-1984." [CrossC] (10:2) 88, p. 10.
3566. MILNE, William S.
"Paradiso, First Canto, in Scots" (Lines 100-143, tr. of Dante). [AntigR] (73) Spr 88, p. 97, 99.
3567. MILNER, Ian
"Black Tiger" (tr. of Sylva Fischerova, w. Jarmila Milner). [Field] (38) Spr 88, p. 10-11.
"Jasmine Wind" (tr. of Sylva Fischerova, w. Jarmila Milner). [Field] (38) Spr 88, p. 9.
"Necessary" (tr. of Sylva Fischerova, w. Jarmila Milner). [Field] (38) Spr 88, p. 13-14.
"The Primer" (tr. of Sylva Fischerova, w. Jarmila Milner). [Field] (38) Spr 88, p. 12.
3568. MILNER, Jarmila
"Black Tiger" (tr. of Sylva Fischerova, w. Ian Milner). [Field] (38) Spr 88, p. 10-11.
"Jasmine Wind" (tr. of Sylva Fischerova, w. Ian Milner). [Field] (38) Spr 88, p. 9.
"Necessary" (tr. of Sylva Fischerova, w. Ian Milner). [Field] (38) Spr 88, p. 13-14.
"The Primer" (tr. of Sylva Fischerova, w. Ian Milner). [Field] (38) Spr 88, p. 12.
3569. MILOSZ, Czeslaw
"1945" (tr. by the author and Robert Hass). [Antaeus] (60) Spr 88, p. 264.
"An Appeal" (Brie-Compte-Robert, 1954, tr. by Robert Hass). [Verse] (5:1) F 88, p. 12-13.
"An Attempt to Describe the Last Skirmish of the Second World War" (to my brother, tr. of Aleksander Wat, w. Leonard Nathan). [Antaeus] (60) Spr 88, p. 62-63.
"Ballad of Levallois" (Barracks for the unemployed . . . , tr. by the author and Robert Hass). [Antaeus] (60) Spr 88, p. 258-259.

"Before a Weimar Portrait of Dürer" (in two variations, tr. of Aleksander Wat, w. Leonard Nathan). [Antaeus] (60) Spr 88, p. 60-61.
"A Chant" (Wilno, 1934, tr. by Robert Haas). [RiverS] (27) 88, p. 69-71.
"Childhood of a Poet" (tr. of Aleksander Wat, w. Leonard Nathan). [Antaeus] (60) Spr 88, p. 48.
"Dawns" (Wilno, 1932, tr. by Robert Haas). [RiverS] (27) 88, p. 67-68.
"Facing Bonnard" (tr. of Aleksander Wat, w. Leonard Nathan). [Antaeus] (60) Spr 88, p. 47.
"From Hesiod" (tr. of Aleksander Wat, w. Leonard Nathan). [Antaeus] (60) Spr 88, p. 64-65.
"How It Should Be in Heaven" (tr. by the author and Robert Hass). [Antaeus] (60) Spr 88, p. 261.
"In Milan" (tr. by the author and Robert Hass). [Antaeus] (60) Spr 88, p. 260.
"Leaves whirl, leaves swirl" (To Paul Eluard, tr. of Aleksander Wat, w. Leonard Nathan). [Antaeus] (60) Spr 88, p. 46.
"Ode III" (To Albert Vallette, tr. of Aleksander Wat, w. Leonard Nathan). [Antaeus] (60) Spr 88, p. 54-57.
"On Parting with My Wife, Janina" (tr. by the author and Robert Hass). [Antaeus] (60) Spr 88, p. 262-263.
"Paris Revisited" (tr. of Aleksander Wat, w. Leonard Nathan). [Antaeus] (60) Spr 88, p. 49-50.
"A Recollection" (tr. of Aleksander Wat, w. Leonard Nathan). [Antaeus] (60) Spr 88, p. 51-52.
"Taking a Walk" (tr. of Aleksander Wat, w. Leonard Nathan). [Antaeus] (60) Spr 88, p. 58-59.
"To a Roman, My Friend" (tr. of Aleksander Wat, w. Leonard Nathan). [Antaeus] (60) Spr 88, p. 53.
"A Treatise on Poetry" (2 fragments, tr. by the author w. Robert Hass). [AmerPoR] (17:3) My-Je 88, p. 7-8.

3570. MILTNER, Robert
"The Test-taker." [EngJ] (77:6) O 88, p. 86.

3571. MILTON, Marianne
"Foldings" (for Carmela Marian Ermilio Careri, 1897-1983). [SinW] (32) Sum 87, p. 105-106.
"You Watch for Me." [SinW] (32) Sum 87, p. 107-108.

MIN, Zhen
See ZHEN, Min

3572. MINAR, Scott
"Surprise." [DenQ] (22:3) Wint 88, p. 174.

3573. MINCZESKI, John
"A Poet in the Schools / Brainard, Minnesota." [Northeast] (ser. 4:7) Sum 88, p. 30-31.

3574. MINHINNICK, Robert
"Epilogue." [Verse] (5:3) N 88, p. 57.

3575. MINOR, James A.
"Haiku and Senryu" (4 poems). [WeberS] (5:2) Fall 88, p. 36.

3576. MINTON, Helena
"By the Merrimack." [TexasR] (9:3/4) Fall-Wint 88, p. 102.
"Turnip." [WestB] (21/22) 88, p. 138-139.

3577. MINTY, Judith
"Bringing My Father to the Yellow Dog." [PassN] (9:1) Wint 88, p. 13.

3578. MIRON, Gaston
"The Reign of Winter" (tr. by John Glassco). [Trans] (20) Spr 88, p. 172.

3579. MIRSKIN, Jerry
"Abandoning a Car in Brooklyn, the Thing about Angels." [PraS] (62:2) Sum 88, p. 64-65.
"End of the Season." [Blueline] (9:1/2) 88, p. 110.
"Grandmother." [PraS] (62:2) Sum 88, p. 63-64.
"Islamorada." [PraS] (62:2) Sum 88, p. 65-67.

3580. MISHKIN, Julia
"Schumann: Answer to Joachim." [PraS] (62:3) Fall 88, p. 19-20.

3581. MISHRA, Dipak
"From the Fortress of Loneliness" (tr. by the author). [Nimrod] (31:2) Spr-Sum 88, p. 94.

3582. MISRA, Soubhagyakumar
"The Crow" (tr. by the author). [Nimrod] (31:2) Spr-Sum 88, p. 92-93.

3583. MITCHAM, Judson
"Driving Home from the Clinic." [GettyR] (1:1) Wint 88, p. 19.
"Explanations." [GettyR] (1:1) Wint 88, p. 20-21.
"From a Young Man." [DenQ] (23:2) Fall 88, p. 52.
"From an Old Woman." [DenQ] (23:2) Fall 88, p. 51.
"On the Otis Redding Bridge" (Macon, Georgia). [AntR] (46:3) Sum 88, p. 358.
"Somewhere in Ecclesiastes." [GeoR] (42:1) Spr 88, p. 23-32.
3584. MITCHELL, Felicia
"Leda and the Swan." [SpoonRQ] (13:3) Sum 88, p. 64.
3585. MITCHELL, Nora
"Replay" (for Judy Couffer, 1955-1986). [Ploughs] (14:1) 88, p. 90-91.
"Stars Sleep on Cheju Island." [HawaiiR] (12:2, #24) Fall 88, p. 110-111.
3586. MITCHELL, Roger
"After the Big Wind." [PoetryNW] (29:2) Sum 88, p. 42-43.
"Early September." [MassR] (29:2) Sum 88, p. 223.
"Fare Well" (for Dean and Cornelia). [MichQR] (27:4) Fall 88, p. 620.
"Loving the Move." [Crazy] (34) Spr 88, p. 53-54.
"The Meadow." [Thrpny] (35) Fall 88, p. 13.
"Once Upon a Time." [Crazy] (34) Spr 88, p. 55.
"Seeing Some Feral Goats." [Ploughs] (14:4) 88, p. 123-124.
"Sneaking Out at Night." [PoetryNW] (29:2) Sum 88, p. 43.
3587. MITCHELL, Stephen
"Tao Te Ching" (Selections: 46, 53, 57, 60, 61, 62, tr. of Lao-tzu). [Zyzzyva] (4:3) Fall 88, p. 87-90.
"Untitled: We say release, and radiance, and roses" (tr. of Rainer Maria Rilke). [Thrpny] (35) Fall 88, p. 14.
3588. MITCHELL, Susan
"Fragment of a Woman from Kos." [Nat] (246:23) 11 Je 88, p. 834.
3589. MITCHELL, Wendy
"Recovery" (Commended, 15th Anniversary Competition). [StoneC] (16:1/2) Fall-Wint 88-89, unpaged front matter.
3590. MITCHNER, Gary
"Louise and Louis, 1932." [NewRep] (198:25) 20 Je 88, p. 34.
"Not Dying on the Morning of the Nativity." [NewRep] (199:11/12) 12-19 S 88, p. 38.
"Shaw Poems." [Shen] (38:3) 88, p. 52-55.
3591. MIZER, Ray
"In the Beginning Was." [BellArk] (4:4) Jl-Ag 88, p. 9.
"My Country, Were It of Thee." [WebR] (13:2) Fall 88, p. 86.
"One to Get Ready." [BellArk] (4:6) N-D 88, p. 10.
"Seemingly Everywhere Desperate." [BellArk] (4:3) My-Je 88, p. 6.
"Seemingly Everywhere Desperate." [BellArk] (4:4) Jl-Ag 88, p. 4.
"To a Partner: Seasonal Report" (as a certain W.S. might have versed it). [BellArk] (4:6) N-D 88, p. 6.
3592. MLADINIC, Peter
"Mother on a Wednesday Afternoon." [MSS] (6:2) 88, p. 93-94.
3593. MOE, H. D.
"At an Intersection Poetry Reading." [RedBass] (13) 88, p. 27.
"Gertrude Fozdick." [RedBass] (13) 88, p. 56.
"On the Guru FunnyFarm." [AlphaBS] (4) D 88, p. 16.
3594. MOEN, Irvin
"Wren." [Spirit] (9:1) 88, p. 101-1105.
3595. MOFFEIT, Tony
"Charley Plymell, the Oxybiotic, & the Buffalo Bebop Blues 9/20/87." [AlphaBS] (4) D 88, p. 2-3.
"Maybe Coyote, Maybe Crow." [Bogg] (59) 88, p. 23.
"Robert Johnson." [AlphaBS] (4) D 88, p. 4.
3596. MOHAN, Devinder
"The Claim Inside Me." [Nimrod] (31:2) Spr-Sum 88, p. 59.
"The Edge." [Nimrod] (31:2) Spr-Sum 88, p. 63.
"Sati: Roop Kanwar." [Nimrod] (31:2) Spr-Sum 88, p. 60-62.
3597. MOHRBACHER, Bob
"Prehistoric Pink." [CrabCR] (5:3) Fall 88, p. 6.
"Underwater Sleep." [CrabCR] (5:3) Fall 88, p. 6.
3598. MOIR, James M.
"The Winter of No Snow." [PraF] (9:4) Wint 88-89, p. 50-51.

3599. MOLDAW, Carol
"64 Panoramic Way." [Agni] (26) 88, p. 51-52.
"Transmarine." [Agni] (26) 88, p. 53.
MOLEN, Robert vander
See VanderMOLEN, Robert
3600. MÖLLER-SOLER, María Lourdes
"A una Naudora d'Estores Bereberes." [LetFem] (14:1/2) Primavera-Otoño 88, p. 120.
"Cicatrius espirituals." [LetFem] (14:1/2) Primavera-Otoño 88, p. 120-121.
"Davant un Anunci per a una Càtedra de Filologia Llatinoamericana." [LetFem] (14:1/2) Primavera-Otoño 88, p. 121.
"Doneu-me la Vostra Veu." [LetFem] (14:1/2) Primavera-Otoño 88, p. 121.
"Els ulls plens." [LetFem] (14:1/2) Primavera-Otoño 88, p. 122.
3601. MOLLOHAN, Terrie
"Nesting" (Womanhood — Phase II: Approaching the Middle). [Pembroke] (20) 88, p. 281.
3602. MOLONEY, Karen Marguerite
"The Truant Officer Recalls Sweet Maggie." [Jacaranda] (3:2) Fall-Wint 88, p. 32-33.
3603. MOLTON, Warren Lane
"Funeral." [ChrC] (105:28) 5 O 88, p. 860.
3604. MONAGHAN, Patricia
"Burials." [NegC] (8:3) 88, p. 140-141.
"Neither Inviting Nor Repelling" (From the letters of Paula Mondersohn-Becker). [NegC] (8:3) 88, p. 72-73.
"Running with Whales." [BellR] (11:1) Spr 88, p. 50-51.
"Still Lives." [BellR] (11:1) Spr 88, p. 51.
3605. MONAHAN, Jean
"Followed by Children Who Threw Stones." [Shen] (38:2) 88, p. 21-22.
3606. MONETTE, Paul
"To GB from Tuscany." [MichQR] (27:4) Fall 88, p. 603-604.
3607. MONROE, Debra Frigen
"Creed." [DenQ] (22:3) Wint 88, p. 101.
"Thanksgiving." [DenQ] (22:3) Wint 88, p. 102.
3608. MONROE, Melissa
"Almanac." [LitR] (31:3) Spr 88, p. 274-275.
"The Fire-Eater" (tr. of Ernst Herbeck). [BlackWR] (14:2) Spr 88, p. 65.
3609. MONTAGUE, John
"Deer Park." [Antaeus] (60) Spr 88, p. 205-206.
"Hearth Song" (For Seamus Heaney). [Antaeus] (60) Spr 88, p. 203-204.
"Migrant Poet" (tr. of Donncha O Corrain). [Antaeus] (60) Spr 88, p. 295.
3610. MONTALE, Eugenio
"Children Dancing" (tr. by Antony Oldknow). [WebR] (13:1) Spr 88, p. 29.
"Don't Ask for Words" (tr. by Antony Oldknow). [WebR] (13:1) Spr 88, p. 28.
"Falsetto" (tr. by Antony Oldknow). [WebR] (13:1) Spr 88, p. 27-28.
"I Know Times" (tr. by Antony Oldknow). [WebR] (13:1) Spr 88, p. 30.
"I've Often Met" (tr. by Antony Oldknow). [WebR] (13:1) Spr 88, p. 29.
"Some Morning Perhaps" (tr. by Antony Oldknow). [WebR] (13:1) Spr 88, p. 30.
3611. MONTEIRO, George
"Ah, a Sonnet" (tr. of Fernando Pessoa). [NewOR] (15:2) Sum 88, p. 41.
"Clearly Non-*Campos*" (tr. of Fernando Pessoa). [NewOR] (15:2) Sum 88, p. 95.
3612. MONTEJO, Victor
"The Dog" (tr. by Victor Perera). [HangL] (52) 88, p. 67.
"El Perro." [HangL] (52) 88, p. 66.
3613. MONTEZ, Susan
"Part Tapestry." [StoneC] (16:1/2) Fall-Wint 88-89, p. 63.
"The Scale from Queens, or, I Refuse a Large World." [ArtfulD] (14/15) Fall 88, p. 103.
"War Memorial for Yugoslav Partisans." [HampSPR] Wint 88, p. 47.
3614. MOODY, Shirley
"The Guardian of Dinosaurs." [SouthernPR] (28:1) Spr 88, p. 59-60.
"The Ties That Bind Us One to Another." [Pembroke] (20) 88, p. 232.
3615. MOOERS, Vernon
"Raiders of the Outport." [PottPort] (9) 88, p. 21.
3616. MOOLTEN, David
"Daybreak in Deer Country." [HawaiiR] (12:1, #23) Spr 88, p. 5.

"Fishing on Sunapee While Darwin's Ghost Watches, Unheeded." [HawaiiR] (12:1, #23) Spr 88, p. 4.
"For Steve." [TarRP] (27:2) Spr 88, p. 13-14.
"Photograph." [Boulevard] (3:2/3) Fall 88, p. 157-158.

3617. MOORE, Abd al-Hayy
"A House Somewhere." [Zyzzyva] (4:1) Spr 88, p. 39-43.

MOORE, Anne Forsythe
See FORSYTHE-MOORE, Anne

3618. MOORE, Barbara
"Imagining Freedom." [MinnR] (NS 30/31) Spr-Fall 88, p. 7-8.
"November." [NoDaQ] (56:3) Sum 88, p. 91.

MOORE, Daniel
See MOORE, Abd al-Hayy

3619. MOORE, Edward
"Ministry of Sound." [NewAW] (4) Fall 88, p. 86.
"Vigil." [NewAW] (4) Fall 88, p. 85.

3620. MOORE, Ellen E.
"Running." [CreamCR] (12:2) Sum 88, p. 231-232.

3621. MOORE, Frank D.
"Language Lesson." [PaintedB] (36) 88, p. 48.
"The Need to Sing." [PaintedB] (36) 88, p. 49.

3622. MOORE, Honor
"Poem for the End." [YellowS] (26) Spr 88, p. 34-36.
"Sitting for Inge Morath." [NewRep] (199:20) 14 N 88, p. 41.

3623. MOORE, Jacqueline
"And There Was Light." [Lactuca] (11) O 88, p. 10.
"Spruce World." [Lactuca] (11) O 88, p. 11.
"We Count the Minutes." [Lactuca] (11) O 88, p. 11.

3624. MOORE, Janice T.
"Sunday Afternoons." [ChatR] (8:2) Wint 88, p. 77.

3625. MOORE, Jonathan
"I was on my way over to 3620 humanities." [Abraxas] (37) 88, p. 52-53.
"Maria Esta Soñando en Tejas." [Abraxas] (37) 88, p. 54.

3626. MOORE, Lenard D.
"Flounders." [Callaloo] (10:4 #33) Fall 87, p. 560.
"Haiku: Pulling the line in" (The 14th Kansas Poetry Contest, Fourth Honorable Mention). [LittleBR] (5:2) Wint 88-89, p. 70.
"Message to Etheridge Knight." [PaintedB] (32/33) 88, p. 139.
"No Fairytale Phobia." [Crosscur] (7:4) 88, p. 149.

3627. MOORE, Lisa
"Dreaming of Immortality." [GrahamHR] (11) Spr 88, p. 12.

3628. MOORE, Marianne
"Ein Grab" (tr. by Paul Celan). [Acts] (8/9) 88, p. 120.
"A Grave." [Acts] (8/9) 88, p. 119.
"A Grave" (tr. of Paul Celan's German translation by Robert Kelly). [Acts] (8/9) 88, p. 121.

3629. MOORE, Mary
"Memorial Day, 1985, San Francisco." [NegC] (8:3) 88, p. 114-117.

3630. MOORE, Miles David
"Nouvelle Cuisine." [Bogg] (59) 88, p. 40.

3631. MOORE, Opal J.
"Magdalene Say." [PoetL] (83:2) Sum 88, p. 36-37.

3632. MOORE, Richard
"Aglow." [Hudson] (41:2) Sum 88, p. 335.
"Aubade." [LightY] ('88/9) 88, p. 113.
"Blimps and Nightingales." [LightY] ('88/9) 88, p. 103-105.
"Dry Season." [CumbPR] (7:2) Spr 88, p. 44.
"The Embrace." [Hudson] (41:2) Sum 88, p. 333.
"For Galileo." [CumbPR] (7:2) Spr 88, p. 43.
"In the Sunset." [Hudson] (41:2) Sum 88, p. 334.
"Spring." [LightY] ('88/9) 88, p. 37.
"The Stunning." [Hudson] (41:2) Sum 88, p. 333-334.
"Symbols." [CumbPR] (7:2) Spr 88, p. 45.
"Transformation." [Hudson] (41:2) Sum 88, p. 334-335.

3633. MOORE, Sheila
"Seventeen." [MinnR] (NS 30/31) Spr-Fall 88, p. 53-54.

3634. MOORE, Todd
"Babe's." [Lactuca] (9) F 88, p. 16.
"Fucking Around." [WormR] (28:1, #109) 88, p. 30.
"Helping My." [Bogg] (60) 88, p. 11.
"Zenith." [Bogg] (59) 88, p. 37-38.
3635. MOORE, Victoria
"Dream Lovers." [WilliamMR] (26:1) Spr 88, p. 19-20.
3636. MOORHEAD, Andrea
"Map of Gold Leaves." [Os] (26) 88, p. 18.
"Migration North." [StoneC] (15:3/4) Spr-Sum 88, p. 20.
"Niagara in Flames." [Os] (27) 88, p. 26.
"Niagara Transformations." [Os] (27) 88, p. 4.
"On the Road to Joliette." [StoneC] (15:3/4) Spr-Sum 88, p. 20.
"Ontario Wind." [Os] (26) 88, p. 17.
"Open Rain." [Os] (27) 88, p. 14.
"A Poem to Dispel Night." [Os] (27) 88, p. 15.
"Shadow of Speech." [Confr] (37/38) Spr-Sum 88, p. 232.
"The Snows of Troy" (A book of poems. A Special Supplement to OSIRIS for 1988). [Os] 88, 93 p.
3637. MOOSE, Ruth
"Artist's Mouth, Found Poem." [Poem] (59) My 88, p. 46.
"Gale River, New Hampshire." [Poem] (59) My 88, p. 44.
"Making the Bed." [Poem] (59) My 88, p. 45.
3638. MORA, Pat
"Tomás Rivera." [BilingR] (13:1/2) Ja-Ag 86, c1988, p. 100-101.
3639. MORALES, Rosario
"Robles, M'Hija, Robles!" [HangL] (52) 88, p. 68.
3640. MORAN, Duncan
"Children's Games." [HiramPoR] (44/45) Spr-Wint 88, p. 34.
3641. MORAN, Mary
"First Admission." [SinW] (36) Wint 88-89, p. 15.
3642. MORDECAI, Pamela
"Certifiable." [Callaloo] (11:2, #35) Spr 88, p. 253-254.
3643. MORDENSKI, Jan
"Morning." [PassN] (9:2) Sum 88, p. 7.
"Singing in the Stone Rook Pub, Desmond Conchobor" (from Sean-nos Singing, a series of poems). [Nimrod] (32:1) Fall-Wint 88, p. 27-28.
"Song of Nora Breege, the Miller's Daughter" (from Sean-nos Singing, a series of poems). [Nimrod] (32:1) Fall-Wint 88, p. 29.
"The Song of the Drayman, Ciaran Cordu" (from Sean-nos Singing, a series of poems). [Nimrod] (32:1) Fall-Wint 88, p. 26.
"Song of the Gypsy, Breena Bothar'" (from Sean-nos Singing, a series of poems). [Nimrod] (32:1) Fall-Wint 88, p. 27.
"Song of the Priest, Mihail Sheamais" (from Sean-nos Singing, a series of poems). [Nimrod] (32:1) Fall-Wint 88, p. 28-29.
"Valentine." [AntigR] (73) Spr 88, p. 41-42.
3644. MOREAU, June
"I Tremble." [StoneC] (16:1/2) Fall-Wint 88-89, p. 12.
3645. MOREHEAD, Barbara
"Good-byes." [LitR] (31:2) Wint 88, p. 234.
3646. MOREHEAD, Maureen
"Walking the Beaches for Michael." [SouthernPR] (28:1) Spr 88, p. 10.
3647. MOREJON, Nancy
"Alluvion" (tr. by Kathleen Weaver). [Callaloo] (11:1, #34) Wint 88, p. 33.
"El Aluvión." [Callaloo] (11:1, #34) Wint 88, p. 32.
"La Ciudad Expuesta." [Callaloo] (11:1, #34) Wint 88, p. 30.
"Encounter" (tr. by Kathleen Weaver). [Callaloo] (11:1, #34) Wint 88, p. 35.
"Encuentro." [Callaloo] (11:1, #34) Wint 88, p. 34.
"Exhibited City" (tr. by Kathleen Weaver). [Callaloo] (11:1, #34) Wint 88, p. 31.
"Ferocious Cage" (tr. by Kathleen Weaver and Robert Baldock). [Callaloo] (11:1, #34) Wint 88, p. 37.
"Jaula Feroz." [Callaloo] (11:1, #34) Wint 88, p. 36.
"Richard Brought His Flute" (tr. by Lois Wright). [Callaloo] (11:1, #34) Wint 88, p. 24-29.
"Richard Trajo su Flauta." [Callaloo] (11:1, #34) Wint 88, p. 18-23.

3648. MORGAN, Edwin
"Dido." [Verse] (5:1) F 88, p. 43-45.
"The Gurney." [Antaeus] (60) Spr 88, p. 242.
3649. MORGAN, Frederick
"The Burial." [TarRP] (28:1) Fall 88, p. 56.
"Washington Square" (The Mary Elinore Smith Poetry Prize). [AmerS] (57:3) Sum 88, p. 369-372.
3650. MORGAN, Jean
"Amanda, Visited from the Mainland." [Pembroke] (20) 88, p. 133.
3651. MORGAN, John
"Approaching the Whitestone Bridge." [NoAmR] (273:3) D 88, p. 46.
"Neptune's Daughter." [KenR] (NS 10:4) Fall 88, p. 19-20.
"The Third Walk: McKinley Park Hotel to Mount Healy Overlook." [KenR] (NS 10:4) Fall 88, p. 20-21.
"Walking Past Midnight" (For Linda Schandelmeier). [KenR] (NS 10:4) Fall 88, p. 18-19.
3652. MORGAN, Robert
"Fire's Feast." [VirQR] (64:3) Sum 88, p. 442-443.
"Hawthornden Castle." [OntR] (28) Spr-Sum 88, p. 97.
"Heaven." [IndR] (11:3) Sum 88, p. 28.
"Mica Country." [Atlantic] (261:5) My 88, p. 58.
"Neighbors." [Atlantic] (261:6) Je 88, p. 83.
"Sidney Lanier Dies in Tryon 1881." [OntR] (28) Spr-Sum 88, p. 98-99.
"Sourwood Honey." [SouthernHR] (22:4) Fall 88, p. 386.
"Uranium." [VirQR] (64:3) Sum 88, p. 441-442.
3653. MORI, Kyoko
"Arriving Through a Dream." [SingHM] (15) 88, p. 15-16.
"Excellent Birds" (for my mother, eighteen years after her death). [SingHM] (15) 88, p. 17-18.
"Family Pictures: For My Cousin Kazumi." [SingHM] (15) 88, p. 24-25.
"Grandmother." [SingHM] (15) 88, p. 23.
"Heat in October." [Calyx] (11:2/3) Fall 88, p. 82-83.
"The Language of Feathers." [SingHM] (15) 88, p. 19.
"Points of Reference." [SingHM] (15) 88, p. 11-14.
"The Progress of Spring." [SingHM] (15) 88, p. 26-27.
"Settling In." [SingHM] (15) 88, p. 33-37.
"Talk-Story." [SingHM] (15) 88, p. 22.
"To My Ancestral Spirits." [SingHM] (15) 88, p. 9-10.
"Toward Harvest." [SingHM] (15) 88, p. 30-32.
"Walking Among Thistles." [SingHM] (15) 88, p. 28-29.
"The Women in My Life." [SingHM] (15) 88, p. 20-21.
3654. MORIARTY, Laura
"Cuenca." [Conjunc] (12) 88, p. 50-52.
"Fitting this shot against one including." [Conjunc] (12) 88, p. 50.
"In the new environment in real time." [Conjunc] (12) 88, p. 49.
"We here become citizens." [Conjunc] (12) 88, p. 49.
3655. MORICE, Sylvia
"You Do Not Know Me." [PottPort] (9) 88, p. 36.
3656. MORIN, Edward
"Bodhisattva" (tr. of Bei Dao, w. Dennis Ding). [WebR] (13:2) Fall 88, p. 18.
"Distance" (tr. of Cai Qi-jiao, w. Dennis Ding). [TriQ] (71) Wint 88, p. 130.
"Going Astray" (tr. of Wang Xiao-ni, w. Dennis Ding). [WebR] (13:2) Fall 88, p. 17.
"The Pearl" (in Chinese and English, tr. of Cai Qi-jiao, w. Dennis Ding). [HawaiiR] (12:1, #23) Spr 88, p. 90-91.
"Poetry" (tr. of Cai Qi-jiao, w. Dai Fang). [TriQ] (72) Spr-Sum 88, p. 171.
"Repairing the Wall" (tr. of Min Zhen, w. Dennis Ding). [WebR] (13:1) Spr 88, p. 40.
"Scenery" (tr. of Gu Cheng, w. Dennis Ding). [WindO] (50) Aut 88, p. 39.
"A Self-Portrait" (tr. of Shu Ting, w. Dennis Ding). [TriQ] (72) Spr-Sum 88, p. 156.
"The Wind Is Roaring" (tr. of Xiao-ni Wang, w. Dennis Ding). [Spirit] (9:1) 88, p. 100.
3657. MORISON, Ted
"Apple Doppleganger." [ChatR] (8:2) Wint 88, p. 102.
"Habit." [SouthernHR] (22:1) Wint 88, p. 47.

3658. MORITZ, A. F.
"The All-Night Café." [Agni] (27) 88, p. 210-211.
"Popular Songs." [YaleR] (78:1) Aut 88, p. 83.
"The Viaduct." [LitR] (31:4) Sum 88, p. 471-472.
3659. MORLEY, Hilda
"As a Wave Rises." [Sequoia] (32:1) Spr-Sum 88, p. 12-13.
"Notes from Easthampton, March." [Sequoia] (32:1) Spr-Sum 88, p. 14.
"Out of Nothing." [Sulfur] (8:1, #22) Spr 88, p. 149-151.
"Under the Maples." [Sequoia] (32:1) Spr-Sum 88, p. 15.
3660. MORLEY, Salvadore
"About 7:00, I Think." [YellowS] (26) Spr 88, p. 8.
3661. MORRILL, Donald
"Little Anodynes." [HighP] (3:2) Fall 88, p. 107.
3662. MORRIS, James Ryan
"The Alley Cat." [Jacaranda] (3:1) Wint 88, p. 109-110.
"The Curse." [Jacaranda] (3:1) Wint 88, p. 110.
3663. MORRIS, Jenny
"Sane, Plain, and Tedious to Know." [LightY] ('88/9) 88, p. 124.
"The Terracotta Flower Pot." [LightY] ('88/9) 88, p. 42.
3664. MORRIS, Leslie
"The Dream (Y Breuddwyd)" (from the Welsh of Dafydd ap Gwilym, fl. 1340). [Atlantic] (261:6) Je 88, p. 92.
3665. MORRIS, Nicky
"A Sunny Day." [SinW] (34) Spr 88, p. 43.
3666. MORRIS, Peter
"Getting Cable." [JINJPo] (10:1/2) 88, p. 30.
"Headlines." [PoetryE] (25) Spr 88, p. 103.
"Imaginary Pains." [PoetryE] (25) Spr 88, p. 105.
"Passengers." [PoetryE] (25) Spr 88, p. 104.
"Pirates Cry" (Special Section: 27 poems). [WormR] (28:4, #112) 88, p. 105-118.
"The Shroud." [JINJPo] (10:1/2) 88, p. 31.
3667. MORRIS, Richard
"Spontaneous Love Song of Round Mountain" (May 14, during the romance and drought of '86). [AlphaBS] (4) D 88, p. 43.
3668. MORRIS, Sawnie
"Through Daylight" (for Sally). [SinW] (33) Fall 87, p. 82-83.
"Your Passing." [SinW] (34) Spr 88, p. 47-48.
3669. MORRISON, Blake
"Him." [PartR] (55:1) Wint 88, p. 59-60.
"Spring." [PartR] (55:3) Sum 88, p. 474.
3670. MORRISON, Carol
"Phoenix." [RagMag] (6:2) Fall 88, p. 60.
"Stains." [RagMag] (6:2) Fall 88, p. 61.
3671. MORRISON, Eliza
"Wading at Cayes." [Prima] (11/12) 88, p. 38.
3672. MORRISON, Lillian
"Goodbye Forever." [LightY] ('88/9) 88, p. 214.
"This Air" (Alfred, New York). [Confr] (37/38) Spr-Sum 88, p. 226.
3673. MORRISON, Madison
"OKC." [CharR] (14:2) Fall 88, p. 96.
3674. MORRISON, R. H.
"8. This body given to me — what shall I do" (tr. of Osip Mandelstam). [SouthernR] (24:3) Sum 88, p. 539.
"9. Sadness beyond expression" (tr. of Osip Mandelstam). [SouthernR] (24:3) Sum 88, p. 540.
"175. You went by through a cloud of mist" (tr. of Osip Mandelstam). [SouthernR] (24:3) Sum 88, p. 540.
"341. Mounds of human heads recede into the distance" (tr. of Osip Mandelstam). [SouthernR] (24:3) Sum 88, p. 541.
"352. Don't make comparisons: what lives" (tr. of Osip Mandelstam). [SouthernR] (24:3) Sum 88, p. 541.
"457 (xv). Prophetic breath of my verses' life-giving spirit" (tr. of Osip Mandelstam). [SouthernR] (24:3) Sum 88, p. 541.
"Here Toads That Fill One with Disgust" (tr. of Osip Mandelstam). [LitR] (31:2) Wint 88, p. 155.
"In My Perception Winter" (tr. of Osip Mandelstam). [LitR] (31:4) Sum 88, p. 449.

"In the Mist I Could Not Feel Your Image" (tr. of Osip Mandelstam). [LitR] (31:2) Wint 88, p. 155.
"Let the Names of Flourishing Cities" (tr. of Osip Mandelstam). [LitR] (31:4) Sum 88, p. 448.
"Light Vapor Was Melting Away in the Frosty Air" (tr. of Osip Mandelstam). [LitR] (31:4) Sum 88, p. 449.
"My Silent Dream, My Every Minute's Dream" (tr. of Osip Mandelstam). [LitR] (31:4) Sum 88, p. 448.

3675. MORRO, Henry J.
"Somoza's Teeth." [Jacaranda] (3:2) Fall-Wint 88, p. 113.

3676. MORROW, Bradford
"Bestiary." [Bomb] (25) Fall 88, p. 68-69.

3677. MORROW, M. E.
"From Your Porch on the Bay" (Naples, Florida — 1987). [AmerS] (57:2) Spr 88, p. 262.

3678. MORSE, Cheryl
"At Point White." [KanQ] (20:1/2) Wint-Spr 88, p. 91.

3679. MORSE, Ruth
"Gambit." [SouthernR] (24:3) Sum 88, p. 554-555.
"Habit." [SouthernR] (24:3) Sum 88, p. 553-554.
"Lover and Cat." [SouthernR] (24:3) Sum 88, p. 555-556.
"Through a Glass, Darkly." [SouthernR] (24:3) Sum 88, p. 552.
"Yahrzeit." [SouthernR] (24:3) Sum 88, p. 553.

3680. MORT, Jo-Ann
"Rachel's Narration." [Stand] (29:1) Wint 87-88, p. 54-55.

3681. MORTUS, Cindy
"The Chorus Is Always Female." [Poem] (59) My 88, p. 12-13.
"Conversation with Jack." [Poem] (59) My 88, p. 11.
"Mr. Morse Remembered." [SpoonRQ] (13:3) Sum 88, p. 48.
"Ruby Red Feather." [SpoonRQ] (13:3) Sum 88, p. 46-47.
"Tuning." [Poem] (59) My 88, p. 10.

3682. MOSDAL, Kathy
"Bleached and peeling dock." [Amelia] (5:2, #13) 88, p. 18.

3683. MOSER, Norm
"Fugue for Rexroth." [Pembroke] (20) 88, p. 195.
"Going and Returning" (Campesino's statement near end of "When Mountains Tremble" film). [AlphaBS] (3) Je 88, p. 62-63.
"El Rito Poem, or, The Sound of One Flapping Door." [Pembroke] (20) 88, p. 196.

3684. MOSES, Daniel David
"Fall Fair Moon." [Event] (17:1) Spr 88, p. 40-41.
"Of Course the Sky Does Not Close." [Dandel] (15:1) Spr-Sum 88, p. 12-13.

3685. MOSES, W. R.
"A Spurt of Literary Criticism." [LightY] ('88/9) 88, p. 183.

3686. MOSLER, Charlie
"New Horror Movies." [Footwork] ('88) 88, p. 71-72.
"Some People Think It's All Right to Kill a Rabbit But Not a Cat." [Lips] (14) 88, p. 21.

3687. MOSLEY, Walter
"Out Behind My House." [Abraxas] (37) 88, p. 73.

3688. MOSS, Greg
"Hide and Seek." [AmerS] (57:3) Sum 88, p. 419-420.

3689. MOSS, Stanley
"April, Beijing." [Poetry] (152:1) Ap 88, p. 28-29.
"The Decadent Poets of Kyoto." [Poetry] (143, i.e. 153:1) O 88, p. 25.
"A Gambler's Story." [Poetry] (152:1) Ap 88, p. 29.
"In Defense of a Friend." [VirQR] (64:3) Sum 88, p. 439.
"The Lace Makers." [Poetry] (143, i.e. 153:1) O 88, p. 26-27.
"The Public Gardens of Munich." [VirQR] (64:3) Sum 88, p. 440-441.

3690. MOSS, Thylias
"Interpretation of a Poem by Frost." [Epoch] (37:2) 88, p. 112.
"Landscape with Saxophonist." [GrahamHR] (11) Spr 88, p. 50.
"One for All Newborns." [Callaloo] (10:4 #33) Fall 87, p. 559.
"Spilled Sugar." [GrahamHR] (11) Spr 88, p. 51.
"The Warmth of Hot Chocolate." [Epoch] (37:2) 88, p. 114-115.
"Washing Bread." [Epoch] (37:2) 88, p. 113.

3691. MOTION, Andrew
"Lovely Day." [YaleR] (77:3) Spr 88, p. 373.
3692. MOTT, Elaine
"The Bumblebee." [MemphisSR] (8:2) Spr 88, p. 95.
"Grandmother's Bureau Drawer." [CreamCR] (12:2) Sum 88, p. 233-234.
"Invitation to the Mountains." [MidwQ] (30:1) Aut 88, p. 78.
"An Opera Broadcast, 1930." [MemphisSR] (8:2) Spr 88, p. 96.
"Persephone." [CreamCR] (12:2) Sum 88, p. 236.
"Planting by Moon Signs." [Spirit] (9:1) 88, p. 83.
"The Vampire's Daughter." [CreamCR] (12:2) Sum 88, p. 235.
3693. MOTT, Michael
"Bergamo." [TarRP] (28:1) Fall 88, p. 14.
"Letter from St. Antonin Noble Val." [TarRP] (28:1) Fall 88, p. 14.
"Nsangweni Cave Paintings." [KenR] (NS 10:2) Spr 88, p. 112.
"Roads." [TarRP] (28:1) Fall 88, p. 13.
"Stendhal's Miss Appleby." [TarRP] (27:2) Spr 88, p. 22.
"Storm Over Lake Como." [WilliamMR] (26:1) Spr 88, p. 107.
"Y'iebo." [KenR] (NS 10:2) Spr 88, p. 112.
3694. MOURÉ, Erin
"Crocuses." [WestCR] (22:4) Spr 87, i.e. 88, p. 37.
"Crocuses, Again." [WestCR] (22:4) Spr 87, i.e. 88, p. 38.
"Crocuses, Lastly." [WestCR] (22:4) Spr 87, i.e. 88, p. 39.
"Order, or Red Ends." [CapilR] (48) 88, p. 34-39.
"Planes Over Iceland, or Modern Travel." [CapilR] (48) 88, p. 45-47.
"The Rainshore." [MalR] (84) S 88, p. 137-157.
"Seebe." [PraF] (9:1) Spr 88, p. 13-15.
"Shutter Door." [CapilR] (48) 88, p. 40-43.
"Style, or Courage." [CapilR] (48) 88, p. 48.
"This Ice, or the Aunts." [CapilR] (48) 88, p. 44.
"The Trepanation" (cinq morceaux en forme de poire). [PraF] (9:3) Aut 88, p. 38-43.
"Trix." [CapilR] (48) 88, p. 49.
3695. MUCHHALA, C. J.
"Looking Back." [Amelia] (4:4, #11) 88, p. 75.
3696. MUELLER, Ilze Klavina
"The Admirer" (tr. of Gunars Salins). [Vis] (26) 88, p. 28.
3697. MUELLER, Jenny
"Memorandum." [TriQ] (72) Spr-Sum 88, p. 164-165.
"Shower and Sun." [TriQ] (72) Spr-Sum 88, p. 166.
3698. MUELLER, Lisel
"After Your Death." [PoetryNW] (29:4) Wint 88-89, p. 8-9.
"Aphasia." [PoetryNW] (29:4) Wint 88-89, p. 9.
"The Artist." [NewL] (55:1) Fall 88, p. 72.
"Balancing Acts." [PoetryNW] (29:4) Wint 88-89, p. 10.
"Cavalleria Rusticana." [Poetry] (151:6) Mr 88, p. 455-456.
"Film Script." [OhioR] (42) 88, p. 72.
"Joy." [GeoR] (42:3) Fall 88, p. 486.
"Missing the Dead." [Poetry] (151:6) Mr 88, p. 453.
"Muse." [NewL] (55:1) Fall 88, p. 73.
"Paul Delvaux: The Village of the Mermaids" (Oil on canvas, 1943). [OhioR] (42) 88, p. 73.
"Poem for My Birthday." [Poetry] (151:6) Mr 88, p. 454-455.
"Pulic Service Announcement." [Poetry] (151:6) Mr 88, p. 456.
"Three Poems About the Voiceless." [PoetryNW] (29:4) Wint 88-89, p. 7-8.
"Triage." [GeoR] (42:3) Fall 88, p. 485.
"Writing in the Eighties." [Poetry] (151:6) Mr 88, p. 454.
3699. MUELLER, Paul Kennedy
"The Cardinal and the Locust" (Vicksburg, Mississippi). [SmPd] (25:3) Fall 88, p. 38.
"Still Life with Nicked Chin." [CarolQ] (41:1) Fall 88, p. 42.
3700. MUISE, Louise A.
"Ode to a First Baseman." [EngJ] (77:3) Mr 88, p. 88.
3701. MUKHOPADHYAY, Vijaya
"Companion" (tr. by Sunil B. Ray and Carolyne Wright, w. the author). [Nimrod] (31:2) Spr-Sum 88, p. 31.

"Monday's Hand on Your Shoulder" (tr. by Sunil B. Ray and Carolyne Wright, w. the author). [Nimrod] (31:2) Spr-Sum 88, p. 32.

3702. MULDOON, Paul
"Disillusion Street" (tr. of Michael Davitt). [Antaeus] (60) Spr 88, p. 296.

3703. MULLIN, Anne
"Walking Too Slowly." [TexasR] (9:3/4) Fall-Wint 88, p. 103-104.

3704. MULLINS, Cecil J.
"Mid-Winter." [CapeR] (23:1) Spr 88, p. 50.

3705. MULLINS, Hilary
"Witness." [SinW] (32) Sum 87, p. 18-22.

3706. MULRANE, Scott H.
"Adieu." [Poem] (59) My 88, p. 31.
"Enough" (for K.). [Poem] (59) My 88, p. 30.
"Fishing on the Gower." [Poem] (59) My 88, p. 29.

3707. MUNFORD, Christopher
"Returning at Night from Far Rockaway." [Footwork] ('88) 88, p. 80.

3708. MUNGANYE
"Black and White." [PraS] (62:4) Wint 88-89, p. 76-77.
"Old Man." [PraS] (62:4) Wint 88-89, p. 74-75.

3709. MUÑIZ, Lucio
"Ahora que hay campanas." [Mairena] (10:25) 88, p. 131.

3710. MUÑOZ, Alira
"Invocacion en Lengua Yoruba" (Spanish tr. of Anonymous work). [Areíto] (1:3) Jl 88, inside front cover.
"Iyuba" (Reiterando homenaje, Spanish tr. of Anonymous work). [Areíto] (1:3) Jl 88, inside back cover.

3711. MUNRO, Darren
"From the Limb." [PottPort] (9) 88, p. 45.

3712. MUNSO, Felix
"On the Job" (After the Labour and Tory Party conferences). [LightY] ('88/9) 88, p. 226-227.

3713. MUOLO, Paul
"Gangsters on Their Holiday." [LittleM] (15:3/4) 88, p. 25.
"Lost in the West." [LittleM] (15:3/4) 88, p. 29.
"The N.Y. — D.C. Line." [MinnR] (NS 30/31) Spr-Fall 88, p. 22.
"Poem: If I take enough pills in the bathroom." [LittleM] (15:3/4) 88, p. 28.
"Poem: They are still here in America." [LittleM] (15:3/4) 88, p. 27.
"The Return of Grace Poole." [LittleM] (15:3/4) 88, p. 26.

3714. MURA, David
"The Architect's Son." [IndR] (12:1) Wint 88, p. 75-76.
"Letters from Poston Relocation Camp (1942-44)" (Letters 2-4). [MissouriR] (11:1) 88, p. 38-40.
"The One Who Tells, the One Who Burns" (Soweto). [IndR] (12:1) Wint 88, p. 71-72.
"These Years Are Obscure, Their Chronicle Uncertain" (for Frank Wilderson). [IndR] (12:1) Wint 88, p. 73-74.
"This Loss, This Brightness." [IndR] (12:1) Wint 88, p. 77-79.

3715. MURATORI, Fred
"Maturity." [Gargoyle] (35) 88, p. 51.
"Vita Poetica." [KanQ] (20:3) Sum 88, p. 47.

3716. MURAWSKI, Elisabeth
"Nerves." [LitR] (31:3) Spr 88, p. 344.
"Our Russian Landlord." [KanQ] (20:3) Sum 88, p. 214-215.
"Slipping Through the Dark." [OhioR] (42) 88, p. 15.

3717. MURDOCK, Suzanne
"The Mathematician Burns Her Bridges" (July, 1986, First Place, Creative Writing Club Contest). [DeKalbLAJ] (21:2) Spr 88, p. 50.

3718. MURDOCK, Tom
"Horses" (Michigan Sesquicentennial Poetry Competition, Third Prize). [PassN] (9:1) Wint 88, p. 3.

3719. MURILLO, Rosario
"Love Until Now" (tr. by Preston Browning and Lang Gomez). [AnotherCM] (18) 88, p. 138.

3720. MURPHY, Bruce
"Estuary, Sunday Evening." [ParisR] (30:109) Wint 88, p. 135.

3721. MURPHY, Gordon
"Greatness & I Went to the Mat Today." [JlNJPo] (10:1/2) 88, p. 32.
3722. MURPHY, Kay
"Shooting Star." [SpoonRQ] (13:2) Spr 88, p. 52-53.
3723. MURPHY, Maureen
"Angel." [Wind] (18:63) 88, p. 29.
3724. MURPHY, Ray
"Adult Movies." [PoetL] (83:2) Sum 88, p. 9-10.
"Debt." [PoetL] (83:2) Sum 88, p. 15-16.
"Holiday." [PoetL] (83:2) Sum 88, p. 11.
"Need." [PoetL] (83:2) Sum 88, p. 7-8.
"Staying On." [PoetL] (83:2) Sum 88, p. 12-14.
3725. MURPHY, Rich
"Bedtime for the Commuter." [LakeSR] (22) 88, p. 36.
"Where Are the Brave." [MidwQ] (29:3) Spr 88, p. 348.
3726. MURPHY, Sheila E.
"Boot Camp." [Bogg] (59) 88, p. 7.
"Fitting." [Paint] (15:29) Spr 88, p. 16.
"For B." [Paint] (15:29) Spr 88, p. 17.
"Unjacketed." [Amelia] (4:4, #11) 88, p. 8.
3727. MURRAY, G. E.
"At the Japanese Baths." [TriQ] (73) Fall 88, p. 101-102.
"At the Tifft Street Dump" (Buffalo, NY). [SenR] (18:1) 88, p. 42-43.
"Double-Dare Dreams at the Hotel Amsterdam." [SenR] (18:1) 88, p. 38-41.
"On Being Disabled by Light at Dawn in the Wilderness" (Boulder Junction, Wisconsin). [AntR] (46:2) Spr 88, p. 241.
"On Getting Unstuck" (at San Francisco Airport). [HawaiiR] (12:1, #23) Spr 88, p. 29.
3728. MURRAY, Jason
"For Etheridge Knight." [PaintedB] (32/33) 88, p. 88.
3729. MURRAY, Joan
"Larkspur." [OntR] (29) Fall-Wint 88-89, p. 88-89.
3730. MURRAY, Joan Baird
"Dietrich Bonhofer in Prison — Reflections." [DeKalbLAJ] (21:2) Spr 88, p. 41-42.
3731. MURRAY, Les (Les A.)
"The 1812 Overture at Topkapi Saray." [PraS] (62:4) Wint 88-89, p. 91-93.
"At Min-Min Camp." [AmerPoR] (17:5) S-O 88, p. 39.
"From the Other Hemisphere." [YaleR] (78:1) Aut 88, p. 32-33.
"The Grandmother's Story." [AmerPoR] (17:5) S-O 88, p. 39.
"Hastings River Cruise" (i.m. Ruth and Harry Liston, d. Port Macquarie, 1826). [YaleR] (78:1) Aut 88, p. 35-36.
"Hearing Impairment." [PraS] (62:4) Wint 88-89, p. 89-90.
"The International Terminal." [YaleR] (78:1) Aut 88, p. 33-34.
"Letters to the Winner." [Atlantic] (261:1) Ja 88, p. 76-77.
"The Tube" (for Rob Crawford). [Verse] (5:2) Jl 88, p. 4.
3732. MURRAY, T. K.
"Spring." [Bogg] (59) 88, p. 43-44.
3733. MURRAY, Thomas A.
"Of Hart Crane." [CinPR] (17) Spr 88, p. 70.
3734. MUSGRAVE, Susan
"Family Plot." [CanLit] (117) Sum 88, p. 113.
"Love, He Said." [CanLit] (117) Sum 88, p. 5.
"This Is the Day." [CanLit] (117) Sum 88, p. 70-71.
3735. MUSIAL, Grzegorz
"Count Rzewuski's Deliberations on Betrayal" (tr. by Richard Chetwynd). [PoetL] (83:4) Wint 88-89, p. 23-24.
"Death of an Actress, Berlin, 1937" (tr. by Richard Chetwynd). [PoetL] (83:4) Wint 88-89, p. 22.
"The End of the World at Breakfast" (tr. by Richard Chetwynd). [PoetL] (83:4) Wint 88-89, p. 25.
"Isadora Duncan Dances in Her Red Scarf, 1918" (for Zbigniew Herbert, tr. by Richard Chetwynd). [PoetL] (83:4) Wint 88-89, p. 20.
"Lotte Lenya Sings Brecht, 1932" (tr. by Richard Chetwynd). [PoetL] (83:4) Wint 88-89, p. 21.
3736. MUSKAT, Timothy
"Shoreline." [CapeR] (23:2) Fall 88, p. 36-37.

"The Stallion Cages." [CapilR] (49) 88, p. 69.
"Weathervane." [CapilR] (49) 88, p. 68.

3737. MUSKE, Carol
"After Care." [AmerPoR] (17:3) My-Je 88, p. 27.
"Box." [AmerPoR] (17:3) My-Je 88, p. 28.
"Dream." [AmerPoR] (17:3) My-Je 88, p. 27.
"Ideal." [Verse] (5:1) F 88, p. 14.
"Monk's House, Rodmell" (for Lynne McMahon). [AntR] (46:4) Fall 88, p. 478-480.
"Skid." [NewYorker] (63:51) 8 F 88, p. 38.

3738. MUTH, Teresa
"1969, My Brother & I on the Farm, Coloma, Mich." [PassN] (9:1) Wint 88, p. 10.

3739. MUTIS, Alvaro
"Una Calle de Córdoba" (Para Leticia y Luis Feduchi). [Inti] (26/27) Otoño 87-Primavera 88, p. 270-272.
"Desde el último piso de un hotel." [Inti] (26/27) Otoño 87-Primavera 88, p. 267-270.
"Nocturno en Valdemosa" (a Jan Zych). [Inti] (26/27) Otoño 87-Primavera 88, p. 266-267.

3740. MYCUE, Edward
"And." [JamesWR] (5:3) Spr-Sum 88, p. 3.
"Gregory." [JamesWR] (5:2) Wint 88, p. 5.
"The I Is You." [JamesWR] (5:3) Spr-Sum 88, p. 3.
"Journeys in Time." [JamesWR] (6:1) Fall 88, p. 11.
"The Leaves of Heaven Are Melting." [JamesWR] (5:3) Spr-Sum 88, p. 3.

3741. MYERS, Ben
"For Etheridge Knight." [PaintedB] (32/33) 88, p. 87.

3742. MYERS, Christopher A.
"Another Sunday Morning." [Amelia] (5:1, #12) 88, p. 70.

3743. MYERS, Douglas
"Bookend." [BellR] (11:2) Fall 88, p. 7.
"Night Watch on Alder Street." [BellR] (11:2) Fall 88, p. 5-6.

3744. MYERS, Gary
"Instructions for Leaving College Without a Degree." [Timbuktu] (2) Sum-Fall 88, p. 37.

3745. MYERS, George, Jr.
"The Secret House." [HighP] (3:2) Fall 88, p. 37-38.
"Zone." [NewAW] (3) Spr 88, p. 78-81.

3746. MYERS, Jack
"Alien." [WillowS] (21) Wint 88, p. 41-42.
"From the Luxury Condo on the Sea" (For Evvie). [SouthwR] (73:1) Wint 88, p. 98-100.
"Out of the Question." [WillowS] (21) Wint 88, p. 43-44.
"Visitation Rites." [Poetry] (152:3) Je 88, p. 145.

3747. MYERS, Joan Rohr
"The Opaqueness of Bodies." [Comm] (115:12) 17 Je 88, p. 374.
"Transition." [Spirit] (9:1) 88, p. 69.

3748. MYERS, Neil
"Two for O'Keeffe." [CharR] (14:2) Fall 88, p. 90-91.

3749. NABOKOV, Dmitri
"Tolstoy" (tr. of Vladimir Nabokov). [NewYRB] (35:3) 3 Mr 88, p. 6.

3750. NABOKOV, Vladimir
"Tolstoy" (tr. by Dmitri Nabokov). [NewYRB] (35:3) 3 Mr 88, p. 6.

3751. NABORS, Claudia
"How Dumb Is He?" [LightY] ('88/9) 88, p. 223.

3752. NACKER-PAUL, Sali
"Letter to Father, on a Photograph." [CentR] (32:3) Sum 88, p. 273-274.

3753. NADEL, Alan
"On Writing a Poem." [JINJPo] (10:1/2) 88, p. 46.

3754. NADELMAN, Cynthia
"Another Flawed Philosopher." [ParisR] (30:106) Spr 88, p. 118-119.
"Men Without Women." [ParisR] (30:106) Spr 88, p. 116-117.

3755. NADERPOUR, Nader
"A Door to Madess" (tr. by Haleh Homayounjam). [Vis] (26) 88, p. 12.
"A Meteor in Darkness" (tr. by Haleh Homayounjam). [Vis] (26) 88, p. 12-13.

"The Rose and the Nightingale" (tr. by Amin Banani and Jascha Kessler). [Vis] (26) 88, p. 11.

3756. NAFFZIGER, Audrey
"Crossing Over." [SpoonRQ] (13:3) Sum 88, p. 44-45.
"Crossing Over." [SpoonRQ] (13:4) Fall 88, p. 95-96.
"The Gardener's Bone." [SpoonRQ] (13:3) Sum 88, p. 36-37.
"The Gardener's Bone." [SpoonRQ] (13:4) Fall 88, p. 88-89.
"Hero with a Wing." [SpoonRQ] (13:3) Sum 88, p. 33-35.
"Hero with a Wing." [SpoonRQ] (13:4) Fall 88, p. 85-87.
"In Triplicate." [SpoonRQ] (13:3) Sum 88, p. 31-32.
"In Triplicate." [SpoonRQ] (13:4) Fall 88, p. 83-84.
"Leaving Home." [SpoonRQ] (13:3) Sum 88, p. 27-28.
"Leaving Home." [SpoonRQ] (13:4) Fall 88, p. 79-80.
"No One Knows What Living in People's Houses Is." [SpoonRQ] (13:3) Sum 88, p. 39.
"On Believing in Ornamentation." [SpoonRQ] (13:3) Sum 88, p. 29-30.
"On Believing in Ornamentation." [SpoonRQ] (13:4) Fall 88, p. 81-82.
"Passage." [SpoonRQ] (13:3) Sum 88, p. 41-42.
"Passage." [SpoonRQ] (13:4) Fall 88, p. 92-93.
"Reflections on a Piltdown Man." [SpoonRQ] (13:3) Sum 88, p. 30.
"Reflections on a Piltdown Man." [SpoonRQ] (13:4) Fall 88, p. 82.
"Storm at Delavan, Illinois." [SpoonRQ] (13:3) Sum 88, p. 43.
"Storm at Delavan, Illinois." [SpoonRQ] (13:4) Fall 88, p. 94.
"Visitation." [SpoonRQ] (13:3) Sum 88, p. 40.
"Visitation." [SpoonRQ] (13:4) Fall 88, p. 91.
"Visitation." [WestB] (21/22) 88, p. 12.
"Whatever the Blood Runs Through." [SpoonRQ] (13:3) Sum 88, p. 38.
"Whatever the Blood Runs Through." [SpoonRQ] (13:4) Fall 88, p. 90.

3757. NAGANAWA, Arlene
"Learning to Swim" (for Allan Braaten, 1968-86). [Calyx] (11:2/3) Fall 88, p. 200.

3758. NAGPAL, Prem
"Else." [MassR] (29:4) Wint 88-89, p. 632.

3759. NAIK, Panna
"Mother." [MassR] (29:4) Wint 88-89, p. 701-702.

3760. NAKULAN
"The Street" (tr. of Gnanakkoothan). [Nimrod] (31:2) Spr-Sum 88, p. 97.

3761. NALLEY, Richard
"Barcelona from Montjuich." [Nat] (246:17) 30 Ap 88, p. 609.
"Easter Week, Cumberland Island." [Nat] (246:18) 7 My 88, p. 654.

3762. NAMEROFF, Rochelle
"A Jealous Ear Hears All Things." [MalR] (85) D 88, p. 48.
"The Present as Fossil." [MidAR] (8:2) 88, p. 80.
"Summertime Lessons." [DenQ] (22:3) Wint 88, p. 63.
"To Lethe." [DenQ] (22:3) Wint 88, p. 62.

3763. NANDAKUMAR, Prema
"In Time of the Breaking of the Worlds" (Oozhi-K-Koothu, tr. of Subramania Bharati). [Nimrod] (31:2) Spr-Sum 88, p. 98-99.

3764. NANI, Christel
"When Your Mother Dies." [WebR] (13:2) Fall 88, p. 87.

3765. NARASIMHASWAMI, K. S.
"Consolation to Empty Pitchers" (in Kannada and English, tr. by A. K. Ramanujan). [Nimrod] (31:2) Spr-Sum 88, p. 80-81.

3766. NARDOZA, Edward
"Pachysandra." [ManhatPR] (10) Ja 88, p. 40.

3767. NASDOR, Marc
"Treni in Partenza" (for Chris Mason). [Temblor] (7) 88, p. 104-119.

3768. NASH, Roger
"Farming on Water." [CanLit] (119) Wint 88, p. 31.

NATALE, Nanci Roth
See ROTH-NATALE, Nanci

3769. NATAMBU, Kofi
"The Semiotics of Apartheid." [Notus] (3:1) Spr 88, p. 17-19.

3770. NATHAN, Leonard
"An Attempt to Describe the Last Skirmish of the Second World War" (to my brother, tr. of Aleksander Wat, w. Czeslaw Milosz). [Antaeus] (60) Spr 88, p. 62-63.

"Before a Weimar Portrait of Dürer" (in two variations, tr. of Aleksander Wat, w. Czeslaw Milosz). [Antaeus] (60) Spr 88, p. 60-61.
"Childhood of a Poet" (tr. of Aleksander Wat, w. Czeslaw Milosz). [Antaeus] (60) Spr 88, p. 48.
"Facing Bonnard" (tr. of Aleksander Wat, w. Czeslaw Milosz). [Antaeus] (60) Spr 88, p. 47.
"For the Many Things That Fall Slowly." [Shen] (38:4) 88, p. 63.
"From Hesiod" (tr. of Aleksander Wat, w. Czeslaw Milosz). [Antaeus] (60) Spr 88, p. 64-65.
"Leaves whirl, leaves swirl" (To Paul Eluard, tr. of Aleksander Wat, w. Czeslaw Milosz). [Antaeus] (60) Spr 88, p. 46.
"Ode III" (To Albert Vallette, tr. of Aleksander Wat, w. Czeslaw Milosz). [Antaeus] (60) Spr 88, p. 54-57.
"Of Human Bondage." [Salm] (80) Fall 88, p. 111.
"Paris Revisited" (tr. of Aleksander Wat, w. Czeslaw Milosz). [Antaeus] (60) Spr 88, p. 49-50.
"Picnic." [Salm] (80) Fall 88, p. 110-111.
"Postcard from Hellas." [Sequoia] (31:2) Wint 88, p. 30.
"A Recollection" (tr. of Aleksander Wat, w. Czeslaw Milosz). [Antaeus] (60) Spr 88, p. 51-52.
"Snow, Red Wine, and Intelligent Gray Eyes." [NewEngR] (10:3) Spr 88, p. 294-297.
"Taking a Walk" (tr. of Aleksander Wat, w. Czeslaw Milosz). [Antaeus] (60) Spr 88, p. 58-59.
"To a Roman, My Friend" (tr. of Aleksander Wat, w. Czeslaw Milosz). [Antaeus] (60) Spr 88, p. 53.

3771. NATHAN, Norman
"According to Their Biographers." [KanQ] (20:1/2) Wint-Spr 88, p. 262.
"After Shock Treatment." [Event] (17:1) Spr 88, p. 78-79.

3772. NÄTTERQVIST-SAWA, Ulla
"Den Ljusa Underjorden" (Excerpt, tr. of Louise Ekelund). [LitR] (31:3) Spr 88, p. 300.

3773. NAUEN, Elinor
"Plane Ride" (for Ted Berrigan). [Talisman] (1) Fall 88, p. 6-9.

3774. NAWAZ, Shuja
"The Stone Buddha" (Taxila, Pakistan). [Vis] (27) 88, p. 6.

3775. NEELIN, David
"Chatting Up." [Shen] (38:1) 88, p. 36.
"Parataxis." [Shen] (38:1) 88, p. 37.
"Petrarchan." [Shen] (38:1) 88, p. 37.

3776. NEGRI, Sharon
"Freelancing Chance." [Vis] (28) 88, p. 42.
"The Kick from Inside." [Vis] (28) 88, p. 41.

3777. NEGRONI, Maria
"El Angel en la Casa." [Inti] (28) Otoño 88, p. 171.
"Badlands." [Inti] (28) Otoño 88, p. 170.
"Mis Reinos Más Oscuros." [Inti] (28) Otoño 88, p. 169.
"Variedades de Frida Khalo." [Inti] (28) Otoño 88, p. 169-170.

NEJAT, Murat Nemet
See NEMET-NEJAT, Murat

3778. NEKRASOV, Vsevolod
"And I Speak of Cosmic Things" (tr. by Daniel Weissbort). [NegC] (8:1/2) 88, p. 25.

3779. NELMS, Sheryl L.
"Bible Belt Wash." [SmPd] (25:2) Spr 88, p. 25.
"Chinook." [BallSUF] (29:4) Aut 88, p. 32.
"Downed Hawk." [DeKalbLAJ] (21:3/4) 88, p. 62.
"Excerpt from Swan Lane." [SmPd] (25:2) Spr 88, p. 25.
"Married 3 Months." [DeKalbLAJ] (21:3/4) 88, p. 62.

3780. NELSON, Crawdad
"A Poem of Conscience." [AmerV] (13) Wint 88, p. 3-4.

3781. NELSON, Elizabeth
"Somari" (tr. of Gustavo Pereira). [Vis] (28) 88, p. 11.

3782. NELSON, Eric
"Everywhere Pregnant Women Appear." [LightY] ('88/9) 88, p. 138.
"Miscarriage." [Poetry] (143, i.e. 153:2) N 88, p. 103-104.

"Thanksgiving." [Poetry] (143, i.e. 153:2) N 88, p. 102.
3783. NELSON, Erik
"In Neighbor and Weigh?" [Amelia] (4:4, #11) 88, p. 46.
3784. NELSON, Greg
"First Promises" (Selection: 21). [MinnR] (NS 30/31) Spr-Fall 88, p. 32.
3785. NELSON, Howard
"Another Small Death." [Blueline] (9:1/2) 88, p. 51.
"Koans." [WestB] (21/22) 88, p. 119.
3786. NELSON, John S.
"The Afternoon Snack." [ColEng] (50:1) Ja 88, p. 53.
"Oahe Dam." [Farm] (5:2) Fall 88, p. 19.
"Swing Low." [Farm] (5:2) Fall 88, p. 18.
"To the Mowers." [ColEng] (50:1) Ja 88, p. 54.
3787. NELSON, Leslie
"In the Hospital." [SoCaR] (21:1) Fall 88, p. 59.
"My Mother's Heart." [SoCaR] (21:1) Fall 88, p. 58.
3788. NELSON, Sabrina
"Come to Florida." [CinPR] (17) Spr 88, p. 33.
3789. NELSON, Sandra
"Do Not Kiss Brancusi." [FloridaR] (16:1) Spr-Sum 88, p. 123.
"He Was Fat Like I Used to Be." [SlipS] (8) 88, p. 33.
"How You Know If It's a Rat." [PoetC] (20:1) Fall 88, p. 11.
"I Love You So Much." [CapeR] (23:2) Fall 88, p. 33.
"Plant Your Butt Square." [CreamCR] (12:2) Sum 88, p. 237.
"The Story of S." [CreamCR] (12:2) Sum 88, p. 238-240.
"You Know the Ones." [SlipS] (8) 88, p. 32.
3790. NELSON, Stanley
"Untitled: At the moment Transitman unlocks the gates." [Turnstile] (1:2) 88, p. 56-58.
3791. NEMEROV, Howard
"Long Distance." [Ploughs] (14:1) 88, p. 36.
3792. NEMET-NEJAT, Murat
"A Blind Cat Black" (tr. of Ece Ayhan). [Trans] (20) Spr 88, p. 286.
"Body Language." [HangL] (53) 88, p. 35.
"Epitafio" (tr. of Ece Ayhan). [Trans] (20) Spr 88, p. 287.
"Epitaph I" (tr. of Orhan Veli). [HangL] (53) 88, p. 38.
"Epitaph II" (tr. of Orhan Veli). [HangL] (53) 88, p. 39.
"Epitaph III" (tr. of Orhan Veli). [HangL] (53) 88, p. 40.
"The Galata Bridge" (tr. of Orhan Veli). [HangL] (53) 88, p. 43.
"The Guest" (tr. of Orhan Veli). [HangL] (53) 88, p. 42.
"I, Orhan Veli" (tr. of Orhan Veli). [HangL] (53) 88, p. 44.
"A Love Song of the Mountains." [HangL] (53) 88, p. 34.
"Masturbation." [HangL] (53) 88, p. 36.
"Photographs on Tombstones." [HangL] (53) 88, p. 32-33.
"To Keep Busy" (tr. of Orhan Veli). [HangL] (53) 88, p. 41.
"Toes." [HangL] (53) 88, p. 36.
"Vila Nicosa Graveyard." [HangL] (53) 88, p. 33.
3793. NEMETH, Richard
"Babyroll." [JINJPo] (10:1/2) 88, p. 33.
3794. NEPO, Mark
"The Engraver" (For Mauberly and His Maker). [ManhatPR] (10) Ja 88, p. 52-53.
"God Separates Light and Dark." [Chelsea] (47) 88, p. 60-64.
"The Rivers Sweeping." [KanQ] (20:1/2) Wint-Spr 88, p. 112.
3795. NEPVEU, Pierre
"Old Archangel You Know It All" (tr. by Donald Winkler). [Trans] (20) Spr 88, p. 116.
"We Have Lost All Trace of Ourselves" (tr. by Larry Shouldice). [Trans] (20) Spr 88, p. 117.
3796. NERUDA, Pablo
"City" (tr. by William O'Daly). [AmerPoR] (17:5) S-O 88, p. 29.
"Everybody" (tr. by William O'Daly). [AmerPoR] (17:5) S-O 88, p. 29.
"Finale" (tr. by William O'Daly). [CrabCR] (5:3) Fall 88, p. 4.
"Port, this port of Valparaíso" (tr. by William O'Daly). [CrabCR] (5:3) Fall 88, p. 3.
"A small animal" (tr. by William O'Daly). [CrabCR] (5:3) Fall 88, p. 4.
"Today, how many hours are falling" (tr. by William O'Daly). [CrabCR] (5:3) Fall 88, p. 3.

3797. NESHEIM, Steven
"The Pitchforkers." [SouthernPR] (28:1) Spr 88, p. 26.
"Stick Seller." [ArtfulD] (14/15) Fall 88, p. 104-105.
3798. NETO, João Cabral de Melo
"The Canefield and the Sea" (tr. by Richard Zenith). [WebR] (13:2) Fall 88, p. 34.
"Cemetery in Alagoas" (Cemitério Alagoano, tr. by Richard Zenith). [NewOR] (15:2) Sum 88, p. 84.
"The Egg (O Ovo de Galinha)" (tr. by Richard Zenith). [Chelsea] (47) 88, p. 93-94.
"Means of Transportation" (tr. by Richard Zenith). [WebR] (13:2) Fall 88, p. 35.
"A Question of Punctuation" (tr. by Richard Zenith). [WebR] (13:2) Fall 88, p. 35.
"Sandbar of the Sirinhaém" (tr. by Richard Zenith). [NewOR] (15:2) Sum 88, p. 29.
"Sandwater" (A Agua de Aréia, tr. by Richard Zenith). [NewOR] (15:2) Sum 88, p. 90.
"Sugar Cane and the Eighteenth Century" (A Cana e o Século Dezoito, tr. by Richard Zenith). [NewOR] (15:2) Sum 88, p. 79.
"The Voice of the Coconut Grove" (tr. by Richard Zenith). [WebR] (13:2) Fall 88, p. 34.
"The Woman and the House" (tr. by Richard Zenith). [WebR] (13:2) Fall 88, p. 33.
"The Word Silk" (tr. by Richard Zenith). [ParisR] (30:106) Spr 88, p. 120-121.
3799. NEUER, Kathleen
"How to Photograph Telephone Poles." [PaintedB] (36) 88, p. 86.
3800. NEUGROSCHEL, Joachim
"Décimale Blanche" (2 poems, English tr. of Jean Daive). [Acts] (8/9) 88, p. 50-53.
"Décimale Blanche" (4 poems, English tr. of Jean Daive). [Acts] (8/9) 88, p. 32-39.
3801. NEVERS, Blanche Clark
"Haiku: January day" (The 14th Kansas Poetry Contest, Second Prize). [LittleBR] (5:2) Wint 88-89, p. 69.
3802. NEVILLE, Tam Lin
"The Body Reading: A Prose Poem in Defense of Others." [AmerPoR] (17:5) S-O 88, p. 28.
"Muse in a Bay Window." [Spirit] (9:1) 88, p. 86-87.
3803. NEW, Elisa
"Angiogram." [Raritan] (7:3) Wint 88, p. 31.
"Nine Sonnets after an August Abortion" (Selections: 1-4). [Raritan] (7:3) Wint 88, p. 28-30.
3804. NEW, Joan
"The Animal That Was." [SpoonRQ] (13:2) Spr 88, p. 48-49.
"Florida Holiday." [SpoonRQ] (13:2) Spr 88, p. 50.
"Mama's Letters." [SpoonRQ] (13:2) Spr 88, p. 47-48.
"Pigeon in the Second Floor Reading Room of Library East." [DenQ] (22:3) Wint 88, p. 177-178.
"Whirlwind." [SpoonRQ] (13:2) Spr 88, p. 51.
3805. NEWBY, Rick
"And a Fresh Sense of Comfort" (For Chou, Pang-ling, Upon leave-taking, December 28, 1988). [CutB] (31/32) 88, p. 107.
"For David S." [CutB] (31/32) 88, p. 106.
"Without Benefit of Atlas" (for Bill, & for Karl). [CutB] (31/32) 88, p. 105.
3806. NEWCOMB, P. F.
"A Body, A Moment." [CapeR] (23:1) Spr 88, p. 1.
3807. NEWCOMB, Richard
"Anita Paige Recites the Alphabet for Jeremy." [BellArk] (4:4) Jl-Ag 88, p. 3.
"While You Were Out, Your Muse Called." [BellArk] (4:3) My-Je 88, p. 6.
3808. NEWINGTON, Nina
"Teacher." [Vis] (27) 88, p. 36, 38.
3809. NEWLOVE, John
"In Progress." [MalR] (82) Mr 88, p. 76-79.
3810. NEWMAN, Michael
"Biscuits." [Bogg] (59) 88, p. 6.
3811. NEWMAN, P. B.
"The Saco River." [KanQ] (20:1/2) Wint-Spr 88, p. 60.
"Young Women." [Pembroke] (20) 88, p. 224.
3812. NEWMARK, Brittany
"A Little Like Death." [MemphisSR] (8:2) Spr 88, p. 83.
"The Squirrel." [MemphisSR] (8:2) Spr 88, p. 82.
"A Story." [Timbuktu] (1) Wint-Spr 88, p. 22.
"Three Battles & One Flight." [MemphisSR] (8:2) Spr 88, p. 81.

3813. NEWSON, Charles
"We Are the People." [AntigR] (73) Spr 88, p. 10.
3814. NGARUKA, Kavazeua
"Private Worlds." [TriQ] (73) Fall 88, p. 106-109.
NGUYEN, Ngoc Bich
See BICH, Nguyen Ngoc
NGUYEN, Quoc Vinh
See VINH, Nguyen Quoc
3815. NIATUM, Duane
"Son, This Is What I Can Tell You." [Chelsea] (47) 88, p. 152-153.
"Song of Breath and Water." [Caliban] (5) 88, p. 22-23.
"Survival Song at Fifty." [Caliban] (5) 88, p. 21.
"A Walk in the Lake District." [Chelsea] (47) 88, p. 154.
3816. NIAZI, Munir
"Horizons" (tr. by Daud Kamal). [Vis] (28) 88, p. 31.
3817. NICEWONGER, Kirk
"From the Black House." [CrabCR] (5:2) Sum 88, p. 20.
"Here and Gone." [IndR] (11:2) Spr 88, p. 53.
"There Is a Tree in Paradise." [IndR] (11:2) Spr 88, p. 54.
3818. NICHOLS, Martha
"Wanda and Her Fishnet, #1." [FiveFR] (6) 88, p. 52.
"Wanda and Her Fishnet, #2." [FiveFR] (6) 88, p. 54.
"Wanda and the Eyebrow." [FiveFR] (6) 88, p. 53.
3819. NICHOLS, Weeden
"Hoofbeats." [KanQ] (20:3) Sum 88, p. 161.
"A Modest Treatise on Death." [KanQ] (20:3) Sum 88, p. 160-161.
3820. NICKLAS, Deborah
"March Snowstorm." [PoetryE] (25) Spr 88, p. 113.
"Piano Concert." [PoetryE] (25) Spr 88, p. 112.
3821. NICOLL, Polly P.
"Note on the History of Style." [Amelia] (5:2, #13) 88, p. 46.
3822. NICOSIA, Gerald
"Blue City" (inspired by a meditation on the question — if Chicago is B-City, what is San Francisco?). [AlphaBS] (4) D 88, p. 41.
3823. NIDITCH, B. Z.
"Attila Josef." [WebR] (13:1) Spr 88, p. 81.
"Attila Joszef." [SpiritSH] (54) Fall-Wint 88, p. 16.
"Boston's First Night Train." [Plain] (8:1) Fall 87, p. 30.
"Checkpoint Charlie." [AnotherCM] (18) 88, p. 139.
"Chekhov." [InterPR] (14:2) Fall 88, p. 97.
"Daydream: It Happens." [WritersF] (14) Fall 88, p. 135.
"Forgetfulness." [Footwork] ('88) 88, p. 79.
"Frau Raven: My Dedicated Piano Teacher." [AnotherCM] (18) 88, p. 140.
"George Santayana." [Wind] (18:62) 88, p. 36.
"Henry James." [Wind] (18:62) 88, p. 36.
"Leo Tolstoy at Yasnaya-Polyana." [InterPR] (14:2) Fall 88, p. 96.
"Liberation: For Primo Levi" (In Memoriam). [WritersF] (14) Fall 88, p. 136.
"Miklos Radnoti." [CrabCR] (5:1) Wint 88, p. 26.
"Poets Underground." [SpiritSH] (54) Fall-Wint 88, p. 18.
"The Real Country." [SpiritSH] (54) Fall-Wint 88, p. 19.
"Return to Budapest." [ArtfulD] (14/15) Fall 88, p. 64.
"A Snow Sparrow." [HawaiiR] (12:2, #24) Fall 88, p. 38.
"Somnambulist Poet." [ColR] (NS 15:1) Spr-Sum 88, p. 41.
"Somnambulist Poet." [Wind] (18:62) 88, p. 36-37.
"Those Who Silence Words." [SpiritSH] (54) Fall-Wint 88, p. 17.
"What Trembles in My Image." [ArtfulD] (14/15) Fall 88, p. 65.
3824. NIGHTINGALE, Eric
"Aftermath." [WritersF] (14) Fall 88, p. 106.
"One of Them." [WritersF] (14) Fall 88, p. 105-106.
"Sex Surrogate Fragment." [WritersF] (14) Fall 88, p. 105.
"Undedicated." [WritersF] (14) Fall 88, p. 104-105.
3825. NIKOLOPOULOU, Kalliopi
"Eleni." [SenR] (18:2) 88, p. 47.
"Sleepwalking." [SenR] (18:2) 88, p. 46.
NILIUNAS, Alfonsas Nyka
See NYKA-NILIUNAS, Alfonsas

3826. NIMMO, Dorothy
"Rondeau Redouble." [Stand] (29:2) Spr 88, p. 45.
3827. NIMNICHT, Nona
"The Toy Maker" (from "Asylum"). [Nimrod] (32:1) Fall-Wint 88, p. 87.
3828. NIMS, John Frederick
"Niagara." [GeoR] (42:4) Wint 88, p. 770-772.
"Occasions of Grace at a Poetry Performance." [LightY] ('88/9) 88, p. 193.
3829. NINGER, Laura
"Passing the Time." [RagMag] (6:2) Fall 88, p. 63.
"Tapestry." [RagMag] (6:2) Fall 88, p. 62.
NIORD, Chard de
See DeNIORD, Chard
3830. NISHIWAKI, Junzaburo
"The Man Who Read Homer" (tr. by Tomoyuki Iino). [Stand] (29:3) Sum 88, p. 22.
3831. NITCHIE, Geroge W.
"For Marjorie Cook." [SoCaR] (21:1) Fall 88, p. 63.
3832. NITIS, Tommy
"December of 1903" (tr. of C. P. Cavafy). [InterPR] (14:1) Spr 88, p. 75.
"Melancholy of Jason Kleander, . . ." (tr. of C. P. Cavafy). [InterPR] (14:1) Spr 88, p. 75.
"Poseidonians" (tr. of C. P. Cavafy). [InterPR] (14:1) Spr 88, p. 73.
3833. NITSCHKE, Günther
"Zeitgehöft" (7 poems from "Timesteaded," tr. of Paul Celan, w. Cid Corman). [Acts] (8/9) 88, p. 123-129.
"Zeitgehöft" (8 poems from "Timesteaded," tr. of Paul Celan, w. Cid Corman). [Acts] (8/9) 88, p. 218-221.
3834. NIXON, Colin
"Take a Trip Down Lonely Street." [Bogg] (59) 88, p. 45.
3835. NIXON, John, Jr.
"Most of My Aprils." [Comm] (115:8) 22 Ap 88, p. 231.
3836. NOBLES, Edward
"The God of Fish (Rejection)." [CarolQ] (41:1) Fall 88, p. 7-8.
"Heart Ear." [Comm] (115:8) 22 Ap 88, p. 251.
"Transmigrations of the Innocent." [YellowS] (27) Aut 88, p. 7.
NOBUO, Ayukawa
See AYUKAWA, Nobuo
3837. NOETHE, Sheryl
"Bedwetter's Lizard Dream" (For JBT). [CutB] (31/32) 88, p. 17.
"Home." [CutB] (31/32) 88, p. 18.
"The International Luncheon." [CutB] (31/32) 88, p. 19.
3838. NOLAN, Husam
"After a Night of Love Making." [SlipS] (8) 88, p. 59-60.
"Prima Ballerina, Return Engagement." [SlipS] (8) 88, p. 59.
3839. NOLAN, Ruth M.
"Kuthulu Rock." [PacificR] (6) Spr 88, p. 41.
"Rattlesnakes (Real and Imagined)." [PacificR] (6) Spr 88, p. 42-43.
3840. NOLLENDORFS, Valters
"Fairytales and Myths" (tr. of Aina Kraujiete). [Vis] (26) 88, p. 27.
3841. NOLLETTI, Loralee
"Nonna's Kitchen." [Turnstile] (1:2) 88, p. 23.
NOORD, Barbara van
See Van NOORD, Barbara
3842. NORBERG, Viktoria
"My Grandfather Would Sleep." [PacificR] (6) Spr 88, p. 13.
3843. NORD, Gennie
"Death of a Migrant Peasant" (based on a painting by Sergei Ivanov, 1889). [PassN] (9:2) Sum 88, p. 27.
"Lamentation with Landscapes." [NoAmR] (273:3) S 88, p. 44.
3844. NORDHAUS, Jean
"Like Wild Geese." [GettyR] (1:3) Sum 88, p. 480.
"Norfolk." [Ascent] (13:3) 88, p. 37-38.
3845. NORINE, William
"Nightwheels." [KanQ] (20:3) Sum 88, p. 199.
3846. NORMAN, Al "Okla Slim"
"My Grandfather." [CrabCR] (5:2) Sum 88, p. 10.

3847. NORMAN, Anita
"Cradling Her Under Your Arm." [Plain] (8:1) Fall 87, p. 11.
"Nature." [SoDakR] (26:3) Aut 88, p. 71.
"Night Crossing." [SoDakR] (26:3) Aut 88, p. 72.
3848. NORRIS, A.
"Summer of 1947." [NegC] (8:3) 88, p. 188.
3849. NORRIS, Kathleen
"The Gift of Tears." [NoDaQ] (56:4) Fall 88, p. 85.
"House Cleaning." [VirQR] (64:1) Wint 88, p. 88-90.
"Physics Defeats Me Once Again, But Wisdom Saves the Day." [Agni] (27) 88, p. 202.
"Pommes de Terre." [ChiR] (36:2) Aut 88, p. 31-32.
"The Wine" (For David). [NoDaQ] (56:4) Fall 88, p. 83-84.
3850. NORRIS, Ken
"Postcards from Oblivion." [PraF] (9:4) Wint 88-89, p. 53.
"The Years." [PraF] (9:4) Wint 88-89, p. 54.
3851. NORRIS, Leslie
"At the Grave of Dylan Thomas." [TarRP] (28:1) Fall 88, p. 5.
"These Hills, These Woods." [TarRP] (28:1) Fall 88, p. 4.
3852. NORTHRUP, Jim
"Grandpa." [RagMag] (6:1) [88], p. 35.
"A Lifetime of Sad." [RagMag] (6:1) [88], p. 33.
"On Being an Indian Marine." [RagMag] (6:1) [88], p. 32.
"Wall Thoughts." [RagMag] (6:1) [88], p. 34.
3853. NORTHUP, Harry E.
"Eros Needed a Brother." [Jacaranda] (3:2) Fall-Wint 88, p. 114-115.
3854. NOSTRAND, Jennifer
"Those two men in the molten pool of sun." [Amelia] (5:2, #13) 88, p. 64.
"The traffic stops and we cross the street." [Amelia] (5:2, #13) 88, p. 64.
3855. NOTLEY, Alice
"Beginning with a stain, as the universe did perhaps" (from a work in progress). [Talisman] (1) Fall 88, p. 48-66.
"Horn Candle Paper Roses" (dedicated to Steve Carey). [Talisman] (1) Fall 88, p. 36-41.
3856. NOTLEY, Kathie
"Ground Is Blue." [KanQ] (20:1/2) Wint-Spr 88, p. 257.
"Southern Exposure." [KanQ] (20:1/2) Wint-Spr 88, p. 258.
3857. NOULLET, Michelle
"Ruth." [NegC] (8:3) 88, p. 159.
3858. NOVAK, Michael Paul
"Crossing Streets in Manhattan." [WebR] (13:1) Spr 88, p. 75.
"The Family" (suggested by "La Familia" of Luis Cernuda). [Confr] (37/38) Spr-Sum 88, p. 192-193.
"A Story to Tell." [NewL] (54:3) Spr 88, p. 60-61.
"View from the Biology Lab." [WebR] (13:1) Spr 88, p. 75.
3859. NOWAK, Nancy
"Evidence." [DenQ] (22:3) Wint 88, p. 122-124.
"The House to Safety." [PoetryNW] (29:1) Spr 88, p. 18-19.
"Partial Knowledge." [BellR] (11:1) Spr 88, p. 10-11.
"Under the Snow" (for Florence Nowak, 1980-1982). [DenQ] (22:3) Wint 88, p. 121-122.
"Walking Through the Heart." [BellR] (11:1) Spr 88, p. 8-9.
3860. NOWATZKI, Robert
"After the Bath." [SmPd] (25:2) Spr 88, p. 26.
"How to Dig a Grave." [SmPd] (25:1) Wint 88, p. 19.
3861. NOWLAN, Michael O.
"Fisher of Words" (for Alistair MacLeod). [AntigR] (73) Spr 88, p. 101.
"Footprints." [AntigR] (73) Spr 88, p. 100.
"Playthings." [AntigR] (73) Spr 88, p. 102.
3862. NOYES, H. F.
"Moroccan dancer." [Amelia] (5:1, #12) 88, p. 88.
"Seaview path." [Amelia] (5:1, #12) 88, p. 6.
3863. NOYES, Steve
"The Golden Bough, Belleville Edition." [PraF] (9:2) Sum 88, p. 25.
3864. NUÑEZ, Manuel
"Adan Devorando Su Madre." [CuadP] (5:14) Enero-Abril 88, p. 43-44.

"Decires." [CuadP] (5:14) Enero-Abril 88, p. 45-46.
"Luna, Diosa de Barro." [CuadP] (5:14) Enero-Abril 88, p. 46.
"La Vida Mediocre." [CuadP] (5:14) Enero-Abril 88, p. 45.

3865. NURKSE, D.
"Civil War." [MassR] (29:2) Sum 88, p. 318.
"Desertion." [MassR] (29:2) Sum 88, p. 317.
"Exile's Child." [WestB] (21/22) 88, p. 123.
"Factions." [MassR] (29:2) Sum 88, p. 317.
"G.E. Nonviolent Action." [WestB] (21/22) 88, p. 124-125.
"Rockaway Point." [Confr] (Special issue: The World of Brooklyn) 88, p. 42.
"Snowbound." [Blueline] (9:1/2) 88, p. 53.
"Tag." [Abraxas] (37) 88, p. 28.
"The Year in Bed." [Blueline] (9:1/2) 88, p. 53.

3866. NYE, Naomi Shihab
"Answering Your Letter." [SwampR] (1:1) Ja 88, p. 7.
"Chiapas." [SwampR] (1:1) Ja 88, p. 8.
"Debris." [PaintedB] (34) 88, p. 22.
"Even at War." [HighP] (3:1) Spr 88, p. 92.
"French Movies" (In memory of Patrick Dewaere). [Gargoyle] (35) 88, p. 198-199.
"Joan's Students." [PaintedB] (34) 88, p. 23.
"Lucia, Your Voice." [SwampR] (1:1) Ja 88, p. 5.
"The Sail Made of Rags." [HighP] (3:1) Spr 88, p. 91.
"Voices." [SwampR] (1:1) Ja 88, p. 6.

3867. NYHART, Nina
"Two Poems After Paul Klee." [Poetry] (152:3) Je 88, p. 141-142.

3868. NYKA-NILIUNAS, Alfonsas
"December Psalm" (tr. by the author). [Vis] (26) 88, p. 31.

3869. NYSTROM, Debra
"Bellini's Madonna of San Giobbe" (Museo Accademia, Venice). [DenQ] (23:2) Fall 88, p. 53-54.
"Flagstop." [MissouriR] (11:1) 88, p. 181.
"Human." [BostonR] (13:1) F 88, p. 4.
"Ordinary Heartbreak." [AmerPoR] (17:6) N-D 88, p. 34.
"Parting." [VirQR] (64:2) Spr 88, p. 277.
"Poem for a Bad Heart." [AmerPoR] (17:6) N-D 88, p. 34.
"Puppets." [TriQ] (73) Fall 88, p. 98-99.
"Relic." [Thrpny] (34) Sum 88, p. 21.
"Silk." [VirQR] (64:2) Spr 88, p. 277-278.
"To Janny." [VirQR] (64:2) Spr 88, p. 278.
"Wordless Hour." [TriQ] (73) Fall 88, p. 100.

3870. NZUJI, Clémentine
"Come See Where I Was Born" (in French and English, tr. by Steven Rubin. Translation Chapbook Series). [MidAR] (8:1) 88, p. 57-75.

3871. O', Joe
"I Wish the Mall." [Wind] (18:62) 88, p. 21.

3872. O CORRAIN, Donncha
"Migrant Poet" (tr. by John Montague). [Antaeus] (60) Spr 88, p. 295.

3873. OAKSMITH, Laura
"Ash-Tails & Fingers (Krefeld, Germany 1938)." [Gargoyle] (35) 88, p. 37-38.
"Warnings." [Gargoyle] (35) 88, p. 36-37.

3874. OATES, Joyce Carol
"The Consolation of Animals." [Ploughs] (14:4) 88, p. 73.
"Haunted." [FourQ] (2d series 2:1) Spr 88, p. 13.
"Late December, New Jersey." [Poetry] (153:3) D 88, p. 159.
"Make-Up Artist." [ParisR] (30:109) Wint 88, p. 88.
"An Ordinary Morning in Las Vegas." [NewRep] (198:8) 22 F 88, p. 30.
"Photography Session" (for Jim Jacobs). [ParisR] (30:109) Wint 88, p. 89.
"Poem in Death Valley." [GeoR] (42:4) Wint 88, p. 751.
"Prenatal." [ParisR] (30:109) Wint 88, p. 90.
"The Silence." [Ploughs] (14:4) 88, p. 72.
"Strait of Magellan." [Nat] (247:13) 7 N 88, p. 472.

3875. OBEJAS, Achy
"The Cat." [BellR] (11:1) Spr 88, p. 36.
"The Fugitives." [BellR] (11:1) Spr 88, p. 35-36.
"The Garrote." [Abraxas] (37) 88, p. 66.

3876. OBENZINGER, Hilton
"Freak Fire: August 21, 1980." [HangL] (52) 88, p. 11-12.
"I Didn't Even Have to Choose Between Right and Left This Time" (LIRR Train Wreck, November 22, 1950). [HangL] (52) 88, p. 9-10.
3877. OBER, Robert
"Messengers from the Vietnam War." [Stand] (29:4) Aut 88, p. 5.
"An Old Friendliness Returns." [Stand] (29:4) Aut 88, p. 6.
"One from 'Le Pouget'." [Stand] (29:4) Aut 88, p. 4.
"Right of Way." [Stand] (29:4) Aut 88, p. 4.
3878. O'BRIEN, Geoffrey
"Cryptograms." [ParisR] (30:108) Fall 88, p. 85.
"Fred Astaire in the Wilderness." [ParisR] (30:108) Fall 88, p. 86-87.
"The Luminous Mammoth." [ParisR] (30:108) Fall 88, p. 81-82.
"The Poetry of the Policeman." [ParisR] (30:108) Fall 88, p. 83-84.
"Provisional Landscapes" (2 Selections). [CentralP] (14) Fall 88, p. 139-140.
3879. O'BRIEN, Katharine
"In Winter." [LightY] ('88/9) 88, p. 154.
"Open Letter to Manufacturers of Bathroom Wallpaper." [LightY] ('88/9) 88, p. 215.
3880. O'BRIEN, Sean
"Cold." [Antaeus] (60) Spr 88, p. 240-241.
"Coming Home" (In Memory of My Father). [Antaeus] (60) Spr 88, p. 238-239.
3881. OCHESTER, Ed
"For the Margrave of Brandenburg." [LightY] ('88/9) 88, p. 67-68.
"Poem for Dr. Spock." [LightY] ('88/9) 88, p. 53.
3882. O'CONNELL, Bill
"How to Catch an Elk." [KanQ] (20:3) Sum 88, p. 148.
3883. O'CONNELL, Patrick
"Here Where the Water Breaks" (for Darlene). [Quarry] (37:4) Aut 88, p. 34.
3884. O'CONNELL, Richard
"Irish Wake Song" (sung by Scotty O'Connor). [LightY] ('88/9) 88, p. 211.
"Lives of the Poets" (Selections: "Sir John Sucking," "Arthur Hugh Clough"). [LightY] ('88/9) 88, p. 186.
3885. O'CONNOR, J. F.
"Accent Schmaccent." [LightY] ('88/9) 88, p. 109.
3886. O'CONNOR, Mark
"The Cuttlefish Bone." [LittleM] (15:3/4) 88, p. 141.
"Love in the Blue Mountains." [PraS] (62:4) Wint 88-89, p. 82-84.
3887. O'CONNOR, Michael
"In Carnegie, Pennsylvania, on the Weekend." [MinnR] (NS 30/31) Spr-Fall 88, p. 24-25.
"In the Morning." [MinnR] (NS 30/31) Spr-Fall 88, p. 27.
"The Patch." [MinnR] (NS 30/31) Spr-Fall 88, p. 26.
"The Union." [MinnR] (NS 30/31) Spr-Fall 88, p. 25-26.
3888. O'DALY, William
"City" (tr. of Pablo Neruda). [AmerPoR] (17:5) S-O 88, p. 29.
"Everybody" (tr. of Pablo Neruda). [AmerPoR] (17:5) S-O 88, p. 29.
"Finale" (tr. of Pablo Neruda). [CrabCR] (5:3) Fall 88, p. 4.
"Port, this port of Valparaíso" (tr. of Pablo Neruda). [CrabCR] (5:3) Fall 88, p. 3.
"A small animal" (tr. of Pablo Neruda). [CrabCR] (5:3) Fall 88, p. 4.
"Today, how many hours are falling" (tr. of Pablo Neruda). [CrabCR] (5:3) Fall 88, p. 3.
3889. ODAM, Joyce
"Anemia." [Bogg] (60) 88, p. 9.
"Busy Mornings Give Us Time to Hide." [Bogg] (60) 88, p. 33.
"Cold." [Bogg] (59) 88, p. 44.
"Home Runs." [SwampR] (1:2/3) D 88, p. 59.
"The June Rain." [CapeR] (23:1) Spr 88, p. 30.
"Late." [Bogg] (60) 88, p. 25.
"Ownership." [StoneC] (15:3/4) Spr-Sum 88, p. 30.
"Poverty." [Interim] (7:2) Fall 88, p. 41.
"Resistance." [PoetC] (19:3) Spr 88, p. 25.
"The Rock Madonna." [ChamLR] (2:1, #3) Fall 88, p. 12.
"The Snow Looks for Me." [ChamLR] (2:1, #3) Fall 88, p. 11.
"Something in the Grass." [Interim] (7:2) Fall 88, p. 42.
"Twinkle Twinkle." [Bogg] (59) 88, p. 13.

3890. O'DELL, John
"Mugs." [Bogg] (59) 88, p. 19.
3891. O'DONNELL, Hugh
"Erosion at Spanish Point." [FourQ] (2d series 2:1) Spr 88, p. 48.
"Gardening in May." [FourQ] (2d series 2:1) Spr 88, p. 49.
3892. O'DRISCOLL, Dennis
"Mistaken Identity." [ParisR] (30:108) Fall 88, p. 35-36.
"Shandyesque." [ParisR] (30:108) Fall 88, p. 34.
3893. OEDEL, Penney
"The Bath." [DenQ] (22:3) Wint 88, p. 103-105.
3894. OFFEN, Ron
"Charlotte." [PikeF] (9) Fall 88, p. 6.
"Going Home." [WritersF] (14) Fall 88, p. 74-75.
"Liebesfugue: Lying in Love's Stupor" (After Celan, tr. of Jacques Dauphin). [Vis] (27) 88, p. 43.
3895. OGDEN, Hugh
"At the Hotel in Delphi While My Daughter Is Out Dancing." [NoDaQ] (56:3) Sum 88, p. 117-119.
"The Blacksmith Tavern." [PoetryNW] (29:3) Aut 88, p. 44-45.
"Earle Park: The Burial Grounds." [PoetryNW] (29:3) Aut 88, p. 43-44.
"In the Evening Looking for History in a Used Bookstore." [PoetryNW] (29:2) Sum 88, p. 33-35.
"Lord, Lord, Do Not Forsake Them" (to the memory of Melanie Hines). [PoetryNW] (29:2) Sum 88, p. 35-38.
3896. OGILVIE, Fan
"Great Audiences." [PoetL] (83:4) Wint 88-89, p. 43.
3897. OGLOZA, Darius
"Schopenhauer." [Bogg] (59) 88, p. 30.
3898. O'GORMAN, Ned
"On Carnal Love." [Raritan] (7:3) Wint 88, p. 25.
"When I Had Thought of Fire." [Raritan] (7:3) Wint 88, p. 26.
"Why I Do Not Fall Down." (Dick Blackmur in mind). [Raritan] (7:3) Wint 88, p. 27.
3899. O'HARRA, Deborah
"Ministering the Chicken." [AnotherCM] (18) 88, p. 141-142.
3900. O'HAY, Charles
"J.B." [RagMag] (6:2) Fall 88, p. 64.
3901. OHE, Brucette
"The East End." [CinPR] (17) Spr 88, p. 75.
3902. OHMAN-YOUNGS, Anne
"Greeting Cards." [MidwQ] (29:3) Spr 88, p. 349-350.
"Requiem." [Vis] (27) 88, p. 26.
3903. OHNESORGE-FICK, Karen
"Twin Planets." [SpoonRQ] (13:3) Sum 88, p. 55.
3904. O'KEEFE, James
"Tituba." [FiveFR] (6) 88, p. 12.
3905. OKTENBERG, Adrian
"North" (Selections. Pablo Neruda Prize for Poetry, Honorable Mention). [Nimrod] (32:1) Fall-Wint 88, p. 77-80.
3906. OKUDZHAVA, Bulat
"The Prayer of François Villon" (tr. by Gerald Stanton Smith). [NegC] (8:1/2) 88, p. 16.
OLAFUR JOHANN SIGURDSSON
See SIGURDSSON, Olafur Johann
3907. OLASON, Sara
"Mesa Verde." [BellArk] (4:2) Mr-Ap 88, p. 9.
3908. OLDER, Julia
"Night of Tepoztlan — One" (To Cecilia, tr. of Jean Clarence Lambert). [Vis] (27) 88, p. 41.
"Night of Tepoztlan — Five" (tr. of Jean Clarence Lambert). [Vis] (27) 88, p. 42.
"The Ossabaw Book of Hours." [NewYorker] (64:10) 25 Ap 88, p. 40.
"RDA (Recommended Daily Addictions)." [LightY] ('88/9) 88, p. 50-51.
3909. OLDKNOW, Antony
"The Bad Weather in Paris." [KanQ] (20:3) Sum 88, p. 37.
"Blackberrying." [SoDakR] (26:3) Aut 88, p. 102-103.
"Children Dancing" (tr. of Eugenio Montale). [WebR] (13:1) Spr 88, p. 29.

"Cliff by the Sea." [SoDakR] (26:1) Spr 88, p. 31-33.
"Come, I'll Give You" (tr. of Francis Jammes). [Antaeus] (60) Spr 88, p. 272.
"Confucius" (tr. of Francis Jammes). [Antaeus] (60) Spr 88, p. 275-276.
"Don't Ask for Words" (tr. of Eugenio Montale). [WebR] (13:1) Spr 88, p. 28.
"Extra Mailman." [NoDaQ] (56:4) Fall 88, p. 117-118.
"Falsetto" (tr. of Eugenio Montale). [WebR] (13:1) Spr 88, p. 27-28.
"Field." [NoDaQ] (56:4) Fall 88, p. 119-120.
"I Know Times" (tr. of Eugenio Montale). [WebR] (13:1) Spr 88, p. 30.
"In Hot Sun" (tr. of Francis Jammes). [Antaeus] (60) Spr 88, p. 271.
"I've Often Met" (tr. of Eugenio Montale). [WebR] (13:1) Spr 88, p. 29.
"Man in the Snow." [SoDakR] (26:3) Aut 88, p. 100-101.
"Miniature Clouds." [CreamCR] (12:1) Wint 88, p. 70.
"Musicians." [CreamCR] (12:1) Wint 88, p. 67-69.
"Some Morning Perhaps" (tr. of Eugenio Montale). [WebR] (13:1) Spr 88, p. 30.
"There Will Be Snow" (tr. of Francis Jammes). [Antaeus] (60) Spr 88, p. 274.
"What Flowers." [KanQ] (20:3) Sum 88, p. 38.
"When Shall I See the Islands" (tr. of Francis Jammes). [Antaeus] (60) Spr 88, p. 273.

3910. OLDS, Sharon
"After Making Love, Winter Solstice." [PoetL] (83:1) Spr 88, p. 33.
"The Beast." [PoetL] (83:1) Spr 88, p. 35-36.
"The Body Remembers." [AmerPoR] (17:3) My-Je 88, p. 5.
"The Cemetery" (for my father). [GettyR] (1:1) Wint 88, p. 126-127.
"Christian Child." [OntR] (29) Fall-Wint 88-89, p. 79-81.
"The Door." [Chelsea] (47) 88, p. 55-56.
"Every Time." [AmerPoR] (17:3) My-Je 88, p. 3.
"For and Against Knowledge" (For Christa McAuliffe). [AmerPoR] (17:3) My-Je 88, p. 4.
"The Immigrants." [OntR] (29) Fall-Wint 88-89, p. 83.
"The Killers." [AmerPoR] (17:3) My-Je 88, p. 3.
"Lament." [ParisR] (30:108) Fall 88, p. 152.
"Last Night." [AmerPoR] (17:3) My-Je 88, p. 6.
"The Morning After Kristallnacht" (November 7, 1938). [PoetL] (83:1) Spr 88, p. 34.
"My Father's Eyes." [Chelsea] (47) 88, p. 52-53.
"My Mother's College." [AmerPoR] (17:3) My-Je 88, p. 5.
"Night Poem to My Mother." [PoetL] (83:1) Spr 88, p. 37-38.
"The Protestor" (for Bob Stein). [ParisR] (30:108) Fall 88, p. 153.
"Sex at College (Celibacy)." [AmerPoR] (17:3) My-Je 88, p. 4.
"The Swimmer." [AmerPoR] (17:3) My-Je 88, p. 6.
"The Underlife." [AmerPoR] (17:3) My-Je 88, p. 6.
"The Waiting Room." [OntR] (29) Fall-Wint 88-89, p. 82.
"The Wellspring." [AmerPoR] (17:3) My-Je 88, p. 5.
"What Shocked Me When My Father Died." [Chelsea] (47) 88, p. 54.
"Where Will Love Go?" [GettyR] (1:1) Wint 88, p. 128.

3911. O'LEARY, Dawn
"At Thirty Five: Running in Place." [JINJPo] (10:1/2) 88, p. 28.
"The Cradle." [NewL] (54:3) Spr 88, p. 91.
"To Warren's Mother." [JINJPo] (10:1/2) 88, p. 29.

3912. O'LEARY, Patrick
"The Astronaut." [Iowa] (18:3) 88, p. 64-65.
"Depression." [LittleM] (15:3/4) 88, p. 72.
"Kudzu." [Iowa] (18:3) 88, p. 61-62.
"Somewhere, like Leonardo, there is a brilliant child." [LittleM] (15:3/4) 88, p. 70.
"True Story." [Iowa] (18:3) 88, p. 63-64.
"We're driving too fast." [LittleM] (15:3/4) 88, p. 71.

3913. OLENICK, Roberta
"Lyell Island" (Editors' First Prize Winner). [CrossC] (10:1) 88, p. 16.

3914. OLES, Carole
"The Finger." [PoetryNW] (29:2) Sum 88, p. 19.
"Four Bones for Late March." [Ploughs] (14:1) 88, p. 104-105.
"How He Celebrated Daily Mass." [Poetry] (151:6) Mr 88, p. 466-467.
"The Interpretation of Baseball." [Poetry] (152:3) Je 88, p. 133.
"Postpartum II" (for B and J). [PoetryNW] (29:2) Sum 88, p. 18.
"The Radioactive Ball." [Ploughs] (14:1) 88, p. 106.
"Small Poem of Thanks for Maxine." [PraS] (62:3) Fall 88, p. 63.

3915. OLIENSIS, Jane
"Shopping Cart's Ditty." [Agni] (26) 88, p. 172-173.
3916. OLINKA, Sharon
"Ace of Spades." [ColR] (NS 15:1) Spr-Sum 88, p. 87-88.
"A Face Not My Own." [FiveFR] (6) 88, p. 64-65.
3917. OLIPHANT, Andries Walter
"A Child Waking from Its Dreams" (For Oswald Mtshali). [CutB] (29/30) 88, p. 64.
"Moist Bread." [CutB] (29/30) 88, p. 60.
"The Raid." [CutB] (29/30) 88, p. 62.
3918. OLIVE, Harry
"Sand Walker." [Amelia] (5:1, #12) 88, p. 57.
3919. OLIVER, Douglas
"The Ferry Pirate (Variations)." [PartR] (55:3) Sum 88, p. 482-483.
"For *Kind*." [Talisman] (1) Fall 88, p. 11.
"Not in Another Photo." [PartR] (55:3) Sum 88, p. 481.
"Snowdonia at a Distance." [PartR] (55:1) Wint 88, p. 65-66.
3920. OLIVER, Louis Littlecoon
"Lens." [Phoenix] (9:1/2) 88, p. 41.
3921. OLIVER, Mary
"Crows." [OhioR] (42) 88, p. 84.
"Death at a Great Distance." [Poetry] (152:4) Jl 88, p. 191.
"The Kingfisher." [Poetry] (152:4) Jl 88, p. 193.
"Lilies." [Atlantic] (261:3) Mr 88, p. 66.
"The Loon on Oak-Head Pond." [Atlantic] (262:1) Jl 88, p. 56.
"Praise." [WestHR] (42:2) Sum 88, p. 91-92.
"Singapore." [Poetry] (152:4) Jl 88, p. 192-193.
"Writing Poems." [Atlantic] (261:1) Ja 88, p. 70.
3922. OLLÉ, Carmen
"Noches de Adrenalina" (6 selections: i, xiii-xvii, tr. by Anne Archer). [AmerPoR] (17:6) N-D 88, p. 41-43.
3923. OLMSTED, Katya
"A horizontal country" (tr. of Aleksandr Eremenko, w. John High). [FiveFR] (6) 88, p. 30.
"Quiet of the Chestnuts" (Excerpts, tr. of Aleksandr Tkachenko, w. John High). [FiveFR] (6) 88, p. 87-88.
3924. OLSEN, David
"Nighthawks, 1942" (After Edward Hopper). [Amelia] (5:2, #13) 88, p. 124.
3925. OLSEN, Lance
"The Last Line of My Geology Textbook" (Found Poem). [CreamCR] (12:2) Sum 88, p. 241.
3926. OLSEN, William
"Godlessness." [GettyR] (1:3) Sum 88, p. 540-541.
"The Oasis Motel." [Shen] (38:2) 88, p. 76.
"Reading Willa Cather." [GettyR] (1:3) Sum 88, p. 537-539.
3927. OLSON, Avalyn
"Haiku: Opening the drapes" (The 14th Kansas Poetry Contest, Second Honorable Mention). [LittleBR] (5:2) Wint 88-89, p. 70.
3928. OLSON, Curtis
"Minor Figures in History and Geography." [Plain] (8:2) Wint 88, p. 19.
3929. OLSON, Kirby
"Summer in Academia (Sumerian Academia)." [LightY] ('88/9) 88, p. 159.
3930. OLSON, Marian
"Coyote Love." [Spirit] (9:1) 88, p. 130.
"The Vigil." [Spirit] (9:1) 88, p. 131.
3931. O'MARA, Philip F.
"For the Wedding of a Historian and a Philosopher." [SpiritSH] (54) Fall-Wint 88, p. 8-9.
3932. O'NEILL, Alexandre
"Gentlemen's Meeting" (tr. by Richard Zenith). [MissR] (16:1, #46) 88, p. 63.
"The Household Gun" (tr. by Richard Zenith). [MissR] (16:1, #46) 88, p. 65.
"Weekend" (tr. by Richard Zenith). [MissR] (16:1, #46) 88, p. 64.
3933. O'NEILL, Brian
"Lucia." [Crazy] (35) Wint 88, p. 43-48.
3934. O'NEILL, Elizabeth Stone
"Coyote Old Man." [BellArk] (4:5) S-O 88, p. 10.
"Loop de Loop." [AlphaBS] (4) D 88, p. 7.

3935. O'NEILL, John
"A Barn Burns Down." [Event] (17:1) Spr 88, p. 29.
3936. O'NEILL, Maureen
"Enter Me." [WeberS] (5:1) Spr 88, p. 74-75.
"I Am Content." [WeberS] (5:1) Spr 88, p. 77.
"In Climbing." [WeberS] (5:1) Spr 88, p. 78.
"My Sister." [WeberS] (5:1) Spr 88, p. 75-76.
3937. ONESS, Chad
"The Poet to His Grandmother." [HighP] (3:3) Wint 88-89, p. 95.
3938. OPENGART, Bea
"At the River." [CinPR] (18) Fall 88, p. 56-57.
"At the Sea." [CinPR] (18) Fall 88, p. 54-55.
"Driving at Night." [CinPR] (18) Fall 88, p. 52-53.
"Living Apart." [CinPR] (18) Fall 88, p. 50-51.
"Ocean." [SouthernHR] (22:3) Sum 88, p. 224.
"Songs of the Body." [Iowa] (18:2) 88, p. 102-107.
"Sunday Drive." [CinPR] (18) Fall 88, p. 48-49.
3939. OPPENHEIMER, Joel
"Breast Poem." [Writ] (20) 88, p. 8-9.
"Celebrating the Peace, 9-15 May 1975." [Writ] (20) 88, p. 12-14.
"Cities This City." [Writ] (20) 88, p. 15-16.
"The Debt." [Agni] (26) 88, p. 174-175.
"Ghosts." [Notus] (3:1) Spr 88, p. 61-64.
"Houses." [Writ] (20) 88, p. 17-27.
"Mother Poem." [Writ] (20) 88, p. 10-11.
"On the Giving of the Tallis" (for Nathaniel Ezra Oppenheimer, his bar mitzvah, 1 December 1979). [Writ] (20) 88, p. 30-31.
"The Root G N." [Notus] (3:1) Spr 88, p. 54-60.
"The Teacher." [Writ] (20) 88, p. 28-29.
3940. OQUENDO DE AMAT, Carlos
"Rain" (tr. by David M. Guss). [AmerV] (10) Spr 88, p. 83.
"Rain" (tr. by David Unger). [AmerV] (10) Spr 88, p. 88.
"Rain" (tr. by Grace Shulman). [AmerV] (10) Spr 88, p. 86.
"Rain" (tr. by Margaret Randall). [AmerV] (10) Spr 88, p. 85.
"Rain" (tr. by Margaret Sayers Peden). [AmerV] (10) Spr 88, p. 84.
"Rain" (tr. by William Jay Smith). [AmerV] (10) Spr 88, p. 87.
3941. ORBAN, Ottó
"Air Granma" (tr. by Jascha Kessler, w. Maria Körösy). [LitR] (31:2) Wint 88, p. 157.
"Ancestors" (tr. by Jascha Kessler, w. Maria Körösy). [LitR] (31:2) Wint 88, p. 159.
"Chile" (tr. by Jascha Kessler, w. Maria Körösy). [MSS] (6:2) 88, p. 83.
"Cradle" (tr. by Jascha Kessler, w. Maria Körösy). [MSS] (6:2) 88, p. 85.
"Earth Granma" (tr. by Jascha Kessler, w. Maria Körösy). [LitR] (31:2) Wint 88, p. 158.
"The Uses of Poetry" (tr. by Jascha Kessler, w. Maria Körösy). [LitR] (31:2) Wint 88, p. 156.
3942. ORDOÑEZ, Heriberto
"Las manos trémulas miraron al cielo." [Mairena] (10:25) 88, p. 144.
3943. ORDOWSKI, Charles
"It was a night in earliest winter." [Writer] (101:6) Je 88, p. 25.
3944. OREN, Miriam
"Father" (tr. by Ruth Whitman). [AmerV] (10) Spr 88, p. 13.
3945. ORLEN, Steve
"The Big Difference." [PoetryE] (25) Spr 88, p. 100.
"The Bridge of Sighs." [Atlantic] (262:6) D 88, p. 48.
"Child Care." [PoetryE] (25) Spr 88, p. 101.
"Standing in Line for *The Pickle Family Circus*." [PoetryE] (25) Spr 88, p. 102.
3946. ORLOWSKY, Dzvinia (Orlovsky, Dzvinia)
"Occupation of the Deceased." [PennR] (4:1) 88, p. 32.
"Piccolo." [Agni] (26) 88, p. 182-183.
"Pontoosuc Lake, Tanglewood" (for Jay). [Agni] (26) 88, p. 180-181.
"Visiting Hours." [Agni] (26) 88, p. 184.
3947. ORMSBY, Eric
"Redwing Blackbird." [Blueline] (9:1/2) 88, p. 5.

3948. ORNSTEIN, Nancy MacDonald
"The Blue Dress." [Footwork] ('88) 88, p. 38.
3949. O'ROURKE, Leigh
"Venice, California Circa 1979." [Writer] (101:12) D 88, p. 24.
3950. ORR, Ed
"Dancer and Dance (Idea for a Movie by Agee)." [SouthernR] (24:3) Sum 88, p. 571-572.
"Ice Glare" (after Burchfield). [SouthernHR] (22:4) Fall 88, p. 385.
"Music (after Matisse)." [SouthernR] (24:3) Sum 88, p. 572.
"Shopping in Chicago." [LightY] ('88/9) 88, p. 162.
"Typical Summer." [SouthernR] (24:3) Sum 88, p. 571.
3951. ORR, Pam
"Orion." [CarolQ] (40:2) Wint 88, p. 65.
3952. ORR, Priscilla
"Aravaipa Canyon" (for Nic). [Footwork] ('88) 88, p. 9-10.
"At the Ranch." [Footwork] ('88) 88, p. 10.
"The Coyote Pup" (for Nic). [Footwork] ('88) 88, p. 10.
"The Living-Room Set" (for Mother). [Footwork] ('88) 88, p. 10.
3953. ORR, Verlena
"I Can't Stop This Scene." [PoetC] (19:3) Spr 88, p. 28-29.
3954. ORTEGA, Arturo
"Amanece." [Mairena] (10:25) 88, p. 168.
3955. ORTEGA, Frank
"Refugee." [ColR] (NS 15:1) Spr-Sum 88, p. 42.
3956. ORTEGA, Julio
"Cuerpo Barroco." [Lyra] (1:4) 88, p. 9.
"Glosa." [Lyra] (1:4) 88, p. 8.
"Gruta de la Sirena." [Lyra] (1:4) 88, p. 8.
3957. ORTEZ, Javier
"Sandino" (tr. by Kent Johnson). [MidAR] (8:1) 88, p. 143.
3958. ORTIZ, Simon (Simon J.)
"Blue Light Changing." [Caliban] (5) 88, p. 94.
"Getting Ready." [Contact] (9:47/48/49) Spr 88, p. 52.
"The Margin's Light." [Caliban] (5) 88, p. 95.
"Mountain / Memory." [Contact] (9:47/48/49) Spr 88, p. 53.
"The Quick." [Contact] (9:47/48/49) Spr 88, p. 53.
"The Unfolding Mystery." [PaintedB] (32/33) 88, p. 30.
ORTIZ COFER, Judith
See COFER, Judith Ortiz
3959. ORTOLANI, Al
"The Day Before Winter." [LittleBR] (5:2) Wint 88-89, p. 93.
3960. OSBEY, Brenda Marie
"Consuela." [Epoch] (37:2) 88, p. 117-119.
"The Evening News" (A letter to Nina Simone). [AmerV] (11) Sum 88, p. 3-11.
"Faubourg Study No. 3: The Seven Sisters of New Orleans." [Callaloo] (11:3, #36) Sum 88, p. 464-476.
3961. OSBORN, Karen
"The Night That Covers Us." [SouthernR] (24:4) Aut 88, p. 950-951.
"A Returning." [KanQ] (20:3) Sum 88, p. 232.
"Summer Vacation, 1930" (for Lois Priest Mays, 1902-1931). [SouthernR] (24:4) Aut 88, p. 949-950.
3962. OSHEROW, Jacqueline
"The Presence of the Lute" (after Vermeer's *Woman with a Wine Glass*i). [GeoR] (42:2) Sum 88, p. 272.
"South for Winter." [DenQ] (23:1) Sum 88, p. 74-76.
3963. OSING, Gordon
"Spirit Houses" (Thailand). [SouthernR] (24:3) Sum 88, p. 581.
3964. OSTASZEWSKI, Krzysztof
"Opus 64, a Comedy" (tr. by Wojtek Stelmaszynski). [Amelia] (5:2, #13) 88, p. 130.
3965. OSTERMAN, Susan
"Cat" (For Grendel). [BallSUF] (29:4) Aut 88, p. 28-29.
"Ophelia." [BallSUF] (29:4) Aut 88, p. 67-68.
OSTOS, Alicia Martínez
See MARTINEZ OSTOS, Alicia

3966. OSTRIKER, Alicia
"American Loneliness." [OntR] (28) Spr-Sum 88, p. 33.
"An Army of Lovers." [DenQ] (22:4) Spr 88, p. 32-34.
"The Bride." [SouthernHR] (22:3) Sum 88, p. 272-273.
"Cat" (for Eve). [OntR] (28) Spr-Sum 88, p. 35.
"From the Moon." [Ploughs] (14:4) 88, p. 99.
"Ghazals." [Iowa] (18:2) 88, p. 117-121.
"Ripping." [JlNJPo] (10:1/2) 88, p. 47.
"Surfer Days." [Ploughs] (14:4) 88, p. 98.
"Three Poems from a Birthday Suite." [Ploughs] (14:1) 88, p. 58-60.
"Wanting to Be in Love As in Sunlight." [OntR] (28) Spr-Sum 88, p. 34-35.
"Watching the Feeder." [Thrpny] (35) Fall 88, p. 30.

3967. O'SULLIVAN, Derry
"Reading History." [Agni] (26) 88, p. 187.
"Where Is Your Judas?" [Agni] (26) 88, p. 185-186.

3968. O'SULLIVAN, Maggie
"In the House of the Shaman" (Excerpts). [Sink] (3) 88, p. 66-70.

3969. O'SULLIVAN, Sibbie
"Calling Wordsworth from His Room for Dinner." [LaurelR] (22:21) Wint 88, p. 9.
"Listening for Trains." [LaurelR] (22:21) Wint 88, p. 10.
"Physical Therapy." [PoetC] (19:3) Spr 88, p. 26-27.

3970. OTEY, H. L.
"Nymph." [Plain] (9:1) Fall 88, p. 24.
"Permutations." [Plain] (8:2) Wint 88, p. 6.
"An Untitled Ode." [Plain] (8:1) Fall 87, p. 35.

3971. OTEY, Wili
"Night time mercy seeking." [Plain] (8:3) Spr-Sum 88, p. 27.

3972. OTHEGUY, Nedda
"Vivir con el asombro." [Mairena] (10:25) 88, p. 131.

3973. OTT, Rita
"Flying Kites in Mid-March at Golden Gardens Beach." [BellArk] (4:4) Jl-Ag 88, p. 4.

3974. OUELLETTE, Fernand
"And We Loved" (tr. by D. G. Jones). [Trans] (20) Spr 88, p. 141-142.
"The Sun" (tr. by D. G. Jones). [Trans] (20) Spr 88, p. 143.

3975. OUGHTON, Libby
"Fragment from Yugoslavia." [PottPort] (10) 88, p. 45.
"Green Boots." [PottPort] (10) 88, p. 45.

3976. OVERTON, Ron
"Kissing." [HangL] (53) 88, p. 45.
"Poets in Their Youth." [MassR] (29:2) Sum 88, p. 332.

3977. OVID
"Amores, I:5" (tr. by Joe Malone). [CharR] (14:1) Spr 88, p. 91.

3978. OWEN, Jan
"Dividend." [PraS] (62:4) Wint 88-89, p. 121.
"Wings." [PraS] (62:4) Wint 88-89, p. 120.
"Zippers." [Verse] (5:3) N 88, p. 41.

3979. OWEN, Sue
"Chilled to the Bone." [SouthernR] (24:4) Aut 88, p. 962-963.
"Needlework." [NewOR] (15:1) Spr 88, p. 47.
"Speak of the Devil." [Sequoia] (32:1) Spr-Sum 88, p. 65.

3980. OWENS, Collie
"John Calvin Redivivus." [ChatR] (8:3) Spr 88, p. 56.

3981. OWENS, Derek
"After a Chinese Dinner." [YellowS] (26) Spr 88, p. 12.

3982. OWENS, Rochelle
"W. C. Fields in French Light" (Selections: "Brooklyn Turf Odessa"). [Bound] (15:3/16:1) Spr-Fall 88, p. 277-281.

3983. OZAROW, Kent Jorgensen
"Big Daddy." [Confr] (37/38) Spr-Sum 88, p. 213.
"Second Story." [Confr] (37/38) Spr-Sum 88, p. 214-215.

3984. OZER, Kemal
"Like Kissing a Wound" (tr. by Talat S. Halman). [Vis] (27) 88, p. 28.

3985. OZKOK, Lutfu
"Ending" (tr. by Talat Halman). [Vis] (28) 88, p. 35.

3986. OZSVATH, Zsuzsanna
"Foamy Sky" (June 8th, 1940, tr. of Miklós Radnoti, w. Frederick Turner). [Poetry] (151:6) Mr 88, p. 491-492.
"Letter to My Wife" (Lager Heidenau, 1944, tr. of Miklós Radnoti, w. Frederick Turner). [Poetry] (151:6) Mr 88, p. 490-491.
"Shimmering, But Darkening" (tr. of Zsuzsa Beney, w. Martha Satz). [LitR] (31:2) Wint 88, p. 160-161.
3987. PACERNICK, Gary
"The Last Visit with My Father." [CapeR] (23:2) Fall 88, p. 21.
"Murray's Story." [CinPR] (18) Fall 88, p. 43.
3988. PACHECO, Carlos
"I Wonder" (tr. by Kent Johnson). [MidAR] (8:1) 88, p. 143.
3989. PACK, Robert
"Are Quarks the End?" [PoetC] (19:3) Spr 88, p. 3-5.
"Big Bang." [Poetry] (151:4) Ja 88, p. 337-339.
"The Black Hole." [MichQR] (27:3) Sum 88, p. 397-399.
"Brotherhood." [Salm] (80) Fall 88, p. 119-121.
"Display." [YaleR] (78:1) Aut 88, p. 144-146.
"Fidelity." [SenR] (18:1) 88, p. 11-13.
"The Invisible Hand." [GeoR] (42:4) Wint 88, p. 716-718.
"Number." [NewEngR] (11:1) Aut 88, p. 63-64.
"Quantum Weirdness." [TexasR] (9:3/4) Fall-Wint 88, p. 105-106.
"Recounting the Past to Come." [CreamCR] (12:2) Sum 88, p. 242-244.
"The Speck in the Soup." [Salm] (80) Fall 88, p. 117-119.
"Table, Chair, Cat." [PoetC] (19:3) Spr 88, p. 6-8.
3990. PACKARD, William
"Sex Poem." [YellowS] (26) Spr 88, p. 4-7.
3991. PACOSZ, Christina
"There Was No Moon." [CreamCR] (12:2) Sum 88, p. 245.
3992. PADGETT, Ron
"Epithalamus for Douglas & Alice." [Talisman] (1) Fall 88, p. 70.
"Talking to Vladimir Mayakovsky." [NewAW] (4) Fall 88, p. 25.
3993. PADGETT, Tom
"The End of Invention." [Amelia] (5:2, #13) 88, p. 112.
"The Ring-Tailed Cats." [WebR] (13:2) Fall 88, p. 99.
"The Useful Half-Wit." [Amelia] (4:4, #11) 88, p. 82-83.
3994. PADHI, Bibhu
"Annual Invitation to the Dead." [TriQ] (73) Fall 88, p. 112.
"Looking for Things." [TriQ] (73) Fall 88, p. 114.
"Stranger in the House." [TriQ] (73) Fall 88, p. 113.
3995. PADIAN, Brian
"A Wall." [PikeF] (9) Fall 88, p. 22.
3996. PADILLA, Heberto
"Autorretrato del Otro." [Inti] (26/27) Otoño 87-Primavera 88, p. 282-283.
"Canción de un Lado a Otro." [Inti] (26/27) Otoño 87-Primavera 88, p. 280.
"Fuera del Juego" (A Yannis Ritzos, en una cárcel de Grecia). [Inti] (26/27) Otoño 87-Primavera 88, p. 278-279.
"El Monólogo de Quevedo." [Inti] (26/27) Otoño 87-Primavera 88, p. 283-284.
"Una Pregunta a la Escuela de Frankfort." [Inti] (26/27) Otoño 87-Primavera 88, p. 281-282.
"El Relevo." [Inti] (26/27) Otoño 87-Primavera 88, p. 280-281.
"A Veces." [Inti] (26/27) Otoño 87-Primavera 88, p. 281.
3997. PAGE, Geoff
"Transparencies" (In memory of Barry Andrews). [Verse] (5:3) N 88, p. 36-40.
3998. PAGE, William
"Brothers." [NoAmR] (273:2) Je 88, p. 53.
3999. PAGIS, Dan
"A Lesson in Weeping" (tr. by Tsipi Edith Keller). [PoetL] (83:4) Wint 88-89, p. 26.
"A True Story" (tr. by Tsipi Edith Keller). [PoetL] (83:4) Wint 88-89, p. 27-28.
4000. PAIR, Grant
"Set Theory." [Jacaranda] (3:1) Wint 88, p. 100.
"Set Theory." [Jacaranda] (3:2) Fall-Wint 88, p. 153.
4001. PALADINO, Lyn
"Chief Joseph." [HolCrit] (25:2) Ap 88, p. 14.

4002. PALADINO, Thomas
"Brueghel and Early Maturity." [InterPR] (14:2) Fall 88, p. 99-100.
"The Greek Philosopher." [InterPR] (14:2) Fall 88, p. 101-102.
"Picasso the Magus." [InterPR] (14:2) Fall 88, p. 98.
4003. PALANDER, John
"Men at Work" (From *Rêves à vendre*, tr. of Félix Leclerc). [AntigR] (73) Spr 88, p. 73.
4004. PALAZZOLA, Benedette
"Transplanted." [Poem] (60) N 88, p. 7.
4005. PALEN, John
"Country Road." [KanQ] (20:3) Sum 88, p. 190-191.
"For Ann on Her 21st Birthday" (Michigan Sesquicentennial Poetry Competition, Second Prize). [PassN] (9:1) Wint 88, p. 3.
4006. PALIJ, Lydia
"Mirrors" (tr. by the author). [Vis] (26) 88, p. 47.
4007. PALMA, Janis
"Evolucion." [LindLM] (7:2/4) Ap-D 88, p. 14.
"Numeral." [LindLM] (7:2/4) Ap-D 88, p. 14.
4008. PALMA, Michael
"The Goat" (tr. of Umberto Saba). [GrandS] (7:3) Spr 88, p. 45.
"The Little Tree" (tr. of Umberto Saba). [ParisR] (30:106) Spr 88, p. 251.
"Sleeplessness on a Summer Night" (tr. of Umberto Saba). [ParisR] (30:106) Spr 88, p. 250.
"To My Daughter" (tr. of Umberto Saba). [ParisR] (30:106) Spr 88, p. 252.
"To My Wife" (tr. of Umberto Saba). [GrandS] (7:3) Spr 88, p. 46-48.
PALMA, Ray di
See DiPALMA, Ray
4009. PALMEIRA, Rosemary
"Trial by Mind." [Stand] (29:3) Sum 88, p. 48.
4010. PALMER, Michael
"Baudelaire Series" (2 excerpts). [Verse] (5:1) F 88, p. 15.
4011. PALMER, William
"Fledgling." [Stand] (29:3) Sum 88, p. 49.
"Son's Teeth." [CentR] (32:1) Wint 88, p. 41-42.
PAN-CH'IAO, Cheng
See CHENG, Pan-ch'iao
4012. PANDIRI, Thalia
"The Great Escape (From the Sink)" (tr. of Athina Papadaki). [MassR] (29:2) Sum 88, p. 314-316.
4013. PANIKER, Ayyappa
"Itch" (tr. by the author). [Nimrod] (31:2) Spr-Sum 88, p. 87.
"The Old Woman in the New House" (tr. by the author). [Nimrod] (31:2) Spr-Sum 88, p. 86.
"Tar and Broom" (tr. of Kadammanitta Ramakrishnan, w. Roy K. Tongue). [Nimrod] (31:2) Spr-Sum 88, p. 84-85.
4014. PANKEY, Eric
"Consolation." [IndR] (11:2) Spr 88, p. 49.
"Debtor of Happiness" (for Robert Crum). [GettyR] (1:1) Wint 88, p. 175-176.
"Eclogue." [RiverS] (26) 88, p. 35.
"For Luck" (For José Del Valle). [Poetry] (152:6) S 88, p. 320.
"Illumination of Heaven and Earth." [CinPR] (18) Fall 88, p. 72.
"Neighbor." [RiverS] (26) 88, p. 36.
"Nightshade." [NewYorker] (64:8) 11 Ap 88, p. 42.
"Ode to Forgetfulness." [DenQ] (23:2) Fall 88, p. 55-56.
"Overcoat." [IndR] (11:2) Spr 88, p. 50.
"The Same Cloth." [PennR] (4:1) 88, p. 82-84.
"Work." [Poetry] (152:6) S 88, p. 319.
4015. PANT, Sumitranandan
"Almora Spring" (tr. by David Rubin). [Nimrod] (31:2) Spr-Sum 88, p. 78.
4016. PANTIN, Yolanda
"Vitral de Mujer Sola" (fragmento). [Mairena] (10:25) 88, p. 64.
4017. PAOLA, Suzanne
"Apothecary Jar." [AntR] (46:4) Fall 88, p. 481.
"Blackbirds." [QW] (27) Sum-Fall 88, p. 90.
"Glass." [SenR] (18:2) 88, p. 10-11.
"Red Riding Hood: Variations." [Thrpny] (34) Sum 88, p. 31.

"Thinking of Mary Magdalene: A Seduction Poem." [SenR] (18:2) 88, p. 12-13.
"Woods in Fall." [GrahamHR] (11) Spr 88, p. 16.

4018. PAPADAKI, Athina
"The Great Escape (From the Sink)" (tr. by Thalia Pandiri). [MassR] (29:2) Sum 88, p. 314-316.

4019. PAPE, Greg
"Aphrodite." [NowestR] (26:1) 88, p. 32.
"The Days and the Joys." [LaurelR] (22:21) Wint 88, p. 50-51.
"Don't Worry." [NowestR] (26:1) 88, p. 33.
"Indian Ruins Along Rio de Flag." [Poetry] (151:4) Ja 88, p. 349-350.
"The Morning Horse, Canyon de Chelly." [Poetry] (151:4) Ja 88, p. 348-349.
"Photograph of Richard Hugo." [NowestR] (26:1) 88, p. 30.
"Swamper." [LaurelR] (22:21) Wint 88, p. 51-52.
"Task." [CutB] (29/30) 88, p. 16-17.
"Totem." [NowestR] (26:1) 88, p. 31.

PAPPAS, Rita Signorelli
See SIGNORELLI-PAPPAS, Rita

4020. PAPPAS, Theresa
"Invisible." [CimR] (84) Jl 88, p. 27.
"Voices and Breath." [LitR] (31:3) Spr 88, p. 343.

4021. PARADIS, Philip
"Critic X on Type-A Poems." [PoetC] (19:2) Wint 88, p. 8.
"Critic Y on Type-B Poems." [PoetC] (19:2) Wint 88, p. 7.
"Mass Ascension" (Hot air balloon festival, Indianola, Iowa). [CharR] (14:2) Fall 88, p. 98.

4022. PARAMESWARAN, Uma
"Trishanku" (Selections). [Nimrod] (31:2) Spr-Sum 88, p. 64-68.

4023. PAREDES, Rigoberto
"Entre Nos." [Mairena] (10:25) 88, p. 27.

4024. PARHAM, Robert
"Catron's Pond." [LitR] (31:3) Spr 88, p. 344.
"Lewis and Boyd." [SoCaR] (20:2) Spr 88, p. 54.
"Moving Behind Hollyhocks." [HampSPR] Wint 88, p. 22.
"Shadows in a Box." [SoCaR] (20:2) Spr 88, p. 54.

4025. PARINI, Jay
"Demonial." [Verse] (5:3) N 88, p. 21.
"Late Winter Ramble in Zasyeka Forest." [TarRP] (28:1) Fall 88, p. 63-64.

4026. PARISH, Barbara Shirk
"The Children's Portrait." [Plain] (8:3) Spr-Sum 88, p. 35.
"Moving Day." [Wind] (18:63) 88, p. 30.
"The Oldest Grandma." [Plain] (8:1) Fall 87, p. 26.
"Partners." [Wind] (18:63) 88, p. 30-31.
"The Visit Home." [Plain] (8:2) Wint 88, p. 29.

4027. PARK, Marian Ford
"I Want to Go Where Poets Go." [Amelia] (5:1, #12) 88, p. 41.

4028. PARK, Song-Jook
"On Such a Day" (tr. by Hyun-Jae Yee Sallee). [Calyx] (11:2/3) Fall 88, p. 130.

4029. PARK, Tony
"Remodeling." [Crosscur] (7:4) 88, p. 150.

4030. PARKE, Catherine N.
"Gertrude Stein in Baltimore Thinking." [WebR] (13:1) Spr 88, p. 71.
"There Is No No in Nature." [WebR] (13:1) Spr 88, p. 70.

4031. PARKER, Alan Michael
"7 Types of Congruity." [NewRep] (199:6/7) 8-15 Ag 88, p. 28.
"Facts and Figures." [Shen] (38:3) 88, p. 34.
"Lullaby." [GrandS] (8:1) Aut 88, p. 198.
"The Summer Home." [Shen] (38:3) 88, p. 35.

4032. PARKER, Arlie
"The New Tool." [LaurelR] (22:21) Wint 88, p. 32.

4033. PARKER, Christopher
"This Is Not a Poem." [JlNJPo] (10:1/2) 88, p. 48.

4034. PARKER, J. P.
"Amazon Sunday." [Amelia] (5:2, #13) 88, p. 133.

4035. PARKER, Lizbeth
"In the Recovery Room." [CapeR] (23:1) Spr 88, p. 44.

4036. PARKER, Martha
"Revelation." [StoneC] (16:1/2) Fall-Wint 88-89, p. 45.
4037. PARKER, Pam A.
"The Quilt." [Cond] (15) 88, p. 1.
"Signature Piece." [Cond] (15) 88, p. 76.
4038. PARKER-LOPEZ, Carolie
"Twice Born." [Jacaranda] (3:2) Fall-Wint 88, p. 150.
4039. PARRIS, P. B.
"The Child in the House, the Lightning in the Attic." [Pembroke] (20) 88, p. 222.
4040. PARRISH, Karen
"A Grandfather's Suicide" (for R. D. V. 1905-1981). [SouthernPR] (28:2) Fall 88, p. 53-54.
4041. PARRY, Marian
"Pale Odile Sings" (from *The Memoirs of a Diva*). [Margin] (7) 88, p. 79-80.
4042. PARRY, Mitchell P.
"After the Explosion." [Grain] (16:4) Wint 88, p. 58-59.
4043. PARSON, Julie
"Bones." [SpoonRQ] (13:1) Wint 88, p. 16-17.
"In the Kitchen One Afternoon Early in May." [Contact] (9:47/48/49) Spr 88, p. 44.
"Song for the Unfaithful Husband." [Spirit] (9:1) 88, p. 134-135.
4044. PARTHASARATHY, Rajagopal
"Eunuchs" (tr. of Ka. Naa. Subramanyam). [Nimrod] (31:2) Spr-Sum 88, p. 100.
"The Latecomer" (tr. of Ka. Naa. Subramanyam). [Nimrod] (31:2) Spr-Sum 88, p. 99.
4045. PARTRIDGE, Dixie
"After Looking Up Lapwing in the Encyclopedia" (for my mother). [Kaleid] (17) Sum-Fall 88, p. 39.
"For My Brother in December." [KanQ] (20:3) Sum 88, p. 117.
"Guide for September" (for one wanting to leave). [Comm] (115:17) 7 O 88, p. 538.
"Her Listening: Autumn on 10th Street." [Comm] (115:17) 7 O 88, p. 538.
4046. PASCOE, Judith
"Vacation." [DenQ] (22:3) Wint 88, p. 84-85.
4047. PASCUAL, Moises
"Bitacora para un Largo Viaje." [Mairena] (10:25) 88, p. 182.
4048. PASS, John
"Attic Definition." [WestCR] (22:4) Spr 87, i.e. 88, p. 56-58.
"Emotional Life of Words, Book I" (9 poems). [CapilR] (47) 88, p. 35-47.
4049. PASSAR, Andrei
"The Sacred Tambourine" (tr. by Natasha Killian). [NegC] (8:1/2) 88, p. 68-69.
4050. PASSER, Jay
"Across the Desert and Into New Mexico." [Caliban] (4) 88, p. 164.
"I Know What He's Thinking." [Caliban] (4) 88, p. 162.
"Love Song." [Caliban] (4) 88, p. 163.
"Not One of Them." [Caliban] (4) 88, p. 163.
"Wireless." [Caliban] (4) 88, p. 162.
4051. PASTAN, Linda
"After an Absence." [Poetry] (151:5) F 88, p. 407-408.
"Beauty Shop." [Poetry] (151:5) F 88, p. 408-410.
"The Deathwatch Beetle." [GettyR] (1:1) Wint 88, p. 62-63.
"Gleaning." [Ploughs] (14:4) 88, p. 132-133.
"Love in the Nuclear Age." [LightY] ('88/9) 88, p. 143.
"Posterity." [NewRep] (198:12) 21 Mr 88, p. 40.
"Something About the Trees." [GettyR] (1:1) Wint 88, p. 61.
"What We Want." [IndR] (11:2) Spr 88, p. 70.
4052. PASTERNAK, Boris
"Define this as you choose" (in Russian). [StoneC] (16:1/2) Fall-Wint 88-89, p. 29.
"Define this as you choose" (tr. by Eugene Dubnov and John Heath-Stubbs). [StoneC] (16:1/2) Fall-Wint 88-89, p. 29.
"God's World" (tr. by Lydia Pasternak Slater). [NegC] (8:1/2) 88, p. 15.
4053. PASTOR, Ned
"Career Women Who Marry Today." [LightY] ('88/9) 88, p. 142-143.
"Double Occupancy — Sahara Style." [LightY] ('88/9) 88, p. 167.
"A long-winded lass rendered skittish." [Amelia] (5:2, #13) 88, p. 93.
"No Regrets." [LightY] ('88/9) 88, p. 155-156.
"Paradise Lost — on Wall Street." [Amelia] (4:4, #11) 88, p. 35.

PASTORINI, Eloísa Perez de
See PEREZ DE PASTORINI, Eloísa
4054. PATEL, Ravaji
"Whirlwind" (tr. by Hansa Jhaveri). [Nimrod] (31:2) Spr-Sum 88, p. 74.
4055. PATHAK, Jagadish
"Haiku: A beak is dipped" (tr. by Sneharashmi). [Nimrod] (31:2) Spr-Sum 88, p. 73.
4056. PATIL, Chandrashekhar
"Freak" (tr. by A. K. Ramanujan). [Nimrod] (31:2) Spr-Sum 88, p. 82-83.
"Harijans" (tr. of Vijay Patil). [Nimrod] (31:2) Spr-Sum 88, p. 79.
4057. PATIL, Vijay
"Harijans" (tr. by Chandrashekhar Patil). [Nimrod] (31:2) Spr-Sum 88, p. 79.
4058. PATRICK, Kathleen
"Trial 1982." [Prima] (11/12) 88, p. 76-77.
4059. PATTERSON, Steven L.
"The Lawn Party." [BellR] (11:1) Spr 88, p. 30.
4060. PATTERSON, Veronica
"Every Year the Elk." [MalR] (84) S 88, p. 21.
"Flying Things." [StoneC] (15:3/4) Spr-Sum 88, p. 22.
"The Pointillist's Wife" (Hon. Mention, 15th Anniversary Competition). [StoneC] (16:1/2) Fall-Wint 88-89, unpaged front matter.
"Wild Horses." [MalR] (84) S 88, p. 22.
4061. PATTINSON, Mike
"From the Antonine Wall." [Stand] (29:2) Spr 88, p. 44.
4062. PAU-LLOSA, Ricardo
"The Beauty of Treason." [LindLM] (7:1) Ja-Mr 88, p. 19.
"Point Blank — The Footbridge." [LindLM] (7:1) Ja-Mr 88, p. 19.
"Seals" (for Marilyn). [LindLM] (7:1) Ja-Mr 88, p. 19.
4063. PAUL, Jay
"She Would Like to Be the Storm." [ChrC] (105:27) 28 S 88, p. 828.
PAUL, Sali Nacker
See NACKER-PAUL, Sali
4064. PAULENICH, Craig
"Coming to Ia at Night." [StoneC] (16:1/2) Fall-Wint 88-89, p. 50.
"Lightning in the Hollow." [SouthernPR] (28:1) Spr 88, p. 23.
"Nightmice." [SoCaR] (21:1) Fall 88, p. 8.
4065. PAULIN, Tom
"Defenester." [Antaeus] (60) Spr 88, p. 216.
"Really Naff." [Antaeus] (60) Spr 88, p. 214-215.
4066. PAULIS, Chris
"A Bedtime Story" (for Erin). [EngJ] (77:7) N 88, p. 98.
4067. PAVLICH, Walter
"Feeding Winter" (Corrected reprint of "We toss our offerings," 24:3 Fall 87). [SmPd] (25:1) Wint 88, p. 24-25.
"Giraffes in Late Afternoon." [Interim] (7:1) Spr 88, p. 13-14.
"Grandmother, Sparrow, Glass" (for Lucien Stryk). [Interim] (7:1) Spr 88, p. 14.
"No Such Thing as Undertow" (for my sister Melinda). [CutB] (29/30) 88, p. 31.
"Pluto." [Zyzzyva] (4:3) Fall 88, p. 73.
4068. PAVLOPOULOS, Yorges
"Hokouzaï and the Wife of the Fisherman" (tr. by Robert Head). [Bogg] (59) 88, p. 52.
4069. PAWLAK, Mark
"Words of Wisdom." [Abraxas] (37) 88, p. 43.
4070. PAZ, Octavio
"January First" (tr. by Eliot Weinberger). [Boulevard] (3:2/3) Fall 88, p. 3-4.
"Little Variation" (tr. by Eliot Weinberger). [Boulevard] (3:2/3) Fall 88, p. 4-5.
"To Talk" (tr. by Eliot Weinberger). [Boulevard] (3:2/3) Fall 88, p. 2.
"Wind, Water, Stone" (tr. by Eliot Weinberger). [Boulevard] (3:2/3) Fall 88, p. 1.
4071. PEABODY, Richard
"The Aging Guitar Player." [Bogg] (60) 88, p. 25.
4072. PEACOCK, Molly
"Altruism." [PoetryE] (25) Spr 88, p. 116.
"Buffalo." [GrahamHR] (11) Spr 88, p. 14.
"Chriseaster." [GrahamHR] (11) Spr 88, p. 15.
"The Dark." [Poetry] (152:5) Ag 88, p. 274.
"Dear Heart." [Sequoia] (32:1) Spr-Sum 88, p. 9.

"The Defect-O-Meter." [SenR] (18:1) 88, p. 27.
"Friends." [MichQR] (27:3) Sum 88, p. 445.
"Good Girl." [Nat] (247:5) 27 Ag-3 S 88, p. 179.
"Painted Desert." [SenR] (18:1) 88, p. 26.
"Say You Love Me." [MichQR] (27:3) Sum 88, p. 443-444.
"Trying to Evangelize a Cut Flower in a Vase." [Sequoia] (32:1) Spr-Sum 88, p. 8.

4073. PEACOCK, Paul
"Incident at the O Roe." [Lactuca] (10) Je 88, p. 17-18.
"Question 20." [Lactuca] (9) F 88, p. 17.
"Sierra Leone 1965." [Lactuca] (10) Je 88, p. 16.

4074. PEARN, Victor
"John's house" (For John Knoepfle). [PikeF] (9) Fall 88, p. 3.

4075. PEARRE, Insley
"Whitman's Death Mask." [StoneC] (15:3/4) Spr-Sum 88, p. 52.

4076. PECK, John
"Frieze from the Gardens of Copenhagen" (Selections: 10-11). [TriQ] (72) Spr-Sum 88, p. 126-131.

4077. PECKENPAUGH, Angela
"Bare Limbs." [SwampR] (1:2/3) D 88, p. 64.

4078. PEDEN, Margaret Sayers
"Rain" (tr. of Carlos Oquendo de Amat). [AmerV] (10) Spr 88, p. 84.

4079. PEDERSON, Cynthia S.
"Evolution." [KanQ] (20:1/2) Wint-Spr 88, p. 162-163.
"The Old Ways." [Vis] (28) 88, p. 35.
"A Recipe from Rio Uruguay" (Geo Catlin, Rio Uruguay, 1852). [RiverS] (25) 88, p. 1-3.
"Untitled: I tighten the threads of evening." [KanQ] (20:1/2) Wint-Spr 88, p. 163.

4080. PEDERSON, Miriam
"New York Cheesecake." [LakeSR] (22) 88, p. 15.
"Taking on the Season." [PassN] (9:1) Wint 88, p. 31.

4081. PEELER, Tim
"Hard Bones." [Amelia] (5:1, #12) 88, p. 115.
"While the Tumor Grows." [Lactuca] (9) F 88, p. 19.
"White terns converging." [Amelia] (5:1, #12) 88, p. 76.

4082. P'EI, Ti
"Pepper Plant Garden" (tr. by Joseph Lisowski). [HiramPoR] (44/45) Spr-Wint 88, p. 30.

4083. PELLETIER, Susann
"For Genevieve" (b. October 5, 1985). [TexasR] (9:3/4) Fall-Wint 88, p. 107.

4084. PELLING, Victoria
"Dishes with Sarah." [Grain] (16:3) Fall 88, p. 26.

PEÑA, Guillermo Gomez
See GOMEZ-PEÑA, Guillermo

4085. PEÑA, Horacio
"Nacimiento del Poema." [CuadP] (6:16) Sept.-Dic. 88, p. 53-54.
"El Poema Que Se Entrega." [CuadP] (6:16) Sept.-Dic. 88, p. 54-55.
"El Poema Que Se Niega." [CuadP] (6:16) Sept.-Dic. 88, p. 55-56.
"El Poema Que Se Pierde." [CuadP] (6:16) Sept.-Dic. 88, p. 56-57.

4086. PEÑA REYES, Myrna
"San Juan." [Calyx] (11:2/3) Fall 88, p. 142.
"Toads Mate and Father Cleans the Pool." [Calyx] (11:2/3) Fall 88, p. 143.

4087. PENFOLD, Nita
"Equinox." [Blueline] (9:1/2) 88, p. 26.

4088. PENNANT, Edmund
"Delete? Yes/No?" [LightY] ('88/9) 88, p. 195.
"The Wildebeest of Carmine Street." [Shen] (38:4) 88, p. 64-65.

4089. PENNEY, Darby
"Late-Marrying Blues." [NegC] (8:3) 88, p. 122.
"Mother Road." [GrahamHR] (11) Spr 88, p. 56.

4090. PENNEY, Scott
"Goods." [AnotherCM] (18) 88, p. 143.

4091. PENNY, Michael
"Pellagra Dreams He's Climbing." [Grain] (16:2) Sum 88, p. 13.
"Pellagra's Dragon." [Grain] (16:2) Sum 88, p. 14.

4092. PEOPLES, Peg
"Ruby." [NewL] (54:3) Spr 88, p. 89.

4093. PEPPER, Jim
"Polar Bear." [Caliban] (5) 88, p. 148-149.
"Witchi Tia To." [Caliban] (5) 88, p. 147.
4094. PERCHIK, Simon
"18. What's left is the stillness." [InterPR] (14:1) Spr 88, p. 104.
"65. This slow-burning stove: your eyes." [PaintedB] (34) 88, p. 44.
"101. New Jersey's oldest abandoned iron mine." [Nimrod] (32:1) Fall-Wint 88, p. 120.
"173. Its light can't reach, let go." [Poem] (60) N 88, p. 30.
"192. The waves you don't see anymore." [InterPR] (14:1) Spr 88, p. 102.
"198. Even this stream and my stride." [InterPR] (14:1) Spr 88, p. 103.
"227. Don't ask the piano player." [Poem] (60) N 88, p. 31.
"227. This lighthouse as waves." [HangL] (52) 88, p. 16.
"228. Again the honored stomp, shards." [Poem] (60) N 88, p. 32.
"All evening by itself." [Sonora] (14/15) Spr 88, p. 25-26.
"Even across a table." [Os] (26) 88, p. 15.
"George, George: two steps." [JINJPo] (10:1/2) 88, p. 49.
"I can't keep my lips off you." [Abraxas] (37) 88, p. 46.
"It must recognize these trees, this rain." [Os] (26) 88, p. 5.
"The mirror a convict holds out." [Abraxas] (37) 88, p. 47.
"My hand struggling inside this tiny fish." [SouthernPR] (28:1) Spr 88, p. 39.
"Poem: I run my fingers, favor granite." [ColEng] (50:5) S 88, p. 512.
"Poem: Our table cracked — every frozen lake." [ColEng] (50:5) S 88, p. 513.
"Poem: The stream we thought extinct." [ColEng] (50:5) S 88, p. 511.
"These plates, cups — a dim bulb." [Gargoyle] (35) 88, p. 246.
"With such a downward stroke." [Os] (27) 88, p. 24.
"You tried to say, *Send distances*." [Os] (27) 88, p. 25.
4095. PEREIRA, Gustavo
"Somari" (tr. by Elizabeth Nelson). [Vis] (28) 88, p. 11.
4096. PERELMAN, Bob
"Captive Audience" (Excerpt). [NewAW] (3) Spr 88, p. 63-67.
"Captive Audience" (Excerpt). [Temblor] (7) 88, p. 18-22.
"Face Value" (Selections: "Purgatory," "Numbers," "Public Address"). [Sink] (3) 88, p. 39-41.
4097. PERERA, Victor
"The Dog" (tr. of Victor Montejo). [HangL] (52) 88, p. 67.
4098. PÉREZ, Camilo
"The Promised Land" (Selection: 29, tr. of Clemente Soto Vélez, w. Martín Espada). [HangL] (52) 88, p. 73, 75.
4099. PEREZ DE PASTORINI, Eloísa
"La Voz de Leño." [LetFem] (14:1/2) Primavera-Otoño 88, p. 138.
4100. PERILLO, Lucia
"Bags." [Pequod] (25) 88, p. 11-13.
"Landfill" (for Margo and the rest of the old gang). [Pequod] (25) 88, p. 9-10.
4101. PERKINS, James Ashbrook
"The Lady in White." [Footwork] ('88) 88, p. 38.
"The Love Song of the Amputee." [HiramPoR] (44/45) Spr-Wint 88, p. 35.
"The Railway Lines Illusion." [Footwork] ('88) 88, p. 38.
"Remembering Through the Blood." [Footwork] ('88) 88, p. 38.
4102. PERKINS, Leialoha Apo
"Variations on Inferred War Themes from the *Kumulipo* and *Mo'olelo Hawai'i*." [HawaiiR] (12:2, #24) Fall 88, p. 82-88.
4103. PERKOFF, Stuart Z.
"Craft Notes: for H.E." [Jacaranda] (3:1) Wint 88, p. 103.
"Poets of the World." [Jacaranda] (3:1) Wint 88, p. 103-104.
4104. PERLBERG, Mark
"Christina's Angel." [PraS] (62:1) Spr 88, p. 100.
"Garden Vision" (After Paul Klee). [Poetry] (143, i.e. 153:1) O 88, p. 13.
"Ivar." [PraS] (62:1) Spr 88, p. 101-102.
4105. PERLONGHER, Néstor
"Anade, Caracoles." [Inti] (26/27) Otoño 87-Primavera 88, p. 293-295.
"Convidada." [Inti] (26/27) Otoño 87-Primavera 88, p. 296-297.
"Daisy." [Inti] (26/27) Otoño 87-Primavera 88, p. 291.
"Ethel." [Inti] (26/27) Otoño 87-Primavera 88, p. 290-291.
"Miché." [Inti] (26/27) Otoño 87-Primavera 88, p. 291-292.
"El Palacio del Cine." [Inti] (26/27) Otoño 87-Primavera 88, p. 295-296.

4106. PERRAULT, Kevin
"She Talks Storms to the Sky Now." [CanLit] (119) Wint 88, p. 82.
"Sirens in Cricket Song." [CanLit] (119) Wint 88, p. 83.
4107. PERREAULT, Dwayne
"The Woman from Santiago." [Event] (17:1) Spr 88, p. 64.
4108. PERREAULT, George
"December Smoke." [WritersF] (14) Fall 88, p. 45.
"Listening to the Seniors." [WritersF] (14) Fall 88, p. 46.
"Werewolf Writes an Ad." [WritersF] (14) Fall 88, p. 46.
4109. PERREAULT, John
"Analog" (for Ana Mendieta). [Sulfur] (8:1, #22) Spr 88, p. 94-100.
4110. PERRINE, Laurence
"Limericks" (3 poems). [LightY] ('88/9) 88, p. 171.
"Riddle." [LightY] ('88/9) 88, p. 110.
4111. PERROT-BISHOP, Annick
"Shared E/space Partagé" (w. Pamela Hodgson). [PottPort] (10) 88, p. 9-10.
4112. PERRY, Aaren Yeatts
"Mudsong for Mawdad." [PaintedB] (32/33) 88, p. 18.
4113. PERRY, Chad
"Phone Rings." [CutB] (29/30) 88, p. 32-33.
4114. PERRY, Elaine
"Explorers." [YellowS] (28) D 88, p. 13.
"New World Symphony." [YellowS] (27) Aut 88, p. 33.
"Scenery." [YellowS] (28) D 88, p. 12.
"Women's Work." [YellowS] (28) D 88, p. 13.
4115. PERRY, Elizabeth
"The Bag Lady." [Interim] (7:2) Fall 88, p. 17.
4116. PERRY, Georgette
"Vampire." [Writer] (101:9) S 88, p. 25.
4117. PERRY, J. Leigh
"Degas in Perspective." [Phoenix] (9:1/2) 88, p. 29.
4118. PERRY, Laurie
"American Wife Opens a Package from Iran." [GreensboroR] (44) Sum 88, p. 85.
"Atlas." [GreensboroR] (44) Sum 88, p. 82-84.
"Street Preacher." [LaurelR] (22:21) Wint 88, p. 56-58.
4119. PERSUN, Terry L.
"Endings." [Wind] (18:62) 88, p. 38.
4120. PESEROFF, Joyce
"November Skin." [TexasR] (9:3/4) Fall-Wint 88, p. 108.
"October." [Writer] (101:11) N 88, p. 17.
"Visit to the Prison Farm." [Ploughs] (14:1) 88, p. 137-138.
4121. PESSOA, Fernando
"Ah, a Sonnet" (tr. by George Monteiro). [NewOR] (15:2) Sum 88, p. 41.
"Autopsychography" (tr. by Edwin Honig and Susan M. Brown). [ConnPR] (7:1) 88, p. 44.
"Clearly Non-*Campos*" (tr. by George Monteiro). [NewOR] (15:2) Sum 88, p. 95.
"I Never Kept Sheep" (From "The Keeper of Sheep": I, tr. by Edwin Honig and Susan M. Brown). [ConnPR] (7:1) 88, p. 41.
"Now Ashen Gray Tinges the Balding Brow" (tr. by Edwin Honig and Susan M. Brown). [ConnPR] (7:1) 88, p. 42.
"Oblique Rain" (Excerpt, II, tr. by Edwin Honig and Susan M. Brown). [ConnPR] (7:1) 88, p. 44.
"Salutation to Walt Whitman" (Excerpt, tr. by Edwin Honig and Susan M. Brown). [ConnPR] (7:1) 88, p. 43.
"Written in a Book Abandoned on the Trip" (tr. by Edwin Honig and Susan M. Brown). [ConnPR] (7:1) 88, p. 43.
"You men who raised stone pillars . . ." (from "Maritime Ode," tr. by Edwin Honig and Susan M. Brown). [ConnPR] (7:1) 88, p. 42.
4122. PETERFREUND, Stuart
"Living in the Mouth." [TexasR] (9:3/4) Fall-Wint 88, p. 109.
4123. PETERS, Nancy
"Children of the Unloved Mother, Orphans All." [Plain] (8:2) Wint 88, p. 34.
"Drawn from the Lost." [Plain] (8:1) Fall 87, p. 17.
4124. PETERS, Robert
"The Victorian Painter Benjamin Haydon Meditates on Horses." [HangL] (52) 88, p. 17.

"The Victorian Painter Benjamin Haydon Meets His Future Wife." [HangL] (52) 88, p. 18.

4125. PETERSEN, Eileen Blacker
"Now and Thin." [LightY] ('88/9) 88, p. 220.

4126. PETERSEN, Karen
"Aurora Explains It All to Earth." [Quarry] (37:1) Wint 88, p. 61.
"Eve Sounds Off." [Quarry] (37:1) Wint 88, p. 62.
"Seeing the Light." [CapilR] (48) 88, p. 72.
"Trees in Menses." [CapilR] (48) 88, p. 71.

4127. PETERSEN, Paulann
"Love Spells." [WeberS] (5:2) Fall 88, p. 37-38.
"Merman." [WeberS] (5:2) Fall 88, p. 40.
"Wildcraft" (for Denise Levertov). [WeberS] (5:2) Fall 88, p. 39-40.

4128. PETERSON, Allan
"An Alternative Nature for Flies." [CapeR] (23:1) Spr 88, p. 47.
"Local Influence." [BlackWR] (15:1) Fall 88, p. 32.
"Nothing But Scapulae." [BlackWR] (15:1) Fall 88, p. 28.
"Repairing Gravity." [CimR] (85) O 88, p. 49.
"Something Fantastic." [Jacaranda] (3:2) Fall-Wint 88, p. 37-38.
"Stars on a Wire." [BlackWR] (15:1) Fall 88, p. 29-30.
"Trout Metaphysical." [NegC] (8:3) 88, p. 130-131.
"Vectors of Change." [BlackWR] (15:1) Fall 88, p. 31.

4129. PETERSON, Jim
"The Face." [StoneC] (16:1/2) Fall-Wint 88-89, p. 24-25.
"The Man in the Tree." [StoneC] (16:1/2) Fall-Wint 88-89, p. 25.
"Paid Vacation." [SouthernPR] (28:2) Fall 88, p. 34-35.
"The Pretender." [Poetry] (152:6) S 88, p. 316-317.

4130. PETERSON, Karen
"Elegy: White Flower Clouds on Tesuque Mountain" (For Denise). [Prima] (11/12) 88, p. 75.
"Nostalgia." [PikeF] (9) Fall 88, p. 15.

4131. PETERSON, Kevin R.
"Early Pioneers." [KanQ] (20:4) Fall 88, p. 61.

4132. PETERSON, Robert
"Half-moon in her slip." [SwampR] (1:1) Ja 88, p. 40-41.

4133. PETIT, Michael
"Many Buddhists." [ChiR] (36:2) Aut 88, p. 63-64.

4134. PETRAKOS, Chris
"It Is Clear." [LittleM] (15:3/4) 88, p. 128.
"On and On." [LittleM] (15:3/4) 88, p. 129.
"Seconds." [LittleM] (15:3/4) 88, p. 130.

4135. PETREMAN, David A.
"The Wall." [NewL] (54:3) Spr 88, p. 99.

4136. PETRIE, Paul
"Chronometrics." [Raritan] (7:4) Spr 88, p. 35-36.
"Eros in Middle Age." [Interim] (7:2) Fall 88, p. 23.
"In the Basement." [Interim] (7:2) Fall 88, p. 22.
"Marriage Homily." [Raritan] (7:4) Spr 88, p. 37-38.
"Memory's End." [Comm] (115:4) 26 F 88, p. 114.
"The Mistake." [ColEng] (50:7) N 88, p. 754.
"Remission" (For Doris, Jim and Pete). [HampSPR] Wint 88, p. 36-38.
"The Revenant" (on Peter Findlay). [ChrC] (105:24) 17-24 Ag 88, p. 733.
"Rings." [KanQ] (20:1/2) Wint-Spr 88, p. 165.
"The Survivors" (For J. C.). [Raritan] (7:4) Spr 88, p. 35.
"The Talisman." [KanQ] (20:1/2) Wint-Spr 88, p. 166.
"The Web." [TexasR] (9:3/4) Fall-Wint 88, p. 110-111.

4137. PETROV, Victor
"A Knock" (tr. by Leonid S. Polevoy). [NegC] (8:1/2) 88, p. 67.

4138. PETROVSKI, Trayan
"At Sunset in the Wood" (tr. by Graham W. Reid). [Lips] (14) 88, p. 26.
"Ballad" (tr. by Graham W. Reid). [Lips] (14) 88, p. 27.

4139. PETTET, Simon
"Hapless Variations." [Talisman] (1) Fall 88, p. 12-13.

4140. PETTIT, Michael
"Full Cry." [KenR] (NS 10:2) Spr 88, p. 63-64.
"Pavlov's Dog." [KenR] (NS 10:2) Spr 88, p. 64-65.

"Star Route, Box 2." [SouthernR] (24:4) Aut 88, p. 970.
4141. PFAFF, John
"Departure." [KanQ] (20:3) Sum 88, p. 198.
4142. PFEIFER, Michael
"Der Blaue Engel" (to M.D.). [GreensboroR] (44) Sum 88, p. 70.
"Card Trick: The Turned Card." [Ascent] (13:2) 88, p. 14.
"The Hokey Pokey." [LaurelR] (22:21) Wint 88, p. 35-36.
"Slapstick." [LaurelR] (22:21) Wint 88, p. 36-37.
4143. PFINGSTON, Roger
"Elysian Fields." [ArtfulD] (14/15) Fall 88, p. 43.
"Elysian Fields." [PoetL] (83:1) Spr 88, p. 24.
"Of Stories Fathers Tell." [LightY] ('88/9) 88, p. 82.
4144. PFLUEGER, Ruth
"Inside the Chrysalis." [Poem] (60) N 88, p. 29.
4145. PHENIX, Tami
"Alabama." [CinPR] (17) Spr 88, p. 34.
4146. PHILBRICK, Stephen
"The Weight." [MassR] (29:3) Fall 88, p. 571-572.
4147. PHILIP, Marlene
"Man." [Dandel] (15:1) Spr-Sum 88, p. 9-11.
4148. PHILIPS, Elizabeth
"In Europe Now My Other Self Is Sleeping." [PraF] (9:4) Wint 88-89, p. 33.
4149. PHILIPS EDWARDS, Luis Carlos
"Esa Cosa Que Nos Duele Todo." [Mairena] (10:25) 88, p. 180.
4150. PHILLIPS, Carl
"After Mountains." [Plain] (9:1) Fall 88, p. 21.
"A Life of Its Own." [Poem] (60) N 88, p. 21.
"My Wife Tells Me Stories, Some Nights." [Poem] (60) N 88, p. 18-19.
"Opening Weekend." [Poem] (60) N 88, p. 17.
"This, the Pattern." [Poem] (60) N 88, p. 20.
4151. PHILLIPS, Chester F.
"Memories of Granddaddy." [EngJ] (77:2) F 88, p. 86.
4152. PHILLIPS, Kathy
"Kuan Yin Hears Cries." [ChamLR] (1) Fall 87, p. 1-2.
4153. PHILLIPS, Louis
"A 5th Stanza for Dr. Johnson, Donald Hall, Louis Phillips, & X. J. Kennedy" (who wrote stanzas 1-4). [LightY] ('88/9) 88, p. 182-183.
"Clerihew." [LightY] ('88/9) 88, p. 76.
"Crazy Sleep" (for Ian and Matthew). [MalR] (84) S 88, p. 25.
"For My Wife, Six Months Pregnant with Twins." [MalR] (84) S 88, p. 24.
"God Teaches Us to Forgive, But We Forget." [WebR] (13:1) Spr 88, p. 82.
"Going to Work on an Infinitive." [HawaiiR] (12:2, #24) Fall 88, p. 6.
"Insomnia." [Footwork] ('88) 88, p. 79.
"The Irrational Impulses of Life." [HiramPoR] (44/45) Spr-Wint 88, p. 36.
"Landscape with Three Human Figures." [Event] (17:1) Spr 88, p. 65-69.
"My Life Conceived as a Distant Country." [WebR] (13:1) Spr 88, p. 83.
"On Being in Exile Within One's Own Country." [Footwork] ('88) 88, p. 79.
"On Marriage." [MalR] (84) S 88, p. 23.
"On National Data Banks." [LightY] ('88/9) 88, p. 213-214.
"Why the Monarchy Will Not Be Saved." [HawaiiR] (12:2, #24) Fall 88, p. 5.
4154. PHILLIPS, Louise Dedman
"He Thinks a Woman." [CentR] (32:1) Wint 88, p. 36.
4155. PHILLIPS, Mary L.
"Eighteen Buzzards over Shiloh, Georgia." [ChatR] (8:3) Spr 88, p. 45.
4156. PHILLIPS, Michael Lee
"Chiaroscuro." [PacificR] (6) Spr 88, p. 32.
"Homecoming Bonfire." [Paint] (15:30) Aut 88, p. 20-21.
"Slo-pitch in Chinook, Wa." [HighP] (3:2) Fall 88, p. 39-40.
4157. PHILLIPS, Robert
"Casualties." [ManhatPR] (10) Ja 88, p. 35.
"The Cutting." [ManhatPR] (10) Ja 88, p. 34.
"Despair" (for George Weiser). [ManhatPR] (10) Ja 88, p. 33-34.
"Forsythia." [ManhatPR] (10) Ja 88, p. 32.
"In Concert." [ManhatR] (4:2) Spr 88, p. 46.
"Late Reading" (April 20, 1966). [HeliconN] (19) 88, p. 44.
"The Lost Boy." [ManhatPR] (10) Ja 88, p. 33.

"The Matched Pair." [ManhatR] (4:2) Spr 88, p. 45.
"Mother's Nerves." [ManhatPR] (10) Ja 88, p. 34.
"The Pool & the Cow." [LightY] ('88/9) 88, p. 93.

4158. PHILLIPS, Rod
"Initiation." [PassN] (9:1) Wint 88, p. 4.

4159. PHILLIPS, Walt
"Appeal." [SlipS] (8) 88, p. 34.
"A Forties Kid Recalls." [SlipS] (8) 88, p. 34.
"From the Album." [Amelia] (5:2, #13) 88, p. 79.
"The Girl Above." [SlipS] (8) 88, p. 34.
"Mementos." [Amelia] (5:2, #13) 88, p. 79.
"Summer 1941." [Amelia] (5:2, #13) 88, p. 80.
"The Unknown Girl." [Amelia] (5:2, #13) 88, p. 78.
"Vantage." [Amelia] (5:2, #13) 88, p. 78.

4160. PHILLIS, Randy
"The Plan." [DenQ] (22:3) Wint 88, p. 253-254.

4161. PHOOKAN, Nilmani
"Poems" (4 selections, tr. by Hiren Gohain). [Nimrod] (31:2) Spr-Sum 88, p. 25-27.

4162. PICANO, Felice
"Going Up" (Excerpt). [ConnPR] (7:1) 88, p. 38-39.

4163. PICARD, M. Dane
"A Cat at Home." [KanQ] (20:3) Sum 88, p. 190.
"Lough Currane." [KanQ] (20:3) Sum 88, p. 189.

4164. PICHÉ, J. Marc
"Song for the Sea-Witch." [Grain] (16:3) Fall 88, p. 60.
"Valkyrie Barmaid." [Grain] (16:3) Fall 88, p. 61.

4165. PICKARD, Deanna
"The Undressing." [DenQ] (23:2) Fall 88, p. 57.

4166. PICKETT, James Carroll
"Dream Man" (A Play in One Act, excerpts). [JamesWR] (5:2) Wint 88, p. 3-4.

4167. PIERCE, Edward
"Among Ruins." [StoneC] (16:1/2) Fall-Wint 88-89, p. 30-31.

4168. PIERCY, Marge
"After the Corn Moon." [ManhatPR] (10) Ja 88, p. 6-7.
"The Answer to All Problems." [LightY] ('88/9) 88, p. 45.
"Available Light." [ManhatPR] (10) Ja 88, p. 4-5.
"Avebury." [ManhatPR] (10) Ja 88, p. 7.
"A Low Perspective." [Lips] (14) 88, p. 1.
"The Truth According to Ludd." [Colum] (13) 88, p. 6.
"Up and Out." [ManhatPR] (10) Ja 88, p. 8-13.

4169. PIERMAN, Carol J.
"The Mecca Court & Grill." [FloridaR] (16:1) Spr-Sum 88, p. 58-59.

PIERO, W. S. di
See Di PIERO, W. S.

4170. PIETRASS, Richard
"Emergency Exit" (tr. by Roderick Iverson). [Trans] (20) Spr 88, p. 259.
"Shadow Algae" (tr. by Roderick Iverson). [Trans] (20) Spr 88, p. 258.

4171. PIGNO, Antonia Quintana
"La Jornada" (corrected reprint). [WritersF] (14) Fall 88, p. 162-190.

4172. PIKE, Earl C.
"Counting." [CentralP] (13) Spr 88, p. 149-154.

4173. PILCHER, Barry Edgar
"Quick." [Bogg] (59) 88, p. 15.
"Writing with width of the page." [Bogg] (59) 88, p. 39.

4174. PILIBOSIAN, Helene
"Curlicues on a Red Dress." [KanQ] (20:3) Sum 88, p. 162.
"To a Child Away at School." [HampSPR] Wint 88, p. 10-11.

4175. PILINSZKY, János
"Admonition" (tr. by Emery George). [AntigR] (73) Spr 88, p. 82.
"Cattle Brand" (tr. by Emery George). [AntigR] (73) Spr 88, p. 81.
"Harbach 1944" (tr. by Jascha Kessler, w. Maria Körösy). [MSS] (6:2) 88, p. 86-87.
"White Pietà" (tr. by Emery George). [AntigR] (73) Spr 88, p. 81.

PILINZSKY, János
See PILINSZKY, János

4177. PILLE, Liza
"Fuhrer's Pharmacy in Livingston Manor." [Lactuca] (9) F 88, p. 23-24.
"I Never Forget." [Lactuca] (9) F 88, p. 4.
4178. PILLER, John Anton
"Rebuilding." [HayF] (3) Spr 88, p. 70.
4179. PIÑERO, Miguel
"And Then Came Freedom to Dream." [Americas] (16:3/4) Fall-Wint 88, p. 37-38.
"Another Day." [Americas] (16:3/4) Fall-Wint 88, p. 31.
"The High Don't Equal the Low." [Americas] (16:3/4) Fall-Wint 88, p. 35-36.
"The Lower East Side." [Americas] (16:3/4) Fall-Wint 88, p. 33.
"This Time." [Americas] (16:3/4) Fall-Wint 88, p. 34.
4180. PINES, Paul
"The Fear." [PraS] (62:2) Sum 88, p. 38-39.
"Reading Cavafy." [PraS] (62:2) Sum 88, p. 39-40.
"Regarding the Percussionist." [PraS] (62:2) Sum 88, p. 37-38.
4181. PING, Chin Woon
"The Awakening." [PaintedB] (34) 88, p. 61.
"For My Mother." [PaintedB] (34) 88, p. 58.
"Grief." [PaintedB] (34) 88, p. 62.
"The Joys of Concrete." [PaintedB] (34) 88, p. 55-56.
"Laughing in the Belly of the Beast." [PaintedB] (34) 88, p. 59-60.
"The Older Country." [PaintedB] (34) 88, p. 52-53.
"Rock and Cloud." [PaintedB] (34) 88, p. 56.
"Toledo, Ohio." [PaintedB] (34) 88, p. 54.
"Unbound Feet." [PaintedB] (34) 88, p. 57-58.
PIÑON, Evangelina Vigil
See VIGIL-PIÑON, Evangelina
4182. PINSKER, Sanford
"Belly Song, for Etheridge Knight." [PaintedB] (32/33) 88, p. 56.
"Local News." [KanQ] (20:1/2) Wint-Spr 88, p. 246.
"The Response of Telemachus" (with apologies to Tennyson). [LightY] ('88/9) 88, p. 160-161.
4183. PINSKY, Robert
"At Pleasure Bay." [Raritan] (7:4) Spr 88, p. 32-34.
"From the Childhood of Jesus." [Sequoia] (31:2) Wint 88, p. 56-57.
"From the Childhood of Jesus." [Verse] (5:1) F 88, p. 16-17.
"An Old Man" (after Cavafy). [YaleR] (77:3) Spr 88, p. 401.
"Three on Luck." [StoneC] (15:3/4) Spr-Sum 88, p. 44-45.
4184. PINSON, Hermine
"All-Around Vampires." [Callaloo] (11:2, #35) Spr 88, p. 273-274.
4185. PINSON, Ken
"This Season." [Nimrod] (32:1) Fall-Wint 88, p. 116.
"Tree." [Nimrod] (32:1) Fall-Wint 88, p. 117.
4186. PINTONELLI, Deborah
"Is the cold sheen, almost salmon pink heart." [NewAW] (3) Spr 88, p. 104.
4187. PIOMBINO, Nick
"The Gentle Instructor" (w. Toni Simon). [CentralP] (14) Fall 88, p. 159-166.
4188. PITT, Alexander
"Poem: Majestic panorama with scenic windows." [NewAW] (4) Fall 88, p. 87.
4189. PITTY, Dimas Lidio
"En la Celda Numero 13" (fragmentos). [Mairena] (10:25) 88, p. 179.
4190. PJERROU, Joseph N.
"The Abbott." [SmPd] (25:3) Fall 88, p. 30.
"The Paramedic." [SmPd] (25:3) Fall 88, p. 28.
"Word Solace." [SmPd] (25:3) Fall 88, p. 29.
4191. PLAICE, Stephen
"Insie Out" (prison poems). [CumbPR] (7:2) Spr 88, p. 46-48.
"The Middle" (for M. M.). [CumbPR] (7:2) Spr 88, p. 49.
4192. PLAIT, Jeff
"The Maid." [HarvardA] (The New Yorker spoof issue) 88?, p. 9.
4193. PLATE, Peter
"Afterwords" (from "An Exploded Time"). [RedBass] (13) 88, p. 62.
"San Bernadino." [RedBass] (13) 88, p. 61.
4194. PLATH, James
"Before They Closed Down Denny's Billiards." [Amelia] (5:2, #13) 88, p. 113.
"Night Crawlers." [KanQ] (20:1/2) Wint-Spr 88, p. 175.

4195. PLATT, Don
"April's Algebra." [Timbuktu] (1) Wint-Spr 88, p. 18-19.
"Children's Game." [Timbuktu] (1) Wint-Spr 88, p. 18.
4196. PLATT, William C.
"Instant." [Writer] (101:9) S 88, p. 24.
4197. PLATTNER, Jennifer
"For Tulips, Dahlias and Mali's Child." [BellArk] (4:2) Mr-Ap 88, p. 7.
4198. PLATZER, Michael
"Island" (tr. of Jorge Pedro Barbosa). [Vis] (27) 88, p. 21.
PLESSIS, Rachel Blau du
See DuPLESSIS, Rachel Blau
4199. PLUMB, Hudson
"For My Father." [Kaleid] (17) Sum-Fall 88, p. 27.
4200. PLUMLY, Stanley
"Claustrophobia." [DenQ] (23:2) Fall 88, p. 58.
"Cloud Building." [Field] (39) Fall 88, p. 55-56.
"Fountain Park." [NewYorker] (64:7) 4 Ap 88, p. 38.
"Infidelity." [Field] (39) Fall 88, p. 57.
"The James Wright Annual Festival." [PartR] (55:4) Fall 88, p. 617-618.
"Two Autumns." [IndR] (11:3) Sum 88, p. 13.
4201. PLUMPP, Sterling
"Mississippi Griot" (for Ann Abadie). [RiverS] (26) 88, p. 70-72.
"Muddy Waters" (for Jerry Ward). [TriQ] (73) Fall 88, p. 117-118.
"Robert Johnson." [TriQ] (73) Fall 88, p. 119-120.
"Saturday Night Decades" (for Langston Hughes, Originator). [TriQ] (73) Fall 88, p. 115-116.
PO, Li
See LI, Po
4202. POBO, Kenneth
"Basketball Hero." [WindO] (50) Aut 88, p. 37.
"The Big Game." [WindO] (50) Aut 88, p. 38.
"Epithalamium." [Grain] (16:3) Fall 88, p. 76.
"Georgia O'Keefe's Flowers." [CapeR] (23:2) Fall 88, p. 2.
"Hunilla Returns to Payta." [CumbPR] (7:2) Spr 88, p. 50-51.
"Money Poem." [WindO] (50) Aut 88, p. 36.
"Owl." [Grain] (16:3) Fall 88, p. 74.
"The Sky Floats, a Piano." [Grain] (16:3) Fall 88, p. 75.
"Smokescreen." [CapeR] (23:2) Fall 88, p. 3.
"Spider in the Drain." [MidwQ] (29:3) Spr 88, p. 351.
"Thoughts of the Ovaltine Factory During a Moment of Hysteria." [HawaiiR] (12:2, #24) Fall 88, p. 43.
"Washing Us." [SlipS] (8) 88, p. 33.
4203. PODGURSKI, Robert
"Jimson's Gift." [Sulfur] (8:2, #23) Fall 88, p. 127.
"Oyster Gem." [Sulfur] (8:2, #23) Fall 88, p. 126.
"Spiderplant." [Sulfur] (8:2, #23) Fall 88, p. 126.
4204. POGODA, Jakub
"Beautiful Is My Mother" (tr. of Anna Frajlich-Zajac). [Vis] (26) 88, p. 36.
4205. POLEVOY, Leonid S.
"Bread" (tr. of Simeon Skoptzov). [NegC] (8:1/2) 88, p. 63-64.
"Flights in a Dream" (tr. of Sergei Korolyov). [NegC] (8:1/2) 88, p. 66.
"A Knock" (tr. of Victor Petrov). [NegC] (8:1/2) 88, p. 67.
"The Sound of Fall" (tr. of Boris Kulikov). [NegC] (8:1/2) 88, p. 65.
4206. POLITO, Robert
"Leland W. Smith." [Agni] (26) 88, p. 108-114.
4207. POLIZZI, Michael
"Bending in the Garden." [Footwork] ('88) 88, p. 76.
"The Halfway House." [Footwork] ('88) 88, p. 76.
"A White Moth." [Footwork] ('88) 88, p. 76.
4208. POLKOWSKI, Jan
"Among Us, the Unclean Ones" (tr. by Stanislaw Baranczak and Clare Cavanagh). [ManhatR] (4:2) Spr 88, p. 40.
"Though Mortal, I Desired You" (tr. by Stanislaw Baranczak and Clare Cavanagh). [ManhatR] (4:2) Spr 88, p. 40-41.
4209. POLLACK, Carrie
"Diorama." [CapeR] (23:1) Spr 88, p. 8.

4210. POLLACK, Frederick
"The Abandoned Man #6." [SouthernR] (24:3) Sum 88, p. 586-592.
4211. POLLAK, Felix
"Autobiography in Ten Lines." [NewL] (54:3) Spr 88, p. 55.
"Refugee." [NewL] (54:3) Spr 88, p. 55.
"Song of the American Indian" (In memory of Woody Guthrie, who might have agreed). [NewL] (54:3) Spr 88, p. 56-57.
"To Each His Own" (Jedem das Seine, Inscription over the Entrance to the Buchenwald Concentration Camp). [NewL] (54:3) Spr 88, p. 54.
4212. POLLET, Sylvester
"Elegy for John Wilborg." [LightY] ('88/9) 88, p. 111-112.
4213. POLLITT, Katha
"Amor Fati." [NewYorker] (64:23) 25 Jl 88, p. 26.
"Dreaming About the Dead." [NewYorker] (64:33) 3 O 88, p. 38.
"Walking in the Mist." [NewRep] (199:9) 29 Ag 88, p. 46.
4214. POND, Judith
"Couple." [MalR] (82) Mr 88, p. 55.
"An Early Day." [MalR] (85) D 88, p. 69-92.
"Morning After." [MalR] (82) Mr 88, p. 57.
"On the Day of My Death." [MalR] (82) Mr 88, p. 56.
"You Call from Bermuda." [MalR] (82) Mr 88, p. 54.
4215. POOLE, Richard
"Polymerlogue." [NewEngR] (10:4) Sum 88, p. 438-439.
4216. POOM, Ritva
"The Forest" (tr. of Eeva-Liisa Manner). [ManhatR] (4:2) Spr 88, p. 43.
"The Moon" (tr. of Eeva-Liisa Manner). [ManhatR] (4:2) Spr 88, p. 44.
"Seeing" (tr. of Eeva-Liisa Manner). [ManhatR] (4:2) Spr 88, p. 44-45.
4217. POP-CORNIS, Marcel
"If I'll Meet Any Fountain" (tr. of Anghel Dumbraveanu, w. Robert J. Ward). [NewRena] (7:2, #22) Spr 88, p. 73.
"The Seaman's Window" (tr. of Anghel Dumbraveanu, w. Robert J. Ward). [NewRena] (7:2, #22) Spr 88, p. 75.
4218. POPE, Deborah
"Another Valentine." [TarRP] (27:2) Spr 88, p. 8.
4219. POPOV, Nikolai B.
"Bulgarian Woman from the Old Days" (tr. of Blaga Dimitrova, w. Heather McHugh). [Antaeus] (60) Spr 88, p. 280.
"Forbidden Sea" (Selections: 14, 16, tr. of Blaga Dimitrova, w. Heather McHugh). [Thrpny] (33) Spr 88, p. 18.
"In the Balance" (tr. of Blaga Dimitrova, w. Heather McHugh). [Antaeus] (60) Spr 88, p. 279.
"Portrait with Soap Bubbles" (tr. of Blaga Dimitrova, w. Heather McHugh). [Antaeus] (60) Spr 88, p. 283-284.
"Who Cares for the Blind Stork" (tr. of Blaga Dimitrova, w. Heather McHugh). [Antaeus] (60) Spr 88, p. 277-278.
"The Women Who Are Poets in My Land" (tr. of Blaga Dimitrova, w. Heather McHugh). [Antaeus] (60) Spr 88, p. 281-282.
4220. PORAD, Francine
"Bella Italia." [Amelia] (4:4, #11) 88, p. 60-61.
"Shakespeare Festival." [Amelia] (5:1, #12) 88, p. 56.
PORTA, Guillermo Rivas
See RIVAS PORTA, Guillermo
4221. PORTER, Anne
"Farmyard by Moonlight." [Comm] (115:10) 20 My 88, p. 307.
"Here on Earth." [Comm] (115:22) 16 D 88, p. 685.
"In Holy Week." [Comm] (115:7) 8 Ap 88, p. 219.
"Looking at the Sky." [Comm] (115:12) 17 Je 88, p. 374.
"The Wall." [Comm] (115:16) 23 S 88, p. 500.
4222. PORTER, Peter
"Die-back." [Antaeus] (60) Spr 88, p. 189-191.
"Under Blencathra." [Antaeus] (60) Spr 88, p. 188.
POSADA, Armando Acosta
See ACOSTA POSADA, Armando
4223. POST, Laura
"Holding In." [SinW] (36) Wint 88-89, p. 21.

4224. POSTER, Carol
"Claws." [Vis] (28) 88, p. 45.
4225. POSWIATOWSKA, Halina
"I cannot be only a human being" (tr. by Marek Labinski). [Rohwedder] (4) [Wint 88-89], p. 31.
"I come from the flowing water" (tr. by Marek Labinski). [Rohwedder] (4) [Wint 88-89], p. 30.
"In My Barbaric Language" (tr. by Marek Labinski). [MidAR] (8:2) 88, p. 8.
"A Mirror" (tr. by Marek Labinski). [Rohwedder] (4) [Wint 88-89], p. 30.
"My shadow is a woman" (tr. by Marek Labinski). [Rohwedder] (4) [Wint 88-89], p. 30.
"The sliver of my imagination" (tr. by Marek Labinski). [Rohwedder] (4) [Wint 88-89], p. 29.
"These words have always been" (tr. by Marek Labinski). [Rohwedder] (4) [Wint 88-89], p. 29.
"We don't believe in hell" (tr. by Marek Labinski). [Rohwedder] (4) [Wint 88-89], p. 29.
4226. POTTER, Carol
"All Six of Us Suspended Above Blue Seats." [MassR] (29:2) Sum 88, p. 369-370.
"An Object Falling from Outer Space" (to Meme). [MassR] (29:2) Sum 88, p. 368-369.
4227. POTTER, Jacklyn
"Permanent Vision" (for Lucky). [PoetL] (83:3) Fall 88, p. 27.
4228. POTTS, Lee W.
"Dark Wood." [PaintedB] (34) 88, p. 91.
"To Avoid with Silence." [PaintedB] (34) 88, p. 92.
"Tonight I whispered to You That." [Gargoyle] (35) 88, p. 127.
4229. POVINELLI, Beth
"Parthenogenesis." [SinW] (34) Spr 88, p. 22.
4230. POWELL, Dannye Romine
"Noises." [Poem] (60) N 88, p. 42.
"On What Would Have Been Our 25th Anniversary." [Poem] (60) N 88, p. 41.
"Why I'm Against Liposuction." [Poem] (60) N 88, p. 40.
4231. POWELL, Jim
"Between the Teeth." [Verse] (5:1) F 88, p. 18.
"Fire Signs." [Verse] (5:1) F 88, p. 19.
"A Glass Blower" (3 poems). [Thrpny] (33) Spr 88, p. 10.
"Housekeeping." [ParisR] (30:106) Spr 88, p. 193-195.
"In the Desert" (after Rilke). [Verse] (5:1) F 88, p. 20.
"Time and Light" (for Mark Goodman, 1951-1980). [ChiR] (36:1) 88, p. 4-9.
4232. POWELL, Joseph
"The Calypso Orchid." [WebR] (13:2) Fall 88, p. 91.
"The Fortunate." [CrabCR] (5:2) Sum 88, p. 24.
"The Great Horned Owl." [Poetry] (143, i.e. 153:2) N 88, p. 96-97.
"Ode to Garlics" (for Don & Carol King). [TarRP] (27:2) Spr 88, p. 17-18.
"Photographing Agate Beach in Spring." [WebR] (13:2) Fall 88, p. 89.
"Tucquala Lake." [Poetry] (152:4) Jl 88, p. 209-210.
4233. POWELL, Marcy S.
"Long Island." [LightY] ('88/9) 88, p. 150.
"Precedented." [LightY] ('88/9) 88, p. 115.
4234. POWER, Marjorie
"At Forty." [TarRP] (27:2) Spr 88, p. 12.
"Chagall after Breakfast." [MalR] (84) S 88, p. 117.
"Her Liberation." [CreamCR] (12:2) Sum 88, p. 246.
"September Sequence" (for Anne McDermott). [HawaiiR] (12:1, #23) Spr 88, p. 9-11.
"Stay." [StoneC] (16:1/2) Fall-Wint 88-89, p. 18.
"While a Friend of Danish Ancestry Studies the Old Testament." [MalR] (84) S 88, p. 118-119.
4235. POWER, Nicholas
"Shop on Sunday." [PottPort] (9) 88, p. 21.
4236. POWERS, Dan
"Moving Under Indirect Fire." [CumbPR] (7:2) Spr 88, p. 53-54.
"Moving Under Indirect Fire." [Vis] (27) 88, p. 25.
"What to Say When We Aren't Speaking." [CumbPR] (7:2) Spr 88, p. 52.

4237. POWERS, John
"Fred's Dead Friend." [LightY] ('88/9) 88, p. 110.
4238. POYNER, Ken
"Additional Hands." [WestB] (21/22) 88, p. 106.
"The Burning of the Barn." [PoetL] (83:2) Sum 88, p. 6.
"Discussing Sex with a Son Coming of Age." [WestB] (21/22) 88, p. 105.
"Leghold Trap." [WestB] (21/22) 88, p. 104.
"Why Henson Is Beating His Wife." [PoetL] (83:2) Sum 88, p. 5.
POZNAK, Joan van
See Van POZNAK, Joan
4239. PRADO, Adélia
"A Fast One" (tr. by Ellen Watson). [Antaeus] (60) Spr 88, p. 290.
"Guide" (tr. by Ellen Watson). [Antaeus] (60) Spr 88, p. 294.
"Homily" (tr. by Ellen Watson). [Antaeus] (60) Spr 88, p. 291.
"Miserere" (tr. by Ellen Watson). [Antaeus] (60) Spr 88, p. 292-293.
4240. PRADO, Holly
"At Fifty." [Jacaranda] (3:2) Fall-Wint 88, p. 116.
"Bring the Unmemorized." [ColR] (NS 15:2) Fall-Wint 88, p. 24.
"The Daughter." [ColR] (NS 15:2) Fall-Wint 88, p. 23.
"El Dia de los Muertos." [ColR] (NS 15:2) Fall-Wint 88, p. 19.
"Every Spring." [ColR] (NS 15:2) Fall-Wint 88, p. 21-22.
"Homes." [ColR] (NS 15:2) Fall-Wint 88, p. 17.
"Never Another Light Than This." [ColR] (NS 15:2) Fall-Wint 88, p. 20.
"The Unremembered." [ColR] (NS 15:2) Fall-Wint 88, p. 18.
4241. PRANGE, Marnie
"Imprimatur." [CutB] (31/32) 88, p. 22.
"The Woman Asleep in Our Bed." [CutB] (31/32) 88, p. 21.
4242. PRAT FERRER, Juan José
"Llanto al Pie del Monte Carmelo." [Mester] (17:1) Spr 88, p. 49.
4243. PRATT, Brian
"Mute (Another Poem of Anger and Frustration)." [CanLit] (117) Sum 88, p. 43.
"Winter Wheat." [CanLit] (117) Sum 88, p. 24.
4244. PRATT, Charles W.
"A Fable in Two Languages." [LightY] ('88/9) 88, p. 102.
4245. PRATT, Minnie Bruce
"#65 Parked Down by the Potomac" (for Joan). [SinW] (35) Sum-Fall 88, p. 37.
"#67 To Be Posted on 21st Street, Between Eye and Pennsylvania" (for Joan). [SinW] (35) Sum-Fall 88, p. 35-36.
4246. PRAY, Toni
"Testing, Testing, for Fran." [EngJ] (77:4) Ap 88, p. 86.
4247. PRESTON, Gordon
"Garden Walk." [MissouriR] (11:2) 88, p. 220-221.
4248. PRICE, Alice L.
"Thinking About an Inuit Shaman Carving in Oklahoma" (For Sam Nahualatuq of Spence Bay). [Phoenix] (9:1/2) 88, p. 27.
4249. PRICE, Elizabeth A.
"Element." [MidAR] (8:2) 88, p. 9-10.
4250. PRICE, Reynolds
"Back." [Poetry] (152:1) Ap 88, p. 26.
"Easter Sunday." [Poetry] (152:1) Ap 88, p. 25.
"Good Friday." [Poetry] (152:1) Ap 88, p. 25.
"Juncture." [Poetry] (152:6) S 88, p. 332-335.
"Spring Takes the Homeplace." [NewYorker] (64:5) 21 Mr 88, p. 34.
4251. PRICE, Ron
"Drought." [SwampR] (1:1) Ja 88, p. 37.
"From the Tallahatchie Bridge" (for E.K.). [PaintedB] (32/33) 88, p. 21.
"Shine's Theology." [PaintedB] (32/33) 88, p. 21.
4252. PRICE-GRESTY, David
"Tuesday, October 6, 1987" (Excerpt, of Foreign Desk). [Amelia] (5:2, #13) 88, p. 61-63.
4253. PRICHARD, Dael
"And My Last Summer Too." [CrabCR] (5:2) Sum 88, p. 4.
"Ultra-Violet Light." [CrabCR] (5:2) Sum 88, p. 4-5.
PRIMA, Diane di
See Di PRIMA, Diane

4254. PRINCE, Heather
"Back Talk." [PottPort] (9) 88, p. 35.
4255. PRITAM, Amrita
"Daily Wages" (tr. by Charles Brasch). [Nimrod] (31:2) Spr-Sum 88, p. 96.
4256. PRIVETT, Katharine
"Dulcimers, Handmade" (shop near Gatlinburg, TN). [Phoenix] (9:1/2) 88, p. 53.
"Hugh Walker." [Wind] (18:63) 88, p. 32-33.
"If Ghosts Come Back." [Phoenix] (9:1/2) 88, p. 54.
"That First Love." [WebR] (13:2) Fall 88, p. 82.
4257. PRIVITERA, Rodolfo
"Curriculum." [CinPR] (17) Spr 88, p. 45.
"In the Afternoon." [CinPR] (17) Spr 88, p. 44.
PROKOPCZYK, Regina Grol
See GROL-PROKOPCZYK, Regina
4258. PROPER, Stan
"Fog Lays." [Lactuca] (9) F 88, p. 28.
"Izabela." [SmPd] (25:2) Spr 88, p. 23.
"The Overcoat." [Lactuca] (9) F 88, p. 28.
"Ravensbrüch Poems" (3 poems). [Lactuca] (10) Je 88, p. 30-31.
4259. PROPERTIUS
"3.24. You are wrong, woman, to trust in that beauty of yours" (tr. by Joseph Salemi). [Spirit] (9:1) 88, p. 156.
4260. PROSPERE, Susan
"Despair." [Field] (38) Spr 88, p. 27-28.
"Ultramundane Traveller." [NewYorker] (64:8) 11 Ap 88, p. 38-39.
4261. PROVENCHER, Richard
"Cathedral." [PottPort] (10) 88, p. 42.
4262. PROVOST, Sarah
"I Didn't Mean To." [VirQR] (64:3) Sum 88, p. 436-437.
"The Three Bears." [VirQR] (64:3) Sum 88, p. 437-438.
4263. PRUITT, Gladys (Gladys M.)
"Girl with Sunflowers." [ChamLR] (2:1, #3) Fall 88, p. 35.
"Progressive Madness." [ChamLR] (1) Fall 87, p. 88.
"To Michael" (from his mainland Tutu). [HawaiiR] (12:1, #23) Spr 88, p. 98-99.
4264. PRUITT, Paul
"Spender." [Wind] (18:62) 88, p. 18.
4265. PRUNTY, Wyatt
"The Blue Umbrella." [KenR] (NS 10:3) Sum 88, p. 46.
"For Don, Who Slept through the War." [KenR] (NS 10:3) Sum 88, p. 45.
"Home." [MissouriR] (11:2) 88, p. 184.
"Late Days." [SouthernR] (24:4) Aut 88, p. 948.
"The Only Child." [SouthwR] (73:4) Aut 88, p. 543.
"Water." [SouthernR] (24:4) Aut 88, p. 947.
4266. PRYNNE, J. H.
"Marzipan." [Notus] (3:2) Fall 88, p. 66-67.
4267. PUCCIA, Enrique
"Artesanía." [Inti] (28) Otoño 88, p. 174-175.
"Orden Cerrado." [Inti] (28) Otoño 88, p. 173-174.
"Otoñal Past." [Inti] (28) Otoño 88, p. 174.
"Suma de Vastedades." [Inti] (28) Otoño 88, p. 173.
4268. PUGH, Sheenagh
"Snooker Exhibition." [NewEngR] (10:4) Sum 88, p. 437.
4269. PUGHE, Bronwyn G.
"Primary Care." [HighP] (3:1) Spr 88, p. 93-96.
4270. PULTZ, Constance
"Mornings Like These." [GettyR] (1:2) Spr 88, p. 295.
"The Outcast." [SpoonRQ] (13:3) Sum 88, p. 63.
"Watercolor of Something Once Dreamed." [StoneC] (15:3/4) Spr-Sum 88, p. 5.
4271. PURDY, James
"Jan Erik Speaks." [Lactuca] (11) O 88, p. 41.
4272. PURPURA, Lia
"Anger." [Colum] (13) 88, p. 108-109.
4273. PURSIFULL, Carmen M.
"Enrique" (1st Husband). [Americas] (16:3/4) Fall-Wint 88, p. 57-59.
"The Flight" (3rd Husband). [Americas] (16:3/4) Fall-Wint 88, p. 60-64.

"Long Beach, California" (4th Husband). [Americas] (16:3/4) Fall-Wint 88, p. 65-68.

QAIS IBN DHARIH, Majnun
See IBN DHARIH, Qais, Majnun

QI-JIAO, Cai
See CAI, Qi-jiao

4274. QUAGLIANO, Tony
"Get Out of Poetry by Sundown." [ChamLR] (1:2, #2) Spr 88, p. 117-118.
"A Jazz Note" (with Artist, Laura Ruby). [ChamLR] (2:1, #3) Fall 88, p. 13.
"An Occasional Poem to Czeslaw Milosz." [ChamLR] (1) Fall 87, p. 96.
"Sure, That's It" (for John Garfield). [ChamLR] (1:2, #2) Spr 88, p. 119-121.
"To See *Shoah*." [ChamLR] (2:1, #3) Fall 88, p. 64.
"The Travelling Regionalist." [ChamLR] (1) Fall 87, p. 97-98.

4275. QUALLS, Suzanne
"Laurie's Mother, Back from the Dead." [Verse] (5:1) F 88, p. 20-21.

4276. QUASHA, George
"If I Knew How to Talk to Myself This Is What I'd Say Only Better." [Notus] (3:1) Spr 88, p. 93.
"Storyscape." [Notus] (3:1) Spr 88, p. 92.

4277. QUAYLE, Amil (Amil D.)
"The Simple Joy of Finding a Twelve-Foot High Sunflower Plant Growing in My Front Yard . . ." [KanQ] (20:3) Sum 88, p. 188-189.
"Stairways." [LitR] (31:2) Wint 88, p. 191.

4278. QUIG, Steven
"Jersey Bounce" (His plane, for Uncle Lou). [BellArk] (4:2) Mr-Ap 88, p. 3.

4279. QUINE, W. V.
"Wayward Passages." [GrandS] (8:1) Aut 88, p. 86-90.

4280. QUINN, Bernetta
"Case Histories." [KanQ] (20:1/2) Wint-Spr 88, p. 43.
"Like the Changing Grass." [Pembroke] (20) 88, p. 200.

4281. QUINN, John
"Easy Pie in Dublin." [LaurelR] (22:21) Wint 88, p. 53.
"The Fox." [LaurelR] (22:21) Wint 88, p. 54-55.
"Night Skiing." [PoetC] (19:2) Wint 88, p. 10.

4282. QUINN, John Robert
"Morning." [KanQ] (20:3) Sum 88, p. 79.

4283. QUINN, Sue
"And by 1980 We'd Made Reagan Prez." [NegC] (8:3) 88, p. 157-158.

4284. RAAB, Lawrence
"Angels." [MissouriR] (11:1) 88, p. 180.
"A Crow." [Poetry] (143, i.e. 153:1) O 88, p. 15.
"Minor Painter, Paris, 1954." [Poetry] (143, i.e. 153:1) O 88, p. 14.
"Three Anecdotes About Death." [MissouriR] (11:1) 88, p. 179.

4285. RABA, György
"A Preface to Dying" (tr. by Jascha Kessler, w. Maria Körösy). [MSS] (6:2) 88, p. 88-89.

4286. RABEARIVELO, Jean-Joseph
"Flute Players" (in Malagasy and English, tr. by Leonard Fox). [InterPR] (14:2) Fall 88, p. 66-67.
"Haute Futaie." [InterPR] (14:2) Fall 88, p. 68, 70.
"Lofty Forest" (tr. by Leonard Fox). [InterPR] (14:2) Fall 88, p. 69, 71.
"The Poem" (tr. by Leonard Fox). [InterPR] (14:2) Fall 88, p. 63.
"Le Poeme." [InterPR] (14:2) Fall 88, p. 62.
"Reading" (in Malagasy and English, tr. by Leonard Fox). [InterPR] (14:2) Fall 88, p. 60-61.
"Traduit de la Nuit" (Selections: 1, 2, 4, 21). [InterPR] (14:2) Fall 88, p. 76-82.
"Translated from the Night" (Selections: 1, 2, 4, 21, tr. by Leonard Fox). [InterPR] (14:2) Fall 88, p. 77-83.
"Valiha" (in Malagasy and English, tr. by Leonard Fox). [InterPR] (14:2) Fall 88, p. 74-75.
"The White Bull" (in Malagasy and English, tr. by Leonard Fox). [InterPR] (14:2) Fall 88, p. 64-65.
"Zebu" (in Malagasy and English, tr. by Leonard Fox). [InterPR] (14:2) Fall 88, p. 72-73.

4287. RABINOWITZ, Anna
"Age." [Sulfur] (8:2, #23) Fall 88, p. 88.

"Descent." [Sulfur] (8:2, #23) Fall 88, p. 86.
"On Seeing Andrew Serban's 'Trojan Women'." [Wind] (18:63) 88, p. 34.
"Sappho Comments on an Exhibition of Expressionist Landscapes." [Sulfur] (8:2, #23) Fall 88, p. 87.

4288. RABORG, Frederick A., Jr.
"Rattling 'cross the Tehachapis." [WindO] (50) Aut 88, p. 47.

4289. RACHEL, Naomi
"Middle April." [CanLit] (119) Wint 88, p. 24.
"Saffron: Crocus Sativus." [HawaiiR] (12:1, #23) Spr 88, p. 80-81.

4290. RADAVICH, David
"Churchyard Blues." [Plain] (9:1) Fall 88, p. 6.
"Installment." [Farm] (5:2) Fall 88, p. 61.
"Refugee." [PoetC] (20:1) Fall 88, p. 27.

4291. RADIGAN, John
"Adirondack Dawn." [Blueline] (9:1/2) 88, p. 52.

4292. RADNOTI, Miklós
"The Angel of Dread." [Sulfur] (7:3, #21) Wint 88, p. 57-58.
"Anxiously Autumn Arrives." [Sulfur] (7:3, #21) Wint 88, p. 56-57.
"Foamy Sky" (June 8th, 1940, tr. by Zsuzsanna Ozsvath and Frederick Turner). [Poetry] (151:6) Mr 88, p. 491-492.
"Forced March." [Sulfur] (7:3, #21) Wint 88, p. 62.
"Letter to My Wife" (Lager Heidenau, 1944, tr. by Zsuzsanna Ozsvath and Frederick Turner). [Poetry] (151:6) Mr 88, p. 490-491.
"Root." [Sulfur] (7:3, #21) Wint 88, p. 60-61.
"Serbian Postcard 1." [Sulfur] (7:3, #21) Wint 88, p. 61.
"Seventh Eclogue." [Sulfur] (7:3, #21) Wint 88, p. 59-60.

4293. RAE, Mary
"End of Seasons." [Poem] (60) N 88, p. 61.
"Sudden Storm." [Poem] (60) N 88, p. 60.
"Water's Edge." [Poem] (60) N 88, p. 59.

4294. RAESCHILD, Sheila
"Somebody's Life." [CentR] (32:3) Sum 88, p. 268.
"Why a Woman Takes a (Married) Lover." [CentR] (32:3) Sum 88, p. 267.

4295. RAFFEL, Burton
"Meditation: Ages and Destinies." [DenQ] (23:2) Fall 88, p. 59.

4296. RAFUL, Tony
"Pronostico Paternal." [Mairena] (10:25) 88, p. 109.

4297. RAGAN, James
"The Holy Ghost as Eighth Grader." [NewL] (54:3) Spr 88, p. 94.

4298. RAHMANN, Pat
"Where the Freeway Cuts Through the City." [Confr] (37/38) Spr-Sum 88, p. 212.

4299. RAINE, Craig
"Frustration." [YaleR] (77:3) Spr 88, p. 368-369.
"Lyric." [PartR] (55:1) Wint 88, p. 64.
"Paradise." [YaleR] (77:3) Spr 88, p. 368.

4300. RAJAN, Tilottama
"Allergy: Late October." [MassR] (29:4) Wint 88-89, p. 768.

4301. RAJU, Cherabanda
"Let Me Get Into the Witness-Box" (tr. by Sri Sri). [Nimrod] (31:2) Spr-Sum 88, p. 101-103.

4302. RALLIS, George
"Utopia's Here." [FiveFR] (6) 88, p. 69.

RAM, Amitai F. Avi
See AVI-RAM, Amitai F.

4303. RAMAKRISHNAN, Kadammanitta
"Tar and Broom" (tr. by Roy K. Tongue and Ayyappa Paniker). [Nimrod] (31:2) Spr-Sum 88, p. 84-85.

4304. RAMANTOANINA
"Distant lightning flickers" (in Malagasy and English, tr. by Leonard Fox). [InterPR] (14:2) Fall 88, p. 58-59.

4305. RAMANUJAN, A. K.
"Consolation to Empty Pitchers" (tr. of K. S. Narasimhaswami). [Nimrod] (31:2) Spr-Sum 88, p. 80-81.
"Freak" (tr. of Chandrashekhar Patil). [Nimrod] (31:2) Spr-Sum 88, p. 82-83.
"The Horse Did Not Come Back" (tr. of Erumai Veliyanar). [PartR] (55:3) Sum 88, p. 519.

4306. RAMKE, Bin
"'Compulsion' As the Critical Element in a Defined Perversion." [AntR] (46:1) Wint 88, p. 74.
"The Erotic Light of Circuses." [AntR] (46:1) Wint 88, p. 75.
"The Future of Supplication." [Ploughs] (14:4) 88, p. 64-65.
"Guilty Silence, Dirty Words." [MissR] (16:1, #46) 88, p. 74.
"Harvard Classics 16, The Arabian Nights." [OhioR] (42) 88, p. 18-20.
"Hierarchy." [MissR] (16:1, #46) 88, p. 71-73.
"The Private Tour: Circle 7, Round 3." [IndR] (11:2) Spr 88, p. 18.
"Taking a Message." [Poetry] (152:3) Je 88, p. 149.

4307. RAMKISSOON-CHEN, Rajandaye
"Father II." [Callaloo] (11:2, #35) Spr 88, p. 251-252.

4308. RAMMELL, George
"Ättehögens Ande" (photographs of sculpture with poems). [CapilR] (48) 88, p. 50-70.

4309. RAMSEY, Jarold
"Family Bible." [Chelsea] (47) 88, p. 80.
"In Vain I Tried to Tell You" (for Dell Hymes). [Chelsea] (47) 88, p. 81.
"The Proof of Atlantis" (after H.D.). [TarRP] (27:2) Spr 88, p. 21.
"Unbidden." [Chelsea] (47) 88, p. 80.

4310. RAMSEY, Martha
"Halloween." [NewL] (55:2) Wint 88-89, p. 5-6.
"It Came About." [NewL] (55:2) Wint 88-89, p. 9.
"My Father Lies in the Valley." [NewL] (55:2) Wint 88-89, p. 10-11.
"Testimony." [NewL] (55:2) Wint 88-89, p. 7-8.

4311. RAMSEY, Paul
"Late Summer Afternoon." [Pembroke] (20) 88, p. 120.
"An Ontology of Time." [Pembroke] (20) 88, p. 120.

4312. RANADIVE, Gail
"Pintura Campesina de Nicaragua" (for Joan). [PoetL] (83:2) Sum 88, p. 27.

4313. RAND, Lydia
"Huckleberry Picking." [Vis] (27) 88, p. 15.

4314. RANDALL, Margaret
"First Footnote." [TriQ] (72) Spr-Sum 88, p. 174.
"Listening." [ConnPR] (7:1) 88, p. 20.
"Rain" (tr. of Carlos Oquendo de Amat). [AmerV] (10) Spr 88, p. 85.
"Second Footnote." [TriQ] (72) Spr-Sum 88, p. 175.
"When It Snows Like This." [ConnPR] (7:1) 88, p. 19.

4315. RANDOLPH, Bob
"My Father's Breathing." [MSS] (6:2) 88, p. 12.

4316. RANDOLPH, Sally
"Twelve Haiku." [YellowS] (28) D 88, p. 22.

4317. RANKIN, Paula
"Before the Second Marriage." [TarRP] (28:1) Fall 88, p. 9.
"Before We Parted." [TarRP] (28:1) Fall 88, p. 8.
"Florida." [TarRP] (28:1) Fall 88, p. 10.

4318. RANKIN, Rush
"Musée des Beaux Arts." [AnotherCM] (18) 88, p. 157.

4319. RANSICK, Christopher
"Backroad Possibilities." [CrabCR] (5:3) Fall 88, p. 18-19.
"Sonata." [CrabCR] (5:3) Fall 88, p. 19.

4320. RAO, P., Sreenivasa
"To J — With Thanks." [FourQ] (2d series 2:2) Fall 88, p. 54.

4321. RAPHAEL, Dan
"A couldnt have gone there without B" (for Philip Whalen, novelist). [Bogg] (59) 88, p. 27.
"The Evolution of Cows." [CentralP] (14) Fall 88, p. 93.
"Never enough to get around." [Sink] (3) 88, p. 42-44.

4322. RAPP, Lea Bayers
"One Last Look." [Amelia] (5:1, #12) 88, p. 104.

4323. RAPP, Rachel
"Itineraries." [Notus] (3:2) Fall 88, p. 51.

4324. RAPTOSH, Diane
"Idaho." [MidAR] (8:1) 88, p. 97.

4325. RASH, Ron
"Photograph of a Relative Taken Two Weeks After His Tobacco Crop Was Lost in a Fire: Dated December, 1962." [SoDakR] (26:3) Aut 88, p. 53.
"A Trout Fisherman at Seventy." [BellR] (11:1) Spr 88, p. 4.
4326. RASHIDIAN, Ziba
"Siftings." [Crosscur] (7:4) 88, p. 133.
4327. RASULA, Jed
"New Rev. on Cell. Path. Porn." [Temblor] (7) 88, p. 92-103.
4328. RATCH, Jerry
"Diminished Songs." [Contact] (9:47/48/49) Spr 88, p. 45.
4329. RATCLIFFE, Stephen
"Eleven" (Excerpt). [NewAW] (3) Spr 88, p. 68-72.
"Nine" (Excerpt). [Sulfur] (8:1, #22) Spr 88, p. 130-134.
"Spaces in the Light Said to Be Where One/ Comes From." [Temblor] (7) 88, p. 120-130.
"Spaces in the Light Said to Be Where One/ Comes From" (Selections: 24-26). [Caliban] (5) 88, p. 74-75.
4330. RATNER, Rochelle
"Sabbath in Jerusalem." [GrahamHR] (11) Spr 88, p. 35.
4331. RATTEE, Michael
"Distances." [PoetL] (83:2) Sum 88, p. 28.
4332. RATTRAY, David
"The Cloud." [Bomb] (26) Wint 88-89, p. 65.
"The Spirit of St. Louis" (for John Speicher). [Bomb] (26) Wint 88-89, p. 64.
4333. RATUSHINSKAYA, Irina
"Lady Godiva" (tr. by Lyn Coffin and Serge Shishkoff). [MichQR] (27:3) Sum 88, p. 395-396.
4334. RAUP, Jonathan
"Letter to Seattle." [PaintedB] (36) 88, p. 72.
4335. RAVELLA, Cara
"Choosing Sides." [CimR] (84) Jl 88, p. 52.
"My Indian Children." [CimR] (84) Jl 88, p. 53.
4336. RAVIKOVICH, Daliah (Ravikovitch, Dahlia)
"From Day to Night" (tr. by Bernhard Frank). [ColR] (NS 15:2) Fall-Wint 88, p. 76.
"Rough Draft" (tr. by Chana Bloch). [GrahamHR] (11) Spr 88, p. 107.
"The Window" (tr. by Chana Bloch). [GrahamHR] (11) Spr 88, p. 106.
4337. RAWLINS, Susan
"Daily Bread." [PoetC] (20:1) Fall 88, p. 18.
4338. RAWORTH, Tom
"A Sequence of 126" (12 selections). [Notus] (3:2) Fall 88, p. 16-19.
"Weather Report." (Excerpts, w. David Ball). [Notus] (3:2) Fall 88, p. 20-21.
4339. RAWSON, Eric
"Photographs for the Tsar." [AmerPoR] (17:3) My-Je 88, p. 22.
"Una Romanza." [Confr] (37/38) Spr-Sum 88, p. 116.
4340. RAY, David
"Another Day of the Vietnam War" (for Robert Bly). [ColR] (NS 15:1) Spr-Sum 88, p. 86.
"The Ashes." [PraS] (62:1) Spr 88, p. 102.
"The Assassin." [PraS] (62:1) Spr 88, p. 103.
"At Emily's in Amherst." [HeliconN] (19) 88, p. 47.
"The Bomb." [MSS] (6:2) 88, p. 58.
"Couplets for the Last Class." [CharR] (14:2) Fall 88, p. 93.
"The Cross in New Zealand." [ColEng] (50:4) Ap 88, p. 402.
"The Entrepreneur" (for Robert Frost). [LightY] ('88/9) 88, p. 187.
"A Feather" (for Sam). [ColEng] (50:4) Ap 88, p. 401.
"Flag." [ColEng] (50:5) S 88, p. 514.
"The Good News Is, The Bad News Is." [LightY] ('88/9) 88, p. 133.
"Green." [ColEng] (50:5) S 88, p. 515.
"Grief." [Event] (17:1) Spr 88, p. 75.
"Hanford." [NewRep] (199:23) 5 D 88, p. 30.
"Henny." [PraS] (62:1) Spr 88, p. 105.
"Home Thoughts From Abroad." [ColEng] (50:5) S 88, p. 516.
"I Recall." [CharR] (14:2) Fall 88, p. 94.
"In the Little French Town." [Amelia] (5:2, #13) 88, p. 25.
"Iron Gates." [MSS] (6:2) 88, p. 59.

"Ironweed" (for William Kennedy). [NewL] (55:1) Fall 88, p. 77.
"Isaac Again." [Ploughs] (14:4) 88, p. 60-63.
"L." [CharR] (14:2) Fall 88, p. 95.
"A Mosaic." [Spirit] (9:1) 88, p. 151-152.
"Prakrit Verses" (tr. of 2 anonymous verses, selected by Amritjit Singh). [Nimrod] (31:2) Spr-Sum 88, p. 17.
"Red Streetcars." [SouthernPR] (28:2) Fall 88, p. 71.
"Returning from the Antipodes." [PoetC] (19:3) Spr 88, p. 47.
"Scientific Management." [PoetC] (19:3) Spr 88, p. 46.
"Searching for Marianne." [HeliconN] (19) 88, p. 46.
"A Statuette Raised from the Seafloor." [NewL] (55:1) Fall 88, p. 76.
"Summer Snapshot." [CharR] (14:2) Fall 88, p. 94.
"Surf." [Spirit] (9:1) 88, p. 151.
"Three Poems for Tom McGrath." [NoDaQ] (56:4) Fall 88, p. 121-122.
"The Tour Group." [Ploughs] (14:1) 88, p. 32-33.
"Twigs." [Poetry] (152:6) S 88, p. 349.
"Upstate." [PraS] (62:1) Spr 88, p. 104.
"Yama." [PraS] (62:1) Spr 88, p. 103-104.

4341. RAY, Elle
"Now the Darkness." [CrabCR] (5:3) Fall 88, p. 21.

4342. RAY, Judy
"Concordances." [PoetC] (19:2) Wint 88, p. 6.
"A Doodlebug in the Basement." [NewL] (54:3) Spr 88, p. 62-63.
"Hospital Exit." [PoetC] (19:2) Wint 88, p. 4-5.
"More Innocents Abroad." [Paint] (15:30) Aut 88, p. 11.
"Seeking." [HeliconN] (19) 88, p. 39.

4343. RAY, Pratima
"The Blaze" (tr. by Paramita Banerjee and Carolyne Wright). [Nimrod] (31:2) Spr-Sum 88, p. 33.
"Simile" (tr. by Paramita Banerjee and Carolyne Wright). [Nimrod] (31:2) Spr-Sum 88, p. 33.

4344. RAY, Sunil B.
"Companion" (tr. of Vijaya Mukhopadhyay, w. Carolyne Wright and the author). [Nimrod] (31:2) Spr-Sum 88, p. 31.
"Monday's Hand on Your Shoulder" (tr. of Vijaya Mukhopadhyay, w. Carolyne Wright and the author). [Nimrod] (31:2) Spr-Sum 88, p. 32.

4345. RAYMOND, Monica
"Limerick." [LightY] ('88/9) 88, p. 171.

4346. RAYNARD, Karen
"Arms Race." [PottPort] (10) 88, p. 37.

4347. RAZ, Hilda
"Lullaby." [Plain] (8:1) Fall 87, p. 12.
"Native" (for Paul Olson). [Plain] (8:1) Fall 87, p. 12.
"Pain." [Plain] (8:3) Spr-Sum 88, p. 26.
"Town / County." [Plain] (8:2) Wint 88, p. 33.

4348. REA, Susan
"Colors" (for Millicent Katz). [SingHM] (15) 88, p. 95.
"Correspondence." [SingHM] (15) 88, p. 78-79.
"Dreaming of Pregnancy." [SingHM] (15) 88, p. 74.
"Eclipse." [SingHM] (15) 88, p. 93.
"Family." [SingHM] (15) 88, p. 85.
"For My Father." [SingHM] (15) 88, p. 87-88.
"Headline: 'Woman Tied Up in Woods 91-1/2 Hours'." [SingHM] (15) 88, p. 81-82.
"Home Movies." [SingHM] (15) 88, p. 83-84.
"Listening to Mozart." [SingHM] (15) 88, p. 72-73.
"The Man Who Waves." [SingHM] (15) 88, p. 80.
"North American Rare Bird Alert." [SingHM] (15) 88, p. 92.
"Nuclear Age." [SingHM] (15) 88, p. 94.
"Playing Candleland." [SingHM] (15) 88, p. 96.
"Stroke." [SingHM] (15) 88, p. 89.
"Thaw" (for my mother). [SingHM] (15) 88, p. 86.
"Watching Fish." [SingHM] (15) 88, p. 90-91.
"Woman in Landscape" (for Nina). [SingHM] (15) 88, p. 75-77.

4349. REA, Tom
"Hunting Season." [SouthernPR] (28:2) Fall 88, p. 64.

"Mr. Stolarevsky Ends Up in a Painting by Marc Chagall." [TarRP] (27:2) Spr 88, p. 25.
"The Painter on Main Street." [TarRP] (27:2) Spr 88, p. 26.

4350. REAGLER, Robin
"Elegy." [AnotherCM] (18) 88, p. 162.
"On the Big Screen." [AnotherCM] (18) 88, p. 163.
"These Signs by Which We Sense the Failure of the Myth." [AnotherCM] (18) 88, p. 158-161.

4351. REARDON, M. A.
"Toward." [Footwork] ('88) 88, p. 79-80.
"El Yunque." [Footwork] ('88) 88, p. 79.

4352. REBAZA SORALUZ, Luis
"La Dama." [Inti] (26/27) Otoño 87-Primavera 88, p. 310.
"Mentira de la Verdad Romántica." [Inti] (26/27) Otoño 87-Primavera 88, p. 310-311.
"El Rey." [Inti] (26/27) Otoño 87-Primavera 88, p. 307-309.

4353. RECIPUTI, Natalie
"Just Say." [BellArk] (4:1) Ja-F 88, p. 6.
"Light Observations." [BellArk] (4:4) Jl-Ag 88, p. 10.
"The Rooster Dreams of Eggs." [BellArk] (4:3) My-Je 88, p. 1.

4354. REDDY, Kathleen
"Captivity." [ColR] (NS 15:2) Fall-Wint 88, p. 52-53.
"The Unidentified Man." [RiverS] (27) 88, p. 16.
"Weather Dog." [RiverS] (27) 88, p. 17.

4355. REDGROVE, Peter
"At Delabole Quarry." [ManhatR] (4:2) Spr 88, p. 62-63.
"Black Candles." [ManhatR] (4:2) Spr 88, p. 69.
"From the Tesla Papers." [ManhatR] (4:2) Spr 88, p. 64-65.
"Menopausa." [ManhatR] (4:2) Spr 88, p. 63-64.
"Opening the Shops." [ManhatR] (4:2) Spr 88, p. 67-68.
"Peaceful Moment with Books." [ManhatR] (4:2) Spr 88, p. 68.
"The Sit-Com." [ManhatR] (4:2) Spr 88, p. 66-67.
"Six Poems in October." [ManhatR] (4:2) Spr 88, p. 59-62.

4356. REDHILL, Michael
"A Certain Belief." [CapilR] (49) 88, p. 4.
"The Groom Is Ugly As the Night." [CapilR] (49) 88, p. 7.
"In bed with a plump girl against my will." [Event] (17:1) Spr 88, p. 77.
"Love Happening Badly." [Grain] (16:1) Spr 88, p. 34.
"Reason Is the Night." [CapilR] (49) 88, p. 5-6.
"The Thin Line" (for Karl Wallenda, of the high-wire family, on the anniversary of his death). [Event] (17:1) Spr 88, p. 76.
"Untitled: Early Sunday morning. Rain." [CapilR] (49) 88, p. 8.

4357. REDMOND, Eugene B.
"Poetic Reflections Enroute to, and during, the Funeral and Burial of Henry Dumas, Poet (May 29, 1968)." [BlackALF] (22:2) Sum 88, p. 333-336.

4358. REECE, Byron Herbert
"The Beetle in the Wood." [ChatR] (8:3) Spr 88, p. 18.
"The Brook." [ChatR] (8:3) Spr 88, p. 24.
"The Haying." [ChatR] (8:3) Spr 88, p. 23.
"In Palestine." [ChatR] (8:3) Spr 88, p. 15.
"The Laboring Man." [ChatR] (8:3) Spr 88, p. 16.
"The Stay-At-Home." [ChatR] (8:3) Spr 88, p. 21.

4359. REED, Alison T.
"Dark." [CimR] (84) Jl 88, p. 37.

4360. REED, Ishmael
"Why the Martinicans Have Beautiful Eyes." [Zyzzyva] (4:4) Wint 88, p. 40-41.

4361. REED, Jeremy
"City Afternoon." [Verse] (5:1) F 88, p. 65.
"Expectation." [Verse] (5:3) N 88, p. 63.
"Marbles." [YaleR] (77:3) Spr 88, p. 375.
"Rockpool." [YaleR] (77:3) Spr 88, p. 373-374.

4362. REED, John R.
"Capuchin Catacombs." [SewanR] (96:3) Sum 88, p. 413.
"Detective Novel." [OntR] (28) Spr-Sum 88, p. 42.
"A High Wind." [SewanR] (96:3) Sum 88, p. 415.
"Lenin's Brain." [SouthernPR] (28:1) Spr 88, p. 7.

"Prodigies." [SewanR] (96:3) Sum 88, p. 414.
"Transported." [Poetry] (152:5) Ag 88, p. 262.
"Treatment." [Poetry] (152:5) Ag 88, p. 263.

4363. REED, Stephen G.
"Pinnacle." [SmPd] (25:1) Wint 88, p. 18.

4364. REES, Elizabeth
"Crows." [CimR] (83) Ap 88, p. 54.
"Electra." [Footwork] ('88) 88, p. 23.
"Reasons for Rhythm." [Vis] (27) 88, p. 10.
"The Society Ladies' Ball." [KanQ] (20:1/2) Wint-Spr 88, p. 61.

4365. REES, Lisa
"Body of Water" (For Virginia Woolf). [GrahamHR] (11) Spr 88, p. 79.

4366. REEVE, F. D.
"Country Voices." [SewanR] (96:1) Wint 88, p. 48.
"The End of the Rainbow." [SewanR] (96:1) Wint 88, p. 48.
"On a Maine Island." [CreamCR] (12:2) Sum 88, p. 247.
"The Theater" (tr. of Bella Akhmadulina). [AmerPoR] (17:3) My-Je 88, p. 40.

4367. REEVES, John
"The Reading." [Footwork] ('88) 88, p. 37-38.

4368. REFFE, Candice
"The Aqua House." [Jacaranda] (3:1) Wint 88, p. 45.
"Paradise." [Agni] (27) 88, p. 223-224.
"Sailing on the Equator." [Jacaranda] (3:1) Wint 88, p. 44.
"Waiting for the Dead to Rise." [Jacaranda] (3:1) Wint 88, p. 46.

4369. REGALBUTO, Gloria
"Orchids." [Farm] (5:2) Fall 88, p. 57-60.

4370. REGAN, J. M.
"The Winter Garden: Gazals." [JamesWR] (5:2) Wint 88, p. 8.

4371. REGAN, Mary J.
"Old Hill Cemeteries Above the City." [GrahamHR] (11) Spr 88, p. 67-71.

4372. REGE, P. S.
"Ajanta, February 1962" (in Marathi and English, tr. by Philip C. Engblom). [Nimrod] (31:2) Spr-Sum 88, p. 88.
"Line" (in Marathi and English, tr. by Philip C. Engblom). [Nimrod] (31:2) Spr-Sum 88, p. 90.
"Lord Thousand-Eyes" (in Marathi and English, tr. by Philip C. Engblom). [Nimrod] (31:2) Spr-Sum 88, p. 89.
"Vision" (in Marathi and English, tr. by Philip C. Engblom). [Nimrod] (31:2) Spr-Sum 88, p. 91.

4373. REGIER, Gail
"The Circus As Sign." [IndR] (12:1) Wint 88, p. 109.
"Dutch Uncle." [IndR] (12:1) Wint 88, p. 110.

4374. REIBER, James T.
"Pearls" (tr. of Leopold Sedar Senghor). [Vis] (28) 88, p. 30.
"The Portrait" (tr. of Leopold Sedar Senghor). [Vis] (27) 88, p. 42.

4375. REID, Bethany
"Ashleigh Feeding Geese." [BellArk] (4:1) Ja-F 88, p. 5.
"Violets, Dream Horses" (for Bruce, after visiting the Elizabeth Sandvig exhibit). [BellArk] (4:4) Jl-Ag 88, p. 10.
"Yeats' Crows" (for N.B.). [BellArk] (4:5) S-O 88, p. 10.

4376. REID, Christopher
"Odyssey." [Verse] (5:3) N 88, p. 3.
"One Star in the Michelin." [GrandS] (7:4) Sum 88, p. 72.
"Tyger." [GrandS] (7:4) Sum 88, p. 71.

4377. REID, D. C.
"It Comes When It Comes." [CapilR] (49) 88, p. 16-19.

4378. REID, Graham W.
"At Sunset in the Wood" (tr. of Trayan Petrovski). [Lips] (14) 88, p. 26.
"Ballad" (tr. of Trayan Petrovski). [Lips] (14) 88, p. 27.

4379. REID, Monty
"Peripatetic." [PraF] (9:4) Wint 88-89, p. 9.
"Sutra for Brinkman in Nepal." [MalR] (85) D 88, p. 31-33.

4380. REILLY, Stephen
"Locust Swarm." [KanQ] (20:1/2) Wint-Spr 88, p. 303.

4381. REIMER, Dolores
"Designing Flowerbeds." [Grain] (16:4) Wint 88, p. 71.

"The Swimming Lesson." [Grain] (16:4) Wint 88, p. 70.
4382. REINERS, Victoria
"March Rain." [Jacaranda] (3:1) Wint 88, p. 69.
4383. REINHARD, John
"Oh, Could Cheryl Ferguson Dangle." [PassN] (9:1) Wint 88, p. 21.
4384. REINSCH, Margo
"Abracadabra." [BellR] (11:1) Spr 88, p. 7.
"Nesting." [BellArk] (4:3) My-Je 88, p. 1.
REIS, Ricardo
See PESSOA, Fernando
4385. REIS, Siri von
"God Said We Should Multiply with Anything That Is Good" (after tapes of Bessie Harvey). [Colum] (13) 88, p. 141-142.
"The Shaker Child." [Colum] (13) 88, p. 139-140.
4386. REISS, James
"Amphitheater Canyon." [LitR] (31:3) Spr 88, p. 296.
"A Call." [SenR] (18:1) 88, p. 28.
"Lake Night Festival" (June 1987). [MissouriR] (11:2) 88, p. 185.
"Supper in Tiberias." [Shen] (38:3) 88, p. 17-18.
4387. REITER, Jendi
"I came in from the daylight that glides among the leaves." [HangL] (52) 88, p. 86.
4388. REITER, Lora K.
"Before Sunrise." [KanQ] (20:1/2) Wint-Spr 88, p. 304.
4389. REITER, Thomas
"Class Bully." [Poetry] (151:6) Mr 88, p. 461-462.
"Creek Fire." [FloridaR] (16:1) Spr-Sum 88, p. 62-63.
"My Grandmother's Saints." [TarRP] (28:1) Fall 88, p. 57-58.
4390. REITZENSTEIN, Gerg
"The Pull Is One of Wool." [Writ] (20) 88, p. 44.
"Things to Do." [Writ] (20) 88, p. 45.
4391. REMINGTON, Daniel
"The Aerobic Shop." [Amelia] (5:2, #13) 88, p. 126.
4392. RENDLEMAN, Danny
"Muskegon." [Abraxas] (37) 88, p. 31.
4393. RENDRICK, Bernice
"The Pastel Child." [KanQ] (20:3) Sum 88, p. 159.
4394. RENEHAN, E. J.
"Family Burying Ground." [AmerS] (57:2) Spr 88, p. 221-222.
4395. RENKL, Margaret
"The Swarming." [PoetryNW] (29:3) Aut 88, p. 5.
"Waiting Room, Cancer Ward." [TexasR] (9:1/2) Spr-Sum 88, p. 94-95.
4396. RENO, Janet
"The Senoritas." [Spirit] (9:1) 88, p. 16.
4397. REPP, John
"Good as Walter John, Good as Mathewson." [NewEngR] (11:1) Aut 88, p. 105-106.
"Watering the Garden." [RiverS] (25) 88, p. 67.
4398. RETTBERG, Georgeann Eskievich
"America's Fist" (for my grandfather). [FiveFR] (6) 88, p. 7.
"A whisper." [DeKalbLAJ] (21:1) Wint 88, p. 65.
4399. REVARD, Carter
"Close Encounters." [RiverS] (25) 88, p. 38-40.
"In the Changing Light." [RiverS] (25) 88, p. 41-42.
4400. REVELL, Donald
"Consenting." [AmerPoR] (17:1) Ja-F 88, p. 22.
"Eumenides." [AmerPoR] (17:1) Ja-F 88, p. 21.
"From the Outside." [Shen] (38:4) 88, p. 75-76.
"Futurist." [AmerPoR] (17:1) Ja-F 88, p. 22.
"Magus." [Shen] (38:2) 88, p. 42-43.
"New Dark Ages." [Shen] (38:2) 88, p. 43-44.
"The Northeast Corridor." [AmerPoR] (17:1) Ja-F 88, p. 20.
"A Parish in the Bronx." [MissouriR] (11:2) 88, p. 62-63.
"The Pastoral Tradition." [Sulfur] (8:2, #23) Fall 88, p. 113.
"Perspective." [NewRep] (199:15) 10 O 88, p. 36.
"Psalmist." [Poetry] (153:3) D 88, p. 154-155.
"The Siege of the City of Gorky." [AmerPoR] (17:1) Ja-F 88, p. 20.

"Trying to Live." [AmerPoR] (17:1) Ja-F 88, p. 21.
"Wartime." [Sulfur] (8:2, #23) Fall 88, p. 115-116.
"White Pastoral." [Sulfur] (8:2, #23) Fall 88, p. 113-115.
"Why History Imitates God." [ParisR] (30:106) Spr 88, p. 197-198.

4401. REVERDY, Pierre
"Love in the Shop" (tr. by Rosanna Warren). [AmerPoR] (17:4) Jl-Ag 88, p. 41.
"Same Taste" (tr. by Rosanna Warren). [AmerPoR] (17:4) Jl-Ag 88, p. 41.
"Verso" (tr. by Rosanna Warren). [AmerPoR] (17:4) Jl-Ag 88, p. 41.

REVUELTA, Pedro Gutierrez
See GUTIERREZ REVUELTA, Pedro

4402. REWAK, William J.
"A Formic Study." [KanQ] (20:1/2) Wint-Spr 88, p. 202.
"I Really Do Love My IBM PC XT." [KanQ] (20:1/2) Wint-Spr 88, p. 201.
"Now an Elephant." [KanQ] (20:1/2) Wint-Spr 88, p. 201.
"The Possible." [DeKalbLAJ] (21:2) Spr 88, p. 42.
"Pterodactyls Are Not Inconsiderate." [KanQ] (20:1/2) Wint-Spr 88, p. 200.
"The Waiting Room." [DeKalbLAJ] (21:2) Spr 88, p. 43.

4403. REXROTH, Kenneth
"Collected Shorter: Further Advantages of Learning." [Contact] (9:47/48/49) Spr 88, p. 24.
"Homecoming — Late at Night" (tr. of Fu Du). [Blueline] (9:1/2) 88, p. 54.

REYES, Myrna Peña
See PEÑA-REYES, Myrna

4404. REYES RIVERA, Louis
"The Broomstick Stallion" (Selection: 3, tr. of Clemente Soto Vélez). [HangL] (52) 88, p. 71.

4405. REYES VAZQUEZ, Radhamés
"El Crepusculo de Ezra Pound" (fragmento). [Mairena] (10:25) 88, p. 109-110.

4406. REYNOLDS, Craig A.
"Late Summer." [Turnstile] (1:2) 88, p. 70.

4407. REYNOLDS, Oliver
"City." [Antaeus] (60) Spr 88, p. 231-233.
"Encyclopedia Cantonnica." [NewEngR] (10:4) Sum 88, p. 421-423.

4408. RHEA, Tom
"The Feel of Things." [GeoR] (42:2) Sum 88, p. 400-401.

4409. RHENISCH, Harold
"Charlie Edenshaw (Tahaygen), Circa 1839-1924." [Grain] (16:3) Fall 88, p. 14.
"Grave Carvings at Tsartslip Reserve." [Grain] (16:3) Fall 88, p. 15.
"Grave Post at Cape Mudge." [Dandel] (15:1) Spr-Sum 88, p. 2021.

4410. RHOADES, Lisa
"Needlepoint." [FloridaR] (16:1) Spr-Sum 88, p. 60.

4411. RHODENBAUGH, Suzanne
"A Bird Lives in My Grocery Store." [TexasR] (9:3/4) Fall-Wint 88, p. 113-114.
"The Marriage Bed." [TexasR] (9:3/4) Fall-Wint 88, p. 112.
"Sire." [Spirit] (9:1) 88, p. 153.

4412. RHODES, Gina
"The Last Supper." [Cond] (15) 88, p. 139.
"Margaret." [Cond] (15) 88, p. 40-41.

4413. RHODES, Martha
"Draining Fox Hill Pond." [Bomb] (25) Fall 88, p. 70.
"Our Bedroom Walls." [Bomb] (25) Fall 88, p. 70.
"These Are the Nights." [Bomb] (25) Fall 88, p. 70.

4414. RICCI, Roy
"Gum Wrapper." [Contact] (9:47/48/49) Spr 88, p. 46.

4415. RICE, Paul
"Pulpwood Train: 5:00 a.m." [ChatR] (8:2) Wint 88, p. 98.

4416. RICH, Adrienne
"Negotiations." [SinW] (33) Fall 87, p. 10.

4417. RICH, Mark
"Amassing Knowledge." [LightY] ('88/9) 88, p. 103.
"A Person of Action Wonders Sometimes." [ManhatR] (4:2) Spr 88, p. 47.

4418. RICH, Morton D.
"Vacation on the River Flatulent." [Footwork] ('88) 88, p. 81.

4419. RICHARDS, Marilee
"Cows Remember." [SouthernR] (24:1) Wint 88, p. 164-165.
"Fly Fishing." [SouthernR] (24:1) Wint 88, p. 165-166.

"Jen." [SouthernPR] (28:1) Spr 88, p. 56-57.
4420. RICHARDS, Tad
"Distant Early Warning." [CarolQ] (40:2) Wint 88, p. 70.
"Female Bigfoot Stole My Baby, Heartbroken Teen Laments." [LaurelR] (22:21) Wint 88, p. 61.
"The Gravel Business." [LaurelR] (22:21) Wint 88, p. 59-61.
4421. RICHES, Brenda
"Book of Hours." [Dandel] (15:2) Fall-Wint 88, p. 35-37.
"Instrumental." [Dandel] (15:2) Fall-Wint 88, p. 34.
"The Walking Place." [CapilR] (49) 88, p. 57-65.
4422. RICHETTI, Peter
"Black Star." [HighP] (3:1) Spr 88, p. 58-59.
"Duet." [AmerPoR] (17:6) N-D 88, p. 33.
"Three Little Nietzsche Poems." [AmerPoR] (17:6) N-D 88, p. 33.
"Where Is It?" [HighP] (3:1) Spr 88, p. 57.
4423. RICHMAN, Elliot
"Another Homecoming — Late at Night." [Blueline] (9:1/2) 88, p. 54.
"Haiku Composed in the Rain." [WindO] (50) Aut 88, p. 4.
"My Dadaist Therapist." [SlipS] (8) 88, p. 76-77.
"Night Basketball in a Baltimore Playground on an April Evening in 1954." [WindO] (50) Aut 88, p. 49.
"The Old Pain Comes Calling" (a found poem. Thanks to Anne). [Spirit] (9:1) 88, p. 140-142.
"Seven Sketches from the Tao." [BelPoJ] (38:4) Sum 88, p. 28-30.
4424. RICHMOND, Steve
"All." [Wind] (18:62) 88, p. 39.
"Gagaku." [Bogg] (59) 88, p. 29-30.
"Gagaku." [Bogg] (60) 88, p. 55.
"Gagaku" (4 poems). [Lactuca] (9) F 88, p. 40-41.
"Gagaku" (6 poems). [Lactuca] (11) O 88, p. 38-41.
"Gagaku: I like hookers hookers understand." [SlipS] (8) 88, p. 65.
4425. RICHSTONE, May
"Constructive Criticism." [LightY] ('88/9) 88, p. 61.
4426. RICKABAUGH, Devon
"For Suzy, the Sow at the Puyallup Fair." [BellArk] (4:1) Ja-F 88, p. 4.
4427. RICKEL, Boyer
"Our Names." [CarolQ] (40:2) Wint 88, p. 32.
RICORD, Elsie Alvarado de
See ALVARADO DE RICORD, Elsie
4428. RIDDELL, Elizabeth
"My Second Cousin." [PraS] (62:4) Wint 88-89, p. 17.
4429. RIDER, Eddie Lee
"Miss Oxygene." [ChatR] (8:3) Spr 88, p. 57.
4430. RIDL, Jack
"After School" (for John Armstrong). [CarolQ] (40:3) Spr 88, p. 73.
"American Suite for a Lost Daughter." [Poetry] (152:3) Je 88, p. 152-154.
"Coach Goes Down the Hall Wondering Where All the Men Went." [PassN] (9:1) Wint 88, p. 12.
"Coach on Vacation." [PoetryE] (25) Spr 88, p. 99.
"Coach Sits in Church Drawing a New Offense on the Front of the Sunday Bulletin." [CarolQ] (41:1) Fall 88, p. 36.
"My Girl's Father Always Changed the Station." [SouthernPR] (28:2) Fall 88, p. 11.
"Tall Tales." [ChamLR] (2:1, #3) Fall 88, p. 34.
4431. RIDLAND, John
"To Helen." [Hudson] (40:4) Wint 88, p. 627.
4432. RIEL, Steven
"Bird's Eye View" (on the 40th anniversary of Hiroshima and Nagasaki). [MinnR] (NS 30/31) Spr-Fall 88, p. 43-45.
4433. RIELLY, Edward J.
"Darkness." [BellR] (11:1) Spr 88, p. 13.
"The Next Assignment." [BellR] (11:1) Spr 88, p. 14.
4434. RIGGS, Dionis Coffin
"Salt" (tr. of Bedri Rahmi Eyuboglu, w. Ozcan Yalim and William A. Fielder). [StoneC] (16:1/2) Fall-Wint 88-89, p. 40.

4435. RILEY, Joanne M.
"Aunt Ruth." [Spirit] (9:1) 88, p. 166.
"The Church That Says Women Cannot Cut Their Hair" (for Judy). [SouthernHR] (22:3) Sum 88, p. 223.
4436. RILEY, Mark S.
"I Remember Wishing I Knew How to Paint." [SmPd] (25:3) Fall 88, p. 18.
4437. RILEY, Michael D.
"The Man in the Brown Shirt." [MinnR] (NS 30/31) Spr-Fall 88, p. 33-35.
4438. RILEY, Tom
"The Charitable Stranger." [LightY] ('88/9) 88, p. 43.
"The Painted Mirror." [Paint] (15:30) Aut 88, p. 22.
"Professional Individual." [LightY] ('88/9) 88, p. 86.
4439. RILKE, Rainer Maria
"1.4. O ihr Zärtlichen, tretet zuweilen." [InterPR] (14:1) Spr 88, p. 18.
"1.4. O, you innocents, go out now and then" (tr. by Steven Lautermilch). [InterPR] (14:1) Spr 88, p. 19.
"Apprehension" (tr. by Edward Snow). [Thrpny] (35) Fall 88, p. 14.
"Die Aschanti" (Jardin d'Acclimatation). [Thrpny] (35) Fall 88, p. 18.
"The Ashanti: Jardin d'Acclimatation" (tr. by Edward Snow). [Thrpny] (35) Fall 88, p. 18.
"Autumn Day" (tr. by Steven Lautermilch). [InterPR] (14:1) Spr 88, p. 15.
"Bangnis." [Thrpny] (35) Fall 88, p. 14.
"Experience of Death" (tr. by Walter Arndt). [Thrpny] (35) Fall 88, p. 14.
"A Festival Play" (For the Inauguration of the Art Center, Bremen, 1902, tr. by John Locke). [Paint] (15:30) Aut 88, p. 26-29.
"Herbsttag." [InterPR] (14:1) Spr 88, p. 14.
"Mariae Verkündigung." [InterPR] (14:1) Spr 88, p. 16.
"Mary's Annunciation" (tr. by Steven Lautermilch). [InterPR] (14:1) Spr 88, p. 17.
"Mein Leben ist nicht diese steile Stunde." [InterPR] (14:1) Spr 88, p. 12.
"My life is not this steep and dizzy hour" (tr. by Steven Lautermilch). [InterPR] (14:1) Spr 88, p. 13.
"To Say While Falling Asleep" (tr. by Steven Lautermilch). [InterPR] (14:1) Spr 88, p. 15.
"Todeserfahrung." [Thrpny] (35) Fall 88, p. 14.
"Untitled: We say release, and radiance, and roses" (tr. by Stephen Mitchell). [Thrpny] (35) Fall 88, p. 14.
"Untitled: Wir sagen Reinheit and wir sagen Rose." [Thrpny] (35) Fall 88, p. 14.
"Zum Einschlafen zu Sagen." [InterPR] (14:1) Spr 88, p. 14.
4440. RINALDI, Nicholas
"It Happens." [TexasR] (9:3/4) Fall-Wint 88, p. 115.
4441. RIND, Sherry
"A Chick Falls Out the Door." [PoetryNW] (29:1) Spr 88, p. 29.
4442. RINGER, Darby
"Flowers That Light the Way." [BellArk] (4:5) S-O 88, p. 10.
4443. RINGOLD, Francine Leffler
"Dear Father." [Phoenix] (9:1/2) 88, p. 30.
"Don't Mention It" (Quartz Mountain, October 12, 1985). [Phoenix] (9:1/2) 88, p. 31.
"Quartz Mountain Divide." [Phoenix] (9:1/2) 88, p. 31.
4444. RIORDAN, Timothy M.
"Overture." [CinPR] (17) Spr 88, p. 71.
4445. RIOS, Alberto
"Concerning an End to His Life." [WestHR] (42:1) Spr 88, p. 71.
"Edith Piaf Dead." [PraS] (62:3) Fall 88, p. 111-112.
"In Second Grade Miss Lee I Promised Never to Forget You and I Never Did." [TampaR] (1) 88, p. 59.
"Leaving Off." [PraS] (62:3) Fall 88, p. 110-111.
"The Lime Orchard Woman." [MissR] (16:1, #46) 88, p. 75-78.
"Lost on September Trail, 1976." [WillowS] (21) Wint 88, p. 11-14.
"Miguelin and His Best Idea" (For Joaquin). [WillowS] (21) Wint 88, p. 15.
"Saints, and Their Care." [AmerPoR] (17:3) My-Je 88, p. 47.
"Sculpting the Whistle." [PraS] (62:3) Fall 88, p. 109-110.
"The Sea by Holding." [WillowS] (21) Wint 88, p. 16.
"Shoreline Horses." [PraS] (62:3) Fall 88, p. 113-114.
"The Sword Eusebio Montero Swallowed, and Kept There." [Crazy] (34) Spr 88, p. 7-10.

4446. RIOS, Catalina
"The Three Tongues." [SinW] (34) Spr 88, p. 58.
4447. RIOS, Frank T.
"The Clown." [Jacaranda] (3:1) Wint 88, p. 107-108.
"Structures Already Charted." [Jacaranda] (3:1) Wint 88, p. 108-109.
RIPER, Craig van
See Van RIPER, Craig
4448. RIPPIN, Kevin
"Witness." [KanQ] (20:3) Sum 88, p. 215.
4449. RISDEN, E. L.
"Introit." [HiramPoR] (44/45) Spr-Wint 88, p. 37.
4450. RISI, Nelo
"Backwards Suite" (3, tr. by Richard Zenith). [LitR] (31:4) Sum 88, p. 469.
"Elementary Thought #21" (tr. by Richard Zenith). [LitR] (31:4) Sum 88, p. 468.
"How Much Longer?" (tr. by Richard Zenith). [LitR] (31:4) Sum 88, p. 468.
4451. RISTAU, Harland
"Enigma # 158." [Northeast] (ser. 4:7) Sum 88, p. 48.
4452. RITCHIE, Elisavietta
"Bumper Brop." [Amelia] (5:1, #12) 88, p. 38.
"Correspondence with a Russian Sailor." [CinPR] (18) Fall 88, p. 16-17.
"Giant Cameroonian Frog." [StoneC] (16:1/2) Fall-Wint 88-89, p. 12.
4453. RITCHINGS, Joan Drew
"April Fool." [LightY] ('88/9) 88, p. 114.
"Nuptial." [LightY] ('88/9) 88, p. 136.
4454. RITSOS, Yannis
"Helen" (tr. by Peter Green and Beverly Bardsley). [GrandS] (8:1) Aut 88, p. 65-85.
4455. RITTY, Joan
"Bonsai." [CentR] (32:3) Sum 88, p. 278.
"Prime Time." [Plain] (8:1) Fall 87, p. 21.
4456. RIVARD, David
"Ariadne." [Agni] (27) 88, p. 20-21.
"Fall River." [NoAmR] (273:1) Mr 88, p. 9.
"Firestone." [Agni] (27) 88, p. 18-19.
4457. RIVARD, Dennis
"Semi-Celebration of Existence." [Plain] (8:2) Wint 88, p. 18.
"Shuttle Disaster." [Plain] (8:3) Spr-Sum 88, p. 23.
4458. RIVARD, Ken
"More Common." [CapilR] (49) 88, p. 13.
"Pulsing Through Their Optimism." [CapilR] (49) 88, p. 15.
"The Tania Carousel" (for Tania Laniel). [CapilR] (49) 88, p. 14.
RIVAS, Carlos Martínez
See MARTINEZ RIVAS, Carlos
4459. RIVAS PORTA, Guillermo
"Silencios de la Honda Herida." [LindLM] (7:2/4) Ap-D 88, p. 5.
4460. RIVERA, Diana
"Heart Doctor." [Paint] (15:29) Spr 88, p. 27.
"May's Rain." [Paint] (15:29) Spr 88, p. 26.
"Returning." [StoneC] (16:1/2) Fall-Wint 88-89, p. 50.
RIVERA, Louis Reyes
See REYES RIVERA, Louis
4461. RIVERA, Tomás
"Always and Other Poems" (12 poems). [BilingR] (13:1/2) Ja-Ag 86, c1988, p. 7-14.
"The Searchers." [BilingR] (13:1/2) Ja-Ag 86, c1988, p. 15-20.
4462. RIVERS, J. W.
"From the German Homeland, Gottlieb Beissel, His Wife Gerda and His Brother Gottrecht Settle . . . ." [SoCaR] (21:1) Fall 88, p. 24-26.
"Hiking with the Old Acorn Lady." [Poetry] (152:4) Jl 88, p. 211-212.
"Reconciliation." [Poetry] (152:4) Jl 88, p. 212-214.
RIVIERE, G. M. La
See LaRIVIERE, G. M.
4463. ROBBINS, Anthony (*See also* Robbins, Anthony J.)
"On the Tropic of Time." [Sulfur] (8:2, #23) Fall 88, p. 39-40.
"Organism As Metaphor." [Sulfur] (8:2, #23) Fall 88, p. 40-41.
"Second Night." [SouthernR] (24:4) Aut 88, p. 968.

"To Genevieve in Her Sickness." [SouthernR] (24:4) Aut 88, p. 969.
4464. ROBBINS, Anthony J. (*See also* Robbins, Anthony)
"Snow, Streetlamp (Philadelphia, February, 1983)." [Wind] (18:62) 88, p. 40-41.
"Totem." [Wind] (18:62) 88, p. 40.
4465. ROBBINS, Martin
"The Angels Around My Bed." [Os] (27) 88, p. 3.
"A City Underpass." [Os] (26) 88, p. 14.
"Going Through Old Photos." [StoneC] (15:3/4) Spr-Sum 88, p. 31.
"Hospital Vigil." [CapeR] (23:2) Fall 88, p. 35.
"Night Watchman." [SewanR] (96:2) Spr 88, p. 216.
"Old Snapshot." [CapeR] (23:1) Spr 88, p. 34.
"One Illness, Long Life: A Cancer Notebook." [WebR] (13:1) Spr 88, p. 5-13.
"Rembrandt's Portrait of His Father." [SewanR] (96:2) Spr 88, p. 216.
"To My Happy Workshop Poets." [CapeR] (23:1) Spr 88, p. 33.
"The Year Chagall Died." [Crosscur] (7:4) 88, p. 93.
4466. ROBBINS, Richard
"Fourth-Person Singular." [PoetryNW] (29:4) Wint 88-89, p. 46.
"How November Comes." [MidAR] (8:1) 88, p. 98.
"The Literalists." [MissouriR] (11:1) 88, p. 151.
"Our Second House." [CharR] (14:2) Fall 88, p. 104.
"Planting Potatoes on Good Friday." [CharR] (14:2) Fall 88, p. 103.
"You Felt Happy." [PoetryNW] (29:4) Wint 88-89, p. 47.
4467. ROBBINS, Robert J.
"For Primo Levi." [Nimrod] (32:1) Fall-Wint 88, p. 125.
4468. ROBBINS, Sandra Morgan
"Magazines and Plastic Capers." [KanQ] (20:1/2) Wint-Spr 88, p. 74.
4469. ROBBINS, Tim
"Answering Machine." [HangL] (53) 88, p. 47.
"Better Homes." [HangL] (53) 88, p. 48.
"Moonlighting." [HangL] (53) 88, p. 47.
"Speeding." [JamesWR] (6:1) Fall 88, p. 3.
"Vesper Service at the Fair." [HangL] (53) 88, p. 46.
4470. ROBERTS, Betty
"Christmas Cabaret." [Bogg] (60) 88, p. 32.
4471. ROBERTS, Charles Stewart
"Cézanne." [AmerPoR] (17:3) My-Je 88, p. 37.
ROBERTS, Cynthia Day
See DAY-ROBERTS, Cynthia
4472. ROBERTS, Dick
"Fishing Trip." [SouthernPR] (28:1) Spr 88, p. 42.
4473. ROBERTS, Johnnie G.
"For Etheridge." [PaintedB] (32/33) 88, p. 17.
4474. ROBERTS, Kim
"Poem Ending with the Thesis Sentence from a Freshman's Comparison/Contrast Essay Assignment." [StoneC] (16:1/2) Fall-Wint 88-89, p. 20.
4475. ROBERTS, Len
"The Black Wings." [CinPR] (18) Fall 88, p. 67.
"The Drivers." [QW] (27) Sum-Fall 88, p. 116.
"He's Alone." [IndR] (12:1) Wint 88, p. 106-107.
"Learning on Olmstead Street." [Poetry] (152:3) Je 88, p. 143.
"Making Galumpkis." [WestB] (21/22) 88, p. 154.
"Ray Shows His Brother the Barn." [PassN] (9:1) Wint 88, p. 16.
"The Red Leaves Remind Me Again." [NoAmR] (273:2) Je 88, p. 31.
"Rising to Work, January, Upstate New York." [NowestR] (26:3) 88, p. 18.
"The Seven Steps." [Poetry] (152:3) Je 88, p. 144.
"Sleighing Down the Clay Hill." [KanQ] (20:1/2) Wint-Spr 88, p. 281.
"Talking on the Telephone." [QW] (27) Sum-Fall 88, p. 117.
"Tine" (for Joshua). [KanQ] (20:1/2) Wint-Spr 88, p. 282.
"Ushering in the New Year at the Cohoes Theater." [WestB] (21/22) 88, p. 155.
"We." [IndR] (12:1) Wint 88, p. 108.
"What Next?" [TarRP] (27:2) Spr 88, p. 5.
"When the Bishop Came." [CinPR] (18) Fall 88, p. 66.
"When the Dead Speak." [NowestR] (26:3) 88, p. 19.
4476. ROBERTS, Michael Symmons
"The Telex." [Verse] (5:3) N 88, p. 59.

4477. ROBERTS, Phil
"Reflections on a Globe." [PottPort] (10) 88, p. 5.
"Return." [PottPort] (10) 88, p. 4.
4478. ROBERTS, Rebecca
"The Singing Bridge" (for my mother). [PassN] (9:1) Wint 88, p. 11.
4479. ROBERTS, Sheila
"The Residents of Clifton Beach Town Houses." [CreamCR] (12:2) Sum 88, p. 248-254.
4480. ROBERTS, Stephen R.
"Larval Stage" (To an abandoned Oliver tractor). [Farm] (5:2) Fall 88, p. 73.
"Nothing Rhymes with Orange." [Farm] (5:2) Fall 88, p. 72.
4481. ROBERTS, Teresa Noelle
"Dancing for My Grandmother." [BellArk] (4:4) Jl-Ag 88, p. 7.
"The Heat at the Heart of the Blizzard." [BellArk] (4:6) N-D 88, p. 9.
"Movement of Water, Movement of Longing." [BellArk] (4:2) Mr-Ap 88, p. 7.
"Rose Medallion" (Chinese New York 1988). [BellArk] (4:3) My-Je 88, p. 8.
"Witch Candles, the Flame." [BellArk] (4:5) S-O 88, p. 16.
"Wolf Moon." [BellArk] (4:6) N-D 88, p. 10.
4482. ROBERTS, Tony
"Watching Trout." [Verse] (5:2) Jl 88, p. 17.
4483. ROBERTSON, Carol Ann
"Circling the Daughter" (for Tandi). [PaintedB] (32/33) 88, p. 91.
"Some Words of Advice." [PaintedB] (32/33) 88, p. 90.
4484. ROBERTSON, Georgia
"Early Rain, Late Rain." [Plain] (8:2) Wint 88, p. 10-11.
"I Expect Nothing to Happen Again." [Plain] (8:3) Spr-Sum 88, p. 20-21.
"Watching the Play" (for Louan). [Plain] (8:1) Fall 87, p. 23.
4485. ROBERTSON, Kell
"Of Bats and Drunks." [SwampR] (1:2/3) D 88, p. 62-63.
4486. ROBERTSON, Kirk
"Hopper." [SwampR] (1:1) Ja 88, p. 15.
"Pollock." [SwampR] (1:1) Ja 88, p. 13.
"Schwitters." [SwampR] (1:1) Ja 88, p. 16-17.
"Seurat." [SwampR] (1:1) Ja 88, p. 14.
4487. ROBERTSON, Robin
"Child Lost." [GrandS] (7:2) Wint 88, p. 25.
"Fugue for Phantoms." [GrandS] (7:2) Wint 88, p. 23.
"Given Time" (i.m. David Jones, 1 November 1895-28 October 1974). [GrandS] (7:2) Wint 88, p. 27-28.
"Pibroch." [GrandS] (7:2) Wint 88, p. 24.
"Stones." [GrandS] (7:2) Wint 88, p. 26.
4488. ROBIDEAUX, Sharon Cockerham
"The Shadow of the Bird." [SouthernPR] (28:2) Fall 88, p. 17-18.
4489. ROBINS, Corinne
"230 Self Portraits" (For Alan Kleinman). [Confr] (37/38) Spr-Sum 88, p. 193.
4490. ROBINSON, Al
"Beyond the Vanishing Point" (for Robert Orsini). [YellowS] (27) Aut 88, p. 22.
"Philip's Dream." [YellowS] (27) Aut 88, p. 22.
4491. ROBINSON, Elizabeth
"October Etudes" (Selections: I, V, VII). [CentralP] (13) Spr 88, p. 103-105.
4492. ROBINSON, James
"Under the Dust of Lions." [ChamLR] (1:2, #2) Spr 88, p. 11-12.
4493. ROBINSON, James Miller
"Caravan" (for Clearence Jordan). [Wind] (18:63) 88, p. 35.
"The Day of the Dead." [SouthernHR] (22:4) Fall 88, p. 388.
"Isidro's Brith." [Poem] (60) N 88, p. 6.
4494. ROBINSON, John D.
"Shakespeare." [Iowa] (18:3) 88, p. 132-135.
"Windfall." [Iowa] (18:3) 88, p. 136-137.
4495. ROBINSON, Kit
"The Champagne of Concrete." [Zyzzyva] (4:3) Fall 88, p. 62-64.
"Zoo." [CinPR] (17) Spr 88, p. 77.
4496. ROBINSON, Leonard Wallace
"Charlotte Waiting before Dying." [Atlantic] (261:2) F 88, p. 61.
"Sicilian Airs." [LightY] ('88/9) 88, p. 114.

4497. ROBINSON, Peter
"Consorts of Phantasms." [Verse] (5:3) N 88, p. 65.
"A Disturbed Night." [Thrpny] (33) Spr 88, p. 25.
4498. ROBINSON, Roland
"Billy Bamboo" (Aboriginal Narrative of New South Wales, Related by Billy Bamboo, Wallaga Lake). [PraS] (62:4) Wint 88-89, p. 18-19.
"The Child Who Had No Father" (Aboriginal Narrative of New South Wales, Related by Fred Biggs). [PraS] (62:4) Wint 88-89, p. 20-21.
"The Song of the Vine" (Aboriginal Narrative of New South Wales, Related by Charlotte Williams). [PraS] (62:4) Wint 88-89, p. 21.
4499. ROBISON, Margaret
"Because of These Things." [SinW] (36) Wint 88-89, p. 9-10.
4500. ROBSON, Ruthann
"Closure." [SinW] (35) Sum-Fall 88, p. 38-42.
"Self-Portrait of Frida Kahlo without a Moustache." [Cond] (15) 88, p. 7-8.
4501. ROBY, G.
"Widower." [MissouriR] (11:1) 88, p. 182.
ROCCA, L. della
See DellaROCCA, L.
4502. ROCHA, Luis
"Mirror" (tr. by Nancy Esposito). [AmerPoR] (17:2) Mr-Ap 88, p. 31.
4503. ROCHE, Joanna
"Flight." [PacificR] (6) Spr 88, p. 60-61.
"Labyrinth." [PacificR] (6) Spr 88, p. 62.
4504. ROCHE, Judith
"The Release." [AmerV] (13) Wint 88, p. 73-74.
4505. RODAS, Ana María
"Explain to Me" (tr. by Zoe Anglesey). [RedBass] (13) 88, p. 16.
"Scab" (tr. by Zoë Anglesey). [CrabCR] (5:1) Wint 88, p. 25.
4506. RODEFER, Stephen
"Drove of Stallions." [CentralP] (13) Spr 88, p. 17.
"Priory." [NewAW] (3) Spr 88, p. 55-57.
4507. RODITI, Edouard
"From the Marble Rose to the Iron Rose" (tr. of Robert Desnos). [Antaeus] (60) Spr 88, p. 265-266.
"Meditation on Robert Burton's 'Anatomy of Melancholy'." [Notus] (3:2) Fall 88, p. 42-43.
4508. RODNING, Charles (Charles B.)
"Late autumn rains." [BallSUF] (29:4) Aut 88, p. 27.
"The river runs." [Amelia] (5:2, #13) 88, p. 22.
"A sparrow's song." [BallSUF] (29:4) Aut 88, p. 27.
4509. RODNING, Susan Alene
"From the Ridge I Call to Her." [PraF] (9:2) Sum 88, p. 26.
4510. RODRIGUESORIANO, René
"Cortaziana con Lluvia y Chocolate." [CuadP] (5:14) Enero-Abril 88, p. 41-42.
"Cuando Se Calló la Ultima Canción en el Cassette." [CuadP] (5:14) Enero-Abril 88, p. 39-40.
"Estrobóscópica i." [CuadP] (5:14) Enero-Abril 88, p. 37-38.
"Estrobóscópica ii." [CuadP] (5:14) Enero-Abril 88, p. 38-39.
"Ni Tanto Huele la Flor." [CuadP] (5:14) Enero-Abril 88, p. 40.
"Tantalia." [CuadP] (5:14) Enero-Abril 88, p. 41.
4511. RODRIGUEZ, Alfonso
"A Tomás Rivera in Memoriam." [BilingR] (13:1/2) Ja-Ag 86, c1988, p. 103-105.
4512. RODRIGUEZ, Blanca.
"Sellados por la anguistia." [Os] (26) 88, p. 19.
RODRIGUEZ, Ernesto Diaz
See DIAZ RODRIGUEZ, Ernesto
4513. RODRIGUEZ, Judith
"Face for Casting" (for Emily Hope). [MalR] (82) Mr 88, p. 51.
"In-Flight Note." [MalR] (82) Mr 88, p. 50.
"The Letter from America." [MalR] (82) Mr 88, p. 48-49.
"Wild Shiners." [MalR] (82) Mr 88, p. 52-53.
4514. RODRIGUEZ-FLORIDO, Jorge J.
"El Alcalde Washington Se Murió de Pronto." [LindLM] (7:1) Ja-Mr 88, p. 6.
"Juramento." [LindLM] (7:1) Ja-Mr 88, p. 6.

4515. ROE, Margie McCreless
"Live Oak Spring." [ChrC] (105:10) 23-30 Mr 88, p. 301.
"Looking Forward: Learning How." [ChrC] (105:25) 31 Ag-7 S 88, p. 760.
4516. ROESER, Dana
"Needing Blessing." [Timbuktu] (2) Sum-Fall 88, p. 41.
"On the Fall Equinox." [Timbuktu] (2) Sum-Fall 88, p. 40.
"Questions." [Timbuktu] (2) Sum-Fall 88, p. 42.
4517. ROETHER, Barbara
"Bell of Nail." [Notus] (3:1) Spr 88, p. 80-81.
"The Formulations." [Temblor] (7) 88, p. 154-158.
4518. ROFFMAN, Rosaly DeMaios
"Aids Victim." [Footwork] ('88) 88, p. 37.
"No One Wants to be Obscure: To M.M." [HeliconN] (19) 88, p. 74.
"On Learning That My First Love Returned to His Job at the Post Office." [Footwork] ('88) 88, p. 36-37.
"Zoology Colleague Exiting a Topless Bar at Four O'Clock in the Afternoon." [Footwork] ('88) 88, p. 37.
4519. ROGAL, Stan
"& The Void Stares Back" (for Friedrich Nietzsche). [CrossC] (10:2) 88, p. 8.
"Gate Crasher" (to be read in a drunken, bluesy tone). [AlphaBS] (4) D 88, p. 27.
"In Search of the Emerald City" (Selections: XII, XXIV). [Grain] (16:2) Sum 88, p. 26-27.
4520. ROGERS, Bertha
"The Ailanthus." [InterPR] (14:1) Spr 88, p. 99.
"The Bowl, the Flowers." [InterPR] (14:1) Spr 88, p. 101.
"Gleaning." [InterPR] (14:1) Spr 88, p. 97.
"Listening to Tchaikovsky." [Vis] (28) 88, p. 29-30.
"Now Clouds Are Everywhere Dancing." [InterPR] (14:1) Spr 88, p. 100.
"Our Eyes." [InterPR] (14:1) Spr 88, p. 98.
"Schubert." [Bogg] (59) 88, p. 20.
4521. ROGERS, Bobby Caudle
"Reading Silently with an Accent: Some Notes on Writing in the South." [GreensboroR] (44) Sum 88, p. 20-21.
"Waiting for the Crescent." [Timbuktu] (2) Sum-Fall 88, p. 6-7.
4522. ROGERS, Bruce P. H.
"Tristan." [RagMag] (6:1) [88], p. 36.
"Ursula." [RagMag] (6:1) [88], p. 37.
4523. ROGERS, Daryl
"Universal Phrase." [WormR] (28:1, #109) 88, p. 27.
"Xmas Bonus." [WormR] (28:1, #109) 88, p. 27.
4524. ROGERS, Del Marie
"The Whole Story" (for George McCaleb, Alabama A&M). [FiveFR] (6) 88, p. 59.
4525. ROGERS, Hoyt
"Mirrors." [InterPR] (14:2) Fall 88, p. 103-106.
"Paragraphs." [LitR] (32:1) Fall 88, p. 108-109.
4526. ROGERS, Jalane
"Departure." [DeKalbLAJ] (21:2) Spr 88, p. 44.
4527. ROGERS, Pattiann
"Approaching the Metropolis." [TriQ] (73) Fall 88, p. 131-132.
"April Coordinator." [CreamCR] (12:2) Sum 88, p. 257-258.
"Because You Understand This." [CutB] (31/32) 88, p. 44.
"Beyond All Ken." [CutB] (31/32) 88, p. 42-43.
"A Common Sight." [Poetry] (151:4) Ja 88, p. 355-356.
"The Dead Never Fight Against Anything." [MissouriR] (11:1) 88, p. 12-13.
"The Family Is All There Is." [TriQ] (73) Fall 88, p. 127-128.
"For Passions Denied: Pineywoods Lily." [TriQ] (73) Fall 88, p. 133.
"How the Old See Death." [Poetry] (151:4) Ja 88, p. 357-358.
"Knot." [NewRep] (198:18) 2 My 88, p. 40.
"The Message." [CreamCR] (12:2) Sum 88, p. 259.
"Playroom: The Visionaries." [CreamCR] (12:2) Sum 88, p. 255-256.
"Predestination." [TriQ] (73) Fall 88, p. 129-130.
"Taking Leave." [MissouriR] (11:1) 88, p. 14-15.
4528. ROGERS, Peter A.
"Sitting in Bed Writing Poetry, Drinking Wine." [SpiritSH] (54) Fall-Wint 88, p. 15.

4529. ROGOFF, Jay
"Visions of Great-Grandmother." [MSS] (6:2) 88, p. 98-99.
4530. ROJAS, Gonzalo
"Cierta Heridilla." [Inti] (26/27) Otoño 87-Primavera 88, p. 318.
"Llámandote Aquí: Cambio." [Inti] (26/27) Otoño 87-Primavera 88, p. 319-320.
"Memoria de Joan Crawford." [Inti] (26/27) Otoño 87-Primavera 88, p. 316.
"Microfilm de Abismo." [Inti] (26/27) Otoño 87-Primavera 88, p. 318-319.
"Ningunos." [Inti] (26/27) Otoño 87-Primavera 88, p. 321-322.
"Paul Celan." [Inti] (26/27) Otoño 87-Primavera 88, p. 315.
"Sebastián Acevedo." [Inti] (26/27) Otoño 87-Primavera 88, p. 320-321.
"Visión de Gwen Kirpatrick." [Inti] (26/27) Otoño 87-Primavera 88, p. 317.
"Zung-guo." [Inti] (26/27) Otoño 87-Primavera 88, p. 316-317.
4531. ROLAND, Greaves
"Something Like the Next Moment." [Descant] (19:2, #61) Sum 88, p. 24.
"Very Shiv, Near at Hand." [Descant] (19:2, #19) Sum 88, p. 25-26.
4532. ROLHEISER, Ken
"Class Reunion." [Grain] (16:3) Fall 88, p. 41.
4533. ROMAINE, E.
"The Lover Mumbles Under His Breath to Heraclitus." [HolCrit] (25:3) Je 88, p. 17.
4534. ROMANO, Edward
"I Hate It." [PaintedB] (34) 88, p. 67.
"New York Poem." [PaintedB] (34) 88, p. 67.
"The Six O'Clock News." [PaintedB] (34) 88, p. 68.
"When I Consider How My Shlong Was Stung." [PaintedB] (34) 88, p. 68.
4535. ROMANO, Ellen
"Poem for My Mother's Eyes." [CentR] (32:3) Sum 88, p. 271.
4536. ROMANO, Rose
"The Chopping of Wood." [Footwork] ('88) 88, p. 36.
"Confirmation." [Footwork] ('88) 88, p. 36.
"Finding Out." [SinW] (35) Sum-Fall 88, p. 58.
"Heart Attack." [SinW] (32) Sum 87, p. 73.
"Not to Be Trusted." [SinW] (33) Fall 87, p. 62-63.
"Poem for Nikki Coletti." [Footwork] ('88) 88, p. 36.
4537. ROMER, Stephen
"Beneath the Tree." [YaleR] (77:3) Spr 88, p. 371-372.
"Not to Neglect." [YaleR] (77:3) Spr 88, p. 369-370.
"Roissy, December 1987." [YaleR] (77:3) Spr 88, p. 370-371.
4538. ROMERO, Armando
"El Arbol Digital." [Inti] (26/27) Otoño 87-Primavera 88, p. 328-329.
"Brisa." [Inti] (26/27) Otoño 87-Primavera 88, p. 333-334.
"Extraños Seres Relucientes Ciudades." [Inti] (26/27) Otoño 87-Primavera 88, p. 329-331.
"Flores de Uranio." [Inti] (26/27) Otoño 87-Primavera 88, p. 329.
"From Chicago to O.G." [Inti] (26/27) Otoño 87-Primavera 88, p. 332-333.
"My Ancestors" (tr. by Constance Lardas). [CinPR] (17) Spr 88, p. 46-47.
"El Pararrayos en el Desierto." [Inti] (26/27) Otoño 87-Primavera 88, p. 334-335.
"Viajera." [Inti] (26/27) Otoño 87-Primavera 88, p. 331.
4539. ROMERO, Leo
"Desert Nights." [Sonora] (14/15) Spr 88, p. 61-62.
"For Our Own Reasons." [Sonora] (14/15) Spr 88, p. 65-66.
"There Was Such Intense Anger in Him." [Sonora] (14/15) Spr 88, p. 59.
"We Slept on the Porch." [Sonora] (14/15) Spr 88, p. 63-64.
4540. ROMTVEDT, David
"Before Wyoming." [Event] (17:3) Fall 88, p. 38.
"Distance." [MSS] (6:2) 88, p. 36.
"Harold's Idea." [Event] (17:3) Fall 88, p. 39.
"Thirteen Snapshots." [HighP] (3:1) Spr 88, p. 97-100.
4541. RONAN, Stephen
"Blue Postcards" (as Gene Kerosene, to Jack Kerouac). [AlphaBS] (4) D 88, p. 33-35.
4542. RONDELL, Rat
"Big Red and Shiny." [ArtfulD] (14/15) Fall 88, p. 38-42.
4543. ROOT, Judith
"Free Will and the River." [Nat] (247:12) 31 O 88, p. 428.
4544. ROOT-McGILL, Deborah
"FDA Approved." [Contact] (9:47/48/49) Spr 88, p. 46.

4545. ROPER, June
"Ocean Eyes." [NewRena] (7:2, #22) Spr 88, p. 63.
ROSA, A. Gomez
See GOMEZ ROSA, A.
4546. ROSALES, Victoria
"The Earth." [SinW] (35) Sum-Fall 88, p. 18.
ROSAZZA, Mercedes Ibañez
See IBAÑEZ ROSAZZA, Mercedes
4547. ROSBERG, Rose
"Cover Up." [CrabCR] (5:2) Sum 88, p. 5.
4548. ROSCHER, Marina L.
"Fiery Oven" (tr. of Sarah Kirsch, w. Charles Fishman). [Rohwedder] (4) [Wint 88-89], p. 8.
"The Geese Flew Inland" (tr. of Sarah Kirsch, w. Charles Fishman). [Rohwedder] (4) [Wint 88-89], p. 6.
"The Geologists" (tr. of Sarah Kirsch, w. Charles Fishman). [Rohwedder] (4) [Wint 88-89], p. 5.
"The Green Double" (tr. of Sarah Kirsch, w. Charles Fishman). [Rohwedder] (4) [Wint 88-89], p. 4.
"Hoarfrost Harvest" (tr. of Sarah Kirsch, w. Charles Fishman). [Rohwedder] (4) [Wint 88-89], p. 7.
"Moorland" (tr. of Sarah Kirsch, w. Charles Fishman). [Rohwedder] (4) [Wint 88-89], p. 8.
"When the Ice Floats" (tr. of Sarah Kirsch, w. Charles Fishman). [Rohwedder] (4) [Wint 88-89], p. 3.
4549. ROSE, Al Israel
"In a Couple of Hours." [WormR] (28:4, #112) 88, p. 126.
"Shoot Em Up Bang Bang." [WormR] (28:4, #112) 88, p. 126.
4550. ROSE, Anne
"No Tears." [Quarry] (37:1) Wint 88, p. 28.
4551. ROSE, Jennifer
"The Italian Rose Garden." [PartR] (55:4) Fall 88, p. 620-621.
4552. ROSE, Mildred A.
"Annihilation." [Grain] (16:3) Fall 88, p. 57.
"Glimpses." [Grain] (16:3) Fall 88, p. 59.
"River Spell." [Grain] (16:3) Fall 88, p. 58.
4553. ROSE, Stan
"Names" (tr. of Jorge Guillen). [CutB] (31/32) 88, p. 78.
"Secret" (tr. of Carlos Drummond de Andrade). [CutB] (31/32) 88, p. 79.
"Untitled: I missed the bus and lost hope" (tr. of Carlos Drummond de Andrade). [CutB] (31/32) 88, p. 80.
4554. ROSE, Wilga
"Windfall." [Bogg] (60) 88, p. 22.
4555. ROSEDAUGHTER, Stefanie Prather
"Silence Is Exciting When It's Loud." [BellArk] (4:5) S-O 88, p. 10.
4556. ROSEN, Kenneth
"Caribou." [NoAmR] (273:3) D 88, p. 17.
"The Castrato." [NoAmR] (273:3) S 88, p. 44.
"Dinosaur." [NewRep] (198:7) 15 F 88, p. 38.
"Soul Flight." [Shen] (38:3) 88, p. 94-95.
4557. ROSEN, Michael J.
"The Reader Falls Asleep in His Library." [CinPR] (18) Fall 88, p. 13-15.
"Traveling in Notions" (Selections: 6 poems). [HampSPR] Wint 88, p. 54-61.
4558. ROSENBERG, Betsy
"Bird Song." [ParisR] (30:106) Spr 88, p. 258.
4559. ROSENBERG, Liz
"Because I Was Dying." [Nat] (246:19) 14 My 88, p. 688.
"The Crucified." [Nat] (246:6) 13 F 88, p. 211.
"Dark Eyes." [AmerPoR] (17:1) Ja-F 88, p. 19.
"For the Earth." [TarRP] (28:1) Fall 88, p. 12.
"In Florida." [TarRP] (28:1) Fall 88, p. 11.
"In Time." [SouthernR] (24:2) Spr 88, p. 330-331.
"Oswald." [SouthernR] (24:2) Spr 88, p. 331.
"Pregnancy, First Trimester." [SouthernR] (24:2) Spr 88, p. 330.
"Susquehanna Country." [AmerPoR] (17:1) Ja-F 88, p. 19.

4560. ROSENBERGER, F. C.
"First Acceptance." [ArizQ] (44:1) Spr 88, p. 61.
4561. ROSENBLATT, Sarah
"Four Facets of Searching for an I." [RagMag] (6:2) Fall 88, p. 46.
4562. ROSENFELD, Natania
"In Lithuania." [CutB] (31/32) 88, p. 66.
"Kalypso." [SenR] (18:2) 88, p. 48-51.
"Krolis Thinking About Water in Oma's Kitchen." [SenR] (18:2) 88, p. 52.
"Opa." [SenR] (18:2) 88, p. 53-54.
"Waking." [CutB] (31/32) 88, p. 64-65.
4563. ROSENQUIST, Karl
"Reading My Mother's Copy of *The Portrait of a Lady*i." [Shen] (38:1) 88, p. 51-52.
"Two Students Talk About Love." [Shen] (38:1) 88, p. 51-52.
4564. ROSENTHAL, Bob
"Grandma and Andry." [Talisman] (1) Fall 88, p. 82-83.
4565. ROSENTHAL, Laura
"Amazing Grace." [NewAW] (4) Fall 88, p. 77.
"Escape from the Alluvial Fan." [NewAW] (4) Fall 88, p. 79.
"O." [NewAW] (4) Fall 88, p. 78.
4566. ROSENTHAL, M. L.
"Into the Valley" (tr. of Primo Levi). [Nat] (246:22) 4 Je 88, p. 802.
4567. ROSENWALD, John
"Smoking People: Encountering the New Chinese Poetry" (Chapbook 19, ed. by John Rosenwald, tr. by John Rosenwald *et al.*). [BelPoJ] (39:2) Wint 88-89, 76 p.
4568. ROSKOS, Dave
"Confession." [Lactuca] (9) F 88, p. 36.
"In the Bowels of Hope." [Lactuca] (9) F 88, p. 36.
4569. ROSSER, J. Allyn
"All But Yours." [GettyR] (1:4) Aut 88, p. 621-622.
"Getting Wise." [Hudson] (41:2) Sum 88, p. 336-338.
"Goose's Jack: Over the Hill?" [GeoR] (42:2) Sum 88, p. 315.
"Last I Remember, 1973." [GeoR] (42:2) Sum 88, p. 316-317.
"Love Lessons." [GettyR] (1:4) Aut 88, p. 623.
"Manichean Middle Game." [GeoR] (42:2) Sum 88, p. 318-319.
"My Father's Palette." [Poetry] (152:4) Jl 88, p. 227-228.
"Ode on the Unsung." [GeoR] (42:2) Sum 88, p. 314.
4570. ROSSINI, Frank
"Parrot's Eye." [CrabCR] (5:3) Fall 88, p. 7.
4571. ROSTEN, Norman
"Brooklyn Bridge." [Confr] (Special issue: The World of Brooklyn) 88, p. 13.
4572. ROSU, Dona
"Ten Prose Poems" (2, 7, 13, 20, 22, 23, 25, 29, 30, 31, tr. by Ann Woodward). [WebR] (13:2) Fall 88, p. 40-42.
4573. ROTH, Laurence
"Compass." [Jacaranda] (3:1) Wint 88, p. 97.
4574. ROTH-NATALE, Nanci
"I Heard the Owl." [BellArk] (4:6) N-D 88, p. 5.
"Solstice." [BellArk] (4:1) Ja-F 88, p. 3.
4575. ROTHENBERG, Jerome
"Domestic Gematria: Home Movies." [Notus] (3:2) Fall 88, p. 35.
"Eighth Gematria: Things." [Caliban] (5) 88, p. 131-135.
"In the Forest of Clocks" (a suite, tr. of Federico Garcia Lorca). [Sulfur] (8:2, #23) Fall 88, p. 141-145.
"Khurban" (Selections: 4 poems). [Temblor] (7) 88, p. 11-17.
"Mirror Suite" (tr. of Federico Garcia Lorca). [Sulfur] (8:2, #23) Fall 88, p. 134-140.
"Peroration for a Lost Town." [Sulfur] (8:2, #23) Fall 88, p. 82-85.
"Poland / 1987." [Sulfur] (7:3, #21) Wint 88, p. 33-43.
"Third Gematria: Lot in Sodom." [Notus] (3:2) Fall 88, p. 36-41.
4576. ROTHMAN, David
"You Have Caught the Screaming Baby." [GettyR] (1:2) Spr 88, p. 392.
4577. ROTHMAN, Susan Noe
"Sleeping Breast to Chest." [SlipS] (8) 88, p. 29.

4578. ROTHOLZ, Susan
"Climb to the High Meadow." [ChamLR] (1) Fall 87, p. 391-392.
4579. ROUBAUD, Jacques
"Some Thing Black" (Selections: 9 poems, tr. by Rosmarie Waldrop). [Temblor] (8) 88, p. 87-90.
4580. ROUMAIN, Jacques
"Madrid" (Commune, 1937, tr. by Jack Hirschman). [RedBass] (13) 88, p. 22-23.
4581. ROUSE, Nancy Frost
"A Poet's Avocations" (for RJF). [InterPR] (14:2) Fall 88, p. 107.
4582. ROY, Lucinda
"Carousel" (For Namba Roy, 1910-1961). [Callaloo] (11:3, #36) Sum 88, p. 549-550.
"Excision." [Callaloo] (11:3, #36) Sum 88, p. 551-552.
"The Ferry." [DenQ] (22:3) Wint 88, p. 49-50.
"If You Know Black Hair." [Callaloo] (11:3, #36) Sum 88, p. 553.
"A Senegalese Student Thinks of His Days in Paris." [DenQ] (22:3) Wint 88, p. 48.
"Thames." [Callaloo] (11:3, #36) Sum 88, p. 547-548.
"Wailing the Dead to Sleep." [Callaloo] (11:3, #36) Sum 88, p. 554.
4583. ROY, Margaret
"Ice Out." [Contact] (9:47/48/49) Spr 88, p. 60.
"Nicholas and Megan Come to the Mountains to Visit Grandma." [Contact] (9:47/48/49) Spr 88, p. 60.
4584. ROYET-JOURNOUD, Claude
"A Descriptive Method" (tr. by Michael Davidson). [Temblor] (7) 88, p. 61-71.
4585. ROZEBOOM, Cindy
"Encounter at 2:30." [Quarry] (37:4) Aut 88, p. 60-61.
4586. ROZEMA, Mark
"Skipping Stones." [CutB] (31/32) 88, p. 37.
4587. ROZHDESTVENSKY, Robert
"On the Far Side of the Clouds" (tr. by Gerald Stanton Smith). [NegC] (8:1/2) 88, p. 45.
4588. RUARK, Gibbons
"Reading the Mail in Early Fall." [Salm] (80) Fall 88, p. 108-109.
4589. RUBIN, David
"Almora Spring" (tr. of Sumitranandan Pant). [Nimrod] (31:2) Spr-Sum 88, p. 78.
4590. RUBIN, Larry
"Cycles." [Wind] (18:62) 88, p. 42.
"Harrisburg, Mon Amour" (Three-Mile Island). [Comm] (115:4) 26 F 88, p. 114.
"In the Lifeguard Stand at Night." [ChatR] (8:3) Spr 88, p. 44.
"Lessons of the Interstate: The Ambiguities." [SouthwR] (73:3) Sum 88, p. 318.
"Love on the Beach" (For My Mother). [HiramPoR] (44/45) Spr-Wint 88, p. 38.
"Remembering the Thirties." [Wind] (18:62) 88, p. 42.
"San Francisco: Predictions." [Wind] (18:62) 88, p. 43.
4591. RUBIN, Mark
"Wheatback Pennies." [IndR] (11:2) Spr 88, p. 14.
4592. RUBIN, Steven
"Come See Where I Was Born" (tr. of Clémentine Nzuji. Translation Chapbook Series). [MidAR] (8:1) 88, p. 57-75.
4593. RUCKER, Trish
"Easter Morning." [MidwQ] (29:2) Wint 88, p. 221.
"Encounters." [LitR] (31:2) Wint 88, p. 235.
"Housesitting on Northside Drive." [KanQ] (20:1/2) Wint-Spr 88, p. 292-293.
"Springdale Park." [KanQ] (20:1/2) Wint-Spr 88, p. 292.
4594. RUCKMAN, Kimberly
"Disappointing General Booth." [Plain] (8:2) Wint 88, p. 7.
"Homesteading." [Plain] (8:3) Spr-Sum 88, p. 31.
4595. RUDEL, Jaufré
"Quant lo Rosignols el Fuoillos" (tr. by Joseph S. Salemi). [Paint] (15:29) Spr 88, p. 60-61.
4596. RUDMAN, Mark
"Almost a Lullaby" (tr. of Bohdan Boychuk). [Pequod] (25) 88, p. 113.
"Anything But." [Epoch] (37:2) 88, p. 110-111.
"Bottles." [PoetryE] (25) Spr 88, p. 79-85.
"Cliff Seen in a New Light." [GrandS] (8:1) Aut 88, p. 175.
"Independence Day." [DenQ] (23:1) Sum 88, p. 77-79.
"The Shoebox." [ParisR] (30:108) Fall 88, p. 210-211.

4597. RUDOLPH, Lee
"A Woman and a Man, Ice Fishing." [NewYorker] (64:9) 18 Ap 88, p. 44.
4598. RUDY, D. L.
"Consciousness Raising." [Footwork] ('88) 88, p. 76-77.
"O to Be a Dragon" (Title of 1959 book of poems by Marianne Moore). [Poem] (60) N 88, p. 39.
4599. RUE, Pilar
"Manifiesto." [LetFem] (14:1/2) Primavera-Otoño 88, p. 140.
"Naufragio" (a mi hijo). [LetFem] (14:1/2) Primavera-Otoño 88, p. 139.
4600. RUEFLE, Mary
"Council of Agde." [Iowa] (18:3) 88, p. 55.
"The Derision of Christ in New England." [GettyR] (1:2) Spr 88, p. 360.
"The Details from Your Last Letter." [GettyR] (1:2) Spr 88, p. 361.
"The Last Supper." [Iowa] (18:3) 88, p. 58.
4601. RUESCHER, Scott
"African Souvenirs." [Agni] (26) 88, p. 152-153.
"Black and White Elegy." [Agni] (26) 88, p. 146-147.
"Dare Me." [Agni] (26) 88, p. 150-151.
"Hot Water." [Agni] (26) 88, p. 148-149.
"Screech Owl." [Agni] (26) 88, p. 142-143.
"Weather Report." [Agni] (26) 88, p. 144-145.
4602. RUFF, John
"The Poet Dreams of His Dead Friend." [MemphisSR] (8:2) Spr 88, p. 16.
"Putting You Into Words." [MemphisSR] (8:2) Spr 88, p. 21-23.
"A Translation: Wordsworth Wrote That." [MemphisSR] (8:2) Spr 88, p. 17.
"While Reading About *French Social Thought During the Years of Desperation*." [MemphisSR] (8:2) Spr 88, p. 18-20.
4603. RUFFIN, Paul
"The Day Billy Franklin Died." [StoneC] (15:3/4) Spr-Sum 88, p. 60.
"Grandma Chooses Her Plot at the County Cemetery." [StoneC] (15:3/4) Spr-Sum 88, p. 60-61.
RUGERIS, C. K. de
See DeRUGERIS, C. K.
4604. RUGGLES, Eugene
"The Rooftops." [PassN] (9:1) Wint 88, p. 15.
"The Rooftops" (corrected reprint). [PassN] (9:2) Sum 88, p. 18.
"The Unemployed Automobile Workers of Detroit Prepare to Share Christmas Standing in Line." [FiveFR] (6) 88, p. 63.
RUISSEAUX, Pierre des
See DesRUISSEAUX, Pierre
4605. RUMENS, Carol
"At the Piskaryovskoye Cemetery." [PartR] (55:1) Wint 88, p. 60-61.
"The Fire Fighter's Widow on Her First Memorial Day Outing." [YaleR] (77:3) Spr 88, p. 377-381.
"The Mostly Happy Returns." [YaleR] (77:3) Spr 88, p. 376-377.
4606. RUNNING, Thorpe
"Flight" (tr. of Jorge Brega). [ColR] (NS 15:1) Spr-Sum 88, p. 76-77.
"Ruben Dario at the Beachhead" (tr. of Alfredo Veiravé). [ColR] (NS 15:1) Spr-Sum 88, p. 80.
"While" (tr. of Gonzalo Millan). [ColR] (NS 15:1) Spr-Sum 88, p. 78-79.
4607. RUO, Guo Mo
"Coal in the Stove" (For my Motherland, tr. by Scott Francis). [Paint] (15:29) Spr 88, p. 58.
"Phoenix Dying: A Chorus of Birds Celebrate" (tr. by Scott Francis). [Paint] (15:29) Spr 88, p. 59.
4608. RUSETSKI, Alyaksei
"Revelation" (tr. by Walter May). [NegC] (8:1/2) 88, p. 30.
4609. RUSS, Biff
"Rodin, in Love, Unmolds His Bronze Statue of Eve." [MidAR] (8:1) 88, p. 99.
4610. RUSS, Don
"Resurrection." [ChatR] (8:2) Wint 88, p. 65.
"Saint Ross and the Rattledragon" (Florida Reptile Institute, Silver Springs). [Poem] (59) My 88, p. 62.
"The Substance of Things Hoped For." [Poem] (59) My 88, p. 61.
4611. RUSS, Lisa
"Packing Shed" (for my father). [PacificR] (6) Spr 88, p. 10-11.

"Watching Lu Junne-Nan Make the Poem 'Night Thoughts' by Li-Po." [PacificR] (6) Spr 88, p. 12.

4612. RUSSAKOFF, Molly
"The Japanese Desire." [PaintedB] (34) 88, p. 42.

4613. RUSSEL, CarolAnn (*See also* Russell, CarolAnn)
Waiting" (for Hidla Raz). [QW] (26) Wint 88, p. 106-107.

4614. RUSSELL, CarolAnn (*See also* Russel, CarolAnn)
The Black Brother Poems" (to Etheridge Knight). [PaintedB] (32/33) 88, p. 67-69.
Changing Color in America." [ColR] (NS 15:1) Spr-Sum 88, p. 17-19.
Cheap Pictures." [LaurelR] (22:21) Wint 88, p. 72-73.
Silver Dollar." [PoetryNW] (29:4) Wint 88-89, p. 29-30.
The Trains we've Missed." [LaurelR] (22:21) Wint 88, p. 70-72.
The Wedding." [Spirit] (9:1) 88, p. 88-90.

4615. RUSSELL, Diana
"Autumn has lowered" (tr. of Ruslan Galimov). [NegC] (8:1/2) 88, p. 46.
"He sat, one leg drawn up" (tr. of Ruslan Galimov). [NegC] (8:1/2) 88, p. 46.
"Today I thought about death" (tr. of Ruslan Galimov). [NegC] (8:1/2) 88, p. 47.

4616. RUSSELL, Dianna L.
"The Dousing." [DenQ] (22:3) Wint 88, p. 217-218.

RUSSELL, Gillian Harding
See HARDING-RUSSELL, Gillian

4617. RUSSELL, Hilary
"The Boy Alone." [Spirit] (9:1) 88, p. 77.
"Jars with Holes." [Boulevard] (3:2/3) Fall 88, p. 118.

4618. RUSSELL, Jonathan
"Cursed Are They in High Places!" [Plain] (9:1) Fall 88, p. 27.
"Uptown Anna." [SmPd] (25:3) Fall 88, p. 35.

4619. RUSSELL, Norman
"Coming Back." [Caliban] (5) 88, p. 72.
"Monster Slayer." [Caliban] (5) 88, p. 73.

4620. RUSSELL, Norman H.
"The Artist." [KanQ] (20:3) Sum 88, p. 65.
"Drought." [Plain] (8:1) Fall 87, p. 21.
"The Great Man." [Pembroke] (20) 88, p. 171.
"My Fear Is My Anger." [KanQ] (20:3) Sum 88, p. 65.
"The Paths of Memory." [Plain] (8:1) Fall 87, p. 9.

4621. RUSSELL, Paul
"A Painting Called 'Scrub'" (for Catherine Murphy). [Sequoia] (32:1) Spr-Sum 88, p. 44.

4622. RUSSELL, Peg
"Clerihew." [LightY] ('88/9) 88, p. 75.

4623. RUSSELL, Peter
"Imagine the Yellow Grass in Wind" (Second Award Poem, 1987/1988). [KanQ] (20:1/2) Wint-Spr 88, p. 14.

4624. RUSSELL, Thomas (Tom)
"The Accident." [CimR] (84) Jl 88, p. 63-65.
"Dictionary Toad." [CreamCR] (12:2) Sum 88, p. 260-261.
"Frank Labo." [SouthernPR] (28:1) Spr 88, p. 57-58.
"Hoods in Repose" (Seaton Honorable Mention Poem 1988). [KanQ] (20:3) Sum 88, p. 36-37.
"Kinning Wheel." [NoDaQ] (56:3) Sum 88, p. 93.
"Since the Eye Is Dumber." [CimR] (84) Jl 88, p. 66.
"Soul Food." [MinnR] (NS 30/31) Spr-Fall 88, p. 23.
"Tarzan 1968." [SouthernPR] (28:2) Fall 88, p. 62-63.

4625. RUSTED, Brian
"Jimmy's Daughter." [CanLit] (119) Wint 88, p. 23-24.

4626. RUTH, Barbara
"I Go to Work in Drag." [SinW] (35) Sum-Fall 88, p. 57.
"Song of the Womon with Rope in Her Hair." [SinW] (36) Wint 88-89, p. 117.
"When Marie Laveau Danced in Congo Square." [SinW] (33) Fall 87, p. 36-40.

4627. RUTSALA, Vern
"Blake in Idaho." [CharR] (14:2) Fall 88, p. 108-109.
"Calling Up the Pain." [TarRP] (28:1) Fall 88, p. 19.
"Change." [SewanR] (96:1) Wint 88, p. 53.
"Fret." [SewanR] (96:1) Wint 88, p. 50-51.
"Grandfather." [SewanR] (96:1) Wint 88, p. 51-53.

"Owning Things." [IndR] (12:1) Wint 88, p. 7-9.
"Reclaiming the House." [SewanR] (96:1) Wint 88, p. 49-50.
"Shame." [AmerS] (57:4) Aut 88, p. 574.
"Surfaces." [TarRP] (28:1) Fall 88, p. 17-18.
"Trust." [CharR] (14:2) Fall 88, p. 107-108.
"Whatever It Is." [IndR] (12:1) Wint 88, p. 10.

4628. RYALS, Mary Jane
"Timucuan Spirits." [FloridaR] (16:1) Spr-Sum 88, p. 121.

4629. RYAN, Gig
"After Hours." [NewAW] (4) Fall 88, p. 95-96.
"By Water." [NewAW] (4) Fall 88, p. 93.
"Cruising." [NewAW] (4) Fall 88, p. 96.
"How I Went." [NewAW] (4) Fall 88, p. 95.
"If I Had a Gun." [NewAW] (4) Fall 88, p. 91-92.
"In the Purple Bar." [NewAW] (4) Fall 88, p. 90.
"January." [NewAW] (4) Fall 88, p. 93-94.
"Kings Cross Pastoral." [NewAW] (4) Fall 88, p. 94.
"Some Women." [NewAW] (4) Fall 88, p. 92.

4630. RYAN, Gregory A.
"The Bathers." [MidwQ] (29:3) Spr 88, p. 352.
"The Window." [LitR] (31:2) Wint 88, p. 236.

4631. RYAN, Kay
"Conversion." [TriQ] (72) Spr-Sum 88, p. 149.
"Journey." [BostonR] (13:6) D 88, p. 3.
"Masterworks of Ming." [Zyzzyva] (4:1) Spr 88, p. 52-53.
"The Most General Trend We Know Is Speciation." [BostonR] (13:1) F 88, p. 15.
"Such Women." [TriQ] (72) Spr-Sum 88, p. 148.

4632. RYAN, Michael
"Boy 'Carrying In' Bottles in Glass Works" (West Virginia, 1911. Photograph by Lewis W. Hine). [TriQ] (72) Spr-Sum 88, p. 153.
"God Hunger." [AmerPoR] (17:2) Mr-Ap 88, p. 4.
"Moonlight." [AmerPoR] (17:2) Mr-Ap 88, p. 3.
"Not the End of the World." [AmerPoR] (17:2) Mr-Ap 88, p. 4.
"One." [AmerPoR] (17:2) Mr-Ap 88, p. 4.
"Palinode." [TriQ] (72) Spr-Sum 88, p. 155.
"Passion." [AmerPoR] (17:2) Mr-Ap 88, p. 3.
"Pedestrian Pastoral." [TriQ] (72) Spr-Sum 88, p. 152.
"Sea Worms." [AmerPoR] (17:2) Mr-Ap 88, p. 5.
"Spider Plant." [AmerPoR] (17:2) Mr-Ap 88, p. 5.
"A Splinter." [AmerPoR] (17:2) Mr-Ap 88, p. 5.
"Through a Crack." [TriQ] (72) Spr-Sum 88, p. 154.

4633. RYEGATE, Lucy
"A Study in Depth." [LitR] (31:2) Wint 88, p. 238.

4634. RYEL, Deborah E.
"Chicago's April Overture." [Writer] (101:3) Mr 88, p. 17.

4635. RYLE, John
"Oh Canada." [Margin] (7) 88, p. 93.

RYUICHI, Tamura
See TAMURA, Ryuichi

RYUSEI, Hasegawa
See HASEGAWA, Ryusei

4636. SAARIKOSKI, Pentti
"Snow Melts" (tr. by Stephen Kuusisto). [SenR] (18:1) 88, p. 21.
"Today I Go by Another Route" (tr. by Stephen Kuusisto). [SenR] (18:1) 88, p. 20.
"You Couldn't See Through the Snow Squall" (tr. by Stephen Kuusisto). [SenR] (18:1) 88, p. 22.

4637. SABA, Umberto
"The Goat" (tr. by Michael Palma). [GrandS] (7:3) Spr 88, p. 45.
"The Little Tree" (tr. by Michael Palma). [ParisR] (30:106) Spr 88, p. 251.
"Sleeplessness on a Summer Night" (tr. by Michael Palma). [ParisR] (30:106) Spr 88, p. 250.
"To My Daughter" (tr. by Michael Palma). [ParisR] (30:106) Spr 88, p. 252.
"To My Wife" (tr. by Michael Palma). [GrandS] (7:3) Spr 88, p. 46-48.

4638. SADOFF, Ira
"After Dreaming." [VirQR] (64:2) Spr 88, p. 281-282.
"Civil Rights" (Biloxi, Freedom Summer, 1964). [VirQR] (64:2) Spr 88, p. 279.

"Emotional Traffic." [VirQR] (64:2) Spr 88, p. 280-281.
"A Production Number." [Sonora] (14/15) Spr 88, p. 21.
"Sonnet to Orifice." [Sonora] (14/15) Spr 88, p. 20.

4639. SADOW, Stephen A.
"Argentina 1983" (tr. of Ricardo Feierstein, w. J. Kates). [MinnR] (NS 30/31) Spr-Fall 88, p. 47.

4640. SAFIR, Natalie
"Approaching the Solstice." [SmPd] (25:2) Spr 88, p. 8.
"Weather Bulletin" (Hudson River Valley). [SmPd] (25:2) Spr 88, p. 7.

4641. SAGOFF, Maurice
"Clerihews" (2 poems). [LightY] ('88/9) 88, p. 76.

SAID, Abu Jafar Ahmad ben
See BEN SAID, Abu Jafar Ahmad

SAINT
See also ST. (filed as spelled)

4642. SAJE, Natasha
"Goodbye to Robert Graves, 1895-1985." [AmerV] (11) Sum 88, p. 23.
"Was It Lucca." [AntR] (46:3) Sum 88, p. 354.

4643. SAKNUSSEMM, Kristopher
"Call to Worship." [Gargoyle] (35) 88, p. 247.
"Epicenter." [PraS] (62:4) Wint 88-89, p. 121-123.
"Galahs." [SmPd] (25:1) Wint 88, p. 9-10.
"Hypothesis." [SmPd] (25:3) Fall 88, p. 25.
"More Joy of Recognition." [SmPd] (25:1) Wint 88, p. 7-8.
"What the Night Brings." [SmPd] (25:3) Fall 88, p. 24.

4644. SAKSENA, Sarveshvar Dayal
"Prayer One" (tr. by Judi Benade). [Nimrod] (31:2) Spr-Sum 88, p. 76.
"Prayer Two" (tr. by Judi Benade). [Nimrod] (31:2) Spr-Sum 88, p. 77.
"The Red Bicycle" (tr. by Vinay Dharwadker). [Nimrod] (31:2) Spr-Sum 88, p. 75.

SAKUTARO, Hagiwara
See HAGIWARA, Sakutaro

4645. SALA, Jerome
"Inside Edmond O'Brien." [NewAW] (3) Spr 88, p. 92.

4646. SALAMONE, Karen
"The Idiom of Sunrise." [BellArk] (4:4) Jl-Ag 88, p. 10.
"Inhabiting the Inhospitable." [Plain] (8:1) Fall 87, p. 16.
"Into the Silence." [BellArk] (4:6) N-D 88, p. 9.
"My Decent Wife." [CapeR] (23:1) Spr 88, p. 42.
"The Need for Something More." [Footwork] ('88) 88, p. 49.
"A Velvet Afternoon." [BellArk] (4:6) N-D 88, p. 10.

4647. SALAMUN, Tomaz
"The Arm" (tr. by John Engels and Michael Biggins). [NewEngR] (10:3) Spr 88, p. 279-280.
"Birds" (tr. by Michael Biggins). [NewEngR] (10:3) Spr 88, p. 278.
"Black Madonna" (tr. by Charles Simic). [AmerPoR] (17:3) My-Je 88, p. 34.
"Black Madonna" (tr. by Charles Simic). [RiverS] (26) 88, p. 21.
"Cantina in Querétaro" (tr. by Charles Simic). [RiverS] (26) 88, p. 20.
"Judas Iscariot" (tr. by Michael Biggins). [Agni] (27) 88, p. 206.
"Lapis Lazuli" (tr. by Charles Simic). [RiverS] (26) 88, p. 18.
"Oops!" (tr. by Michael Biggins). [Agni] (27) 88, p. 205.
"Rabbit Oaxaqueño" (tr. by Charles Simic). [AmerPoR] (17:3) My-Je 88, p. 34.
"Red Cliff" (tr. by Michael Biggins). [NewEngR] (10:3) Spr 88, p. 278.
"Sky Above Querétaro" (tr. by Charles Simic). [RiverS] (26) 88, p. 19.
"To the Traveller" (tr. by Charles Simic). [RiverS] (26) 88, p. 22.
"The Window" (tr. by Charles Simic). [AmerPoR] (17:3) My-Je 88, p. 34.

4648. SALASIN, Sal
"Brought in on a five-fifteen." [HangL] (53) 88, p. 49.
"Dearly deported." [LittleM] (15:3/4) 88, p. 120.
"Everyone so hateful." [LittleM] (15:3/4) 88, p. 122.
"The ghost of Count Basie." [LittleM] (15:3/4) 88, p. 121.
"If I were rich." [HangL] (53) 88, p. 50.
"Intelligible." [LittleM] (15:3/4) 88, p. 117.
"Mr. Khrushchev." [LittleM] (15:3/4) 88, p. 118.
"The nation is full of slime." [LittleM] (15:3/4) 88, p. 119.
"So this is my life in the steno pool." [NewAW] (3) Spr 88, p. 105.
"This is a poem about immigration and baptism." [NewAW] (3) Spr 88, p. 105.

4649. SALAZAR, Deborah
"For Lisa Wielding a Comb." [Cond] (15) 88, p. 74.
"They Were Sobbing." [Cond] (15) 88, p. 42.
"Two Sonnets" (for Carrie). [DenQ] (22:3) Wint 88, p. 252.

4650. SALDAÑA, Silvina
"This Song Be Your Shroud" (tr. by Frederick H. Fornoff). [MichQR] (27:2) Spr 88, p. 240-241.
"To Dream Death" (tr. by Frederick H. Fornoff). [MichQR] (27:2) Spr 88, p. 242-244.

4651. SALEH, Dennis
"Cat's Prayer" (for December). [LittleM] (15:3/4) 88, p. 46-47.
"Doing Nothing." [LightY] ('88/9) 88, p. 53-54.

4652. SALEMI, Joseph (Joseph S.)
"3.24. You are wrong, woman, to trust in that beauty of yours" (tr. of Propertius). [Spirit] (9:1) 88, p. 156.
"I.23. You shun me, Chloe, like a young fawn" (tr. of Horace). [HolCrit] (25:5) D 88, p. 15.
"Quant lo Rosignols el Fuoillos" (tr. of Jaufré Rudel). [Paint] (15:29) Spr 88, p. 60-61.

4653. SALERNO, Mark
"An Alba." [SmPd] (25:3) Fall 88, p. 23.
"Now's the Time." [StoneC] (16:1/2) Fall-Wint 88-89, p. 60.
"Untitled XII." [RagMag] (6:2) Fall 88, p. 39.
"What We Are." [StoneC] (16:1/2) Fall-Wint 88-89, p. 60-61.
"What We Learn." [SmPd] (25:3) Fall 88, p. 22.

4654. SALINAS, Raul R.
"Lady Jean" (a la memoria de jean garavente). [RiverS] (27) 88, p. 44-45.

4655. SALING, Joseph
"The Son." [BallSUF] (29:4) Aut 88, p. 40.

4656. SALINS, Gunars
"The Admirer" (tr. by Ilze Klavina Mueller). [Vis] (26) 88, p. 28.
"Spring in the City" (tr. by the author). [Vis] (26) 88, p. 28.

SALLE, Peter la
See LaSALLE, Peter

4657. SALLEE, Hyun-Jae Yee
"On Such a Day" (tr. of Song-Jook Park). [Calyx] (11:2/3) Fall 88, p. 130.

4658. SALLEE, Wayne Allen
"Linda Hamilton Reminds." [SlipS] (8) 88, p. 66.
"Terra Strains 47." [SlipS] (8) 88, p. 66.

4659. SALLI, Donna
"Moving for Cover." [KanQ] (20:3) Sum 88, p. 191.
"Wishful Thinking." [LittleM] (15:3/4) 88, p. 81.
"The Word Silk." [LittleM] (15:3/4) 88, p. 80.

4660. SALLI, Doreen
"Thickening." [KanQ] (20:1/2) Wint-Spr 88, p. 114.

4661. SALLIS, James
"In the Realm" (for Kierkegaard). [SoDakR] (26:1) Spr 88, p. 7.
"Salvador." [MinnR] (NS 30/31) Spr-Fall 88, p. 48.
"The Surrealist, Married." [SoDakR] (26:1) Spr 88, p. 9.
"The Surrealist Works at His Novel." [SoDakR] (26:1) Spr 88, p. 8.

4662. SALMOIRAGHI, Franco
"Like dreams." [ChamLR] (2:1, #3) Fall 88, p. 74.

4663. SALOM, Philip
"Spirit to the Body." [PraS] (62:4) Wint 88-89, p. 123-124.

4664. SALOMON, Jorge
"Encuentro." [Mairena] (10:25) 88, p. 169.

4665. SALTER, Mary Jo
"A Case of Netsuke." [NewYorker] (64:38) 7 N 88, p. 38.
"Etsuko: An Elegy." [GrandS] (7:4) Sum 88, p. 50-55.
"Spring Thaw in South Hadley." [NewYorker] (64:2) 29 F 88, p. 30.
"Summer 1983." [NewYorker] (64:28) 29 Ag 88, p. 47.

4666. SALTMAN, Benjamin
"Going Away." [Event] (17:1) Spr 88, p. 39.
"The Summer Drowning." [Pembroke] (20) 88, p. 247.

4667. SAMMONS, Toni
"21 Beans." [LitR] (32:1) Fall 88, p. 110.

"The Hands and Mind Still Try." [KanQ] (20:1/2) Wint-Spr 88, p. 248.
"If We're Not Drowned." [CapilR] (49) 88, p. 9-10.
"New Love Is Old." [KanQ] (20:1/2) Wint-Spr 88, p. 255.
"Poem for a Hiatus." [CapilR] (49) 88, p. 11-12.

4668. SAMPSON, Dennis
"1959." [Hudson] (40:4) Wint 88, p. 622-623.
"An Actual Wife." [Hudson] (40:4) Wint 88, p. 623-624.
"The Commandment." [Ploughs] (14:4) 88, p. 152-154.
"Forgiveness." [OhioR] (41) 88, p. 100-104.
"When the Power Goes Out in the Supermarket." [PoetryNW] (29:3) Aut 88, p. 25.

4669. SAMSON, Sue
"Custom Cutters." [Farm] (4:1, i.e. 5:1) Wint 88, p. 14.
"Ghost, Owl, Dew." [Farm] (4:1, i.e. 5:1) Wint 88, p. 16.
"Picking Wild Plums." [Farm] (4:1, i.e. 5:1) Wint 88, p. 15.
"Scythe into Night." [Farm] (4:1, i.e. 5:1) Wint 88, p. 12-13.

4670. SANADI, Mary Jane
"The Morrison's Living Room." [NewRena] (7:2, #22) Spr 88, p. 58.
"Our Daughter Is Getting Married, She Tells Us." [NewRena] (7:2, #22) Spr 88, p. 56-57.

4671. SANAZARO, Leonard
"Winter Harvest." [AntR] (46:3) Sum 88, p. 346-347.

SANCHEZ, Ernesto Mejía
See MEJIA SANCHEZ, Ernesto

4672. SANCHO, Briseida
"Deja Vu." [Spirit] (9:1) 88, p. 74.
"A Sadness." [Spirit] (9:1) 88, p. 74.

4673. SANDERS, B. B.
"Over a Cottonwood Grove." [SoDakR] (26:1) Spr 88, p. 91-92.

4674. SANDERS, Jo
"Like Water, Love." [CentR] (32:1) Wint 88, p. 37.
"Slat Talk." [GreensboroR] (45) Wint 88-89, p. 93.

4675. SANDERS, Mark
"Anniversary." [KanQ] (20:4) Fall 88, p. 47.
"Cutting Firewood." [NoDaQ] (56:1) Wint 88, p. 152-153.
"The Death of the Vaudevillian." [LightY] ('88/9) 88, p. 88-89.
"Elms." [Plain] (8:1) Fall 87, p. 14.
"Elms." [SoDakR] (26:1) Spr 88, p. 142.
"Pierce County Summer." [PraF] (9:4) Wint 88-89, p. 14-15.
"When the Honeymoon Is Over." [Plain] (8:3) Spr-Sum 88, p. 35.

4676. SANDOR, Andras
"Grape." [Vis] (26) 88, p. 26.
"Ordinary Story." [Vis] (26) 88, p. 26.

4677. SANDRICH, Nina
"Graven Image." [Confr] (37/38) Spr-Sum 88, p. 168.

4678. SANDY, Stephen
"Allegheny Front." [AmerPoR] (17:2) Mr-Ap 88, p. 44-45.
"Egyptian Onions." [TexasR] (9:3/4) Fall-Wint 88, p. 116.
"Zebra Skins." [SouthernPR] (28:2) Fall 88, p. 65-66.

4679. SANER, Reg
"Come with Me." [LaurelR] (22:21) Wint 88, p. 76.
"Field Notes." [Chelsea] (47) 88, p. 135.
"Forest Fire." [Field] (38) Spr 88, p. 29.
"Mexican Hat." [LaurelR] (22:21) Wint 88, p. 75.
"Near Mishongnovi." [SouthwR] (73:2) Spr 88, p. 249.
"The Neutrinos." [Field] (38) Spr 88, p. 30-31.
"Nobodies from Nowhere." [Crazy] (34) Spr 88, p. 40.
"Waiting Out Rain, Sheltered by Overhang." [Field] (38) Spr 88, p. 32-33.
"Walking into the Moon." [GettyR] (1:2) Spr 88, p. 387-388.
"What to Do When Not Being Useful." [Chelsea] (47) 88, p. 134.
"Winter Stars over Volterra." [GettyR] (1:2) Spr 88, p. 386.

4680. SANFORD, Christy Sheffield
"Imperfections in Various Sizes" (New York City). [ColR] (NS 15:2) Fall-Wint 88, p. 54.
"Looking at Paris and the Moon in 1922 (With Phrases from Mina Loy's Lunar Guide)." [QW] (27) Sum-Fall 88, p. 111-114.
"Scenario for Marion and Gregory" (Stories). [NegC] (8:3) 88, p. 160-162.

"Valerie, Touring 'V's' in Florida." [Sonora] (16) Fall 88, p. 64-65.
4681. SANGE, Gary
"Personal Belonging." [HampSPR] Wint 88, p. 17-19.
"Sex Tours Are Killing the Elderly." [HampSPR] Wint 88, p. 16-17.
SANTAREN, Ben Sara of
See BEN SARA OF SANTAREN
4682. SANTEK, Jerry
"The Lillian That Remains." [HayF] (3) Spr 88, p. 76-77.
SANTOS, Julio Iraheta
See IRAHETA SANTOS, Julio
4683. SANTOS, Sherod
"Abandoned Railway Station." [NewYorker] (64:22) 18 Jl 88, p. 26.
"The Air Base at Chateauroux, France." [AntR] (46:1) Wint 88, p. 68.
"The Dairy Cows of María Cristina Cortés." [NewYorker] (64:10) 25 Ap 88, p. 36.
"Empire" (Luxembourg Gardens, 1986). [NewRep] (198:14) 4 Ap 88, p. 38.
"The Houses of the Rich." [AntR] (46:1) Wint 88, p. 69.
"In the Rainy Season." [AntR] (46:1) Wint 88, p. 66-67.
"Jeffers Country." [WestHR] (42:2) Sum 88, p. 137.
"A Late Elegy" (for my niece, d. Oct. 6, 1967). [AntR] (46:1) Wint 88, p. 70-71.
"The Lost Hour." [WestHR] (42:2) Sum 88, p. 135-136.
"Of Haloes and Saintly Aspects." [Nat] (247:16) 28 N 88, p. 580.
4684. SARAVIA, Juan Ramon
"De Como las Piedras, el Bambu y Otros Supuestos Desperdicios Han Demostrado Ser Excelente . . ." [Mairena] (10:25) 88, p. 26.
4685. SARGENT, Robert
"The Gospel Writers." [Pembroke] (20) 88, p. 173-174.
"Something From Milosz." [HolCrit] (25:5) D 88, p. 19.
"Three Biblical Views." [BallSUF] (29:4) Aut 88, p. 37-39.
4686. SARKAR, Subodh
"Comb" (tr. by the author). [SenR] (18:2) 88, p. 23.
"I Regret" (tr. by the author). [SenR] (18:2) 88, p. 22.
"A Killer Meets a Killer" (tr. by the author). [SenR] (18:2) 88, p. 20.
"The One Whom You Loved" (tr. by the author). [SenR] (18:2) 88, p. 21.
"Water Ends Nowhere" (tr. by the author). [SenR] (18:2) 88, p. 19.
4687. SARTON, May
"Of Havens." [TexasR] (9:3/4) Fall-Wint 88, p. 117.
4688. SARVER, E. B.
"The Spider and the Man." [RagMag] (6:1) [88], p. 39.
4689. SASANOV, Catherine
"The American in Brazil Watches a French Film" (Subtitles in English). [CharR] (14:1) Spr 88, p. 92.
"History." [LittleM] (15:3/4) 88, p. 104.
"The Mother Next Door to the Murderer's House." [LittleM] (15:3/4) 88, p. 105.
"Recognizing Little Tortures." [AnotherCM] (18) 88, p. 164.
"Traditions of Bread and Violence." [LittleM] (15:3/4) 88, p. 103.
"When We Absorb Sound." [Sonora] (16) Fall 88, p. 58.
4690. SASSO, Laurence J. (*See also* Sasso, Laurence J., Jr.)
"Doe." [Wind] (18:63) 88, p. 12.
4691. SASSO, Laurence J., Jr. (*See also* Sasso, Laurence J.)
"Majorette at Dusk." [TexasR] (9:3/4) Fall-Wint 88, p. 118-119.
4692. SASSOR, Tanja
"Separate Development" (tr. by Lauris Edmond). [Verse] (5:3) N 88, p. 68.
4693. SATEL, Sally
"Salt." [Prima] (11/12) 88, p. 16-17.
4694. SATER, Steven
"On Munch's Woodprint 'The Kiss'." [SpiritSH] (54) Fall-Wint 88, p. 22.
"To the Stones." [SpiritSH] (54) Fall-Wint 88, p. 22.
4695. SATTERFIELD, Ben
"Voice of America." [LightY] ('88/9) 88, p. 229.
4696. SATYAMURTI, Carole
"Night Harvest." [Verse] (5:2) Jl 88, p. 12.
4697. SATZ, Martha
"Shimmering, But Darkening" (tr. of Zsuzsa Beney, w. Zsuzsanna Ozsvath). [LitR] (31:2) Wint 88, p. 160-161.
4698. SAUTTER, Diane Moon
"Blue Corn." [MidwQ] (29:3) Spr 88, p. 353.

4699. SAVAGE, Tom
"Magda Taliaferro?" [LittleM] (15:3/4) 88, p. 36.
"Mouth Play One." [NewAW] (3) Spr 88, p. 82-89.
4700. SAVARD, Jeannine
"Stealing Away." [WestHR] (42:1) Spr 88, p. 70.
4701. SAVERY, Pancho
"Going to the Hoop in Chinatown." [HangL] (52) 88, p. 20.
"Racism in Boston." [HangL] (52) 88, p. 19.
"Woman and Death #23 (1910)." [HangL] (52) 88, p. 21.
4702. SAVIN, Jody L.
"Breakfast at 9:40." [Amelia] (5:1, #12) 88, p. 15.
4703. SAVITT, Lynne
"Six Things to Know If You Love a Convict." [PaintedB] (32/33) 88, p. 53.
4704. SAVVAS, Minas
"The Cemetery in Kukuvaunes." [Footwork] ('88) 88, p. 28.
"Vanity." [Interim] (7:2) Fall 88, p. 36.
"Women at Fifty." [Interim] (7:2) Fall 88, p. 35.
SAWA, Ulla Nätterqvist
See NÄTTERQVIST-SAWA, Ulla
4705. SAWYER, Paul
"Garage Sales." [LightY] ('88/9) 88, p. 215.
4706. SAYRES, William
"Jason S. Finch." [KanQ] (20:3) Sum 88, p. 79.
4707. SCACCIA, Kathy
"Free Fall." [Bogg] (60) 88, p. 21.
4708. SCALAPINO, Leslie
"Busby Berkeley: Formation or Follies." [Temblor] (8) 88, p. 27-35.
"From a Novel Titled: The Return of Painting." [Talisman] (1) Fall 88, p. 45.
"Sweet." [Sink] (3) 88, p. 3-8.
4709. SCALF, Sue
"The Baptist Ladies Travel to the Factory Outlets." [SouthernR] (24:4) Aut 88, p. 967.
4710. SCAMMACCA, Nat
"Play with Silence." [Footwork] ('88) 88, p. 85.
4711. SCANLON, Mara Noëlle
"In the Steel City." [HangL] (52) 88, p. 87-88.
4712. SCARBROUGH, George
"Afternoon by the River" (For Seamus Heaney). [SpiritSH] (54) Fall-Wint 88, p. 4.
"Indian Summer." [SpiritSH] (54) Fall-Wint 88, p. 5-6.
"Letter to the Editors" (Prompted by a Dream of Van Gogh's Other Bedroom). [SpiritSH] (54) Fall-Wint 88, p. 1-3.
4713. SCARRON, Paul
"Philosophiae Consolationis" (tr. by G. N. Gabbard). [LightY] ('88/9) 88, p. 70.
4714. SCATES, Maxine
"Salem: Two Windows." [MissouriR] (11:2) 88, p. 222-223.
"We Never Knew You" (for my grandmother, Helen Greeley, 1898-1986). [AmerPoR] (17:5) S-O 88, p. 40.
4715. SCHACHT, Hans-Jurgen
"Questions Posed to the Foreigners Out Germans" (tr. of Peter Schneider, w. Colin MacLeod). [Rohwedder] (4) [Wint 88-89], p. 13.
4716. SCHACHTER, Sandy Rochelle
"On the Beach." [Vis] (28) 88, p. 28.
4717. SCHAEFER, Ted
"Natural Protection." [CreamCR] (12:2) Sum 88, p. 262.
4718. SCHAEFFER, Susan Fromberg
"Gifts." [Confr] (37/38) Spr-Sum 88, p. 42-44.
"Hooves." [Confr] (37/38) Spr-Sum 88, p. 41.
"Knees." [OntR] (29) Fall-Wint 88-89, p. 105.
"Monday." [NewL] (54:3) Spr 88, p. 17.
"Mouth." [OntR] (29) Fall-Wint 88-89, p. 106-107.
"Saturday." [NewL] (54:3) Spr 88, p. 20-21.
"Tuesday." [NewL] (54:3) Spr 88, p. 18-19.
4719. SCHAFFER, Teya
"Four Poems" (I, II "Haircuts," III, "As If the Sun"). [SinW] (32) Sum 87, p. 100-103.
"We Learn." [SinW] (33) Fall 87, p. 43.

4720. SCHAIN, Eliot
"The Birth of Charlie Parker." [StoneC] (15:3/4) Spr-Sum 88, p. 68-70.
"The Scout" (Penn Valley Park, Kansas City, 1936). [Ploughs] (14:1) 88, p. 78-80.
4721. SCHECHTER, Ruth Lisa
"Meteors Over Haverstraw Bay." [Footwork] ('88) 88, p. 52.
4722. SCHEELE, Roy
"Again." [Plain] (8:1) Fall 87, p. 31.
"Elder Blossom." [SewanR] (96:2) Spr 88, p. 217.
"Gong." [PraS] (62:3) Fall 88, p. 87.
"Hopper's *Early Sunday Morning*." [PraS] (62:3) Fall 88, p. 86-87.
"The Hunter, Home." [EngJ] (77:8) D 88, p. 81.
"A Kill." [PraS] (62:3) Fall 88, p. 85.
"Seashells" (A Book of Stamps). [Plain] (8:3) Spr-Sum 88, p. 8-9.
"Small Gray-Toned Portrait, Circa 1910." [SewanR] (96:2) Spr 88, p. 218-219.
"Tabula Rasa." [Plain] (9:1) Fall 88, p. 31.
"The Water Meadows, Winchester." [SewanR] (96:2) Spr 88, p. 217.
"Woman Feeding Chickens." [PraS] (62:3) Fall 88, p. 86.
4723. SCHEER, Linda
"19. The bed slides through a sleepless sea" (tr. of Francisco Hernandez). [Caliban] (5) 88, p. 97.
"About How Robert Schumann Was Defeated by His Demons" (tr. of Francisco Hernandez). [Caliban] (5) 88, p. 96.
"November Notebook — 1976" (Excerpt, tr. of David Huerta). [Caliban] (5) 88, p. 98-99.
SCHENDEL, Michel van
See Van SCHENDEL, Michel
4724. SCHENDLER, Revan
"I See." [NewYorker] (64:11) 2 My 88, p. 56.
4725. SCHENKER, Donald
"As I Snarl Back at Her Eyes in the Dark." [WormR] (28:4, #112) 88, p. 98-99.
"Clouds." [Caliban] (5) 88, p. 63.
"Coyote." [Caliban] (5) 88, p. 62.
"Dawn Rain." [WormR] (28:4, #112) 88, p. 97-98.
"The Enigma of Arrival." [WormR] (28:4, #112) 88, p. 102-103.
"Hard Moon." [HangL] (52) 88, p. 22-23.
"Hurd's Gulch Poem." [Zyzzyva] (4:1) Spr 88, p. 75.
"The Immortality Game." [WormR] (28:4, #112) 88, p. 103-104.
"The Lineup." [WormR] (28:4, #112) 88, p. 101-102.
"M. Rousseau." [WormR] (28:4, #112) 88, p. 102.
"The Neanderthal Man." [WormR] (28:4, #112) 88, p. 99-100.
"Portrait of a Lamplit Interior Suspended Over a Hillside with Oaks at Dusk." [WormR] (28:4, #112) 88, p. 97.
"The Rat in a Trap." [WormR] (28:4, #112) 88, p. 100-101.
"Signs." [Abraxas] (37) 88, p. 7.
"Third Ear." [Abraxas] (37) 88, p. 8.
"This Light." [WormR] (28:4, #112) 88, p. 97.
4726. SCHERTZER, Mike
"Flag." [Dandel] (15:2) Fall-Wint 88, p. 25.
"If You Don't Phone Me." [Grain] (16:2) Sum 88, p. 52.
SCHERTZER, Miles
See SCHERTZER, Mike
4727. SCHIFF, Harris
"Steppin' Out" (for John Godfrey). [Talisman] (1) Fall 88, p. 42-44.
4728. SCHIFF, Jeff
"A Learned Gesture." [HawaiiR] (12:1, #23) Spr 88, p. 119.
"My Own Fears, For Instance, Are Many" (For Shirley Anderson). [HighP] (3:3) Wint 88-89, p. 51-52.
"Resistance." [StoneC] (16:1/2) Fall-Wint 88-89, p. 39.
"Salvage." [CarolQ] (41:1) Fall 88, p. 59-60.
"Swallows." [StoneC] (16:1/2) Fall-Wint 88-89, p. 38.
4729. SCHJELDAHL, Peter
"Korea." [NewAW] (4) Fall 88, p. 27.
"When Good Things Happen to Bad People." [NewAW] (4) Fall 88, p. 26.
4730. SCHLOSS, David
"Her Date with Destiny." [CinPR] (17) Spr 88, p. 56-57.

4731. SCHMIDT, Paul
"The Operation" ("circumcised at six by mother and grandmother on the dining room table"). [Shen] (38:1) 88, p. 75-78.
4732. SCHMIDT, Steven
"Withershins." [ChatR] (9:1) Fall 88, p. 36-37.
4733. SCHMITT, Peter
"First Art Lessons." [PassN] (9:1) Wint 88, p. 18.
"Grave-Rubbing in a New England Cemetery." [Nat] (246:17) 30 Ap 88, p. 610.
"Jonathan Edwards and the Quaking Bog" (Hawley Bog, Hawley, Mass.). [Nat] (246:19) 14 My 88, p. 692.
4734. SCHMITZ, Barbara
"A Fantasy for Mona Neihardt." [KanQ] (20:4) Fall 88, p. 114-115.
"Grudges." [Plain] (8:3) Spr-Sum 88, p. 10.
"Help the Poor." [Plain] (8:3) Spr-Sum 88, p. 7.
4735. SCHMITZ, Dennis
"Farney's Sister." [HayF] (3) Spr 88, p. 79-80.
"Good Friday." [AmerPoR] (17:6) N-D 88, p. 21.
"The Grand Egress." [Field] (38) Spr 88, p. 52-53.
"Halloween." [AmerPoR] (17:6) N-D 88, p. 21.
"Harness." [Field] (38) Spr 88, p. 50-51.
"Italy: Carrara #8" (for Roger Vail). [Field] (38) Spr 88, p. 48-49.
"Sterno." [AmerPoR] (17:6) N-D 88, p. 22.
"The Three-Legged Dog." [HayF] (3) Spr 88, p. 78.
"U.S. Considers War with Libya." [AmerPoR] (17:6) N-D 88, p. 20.
"Zoo." [AmerPoR] (17:6) N-D 88, p. 20.
4736. SCHNEEMANN, Carolee
"Hand / Heart for Ana." [Sulfur] (8:1, #22) Spr 88, p. 104-106.
4737. SCHNEIDER, Peter
"Fragen an die Ausländer-Raus-Deutschen." [Rohwedder] (4) [Wint 88-89], p. 13.
"Questions Posed to the Foreigners Out Germans" (tr. by Hans-Jurgen Schacht and Colin MacLeod). [Rohwedder] (4) [Wint 88-89], p. 13.
4738. SCHOEBERLEIN, Marion
"The Mexican Girl." [Writer] (101:6) Je 88, p. 24.
4739. SCHOENBERGER, Nancy
"The Great Indifference: Clouds Billowing Up." [Ploughs] (14:4) 88, p. 22-23.
"Long Like a River." [NewYorker] (64:32) 26 S 88, p. 40.
"Men Were Swimming." [Ploughs] (14:4) 88, p. 21.
4740. SCHOFIELD, Don
"Summer Rain." [Amelia] (4:4, #11) 88, p. 69.
4741. SCHOONOVER, Amy Jo
"Encyclopedia." [KanQ] (20:1/2) Wint-Spr 88, p. 197.
4742. SCHORR, Laurie
"After a Post Card She Sent Me Showing *The Hen Wife in the Story of the Hells*." [PennR] (4:1) 88, p. 14-16.
4743. SCHOTT, Penelope Scambly
"At Princeton Airport." [Footwork] ('88) 88, p. 35.
"Her Daughter's Neck." [Footwork] ('88) 88, p. 35.
"Next Time" (2nd Prize, 15th Anniversary Competition). [StoneC] (16:1/2) Fall-Wint 88-89, unpaged front matter.
4744. SCHRAUFNAGEL, Lynda
"The Hay Field." [PaintedB] (34) 88, p. 11.
"Measures." [PaintedB] (34) 88, p. 10.
4745. SCHREIBER, Alvin L.
"There once was a playwright named Pinter." [Amelia] (5:2, #13) 88, p. 70.
4746. SCHREIBER, Dale A.
"Cool Mule." [LightY] ('88/9) 88, p. 93.
"Great Vocabulary." [LightY] ('88/9) 88, p. 200.
4747. SCHREIBER, Jan
"Desire." [TexasR] (9:3/4) Fall-Wint 88, p. 120-121.
4748. SCHREIBER, Ron
"The Birds of Sorrow" (11-1-86). [Agni] (27) 88, p. 194.
"French Tulips." [Abraxas] (37) 88, p. 38.
"Moving Towards Memory (4-22-86)." [Colum] (13) 88, p. 14.
"Preparing to Visit (4-30-86)." [Colum] (13) 88, p. 15.
"A Sequence." [Spirit] (9:1) 88, p. 112-116.

4749. SCHREIBMAN, Susan
"Ahoy" (For Michael Bellew). [Footwork] ('88) 88, p. 22.
"Rooms" (for Michael Bellow). [Footwork] ('88) 88, p. 22-23.
"The Stroke" (for Marianne Andrea). [Footwork] ('88) 88, p. 23.
4750. SCHREINER, Steven
"The Crabapple Tree" (for my brother). [MalR] (84) S 88, p. 109-110.
"Crossing the Country." [PraS] (62:3) Fall 88, p. 105-108.
"Radio." [PraS] (62:3) Fall 88, p. 108-109.
"This Dawn a Spectral Whiteness." [MalR] (84) S 88, p. 111.
"White Branch." [IndR] (11:2) Spr 88, p. 34.
4751. SCHROEDER, Krista
"Upside-Down Brown / Upside-Right White." [Plain] (8:2) Wint 88, p. 9.
4752. SCHUETZ, William
"Au Naturel." [NegC] (8:3) 88, p. 163.
4753. SCHULER, Robert
"Be-Bopping It Out" (for Jody). [Caliban] (4) 88, p. 91.
"Winter Blues" (for Pink Floyd). [Caliban] (4) 88, p. 91.
4754. SCHULER, Ruth Wildes
"Morning Breakdown." [Amelia] (5:2, #13) 88, p. 128.
4755. SCHULMAN, John
"Illinois." [Abraxas] (37) 88, p. 77.
4756. SCHULTE, Ray
"Before Parting." [CharR] (14:2) Fall 88, p. 75.
"Finding a Photograph of a Chinese Friend in an Anthology of American Poetry." [CharR] (14:2) Fall 88, p. 75.
"Mass Grave." [CharR] (14:2) Fall 88, p. 74.
"Phoning Geo Chi-Hwe in Doulio." [CharR] (14:2) Fall 88, p. 75.
4757. SCHULTZ, Dagmar
"My Germany." [Cond] (15) 88, p. 92-94.
"A Pound of Cherries." [Cond] (15) 88, p. 129-130.
4758. SCHULTZ, Lee
"On the Sixty-Three-Yard Black Hunter Round Target, the Young Mystic Falls into His New Name." [PacificR] (6) Spr 88, p. 58-59.
4759. SCHULTZ, Leslie
"Cassatt: Lady at the Tea Table." [PacificR] (6) Spr 88, p. 6.
4760. SCHULTZ, Philip
"The Answering Machine." [Poetry] (151:5) F 88, p. 414-415.
4761. SCHULTZ, Robert
"In this Dark Pool, Our Marriage Bed." [Hudson] (40:4) Wint 88, p. 615-616.
"January 1, 1987." [Hudson] (40:4) Wint 88, p. 615.
"The Morning News." [VirQR] (64:2) Spr 88, p. 282.
"Two or Three Dreams of Spring." [Hudson] (40:4) Wint 88, p. 616-618.
4762. SCHULTZ, Robert O'Neal
"Eggshells and Hourglass." [CreamCR] (12:1) Wint 88, p. 88.
"Sound Boulder." [Plain] (8:3) Spr-Sum 88, p. 27.
"Sun Frown." [BallSUF] (29:4) Aut 88, p. 35.
4763. SCHUMACHER, Rose
"Arabia IV." [RagMag] (6:2) Fall 88, p. 65.
"A Luxury for Which the Artist Pays." [Pembroke] (20) 88, p. 188.
4764. SCHUSTER, Cindy
"Interstate." [CarolQ] (41:1) Fall 88, p. 61.
4765. SCHWARTZ, Hillel
"American Foul Brood." [CrabCR] (5:1) Wint 88, p. 19-20.
"Birth Certificate, Tiberias, '48." [BelPoJ] (38:4) Sum 88, p. 11-13.
"Buz Loves Donna Forever, All in Caps, Outside Trenton." [BelPoJ] (38:4) Sum 88, p. 8-10.
"Captions." [LitR] (32:1) Fall 88, p. 88.
"The Closing Tao." [LitR] (32:1) Fall 88, p. 89.
"Conversations with the Dead, Part III." [MalR] (82) Mr 88, p. 37.
"h = 2000" (the last line in Che Guevara's diary). [LitR] (31:2) Wint 88, p. 240-241.
"He Goes at Last to Antarctica." [Salm] (78/79) Spr-Sum 88, p. 161.
"Killer Kowalsky Who You Last Saw on a Saturday So Many Years Ago." [Farm] (4:1, i.e. 5:1) Wint 88, p. 54-55.
"Last, I Suppose, Sextets." [MalR] (82) Mr 88, p. 35-36.
"Marquis Photographers, Inc.." [PoetL] (83:3) Fall 88, p. 32.
"Named Perils." [HampSPR] Wint 88, p. 27.

"A New Man." [CrabCR] (5:2) Sum 88, p. 28.
"Outside Wrigley Field Long Ago Last Dollar Day." [PoetryNW] (29:4) Wint 88-89, p. 15-16.
"Second Sight." [PoetryNW] (29:3) Aut 88, p. 19-20.
"Whether There Be Any Substance to the Milk of Human Kindness." [NoDaQ] (56:3) Sum 88, p. 120.
"Wonders of the World: Last Wonder." [Thrpny] (34) Sum 88, p. 8.

4766. SCHWARTZ, Howard
"City of the Dead" (In Memory of Rabbi Arnold Asher). [RiverS] (26) 88, p. 73.
"Salt." [RiverS] (26) 88, p. 74.

4767. SCHWARTZ, Leonard
"As You Run Up the Stairs." [CentralP] (14) Fall 88, p. 154-155.

4768. SCHWARTZ, Lloyd
"Goodnight, Gracie" (For Gracie Allen, 1906-1964). [GrandS] (7:4) Sum 88, p. 137-139.

4769. SCHWARTZ, Naomi
"Tomb in the Chang Sha — 1974" (last decade of 3rd c. B.C.). [Verse] (5:1) F 88, p. 22.

4770. SCHWARTZ, Perla
"Al Tocar el Viento." [LetFem] (14:1/2) Primavera-Otoño 88, p. 123.
"Demasiado Tarde" (A mi abuelo Zelig). [LetFem] (14:1/2) Primavera-Otoño 88, p. 123.
"Y Jamás." [LetFem] (14:1/2) Primavera-Otoño 88, p. 123-124.

4771. SCHWARZ, Robin
"Summer Cottage." [HampSPR] Wint 88, p. 48-49.

4772. SCIBELLA, Tony
"Fair Exchange." [Jacaranda] (3:1) Wint 88, p. 105.
"Never Ezy Love Isnt." [Jacaranda] (3:1) Wint 88, p. 106.

4773. SCONZA, Gina
"Departure for Cythera" (tr. of Guillermo Carnero, w. Alexis Levitin). [WebR] (13:1) Spr 88, p. 34.

4774. SCOTELLARO, Robert
"Among Men" (for my father). [LaurelR] (22:21) Wint 88, p. 46.
"Foreign Tongues." [Vis] (28) 88, p. 15.

4775. SCOTT, F. R.
"Bird Cage" (tr. of Saint-Denys Garneau). [Trans] (20) Spr 88, p. 156.
"Greener Than Nature" (tr. of Roland Giguere). [Trans] (20) Spr 88, p. 107.
"Landscape Estranged" (tr. of Roland Giguere). [Trans] (20) Spr 88, p. 108.
"Manor Life" (tr. of Anne Hebert). [Trans] (20) Spr 88, p. 132.
"Rue Saint-Denis" (tr. of Jacques Brault). [Trans] (20) Spr 88, p. 173-174.
"Spectacle of the Dance" (tr. of Saint-Denys Garneau). [Trans] (20) Spr 88, p. 154-155.
"The Tomb of the Kings" (tr. of Anne Hebert). [Trans] (20) Spr 88, p. 133-135.

4776. SCOTT, Herb (*See also* Scott, Herbert)
"The Minister." [Caliban] (4) 88, p. 118.
"She Dreams a Letter from Her Son." [Caliban] (4) 88, p. 117.

4777. SCOTT, Herbert (*See also* Scott, Herb)
"A Brief Reversal: 1941." [PassN] (9:1) Wint 88, p. 15.
"The Husband." [BlackWR] (14:2) Spr 88, p. 48.
"Invocation." [BlackWR] (14:2) Spr 88, p. 45.
"The Neighbor." [BlackWR] (14:2) Spr 88, p. 47.
"The Sea of Despair." [BlackWR] (14:2) Spr 88, p. 46.

4778. SCOTT, John A.
"Changing Room." [NewAW] (4) Fall 88, p. 117-118.
"The Dog Becomes a Waterfall." [NewAW] (4) Fall 88, p. 114.
"Man in Petersham." [NewAW] (4) Fall 88, p. 116.
"Polka." [NewAW] (4) Fall 88, p. 116.
"Pride of Erin." [NewAW] (4) Fall 88, p. 115.
"Wine-Dark." [NewAW] (4) Fall 88, p. 117.

4779. SCOTT, Paul
"Everything But Pedersen's Hill." [RagMag] (6:2) Fall 88, p. 47.

4780. SCOTT, Peter Dale
"Coming to Jakarta: a Poem About Terror" (Three Sections). [Epoch] (37:3) 88, p. 133-140.

4781. SCOTT, Shelley
"Bergen-Belsen 1945." [Lactuca] (11) O 88, p. 6.

4782. SCOVILLE, Jane (Jane A.)
"Education." [BellArk] (4:1) Ja-F 88, p. 1.
"Faith." [BellArk] (4:1) Ja-F 88, p. 8.
"Like the Flowers." [BellArk] (4:5) S-O 88, p. 10.
4783. SCRIMGEOUR, J. D.
"Two Lies About My Family ." [Poetry] (143, i.e. 153:2) N 88, p. 87-88.
4784. SCUTELLARO, Guy (Guy E.)
"The Dreamers." [Amelia] (5:1, #12) 88, p. 108.
"Who Remembers Norman Morrison?" [AnotherCM] (18) 88, p. 165-166.
SE, Lan
See LAN, Se
4785. SEA, Gary
"A Beggar Sings" (tr. of Jesse Thoor). [Paint] (15:30) Aut 88, p. 38.
"Oo La La" (tr. of Jesse Thoor). [Paint] (15:30) Aut 88, p. 38.
4786. SEABURG, Alan
"Applesauce!" [HawaiiR] (12:2, #24) Fall 88, p. 57.
"Be Wondrous." [KanQ] (20:1/2) Wint-Spr 88, p. 263.
"By These Good Images." [CapeR] (23:1) Spr 88, p. 49.
"Looking Away from Death." [BallSUF] (29:4) Aut 88, p. 26.
4787. SEALE, Jan Epton
"Still Life with Quadruped: A Painting of Chang-Eng." [NegC] (8:3) 88, p. 44-53.
4788. SEARS, Vickie
"Ceremony." [SinW] (32) Sum 87, p. 122.
"On Father's Death." [SinW] (32) Sum 87, p. 43-45.
4789. SEATON, Maureen
"Letter to Kate's Son." [Footwork] ('88) 88, p. 42.
"Preposition." [Sonora] (16) Fall 88, p. 49.
"Toward Burton's Bridge." [Footwork] ('88) 88, p. 42.
4790. SECREAST, Donald
"Weekend Clouds." [SouthernPR] (28:2) Fall 88, p. 33.
4791. SEETCH, Beth
"Mission Control." [RiverS] (26) 88, p. 12-13.
"Rain in April: Naked City." [RiverS] (26) 88, p. 11.
4792. SEGALL, Pearl Bloch
"Pie Are Square." [LightY] ('88/9) 88, p. 219.
4793. SEIBLES, Timothy S.
"Prayer" (after W. S. Merwin). [WorldO] (20:3/4) Spr-Sum 86, c89, p. 25.
4794. SEIDEL, Frederick
"AIDS Days." [Raritan] (8-1) Sum 88, p. 28-31.
"Early Sunday Morning in the Cher." [Raritan] (8-1) Sum 88, p. 32-35.
4795. SEIDMAN, Hugh
"A Day." [ParisR] (30:106) Spr 88, p. 122.
"E Train — 8:32 AM." [ParisR] (30:106) Spr 88, p. 123.
"The Null Geodesics." [ParisR] (30:106) Spr 88, p. 124.
4796. SEIFERLE, Rebecca
"The Death of Compassion: To Robert Desnos." [AmerPoR] (17:3) My-Je 88, p. 35.
"In the Kidding Pen." [NegC] (8:3) 88, p. 123-124.
4797. SEIFERT, Jaroslav
"Old Shop Signs" (tr. by Donald Mager). [MidAR] (8:1) 88, p. 102-103.
"Song at Evening" (tr. by Donald Mager). [MidAR] (8:1) 88, p. 102-104.
"Whale's Song" (tr. by Lyn Coffin). [Spirit] (9:1) 88, p. 157-160.
4798. SEINE, Ute M.
"Annie Wauneka's Story." [SinW] (35) Sum-Fall 88, p. 16-17.
4799. SEITZER, Carol
"Aiming for the Mouth." [Interim] (7:1) Spr 88, p. 24.
"Defrosting." [Interim] (7:1) Spr 88, p. 23.
"He Was Fed Up." [CentR] (32:2) Spr 88, p. 151-152.
"A Latin Problem." [Wind] (18:63) 88, p. 36.
"An Obvious Overture to a Research Associate in the Applied Math Department." [HampSPR] Wint 88, p. 52-53.
4800. SELAWSKY, John T.
"August." [WestB] (21/22) 88, p. 153.
"The Relic." [SoDakR] (26:3) Aut 88, p. 154.
"Windfall." [SoDakR] (26:3) Aut 88, p. 155.

4801. SELBY, Martha Ann
"Gathasaptashati" (Selections: tr. of 3 anonymous Prakrit Verses). [Nimrod] (31:2) Spr-Sum 88, p. 16.
"Subhashitaratnakosha" (Selections: tr. of 2 anonymous Sanskrit poems collected by Vidyakara). [Nimrod] (31:2) Spr-Sum 88, p. 18.
4802. SELCH, A. H.
"After Many Years of Backyard Ball." [GreensboroR] (45) Wint 88-89, p. 90-91.
4803. SELLARI, T. J.
"Anna Asleep on the Couch." [PoetryE] (25) Spr 88, p. 64.
4804. SELTZER, Joanne
"Upon Reading a Poem by Etheridge Knight." [PaintedB] (32/33) 88, p. 80.
4805. SEMANSKY, Chris
"Sleeping with Grandfather." [SpoonRQ] (13:3) Sum 88, p. 8-9.
4806. SEMENOVICH, Joseph
"Afterthought." [SlipS] (8) 88, p. 76.
"Dead Love." [Footwork] ('88) 88, p. 51.
4807. SEMONES, Charles
"Backcountry." [AmerV] (11) Sum 88, p. 88-89.
"Full Moon." [KanQ] (20:3) Sum 88, p. 20.
4808. SEN, Nabaneeta Dev
"The Poor Fund" (tr. by Paramita Banerjee and Carolyne Wright, w. the author). [Nimrod] (31:2) Spr-Sum 88, p. 37.
"Recovery" (tr. by Paramita Banerjee and Carolyne Wright, w. the author). [Nimrod] (31:2) Spr-Sum 88, p. 36.
4809. SENECHAL, Diana
"Another" (tr. of Bella Akhmadulina). [Trans] (20) Spr 88, p. 208.
"Don't Devote Much Time to Me" (tr. of Bella Akhmadulina). [Trans] (20) Spr 88, p. 207.
"A New Notebook" (tr. of Bella Akhmadulina). [Trans] (20) Spr 88, p. 209.
"Who Knows If I May Roam the Earth" (tr. of Bella Akhmadulina). [Trans] (20) Spr 88, p. 208.
4810. SENGHOR, Leopold Sedar
"Pearls" (tr. by James T. Reiber). [Vis] (28) 88, p. 30.
"The Portrait" (tr. by James T. Reiber). [Vis] (27) 88, p. 42.
4811. SENGUPTA, Mallika
"Man" (tr. by Paramita Banerjee and Carolyne Wright). [SenR] (18:2) 88, p. 29.
"Month of Honey" (tr. by Paramita Banerjee and Carolyne Wright). [SenR] (18:2) 88, p. 25-26.
"Son of Air" (tr. by Paramita Banerjee and Carolyne Wright). [SenR] (18:2) 88, p. 28.
"Two Golden Airplanes" (tr. by Paramita Banerjee and Carolyne Wright). [SenR] (18:2) 88, p. 27.
"Worshipping the Tree" (tr. by Paramita Banerjee and Carolyne Wright). [SenR] (18:2) 88, p. 24.
4812. SENIOR, Olive
"X. December that year started out" (from *Talking of Trees*). [Callaloo] (11:3, #36) Sum 88, p. 534.
"And What of the Headlines?" [Callaloo] (11:3, #36) Sum 88, p. 528-529.
"Cockpit Country Dreams." [Callaloo] (11:3, #36) Sum 88, p. 519-520.
"Letter from the Lesser World." [Callaloo] (11:3, #36) Sum 88, p. 523-524.
"Nansi 'Tory." [Callaloo] (11:3, #36) Sum 88, p. 531-533.
"Reaching My Station." [Callaloo] (11:3, #36) Sum 88, p. 525-527.
"Searching for Grandfather." [Callaloo] (11:3, #36) Sum 88, p. 521-522.
"To the Madwoman in My Yard." [Callaloo] (11:3, #36) Sum 88, p. 530.
4813. SEQUEIRA, Jose
"Young Nights." [Wind] (18:63) 88, p. 37.
4814. SEQUIN, Iliassa
"Chance having relinquished 'shuttles of dreams'." [Conjunc] (12) 88, p. 138-140.
"Self-circumvented." [Conjunc] (12) 88, p. 135-136.
"While wallowing famine relished its own — gray, unriddled feathers." [Conjunc] (12) 88, p. 136-138.
4815. SERGEYEV, Mark
"Irkutsk — Three Centuries" (tr. by Natasha Killian). [NegC] (8:1/2) 88, p. 70-71.
4816. SERPAS, Martha
"Port Fourchon." [SouthernPR] (28:1) Spr 88, p. 15-16.
"St. Charles Crossing" (for my father). [SouthernPR] (28:1) Spr 88, p. 16-17.

"Xenophile." [SinW] (34) Spr 88, p. 83.

4817. SESHADRI, Vijay
"My Esmeralda." [Shen] (38:1) 88, p. 22.

4818. SETHI, Suresh
"Monsoon." [NewL] (55:1) Fall 88, p. 50.

4819. SETIAN, Ralph
"Chimera" (tr. by the author). [Vis] (26) 88, p. 10.
"Mal du Pays" (Beirut: July 1971, tr. by the author). [Vis] (26) 88, p. 10.

4820. SEXTON, Tom
"Candle Fish." [ArtfulD] (14/15) Fall 88, p. 6.
"Compass Rose." [Interim] (7:2) Fall 88, p. 9.
"Sweet Spring Grasses." [Interim] (7:2) Fall 88, p. 9.
"Väinämöinen's Bride." [Interim] (7:2) Fall 88, p. 10.

4821. SEYFRIED, Robin
"Bedtime Stories" (for my father). [HangL] (52) 88, p. 31.
"Jigsaw Puzzles." [AmerS] (57:2) Spr 88, p. 219-220.
"Serious Suicide." [HangL] (52) 88, p. 29-30.

4822. SHADOIAN, Jack
"Bowlerama Erection." [SlipS] (8) 88, p. 29.
"Checkup." [RagMag] (6:1) [88], p. 40.
"No Etiquette." [SlipS] (8) 88, p. 28.
"Sal Says O.K. to Bernice." [RagMag] (6:1) [88], p. 41.
"Sarcophagus." [SlipS] (8) 88, p. 28.
"The Water Loves Your Song." [StoneC] (15:3/4) Spr-Sum 88, p. 40.

4823. SHAFFER, Kenneth
"Rain." [MidwQ] (29:3) Spr 88, p. 354.

4824. SHAHRYAR
"Call from Above" (tr. by Muhammad Umar Memon). [Nimrod] (31:2) Spr-Sum 88, p. 107.

4825. SHANG, Ch'in
"The Turkey" (tr. by John Balcom). [NowestR] (26:3) 88, p. 56.
"Water Hyacinths" (tr. by John Balcom). [NowestR] (26:3) 88, p. 57.

SHANG-YIN, Li
See LI, Shang-yin

4826. SHANKAR, S.
"After Konarak Sun Temple, 1987." [MassR] (29:4) Wint 88-89, p. 742-743.

4827. SHAPIRO, Alan
"At the Dump." [Agni] (26) 88, p. 45-46.
"Cold Wood" (for W. S. Di Piero). [Thrpny] (33) Spr 88, p. 20.
"Covenant." [YaleR] (77:4) Sum 88, p. 568-572.
"The Dawn of Time." [Thrpny] (35) Fall 88, p. 4.
"The Experiment." [TriQ] (72) Spr-Sum 88, p. 181-182.
"Kinship." [TriQ] (72) Spr-Sum 88, p. 180.
"Night Watch." [TriQ] (72) Spr-Sum 88, p. 178-179.
"Owl." [TriQ] (72) Spr-Sum 88, p. 176-177.
"Sunday at the Dump." [Agni] (26) 88, p. 43-44.

4828. SHAPIRO, Daniel E.
"Voyeurs." [ConnPR] (7:1) 88, p. 23.

4829. SHAPIRO, David
"After 'Asturiana'." [NewAW] (4) Fall 88, p. 14.
"All Night Shows Are Called Transfigured Night" (dedicated to Joseph Ceravolo). [Notus] (3:2) Fall 88, p. 65.
"The Boy Who Loved Bubbles" (dedicated to Joseph Ceravolo). [Notus] (3:2) Fall 88, p. 62.
"A Fragile Art" (dedicated to Joseph Ceravolo). [Notus] (3:2) Fall 88, p. 64.
"In Germany." [NewAW] (4) Fall 88, p. 13.
"To a Swan" (dedicated to Joseph Ceravolo). [Notus] (3:2) Fall 88, p. 63.
"Walter Benjamin: A Lost Poem." [NewAW] (4) Fall 88, p. 12.

4830. SHAPIRO, Gregg
"Suspicious Honeymoon." [Gargoyle] (35) 88, p. 118.

4831. SHAPIRO, Harvey
"1943." [OntR] (28) Spr-Sum 88, p. 100.
"Blue Eyes." [Confr] (Special issue: The World of Brooklyn) 88, p. 29.
"Every Day." [HangL] (52) 88, p. 33.
"Natural History." [HangL] (52) 88, p. 34.
"New York Summer." [OntR] (28) Spr-Sum 88, p. 101.

"Sure." [HangL] (52) 88, p. 32.
4832. SHAPIRO, Karl
"Down Under." [Chelsea] (47) 88, p. 49.
"Mencken." [Chelsea] (47) 88, p. 50.
"A Room in Rome" (For Vera Cacciatore). [Poetry] (152:1) Ap 88, p. 30-31.
"Ruby Bates." [Chelsea] (47) 88, p. 51.
"The Sparrows." [Chelsea] (47) 88, p. 48.
"Tennyson." [NewYorker] (64:37) 31 O 88, p. 34.
4833. SHAPIRO, Martin
"In a Dream Reservoir." [KanQ] (20:1/2) Wint-Spr 88, p. 223.
4834. SHAPIRO, Myra
"On an Island." [OhioR] (42) 88, p. 76-77.
"The Poker Game." [PaintedB] (32/33) 88, p. 66.
SHARAT CHANDRA, G. S.
See CHANDRA, G. S. Sharat
4835. SHARE, Don
"I Have Walked Down Many Roads" (tr. of Antonio Machado). [Agni] (27) 88, p. 9-10.
"Lullaby of the Onion" (Dedicated to his son, tr. of Miguel Hernandez). [ParisR] (30:107) Sum 88, p. 198-200.
4836. SHARFMAN, Bern
"Raw Cowardice." [LightY] ('88/9) 88, p. 217.
4837. SHARTSE, Olga
"In Moments Rare of Inspiration" (tr. of Gevork Emin). [NegC] (8:1/2) 88, p. 49.
4838. SHAVIT, Dean D.
"Pottery Workshop." [PikeF] (9) Fall 88, p. 3.
4839. SHAW, Alan
"Pinball Paradise." [GrandS] (7:2) Wint 88, p. 218.
4840. SHAW, Amanda
"Silently Happy." [PottPort] (10) 88, p. 44.
4841. SHAW, Catherine
"The Parrot Child." [CentR] (32:3) Sum 88, p. 271-272.
4842. SHAW, Catherine Harnett
"The Anthropologist Speaks to the Pilot's Remains." [Gargoyle] (35) 88, p. 158-159.
SHAW, Jacquelyn
See SHAWH, Jacquelyn
4843. SHAW, Jeanne Osborne
"To AC-9, Ivan, Last Wild Condor." [DeKalbLAJ] (21:3/4) 88, p. 63.
4844. SHAW, John
"Elmer Jagow: on His 60th Birthday." [HiramPoR] (Suppl. #8) 88, p. 12.
"For Grace Gruenler on Her Birthday, 1974: A House Built on a Rock." [HiramPoR] (Suppl. #8) 88, p. 13.
"(Here's a Character from 'Hiram, Ohio,' Not *Winesburg, Ohio*)." [HiramPoR] (Suppl. #8) 88, p. 1.
"A New Typewriter Ribbon." [HiramPoR] (Suppl. #8) 88, p. 2.
"On Julia's Birthday." [HiramPoR] (Suppl. #8) 88, p. 6.
"On the detraction which followed upon my making a certain assignment." [HiramPoR] (Suppl. #8) 88, p. 3.
"Sonnet: This British Lit. Survey is quite sold out." [HiramPoR] (Suppl. #8) 88, p. 4.
"Spots of Time: Christmas, 1976" (For the Cambridge 1976 wonderful class of students). [HiramPoR] (Suppl. #8) 88, p. 5.
"To David Anderson." [HiramPoR] (Suppl. #8) 88, p. 11.
"To Kimon Giocarinis." [HiramPoR] (Suppl. #8) 88, p. 7-8.
"To Mary Louise Vincent: Her Birthday." [HiramPoR] (Suppl. #8) 88, p. 9.
"Upon Charles McKinley's Retirement, 1976." [HiramPoR] (Suppl. #8) 88, p. 10.
4845. SHAW, Robert B.
"Parting gift." [CreamCR] (12:2) Sum 88, p. 263.
4846. SHAW-MacKINNON, Margaret
"The Ones That Bless You." [PraF] (9:3) Aut 88, p. 84-85.
4847. SHAWGO, Lucy
"Ordination." [KenR] (NS 10:4) Fall 88, p. 82-83.
"The Pruning." [KenR] (NS 10:4) Fall 88, p. 82.
4848. SHAWH, Jacquelyn
"Dog Days." [TarRP] (27:2) Spr 88, p. 33-34.

4849. SHCHERBINA, Tatyana
"Still-Life" (tr. by J. Kates). [MinnR] (NS 30/31) Spr-Fall 88, p. 46.
4850. SHEA, John
"Baby." [LightY] ('88/9) 88, p. 174.
4851. SHEA, Marilyn
"The Abbey at Bath." [Amelia] (5:2, #13) 88, p. 111.
"Cleanliness Is Next." [Vis] (28) 88, p. 18.
"The Painter's Notebook" (August-September, circa 1623. 1987 John Williams Andrews Prize Winner). [PoetL] (83:1) Spr 88, p. 7-13.
4852. SHEARD, Norma Voorhees
"All Things Wear Thin with Time." [Footwork] ('88) 88, p. 13.
"Open Window." [Footwork] ('88) 88, p. 12-13.
"Reflections on a Male Cardinal." [Footwork] ('88) 88, p. 13.
"Under the Full Red Moon." [Footwork] ('88) 88, p. 13.
4853. SHEBELSKI, R. C.
"Out of Sight." [LightY] ('88/9) 88, p. 84.
4854. SHECK, Laurie
"Io." [NewYorker] (64:18) 20 Je 88, p. 36.
"To Softness." [NewYorker] (64:12) 9 My 88, p. 42.
4855. SHEEHAN, Marc J.
"With Three Young Women in the Darkness." [HighP] (3:1) Spr 88, p. 106-107.
"Writing the Limbo Rock." [HighP] (3:1) Spr 88, p. 108-109.
4856. SHEEHAN, Thomas
"Morning at the Bare Display." [Pembroke] (20) 88, p. 119-120.
4857. SHEIKH, Mansoor Y.
"Shalimar." [Vis] (27) 88, p. 19.
4858. SHEIRER, John
"The Meaning of Elevators." [RagMag] (6:2) Fall 88, p. 48-49.
"Some Days." [RagMag] (6:2) Fall 88, p. 49.
4859. SHEK, Ben-Zion
"About a Sum and a Remainder" (tr. of Michel Van Schendel). [CanLit] (117) Sum 88, p. 47.
"Another Ellipsis" (tr. of Michel Van Schendel). [CanLit] (117) Sum 88, p. 51.
"Brief" (tr. of Michel Van Schendel). [CanLit] (117) Sum 88, p. 46.
"Conversation" (tr. of Michel Van Schendel). [CanLit] (117) Sum 88, p. 55-56.
"Discreet" (tr. of Michel Van Schendel). [CanLit] (117) Sum 88, p. 51.
"Frail" (tr. of Michel Van Schendel). [CanLit] (117) Sum 88, p. 46.
"The heterogeneous is a laugh, a lack of order" (tr. of Michel Van Schendel). [CanLit] (117) Sum 88, p. 49-50.
"Imagines Possessing" (tr. of Michel Van Schendel). [CanLit] (117) Sum 88, p. 46.
"The musical flows from silence" (tr. of Michel Van Schendel). [CanLit] (117) Sum 88, p. 56-57.
"A (Nearly) Unretouched Portrait" (tr. of Michel Van Schendel). [CanLit] (117) Sum 88, p. 54-55.
"On the Line" (tr. of Michel Van Schendel). [CanLit] (117) Sum 88, p. 54.
"A Pinch of Ink Is Just Too Much" (tr. of Michel Van Schendel). [CanLit] (117) Sum 88, p. 52-53.
"Poem-drawing" (tr. of Michel Van Schendel). [CanLit] (117) Sum 88, p. 51.
"The proverbial is an obelisk" (tr. of Michel Van Schendel). [CanLit] (117) Sum 88, p. 48-49.
"A Request to My Trade-Union Comrades" (tr. of Michel Van Schendel). [CanLit] (117) Sum 88, p. 48.
"The sensual: a knit of forms" (tr. of Michel Van Schendel). [CanLit] (117) Sum 88, p. 45.
"She'd love the branch of slate" (tr. of Michel Van Schendel). [CanLit] (117) Sum 88, p. 57.
"Sketch" (tr. of Michel Van Schendel). [CanLit] (117) Sum 88, p. 45-46.
"Support" (tr. of Michel Van Schendel). [CanLit] (117) Sum 88, p. 47.
"The Tea-Rose Unties the Tongue" (tr. of Michel Van Schendel). [CanLit] (117) Sum 88, p. 56.
"Three Words Three Points" (tr. of Michel Van Schendel). [CanLit] (117) Sum 88, p. 51-52.
"We Shall Go All the Way to the Star Beamed by the City" (tr. of Michel Van Schendel). [CanLit] (117) Sum 88, p. 45.
"Written on Rue Danton near Fertile Eyes or Homage to a Book" (tr. of Michel Van Schendel). [CanLit] (117) Sum 88, p. 51.

"Written with a New Pen" (tr. of Michel Van Schendel). [CanLit] (117) Sum 88, p. 53-54.

SHEKERJIAN, Regina deCormier
See DeCORMIER-SHEKERJIAN, Regina

4860. SHELDON, Glenn
"For Stevie." [SlipS] (8) 88, p. 72.
"Masturbating in San Juan." [SlipS] (8) 88, p. 72.

4861. SHELDON, Roy A.
"Sappers." [KanQ] (20:3) Sum 88, p. 193.
"What Happens to a Dream Deferred?" [KanQ] (20:3) Sum 88, p. 192-193.

4862. SHELLER, Gayle Hunter
"Mount Pisgah Morning." [BellArk] (4:6) N-D 88, p. 3.

4863. SHELNUTT, Eve
"Daughters Weighing Their Legacy." [BellR] (11:1) Spr 88, p. 33.
"Labor at Our Mother's Death." [CreamCR] (12:2) Sum 88, p. 265.
"Little Beach" (for Joe). [CreamCR] (12:2) Sum 88, p. 264.
"The Long Mourning." [CreamCR] (12:2) Sum 88, p. 267-268.
"'Luxe, Calme and Volupte,' by Matisse." [CreamCR] (12:2) Sum 88, p. 266.

4864. SHELTON, Richard
"The Creep." [Atlantic] (261:2) F 88, p. 61.

4865. SHEPARD, Neil
"Autumn at the Farm." [TexasR] (9:3/4) Fall-Wint 88, p. 122-123.
"Carleton's Hill." [TexasR] (9:3/4) Fall-Wint 88, p. 126-127.
"Late Spring at the Farm." [TexasR] (9:3/4) Fall-Wint 88, p. 124-125.

4866. SHEPHERD, Elisa Louise
"Yes." [BellArk] (4:4) Jl-Ag 88, p. 9.

4867. SHEPHERD, J. Barrie
"Cana." [ChrC] (105:20) 22-29 Je 88, p. 604.
"The Coming of the Light." [ChrC] (105:39) 21-28 D 88, p. 1181.
"Marking." [ChrC] (105:5) 17 F 88, p. 157.
"The Morning After." [ChrC] (105:39) 21-28 D 88, p. 1183.
"Retrospective Halloween." [ChrC] (105:31) 26 O 88, p. 949.
"Thanksgiving in Advance." [ChrC] (105:35) 23 N 88, p. 1067.

4868. SHERMAN, Alana
"What the Frog's Eye Tells the Frog's Brain." [ManhatPR] (10) Ja 88, p. 59.

4869. SHERMAN, Kenneth
"Mary." [CrossC] (10:3) 88, p. 12.
"Pilate." [CrossC] (10:3) 88, p. 12.

4870. SHERRILL, Jan-Mitchell
"Courtship in Plague Years." [JamesWR] (6:1) Fall 88, p. 8.

4871. SHERRY, Pearl Andelson
"Pinwheels." [SouthernR] (24:3) Sum 88, p. 580.

4872. SHEVIN, David
"Growl" (Excerpt, by Solomon, Allen Ginsberg's husky). [LightY] ('88/9) 88, p. 178-180.
"'Hope' Is the Thing with Whiskers" (by Higginson, Emily Dickinson's hamster). [LightY] ('88/9) 88, p. 177.
"On the Late Mass of Curs in Piedmont" (by Samson, John Milton's mastiff). [LightY] ('88/9) 88, p. 176-177.
"A Valediction: Forbidding Whining" (by Dorset, John Donne's hound). [LightY] ('88/9) 88, p. 175-176.

4873. SHIELDS, Bill (William)
"8 Years Ago." [CutB] (31/32) 88, p. 81.
"Geography." [Contact] (9:47/48/49) Spr 88, p. 50.
"The Horse You Rode In On." [Contact] (9:47/48/49) Spr 88, p. 50.
"In Country." [HangL] (53) 88, p. 51.
"Post Vietnam Stress Syndrome." [HangL] (53) 88, p. 51.
"A Tune About War." [Contact] (9:47/48/49) Spr 88, p. 51.
"Vietnam Veteran." [Contact] (9:47/48/49) Spr 88, p. 51.

SHIGEJI, Tsuboi
See TSUBOI, Shigeji

4874. SHIKATANI, Gerry
"Domenico." [Dandel] (15:2) Fall-Wint 88, p. 18.

4875. SHIKIBU, Izumi
"If the one I've waited for" (tr. by Jane Hirshfield, w. Mariko Aratani). [AmerPoR] (17:1) Ja-F 88, p. 16.

"Love-soaked, rain soaked" (tr. by Jane Hirshfield, w. Mariko Aratani). [AmerPoR] (17:1) Ja-F 88, p. 16.
"Lying alone" (tr. by Jane Hirshfield, w. Mariko Aratani). [AmerPoR] (17:1) Ja-F 88, p. 16.
"The way I must enter" (tr. by Jane Hirshfield, w. Mariko Aratani). [AmerPoR] (17:1) Ja-F 88, p. 16.
"We live in a tide-swept inlet" (tr. by Jane Hirshfield, w. Mariko Aratani). [AmerPoR] (17:1) Ja-F 88, p. 16.

4876. SHIMOSE, Pedro
"La Patria Arde Como un Leño en Mi Memoria." [Mairena] (10:25) 88, p. 76.

4877. SHIN, Dong-Jip
"Dizziness" (tr. by Chang Soo Ko). [WebR] (13:2) Fall 88, p. 14.
"Peasant and Ox" (tr. by Chang Soo Ko). [WebR] (13:2) Fall 88, p. 15.
"The Sea" (tr. by Chang Soo Ko). [WebR] (13:2) Fall 88, p. 16.
"Suburbs on Spring Day" (tr. by Chang Soo Ko). [WebR] (13:2) Fall 88, p. 15.

4878. SHIPLEY, Betty
"High." [Phoenix] (9:1/2) 88, p. 12.
"Rabid, 1893." [Phoenix] (9:1/2) 88, p. 13.
"Raccoons Worth the Name." [Phoenix] (9:1/2) 88, p. 11.
"Weekend." [Phoenix] (9:1/2) 88, p. 10.

4879. SHIPLEY, Vivian
"It Hurts to Burn." [SwampR] (1:2/3) D 88, p. 40-42.
"Outside Cecelia, Kentucky." [SwampR] (1:2/3) D 88, p. 44-45.
"Untitled: We would wake to hoe." [SwampR] (1:2/3) D 88, p. 46.

4880. SHIRLEY, Aleda
"The Glass Lotus." [Poetry] (152:6) S 88, p. 338-339.
"The Last Dusk of August." [Poetry] (152:6) S 88, p. 339-340.

4881. SHISHKOFF, Serge
"Lady Godiva" (tr. of Irina Ratushinskaya, w. Lyn Coffin). [MichQR] (27:3) Sum 88, p. 395-396.

4882. SHOAF, Diann Blakely
"A celebrity in Brownsville!" [WebR] (13:2) Fall 88, p. 81-82.
"The Christmas Party." [HampSPR] Wint 88, p. 50-51.
"The Closed Eye of the Dirt" (after a line by Donald Hall). [SouthernHR] (22:1) Wint 88, p. 62.
"Crow in Cambridge." [DeKalbLAJ] (21:2) Spr 88, p. 44.
"The Doll-Box." [PoetL] (83:3) Fall 88, p. 28.
"The Golden Bird." [CumbPR] (7:2) Spr 88, p. 55.
"Leaving the Church" (Christ Episcopal Church, est. 1761, Cambridge, Mass.). [SouthernR] (24:4) Aut 88, p. 956-957.
"The Rest Home." [HolCrit] (25:3) Je 88, back cover.
"Running a Pig." [LittleM] (15:3/4) 88, p. 136.
"Witch." [Agni] (27) 88, p. 203-204.

4883. SHOLL, Betsy
"Amoco." [WestB] (21/22) 88, p. 8-9.

4884. SHOMER, Enid
"Fishing Seahorse Reef." [Ploughs] (14:1) 88, p. 109-110.
"For Those Who Are No Longer Young." [Poetry] (152:5) Ag 88, p. 271-272.
"Villa Maria." [Poetry] (152:5) Ag 88, p. 272-273.

4885. SHOPTAW, John
"Unfurling" (after Friedrich's *On the Sailing Ship*i). [Notus] (3:2) Fall 88, p. 75.

4886. SHOR, Cynthia Lynch
"My Dog." [Confr] (37/38) Spr-Sum 88, p. 241.
"Polite Conversation." [Confr] (37/38) Spr-Sum 88, p. 241.

4887. SHORE, Jane
"Monday." [Ploughs] (14:4) 88, p. 74-75.

4888. SHORT, Clarice
"Birds of Prey." [WestHR] (42:2) Sum 88, p. 141.
"Carved Door." [WeberS] (5:1) Spr 88, p. 30.
"Credo: Museum." [WeberS] (5:1) Spr 88, p. 31.
"The Elusive." [WeberS] (5:1) Spr 88, p. 31.
"'Mostly Nocturnal' (At the Zoo)." [WestHR] (42:2) Sum 88, p. 140.
"On the Shore of Crete." [WeberS] (5:1) Spr 88, p. 33.
"Said to the Wolf." [WeberS] (5:1) Spr 88, p. 32.

4889. SHORT, Gary
"Dust." [CharR] (14:2) Fall 88, p. 47.

"Farnes Egbert: Water Dowser." [Interim] (7:2) Fall 88, p. 34.

4890. SHORT, Steve
"First Sunday in Advent." [NewEngR] (10:4) Sum 88, p. 475.

4891. SHOULDICE, Larry
"We Have Lost All Trace of Ourselves" (tr. of Pierre Nepveu). [Trans] (20) Spr 88, p. 117.

4892. SHROFF, Beheroze F.
"For a Seventeen-Year-Old Bride." [MassR] (29:4) Wint 88-89, p. 707-708.

4893. SHU, Ting
"Between" (in Chinese & English). [BelPoJ] (39:2) Wint 88-89, p. p. 24-25.
"Love Poem Earth" (in Chinese & English). [BelPoJ] (39:2) Wint 88-89, p. p. 20-21.
"Motherland, My Dear Motherland" (in Chinese & English). [BelPoJ] (39:2) Wint 88-89, p. p. 22-23.
"Resurrection" (in Chinese & English). [BelPoJ] (39:2) Wint 88-89, p. p. 26-29.
"A Self-Portrait" (tr. by Edward Morin and Dennis Ding). [TriQ] (72) Spr-Sum 88, p. 156.
"This Is Also Everything in Reply to a Young Friend's Everything" (in Chinese & English). [BelPoJ] (39:2) Wint 88-89, p. 18-19.

4894. SHUGRUE, Jim
"At Chichen Itza." [Lactuca] (11) O 88, p. 7.
"Package Vacation." [Lactuca] (11) O 88, p. 8.

4895. SHULMAN, Grace
"Rain" (tr. of Carlos Oquendo de Amat). [AmerV] (10) Spr 88, p. 86.

4896. SHUMAKER, Peggy
"After Talking to My Husband's Lover." [MSS] (6:2) 88, p. 64.

4897. SHUMWAY, Mary
"Occasions." [Northeast] (ser. 4:7) Sum 88, p. 20.

SHUNTARO, Tanikawa
See TANIKAWA, Shuntaro

4898. SHURIN, Aaron
"All That." [Sulfur] (8:2, #23) Fall 88, p. 42.
"Below Ground Level." [Temblor] (8) 88, p. 86.
"Reaching Particle." [Notus] (3:2) Fall 88, p. 44.
"Saturated." [Sulfur] (8:2, #23) Fall 88, p. 42-43.

4899. SHUTT, Cary
"Alone in the House." [PikeF] (9) Fall 88, p. 20.

4900. SHUTTLE, Penelope
"Adventures with My Horse." [Stand] (29:2) Spr 88, p. 4-5.
"Dream Dance." [Stand] (29:2) Spr 88, p. 6.
"Ghost of a Housewife." [ManhatR] (4:2) Spr 88, p. 56.
"Killiow Pigs." [ManhatR] (4:2) Spr 88, p. 55-56.
"Tattooed Hand." [ManhatR] (4:2) Spr 88, p. 57.
"Thief." [ManhatR] (4:2) Spr 88, p. 57-59.

4901. SHUTTLEWORTH, Paul
"Candles." [Plain] (8:1) Fall 87, p. 34.
"I Feel This Thing Behind Me." [OntR] (28) Spr-Sum 88, p. 99.
"It Will Never Be Noon Again for So Many of Us: An Exploded Sonnet" (A Plainsongs Award Poem). [Plain] (8:1) Fall 87, p. 4-7.
"This Song and Others." [KanQ] (20:3) Sum 88, p. 34.
"Without Saying Another Word." [Plain] (8:2) Wint 88, p. 32.

4902. SICOLI, Dan
"Dinner." [SlipS] (8) 88, p. 93.

4903. SIEGEL, Bill
"Can You?" (tr. of Nicolás Guillén). [InterPR] (14:1) Spr 88, p. 63, 65.
"The Grandfather" (tr. of Nicolás Guillén). [InterPR] (14:1) Spr 88, p. 67.
"Sensemayá: A Chant for Killing a Snake" (tr. of Nicolás Guillén). [InterPR] (14:1) Spr 88, p. 69.

4904. SIEGEL, Joan I.
"Canada Geese." [InterPR] (14:1) Spr 88, p. 86.
"Dolphins." [InterPR] (14:1) Spr 88, p. 85.
"Piano Lesson" (for Alexander Lipsky). [InterPR] (14:1) Spr 88, p. 88.
"Summer Solstice." [InterPR] (14:1) Spr 88, p. 87.

4905. SIEGEL, June
"Apologia Pro Vita." [LightY] ('88/9) 88, p. 201-202.

4906. SIEGEL, Mary Reinhard
"Beloved Child." [ChatR] (8:2) Wint 88, p. 33.
4907. SIEGEL, Robert
"Bronze Horses." [CreamCR] (12:1) Wint 88, p. 82.
"Mussel." [CreamCR] (12:2) Sum 88, p. 272-274.
"The Sea." [CreamCR] (12:1) Wint 88, p. 83.
"Slug." [CreamCR] (12:2) Sum 88, p. 275-276.
"Sunfish." [CreamCR] (12:2) Sum 88, p. 270-271.
"Swimming Snake." [CreamCR] (12:2) Sum 88, p. 269.
4908. SIEMS, Lawrence
"From Beirut, to His Former Wife." [SouthernPR] (28:2) Fall 88, p. 12-14.
"Thirteen Falls." [Agni] (26) 88, p. 170-171.
4909. SIENRA, Vera
"Hay días en que una sola ciudad." [Mairena] (10:25) 88, p. 130.
4910. SIGNORELLI-PAPPAS, Rita
"Daybook: Leonard Woolf" (March 28, 1941). [Crosscur] (7:4) 88, p. 12-13.
"House of Refuge." [SouthernPR] (28:1) Spr 88, p. 36.
4911. SIGURDSSON, Olafur Johann
"Primal Symbol" (tr. by Alan Boucher). [Vis] (27) 88, p. 6.
4912. SILAS, Paul N.
"Pieces of Night Poems from Prison" (Selection: 23). [SouthernPR] (28:2) Fall 88, p. 36.
"Pieces of Night: Poems from Prison" (Selections: 67, 77, 91). [Poem] (60) N 88, p. 33-35.
4913. SILBERT, Layle
"Crowd." [Footwork] ('88) 88, p. 47.
4914. SILESKY, Barry
"The Morning Bath." [SpoonRQ] (13:1) Wint 88, p. 14-15.
"State of War: Siege 1" (after Phyllis Bramson). [CentralP] (13) Spr 88, p. 155-156.
4915. SILK, Dennis
"In Memoriam" (After Ungaretti). [AmerV] (13) Wint 88, p. 16-17.
"Truant." [Shen] (38:4) 88, p. 78.
4916. SILKIN, Jon
"Durham Bread" (for Jackie Levitas and Dave Bell). [AntR] (46:1) Wint 88, p. 86-87.
"The Levels." [KenR] (NS 10:4) Fall 88, p. 62-63.
"The Silence." [KenR] (NS 10:4) Fall 88, p. 61-62.
4917. SILLIMAN, Ron
"The Alphabet" (Jessie's book, selection: "Ink"). [Temblor] (8) 88, p. 11-24.
"Hidden" (Exceprt: "Lucky"). [Conjunc] (12) 88, p. 248-251.
4918. SILVA, Beverly
"For Naomi Who Asked for an Erotic Poem & for Ray Who Asked for Me." [SlipS] (8) 88, p. 35-36.
"A Piece of Ass." [SlipS] (8) 88, p. 36-37.
4919. SILVA, Fernando Antonio
"November" (tr. by Nancy Esposito). [AmerPoR] (17:2) Mr-Ap 88, p. 28.
4920. SILVA, Paul
"Tomás." [BilingR] (13:1/2) Ja-Ag 86, c1988, p. 85.
"When I See Him." [BilingR] (13:1/2) Ja-Ag 86, c1988, p. 85.
4921. SILVA ESTRADA, Alfredo
"Los Dias Han Ido Lentamente Perdiendo." [Mairena] (10:25) 88, p. 61.
4922. SILVER-LILLYWHITE, Eileen
"The Journey." [PoetryE] (25) Spr 88, p. 109-110.
"Portrait of Mother and Daughter." [PoetryE] (25) Spr 88, p. 111.
"The River." [OhioR] (42) 88, p. 21.
"A Sky." [PoetryE] (25) Spr 88, p. 108.
4923. SILVERIO, Nicasio
"No He Roto Nada Hoy." [LindLM] (7:1) Ja-Mr 88, p. 16.
4924. SILVERSTEIN, David
"The Brick." [YellowS] (27) Aut 88, p. 38.
"Dreaming of Fire, Waking with Burns." [ChiR] (36:2) Aut 88, p. 80.
"Ginger Mousse." [YellowS] (27) Aut 88, p. 38.
4925. SIMAS, Joseph
"Emblematic Series" (Photos: Tim Trompeter). [Acts] (8/9) 88, p. 23-31.
"Kinderpart" (6 selections). [Notus] (3:1) Spr 88, p. 74-79.

4926. SIMBECK, Rob
"The Last Offering." [KanQ] (20:3) Sum 88, p. 181.
4927. SIMIC, Charles
"The Betrothal." [GeoR] (42:4) Wint 88, p. 794.
"Black Madonna" (tr. of Tomaz Salamun). [AmerPoR] (17:3) My-Je 88, p. 34.
"Black Madonna" (tr. of Tomaz Salamun). [RiverS] (26) 88, p. 21.
"Book of Magic." [GettyR] (1:1) Wint 88, p. 146.
"Breakfast." [IndR] (11:3) Sum 88, p. 21.
"Cabbage." [GrandS] (8:1) Aut 88, p. 219.
"Cantina in Querétaro" (tr. of Tomaz Salamun). [RiverS] (26) 88, p. 20.
"Chairs." [GettyR] (1:1) Wint 88, p. 148.
"Childhood Story." [Field] (38) Spr 88, p. 6.
"Evening Talk." [GettyR] (1:1) Wint 88, p. 147.
"Heights of Folly." [ParisR] (30:109) Wint 88, p. 25.
"Lapis Lazuli" (tr. of Tomaz Salamun). [RiverS] (26) 88, p. 18.
"Marching Music." [GeoR] (42:4) Wint 88, p. 793.
"The Meaning." [Field] (38) Spr 88, p. 5.
"The Pieces of the Clock Lie Scattered." [WestHR] (42:4) Wint 88, p. 307.
"Rabbit Oaxaqueño" (tr. of Tomaz Salamun). [AmerPoR] (17:3) My-Je 88, p. 34.
"Six Prose Poems." [WestHR] (42:1) Spr 88, p. 19-20.
"Sky Above Querétaro" (tr. of Tomaz Salamun). [RiverS] (26) 88, p. 19.
"These Homemade Dolls Are No Good." [ParisR] (30:109) Wint 88, p. 23.
"To the Traveller" (tr. of Tomaz Salamun). [RiverS] (26) 88, p. 22.
"Two Dogs." [ParisR] (30:109) Wint 88, p. 22.
"Weather of the Soul." [ParisR] (30:109) Wint 88, p. 21.
"Wherein Obscurely." [TexasR] (9:3/4) Fall-Wint 88, p. 128.
"The Window" (tr. of Tomaz Salamun). [AmerPoR] (17:3) My-Je 88, p. 34.
"Windy Evening." [ParisR] (30:109) Wint 88, p. 24.
"Winter Sunset." [Field] (38) Spr 88, p. 7.
"With Eyes Veiled." [OntR] (29) Fall-Wint 88-89, p. 85.
"The Woman at the Bar." [OntR] (29) Fall-Wint 88-89, p. 84.
"The World." [Field] (38) Spr 88, p. 8.
4928. SIMMERMAN, Jim
"Just to Love the Dog." [Poetry] (152:6) S 88, p. 315.
"Moon Go Away, I Don't Love You No More." [Poetry] (152:6) S 88, p. 314-315.
4929. SIMMONS, Jes
"Looking at Baby through Magnifying Glass." [ColEng] (50:2) F 88, p. 159.
4930. SIMMONS, Thomas
"Bird Dog." [PraS] (62:2) Sum 88, p. 42-43.
"Birthday Poems." [PraS] (62:2) Sum 88, p. 40-42.
4931. SIMMS, Norman
"Love Light." [Bogg] (59) 88, p. 13.
4932. SIMON, Greg
"Abandoned Church" (Ballad of the Great War, tr. of Federico Garcia Lorca, w. Steven F. White). [NowestR] (26:1) 88, p. 88.
"Childhood and Death" (tr. of Federico Garcia Lorca, w. Steven F. White). [Antaeus] (60) Spr 88, p. 254-255.
"Christmas on the Hudson" (tr. of Federico Garcia Lorca, w. Steven F. White). [NowestR] (26:1) 88, p. 89.
"Earth and Moon" (tr. of Federico Garcia Lorca, w. Steven F. White). [Antaeus] (60) Spr 88, p. 252-253.
"Fable of Three Friends, to Be Sung in Rounds" (tr. of Federico Garcia Lorca, w. Steven F. White). [NowestR] (26:1) 88, p. 86-87.
"Little Infinite Poem" (For Luis Cardoza y Aragón, tr. of Federico Garcia Lorca, w. Steven F. White). [Antaeus] (60) Spr 88, p. 256-257.
4933. SIMON, John Oliver
"Black Tryptich" (tr. of Alberto Blanco). [Rohwedder] (3) Spr 88, p. 17.
"Does Anyone Know Where Roque Dalton Spent His Final Night?" (tr. of Gaspar Aguilar Díaz). [Rohwedder] (3) Spr 88, p. 8-9.
"I Say Inside Me" (tr. of Jorge Boccanera). [Rohwedder] (3) Spr 88, p. 32.
"A Skeptical Noah" (tr. of Alberto Blanco). [Zyzzyva] (4:3) Fall 88, p. 129-130.
"Sketch of Ingmar Bergman" (tr. of Adrian Desiderato). [Rohwedder] (3) Spr 88, p. 28.
"To Your Light, To Your People, To your Galaxy" (tr. of Fayad Jamis). [Rohwedder] (3) Spr 88, p. 26.

4934. SIMON, Maurya
"The Abandoned Church." [OntR] (29) Fall-Wint 88-89, p. 98.
"Boy Crazy." [Hudson] (40:4) Wint 88, p. 631-632.
"The Dybbuk's Wedding." [Vis] (28) 88, p. 7-8.
"The Future." [GeoR] (42:2) Sum 88, p. 313.
"In the Valley of Ether." [SenR] (18:1) 88, p. 19.
"Marriage." [PacificR] (6) Spr 88, p. 63.
"Mysteries of the Present" (for Robert Pinsky). [OntR] (29) Fall-Wint 88-89, p. 96-97.
"Origins." [GettyR] (1:1) Wint 88, p. 69-78.
"Shadow Talk." [Spirit] (9:1) 88, p. 149-150.
"Survival" (International Poetry Contest, First Prize). [WestB] (21/22) 88, p. 38.
"Villanelle." [Verse] (5:2) Jl 88, p. 5.
4935. SIMON, Toni
"The Gentle Instructor" (w. Nick Piombino). [CentralP] (14) Fall 88, p. 159-166.
4936. SIMONDET, Helen
"New York 1938." [AmerS] (57:4) Aut 88, p. 548.
4937. SIMONE, Roberta
"Clerihew." [LightY] ('88/9) 88, p. 73.
"The Nicolsons." [LightY] ('88/9) 88, p. 77.
4938. SIMONS, Mary Crescenzo
"Between Puzzle Cracks on the Wall." [Phoenix] (9:1/2) 88, p. 56.
"Grave Sight" (for David Leak). [Phoenix] (9:1/2) 88, p. 56.
4939. SIMONS, Michelle Blake
"Prayer for the Unborn." [SouthernR] (24:2) Spr 88, p. 347-348.
"Thanksgiving." [SouthernR] (24:2) Spr 88, p. 346.
4940. SIMPSON, Betty Jane
"Around the Weather Vane" (The 14th Kansas Poetry Contest, Third Prize). [LittleBR] (5:2) Wint 88-89, p. 64.
4941. SIMPSON, Louis
"Herons and Water Lilies." [KenR] (NS 10:1) Wint 88, p. 19-22.
"His and Hers." [TarRP] (28:1) Fall 88, p. 23.
"It Figures." [TarRP] (28:1) Fall 88, p. 24.
"Neighbors" (expanded version). [TarRP] (28:1) Fall 88, p. 25-26.
"The People Next Door." [Poetry] (152:2) My 88, p. 63-65.
"Santa Monica Boulevard." [GettyR] (1:2) Spr 88, p. 296-298.
"Saudi Arabia." [Sequoia] (31:2) Wint 88, p. 12.
"A Visitor." [Hudson] (40:4) Wint 88, p. 629-630.
4942. SIMPSON, R. A.
"Australian History." [PraS] (62:4) Wint 88-89, p. 118-119.
"Goya in Old Age." [PraS] (62:4) Wint 88-89, p. 118.
4943. SIMS, John
"From Manners of Speaking." [PartR] (55:3) Sum 88, p. 479.
4944. SINCLAIR, Marjorie
"Building." [ChamLR] (1) Fall 87, p. 32.
"Hermit Crab." [HawaiiR] (12:2, #24) Fall 88, p. 25.
"In Lava Country." [ChamLR] (1) Fall 87, p. 33-34.
"Old Woman Waking." [HawaiiR] (12:2, #24) Fall 88, p. 27.
"Origins." [HawaiiR] (12:2, #24) Fall 88, p. 26.
"Winter Song." [ChamLR] (1) Fall 87, p. 31.
4945. SINDOLIC, Vojo
"Three Spontaneous Poems for Michael McClure." [AlphaBS] (4) D 88, p. 17.
4946. SINGER, Frieda
"Chagall and the Village." [NegC] (8:3) 88, p. 146-147.
4947. SINGH, Kedarnath
"Direction" (tr. by Ghanshyam Asthana). [Nimrod] (31:2) Spr-Sum 88, p. 78.
4948. SINGLETON, Martin
"Elegies for Three Poets." [AntigR] (73) Spr 88, p. 61-64.
4949. SINGLETON, Maura
"Autumn: Departures." [Vis] (27) 88, p. 20.
4950. SINHA, Kabita
"To a Cowherd Boy" (tr. by Enakshi Chatterjee and Carolyne Wright). [Nimrod] (31:2) Spr-Sum 88, p. 30.
4951. SINISGALLI, Leonardo
"December at Porta Nuova" (tr. by Rina Ferrarelli). [WebR] (13:1) Spr 88, p. 31.

"Where the Age of the Rose Burned Proudly" (In Italian. Translation Chapbook Series). [MidAR] (8:2) 88, p. 129-153.
"Where the Age of the Rose Burned Proudly" (tr. by Rina Ferrarelli. Translation Chapbook Series). [MidAR] (8:2) 88, p. 129-153.

4952. SISSON, C. H.
"Sonnet: Read me or not: I am nobody." [PartR] (55:1) Wint 88, p. 62.
"Things." [PartR] (55:3) Sum 88, p. 480-481.

4953. SITTERLY, Cassandra
"Black Willow, Arborescent." [Epoch] (37:3) 88, p. 142.
"Precious Metals." [Epoch] (37:3) 88, p. 143.
"Slant." [Epoch] (37:3) 88, p. 141.
"What Models Teach Us About the Globe." [Epoch] (37:3) 88, p. 144.

4954. SJOBERG, Leif
"Below the Stars' Distant Glow" (tr. of Harry Martinson, w. William Jay Smith). [PaintedB] (36) 88, p. 27.
"The Butterfly" (tr. of Harry Martinson, w. William Jay Smith). [PaintedB] (36) 88, p. 24.
"The Forest of Childhood" (tr. of Harry Martinson, w. William Jay Smith). [PaintedB] (36) 88, p. 26.
"The Henhouse" (tr. of Harry Martinson, w. William Jay Smith). [PaintedB] (36) 88, p. 28.
"Late-Born Swarms of Flying Beings" (tr. of Harry Martinson, w. William Jay Smith). [PaintedB] (36) 88, p. 29.
"Leaf-Fall" (tr. of Harry Martinson, w. William Jay Smith). [PaintedB] (36) 88, p. 30.
"The Song of the Meadow" (tr. of Harry Martinson, w. William Jay Smith). [PaintedB] (36) 88, p. 25.

4955. SKAU, Michael
"Winter at Ram's Horn Mountain." [Paint] (15:30) Aut 88, p. 23.

4956. SKEATH, Meredith Briggs
"The Two Doors at Either End of the Hall." [TriQ] (71) Wint 88, p. 163-164.
"Who Wakes Up?" [TriQ] (71) Wint 88, p. 165.

4957. SKILLMAN, Judith
"All the Would Be Dancers." [SpoonRQ] (13:2) Spr 88, p. 19-20.
"A Bouquet for the Sleepless." [NowestR] (26:3) 88, p. 22.
"For the Women Who Wore Muslin." [LaurelR] (22:2) Sum 88, p. 44-45.
"Growing Her Hair." [Colum] (13) 88, p. 105-106.
"Harbor Song." [Iowa] (18:3) 88, p. 129-130.
"The House That Owns Us." [SouthernPR] (28:2) Fall 88, p. 58.
"The Housewife Dreams of Order." [Iowa] (18:3) 88, p. 130.
"Notes on the Vanishing Point." [BellR] (11:2) Fall 88, p. 43.
"The Stoneware Women." [SpoonRQ] (13:2) Spr 88, p. 21-22.
"The Thin Wash of Northwest Autumn." [CreamCR] (12:1) Wint 88, p. 85-86.
"To See Shadows." [NowestR] (26:3) 88, p. 23.

4958. SKINNER, Jeffrey
"Ars Poetica, September." [KanQ] (20:3) Sum 88, p. 116.
"The Company of Heaven." [Poetry] (152:6) S 88, p. 344-348.
"Greetings from the Edge of Ridicule." [CutB] (31/32) 88, p. 41.
"Rescuing the Angel." [TexasR] (9:3/4) Fall-Wint 88, p. 129.
"Shore Report." [CutB] (31/32) 88, p. 40.
"Wheel of Fortune." [KanQ] (20:3) Sum 88, p. 116-117.

4959. SKINNER, Knute
"Images." [Confr] (37/38) Spr-Sum 88, p. 229.
"Introduction to a Pub in Limerick." [LightY] ('88/9) 88, p. 90.

4960. SKLAN, Susan
"Express Mail." [CentR] (32:2) Spr 88, p. 153-154.
"On Passing an Old Lover's Address." [Spirit] (9:1) 88, p. 171.

4961. SKLOOT, Floyd
"Closer to Home." [GreensboroR] (45) Wint 88-89, p. 39.
"Holman Meadow." [WritersF] (14) Fall 88, p. 54.
"I Am Getting a Mountain View." [LightY] ('88/9) 88, p. 152-153.
"Leavings." [WritersF] (14) Fall 88, p. 52.
"The Mill." [SouthernPR] (28:2) Fall 88, p. 38.
"The New and Used Bookstore." [WritersF] (14) Fall 88, p. 53.
"Shoreline Life." [Comm] (115:13) 15 Jl 88, p. 405.
"You Asked for It." [Harp] (276:1652) Ja 88, p. 31.

4962. SKOPTZOV, Simeon
"Bread" (tr. by Leonid S. Polevoy). [NegC] (8:1/2) 88, p. 63-64.
4963. SKRANDE, Eva
"The Sea's Monologue." [AmerPoR] (17:4) Jl-Ag 88, p. 20.
4964. SKYNNER, Robin
"I could never understand why pain and suffering." [Margin] (6) Sum 88, p. 30-31.
4965. SLATER, Dashka
"Heirloom." [BelPoJ] (38:4) Sum 88, p. 1.
4966. SLATER, Lydia Pasternak
"God's World" (tr. of Boris Pasternak). [NegC] (8:1/2) 88, p. 15.
4967. SLAUERHOFF, J.
"Arcadia" (in Dutch). [KanQ] (20:1/2) Wint-Spr 88, p. 75.
"Arcadia" (tr. by Gerald George). [KanQ] (20:1/2) Wint-Spr 88, p. 75.
4968. SLAUGHTER, William
"Climbing Tai Shan" (National Day, 1 October 1987). [Poetry] (143, i.e. 153:1) O 88, p. 28-29.
4969. SLAVITT, David (David R.)
"Circus Costumes." [FourQ] (2d series 2:1) Spr 88, p. 53-57.
"Intermission Greetings at the Paris Opera — 1898." [LightY] ('88/9) 88, p. 69.
"Matisse's Tablecloth." [GeoR] (42:2) Sum 88, p. 236-237.
"Nevelson." [PaintedB] (34) 88, p. 28.
"Snowfall." [PaintedB] (34) 88, p. 27.
"Used Furniture." [WestB] (21/22) 88, p. 24-25.
4970. SLAVOV, Atanas
"The Flesh of Air" (tr. of Svezha Dacheva). [Vis] (26) 88, p. 18, 20.
"Spring Promenade." [Vis] (26) 88, p. 20.
4971. SLEIGH, Tom
"The Last Word." [ParisR] (30:107) Sum 88, p. 128-129.
"Vows." [ParisR] (30:107) Sum 88, p. 125-127.
4972. SLOAN, Gerry
"John Anderson's Lament." [KanQ] (20:1/2) Wint-Spr 88, p. 247.
"Little Elegy." [KanQ] (20:1/2) Wint-Spr 88, p. 246-247.
"Message Found in a Typewriter." [NoDaQ] (56:2) Spr 88, p. 89.
"Petoskey Stone from Rebecca." [Poem] (60) N 88, p. 38.
4973. SLOANE, Arlac (Arlac P.)
"Early Suburban Rigormortis." [Lactuca] (10) Je 88, p. 42.
"Rapid Eye Movement." [SlipS] (8) 88, p. 17.
"What's Doin', Mr. McLuhan?" [Lactuca] (9) F 88, p. 39.
4974. SLONIMSKY, Lee
"Trees." [ManhatPR] (10) Ja 88, p. 58.
4975. SLYMAN, Ernest
"Chinese Restaurant." [LightY] ('88/9) 88, p. 217.
"Lightning Bugs." [LightY] ('88/9) 88, p. 42.
"Scoop." [LightY] ('88/9) 88, p. 226.
4976. SMALL, Judith
"Jackson the Pirate" (Excerpts). [FiveFR] (6) 88, p. 77-80.
4977. SMITH, Annette
"Genesis for Wilfredo" (tr. of Aimé Césaire, w. Clayton Eshleman). [Caliban] (5) 88, p. 18.
"Leon G. Damas Somber Fire Always" (in memoriam, tr. of Aimé Césaire, w. Clayton Eshleman). [Epoch] (37:2) 88, p. 105.
"Let Us Offer Its Heart to the Sun" (tr. of Aimé Césaire, w. Clayton Eshleman). [Caliban] (5) 88, p. 19.
"Link of the Chain-Gang" (tr. of Aimé Césaire, w. Clayton Eshleman). [Epoch] (37:2) 88, p. 109.
"Macumba Word" (tr. of Aimé Césaire, w. Clayton Eshleman). [Caliban] (5) 88, p. 15.
"Mangrove Swamp" (tr. of Aimé Césaire, w. Clayton Eshleman). [Caliban] (5) 88, p. 14.
"Nights" (tr. of Aimé Césaire, w. Clayton Eshleman). [Caliban] (5) 88, p. 16.
"Ribbon" (tr. of Aimé Césaire, w. Clayton Eshleman). [Caliban] (5) 88, p. 17.
"Testing" (tr. of Aimé Césaire, w. Clayton Eshleman). [Epoch] (37:2) 88, p. 107.
4978. SMITH, Arthur
"Happy Little Love Poem." [IndR] (11:3) Sum 88, p. 24.
"Her Shoes." [MSS] (6:2) 88, p. 11.
"Outdoor Theater." [NewEngR] (10:3) Spr 88, p. 353-354.

4979. SMITH, Bobbie Jean
"Jeannie." [Quarry] (37:1) Wint 88, p. 48-50.
"Offspring." [Quarry] (37:1) Wint 88, p. 46-47.
4980. SMITH, Bruce
"Something of Consolation." [Agni] (26) 88, p. 115-118.
4981. SMITH, Carolyn Reams
"Geophysical." [MidAR] (8:1) 88, p. 100-101.
4982. SMITH, Charlie
"Ageling." [Chelsea] (47) 88, p. 79.
"The Banquet." [ParisR] (30:107) Sum 88, p. 224-225.
"Beauty Kills." [Crazy] (34) Spr 88, p. 20-21.
"Cycles." [ParisR] (30:107) Sum 88, p. 226.
"The defiance of Heroes." [SouthernPR] (28:2) Fall 88, p. 27.
"An Explanation." [Sonora] (16) Fall 88, p. 56-57.
"Gosnold Pond." [BlackWR] (14:2) Spr 88, p. 18-20.
"Heads of Fire." [Crazy] (34) Spr 88, p. 18-19.
"How I Smack My Head." [Chelsea] (47) 88, p. 77.
"Kogane No Nami." [BlackWR] (14:2) Spr 88, p. 21.
"R.I.P." [Sonora] (16) Fall 88, p. 55.
"Raison d'être." [NoAmR] (273:3) S 88, p. 29.
"Sonnet: At the track." [Chelsea] (47) 88, p. 76.
"Testament of White, Part Two: The Past." [Crazy] (34) Spr 88, p. 22-23.
"Too Much, Never Enough." [Chelsea] (47) 88, p. 78.
4983. SMITH, Clark
"How I Learned to Cook." [WritersF] (14) Fall 88, p. j92-93.
4984. SMITH, Dave
"1957 Belaire." [Verse] (5:3) N 88, p. 23.
"Baptism by Personal Choice." [Verse] (5:3) N 88, p. 24.
"Clay" (A Valentine). [Poetry] (152:4) Jl 88, p. 226.
"The Futility of Criticism." [CreamCR] (12:2) Sum 88, p. 277.
"Lynwood & Two-on-One." [Verse] (5:3) N 88, p. 25.
"Pallbearers at the Mausoleum." [CreamCR] (12:2) Sum 88, p. 278-279.
"Sugar." [Poetry] (152:4) Jl 88, p. 223.
"The Virginian." [Poetry] (152:4) Jl 88, p. 224.
"Writing Spider." [Poetry] (152:4) Jl 88, p. 225.
4985. SMITH, David
"Little Birds." [PoetL] (83:4) Wint 88-89, p. 36.
4986. SMITH, David-Glen
"In Darkness You Slept, a Grandfalloon for Mark Whose Last Name Remains Hidden. . . ." [RagMag] (6:2) Fall 88, p. 32-33.
"On the Last Hour" (for Ruth who braids her hair in silence). [RagMag] (6:2) Fall 88, p. 29.
"Robyn As Celestina." [YellowS] (28) D 88, p. 36.
"Season." [YellowS] (27) Aut 88, p. 13.
"Suddenly He Was a Man of Clay." [RagMag] (6:2) Fall 88, p. 30-31.
"Your Son's IO Eyes Shine as Copper." [YellowS] (27) Aut 88, p. 12.
4987. SMITH, Gerald Stanton
"Ginger Moll" (tr. of Vladimir Vysotsky). [NegC] (8:1/2) 88, p. 43.
"On the Far Side of the Clouds" (tr. of Robert Rozhdestvensky). [NegC] (8:1/2) 88, p. 45.
"The Prayer of François Villon" (tr. of Bulat Okudzhava). [NegC] (8:1/2) 88, p. 16.
4988. SMITH, Iain Crichton
"The Island." [Verse] (5:3) N 88, p. 6-10.
4989. SMITH, J.
"Jack Smith." [LitR] (31:3) Spr 88, p. 295.
4990. SMITH, J. D.
"First Grade." [SmPd] (25:2) Spr 88, p. 13.
"Wire Fishing." [SpoonRQ] (13:1) Wint 88, p. 56-57.
4991. SMITH, James Steel
"Dog Story." [LightY] ('88/9) 88, p. 94.
SMITH, James Sutherland
See SUTHERLAND-SMITH, James
4992. SMITH, Jared
"Of Fire." [PoetL] (83:2) Sum 88, p. 45.
"The Wall." [DeKalbLAJ] (21:2) Spr 88, p. 45.

4993. SMITH, John
"All Things Sacred and Forgotten." [Footwork] ('88) 88, p. 61.
"Blue Shirt" (for joey). [InterPR] (14:1) Spr 88, p. 92.
"Jack Smith." [InterPR] (14:1) Spr 88, p. 92.
"Lauren." [InterPR] (14:1) Spr 88, p. 93.
"Snow." [Vis] (27) 88, p. 21.
"Tragic Update." [InterPR] (14:1) Spr 88, p. 91.
4994. SMITH, Jordan
"For George Oppen." [Agni] (26) 88, p. 176.
"That Orchard That They're Cutting Down." [TampaR] (1) 88, p. 79.
4995. SMITH, Ken
"Carteret Plage" (For Judi). [Antaeus] (60) Spr 88, p. 217-219.
"The Night Whispers" (For John, and all the men in the world called John). [Antaeus] (60) Spr 88, p. 220-222.
4996. SMITH, Lawrence R.
"Cheap Teflon." [Caliban] (5) 88, p. 84.
"Monkey in the Moonlight, with Birds." [Caliban] (5) 88, p. 85.
"Ruby My Dear." [Caliban] (5) 88, p. 83.
"State of the Union." [Caliban] (5) 88, p. 82.
4997. SMITH, LeRoy
"Legacies." [Comm] (115:5) 11 Mr 88, p. 142.
4998. SMITH, Maggie
"For Jonathon." [JlNJPo] (10:1/2) 88, p. 35.
"Stigma." [JlNJPo] (10:1/2) 88, p. 34.
4999. SMITH, Marion H.
"Lady to Archaeologist, Royal Cemetery at Ur." [KeyWR] (1:1) Spr 88, p. 32-33.
5000. SMITH, Maurine
"Full Circle." [Phoenix] (9:1/2) 88, p. 46.
5001. SMITH, Michael C.
"Yard Sale." [Jacaranda] (3:1) Wint 88, p. 92-93.
5002. SMITH, Pat
"4:00 a m" (from "A Book of Ours"). [Notus] (3:2) Fall 88, p. 30-34.
5003. SMITH, R. T.
"Apple Hymn and Dog's Promise for Blair." [Poem] (59) My 88, p. 1-3.
"Curio." [NegC] (8:3) 88, p. 138.
"Friday 13, a Fascination." [CreamCR] (12:2) Sum 88, p. 280.
"Marriage." [NegC] (8:3) 88, p. 62-64.
"Mending." [Pembroke] (20) 88, p. 117.
"Rushlight." [Poetry] (152:6) S 88, p. 329-330.
"Scott Ward, Explaining History, Goes One Up on Gibbon." [PaintedB] (36) 88, p. 33.
"Self As Trout." [Poetry] (152:6) S 88, p. 330-331.
"Shrine." [SouthernPR] (28:1) Spr 88, p. 64-65.
"Souvenir." [Poem] (59) My 88, p. 4.
"Spackling." [SoCaR] (20:2) Spr 88, p. 17.
"Vernacular." [PaintedB] (36) 88, p. 31-32.
5004. SMITH, Robert L. (*See also* Smith, Robert Lavett)
"One Hundred-Two Lbs. of Bluefish." [StoneC] (16:1/2) Fall-Wint 88-89, p. 32-33.
5005. SMITH, Robert Lavett (*See also* Smith, Robert L.)
"The Bo Tree" (for John and Madhavi). [JlNJPo] (10:1/2) 88, p. 36.
"Old Men in Shirtsleeves." [JlNJPo] (10:1/2) 88, p. 37.
"Thirty Years After the War" (Palau, 1971). [PikeF] (9) Fall 88, p. 15.
"Unlike Hiroshima." [PikeF] (9) Fall 88, p. 7.
"Waiting for the Thaw" (For Mekeel McBride). [BallSUF] (29:4) Aut 88, p. 43.
5006. SMITH, Ron
"Gatlinburg." [WilliamMR] (26:1) Spr 88, p. 40.
"Henry James and the Future of Photography." [VirQR] (64:3) Sum 88, p. 438-439.
"Jacob, Swinging." [PoetryNW] (29:4) Wint 88-89, p. 28-29.
"Knock." [KanQ] (20:1/2) Wint-Spr 88, p. 77.
"Morning: Two Dogs on a Winter Field." [KenR] (NS 10:2) Spr 88, p. 67.
"Oxford, 1975." [KenR] (NS 10:2) Spr 88, p. 66-67.
"Sleeping on the North Rim." [PoetryNW] (29:4) Wint 88-89, p. 27.
"So Long Since I Have Put My Hand on You with This Pleasure." [PoetryNW] (29:4) Wint 88-89, p. 26-27.
"The Southern Poet Reads Emerson." [NewEngR] (11:1) Aut 88, p. 103-104.
"Starting Over at Boot Hill." [Timbuktu] (2) Sum-Fall 88, p. 8.

"Striking Out My Son in the Father-Son Game." [KanQ] (20:1/2) Wint-Spr 88, p. 76-77.

5007. SMITH, Russell C.
"Jesse James Was a Virgo." [LittleM] (15:3/4) 88, p. 50.
"Springtime in New York." [LittleM] (15:3/4) 88, p. 48.
"The Zookeeper's Dream." [LittleM] (15:3/4) 88, p. 49.

5008. SMITH, Sherry
"Sour Grapes." [Phoenix] (9:1/2) 88, p. 57.

5009. SMITH, Stephen E.
"The Poet's Photograph." [LightY] ('88/9) 88, p. 190-192.

5010. SMITH, Steven
"Medici Fountain. 1928." [Grain] (16:4) Wint 88, p. 57.
"Rue des Ursins. 1931." [Grain] (16:4) Wint 88, p. 56.

SMITH, Sybil Woods
See WOODS-SMITH, Sybil

5011. SMITH, Thomas R.
"After Seeing an Exhibit of Maori Art." [LakeSR] (22) 88, p. 12.
"Cherry Harvest in Wenatchee." [Northeast] (ser. 4:7) Sum 88, p. 23.
"Palmina." [LakeSR] (22) 88, p. 13.

5012. SMITH, Tom
"Glass." [Blueline] (9:1/2) 88, p. 70.
"Song of Solomon 2:13." [SpiritSH] (54) Fall-Wint 88, p. 23-24.
"Song of Solomon 4:12." [SpiritSH] (54) Fall-Wint 88, p. 24-25.
"Song of Solomon 6:10." [SpiritSH] (54) Fall-Wint 88, p. 25-26.
"Song of Solomon 8:4." [SpiritSH] (54) Fall-Wint 88, p. 26-27.
"Weeding." [Blueline] (9:1/2) 88, p. 69.
"A Young Raccoon." [Blueline] (9:1/2) 88, p. 71.

5013. SMITH, William Jay
"At the End of Life" (tr. of Sándor Weöres). [AmerPoR] (17:2) Mr-Ap 88, p. 32.
"Below the Stars' Distant Glow" (tr. of Harry Martinson, w. Leif Sjoberg). [PaintedB] (36) 88, p. 27.
"The Butterfly" (tr. of Harry Martinson, w. Leif Sjoberg). [PaintedB] (36) 88, p. 24.
"The Christmas Tree in the Hospital Corridor" (tr. of Bella Akhmadulina, w. Svetlana Kluge). [AmerPoR] (17:3) My-Je 88, p. 40.
"The Death of the Owl" (tr. of Bella Akhmadulina, w. Svetlana Kluge). [AmerPoR] (17:3) My-Je 88, p. 38.
"The Forest of Childhood" (tr. of Harry Martinson, w. Leif Sjoberg). [PaintedB] (36) 88, p. 26.
"The Henhouse" (tr. of Harry Martinson, w. Leif Sjoberg). [PaintedB] (36) 88, p. 28.
"Late-Born Swarms of Flying Beings" (tr. of Harry Martinson, w. Leif Sjoberg). [PaintedB] (36) 88, p. 29.
"Leaf-Fall" (tr. of Harry Martinson, w. Leif Sjoberg). [PaintedB] (36) 88, p. 30.
"The Lunatic Cyclist" (tr. of Sándor Weöres). [AmerPoR] (17:2) Mr-Ap 88, p. 32.
"Rain" (tr. of Carlos Oquendo de Amat). [AmerV] (10) Spr 88, p. 87.
"Raphael Day" (tr. of Bella Akhmadulina, w. Svetlana Kluge). [AmerPoR] (17:3) My-Je 88, p. 39.
"The Resort" (tr. of Bella Akhmadulina, w. Svetlana Kluge). [AmerPoR] (17:3) My-Je 88, p. 39.
"The Song of the Meadow" (tr. of Harry Martinson, w. Leif Sjoberg). [PaintedB] (36) 88, p. 25.

5014. SMITH-BOWERS, Cathy
"Hanging the Screens." [GeoR] (42:1) Spr 88, p. 93-94.
"Stars." [HiramPoR] (44/45) Spr-Wint 88, p. 39.
"Wanting Them Back." [SouthernPR] (28:2) Fall 88, p. 50.
"The Worst a Good Man Dan Do." [GeoR] (42:1) Spr 88, p. 92-93.

5015. SMITH-MANCERON, Katherine
"Landscape." [Vis] (27) 88, p. 15.

5016. SMOCK, Frederick
"Irkutsk Station." [Iowa] (18:1) 88, p. 125.

5017. SMOKEWOOD, Elaine
"Flashflood." [AmerPoR] (17:4) Jl-Ag 88, p. 17.
"Love Song" (for my grandparents). [AmerPoR] (17:4) Jl-Ag 88, p. 17.
"Pink Dolphins." [AmerPoR] (17:4) Jl-Ag 88, p. 17.

5018. SMYTH, Paul
"Ashes." [TexasR] (9:3/4) Fall-Wint 88, p. 130.
5019. SMYTH, Richard
"Continent." [MidwQ] (29:4) Sum 88, p. 460.
"Moment of Silence." [MidwQ] (29:4) Sum 88, p. 459.
5020. SNEED, Pamela
"Eyes on the Prize" (for Bernhard Goetz). [Cond] (15) 88, p. 33-34.
"Rapunzel." [Cond] (15) 88, p. 73.
5021. SNEFF, Priscilla
"Antarctica." [Timbuktu] (1) Wint-Spr 88, p. 3.
"For the Skeleton Elk." [Timbuktu] (1) Wint-Spr 88, p. 4.
"For Want of the Golden City" (Selections: 1-4). [Timbuktu] (1) Wint-Spr 88, p. 1-2.
"Once More with Spriit." [Timbuktu] (1) Wint-Spr 88, p. 76.
5022. SNEHARASHMI
"Haiku" (2 poems, tr. of Ushanas). [Nimrod] (31:2) Spr-Sum 88, p. 73.
"Haiku" (3 poems, tr. by the author). [Nimrod] (31:2) Spr-Sum 88, p. 72.
"Haiku: A beak is dipped" (tr. of Jagadish Pathak). [Nimrod] (31:2) Spr-Sum 88, p. 73.
"Haiku: Full of honey" (tr. of the anonymous Gujarati). [Nimrod] (31:2) Spr-Sum 88, p. 72.
5023. SNIDER, Grant
"Our Grandfather's House." [LaurelR] (22:2) Sum 88, p. 7-8.
"Thunderbird Wine — Flagstaff AZ." [LaurelR] (22:2) Sum 88, p. 8-9.
5024. SNODGRASS, Ann
"A Distance." [PartR] (55:4) Fall 88, p. 622-623.
5025. SNODGRASS, W. D.
"Cock Robin Escapes from the Alizarin of Evening" (after the painting by DeLoss McGraw). [NoDaQ] (56:3) Sum 88, p. 21.
"The Forces of Love Re-assemble W.D." (after the painting by DeLoss McGraw). [NoDaQ] (56:3) Sum 88, p. 20-21.
"Fox Trot: The Whisper, the Whistle and the Song" (For John and Carol Wood). [MichQR] (27:3) Sum 88, p. 439.
"The Memory of Cock Robin Dwarfs W. D." (after the painting by DeLoss McGraw). [MichQR] (27:3) Sum 88, p. 441-442.
"Mr. Evil Disguises Himself As Herself — with Murder in Her Heart for W. D." [Salm] (78/79) Spr-Sum 88, p. 208.
"Mr. Evil Humiliates W. D. with Child-Like Toys" (after the painting by DeLoss McGraw). [Salm] (78/79) Spr-Sum 88, p. 205.
"Mr. Evil Waltzes W. D.'s Thought Away from Cock Robin" (after the painting by DeLoss McGraw). [Salm] (78/79) Spr-Sum 88, p. 206.
"W. D. and the Dark Comedian Search for Happy Families." [Salm] (78/79) Spr-Sum 88, p. 207.
"W.D. Sees Himself Animated" (after the painting by DeLoss McGraw). [NoDaQ] (56:3) Sum 88, p. 19-20.
5026. SNOOK, Kirsten
"Human Nature." [HangL] (53) 88, p. 66.
5027. SNOW, Carol
"Artist and Model III: The Morning Exercise." [DenQ] (23:2) Fall 88, p. 60.
"Artist and Model IV: From the Model." [DenQ] (23:2) Fall 88, p. 61.
"Artist and Model V: Likeness." [DenQ] (23:2) Fall 88, p. 62.
"The Back of the White Blouse." [Verse] (5:1) F 88, p. 23.
"Le Déjeuner." [Verse] (5:1) F 88, p. 23-24.
"Trees We Pass." [Verse] (5:1) F 88, p. 23.
5028. SNOW, Edward
"Apprehension" (tr. of Rainer Maria Rilke). [Thrpny] (35) Fall 88, p. 14.
"The Ashanti: Jardin d'Acclimatation" (tr. of Rainer Maria Rilke). [Thrpny] (35) Fall 88, p. 18.
5029. SNOW, Robert M.
"Night March." [StoneC] (16:1/2) Fall-Wint 88-89, p. 36.
5030. SNYDAL, James
"Poetry Editor for a London Publisher." [Bogg] (60) 88, p. 29-30.
5031. SNYDAL, Laurence
"April." [SpoonRQ] (13:2) Spr 88, p. 64.
"Chef's Knife." [SpoonRQ] (13:2) Spr 88, p. 64.

5032. SNYDER, Gary
"The Bear Mother" (Brooks Range, VIII: 86). [Sulfur] (8:1, #22) Spr 88, p. 115.
"Jackrabbit" (for Mts. & Rivers, V: 87). [Sulfur] (8:1, #22) Spr 88, p. 115-116.
"Kusiwoqqóbi" (VII: 82 - VII: 87 Trip with Kai down the east side near Mammoth . . .). [Sulfur] (8:1, #22) Spr 88, p. 116-117.
"Raven's Beak River at the End" (Mountains and Rivers without End, . . . July 86). [Sulfur] (8:1, #22) Spr 88, p. 118-119.
"Surrounded by Wild Turkeys." [Verse] (5:1) F 88, p. 24.
"Surrounded by Wild Turkeys" (4 IX: 87, for the teachings of the wild turkey flock). [Sulfur] (8:1, #22) Spr 88, p. 117.
"The Sweat" (For John and Jan Straley after all the meetings were over). [Zyzzyva] (4:2) Sum 88, p. 95-97.
"Waikiki." [ChamLR] (1) Fall 87, p. 38.
5033. SOBIN, Anthony
"Astounded by Breasts." [PoetryNW] (29:3) Aut 88, p. 28.
"How I Became a San Francisco Poet." [BelPoJ] (39:1) Fall 88, p. 35-36.
"Revolutions." [Poetry] (153:3) D 88, p. 141-142.
"The Word Sanctuary" (for Phil Dacey). [PoetryNW] (29:3) Aut 88, p. 26-27.
5034. SOBIN, Gustaf
"Of the Four-Winged Cherubim as Signature" (from "Voyaging Portraits"). [Temblor] (7) 88, p. 30-43.
5035. SOBSEY, Cynthia
"Winter Weeds." [SwampR] (1:2/3) D 88, p. 66.
5036. SOFRANKO, Michael
"Near Lone Tree." [Ploughs] (14:4) 88, p. 102.
5037. SOIFER, Mark
"Words Without a Subject." [Pembroke] (20) 88, p. 248.
5038. SOLARCZYK, Bart
"I Hear We're Floating Apart." [Bogg] (59) 88, p. 42.
SOLER, María Lourdes Möller
See MÖLLER-SOLER, María Lourdes
5039. SOLHEIM, James
"Born into the Wry, Eocenic Tomfoolery of a Kemmerer, Wyoming Magician's Family . . ." [Iowa] (18:3) 88, p. 48-51.
"Echocardiogram." [Poetry] (152:5) Ag 88, p. 264.
"Ev Pangborn's Bridge." [QW] (27) Sum-Fall 88, p. 115.
"Fluffy in Heaven." [KenR] (NS 10:1) Wint 88, p. 97.
"Growth Rings." [Iowa] (18:3) 88, p. 52-54.
"My Father Playing Pool." [KenR] (NS 10:1) Wint 88, p. 98.
"Roughing-In a House." [Poetry] (152:5) Ag 88, p. 265.
5040. SOLI, Sandra
"Getting There" (Written after viewing a model of Marc Chagall's Jerusalem Windows). [Phoenix] (9:1/2) 88, p. 40.
"Tet in the Afternoon." [Phoenix] (9:1/2) 88, p. 39.
5041. SOLIS, Mercedes
"Abruptamente irrumpí en el mundo." [Mairena] (10:25) 88, p. 142.
5042. SOLOGUREN, Javier
"A la Sombra de las Primicias del Verano." [Inti] (26/27) Otoño 87-Primavera 88, p. 345.
"La Hora." [Inti] (26/27) Otoño 87-Primavera 88, p. 345-354.
"Museo." [Inti] (26/27) Otoño 87-Primavera 88, p. 344.
"El Pan." [Inti] (26/27) Otoño 87-Primavera 88, p. 344-345.
"Tema Garcileño." [Inti] (26/27) Otoño 87-Primavera 88, p. 343-344.
5043. SOLOMON, Carl
"In Which I Take It on the Chin for Having Been 4F, or, Local Woody Allen Fan Meets Viet Nam Vet." [AlphaBS] (4) D 88, p. 1.
5044. SOLOMON, Sandy
"After Qu Yuan." [VirQR] (64:4) Aut 88, p. 621-622.
"Praying Mantis." [VirQR] (64:4) Aut 88, p. 620-621.
5045. SOLOMON, Stanley J.
"Matthew Arnold Takes My Wife to Atlantic City." [HampSPR] Wint 88, p. 44-45.
"Strictures for a Young Man Entering the College Teaching Profession." [HampSPR] Wint 88, p. 45-46.
5046. SOLONCHE, J. R.
"Diary of 56 Days in an Israeli Psychiatric Hospital." [Salm] (78/79) Spr-Sum 88, p. 168-169.

"Eglantine." [PoetryNW] (29:1) Spr 88, p. 14-16.
"My Favorite Photograph." [CrabCR] (5:1) Wint 88, p. 15.
"The Sugar Loaf Mastodon." [Salm] (78/79) Spr-Sum 88, p. 167-168.

5047. SOMERVILLE, Jane
"Evidence." [TarRP] (28:1) Fall 88, p. 45.
"Grace." [LaurelR] (22:2) Sum 88, p. 30-31.
"Loss." [LaurelR] (22:2) Sum 88, p. 31.
"The Map." [TarRP] (28:1) Fall 88, p. 44.
"The Robin." [OhioR] (41) 88, p. 110-111.
"The Sleepwalker." [CreamCR] (12:2) Sum 88, p. 281.
"Visiting in the Home of a Blind Man." [CreamCR] (12:2) Sum 88, p. 282-284.
"Whitefly." [OhioR] (41) 88, p. 112.
"The Woman Contemplates Syntax." [GettyR] (1:3) Sum 88, p. 444.

5048. SOMMER, Piotr
"A Filmframe" (in Polish and English, tr. by Andrew Gorski). [Os] (27) 88, p. 8-9.
"Fragility" (in Polish and English, tr. by Andrew Gorski). [Os] (27) 88, p. 28-31.
"Landscape with a Branch" (in Polish and English, tr. by Andrew Gorski). [Os] (27) 88, p. 6-7.
"Medicine" (in Polish and English, tr. by Andrew Gorski). [Os] (27) 88, p. 12-13.
"Street Songs" (in Polish and English, tr. by Andrew Gorski). [Os] (27) 88, p. 10-11.

5049. SONDE, Susan
"The Campaign of White." [SouthernPR] (28:1) Spr 88, p. 29.
"Letters from the Baja" (Selections). [BallSUF] (29:4) Aut 88, p. 11.

5050. SONG, Cathy
"Frameless Windows, Squares of Light." [ChamLR] (2:1, #3) Fall 88, p. 6-8.
"Points of Reference." [Poetry] (153:3) D 88, p. 134-135.
"School Figures." [Poetry] (153:3) D 88, p. 135-137.
"Shadow Figures." [ChamLR] (1) Fall 87, p. 63-67.
"Stamp Collecting." [MissouriR] (11:2) 88, p. 102-103.
"What Belongs to You." [ChamLR] (2:1, #3) Fall 88, p. 9-10.

5051. SONIAT, Katherine
"From a Vantage Point Overlooking the Battle of Hanging Rock." [NoDaQ] (56:2) Spr 88, p. 90.
"Learning in Time." [YaleR] (78:1) Aut 88, p. 80.
"Secrets About Nothing." [Poetry] (152:4) Jl 88, p. 217-218.
"Think About It." [GreensboroR] (45) Wint 88-89, p. 57-58.
"War." [PoetL] (83:3) Fall 88, p. 21.

5052. SONNENSCHEIN, Dana
"At Midnight." [DenQ] (22:3) Wint 88, p. 137.

5053. SONNEVI, Göran
"The Center of Unheard-Of" (tr. by Rika Lesser). [MissouriR] (11:1) 88, p. 41.
"Poems with No Order" (Excerpt, tr. by Rika Lesser). [Boulevard] (3:2/3) Fall 88, p. 180.
"There Is Life That" (tr. by Rika Lesser). [MissouriR] (11:1) 88, p. 37.
"Unfinished Poems" (Excerpt, tr. by Rika Lesser). [Boulevard] (3:2/3) Fall 88, p. 179-180.

5054. SONTAG, Kate
"As I Stand Here Reeling in the Afternoon Like a White Thread Suspended Endlessly . . ." [Nimrod] (32:1) Fall-Wint 88, p. 124-125.

5055. SOPOV, Vladimir A. B.
"Gay Poem" (University Missouri Kansas City, January 17, 1988). [Lips] (14) 88, p. 42-43.
"I Hate" ("McGillacuty's" Kansas City, January 1988). [Lips] (14) 88, p. 41.

SORALUZ, Luis Rebaza
See REBAZA SORALUZ, Luis

5056. SORENSEN, Sally Jo
"Another Common Prayer." [PaintedB] (34) 88, p. 88.
"Middle Lake." [PaintedB] (34) 88, p. 89.
"The Rye Wolf." [WestB] (21/22) 88, p. 26-27.

5057. SORESTAD, Glen
"Early Morning Bracers." [PraF] (9:4) Wint 88-89, p. 52.
"Lunar Considerations." [Grain] (16:2) Sum 88, p. 45.
"Summer Nights" (for Vera). [Grain] (16:2) Sum 88, p. 44.
"Tomato Challenge." [CrossC] (10:1) 88, p. 11.
"West German Beer Break." [PraF] (9:4) Wint 88-89, p. 53.

5058. SORKIN, Adam J.
"Dreaming with Snow" (for Adam Puslojic, tr. of Anghel Dumbraveanu, w. Irina Grigorescu). [NowestR] (26:3) 88, p. 53.
"The News from Chimaera Land" (tr. of Anghel Dumbraveanu, w. Irina Grigorescu). [NowestR] (26:3) 88, p. 54.
5059. SORNBERGER, Judith
"The Absence of Color." [SpoonRQ] (13:1) Wint 88, p. 11-12.
"The Blue Hour" (for Linnea, who sent me three cards). [SpoonRQ] (13:1) Wint 88, p. 9-10.
"A Clash of Bone: a Painting of Pachycephalosauri" (for my twin sons). [LaurelR] (22:2) Sum 88, p. 114-115.
"Poem in September, on My Mother's Birthday." [PraS] (62:1) Spr 88, p. 113-114.
5060. SOSA, Roberto
"The Brutal Lovers" (To F. Díaz Chávez, J. A. Medina Durón & C. S. Toro, tr. by Jo Anne Engelbert). [Bomb] (24) Sum 88, p. 70.
"Military Secret" (Answer to Rafael Heliodoro Valle, tr. by Jo Anne Engelbert). [Bomb] (24) Sum 88, p. 70.
"Stroessner or the Mask" (tr. by Jo Anne Engelbert). [Bomb] (24) Sum 88, p. 70.
"Tegucigalpa." [Mairena] (10:25) 88, p. 25.
"Urgent" (tr. by Jo Anne Engelbert). [Bomb] (24) Sum 88, p. 70.
5061. SOSNORA, Viktor
"The Contours of the Owl" (tr. by John Statathos). [NewYRB] (35:15) 13 O 88, p. 47.
"Fir Trees Clanked Like Green Metal!" (tr. by Darra Goldstein and Kathryn Hellerstein). [NewYRB] (35:15) 13 O 88, p. 47.
"Letter" (tr. by Darra Goldstein and Kathryn Hellerstein). [NewYRB] (35:15) 13 O 88, p. 47.
5062. SOTELO, Sandra
"Hope." [Amelia] (4:4, #11) 88, p. 54.
5063. SOTO, Gary
"Elegy" (For Sadao Oda). [Poetry] (152:2) My 88, p. 76.
"Feeding Time at the Roeding Zoo." [Zyzzyva] (4:3) Fall 88, p. 93-94.
"The History of Karate." [Caliban] (4) 88, p. 29-34.
"Inventory of a Vacant Lot." [Nat] (247:16) 28 N 88, p. 576.
"Provisions." [OntR] (29) Fall-Wint 88-89, p. 102.
"The Red Palm." [OntR] (29) Fall-Wint 88-89, p. 101-102.
"Settling Matters at a Yugoslavian Bar." [OntR] (29) Fall-Wint 88-89, p. 103-104.
"Taking the Movies to the Streets." [Thrpny] (32) Wint 88, p. 32.
"Target Practice." [OntR] (29) Fall-Wint 88-89, p. 99-100.
"Worry at the End of the Month." [Poetry] (152:2) My 88, p. 74-75.
5064. SOTO VÉLEZ, Clemente
"The Broomstick Stallion" (Selection: 3, tr. by Louis Reyes Rivera). [HangL] (52) 88, p. 71.
"Caballo de Palo" (The Broomstick Stallion, Selection: 3). [HangL] (52) 88, p. 70.
"The Promised Land" (Selection: 29, tr. by Martín Espada and Camilo Pérez). [HangL] (52) 88, p. 73, 75.
"La Tierra Prometida" (The Promised Land, Selection: 29). [HangL] (52) 88, p. 72, 74.
5065. SOUSTER, Raymond
"My Wild Alberta Rose." [CrossC] (10:1) 88, p. 4.
"Our New Climbing Rose Bush." [CrossC] (10:1) 88, p. 4.
"Some Morning I Know." [CrossC] (10:1) 88, p. 4.
"When the Day of the Cornroast Came." [CrossC] (10:1) 88, p. 4.
"When You Are Gone." [CrossC] (10:1) 88, p. 4.
5066. SOUTHWICK, Marcia
"Dirty Stockings." [LaurelR] (22:2) Sum 88, p. 118-119.
"The Gaze." [LaurelR] (22:2) Sum 88, p. 119-120.
"Red Light, Green Light." [MissouriR] (11:1) 88, p. 51.
"The Ruins." [AmerPoR] (17:3) My-Je 88, p. 33.
"The Sun Speaks." [AmerPoR] (17:3) My-Je 88, p. 33.
5067. SOYINKA, Wole
"After the Deluge." [TriQ] (73) Fall 88, p. 143-144.
"Apollodorus on the Niger" (The sale of a continent yet again in Lagos, . . . 1977 Black Arts Festival). [TriQ] (73) Fall 88, p. 145.
"The Apotheosis of Master-Sergeant Doe." [TriQ] (73) Fall 88, p. 146-147.

"My Tongue Does Not Marry Slogans" (for Odia Ofeimun). [TriQ] (73) Fall 88, p. 149-153.
"So Now They Burn the Roof Above Her Head" (for Winnie). [TriQ] (73) Fall 88, p. 139-142.
"Your Logic Frightens Me Mandela." [ParisR] (30:107) Sum 88, p. 130-132.

5068. SPACKS, Barry
"Autumn Poem." [NoDaQ] (56:1) Wint 88, p. 194.
"The Catch" (in memory of James Wright). [PoetC] (20:1) Fall 88, p. 26.
"Inheritors." [Hudson] (40:4) Wint 88, p. 633-634.
"Miles Davis Plays 'Sketches of Spain'." [TarRP] (28:1) Fall 88, p. 76.
"Two Moons." [PoetC] (20:1) Fall 88, p. 25.

5069. SPAHR, Juliana
"It is the legs going up over around the body." [Notus] (3:2) Fall 88, p. 12.

5070. SPALDING, Philip, III
"Deathsweat." [ChamLR] (1:2, #2) Spr 88, p. 54.
"Dust." [ChamLR] (1:2, #2) Spr 88, p. 55.
"An Early Morning in the Winter of 1985." [ChamLR] (1:2, #2) Spr 88, p. 53.
"Pu'u Nana." [ChamLR] (1:2, #2) Spr 88, p. 52.

5071. SPARKS, Amy Bracken
"Frida Kahlo." [DenQ] (23:2) Fall 88, p. 63-64.
"The God of Asthma." [Nimrod] (32:1) Fall-Wint 88, p. 88.

5072. SPEAKES, Richard
"The Cadillac on Fire in the Columbia Gorge." [PoetryE] (25) Spr 88, p. 25.
"The One with the Flaubert Epigraph." [PoetryE] (25) Spr 88, p. 20-21.
"Paul Butterfield" (Tipitina's, New Orleans, 1984). [PoetryE] (25) Spr 88, p. 26-27.
"The Photograph." [PoetryE] (25) Spr 88, p. 28.
"Sweeping Up" (for Susan Moncada). [PoetryE] (25) Spr 88, p. 22-23.
"West Texas Seven-Eleven." [PoetryE] (25) Spr 88, p. 24.

5073. SPEAR, Roberta
"Conversions" (for Ignacio and Norman). [Ploughs] (14:4) 88, p. 100-101.
"Geraniums." [Field] (39) Fall 88, p. 52.
"The Old Ones at Dawn." [Poetry] (143, i.e. 153:2) N 88, p. 67-68.

5074. SPEARS, Heather
"Instantly It Was a Word" (for Ahmad). [Event] (17:3) Fall 88, p. 41.
"Write a Poem About Angels." [Event] (17:3) Fall 88, p. 40.

5075. SPEARS, Monroe K.
"Academic Distinctions (or, Not Like Some)." [SewanR] (96:4) Fall 88, p. 608-609.
"A Dream." [SewanR] (96:4) Fall 88, p. 609.

5076. SPECTOR, Al
"Father Business." [Bogg] (60) 88, p. 52.
"Independent Study." [RagMag] (6:2) Fall 88, p. 59.
"Mates." [Bogg] (59) 88, p. 44.

5077. SPECTOR, Joel
"The Mill of Death" (tr. of Yvan Goll). [Agni] (27) 88, p. 43-44.
"The Sacred Body" (tr. of Yvan Goll). [Agni] (27) 88, p. 45.

5078. SPEER, Laurel
"8 Steps in Search of MM." [HeliconN] (19) 88, p. 38.
"Another Cowboy." [CrabCR] (5:3) Fall 88, p. 15.
"The Beautiful City of Prague." [CrabCR] (5:3) Fall 88, p. 17.
"The Blind Man Tells His Secret of Winning Brawls." [CrabCR] (5:3) Fall 88, p. 16.
"'But Don't You Think People Want the Truth?' 'If They Did They Wouldn't Eat Out'" (The 1 Minute President). [Footwork] ('88) 88, p. 34.
"H. Finn." [NewL] (54:3) Spr 88, p. 96.
"Hag-Light." [PoetC] (19:3) Spr 88, p. 18.
"The Juilliard Mother." [MidAR] (8:2) 88, p. 78.
"Mules." [SwampR] (1:2/3) D 88, p. 47.
"An Obscene Version of Beatrix Potter." [CrabCR] (5:3) Fall 88, p. 15.
"Red-Eyed Tailors." [ConnPR] (7:1) 88, p. 37.
"The Single Woman Laureate." [Pembroke] (20) 88, p. 275.
"Some Blood." [Cond] (15) 88, p. 91.
"Stunning First Lines." [CrabCR] (5:3) Fall 88, p. 15-16.
"Well, Ondine, You're Not Sixteen and Lost Your Pearls." [Spirit] (9:1) 88, p. 24.

5079. SPENCE, Michael
"The Bengal Tiger." [LightY] ('88/9) 88, p. 98.
"A Little Golden Book of Dinosaurs." [SouthernR] (24:3) Sum 88, p. 549-550.

"Proper Heroes: Driving Kansas City to Kirksville." [CharR] (14:1) Spr 88, p. 29.
"The Roxy Closes." [SouthernR] (24:3) Sum 88, p. 550-551.

5080. SPENCER, Robert
"The Poet Is Interrupted by His Young Son." [Confr] (37/38) Spr-Sum 88, p. 264.

5081. SPENDER, Stephen
"Farewell to My Student." [Stand] (29:1) Wint 87-88, p. 24.
"Her House." [Stand] (29:1) Wint 87-88, p. 25.

5082. SPERANZA, Anthony
"The Snow Letter." [Plain] (8:2) Wint 88, p. 26.

5083. SPHERES, Duane
"Cancer" (for Gary Otto). [BellArk] (4:6) N-D 88, p. 6.
"Crow." [BellArk] (4:5) S-O 88, p. 10.
"Geese Nights." [BellArk] (4:6) N-D 88, p. 10.
"Riverpool." [Turnstile] (1:2) 88, p. 69.

5084. SPICER, David
"Port Wine and Beet Sandwiches." [AmerPoR] (17:4) Jl-Ag 88, p. 21.

5085. SPICKERMAN, Frances
"Satisfying the Appetite" (for my daughter). [HampSPR] Wint 88, p. 42.
"What the Duckling Learns to Follow." [CumbPR] (7:2) Spr 88, p. 56-57.

5086. SPIEGEL, Erika
"Tracing Paper." [HangL] (53) 88, p. 67.

5087. SPIEGEL, Robert
"See These Eyes So Green." [Wind] (18:63) 88, p. 38.

5088. SPIELMAN, Tamarie
"Breaking Superstition" (for Grandma). [PassN] (9:1) Wint 88, p. 25.

5089. SPIERS, M. Ann
"Cheap Motel." [CrabCR] (5:1) Wint 88, p. 13.

5090. SPINELLI, Elleen
"For a Teenaged Daughter." [Footwork] ('88) 88, p. 63.
"For My Grandfather." [Footwork] ('88) 88, p. 63.
"In Lieu of Flowers" (For Helen). [Footwork] ('88) 88, p. 63.
"The Old People." [Footwork] ('88) 88, p. 63.

5091. SPINGARN, Lawrence P.
"Chappaquiddick, Martha's Vineyard." [Salm] (78/79) Spr-Sum 88, p. 156.
"Keeping Kosher." [Salm] (78/79) Spr-Sum 88, p. 157.
"The Patroons." [Amelia] (4:4, #11) 88, p. 53-54.
"Termites." [PikeF] (9) Fall 88, p. 7.

5092. SPIRES, Elizabeth
"The Bells." [GrandS] (7:3) Spr 88, p. 166-167.
"Black Fairy Tale." [Poetry] (143, i.e. 153:2) N 88, p. 73-74.
"The Comb and the Mirror" (based on the Cornish legend of the mermaid of Zennor). [GrandS] (7:3) Spr 88, p. 164-165.
"Fabergé's Egg" (Switzerland, 1920). [Poetry] (143, i.e. 153:2) N 88, p. 72-73.
"Mutoscope." [NoAmR] (273:3) S 88, p. 46.
"Sunday Afternoon at Fulham Palace." [Iowa] (18:2) 88, p. 50-52.

5093. SPIRO, Peter
"Literature Professor." [Bogg] (59) 88, p. 43.

5094. SPISAK, Dagmar Jill
"At Home with Rachel." [BellR] (11:1) Spr 88, p. 12.

5095. SPIVACK, Kathleen
"The Double Wedding Ring Quilt." [Spirit] (9:1) 88, p. 92-93.
"The Great Railroad Train of Art." [LitR] (31:4) Sum 88, p. 485-489.
"Hidden Nature." [StoneC] (16:1/2) Fall-Wint 88-89, p. 67.
"Over the Connecticut River." [PoetL] (83:3) Fall 88, p. 42-43.
"Roethke at Harvard." [NewL] (55:2) Wint 88-89, p. 79.

5096. SPIVACK, Susan Fantl
"Love Is a Form of Victory." [Spirit] (9:1) 88, p. 98.

5097. SPRAYBERRY, Sandra
"For What." [CarolQ] (40:3) Spr 88, p. 90.
"Postoperative." [PacificR] (6) Spr 88, p. 53.

5098. SPRING, Anne
"Stone Boats." [DeKalbLAJ] (21:1) Wint 88, p. 67.

5099. SPROUSE, James
"The Gap" (for Andy Andrei). [Spirit] (9:1) 88, p. 143.

5100. SQUIER, Charles
"No Se Van los Pastores" (after Dudley Fitts). [LightY] ('88/9) 88, p. 165.

5101. SRI, Sri
"Let Me Get Into the Witness-Box" (tr. of Cherabanda Raju). [Nimrod] (31:2) Spr-Sum 88, p. 101-103.

ST. . . .
See also SAINT . . .

5102. ST. ANDREWS, B. A.
"The Boy Who Sang Along." [CapeR] (23:1) Spr 88, p. 11.
"Icarus Rising." [ChamLR] (2:1, #3) Fall 88, p. 116.
"Of Love and War and the Messenger." [GettyR] (1:3) Sum 88, p. 498-500.
"On Witnessing Open-Heart Surgery." [ParisR] (30:109) Wint 88, p. 52-53.

5103. ST. CLAIR, Philip
"Late." [Interim] (7:2) Fall 88, p. 6.
"Letter." [Interim] (7:2) Fall 88, p. 8.
"Thunder." [Interim] (7:2) Fall 88, p. 7.
"Walk." [Interim] (7:2) Fall 88, p. 5.

5104. ST. CYR, Napoleon
"Her Yarn, His Yarns." [SmPd] (25:1) Wint 88, p. 35.

5105. ST. GERMAIN, Sheryl
"For One Who Has Known Grief." [Lips] (14) 88, p. 35.
"In California, Thinking of a Lover." [Footwork] ('88) 88, p. 14.
"The Lake." [GrahamHR] (11) Spr 88, p. 86.
"Medusa Looks Out Her Window in January." [Lips] (14) 88, p. 34.

5106. ST. JOHN, David
"Looking Back." [Jacaranda] (3:2) Fall-Wint 88, p. 117.
"My Days at the University." [WestHR] (42:1) Spr 88, p. 48-49.

5107. ST. LOUIS, Ralph
"The Attic Window." [KanQ] (20:3) Sum 88, p. 48.

5108. STAFFORD, William
"Amounting to Something." [ChamLR] (1) Fall 87, p. 70.
"Anchor Message #1." [HawaiiR] (12:2, #24) Fall 88, p. 113.
"Anchor Message #2." [HawaiiR] (12:2, #24) Fall 88, p. 114.
"An Archival Print." [Field] (39) Fall 88, p. 66.
"Coming Back." [Poetry] (152:1) Ap 88, p. 27.
"Conducting a Meeting." [Footwork] ('88) 88, p. 8.
"Finding Our Way" (8 poems). [OhioR] (40) 88, p. 25-33.
"For My *Vita*." [CutB] (31/32) 88, p. 108.
"Harvest in the Furrows." [Footwork] ('88) 88, p. 8.
"In Any Country." [TarRP] (28:1) Fall 88, p. 43.
"It's All Right." [CutB] (31/32) 88, p. 109.
"The Old Way." [Caliban] (5) 88, p. 11.
"The Old Writers' Welcome to the New." [CreamCR] (12:2) Sum 88, p. 285.
"On the Quiet." [Field] (39) Fall 88, p. 67.
"Report from K9 Operator Rover on the Motel at Grand Island." [LightY] ('88/9) 88, p. 37.
"Roll Call." [NowestR] (26:3) 88, p. 24.
"Security." [HawaiiR] (12:2, #24) Fall 88, p. 112.
"Tracker Dog." [Abraxas] (37) 88, p. 6.
"Transcending Earth." [TampaR] (1) 88, p. 34.
"The Trouble with Reading." [Field] (39) Fall 88, p. 68.
"Who Is Richest Along Our Street?" [TarRP] (28:1) Fall 88, p. 43.

5109. STAINSBY, Martha
"Inside." [Event] (17:1) Spr 88, p. 43-44.
"Why Hummingbird and Spider Are Angry." [Event] (17:1) Spr 88, p. 42-43.

5110. STANDING, Sue
"The Elegy of Doubt." [Agni] (27) 88, p. 195.
"Gravida." [TexasR] (9:3/4) Fall-Wint 88, p. 132.
"How to Make a Planet." [TexasR] (9:3/4) Fall-Wint 88, p. 131.
"Six Values of Neutral Gray." [Agni] (27) 88, p. 196.
"Windfall." [GrahamHR] (11) Spr 88, p. 76.

5111. STANHOPE, Patrick
"Seven Vessels." [KanQ] (20:1/2) Wint-Spr 88, p. 88.

5112. STANHOPE, Rosamund
"Collage." [WebR] (13:2) Fall 88, p. 96.
"Mushroom Farm." [WebR] (13:2) Fall 88, p. 97.

5113. STANIZZI, John L.
"Another Quest" (after James Wright). [Wind] (18:62) 88, p. 8.

5114. STANLEY, Jean W.
"The Laminated Whale." [CapeR] (23:2) Fall 88, p. 42-43.
"Old Salt." [CapeR] (23:2) Fall 88, p. 41.
5115. STANSBERGER, Richard
"Crossed sticks." [CinPR] (17) Spr 88, p. 68.
5116. STANTON, Joseph
"6. Atsumori" (from *Noh Variations*). [ChamLR] (1) Fall 87, p. 3.
"7. Komachi" (from *Noh Variations*). [ChamLR] (1) Fall 87, p. 4.
"Basho" (from *Noh Variations*). [ChamLR] (1) Fall 87, p. 5.
"Edward Hopper's *New York Movie*." [ChamLR] (1:2, #2) Spr 88, p. 124-125.
"Giorgione's The Tempest." [ChamLR] (1:2, #2) Spr 88, p. 128-130.
"The Hour of Cézanne." [ChamLR] (1) Fall 87, p. 6.
"The House" (for Chris Van Allsburg). [ChamLR] (2:1, #3) Fall 88, p. 86-87.
"The Ship of Laughter." [ChamLR] (2:1, #3) Fall 88, p. 85.
"Twelve Dancing Princesses." [ChamLR] (1:2, #2) Spr 88, p. 126-127.
"Watteau's *Italian Comedians*." [ChamLR] (1) Fall 87, p. 7-8.
5117. STANTON, Maura
"At the Salmon Feast." [HayF] (3) Spr 88, p. 75.
"The Courthouse." [Chelsea] (47) 88, p. 143.
"Diana and Her Companions" (Vermeer. Oil on Canvas). [Chelsea] (47) 88, p. 140-141.
"Keepsakes." [HayF] (3) Spr 88, p. 71-72.
"Parable." [HayF] (3) Spr 88, p. 73-74.
"Paradise." [Chelsea] (47) 88, p. 144-145.
"Persephone." [Chelsea] (47) 88, p. 142.
5118. STARBUCK, George
"Dame Edith's Hundredth." [Poetry] (152:1) Ap 88, p. 11.
"Dogs' Golfballs." [Poetry] (152:1) Ap 88, p. 13.
"Fifty Years of No George Gershwin Rag." [Poetry] (152:1) Ap 88, p. 12.
"Fifty Years of No George Gershwin Rag Part Two." [Poetry] (152:1) Ap 88, p. 12.
"Gastarbeiter." [Poetry] (152:1) Ap 88, p. 10.
"Last Straw." [LightY] ('88/9) 88, p. 81.
"Magnificat. Brave Cat at Snifter Fishbowl" (For May Swenson). [Poetry] (152:1) Ap 88, p. 14.
"Nineteenfifties Vogue Rorschach." [KeyWR] (1:2) Fall 88, p. 27.
"Pilgrim Tale." [Poetry] (152:1) Ap 88, p. 13.
"Pleasures of the Voyageurs." [Ploughs] (14:1) 88, p. 115-116.
"Purple Goatee." [LightY] ('88/9) 88, p. 171-172.
"Quatrain for Kathy." [PartR] (55:4) Fall 88, p. 615-616.
"Reading the Facts About Frost in the *Norton Anthology*." [Poetry] (152:1) Ap 88, p. 9.
"S.L.A.B.S., for George Herbert" (Standard Length and Breadth Sonnet). [LightY] ('88/9) 88, p. 80.
"Scat." [KeyWR] (1:2) Fall 88, p. 27.
"Session." [Poetry] (152:1) Ap 88, p. 11.
"Six Things: Lament." [OhioR] (41) 88, p. 113.
"Spin Control." [LightY] ('88/9) 88, p. 225.
"Standard Length and Breadth Sonnets." [OhioR] (41) 88, p. 114-115.
"The T.S. Eliot 22¢ Portrait Postage Stamp." [KeyWR] (1:2) Fall 88, p. 28.
"Things Keep Dawning on President Joshua." [LightY] ('88/9) 88, p. 225.
"Two SLABS (Standard-Length-and-Breadth Sonnets)." [Ploughs] (14:1) 88, p. 117-118.
5119. STARKEY, David
"At the Blue Mango They Play the Saw." [BellArk] (4:6) N-D 88, p. 1.
"Listening to Blues Artist John Hartman in a Bar in Sacramento." [BellArk] (4:3) My-Je 88, p. 9.
"New Frontiers" (Ely, Nevada). [BellArk] (4:5) S-O 88, p. 3.
5120. STARZEC, Larry
"An Evening Walk." [CapeR] (23:2) Fall 88, p. 28.
"Takeoff." [SpoonRQ] (13:1) Wint 88, p. 8.
"To a Pickpocket." [CreamCR] (12:1) Wint 88, p. 91.
5121. STATATHOS, John
"The Contours of the Owl" (tr. of Viktor Sosnora). [NewYRB] (35:15) 13 O 88, p. 47.
5122. STEDLER, Harding
"Changing Course." [InterPR] (14:1) Spr 88, p. 90.

"No Greater Gift." [InterPR] (14:1) Spr 88, p. 89.
"Taste of April Green." [InterPR] (14:1) Spr 88, p. 89.
5123. STEDMAN, Judy
"The (Vast) Wasteland." [Bogg] (60) 88, p. 21.
5124. STEELE, Leighton
"City of the Strait." [PraF] (9:1) Spr 88, p. 46.
"The Dinosaurs." [PraF] (9:1) Spr 88, p. 47.
5125. STEELE, Paul Curry
"Clerihew." [LightY] ('88/9) 88, p. 76.
5126. STEELE, Peggy
"At the Cosmetics Counter." [AmerV] (10) Spr 88, p. 113-114.
5127. STEELE, Timothy
"Scrapbook for My Sister." [Jacaranda] (3:2) Fall-Wint 88, p. 118.
STEFANO, John di
See Di STEFANO, John
5128. STEFENHAGENS, Lyn
"Dyslexic." [CapeR] (23:2) Fall 88, p. 40.
5129. STEFFENS, Bradley
"Crocus Hill." [Farm] (5:2) Fall 88, p. 55.
"Succubus." [BellR] (11:1) Spr 88, p. 45.
"Two Weeks Ago." [Crosscur] (7:4) 88, p. 9-10.
5130. STEFFLER, John
"Cannibals of Different Kinds." [Event] (17:3) Fall 88, p. 78-79.
"The Cobs Fatten, But Every So Often." [CanLit] (117) Sum 88, p. 10.
"Green Giving." [CanLit] (117) Sum 88, p. 113.
"Walls of Sound." [CanLit] (117) Sum 88, p. 107.
5131. STEIN, Charles
"The Hounds" (from "the forestforthetrees"). [Notus] (3:1) Spr 88, p. 33-36.
"Language Generated While Hearing Lama Norla Discourse on Atisa's Seven Points of Mind Training . . ." [Notus] (3:2) Fall 88, p. 4-7.
"Theforestforthetrees" (Selection: 3 poems). [Bound] (15:3/16:1) Spr-Fall 88, p. 305-311.
5132. STEIN, Dona
"Driving to Fitchburg with Elsey." [ColR] (NS 15:1) Spr-Sum 88, p. 81-84.
"How It Is." [StoneC] (15:3/4) Spr-Sum 88, p. 57.
"Russian River." [StoneC] (15:3/4) Spr-Sum 88, p. 56-57.
"El Santuario de Chimayo." [WritersF] (14) Fall 88, p. 62-63.
5133. STEIN, Donna Baier
"Wooing Lady Luck in Philipsburg." [Spirit] (9:1) 88, p. 106.
5134. STEIN, Hannah
"The Ladder." [MSS] (6:2) 88, p. 57.
"Lockout." [MSS] (6:2) 88, p. 55-56.
"The Turning." [AntR] (46:3) Sum 88, p. 344.
"Walking Up the Hill." [PassN] (9:1) Wint 88, p. 31.
5135. STEIN, Julia
"Coordinates" (tr. of Sara Martinez). [RedBass] (13) 88, p. 28.
5136. STEIN, Kevin
"Gratitude." [Crazy] (34) Spr 88, p. 62-63.
"How Things Fall." [Crazy] (34) Spr 88, p. 60-61.
"A Prayer for the Body." [OhioR] (40) 88, p. 46-47.
"Rites for the End of a Drought." [PoetryNW] (29:4) Wint 88-89, p. 11-12.
5137. STEIN, M. D.
"The Smallest Dance Floor." [SouthwR] (73:4) Aut 88, p. 524.
5138. STEIN, Michael
"Philomorph." [Boulevard] (3:2/3) Fall 88, p. 119-120.
5139. STEINARR, Steinn
"Words Fell" (tr. by Alan Boucher). [Vis] (28) 88, p. 28.
5140. STEINGASS, David
"Basement Catechism." [PoetryNW] (29:1) Spr 88, p. 43-44.
"Bride of the Prairie." [Abraxas] (37) 88, p. 57.
"The Day Lightning Called." [PoetryNW] (29:4) Wint 88-89, p. 32-33.
"My Grimm Grandmother's Hands." [PoetryNW] (29:4) Wint 88-89, p. 33-34.
"Redbone." [Northeast] (ser. 4:7) Sum 88, p. 27-28.
"Snapper, Python." [Northeast] (ser. 4:7) Sum 88, p. 26.
"Strong Science." [PoetryNW] (29:1) Spr 88, p. 41-42.

5141. STEINGLASS, Matt
"Sleep in Jerusalem" (tr. of Yehuda Amichai). [HarvardA] (122:4) My 88, p. 27.
5142. STEINGRABER, Sandra
"A Letter to the City." [HiramPoR] (44/45) Spr-Wint 88, p. 40-41.
5143. STEINKE, Rene
"Insomiac Landscape." [SouthernPR] (28:2) Fall 88, p. 34.
"Waitress in a Black and White Movie." [CarolQ] (40:3) Spr 88, p. 74-75.
5144. STEINMAN, Lisa (*See also* Steinman, Lisa M.)
"Drafting a New Life." [Boulevard] (3:2/3) Fall 88, p. 185-186.
5145. STEINMAN, Lisa M. (*See also* Steinman, Lisa)
"Greeks Bearing Gifts." [SpoonRQ] (13:2) Spr 88, p. 8.
"Relatives." [SpoonRQ] (13:2) Spr 88, p. 9.
STEINN STEINARR
See STEINARR, Steinn
5146. STELMASZYNSKI, Wojtek
"Opus 64, a Comedy" (tr. of Krzysztof Ostaszewski). [Amelia] (5:2, #13) 88, p. 130.
5147. STEPANCHEV, Stephen
"Byzantine." [Interim] (7:1) Spr 88, p. 7.
"Dust." [Interim] (7:1) Spr 88, p. 8.
"Japanese." [LightY] ('88/9) 88, p. 164.
"Tenochtitlán." [Interim] (7:1) Spr 88, p. 9.
5148. STEPHAN, Nancy
"There Is Another World And It Is In This One." [Footwork] ('88) 88, p. 23.
5149. STEPHENS, Genevieve
"Superstition." [Plain] (8:2) Wint 88, p. 8.
5150. STEPHENS, Michael
"What's Going On." [HangL] (52) 88, p. 35.
5151. STEPHENSON, Shelby
"Farm: A Trilogy." [ManhatR] (4:2) Spr 88, p. 49-51.
"Push On." [ManhatR] (4:2) Spr 88, p. 48.
"A Rose and a Baby Ruth" (for Stephen E. Smith). [LightY] ('88/9) 88, p. 122.
"The Soda Sower." [ManhatR] (4:2) Spr 88, p. 52.
5152. STEPPE, Teresa
"Love Sestina for a Two Income Family." [Pembroke] (20) 88, p. 282.
5153. STEPTOE, Lamont B.
"Dust and Sunshine." [PaintedB] (34) 88, p. 32.
"For Etheridge Knight." [PaintedB] (32/33) 88, p. 82.
"Poem for the New Age." [PaintedB] (32/33) 88, p. 83-84.
"Toxic Waste." [PaintedB] (36) 88, p. 50.
5154. STERLE, Francine
"After the Cremation." [Wind] (18:63) 88, p. 39.
"Fever." [Ascent] (13:2) 88, p. 31.
5155. STERLING, Cary
"Trochaic Sonnet for My Stepfather" (Coronach: Norman Wicklund Macleod, 1906-1985). [Pembroke] (20) 88, p. 245.
5156. STERLING, Phillip
"The Forgiveness of Sins." [PassN] (9:1) Wint 88, p. 5.
5157. STERLING, Sarge
"On the Steps." [Iowa] (18:3) 88, p. 131.
5158. STERN, Cathy
"At the (Misses) Voskamp's Market, New Ulm, Texas." [Shen] (38:3) 88, p. 33.
5159. STERN, Gerald
"The Age of Strolling." [PoetryE] (26) Fall 88, p. 12-14.
"Behaving Like a Jew." [PoetryE] (26) Fall 88, back cover.
"The Bull-Roarer." [Poetry] (151:6) Mr 88, p. 480-482.
"The First Lewd Offering." [PoetryE] (26) Fall 88, p. 7.
"Love Is the Opposite." [PoetryE] (26) Fall 88, p. 15-16.
"My Death for Now." [PoetryE] (26) Fall 88, p. 8-9.
"Neither English Nor Spanish" (for Heidi Kalafski). [MissouriR] (11:1) 88, p. 34-36.
"Nice Mountain." [PoetryE] (26) Fall 88, p. 10-11.
"One Gift." [PoetryE] (26) Fall 88, p. 17-16.
"Sending Back the Gloom." [PoetryE] (26) Fall 88, p. 19-20.
5160. STERN, Joan
"Afternoon in Bermuda." [LittleM] (15:3/4) 88, p. 112.

"Dear John." [LittleM] (15:3/4) 88, p. 113.
5161. STERN, Robert
"Dear Mr. Kanaya." [AntigR] (73) Spr 88, p. 89-90.
"Moon Goddess." [AntigR] (73) Spr 88, p. 90.
5162. STERNBACH, Mary Egan
"How Hurricanes Get Their Names" (for D.A.). [Notus] (3:1) Spr 88, p. 50.
"The Place Which No One Believed Was Truly a Place." [Notus] (3:1) Spr 88, p. 51.
5163. STERNLIEB, Barry
"Photograph of Geronimo, 1906." [StoneC] (15:3/4) Spr-Sum 88, p. 63.
"Shi Huang Ti" (d. 210 B.C.). [StoneC] (15:3/4) Spr-Sum 88, p. 62.
5164. STEUER, Lee
"Poem for Heie." [ChatR] (9:1) Fall 88, p. 39.
5165. STEVENS, Alex
"Homage to Pico Della Mirandola." [Shen] (38:2) 88, p. 72-73.
"Museum Piece: Pioneer Bible at Austin, Texas." [NewRep] (198:13) 28 Mr 88, p. 36.
"Natural History." [NewYorker] (64:32) 26 S 88, p. 98.
5166. STEVENS, Annie E.
"Ephphatha: On Hearing" (Mark 7:31-37). [ChrC] (105:28) 5 O 88, p. 868.
5167. STEVENS, C. J.
"1939." [Bogg] (59) 88, p. 16.
5168. STEVENSON, Anne
"Study for a Portrait of Van Gogh After Francis Bacon." [PartR] (55:1) Wint 88, p. 55-56.
"Wounds." [PartR] (55:3) Sum 88, p. 478.
5169. STEVENSON, Diane
"Afterimage." [SouthernPR] (28:1) Spr 88, p. 67-68.
5170. STEVER, Margo
"On the Posession of Horses." [Chelsea] (47) 88, p. 131.
5171. STEWARD, D. E.
"Chroma" (Selections: 5 months). [Temblor] (8) 88, p. 155-171.
"September." [Sulfur] (8:2, #23) Fall 88, p. 151-159.
5172. STEWART, Christine
"A Wet Dream" (Concrete Poem). [Dandel] (15:2) Fall-Wint 88, p. 19.
5173. STEWART, Dolores
"Mother Shipton." [BallSUF] (29:4) Aut 88, p. 18-20.
"New Moon of July." [Vis] (27) 88, p. 12.
"The People Who Have Gone Away." [BallSUF] (29:4) Aut 88, p. 54.
5174. STEWART, Frank
"Above June Lake." [ChamLR] (1) Fall 87, p. 68-69.
"A Christmas Toast" (For Dean and Julie, Honolulu 1986). [SwampR] (1:1) Ja 88, p. 20-21.
"The Diary." [MissouriR] (11:1) 88, p. 183.
"Marriage to You Was Like Michigan." [SwampR] (1:1) Ja 88, p. 19.
5175. STEWART, Gerry
"Pianoman." [Quarry] (37:1) Wint 88, p. 63.
"Sax." [Margin] (7) 88, p. 26.
"Sax." [Quarry] (37:1) Wint 88, p. 64.
"Saxaphone." [Margin] (7) 88, p. 26.
5176. STEWART, Jack
"The Age of Bronze." [Poem] (59) My 88, p. 36.
"Jerome." [BlackWR] (14:2) Spr 88, p. 91-92.
"Songs of the Earth." [Poem] (59) My 88, p. 39.
"Spielraum." [Poem] (59) My 88, p. 37-38.
5177. STEWART, Pamela
"Good Friday." [HighP] (3:3) Wint 88-89, p. 88-89.
"Infrequent Mysteries." [HighP] (3:2) Fall 88, p. 83-87.
5178. STEWART, Pat
"The Mirror's Tale." [Amelia] (5:2, #13) 88, p. 110.
5179. STEWART, Susan
"1931." [VirQR] (64:4) Aut 88, p. 617.
"1936. Her Mother in the Daylight Hours." [VirQR] (64:4) Aut 88, p. 617-618.
"1937. The Arbor." [MichQR] (27:2) Spr 88, p. 282-283.
"1956. The Coincidence." [VirQR] (64:4) Aut 88, p. 618.
"1960. The Memory Cabinet of Mrs. K." [VirQR] (64:4) Aut 88, p. 619.

5180. STEWART, W. Gregory
"Pick It Up." [Amelia] (5:1, #12) 88, p. 56.
"Tribal Postures: Fame." [Amelia] (4:4, #11) 88, p. 45.
"Who Ordered That?" [LightY] ('88/9) 88, p. 71.
5181. STIBOR, Bill
"Autumn, by Your Leave" (A Plainsongs Award Poem).). [Plain] (9:1) Fall 88, p. 12-13.
5182. STILLMAN, Clark
"David and Delilah." [LightY] ('88/9) 88, p. 127.
"The Grotto" (Robert Frost's "The Pasture" more classically rendered). [LightY] ('88/9) 88, p. 175.
"Life." [LightY] ('88/9) 88, p. 97.
"Your Eyes and Swiveling Members." [LightY] ('88/9) 88, p. 123.
5183. STILLWELL, Marie
"An Afternoon at Cape Sable." [WebR] (13:2) Fall 88, p. 93.
"Ice Caves of Haleakala." [WebR] (13:2) Fall 88, p. 94.
5184. STILLWELL, Mary Kathryn
"The Mountain." [Wind] (18:63) 88, p. 40-41.
"This Is Brooklyn" (for Frank). [NoDaQ] (56:3) Sum 88, p. 145.
"The Three Sisters." [Confr] (37/38) Spr-Sum 88, p. 238.
5185. STINSON, Susan
"The Cool Reticence of Privilege Covering Its Ass." [SinW] (33) Fall 87, p. 94.
"The Lesson." [SinW] (33) Fall 87, p. 94.
5186. STIRNEMANN, S. A.
"Dust Motes." [Ploughs] (14:4) 88, p. 11.
"How Angel Came to Be Born in September." [Ploughs] (14:4) 88, p. 12-13.
"Lights from Belle Isle." [Ploughs] (14:4) 88, p. 14-15.
5187. STITT, Linda
"The Poet As Petitioner, or, The Reading as Pleading." [KeyWR] (1:1) Spr 88, p. 57.
"Time Is Wealth and Time Is Treasure." [KeyWR] (1:1) Spr 88, p. 56.
"Winds." [KeyWR] (1:1) Spr 88, p. 55.
5188. STOCK, Norman
"Chicken Love." [ColEng] (50:4) Ap 88, p. 399.
"Duck Hunting." [ColEng] (50:7) N 88, p. 753.
"The First Time I Robbed Tiffany's." [ColEng] (50:7) N 88, p. 752.
"The Funeral." [ColEng] (50:4) Ap 88, p. 397.
"A Giant Woman Is Talking to Me." [ColEng] (50:4) Ap 88, p. 396.
"The Insect Conspiracy." [ColEng] (50:4) Ap 88, p. 399.
"The Man with the Skewered Lip." [ColEng] (50:4) Ap 88, p. 398.
"The Stone House." [ColEng] (50:4) Ap 88, p. 400.
5189. STODDART, William R.
"Reflective Wall." [Writer] (101:3) Mr 88, p. 19-20.
5190. STOKES, Terry
"Havana's Light." [CinPR] (17) Spr 88, p. 42.
"Photos from the Dream." [CinPR] (17) Spr 88, p. 43.
5191. STOLOFF, Carolyn
"Animal, Vegetable, Mineral." [Paint] (15:30) Aut 88, p. 5.
"A Built Bridge, Footnotes." [LightY] ('88/9) 88, p. 169.
"Master Fashioner." [Paint] (15:30) Aut 88, p. 6.
"A Wilderness in the Veins." [Paint] (15:30) Aut 88, p. 7.
5192. STONE, Alison
"Not Seeking New Worlds." [Poetry] (151:6) Mr 88, p. 457-458.
"Snapshot." [Amelia] (5:2, #13) 88, p. 106.
5193. STONE, Carole
"Loving an Old Man" (Third Place, 1987 Eve of Saint Agnes Poetry Competition). [NegC] (8:3) 88, p. 29-34.
5194. STONE, James
"The End of the Day" (tr. of Yannis Kondos). [Agni] (27) 88, p. 209.
5195. STONE, Jennifer
"1974 — Historical Footnote: Nemesis." [WormR] (28:1, #109) 88, p. 2-3.
"End of April, 1975." [WormR] (28:1, #109) 88, p. 1-2.
5196. STONE, Joan
"Aubade" (from *Our Lady of the Harbor*). [ChamLR] (1) Fall 87, p. 24.
"In the Neighborhood" (from *Our Lady of the Harbor*). [ChamLR] (1) Fall 87, p. 26.

"Morning Market: Lisbon" (from *Our Lady of the Harbor*). [ChamLR] (1) Fall 87, p. 23.
"Our Lady of Rossio Square" (from *Our Lady of the Harbor*). [ChamLR] (1) Fall 87, p. 25.
"Our Lady of the Harbor" (from *Our Lady of the Harbor*). [ChamLR] (1) Fall 87, p. 27-30.
"Poem for a Zoo Owl." [ChamLR] (1) Fall 87, p. 20.
"Returning." [ChamLR] (1) Fall 87, p. 22.
"Triolet." [ChamLR] (1) Fall 87, p. 21.

5197. STONE, Lois Greene
"Stanislavsky's Unit." [Writer] (101:12) D 88, p. 25.

5198. STONE, Myrna J.
"Buying Thornton House." [Event] (17:3) Fall 88, p. 76-77.
"Gone." [Event] (17:3) Fall 88, p. 75.

5199. STORACE, Patricia
"Movie." [NewYRB] (35:20) 22 D 88, p. 12.

5200. STOVER, Dean
"A Circuit Rider's Winter." [Farm] (5:2) Fall 88, p. 37.
"God Bless You." [PassN] (9:1) Wint 88, p. 29.
"The Human Season." [Farm] (5:2) Fall 88, p. 36.

5201. STOWELL, Phyllis
"Denial." [Ascent] (13:3) 88, p. 27.
"Leda." [NewL] (54:3) Spr 88, p. 88.
"Look at All You Can Trust." [Ascent] (13:2) 88, p. 16-17.
"One Day You Put on Your Shoes." [Ascent] (13:2) 88, p. 15-16.
"The Question." [Ascent] (13:3) 88, p. 25-26.

5202. STRAHAN, Bradley R.
"Blue Jean Blues." [Wind] (18:63) 88, p. 42.
"The Seasons Last Apples." [Wind] (18:63) 88, p. 42-43.

5203. STRANAHAN, Ann Anderson
"Superior Street People" (Selections: 7 prose poems). [RiverS] (26) 88, p. 27-34.

5204. STRAND, Mark
"A.M." [NewYorker] (64:26) 15 Ag 88, p. 38.
"Fear of the Night" (after Leopardi). [WestHR] (42:4) Wint 88, p. 274.
"One Winter Night." [NewRep] (198:21) 23 My 88, p. 32.
"Reading in Place." [GrandS] (7:4) Sum 88, p. 34.
"Se la Vita É Sventura?" [GrandS] (7:4) Sum 88, p. 35.

5205. STRATFORD, Philip
"Beginning of Summer" (tr. of Robert Melançon). [Trans] (20) Spr 88, p. 151.
"Blind Painting II" (tr. of Robert Melançon). [Trans] (20) Spr 88, p. 152.

5206. STRATTON, R. E.
"Nebraska Express" (for William Kloefkorn). [Plain] (8:2) Wint 88, p. 31.
"The Two of Us." [Plain] (8:3) Spr-Sum 88, p. 18.

5207. STRAUS, Austin
"Guts." [Jacaranda] (3:2) Fall-Wint 88, p. 119-120.
"Ruint" (For Wanda C.). [SlipS] (8) 88, p. 24.

STRAUSS, David Levi
See LEVI STRAUSS, David

5208. STRAUSS, Gwen
"Endurance." [PoetryNW] (29:3) Aut 88, p. 13.
"Their Father." [NewRep] (199:24) 12 D 88, p. 40.

5209. STRAW, Silvana R.
"No Mercy: A Love Poem." [Gargoyle] (35) 88, p. 142-143.

5210. STREVER, Linda
"While You Slept." [BelPoJ] (38:3) Spr 88, p. 1.

5211. STRICKER, Meredith
"Arriving at the Mississippi." [PoetC] (19:2) Wint 88, p. 19-20.
"For the Blue Lady." [PoetC] (19:2) Wint 88, p. 20-21.

5212. STRICKLAND, Stephanie
"Jus Suum: What Can Never Be Taken." [AmerV] (12) Fall 88, p. 66-67.

5213. STRINGER, A. E.
"Cargo Worship, 1947." [TampaR] (1) 88, p. 90.
"The Incomplete Is Unforgiving." [OhioR] (41) 88, p. 97.
"Model in the Round." [DenQ] (23:2) Fall 88, p. 66.
"No Moon in the Ruins." [DenQ] (23:2) Fall 88, p. 65.

5214. STRINGER, David
"Drownings." [PassN] (9:1) Wint 88, p. 11.
5215. STROUS, Allen
"Cobra Report." [OhioR] (40) 88, p. 92-93.
"February." [KanQ] (20:1/2) Wint-Spr 88, p. 265.
"The First Warm Day." [OhioR] (40) 88, p. 91.
"Recluse." [KanQ] (20:1/2) Wint-Spr 88, p. 264.
"Winter Afternoon." [KanQ] (20:1/2) Wint-Spr 88, p. 265.
5216. STRUNK, Orlo, Jr.
"Recalling a Bombing Mission" (England, December 1944). [Bogg] (60) 88, p. 31.
5217. STRUTHERS, Ann
"False Maps." [PoetC] (20:1) Fall 88, p. 20.
"God, Ronald Reagan, and the Cosmic Pinball Machine." [MinnR] (NS 30/31) Spr-Fall 88, p. 52.
"Henry Wadsworth Longfellow." [Iowa] (18:2) 88, p. 111.
"Indian Baskets." [PoetC] (20:1) Fall 88, p. 19.
5218. STRYK, Dan
"Home of Country Music" (Bristol, Virginia). [CharR] (14:2) Fall 88, p. 85.
"The Mountains Change Aspect Like Our Moods." [CharR] (14:2) Fall 88, p. 84-85.
"Nutgatherers." [Paint] (15:30) Aut 88, p. 13.
"An Old Milkman 'Returns'." [Paint] (15:30) Aut 88, p. 12.
"They Will Stay." [SouthernHR] (22:1) Wint 88, p. 32-33.
5219. STRYK, Lucien
"Bacchus." [CreamCR] (12:2) Sum 88, p. 287.
"Drama." [MidAR] (8:2) 88, p. 73.
"Dreaming to Music." [Poetry] (152:6) S 88, p. 313.
"Images." [CharR] (14:1) Spr 88, p. 90.
"June 5, 1987." [CreamCR] (12:2) Sum 88, p. 286.
"Modern Art." [MidAR] (8:2) 88, p. 72.
5220. STUART, Dabney
"The End of the Century." [GettyR] (1:1) Wint 88, p. 155.
"The Man in the Black Bear." [Chelsea] (47) 88, p. 136.
"Moving Pictures." [Chelsea] (47) 88, p. 137-139.
"Tane Mahuta" (Waipoua Forest, New Zealand). [TarRP] (28:1) Fall 88, p. 65-66.
STUBBS, John Heath
See HEATH-STUBBS, John
5221. STUDEBAKER, William
"Prelude to a Good Time in Nevada." [SoDakR] (26:1) Spr 88, p. 109.
5222. STUDER, Constance
"Climbing." [Kaleid] (17) Sum-Fall 88, p. 20.
"Wooden Leg." [Kaleid] (16) Wint-Spr 88, p. 28.
5223. STULL, Richard
"Autumn Exercise" (Memento Mori). [Boulevard] (3:2/3) Fall 88, p. 125-126.
5224. STUMP, Sheldon
"The Color of the Wall." [Sonora] (14/15) Spr 88, p. 22-23.
5225. STURGIS, Susanna J.
"The Bullfight Sonnets." [SinW] (35) Sum-Fall 88, p. 55-56.
5226. SUAREZ, Jorge
"Del Cuerpo al Alma." [Mairena] (10:25) 88, p. 79.
5227. SUBLETT, Dyan
"Summer on the River." [IndR] (11:2) Spr 88, p. 19-20.
5228. SUBRAMAN, Belinda
"Blessings." [AlphaBS] (4) D 88, p. 46.
"Genesis According to Charlie." [Lactuca] (9) F 88, p. 19.
"A Helping Hand" (Or, Browning the Meat). [Bogg] (59) 88, p. 6.
"His Mouth Must Be on Women." [SlipS] (8) 88, p. 21.
"I Like Being Published" (The Way a Male Chauvinist Likes His Women). [Bogg] (60) 88, p. 13.
"Mute." [Amelia] (5:1, #12) 88, p. 113.
"New Line." [AlphaBS] (4) D 88, p. 47.
"On the Street." [Amelia] (5:1, #12) 88, p. 112.
"Orissa Truck Stop." [AlphaBS] (4) D 88, p. 45.
"Quick." [SlipS] (8) 88, p. 21.
"Sun Rite / Other Ways." [AlphaBS] (4) D 88, p. 44.
"The Zoo." [Amelia] (5:1, #12) 88, p. 112.

5229. SUBRAMANYAM, Ka. Naa.
"Eunuchs" (tr. by Rajagopal Parthasarathy). [Nimrod] (31:2) Spr-Sum 88, p. 100.
"The Latecomer" (tr. by Rajagopal Parthasarathy). [Nimrod] (31:2) Spr-Sum 88, p. 99.

5230. SUDERMAN, Elmer
"Highway 77, Eastern Nebraska." [SoDakR] (26:3) Aut 88, p. 27.

5231. SUGIOKA, Stephanie
"Legacy." [Calyx] (11:2/3) Fall 88, p. 88-90.

5232. SUK, Julie
"Chickens and Dragons." [MemphisSR] (8:2) Spr 88, p. 38-39.
"The Dead Come Back." [MemphisSR] (8:2) Spr 88, p. 40.
"Early and Late." [MemphisSR] (8:2) Spr 88, p. 42.
"Not a Place We Own." [MemphisSR] (8:2) Spr 88, p. 41.
"Photographs Taken from a Distance" (International Poetry Contest, Fourth Prize). [WestB] (21/22) 88, p. 42-43.
"Smoldering." [NewL] (55:2) Wint 88-89, p. 75.

5233. SULLAM, Elizabeth
"Night Walks Unaware." [DeKalbLAJ] (21:1) Wint 88, p. 69.

5234. SULLIVAN, William A.
"Late November." [TexasR] (9:1/2) Spr-Sum 88, p. 84.

5235. SUMRALL, Amber Coverdale
"Eagle Woman." [SinW] (32) Sum 87, p. 113.
"Intruder" (for Joseph M. Park). [NegC] (8:3) 88, p. 88-89.
"Questions." [SinW] (32) Sum 87, p. 74-75.
"Tailings." [Kaleid] (17) Sum-Fall 88, p. 55.

5236. SUN, Li
"Smoking People: Encountering the New Chinese Poetry" (Chapbook 19, tr. by Sun Li et al.). [BelPoJ] (39:2) Wint 88-89, 76 p.

5237. SUN, Wu-jun
"What Else Am I Afraid Of?" (in Chinese & English). [BelPoJ] (39:2) Wint 88-89, p. 32-33.

5238. SUND, Robert
"Shack Medicine." [SwampR] (1:2/3) D 88, p. 74-76.

5239. SUNDAHL, Daniel (*See also* Sundahl, Daniel James)
"Interjections I-IV: Thoreau in South America." [HolCrit] (25:3) Je 88, p. 16.

5240. SUNDAHL, Daniel James (*See also* Sundahl, Daniel)
"A Change of Climate." [FourQ] (2d series 2:2) Fall 88, p. 24.
"In Late Autumn, the Devil's Wind Visits Mrs. Vigo Miller's Husband." [WritersF] (14) Fall 88, p. 91-92.
"Pyrrhonian Doubt." [FloridaR] (16:1) Spr-Sum 88, p. 120.

5241. SUNDSTROM, Kay
"Beasts." [Thrpny] (35) Fall 88, p. 22.

5242. SURDAS
"Worshipping God As a Baby" (3 poems, tr. by Judi Benade). [Nimrod] (31:2) Spr-Sum 88, p. 21-23.

5243. SURVANT, Joe
"Navarathri." [Stand] (29:4) Aut 88, p. 70-71.

5244. SURYA, Vasantha
"The Stalk of Time" (Excerpts). [Nimrod] (31:2) Spr-Sum 88, p. 68-69.

5245. SUSSKIND, Harriet
"The Gift of Reason." [NegC] (8:3) 88, p. 179-182.
"The Mind Dislikes Surprises" (At Sigmund Freud's, 1919). [MSS] (6:2) 88, p. 32-33.

5246. SUTHERLAND, W. Mark
"Portrait of Kid Novocaine's Skeleton." [AlphaBS] (4) D 88, p. 5-6.

5247. SUTHERLAND-SMITH, James
"A Collection of Clocks: The British Museum." [LitR] (31:3) Spr 88, p. 293.
"Dante at the Seaside." [StoneC] (16:1/2) Fall-Wint 88-89, p. 41.
"Graffito." [StoneC] (16:1/2) Fall-Wint 88-89, p. 43.
"Grünewald's 'Pair of Lovers'." [KanQ] (20:1/2) Wint-Spr 88, p. 187.
"Mist and Horses Outside Sittingbourne." [StoneC] (16:1/2) Fall-Wint 88-89, p. 42-43.
"Nemesis" (for Guy Carter). [CumbPR] (7:2) Spr 88, p. 58-59.
"Surrman Lagoon in July." [LitR] (31:3) Spr 88, p. 294.
"A Viola Solo." [LitR] (31:2) Wint 88, p. 185.
"Wasps." [KanQ] (20:3) Sum 88, p. 178-179.

"A Widow in Her Bedroom." [KanQ] (20:3) Sum 88, p. 179.
5248. SUTTON, Catherine
"Kate Glenn." [AmerV] (13) Wint 88, p. 6.
5249. SUTTON, Dorothy Moseley
"Gymnastics." [Wind] (18:62) 88, p. 44-45.
"On the Spanish Steps in Rome." [Wind] (18:62) 88, p. 44.
5250. SUTTON, Maureen D.
"Late for a Spaying Appointment." [Pembroke] (20) 88, p. 248.
5251. SUTZKEVER, Abraham
"Because I Was Drinking Wine: IV" (tr. by C. K. Williams). [AmerPoR] (17:6) N-D 88, p. 28.
"Charred Pearls" (tr. by C. K. Williams). [AmerPoR] (17:6) N-D 88, p. 30.
"Faces in the Mire: I" (tr. by C. K. Williams). [AmerPoR] (17:6) N-D 88, p. 27.
"I Lie in This Coffin" (tr. by C. K. Williams). [AmerPoR] (17:6) N-D 88, p. 28.
"In the Cell: II" (tr. by C. K. Williams). [AmerPoR] (17:6) N-D 88, p. 27.
"Leaves of Ash: III" (tr. by C. K. Williams). [AmerPoR] (17:6) N-D 88, p. 28.
"A Load of Shoes" (tr. by C. K. Williams). [AmerPoR] (17:6) N-D 88, p. 29.
"Pray" (tr. by C. K. Williams). [AmerPoR] (17:6) N-D 88, p. 28.
"Song for the Last" (tr. by C. K. Williams). [AmerPoR] (17:6) N-D 88, p. 30.
"To My Child" (tr. by C. K. Williams). [AmerPoR] (17:6) N-D 88, p. 29.
"A Voice from the Heart: V" (tr. by C. K. Williams). [AmerPoR] (17:6) N-D 88, p. 28.
5252. SVEHLA, John
"Dawn." [DeKalbLAJ] (21:2) Spr 88, p. 46.
"Nereids." [DeKalbLAJ] (21:2) Spr 88, p. 46.
5253. SVOBODA, Teresa (Terese)
"Angelus" (after Millet). [Chelsea] (47) 88, p. 155.
"Do Machines Bleed?" [Pequod] (25) 88, p. 25-26.
"No Historical Marker" (An anthropologist takes us to the highest point of Waiheke Island, New Zealand). [Pequod] (25) 88, p. 27-28.
"On That Day." [Colum] (13) 88, p. 10.
"The Root of Mother Is Moth." [ParisR] (30:106) Spr 88, p. 259.
"A Scarlet Bird." [GettyR] (1:4) Aut 88, p. 751.
"Shell." [GettyR] (1:4) Aut 88, p. 750.
"Spiders." [Colum] (13) 88, p. 11-13.
5254. SWANBERG, Christine
"Finding the Floor." [Farm] (4:1, i.e. 5:1) Wint 88, p. 68.
"In Genoa, Near Relatives." [SpoonRQ] (13:1) Wint 88, p. 21.
"The Portland Roses." [SpoonRQ] (13:1) Wint 88, p. 22-23.
"Sonnet Before Grooming the Horse in Winter." [SpoonRQ] (13:1) Wint 88, p. 20.
"To Tend My Horse." [BelPoJ] (38:3) Spr 88, p. 20-21.
"Witch's Red Onion." [Farm] (5:2) Fall 88, p. 64.
5255. SWANDER, Mary
"Heaven and Earth House." [NewYorker] (64:44) 19 D 88, p. 42.
5256. SWANGER, David
"We Have Faced Night and Warmed Each Other." [CharR] (14:1) Spr 88, p. 89.
5257. SWANN, Brian
"Aftermath." [ColEng] (50:3) Mr 88, p. 287.
"Arabian Nights and Days" (to Leo and Nora Lionni). [LitR] (31:2) Wint 88, p. 201.
"Breakdown." [Salm] (78/79) Spr-Sum 88, p. 166.
"Burials." [Salm] (78/79) Spr-Sum 88, p. 165.
"Carthage." [KenR] (NS 10:1) Wint 88, p. 84.
"Dying." [CharR] (14:1) Spr 88, p. 84.
"Entropy." [YaleR] (78:1) Aut 88, p. 81-82.
"Fire" (to Leo and Nora Lionni). [LitR] (31:2) Wint 88, p. 200-201.
"For Adolf Eichmann" (tr. of Primo Levi, w. Ruth Feldman). [ParisR] (30:108) Fall 88, p. 206.
"The Heart." [CharR] (14:1) Spr 88, p. 84.
"Magic." [Caliban] (5) 88, p. 146.
"Magic." [ColEng] (50:3) Mr 88, p. 285.
"Marriage." [KenR] (NS 10:1) Wint 88, p. 83.
"Of Coal." [YaleR] (78:1) Aut 88, p. 80-81.
"Papago Deer Songs" (tr. of anonymous songs, w. Donald Bahr). [SouthernHR] (22:3) Sum 88, p. 238-240.
"Scorpions." [ColEng] (50:3) Mr 88, p. 286.
"Singing." [ColEng] (50:3) Mr 88, p. 284-285.

"Stopping at Night." [ColEng] (50:3) Mr 88, p. 288.
"Upstate Vignette." [CharR] (14:1) Spr 88, p. 85.
"Worlds" (To Leo and Nora Lionni). [KenR] (NS 10:1) Wint 88, p. 84.

5258. SWANNELL, Anne
"The Diamond" (For Phyllis Webb). [CanLit] (118) Aut 88, p. 114.
"Never." [Event] (17:1) Spr 88, p. 37.
"Obfuscation with Mirrors." [CanLit] (118) Aut 88, p. 115.
"The Scent of Freshcut Grass." [Event] (17:1) Spr 88, p. 36.

5259. SWANSON, Catherine
"The Pioneer Wife's Canary." [ArtfulD] (14/15) Fall 88, p. 70.

5260. SWANSON, Eleanor
"Man Waves at Train." [BlackWR] (14:2) Spr 88, p. 43-44.
"The Secrets of Children." [CumbPR] (7:2) Spr 88, p. 60.
"Speaking to My Child." [HighP] (3:3) Wint 88-89, p. 65-66.

5261. SWANSON, James L.
"The Almagest." [CapilR] (46) 88, p. 15-16.
"On the Lodestone and Magnetic Bodies." [CapilR] (46) 88, p. 19-21.
"On the Revolutions of the Heavenly Spheres." [CapilR] (46) 88, p. 17-18.

5262. SWANSON, Mark
"Iron." [VirQR] (64:2) Spr 88, p. 289.
"The Stand." [VirQR] (64:2) Spr 88, p. 288-289.
"Thirst." [VirQR] (64:2) Spr 88, p. 290.

5263. SWANSON, Susan Marie
"The Lake and the Shooting Star." [Prima] (11/12) 88, p. 96-97.
"The Woods at Nerstrand." [Prima] (11/12) 88, p. 28-32.

5264. SWARTWOUT, Susan
"Nightmoves." [BelPoJ] (39:1) Fall 88, p. 31.

5265. SWEENEY, Gael
"In Amish Country." [HiramPoR] (44/45) Spr-Wint 88, p. 71-72.
"In the Kremlin: an Egg by Fabergé." [HiramPoR] (44/45) Spr-Wint 88, p. 73.

5266. SWEENEY, Teresa
"Desire." [RiverS] (26) 88, p. 75.

5267. SWEET, Mary Logan
"Old Men." [BallSUF] (29:4) Aut 88, p. 44.

5268. SWENSON, Karen
"The Beast." [Salm] (78/79) Spr-Sum 88, p. 163-164.
"Diorama Painter at the Museum of Natural History." [PraS] (62:3) Fall 88, p. 116.
"Flight from Minneapolis to Fargo." [KanQ] (20:3) Sum 88, p. 202-203.
"Madness." [Salm] (78/79) Spr-Sum 88, p. 162.
"Malacca." [Salm] (78/79) Spr-Sum 88, p. 162-163.
"Sarah's Monsters." [PraS] (62:3) Fall 88, p. 117.
"Spring's Nebraska." [CreamCR] (12:2) Sum 88, p. 288.
"A Yellow Coin." [KanQ] (20:3) Sum 88, p. 202.

5269. SWENSON, May
"The Hole Seen." [LightY] ('88/9) 88, p. 116-117.
"Look Closer." [NewYorker] (64:43) 12 D 88, p. 48.
"My Name Was Called." [NewYorker] (64:17) 13 Je 88, p. 32.
"The Rest of My Life." [Poetry] (151:5) F 88, p. 394-397.

5270. SWIFT, Michael
"Summer Night in the Country." [HolCrit] (25:1) F 88, p. 17.

5271. SWIGART, Rob
"Bedtime." [PoetryNW] (29:1) Spr 88, p. 37.
"Telephone Sonnet." [PoetryNW] (29:1) Spr 88, p. 36-37.

5272. SWIST, Wally
"Budding." [Os] (26) 88, p. 4.
"Coyotes." [Os] (26) 88, p. 8.
"Setting Type" (for Gary Metras). [PoetryE] (25) Spr 88, p. 68.
"What Was Said." [Os] (26) 88, p. 9.

5273. SYLVESTER, Janet
"Good Luck Len Fuller." [SouthernR] (24:3) Sum 88, p. 574-575.
"Illumination Rounds." [GettyR] (1:2) Spr 88, p. 362-362.
"On Bent Grounds." [QW] (27) Sum-Fall 88, p. 103.
"The Road Between Walls." [SouthernR] (24:3) Sum 88, p. 573-574.
"The Village Pacified." [TampaR] (1) 88, p. 78.

5274. SYVERTSEN, Paul
"Oslo Meat Market." [Amelia] (5:1, #12) 88, p. 71.

"Teaching Health Science." [StoneC] (16:1/2) Fall-Wint 88-89, p. 19.
5275. SZE, Arthur
"The Solderer." [RiverS] (26) 88, p. 77.
"Wasabi." [RiverS] (26) 88, p. 76.
5276. SZOCS, Geza
"Commentary on an Old Review." [Sulfur] (7:3, #21) Wint 88, p. 96-100.
5277. SZPORLUK, Jarissa
"Things." [Plain] (8:2) Wint 88, p. 37.
5278. SZYMBORSKA, Wislawa
"Archaeology" (tr. by Stanislaw Baranczak and Clare Cavanagh). [TriQ] (71) Wint 88, p. 147-148.
"Funeral" (tr. by Stanislaw Baranczak and Clare Cavanagh). [TriQ] (71) Wint 88, p. 150.
"Hitler's First Photograph" (tr. by Stanislaw Baranczak and Clare Cavanagh). [TriQ] (71) Wint 88, p. 149.
"Plotting with the Dead" (tr. by Stanislaw Baranczak and Clare Cavanagh). [ManhatR] (4:2) Spr 88, p. 33-34.
"Stage Fright" (tr. by Stanislaw Baranczak and Clare Cavanagh). [ManhatR] (4:2) Spr 88, p. 31-32.
"View with a Grain of Sand" (tr. by Stanislaw Baranczak and Clare Cavanagh). [ManhatR] (4:2) Spr 88, p. 32-33.
5279. SZYPER, Adam
"After Reading About Writers Workshop at Arizona State Prison." [Spirit] (9:1) 88, p. 56.
5280. TABAKOW, Phil
"Some Night, Maybe." [CinPR] (17) Spr 88, p. 29.
"Walt Whitman at Pfaff's: A Fantasy." [CinPR] (17) Spr 88, p. 28.
5281. TABLADA, José Juan
"Insomnia" (tr. by Michael L. Johnson). [WebR] (13:2) Fall 88, p. 32.
"Peacock" (tr. by Michael L. Johnson). [WebR] (13:2) Fall 88, p. 32.
5282. TAFDRUP, Pia
"Anyway" (tr. by Thomas E. Kennedy and Monique M. Kennedy). [Spirit] (9:1) 88, p. 165.
"Came to You" (tr. by Thomas E. Kennedy and Monique M. Kennedy). [StoneC] (16:1/2) Fall-Wint 88-89, p. 54.
"The Dream about the Reader" (tr. by Monique M. Kennedy and Thomas E. Kennedy). [Rohwedder] (4) [Wint 88-89], p. 36.
"Fevered Lillies" (tr. by Thomas E. Kennedy). [Vis] (28) 88, p. 32.
"Glazed Eyes" (tr. by Thomas E. Kennedy and Monique M. Kennedy). [ColR] (NS 15:2) Fall-Wint 88, p. 78.
"Kom til Dig" (in Danish). [StoneC] (16:1/2) Fall-Wint 88-89, p. 54.
"The Many Lives" (tr. by Monique M. Kennedy and Thomas E. Kennedy). [Rohwedder] (4) [Wint 88-89], p. 36.
"Panorama" (tr. by Thomas E. Kennedy and Monique M. Kennedy). [ColR] (NS 15:2) Fall-Wint 88, p. 79.
"Silent Explosion" (tr. by Thomas E. Kennedy and Monique M. Kennedy). [ColR] (NS 15:2) Fall-Wint 88, p. 77.
"Snowpins" (tr. by Thomas E. Kennedy and Monique M. Kennedy). [Spirit] (9:1) 88, p. 164.
"Vanishing Days" (tr. by Anne Born). [ColR] (NS 15:2) Fall-Wint 88, p. 80-81.
5283. TAGGART, John
"All the Steps." [Temblor] (8) 88, p. 65-70.
"Last Train." [NewAW] (4) Fall 88, p. 59-62.
5284. TAGLIABUE, John
"Italy Travel Journal" (Selections: 1-4). [Chelsea] (47) 88, p. 72-74.
"Just Keep Talking Until It Becomes You." [TexasR] (9:3/4) Fall-Wint 88, p. 133.
5285. TAKACS, Nancy
"Depth." [Plain] (8:3) Spr-Sum 88, p. 28.
"February Sky." [Plain] (9:1) Fall 88, p. 23.
"Losing the Rio Grande." [Plain] (8:1) Fall 87, p. 27.
"The Pheasant." [QW] (26) Wint 88, p. 104-105.
5286. TAKARA, Kathryn
"Halawa Falls." [HawaiiR] (12:1, #23) Spr 88, p. 100-101.
"Hunting." [ChamLR] (2:1, #3) Fall 88, p. 47.
"Magnolias & Memories." [HawaiiR] (12:2, #24) Fall 88, p. 40-41.
"Samantha." [ChamLR] (2:1, #3) Fall 88, p. 48.

TAKASHI, Hiraide
See HIRAIDE, Takashi
5287. TAKSA, Mark
"Bargaining the Collective Hello." [PikeF] (9) Fall 88, p. 11.
"Jailed Sharks, Appointments." [Plain] (9:1) Fall 88, p. 9.
"Rope Shreds." [ConnPR] (7:1) 88, p. 29.
5288. TALAL, Marilynn
"Motion in One Direction." [SouthernPR] (28:1) Spr 88, p. 47.
5289. TALL, Deborah
"First Night, Tuscany." [GettyR] (1:2) Spr 88, p. 373.
"The Last Horseman." [GettyR] (1:2) Spr 88, p. 372.
5290. TALLEY, Carole Flegal
"A Birthday." [Writer] (101:3) Mr 88, p. 18.
5291. TAM, Reuben
"Adjectives for Sand." [HawaiiR] (12:2, #24) Fall 88, p. 115.
"At Lae Lipoa." [ChamLR] (1:2, #2) Spr 88, p. 71.
"Dark." [HawaiiR] (12:1, #23) Spr 88, p. 38.
"A Day at Ten-C." [ChamLR] (2:1, #3) Fall 88, p. 18.
"Ghost Dogs of Halaula." [ChamLR] (2:1, #3) Fall 88, p. 19.
"Groundwater." [ChamLR] (1:2, #2) Spr 88, p. 72.
"The Hills of East Kauai." [HawaiiR] (12:2, #24) Fall 88, p. 118.
"The Ironwoods." [HawaiiR] (12:1, #23) Spr 88, p. 37.
"Sandbars." [ChamLR] (1:2, #2) Spr 88, p. 70.
"Ways to the Sea." [HawaiiR] (12:2, #24) Fall 88, p. 116-117.
"Where the Island Ended." [HawaiiR] (12:1, #23) Spr 88, p. 36.
5292. TAMMARO, Thom
"Grandmother's Song." [SoDakR] (26:2) Sum 88, p. 75-76.
"Nighthawks." [SoDakR] (26:2) Sum 88, p. 73-74.
"That John Garfield Feeling." [SoDakR] (26:2) Sum 88, p. 71-72.
5293. TAMURA, Ryuichi
"In the Morning, Why?" (tr. by Tomoyuki Iino). [Stand] (29:3) Sum 88, p. 21.
"Summer Letter" (tr. by Tomoyuki Iino). [Stand] (29:3) Sum 88, p. 20.
TAN, Cao
See CAO, Tan
5294. TANENBAUM, Leora
"Submersion." [HangL] (53) 88, p. 68.
5295. TANG, Zhao-jian
"In Autumn Days" (tr. of Geng Wei). [MidAR] (8:1) 88, p. 14-15.
5296. TANGORRA, Joanne
"Blueprint." [PoetC] (20:1) Fall 88, p. 14-15.
"Instead of a Letter" (for L.J.T.). [IndR] (12:1) Wint 88, p. 65-66.
"Leda Speaks." [PoetC] (20:1) Fall 88, p. 16-17.
"My Daughter" (after a theme by Carlos Drummond de Andrade). [PoetL] (83:2) Sum 88, p. 43-44.
"Separation." [PoetL] (83:2) Sum 88, p. 42.
5297. TANIKAWA, Shuntaro
"Hymn" (tr. by William I. Elliott and Kazuo Kawamura). [CrabCR] (5:2) Sum 88, p. 14.
"Some Questions" (tr. by William I. Elliott and Kazuo Kawamura). [CrabCR] (5:2) Sum 88, p. 15-16.
"A Study of the Tactile Sense" (tr. by William I. Elliott and Kazuo Kawamura). [CrabCR] (5:2) Sum 88, p. 16-19.
"The Window" (tr. by William I. Elliott and Kazuo Kawamura). [CrabCR] (5:2) Sum 88, p. 14.
5298. TANNENBAUM, Judith
"California North Coast." [Amelia] (5:1, #12) 88, p. 117.
5299. TANNER, Sara
"Lexicon: Helen Keller." [Vis] (28) 88, p. 28.
5300. TANNY, Marlaina
"Wisdom." [PoetryE] (25) Spr 88, p. 66.
5301. TAPAHONSO, Lucy
"What Danger We Court." [Caliban] (5) 88, p. 100.
5302. TAPSCOTT, Stephen
"Nocturne." [TarRP] (27:2) Spr 88, p. 2-3.
"Prehistoric Horses." [Agni] (27) 88, p. 68-75.

5303. TARN, Nathaniel
"Architextures." [Temblor] (8) 88, p. 71-77.
5304. TATARUNIS, Paula
"47 Exchange Street." [LitR] (32:1) Fall 88, p. 121-122.
"Cellar Door." [CreamCR] (12:1) Wint 88, p. 89-90.
5305. TATE, James
"The Banner." [AmerPoR] (17:4) Jl-Ag 88, p. 4.
"Bewitched." [AmerPoR] (17:4) Jl-Ag 88, p. 5.
"Burn Down the Town, No survivors." [AmerPoR] (17:4) Jl-Ag 88, p. 5.
"The Condemned Man." [AmerPoR] (17:4) Jl-Ag 88, p. 4.
"Editor." [AmerPoR] (17:4) Jl-Ag 88, p. 4.
"How Was Your Day?" [AmerPoR] (17:4) Jl-Ag 88, p. 3.
"Indivisible." [AmerPoR] (17:4) Jl-Ag 88, p. 6.
"The Less Said." [NewL] (55:1) Fall 88, p. 75.
"A Little Skull." [AmerPoR] (17:4) Jl-Ag 88, p. 3.
"Pastoral." [AmerPoR] (17:4) Jl-Ag 88, p. 6.
"Quabbin Reservoir." [AmerPoR] (17:4) Jl-Ag 88, p. 3.
"Saturdays Are for Bathing Betsy." [AmerPoR] (17:4) Jl-Ag 88, p. 5.
"You Are My Destination and Desire, Fading." [AmerPoR] (17:4) Jl-Ag 88, p. 4.
5306. TAYKO, Gail
"Two Brothers' Guilt." [PaintedB] (34) 88, p. 83-84.
5307. TAYLOR, Alexander
"Journey North with Voices." [NegC] (8:3) 88, p. 94-101.
5308. TAYLOR, Brian
"Easing Home across Illinois" (For Jeanne Beaumont). [NewEngR] (11:2) Wint 88, p. 128.
"Requiem for Orpheus." [NewEngR] (11:2) Wint 88, p. 127.
5309. TAYLOR, Brigham
"Independence Pass." [SenR] (18:2) 88, p. 63.
5310. TAYLOR, Bruce
"He Shouts Peas." [MalR] (82) Mr 88, p. 67.
"Mandrakes." [CanLit] (117) Sum 88, p. 30.
"Nile." [MalR] (82) Mr 88, p. 66.
5311. TAYLOR, Craig
"The Creosote Bush." [CapeR] (23:2) Fall 88, p. 18.
"Empty Shells." [CapeR] (23:2) Fall 88, p. 19.
"The Fence." [KanQ] (20:1/2) Wint-Spr 88, p. 210-211.
"Gilbert King." [Lactuca] (11) O 88, p. 7.
"The Men in Dark Glasses." [Lactuca] (11) O 88, p. 6-7.
5312. TAYLOR, Eleanor Ross
"Harvest, 1925." [SenR] (18:1) 88, p. 9-10.
"The Plot Behind the Church." [Ploughs] (14:1) 88, p. 37.
5313. TAYLOR, Granville
"For Peggy." [EngJ] (77:4) Ap 88, p. 86.
5314. TAYLOR, Joan Crate
"Letters in Colour to Father." [Quarry] (37:4) Aut 88, p. 19-20.
"Thoughts of Charles." [Quarry] (37:4) Aut 88, p. 21.
5315. TAYLOR, Jonathan
"The Clapham Omnibus and the Man on It." [CumbPR] (7:2) Spr 88, p. 61-64.
5316. TAYLOR, Josephine
"Chemo Ladies." [Stand] (29:1) Wint 87-88, p. 47.
5317. TAYLOR, Kent
"April." [SwampR] (1:2/3) D 88, p. 16.
"Art Pepper." [SwampR] (1:1) Ja 88, p. 31.
"Carnival Masks." [SwampR] (1:2/3) D 88, p. 21.
"Chasing Helen." [SwampR] (1:2/3) D 88, p. 10.
"Dancer" (for Helen). [SwampR] (1:2/3) D 88, p. 11.
"Fugitive." [SwampR] (1:2/3) D 88, p. 17.
"Late Show." [SwampR] (1:1) Ja 88, p. 30.
"Lifelines." [PaintedB] (36) 88, p. 87.
"Lifelines." [SwampR] (1:2/3) D 88, p. 19.
"Lightning Bugs." [PaintedB] (36) 88, p. 89.
"March." [SwampR] (1:2/3) D 88, p. 23.
"Note to My Wife." [Abraxas] (37) 88, p. 32-33.
"One-Way." [Abraxas] (37) 88, p. 32.
"Ordinary Stars." [SwampR] (1:2/3) D 88, p. 15.

"Pantomime at My Wife's Grave." [SwampR] (1:2/3) D 88, p. 13.
"Passing Time." [SwampR] (1:2/3) D 88, p. 22.
"Requiem." [SwampR] (1:2/3) D 88, p. 18.
"Returning to Cleveland with an Olive Branch." [SwampR] (1:2/3) D 88, p. 20.
"Silence" (in memory of my wife). [SwampR] (1:2/3) D 88, p. 12.
"Silhouette." [SwampR] (1:1) Ja 88, p. 32.
"Solo." [SwampR] (1:2/3) D 88, p. 14.
"There Was Too Much to Hold" (in memory of my father). [PaintedB] (36) 88, p. 88.

5318. TAYLOR, Linda
"The Bear Woman." [KenR] (NS 10:4) Fall 88, p. 64.
"Heating Up the Snow." [TarRP] (27:2) Spr 88, p. 6-7.
"Notre Dame." [MinnR] (NS 30/31) Spr-Fall 88, p. 11.
"Pioneer Women" (for Susan Ludvigson). [MidwQ] (30:1) Aut 88, p. 75.
"Spring Sunset in the Suburbs." [MidwQ] (30:1) Aut 88, p. 76.
"Supper at LaPush." [KenR] (NS 10:4) Fall 88, p. 65-66.

5319. TAYLOR, Marilyn
"At Pompano." [CreamCR] (12:1) Wint 88, p. 76.
"Earth Mother." [CreamCR] (12:1) Wint 88, p. 77.
"A Short History of Art in the Western World." [CreamCR] (12:1) Wint 88, p. 78.

5320. TAYLOR, Robert M.
"Educational Research." [EngJ] (77:4) Ap 88, p. 87.

5321. TAYLOR, Ross
"Derwent Water: Words Re. Tranquillity." [VirQR] (64:4) Aut 88, p. 620.
"Re-thinking the Black Raincoat." [WestHR] (42:3) Aut 88, p. 219.

5322. TAYLOR, Sheila Ortiz
"Southern Exposure." [SinW] (34) Spr 88, p. 67-69.

5323. TEIGEN, Sue
"The White Snake." [IndR] (12:1) Wint 88, p. 111.

5324. TEILLIER, Jorge
"Camino Rural." [BlackWR] (15:1) Fall 88, p. 94.
"Country Road" (tr. by Mary Crow). [BlackWR] (15:1) Fall 88, p. 95.
"The Key" (tr. by Mary Crow). [BlackWR] (15:1) Fall 88, p. 93.
"La Llave." [BlackWR] (15:1) Fall 88, p. 92.

5325. TELLER, Gayl
"Menstruation" (Hanuka Scenario). [PikeF] (9) Fall 88, p. 25.

5326. TELLMAN, Susan
"Another Eve." [BallSUF] (29:4) Aut 88, p. 51-52.
"Elements in a Dream Place." [BallSUF] (29:4) Aut 88, p. 9.

5327. TEMPLE, M. K.
"Pass Christian." [CinPR] (18) Fall 88, p. 28.

5328. TENENBAUM, Molly
"Always More to Be Erased." [PoetryNW] (29:4) Wint 88-89, p. 21-22.
"Degrees." [PoetryNW] (29:4) Wint 88-89, p. 20.
"Groundskeepers." [PoetryNW] (29:4) Wint 88-89, p. 19.
"'Indirect Object' Is an Oxymoron." [PoetryNW] (29:2) Sum 88, p. 44.
"Song of the Bridge Tender." [PoetryNW] (29:2) Sum 88, p. 45-46.

5329. TENER, Robert L.
"Blemished Face." [Kaleid] (17) Sum-Fall 88, p. 54.
"Early Morning at St. Thomas Hospital: Waiting for Dr. Lehocz." [Kaleid] (17) Sum-Fall 88, p. 54.

5330. TENNENT, Cheryl Ervin
"Labyrinth." [CimR] (85) O 88, p. 34.
"The Ripening." [Plain] (9:1) Fall 88, p. 30.

5331. TEPLITSKY, Linda
"Winter." [CrabCR] (5:1) Wint 88, p. 14.

5332. TERADA, Rei
"Charlotte Champe Eliot (1929)." [GrandS] (7:2) Wint 88, p. 71-72.

5333. TERASHIMA, Robert
"The Dance." [HangL] (52) 88, p. 36-37.

5334. TERRANOVA, Elaine
"For Arlene." [Footwork] ('88) 88, p. 61.
"Newlywed." [Footwork] ('88) 88, p. 60-61.
"On Market Street." [SouthernPR] (28:2) Fall 88, p. 51.
"A Schoolgirl Writes to a Prisoner" (for Etheridge Knight). [PaintedB] (32/33) 88, p. 49-50.

5335. TERRIS, Virginia R.
"After the Prom." [HampSPR] Wint 88, p. 12.
"Against Requests." [ManhatPR] (10) Ja 88, p. 41-42.
"Autumn." [WindO] (50) Aut 88, p. 30.
"Bravado." [HampSPR] Wint 88, p. 12.
"Cold Front." [WindO] (50) Aut 88, p. 31.
"The Field." [ManhatPR] (10) Ja 88, p. 41.
"Love Song, 1." [ManhatPR] (10) Ja 88, p. 42.
"Marriage in the Suburbs." [ManhatPR] (10) Ja 88, p. 42-43.
5336. TETI, Zona
"Among Hellenistic Fragments." [Iowa] (18:1) 88, p. 49.
"By the Waters of Bic." [Quarry] (37:4) Aut 88, p. 71.
"Elevators" (for GW). [AmerPoR] (17:5) S-O 88, p. 19.
"Equinox." [Ascent] (13:3) 88, p. 12.
"Erosion." [Ploughs] (14:4) 88, p. 71.
"Next Door." [Iowa] (18:1) 88, p. 51.
"On a Low Porch." [Quarry] (37:4) Aut 88, p. 72.
"Passage Through Zola's *The Earth.*" [Iowa] (18:1) 88, p. 50.
"Una Vecchia." [Iowa] (18:1) 88, p. 48.
5337. THACKREY, Susan
"Untitled: No there's no story." [Verse] (5:1) F 88, p. 25.
5338. THELEN, Erik
"Algebra for Ethnographers." [CreamCR] (12:2) Sum 88, p. 289.
5339. THESEN, Sharon
"The Art of Love." [MalR] (83) Je 88, p. 64.
"Elegy, the Fertility Specialist." [MalR] (83) Je 88, p. 59-60.
"Estimates for the Painting." [MalR] (83) Je 88, p. 69-70.
"The Future." [MalR] (83) Je 88, p. 65-66.
"Greece, Birthplace of Modern Culture." [MalR] (83) Je 88, p. 63.
"Head in the Clouds." [MalR] (83) Je 88, p. 67.
"In Memory of a Brief Husband." [MalR] (83) Je 88, p. 62.
"Island New Year." [MalR] (83) Je 88, p. 71-72.
"Joie de Vivre." [Trans] (20) Spr 88, p. 79.
"Matisse Series" (Selections: 10 poems). [MalR] (83) Je 88, p. 73-82.
"Poem for Norbert's Thesis." [MalR] (83) Je 88, p. 68.
"The Same Trophy." [Trans] (20) Spr 88, p. 80-81.
"September, Turning, the Long Road Down to Love." [MalR] (83) Je 88, p. 57-58.
"The Shroud of Turin." [Trans] (20) Spr 88, p. 77-78.
"Winter and Then Summer." [MalR] (83) Je 88, p. 61.
5340. THIERS, Naomi
"Your Bed a Warm River Bottom." [PacificR] (6) Spr 88, p. 48.
5341. THOMAE, Edie
"Ann." [Crazy] (35) Wint 88, p. 52-53.
5342. THOMAS, Barbara
"Leona Florence Rice Blakely, 1879-1963." [StoneC] (15:3/4) Spr-Sum 88, p. 72.
5343. THOMAS, Denise
"El Paso." [SoDakR] (26:2) Sum 88, p. 132.
"San Antonio, the Missions." [SoDakR] (26:2) Sum 88, p. 131.
"Texas." [SoDakR] (26:2) Sum 88, p. 30.
5344. THOMAS, Elizabeth
"Cerrillos Petting Zoo." [WillowS] (21) Wint 88, p. 80-82.
"Inside the Heart." [WestB] (21/22) 88, p. 120-122.
5345. THOMAS, F. Richard
"After Sin, Penitence." [LightY] ('88/9) 88, p. 216.
5346. THOMAS, Hazel Foster
"Molly Petty Passes." [Pembroke] (20) 88, p. 120.
5347. THOMAS, Jim
"Enduring a Fall Rain." [KanQ] (20:3) Sum 88, p. 128.
"Fall Murrain." [KanQ] (20:1/2) Wint-Spr 88, p. 174.
"Ghost." [KanQ] (20:3) Sum 88, p. 28.
"The Honey Man." [KanQ] (20:1/2) Wint-Spr 88, p. 174.
"In Praise of Kestrels." [Paint] (15:29) Spr 88, p. 12.
5348. THOMAS, John
"In the Coming Conflict Between the Two Great Powers." [Jacaranda] (3:2) Fall-Wint 88, p. 121.
"Lost Inventions of the Night" (11 poems). [Temblor] (8) 88, p. 107-112.

5349. THOMAS, Joyce
"DES Daughter." [NegC] (8:3) 88, p. 55-57.
"Ice-Fishing." [Blueline] (9:1/2) 88, p. 82.
5350. THOMAS, Larry D.
"Each Color." [DeKalbLAJ] (21:1) Wint 88, p. 71.
"For Bright Candy." [PoetL] (83:3) Fall 88, p. 37.
"For Hints of Fullness." [YellowS] (26) Spr 88, p. 13.
"These Blooms." [PoetL] (83:3) Fall 88, p. 36.
5351. THOMAS, Linda
"When Angels Clap." [ChamLR] (2:1, #3) Fall 88, p. 60.
5352. THOMAS, Mike
"Once, Because She Smiled at Him." [Wind] (18:62) 88, p. 43.
5353. THOMAS, R. S.
"A Wish." [NewEngR] (10:4) Sum 88, p. 474.
5354. THOMAS, Robert
"December Matinee." [YaleR] (78:1) Aut 88, p. 115-116.
"Fast Angel." [CapilR] (46) 88, p. 4.
"Mortal Light." [CapilR] (46) 88, p. 5.
"Wolf Point." [SenR] (18:2) 88, p. 76.
5355. THOMAS-HAYES, Reine
"Old Maid." [DenQ] (22:3) Wint 88, p. 250.
5356. THOMASON, Melody Collins
"Gloria Mundi." [Dandel] (15:2) Fall-Wint 88, p. 12.
5357. THOMPSON, Catherine
"If You Could Just Get Beyond Your Own Noise." [Crosscur] (7:4) 88, p. 33.
"White Zinfandel." [PassN] (9:2) Sum 88, p. 25.
5358. THOMPSON, Clark
"Peace Talks." [Rohwedder] (3) Spr 88, p. 38.
5359. THOMPSON, Gary
"House." [Abraxas] (37) 88, p. 65.
5360. THOMPSON, Jerry
"Smoking." [JamesWR] (6:1) Fall 88, p. 3.
5361. THOMPSON, John A., Sr.
"Dedicated to Quality." [Wind] (18:63) 88, p. 28.
5362. THOMPSON, Margareta O.
"By Right of Memory" (tr. of Alexander Tvardovsky). [NegC] (8:1/2) 88, p. 72-91.
5363. THOMPSON, Phyllis Hoge
"Apparitions." [ChamLR] (1:2, #2) Spr 88, p. 27.
"El Paso" (At the Immigration and Naturalization Processing Center Court). [ChamLR] (1:2, #2) Spr 88, p. 26.
"The House." [ChamLR] (1:2, #2) Spr 88, p. 28-29.
"The Shape of Things." [NewEngR] (10:3) Spr 88, p. 293.
"The Silence Overriding" (for Al Attanasio). [HawaiiR] (12:1, #23) Spr 88, p. 107-110.
"Waiting" (In Memory: Joan G. Kirtley). [HawaiiR] (12:1, #23) Spr 88, p. 106.
"What Ezra Said in Meeting." [PraS] (62:1) Spr 88, p. 108-109.
5364. THOMPSON, Sue Ellen
"Easier" (Guy Owen Poetry Prize Winner, Gerald Stern, Judge). [SouthernPR] (28:2) Fall 88, p. 5.
"Thaw." [TexasR] (9:3/4) Fall-Wint 88, p. 134.
5365. THOOR, Jesse
"A Beggar Sings" (tr. by Gary Sea). [Paint] (15:30) Aut 88, p. 38.
"Oo La La" (tr. by Gary Sea). [Paint] (15:30) Aut 88, p. 38.
5366. THORNE, Hooper
"Loitering with Intent." [Iowa] (18:2) 88, p. 36-45.
5367. THORNTON, Don
"Meeting at the Houston Contemporary Museum, Erotica Exhibition." [SlipS] (8) 88, p. 60.
5368. THORPE, Michael
"Gull in a Storm" (For David Silverberg). [AntigR] (73) Spr 88, p. 120.
"Ruskin's Pine." [PottPort] (10) 88, p. 39.
"To an Individualist." [AntigR] (73) Spr 88, p. 121.
5369. TIBBETTS, Frederick
"Beginning Aristotle." [Crosscur] (7:4) 88, p. 69.
"First Reader." [Crosscur] (7:4) 88, p. 68.
"Il Rè Pastore." [Crosscur] (7:4) 88, p. 67.

"Imaginary Classics." [ChiR] (36:2) Aut 88, p. 78.
"Objects of Vertu." [ChiR] (36:2) Aut 88, p. 77.
"The Port-Royal Grammar." [Verse] (5:3) N 88, p. 19.
"Storm Meadows." [Verse] (5:3) N 88, p. 19.
"To Morisot." [Contact] (9:47/48/49) Spr 88, p. 47.
"The Wild Swans." [Contact] (9:47/48/49) Spr 88, p. 47.

5370. TIBBETTS, Tara
"The Junto." [Phoenix] (9:1/2) 88, p. 55.

5371. TICHY, Susan
"Barrio Fiesta, Philippines: A Captain" (For My Husband). [HighP] (3:1) Spr 88, p. 54-56.
"Inheritance: the Water Cure" (Selection: Part Five, "Montana and Dakota Territories, 1876"). [NowestR] (26:1) 88, p. 48-52.

5372. TICKLE, Phyllis
"For Etheridge's Hat." [PaintedB] (32/33) 88, p. 89.

5373. TIFFANY, Daniel
"Black Genoa." [QW] (27) Sum-Fall 88, p. 105.
"Native Spring." [QW] (27) Sum-Fall 88, p. 106.

5374. TIFFANY, Jim
"Smashing Poem." [Bogg] (60) 88, p. 40.

5375. TIGER, Madeline (Madeline J.)
"The Birds" (after the words of Katharyn Machal Aal & Marge Piercy & Charlotte Gilman Perkins . . .). [Footwork] ('88) 88, p. 44-45.
"Elegy for David Hamburg" (b. 1878 - d. 1915). [Footwork] ('88) 88, p. 44.
"Forgiving the Husband." [Spirit] (9:1) 88, p. 136-139.
"Mercy" (Honorable Mention, 15th Anniversary Competition). [StoneC] (16:1/2) Fall-Wint 88-89, unpaged front matter.
"Water Has No Color." [Vis] (27) 88, p. 24.

5376. TIHANYI, Eva
"You Wondered How." [CrossC] (10:1) 88, p. 11.

5377. TILLINGHAST, David
"Blood Risen." [SoCaR] (20:2) Spr 88, p. 49.
"Passion." [SoCaR] (20:2) Spr 88, p. 48.

5378. TIMMONS, Susie
"Grecian Formula." [Bomb] (26) Wint 88-89, p. 58.
"On the Daily Monument." [Bomb] (26) Wint 88-89, p. 58.
"The Plane Is Landing." [Bomb] (26) Wint 88-89, p. 58.
"Poem: Days are short." [Bomb] (26) Wint 88-89, p. 58.

5379. TINDAL, Douglas L.
"Of Air." [RagMag] (6:2) Fall 88, p. 36.

TING, Shu
See SHU, Ting

5380. TIPTON, David
"Missing Bets." [WormR] (28:4, #112) 88, p. 125.
"Sue's Past & Mine." [WormR] (28:4, #112) 88, p. 124-125.

5381. TITTLER, Nancy
"Anguish of White Stone" (tr. of Innokenty Annensky, w. Devon Miller-Duggan). [Paint] (15:30) Aut 88, p. 31.
"January Fairy Tale" (tr. of Innokenty Annensky, w. Devon Miller-Duggan). [Paint] (15:30) Aut 88, p. 30.

5382. TKACHENKO, Aleksandr
"Quiet of the Chestnuts" (Excerpts, tr. by John High and Katya Olmsted). [FiveFR] (6) 88, p. 87-88.

5383. TOBE, Dorothy
"Wabash." [KanQ] (20:1/2) Wint-Spr 88, p. 284.

5384. TOBIN, Daniel
"A Dragonfly." [Jacaranda] (3:2) Fall-Wint 88, p. 36.

5385. TODD, Theodora
"Four Lakes Basin, the Uintas." [CinPR] (18) Fall 88, p. 60.
"Your Dream." [CinPR] (18) Fall 88, p. 61.

5386. TOKUNO, Ken
"Poems of Character." [BellArk] (4:6) N-D 88, p. 1.
"When Evening Seemed Morning." [BellArk] (4:6) N-D 88, p. 10.

5387. TOMLINSON, Charles
"Anniversary" (for Beatrice). [PartR] (55:3) Sum 88, p. 477.
"The Butterflies." [Hudson] (41:1) Spr 88, p. 156-157.

"The Cycle." [Hudson] (41:1) Spr 88, p. 160.
"Far Point." [Hudson] (41:1) Spr 88, p. 157-159.
"Ode to Dmitri Shostakovich." [PartR] (55:1) Wint 88, p. 56-57.
"Parking Lot" (Albuquerque). [Hudson] (41:1) Spr 88, p. 159.
"Pines." [Hudson] (41:1) Spr 88, p. 156.
"The Plaza." [Antaeus] (60) Spr 88, p. 209-211.
"The Santa Fe Railroad." [Hudson] (41:1) Spr 88, p. 160.
"Variant on a Line of Hughes." [PartR] (55:3) Sum 88, p. 478.

5388. TOMLINSON, Rawdon
"Ballad of a Road Boy." [ColEng] (50:3) Mr 88, p. 290-291.
"Easter 1954." [WeberS] (5:2) Fall 88, p. 74.
"Insomnia." [WeberS] (5:2) Fall 88, p. 75.
"Make-Believe, Ukraine 1932-33." [WritersF] (14) Fall 88, p. 75-77.
"Of an Evening." [WeberS] (5:2) Fall 88, p. 72.
"Open Swim." [HolCrit] (25:1) F 88, p. 19.
"Riding Home with Them." [ColEng] (50:3) Mr 88, p. 289.
"Sunday After the Tornado." [WeberS] (5:2) Fall 88, p. 73-74.
"Under the Hackberry." [LitR] (31:4) Sum 88, p. 434.

TOMOYUKI, Iino
See IINO, Tomoyuki

5389. TONGUE, Margaret
"Fathers / Daughters." [SinW] (33) Fall 87, p. 60-61.

5390. TONGUE, Roy K.
"Tar and Broom" (tr. of Kadammanitta Ramakrishnan, w. Ayyappa Paniker). [Nimrod] (31:2) Spr-Sum 88, p. 84-85.

5391. TOPAL, Carine
"Edging the Nile." [Pembroke] (20) 88, p. 229.
"Violinist in the Snow" (after a painting by Marc Chagall). [Pembroke] (20) 88, p. 230.
"What Passes." [PacificR] (6) Spr 88, p. 46-47.

5392. TOPP, Mike
"Three Quips." [Colum] (13) 88, p. 69-70.

5393. TORNES, Elizabeth
"The Story." [NewRep] (199:8) 22 Ag 88, p. 30.

5394. TÖRNLUND, Niklas
"The Blind Spot" (tr. by John Tritica). [WebR] (13:2) Fall 88, p. 22.
"Train-Rattle" (tr. by John Tritica). [WebR] (13:2) Fall 88, p. 19-20.
"Zooming Out, Nepal" (tr. by John Tritica). [WebR] (13:2) Fall 88, p. 21.

5395. TOROP, Karen
"The Orb Weaver." [Wind] (18:63) 88, p. 44-45.

5396. TORRA, Joseph
"Expressway North." [Wind] (18:63) 88, p. 41.

5397. TORRE, Stephan
"Behind the House." [Zyzzyva] (4:4) Wint 88, p. 43.
"Hayfield." [AmerPoR] (17:4) Jl-Ag 88, p. 34.
"The Sinker: Navarro Journal." [AmerPoR] (17:4) Jl-Ag 88, p. 34.

5398. TORREN, Asher
"The Past." [Lactuca] (9) F 88, p. 16.
"Saleh-al-Din." [BallSUF] (29:4) Aut 88, p. 55.
"Syrian Serenade 1986." [RagMag] (6:2) Fall 88, p. 17.

5399. TORRES, Daniel
"Buscamos." [CuadP] (6:16) Sept.-Dic. 88, p. 59.
"Esta noche soy Maga." [CuadP] (6:16) Sept.-Dic. 88, p. 59-60.

5400. TORRESON, Rodney
"Japheth Considers the Ruins." [ChatR] (8:2) Wint 88, p. 89.

5401. TORRICO, Alcira Cardona
"Santos Mayta." [Mairena] (10:25) 88, p. 77.

5402. TOSTESON, Heather
"Birdnesters." [SouthernPR] (28:1) Spr 88, p. 32-33.

TOV, S. Ben
See BEN-TOV, S.

5403. TOWLE, Andrew
"Between Stations." [Poetry] (152:4) Jl 88, p. 197-198.
"The Dead Sea at Dinner." [Poetry] (143, i.e. 153:2) N 88, p. 93.
"Nocturne." [Poetry] (152:4) Jl 88, p. 198-199.

5404. TOWLE, Parker
"Roofer." [DenQ] (22:3) Wint 88, p. 176-177.
5405. TOWNS, Jeanne R.
"Words of Wisdom, Passed On." [MinnR] (NS 30/31) Spr-Fall 88, p. 20.
5406. TOWNSEND, Alison
"Spring Geography." [Spirit] (9:1) 88, p. 167-170.
5407. TOWNSEND, Ann
"Elegy for My Father." [KanQ] (20:1/2) Wint-Spr 88, p. 124-125.
"Plain Song." [NewEngR] (11:2) Wint 88, p. 207-208.
"Winter Mine." [NewEngR] (11:2) Wint 88, p. 207.
5408. TOWNSEND, Cheryl
"Shower Massage." [SlipS] (8) 88, p. 37.
"Taboo." [SlipS] (8) 88, p. 38.
5409. TOYAMA, Jean Yamasaki
"Beyond the Intimate." [ChamLR] (2:1, #3) Fall 88, p. 41.
"Red." [Calyx] (11:2/3) Fall 88, p. 201.
TRAN, Kha
See KHA, Tran
5410. TRANBARGER, Ossie E.
"Iambus." [LittleBR] (5:2) Wint 88-89, p. 61.
"In the museum." [Amelia] (5:1, #12) 88, p. 10.
"Summer watch ended." [Amelia] (5:2, #13) 88, p. 20.
5411. TRANTER, John
"Backyard." [NewAW] (4) Fall 88, p. 127.
"Laminex." [NewAW] (4) Fall 88, p. 128.
"Lufthansa." [NewAW] (4) Fall 88, p. 132-133.
"Modern Art." [NewAW] (4) Fall 88, p. 130.
"The Pool." [PraS] (62:4) Wint 88-89, p. 65-66.
"Poolside." [NewAW] (4) Fall 88, p. 131.
"Shadow Detail." [NewAW] (4) Fall 88, p. 131-132.
"Voodoo." [NewAW] (4) Fall 88, p. 129-130.
"Widower." [PraS] (62:4) Wint 88-89, p. 64.
5412. TRAWICK, Leonard
"At the Flying School." [LightY] ('88/9) 88, p. 190.
"Suthun Accent." [LightY] ('88/9) 88, p. 61-62.
"Where Are the Snows?" [LightY] ('88/9) 88, p. 121.
5413. TREGEBOV, Rhea
"Dialectical Materialism." [MalR] (85) D 88, p. 28.
"The Good Bone." [MalR] (85) D 88, p. 24.
"The Habit of Seeing." [MalR] (85) D 88, p. 25.
"The Right Thing." [Grain] (16:1) Spr 88, p. 12.
"Vital Signs." [MalR] (85) D 88, p. 26-27.
5414. TREITEL, Margot
"Domestic Detail." [WindO] (50) Aut 88, p. 16.
5415. TREITEL, Renata
"Eurydice" (To the poet Phoebus Delphi, in remembrance of his Marie, tr. of Margherita Guidacci). [InterPR] (14:1) Spr 88, p. 59.
"For a Gift of Loukoumi" (tr. of Margherita Guidacci). [InterPR] (14:1) Spr 88, p. 61.
"In the Midst of the Telchines" (tr. of Margherita Guidacci). [InterPR] (14:1) Spr 88, p. 57.
"Oklahoma Baroque." [Phoenix] (9:1/2) 88, p. 68.
"Slava Raskaj" (tr. of Margherita Guidacci, w. Manly Johnson). [GrahamHR] (11) Spr 88, p. 98-99.
"To Phoebus for Lefteris's Friendship" (tr. of Margherita Guidacci). [InterPR] (14:1) Spr 88, p. 61.
"Virius" (tr. of Margherita Guidacci, w. Manly Johnson). [GrahamHR] (11) Spr 88, p. 97.
5416. TREJO, Ernesto
"One Summer." [Zyzzyva] (4:1) Spr 88, p. 130-131.
"Today I'll Sit Still." [AntR] (46:3) Sum 88, p. 355.
5417. TRETHEWEY, Eric
"The Cold Child." [ColEng] (50:2) F 88, p. 154-155.
"In a Cocked Hat." [NoDaQ] (56:3) Sum 88, p. 70.
"The Man in the Boot." [CanLit] (118) Aut 88, p. 96.
"Prayer at Evening." [NoDaQ] (56:3) Sum 88, p. 69.

"Prospective." [PoetL] (83:4) Wint 88-89, p. 31.
"Reading the Signs." [ChrC] (105:36) 30 N 88, p. 1092.

5418. TRIANA, José
"Cuaderno de Familia: Instantáneas" (Selections: 3 poems). [Lyra] (1:4) 88, p. 20-21.
"Family Album: Snapshots" (Selections: 3 poems, tr. by Iraida Iturralde and Lourdes Gil). [Lyra] (1:4) 88, p. 22-23.

5419. TRIER, Jan
"If the Men." [EngJ] (77:7) N 88, p. 98.

5420. TRIGGS, Jeffery
"'Carnation, Lily, Lily, Rose,' Sargent — 1885-86." [InterPR] (14:2) Fall 88, p. 108.
"Lear's Wife." [Interim] (7:1) Spr 88, p. 16.
"Rose of Sharon." [InterPR] (14:2) Fall 88, p. 109.

5421. TRINIDAD, David
"Hand Over Heart." [ParisR] (30:106) Spr 88, p. 200-202.
"Oscar Night." [Jacaranda] (3:2) Fall-Wint 88, p. 122.

5422. TRITICA, John
"The Blind Spot" (tr. of Niklas Törnlund). [WebR] (13:2) Fall 88, p. 22.
"Train-Rattle" (tr. of Niklas Törnlund). [WebR] (13:2) Fall 88, p. 19-20.
"Zooming Out, Nepal" (tr. of Niklas Törnlund). [WebR] (13:2) Fall 88, p. 21.

5423. TRIVELPIECE, Laurel
"Ceres." [Poetry] (152:6) S 88, p. 323.
"Grazing." [Poetry] (152:6) S 88, p. 324.
"Red-Tailed Hawks." [SouthernPR] (28:2) Fall 88, p. 24.

5424. TROSCHAK, William
"Thoughts on Viewing Recent American History on Television." [ChatR] (8:3) Spr 88, p. 43.

5425. TROTSKY, Dana
"Fireflies." [DeKalbLAJ] (21:1) Wint 88, p. 72.
"For Henna." [DeKalbLAJ] (21:2) Spr 88, p. 73.
"Holes." [DeKalbLAJ] (21:2) Spr 88, p. 74.
"An Idealist's Reverie" (Second Place, Creative Writing Club Contest). [DeKalbLAJ] (21:2) Spr 88, p. 51-52.

5426. TROWBRIDGE, William
"Bulk Mail." [PraS] (62:1) Spr 88, p. 89.
"Hope." [PraS] (62:1) Spr 88, p. 88.
"Kong Hits the Road with Dan-Dee Carnivals, Inc." [LightY] ('88/9) 88, p. 158.
"Little Boy." [TarRP] (28:1) Fall 88, p. 36.
"Suppose." [LightY] ('88/9) 88, p. 209.

5427. TRUDELL, Dennis
"Viet Man." [PraS] (62:2) Sum 88, p. 95-98.

5428. TRUEMAN, Terry
"Back to School." [Amelia] (4:4, #11) 88, p. 10.

5429. TRUITT, Samuel
"Alter" (Selections: 4 poems). [Gargoyle] (35) 88, p. 52-53.

5430. TRUJILLO, Paul
"A Child Was Born" (For Tomás Rivera). [BilingR] (13:1/2) Ja-Ag 86, c1988, p. 96-97.

5431. TRUSSELL, Donna
"A Deeper Well." [TarRP] (27:2) Spr 88, p. 18.
"Paris and Palo Alto." [MassR] (29:2) Sum 88, p. 287-288.

5432. TSUBOI, Shigeji
"Sky" (tr. by Graeme Wilson). [Jacaranda] (3:1) Wint 88, p. 5.

5433. TSUJIMOTO, Joseph (Joseph I.)
"Double Kill." [HawaiiR] (12:1, #23) Spr 88, p. 30-31.
"Mighty Joe Young" (for the living and dead of the CDR). [ChamLR] (2:1, #3) Fall 88, p. 110.
"A Preference for Order." [ChamLR] (2:1, #3) Fall 88, p. 111-112.

5434. TSVETAYEVA, Marina
"Poem of the End" (tr. by John Dolan). [Sulfur] (8:2, #23) Fall 88, p. 6-30.

TU, Fu
See DU, Fu

5435. TUCKER, Camille
"Homecoming. By a Girl Who Really Knows." [Jacaranda] (3:2) Fall-Wint 88, p. 152.

5436. TUCKER, Jim
"New York Morning." [Gargoyle] (35) 88, p. 141.
5437. TUCKER, Liza
"Northern Elegies" (Selection: "Four," tr. of Anna Akhmatova). [Field] (39) Fall 88, p. 32-33.
5438. TUCKER, Martin
"Alfred University on a Tuesday." [Confr] (37/38) Spr-Sum 88, p. 225.
"Brooklyn and the World." [Confr] (Special issue: The World of Brooklyn) 88, p. 53.
5439. TUDORAN, Dorin
"Apprenticeship" (tr. by M. Calinescu and Willis Barnstone). [Vis] (26) 88, p. 41.
"The Girth." [Vis] (26) 88, p. 42.
"Notes from an Underground" (tr. by the author). [Vis] (26) 88, p. 42.
5440. TULLOS, Rod
"The Wonder Bread Horror" (A Radio Play for Mark who suggested it). [JINJPo] (10:1/2) 88, p. 50-51.
5441. TULLY, John
"As It Is." [Blueline] (9:1/2) 88, p. 98.
5442. TUMA, Keith
"On the Chain." [ChiR] (36:1) 88, p. 52.
"Rime." [ChiR] (36:1) 88, p. 51.
5443. TUPPER, Barbara
"Gleaning from My East Patio." [Plain] (9:1) Fall 88, p. 39.
5444. TURCO, Lewis
"Joseph Carr (1917-)." [Ploughs] (14:1) 88, p. 139-140.
"The Last Subway" (For Tony Walters, d. October 17, 1977). [CentR] (32:3) Sum 88, p. 270.
"Three Poems from Lines in Emily Dickinson's Letters." [LaurelR] (22:21) Wint 88, p. 63-64.
5445. TURGEON, Gregoire
"History." [MidAR] (8:1) 88, p. 106.
"The Kill." [MidAR] (8:1) 88, p. 105.
5446. TURNBULL, Becky
"Elegy." [PraS] (62:1) Spr 88, p. 74-75.
"Surrender and Other Small Talk." [PraS] (62:1) Spr 88, p. 75-76.
5447. TURNER, Alberta
"In Place." [OhioR] (42) 88, p. 81.
"Monochrome." [ColR] (NS 15:2) Fall-Wint 88, p. 57.
5448. TURNER, Brian
"Naming the Lost." [NewL] (54:3) Spr 88, p. 76.
"Under the Hawkduns" (for W. S. Merwin). [NewL] (54:3) Spr 88, p. 77.
5449. TURNER, Donna
"Mushrooms in the Salad." [LittleBR] (5:2) Wint 88-89, p. 23.
5450. TURNER, Frederick
"Foamy Sky" (June 8th, 1940, tr. of Miklós Radnoti, w. Zsuzsanna Ozsvath). [Poetry] (151:6) Mr 88, p. 491-492.
"Letter to My Wife" (Lager Heidenau, 1944, tr. of Miklós Radnoti, w. Zsuzsanna Ozsvath). [Poetry] (151:6) Mr 88, p. 490-491.
"On Gibbs' Law." [Poetry] (153:3) D 88, p. 143.
5451. TURNER, Gordon
"In a Moment / Become Life." [CapilR] (48) 88, p. 5.
"Metaphors Where Coho." [CapilR] (48) 88, p. 4.
5452. TURNER, Lillian
"Cracklepatter." [CarolQ] (40:2) Wint 88, p. 90.
5453. TURNER, Marjorie L.
"The Redwoods." [Writer] (101:6) Je 88, p. 23.
5454. TURNER, Seneca
"Opus VI" (for Henry Dumas). [BlackALF] (22:2) Sum 88, p. 384-385.
5455. TUSSING, Raleigh
"Shit Kids." [HangL] (53) 88, p. 69.
5456. TVARDOVSKY, Alexander
"By Right of Memory" (tr. by Margareta O. Thompson). [NegC] (8:1/2) 88, p. 72-91.
5457. TWICHELL, Chase
"Chanel No. 5." [OhioR] (41) 88, p. 98-99.
"The Imaginary Land." [IndR] (11:3) Sum 88, p. 17.

"Lapses of Turquoise Sea." [Poetry] (152:4) Jl 88, p. 205-207.
"Worldliness." [AntR] (46:2) Spr 88, p. 250-253.

5458. TYLER, Robert L.
"From the Global Village." [Vis] (28) 88, p. 20.
"Sailing to Medicare." [WindO] (50) Aut 88, p. 25.

5459. TYLER, Steve
"My Cockroach." [Gargoyle] (35) 88, p. 154-155.

5460. TYNES, Maxine (Maxine N.)
"As the Book Begins." [PottPort] (9) 88, p. 51.
"Chameleon Silence." [CrossC] (10:2) 88, p. 3.

5461. TZARA, Tristan
"The Great Complaint of My Obscurity Three" (tr. by Marilyn Kallet). [Sonora] (14/15) Spr 88, p. 11.
"Wheat and Chaff" (A Partially Recovered Proclamation, tr. by Marilyn Kallet). [Sonora] (14/15) Spr 88, p. 12-13.

5462. ULLAH, Emdad
"The Empty Pitcher Lying Over Dry Ground" (tr. of Keshab Mahanta). [Nimrod] (31:2) Spr-Sum 88, p. 28.

5463. UMPHREY, Michael
"Black Ice." [CutB] (29/30) 88, p. 28-29.
"Resistance Is the Opposite of Escape." [CrabCR] (5:3) Fall 88, p. 24.

5464. UNDERWOOD, Jane
"Action." [FiveFR] (6) 88, p. 51.
"Of Returning." [FiveFR] (6) 88, p. 50.

5465. UNDERWOOD, Robert
"Bosch's *Mandragora by the Pool*." [PacificR] (6) Spr 88, p. 24.

5466. UNGAR, Barbara Louise
"Nonalogy (or, Myth of the Magic Grandma)." [CreamCR] (12:2) Sum 88, p. 290-291.

5467. UNGER, David
"Rain" (tr. of Carlos Oquendo de Amat). [AmerV] (10) Spr 88, p. 88.

5468. UNTERECKER, John
"Atoll." [HawaiiR] (12:2, #24) Fall 88, p. 32.
"Cross-Country." [ChamLR] (1:2, #2) Spr 88, p. 133.
"Elmwood Avenue" (the New Addition to Albright Art Gallery . . .). [ChamLR] (1:2, #2) Spr 88, p. 131-132.
"The Gift." [HawaiiR] (12:2, #24) Fall 88, p. 33-36.
"Midnight Guava: April 21." [HawaiiR] (12:2, #24) Fall 88, p. 31.
"Oahu: Midday Concert in Orange Air." [ChamLR] (1) Fall 87, p. 73.
"Passage." [HangL] (52) 88, p. 39-41.
"Praise." [MichQR] (27:4) Fall 88, p. 621.
"Preparing the Seed Bed." [HangL] (52) 88, p. 38.
"The White Stone Beach." [ChamLR] (2:1, #3) Fall 88, p. 3-5.

5469. UPDIKE, John
"Condo Moon." [NewYorker] (64:41) 28 N 88, p. 44.
"Déjà, Indeed." [LightY] ('88/9) 88, p. 84.
"Hot Water." [Shen] (38:2) 88, p. 41.
"Hymn to These Newly Abbreviated States" (Including Puerto Rico, the Virgin Islands, . . .). [LightY] ('88/9) 88, p. 150.
"Klimt and Schiele Confront the Cunt" (Reflections after Viewing the Vienna Show in Paris, 1986). [ParisR] (30:106) Spr 88, p. 203-204.
"Mites." [NewYorker] (64:22) 18 Jl 88, p. 30.
"Sails on All-Saints Day." [Shen] (38:2) 88, p. 40.
"Solitaire." [LightY] ('88/9) 88, p. 64.
"Tulsa." [OntR] (29) Fall-Wint 88-89, p. 18.
"Two Limericks After Lear." [LightY] ('88/9) 88, p. 170.
"Video." [OntR] (29) Fall-Wint 88-89, p. 18.
"Washington: Tourist View." [OntR] (29) Fall-Wint 88-89, p. 16-17.

5470. UPHAM, Sondra
"The Cellar." [PraS] (62:1) Spr 88, p. 76-77.
"The Lady's Slipper." [PraS] (62:1) Spr 88, p. 78.
"Meeting My Son's Girl." [PraS] (62:1) Spr 88, p. 77-78.

5471. UPTON, Lee
"The Faithful Wife." [WillowS] (21) Wint 88, p. 19.
"Invitation to Health." [Field] (39) Fall 88, p. 69-70.
"Jims Hairball." [Field] (39) Fall 88, p. 72-73.

"Narratives." [DenQ] (23:1) Sum 88, p. 81.
"Sold." [WillowS] (21) Wint 88, p. 17-18.
"Thank You Too Much." [DenQ] (23:1) Sum 88, p. 80.
"Unhappiness." [LitR] (31:2) Wint 88, p. 237.
"Water Gardening." [Field] (39) Fall 88, p. 71.

5472. USCHUK, Pamela
"Calendar of Thirst." [Ascent] (14:2) 88, p. 24-27.
"A Donde Vas?" [DenQ] (22:3) Wint 88, p. 139-140.
"With Its Toll of Char." [Pequod] (25) 88, p. 18-19.

5473. USHANAS
"Haiku" (2 poems, tr. by Sneharashmi). [Nimrod] (31:2) Spr-Sum 88, p. 73.

VALENCIA, Ali ben Hariq of
See BEN HARIQ OF VALENCIA, Ali

5474. VALENTINE, Jean
"The Counsellor Retires, and Then He Dies." [NewYorker] (63:49) 25 Ja 88, p. 34.
"Everything Starts with a Letter." [NewYorker] (63:49) 25 Ja 88, p. 34.
"High School Boyfriend." [AmerPoR] (17:2) Mr-Ap 88, p. 56.
"The King." [NewYorker] (64:20) 4 Jl 88, p. 22.
"Spring and Its Flowers." [Boulevard] (3:2/3) Fall 88, p. 40.
"Trust Me." [Boulevard] (3:2/3) Fall 88, p. 39.

5475. VALERO, Roberto
"Oír Crecer la Hierba." [Lyra] (1:4) 88, p. 29.
"Plymouth, 1657." [Lyra] (1:4) 88, p. 28.

5476. VALIS, Noël
"Ugly Duckling." [CentR] (32:1) Wint 88, p. 35-36.

VALLE, Pompeyo del
See Del VALLE, Pompeyo

5477. VALLE, Victor
"Teófilo." [Rohwedder] (3) Spr 88, p. 21-23.

5478. VALLEJO, César
"Trilce XXXIII" (Accompanying English "version" by Joe Bolton). [StoneC] (16:1/2) Fall-Wint 88-89, p. 22.

5479. VALLS ARANGO, Jorge
"The Nightingale" (tr. by Emilio Bernal Labrada). [Vis] (26) 88, p. 51.
"There Is No Light" (tr. by Emilio Bernal Labrada). [Vis] (26) 88, p. 51.

Van . . .
See also names beginning with "Van" without the following space, filed below in their alphabetic positions.

Van BRUNT, H. L.
See Van BRUNT, Lloyd

5480. Van BRUNT, Lloyd
"The Girl Who Learned to Pose for Photographers." [Blueline] (9:1/2) 88, p. 95-96.
"I Fall in Love with Nancy Drew." [SouthernPR] (28:1) Spr 88, p. 27.
"Quartered with the Sun." [SouthernPR] (28:1) Spr 88, p. 28-29.
"The Stars Like Minstrels Sing to Blake." [SoDakR] (26:2) Sum 88, p. 100-101.

5481. Van DOREN, John
"Alive." [CumbPR] (7:2) Spr 88, p. 65-66.

5482. Van DUYN, Mona
"Double Sonnet for Minimalists." [NewRep] (199:26) 26 D 88, p. 36.
"Falling in Love at Sixty-Five." [Poetry] (151:5) F 88, p. 411-412.
"Journal Jottings" (for Eli). [YaleR] (77:4) Sum 88, p. 574-575.
"Last Words of Pig No. 6707." [GrandS] (7:3) Spr 88, p. 140-142.
"Memoir" (for Harry Ford). [YaleR] (77:4) Sum 88, p. 576-577.
"Pigeon Eggs" (for Peggy). [YaleR] (77:4) Sum 88, p. 572-574.
"To a Friend Who Threw Away Hair Dyes." [Poetry] (151:5) F 88, p. 411.

5483. Van HOUTEN, Lois
"Flesh." [Footwork] ('88) 88, p. 69.
"The Games That Sisters Play." [Footwork] ('88) 88, p. 69.
"Presence of Magic." [Footwork] ('88) 88, p. 69.
"The Room." [StoneC] (15:3/4) Spr-Sum 88, p. 53.

5484. Van METER, Suzanne
"Rejection." [Plain] (8:2) Wint 88, p. 37.

5485. Van NOORD, Barbara
"The Eye of the Beholder." [Vis] (28) 88, p. 12-13.

5486. Van POZNAK, Joan
"Euro-Squawk." [LightY] ('88/9) 88, p. 102.

"Sun Dance in St. Lucia." [LightY] ('88/9) 88, p. 63.

5487. Van RIPER, Craig
"Between Acts of Love." [SpoonRQ] (13:3) Sum 88, p. 49-50.
"Instructions for Desert Survival." [PassN] (9:2) Sum 88, p. 27.
"Morning." [Lactuca] (11) O 88, p. 20.
"La Vie Ordinaire." [Lactuca] (11) O 88, p. 19-20.

5488. Van SCHENDEL, Michel
"About a Sum and a Remainder" (tr. by Ben-Zion Shek). [CanLit] (117) Sum 88, p. 47.
"Another Ellipsis" (tr. by Ben-Zion Shek). [CanLit] (117) Sum 88, p. 51.
"Brief" (tr. by Ben-Zion Shek). [CanLit] (117) Sum 88, p. 46.
"Conversation" (tr. by Ben-Zion Shek). [CanLit] (117) Sum 88, p. 55-56.
"Discreet" (tr. by Ben-Zion Shek). [CanLit] (117) Sum 88, p. 51.
"Frail" (tr. by Ben-Zion Shek). [CanLit] (117) Sum 88, p. 46.
"The heterogeneous is a laugh, a lack of order" (tr. by Ben-Zion Shek). [CanLit] (117) Sum 88, p. 49-50.
"Imagines Possessing" (tr. by Ben-Zion Shek). [CanLit] (117) Sum 88, p. 46.
"The musical flows from silence" (tr. by Ben-Zion Shek). [CanLit] (117) Sum 88, p. 56-57.
"A (Nearly) Unretouched Portrait" (tr. by Ben-Zion Shek). [CanLit] (117) Sum 88, p. 54-55.
"On the Line" (tr. by Ben-Zion Shek). [CanLit] (117) Sum 88, p. 54.
"A Pinch of Ink Is Just Too Much" (tr. by Ben-Zion Shek). [CanLit] (117) Sum 88, p. 52-53.
"Poem-drawing" (tr. by Ben-Zion Shek). [CanLit] (117) Sum 88, p. 51.
"The proverbial is an obelisk" (tr. by Ben-Zion Shek). [CanLit] (117) Sum 88, p. 48-49.
"A Request to My Trade-Union Comrades" (tr. by Ben-Zion Shek). [CanLit] (117) Sum 88, p. 48.
"The sensual: a knit of forms" (tr. by Ben-Zion Shek). [CanLit] (117) Sum 88, p. 45.
"She'd love the branch of slate" (tr. by Ben-Zion Shek). [CanLit] (117) Sum 88, p. 57.
"Sketch" (tr. by Ben-Zion Shek). [CanLit] (117) Sum 88, p. 45-46.
"Support" (tr. by Ben-Zion Shek). [CanLit] (117) Sum 88, p. 47.
"The Tea-Rose Unties the Tongue" (tr. by Ben-Zion Shek). [CanLit] (117) Sum 88, p. 56.
"Three Words Three Points" (tr. by Ben-Zion Shek). [CanLit] (117) Sum 88, p. 51-52.
"We Shall Go All the Way to the Star Beamed by the City" (tr. by Ben-Zion Shek). [CanLit] (117) Sum 88, p. 45.
"Written on Rue Danton near Fertile Eyes or Homage to a Book" (tr. by Ben-Zion Shek). [CanLit] (117) Sum 88, p. 51.
"Written with a New Pen" (tr. by Ben-Zion Shek). [CanLit] (117) Sum 88, p. 53-54.

5489. Van WALLEGHEN, Michael
"Atlantis." [MidwQ] (30:1) Aut 88, p. 85-86.
"Bowling Alley." [Colum] (13) 88, p. 146-147.
"The Cat's Meow." [MidwQ] (30:1) Aut 88, p. 89-91.
"Mother Bear, Father Bear." [MidwQ] (30:1) Aut 88, p. 92.
"The Other World" (For O.S.-B., tr. of Dmitry Bobyshev). [Vis] (26) 88, p. 44.
"Return" (tr. of Dmitry Bobyshev). [Vis] (26) 88, p. 45, 47.
"Sneaky." [MidwQ] (30:1) Aut 88, p. 87-88.
"Tranquil Acres." [Boulevard] (3:2/3) Fall 88, p. 95-96.
"Trotsky in Mexico" (tr. of Dmitry Bobyshev). [Vis] (26) 88, p. 43.
"Worry." [Colum] (13) 88, p. 144-145.

5490. Van WIENEN, Mark
"The Second Eve." [Ascent] (13:2) 88, p. 17.

5491. Van WINCKEL, Nance
"Boy with Squirrel" (after the portrait by John Singleton Copley). [AnotherCM] (18) 88, p. 173.
"Calvary Baptist Church, 1957." [PoetryNW] (29:4) Wint 88-89, p. 24.
"Drill, 1957." [PoetryNW] (29:2) Sum 88, p. 20.
"Infidel." [NoAmR] (273:3) S 88, p. 45.
"Snowpeople." [Ascent] (13:3) 88, p. 36-37.
"Subterranean Gossip" (for Anita Endrezze). [PennR] (4:1) 88, p. 17-18.

"Trials." [CutB] (31/32) 88, p. 38-39.
"Two-Room Schoolhouse" (Mt. Vernon, Virginia 1958). [PennR] (4:1) 88, p. 19.

Vander . . .
See also names beginning with "Vander" without the following space, filed below in their alphabetic positions, e.g. VanderMOLEN.

5492. VANDERLIP, Brian
"Father Time." [MalR] (84) S 88, p. 116.
"Grandmother Turnip." [MalR] (84) S 88, p. 112.
"A Groundskeeper's Notebook." [MalR] (84) S 88, p. 113-115.

5493. VanderMOLEN, Robert
"The Gypsum Mines." [HawaiiR] (12:2, #24) Fall 88, p. 60.

5494. VANGELISTI, Paul
"Untitled (35 Lines, 1981-1987)." [Jacaranda] (3:2) Fall-Wint 88, p. 123.

5495. VANNATTA, Dennis
"From End to End the King." [Footwork] ('88) 88, p. 34.

5496. VARGA, Jon
"Notes for an Ancient Gardenia." [Wind] (18:63) 88, p. 43.

5497. VASQUEZ, Robert
"Coyotes." [Ploughs] (14:4) 88, p. 109-110.

5498. VAUGHAN, Judith
"At the Key West Lighthouse." [KeyWR] (1:2) Fall 88, p. 73-74.
"Descent." [KeyWR] (1:2) Fall 88, p. 71-72.
"Of Time and the Sea." [KeyWR] (1:2) Fall 88, p. 70.

5499. VAZQUEZ MENDEZ, Gonzalo
"Mi Pais." [Mairena] (10:25) 88, p. 78.

5500. VECCHIONE, Patrice
"Moving House." [YellowS] (26) Spr 88, p. 10.

5501. VEGA, Janine Pommy
"Catskill Drought." [AlphaBS] (4) D 88, p. 49.
"Madre Selva." [AlphaBS] (4) D 88, p. 48.

5502. VEGA, Suzanne
"Undertow." [ClockR] (4:2) 88, p. 19.

5503. VEIGA, Marisella L.
"Offering." [Americas] (16:2) Sum 88, p. 46.
"The Working Artist in the World: A Portrait." [Americas] (16:2) Sum 88, p. 47-48.

5504. VEINBERG, Jon
"The Hand That Once Held Fire." [GettyR] (1:2) Spr 88, p. 389.

5505. VEIRAVÉ, Alfredo
"Ruben Dario at the Beachhead" (tr. by Thorpe Running). [ColR] (NS 15:1) Spr-Sum 88, p. 80.

5506. VELA, Ruben
"America" (tr. by Zoe Anglesey). [ColR] (NS 15:2) Fall-Wint 88, p. 88.

VÉLEZ, Clemente Soto
See SOTO VÉLEZ, Clemente

5507. VELI, Orhan
"Epitaph I" (tr. by Murat Nemet-Nejat). [HangL] (53) 88, p. 38.
"Epitaph II" (tr. by Murat Nemet-Nejat). [HangL] (53) 88, p. 39.
"Epitaph III" (tr. by Murat Nemet-Nejat). [HangL] (53) 88, p. 40.
"The Galata Bridge" (tr. by Murat Nemet-Nejat). [HangL] (53) 88, p. 43.
"The Guest" (tr. by Murat Nemet-Nejat). [HangL] (53) 88, p. 42.
"I, Orhan Veli" (tr. by Murat Nemet-Nejat). [HangL] (53) 88, p. 44.
"To Keep Busy" (tr. by Murat Nemet-Nejat). [HangL] (53) 88, p. 41.

5508. VELIYANAR, Erumai
"The Horse Did Not Come Back" (tr. by A. K. Ramanujan). [PartR] (55:3) Sum 88, p. 519.

5509. VERNON, William J.
"The Bookstacks in Krogers." [FiveFR] (6) 88, p. 71.
"Kingfishers." [CapeR] (23:2) Fall 88, p. 44.
"Sugar Bird." [Blueline] (9:1/2) 88, p. 3.

5510. VERSENYI, Sue Lipsiner
"Death of the Rhine." [PaintedB] (34) 88, p. 94.
"Eulogy" (to Geogia O'Keefe [sic]). [PaintedB] (34) 88, p. 93.
"Jitterbug." [BellArk] (4:1) Ja-F 88, p. 6.
"New Teeth." [DenQ] (22:3) Wint 88, p. 178-179.

5511. VERSTEEG, Tom
"Entrance." [KanQ] (20:1/2) Wint-Spr 88, p. 212.

5512. VERTREACE, Martha M.
"Aborigine." [SpoonRQ] (13:1) Wint 88, p. 35.
"Aborigine." [SpoonRQ] (13:4) Fall 88, p. 38.
"American Impressionism." [SpoonRQ] (13:1) Wint 88, p. 36-37.
"Black Tulips." [SpoonRQ] (13:1) Wint 88, p. 45.
"Black Tulips." [SpoonRQ] (13:4) Fall 88, p. 46.
"Bookmarks." [SpoonRQ] (13:1) Wint 88, p. 34.
"Bookmarks." [SpoonRQ] (13:4) Fall 88, p. 37.
"Breakwater." [SpoonRQ] (13:1) Wint 88, p. 46.
"Breakwater." [SpoonRQ] (13:4) Fall 88, p. 47.
"Clotho." [SpoonRQ] (13:1) Wint 88, p. 47.
"Clotho." [SpoonRQ] (13:4) Fall 88, p. 48.
"Dublin, Cloudy." [SpoonRQ] (13:1) Wint 88, p. 33-34.
"Dublin, Cloudy." [SpoonRQ] (13:4) Fall 88, p. 36-37.
"Earthbound." [SpoonRQ] (13:1) Wint 88, p. 39.
"Earthbound." [SpoonRQ] (13:4) Fall 88, p. 40.
"Entering the Dream." [SpoonRQ] (13:1) Wint 88, p. 50-51.
"Entering the Dream." [SpoonRQ] (13:4) Fall 88, p. 51-52.
"Foreground Reversal." [SpoonRQ] (13:1) Wint 88, p. 40.
"Foreground Reversal." [SpoonRQ] (13:4) Fall 88, p. 41.
"Letter from France" (Auvers-sur-Oise, July, 1890). [SpoonRQ] (13:1) Wint 88, p. 43.
"Letter from France" (Auvers-sur-Oise, July, 1890). [SpoonRQ] (13:4) Fall 88, p. 44.
"On the Road to Lauves." [SpoonRQ] (13:1) Wint 88, p. 48.
"On the Road to Lauves." [SpoonRQ] (13:4) Fall 88, p. 49.
"Pelvis with the Moon." [SpoonRQ] (13:1) Wint 88, p. 38.
"Pelvis with the Moon." [SpoonRQ] (13:4) Fall 88, p. 39.
"Self-Portrait." [SpoonRQ] (13:1) Wint 88, p. 44.
"Self-Portrait." [SpoonRQ] (13:4) Fall 88, p. 45.
"Study from an Antique Cast, 1886." [SpoonRQ] (13:1) Wint 88, p. 41-42.
"Study from an Antique Cast, 1886." [SpoonRQ] (13:4) Fall 88, p. 42-43.
"Time Is a River Without Banks" (after Chagall). [SpoonRQ] (13:1) Wint 88, p. 49-50.
"Time Is a River Without Banks" (after Chagall). [SpoonRQ] (13:4) Fall 88, p. 50-51.
"Vincent in Flames." [SpoonRQ] (13:1) Wint 88, p. 42.
"Vincent in Flames." [SpoonRQ] (13:4) Fall 88, p. 43.

5513. VEST, Debra Kay
"Key Words." [CreamCR] (12:2) Sum 88, p. 295-297.
"The Last Word." [CreamCR] (12:2) Sum 88, p. 292-294.

5514. VETTER, Robert
"Burley Harvest, NYC." [Contact] (9:47/48/49) Spr 88, p. 37.

5515. VICENTE, Luis Miguel
"Delirio." [Mester] (17:1) Spr 88, p. 51.
"Paisaje." [Mester] (17:1) Spr 88, p. 52.
"Pensando en Cernuda." [Mester] (17:1) Spr 88, p. 50.

5516. VICONDOA, Brenda
"After August." [Writer] (101:3) Mr 88, p. 19.

5517. VICTOR, David A.
"Independence Lake." [PassN] (9:1) Wint 88, p. 12.

5518. VIDALES, Luis
"Paisaje Junto a las Fabricas." [Mairena] (10:25) 88, p. 43.

5519. VIERECK, Peter
"The Planted Poet." [TexasR] (9:3/4) Fall-Wint 88, p. 135-137.

5520. VIGIL-PIÑON, Evangelina
"Blessing." [Americas] (16:1) Spr 88, p. 114.
"Camposanto." [Americas] (16:1) Spr 88, p. 112-113.
"Cuando el Destino" (for Ernie Olivares). [Americas] (16:3/4) Fall-Wint 88, p. 45-47.
"Día de los Muertos." [Americas] (16:1) Spr 88, p. 109-111.
"Dumb Broad!" [Americas] (16:1) Spr 88, p. 103-105.
"Space City" (to the architects of the future). [Americas] (16:1) Spr 88, p. 101-102.
"They're Everywhere." [Americas] (16:1) Spr 88, p. 106-108.

5521. VILLAFUERTE, Ovidio
"Cancion de Amor a la Patria." [Mairena] (10:25) 88, p. 156-157.

5522. VILLANI, Jim
"Stars on Lake." [CinPR] (18) Fall 88, p. 30.
5523. VILLANUEVA, Tino
"El Angosto Marco de Mi Tiempo." [HangL] (52) 88, p. 76.
"In My Narrow Frame of Time" (tr. by the author). [HangL] (52) 88, p. 77.
5524. VILLANUEVA-COLLADO, Alfredo
"IV. Cómo me dan pena los machos al cuadrado." [Inti] (28) Otoño 88, p. 178.
"Arte Poética." [Inti] (28) Otoño 88, p. 177.
"Invocación desde el Pentáculo." [Inti] (28) Otoño 88, p. 178-179.
"Liber Escriptus." [Inti] (28) Otoño 88, p. 179-180.
5525. VILLARINO, José
"Corrido, Homenaje a Tomás Rivera" (Y no se lo tragó la tierra). [BilingR] (13:1/2) Ja-Ag 86, c1988, p. 89-91.
5526. VILLON, François
"Villon's Quatrain" (tr. by David Lunde). [LightY] ('88/9) 88, p. 70.
5527. VINCIGUERRA, Theresa
"The Meadow." [YellowS] (28) D 88, p. 28.
VINCK, Christopher de
See De VINCK, Christopher
5528. VINH, Nguyen Quoc
"Autumn Inspiration" (in English and Vietnamese, tr. by the author). [InterPR] (14:1) Spr 88, p. 71.
"Autumn Inspiration" (in Vietnamese and English, tr. by the author). [Os] (26) 88, p. 22-23.
"Escape by Crossing the Ocean" (in English and Vietnamese, tr. by the author). [InterPR] (14:1) Spr 88, p. 71.
"Escape by Crossing the Ocean" (in Vietnamese and English, tr. by the author). [Os] (26) 88, p. 20-21.
5529. VINOGRAD, Julia
"Inheritance." [FiveFR] (6) 88, p. 84.
"Inhuman Atrocities." [FiveFR] (6) 88, p. 83.
5530. VINZ, Mark
"The Blues." [NoDaQ] (56:4) Fall 88, p. 82.
"Call of the Wild." [SoDakR] (26:2) Sum 88, p. 79.
"Country Roads." [NoDaQ] (56:4) Fall 88, p. 81-82.
"Driving with Hugo in the Rain." [Abraxas] (37) 88, p. 76.
"First Snow." [NoDaQ] (56:4) Fall 88, p. 81.
"The Last Time." [Abraxas] (37) 88, p. 75.
"Late Night Calls." [NoDaQ] (56:4) Fall 88, p. 82.
"A Mighty Fortress." [SoDakR] (26:2) Sum 88, p. 78.
"Testing the Water." [SoDakR] (26:2) Sum 88, p. 77.
VIOLA, Hugo Giovanetti
See GIOVANETTI VIOLA, Hugo
5531. VIOLI, Paul
"Little Testament" (Excerpt). [Epoch] (37:2) 88, p. 120-124.
"Little Testament" (Excerpt). [NewAW] (3) Spr 88, p. 31-41.
5532. VIRGIN, Daniil
"Verses" (tr. by Daniel Weissbort). [NegC] (8:1/2) 88, p. 41-42.
5533. VITALE, Ida
"Amanecer del Solo." [Inti] (26/27) Otoño 87-Primavera 88, p. 361.
"La Batalla." [Inti] (26/27) Otoño 87-Primavera 88, p. 359.
"Naturalismo." [Inti] (26/27) Otoño 87-Primavera 88, p. 361.
"Pálidas Señas." [Inti] (26/27) Otoño 87-Primavera 88, p. 360-361.
"Reunión." [Inti] (26/27) Otoño 87-Primavera 88, p. 359-360.
"Sala de Profesores." [Inti] (26/27) Otoño 87-Primavera 88, p. 360.
5534. VITKA, Vasil
"Rye" (tr. by Walter May). [NegC] (8:1/2) 88, p. 37.
VITO, E. B. de
See De VITO, E. B.
5535. VOEGE, Jeanne
"Willie, Is That You?" [Spirit] (9:1) 88, p. 118.
5536. VOGEL, S.
"A Substitute Need Not Explain." [EngJ] (77:1) Ja 88, p. 102.
5537. VOGELSANG, Arthur
"The Companion." [WestHR] (42:3) Aut 88, p. 247-248.
"Fate Awake, Dreams Accidents." [MSS] (6:2) 88, p. 96-97.

"Glass Breaking in the Night." [PartR] (55:2) Spr 88, p. 284-285.
"The Hebrus River." [Verse] (5:1) F 88, p. 26.
"Photo from Memory." [AntR] (46:1) Wint 88, p. 76-77.
"Rain." [MSS] (6:2) 88, p. 95.
"Where? There. Where? Here." [AntR] (46:1) Wint 88, p. 78.

5538. VOIGT, Ellen Bryant
"Jug Brook." [TexasR] (9:3/4) Fall-Wint 88, p. 138.

5539. VOLDSETH, Beverly
"Road Song." [RagMag] (6:2) Fall 88, p. 51.
"We Walk the Beach on Lake Michigan." [RagMag] (6:1) [88], p. 42.

5540. VOLEK, Bronislava
"American Now." [Vis] (26) 88, p. 22.
"Winter Came" (tr. by the author and Willis Barnstone). [Vis] (26) 88, p. 21.

VOLKOVA, Bronislava
See VOLEK, Bronislava

5541. VOLLMER, Judith
"Motel, on the Anniversary of the Death of John Belushi." [SouthernPR] (28:1) Spr 88, p. 11-12.

Von HOFMANNSTHAL, Hugo
See HOFMANNSTHAL, Hugo von

Von REIS, Siri
See REIS, Siri von

5542. VOSS, Sarah
"Restraint." [Plain] (8:3) Spr-Sum 88, p. 16.
"The Stories He Tells." [Plain] (9:1) Fall 88, p. 33.

5543. VOURVOULIAS, Sabrina
"Suite for Rosario Godoy de Cuevas." [GrahamHR] (11) Spr 88, p. 31-33.

5544. VYARTSINSKI, Anatol
"Requiem for Every Fourth" (tr. by Walter May). [NegC] (8:1/2) 88, p. 33-36.

5545. VYSOTSKY, Vladimir
"Ginger Moll" (tr. by Gerald Stanton Smith). [NegC] (8:1/2) 88, p. 43.

5546. WAAGE, Fred
"To Sleeping Children — Labor Day, '85." [Lactuca] (11) O 88, p. 3.

5547. WADDINGTON, J.
"Long Distance." [Grain] (16:2) Sum 88, p. 28.

5548. WADE, Cheryl Marie
"I Am Not One of The." [SinW] (35) Sum-Fall 88, p. 24.

5549. WADE, Seth
"A Little Confession." [Bogg] (59) 88, p. 38.

5550. WADE, Sidney
"In Praise of Degeneration." [GrandS] (7:2) Wint 88, p. 182-184.
"In Praise of Degeneration." [Harp] (277:1658) Jl 88, p. 37.

5551. WADSWORTH, William
"The Authority of Elsewhere." [GrandS] (7:4) Sum 88, p. 161-162.

5552. WAGNER, Anneliese
"Break." [HiramPoR] (44/45) Spr-Wint 88, p. 43.
"Everything." [WestB] (21/22) 88, p. 136.
"Gate." [WestB] (21/22) 88, p. 137.
"Hot September Day." [HiramPoR] (44/45) Spr-Wint 88, p. 42.
"Imaginary Friends: Schuli and Bubi." [WestB] (21/22) 88, p. 137.
"Stopover in India" (The Goulds take a trip around the world). [Confr] (37/38) Spr-Sum 88, p. 117.
"Yes, it's true, at midnight" (tr. of Elisabeth Borchers). [StoneC] (16:1/2) Fall-Wint 88-89, p. 64.
"You Are Far Away." [StoneC] (15:3/4) Spr-Sum 88, p. 70.

5553. WAGNER, D. R.
"Ambulances to the Heart." [Abraxas] (37) 88, p. 13.
"Burning the Stairs." [Abraxas] (37) 88, p. 10.
"Promise me that you will tell no one about this poem." [Abraxas] (37) 88, p. 11.
"When the Imagination Is Unleashed." [Abraxas] (37) 88, p. 12.

5554. WAGNER, Kathy
"On the Washington D.C. Metro." [Sequoia] (31:2) Wint 88, p. 64.
"Quaker Neck Public Landing." [Sequoia] (31:2) Wint 88, p. 65.

5555. WAGNER, Robert
"Letter to Paul." [Abraxas] (37) 88, p. 39.

5556. WAGNER, Shari
"Family Tree (Kenya, 1973)." [ArtfulD] (14/15) Fall 88, p. 7.
"The Farmer's Wife." [BlackWR] (14:2) Spr 88, p. 77.
5557. WAGONER, David
"Come with Me." [Poetry] (152:4) Jl 88, p. 221-222.
"Dizzy." [Poetry] (152:4) Jl 88, p. 221.
"My Vision." [WestHR] (42:2) Sum 88, p. 142-144.
5558. WAHLE, F. Keith
"Car Crash." [CinPR] (17) Spr 88, p. 13.
5559. WAID, Mark
"Optimal Bull." [Sink] (3) 88, p. 12-13.
"Shakes." [Sink] (3) 88, p. 9-11.
5560. WAINWRIGHT, Sonny
"For Those of Us Who Know We're Dying." [Cond] (15) 88, p. 2-6.
5561. WAISANEN, Michael
"Flowers from Various Angles." [Plain] (8:2) Wint 88, p. 14.
5562. WAKEFIELD, Kathleen
"She Sings to Her Child." [Amelia] (4:4, #11) 88, p. 65.
5563. WAKOSKI, Diane
"All the Paperweights I've Never Bought for You" (to Bernie Paris). [ManhatPR] (10) Ja 88, p. 18-19.
"Clearing the Palette (sic), In Lieu of an Essay." [ManhatPR] (10) Ja 88, p. 22-23.
"Listening to Whales." [ManhatPR] (10) Ja 88, p. 21-22.
"Red in the Morning." [PassN] (9:2) Sum 88, p. 18.
"Through the Looking Glass." [ManhatPR] (10) Ja 88, p. 20-21.
"Waiting for the Morning Glories." [CreamCR] (12:1) Wint 88, p. 71-72.
5564. WALCOTT, Derek
"Omeros" (Selections: Chapter XXV-XXVI). [WestHR] (42:4) Wint 88, p. 275-280.
5565. WALDMAN, Anne
"A Name As Revery." [Talisman] (1) Fall 88, p. 67.
"Under My Breatjh." [AmerPoR] (17:6) N-D 88, p. 56.
5566. WALDMAN, Marianne Wolfe
"Quilts." [Spirit] (9:1) 88, p. 91.
5567. WALDROP, Keith
"Instances of Echoes." [Sink] (3) 88, p. 14.
"Internal Evidence." [Sink] (3) 88, p. 15.
"An Involuntary Winter." [Sink] (3) 88, p. 16.
5568. WALDROP, Rosmarie
"Lawn of Excluded Middle" (4 selections). [Notus] (3:2) Fall 88, p. 8-11.
"Some Thing Black" (Selections: 9 poems, tr. of Jacques Roubaud). [Temblor] (8) 88, p. 87-90.
5569. WALKER, Brenda
"Temptation" (tr. of Nina Cassian, w. Andrea Deletant). [AmerPoR] (17:2) Mr-Ap 88, p. 48.
5570. WALKER, Jeanne Murray
"American Tourist at Covent Garden." [PraS] (62:3) Fall 88, p. 22-23.
"Cold War." [PraS] (62:3) Fall 88, p. 26-27.
"Cutpurse." [PraS] (62:3) Fall 88, p. 24.
"Driving by Westminster Abbey after Midnight." [PraS] (62:3) Fall 88, p. 25.
"Extravagance." [CreamCR] (12:2) Sum 88, p. 300.
"How Labor Starts." [AmerV] (12) Fall 88, p. 34-35.
"Journal Entry: Remembering the Tate Gallery." [CreamCR] (12:2) Sum 88, p. 298-299.
"London Underground." [PraS] (62:3) Fall 88, p. 28-29.
"The *National Enquirer* Headline Writer Calls Etheridge Knight to Interview Him About Gravity." [PaintedB] (32/33) 88, p. 37.
"Paddington Station at Midnight." [PraS] (62:3) Fall 88, p. 27-28.
5571. WALKER, Leon
"Playing Alone." [Plain] (8:2) Wint 88, p. 30.
"Well, Here I Go Again." [Plain] (8:1) Fall 87, p. 29.
5572. WALKER, Sue
"Carson McCullers' Fevered Heart." [Pembroke] (20) 88, p. 8.
"Little Precious." [Pembroke] (20) 88, p. 9.
5573. WALL, Janine L.
"The Day I Threw the Oats." [PoetryNW] (29:3) Aut 88, p. 9-10.

5574. WALLACE, Bruce
"June 21st: Teach Me, Quick, the Moon Is Falling." [Plain] (9:1) Fall 88, p. 19.
"The Leap." [Plain] (8:2) Wint 88, p. 23.
"No Stone Wings Allowed." [Plain] (8:1) Fall 87, p. 14.
"Pausing in the Woods at Midnight by a Forgotten Cemetery." [WindO] (50) Aut 88, p. 48.
"The Water Boy." [Plain] (9:1) Fall 88, p. 19.
5575. WALLACE, Jan
"Anima." [BellArk] (4:3) My-Je 88, p. 3.
"Meditation As I Lose My Brakes on Aurora." [BellArk] (4:1) Ja-F 88, p. 20.
"Serious Underwear." [BellArk] (4:1) Ja-F 88, p. 1.
5576. WALLACE, Mark
"On the Veranda." [HawaiiR] (12:1, #23) Spr 88, p. 33.
5577. WALLACE, Robert
"Dig for Her the Narrow Bed." [LightY] ('88/9) 88, p. 187.
"For a Long Time." [NoDaQ] (56:3) Sum 88, p. 53.
"Goats in the Road." [NoDaQ] (56:3) Sum 88, p. 52-53.
"The Poem." [LaurelR] (22:21) Wint 88, p. 27.
"Riding in a Stranger's Funeral." [TarRP] (27:2) Spr 88, p. 38.
"Tell the Chipmunk." [LaurelR] (22:21) Wint 88, p. 26-27.
"Thinking About Gravesites." [TarRP] (27:2) Spr 88, p. 39.
5578. WALLACE, Ronald
"Apple Cider." [Poetry] (152:6) S 88, p. 321.
"Astronomy." [TarRP] (28:1) Fall 88, p. 31.
"At Forty." [TarRP] (28:1) Fall 88, p. 32.
"Building an Outhouse." [CreamCR] (12:2) Sum 88, p. 301.
"The Fat of the Land." [Poetry] (152:6) S 88, p. 322.
"Florida." [Poem] (59) My 88, p. 64.
"Flying the Friendly Skies." [Poem] (59) My 88, p. 63.
"The Fox in the Berry Patch." [LaurelR] (22:2) Sum 88, p. 51.
"Hairpin." [CreamCR] (12:2) Sum 88, p. 302.
"The Hell Mural" (2 poems with same title). [PraS] (62:1) Spr 88, p. 106-108.
"The Makings of Happiness." [PoetryNW] (29:3) Aut 88, p. 15.
"Migrations." [Poem] (59) My 88, p. 65.
"Natives." [Poem] (59) My 88, p. 66.
"Off the Record." [PoetryNW] (29:3) Aut 88, p. 14.
"Speeding." [LaurelR] (22:21) Wint 88, p. 69.
"Staked." [TarRP] (28:1) Fall 88, p. 33.
5579. WALLACE, T. S.
"The Author Writes Himself a Short History of the Heartland." [Footwork] ('88) 88, p. 14.
"From the Cities of Appetite." [NegC] (8:3) 88, p. 113.
"Garden Party." [CumbPR] (7:2) Spr 88, p. 67-68.
"So the Old Beggar with the Bow Can Shoot as Straight as Death." [Footwork] ('88) 88, p. 13.
5580. WALLACE-CRABBE, Chris
"An Elegy." [PraS] (62:4) Wint 88-89, p. 34-35.
"The Fire-Bringers" (from a Tasmanian legend). [PraS] (62:4) Wint 88-89, p. 35-36.
"Innocence." [PraS] (62:4) Wint 88-89, p. 32-33.
"Spa." [PraS] (62:4) Wint 88-89, p. 33-34.
WALLEGHEN, Michael van
See Van WALLEGHEN, Michael
5581. WALLENFELS, Immy
"Cat Sonnet." [Amelia] (5:2, #13) 88, p. 41.
"October." [Vis] (28) 88, p. 31.
5582. WALLENSTEIN, Barry
"Boy Up a Tree." [Pembroke] (20) 88, p. 171.
5583. WALLER, Kim
"Kim's Dreamsong, 1987" (w. Philip Booth, in memory of Gabrielle Ladd, 1937-1960). [CreamCR] (12:2) Sum 88, p. 303.
5584. WALLS, Doyle Wesley
"Found Poem." [Abraxas] (37) 88, p. 62.
5585. WALSH, Michael
"Prehistoric Flowers." [ChamLR] (2:1, #3) Fall 88, p. 36.

5586. WALSH, Phyllis
"August Hail." [KanQ] (20:3) Sum 88, p. 50.
5587. WALSH, William
"The Tyburn Tree." [DeKalbLAJ] (21:1) Wint 88, p. 73.
5588. WALTER, Eugene
"Poetry in Various Modes, 1935-1988." [NegC] (8:4, Special Number: the polyfarious Eugene Walter) 88, p. 21-38.
5589. WALTERS, Madonna
"Poem for My Father." [PassN] (9:1) Wint 88, p. 5.
5590. WALTHALL, Hugh
"Frantic Ease: An Examination." [Shen] (38:3) 88, p. 75-76.
"The Perfect Name for a Racehorse" (for Joan Retallack). [Shen] (38:2) 88, p. 44-45.
"Revodneb" (Bendover, backwards). [Shen] (38:3) 88, p. 74.
5591. WALTON, Gary
"Dusk in Norwood, Ohio (or Song to Life on a One-Way, Dead-End)." [CinPR] (17) Spr 88, p. 69.
5592. WALTON, Judith Ames
"A Tour of Eastern State Mental Hospital." [Phoenix] (9:1/2) 88, p. 37.
5593. WALWICZ, Ania
"The Abattoir." [NewAW] (4) Fall 88, p. 135.
"Big Red." [NewAW] (4) Fall 88, p. 138-139.
"Big Tease." [NewAW] (4) Fall 88, p. 134.
"Daredevil." [NewAW] (4) Fall 88, p. 134.
"Evening." [NewAW] (4) Fall 88, p. 135-137.
"Max, the Axe." [NewAW] (4) Fall 88, p. 137-138.
5594. WAMPLER, Pamela
"Adultery." [PraS] (62:3) Fall 88, p. 78-79.
"Anniversary." [BlackWR] (15:1) Fall 88, p. 11.
"Girls Watching Pubescent Boys in the River." [BlackWR] (15:1) Fall 88, p. 9.
"The Morning Song." [BlackWR] (15:1) Fall 88, p. 10.
"September 19th." [PraS] (62:3) Fall 88, p. 77-78.
"What She Wished for When She Blew Out the Candles on Her Sixteenth Birthday." [CutB] (29/30) 88, p. 84.
"Words for a Daughter." [BlackWR] (15:1) Fall 88, p. 12.
5595. WANG, Qing-ling
"In Autumn Days" (tr. of Geng Wei). [MidAR] (8:1) 88, p. 14-15.
5596. WANG, Wei
"About Old Age, in Answer to a Poem by Zhang Shaofu" (tr. by Tony Barnstone, Willis Barnstone, and Xu Haixin). [ArtfulD] (14/15) Fall 88, p. 81.
"Drifting on the Lake" (tr. by Tony Barnstone, Willis Barnstone, and Xu Haixin). [ArtfulD] (14/15) Fall 88, p. 81.
"East River Moon" (tr. by Tony Barnstone, Willis Barnstone, and Xu Haixin). [ArtfulD] (14/15) Fall 88, p. 80.
"Lazy about Writing Poems" (tr. by Tony Barnstone, Willis Barnstone, and Xu Haixin). [ArtfulD] (14/15) Fall 88, p. 80.
"Pepper Plant Garden" (tr. by Joseph Lisowski). [HiramPoR] (44/45) Spr-Wint 88, p. 31.
"Red Peonies" (tr. by Tony Barnstone, Willis Barnstone, and Xu Haixin). [ArtfulD] (14/15) Fall 88, p. 81.
5597. WANG, Xiao-long
"In Memoriam" (Dedicated respectfully before my father's funeral urn, " (in Chinese & English). [BelPoJ] (39:2) Wint 88-89, p. 50-53.
"In Memory of the Space Ship Challenger" (in Chinese & English). [BelPoJ] (39:2) Wint 88-89, p. 54-61.
"The Third Eye" (in Chinese & English). [BelPoJ] (39:2) Wint 88-89, p. 48-49.
5598. WANG, Xiao-ni
"Going Astray" (tr. by Edward Morin and Dennis Ding). [WebR] (13:2) Fall 88, p. 17.
"The Wind Is Roaring" (tr. by Edward Morin and Dennis Ding). [Spirit] (9:1) 88, p. 100.
5599. WANG, Zhihuan
"Bamboo Growing Out of a Rock" (1693-1765 — Ch'ing Dynasty, tr. of Cheng Pan-ch'iao). [AntR] (46:2) Spr 88, p. 221.
"Untitled: So hard for us to meet" (A.D. 813-858 — T'ang Dynasty, tr. of Li Shang-yin). [AntR] (46:2) Spr 88, p. 203.

"Written During a Storm" (A.D. 1192, at 68 years of age, in retirement in Chekiang Prov., tr. of Lu Yiu). [AntR] (46:2) Spr 88, p. 196.

5600. WANICK, Marilyn
"Space Dog" (tr. of Thorkild Bjornvig). [ColR] (NS 15:2) Fall-Wint 88, p. 72-73.

5601. WARD, Dave
"A dove lives in her belly." [Bogg] (60) 88, p. 10.
"Her body fades." [Bogg] (59) 88, p. 28.
"She is a photograph of herself." [Bogg] (60) 88, p. 10.
"A street in black and white." [Bogg] (60) 88, p. 10.

5602. WARD, David Scott
"The Fire." [ChatR] (9:1) Fall 88, p. 34-35.
"Hunting in Twilight." [TexasR] (9:1/2) Spr-Sum 88, p. 86-87.

5603. WARD, Deborah
"The Scream" (after the woodcut by Edvard Munch). [NoAmR] (273:3) D 88, p. 51.

5604. WARD, Diane
"Gone So." [Temblor] (8) 88, p. 40-41.

5605. WARD, Gene Denys
"City Sizzle." [Amelia] (5:2, #13) 88, p. 29-30.
"Down the Do-Wop Street." [Amelia] (5:2, #13) 88, p. 28-29.
"July Night." [Amelia] (5:2, #13) 88, p. 31-32.
"Rolla Skatin Boy." [Amelia] (5:2, #13) 88, p. 27.
"Summer." [Amelia] (5:2, #13) 88, p. 30.

5606. WARD, Philip
"Arise, Dear Neighbor" (from Bogg 30, 1975). [Bogg] (59) 88, p. 41.

5607. WARD, Robert
"Death." [AnotherCM] (18) 88, p. 174-177.

5608. WARD, Robert J.
"If I'll Meet Any Fountain" (tr. of Anghel Dumbraveanu, w. Marcel Pop-Cornis). [NewRena] (7:2, #22) Spr 88, p. 73.
"The Seaman's Window" (tr. of Anghel Dumbraveanu, w. Marcel Pop-Cornis). [NewRena] (7:2, #22) Spr 88, p. 75.

5609. WARD, Robert R.
"Kelcema Lake, October, 1987." [BellArk] (4:6) N-D 88, p. 4.
"Listen to the Music: It's Part of the Dance." [BellArk] (4:1) Ja-F 88, p. 5.
"Some Day, Even Numbers Will Play." [BellArk] (4:1) Ja-F 88, p. 5.
"Stumping." [Farm] (5:2) Fall 88, p. 70-71.

5610. WARD, Scott
"Driving in a Thunderstorm" (for M. B. E.). [SouthernPR] (28:1) Spr 88, p. 25.
"My Brothers Make a Lantern." [SouthernPR] (28:1) Spr 88, p. 24-25.

5611. WARE, Karen
"Melodies vs Anthems." [PottPort] (10) 88, p. 36.

WARHAFT, Gail Holst
See HOLST-WARHAFT, Gail

5612. WARNER, Barrett
"After the Closing." [Turnstile] (1:2) 88, p. 60.

5613. WARREN, Charlotte Gould
"Choices." [StoneC] (15:3/4) Spr-Sum 88, p. 29.
"Old Tree with Plum Blossoms." [BellArk] (4:3) My-Je 88, p. 9.

5614. WARREN, Chris
"Jerusalem." [CapilR] (48) 88, p. 10-11.
"Red Rocket." [CapilR] (48) 88, p. 9.

5615. WARREN, Rebecca
"Siberia." [SouthernPR] (28:2) Fall 88, p. 43.

5616. WARREN, Rosanna
"Child Model" (Greenland Eskimo mummy, boy, four years old,... February 1985. For Rosalie Carlson). [SouthwR] (73:2) Spr 88, p. 208.
"The Cost." [NewRep] (199:18) 31 O 88, p. 35.
"Country Music." [Verse] (5:1) F 88, p. 59.
"Eskimo Widow." [Verse] (5:1) F 88, p. 60.
"Love in the Shop" (tr. of Pierre Reverdy). [AmerPoR] (17:4) Jl-Ag 88, p. 41.
"Sacrament." [Verse] (5:1) F 88, p. 60.
"Same Taste" (tr. of Pierre Reverdy). [AmerPoR] (17:4) Jl-Ag 88, p. 41.
"Tide-Pickers." [SouthwR] (73:2) Spr 88, p. 209.
"Verso" (tr. of Pierre Reverdy). [AmerPoR] (17:4) Jl-Ag 88, p. 41.

5617. WARSAW, Irene
"Slither Thither." [LightY] ('88/9) 88, p. 99-100.

5618. WARSH, Lewis
"Athens '69." [Notus] (3:2) Fall 88, p. 55.
"By the Fire." [Notus] (3:2) Fall 88, p. 52-53.
"No Victims." [Notus] (3:2) Fall 88, p. 56.
"Sister Agatha's Lament." [Notus] (3:2) Fall 88, p. 54.
5619. WARSHAWSKI, Morrie
"Going to Sleep." [CutB] (31/32) 88, p. 103.
"In the Cards." [CutB] (31/32) 88, p. 104.
"The Question of Live Hides." [YellowS] (27) Aut 88, p. 29.
5620. WARTH, Robert
"The Butter Festival of Choni." [HawaiiR] (12:2, #24) Fall 88, p. 56.
"Lirazel." [Plain] (8:3) Spr-Sum 88, p. 9.
5621. WARWICK, Joanna-Veronika (Joanne, Ioanna-Veronika)
"Blood Soup." [Vis] (26) 88, p. 34.
"Captain Cook Encounters the Natives of New Holland." [PacificR] (6) Spr 88, p. 64-65.
"Europe After the Rain" (after Max Ernst). [Rohwedder] (4) [Wint 88-89], p. 18.
"Exile" (for Robert Pinsky). [Jacaranda] (3:2) Fall-Wint 88, p. 126-128.
"Fish" (tr. of Zbigniew Herbert). [Thrpny] (35) Fall 88, p. 26.
"The High Diver" (for Charles). [Jacaranda] (3:2) Fall-Wint 88, p. 128-130.
"The Ice Palace." [SouthernPR] (28:1) Spr 88, p. 5-6.
"The Lady Knows How to Die" (a French officer at the execution of Mata Hari). [SoDakR] (26:3) Aut 88, p. 107-109.
"Letter from Kafka." [Jacaranda] (3:2) Fall-Wint 88, p. 124-126.
"Letter from Kafka." [Rohwedder] (4) [Wint 88-89], p. 18-19.
"Letter to Anna Karenina." [SoDakR] (26:3) Aut 88, p. 110-111.
"Member of the Church." [PoetC] (20:1) Fall 88, p. 5-7.
"Moje Serce." [PacificR] (6) Spr 88, p. 66-67.
"Mushroom Picking." [SoDakR] (26:3) Aut 88, p. 104-106.
"My Real Life" (for Steven). [Rohwedder] (3) Spr 88, p. 25.
"Witch." [NegC] (8:3) 88, p. 74-75.
5622. WAS, Elizabeth
"Every Lines Other" (Selection: ii. Re: Turn). [Sink] (3) 88, p. 26-31.
5623. WASNER, Alinda Dickinson
"Thin Ice." [PassN] (9:2) Sum 88, p. 30.
"Untitled: After the sun goes down." [Amelia] (4:4, #11) 88, p. 81.
5624. WASSERMAN, E. H.
"Joseph" (1885-1983). [ChatR] (8:3) Spr 88, p. 61-62.
5625. WASSERMAN, Rosanne
"Pillow Dreams of a Woman She Loves." [Caliban] (4) 88, p. 161.
5626. WASSON, Kirsten
"In the Right Hands." [Ascent] (13:2) 88, p. 32.
5627. WAT, Aleksander
"An Attempt to Describe the Last Skirmish of the Second World War" (to my brother, tr. by Czeslaw Milosz and Leonard Nathan). [Antaeus] (60) Spr 88, p. 62-63.
"Before a Weimar Portrait of Dürer" (in two variations, tr. by Czeslaw Milosz and Leonard Nathan). [Antaeus] (60) Spr 88, p. 60-61.
"Childhood of a Poet" (tr. by Czeslaw Milosz and Leonard Nathan). [Antaeus] (60) Spr 88, p. 48.
"Facing Bonnard" (tr. by Czeslaw Milosz and Leonard Nathan). [Antaeus] (60) Spr 88, p. 47.
"From Hesiod" (tr. by Czeslaw Milosz and Leonard Nathan). [Antaeus] (60) Spr 88, p. 64-65.
"Leaves whirl, leaves swirl" (To Paul Eluard, tr. by Czeslaw Milosz and Leonard Nathan). [Antaeus] (60) Spr 88, p. 46.
"Ode III" (To Albert Vallette, tr. by Czeslaw Milosz and Leonard Nathan). [Antaeus] (60) Spr 88, p. 54-57.
"Paris Revisited" (tr. by Czeslaw Milosz and Leonard Nathan). [Antaeus] (60) Spr 88, p. 49-50.
"A Recollection" (tr. by Czeslaw Milosz and Leonard Nathan). [Antaeus] (60) Spr 88, p. 51-52.
"Taking a Walk" (tr. by Czeslaw Milosz and Leonard Nathan). [Antaeus] (60) Spr 88, p. 58-59.
"To a Roman, My Friend" (tr. by Czeslaw Milosz and Leonard Nathan). [Antaeus] (60) Spr 88, p. 53.

5628. WATERHOUSE, Philip Anthony
"A Favoring Night Wind." [CrabCR] (5:2) Sum 88, p. 20.
5629. WATERS, Chocolate
"Sergi's Surgery." [SinW] (32) Sum 87, p. 79-82.
5630. WATERS, Deborah
"Fish" (tr. of Paul Eluard). [StoneC] (15:3/4) Spr-Sum 88, p. 27.
5631. WATERS, Mary Ann
"Bath." [Poetry] (152:2) My 88, p. 84-85.
"Car." [Poetry] (152:2) My 88, p. 81-83.
5632. WATERS, Michael
"Betta Splendens." [OhioR] (42) 88, p. 74-75.
"Bountiful." [Poetry] (152:4) Jl 88, p. 202-203.
"Country Post Office " (Quantico, Maryland). [TarRP] (28:1) Fall 88, p. 49.
"The Difference Between a Rooster and a Whore." [GeoR] (42:1) Spr 88, p. 160.
"The Fox." [MissouriR] (11:2) 88, p. 34-35.
"Homo Sapiens." [Poetry] (151:4) Ja 88, p. 344-345.
"The Inarticulate." [Poetry] (152:4) Jl 88, p. 202.
"Lace." [Crazy] (34) Spr 88, p. 16-17.
"Monsoon" (Koh Samui, Thailand). [TarRP] (28:1) Fall 88, p. 48.
"The Prince of Geese." [TarRP] (28:1) Fall 88, p. 47.
"Scorpions" (Ios, 1987). [Poetry] (152:4) Jl 88, p. 203-204.
"Shadow Boxes" (in memoriam Joseph Cornell). [MissouriR] (11:2) 88, p. 31-33.
5633. WATKINS, Edward
"Carrot Crazy." [LightY] ('88/9) 88, p. 217.
5634. WATKINS, William John
"Answer to a Wifely Question." [PoetC] (20:1) Fall 88, p. 21.
"Four of Us in Bed." [HolCrit] (25:4) O 88, p. 19.
"How to Write a Literate Poem." [Poem] (59) My 88, p. 47.
"I Have an Ear for Grief." [SouthernPR] (28:2) Fall 88, p. 55.
"Parkway Sonnet: November." [PoetC] (20:1) Fall 88, p. 22.
"Route 84 in a Freezing Drizzle." [Vis] (28) 88, p. 38.
"Sleep Packs You." [KanQ] (20:1/2) Wint-Spr 88, p. 314.
"Some Lines Lie Too Deep for Grief." [KanQ] (20:1/2) Wint-Spr 88, p. 313.
"We have kissed the loving demon." [Poem] (59) My 88, p. 49.
"You are not the first poem." [Poem] (59) My 88, p. 48.
5635. WATSON, Craig
"Gravity" (Letter to M.E.B.). [Notus] (3:1) Spr 88, p. 28-32.
5636. WATSON, Ellen
"Around Noon." [MidwQ] (30:1) Aut 88, p. 79-80.
"Black Garments" (tr. of Jan Arb). [Antaeus] (60) Spr 88, p. 285.
"Dictionary of the Rose-Colored Wizard" (tr. of Jotamario). [Antaeus] (60) Spr 88, p. 286-289.
"A Fast One" (tr. of Adélia Prado). [Antaeus] (60) Spr 88, p. 290.
"Guide" (tr. of Adélia Prado). [Antaeus] (60) Spr 88, p. 294.
"Homily" (tr. of Adélia Prado). [Antaeus] (60) Spr 88, p. 291.
"Miserere" (tr. of Adélia Prado). [Antaeus] (60) Spr 88, p. 292-293.
5637. WATSON, Lawrence
"Cheap Shoes." [GettyR] (1:4) Aut 88, p. 706-707.
5638. WATSON, Ron
"Ghost." [Vis] (28) 88, p. 38.
5639. WATSON, Susan
"Snow." [TexasR] (9:3/4) Fall-Wint 88, p. 139.
5640. WATT, D.
"Dreams." [PaintedB] (36) 88, p. 75.
5641. WATTS, David
"Visit." [Footwork] ('88) 88, p. 33.
5642. WAUGAMAN, Charles A.
"Even Before Frost." [CapeR] (23:2) Fall 88, p. 29.
5643. WAUGH, Robert H.
"Delivery." [InterPR] (14:2) Fall 88, p. 110.
"My Father Looks In." [LaurelR] (22:21) Wint 88, p. 25.
"Optic Neuritis." [InterPR] (14:2) Fall 88, p. 110.
5644. WAYMAN, Tom
"After Failure." [Event] (17:3) Fall 88, p. 28.
"Canadian Culture: Another Riel Poem." [Event] (17:3) Fall 88, p. 30-31.
"Defective Parts of Speech: Mediaburn." [LittleM] (15:3/4) 88, p. 82.

"Greed Suite: The Climate." [OntR] (28) Spr-Sum 88, p. 36-37.
"In a Small House on the Outskirts of Heaven" (after Zbigniew Herbert). [TriQ] (72) Spr-Sum 88, p. 184-185.
"Picnic in a Runaway Lane." [OntR] (28) Spr-Sum 88, p. 38-39.
"A Political Economy of Poets." [Event] (17:3) Fall 88, p. 29.
"The Thread." [MalR] (84) S 88, p. 71-73.
"What the House Windows See." [LittleM] (15:3/4) 88, p. 83-84.

5645. WEAVER, Kathleen
"Alluvion" (tr. of Nancy Morejon). [Callaloo] (11:1, #34) Wint 88, p. 33.
"Encounter" (tr. of Nancy Morejon). [Callaloo] (11:1, #34) Wint 88, p. 35.
"Exhibited City" (tr. of Nancy Morejon). [Callaloo] (11:1, #34) Wint 88, p. 31.
"Ferocious Cage" (tr. of Nancy Morejon, w. Robert Baldock). [Callaloo] (11:1, #34) Wint 88, p. 37.

5646. WEAVER, Michael S.
"A Life in a Steel Mill." [PaintedB] (32/33) 88, p. 28.

5647. WEAVER, Roger
"Poem for Parents." [StoneC] (16:1/2) Fall-Wint 88-89, p. 49.
"Watershed Moment." [Plain] (8:3) Spr-Sum 88, p. 16.

5648. WEBB, Bernice Larson
"Persimmon Day." [NewOR] (15:1) Spr 88, p. 99.
"Scarecrow." [NewOR] (15:1) Spr 88, p. 14.

5649. WEBB, Charles
"According to the Rule." [PoetL] (83:3) Fall 88, p. 35.
"All the Guys Who Sold Us Bait in Galveston." [Jacaranda] (3:2) Fall-Wint 88, p. 131-132.
"Curmudgeon-Man." [WormR] (28:1, #109) 88, p. 34-36.
"Girl Across the Room." [SlipS] (8) 88, p. 27.

5650. WEBB, Phyllis
"Ambrosia." [PraF] (9:3) Aut 88, p. 12.
"The Unbearable Lightness of Being" (Milan Kundera). [PraF] (9:3) Aut 88, p. 13.

5651. WEBER, Elizabeth
"Breslau, 1945: For Oma." [FloridaR] (16:1) Spr-Sum 88, p. 112-113.
"Myth." [GrahamHR] (11) Spr 88, p. 37-38.

5652. WEBER, Joanne
"The Lie." [Grain] (16:3) Fall 88, p. 42.

5653. WEBER, Maria
"In Late Life." [Footwork] ('88) 88, p. 66.
"The Loser." [Footwork] ('88) 88, p. 66.

5654. WEBER, Mark
"When the Chips Are Down." [WormR] (28:1, #109) 88, p. 30-31.
"While Mopping." [WormR] (28:1, #109) 88, p. 31.

5655. WEBER, Tom
"On 'Science Fiction Poetry'." [LittleM] (15:3/4) 88, p. 139.

5656. WECHSLER, Shoshana
"Invocation to the Forces of Chance." [Sequoia] (32:1) Spr-Sum 88, p. 64.

5657. WEDGE, George F.
"Cold Night in Spring." [HighP] (3:3) Wint 88-89, p. 63.

5658. WEDGE, Philip
"Deaf and Blind" (For Jack and Ruth Clemo). [AmerS] (57:2) Spr 88, p. 261.
"Hunter." [Wind] (18:62) 88, p. 46.
"Monet's Fields" (Chicago Art Institute, 1976). [Wind] (18:62) 88, p. 46.

5659. WEED, David Milo
"Bruised Hands." [KanQ] (20:1/2) Wint-Spr 88, p. 327.
"Salamander." [KanQ] (20:1/2) Wint-Spr 88, p. 327.

5660. WEEDON, Syd
"Litany." [RagMag] (6:2) Fall 88, p. 65.

5661. WEEKES, Barbara
"Shadows." [StoneC] (16:1/2) Fall-Wint 88-89, p. 59.

5662. WEEKLEY, Richard J.
"He Was a Curve." [HiramPoR] (44/45) Spr-Wint 88, p. 44.
"How I Long to Write a Poem." [DeKalbLAJ] (21:1) Wint 88, p. 75.
"I Have Moved Out of My House." [Quarry] (37:1) Wint 88, p. 44-45.
"Pastel Raving." [LitR] (31:2) Wint 88, p. 242-243.

5663. WEEKS, Ramona
"Uninvited Visitor and Charms." [HolCrit] (25:5) D 88, p. 16.

5664. WEEKS, Robert Lewis
"A Body of Earth." [CapeR] (23:2) Fall 88, p. 6-7.
"Cry." [HampSPR] Wint 88, p. 32.
"Evocation." [Pembroke] (20) 88, p. 106.
"Forever, Exactly." [BelPoJ] (38:3) Spr 88, p. 3.
"Nanking Cherry." [KanQ] (20:3) Sum 88, p. 50.
"O's." [Crosscur] (7:4) 88, p. 147.
"Political Poem." [BelPoJ] (38:3) Spr 88, p. 2.
"Professor." [HampSPR] Wint 88, p. 31.
"The Real One." [LitR] (31:2) Wint 88, p. 184.
"Say Those Quiet and Humble Words." [BelPoJ] (38:3) Spr 88, p. 4.
"Tell Us." [KanQ] (20:3) Sum 88, p. 49.
WEI, Geng
See GENG, Wei
5665. WEIDMAN, Phil
"Escape the Music." [WormR] (28:4, #112) 88, p. 90.
"Fiftyone." [WormR] (28:4, #112) 88, p. 90.
"Freeze." [WormR] (28:4, #112) 88, p. 90.
"Gretel." [WormR] (28:4, #112) 88, p. 90.
"My Job." [WormR] (28:4, #112) 88, p. 90.
"Nine Daffodils." [WormR] (28:4, #112) 88, p. 91.
"Our Ideal." [WormR] (28:4, #112) 88, p. 91.
"Postcard from Lisa." [WormR] (28:4, #112) 88, p. 91.
"Scratching My Head." [WormR] (28:4, #112) 88, p. 91.
"Trick." [WormR] (28:4, #112) 88, p. 90.
"Worrier." [WormR] (28:4, #112) 88, p. 89.
"Zoo Visit." [WormR] (28:4, #112) 88, p. 90.
5666. WEIGEL, Tom
"One Night in Mystic." [LittleM] (15:3/4) 88, p. 79.
"Walking after Midnight." [LittleM] (15:3/4) 88, p. 79.
5667. WEIGL, Bruce
"Apparition of the Exile." [TriQ] (72) Spr-Sum 88, p. 160.
"April." [TriQ] (72) Spr-Sum 88, p. 163.
"Autumn in the New Town." [OhioR] (41) 88, p. 94-95.
"Blues at the Equinox." [TriQ] (72) Spr-Sum 88, p. 159.
"Dialectical Materialism." [Harp] (277:1660) S 88, p. 34.
"Elegy." [ParisR] (30:107) Sum 88, p. 201.
"In the Days Before Insurrection." [TriQ] (72) Spr-Sum 88, p. 161.
"In the House of Immigrants." [TriQ] (72) Spr-Sum 88, p. 162.
"Meditation at Pearl Street." [OhioR] (41) 88, p. 93.
"On the Anniversary of Her Grace." [PraS] (62:2) Sum 88, p. 98-99.
"On the Evening Before His Departure." [WestHR] (42:2) Sum 88, p. 118.
"The Sky in Daduza Township." [WestHR] (42:2) Sum 88, p. 117.
"The Way of Tet." [PraS] (62:2) Sum 88, p. 100-101.
"What Saves Us." [ColR] (NS 15:1) Spr-Sum 88, p. 94.
5668. WEIL, James L.
"Cherries" (to Hnizdovsky's painting). [Confr] (37/38) Spr-Sum 88, p. 194.
5669. WEINBERGER, Eliot
"January First" (tr. of Octavio Paz). [Boulevard] (3:2/3) Fall 88, p. 3-4.
"Little Variation" (tr. of Octavio Paz). [Boulevard] (3:2/3) Fall 88, p. 4-5.
"To Talk" (tr. of Octavio Paz). [Boulevard] (3:2/3) Fall 88, p. 2.
"Wind, Water, Stone" (tr. of Octavio Paz). [Boulevard] (3:2/3) Fall 88, p. 1.
5670. WEINBERGER, Florence
"Dear Jessie." [Jacaranda] (3:2) Fall-Wint 88, p. 133.
5671. WEINGARTEN, Roger
"Fathers and Sons." [MissR] (16:1, #46) 88, p. 96-97.
"The Forever Bird." [Poetry] (152:5) Ag 88, p. 268-269.
"Infant Bonds of Joy." [MissouriR] (11:2) 88, p. 106-108.
"Late One Night." [AmerPoR] (17:1) Ja-F 88, p. 46.
"Lunch at the Russian Tea Room." [Shen] (38:2) 88, p. 22-23.
"Red Cars." [NewRep] (199:13) 26 S 88, p. 37.
5672. WEINMAN, Paul
"Bait in Wait." [WindO] (50) Aut 88, p. 34.
"Hair There" (booklet issued as an insert). [SlipS] (8) 88, 52 p.
"Maybe Not So Bad." [DeKalbLAJ] (21:2) Spr 88, p. 47.
"Misty Seen." [CimR] (85) O 88, p. 41.

"Our Tomatoes Touched." [WindO] (50) Aut 88, p. 35.
"Rafting." [MidAR] (8:2) 88, p. 71.
5673. WEISMILLER, Edward
"Armida." [GeoR] (42:4) Wint 88, p. 821.
5674. WEISS, David
"Drumlins." [IndR] (11:2) Spr 88, p. 35.
"Husbands." [SenR] (18:1) 88, p. 31-32.
"The Messenger of Space." [SenR] (18:1) 88, p. 33.
"Wives." [SenR] (18:1) 88, p. 29-30.
5675. WEISS, R. (Renée)
"A Company" (with T. Weiss). [NewRep] (199:25) 19 D 88, p. 32.
5676. WEISS, Sigmund
"Beauty Walks in Changing Colors." [Lactuca] (9) F 88, p. 21.
"City of Rocking Stones." [Lactuca] (9) F 88, p. 31.
5677. WEISS, T. (Theodore)
"A Company" (with R. Weiss). [NewRep] (199:25) 19 D 88, p. 32.
"A Lamp of Sorts." [JINJPo] (10:1/2) 88, p. 53.
"Lately." [CreamCR] (12:2) Sum 88, p. 304.
5678. WEISSBORT, Daniel
"And I Speak of Cosmic Things" (tr. of Vsevolod Nekrasov). [NegC] (8:1/2) 88, p. 25.
"In Memory of Dima Leontev" (2 excerpts, tr. of Irina Grivnina). [NegC] (8:1/2) 88, p. 53-56.
"Khikhimora" (Excerpt, tr. of Nikolai Glazkov). [NegC] (8:1/2) 88, p. 20-22.
"Parting" (tr. of Irina Grivnina). [NegC] (8:1/2) 88, p. 57-59.
"Poetograd" (Selections: 1-2, tr. of Nikolai Glazkov). [NegC] (8:1/2) 88, p. 17-19.
"The Raven" (tr. of Nikolai Glazkov). [NegC] (8:1/2) 88, p. 23.
"Suicide Is a Duel With Yourself" (tr. of Sergei Chudakov). [NegC] (8:1/2) 88, p. 24.
"To J.D. Salinger — One Who Understood the Vanity of Human Relations . . ." (tr. of Irina Grivnina). [NegC] (8:1/2) 88, p. 62.
"To V. Bukovsky" (tr. of Irina Grivnina). [NegC] (8:1/2) 88, p. 60-61.
"Verses" (tr. of Daniil Virgin). [NegC] (8:1/2) 88, p. 41-42.
"Verses on the Back of a Photograph of an Old Town" (dedicated to B.V., tr. of Irina Grivnina). [NegC] (8:1/2) 88, p. 52.
"A word in your ear" (tr. of Irina Grivnina). [NegC] (8:1/2) 88, p. 50-51.
5679. WEISTER, Darlene T.
"The Color of Sin." [CentR] (32:3) Sum 88, p. 276-277.
"Paper Cycle." [CentR] (32:3) Sum 88, p. 275.
5680. WEKA, Mogens
"Absurdity Offsets Lost Charms." [JamesWR] (5:2) Wint 88, p. 5.
5681. WELBOURN, Cynthia
"Corporate Board Meeting." [DeKalbLAJ] (21:1) Wint 88, p. 76.
"The Exchange." [DeKalbLAJ] (21:1) Wint 88, p. 76.
"The Sidewalk, 1955." [DeKalbLAJ] (21:1) Wint 88, p. 77.
"Telephone Wires." [DeKalbLAJ] (21:1) Wint 88, p. 77.
5682. WELBURN, Ron
"Serial Composition to Miss Blake Avenue." [Abraxas] (37) 88, p. 16-17.
5683. WELCH, Don
"The Vice-President of the Universe." [LightY] ('88/9) 88, p. 223-224.
5684. WELCH, Liliane
"March." [PottPort] (9) 88, p. 41.
"Stone Gods." [StoneC] (15:3/4) Spr-Sum 88, p. 12.
5685. WELIN, Richard
"Stretch." [BellArk] (4:5) S-O 88, p. 20.
5686. WELISH, Marjorie
"Blood or Color." [Sulfur] (7:3, #21) Wint 88, p. 112-113.
"Greeting." [ParisR] (30:106) Spr 88, p. 199.
"Publicly Silent." [Sulfur] (7:3, #21) Wint 88, p. 111.
"Two Lines from Redon." [Sulfur] (7:3, #21) Wint 88, p. 111-112.
5687. WELLS, Stan
"Winter Content." [Bogg] (59) 88, p. 40.
5688. WELLS, Will
"Stealing Fire." [WebR] (13:2) Fall 88, p. 60.
"Two Potatoes." [WebR] (13:2) Fall 88, p. 59.

5689. WELTNER, Peter
"Beachside Entries" (Excerpt). [JamesWR] (6:1) Fall 88, p. 11.

WEN, Lu
See LU, Wen

WEN-YING, Wu
See WU, Wen-ying

5690. WENDELL, Julia
"Hatteras." [PraS] (62:2) Sum 88, p. 114-115.
"Holding Pattern." [SouthernPR] (28:1) Spr 88, p. 45-46.

5691. WENDT, Ingrid
"On the Pleasure of Plain White Bread." [CutB] (29/30) 88, p. 96.
"Singing the B Minor Mass." [CutB] (29/30) 88, p. 97.

5692. WENTHE, William
"The Birds of Hoboken." [GeoR] (42:4) Wint 88, p. 752-753.

5693. WEÖRES, Sándor
"At the End of Life" (tr. by William Jay Smith). [AmerPoR] (17:2) Mr-Ap 88, p. 32.
"The Lunatic Cyclist" (tr. by William Jay Smith). [AmerPoR] (17:2) Mr-Ap 88, p. 32.
"A Poem on Theater" (tr. by Jascha Kessler, w. Maria Körösy). [Nimrod] (32:1) Fall-Wint 88, p. 141.
"A Strange City" (tr. by Jascha Kessler, w. Maria Körösy). [MSS] (6:2) 88, p. 84.
"A Vision" (tr. by Jascha Kessler, w. Maria Körösy). [Nimrod] (32:1) Fall-Wint 88, p. 140.

5694. WERDINGER, Roberta
"Horizon, Hum." [YellowS] (27) Aut 88, p. 29.

5695. WESLOWSKI, Dieter
"Ann B. Holds Forth on Angels." [Caliban] (4) 88, p. 116.
"During an Evening Walk in Late March." [SouthernHR] (22:2) Spr 88, p. 112.
"The Era of Bread." [AntigR] (73) Spr 88, p. 128.
"Feeling My Exile Before a Silver Maple Branch." [KanQ] (20:3) Sum 88, p. 132.
"A Few Slits of Blue." [PaintedB] (34) 88, p. 24.
"I Have No Problem." [Caliban] (4) 88, p. 115.
"Il Vento, Il Vento." [SouthernHR] (22:4) Fall 88, p. 322.
"Ma Non Fatto." [Caliban] (5) 88, p. 71.
"A Note to the Curator of the Prado." [GreensboroR] (44) Sum 88, p. 66.
"Sainthood." [GreensboroR] (44) Sum 88, p. 66.
"Sunday Beginning with a Motet by Giovanni Gabrieli." [Grain] (16:2) Sum 88, p. 29.
"Which Life?" [Caliban] (5) 88, p. 70.

5696. WEST, Charles
"Autumn in California." [LightY] ('88/9) 88, p. 152.
"The Blind Man Dresses." [Amelia] (5:2, #13) 88, p. 6.

5697. WEST, John Foster
"Hog Heaven." [Pembroke] (20) 88, p. 123.

5698. WEST, Michael Lee
"Making Grape Jelly in August." [Spirit] (9:1) 88, p. 125-126.

5699. WEST, Richard W.
"Maggie & Jiggs, or a Suggested Cure for Two Cases of Necrophilia." [WormR] (28:4, #112) 88, p. 98.

5700. WEST, Ruth Green
"Time in January." [Wind] (18:63) 88, p. 46.

5701. WESTERBEKE, Paul
"Annuity." [Writer] (101:3) Mr 88, p. 20.

5702. WESTERFIELD, Nancy G.
"Amortization." [LightY] ('88/9) 88, p. 50.
"The Convent in Winter." [BallSUF] (29:4) Aut 88, p. 42.
"The Game with the Beast." [NegC] (8:3) 88, p. 110.
"Headstone." [Plain] (9:1) Fall 88, p. 29.
"A Light Touch of Love." [ChrC] (105:11) 6 Ap 88, p. 335.
"The Mock-Orange." [BallSUF] (29:4) Aut 88, p. 30.
"The Partial." [BostonR] (13:3 [sic]) O 88, p. 3.
"Streets." [Plain] (8:1) Fall 87, p. 20.

5703. WESTERGAARD, Diane
"November Apples." [CapeR] (23:2) Fall 88, p. 15.
"What to Do on a Day When You Feel You Cannot Meet the Standard Set by Melville." [CapeR] (23:2) Fall 88, p. 14.

5704. WESTFALL, Marilyn
"Storm Warnings." [Plain] (8:2) Wint 88, p. 26.
5705. WESTON, Ruth
"Homage to John Hollander." [Nimrod] (32:1) Fall-Wint 88, p. 123.
5706. WETTERAU, John
"April, Maine." [Spirit] (9:1) 88, p. 120.
"Spring Dream" (of SueSue). [Spirit] (9:1) 88, p. 120.
5707. WETTEROTH, Bruce
"Arboretum." [MassR] (29:1) Spr 88, p. 41.
"Missouri River Trail." [PraS] (62:2) Sum 88, p. 120-121.
"San Luis Pass." [MassR] (29:1) Spr 88, p. 42.
"Townhome." [PraS] (62:2) Sum 88, p. 121-122.
5708. WEXELBLATT, R. (Robert)
"The Excellence of Afternoons." [Poem] (60) N 88, p. 58.
"Going to Bed with Jane Austen." [LitR] (31:3) Spr 88, p. 299.
"In November." [Poem] (60) N 88, p. 56-57.
"A Mosquito Bite." [StoneC] (16:1/2) Fall-Wint 88-89, p. 15.
5709. WEXLER, Evelyn
"Parting." [Spirit] (9:1) 88, p. 71.
5710. WEXLER, Philip
"Became of Him." [Lactuca] (11) O 88, p. 9.
"Contrary to Rumor." [Lactuca] (11) O 88, p. 8.
5711. WHALEN, John
"Turned Into a Bird" (For Kevin). [CutB] (31/32) 88, p. 102.
5712. WHALEN, Tom
"Travellers." [Vis] (28) 88, p. 26.
5713. WHALLEY, Karen
"Drought." [BellArk] (4:1) Ja-F 88, p. 4.
"Nesting." [BellArk] (4:6) N-D 88, p. 9.
"Ripening As a Measure of Time." [BellArk] (4:1) Ja-F 88, p. 3.
5714. WHARTON, Gordon
"Interior." [Stand] (29:3) Sum 88, p. 49.
5715. WHATLEY, Wallace
"Talking in the Shade." [Spirit] (9:1) 88, p. 76.
5716. WHEDON, Tony
"March Poem." [TexasR] (9:3/4) Fall-Wint 88, p. 140.
5717. WHEELER, Charles B.
"My Father." [HiramPoR] (44/45) Spr-Wint 88, p. 45-46.
5718. WHEELER, Susan
"105 Mulberry" (for Pat Steir). [NewAW] (3) Spr 88, p. 29.
"Let's Talk About It Again, Please." [NewAW] (3) Spr 88, p. 30.
"The Privilege of Feet" (for Daniel Wheeler). [NewAW] (3) Spr 88, p. 28.
"Ruinous Disbelief." [NewAW] (3) Spr 88, p. 27.
5719. WHELAN, Benjamin
"Requiem." [HangL] (52) 88, p. 89-92.
5720. WHISLER, Robert F.
"Weighed in the Balance." [DeKalbLAJ] (21:2) Spr 88, p. 47-48.
5721. WHISNANT, Luke
"Poem on a Line from Kafka." [WebR] (13:1) Spr 88, p. 62.
"Vision." [WebR] (13:1) Spr 88, p. 63.
5722. WHITE, Boyd
"Where We've Already Been." [SouthernPR] (28:1) Spr 88, p. 21-23.
5723. WHITE, Calvin
"Afternoon on the Reserve." [Grain] (16:2) Sum 88, p. 60.
"The Stone Creek Hotel Fire." [Grain] (16:2) Sum 88, p. 61.
5724. WHITE, Clark E.
"The Stone Rollers" (for Little Jimmy Scott and Etheridge Knight). [PaintedB] (32/33) 88, p. 110.
5725. WHITE, Gail
"Choosing the Falls." [NegC] (8:3) 88, p. 164-166.
5726. WHITE, J. K.
"Etude: For the Lark." [SpoonRQ] (13:1) Wint 88, p. 27-29.
"Three Years Our Sister." [SpoonRQ] (13:1) Wint 88, p. 26.
5727. WHITE, J. P.
"Boy at the Bow of a Sailboat." [MemphisSR] (8:2) Spr 88, p. 84.
"In the Eye of the Barracuda." [MemphisSR] (8:2) Spr 88, p. 85-86.

5728. WHITE, Julie Herrick
"Healing the Dog." [PoetryNW] (29:1) Spr 88, p. 34-35.
"The Hour of Charm." [PoetryNW] (29:1) Spr 88, p. 35-36.
5729. WHITE, Mary Jane
"Here." [WillowS] (22) Spr 88, p. 31.
5730. WHITE, Mike
"The River" (for Larry Levis). [MissouriR] (11:2) 88, p. 25-30.
5731. WHITE, Patrick
"The Benjamin Chee Chee Elegies" (Selection: XII). [CrossC] (10:3) 88, p. 8.
5732. WHITE, Sarah
"Threaded Itineraries" (for Matilda Bruckner). [WestB] (21/22) 88, p. 140-141.
5733. WHITE, Steven F.
"Abandoned Church" (Ballad of the Great War, tr. of Federico Garcia Lorca, w. Greg Simon). [NowestR] (26:1) 88, p. 88.
"Childhood and Death" (tr. of Federico Garcia Lorca, w. Greg Simon). [Antaeus] (60) Spr 88, p. 254-255.
"Christmas on the Hudson" (tr. of Federico Garcia Lorca, w. Greg Simon). [NowestR] (26:1) 88, p. 89.
"Earth and Moon" (tr. of Federico Garcia Lorca, w. Greg Simon). [Antaeus] (60) Spr 88, p. 252-253.
"Fable of Three Friends, to Be Sung in Rounds" (tr. of Federico Garcia Lorca, w. Greg Simon). [NowestR] (26:1) 88, p. 86-87.
"Little Infinite Poem" (For Luis Cardoza y Aragón, tr. of Federico Garcia Lorca, w. Greg Simon). [Antaeus] (60) Spr 88, p. 256-257.
5734. WHITE, William M.
"Adam." [TexasR] (9:1/2) Spr-Sum 88, p. 85.
"Sunday Circus." [Paint] (15:30) Aut 88, p. 9.
"Sunday on the Mountaintop." [Paint] (15:30) Aut 88, p. 8.
5735. WHITEBIRD, J.
"Twins." [Crosscur] (7:4) 88, p. 94-95.
5736. WHITEHEAD, Jeffrey
"Building the Soil." [PoetryNW] (29:3) Aut 88, p. 18-19.
"Hologram." [SouthernPR] (28:1) Spr 88, p. 44.
"Landscape with Skidding Dove." [WillowS] (22) Spr 88, p. 67.
5737. WHITEHEAD, Thomas
"Muttering in Unamerican." [HampSPR] Wint 88, p. 28-29.
5738. WHITELAW, Scot
"Boreal Ancestors." [PottPort] (10) 88, p. 8.
5739. WHITEMAN, Bruce
"The hard clarity of speech pushes the body into the world." [CrossC] (10:1) 88, p. 8.
"A woman's voice speaks of the beautiful fatalities of consciousness." [CrossC] (10:1) 88, p. 8.
5740. WHITING, Nathan
"In Dog Tongue." [HawaiiR] (12:2, #24) Fall 88, p. 76-77.
"Second Firing of the Starter's Gun." [BellArk] (4:1) Ja-F 88, p. 8.
5741. WHITLEDGE, Jane
"Repeating Patterns." [WebR] (13:1) Spr 88, p. 64-65.
5742. WHITMAN, Ruth
"The Drowned Mountain" (Selection: "1. The Mountain," for CHW, 1916-1979). [Ploughs] (14:1) 88, p. 133-134.
"Father" (tr. of Miriam Oren). [AmerV] (10) Spr 88, p. 13.
"Hanna Senesh." [TexasR] (9:3/4) Fall-Wint 88, p. 141.
5743. WHITMAN, Walt
"Crossing Brooklyn Ferry" (Excerpt). [Confr] (Special issue: The World of Brooklyn) 88, p. 3.
5744. WHITMIRE, Mary Anna
"The Offering." [TexasR] (9:1/2) Spr-Sum 88, p. 47.
5745. WHITT, Laurie Anne
"It Came to This." [MalR] (85) D 88, p. 22-23.
5746. WHITTEMORE, Reed
"The Crow and the Fox." [AmerPoR] (17:5) S-O 88, p. 37-38.
5747. WHITTINGTON, Janice D.
"Expensive Harvest." [KanQ] (20:1/2) Wint-Spr 88, p. 141.
5748. WIDERKEHR, Richard
"Looking for My Sister." [CrabCR] (5:2) Sum 88, p. 26.

"Where the Voices Took Her" (for my sister). [CrabCR] (5:2) Sum 88, p. 27.

5749. WIDNER, Jill
"Broodmare." [ChamLR] (1) Fall 87, p. 53.
"Finding Schopenhauer in Spain." [ChamLR] (1:2, #2) Spr 88, p. 22-25.
"The Lost." [CimR] (83) Ap 88, p. 70.
"My Baby Thinks He's a Train" (— Rosanne Cash). [ChamLR] (1:2, #2) Spr 88, p. 20-21.
"Water from the Moon." [ChamLR] (1) Fall 87, p. 54.

5750. WIEBE, Armin
"What the Kroetsch Said, or Amber Liquid Is Beer, Aritha." [PraF] (9:1) Spr 88, p. 56-57.

5751. WIELAND, Liza
"Lie Near." [Ploughs] (14:4) 88, p. 129-131.

WIENEN, Mark van
See Van WIENEN, Mark

5752. WIER, Dara
"Eidetic." [CutB] (31/32) 88, p. 58.
"Little Black Tangrams" (1959). [WillowS] (21) Wint 88, p. 68-71.
"A Long Time More." [CutB] (31/32) 88, p. 59.
"Nude Descending a Staircase." [WillowS] (21) Wint 88, p. 72-73.
"Update on Jekyll and Hyde." [AmerPoR] (17:3) My-Je 88, p. 22.

5753. WIGGIN, Neurine
"A Clump of White-Haired Ladies." [SmPd] (25:2) Spr 88, p. 30.
"Cornstarch Cake." [PoetryNW] (29:2) Sum 88, p. 27-28.
"The Growing Season." [BellArk] (4:4) Jl-Ag 88, p. 4.
"Man of My Dreams." [BellArk] (4:2) Mr-Ap 88, p. 7.
"The Man She Loves." [BellArk] (4:5) S-O 88, p. 3.
"Sad in the Best of Days." [Ascent] (14:2) 88, p. 22-23.
"Some Laws of Chemistry ." [PoetryNW] (29:2) Sum 88, p. 26-27.

5754. WIGGINS, Jean
"The Priest." [Plain] (8:1) Fall 87, p. 30.
"Words Unspoken." [Wind] (18:63) 88, p. 48.

5755. WILBORN, Rob
"Rag Rug." [LightY] ('88/9) 88, p. 144-145.

5756. WILBORN, William
"Guitar Wife" (for Carol Loranger). [Margin] (7) 88, p. 45.
"In the Garden." [CumbPR] (7:2) Spr 88, p. 70-71.
"Juice" (for George Herman). [DenQ] (23:2) Fall 88, p. 67-69.
"Ten To." [CumbPR] (7:2) Spr 88, p. 69.

5757. WILBUR, Richard
"More Opposites." [KeyWR] (1:1) Spr 88, p. 7-8.
"Three Riddles from Symphosius." [Poetry] (152:1) Ap 88, p. 1.
"Under a Tree." [Poetry] (152:1) Ap 88, p. 2.
"Worlds." [Poetry] (152:1) Ap 88, p. 2.

5758. WILD, Peter
"Addictions." [Ascent] (14:2) 88, p. 13.
"Astronomers." [HiramPoR] (44/45) Spr-Wint 88, p. 47.
"Being Good." [ChatR] (9:1) Fall 88, p. 38.
"Birds." [LittleM] (15:3/4) 88, p. 99.
"The Book of Proverbs." [NoDaQ] (56:1) Wint 88, p. 108.
"Demurrage." [Abraxas] (37) 88, p. 67.
"Dirigibles." [LaurelR] (22:2) Sum 88, p. 36.
"Heaven." [HawaiiR] (12:2, #24) Fall 88, p. 59.
"Holy Ghost." [Wind] (18:62) 88, p. 48.
"Lewis and Clark." [CinPR] (18) Fall 88, p. 73.
"Marriage." [Wind] (18:62) 88, p. 47.
"Meteorologist." [TarRP] (27:2) Spr 88, p. 30.
"A Movie About Brazil." [MissR] (16:1, #46) 88, p. 106-107.
"Newlyweds." [LaurelR] (22:2) Sum 88, p. 35.
"Night Shifts." [AnotherCM] (18) 88, p. 178.
"Novelists." [AnotherCM] (18) 88, p. 179.
"Novelists." [LaurelR] (22:2) Sum 88, p. 34.
"Old Novitiates." [CutB] (29/30) 88, p. 34.
"Parsnips." [LitR] (31:4) Sum 88, p. 433.
"Piano Player." [AmerPoR] (17:2) Mr-Ap 88, p. 25.
"Smoke Jumpers." [TarRP] (27:2) Spr 88, p. 29.

"Splendid Order." [LittleM] (15:3/4) 88, p. 100.
"Sunlight in a Violin Case." [LittleM] (15:3/4) 88, p. 98.

5759. WILDS, Michael
"Comes the Rhinoceros." [LitR] (31:3) Spr 88, p. 330.

5760. WILK, Melvin
"Eviction Still Life." [MSS] (6:2) 88, p. 8.

5761. WILKERSON, Robin
"Message in a Bottle." [Wind] (18:62) 88, p. 49.

5762. WILKES, Kennette H. (Kennette Harrison)
"Deep into Feathers." [Nimrod] (32:1) Fall-Wint 88, p. 115.
"More Light." [Phoenix] (9:1/2) 88, p. 34.
"One Wing." [Phoenix] (9:1/2) 88, p. 36.
"This July." [Phoenix] (9:1/2) 88, p. 35.
"This Letter." [Phoenix] (9:1/2) 88, p. 33.
"Weatherwatch." [Nimrod] (32:1) Fall-Wint 88, p. 114-115.

5763. WILKINSON, Robin
"Confessionaries." [KanQ] (20:1/2) Wint-Spr 88, p. 232=233.
"Counterpoint for Cellos." [KanQ] (20:1/2) Wint-Spr 88, p. 233.
"Memo to My Daughter." [QW] (27) Sum-Fall 88, p. 104.

5764. WILKOWSKI, Jillian
"Hunting Season." [SinW] (32) Sum 87, p. 23.

5765. WILKS, Jonathan
"Walking on a Sleepless Night." [PoetryNW] (29:2) Sum 88, p. 12-13.

5766. WILLARD, Nancy
"For Karen." [Sequoia] (31:2) Wint 88, p. 80.

5767. WILLARD, Nona
"Equity." [Grain] (16:4) Wint 88, p. 61.
"An Ideal Beauty." [Grain] (16:4) Wint 88, p. 61.
"Visiting" (For Roy). [Grain] (16:4) Wint 88, p. 60.

5768. WILLIAMS, Barbara
"Process." [CrossC] (10:2) 88, p. 10.

5769. WILLIAMS, C. K.
"Alma Mater" (tr. of Adam Zagajewski, w. Renata Gorczynski). [TriQ] (71) Wint 88, p. 142.
"Because I Was Drinking Wine: IV" (tr. of Abraham Sutzkever). [AmerPoR] (17:6) N-D 88, p. 28.
"Charred Pearls" (tr. of Abraham Sutzkever). [AmerPoR] (17:6) N-D 88, p. 30.
"Faces in the Mire: I" (tr. of Abraham Sutzkever). [AmerPoR] (17:6) N-D 88, p. 27.
"I Lie in This Coffin" (tr. of Abraham Sutzkever). [AmerPoR] (17:6) N-D 88, p. 28.
"In the Cell: II" (tr. of Abraham Sutzkever). [AmerPoR] (17:6) N-D 88, p. 27.
"Leaves of Ash: III" (tr. of Abraham Sutzkever). [AmerPoR] (17:6) N-D 88, p. 28.
"A Load of Shoes" (tr. of Abraham Sutzkever). [AmerPoR] (17:6) N-D 88, p. 29.
"Pray" (tr. of Abraham Sutzkever). [AmerPoR] (17:6) N-D 88, p. 28.
"September Afternoon in the Abandoned Barracks" (tr. of Adam Zagajewski, w. Renata Gorczynski). [TriQ] (71) Wint 88, p. 141.
"Song for the Last" (tr. of Abraham Sutzkever). [AmerPoR] (17:6) N-D 88, p. 30.
"To My Child" (tr. of Abraham Sutzkever). [AmerPoR] (17:6) N-D 88, p. 29.
"A Voice from the Heart: V" (tr. of Abraham Sutzkever). [AmerPoR] (17:6) N-D 88, p. 28.
"When Death Came" (tr. of Adam Zagajewski, w. Renata Gorczynski). [TriQ] (71) Wint 88, p. 139-140.

5770. WILLIAMS, Charlotte
"The Song of the Vine" (Aboriginal Narrative of New South Wales, Collected by Roland Robinson). [PraS] (62:4) Wint 88-89, p. 21.

5771. WILLIAMS, David
"Breath." [PoetryE] (25) Spr 88, p. 31.
"Collusion." [PoetryE] (25) Spr 88, p. 29-30.
"Constellations." [PoetryE] (25) Spr 88, p. 35.
"Further Arguments Against the War" (Nicaragua). [PoetryE] (25) Spr 88, p. 33.
"Looking at a Mural in Grenada, Nicaragua, 1982." [PoetryE] (25) Spr 88, p. 34.
"My Great-Uncle's Broken Song." [PoetryE] (25) Spr 88, p. 32.

5772. WILLIAMS, Donna Glee
"For Steve and the Seventeen-Year-Old Girl." [BellR] (11:2) Fall 88, p. 28.
"In Honor of Franz Joseph Gall (1758-1828)." [BellR] (11:2) Fall 88, p. 29.
"Shapes and Changes." [BellR] (11:1) Spr 88, p. 54-55.

5773. WILLIAMS, James D., Jr.
"Retrospect: 3 A.M." [Phoenix] (9:1/2) 88, p. 14.
5774. WILLIAMS, Joe
"South Africa." [Bogg] (60) 88, p. 23.
5775. WILLIAMS, John
"Key West, 1945." [KeyWR] (1:1) Spr 88, p. 53-54.
5776. WILLIAMS, Leslita
"Non-violence." [SinW] (33) Fall 87, p. 32-34.
"Purple Garlic." [SinW] (33) Fall 87, p. 81.
5777. WILLIAMS, Lisa
"A Poet's Death" (for Keats). [Phoenix] (9:1/2) 88, p. 32.
5778. WILLIAMS, Marcelle
"Cab Poem #7." [LakeSR] (22) 88, p. 14.
5779. WILLIAMS, Mark
"Particulates." [Hudson] (40:4) Wint 88, p. 620-621.
"Refrigerator Queen." [Hudson] (40:4) Wint 88, p. 619.
5780. WILLIAMS, Merryn
"The Masterpiece." [Crosscur] (7:4) 88, p. 131.
5781. WILLIAMS, Otis
"Blues for Henry Dumas." [BlackALF] (22:2) Sum 88, p. 406-407.
"For Henry Dumas" (Hoo Doo Blues God). [BlackALF] (22:2) Sum 88, p. 405-406.
5782. WILLIAMS, Stephen Jarrell
"Worst Flood in Forty Years." [HawaiiR] (12:2, #24) Fall 88, p. 58.
5783. WILLIAMSON, Don T.
"Moonlight." [Plain] (8:3) Spr-Sum 88, p. 10.
"My Father's Dump." [WebR] (13:1) Spr 88, p. 68-69.
5784. WILLIAMSON, Tharin
"The Quotients Are All Sums." [HolCrit] (25:5) D 88, p. 19.
5785. WILLIS, Clara Gehron
"Haiku: February snow" (The 14th Kansas Poetry Contest, Third Honorable Mention). [LittleBR] (5:2) Wint 88-89, p. 70.
5786. WILLSON, Robert F., Jr.
"Closet Poet." [NewL] (54:3) Spr 88, p. 83.
5787. WILMARTH, Richard
"Yin and Yang." [RagMag] (6:2) Fall 88, p. 37.
5788. WILMER, Clive
"Found Images" (tr. of George Gomori, w. the author). [Vis] (26) 88, p. 25.
5789. WILMOT, Jeanne
"Madonna: A Story." [AntR] (46:2) Spr 88, p. 242-245.
5790. WILNER, Eleanor
"As Far As It Goes and Back." [NewYorker] (64:39) 14 N 88, p. 44.
"A Green Aubade for Etheridge." [PaintedB] (32/33) 88, p. 19-20.
5791. WILSON, Alan R.
"Counting to 100" (Selections: 71-80). [PraF] (9:3) Aut 88, p. 59-63.
"Newton's Laws." [MalR] (85) D 88, p. 114-115.
"Radio Waves." [Dandel] (15:2) Fall-Wint 88, p. 26-27.
"Thirteen Ways of Looking at Pepper." [MalR] (85) D 88, p. 111-113.
5792. WILSON, Barbara (Barbara H.)
"The Age Inside." [PoetL] (83:3) Fall 88, p. 33.
"Still Life in the Rhododendrons." [StoneC] (15:3/4) Spr-Sum 88, p. 43.
5793. WILSON, David
"Tara." [Bogg] (60) 88, p. 31.
5794. WILSON, Graeme
"Cracksman" (tr. of Sakutaro Hagiwara). [SenR] (18:2) 88, p. 42.
"Dancing Girl" (tr. of Wu Wen-ying). [Jacaranda] (3:2) Fall-Wint 88, p. 145.
"Estuary Anchorage" (tr. of Kaoru Maruyama). [Jacaranda] (3:1) Wint 88, p. 7.
"Expanding the Frontiers" (tr. of Du Fu). [Jacaranda] (3:2) Fall-Wint 88, p. 144.
"First Born" (tr. of Hiroshi Yoshino). [Jacaranda] (3:1) Wint 88, p. 4.
"Green Mountain Mind" (tr. of Li Po). [Jacaranda] (3:2) Fall-Wint 88, p. 145.
"Howling at the Moon" (tr. of Sakutaro Hagiwara). [SenR] (18:2) 88, p. 45.
"Kindlings" (tr. of anonymous Korean poem). [LitR] (32:1) Fall 88, p. 68.
"Master Fall" (tr. of Hakushu Kitahara). [Jacaranda] (3:1) Wint 88, p. 6-7.
"Memento" (tr. of anonymous Korean poet). [Jacaranda] (3:2) Fall-Wint 88, p. 144.
"People Who Get Off" (tr. of Ryusei Hasegawa). [Jacaranda] (3:1) Wint 88, p. 5.
"Rotten Chrysanthemum" (tr. of Sakutaro Hagiwara). [SenR] (18:2) 88, p. 44.

"Scene of the Crime" (tr. of Sakutaro Hagiwara). [SenR] (18:2) 88, p. 41.
"Sky" (tr. of Shigeji Tsuboi). [Jacaranda] (3:1) Wint 88, p. 5.
"Sparrows" (tr. of Sakutaro Hagiwara). [SenR] (18:2) 88, p. 43.

5795. WILSON, Joseph
"How Many Clouds Are There?" (For Andrew, 6). [Vis] (28) 88, p. 30.
"My Father's Birthday." [StoneC] (15:3/4) Spr-Sum 88, p. 59.

5796. WILSON, Larry
"Garden Tender." [Epoch] (37:3) 88, p. 149.
"The Whole Prose Scene." [Epoch] (37:3) 88, p. 150-151.

5797. WILSON, Leonore
"Afterbirth." [FiveFR] (6) 88, p. 73.

5798. WILSON, Miles
"Bear on the Stump." [KanQ] (20:1/2) Wint-Spr 88, p. 62-63.

5799. WILSON, Patricia
"All in the Family." [PassN] (9:2) Sum 88, p. 19.

5800. WILSON, Reed
"Coming Back" (for Adina Lawson). [Jacaranda] (3:1) Wint 88, p. 70-71.

5801. WILSON, Rob
"Come Back." [NewRep] (199:22) 28 N 88, p. 25.
"By the Temple at Lahaina." [ChamLR] (1) Fall 87, p. 39.
"The Fires of Kilauea." [ChamLR] (1) Fall 87, p. 40.
"Meditation at Kilauea Iki." [ChamLR] (1) Fall 87, p. 41.

5802. WILSON, Robley, Jr.
"Company Cafeteria." [Poetry] (151:5) F 88, p. 401.

5803. WILSON, Steve
"Field Study" (for William Stafford). [MidwQ] (29:4) Sum 88, p. 461.
"This Poem Can't Be Published." [WebR] (13:2) Fall 88, p. 98.

5804. WINANS, A. D.
"For Kenneth Patchen." [Footwork] ('88) 88, p. 66.
"For Lawrence Ferlinghetti and the Old Revolution." [Abraxas] (37) 88, p. 42.
"For Neal Cassady." [AlphaBS] (4) D 88, p. 28.
"Sitting Here Alone." [StoneC] (16:1/2) Fall-Wint 88-89, p. 69.

5805. WINANS, Janet
"As We Were and Are." [MemphisSR] (8:2) Spr 88, p. 48.
"Dear Esme." [Footwork] ('88) 88, p. 33.
"Half Day." [MemphisSR] (8:2) Spr 88, p. 49.
"The Old Ones." [MemphisSR] (8:2) Spr 88, p. 46.
"Running Trains." [Footwork] ('88) 88, p. 33.
"South Fork, Yuba, 1964." [MemphisSR] (8:2) Spr 88, p. 47.

5806. WINBURN, Rae
"Fish Eye." [Amelia] (4:4, #11) 88, p. 14.

WINCKEL, Nance van
See Van WINCKEL, Nance

5807. WINDER, Barbara
"El Campo Santo." [NegC] (8:3) 88, p. 106-107.
"The Destroying Angel" (International Poetry Contest, Second Prize). [WestB] (21/22) 88, p. 39-40.
"A Fine Two Carat Stone in a Bed of Emeralds." [NegC] (8:3) 88, p. 104-105.

5808. WINFIELD, William
"Desire." [MidwQ] (29:3) Spr 88, p. 356.
"Halo." [MidwQ] (29:3) Spr 88, p. 355.

WING, Tek Lum
See LUM, Wing Tek

5809. WINKLER, Donald
"Old Archangel You Know It All" (tr. of Pierre Nepveu). [Trans] (20) Spr 88, p. 116.
"Rose and Thorn" (tr. of Roland Giguere). [Trans] (20) Spr 88, p. 103-105.

5810. WINN, Howard
"The Undiscovered Country." [MidwQ] (29:4) Sum 88, p. 462.
"Wallace Stevens Escapes Connecticut." [BallSUF] (29:4) Aut 88, p. 46-47.

WINTER, Corrine de
See DeWINTER, Corrine

5811. WINTER, Jonah
"Amnesia: I forget what happens next." [Timbuktu] (2) Sum-Fall 88, p. 22.
"Amnesia: I like that movie." [Timbuktu] (2) Sum-Fall 88, p. 23.
"Amnesia: I see 'Astronauts'." [Timbuktu] (2) Sum-Fall 88, p. 24.

"Conversation with Inflatable Doll." [Timbuktu] (2) Sum-Fall 88, p. 20.
"Cowboys and Indians." [Timbuktu] (1) Wint-Spr 88, p. 51.
"December Mosaic." [Timbuktu] (1) Wint-Spr 88, p. 53.
"Girl Accuses Father of Taping Her Mouth Shut." [Timbuktu] (1) Wint-Spr 88, p. 49.
"Mollusks and Mankind." [Timbuktu] (1) Wint-Spr 88, p. 52.
"Soliloquy Beginning in Anger." [Timbuktu] (2) Sum-Fall 88, p. 21.
"Whoopy Tie Yie Yoe." [Timbuktu] (1) Wint-Spr 88, p. 50.

5812. WINTER-DAMON, T.
"Hellequins." [Bogg] (59) 88, p. 18.

5813. WINWOOD, David
"Roots and Politics." [LitR] (31:2) Wint 88, p. 239.

5814. WISECHILD, Louise
"Patience Becomes a Dragon" (for an imaginary client of Freud's, excerpt). [SinW] (36) Wint 88-89, p. 116.

5815. WISEMAN, Christopher
"Against the Dying of the Light" (for Stephen). [CanLit] (118) Aut 88, p. 184.
"Bedside Manners." [Trans] (20) Spr 88, p. 25.
"Beneath the Visiting Moon." [Trans] (20) Spr 88, p. 27.
"The Fall and After." [Trans] (20) Spr 88, p. 29.
"Incident in Oxford Street." [Trans] (20) Spr 88, p. 26.
"Thinking About AIDS." [Trans] (20) Spr 88, p. 24.

5816. WIT, Johan de
"Understanding Prohibited." [Bogg] (59) 88, p. 27.

5817. WITEK, Terri
"The Problem." [NowestR] (26:3) 88, p. 20-21.

5818. WITHERUP, William
"Egret: Bolinas Lagoon: 4/27/86." [SwampR] (1:1) Ja 88, p. 38-39.

5819. WITT, Harold
"All My Sons." [BellArk] (4:6) N-D 88, p. 1.
"American Lit." [Wind] (18:63) 88, p. 47-48.
"American Lit: A Cask of Amontillado." [WritersF] (14) Fall 88, p. 44.
"American Lit: Susan Glaspell's 'The Verge' at Coleville." [WritersF] (14) Fall 88, p. 44-45.
"American Lit: Walden." [WebR] (13:2) Fall 88, p. 58.
"An American Tragedy." [LitR] (31:2) Wint 88, p. 170.
"Auden." [Bogg] (59) 88, p. 9.
"Billy Budd." [Amelia] (5:2, #13) 88, p. 32.
"The Glass Menagerie." [BellArk] (4:1) Ja-F 88, p. p. 9.
"The Great Gatsby." [Wind] (18:63) 88, p. 47.
"The Heart Is a Lonely Hunter." [Wind] (18:63) 88, p. 47.
"Main-Travelled Roads" (American Lit). [HiramPoR] (44/45) Spr-Wint 88, p. 48.
"Modern American Poetry." [BellArk] (4:4) Jl-Ag 88, p. 3.
"O William Carlos." [BallSUF] (29:4) Aut 88, p. 45.
"The Plumber." [Interim] (7:1) Spr 88, p. 19.
"The Red Badge of Courage." [LitR] (31:2) Wint 88, p. 170.
"Roethke." [BellArk] (4:5) S-O 88, p. 10.
"To Build a Fire" (American Lit). [Interim] (7:2) Fall 88, p. 3.
"Vachel" (American Lit). [Interim] (7:2) Fall 88, p. 4.
"Winesburg by the Sea" (American Lit). [Interim] (7:1) Spr 88, p. 20.

5820. WITT, Sandra
"Composing Photos." [CreamCR] (12:2) Sum 88, p. 305.
"The Grass." [Vis] (27) 88, p. 32.

WITT, Susan Kelly de
See KELLY-DeWITT, Susan

5821. WITTE, Francine
"The Magic in the Streets." [HiramPoR] (44/45) Spr-Wint 88, p. 50.
"Only." [HiramPoR] (44/45) Spr-Wint 88, p. 49.

5822. WITTE, George
"The Covered Well." [SouthwR] (73:3) Sum 88, p. 373-374.

5823. WITTE, John
"Breast Poem." [NewEngR] (11:2) Wint 88, p. 194.
"Elva." [NewEngR] (11:2) Wint 88, p. 195.
"The White Wall." [Iowa] (18:1) 88, p. 124.

5824. WITTLINGER, Ellen
"Bedtime." [Iowa] (18:1) 88, p. 53-54.

"The Egg." [AmerV] (13) Wint 88, p. 54-55.
"Flesh." [Iowa] (18:1) 88, p. 52-53.
"Mother's Incurable Wish." [Iowa] (18:1) 88, p. 54-55.
"A Thing Like a Baby." [MidwQ] (30:1) Aut 88, p. 81-83.

5825. WOERTH, John S.
"Love Love Love." [RagMag] (6:2) Fall 88, p. 46.

5826. WOESSNER, Warren
"Cedar Waxwings." [SwampR] (1:2/3) D 88, p. 72.
"Clearwater." [SwampR] (1:2/3) D 88, p. 73.
"Entrance." [LakeSR] (22) 88, p. 11.
"High Summer." [LakeSR] (22) 88, p. 11.
"Inventory of Fear" (w. Ed Janes). [Lips] (14) 88, p. 25.
"Magnificent Frigatebird." [Abraxas] (37) 88, p. 27.

WOFFORD, Jan Bailey
See BAILEY-WOFFORD, Jan

5827. WOHLFELD, Valerie
"The Philosophy of Anatomy" (from *An Echo of Crows*). [Epoch] (37:1) 88, p. 13-17.
"The Uccello." [NewYorker] (64:12) 9 My 88, p. 36.

5828. WOJAHN, David
"Futures." [DenQ] (22:4) Spr 88, p. 72-73.
"Professor Cameron." [MissouriR] (11:2) 88, p. 64-65.
"The Trans-Siberian." [DenQ] (22:4) Spr 88, p. 74-76.

WOLF, Elizabeth
See WOLF, Janis T. B.

5829. WOLF, Janis T. B.
"Mother (2)." [Kaleid] (16) Wint-Spr 88, p. 59.
"Priorities." [Kaleid] (16) Wint-Spr 88, p. 59.

5830. WOLF, Michele
"Fisherman." [Confr] (37/38) Spr-Sum 88, p. 276.

5831. WOLFF, Daniel
"Sweet Beads of Sweat." [Sequoia] (32:1) Spr-Sum 88, p. 45.
"Two Work Sonnets." [Thrpny] (34) Sum 88, p. 24.

5832. WOLFF, Jurgen
"Choices." [Crosscur] (7:4) 88, p. 71-72.
"The Rest Home." [Crosscur] (7:4) 88, p. 70.

WOLHEE, Choe
See CHOE, Wolhee

5833. WOLPER, Page Kerry
"The Foundling." [StoneC] (15:3/4) Spr-Sum 88, p. 21.

5834. WOLVERTON, Terry
"Black Slip." [Jacaranda] (3:2) Fall-Wint 88, p. 134-135.

5835. WONG, Nellie
"For an Asian Woman Who Says My Poetry Gives Her a Stomachache." [Calyx] (11:2/3) Fall 88, p. 86-87.

5836. WOO, Merle
"Untitled: In the deepest night and a full moon." [Calyx] (11:2/3) Fall 88, p. 131.
"Whenever You're Cornered, the Only Way Out Is to Fight." [Calyx] (11:2/3) Fall 88, p. 132-133.

5837. WOOD, Eve E. M.
"Come to the Mission." [Plain] (8:2) Wint 88, p. 24.

5838. WOOD, Peter
"I Know a Woman." [HangL] (52) 88, p. 43.
"Mad Chat." [HangL] (52) 88, p. 44.
"Meta's Daughters." [StoneC] (15:3/4) Spr-Sum 88, p. 25.
"Mr. Bartolino." [HangL] (52) 88, p. 42.

5839. WOOD, Renate
"The Chill." [SenR] (18:1) 88, p. 54-55.
"The Glass House." [MassR] (29:3) Fall 88, p. 538.
"Man and Boy." [NewEngR] (11:1) Aut 88, p. 74.

5840. WOOD, Susan
"Knowing the End" (for Lee Abbott). [TampaR] (1) 88, p. 92-93.
"Matinee." [IndR] (11:3) Sum 88, p. 10-11.

5841. WOODFORD, Keisha Lynette
"Black." [Footwork] ('88) 88, p. 55-56.

"Black Bodies" (Lyrics for Billie Holiday, In Reminder of "Strange Fruit"). [Footwork] ('88) 88, p. 56-57.
"Black Bottoms on a Hot Summer Day." [Footwork] ('88) 88, p. 55.
"How bout if we migrate?" [Footwork] ('88) 88, p. 58.
"I started at the tender age of sixteen." [Footwork] ('88) 88, p. 58.
"It's SUE I CIDE baybee." [Footwork] ('88) 88, p. 57.
"Maybe If." [Footwork] ('88) 88, p. 55.
"Sherade" (Written with Matheu Hinton). [Footwork] ('88) 88, p. 54-55.
"Street People." [Footwork] ('88) 88, p. 54.
"A Thank You Note to Mama." [Footwork] ('88) 88, p. 56.

5842. WOODRUFF, Jennifer Lynn
"Dedicated to the Crew." [PikeF] (9) Fall 88, p. 20.

5843. WOODRUFF, William
"Meaning and Purpose." [Lactuca] (11) O 88, p. 33.

5844. WOODS, Brien
"City Limits." [CharR] (14:2) Fall 88, p. 54.

5845. WOODS, Christopher
"Alphonso." [PaintedB] (34) 88, p. 86.
"Waking, Going On." [CutB] (29/30) 88, p. 30.

5846. WOODS, John
"Cursing the First Book." [LightY] ('88/9) 88, p. 194.
"Digging Up Small Coffins." [PoetryNW] (29:4) Wint 88-89, p. 12-13.
"Knowing." [PoetryNW] (29:4) Wint 88-89, p. 13.
"Living in the Ground." [PassN] (9:1) Wint 88, p. 14.
"The Long-Head Poem." [GettyR] (1:3) Sum 88, p. 508.
"The Long-Head Poem." [LightY] ('88/9) 88, p. 166-167.
"Resolutions: Ice Storm" (Dec. 31, 1986). [PoetryNW] (29:4) Wint 88-89, p. 14.

5847. WOODS-SMITH, Sybil
"A Nurse's Advice on Dust Mites." [SpoonRQ] (13:3) Sum 88, p. 10-11.

5848. WOODWARD, Ann
"Ten Prose Poems" (2, 7, 13, 20, 22, 23, 25, 29, 30, 31, tr. of Dona Rosu). [WebR] (13:2) Fall 88, p. 40-42.

5849. WOON, Koon
"A = L. + O.E." [BellArk] (4:1) Ja-F 88, p. 4.
"At the Bus Stop." [Contact] (9:47/48/49) Spr 88, p. 43.
"Centering." [BellArk] (4:6) N-D 88, p. 17.
"Egg Tarts." [BellArk] (4:6) N-D 88, p. 5.
"Gillette Boxing." [BellArk] (4:5) S-O 88, p. 3.
"In Water Buffalo Time." [BellArk] (4:3) My-Je 88, p. 4-5.
"An Old Hotel Dweller." [Contact] (9:47/48/49) Spr 88, p. 43.
"Windows After a Rain." [BellArk] (4:4) Jl-Ag 88, p. 10.

5850. WORLEY, James
"Adam's Revenge." [ChrC] (105:20) 22-29 Je 88, p. 598.
"The Gravedigger." [ChrC] (105:22) 20-27 Jl 88, p. 660.
"Maculate Conception." [ChrC] (105:33) 9 N 88, p. 1006.

5851. WORLEY, Jeff
"Dropping." [CarolQ] (41:1) Fall 88, p. 20.
"Elated by Rereading a Book of James Wright's Poetry, I Get Drunk . . ." (for J.W.). [PoetryNW] (29:4) Wint 88-89, p. 35-36.
"Ezra" (for Craig Anderson). [PoetryNW] (29:4) Wint 88-89, p. 34-35.
"Griswald, Last House on the Block." [CarolQ] (41:1) Fall 88, p. 21-22.
"Homecoming." [FloridaR] (16:1) Spr-Sum 88, p. 82-83.
"Insider Trading." [BelPoJ] (39:1) Fall 88, p. 1.
"Kokkari" (for Chuck and Ruth). [HawaiiR] (12:1, #23) Spr 88, p. 92-93.
"Moles." [Thrpny] (35) Fall 88, p. 7.
"Morning." [MalR] (82) Mr 88, p. 80-81.
"Shopping at Mueller's Variety with Uncle Harley" (The Seaton First Award Poem 1988). [KanQ] (20:3) Sum 88, p. 9-10.
"To My Brother, Terrified of Wasps" (for Mike). [MidwQ] (30:1) Aut 88, p. 73-74.
"Vasectomy." [PoetryNW] (29:3) Aut 88, p. 46.

5852. WORMHOUDT, Arthur
"Lubna's Word" (tr. of Qais ibn Dharih, Majnun). [Paint] (15:30) Aut 88, p. 42.
"On Death" (tr. of Al-Shaddakh al-Kinani). [Paint] (15:30) Aut 88, p. 43.

5853. WORMHOUDT, Sarah
"Amaryllis." [Paint] (15:29) Spr 88, p. 30.

5854. WOROSZYLSKI, Wiktor
"In this slough becoming stone" (tr. by Stanislaw Baranczak and Clare Cavanagh). [ManhatR] (4:2) Spr 88, p. 38.
"Roommates" (tr. by Stanislaw Baranczak and Clare Cavanagh). [TriQ] (71) Wint 88, p. 155-156.
"What a Poem Is Allowed" (tr. by Stanislaw Baranczak and Clare Cavanagh). [ManhatR] (4:2) Spr 88, p. 37.
5855. WOROZBYT, Theodore (Theodore, Jr.)
"For Your Sins." [MinnR] (NS 30/31) Spr-Fall 88, p. 29-31.
"The Mug." [KanQ] (20:1/2) Wint-Spr 88, p. 328.
"Photograph of the Bruised Child." [CutB] (31/32) 88, p. 63.
5856. WORTH, Douglas
"Maybe We Had to Come This Far" (for Irwin). [TexasR] (9:3/4) Fall-Wint 88, p. 142.
5857. WORTH, Jan
"Easter Sunday." [Nimrod] (32:1) Fall-Wint 88, p. 112.
"My Mother's First Manicure." [PassN] (9:1) Wint 88, p. 10.
"World Travelers." [PassN] (9:2) Sum 88, p. 29.
5858. WREGGITT, Andrew
"Alaska Highway, 1965." [Dandel] (15:2) Fall-Wint 88, p. 7-8.
"Brothers." [Event] (17:2) Sum 88, p. 40-45.
"Inverness Passage." [CrossC] (10:3) 88, p. 3.
"Visible." [Dandel] (15:2) Fall-Wint 88, p. 9-12.
"Weeds." [CanLit] (119) Wint 88, p. 5-7.
5859. WRIGHT, C. D.
"Mons Venus." [Field] (39) Fall 88, p. 77.
"More Blues and the Abstract Truth." [ParisR] (30:109) Wint 88, p. 94-95.
"Our Dust." [ParisR] (30:109) Wint 88, p. 91-93.
"Planks." [Field] (39) Fall 88, p. 74-75.
"Self Portrait on a Rocky Mount." [Field] (39) Fall 88, p. 76.
5860. WRIGHT, Carolyne
"After All Is Said and Done." [SouthernPR] (28:2) Fall 88, p. 14-16.
"Another Look at 'Albion on the Rock': Plate 38 of Blake's *Milton*." [Chelsea] (47) 88, p. 68-69.
"The Blaze" (tr. of Pratima Ray, w. Paramita Banerjee). [Nimrod] (31:2) Spr-Sum 88, p. 33.
"Companion" (tr. of Vijaya Mukhopadhyay, w. Sunil B. Ray and the author). [Nimrod] (31:2) Spr-Sum 88, p. 31.
"A Conjectural Guide to Dunstanburgh Castle" (Northumberland Coast). [Chelsea] (47) 88, p. 70-71.
"Escape from the Museum: Boston" (for Jeanne). [AmerV] (10) Spr 88, p. 24-25.
"Man" (tr. of Mallika Sengupta, w. Paramita Banerjee). [SenR] (18:2) 88, p. 29.
"Monday's Hand on Your Shoulder" (tr. of Vijaya Mukhopadhyay, w. Sunil B. Ray and the author). [Nimrod] (31:2) Spr-Sum 88, p. 32.
"Month of Honey" (tr. of Mallika Sengupta, w. Paramita Banerjee). [SenR] (18:2) 88, p. 25-26.
"Peace" (tr. of Anuradha Mahapatra, w. Paramita Banerjee). [Nimrod] (31:2) Spr-Sum 88, p. 35.
"The Poor Fund" (tr. of Nabaneeta Dev Sen, w. Paramita Banerjee and the author). [Nimrod] (31:2) Spr-Sum 88, p. 37.
"Recovery" (tr. of Nabaneeta Dev Sen, w. Paramita Banerjee and the author). [Nimrod] (31:2) Spr-Sum 88, p. 36.
"Second Planet Earth" (tr. of Anuradha Mahapatra, w. Jyotirmoy Datta). [Nimrod] (31:2) Spr-Sum 88, p. 34.
"Simile" (tr. of Pratima Ray, w. Paramita Banerjee). [Nimrod] (31:2) Spr-Sum 88, p. 33.
"Son of Air" (tr. of Mallika Sengupta, w. Paramita Banerjee). [SenR] (18:2) 88, p. 28.
"Spell" (tr. of Anuradha Mahapatra, w. Jyotirmoy Datta). [Nimrod] (31:2) Spr-Sum 88, p. 34.
"To a Cowherd Boy" (tr. of Kabita Sinha, w. Enakshi Chatterjee). [Nimrod] (31:2) Spr-Sum 88, p. 30.
"Two Golden Airplanes" (tr. of Mallika Sengupta, w. Paramita Banerjee). [SenR] (18:2) 88, p. 27.
"Worshipping the Tree" (tr. of Mallika Sengupta, w. Paramita Banerjee). [SenR] (18:2) 88, p. 24.

5861. WRIGHT, Charles
"Bicoastal Journal." [Poetry] (143, i.e. 153:1) O 88, p. 16-17.
"China Journal." [NewYorker] (64:32) 26 S 88, p. 46.
"Chinese Journal." [GettyR] (1:1) Wint 88, p. 32.
"A Journal of Southern Rivers." [NewYorker] (64:20) 4 Jl 88, p. 28-29.
"Light Journal." [GettyR] (1:1) Wint 88, p. 31.
"Local Journal." [NewYorker] (64:41) 28 N 88, p. 38-39.
"Primitive Journal II." [NewRep] (198:17) 25 Ap 88, p. 36.
"Sinology." [Verse] (5:3) N 88, p. 23.
"To Raymond Carver in Heaven." [Field] (39) Fall 88, p. 95-97.
"Vesper Journal." [Poetry] (143, i.e. 153:1) O 88, p. 16.
5862. WRIGHT, Constance
"Palolo Day." [ChamLR] (1:2, #2) Spr 88, p. 73.
"Palolo Night." [ChamLR] (1:2, #2) Spr 88, p. 74.
5863. WRIGHT, James
"On a Phrase from Southern Ohio" (for Etheridge Knight). [PaintedB] (32/33) 88, p. 63-64.
5864. WRIGHT, Jay
"Madrid." [YaleR] (77:2) Wint 88, p. 293-294.
5865. WRIGHT, Jeff
"Forever Young." [Talisman] (1) Fall 88, p. 5.
5866. WRIGHT, Lois
"Richard Brought His Flute" (tr. of Nancy Morejon). [Callaloo] (11:1, #34) Wint 88, p. 24-29.
5867. WRIGHT, Margaret Borron
"Lunar Eclipse." [StoneC] (16:1/2) Fall-Wint 88-89, p. 56-57.
5868. WRIGLEY, Robert
"American Manhood." [Poetry] (152:3) Je 88, p. 155-156.
"Camping." [Poetry] (152:3) Je 88, p. 159-160.
"Creel." [Poetry] (152:4) Jl 88, p. 195.
"Economics." [GeoR] (42:1) Spr 88, p. 103-105.
"The Emblem." [Poetry] (152:3) Je 88, p. 156-158.
"For the Last Summer." [Poetry] (152:4) Jl 88, p. 195-196.
"What My Father Believed." [Poetry] (152:3) Je 88, p. 158-159.
"The Wishing Tree" (For Phillip, September, 1987). [NewEngR] (11:2) Wint 88, p. 125-126.
5869. WU, Wen-ying
"Dancing Girl" (tr. by Graeme Wilson). [Jacaranda] (3:2) Fall-Wint 88, p. 145.
WU-JUN, Sun
See SUN, Wu-jun
5870. WYGAL, Jane
"Bridge of the Nose." [DenQ] (22:3) Wint 88, p. 89-90.
5871. WYNAND, Derk
"Sea Wall." [Event] (17:1) Spr 88, p. 38.
"The Sign of Our Prosperity." [Quarry] (37:1) Wint 88, p. 20-21.
5872. WYSE, Bruce David
"I Am No tiger." [Grain] (16:4) Wint 88, inside back cover.
5873. WYTTENBERG, Victoria
"Lora at Ten." [PoetryNW] (29:1) Spr 88, p. 32.
"Lot's Wife." [PoetryNW] (29:1) Spr 88, p. 33.
XIAO-LONG, Wang
See WANG, Xiao-long
XIAO-NI, Wang
See WANG, Xiao-ni
5874. XIE, Ye
"At Last I Turn My Back" (in Chinese & English). [BelPoJ] (39:2) Wint 88-89, p. p. 30-31.
5875. XING, Yong-zhen
"In Autumn Days" (tr. of Geng Wei). [MidAR] (8:1) 88, p. 14-15.
5876. XU, Haixin
"About Old Age, in Answer to a Poem by Zhang Shaofu" (tr. of Wang Wei, w. Tony Barnstone and Willis Barnstone). [ArtfulD] (14/15) Fall 88, p. 81.
"Drifting on the Lake" (tr. of Wang Wei, w. Tony Barnstone and Willis Barnstone). [ArtfulD] (14/15) Fall 88, p. 81.
"East River Moon" (tr. of Wang Wei, w. Tony Barnstone and Willis Barnstone). [ArtfulD] (14/15) Fall 88, p. 80.

"Lazy about Writing Poems" (tr. of Wang Wei, w. Tony Barnstone and Willis Barnstone). [ArtfulD] (14/15) Fall 88, p. 80.
"Red Peonies" (tr. of Wang Wei, w. Tony Barnstone and Willis Barnstone). [ArtfulD] (14/15) Fall 88, p. 81.

XUEFEI, Jin
See JIN, Ha

5877. YALE, Jo-Ellen
"Shock." [SinW] (36) Wint 88-89, p. 18.

5878. YALIM, Ozcan
"Salt" (tr. of Bedri Rahmi Eyuboglu, w. William A. Fielder and Dionis Coffin Riggs). [StoneC] (16:1/2) Fall-Wint 88-89, p. 40.

5879. YAMADA, Leona
"Ash Room." [HawaiiR] (12:2, #24) Fall 88, p. 9.
"I Thought." [HawaiiR] (12:2, #24) Fall 88, p. 7-8.
"Mail Order" (for Jack). [HawaiiR] (12:2, #24) Fall 88, p. 10.
"Roof Pipes." [ChamLR] (2:1, #3) Fall 88, p. 109.

5880. YAMADA, Mitsuye
"The Club." [Calyx] (11:2/3) Fall 88, p. 84-85.

5881. YAMRUS, John
"Picture This." [Bogg] (59) 88, p. 15.

5882. YANDELL, Ben
"On Reading the Feynman Lectures." [Nimrod] (32:1) Fall-Wint 88, p. 43-51.

5883. YANISHCHITS, Yaugenia
"Our Neighbor Pelagea" (tr. by Walter May). [NegC] (8:1/2) 88, p. 38.

5884. YASHASCHANDRA, Sitanshu
"A Tree" (tr. by the author). [Nimrod] (31:2) Spr-Sum 88, p. 70.

5885. YATES, Ernest
"Song for a Holiday." [KanQ] (20:1/2) Wint-Spr 88, p. 141.

5886. YATES, J. Michael
"5. The numberlessness of northern green." [CapilR] (48) 88, p. 6.
"6. Photograph of me holding in both hands the pierced heart of a grizzly bear." [CapilR] (48) 88, p. 7.
"14. Wet you can bear being wet." [CapilR] (48) 88, p. 8.

YE, Xie
See XIE, Ye

5887. YEE, Marian
"The Handbook of Sex of the Plain Girl." [Calyx] (11:2/3) Fall 88, p. 78-79.
"Wintermelons." [Calyx] (11:2/3) Fall 88, p. 80-81.

5888. YENSER, Pamela
"Calling the Dog." [Spirit] (9:1) 88, p. 99.
"Pentacles: A Tarot Reading." [MidwQ] (29:4) Sum 88, p. 463-468.
"Questions for Travel on Route 66" (in Memory of Elizabeth Bishop). [KanQ] (20:3) Sum 88, p. 212-213.

5889. YERBURGH, Rhoda
"Deaf." [TexasR] (9:3/4) Fall-Wint 88, p. 143.

5890. YGLESIAS, Luis E.
"The Magic Drum" (Inuit / Copper Eskimo). [LindLM] (7:2/4) Ap-D 88, p. 16-17.

YI-DONG, Li
See LI, Yi-dong

YIU, Lu
See LU, Yiu

5891. YORK, Cathryn
"Travel Brochure." [PacificR] (6) Spr 88, p. 49.

5892. YORTON, Linda
"Civil Wedding at High Water" (St. Louis, 1986). [WebR] (13:1) Spr 88, p. 79-81.

5893. YOSHINO, Hiroshi
"First Born" (tr. by Graeme Wilson). [Jacaranda] (3:1) Wint 88, p. 4.

5894. YOSHINO, Kenji
"Alignments" (Poetry Contest Honorable Mention). [HarvardA] (122:3) Mr 88, p. 12.

5895. YOTS, Michael
"Reading Dead Poets." [KanQ] (20:1/2) Wint-Spr 88, p. 188.

5896. YOUMANS, Marlene
"A Lawn Colonized by Orb Spiders." [Blueline] (9:1/2) 88, p. 39.

5897. YOUNG, Dean
"Age of Discovery." [Poetry] (151:4) Ja 88, p. 341-342.

"Elegy for My Cat." [OhioR] (40) 88, p. 98-99.
"Germinations." [Crazy] (34) Spr 88, p. 13.
"Interference & Delivery." [Poetry] (151:4) Ja 88, p. 340-341.
"Memories of the Invisible Man." [Ploughs] (14:4) 88, p. 111-112.
"My Life with Litter." [Crazy] (34) Spr 88, p. 11-12.
"Thine Is the Kingdom." [Crazy] (34) Spr 88, p. 14-15.

5898. YOUNG, Gary
"The Orchard in Oils." [AntR] (46:3) Sum 88, p. 341.

5899. YOUNG, George
"Creating the Universe." [PaintedB] (34) 88, p. 15.
"Damien." [PaintedB] (34) 88, p. 13-14.
"Shiloh." [PoetL] (83:4) Wint 88-89, p. 37.

5900. YOUNG, Jim
"Chimney." [Wind] (18:62) 88, p. 50-51.
"The La Salle." [Wind] (18:62) 88, p. 50.
"The Latest Diet." [LightY] ('88/9) 88, p. 221.

5901. YOUNG, Kathryn
"Stowaways in the Dusty Rose" (for C. Carpenter). [SpoonRQ] (13:2) Spr 88, p. 10-12.

5902. YOUNG, Libby
"The Secret." [ChamLR] (1) Fall 87, p. 10-11.
"A Visit to the Gallery." [ChamLR] (1) Fall 87, p. 9.

5903. YOUNG, Patricia
"Connie, Marlene and Me, Shimmering." [Quarry] (37:4) Aut 88, p. 76.
"First Day Warm Enough to Wear Bathingsuits." [Quarry] (37:4) Aut 88, p. 75.
"Holloween." [CrossC] (10:1) 88, p. 11.
"Yesterday Hotel." [CrossC] (10:1) 88, p. 11.

5904. YOUNG, Ree
"Episodes." [Vis] (28) 88, p. 10.

5905. YOUNG, Tom
"Tubs 2." [JamesWR] (5:2) Wint 88, p. 5.

5906. YOUNG, Virginia Brady
"Back to County Cork." [TexasR] (9:3/4) Fall-Wint 88, p. 144.

5907. YOUNG BEAR, Ray A.
"Always Is He Criticized." [Sonora] (14/15) Spr 88, p. 52-54.
"The Handcuff Symbol." [VirQR] (64:4) Aut 88, p. 629-632.
"The Rock Island Hiking Club." [VirQR] (64:4) Aut 88, p. 624-625.
"A Woman's Name Is In the Second Verse: Earthquakes and Parallels." [VirQR] (64:4) Aut 88, p. 626-629.

YOUNGS, Anne Ohman
See OHMAN-YOUNGS, Anne

5908. YOUNT, Lisa
"Navel Orange." [Interim] (7:1) Spr 88, p. 18.
"Owlnight." [Interim] (7:1) Spr 88, p. 17.
"White Stones." [Interim] (7:1) Spr 88, p. 17.

5909. YOWS, Kristina
"Gin." [HighP] (3:3) Wint 88-89, p. 96-97.
"Terminus: the First Unusual Day." [HighP] (3:3) Wint 88-89, p. 98-99.

YUHN-BOK, Kim
See KIM, Yuhn-Bok

5910. YUNGKANS, Jonathan
"Paris Meets Japan, 1890-1930." [PoetL] (83:4) Wint 88-89, p. 45-48.

5911. YURKIEVICH, Saul
"Autocrítica." [Inti] (26/27) Otoño 87-Primavera 88, p. 369-371.
"Para Qué Leerlos." [Inti] (26/27) Otoño 87-Primavera 88, p. 371-372.

5912. YURMAN, R.
"Waiting for One on One." [Amelia] (5:1, #12) 88, p. 21.

5913. ZABLE, Jeffrey
"At the End." [Wind] (18:62) 88, p. 52.
"The class of 39." [Wind] (18:62) 88, p. 52.
"The Come On." [SlipS] (8) 88, p. 38.
"The Promise." [SlipS] (8) 88, p. 38-39.

5914. ZAGAJEWSKI, Adam
"Alma Mater" (tr. by C. K. Williams and Renata Gorczynski). [TriQ] (71) Wint 88, p. 142.

"September Afternoon in the Abandoned Barracks" (tr. by C. K. Williams and Renata Gorczynski). [TriQ] (71) Wint 88, p. 141.
"Seventeen Years Old" (tr. by Renata Gorczynski). [WestHR] (42:4) Wint 88, p. 273.
"When Death Came" (tr. by C. K. Williams and Renata Gorczynski). [TriQ] (71) Wint 88, p. 139-140.
"Without Shape" (tr. by the author). [WestHR] (42:4) Wint 88, p. 272.

5915. ZAHLLER, Elaine
"The Fuzzy Child." [DeKalbLAJ] (21:3/4) 88, p. 64.

ZAJAC, Anna Frajlich
See FRAJLICH-ZAJAC, Anna

5916. ZALAN, Tibor
"Before Long You'll Turn 28. You'll Live to See the Axe" (tr. by Nicholas Kolumban). [CharR] (14:2) Fall 88, p. 101.
"I'm with My Most Supple Poems Now When You Don't Love Me" (tr. by Nicholas Kolumban). [CharR] (14:2) Fall 88, p. 102-103.
"When It's Not Fashionable to Write Silence, I'll Portray Your Silence" (tr. by Nicholas Kolumban). [CharR] (14:2) Fall 88, p. 102.
"You Can Do Anything to Me But One Thing: Don't Love Me" (tr. by Nicholas Kolumban). [CharR] (14:2) Fall 88, p. 100.

5917. ZAMORA, Daisy
"It Was a Scattered Squadron (September, 1978)" (tr. by Preston Browning and Lang Gomez). [AnotherCM] (18) 88, p. 195.
"Reflection About My Feet" (tr. by Nancy Esposito). [AmerPoR] (17:2) Mr-Ap 88, p. 30.
"What Hands in My Hands" (tr. by Nancy Esposito). [AmerPoR] (17:2) Mr-Ap 88, p. 30.

5918. ZANA
"Wrap Me in Violets." [Kaleid] (16) Wint-Spr 88, p. 55.

5919. ZANDER, William
"The Christmas Journey" (for 1983). [PoetryNW] (29:1) Spr 88, p. 24-25.

5920. ZARAK, Ricardo
"No hay tierra." [Mairena] (10:25) 88, p. 182.

5921. ZARIN, Cynthia
"The Box Turtle." [NewYorker] (64:31) 19 S 88, p. 42.
"The June Beetle." [GrandS] (7:3) Spr 88, p. 78-79.
"Klex." [YaleR] (77:3) Spr 88, p. 436-438.
"Pears Soap." [GrandS] (7:3) Spr 88, p. 80.
"Snail." [SouthwR] (73:3) Sum 88, p. 400.
"The Swordfish Tooth." [GrandS] (8:1) Aut 88, p. 143-144.

5922. ZARZYSKI, Paul
"Antipasto!" [WestB] (21/22) 88, p. 54.

5923. ZAUHAR, David
"Understanding Media." [RiverS] (27) 88, p. 74.

5924. ZAWADIWSKY, Christina
"Stranglehold." [Sonora] (14/15) Spr 88, p. 17.

5925. ZAZUYER, Leah
"Nuptial Flight." [Blueline] (9:1/2) 88, p. 38.
"Town Historian." [NegC] (8:3) 88, p. 102-103.

ZBLOKI, Chiah Heller
See HELLER-ZBLOKI, Chiah

5926. ZDANYS, Jonas
"Chiaroscuro." [Vis] (26) 88, p. 33.
"February Snow." [Crosscur] (7:4) 88, p. 29-30.
"Spring Blessing." [Crosscur] (7:4) 88, p. 31-32.
"This Hard Light: Fragments." [Vis] (26) 88, p. 32.

5927. ZEGERS, Kip
"Night Flight to Chicago." [NoDaQ] (56:3) Sum 88, p. 102.
"A Promise." [HangL] (52) 88, p. 45.

5928. ZEIDENSTEIN, Sondra
"To an Old Lover." [PoetL] (83:1) Spr 88, p. 29-30.

5929. ZEIDNER, Lisa
"Baltimore Avenue." [MissR] (16:1, #46) 88, p. 116.
"Dying in Your Dreams." [MissR] (16:1, #46) 88, p. 113-115.
"Lesson." [MissR] (16:1, #46) 88, p. 108-110.
"The Mesopotamian Tool Room." [PaintedB] (34) 88, p. 25-26.

"Sweeping." [MissR] (16:1, #46) 88, p. 111-112.
5930. ZEIGER, Gene
"4 P.M." [TarRP] (27:2) Spr 88, p. 31.
"First Day, November 1, 1987" (for Bill). [YellowS] (28) D 88, p. 40.
5931. ZEIGER, L. L.
"Bargemusic" (For Olga Bloom). [Confr] (Special issue: The World of Brooklyn) 88, p. 28.
5932. ZEIGER, Lila
"Bargain." [PassN] (9:1) Wint 88, p. 18.
"Clerihews" (2 poems). [LightY] ('88/9) 88, p. 74-75.
"River Rhyme." [LightY] ('88/9) 88, p. 111.
5933. ZEMAIDUK, Nick R.
"Doing Without." [BallSUF] (29:4) Aut 88, p. 21.
"Inflections." [Plain] (8:1) Fall 87, p. 29.
5934. ZEMELMAN, Susan
"An English Teacher Revisited." [EngJ] (77:7) N 88, p. 99.
5935. ZENITH, Richard
"And I'm Wearing Myself Out Standing" (tr. of Roger Giroux). [WebR] (13:1) Spr 88, p. 32-33.
"Backwards Suite" (3, tr. of Nelo Risi). [LitR] (31:4) Sum 88, p. 469.
"The Canefield and the Sea" (tr. of João Cabral de Melo Neto). [WebR] (13:2) Fall 88, p. 34.
"Catechism for a Cathedral Concert." [SoDakR] (26:3) Aut 88, p. 150-151.
"Cemetery in Alagoas" (Cemitério Alagoano, tr. of João Cabral de Melo Neto). [NewOR] (15:2) Sum 88, p. 84.
"The Egg (O Ovo de Galinha)" (tr. of João Cabral de Melo Neto). [Chelsea] (47) 88, p. 93-94.
"Elementary Thought #21" (tr. of Nelo Risi). [LitR] (31:4) Sum 88, p. 468.
"Envy and the Violin." [GeoR] (42:4) Wint 88, p. 783.
"Gentlemen's Meeting" (tr. of Alexandre O'Neill). [MissR] (16:1, #46) 88, p. 63.
"The Household Gun" (tr. of Alexandre O'Neill). [MissR] (16:1, #46) 88, p. 65.
"How Much Longer?" (tr. of Nelo Risi). [LitR] (31:4) Sum 88, p. 468.
"Legacy" (tr. of Roger Giroux). [WebR] (13:1) Spr 88, p. 33.
"Means of Transportation" (tr. of João Cabral de Melo Neto). [WebR] (13:2) Fall 88, p. 35.
"Pebbles at the Window" (tr. of Mario Benedetti). [ColR] (NS 15:2) Fall-Wint 88, p. 85.
"A Question of Punctuation" (tr. of João Cabral de Melo Neto). [WebR] (13:2) Fall 88, p. 35.
"Sandbar of the Sirinhaém" (tr. of João Cabral de Melo Neto). [NewOR] (15:2) Sum 88, p. 29.
"Sandwater" (A Agua de Aréia, tr. of João Cabral de Melo Neto). [NewOR] (15:2) Sum 88, p. 90.
"Sugar Cane and the Eighteenth Century" (A Cana e o Século Dezoito, tr. of João Cabral de Melo Neto). [NewOR] (15:2) Sum 88, p. 79.
"The Voice of the Coconut Grove" (tr. of João Cabral de Melo Neto). [WebR] (13:2) Fall 88, p. 34.
"Weekend" (tr. of Alexandre O'Neill). [MissR] (16:1, #46) 88, p. 64.
"The Woman and the House" (tr. of João Cabral de Melo Neto). [WebR] (13:2) Fall 88, p. 33.
"The Word Silk" (tr. of João Cabral de Melo Neto). [ParisR] (30:106) Spr 88, p. 120-121.
5936. ZEPEDA, Rafael
"The Man Who Knew William Faulkner." [WormR] (28:4, #112) 88, p. 92.
"The Man with a Bad Habit." [WormR] (28:4, #112) 88, p. 92-93.
5937. ZETZEL, Geraldine
"You Only Fall If You Imagine Falling" (Hon. Mention, 15th Ann. Comp.). [StoneC] (16:1/2) Fall-Wint 88-89, unpaged front matter.
5938. ZHEN, Min
"Repairing the Wall" (tr. by Edward Morin and Dennis Ding). [WebR] (13:1) Spr 88, p. 40.
ZHIHUAN, Wang
See WANG, Zhihuan
5939. ZIEROTH, Dale
"1. The Mother Prone." [WestCR] (23:2) Fall 88, p. 23-24.
"2. Advising." [WestCR] (23:2) Fall 88, p. 25-26.

"The Bath." [WestCR] (23:2) Fall 88, p. 21-22.
"Free Trade Debate." [WestCR] (23:2) Fall 88, p. 17.
"Letter from Africa." [WestCR] (23:2) Fall 88, p. 19-20.
"New Dispatches." [WestCR] (23:2) Fall 88, p. 18.
"Pariah on Main." [WestCR] (23:2) Fall 88, p. 15-16.
"Poem Facing Evening." [WestCR] (23:2) Fall 88, p. 5-13.
"Postscript: Sarah." [WestCR] (23:2) Fall 88, p. 31-32.
"Reading Late." [WestCR] (23:2) Fall 88, p. 27-28.
"Remembering Frank." [WestCR] (23:2) Fall 88, p. 29-30.
"This Writer." [WestCR] (23:2) Fall 88, p. 14.

5940. ZIMMER, Paul
"Dear Wanda." [BallSUF] (29:3) Sum 88, p. 62-63.
"The Eisenhower Years" (for my father). [BallSUF] (29:3) Sum 88, p. 58-59.
"An Enzyme Poem for Suzanne." [BallSUF] (29:3) Sum 88, p. 68-69.
"How Zimmer Will be Reborn." [GettyR] (1:4) Aut 88, p. 633.
"The Origins of Love." [GettyR] (1:4) Aut 88, p. 634.
"Wanda Being Beautiful." [BallSUF] (29:3) Sum 88, p. 64.
"Wounds." [GeoR] (42:3) Fall 88, p. 510.
"Zimmer Warns Himself with Vivid Images Against Old Age." [BallSUF] (29:3) Sum 88, p. 70.

5941. ZIMMERMAN, H. A.
"The Moments We Choose to Play." [Ascent] (13:3) 88, p. 43.

5942. ZIMMERMAN, Jean
"The Afterlife." [Nimrod] (32:1) Fall-Wint 88, p. 132.
"The Weather at Birthday." [ParisR] (30:108) Fall 88, p. 207.

5943. ZIMMERMAN, Lisa
"Visitor." [Spirit] (9:1) 88, p. 127.

5944. ZIMMERMAN, Richard
"Taking Flight." [Phoenix] (9:1/2) 88, p. 64.

5945. ZIMMERMAN, Thomas
"A Pagan God's Decline." [Plain] (8:2) Wint 88, p. 30.

5946. ZIMROTH, Evan
"Breathing." [LittleM] (15:3/4) 88, p. 10.
"Café." [LittleM] (15:3/4) 88, p. 11.
"City Blizzard." [Atlantic] (261:2) F 88, p. 58.
"Each Summer." [LittleM] (15:3/4) 88, p. 13.
"Just Another Love Affair." [LittleM] (15:3/4) 88, p. 9.
"A Note to the Free World." [LittleM] (15:3/4) 88, p. 12.

5947. ZIOLKOWSKI, Thad
"Untitled: Moreover, said of a stream." [Caliban] (4) 88, p. 154.
"Untitled: Sills, and in the breath between tracks." [Caliban] (4) 88, p. 153.

5948. ZIRLIN, Larry
"36 Today." [HangL] (53) 88, p. 54.
"Chronic." [HangL] (53) 88, p. 53.
"New Year's Day." [HangL] (53) 88, p. 52.
"Weegee." [HangL] (53) 88, p. 55.

5949. ZIVANCEVIC, Nina
"Dawn." [NewAW] (4) Fall 88, p. 72.
"Jimmy." [NewAW] (4) Fall 88, p. 71.
"On Impermanence." [NewAW] (4) Fall 88, p. 68.
"Small Town." [NewAW] (4) Fall 88, p. 67.
"Ted Berrigan." [NewAW] (4) Fall 88, p. 73.
"That Happened." [NewAW] (4) Fall 88, p. 69.

5950. ZOLLER, Ann (Ann L.)
"Along the Way." [Phoenix] (9:1/2) 88, p. 71.
"The Grotto." [Phoenix] (9:1/2) 88, p. 72.
"Home Fire." [Phoenix] (9:1/2) 88, p. 69.
"Hybrid of Birds, of Water." [Phoenix] (9:1/2) 88, p. 73.
"Inside the Candle." [MidwQ] (29:2) Wint 88, p. 220.
"Night Garden." [Phoenix] (9:1/2) 88, p. 69.
"Night Mower." [Vis] (27) 88, p. 11.
"Reflection." [Phoenix] (9:1/2) 88, p. 70.
"To an Old Board." [Vis] (28) 88, p. 27.

5951. ZUCKER, Jack
"On Durer's Hill." [WebR] (13:2) Fall 88, p. 66.

5952. ZULAUF, Sander
"One for the Old Roosters." [JlNJPo] (10:1/2) 88, p. 52.
5953. ZUO, Hong
"Smoking People: Encountering the New Chinese Poetry" (Chapbook 19, tr. by Zuo Hong et al.). [BelPoJ] (39:2) Wint 88-89, 76 p.
5954. ZUYONAK, Vasil
"Arise, Dead Tyrants" (tr. by Walter May). [NegC] (8:1/2) 88, p. 31-32.
5955. ZWEIG, Martha
"Fidelity." [MassR] (29:1) Spr 88, p. 40.
5956. ZWICKY, Jan
"Last Steps." [MalR] (82) Mr 88, p. 28-32.
"Leaving Home." [Dandel] (15:1) Spr-Sum 88, p. 26-33.
"Pacific Rim." [MalR] (82) Mr 88, p. 25-27.
"St. Vincent de Paul's" (for my father). [MalR] (82) Mr 88, p. 23-24.
5957. ZYCHLINSKA, Rajzel
"A Black Man Has Fallen Asleep" (tr. by Aaron Kramer). [Vis] (27) 88, p. 26.
"I Look into Rembrandt's Eyes" (tr. by Aaron Kramer). [Vis] (26) 88, p. 35.
"A Snow Falls" (tr. by Aaron Kramer). [Vis] (26) 88, p. 35.
"This Is Not the Road" (Book of Kings II, tr. by Aaron Kramer). [Vis] (26) 88, p. 35.
"Two Stones" (tr. by Aaron Kramer). [Vis] (27) 88, p. 27.
5958. ZYDEK, Fredrick (Frederick)
"Echoes from the State Institution for the Mentally Retarded." [CimR] (82) Ja 88, p. 50.
"A Fear of Evil." [Event] (17:2) Sum 88, p. 63.
"In Praise of Grandma's Pantry." [HawaiiR] (12:1, #23) Spr 88, p. 8.
"Old Man." [Event] (17:2) Sum 88, p. 62.
"Shooting Bear." [HiramPoR] (44/45) Spr-Wint 88, p. 51.

Title Index

Titles are arranged alphanumerically, with numerals filed in numerical order before letters. Each title is followed by one or more author entry numbers, which refer to the numbered entries in the first part of the volume. Poems which were untitled are represented by first lines.